Lecture Notes in Computer Science   12111

More information about this series at http://www.springer.com/series/7410

Aggelos Kiayias · Markulf Kohlweiss ·
Petros Wallden · Vassilis Zikas (Eds.)

Public-Key Cryptography – PKC 2020

23rd IACR International Conference
on Practice and Theory of Public-Key Cryptography
Edinburgh, UK, May 4–7, 2020
Proceedings, Part II

 Springer

Editors
Aggelos Kiayias
University of Edinburgh
Edinburgh, UK

Markulf Kohlweiss
University of Edinburgh
Edinburgh, UK

Petros Wallden
University of Edinburgh
Edinburgh, UK

Vassilis Zikas
University of Edinburgh
Edinburgh, UK

ISSN 0302-9743   ISSN 1611-3349 (electronic)
Lecture Notes in Computer Science
ISBN 978-3-030-45387-9   ISBN 978-3-030-45388-6 (eBook)
https://doi.org/10.1007/978-3-030-45388-6

LNCS Sublibrary: SL4 – Security and Cryptology

This Springer imprint is published by the registered company Springer Nature Switzerland AG
The registered company address is: Gewerbestrasse 11, 6330 Cham, Switzerland

Preface

The 23rd IACR International Conference on Practice and Theory of Public-Key Cryptography (PKC 2020) was held during May 4–7, 2020, in Edinburgh, Scotland, UK. This conference series is organized annually by the International Association of Cryptologic Research (IACR). It is the main annual conference with an explicit focus on public-key cryptography sponsored by IACR. The proceedings are comprised of two volumes and include the 44 papers that were selected by the Program Committee.

A total of 180 submissions were received for consideration for this year's program. Three submissions were table rejected due to significant deviations from the instructions of the call for papers. Submissions were assigned to at least three reviewers, while submissions by Program Committee members received at least four reviews.

The review period was divided in three stages, the first one reserved for individual reviewing that lasted five weeks. It was followed by the second stage, where the authors were given the opportunity to respond to the reviews. Finally in the third stage, which lasted about 5 weeks, the Program Committee members engaged in discussion taking into account the rebuttal comments submitted by the authors. In addition to the rebuttal, in a number of occasions, the authors of the papers were engaged with additional questions and clarifications. Seven of the papers were conditionally accepted and received a final additional round of reviewing. The reviewing and paper selection process was a difficult task and I am deeply grateful to the members of the Program Committee for their hard and thorough work. Additionally, my deep gratitude is extended to the 252 external reviewers who assisted the Program Committee. The submissions included two papers with which the program chair had a soft conflict of interest (they included in their author list researchers based at the University of Edinburgh). For these two papers, the chair abstained from the management of the discussion and delegated this task to a Program Committee member. I am grateful to Helger Lipmaa for his help in managing these two papers. I would like to also thank Shai Halevi for his web submission and review software which we used for managing the whole process very successfully.

The invited talk at PKC 2020, entitled "How low can we go?" was delivered by Yuval Ishai. I would like to thank Yuval for accepting the invitation and contributing to the program this year as well as all the authors who submitted their work. I would like to also thank my good colleagues and co-editors of these two volumes, Markulf Kohlweiss, Petros Wallden, and Vassilis Zikas who served as general co-chairs this year. A special thanks is also due to Dimitris Karakostas who helped with the website of the conference, Gareth Beedham who assisted in various administrative tasks, and all

---

This proceedings volume was prepared before the conference took place and it reflects its original planning, irrespective of the disruption caused by the COVID-19 pandemic.

PhD students at the School of Informatics who helped with the conference organization. Finally, I am deeply grateful to our industry sponsors, listed in the conference's website, who provided generous financial support.

May 2020   Aggelos Kiayias

Organization

The 23rd IACR International Conference on Practice and Theory in Public-Key Cryptography (PKC 2020) was organized by the International Association for Cryptologic Research and sponsored by the Scottish Informatics and Computer Science Alliance.

General Chairs

Markulf Kohlweiss   University of Edinburgh, UK
Petros Wallden   University of Edinburgh, UK
Vassilis Zikas   University of Edinburgh, UK

Program Chair

Aggelos Kiayias   University of Edinburgh, UK

Program Committee

Gorjan Alagic	UMD, USA
Gilad Asharov	Bar-Ilan University, Israel
Nuttapong Attrapadung	AIST, Japan
Joppe Bos	NXP, Germany
Chris Bruszka	TU Hamburg, Germany
Liqun Chen	University of Surrey, UK
Kai-Min Chung	Academia Sinica, Taiwan
Dana Dachman-Soled	UMD, USA
Sebastian Faust	TU Darmstadt, Germany
Dario Fiore	IMDEA Software Institute, Spain
Marc Fischlin	TU Darmstadt, Germany
Georg Fuchsbauer	ENS Paris, France
Steven Galbraith	Auckland University, New Zealand
Junqing Gong	CNRS and ENS, France
Kyoohyung Han	Coinplug, South Korea
Aggelos Kiayias	University of Edinburgh, UK
Stephan Krenn	AIT, Austria
Benoît Libert	CNRS and ENS de Lyon, France
Helger Lipmaa	Simula UiB, Norway
Ryo Nishimaki	NTT Secure Platform Lab, Japan
Miyako Okhubo	NICT, Japan
Emmanuela Orsini	KUL, Belgium
Omkant Pandey	Stonybrook University, USA

Charalampos Papamanthou	UMD, USA
Christophe Petit	University of Birmingham, UK
Thomas Prest	PQ Shield Ltd., USA
Carla Ràfols	University of Bristol, UK
Arnab Roy	Universitat Pompeu Fabra, Spain
Simona Samardjiska	Radboud University, The Netherlands
Yongsoo Song	Microsoft Research, USA
Rainer Steinwandt	Florida Atlantic University, USA
Berk Sunar	Worcester Polytechnic Institute, USA
Atsushi Takayasu	University of Tokyo, Japan
Serge Vaudenay	EPFL, Switzerland
Daniele Venturi	Sapienza Università di Roma, Italy
Frederik Vercauteren	KUL, Belgium
Chaoping Xing	Nanyang Technological University, Singapore
Thomas Zacharias	University of Edinburgh, UK
Hong Sheng Zhou	VCU, USA

External Reviewers

Aydin Abadi
Behzad Abdolmaleki
Masayuki Abe
Kamalesh Acharya
Shashank Agrawal
Younes Talibi Alaoui
Erdem Alkim
Miguel Ambrona
Myrto Arapinis
Thomas Attema
Shi Bai
Foteini Baldimtsi
Fatih Balli
Subhadeep Banik
Khashayar Barooti
Andrea Basso
Balthazar Bauer
Carsten Baum
Ward Beullens
Rishiraj Bhattacharyya
Nina Bindel
Olivier Blazy
Carl Bootland
Colin Boyd
Andrea Caforio
Sergiu Carpov

Ignacio Cascudo
Wouter Castryck
Andrea Cerulli
Rohit Chatterjee
Hao Chen
Long Chen
Rongmao Chen
Jung Hee Cheon
Ilaria Chillotti
Gwangbae Choi
Heewon Chung
Michele Ciampi
Aloni Cohen
Ran Cohen
Alexandru Cojocaru
Simone Colombo
Anamaria Costache
Craig Costello
Wei Dai
Dipayan Das
Poulami Das
Thomas Debris-Alazard
Thomas Decru
Ioannis Demertzis
Amit Deo
Yarkin Doroz

Yfke Dulek
F. Betül Durak
Stefan Dziembowski
Fabian Eidens
Thomas Eisenbarth
Naomi Ephraim
Andreas Erwig
Leo Fan
Xiong Fan
Antonio Faonio
Pooya Farshim
Prastudy Fauzi
Tamara Finogina
Danilo Francati
Cody Freitag
Eiichiro Fujisaki
Jun Furukawa
Ameet Gadekar
Chaya Ganesh
Wei Gao
Pierrick Gaudry
Romain Gay
Huijing Gong
Alonso Gonzalez
Alonso González
Cyprien de Saint Guilhem
Mohammad Hajiabadi
Shuai Han
Abida Haque
Patrick Harasser
Carmit Hazay
Javier Herranz
Kristina Hostakova
Dongping Hu
Loïs Huguenin-Dumittan
Shih-Han Hung
Ilia Iliashenko
Mitsugu Iwamoto
Kiera Jade
Aayush Jain
Christian Janson
David Jao
Jinhyuck Jeong
Dingding Jia
Yanxue Jia
Charanjit Jutla

Dimitris Karakostas
Nada El Kassem
Shuichi Katsumata
Marcel Keller
Thomas Kerber
Nguyen Ta Toan Khoa
Ryo Kikuchi
Allen Kim
Dongwoo Kim
Duhyeong Kim
Jiseung Kim
Miran Kim
Taechan Kim
Mehmet Kiraz
Elena Kirshanova
Fuyuki Kitagawa
Susumu Kiyoshima
Karen Klein
Dimitris Kolonelos
Ilan Komargodski
Venkata Koppula
Toomas Krips
Mukul Kulkarni
Péter Kutas
Norman Lahr
Nikolaos Lamprou
Fei Li
Jiangtao Li
Zengpeng Li
Zhe Li
Xiao Liang
Wei-Kai Lin
Yeo Sze Ling
Orfeas Thyfronitis Litos
Julian Loss
Zhenliang Lu
Vadim Lyubashevsky
Fermi Ma
Yi-Hsin Ma
Bernardo Magri
Christian Majenz
Nathan Manohar
William J. Martin
Chloe Martindale
Ramiro Martínez
Daniel Masny

Simon Masson
Takahiro Matsuda
Sogol Mazaheri
Simon-Philipp Merz
Peihan Miao
Takaaki Mizuki
Fabrice Mouhartem
Yi Mu
Pratyay Mukherjee
Koksal Mus
Michael Naehrig
Khoa Nguyen
Ariel Nof
Luca Notarnicola
Adam O'Neill
Erdinc Ozturk
Tapas Pal
Alain Passelègue
Alice Pellet–Mary
Ray Perlner
Thomas Peters
Zaira Pindado
Rafael del Pino
Federico Pintore
Antoine Plouviez
Yuriy Polyakov
Chen Qian
Luowen Qian
Yuan Quan
Sebastian Ramacher
Joost Renes
Thomas Ricosset
Felix Rohrbach
Mélissa Rossi
Dragos Rotaru
Sujoy Sinha Roy
Cyprien Delpech de Saint-Guilhem
Yusuke Sakai
Katerina Samari
Kai Samelin
Olivier Sanders
Benjamin Schlosser
Jacob Schuldt
Peter Schwabe
Jae Hong Seo
Ido Shahaf

Yu-Ching Shen
Kazumasa Shinagawa
Janno Siim
Javier Silva
Luisa Siniscalchi
Daniel Slamanig
Azam Soleimanian
Yongha Son
Claudio Soriente
Pierre-Jean Spaenlehauer
Florian Speelman
Akshayaram Srinivasan
Shravan Srinivasan
Martijn Stam
Igors Stephanovs
Noah Stephens-Davidowitz
Christoph Striecks
Shifeng Sun
Koutarou Suzuki
Alan Szepieniec
Katsuyuki Takashima
Rajdeep Talapatra
Qiang Tang
Titouan Tanguy
Phuc Thai
Radu Titiu
Junichi Tomida
Nikos Triandopoulos
Yiannis Tselekounis
Jorge L. Villar
Christine van Vredendaal
Sameer Wagh
Michael Walter
Yuntao Wang
Yuyu Wang
Yohei Watanabe
Gaven Watson
Florian Weber
Charlotte Weitkämper
Weiqiang Wen
Benjamin Wesolowski
Jeroen van Wier
Jan Winkelmann
Fredrik Winzer
Keita Xagawa
Chaoping Xing

Shota Yamada
Takashi Yamakawa
Avishay Yanai
Rupeng Yang
Eylon Yogev
Kazuki Yoneyama
Chen Yuan
Alexandros Zacharakis

Michal Zajac
Bingsheng Zhang
Yupeng Zhang
Zhenfei Zhang
Yi Zhao
Haibin Zheng
Arne Tobias Ødegaard
Morten Øygarden

This proceedings volume was prepared before the conference took place and it reflects its original planning, irrespective of the disruption caused by the COVID-19 pandemic.

Contents – Part II

Secure Computation and Related Primitives

Post-Quantum Primitives

Cryptanalysis and Concrete Security

Privacy-Preserving Schemes

Contents – Part I

Lattice-Based Cryptography

Lattice-Based Cryptography

The Randomized Slicer for CVPP: Sharper, Faster, Smaller, Batchier

Léo Ducas[1], Thijs Laarhoven[2], and Wessel P. J. van Woerden[1(✉)]

[1] CWI, Amsterdam, The Netherlands
wvw@cwi.nl
[2] TU/e, Eindhoven, The Netherlands

Abstract. Following the recent line of work on solving the closest vector problem with preprocessing (CVPP) using approximate Voronoi cells, we improve upon previous results in the following ways:

- We derive sharp asymptotic bounds on the success probability of the randomized slicer, by modelling the behaviour of the algorithm as a random walk on the coset of the lattice of the target vector. We thereby solve the open question left by Doulgerakis–Laarhoven–De Weger [PQCrypto 2019] and Laarhoven [MathCrypt 2019].
- We obtain better trade-offs for CVPP and its generalisations (strictly, in certain regimes), both with and without nearest neighbour searching, as a direct result of the above sharp bounds on the success probabilities.
- We show how to reduce the memory requirement of the slicer, and in particular the corresponding nearest neighbour data structures, using ideas similar to those proposed by Becker–Gama–Joux [Cryptology ePrint Archive, 2015]. Using $2^{0.185d+o(d)}$ memory, we can solve a single CVPP instance in $2^{0.264d+o(d)}$ time.
- We further improve on the per-instance time complexities in certain memory regimes, when we are given a sufficiently large batch of CVPP problem instances for the same lattice. Using $2^{0.208d+o(d)}$ memory, we can heuristically solve CVPP instances in $2^{0.234d+o(d)}$ amortized time, for batches of size at least $2^{0.058d+o(d)}$.

Our random walk model for analysing arbitrary-step transition probabilities in complex step-wise algorithms may be of independent interest, both for deriving analytic bounds through convexity arguments, and for computing optimal paths numerically with a shortest path algorithm. As a side result we apply the same random walk model to graph-based nearest neighbour searching, where we improve upon results of Laarhoven [SOCG 2018] by deriving sharp bounds on the success probability of the corresponding greedy search procedure.

Keywords: Lattices · Closest vector problem with preprocessing · Approximate Voronoi cells · Iterative slicer · Graph-based nearest neighbours

© International Association for Cryptologic Research 2020
A. Kiayias et al. (Eds.): PKC 2020, LNCS 12111, pp. 3–36, 2020.
https://doi.org/10.1007/978-3-030-45388-6_1

1   Introduction

Lattice Problems. Following Shor's breakthrough work on efficient quantum algorithms for problems previously deemed sufficiently hard to base cryptography on [26], researchers have began looking for alternatives to "classical" cryptosystems such as RSA [25] and Diffie–Hellman [10]. Out of these candidates for "post-quantum" cryptography [8], lattice-based cryptography has emerged as a leading candidate, due to its efficiency, versatility, and the conjecture that the underlying lattice problems may be hard to solve quantumly as well [23]. The security of most lattice-based cryptographic schemes can be traced back to either the shortest vector problem (SVP) or variants of the closest vector problem (CVP), which ask to either return the shortest non-zero vector in a lattice, or the closest lattice vector to a given target vector. These variants include approx-CVP, where we need to return a somewhat close lattice vector, and bounded distance decoding (BDD), where we are guaranteed that the target lies close to the lattice. As parameters for cryptographic schemes are commonly based on the estimated complexities of state-of-the-art methods for these problems, it is important to obtain a good understanding of the true hardness of these and other lattice problems. The current fastest approaches for solving these problems are based on lattice sieving [1,2,6] and lattice enumeration [3,4,14,15,17], where the former offers a better asymptotic scaling of the time complexity in terms of the lattice dimension, at the cost of an exponentially large memory consumption.

The Closest Vector Problem with Preprocessing (CVPP). The closest vector problem with preprocessing (CVPP) is a variant of CVP, where the solver is allowed to perform some preprocessing on the lattice at no additional cost, before being given the target vector. Closely related to this is batch-CVP, where many CVP instances on the same lattice are to be solved; if an efficient global preprocessing procedure can be performed using only the lattice as input, and that would help reduce the costs of single CVP instances, then this preprocessing cost can be amortized over many problem instances to obtain a faster algorithm for batch-CVP. This problem of batch-CVP most notably appears in the context of lattice enumeration for solving SVP or CVP, as a fast batch-CVP algorithm would potentially imply faster SVP and CVP algorithms based on a hybrid of enumeration and such a CVPP oracle [13,15].

Voronoi Cells and the Iterative Slicer. One method for solving CVPP is the iterative slicer by Sommer–Feder–Shalvi [27]. Preprocessing consists of computing a large list of lattice vectors, and a query is processed by "reducing" the target vector t with this list, i.e. repeatedly translating the target by some lattice vector until the shortest representative t' in the coset of the target vector is found. The closest lattice vector to t is then given by $t - t'$, which lies at distance $\|t'\|$ from t. For this method to provably succeed, the preprocessed list needs to contain all $O(2^d)$ so-called Voronoi relevant vectors of the lattice, which together define the boundaries of the Voronoi cell of the lattice. This leads to a $4^{d+o(d)}$ algorithm by bounding the number of reduction steps by $2^{d+o(d)}$ [21], which was later improved to an expected time of $2^{d+o(d)}$ by randomizing the algorithm such that the number of expected steps is polynomially bounded [9].

Approximate Voronoi Cells and the Randomized Slicer. The large number of Voronoi relevant vectors of a lattice, needed for the iterative slicer to be provably successful, makes the straightforward application of this method impractical and does not result in an improvement over the best (heuristic) CVP complexities without preprocessing. Therefore we fall back on heuristics to analyse lattice-based algorithms, as they often better represent the practical complexities of the algorithms than the proven worst-case bounds. For solving CVPP more efficiently than CVP, Laarhoven [18] proposed to use a smaller preprocessed list of size $2^{d/2+o(d)}$ containing all lattice vectors up to some radius, while heuristically retaining a constant success probability of finding the closest vector with the iterative slicer. Doulgerakis–Laarhoven–De Weger [12] formalized this method in terms of approximate Voronoi cells, and proposed an improvement based on rerandomizations; rather than hoping to find the shortest representative in the coset of the target in one run of the iterative slicer, which would require a preprocessed list of size at least $2^{d/2+o(d)}$, the algorithm uses a smaller list and runs the same reduction procedure many times starting with randomly sampled members from the coset of the target vector. The success probability of this randomized slicing procedure, which depends on the size of the list, determines how often it has to be restarted, and thus plays an important role in the eventual time complexity of the algorithm. Doulgerakis–Laarhoven–De Weger (DLW) only obtained a heuristic lower bound on the success probability of this randomized slicer, and although Laarhoven [20] later improved upon this lower bound in the low-memory regime, the question remained open what is the actual asymptotic success probability of this randomized slicing procedure, and therefore what is the actual asymptotic time complexity of the current state-of-the-art heuristic method for solving CVPP.

1.1 Contributions

Success Probability Asymptotics via Random Walks. Our main contribution is solving the central open problem resulting from the approximate Voronoi cells line of work – finding sharp asymptotics on the success probability of the randomized slicer. To find these sharp bounds, in Sect. 3 we show how to model the flow of the algorithm as a random walk on the coset of the lattice corresponding to the target vector, and we heuristically characterise transition probabilities between different states in this infinite graph when using a list of the $\alpha^{d+o(d)}$ shortest lattice vectors. The aforementioned problem of finding the success probability of the slicer then translates to: what is the probability in this graph of starting from a given initial state and ending at any target state of norm at most γ? From DLW [12] we know that we almost always reach a state of norm at most some $\beta = f(\alpha) \geq \gamma$ – reaching this state occurs with probability at least $1/\text{poly}(d)$. However, reaching a state $\beta' < \beta$ occurs only with exponentially small probability $2^{-\Theta(d)}$. Now, whereas the analysis of DLW

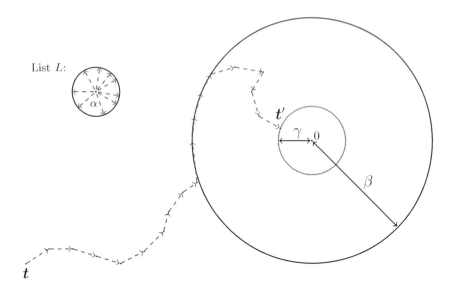

Fig. 1. The iterative slicer as a random walk over the coset $t + \mathcal{L}$ using the list of lattice vectors $L = \mathcal{L} \cap \mathcal{B}(\mathbf{0}, \alpha)$.

can be interpreted as lower-bounding the success probability by attempting to reach the target norm in a single step after reaching radius β, we are interested in the arbitrary-step transition probabilities from β to at most γ, so as to obtain sharp bounds (Fig. 1).

As every path in our graph from β to γ has an exponentially small probability in d, the total success probability is dominated by that of the highest probable path for large d; which after an appropriate log-transform boils down to a shortest path in a graph. Therefore obtaining the success probability of the randomized slicer is reduced to determining a shortest path in this infinite graph. We show in Sect. 4 how we can approximately compute this shortest path numerically, using a suitably dense discretization of the search space or using convex optimization. In Sect. 5 we go a step further by proving an exact analytic expression of the shortest path, which results in sharp asymptotics on the success probability of the randomized slicer for the general case of approx-CVP.

Heuristic claim 1 (Success probability of the randomized slicer). *Given a list L of the $\alpha^{d+o(d)}$ shortest lattice vectors as input, the success probability of one iteration of the randomized slicer for γ-CVPP equals:*

$$\mathbb{P}_{\alpha^2, \gamma^2} = \prod_{i=1}^{n} \left(\alpha^2 - \frac{(\alpha^2 + x_{i-1} - x_i)^2}{2x_{i-1}} \right)^{d/2 + o(d)} \tag{1}$$

with n defined by Eq. (39) and x_i as in Definition 7 depending only on α and γ.

Running the randomized slicer for $O(\mathbb{P}_{\alpha^2, \gamma^2}^{-1})$ iterations, we expect to solve γ-CVPP with constant probability. Together with a (naive) linear search over the

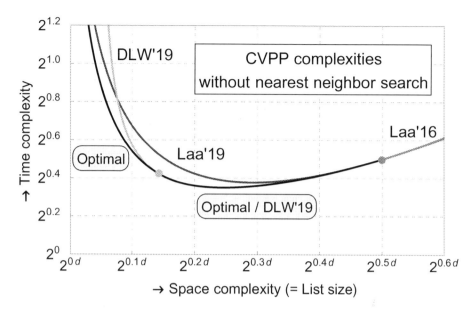

Fig. 2. Query complexities for solving CVPP **without** nearest neighbour techniques. The blue curve refers to [20], the red curve to [12], the green curve to [18], and the black curve is the result of our refined analysis. The red point indicates the point where red and black curves merge into one. (Color figure online)

preprocessed list, this directly leads to explicit time and space complexities for a plain version of the randomized slicer for solving CVPP, described in Fig. 2. When using a large list of size at least $2^{0.1437d+o(d)}$ from the preprocessing phase of CVPP, we derive that one step is optimal, thus obtaining the same asymptotic complexity as DLW. When using less than $2^{0.1437d+o(d)}$ memory we gradually see an increase in the optimal number of steps in the shortest path, resulting in ever-increasing improvements in the resulting asymptotic complexities for CVPP as compared to DLW.

Using a similar methodology the asymptotic scaling of our exact analysis when using $\text{poly}(d)$ memory matches the $2^{\frac{1}{2}d\log_2 d+o(d\log d)}$ time complexity lower bound of Laarhoven [20]. We do stress that to make this rigorous one should do a more extensive analysis of the lower order terms.

In Sect. 7 we further show how to adapt the graph slightly to analyse the success probability of the iterative slicer for the BDD-variant of CVP, where the target lies unusually close to the lattice.

Improved Complexities with Nearest Neighbour Searching. The main subroutine of the iterative slicer is to find lattice vectors close to a target in a large list, also known as the nearest-neighbour search problem (NNS). By preprocessing the list and storing more data we could find a close vector much

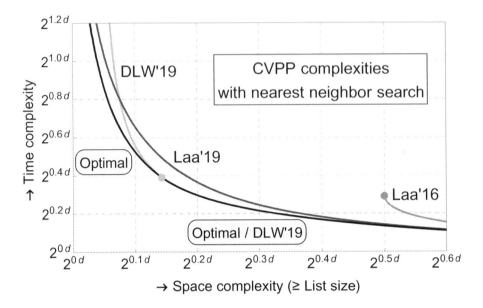

Fig. 3. Query complexities for solving CVPP **with** nearest neighbour techniques, but **without** the improved memory management described in Sect. 6. Similar to Fig. 2 the curves meet at a memory complexity of approximately $2^{0.1436d}$.

faster than the naive way of trying them all. Here we obtain a trade-off between the size of the NNS data structure and the eventual query complexity.

Heuristic claim 2 (Improved complexities for γ-CVPP). *Given a list L of the $\alpha^{d+o(d)}$ shortest lattice vectors as input and a nearest neighbour parameter $u \in (\sqrt{(\alpha^2 - 1)/\alpha^2}, \sqrt{\alpha^2/(\alpha^2 - 1)})$, we can solve CVPP in space and time S and T, where:*

$$S = \left(\frac{\alpha}{\alpha - (\alpha^2 - 1)(\alpha u^2 - 2u\sqrt{\alpha^2 - 1} + \alpha)} \right)^{d/2 + o(d)}, \tag{2}$$

$$T = \frac{1}{\mathbb{P}_{\alpha^2, \gamma^2}} \cdot \left(\frac{\alpha + u\sqrt{\alpha^2 - 1}}{-\alpha^3 + \alpha^2 u\sqrt{\alpha^2 - 1} + 2\alpha} \right)^{d/2 + o(d)}. \tag{3}$$

Figure 3 shows the resulting exact trade-offs for exact CVPP, as well as the previous lower bounds of [12,20].

Improved Memory Usage for the NNS Data Structure. When the number of NNS queries matches the list size there is a way to do the NNS preprocessing on the fly; obtaining significantly lower query times while using negligible extra memory [6,7]. Normally this observation is only helpful for batch-CVPP and not for a single CVPP instance, however the randomized slicer naturally reduces to batch-CVPP by considering all target rerandomizations as a batch of targets. In Sect. 6 we exploit this to obtain better CVPP complexities when using NNS; improving significantly on the state-of-the-art as shown in Fig. 4.

Heuristic claim 3 (Improved memory usage for CVPP with NNS).
Given a list L of the $\alpha^{d+o(d)} \leq 2^{0.185d}$ shortest lattice vectors as input we can solve a single CVPP instance with the following complexities:

$$S = \alpha^{d+o(d)}, \qquad T = \frac{1}{\mathbb{P}_{\alpha^2,1}} \cdot \left(\alpha \cdot \sqrt{1 - \frac{2 \cdot (1 - 1/\alpha^2)}{1 + \sqrt{1 - 1/\alpha^2}}} \right)^{-d+o(d)}. \qquad (4)$$

Heuristic claim 4 (Improved memory usage for batch-CVPP). *Given a list L of the $\alpha^{d+o(d)}$ shortest lattice vectors and a batch of at least B CVPP instances, with*

$$B = \max(1, \alpha^d \cdot \mathbb{P}_{\alpha^2,1}). \qquad (5)$$

Then we can solve this entire batch of CVPP instances with the following amortized complexities per CVPP instance:

$$S = \alpha^{d+o(d)}, \qquad T = \frac{1}{\mathbb{P}_{\alpha^2,1}} \cdot \left(\alpha \cdot \sqrt{1 - \frac{2 \cdot (1 - 1/\alpha^2)}{1 + \sqrt{1 - 1/\alpha^2}}} \right)^{-d+o(d)}. \qquad (6)$$

In particular, one can heuristically solve a batch of $2^{0.058d+o(d)}$ CVP instances in time $2^{0.292d+o(d)}$ and space $2^{0.208d+o(d)}$.

Note that this is a stronger result than DLW, which claimed it is possible to solve $2^{\Theta(d)}$ CVP instances in time and space $2^{0.292d+o(d)}$. In contrast, the best complexities for a single instance of CVP are time $2^{0.292d+o(d)}$ and space $2^{0.208d+o(d)}$, thus the algorithm proposed by DLW significantly increases the memory requirement for the batch of CVP instances. We show that we can also solve an exponential-sized batch of CVP instances without significantly increasing either the time or the memory.

Application to Graph-Based Nearest Neighbour Searching. Besides deriving sharp asymptotics for the randomized slicer, the random walk model may well be of independent interest in the context of analysing asymptotics of other complex step-wise algorithms, and we illustrate this by applying the same model to solve a problem appearing in the analysis of graph-based nearest neighbour searching in [19]: what is the success probability of performing a greedy walk on the k-nearest neighbour graph, attempting to converge to the actual nearest neighbour of a random query point? We formalize the transition probabilities in this context, and show how this leads to improved complexities for lattice sieving with graph-based nearest neighbour searching for solving SVP.

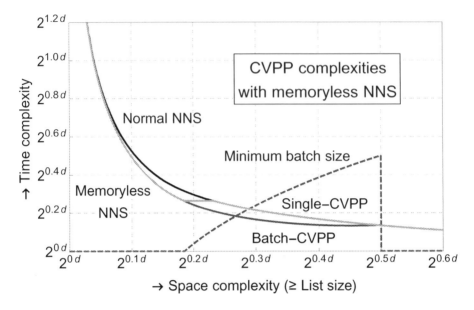

Fig. 4. Query complexities for solving CVPP and batch-CVPP **with** nearest neighbour techniques, and **with** the improved memory management outlined in Sect. 6, making the memory-wise overhead of the nearest neighbour data structure negligible, either for a single target (below space $2^{0.185d}$) or for batch-CVPP for sufficiently large batches (between space $2^{0.185d}$ and $2^{0.5d}$). The black curve equals the black curve from Fig. 3, the orange curve shows optimized complexities for CVPP using memoryless NNS whenever possible, and the red curve shows the optimized per-instance complexities for batch-CVPP for sufficiently large batch sizes; if the batch size exceeds the quantity indicated by the dashed red curve, then the amortized complexity is given by the solid red curve. (Color figure online)

1.2 Working Heuristics

While some of our intermediate results are entirely formal, the eventual conclusion on the behaviour of the iterative slicer also relies on heuristics. We restrict the use of "Theorem", "Lemma", and "Corollary" to the formal claims, and refer to "Heuristic claims" for the rest.

The first heuristic which we use is the commonly used Gaussian heuristic, which predicts the number of lattice vectors and their density within certain regions based on the lattice volume. Its use for analysing sieve-type algorithms is well established [6,7,18,22] and seems consistent with various experiments conducted in the past.

The second heuristic assumption we use is also central in previous work on the randomized iterative slicer [12,20], and consists of assuming that the input target can be randomized, yielding essentially independent experiments each time we randomize the input over the coset of the target vector. Practical experiments from DLW [12] seem to support this assumption.

The third heuristic is specific to this work, and consists of assuming that in our graph, the density over all successful paths taken by the slicing procedure is asymptotically equal to the density given by the most probable successful path. We suspect that this heuristic assumption can be formalized and justified following an analysis similar to the concentration bound result of Herold and Kirshanova [16]. We leave this question open for future work. Note that this heuristic is only needed to justify the sharpness of our analysis; even without it our results give lower bounds on the success probability of the iterative slicer.

2   Preliminaries

2.1   Notation

Let us first describe some basic notation. Throughout we will write $\|\cdot\|$ for Euclidean norms, and $\langle\cdot,\cdot\rangle$ for the standard dot product. Dimensions of vector spaces are commonly denoted by d. Vectors are written in boldface notation (e.g. $\boldsymbol{x}$). We denote d-dimensional volumes by $\mathrm{Vol}(\cdot)$.

2.2   Spherical Geometry

We write $\mathcal{B} = \mathcal{B}^d \subset \mathbb{R}^d$ for the unit ball, consisting of all vectors with Euclidean norm at most 1, and we write $\mathcal{S} = \mathcal{S}^{d-1} \subset \mathbb{R}^d$ for the unit sphere, i.e. the boundary of $\mathcal{B}^d$. More generally we denote by $\mathcal{B}(\boldsymbol{x}, \alpha)$ the ball of radius α around $\boldsymbol{x}$. Within the unit ball, we denote spherical caps by $\mathcal{C}_{\boldsymbol{x},\alpha} = \{\boldsymbol{v} \in \mathcal{B} : \langle \boldsymbol{x}, \boldsymbol{v} \rangle \geq \alpha\}$ for $\boldsymbol{x} \in \mathcal{S}$ and $\alpha \in (0,1)$, and we denote spherical wedges by $\mathcal{W}_{\boldsymbol{x},\alpha,\boldsymbol{y},\beta} = \mathcal{C}_{\boldsymbol{x},\alpha} \cap \mathcal{C}_{\boldsymbol{y},\beta}$ where $\boldsymbol{x}, \boldsymbol{y} \in \mathcal{S}$ and $\alpha, \beta \in (0,1)$. Note that due to spherical symmetry, the volume of $\mathcal{C}_{\boldsymbol{x},\alpha}$ is independent of the choice of $\boldsymbol{x}$, and the volume of $\mathcal{W}_{\boldsymbol{x},\alpha,\boldsymbol{y},\beta}$ only depends on the angle between $\boldsymbol{x}$ and $\boldsymbol{y}$. To obtain the relevant probability distributions for the treated algorithms we need the following asymptotic volumes.

Lemma 1 (Volume spherical cap). *Let $\alpha \in (0,1)$ and let $\boldsymbol{x} \in \mathcal{S}$. Then the volume of a spherical cap $\mathcal{C}_{\boldsymbol{x},\alpha}$ relative to the unit ball $\mathcal{B}$ is*

$$\mathcal{C}(\alpha) := (1 - \alpha^2)^{d/2 + o(d)}. \tag{7}$$

Lemma 2 (Volume spherical wedge). *Let $\alpha, \beta \in (0,1)$, let $\boldsymbol{x}, \boldsymbol{y} \in \mathcal{S}$, and let $\gamma = \langle \boldsymbol{x}, \boldsymbol{y} \rangle$. Then the volume of the spherical wedge $\mathcal{W}_{\boldsymbol{x},\alpha,\boldsymbol{y},\beta}$ relative to $\mathcal{B}$ is*

$$\mathcal{W}(\alpha, \beta, \gamma) := \begin{cases} \left(\frac{1 - \alpha^2 - \beta^2 - \gamma^2 + 2\alpha\beta\gamma}{1 - \gamma^2}\right)^{d/2 + o(d)}, & \text{if } 0 < \gamma < \min\left(\frac{\alpha}{\beta}, \frac{\beta}{\alpha}\right); \\ (1 - \alpha^2)^{d/2 + o(d)}, & \text{if } \frac{\beta}{\alpha} \leq \gamma < 1; \\ (1 - \beta^2)^{d/2 + o(d)}, & \text{if } \frac{\alpha}{\beta} \leq \gamma < 1. \end{cases} \tag{8}$$

2.3 Lattices

Given a set of linearly independent vectors $\mathbf{B} = \{\mathbf{b}_1, \ldots, \mathbf{b}_d\} \subset \mathbb{R}^d$, we define the lattice generated by the basis $\mathbf{B}$ as $\mathcal{L} = \mathcal{L}(\mathbf{B}) := \{\sum_{i=1}^d \lambda_i \mathbf{b}_i : \lambda_i \in \mathbb{Z}\}$. We denote the volume $\det(\mathbf{B})$ of the parallelepiped $\mathbf{B} \cdot [0,1]^d$ by $\det(\mathcal{L})$; this volume is independent of the choice of basis for a lattice. Given a basis of a lattice, the shortest vector problem (SVP) asks to find a lattice vector of minimum (non-zero) Euclidean norm in this lattice: if we let $\lambda_1(\mathcal{L}) = \min_{\boldsymbol{x} \in \mathcal{L} \setminus \{\boldsymbol{0}\}} \|\boldsymbol{x}\|$, then solving SVP corresponds to finding a vector $\boldsymbol{x} \in \mathcal{L}$ of norm $\lambda_1(\mathcal{L})$.

The analysis of lattice algorithms heavily depends on the Gaussian heuristic, as it better represents the practical complexity of the algorithms than their provable counterparts.

Heuristic 1 (The Gaussian heuristic (GH)). *Let $K \subset \mathbb{R}^d$ be a measurable body, then the number $|K \cap \mathcal{L}|$ of lattice points in K is approximately equal to $\mathrm{Vol}(K)/\det(\mathcal{L})$.*

Assuming this heuristic with K a Euclidean d-ball we obtain that $\lambda_1(\mathcal{L})$ has expected value $\sqrt{d/(2\pi e)} \cdot \det(\mathcal{L})^{1/d}$. For random lattices, which are the main target in the context of cryptanalysis, the Gaussian heuristic is widely verified and the following statement can be observed in practice.

Heuristic 2 (Lattice points in a ball, consequence of GH). *Let $\boldsymbol{t} \in \mathbb{R}^d$ be random. Under the Gaussian heuristic the ball of radius $\alpha \cdot \lambda_1(\mathcal{L})$ contains $\alpha^{d+o(d)}$ lattice points that we treat as being uniformly distributed over the ball.*

As a direct result a random target $\boldsymbol{t} \in \mathbb{R}^d$ is expected to lie at distance $\approx \lambda_1(\mathcal{L})$ from the lattice. This gives the following alternative statements for the common variants of the closest vector problem (CVP).

Definition 1 (Closest Vector Problem (CVP)). *Given a basis $\mathbf{B}$ of a lattice $\mathcal{L}$ and a target vector $\boldsymbol{t} \in \mathbb{R}^d$, find a vector $\boldsymbol{v} \in \mathcal{L}$ such that $\|\boldsymbol{t} - \boldsymbol{v}\| \leq \lambda_1(\mathcal{L})$.*

The hardness of most lattice-based cryptographic schemes actually depends on one of the following two easier variants.

Definition 2 (Approximate Closest Vector Problem (γ-CVP)). *Given a basis $\mathbf{B}$ of a lattice $\mathcal{L}$, a target vector $\boldsymbol{t} \in \mathbb{R}^d$ and an approximation factor $\gamma \geq 1$, find a vector $\boldsymbol{v} \in \mathcal{L}$ such that $\|\boldsymbol{t} - \boldsymbol{v}\| \leq \gamma \cdot \lambda_1(\mathcal{L})$.*

Definition 3 (Bounded Distance Decoding (δ-BDD)). *Given a basis $\mathbf{B}$ of a lattice $\mathcal{L}$, a target vector $\boldsymbol{t} \in \mathbb{R}^d$ and a distance guarantee $\delta \in (0,1)$ such that $\min_{\boldsymbol{v} \in \mathcal{L}} \|\boldsymbol{t} - \boldsymbol{v}\| \leq \delta \cdot \lambda_1(\mathcal{L})$, find a vector $\boldsymbol{v} \in \mathcal{L}$ such that $\|\boldsymbol{t} - \boldsymbol{v}\| \leq \delta \cdot \lambda_1(\mathcal{L})$.*

The preprocessing variants CVPP, γ-CVPP and δ-BDDP additionally allow to do any kind of preprocessing given only a description of the lattice $\mathcal{L}$ (and not the target $\boldsymbol{t}$). The size of the final preprocessing advice is counted in the eventual space complexity of the CVPP algorithm or variants thereof. In the remainder we assume without loss of generality that $\lambda_1(\mathcal{L}) = 1$.

Algorithm 1. The iterative slicer of [27]

    Input: A target vector $t \in \mathbb{R}^d$, a list $L \subset \mathcal{L}$.
    Output: A close vector $v \in L$ to t.
1 **Function** IterativeSlicer(L, t):
2     $t_0 \leftarrow t$;
3   **for** $i \leftarrow 0, 1, 2, \ldots$ **do**
4         $t_{i+1} \leftarrow \min\limits_{v \in L \cup \{0\}} \{t_i - v\}$;
5   **if** $t_{i+1} = t_i$ **then return** $t_0 - t_i$;

2.4   Solving CVPP with the Randomized Slicer

The (Randomized) Iterative Slicer. The iterative slicer (Algorithm 1) is a simple but effective algorithm that aims to solve the closest vector problem or variants thereof. The preprocessing consists of finding and storing a list $L \subset \mathcal{L}$ of lattice vectors. Then given a target point $t \in \mathbb{R}^d$ the iterative slicer tries to reduce the target t by the list L to some smaller representative $t' \in t + \mathcal{L}$ in the same coset of the lattice. This is repeated until the reduction fails or until the algorithm succeeds, i.e. when $\|t'\| \leq \gamma$. We then obtain the lattice point $t - t'$ that lies at distance at most γ to t. Observe that t' is the shortest vector in $t + \mathcal{L}$ if and only if $v = t - t' \in \mathcal{L}$ is the closest lattice vector to t.

To provably guarantee that the closest vector is found we need the preprocessed list L to contain all the Voronoi-relevant vectors; the vectors that define the Voronoi cell of the lattice. However most lattices have $O(2^d)$ relevant vectors, which is too much to be practically viable. Under the Gaussian heuristic, Laarhoven [18] showed that $2^{d/2+o(d)}$ short vectors commonly suffice for the iterative slicer to succeed with high probability, but this number of vectors is still too large for any practical algorithm. The randomized slicer (Algorithm 2) of Doulgerakis–Laarhoven–De Weger [12] attempts to overcome this large list requirement by using a smaller preprocessed list together with rerandomizations to obtain a reasonable probability of finding a close vector – the success probability of one run of the iterative slicer might be small, but repeating the algorithm many times using randomized inputs from $t + \mathcal{L}$, the algorithm then succeeds with high probability, without requiring a larger preprocessed list.

Because we can only use a list of limited size, one can ask the question which lattice vectors to include in this list L. Later in the analysis it will become clear that short vectors are more useful to reduce a random target, so it is natural to let L consist of all short vectors up to some radius. Let $\alpha > 1$ be this radius and denote its square by $a := \alpha^2$. The preprocessed list then becomes

$$L_a := \{x \in \mathcal{L} : \|x\|^2 \leq a\}. \tag{9}$$

Recall that we normalized to $\lambda_1(\mathcal{L}) = 1$ and thus under the Gaussian heuristic this list consists of $|L_a| = \alpha^{d+o(d)}$ lattice points, which determines (ignoring nearest neighbour data structures) the space complexity of the algorithm and

---

Algorithm 2. The randomized iterative slicer of [12]

Input: A target vector $t \in \mathbb{R}^d$, a list $L \subset \mathcal{L}$, a target distance $\gamma \in \mathbb{R}$.
Output: A close vector $v \in \mathcal{L}$, s.t. $\|t - v\| \leq \gamma$.

1 **Function** RandomizedSlicer(L, t, γ):
2   **repeat**
3         $t' \leftarrow$ Sample($t + \mathcal{L}$);
4         $v \leftarrow$ IterativeSlicer(L, t');
5   **until** $\|t' - v\| \leq \gamma$;
6   **return** $v + (t - t')$;

---

also determines the time complexity of each iteration. Until Sect. 7 we restrict our attention to the approximate case γ-CVPP where we have $\gamma \geq 1$, with $\gamma = 1$ corresponding to (average-case) exact CVPP. Throughout we will write $c := \gamma^2$.

Success Probability. The iterative slicer is not guaranteed to succeed as the list does not contain all relevant vectors. However, suppose that the iterative slicer has a success probability of $\mathbb{P}_{a,c}$ given a random target. It is clear that having a larger preprocessed list increases the success probability, but in general it is hard to concretely analyse the success probability for a certain list. Under the Gaussian heuristic we can actually derive bounds on $\mathbb{P}_{a,c}$, as was first done by DLW [12]. They obtained the following two regimes for the success probability as $d \to \infty$:

- For $a \geq 2c - 2\sqrt{c^2 - c}$ we have $\mathbb{P}_{a,c} \to 1$.
- For $a < 2c - 2\sqrt{c^2 - c}$ we have $\mathbb{P}_{a,c} = \exp(-C \cdot d + o(d))$ for $C > 0$.

The second case above illustrates that for a small list size the algorithm needs to be repeated a large number of times with fresh targets to guarantee a high success probability. This gives us the randomized slicer algorithm. To obtain a fresh target the idea is to sample randomly a not too large element from the coset $t + \mathcal{L}$, and assume that the reduction of this new target is independent from the initial one. Experiments from DLW suggest that this is a valid assumption to make, and given a success probability $\mathbb{P}_{a,c} \ll 1$ it is enough to repeat the algorithm $O(1/\mathbb{P}_{a,c})$ times to find the closest lattice point. However this success probability in the case $a < 2c - 2\sqrt{c^2 - c}$ is not yet fully understood. Two heuristic lower bounds [12,20] are known and are shown in Fig. 5. None of these lower bounds fully dominates the other, which implies that neither of the bounds is sharp. In the remainder of this work we consider this case where we have a small success probability.

3 The Random Walk Model

To interpret the iterative slicer algorithm as a random walk we first look at the probability that a target t is reduced by a random lattice point from the preprocessed list L_a. By the Gaussian heuristic this lattice point is distributed uniformly over the ball of radius α. To reduce $\|t\|^2$ from x to $y \in [(\sqrt{x} - \alpha)^2, x]$ by some v with $\|v\|^2 = a$, their inner product must satisfy:

$$\langle t, v \rangle < -(a + x - y)/2.$$

Using the formulas for the volume of a spherical cap we then deduce the following probability:

$$\mathbb{P}_{v \in \alpha \cdot \mathcal{B}^d} \left(\|t + v\|^2 \leq y \ \Big| \ \|t\|^2 = x \right) = \left(1 - \frac{(a + x - y)^2}{4ax} \right)^{d/2 + o(d)}. \tag{10}$$

Clearly any reduction to $y < (\sqrt{x} - \alpha)^2$ is unreachable by a vector in $\alpha \cdot \mathcal{B}^d$. The probability that the target norm is successfully reduced to some $y \leq \|t\|^2$ decreases in α and thus we prefer to have short vectors in our list. As the list L_a does not contain just one, but $a^{d/2}$ lattice vectors we obtain the following reduction probability for a single iteration of the iterative slicer:

$$\mathbb{P} \left(\exists v \in L_a : \|t + v\|^2 \leq y \ \Big| \ \|t\|^2 = x \right)^{2/d} \to \min \left\{ 1, a \cdot \left(1 - \frac{(a + x - y)^2}{4ax} \right) \right\}$$

as $d \to \infty$. Note that the reduction probability takes the form $\exp(-Cd + o(d))$ for some constant $C \geq 0$ that only depends on a, x and y. As we are interested in the limit behaviour as $d \to \infty$ we focus our attention to this base $\exp(-C)$, which we call the base-probability of this reduction and denote it by $p_a(x, y)$. Although these transition probabilities represent a reduction to any square norm $\leq y$, they should asymptotically be interpreted as a reduction to $\approx y$, as for any fixed $\varepsilon > 0$ we have that $p_a(x, y - \epsilon)^d / p_a(x, y)^d = 2^{-\Theta(d)} \to 0$ as $d \to \infty$. If $\|t\|^2 = x$ is large enough we can almost certainly find a lattice point in L_a that reduces this norm successfully. In fact a simple computation shows that this is the case for any $x > b := a^2/(4a - 4)$ as $d \to \infty$. So in our analysis we can assume that our target is already reduced to square norm b, and the interesting part is how probable the remaining reduction from b to c is.

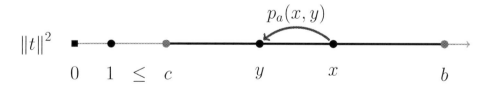

Definition 4 (Transition probability). *The transition base-probability* $p_a(x, y)$ *to reduce* $\|t\|^2$ *from* $x \in [c, b]$ *to* $y \in [c, x]$ *is given by*

$$p_a(x, y) : S_a \to (0, 1], \tag{11}$$

$$(x, y) \mapsto \left(a - \frac{(a + x - y)^2}{4x} \right)^{1/2}, \tag{12}$$

with $S_a = \{(x, y) \in [c, b]^2 : b \geq x \geq y \text{ and } \sqrt{x} - \sqrt{y} < \alpha\}$ the allowed transitions.

Using the above reduction probabilities we model the iterative slicer as a random walk over an infinite graph where each node $x_i \in [c, b]$ is associated with the squared norm $\|t_i\|^2$ of the partly reduced target. Note that each possible successful random walk $b = x_0 \to x_1 \to \cdots \to x_n = c$ has a certain success probability. Assuming the different steps are independent this success probability is just the product of the individual reduction probabilities. For an n-step path we could split our list L_a in n parts, one for each step, to obtain this independence without changing the asymptotic size of these lists. Again this success probability is of the form $\exp(-Cd + o(d))$ for some constant $C \geq 0$ that only depends on $x_0, \ldots, x_n$ and a.

Definition 5 (Path). *All decreasing n-step paths $x_0 \to x_1 \to \cdots \to x_n$ with positive probability from b to c are given by the set:*

$$S_a[b \xrightarrow{n} c] := \{(b = x_0, x_1, \ldots, x_n = c) \in \mathbb{R}^{n+1} : \forall i \; (x_{i-1}, x_i) \in S_a\}. \tag{13}$$

The transition base-probability of such a path is given by

$$P_a[b \xrightarrow{n} c] : S_a[b \xrightarrow{n} c] \to (0, 1], \tag{14}$$

$$\boldsymbol{x} \mapsto \prod_{i=1}^{n} p_a(x_{i-1}, x_i). \tag{15}$$

The success probability of reaching c from b is determined by the total probability of all successful paths. Note that all these paths have some probability of the form $\exp(-Cd + o(d))$ and thus the probability for the path with the smallest $C \geq 0$ will dominate all other paths for large d. As a result, almost all successful walks will go via the highest probable path, i.e. the one with the highest base-probability. After applying a log-transform this becomes equivalent to finding the shortest path in a weighted graph.

Definition 6 (Transition graph). *Let $V = [c, b]$ and $E = [c, b]^2$ be an infinite graph $G = (V, E)$ with weight function $w : E \to \mathbb{R}_{\geq 0} \cup \{\infty\}$ given by:*

$$w(x, y) = \begin{cases} -\log p_a(x, y), & \text{if } (x, y) \in S_a; \\ \infty, & \text{otherwise.} \end{cases} \tag{16}$$

One can associate n-step paths in this graph from b to c with the space $S_a[b \xrightarrow{n} c]$. The length of a path $\boldsymbol{x} \in S_a[b \xrightarrow{n} c]$ is denoted by $\ell_a[b \xrightarrow{n} c](\boldsymbol{x})$ and the shortest path length by

$$\ell_{a,opt}[b \to c] = \inf_{n \in \mathbb{Z}_{\geq 1}} \inf_{\boldsymbol{x} \in S_a[b \xrightarrow{n} c]} \ell_a[b \xrightarrow{n} c](\boldsymbol{x}). \tag{17}$$

Obtaining the success probability in this model therefore becomes equivalent to obtaining the length of the shortest path $\ell_{a,\text{opt}}[b \to c]$ as we have $P_a[b \xrightarrow{n} c](\boldsymbol{x}) = \exp(-\ell_a[b \xrightarrow{n} c](\boldsymbol{x}))$.

Algorithm 3. A discretized shortest path algorithm [11]

Input: Parameters a, b, c describing the graph, a discretization value k.
Output: A shortest path on the discretized graph from b to c.
1 **Function** DiscretizedDijkstra(a, b, c, k):
2   Compute $V_d = \{c + \frac{i \cdot (b-c)}{k} : i = 0, \ldots, k\}$;
3   Compute $E_d = \{(x, y) \in V_d^2 \cap S_a\}$ and the weights $w_a(x, y)$;
4   Compute shortest path on $G_d = (V_d, E_d)$ from b to c.

---

4 Numerical Approximations

We reduced the problem of obtaining the success probability of the iterative slicer to the search of a shortest path in a specially constructed weighted infinite graph. We might not always be able to find an exact solution in the input variables to the length of the shortest path. However for fixed parameters we can always try to numerically approximate the success probability, by approximating the shortest path in our infinite graph. We present two fairly standard methods for doing so. The first method first discretizes the infinite graph and then determines the shortest path using standard algorithms such as Dijkstra's algorithm [11]. The second method uses the fact that the weight function $w_a : S_a \to \mathbb{R}_{\geq 0}$ is convex.

4.1 Discretization

A natural way to approximate the shortest path in an infinite graph is to first discretize to a finite subgraph. Then one can determine the shortest path in this subgraph using standard methods to obtain a short path in the infinite graph. The details of this approach are shown in Algorithm 3.

Using any optimized Dijkstra implementation the time and space complexity of Algorithm 3 is $O(|E_d| + |V_d| \log |V_d|) = O(k^2)$. In general this method gives a lower bound on the success probability for any fixed a and c. Because the weight function $w_a : S_a \to \mathbb{R}_{\geq 0}$ is continuous Algorithm 3 converges to the optimal path length as $k \to \infty$. The C++ implementation of this method used for the experiments is attached in the complementary material of this work.

For this method to converge to the shortest path in the full graph we only need a continuous weight function. Furthermore the number of steps does not have to be specified a priori. The high memory usage of $O(k^2)$ could limit the fineness of our discretization. To circumvent this we can generate the edges (and their weight) on the fly when needed, which reduces the memory consumption to $O(k)$.

4.2 Convex Optimization

Where the first method only needed $w_a : S_a \to \mathbb{R}_{\geq 0}$ to be continuous, the second method makes use of the convexity of this function.

Lemma 3 (Convexity of S_a and w_a). *The set of allowed transitions S_a is convex and the weight function w_a is strictly convex on S_a.*

Proof. The convexity of $S_a = \{(x,y) \in [c,b]^2 : b \geq x \geq y$ and $\sqrt{x} - \sqrt{y} < \alpha\}$ follows immediately from the fact that $x \mapsto \sqrt{x}$ is concave on $[0, \infty)$. Remember that for $(x,y) \in S_a$

$$w_a(x,y) = -\log p_a(x,y) = -\frac{1}{2}\log\left(a - \frac{(a+x-y)^2}{4x}\right), \tag{18}$$

and thus we have

$$\frac{d^2}{dx^2}w_a(x,y) = \frac{8xp_a(x,y)^2 + (4a - 2(a+x-y))^2 - 16p_a(x,y)^4}{32x^2p_a(x,y)^4}, \tag{19}$$

$$\frac{d}{dy}\frac{d}{dx}w_a(x,y) = \frac{-8xp_a(x,y)^2 + (4a - 2(a+x-y)) \cdot 2(a+x-y)}{32x^2p_a(x,y)^4}, \tag{20}$$

$$\frac{d^2}{dy^2}w_a(x,y) = \frac{8xp_a(x,y)^2 + 4(a+x-y)^2}{32x^2p_a(x,y)^4}. \tag{21}$$

As $p_a(x,y) > 0$ and $a + x - y \geq a > 0$ for $(x,y) \in S_a$ we have $\frac{d^2}{dy^2}w_a(x,y) > 0$. We consider the Hessian H of w_a. Computing the determinant gives:

$$\det(H) = \frac{2(a+x-y)^4 \cdot (4ax - (a+x-y)^2)}{1024x^6p_a(x,y)^8} \tag{22}$$

and we can conclude that $\det(H) > 0$ from the fact that $4ax - (a+x-y)^2 > 0$ and $(a+x-y)^4 > 0$ for $(x,y) \in S_a$. So H is positive definite, which makes w_a strictly convex on S_a. □

Corollary 1 (Convexity of $S_a[b \xrightarrow{n} c]$ and $\ell_a[b \xrightarrow{n} c]$). *The space of n-step paths $S_a[b \xrightarrow{n} c]$ is convex and the length function $\ell_a[b \xrightarrow{n} c]$ is strictly convex on $S_a[b \xrightarrow{n} c]$ for any $n \geq 1$.*

Proof. The convexity of $S_a[b \xrightarrow{n} c]$ follows immediately from that of S_a. Note that $\ell_a[b \xrightarrow{n} c](\boldsymbol{x}) = \sum_{i=1}^{n} w_a(x_{i-1}, x_i)$ and thus it is convex as a sum of convex functions. Furthermore for each variable at least one of these functions is strictly convex and thus the sum is strictly convex. □

So for any fixed $n \geq 1$ we can use convex optimization to numerically determine the optimal path of n steps. In fact, because of the strict convexity, we know that this optimal path of n steps (if it exists) is unique. However the question remains what the optimal number of steps is, i.e. for which n we should run the convex optimization algorithm. We might miss the optimal path if we do not guess the optimal number of steps correctly. Luckily because $w_a(b,b) = 0$ by definition, we can increase n without being afraid to skip some optimal path.

Lemma 4 (Longer paths are not worse). *If $\ell_a[b \overset{n}{\to} c]$ and $\ell_a[b \overset{n+k}{\to} c]$ for $n, k \geq 0$ both attain a minimum, then*

$$\min_{\boldsymbol{x} \in S_a[b \overset{n}{\to} c]} \ell_a[b \overset{n}{\to} c](\boldsymbol{x}) \geq \min_{\boldsymbol{x} \in S_a[b' \overset{n+k}{\to} c]} \ell_a[b \overset{n+k}{\to} c](\boldsymbol{x}). \tag{23}$$

Proof. Suppose $\ell_a[b \overset{n}{\to} c]$ attains its minimum at $\boldsymbol{y} = (b = y_0, y_1, \ldots, y_n = c) \in S_a[b \overset{n}{\to} c]$. Using that $w_a(b, b) = 0$ we get that:

$$\min_{\boldsymbol{x} \in S_a[b' \overset{n+k}{\to} c]} \ell_a[b \overset{n+k}{\to} c](\boldsymbol{x}) \leq \ell_a[b \overset{n+k}{\to} c](b, \ldots, b = y_0, \ldots, y_n = c) \tag{24}$$

$$= k \cdot w_a(b, b) + \ell_a[b \overset{n}{\to} c](\boldsymbol{y}) \tag{25}$$

$$= \ell_a[b \overset{n}{\to} c](\boldsymbol{y}). \tag{26}$$

This completes the proof. □

So increasing n can only improve the optimal result. When running a numerical convex optimization algorithm one could start with a somewhat small n and increase it (e.g. double it) until the result does not improve any more.

4.3   Numerical Results

We ran both numerical algorithms and got similar results. Running the convex optimization algorithm gave better results for small $a = 1 + \varepsilon$ as the fineness of the discretization is not enough to represent the almost shortest paths in this regime. This is easily explained as $b \approx \frac{1}{4\varepsilon}$ and thus for fixed c the distance between b and c, i.e. the interval to be covered by the discretization quickly grows as $\varepsilon \to 0$.

The new lower bound that we obtained numerically for exact CVPP ($c = 1$) is shown in Fig. 5. For $\alpha \leq 1.1047$ we observe that the new lower bound is strictly better than the two previous lower bounds. For $\alpha > 1.1047$ the new lower bound is identical to the lower bound from [12]. Taking a closer look at the short paths we obtained numerically we see that $\alpha \approx 1.1047$ is exactly the moment where this path switches from a single step to at least 2 steps. This makes sense as in our model the lower bound from [12] can be interpreted as a 'single step' analysis. This also explains the asymptote for this lower bound as for $\alpha \leq 1.0340$ it is not possible to walk from b to $c = 1$ in a single step.

When inspecting these short paths $b = x_0 \to x_1 \to \cdots \to x_n = c$ further we observed an almost perfect fit with a quadratic formula $x_i = u \cdot i^2 + v \cdot i + b$ for some constants u, v. In the next section we show how we use this to obtain an exact analytic solution for the shortest path.

5   An Exact Solution for the Randomized Slicer

In order to determine an exact solution of the shortest path, and thus an exact solution of the success probability of the iterative slicer we use some observations

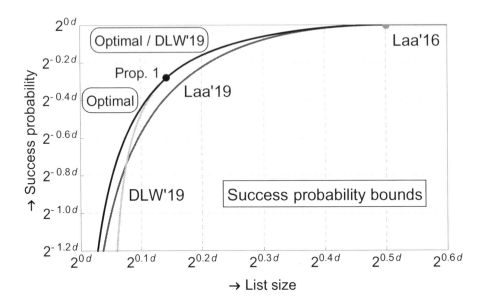

Fig. 5. Lower bounds on success probability of the iterative slicer for CVPP ($c = 1$) computed with a discretization parameter of $k = 5000$.

from the numerical results. Due to Corollary 1 we know that for any fixed $n \geq 1$ our minimization problem is strictly convex. As a result there can be at most one local minimum which, if it exists, is immediately also the unique global minimum.

In order to find an exact solution we explicitly construct the shortest n-step path using observations from the numerical section. Then showing that this path is a local minimum is enough to prove that it is optimal. We recall from Sect. 4.3 that the optimal path $x_0 \to \cdots \to x_n$ seems to take the shape $x_i = u \cdot i^2 + v \cdot i + b$ with $x_n = c$. So for our construction we assume this shape, which reduces the problem to determining the constants u, v. Furthermore, as we are trying to construct a local minimum, we assume that all partial derivatives in the non-constant variables are equal to 0. This gives enough restrictions to obtain an explicit solution.

Definition 7 (Explicit construction). *Let $n \geq 1$ and let*

$$x_i = u_a[b \xrightarrow{n} c] \cdot i^2 + v_a[b \xrightarrow{n} c] \cdot i + b, \tag{27}$$

with $u_a[b \xrightarrow{1} c] := 0$, $v_a[b \xrightarrow{1} c] := c - b$ and for $n \geq 2$:

$$u_a[b \xrightarrow{n} c] := \frac{(b + c - a)n - \sqrt{(an^2 - (b+c))^2 + 4bc(n^2 - 1)}}{n^3 - n}, \tag{28}$$

$$v_a[b \xrightarrow{n} c] := \frac{(a - 2b)n^2 + (b - c) + \sqrt{(an^2 - (b+c))^2 + 4bc(n^2 - 1)}\,n}{n^3 - n}. \tag{29}$$

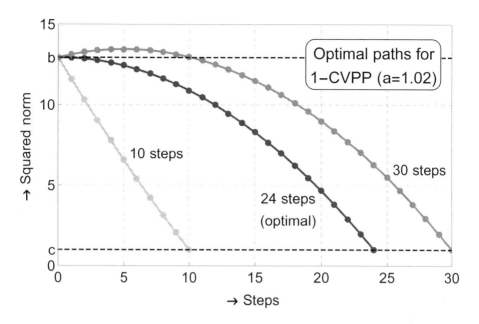

Fig. 6. Some examples of the constructed paths in Definition 7 for $a = 1.02, c = 1$.

Lemma 5. *By construction we have $x_n = c$ and*

$$\frac{\partial}{\partial x_i} \sum_{j=1}^{n} -\log p_a(x_{j-1}, x_j) = 0 \tag{30}$$

for all $i \in \{1, \ldots, n-1\}$.

Proof. Note that the partial derivative constraints can be reduced to the single constraint $\frac{\partial}{\partial x_i}\left(-\log p_a(x_{i-1}, x_i) - \log p_a(x_i, x_{i+1})\right) = 0$ for a symbolic i. Together with the constraint $x_n = c$ one can solve for u, v in $x_i = u \cdot i^2 + v \cdot i + b$. For a symbolic verification see the Sage script in Appendix A. □

What remains is to show that the explicit construction indeed gives a valid path, i.e. one that is in the domain $S_a[b \xrightarrow{n} c]$. An example of how these constructed paths look are given in Fig. 6. We observe that if n becomes too large these constructed paths are invalid as they walk outside the interval $[c, b]$. This is an artefact of our simplification that $w_a(x, y) = -\log p_a(x, y)$ which does not hold for $(x, y) \notin S_a$. We can still ask the question for which n this construction is actually valid.

Lemma 6 (Valid constructions). *Let $\frac{b-c}{a} \leq n < \frac{1}{2} + \frac{\sqrt{(4b-a)^2 - 8(2b-a)c}}{2a}$ and*

$$x_i = u_a[b \xrightarrow{n} c] \cdot i^2 + v_a[b \xrightarrow{n} c] \cdot i + b. \tag{31}$$

Then $\boldsymbol{x} = (x_0, \ldots, x_n) \in S_a[b \xrightarrow{n} c]$ and $\boldsymbol{x}$ is the unique minimum of $\ell_a[b \xrightarrow{n} c]$.

Proof. We have to check that $\boldsymbol{x}$ satisfies the two conditions

$$x_{i-1} \geq x_i \qquad \text{and} \qquad \sqrt{x_{i-1}} - \sqrt{x_i} < \alpha, \qquad (32)$$

for all $i \in \{1, \dots, n\}$. Note that for $n = 0$ we must have $b = c$ and the statement becomes trivial. For $n = 1$ we have $\boldsymbol{x} = (b, c)$ and the conditions follows from $0 \leq b - c \leq na \leq a$. So we can assume that $n \geq 2$. First we rewrite $u_a[b \xrightarrow{n} c]$ to:

$$u_a[b \xrightarrow{n} c] = \frac{(b + c - a)n - \sqrt{((b + c - a)n)^2 + (a^2 n^2 - (b - c)^2)(n^2 - 1)}}{n^3 - n}, \quad (33)$$

which makes it clear that $u_a[b \xrightarrow{n} c] \leq 0$ when $an \geq b - c$. As a result the differences

$$x_{i-1} - x_i = (1 - 2i) \cdot u_a[b \xrightarrow{n} c] - v_a[b \xrightarrow{n} c], \qquad (34)$$

are increasing in $i \in \{1, \dots, n\}$. Therefore for the first condition it is enough to check that

$$x_0 - x_1 = \frac{(b - c) + (2b - a)n - \sqrt{(an^2 - (b + c))^2 + 4bc(n^2 - 1)}}{n^2 + n} \geq 0. \quad (35)$$

In fact a solution with $x_0 = x_1 = b$ is not so interesting, so solving for $x_0 - x_1 > 0$ gives for $n \geq 2$ the sufficient condition

$$n < \frac{1}{2} + \frac{\sqrt{(4b - a)^2 - 8(2b - a)c}}{2a}. \qquad (36)$$

For the second condition we first show the stronger property that $x_{i-1} - x_i \leq a$, and again by the increasing differences it is enough to show that $x_{n-1} - x_n \leq a$; rewriting gives the following sufficient statement for $n \geq 2$:

$$-an + b - c \leq 0. \qquad (37)$$

Now we prove that $\sqrt{x_{i-1}} - \sqrt{x_i} < \alpha$. If $x_{i-1} = x_i$ the condition holds trivially, else $x_{i-1} > x_i$ and we get

$$(\sqrt{x_{i-1}} - \sqrt{x_i})^2 < (\sqrt{x_{i-1}} - \sqrt{x_i})(\sqrt{x_{i-1}} + \sqrt{x_i}) = x_{i-1} - x_i \leq a. \quad (38)$$

We conclude that $\boldsymbol{x} \in S_a[b \xrightarrow{n} c]$. As $\ell_a[b \xrightarrow{n} c](\boldsymbol{x}) = \sum_{i=1}^{n} -\log p_a(x_{i-1}, x_i)$ on $S_a[b \xrightarrow{n} c]$, the claim that this is a global minimum follows from Definition 7 and Lemma 1. $\qquad \square$

So by Lemma 7 there exists some $s \in \mathbb{N}$ such that for all $(b - c)/a \leq n \leq s$ we have an explicit construction for the optimal n-step path. By Lemma 4 we know that of these paths the one with $n = s$ steps must be the shortest. However for $n > s$ our construction did not work and thus we do not know if any shorter path exists. Inspired by Lemma 4 and numerical results we obtain the following alternative exact solution for $n > s$.

Theorem 1 (Optimal arbitrary-step paths). *Let n satisfy*

$$n = \left\lceil -\frac{1}{2} + \frac{1}{2a}\sqrt{(4b-a)^2 - 8(2b-a)c} \right\rceil. \tag{39}$$

For $k \geq n$ the unique global minimum of $\ell_a[b \xrightarrow{k} c]$ is given by

$$\boldsymbol{x} = (b, \ldots, b, b = y_0, \ldots, y_n = c) \in S_a[b \xrightarrow{k} c] \tag{40}$$

with $y_i = u_a[b \xrightarrow{n} c] \cdot i^2 + v_a[b \xrightarrow{n} c] \cdot i + b$ and the length is equal to $\ell_a[b \xrightarrow{n} c](\boldsymbol{y})$.

Proof. By Corollary 1 it is enough to show that $\boldsymbol{x}$ is a local minimum, therefore we check the partial derivatives. For $i > k-n$ we have $\frac{\partial}{\partial x_i}\ell_a[b \xrightarrow{k} c](\boldsymbol{x}) = \frac{\partial}{\partial x_i}\ell_a[b \xrightarrow{n} c](\boldsymbol{y}) = 0$ by construction. For $i < k-n$ we have $x_{i-1} = x_i = x_{i+1} = b$, which results in $\frac{\partial}{\partial x_i}\ell_a[b \xrightarrow{k} c](\boldsymbol{x}) = -\frac{a-1}{2b} < 0$. For the most interesting case $i = k-n$ we need that $n \geq -\frac{1}{2} + \frac{\sqrt{(4b-a)^2-8(2b-a)c}}{2a}$. Because as a result we get $y_0 - y_1 \leq \frac{a^2}{2b-a}$, which together with $y_0 - y_1 \leq b - c \leq b - 1$ is precisely enough to show that $\frac{\partial}{\partial x_{k-n}}\ell_a[b \xrightarrow{k} c](\boldsymbol{x}) \leq 0$.

To conclude let $\boldsymbol{z} \neq \boldsymbol{x} \in S_a[b \xrightarrow{n} c]$, then by Corollary 1 and using that $z_i - x_i = z_i - b \leq 0$ for all $0 \leq i \leq k-n$ we have:

$$\ell_a[b \xrightarrow{k} c](\boldsymbol{z}) > \ell_a[b \xrightarrow{k} c](\boldsymbol{x}) + \langle \boldsymbol{y} - \boldsymbol{x}, \nabla \ell_a[b \xrightarrow{k} c](\boldsymbol{x}) \rangle \tag{41}$$

$$= \ell_a[b \xrightarrow{k} c](\boldsymbol{x}) + \sum_{i \leq k-n} (z_i - x_i) \cdot \frac{\partial}{\partial x_i}\ell_a[b \xrightarrow{k} c](\boldsymbol{x}) \geq \ell_a[b \xrightarrow{k} c](\boldsymbol{x}). \tag{42}$$

and thus $\boldsymbol{x}$ is the unique global minimum of $\ell_a[b \xrightarrow{k} c]$. □

Corollary 2 (Optimal minimum-step paths). *The optimal path from b to c consists of n steps, with n defined by Eq. (39). The optimal path is of the form $b = x_0 \to x_1 \to \cdots \to x_n = c$ with $x_i = u_a[b \xrightarrow{n} c] \cdot i^2 + v_a[b \xrightarrow{n} c] \cdot i + b$.*

Heuristic claim 5. *Given the optimal path $b = x_0 \to \cdots \to x_n = c$ from Corollary 2, the success probability of the iterative slice algorithm for γ-CVPP is given by*

$$\exp\left(\sum_{i=1}^{n} w_a(x_{i-1}, x_i)d + o(d)\right). \tag{43}$$

As we have an exact formula for the optimal number of steps, and the lower bound from DLW [12] uses a 'single-step' analysis we know exactly in which regime Corollary 2 improves on theirs. Namely for those $a > 1$ and $c \geq 1$ such that for n defined by Eq. (39) we have $n > 1$. For exact CVPP we obtain

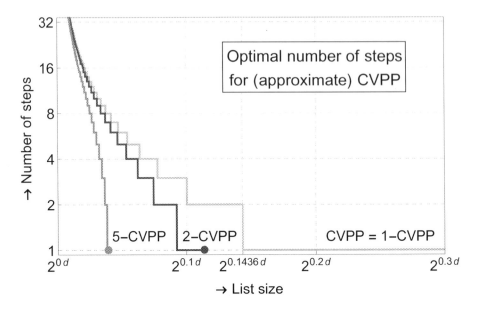

Fig. 7. Optimal number of steps n against the list size $|L| = \alpha^{d+o(d)} = a^{d/2+o(d)}$. We improve upon DLW whenever $n > 1$. For large list sizes the optimal number of steps of cost $\exp(-Cd + o(d))$ drops to 0, as then the success probability of the iterative slicer equals $2^{-o(d)}$.

improvements for $a < 1.22033$. This improvement can also be visualized through Fig. 7, which plots the optimal number of steps against the size of the preprocessed list. Whenever the optimal strategy involves taking more than one step, we improve upon DLW. For the crossover points where the number of optimal steps changes we have a more succinct formula for the shortest path and the success probability.

Lemma 7 (Success probability for integral n). *If n defined similar to Eq. (39), but without rounding up, is integral, then the optimal path from b to c has probability*

$$\left(\left(\frac{a}{2-a} \right)^n \cdot \left(1 - \frac{2n(a-1)}{2-a} \right) \right)^{d/2+o(d)} . \tag{44}$$

Proof. For such n we obtain the expression $x_i = b - (i+1) \cdot i \cdot \frac{a^2-a}{2-a}$. The result follows from simplifying the remaining expression. $\qquad\square$

Using this special case we can easily analyse the success probability in the low-memory regime.

Corollary 3 (Low-memory asymptotics). *For a fixed $\epsilon > 0$ and $a = 1 + \varepsilon$, the success probability of the optimal path from b to c equals $(2e\varepsilon + o(\varepsilon))^{d/2+o(d)}$.*

The above improves upon the lower bound of $(4\varepsilon + o(\varepsilon))^{d/2+o(d)}$ of Laarhoven [20]. Using a similar methodology to [20], to obtain a polynomial space complexity $a^{d/2+o(d)} = d^{\Theta(1)}$ we set $\varepsilon = \Theta(\frac{1}{d}\log d)$, resulting in a success probability of $e^{-\frac{1}{2}d\ln d + o(d\ln d)}$.

We nevertheless stress that drawing conclusions on the iterative slicer efficiency for $\epsilon = o(1)$ is far from rigorous: first the analysis assumes a space complexity of $a^{d/2+o(d)}$ for a constant $a > 1$; second, the optimal path now requires an non-constant number of steps, and the $o(d)$ terms in the exponent may accumulate to linear or super-linear terms. To make this more rigorous one would require do a more extensive analysis of the lower order terms.

6   Memoryless Nearest Neighbour Searching

Nearest Neighbour Searching Techniques. The main subroutine of the iterative slicer is to find lattice vectors close to a target t in a large list L, also known as the nearest neighbour search problem (NNS). By preprocessing the list and storing them in certain query-friendly data structures, we can find a close vector much faster than through the naive way of going through all vectors in the list. Generally we obtain a trade-off between the size of the NNS data structure (and the time to generate and populate this data structure) and the eventual query complexity of finding a nearest neighbour given a target vector.

A well known technique for finding near neighbours is locality-sensitive hashing (LSH). The idea is that a hash function partitions the space into buckets, such that two vectors that are near neighbours are more likely to fall in the same bucket than a general pair of vectors. Preprocessing then consists of indexing the list L in these buckets, for each of several hash functions. Using a hash table we then perform a quick lookup of all list vectors that lie in the same bucket as our query vector, to find candidate near neighbours. A query t is then answered by searching for a close vector in these buckets, one for each hash function, that corresponds to t. Given the correct parameters this leads to a query time of $|L|^{\rho+o(1)}$ for some $\rho < 1$. More hash functions giving finer partitions can reduce the query time at the cost of extra storage for the required number of hash tables.

Locality-sensitive filters (LSF) were later proposed as a generalization of LSH, where the space is not necessarily partitioned into buckets, but where regions can overlap – some vectors may end up in multiple buckets for one hash function, and some may end up in none of them. Currently the best nearest neighbour complexities for large lists are achieved by using spherical locality-sensitive filters [6].

Nearest Neighbour Search in Batches. The drawback of NNS data structures is that it can increase the memory usage significantly. As for the iterative slicer this memory could also be used for a larger list L, and thus giving a higher success probability, the current optimal time-memory trade-offs only spend a small amount of memory on the NNS data structure.

However as already introduced in [7] and later applied in [12,18] and [6], we can reduce the query time significantly without any extra memory in case we process multiple queries at the same time. Suppose we have $|L|$ targets, then to process all these queries we need as many hash computations as one would need for the precomputation of the list. As a result we could just process each hash function one by one on our list L and our list of targets. We immediately process the list and target vectors that fall in the same bucket. In the end this is equivalent to first preprocessing the list L and then running all queries one by one, however without using more than $\tilde{O}(|L|)$ memory. So we can achieve low amortized query times for large batches, without using any extra memory.

Lemma 8 (Batch NNS [6]). *Given a list of size* $|L| = \alpha^{d+o(d)}$ *uniformly distributed over* $\mathcal{S}^{d-1}$ *and a batch of targets of size* $|B| \geq |L|$, *we can solve the nearest-neighbour problem with an amortized cost per target of*

$$T = \left(a - \frac{2 \cdot (a-1)}{1 + \sqrt{1 - 1/a}} \right)^{-d/2} \tag{45}$$

using only $\alpha^{d+o(d)}$ *space.*

Batches from Rerandomization. Note that for the randomized slicer we naturally obtain a batch of rerandomized targets of size $|B| = O(1/\mathbb{P}_{a,c})$. In the case that the number of rerandomized targets is larger than the list size $|L|$ we could generate and process these targets in batches of $|L|$ at a time, therefore making use of optimal NNS parameters without any extra memory. This idea significantly improves the time-memory trade-off compared to the current state-of-the-art as shown in Fig. 4. Also note that in the higher memory regimes where we do not have enough rerandomized targets to do this, we still lower the necessary batch sizes for this technique to work by a factor one over the success probability.

Heuristic claim 6 (Improved memory usage for batch-CVPP with NNS). *Suppose we have a list of size* $|L| = \alpha^{d+o(d)}$, *and suppose we are given a batch of at least B γ-CVPP instances, with*

$$B = \max(1, \alpha^{d+o(d)} \cdot \mathbb{P}_{a,c}) \tag{46}$$

Then we can heuristically solve this entire batch of γ-CVPP instances with the following amortized complexities per CVPP instance:

$$S = \alpha^{d+o(d)}, \qquad T = \frac{1}{\mathbb{P}_{a,c}} \cdot \left(a - \frac{2 \cdot (a-1)}{1 + \sqrt{1 - 1/a}} \right)^{-d/2+o(d)}. \tag{47}$$

7   Bounded Distance Decoding with Preprocessing

We consider the success probability of the iterative slicer for bounded distance decoding. Instead of assuming that our target lies at distance $\lambda_1(\mathcal{L})$ of the lattice we get the guarantee that our target lies at distance $\delta \cdot \lambda_1(\mathcal{L})$ of the lattice. To incorporate this into our model we start with the same graph $G = (V, E)$ with $V = [1, b]$ and weight function w_a from Definition 6. However we add a single extra node $V' = V \cup \{\delta^2\}$ to the graph that represents our goal, i.e. the reduced target $\boldsymbol{t}'$ with norm δ.

We have to determine the base-probability of transitioning from a target $\boldsymbol{t}$ of squared norm x to our goal $\boldsymbol{t}'$ of norm at most δ using a lattice vector $\boldsymbol{v} \in L_a$. Because the reduction vector $\boldsymbol{v} = \boldsymbol{t} - \boldsymbol{t}'$ can assumed to be uniformly distributed over $\mathcal{B}(t, \delta)$ we obtain the following base-probability of the reduction:

$$
\mathbb{P}_{\boldsymbol{v} \in \mathcal{B}(t,\delta)}(\boldsymbol{v} \in L_a)^{2/d} \rightarrow
\begin{cases}
1, & \text{if } x \leq a - \delta^2, \\
\frac{-x^2 + 2x(\delta^2 + a) - (a - \delta^2)^2}{4x\delta^2}, & \text{if } a - \delta^2 < x < (\alpha + \delta)^2, \\
0, & \text{otherwise.}
\end{cases}
$$

as $d \rightarrow \infty$.

Given the base-probability that we can transition from a target $\boldsymbol{t}$ to our goal $\boldsymbol{t}'$ we extend the weight function on the edges (x, δ^2) in the natural way. As before we can now run the numerical approximation algorithm from Sect. 4.1 to obtain a lower bound on the success probability. The results are shown in Fig. 8 and improve on those from [12] in the low-memory regime. We do not see any restrictions for doing an exact analysis for BDDP similar to that of Sect. 5, but it is out of the scope of this paper. Also we expect these numerical results to be sharp, just as shown in the approximate CVPP case.

In Fig. 9 we show the resulting δ-BDDP time-memory trade-off with memory-intensive NNS, similar to Fig. 3. The memoryless NNS technique from Sect. 6 could also directly be applied for (batch-)BDDP, to obtain even better amortized complexities. We also note from Fig. 9 that, our bound for the time complexity δ-BDDP is always smaller than δ'-BDDP for $\delta < \delta'$, as one would naturally expect. This resolves another mystery left by the analysis of [12], for which this wasn't the case.

We observe that the BDD guarantee does not improve the success probabilities that much, certainly not in the low-memory regime. The iterative slicer algorithm does not seem to fully exploit the BDD guarantee. An explanation for this in the low-memory regime is that only the 'last' step can improve by the BDD guarantee. For all other steps, of which there are many in the low-memory regime, the BDD guarantee does not improve the transition probabilities. Therefore we cannot expect that the algorithm performs significantly better in the low-memory regime with that BDD guarantee than without. An open problem would be to adapt the iterative slicer to make better use of this guarantee.

8   Application to Graph-Based NNS

Besides nearest-neighbour search data structures based on locality-sensitive hashing or filters, as seen in Sect. 6, there also exists a graph based variant. Although graph based nearest-neighbour data structures have proven to be very

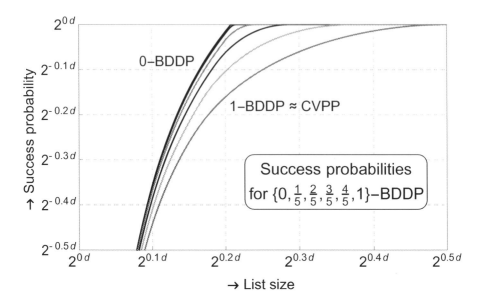

Fig. 8. Success probability of the iterative slicer for δ-BDDP with $\delta \in \{0, 0.2, 0.4, 0.6, 0.8, 1\}$, computed with a discretization parameter of $k = 5000$.

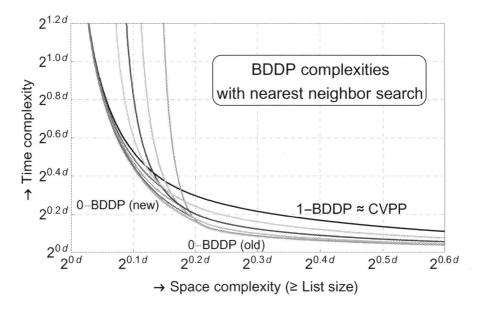

Fig. 9. Time complexities for δ-BDDP with memory-intensive nearest neighbour searching.

efficient in practice [5], the theoretical analysis has only been considered very recently [19,24]. Preprocessing consists out of constructing a nearest-neighbour graph of the list L and the query phase consists out of a greedy walk on this graph that hopefully ends at the closest vector to the given target.

Definition 8 (α-near neighbour graph). *Let $L \subset \mathcal{S}^{d-1}$ and $\alpha \in (0,1)$, we define the α-near neighbour graph $G = (V, E)$ with $V = L$ and $(\boldsymbol{x}, \boldsymbol{y}) \in E$ if and only if $\langle x, y \rangle \geq \alpha$.*

Given a target t, the query phase starts at some random node $\boldsymbol{x} \in L$ of the α-near neighbour graph. Then it tries to find a neighbour $\boldsymbol{y}$ of $\boldsymbol{x}$ in the graph that lies closer to t. This is repeated until such a closer neighbour does not exist any more or if a close enough neighbour is found. Note that for $\alpha \approx 0$ this is equivalent to a brute-force algorithm with time $O(N)$, however for larger α the number of neighbours can be much lower than N, possibly resulting in lower query times.

Just as for the iterative slicer there is no guarantee that the nearest neighbour of t is found. This success probability decreases as the graph becomes sparser, and just as for the iterative slicer we achieve a good probability of answering the query successfully by repeating the algorithm. The rerandomization in this case is achieved by starting the greedy walk at a different node of the graph.

In the context of lattice problems we are mainly interested in NNS in the setting that $|L| = (4/3)^{d/2}$, and thus we will focus on that, but our model is certainly not limited by this. In this setting the points in our list are uniformly distributed over the sphere. Laarhoven [19] was the first to formalize the success probability and this resulted in a lower bound using similar techniques as those used for DLW [12]. We show that this lower bound on the success probability is not sharp for all parameters α and our analysis gives the real asymptotic success probability, again using the random walk model.

In this case the distance measure is taken as the cosine of the angle $\langle v, t \rangle$ between the vector and the target. Note that in this setting the goal is to find a $v \in L$ such that $\langle v, t \rangle \geq \frac{1}{2}$ by greedily walking over the graph, decreasing this angle in each step if possible. Again given α we have some $\beta \leq \frac{1}{2}$ such that with high probability we end up at the some $v \in L$ with $\langle v, t \rangle \approx \beta$. So just as in Sect. 3 the success probability is determined by the highest probable path from β to $\frac{1}{2}$. The transition probability from x to y is equal to $(4/3)^{d/2} \cdot \mathcal{W}(\alpha, y, x)$ [19].

Heuristic claim 7 (Success probability of graph-NNS). *Let $L \subset \mathcal{S}^{d-1}$ be a uniformly distributed list of size $(4/3)^{d+o(d)}$. Let $\alpha \in (0, \frac{1}{2})$ and $\beta = \max\left(\frac{1}{2}, \sqrt{(1 - 4\alpha^2)/(5 - 8\alpha)}\right)$. Let $G = (V, E)$ be an infinite graph with $V = [\beta, \frac{1}{2}]$ and weight function*

$$w_{\alpha,nns}(x, y) = \min\left(0, -\frac{1}{2}\log\left(\frac{4}{3} - \frac{4}{3} \cdot \frac{\alpha^2 + y^2 - 2\alpha xy}{1 - x^2}\right)\right). \tag{48}$$

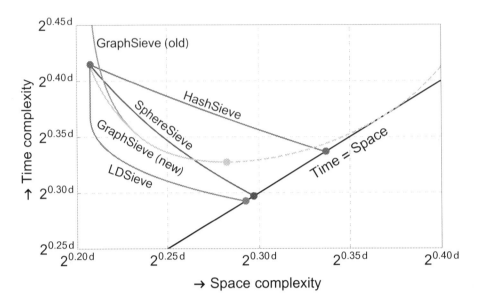

Fig. 10. Asymptotic exponents for heuristic lattice sieving methods for solving SVP in dimension d, using near neighbour techniques.

Let $x_0 \to \cdots \to x_n$ be the shortest path in G from β to $\frac{1}{2}$, then success probability of a single greedy walk in the α-near neighbour graph of L is given by

$$\exp\left(-\sum_{i=1}^{n} w_{\alpha,nns}(x_{i-1}, x_i)d + o(d)\right). \tag{49}$$

We do not see major problems in finding an exact solution for the shortest path, but this is out of the scope of this paper. The results from a numerical approximation using the techniques from Sect. 4 are shown in Fig. 10.

Acknowledgements. Leo Ducas was supported by the European Union H2020 Research and Innovation Program Grant 780701 (PROMETHEUS) and the Veni Innovational Research Grant from NWO under project number 639.021.645. Thijs Laarhoven was supported by a Veni Innovational Research Grant from NWO under project number 016.Veni.192.005. Wessel van Woerden was supported by the ERC Advanced Grant 740972 (ALGSTRONGCRYPTO).

Appendix A: Sage Code for Symbolic Verification

Sage code for the symbolic verification of the statements in this paper.

```
[1]: var('k','a', 'b', 'c', 'd', 'u', 'v', 'm', 'n', 'x', 'y', 'z')
     p(x,y) = a - (a+x-y)^2/(4*x)
     logp(x,y) = -log(p(x,y))/2
```

A.1 Lemma (Strict Convexity)

We check that the given partial derivatives in the Lemma are correct.

```
[2]:   d2x2 = (8*x*p(x,y) + (4*a-2*(a+x-y))^2 - 16*p(x,y)^2)/(2*(4*x*p(x,y))^2)
       dydx = (-8*x*p(x,y)+(4*a-2*(a+x-y))*2*(a+x-y))/(2*(4*x*p(x,y))^2)
       d2y2 = (8*x*p(x,y) + 4*(a+x-y)^2)/(2*(4*x*p(x,y))^2)
       detH = (2*(a+x-y)^4*(4*a*x-(a+x-y)^2))/(1024*x^6*p(x,y)^4)
       print 'd2x2 logp correct: ', (d2x2-logp.derivative(x).derivative(x)).is_zero()
       print 'd2y2 logp correct: ', (d2y2-logp.derivative(y).derivative(y)).is_zero()
       print 'dydx logp correct: ', (dydx-logp.derivative(x).derivative(y)).is_zero()
       print 'detH logp correct: ', (detH-d2x2*d2y2+dydx^2).is_zero()
```

```
       d2x2 logp correct:    True
       d2y2 logp correct:    True
       dydx logp correct:    True
       detH logp correct:    True
```

A.2 Definition (Explicit Constructions)

We check that the explicit construction indeed satisfies the mentioned properties.

```
[3]:   xx(k) = u*k^2 + v*k + b
       ly(x,y,z) = (logp(x,y) + logp(y,z))
       dlydy(x,y,z) = ly(x,y,z).derivative(y)
       sols = solve([dlydy(x=xx(k-1), y=xx(k), z=xx(k+1)) == 0, xx(m) == c], u,v)[0]
       uu = ((b+c-a)*m - sqrt((a*m^2-(b+c))^2+4*b*c*(m^2-1)))/(m^3-m)
       vv = ((a-2*b)*m^2+(b-c)+sqrt((a*m^2-(b+c))^2+4*b*c*(m^2-1))*m)/(m^3-m)
       print 'u correct: ', (sols[0].right()-uu).is_zero()
       print 'v correct: ', (sols[1].right()-vv).is_zero()
       print 'xx(m)==c: ', (xx(m)(u=uu,v=vv)-c).is_zero()
       print 'd/dy (logp(x,y)+logp(y,z)) (x=xx(k-1),y=xx(k),z=xx(k+1))(u=uu,v=vv)==0:
       ↪ ', dlydy(x=xx(k-1),y=xx(k),z=xx(k+1))(u=uu,v=vv).is_zero()
```

```
       u correct:    True
       v correct:    True
       xx(m)==c:    True
       d/dy (logp(x,y)+logp(y,z))  (x=xx(k-1),y=xx(k),z=xx(k+1))(u=uu,v=vv)==0:  True
```

A.3 Lemma (Valid Construction)

We check that the explicit construction is valid for

$$\frac{b-c}{a} \leq n < \frac{1}{2} + \frac{\sqrt{(4b-a)^2 - 8(2b-a)c}}{2\,a}$$

We first need to verify that $x_0 - x_1 > 0$. We do this by rewriting the problem to
that of showing that a degree 3 polynomial in n with positive leading coefficient
is negative. Our n is between the second and third root and thus we can conclude.

```
[4]: uu_rewritten = ((b+c-a)*m-sqrt(((b+c-a)*m)^2+(a^2*m^2-(b-c)^2)*(m^2-1)))/
     ↪(m^3-m)
     C = (b-c)+(2*b-a)*m
     D = (a*m^2-(b+c))^2+4*b*c*(m^2-1)
     print 'We define C = ', C(m=n), ', and D = ', D(m=n)
     x0subx1 = ((b-c)+(2*b-a)*m - sqrt((a*m^2-(b+c))^2+4*b*c*(m^2-1)))/(m^2+m)
     print 'u == u_rewritten', (uu-uu_rewritten).is_zero()
     print 'x_0 - x_1 == (C-sqrt(D))/(n^2+n)', (xx(0)-xx(1)-(C-sqrt(D))/
     ↪(m^2+m))(u=uu,v=vv).is_zero()
     DC = ((D-C^2)/m).simplify_full()
     print 'x_0 - x_1 > 0 is equivalent to (D-C^2)/n < 0', '(D-C^2)/n=', DC(m=n)
     E = sqrt((4*b-a)^2-8*(2*b-a)*c)/(2*a)
     print 'Let E=', E
     print '(D-C^2)/n has zeros n=1/2-E, n=-1, n=1/2+E', (DC(m=1/2-E).is_zero(),␣
     ↪DC(m=-1).is_zero(), DC(m=1/2+E).is_zero())
     print 'Because 1/2+E > n >= 2 we have n >= 2 > 1/2-E, so n is between the␣
     ↪second and third root of (D-C^2)/n'
     print 'We conclude that x_0 - x_1 > 0 for all 2 <= n < 1/2+E'
```

```
We define C =  -(a - 2*b)*n + b - c , and D =  4*(n^2 - 1)*b*c + (a*n^2 - b -
c)^2
u == u_rewritten True
x_0 - x_1 == (C-sqrt(D))/(n^2+n) True
x_0 - x_1 > 0 is equivalent to (D-C^2)/n < 0 (D-C^2)/n= a^2*n^3 + 2*a*b - 4*b^2
- 2*(a - 2*b)*c - (a^2 - 2*a*b + 4*b^2 + 2*(a - 2*b)*c)*n
Let E= 1/2*sqrt((a - 4*b)^2 + 8*(a - 2*b)*c)/a
(D-C^2)/n has zeros n=1/2-E, n=-1, n=1/2+E (True, True, True)
Because 1/2+E > n >= 2 we have n >= 2 > 1/2-E, so n is between the second and
third root of (D-C^2)/n
We conclude that x_0 - x_1 > 0 for all 2 <= n < 1/2+E
```

Next we check that $x_n - 1 - x_n <= a$ for $n >= \max(2, (b - c)/a)$, again by rewriting the equations.

```
[5]: xmsub = ((a - 2*c)*m + b - c + sqrt(a^2*m^4 - 2*(a*b + (a - 2*b)*c)*m^2 +␣
     ↪b^2 - 2*b*c + c^2))/(m^2 + m)
     eq = (xmsub <= a)
     eq2 = (eq * (m^2+m) - ((a-2*c)*m+b-c))
     print 'x_n-1 - x_n <= a is for n > 1 equivalent to', eq2.left().
     ↪simplify_full()(m=n), '<=', eq2.right().simplify_full()(m=n)
     print 'Using that n<=(b-c)/a and b+c >= 2 >= a the right hand side is␣
     ↪non-negative, so we can square both sides. Further rewriting gives us'
     eq3 = ((eq2)^2 - ((m^2 + m)*a - (a - 2*c)*m - b + c)^2)/(m*(m+1)*4*c)
     print 'the equivalent statement', eq3.left().simplify_full()(m=n), '<=', eq3.
     ↪right(), 'and we can conclude.'
```

```
x_n-1 - x_n <= a is for n > 1 equivalent to sqrt(a^2*n^4 - 2*(a*b + (a -
2*b)*c)*n^2 + b^2 - 2*b*c + c^2) <= a*n^2 + 2*c*n - b + c
Using that n<=(b-c)/a and b+c >= 2 >= a the right hand side is non-negative, so
we can square both sides. Further rewriting gives us
the equivalent statement -a*n + b - c <= 0 and we can conclude.
```

A.4 Theorem (Optimal Arbitrary-Length Paths)

The case $i < k - n$ is easily verified

```
[6]: print 'd/dy (logp(x,y)+logp(y,z))(x=b,y=b,z=b) == -(a-1)/
     ↪(2*b)',(dlydy(x=b,y=b,z=b) - (-(a-1)/(2*b)))(b=a^2/(4*a-4)).is_zero()
```

```
d/dy (logp(x,y)+logp(y,z))(x=b,y=b,z=b) == -(a-1)/(2*b) True
```

For the case $i = k - n$ we first show that $y_0 - y_1 <= a^2/(2b - a)$.

```
[7]: Y=m^2+m
     X=a^2/(2*b-a)
     print 'We define X = ', X, ', and Y = ', Y
     print 'y_0-y_1 = (C-sqrt(D))/Y <= X is equivalent to (C-XY)^2 <= D'
     df = ((C-X*Y)^2-D).simplify_full()
     print '(C-XY)^2-D =', df
     print '(C-XY)^2-D is of degree 4 and has roots -1/2-E, -1,0, -1/2+E', df(m=-1/
     ↪2-E).is_zero(), df(m=-1).is_zero(), df(m=0).is_zero(), df(m=-1/2+E).
     ↪is_zero()
     print 'If n>=2 and n>=-1/2+E, than n is larger than all roots, so␣
     ↪(C-XY)^2-D<=0 because the leading coeff is negative and we can conclude.'
```

```
We define X =   -a^2/(a - 2*b) , and Y =   m^2 + m
y_0-y_1 = (C-sqrt(D))/Y <= X is equivalent to (C-XY)^2 <= D
(C-XY)^2-D = 4*((a^3*b - a^2*b^2)*m^4 + 2*(a^3*b - a^2*b^2)*m^3 + (a^3*b +
a^2*b^2 - 6*a*b^3 + 4*b^4 - 2*(a^2*b - 3*a*b^2 + 2*b^3)*c)*m^2 + 2*(a^2*b^2 -
3*a*b^3 + 2*b^4 - (a^2*b - 3*a*b^2 + 2*b^3)*c)*m)/(a^2 - 4*a*b + 4*b^2)
(C-XY)^2-D is of degree 4 and has roots -1/2-E, -1,0, -1/2+E True True True␣
↪True
If n>=2 and n>=-1/2+E, than n is larger than all roots, so (C-XY)^2-D<=0␣
↪because
the leading coeff is negative and we can conclude.
```

Now we show that $d := y_0 - y_1 \le \min(a^2/(2b - a), b - 1)$ is sufficient to show that the partial derivative at $i = n - k$ is non-positive.

```
[8]:  print('We want to show that d/dy (logp(x,y)+logp(y,z))(x=b,y=b,z=b-d) <= 0
      ↪for d <= min(X, b-1)')
      F = -(2*a^4 - 4*a^3 - (a^3 - 4*a^2 + 5*a - 2)*d^2 + 2*a^2 - (2*a^4 - 7*a^3 +
      ↪9*a^2 - 4*a)*d)
      G = (a^4 - (a^3 - a^2)*d^2 - 2*(a^4 - a^3)*d)
      print 'We have d/dy (logp(x,y)+logp(y,z))(x=b,y=b,z=b-d) = F/G with'
      print 'F=', F
      print 'G=', G
      print (dlydy(x=b,y=b,z=b-d)(b=a^2/(4*a-4)).simplify_full()-F/G).is_zero()
      print 'We first show that G > 0. Note that G is decreasing in d>0.'
      print 'If a < 4/3, then b>a and thus d <= a^2/(2*b-a) < a^2/(2*a-a) = a.'
      print 'We get G >= G(d=a) > 0 in the interval', solve([G(d=a)>0], a)[1]
      print 'If a >= 4/3, then b<=4/3 and thus d <= b-1 <= 1/3. '
      print 'We get G >= G(d=1/3) > 0 in the interval', solve([G(d=1/3)>0], a)[2]
      print 'Note that F is of degree 2 with roots X and a/(a-1)', F(d=X)(b=a^2/
      ↪(4*a-4)).is_zero(), F(d=a/(a-1)).is_zero()
      print 'F has leading coefficient (a^3 - 4*a^2 + 5*a - 2) which is negative
      ↪in the interval', solve([(a^3 - 4*a^2 + 5*a - 2)<0],a)[1]
      print 'As d <= min(X, b-1) <= min(X, a/(a-1)) is smaller than both roots in
      ↪the interval', solve([a^2/(4*a-4)-1 < a/(a-1)], a)[1],'we have F(d) <= 0
      ↪and we can conclude.'
```

```
We want to show that d/dy (logp(x,y)+logp(y,z))(x=b,y=b,z=b-d) <= 0 for d <=
min(X, b-1)
We have d/dy (logp(x,y)+logp(y,z))(x=b,y=b,z=b-d) = F/G with
F= -2*a^4 + 4*a^3 + (a^3 - 4*a^2 + 5*a - 2)*d^2 - 2*a^2 + (2*a^4 - 7*a^3 +
↪9*a^2
- 4*a)*d
G= a^4 - (a^3 - a^2)*d^2 - 2*(a^4 - a^3)*d
True
We first show that G > 0. Note that G is decreasing in d>0.
If a < 4/3, then b>a and thus d <= a^2/(2*b-a) < a^2/(2*a-a) = a.
We get G >= G(d=a) > 0 in the interval [a > 0, a < (4/3)]
If a >= 4/3, then b<=4/3 and thus d <= b-1 <= 1/3.
We get G >= G(d=1/3) > 0 in the interval [a > 0]
Note that F is of degree 2 with roots X and a/(a-1) True True
F has leading coefficient (a^3 - 4*a^2 + 5*a - 2) which is negative in the
interval [a > 1, a < 2]
As d <= min(X, b-1) <= min(X, a/(a-1)) is smaller than both roots in the
interval [a > 1, a < 2*sqrt(3) + 4] we have F(d) <= 0 and we can conclude.
```

A.5 Proposition (Low-Memory Asymptotics)

```
[9]:  A.<z> = AsymptoticRing(growth_group='z^QQ', coefficient_ring=ZZ);
      a = 1+1/z
      b = a^2/(4*a-4)
      n = -1/2 + sqrt((4*b-a)^2-8*(2*b-a))/(2*a)
      print'asymptotic cost with c=1 as a=1+eps for eps = 1/z -> 0.'
      print'n - 1/(2*eps) + O(1) = ', n - 1/2*z + O(z^0)
      print'So (a/(2-a))^n = ((1+eps)/(1-eps))^(1/(2*eps)) = e + O(eps)'
      print'1-(2*n*(a-1))/(2-a) - 2*eps + O(eps^2) = ', (1-(2*n*(a-1))/(2-a)) - 2/
      ↪z + O(1/z^2)
      print'So success probability ~(2*e*eps)^(d/2)'
```

```
asymptotic cost with c=1 as a=1+eps for eps = 1/z -> 0.
n - 1/(2*eps) + O(1) =  O(1)
So (a/(2-a))^n = ((1+eps)/(1-eps))^(1/(2*eps)) = e + O(eps)
1-(2*n*(a-1))/(2-a) - 2*eps + O(eps^2) =  O(z^(-2))
So success probability ~(2*e*eps)^(d/2)
```

References

1. Ajtai, M., Kumar, R., Sivakumar, D.: A sieve algorithm for the shortest lattice vector problem. In: STOC, pp. 601–610 (2001)
2. Albrecht, M.R., Ducas, L., Herold, G., Kirshanova, E., Postlethwaite, E.W., Stevens, M.: The general sieve kernel and new records in lattice reduction. In: Ishai, Y., Rijmen, V. (eds.) EUROCRYPT 2019. LNCS, vol. 11477, pp. 717–746. Springer, Cham (2019). https://doi.org/10.1007/978-3-030-17656-3_25
3. Aono, Y., Nguyen, P.Q.: Random sampling revisited: lattice enumeration with discrete pruning. In: Coron, J.-S., Nielsen, J.B. (eds.) EUROCRYPT 2017. LNCS, vol. 10211, pp. 65–102. Springer, Cham (2017). https://doi.org/10.1007/978-3-319-56614-6_3
4. Aono, Y., Nguyen, P.Q., Shen, Y.: Quantum lattice enumeration and tweaking discrete pruning. In: Peyrin, T., Galbraith, S. (eds.) ASIACRYPT 2018. LNCS, vol. 11272, pp. 405–434. Springer, Cham (2018). https://doi.org/10.1007/978-3-030-03326-2_14
5. Aumüller, M., Bernhardsson, E., Faithfull, A.: ANN-benchmarks: a benchmarking tool for approximate nearest neighbor algorithms. Inf. Syst. **87**, 1–13 (2020)
6. Becker, A., Ducas, L., Gama, N., Laarhoven, T.: New directions in nearest neighbor searching with applications to lattice sieving. In: SODA, pp. 10–24 (2016)
7. Becker, A., Gama, N., Joux, A.: Speeding-up lattice sieving without increasing the memory, using sub-quadratic nearest neighbor search. IACR Cryptology ePrint Archive 2015, p. 522 (2015)
8. Bernstein, D.J., Buchmann, J., Dahmen, E. (eds.): Post-Quantum Cryptography. Springer, Heidelberg (2009). https://doi.org/10.1007/978-3-540-88702-7
9. Dadush, D., Bonifas, N.: Short paths on the Voronoi graph and closest vector problem with preprocessing. In: Proceedings of the Twenty-Sixth Annual ACM-SIAM Symposium on Discrete Algorithms, pp. 295–314. Society for Industrial and Applied Mathematics (2015)
10. Diffie, W., Hellman, M.E.: New directions in cryptography. IEEE Trans. Inf. Theory **22**(6), 644–654 (1976)
11. Dijkstra, E.W.: A note on two problems in connexion with graphs. Numer. Math. **1**(1), 269–271 (1959)
12. Doulgerakis, E., Laarhoven, T., de Weger, B.: Finding closest lattice vectors using approximate Voronoi cells. In: Ding, J., Steinwandt, R. (eds.) PQCrypto 2019. LNCS, vol. 11505, pp. 3–22. Springer, Cham (2019). https://doi.org/10.1007/978-3-030-25510-7_1
13. Doulgerakis, E., Laarhoven, T., de Weger, B.: A lattice enumeration-sieving hybrid for SVP based on batch-CVP. Draft (2019)
14. Fincke, U., Pohst, M.: Improved methods for calculating vectors of short length in a lattice. Math. Comput. **44**(170), 463–471 (1985)
15. Gama, N., Nguyen, P.Q., Regev, O.: Lattice enumeration using extreme pruning. In: Gilbert, H. (ed.) EUROCRYPT 2010. LNCS, vol. 6110, pp. 257–278. Springer, Heidelberg (2010). https://doi.org/10.1007/978-3-642-13190-5_13
16. Herold, G., Kirshanova, E.: Improved algorithms for the approximate k-list problem in Euclidean norm. In: Fehr, S. (ed.) PKC 2017. LNCS, vol. 10174, pp. 16–40. Springer, Heidelberg (2017). https://doi.org/10.1007/978-3-662-54365-8_2
17. Kannan, R.: Improved algorithms for integer programming and related lattice problems. In: STOC, pp. 193–206 (1983)

18. Laarhoven, T.: Sieving for closest lattice vectors (with preprocessing). In: Avanzi, R., Heys, H. (eds.) SAC 2016. LNCS, vol. 10532, pp. 523–542. Springer, Cham (2017). https://doi.org/10.1007/978-3-319-69453-5_28
19. Laarhoven, T.: Graph-based time-space trade-offs for approximate near neighbors. In: SOCG (2018)
20. Laarhoven, T.: Approximate Voronoi cells for lattices, revisited. In: MathCrypt (2019)
21. Micciancio, D., Voulgaris, P.: A deterministic single exponential time algorithm for most lattice problems based on Voronoi cell computations. SIAM J. Comput. **42**(3), 1364–1391 (2013)
22. Nguyen, P.Q., Vidick, T.: Sieve algorithms for the shortest vector problem are practical. J. Math. Cryptol. **2**(2), 181–207 (2008)
23. Peikert, C.: A decade of lattice cryptography. Found. Trends Theor. Comput. Sci. **10**, 283–424 (2016)
24. Prokhorenkova, L.: Graph-based nearest neighbor search: from practice to theory (2019). arXiv:1907.00845 [cs.DS]
25. Rivest, R.L., Shamir, A., Adleman, L.: A method for obtaining digital signatures and public-key cryptosystems. Commun. ACM **21**(2), 120–126 (1978)
26. Shor, P.W.: Algorithms for quantum computation: discrete logarithms and factoring. In: FOCS, pp. 124–134 (1994)
27. Sommer, N., Feder, M., Shalvi, O.: Finding the closest lattice point by iterative slicing. SIAM J. Discret. Math. **23**(2), 715–731 (2009)

Tweaking the Asymmetry
of Asymmetric-Key Cryptography
on Lattices: KEMs and Signatures
of Smaller Sizes

Jiang Zhang[1]($\boxtimes$), Yu Yu[2]($\boxtimes$), Shuqin Fan[1]($\boxtimes$), Zhenfeng Zhang[3]($\boxtimes$),
and Kang Yang[1]($\boxtimes$)

[1] State Key Laboratory of Cryptology, P.O. Box 5159, Beijing 100878, China
jiangzhang09@gmail.com, shuqinfan78@163.com, yangk@sklc.org
[2] Department of Computer Science and Engineering,
Shanghai Jiao Tong University, Shanghai, China
yuyu@yuyu.hk
[3] Trusted Computing and Information Assurance Laboratory,
Institute of Software, Chinese Academy of Sciences, Beijing, China
zfzhang@tca.iscas.ac.cn

Abstract. Currently, lattice-based cryptosystems are less efficient than their number-theoretic counterparts (based on RSA, discrete logarithm, etc.) in terms of key and ciphertext (signature) sizes. For adequate security the former typically needs thousands of bytes while in contrast the latter only requires at most hundreds of bytes. This significant difference has become one of the main concerns in replacing currently deployed public-key cryptosystems with lattice-based ones. Observing the inherent asymmetries in existing lattice-based cryptosystems, we propose asymmetric variants of the (module-)LWE and (module-)SIS assumptions, which yield further size-optimized KEM and signature schemes than those from standard counterparts.

Following the framework of Lindner and Peikert (CT-RSA 2011) and the Crystals-Kyber proposal (EuroS&P 2018), we propose an IND-CCA secure KEM scheme from the hardness of the asymmetric module-LWE (AMLWE), whose asymmetry is fully exploited to obtain shorter public keys and ciphertexts. To target at a 128-bit quantum security, the public key (resp., ciphertext) of our KEM only has 896 bytes (resp., 992 bytes).

Our signature scheme bears most resemblance to and improves upon the Crystals-Dilithium scheme (ToCHES 2018). By making full use of the underlying asymmetric module-LWE and module-SIS assumptions and carefully selecting the parameters, we construct an SUF-CMA secure signature scheme with shorter public keys and signatures. For a 128-bit quantum security, the public key (resp., signature) of our signature scheme only has 1312 bytes (resp., 2445 bytes).

We adapt the best known attacks and their variants to our AMLWE and AMSIS problems and conduct a comprehensive and thorough analysis of several parameter choices (aiming at different security strengths) and their impacts on the sizes, security and error probability of

© International Association for Cryptologic Research 2020
A. Kiayias et al. (Eds.): PKC 2020, LNCS 12111, pp. 37–65, 2020.
https://doi.org/10.1007/978-3-030-45388-6_2

lattice-based cryptosystems. Our analysis demonstrates that AMLWE and AMSIS problems admit more flexible and size-efficient choices of parameters than the respective standard versions.

1   Introduction

Despite the tremendous success of traditional public-key cryptography (also known as asymmetric-key cryptography), the typical public-key cryptosystems in widespread deployment on the Internet are based on number-theoretic hardness assumptions such as factoring and discrete logarithms, and thus are susceptible to quantum attacks [31] if large-scale quantum computers become a reality. With the advancement of quantum computing technology in recent years [19], developing post-quantum cryptography (PQC) with resistance to both classical and quantum computers has become a primary problem as well as a priority issue for the crypto community. Actually, several government agencies and standardization organizations have announced plans to solicit and standardize PQC algorithms. In 2015, the NSA [28] has announced its schedule for migration to PQC. In 2016, the NIST initiated its standardization process for post-quantum public-key encryption (PKE), key-establishment (KE) and digital signatures. Among the 69 PQC submissions received worldwide, 17 candidate PKE and KE algorithms (e.g., Kyber [6]), and 9 candidate signature schemes (e.g., Dilithium [12]) have been selected to the 2nd round of the NIST PQC standardization, where 12 out of the total 26 2nd-round candidates are lattice-based algorithms.

Most lattice-based cryptosystems base their security on the conjectured quantum hardness of the Short Integer Solution (SIS) problem [1,27] and the Learning With Errors (LWE) problem [30]. Informally speaking, the two problems are both related to solving systems of linear congruences (and are in some sense dual to each other). Let n, m, q be integers and α, β be reals, and let χ_α be some distribution (e.g., a Gaussian distribution) with parameter α defined over $\mathbb{Z}$. The SIS problem $\mathrm{SIS}_{n,m,q,\beta}^\infty$ in the infinity norm asks to find out a non-zero vector $\mathbf{x} \in \mathbb{Z}^m$, given a random matrix $\mathbf{A} \xleftarrow{\$} \mathbb{Z}_q^{n \times m}$, such that $\mathbf{A}\mathbf{x} = \mathbf{0} \bmod q$ and $\|\mathbf{x}\|_\infty \leq \beta$. Correspondingly, the search LWE problem $\mathrm{LWE}_{n,m,q,\alpha}$ searches for $\mathbf{s} \in \mathbb{Z}_q^n$ from samples $(\mathbf{A}, \mathbf{b} = \mathbf{A}\mathbf{s} + \mathbf{e}) \in \mathbb{Z}_q^{m \times n} \times \mathbb{Z}_q^m$, where $\mathbf{A} \xleftarrow{\$} \mathbb{Z}_q^{m \times n}$, $\mathbf{s} \xleftarrow{\$} \mathbb{Z}_q^n$ and $\mathbf{e} \xleftarrow{\$} \chi_\alpha^m$. Decisional LWE problem asks to distinguish $(\mathbf{A}, \mathbf{b} = \mathbf{A}\mathbf{s} + \mathbf{e})$ from uniform distribution over $\mathbb{Z}_q^{m \times n} \times \mathbb{Z}_q^m$. For certain parameters the two (search and decisional) LWE problems are polynomially equivalent [25,30].

It has been shown that the two average-case problems SIS and LWE are at least as hard as some worst-case lattice problems (e.g., Gap-SIVP) for certain parameter choices [27,30]. Moreover, quantum algorithms are not known to have substantial advantages (beyond polynomial speedup) over classical ones in solving these problems, which makes SIS and LWE ideal candidates for post-quantum cryptography. We mention a useful variant of LWE, called the (Hermite) normal form of LWE, where the secret $\mathbf{s}$ is sampled from noise distribution χ_α^n (instead of uniform). The standard LWE and its normal form were known to be equivalent up to a polynomial number of samples [4]. Furthermore, the use of a "small" secret in LWE comes in handy in certain application scenarios, e.g., for better managing the growth of the noise in fully homomorphic encryption [7,10].

SIS is usually used in constructing signature schemes, and LWE is better suited for PKE schemes. However, the standard LWE and SIS problems seem to suffer some constraints in choosing parameters for some practical cryptographic schemes. For example, the LWE parameter for achieving a 128-bit (quantum) security typically cannot provide a matching decryption failure probability ν (say $\nu = 2^{-128}$) for the resulting LWE-based PKE scheme. Note that a larger ν (i.e., $\nu > 2^{-128}$) may sacrifice the security, and a smaller ν (i.e., $\nu < 2^{-128}$) may compromise the performance. To this end, we introduce special variants of SIS and LWE, referred to as asymmetric SIS (ASIS) and asymmetric LWE (ALWE).

Informally, the ASIS problem $\mathrm{ASIS}^{\infty}_{n,m_1,m_2,q,\beta_1,\beta_2}$ refers to the problem that, given a random $\mathbf{A} \xleftarrow{\$} \mathbb{Z}_q^{n \times (m_1+m_2)}$, find out a non-zero $\mathbf{x} = (\mathbf{x}_1^T, \mathbf{x}_2^T)^T \in \mathbb{Z}^{m_1+m_2}$ satisfying $\mathbf{A}\mathbf{x} = \mathbf{0} \bmod q$, $\|\mathbf{x}_1\|_\infty \leq \beta_1$ and $\|\mathbf{x}_2\|_\infty \leq \beta_2$. It is easy to see that $\mathrm{ASIS}^{\infty}_{n,m_1,m_2,q,\beta_1,\beta_2}$ is at least as hard as $\mathrm{SIS}^{\infty}_{n,m_1+m_2,q,\max(\beta_1,\beta_2)}$. Thus, we have

$$\mathrm{SIS}^{\infty}_{n,m_1+m_2,q,\max(\beta_1,\beta_2)} \preceq \mathrm{ASIS}^{\infty}_{n,m_1,m_2,q,\beta_1,\beta_2} \preceq \mathrm{SIS}^{\infty}_{n,m_1+m_2,q,\min(\beta_1,\beta_2)}.$$

This lays the theoretical foundation for constructing secure signatures based on the ASIS problem. In addition, we investigate a class of algorithms for solving the ASIS problem, and provide a method for selecting appropriate parameters for different security levels with reasonable security margin.

Correspondingly, the ALWE problem $\mathrm{ALWE}_{n,m,q,\alpha_1,\alpha_2}$ asks to find out $\mathbf{s} \in \mathbb{Z}_q^n$ from samples $(\mathbf{A}, \mathbf{b} = \mathbf{A}\mathbf{s} + \mathbf{e}) \in \mathbb{Z}_q^{m \times n} \times \mathbb{Z}_q^m$, where $\mathbf{A} \xleftarrow{\$} \mathbb{Z}_q^{m \times n}, \mathbf{s} \xleftarrow{\$} \chi_{\alpha_1}^n, \mathbf{e} \xleftarrow{\$} \chi_{\alpha_2}^m$. The hardness of ALWE may depend on the actual distribution from which $\mathbf{s}$ (or $\mathbf{e}$) is sampled, and thus we cannot simply compare the hardness of LWE and ALWE like we did for SIS and ASIS. However, the relation below remains valid for our parameter choices in respect to all known solving algorithms despite the lack of a proof in general:[1]

$$\mathrm{LWE}_{n,m,q,\min(\alpha_1,\alpha_2)} \preceq \mathrm{ALWE}_{n,m,q,\alpha_1,\alpha_2} \preceq \mathrm{LWE}_{n,m,q,\max(\alpha_1,\alpha_2)}.$$

More importantly, the literature [9,16,26] suggests that ALWE can reach comparable hardness to standard LWE as long as the secret is sampled from a distribution (i.e., $\chi_{\alpha_1}^n$) with sufficiently large entropy (e.g., uniform distribution over $\{0,1\}^n$) and appropriate values are chosen for other parameters. This shows the possibility of constructing secure cryptographic schemes based on the ALWE problem. We also note that Cheon et al. [11] introduced a variant of LWE that is quite related to ALWE, where $\mathbf{s}$ and $\mathbf{e}$ are sampled from different distributions (notice that $\mathbf{s}$ and $\mathbf{e}$ in the ALWE problem are sampled from the same distribution χ, albeit with different parameters α_1 and α_2). By comprehensively comparing, analyzing and optimizing the state-of-the-art LWE solving algorithms, we establish approximate relations between parameters of ALWE and LWE, and suggest practical parameter choices for several levels of security strength intended for ALWE.

---

[1] In the full version, we show that the relations actually hold for discrete Gaussian distributions and binomial distributions under certain choices of parameters.

The definitions of the aforementioned variants can be naturally generalized to the corresponding ring and module versions, i.e., ring-LWE/SIS and module-LWE/SIS. As exhibited in [6,12], module-LWE/SIS allows for better trade-off between security and performance. We will use the asymmetric module-LWE problem (AMLWE) and the asymmetric module-SIS problem (AMSIS) to build a key encapsulation mechanism (KEM) and a signature scheme of smaller sizes.

Technically, our KEM scheme is mainly based on the PKE schemes in [6,22], except that we make several modifications to utilize the inherent asymmetry of the (M)LWE secret and noise in contributing to the decryption failure probabilities, which allow us to obtain smaller public keys and ciphertexts. In Sect. 3.1, we will further discuss this asymmetry in the design of existing schemes, and illustrate our design rationale in more details. For a targeted 128-bit security, the public key (resp., ciphertext) of our KEM only has 896 bytes (resp., 992 bytes).

Our signature scheme bears most resemblance to Dilithium in [12]. The main difference is that we make several modifications to utilize the asymmetric parameterization of the (M)LWE and (M)SIS to reach better trade-offs among computational costs, storage overhead and security, which yields smaller public keys and signatures without sacrificing the security or computational efficiency. In Sect. 4.1, we will further discuss the asymmetries in existing constructions, and illustrate our design rationale in more details. For a targeted 128-bit quantum security, the public key (resp., signature) of our signature scheme only has 1312 bytes (resp., 2445 bytes).

We make a comprehensive and in-depth study on the concrete hardness of AMLWE and AMSIS by adapting the best known attacks (that were originally intended for MLWE and MSIS respectively) and their variants (that were modified to solve AMLWE and AMSIS respectively), and provide several choices of parameters for our KEM and signature schemes aiming at different security strengths. The implementation of our schemes (and its comparison with the counterparts) confirms that our schemes are practical and competitive. We compare our KEM with NIST round2 lattice-based PKEs/KEMs in Sect. 1.1, and compare our signature with NIST round2 lattice-based signatures in Sect. 1.2.

1.1 Comparison with NIST Round2 Lattice-Based PKEs/KEMs

As our KEM is built upon Kyber [6], we would like to first give a slightly detailed comparison between our KEM and Kyber-round2 [6] in Table 1. Our software is implemented in C language with optimized number theory transform (NTT) and vector multiplication using AVX2 instructions. The running times of KeyGen, Encap and Decap algorithms are measured in averaged CPU cycles of 10000 times running on a 64-bit Ubuntu 14.4 LTS ThinkCenter desktop (equipped with Intel Core-i7 4790 3.6 GHz CPU and 4 GB memory). The sizes of public key $|pk|$, secret key $|sk|$, ciphertext $|C|$ are measured in terms of bytes. The column $|ss|$ gives the size of the session key that is encapsulated by each ciphertext. The column "Dec. Failure" lists the probabilities of decryption failure. The last column "Quant. Sec." gives the estimated quantum security level expressed in bits.

Note that for $X \in \{512, 768, 1024\}$ aiming at NIST Category I, III and V, the estimated quantum security of our KEM Π_{KEM}-X is slightly lower than that

Table 1. Comparison between Our KEM Π_{KEM} and Kyber-round2

Schemes	$|pk|$ (Bytes)	$|sk|$ (Bytes)	$|C|$ (Bytes)	$|ss|$ (Bytes)	KeyGen (AVX2)	Encap (AVX2)	Decap	Dec. failure	Quant. Sec.
Kyber-512	800	1632	736	32	37 792	54 465	41 614	2^{-178}	100
Π_{KEM}-512	**672**	**1568**	**672**	32	66 089	70 546	56 385	2^{-82}	102
Π_{KEM}-512†	800	1632	**640**	32	-	-	-	2^{-82}	99
Kyber-768	1184	2400	1088	32	66 760	86 608	69 449	2^{-164}	164
Π_{KEM}-768	**896**	**2208**	**992**	32	84 504	93 069	76 568	2^{-128}	147
Π_{KEM}-768†	1184	2400	**960**	32	-	-	-	2^{-130}	157
Kyber-1024	1568	3168	1568	32	88 503	116 610	96 100	2^{-174}	230
Π_{KEM}-1024	**1472**	3392	**1536**	**64**	115 268	106 740	92 447	2^{-211}	213
Π_{KEM}-1024†	1728	3648	**1472**	**64**	-	-	-	2^{-198}	206

of Kyber-X, but we emphasize that our parameter choices have left out sufficient security margin reserved for further development of attacks. For example, our Π_{KEM}-768 reaches an estimated quantum security of 147 bits and a 2^{-128} decryption failure probability, which we believe is sufficient to claim the same targeted 128-bit quantum security (i.e., NIST Category III) as Kyber-768. We also note that the parameter choice of Π_{KEM}-1024 is set to encapsulate a 64-byte session key, which is twice the size of that achieved by Kyber-1024. This decision is based on the fact that a 32-byte session key may not be able to provide a matching security strength, say, more than 210-bit quantum security (even if the Grover algorithm [17] cannot provide a real quadratic speedup over classical algorithms in practice).

We note that the Kyber team [6] removed the public-key compression to purely base their Kyber-round2 scheme on the standard MLWE problem and obtained (slightly) better computational efficiency (for saving several operations such as NTT). On the first hand, as commented by the Kyber team that "we strongly believe that this didn't lower actual security", we prefer to use the public-key compression to obtain smaller public key sizes (with the cost of a slightly worse computational performance). On the other hand, one can remove the public-key compression and still obtain a scheme with shorter ciphertext size (see Π_{KEM}-X† in Table 1), e.g., a reduction of 128 bytes in the ciphertext size over Kyber-768 at the targeted 128-bit quantum security by using a new parameter set $(n, k, q, \eta_1, \eta_2, d_u, d_v) = (256, 3, 3329, 1, 2, 9, 3)$ (see Π_{KEM}-X† in Table 5).

We also give a comparison between our KEM and NIST round2 lattice-based PKEs/KEMs in Table 2. For simplicity, we only compare those schemes under the parameter choices targeted at IND-CCA security and 128-bit quantum security in terms of space and time (measured in averaged CPU cycles of running 10000 times) on the same computer. We failed to run the softwares of the schemes marked with '*' on our experiment computer (but a public evaluation on the Round1 submissions suggests that Three-Bears may have better computational efficiency than Kyber and ours). As shown in Table 2, our Π_{KEM} has a very competitive performance in terms of both sizes and computational efficiency.

Table 2. Comparison between Π_{KEM} and NIST Round2 lattice-based PKEs/KEMs

Schemes	$\|pk\|$ (Bytes)	$\|sk\|$ (Bytes)	$\|C\|$ (Bytes)	KeyGen (AVX2)	Encap (AVX2)	Decap (AVX2)	Problems
Frodo*	15 632	31 296	15 744	-	-	-	LWE
Kyber	1184	2400	1088	66 760	86 608	69 449	MLWE
LAC	1056	2080	1188	108 724	166 458	208 814	RLWE
Newhope	1824	3680	2208	146 909	233 308	237 619	RLWE
NTRU-Prime*	1158	1763	1039	-	-	-	NTRU variant
NTRU	1138	1450	1138	378 728	109 929	75 905	NTRU
Round5*	983	1031	1119	-	-	-	GLWR
Saber	992	2304	1088	117 504	139 044	133 875	MLWER
Three-Bears*	1194	40	1307	-	-	-	MLWE variant
Π_{KEM}-768	**896**	2208	**992**	84 504	93 069	76 568	AMLWE

1.2 Comparison with NIST Round2 Lattice-Based Signatures

We first give a slightly detailed comparison between our signature Π_{SIG} with Dilithium-round2 [12] in Table 3. Similarly, the running times of the KeyGen, Sign and Verify algorithms are measured in the average number of CPU cycles (over 10000 times) on the same machine configuration as before. The sizes of public key $|pk|$, secret key $|sk|$, signature $|\sigma|$ are counted in bytes. As shown in Table 3, the estimated quantum security of Π_{SIG}-1024 is slightly lower than that of Dilithium-1024, but those at Π_{SIG}-1280 and Π_{SIG}-1536 are slightly higher. In all, our scheme has smaller public key and signatures while still providing comparable efficiency to (or even slightly faster than) Dilithium-round2.

Table 3. Comparison between Our Signature Π_{SIG} and Dilithium-round2

Schemes	$\|pk\|$ (Bytes)	$\|sk\|$ (Bytes)	$\|\sigma\|$ (Bytes)	KeyGen (AVX2)	Sign (AVX2)	Verify (AVX2)	Quantum Sec.
Dilithium-1024	1184	2800	2044	140 181	476 598	129 256	91
Π_{SIG}-1024	**1056**	**2448**	**1852**	126 719	407 981	113 885	90
Dilithium-1280	1472	3504	2701	198 333	657 838	187 222	125
Π_{SIG}-1280	**1312**	**3376**	**2445**	198 876	634 128	170 283	128
Dilithium-1536	1760	3856	3366	269 430	639 966	260 503	158
Π_{SIG}-1536	**1568**	3888	**3046**	296 000	800 831	259 855	163

We also compare our signature with NIST round2 lattice-based signatures: Falcon, qTESLA and Dilithium, where the first one is an instantiation of full-domain hash and trapdoor sampling [15] on NTRU lattices (briefly denoted as FDH-like methodology), and the last two follows the more efficient Fiat-Shamir heuristic with rejection sampling (briefly denoted as FS-like methodology) [24].

As we failed to run the softwares of Falcon and qTESLA on our experiment computer (but a public evaluation on the round1 submissions suggests that Falcon and qTESLA are probably much slower than Dilithium), we only compare the sizes of those schemes at all parameter choices in Table 4. Note that the qTESLA team had dropped all the parameter sets of qTESLA-round2, the figures in Table 4 corresponds to their new choices of parameter sets.

Table 4. Comparison between Π_{SIG} and NIST Round2 lattice-based signatures

NIST category	Schemes	$|pk|$ (Bytes)	$|sk|$ (Bytes)	$|\sigma|$ (Bytes)	Problems	Methodology
I	Falcon-512	897	4097	690	NTRU	FDH-like
	qTESLA-1024	14 880	5 184	2 592	RLWE	FS-like
	Dilithium-1024	1184	2800	2044	MLWE, MSIS	
	Π_{SIG}-1024	1056	2448	1852	AMLWE, AMSIS	
II	Dilithium-1280	1472	3504	2701	MLWE, MSIS	FS-like
	Π_{SIG}-1280	1312	3376	2445	AMLWE, AMSIS	
III	Falcon-1024	1793	8193	1330	NTRU	FDH-like
	qTESLA-2048	38 432	12 352	5 664	RLWE	FS-like
	Dilithium-1536	1760	3856	3366	MLWE, MSIS	
	Π_{SIG}-1536	1568	3888	3046	AMLWE, AMSIS	

1.3 Organizations

Section 2 gives the preliminaries and background information. Section 3 describes the KEM scheme from AMLWE. Section 4 presents the digital signature scheme from AMLWE and AMSIS. Section 5 analyzes the concrete hardness of AMLWE and AMSIS by adapting the best known attacks.

2 Preliminaries

2.1 Notation

We use κ to denote the security parameter. For a real number $x \in \mathbb{R}$, $\lceil x \rfloor$ denotes the closest integer to x (with ties being rounded down, i.e., $\lceil 0.5 \rfloor = 0$). We denote by R the ring $R = \mathbb{Z}[X]/(X^n + 1)$ and by R_q the ring $R_q = \mathbb{Z}_q[X]/(X^n + 1)$, where n is a power of 2 so that $X^n + 1$ is a cyclotomic polynomial. For any positive integer η, S_η denotes the set of ring elements of R that each coefficient is taken from $\{-\eta, -\eta + 1 \ldots, \eta\}$. The regular font letters (e.g., a, b) represent elements in R or R_q (including elements in $\mathbb{Z}$ or $\mathbb{Z}_q$), and bold lower-case letters (e.g., $\mathbf{a}$, $\mathbf{b}$) denote vectors with coefficients in R or R_q. By default, all vectors will be column vectors. Bold upper-case letters (e.g., $\mathbf{A}$, $\mathbf{B}$) represent matrices. We denote by $\mathbf{a}^T$ and $\mathbf{A}^T$ the transposes of vector $\mathbf{a}$ and matrix $\mathbf{A}$ respectively.

We denote by $x \xleftarrow{\$} D$ sampling x according to a distribution D and by $x \xleftarrow{\$} S$ denote sampling x from a set S uniformly at random. For two bit-strings s and t, $s\|t$ denotes the concatenation of s and t. We use $\log_b$ to denote the logarithm function in base b (e.g., 2 or natural constant e) and log to represent $\log_e$. We say that a function $f : \mathbb{N} \to [0,1]$ is *negligible*, if for every positive c and all sufficiently large κ it holds that $f(\kappa) < 1/\kappa^c$. We denote by $\mathsf{negl} : \mathbb{N} \to [0,1]$ an (unspecified) negligible function. We say that f is *overwhelming* if $1 - f$ is negligible.

2.2 Definitions

Modular Reductions. For an even positive integer α, we define $r' = r \bmod^{\pm} \alpha$ as the unique element in the range $(-\frac{\alpha}{2}, \frac{\alpha}{2}]$ such that $r' = r \bmod \alpha$. For an odd positive integer α, we define $r' = r \bmod^{\pm} \alpha$ as the unique element in the range $[-\frac{\alpha-1}{2}, \frac{\alpha-1}{2}]$ such that $r' = r \bmod \alpha$. For any positive integer α, we define $r' = r \bmod^+ \alpha$ as the unique element in the range $[0, \alpha)$ such that $r' = r \bmod \alpha$. When the exact representation is not important, we simply write $r \bmod \alpha$.

Sizes of Elements. For an element $w \in \mathbb{Z}_q$, we write $\|w\|_\infty$ to mean $|w \bmod^{\pm} q|$. The ℓ_∞ and ℓ_2 norms of a ring element $w = w_0 + w_1 X + \cdots + w_{n-1} X^{n-1} \in R$ are defined as follows:

$$\|w\|_\infty = \max_i \|w_i\|_\infty, \ \|w\| = \sqrt{\|w_0\|_\infty^2 + \ldots + \|w_{n-1}\|_\infty^2}.$$

Similarly, for $\mathbf{w} = (w_1, \ldots, w_k) \in R^k$, we define

$$\|\mathbf{w}\|_\infty = \max_i \|w_i\|_\infty, \ \|\mathbf{w}\| = \sqrt{\|w_1\|^2 + \ldots + \|w_k\|^2}.$$

Modulus Switching. For any positive integers p, q, we define the modulus switching function $\lceil \cdot \rfloor_{q \to p}$ as:

$$\lceil x \rfloor_{q \to p} = \lceil (p/q) \cdot x \rfloor \bmod^+ p.$$

It is easy to show that for any $x \in \mathbb{Z}_q$ and $p < q \in \mathbb{N}$, $x' = \lceil \lceil x \rfloor_{q \to p} \rfloor_{p \to q}$ is an element close to x, i.e,

$$|x' - x \bmod^{\pm} q| \leq \left\lceil \frac{q}{2p} \right\rfloor.$$

When $\lceil \cdot \rfloor_{q \to p}$ is used to a ring element $x \in R_q$ or a vector $\mathbf{x} \in R_q^k$, the procedure is applied to each coefficient individually.

Binomial Distribution. The centered binomial distribution B_η with some positive integer η is defined as follows:

$$B_\eta = \left\{ \sum_{i=1}^{\eta} (a_i - b_i) : (a_1, \ldots, a_\eta, b_1, \ldots, b_\eta) \stackrel{\$}{\leftarrow} \{0,1\}^{2\eta} \right\}$$

When we write that sampling a polynomial $g \stackrel{\$}{\leftarrow} B_\eta$ or a vector of such polynomials $\mathbf{g} \stackrel{\$}{\leftarrow} B_\eta$, we mean that sampling each coefficient from B_η individually.

2.3 High/Low Order Bits and Hints

Our signature scheme will adopt several simple algorithms proposed in [12] to extract the "higher-order" bits and "lower-order" bits from elements in $\mathbb{Z}_q$. The goal is that given an arbitrary element $r \in \mathbb{Z}_q$ and another small element $z \in \mathbb{Z}_q$, we would like to recover the higher order bits of $r + z$ without needing to store z. Ducas et al. [12] define algorithms that take r, z and generate a 1-bit hint h that allows one to compute the higher order bits of $r + z$ just using r and h. They consider two different ways which break up elements in $\mathbb{Z}_q$ into their "higher-order" bits and "lower-order" bits. The related algorithms are described in Algorithms 1–6. We refer the reader to [12] for the illustration of the algorithms.

The following lemmas claim some crucial properties of the above supporting algorithms, which are necessary for the correctness and security of our signature scheme. We refer to [12] for their proofs.

Lemma 1. *Let q and α be positive integers such that $q > 2\alpha$, $q \bmod \alpha = 1$ and α is even. Suppose that $\mathbf{r}, \mathbf{z}$ are vectors of elements in R_q, where $\|\mathbf{z}\|_\infty \leq \alpha/2$. Let $\mathbf{h}, \mathbf{h}'$ be vectors of bits. Then, algorithms $\mathsf{HighBits}_q$, $\mathsf{MakeHint}_q$ and $\mathsf{UseHint}_q$ satisfy the following properties:*

- *$\mathsf{UseHint}_q(\mathsf{MakeHint}_q(\mathbf{z}, \mathbf{r}, \alpha), \mathbf{r}, \alpha) = \mathsf{HighBits}_q(\mathbf{r} + \mathbf{z}, \alpha)$.*
- *Let $\mathbf{v}_1 = \mathsf{UseHint}_q(\mathbf{h}, \mathbf{r}, \alpha)$. Then $\|\mathbf{r} - \mathbf{v}_1 \cdot \alpha\|_\infty \leq \alpha + 1$. Furthermore, if the number of 1's in $\mathbf{h}$ is at most ω, then all except for at most ω coefficients of $\mathbf{r} - \mathbf{v}_1 \cdot \alpha$ will have magnitude at most $\alpha/2$ after centered reduction modulo q.*
- *For any $\mathbf{h}, \mathbf{h}'$, if $\mathsf{UseHint}_q(\mathbf{h}, \mathbf{r}, \alpha) = \mathsf{UseHint}_q(\mathbf{h}', \mathbf{r}, \alpha)$, then $\mathbf{h} = \mathbf{h}'$.*

Lemma 2. *If $\|\mathbf{s}\|_\infty \leq \beta$ and $\|\mathsf{LowBits}_q(\mathbf{r}, \alpha)\|_\infty < \alpha/2 - \beta$, then we have:*

$$\mathsf{HighBits}_q(\mathbf{r}, \alpha) = \mathsf{HighBits}_q(\mathbf{r} + \mathbf{s}, \alpha).$$

3   An Improved KEM from AMLWE

Our scheme is based on the key encapsulation mechanism in [6,22]. The main difference is that our scheme uses a (slightly) different hardness problem, which gives us a flexible way to set the parameters for both performance and security.

Algorithm 1: Power2Round$_q(r, d)$

---

1   $r := r \bmod^+ q$;
2   $r_0 := r \bmod^\pm 2^d$;
3   $r_1 := (r - r_0)/2^d$;
4   **return** (r_1, r_0);

Algorithm 2: Decompose$_q(r, \alpha)$

---

1   $r := r \bmod^+ q$;
2   $r_0 := r \bmod^\pm \alpha$;
3   **if** $r - r_0 = q - 1$ **then**
4      $r_1 := 0$;
5      $r_0 := r_0 - 1$;
6   **else**
7      $r_1 := (r - r_0)/\alpha$;
8   **end**
9   **return** (r_1, r_0);

Algorithm 3: HighBits$_q(r, \alpha)$

---

1   $(r_1, r_0) := \mathsf{Decompose}_q(r, \alpha)$;
2   **return** r_1;

Algorithm 4: LowBits$_q(r, \alpha)$

---

1   $(r_1, r_0) := \mathsf{Decompose}_q(r, \alpha)$;
2   **return** r_0;

Algorithm 5: MakeHint$_q(z, r, \alpha)$

---

1   $r_1 := \mathsf{HighBits}_q(r, \alpha)$;
2   $v_1 := \mathsf{HighBits}_q(r + z, \alpha)$;
3   **if** $r_1 \neq v_1$ **then**
4      $h := 1$;
5   **else**
6      $h := 0$;
7   **end**
8   **return** h;

3.1   Design Rationale

For simplicity and clarity, we explain the core idea using the (A)LWE-based public-key encryption (PKE) scheme as an example. Note that most LWE-based

---

Algorithm 6: UseHint$_q(h, r, \alpha)$

---

1 $k := (q-1)/\alpha$;
2 $(r_1, r_0) := \mathsf{Decompose}_q(r, \alpha)$;
3 **if** $h = 1$ *and* $r_0 > 0$ **then**
4      $r_1 := (r_1 + 1) \bmod^+ k$;
5 **end**
6 **if** $h = 1$ *and* $r_0 \leq 0$ **then**
7      $r_1 := (r_1 - 1) \bmod^+ k$;
8 **end**
9 **return** r_1;

PKE schemes mainly follow the framework in [22] up to the choices of parameters and noise distributions. Let $n, q \in \mathbb{Z}$ be positive integers, and let $\chi_\alpha \subset \mathbb{Z}$ be a discrete Gaussian distribution with standard variance $\alpha \in \mathbb{R}$. The LWE-based PKE works as follows:

- **Key generation**: randomly choose $\mathbf{A} \xleftarrow{\$} \mathbb{Z}_q^{n \times n}$, $\mathbf{s}, \mathbf{e} \xleftarrow{\$} \chi_\alpha^n$ and compute $\mathbf{b} = \mathbf{As} + \mathbf{e}$. Return the public key $pk = (\mathbf{A}, \mathbf{b})$ and secret key $sk = \mathbf{s}$.
- **Encryption**: given the public key $pk = (\mathbf{A}, \mathbf{b})$ and a plaintext $\mu \in \{0, 1\}$, randomly choose $\mathbf{r}, \mathbf{x}_1 \xleftarrow{\$} \chi_\alpha^n, x_2 \xleftarrow{\$} \chi_\alpha$ and compute $\mathbf{c}_1 = \mathbf{A}^T \mathbf{r} + \mathbf{x}_1$, $c_2 = \mathbf{b}^T \mathbf{r} + x_2 + \mu \cdot \lceil \frac{q}{2} \rceil$. Finally, return the ciphertext $C = (\mathbf{c}_1, c_2)$.
- **Decryption**: given the secret key $sk = \mathbf{s}$ and a ciphertext $C = (\mathbf{c}_1, c_2)$, compute $z = c_2 - \mathbf{s}^T \mathbf{c}_1$ and output $\lceil z \cdot \frac{2}{q} \rfloor \bmod 2$ as the decryption result.

For a honestly generated ciphertext $C = (\mathbf{c}_1, c_2)$ that encrypts plaintext $\mu \in \{0, 1\}$, we have:

$$z = c_2 - \mathbf{s}^T \mathbf{c}_1 = \mu \cdot \left\lceil \frac{q}{2} \right\rceil + \underbrace{\mathbf{e}^T \mathbf{r} - \mathbf{s}^T \mathbf{x}_1 + x_2}_{\text{noise } e'}. \tag{1}$$

Thus, the decryption algorithm is correct as long as $|e'| < \frac{q}{4}$. Since $|x_2| \ll |\mathbf{e}^T \mathbf{r} - \mathbf{s}^T \mathbf{x}_1|$, the magnitude of $|e'|$ mainly depends on $|\mathbf{e}^T \mathbf{r} - \mathbf{s}^T \mathbf{x}_1|$. That is, the LWE secret $(\mathbf{s}, \mathbf{r})$ and the noise $(\mathbf{e}, \mathbf{x}_1)$ contribute almost equally to the magnitude of $|e'|$. Moreover, for a fixed n the expected magnitude of $|\mathbf{e}^T \mathbf{r} - \mathbf{s}^T \mathbf{x}_1|$ is a monotonically increasing function of α:

$$\text{larger } \alpha \Rightarrow \text{ larger } |\mathbf{e}^T \mathbf{r} - \mathbf{s}^T \mathbf{x}_1| \Rightarrow \text{ larger } |e'|.$$

Let ν be the probability that the decryption algorithm fails, and let λ be the complexity of solving the underlying LWE problem. Ideally, for a targeted security strength κ, we hope that $\nu = 2^{-\kappa}$ and $\lambda = 2^\kappa$, since a large ν (i.e., $\nu > 2^{-\kappa}$) will sacrifice the overall security, and a large λ (i.e., $\lambda > 2^\kappa$) may compromise the overall performance. Since both ν and λ are strongly related to the ratio α/q of the Gaussian parameter α and the modulus q, it is hard to come up with an appropriate choice of (α, q) to simultaneously achieve the best of the two worlds.

To obtain smaller public keys and ciphertexts (and thus improve the communication efficiency), many schemes use the modulus switching technique [8,10] to compress public keys and ciphertexts. We refer to the following scheme that adopts modulus switching technique to compress public keys and ciphertexts, where $p_1, p_2, p_3 \in \mathbb{Z}$ are parameters for compression (p_1 for the public key and p_2, p_3 for ciphertexts).

- **Key generation**: pick $\mathbf{A} \overset{\$}{\leftarrow} \mathbb{Z}_q^{n \times n}$ and $\mathbf{s}, \mathbf{e} \overset{\$}{\leftarrow} \chi_\alpha^n$ and compute $\mathbf{b} = \mathbf{As} + \mathbf{e}$. Then, return the public key $pk = (\mathbf{A}, \bar{\mathbf{b}} = \lceil \mathbf{b} \rfloor_{q \to p_1})$ and the secret key $sk = \mathbf{s}$.
- **Encryption**: given the public key $pk = (\mathbf{A}, \bar{\mathbf{b}})$ and a plaintext $\mu \in \{0, 1\}$, randomly choose $\mathbf{r}, \mathbf{x}_1 \overset{\$}{\leftarrow} \chi_\alpha^n, x_2 \overset{\$}{\leftarrow} \chi_\alpha$, and compute $\mathbf{c}_1 = \mathbf{A}^T \mathbf{r} + \mathbf{x}_1$ and $c_2 = \lceil \bar{\mathbf{b}} \rfloor_{p_1 \to q}^T \mathbf{r} + x_2 + \mu \cdot \lceil \frac{q}{2} \rfloor$. Return the ciphertext $C = (\bar{\mathbf{c}}_1 = \lceil \mathbf{c}_1 \rfloor_{q \to p_2}, \bar{\mathbf{c}}_2 = \lceil c_2 \rfloor_{q \to p_3})$.
- **Decryption**: given the secret key $sk = \mathbf{s}$ and a ciphertext $C = (\bar{\mathbf{c}}_1, \bar{\mathbf{c}}_2)$, compute $z = \lceil \bar{\mathbf{c}}_2 \rfloor_{p_3 \to q} - \mathbf{s}^T \lceil \bar{\mathbf{c}}_1 \rfloor_{p_2 \to q}$ and output $\lceil z \rfloor_{q \to 2} = \lceil z \cdot \frac{2}{q} \rfloor \bmod 2$ as the decryption result.

Let

$$\bar{\mathbf{e}} = \lceil \lceil \mathbf{b} \rfloor_{q \to p_1} \rfloor_{p_1 \to q} - \mathbf{b}, \bar{\mathbf{x}}_1 = \lceil \lceil \mathbf{c}_1 \rfloor_{q \to p_2} \rfloor_{p_2 \to q} - \mathbf{c}_1, \bar{x}_2 = \lceil \lceil c_2 \rfloor_{q \to p_3} \rfloor_{p_3 \to q} - c_2.$$

It is easy to verify $\|\bar{\mathbf{e}}\|_\infty \le \frac{q}{2p_1}, \|\bar{\mathbf{x}}_1\|_\infty \le \frac{q}{2p_2}$, and $|\bar{x}_2| \le \frac{q}{2p_3}$. For any valid ciphertext $C = (\bar{\mathbf{c}}_1, \bar{\mathbf{c}}_2)$ that encrypts $\mu \in \{0, 1\}$ we have

$$\begin{aligned}
z &= \lceil \bar{\mathbf{c}}_2 \rfloor_{p_3 \to q} - \mathbf{s}^T \lceil \bar{\mathbf{c}}_1 \rfloor_{p_2 \to q} \\
&= \mu \cdot \lceil \tfrac{q}{2} \rfloor + \underbrace{(\mathbf{e} + \bar{\mathbf{e}})^T \mathbf{r} - \mathbf{s}^T (\mathbf{x}_1 + \bar{\mathbf{x}}_1) + (x_2 + \bar{x}_2)}_{\text{noise } e'}
\end{aligned} \tag{2}$$

Apparently, the smaller values for p_1, p_2, p_3 the better compression rate is achieved for public keys and ciphertexts. At the same time, however, by the definitions of $\bar{\mathbf{e}}, \bar{\mathbf{x}}_1, \bar{x}_2$ we know that smaller p_1, p_2, p_3 also result in a larger noise e'. Notice that when p_1, p_2, p_3 are much smaller than q, we will have $\|\bar{\mathbf{e}}\|_\infty \gg \|\mathbf{e}\|_\infty$, $\|\bar{\mathbf{x}}_1\|_\infty \gg \|\mathbf{x}_1\|_\infty$ and $|\bar{x}_2| \gg |x_2|$, which further leads to asymmetric roles of $(\mathbf{e}, \mathbf{x}_1, x_2)$ and $(\mathbf{s}, \mathbf{r})$ in contributing to the resulting size of $|e'|$, i.e., for specific (p_1, p_2, p_3) decreasing (resp., increasing) $\|\mathbf{s}\|_\infty$ or $\|\mathbf{r}\|_\infty$ would significantly reducing (resp., enlarging) the noise $|e'|$, and in contrast, changing the size of $\|\mathbf{e}\|_\infty, \|\mathbf{x}_1\|_\infty$ and $|x_2|$ would not result in substantial change to $|e'|$.

The asymmetry observed above motivates the design of our ALWE-based PKE, which uses different noise distributions χ_{α_1} and χ_{α_2} (i.e., same distribution with different parameters α_1 and α_2) for the secrets (i.e., $\mathbf{s}$ and $\mathbf{r}$) and the errors (i.e., $\mathbf{e}, \mathbf{x}_1, x_2$), respectively.

- **Key generation**: pick $\mathbf{A} \overset{\$}{\leftarrow} \mathbb{Z}_q^{n \times n}$, $\mathbf{s} \overset{\$}{\leftarrow} \chi_{\alpha_1}^n$ and $\mathbf{e} \overset{\$}{\leftarrow} \chi_{\alpha_2}^n$, compute $\mathbf{b} = \mathbf{As} + \mathbf{e}$. Then, return the public key $pk = (\mathbf{A}, \bar{\mathbf{b}} = \lceil \mathbf{b} \rfloor_{q \to p_1})$ and the secret key $sk = \mathbf{s}$.

- **Encryption**: given the public key $pk = (\mathbf{A}, \bar{\mathbf{b}})$ and a plaintext $\mu \in \{0, 1\}$, randomly choose $\mathbf{r} \overset{\$}{\leftarrow} \chi_{\alpha_1}^n, \mathbf{x}_1 \overset{\$}{\leftarrow} \chi_{\alpha_2}^n, x_2 \overset{\$}{\leftarrow} \chi_{\alpha_2}$, compute $\mathbf{c}_1 = \mathbf{A}^T \mathbf{r} + \mathbf{x}_1$ and $c_2 = \lceil \mathbf{b} \rfloor_{p_1 \rightarrow q}^T \mathbf{r} + x_2 + \mu \cdot \lceil \frac{q}{2} \rfloor$, and return the ciphertext $C = (\bar{\mathbf{c}}_1 = \lceil \mathbf{c}_1 \rfloor_{q \rightarrow p_2}$ and $\bar{\mathbf{c}}_2 = \lceil c_2 \rfloor_{q \rightarrow p_3})$.
- **Decryption**: Given the secret key $sk = \mathbf{s}$ and the ciphertext $C = (\bar{\mathbf{c}}_1, \bar{\mathbf{c}}_2)$, compute $z = \lceil \bar{\mathbf{c}}_2 \rfloor_{p_3 \rightarrow q} - \mathbf{s}^T \lceil \bar{\mathbf{c}}_1 \rfloor_{p_2 \rightarrow q}$ and output $\lceil z \rfloor_{q \rightarrow 2} = \lceil z \cdot \frac{2}{q} \rfloor \mod 2$ as the decryption result.

Similarly, for ciphertext $C = (\bar{\mathbf{c}}_1, \bar{\mathbf{c}}_2)$ we have the same z and e' as defined in (2), where the difference is that now $\|\mathbf{s}\|_\infty$ and $\|\mathbf{r}\|_\infty$ are determined by α_1, and that $\|\mathbf{e}\|_\infty, \|\mathbf{x}_1\|_\infty$ and $|x_2|$ are determined by α_2. Intuitively, we wish to use small α_1 in order to keep $|e'|$ small, and at the same time choose relatively large α_2 to remedy the potential security loss due to the choice of a small α_1.

While the intuition seems reasonable, it does not shed light on the choices of parameters, in particular, how parameters α_1 and α_2 (jointly) affect security. To this end, we consider the best known attacks and their variants against (A)LWE problems, and obtain the following conclusions: Let χ_{α_1} and χ_{α_2} be subgaussians with standard variances $\alpha_1, \alpha_2 \in \mathbb{R}$ respectively, then we have the following approximate relation between the hardness of ALWE and LWE: the hardness of ALWE with subgaussian standard variances $\alpha_1, \alpha_2 \in \mathbb{R}$ is polynomially equivalent to the hardness of LWE with subgaussian standard variance $\sqrt{\alpha_1 \alpha_2}$. Clearly, the equivalence is trivial for $\alpha_1 = \alpha_2$. This confirms the feasibility of our idea: use a small α_1 to keep the probability ν of decryption failures small while pick a relatively larger α_2 remain the security of the resulting PKE scheme.

The above idea can be naturally generalized to the schemes based on the ring and module versions of LWE. Actually, we will use AMLWE for achieving a better trade-off between computational and communication costs.

3.2 The Construction

We now formally describe a CCA-secure KEM from AMLWE (and AMLWE-R). For ease of implementation, we will use centered binomial distributions instead of Gaussian distributions as in [3,6]. We first give an intermediate IND-CPA secure PKE, which is then transformed into an IND-CCA secure KEM by applying a tweaked Fujisaki-Okamoto (FO) transformation [14,18].

An IND-CPA Secure PKE. Let $n, q, k, \eta_1, \eta_2, d_t, d_u, d_v$ be positive integers. Let $\mathcal{H} : \{0, 1\}^n \rightarrow R_q^{k \times k}$ be a hash function, which is modeled as a random oracle. The PKE scheme Π_{PKE} consists of three algorithms (KeyGen, Enc, Dec):

- $\Pi_{\text{PKE}}.\text{KeyGen}(\kappa)$: randomly choose $\rho \overset{\$}{\leftarrow} \{0, 1\}^n, \mathbf{s} \overset{\$}{\leftarrow} B_{\eta_1}^k, \mathbf{e} \overset{\$}{\leftarrow} B_{\eta_2}^k$, compute $\mathbf{A} = \mathcal{H}(\rho) \in R_q^{k \times k}, \mathbf{t} = \mathbf{A}\mathbf{s} + \mathbf{e} \in R_q^k$ and $\bar{\mathbf{t}} = \lceil \mathbf{t} \rfloor_{q \rightarrow 2^{d_t}}$. Then, return the public key $pk = (\rho, \bar{\mathbf{t}})$ and the secret key $sk = \mathbf{s}$.

– $\Pi_{\text{PKE}}.\text{Enc}(pk, \mu)$: given the public key $pk = (\rho, \bar{\mathbf{t}})$ and a plaintext $\mu \in R_2$, randomly choose $\mathbf{r} \xleftarrow{\$} B_{\eta_1}^k, \mathbf{e}_1 \xleftarrow{\$} B_{\eta_2}^k, e_2 \xleftarrow{\$} B_{\eta_2}$, compute $\mathbf{A} = \mathcal{H}(\rho)$, $\mathbf{u} = \mathbf{A}^T \mathbf{r} + \mathbf{e}_1$, $v = \lceil \bar{\mathbf{t}} \rceil_{2^{d_t} \to q}^T \mathbf{r} + e_2$, and return the ciphertext

$$C = (\bar{\mathbf{u}} = \lceil \mathbf{u} \rfloor_{q \to 2^{d_u}}, \bar{v} = \lceil v + \mu \cdot \lceil \tfrac{q}{2} \rfloor \rfloor_{q \to 2^{d_v}}).$$

– $\Pi_{\text{PKE}}.\text{Dec}(sk, C)$: given the secret key $sk = \mathbf{s}$ and a ciphertext $C = (\bar{\mathbf{u}}, \bar{v})$, compute $z = \lceil \bar{v} \rfloor_{2^{d_v} \to q} - \mathbf{s}^T \lceil \bar{\mathbf{u}} \rfloor_{2^{d_u} \to q}$, output $\lceil z \rfloor_{q \to 2} = \lceil z \cdot \tfrac{2}{q} \rfloor \bmod 2$.

Let $\mathbf{c}_t \in R^k$ satisfy that

$$\lceil \bar{\mathbf{t}} \rfloor_{2^{d_t} \to q} = \lceil \lceil \mathbf{A}\mathbf{s} + \mathbf{e} \rfloor_{q \to 2^{d_t}} \rfloor_{2^{d_t} \to q} = \mathbf{A}\mathbf{s} + \mathbf{e} - \mathbf{c}_t.$$

Let $\mathbf{c}_u \in R^k$ satisfy that

$$\lceil \bar{\mathbf{u}} \rfloor_{2^{d_u} \to q} = \lceil \lceil \mathbf{A}^T \mathbf{r} + \mathbf{e}_1 \rfloor_{q \to 2^{d_u}} \rfloor_{2^{d_u} \to q} = \mathbf{A}^T \mathbf{r} + \mathbf{e}_1 - \mathbf{c}_u.$$

Let $c_v \in R$ satisfy that

$$\begin{aligned}
\lceil \bar{v} \rfloor_{2^{d_v} \to q} &= \lceil \lceil \lceil \bar{\mathbf{t}} \rfloor_{2^{d_t} \to q}^T \mathbf{r} + e_2 + \lceil q/2 \cdot \mu \rfloor_{q \to 2^{d_v}} \rfloor_{2^{d_v} \to q} \\
&= \lceil \bar{\mathbf{t}} \rfloor_{2^{d_t} \to q}^T \mathbf{r} + e_2 + \lceil q/2 \rfloor \cdot \mu - c_v \\
&= (\mathbf{A}\mathbf{s} + \mathbf{e} - \mathbf{c}_t)^T \mathbf{r} + e_2 + \lceil q/2 \rfloor \cdot \mu - c_v \\
&= (\mathbf{A}\mathbf{s} + \mathbf{e})^T \mathbf{r} + e_2 + \lceil q/2 \rfloor \cdot \mu - c_v - \mathbf{c}_t^T \mathbf{r}.
\end{aligned}$$

Using the above equations, we have

$$\begin{aligned}
z &= \lceil \bar{v} \rfloor_{2^{d_v} \to q} - \mathbf{s}^T \lceil \bar{\mathbf{u}} \rfloor_{2^{d_u} \to q} \\
&= \underbrace{\mathbf{e}^T \mathbf{r} + e_2 - c_v - \mathbf{c}_t^T \mathbf{r} - \mathbf{s}^T \mathbf{e}_1 + \mathbf{s}^T \mathbf{c}_u}_{= \, w} + \lceil q/2 \rfloor \cdot \mu \\
&= w + \lceil q/2 \rfloor \cdot \mu.
\end{aligned}$$

It is easy to check that for any odd number q, we have that $\mu = \lceil z \rfloor_{q \to 2}$ holds as long as $\|w\|_\infty < \lceil q/4 \rfloor$. In Sect. 3.4, we will choose the parameters such that the decryption algorithm succeeds with overwhelming probability.

IND-CCA Secure KEM. Let $G : \{0,1\}^* \to \{0,1\}^n$, and $H : \{0,1\}^* \to \{0,1\}^n \times \{0,1\}^n$ be two hash functions, which are modeled as random oracles. By applying a slightly tweaked Fujisaki-Okamoto (FO) transformation [14,18], we can transform the above IND-CPA secure PKE Π_{PKE} into an IND-CCA secure KEM (with implicit rejection) $\Pi_{\text{KEM}} = (\text{KeyGen}, \text{Encap}, \text{Decap})$ as follows.

– $\Pi_{\text{KEM}}.\text{KeyGen}(\kappa)$: choose $z \xleftarrow{\$} \{0,1\}^n$, compute $(pk', sk') = \Pi_{\text{PKE}}.\text{KeyGen}(\kappa)$. Then, return the public key $pk = pk'$ and the secret key $sk = (pk', sk', z)$.

- $\Pi_{\text{KEM}}.\text{Encap}(pk)$: given the public key pk, randomly choose $\mu \xleftarrow{\$} \{0,1\}^n$, compute $\mu' = \mathsf{H}(\mu), (\bar{K}, r) = \mathsf{G}(\mu' \| \mathsf{H}(pk))$ $C = \Pi_{\text{PKE}}.\text{Enc}(pk, \mu'; r)$ and $K = \mathsf{H}(\bar{K} \| \mathsf{H}(C))$, where the notation $\Pi_{\text{PKE}}.\text{Enc}(pk, \mu'; r)$ denotes running the algorithm $\Pi_{\text{PKE}}.\text{Enc}(pk, \mu')$ with fixed randomness r. Finally, return the ciphertext C and the encapsulated key K.
- $\Pi_{\text{KEM}}.\text{Decap}(sk, C)$: given the secret key $sk = (pk', sk', z)$ and a ciphertext C, compute $\mu' = \Pi_{\text{KEM}}.\text{Dec}(sk', C)$ and $(\bar{K}', r') = \mathsf{G}(\mu' \| \mathsf{H}(pk')), C' = \Pi_{\text{KEM}}.\text{Enc}(pk, \mu'; r')$. If $C = C'$, return $K = \mathsf{H}(\bar{K}' \| \mathsf{H}(C))$, else return $\mathsf{H}(z \| \mathsf{H}(C))$.

3.3   Provable Security

In the full version [32], we will show that under the hardness of the AMLWE problem and its rounding variant AMLWE-R (which is needed for compressing the public key, see Appendix A), our scheme Π_{PKE} is provably IND-CPA secure. Formally, we have the following theorem.

Theorem 1. *Let $\mathcal{H} : \{0,1\}^n \to R_q^{k \times k}$ be a random oracle. If both problems AMLWE$_{n,q,k,k,\eta_1,\eta_2}$ and AMLWE-R$_{n,q,2^{d_t},k,k,\eta_1,\eta_2}$ are hard, then the scheme Π_{PKE} is IND-CPA secure.*

Since Π_{KEM} is obtained by applying a slightly tweaked Fujisaki-Okamoto (FO) transformation [14,18] to the PKE scheme Π_{PKE}, given the results in [6,18] and Theorem 1, we have the following theorem.

Theorem 2. *Under the AMLWE assumption and the AMLWE-R assumption, Π_{KEM} is IND-CCA secure in the random oracle model.*

Notice that the algorithm Decap will always return a random "session key" even if the check fails (i.e., implicit rejection). Furthermore, the paper [20] showed that if the underlying PKE is IND-CPA secure, then the resulting KEM with implicit rejection obtained by using the FO transformation is also IND-CCA secure in the quantum random oracle model (QROM). Given the results in [20] and Theorem 1, we have the following theorem.

Theorem 3. *Under the AMLWE assumption and the AMLWE-R assumption, Π_{KEM} is IND-CCA secure in the QROM.*

3.4   Choices of Parameters

In Table 5, we give three sets of parameters (namely, Π_{KEM}-512, Π_{KEM}-768 and Π_{KEM}-1024) for Π_{KEM}, aiming at providing quantum security of at least 80, 128 and 192 bits, respectively. These parameters are carefully chosen such that the decryption failure probabilities (i.e., 2^{-82}, 2^{-128} and 2^{-211}, respectively) are commensurate with the respective targeted security strengths. A concrete estimation of the security strength provided by the parameter sets will be given

Table 5. Parameters sets for Π_{KEM}

Parameters	(n, k, q)	(η_1, η_2)	(d_t, d_u, d_v)	$|pk|$	$|sk|$	$|C|$	$|ss|$	Dec. Fail.	Quant. Sec.
Π_{KEM}-512	$(256, 2, 7681)$	$(2, 12)$	$(10, 9, 3)$	672	1568	672	32	2^{-82}	100
Π_{KEM}-512†	$(256, 2, 3329)$	$(1, 4)$	$(-, 8, 4)$	800	1632	640	32	2^{-82}	99
Π_{KEM}-768	$(256, 3, 7681)$	$(1, 4)$	$(9, 9, 4)$	896	2208	992	32	2^{-128}	147
Π_{KEM}-768†	$(256, 3, 3329)$	$(1, 2)$	$(-, 9, 3)$	1184	2400	960	32	2^{-130}	157
Π_{KEM}-1024	$(512, 2, 12289)$	$(2, 8)$	$(11, 10, 4)$	1472	3392	1536	64	2^{-211}	213
Π_{KEM}-1024†	$(512, 2, 7681)$	$(1, 4)$	$(-, 9, 5)$	1728	3648	1472	64	2^{-198}	206

in Sect. 5. Among them, Π_{KEM}-768 is the recommended parameter set. By the quantum searching algorithm [17], 2κ-bit randomness/session key can only provide at most κ security. Even if the Grover algorithm cannot provide a quadratic speedup over classical algorithms in practice, we still set Π_{KEM}-1024 to support an encryption of 64-bytes (512-bit) randomness/session key, aiming at providing a matching security strength, say, more than 210-bit estimated quantum security. Note that Π_{KEM}-512 and Π_{KEM}-768 only support an encryption of 32-byte (256-bit) session key.

We implemented our Π_{KEM} on a 64-bit Ubuntu 14.4 LTS ThinkCenter desktop (equipped with Intel Core-i7 4790 3.6 GHz CPU and 4 GB memory). Particularly, the codes are mainly written using the C language, with partially optimized codes using AVX2 instructions to speedup some basic operations such as NTT operation and vector multiplications. The average number of CPU cycles (averaged over 10000 times) for running each algorithm is given in Table 1.

4   An Improved Signature from AMLWE and AMSIS

Our signature scheme is based on the "Fiat-Shamir with Aborts" technique [23], and bears most resemblance to Dilithium in [12]. The main difference is that our scheme uses the asymmetric MLWE and MSIS problems, which provides a flexible way to make a better trade-off between performance and security.

4.1   Design Rationale

Several lattice-based signature schemes were obtained by applying the Fiat-Shamir heuristic [13] to three-move identification schemes. For any positive integer n and q, let $R = \mathbb{Z}[x]/(x^n + 1)$ (resp., $R_q = \mathbb{Z}_q[x]/(x^n + 1)$). Let $H : \{0, 1\}^* \to R_2$ be a hash function. Let k, ℓ, η be positive integers, and $\gamma, \beta > 0$ be reals. We first consider an identification protocol between two users A and B based on the $\text{MSIS}_{n,q,k,\ell,\beta}^\infty$ problem. Formally, user A owns a pair of public key $pk = (\mathbf{A}, \mathbf{t} = \mathbf{Ax}) \in R_q^{k \times \ell} \times R_q^k$ and secret key $sk = \mathbf{x} \in R_q^\ell$. In order to convince another user B (who knows the public key pk) of his ownership of sk, A and B can execute the following protocol: (1) A first chooses a vector $\mathbf{y} \in R^\ell$ from some distribution, and sends $\mathbf{w} = \mathbf{Ay}$ to user B; (2) B randomly chooses a bit $c \in R_q$, and sends it as a challenge to A; (3) A computes $\mathbf{z} := \mathbf{y} + c\mathbf{x}$ and sends it back to B; B will accept the response $\mathbf{z}$ by check if $\mathbf{Az} = \mathbf{w} + c\mathbf{t}$.

For the soundness (i.e., user A cannot cheat user B), B also has to make sure that $\beta_2 = \|\mathbf{z}\|_\infty$ is sufficiently small (to ensure that the $\mathrm{MSIS}^\infty_{n,q,k,\ell,\beta}$ problem is hard), otherwise anyone can easily complete the proof by solving a linear equation. Moreover, we require that $\beta_1 = \|\mathbf{x}\|_\infty$ is sufficiently small and $\|\mathbf{y}\|_\infty \gg \|\mathbf{x}\|_\infty$ (and thus $\beta_2 \gg \beta_1$) holds to prevent user B from recovering the secret $\mathbf{x}$ from the public key pk or the response $\mathbf{z}$. Typically, we should require $\beta_2/\beta_1 > 2^{\omega(\log \kappa)}$, where κ is the security parameter. This means that the identification protocol as well as its derived signature from the Fiat-Shamir heuristic will have a very large parameter size. To solve this problem, Lyubashevsky [23, 24] introduce the rejection sampling, which allows A to abort and restart the protocol (by choosing another $\mathbf{y}$) if he thinks $\mathbf{z}$ might leak the information of $\mathbf{x}$. This technique could greatly reduce the size of $\mathbf{z}$ (since it allows to set $\beta_2/\beta_1 = \mathsf{poly}(\kappa)$), but the cost is painful for an interactive identification protocol. Fortunately, this technique will only increase the computation time of the signer when we transform the identification protocol into a signature scheme.

For any positive integer η, S_η denotes the set of elements of R that each coefficient is taken from $\{-\eta, -\eta + 1 \ldots, \eta\}$. By the Fiat-Shamir heuristic, one can construct a signature scheme from the MSIS problem as follows:

- **Key generation**: randomly choose $\mathbf{A} \xleftarrow{\$} R_q^{k \times \ell}, \mathbf{x} \xleftarrow{\$} S_\eta^\ell$, and compute $\mathbf{t} = \mathbf{Ax}$. Return the public key $pk = (\mathbf{A}, \mathbf{t})$ and secret key $sk = (\mathbf{x}, pk)$.
- **Signing**: given the secret key $sk = (\mathbf{x}, pk)$ and a message $\mu \in \{0,1\}^*$,
  1. randomly choose $\mathbf{y} \xleftarrow{\$} S_{\gamma-1}^\ell$;
  2. compute $\mathbf{w} = \mathbf{Ay}$ and $c = \mathsf{H}(\mathbf{w} \| \mu)$;
  3. compute $\mathbf{z} = \mathbf{y} + c\mathbf{x}$;
  4. If $\|\mathbf{z}\|_\infty \geq \gamma - \beta$, restart the computation from step 1), where β is a bound such that $\|c\mathbf{x}\|_\infty \leq \beta$ for all possible c and $\mathbf{x}$. Otherwise, return the signature $\sigma = (\mathbf{z}, c)$.
- **Verification**: given the public key $pk = (\mathbf{A}, \mathbf{t})$, a message $\mu \in \{0,1\}^*$ and a signature $\sigma = (\mathbf{z}, c)$, return 1 if $\|\mathbf{z}\|_\infty < \gamma - \beta$ and $c = \mathsf{H}(\mathbf{Az} - c\mathbf{t} \| \mu)$, and 0 otherwise.

Informally, we require the $\mathrm{MSIS}^\infty_{n,q,k,\ell,\eta}$ problem to be hard for the security of the secret key (i.e., it is computationally infeasible to compute sk from pk). Moreover, we also require the $\mathrm{MSIS}^\infty_{n,q,k,\ell,2\gamma}$ problem to be hard for the unforgeability of signatures (i.e., it is computationally infeasible to forge a valid signature). Since $\|c\mathbf{x}\|_\infty \leq \beta$, for any $(c, \mathbf{x})$ and $\mathbf{z}$ output by the signing algorithm there always exists a $\mathbf{y} \in S_\gamma^\ell$ such that $\mathbf{z} = \mathbf{y} + c\mathbf{x}$, which guarantees that the signature will not leak the information of the secret key. In terms of efficiency, the signing algorithm will repeat about $\left(\frac{2(\gamma - \beta) - 1}{2\gamma - 1} \right)^{-n \cdot \ell}$ times to output a signature, and the signature size is about $n\ell \lceil \log_2(2(\gamma - \beta) - 1) \rceil + n$. Clearly, we wish to use a small ℓ for better efficiency, but the hardness of the underlying MSIS problems require a relatively large ℓ.

To mediate the above conflict, one can use the MLWE problem, which can be seen as a special MSIS problem, to reduce the size of the key and signature. Formally, we can obtain the following improved signature scheme:

- **Key generation**: randomly choose $\mathbf{A} \xleftarrow{\$} R_q^{k \times \ell}$, and $\mathbf{s}_1 \xleftarrow{\$} S_\eta^\ell, \mathbf{s}_2 \xleftarrow{\$} S_\eta^k$, compute $\mathbf{t} = \mathbf{A}\mathbf{s}_1 + \mathbf{s}_2$. Return the public key $pk = (\mathbf{A}, \mathbf{t})$ and secret key $sk = (\mathbf{s}_1, \mathbf{s}_2, pk)$.
- **Signing**: given the secret key $sk = (\mathbf{s}_1, \mathbf{s}_2, pk)$ and a message $\mu \in \{0,1\}^*$,
    1. randomly choose $\mathbf{y} \xleftarrow{\$} S_{\gamma-1}^{\ell+k}$;
    2. compute $\mathbf{w} = (\mathbf{A}\|\mathbf{I}_k)\mathbf{y}$ and $c = \mathsf{H}(\mathbf{w}\|\mu)$;
    3. compute $\mathbf{z} = \mathbf{y} + c\begin{pmatrix} \mathbf{s}_1 \\ \mathbf{s}_2 \end{pmatrix}$;
    4. If $\|\mathbf{z}\|_\infty \geq \gamma - \beta$, restart the computation from step (1), where β is a bound such that $\left\| c\begin{pmatrix} \mathbf{s}_1 \\ \mathbf{s}_2 \end{pmatrix} \right\|_\infty \leq \beta$ holds for all possible $c, \mathbf{s}_1, \mathbf{s}_2$. Otherwise, output the signature $\sigma = (\mathbf{z}, c)$.
- **Verification**: given the public key $pk = (\mathbf{A}, \mathbf{t})$, a message $\mu \in \{0,1\}^*$ and a signature $\sigma = (\mathbf{z}, c)$, return 1 if $\|\mathbf{z}\|_\infty < \gamma - \beta$ and $c = \mathsf{H}((\mathbf{A}\|\mathbf{I}_k)\mathbf{z} - c\mathbf{t}\|\mu)$, otherwise return 0.

Furthermore, since $\mathbf{w} = (\mathbf{A}\|\mathbf{I}_k)\mathbf{y} = \mathbf{A}\mathbf{y}_1 + \mathbf{y}_2$ where $\mathbf{y} = (\mathbf{y}_1^T, \mathbf{y}_2^T)$ and $\gamma \ll q$, we have that the higher bits of (each coefficient of) $\mathbf{w}$ is almost determined by high order bits of (the corresponding coefficient of) $\mathbf{A}\mathbf{y}_1$. This fact has been utilized by [5,12] to compress the signature size. Formally, denote $\mathsf{HighBits}(\mathbf{z}, 2\gamma_2)$ and $\mathsf{LowBits}(\mathbf{z}, 2\gamma_2)$ be polynomial vector defined by the high order bits and low order bits of a polynomial vector $\mathbf{z} \in R_q^k$ related to a parameter γ_2. We can obtain the following signature scheme:

- **Key generation**: randomly choose $\mathbf{A} \xleftarrow{\$} R_q^{k \times \ell}$, and $\mathbf{s}_1 \xleftarrow{\$} S_\eta^\ell, \mathbf{s}_2 \xleftarrow{\$} S_\eta^k$, compute $\mathbf{t} = \mathbf{A}\mathbf{s}_1 + \mathbf{s}_2$. Return the public key $pk = (\mathbf{A}, \mathbf{t})$ and secret key $sk = (\mathbf{s}_1, \mathbf{s}_2, pk)$.
- **Signing**: given the secret key $sk = (\mathbf{s}_1, \mathbf{s}_2, pk)$ and a message $\mu \in \{0,1\}^*$,
    1. randomly choose $\mathbf{y} \xleftarrow{\$} S_{\gamma_1-1}^\ell$;
    2. compute $\mathbf{w} = \mathbf{A}\mathbf{y}$ and $c = \mathsf{H}(\mathsf{HighBits}(\mathbf{w}, 2\gamma_2)\|\mu)$;
    3. compute $\mathbf{z} = \mathbf{y} + c\mathbf{s}_1$;
    4. If $\|\mathbf{z}\|_\infty \geq \gamma_1 - \beta$ or $\mathsf{LowBits}(\mathbf{A}\mathbf{y} - c\mathbf{s}_2, 2\gamma_2) \geq \gamma_2 - \beta$, restart the computation from step 1), where β is a bound such that $\|c\mathbf{s}_1\|_\infty, \|c\mathbf{s}_2\|_\infty \leq \beta$ hold for all possible $c, \mathbf{s}_1, \mathbf{s}_2$. Otherwise, output the signature $\sigma = (\mathbf{z}, c)$.
- **Verification**: given the public key $pk = (\mathbf{A}, \mathbf{t})$, a message $\mu \in \{0,1\}^*$ and a signature $\sigma = (\mathbf{z}, c)$, return 1 if $\|\mathbf{z}\|_\infty < \gamma_1 - \beta$ and $c = \mathsf{H}(\mathsf{HighBits}(\mathbf{A}\mathbf{z} - c\mathbf{t}, 2\gamma_2)\|\mu)$, otherwise return 0.

Essentially, the checks in step (4) are used to ensure that (1) the signature $(\mathbf{z}, c)$ will not leak the information of $\mathbf{s}_1$ and $\mathbf{s}_2$; and (2) $\mathsf{HighBits}(\mathbf{A}\mathbf{z} - c\mathbf{t}, 2\gamma_2) = \mathsf{HighBits}(\mathbf{A}\mathbf{y} - c\mathbf{s}_2, 2\gamma_2) = \mathsf{HighBits}(\mathbf{w}, 2\gamma_2)$ (note that $\mathbf{w} = \mathbf{A}\mathbf{y} = \mathbf{A}\mathbf{y} - c\mathbf{s}_2 + $

$c\mathbf{s}_2$, $\mathsf{LowBits}(\mathbf{Ay} - c\mathbf{s}_2, 2\gamma_2) < \gamma_2 - \beta$ and $\|c\mathbf{s}_2\|_\infty \le \beta$). By setting $\gamma_1 = 2\gamma_2$, we require the $\mathsf{MLWE}_{n,k,\ell,q,\eta}$ problem and the (variant of) $\mathsf{MSIS}^\infty_{n,k,(\ell+k+1),q,2\gamma_1+2}$ problem to be hard to ensure the security of the secret key and the unforgeability of the signature, respectively.

By a careful examination on the above scheme, one can find that the computational efficiency of the signing algorithm is determined by the expected number of repetitions in step (4):

$$\underbrace{\left(\frac{2(\gamma_1 - \beta) - 1}{2\gamma_1 - 1}\right)^{-n\cdot\ell}}_{=N_1} \cdot \underbrace{\left(\frac{2(\gamma_2 - \beta) - 1}{2\gamma_2 - 1}\right)^{-n\cdot k}}_{=N_2},$$

where N_1 and N_2 are determined by the first and second checks in step (4), respectively. Clearly, it is possible to modify N_1 and N_2 while keeping the total number of repetitions $N = N_1 \cdot N_2$ unchanged. Note that the size of the signature is related to γ_1 and is irrelevant to γ_2, which means that a shorter signature can be obtained by using a smaller γ_1. However, simply using a smaller γ_1 will also give a bigger N_1, and thus a worse computational efficiency. In order to obtain a short signature size without (significantly) affecting the computational efficiency:

– We use the AMLWE problem for the security of the secret key, which allows us to use a smaller γ_1 by reducing $\|\mathbf{s}_1\|_\infty$ (and thus $\beta = \|c\mathbf{s}_1\|_\infty$ in the expression of N_1);
– We use the AMSIS problem for the unforgeability of the signatures, which further allows us to use a smaller γ_1 by increasing γ_2 to keep $N = N_1 \cdot N_2$ unchanged.

Note that reducing $\|\mathbf{s}_1\|_\infty$ (by choosing a smaller η_1) may weaken the hardness of the underlying AMLWE problem (if we do not change other parameters). We choose to increase η_2 (and thus $\|\mathbf{s}_2\|_\infty$) to remain the hardness. Similarly, increasing γ_2 will weaken the hardness of the underlying AMSIS problem, and we choose to reduce γ_1 to remain the hardness. Both strategies crucially rely on the asymmetries of the underlying problems.

4.2 The Construction

Let $n, k, \ell, q, \eta_1, \eta_2, \beta_1, \beta_2, \gamma_1, \gamma_2, \omega \in \mathbb{Z}$ be positive integers. Let $R = \mathbb{Z}[x]/(x^n + 1)$ and $R_q = \mathbb{Z}_q[x]/(x^n + 1)$. Denote B_{60} as the set of elements of R that have 60 coefficients are either -1 or 1 and the rest are 0, and $|B_{60}| = 2^{60} \cdot \binom{n}{60}$. When $n = 256$, $|B_{60}| > 2^{256}$. Let $H_1 : \{0,1\}^{256} \to R_q^{k\times\ell}$, $H_2 : \{0,1\}^* \to \{0,1\}^{384}$, $H_3 : \{0,1\}^* \to S^\ell_{\gamma_1-1}$ and $H_4 : \{0,1\}^* \to B_{60}$ be four hash functions. We now present the description of our scheme $\Pi_{\mathsf{SIG}} = (\mathsf{KeyGen}, \mathsf{Sign}, \mathsf{Verify})$:

– $\Pi_{\mathsf{SIG}}.\mathsf{KeyGen}(\kappa)$: first randomly choose $\rho, K \xleftarrow{\$} \{0,1\}^{256}$, $\mathbf{s}_1 \xleftarrow{\$} S^\ell_{\eta_1}, \mathbf{s}_2 \xleftarrow{\$} S^k_{\eta_2}$. Then, compute $\mathbf{A} = H_1(\rho) \in R_q^{k\times\ell}$, $\mathbf{t} = \mathbf{As}_1 + \mathbf{s}_2 \in R_q^k$, $(\mathbf{t}_1, \mathbf{t}_0) = \mathsf{Power2Round}_q(\mathbf{t}, d)$ and $tr = H_2(\rho\|\mathbf{t}_1) \in \{0,1\}^{384}$. Finally, return the public key $pk = (\rho, \mathbf{t}_1)$ and secret key $sk = (\rho, K, tr, \mathbf{s}_1, \mathbf{s}_2, \mathbf{t}_0)$.

- $\Pi_{\text{SIG}}.\text{Sign}(sk, M)$: given $sk = (\rho, K, tr, \mathbf{s}_1, \mathbf{s}_2, \mathbf{t}_0)$ and a message $M \in \{0,1\}^*$, first compute $\mathbf{A} = \mathsf{H}_1(\rho) \in R_q^{k \times \ell}$, $\mu = \mathsf{H}_2(tr\|M) \in \{0,1\}^{384}$, and set $ctr = 0$. Then, perform the following computations:
  1. $\mathbf{y} = \mathsf{H}_3(K\|\mu\|ctr) \in S_{\gamma_1 - 1}^{\ell}$ and $\mathbf{w} = \mathbf{A}\mathbf{y}$;
  2. $\mathbf{w}_1 = \mathsf{HighBits}_q(\mathbf{w}, 2\gamma_2)$ and $c = \mathsf{H}_4(\mu\|\mathbf{w}_1) \in B_{60}$;
  3. $\mathbf{z} = \mathbf{y} + c\mathbf{s}_1$ and $\mathbf{u} = \mathbf{w} - c\mathbf{s}_2$;
  4. $(\mathbf{r}_1, \mathbf{r}_0) = \mathsf{Decompose}_q(\mathbf{u}, 2\gamma_2)$;
  5. if $\|\mathbf{z}\|_\infty \geq \gamma_1 - \beta_1$ or $\|\mathbf{r}_0\|_\infty \geq \gamma_2 - \beta_2$ or $\mathbf{r}_1 \neq \mathbf{w}_1$, then set $ctr = ctr + 1$ and restart the computation from step (1);
  6. compute $\mathbf{v} = c\mathbf{t}_0$ and $\mathbf{h} = \mathsf{MakeHint}_q(-\mathbf{v}, \mathbf{u} + \mathbf{v}, 2\gamma_2)$;
  7. if $\|\mathbf{v}\|_\infty \geq \gamma_2$ or the number of 1's in $\mathbf{h}$ is greater than ω, then set $ctr = ctr + 1$ and restart the computation from step 1);
  8. return the signature $\sigma = (\mathbf{z}, \mathbf{h}, c)$.
- $\Pi_{\text{SIG}}.\text{Verify}(pk, M, \sigma)$: given the public key $pk = (\rho, \mathbf{t}_1)$, a message $M \in \{0,1\}^*$ and a signature $\sigma = (\mathbf{z}, \mathbf{h}, c)$, first compute $\mathbf{A} = \mathsf{H}_1(\rho) \in R_q^{k \times \ell}$, $\mu = \mathsf{H}_2(\mathsf{H}_2(pk)\|M) \in \{0,1\}^{384}$. Let $\mathbf{u} = \mathbf{A}\mathbf{z} - c\mathbf{t}_1 \cdot 2^d$, $\mathbf{w}_1' = \mathsf{UseHints}_q(\mathbf{h}, \mathbf{u}, 2\gamma_2)$ and $c' = \mathsf{H}_4(\mu\|\mathbf{w}_1')$. Finally, return 1 if $\|\mathbf{z}\|_\infty < \gamma_1 - \beta_1$, $c = c'$ and the number of 1's in $\mathbf{h}$ is $\leq \omega$, otherwise return 0.

We note that the hash function H_3 is basically used to make the signing algorithm Sign deterministic, which is needed for a (slightly) tighter security proof in the quantum random oracle model. One can remove H_3 by directly choosing $\mathbf{y} \xleftarrow{\$} S_{\gamma_1 - 1}^{\ell}$ at random, and obtain a probabilistic signing algorithm. We also note that the hash function H_4 can be constructed by using an extendable output function such as SHAKE-256 [29] and a so-called "inside-out" version of Fisher-Yates shuffle algorithm [21]. The detailed constructions of hash functions H_3 and H_4 can be found in [12].

Correctness. Note that if $\|c\mathbf{t}_0\|_\infty < \gamma_2$, by Lemma 1 we have $\mathsf{UseHint}_q(\mathbf{h}, \mathbf{w} - c\mathbf{s}_2 + c\mathbf{t}_0, 2\gamma_2) = \mathsf{HighBits}_q(\mathbf{w} - c\mathbf{s}_2, 2\gamma_2)$. Since $\mathbf{w} = \mathbf{A}\mathbf{y}$ and $\mathbf{t} = \mathbf{A}\mathbf{s}_1 + \mathbf{s}_2$, we have that

$$\mathbf{w} - c\mathbf{s}_2 = \mathbf{A}\mathbf{y} - c\mathbf{s}_2 = \mathbf{A}(\mathbf{z} - c\mathbf{s}_1) - c\mathbf{s}_2 = \mathbf{A}\mathbf{z} - c\mathbf{t},$$
$$\mathbf{w} - c\mathbf{s}_2 + c\mathbf{t}_0 = \mathbf{A}\mathbf{z} - c\mathbf{t}_1 \cdot 2^d,$$

where $\mathbf{t} = \mathbf{t}_1 \cdot 2^d + \mathbf{t}_0$. Therefore, the verification algorithm computes

$$\mathsf{UseHint}_q(\mathbf{h}, \mathbf{A}\mathbf{z} - c\mathbf{t}_1 \cdot 2^d, 2\gamma_2) = \mathsf{HighBits}_q(\mathbf{w} - c\mathbf{s}_2, 2\gamma_2).$$

As the signing algorithm checks that $\mathbf{r}_1 = \mathbf{w}_1$, this is equivalent to

$$\mathsf{HighBits}_q(\mathbf{w} - c\mathbf{s}_2, 2\gamma_2) = \mathsf{HighBits}_q(\mathbf{w}, 2\gamma_2).$$

Hence, the $\mathbf{w}_1$ computed by the verification algorithm is the same as that of the signing algorithm, and thus the verification algorithm will always return 1.

Number of Repetitions. Since our signature scheme uses the rejection sampling [23,24] to generate $(\mathbf{z}, \mathbf{h})$, the efficiency of the signing algorithm is determined by the number of repetitions that will be caused by steps (5) and (7) of the signing algorithm. We first estimate the probability that $\|\mathbf{z}\|_\infty < \gamma_1 - \beta_1$ holds in step (5). Assuming that $\|c\mathbf{s}_1\|_\infty \le \beta_1$ holds, then we always have $\|\mathbf{z}\|_\infty \le \gamma_1 - \beta_1 - 1$ whenever $\|\mathbf{y}\|_\infty \le \gamma_1 - 2\beta_1 - 1$. The size of this range is $2(\gamma_1 - \beta_1) - 1$. Note that each coefficient of $\mathbf{y}$ is chosen randomly from $2\gamma_1 - 1$ possible values. That is, for a fixed $c\mathbf{s}_1$, each coefficient of vector $\mathbf{z} = \mathbf{y} + c\mathbf{s}_1$ has $2\gamma_1 - 1$ possibilities. Therefore, the probability that $\|\mathbf{z}\|_\infty \le \gamma_1 - \beta_1 - 1$ is

$$\left(\frac{2(\gamma_1 - \beta_1) - 1}{2\gamma_1 - 1}\right)^{n\cdot\ell} = \left(1 - \frac{\beta_1}{\gamma_1 - 1/2}\right)^{n\cdot\ell} \approx e^{-n\ell\beta_1/\gamma_1}.$$

Now, we estimate the probability that

$$\|\mathbf{r}_0\|_\infty = \|\mathsf{LowBits}_q(\mathbf{w} - c\mathbf{s}_2, 2\gamma_2)\|_\infty < \gamma_2 - \beta_2$$

holds in step (5). If we (heuristically) assume that each coefficient of $\mathbf{r}_0$ is uniformly distributed modulo $2\gamma_2$, the probability that $\|\mathbf{r}_0\|_\infty < \gamma_2 - \beta_2$ is

$$\left(\frac{2(\gamma_2 - \beta_2) - 1}{2\gamma_2}\right)^{n\cdot k} \approx e^{-nk\beta_2/\gamma_2}.$$

By Lemma 2, if $\|c\mathbf{s}_2\|_\infty \le \beta_2$, then $\|\mathbf{r}_0\|_\infty < \gamma_2 - \beta_2$ implies that $\mathbf{r}_1 = \mathbf{w}_1$. This means that the overall probability that step (5) will not cause a repetition is

$$\approx e^{-n(\ell\beta_1/\gamma_1 + k\beta_2/\gamma_2)}.$$

Finally, under our choice of parameters, the probability that step (7) of the signing algorithm will cause a repetition is less than 1%. Thus, the expected number of repetitions is roughly $e^{n(\ell\beta_1/\gamma_1 + k\beta_2/\gamma_2)}$.

4.3 Provable Security

In the full version [32], we show that under the hardness of the AMLWE problem and a rounding variant AMSIS-R of AMSIS (which is needed for compressing the public key, see Appendix A), our scheme Π_{SIG} is provably SUF-CMA secure in the ROM. Formally, we have the following theorem.

Theorem 4. *If* $\mathsf{H}_1 : \{0,1\}^{256} \to R_q^{k\times\ell}$ *and* $\mathsf{H}_4 : \{0,1\}^* \to B_{60}$ *are random oracles, the outputs of* $\mathsf{H}_3 : \{0,1\}^* \to S_{\gamma_1-1}^\ell$ *are pseudo-random, and* $\mathsf{H}_2 : \{0,1\}^* \to \{0,1\}^{384}$ *is a collision-resistant hash function, then* Π_{SIG} *is SUF-CMA secure under the* $\mathsf{AMLWE}_{n,q,k,\ell,\eta_1,\eta_2}$ *and* $\mathsf{AMSIS\text{-}R}_{n,q,d,k,\ell,4\gamma_2+2,2\gamma_1}^\infty$ *assumptions.*

Furthermore, under an interactive variant SelfTargetAMSIS of the AMSIS problem (which is an asymmetric analogue of the SelfTargetMSIS problem introduced by Ducas et al. [12]), we can also prove that our scheme Π_{SIG} is provably SUF-CMA secure. Formally, we have that following theorem.

Theorem 5. *In the quantum random oracle model (QROM), signature scheme* Π_{SIG} *is SUF-CMA secure under the following assumptions:* $\mathrm{AMLWE}_{n,q,k,\ell,\eta_1,\eta_2}$, $\mathrm{AMSIS}^{\infty}_{n,q,d,k,\ell,4\gamma_2+2,2(\gamma_1-\beta_1)}$ *and* $\mathrm{SelfTargetAMSIS}^{\infty}_{\mathrm{H}_4,n,q,k,\ell_1,\ell_2,4\gamma_2,(\gamma_1-\beta_1)}$.

4.4 Choices of Parameters

In Table 6, we provide three sets of parameters (i.e., Π_{SIG}-1024, Π_{SIG}-1280 and Π_{SIG}-1536) for our signature scheme Π_{SIG}, which provide 80-bit, 128-bit and 160-bit quantum security, respectively (corresponding to 98-bit, 141-bit and 178-bit classical security, respectively). A concrete estimation of the security provided by the parameter sets will be given in Sect. 5. Among them, Π_{SIG}-1280 is the recommended parameter set.

Table 6. Parameters for Π_{SIG} (The column "Reps." indicates the excepted number of repetitions that the signing algorithm takes to output a valid signature)

Parameters	(k,ℓ,q,d,ω)	(η_1,η_2)	(β_1,β_2)	(γ_1,γ_2)	Reps.	Quant. Sec.
Π_{SIG}-1024	$(4,3,2021377,13,80)$	$(2,3)$	$(120,175)$	$(131072,168448)$	5.86	90
Π_{SIG}-1280	$(5,4,3870721,14,96)$	$(2,5)$	$(120,275)$	$(131072,322560)$	7.61	128
Π_{SIG}-1536	$(6,5,3870721,14,120)$	$(1,5)$	$(60,275)$	$(131072,322560)$	6.67	163

Our scheme Π_{SIG} under the same machine configuration as in Sect. 3.4 is implemented using standard C, where some partial optimization techniques (e.g., AVX2 instructions) are adopted to speedup basic operations such as NTT operation. The average CPU cycles (averaged over 10000 times) needed for running the algorithms are given in Table 3.

5 Known Attacks Against AMLWE and AMSIS

Solvers for LWE mainly include primal attacks, dual attacks (against the underlying lattice problems) and direct solving algorithms such as BKW and Arora-Ge [2]. BKW and Arora-Ge attacks need sub-exponentially (or even exponentially) many samples, and thus they are not relevant to the public-key cryptography scenario where only a restricted amount of samples is available. Therefore, for analyzing and evaluating practical lattice-based cryptosystems, we typically consider only primal attacks and dual attacks. Further, these two attacks, which are the currently most relevant and effective, seem not to have additional advantages in solving RLWE/MLWE over standard LWE. Thus, when analyzing RLWE or MLWE based cryptosystems, one often translates RLWE/MLWE instances to the corresponding LWE counterparts [6,12] and then applies the attacks. In particular, one first transforms $\mathrm{AMLWE}_{n,q,k,\ell,\alpha_1,\alpha_2}$ into $\mathrm{ALWE}_{nk,q,k\ell,\alpha_1,\alpha_2}$, and then applies, generalizes and optimizes the LWE solving algorithms to ALWE. Since any bounded centrally symmetric distribution can be regarded as sub-gaussian for a certain parameter, for simplicity and without loss of generality, we consider the case that secret vector and error vector in $\mathrm{ALWE}_{n,q,m,\alpha_1,\alpha_2}$ are sampled from subgaussians with parameters α_1 and α_2 respectively. Formally, the problem is to recover $\mathbf{s}$ from samples

$$(\mathbf{A}, \mathbf{b} = \mathbf{As} + \mathbf{e}) \in \mathbb{Z}_q^{m \times n} \times \mathbb{Z}_q^m,$$

where $\mathbf{A} \xleftarrow{\$} \mathbb{Z}_q^{m \times n}$, $\mathbf{s} \leftarrow \chi_{\alpha_1}^n$ and $\mathbf{e} \leftarrow \chi_{\alpha_2}^m$.

In the full version [32], we will not only consider the traditional primal attack and dual attack against ALWE, but also consider two variants of primal attack and three variants of dual attack, which are more efficient to solve the ALWE problem by taking into account the asymmetry of ALWE.

As for the best known attacks against (A)SIS, the BKZ lattice basis reduction algorithm and its variants are more useful for solving the ℓ_2-norm (A)SIS problem than the ℓ_∞-norm counterpart. Note that a solution $\mathbf{x} = (\mathbf{x}_1^T, \mathbf{x}_2^T)^T \in \mathbb{Z}^{m_1+m_2}$ to the infinity-norm ASIS instance $\mathbf{A} \in \mathbb{Z}_q^{n \times (m_1+m_2-n)}$, where $(\mathbf{I}_n \| \mathbf{A})\mathbf{x} = \mathbf{0} \bmod q$ and $\|\mathbf{x}\|_\infty \leq \max(\beta_1, \beta_2) < q$, may have $\|\mathbf{x}\| > q$, whose ℓ_2-norm is even larger than that of a trivial solution $\mathbf{u} = (q, 0, \ldots, 0)^T$. We will follow [12] to solve the ℓ_∞-norm SIS problem. Further, we can always apply an ℓ_2-norm SIS solve to the ℓ_∞-norm SIS problem due to the relation $\|\mathbf{x}\|_\infty \leq \|\mathbf{x}\|$. Hereafter we refer to the above two algorithms as ℓ_∞-norm and ℓ_2-norm attacks respectively, and use them to estimate the concrete complexity of solving $\mathrm{ASIS}_{n,q,m_1,m_2,\beta_1,\beta_2}^\infty$. As before, when analyzing RSIS or MSIS based cryptosystems, one often translates RSIS/MSIS instances to the corresponding SIS counterparts [12] and then applies the attacks.

In the full version [32], we will not only consider the traditional ℓ_2 norm attack and ℓ_∞ norm attack against ASIS, but also consider one variant of ℓ_2 norm attack and two variants of ℓ_∞ norm attack, which are more efficient to solve the ASIS problem by taking into consideration the asymmetry of ASIS.

In the following two subsections, we will summarize those attacks against our Π_{KEM} and Π_{SIG} schemes.

5.1   Concrete Security of Π_{KEM}

The complexity varies for the type of attacks, the number m of samples used and choice of $b \in \mathbb{Z}$ to run the BKZ-b algorithm. Therefore, in order to obtain an overall security estimation sec of the Π_{KEM} under the three proposed parameter settings, we enumerate all possible values of m (the number of ALWE samples) and b to reach a conservative estimation about the computational complexity of primal attacks and dual attacks, by using a python script (which is planned to be uploaded together with the implementation of our schemes to a public repository later). Tables 7 and 8 estimate the complexities of the three parameter sets against primal attacks and dual attacks by taking the minimum of sec over all possible values of (m, b). Taking into account the above, Table 9 shows the overall security of Π_{KEM}.

Table 7. The security of Π_{KEM} against primal attacks

Parameters	Attack model	Traditional (m, b, sec)	Variant 1 (m, b, sec)	Variant 2 (m, b, sec)
Π_{KEM}-512	Classical	$(761, 390, 114)$	$(531, 405, 118)$	$(\mathbf{476}, \mathbf{385}, \mathbf{112})$
	Quantum	$(761, 390, 103)$	$(531, 405, 107)$	$(\mathbf{476}, \mathbf{385}, \mathbf{102})$
Π_{KEM}-768	Classical	$(1021, 640, 187)$	$(646, 575, 168)$	$(\mathbf{556}, \mathbf{560}, \mathbf{163})$
	Quantum	$(1021, 640, 169)$	$(646, 575, 152)$	$(\mathbf{556}, \mathbf{560}, \mathbf{148})$
Π_{KEM}-1024	Classical	$(1526, 825, 241)$	$(886, 835, 244)$	$(\mathbf{786}, \mathbf{815}, \mathbf{238})$
	Quantum	$(1531, 825, 218)$	$(886, 835, 221)$	$(\mathbf{786}, \mathbf{815}, \mathbf{216})$

Table 8. The security of Π_{KEM} against dual attacks

Parameters	Attack model	Traditional (m, b, sec)	Variation 1 (m, b, sec)	Variation 2 (m, b, sec)	Variation 3 (m, b, sec)
Π_{KEM}-512	Classical	$(766, 385, 112)$	$(736, 395, 115)$	$(595, 380, 111)$	$(\mathbf{711}, \mathbf{380}, \mathbf{111})$
	Quantum	$(766, 385, 102)$	$(736, 395, 104)$	$(\mathbf{596}, \mathbf{380}, \mathbf{100})$	$(\mathbf{711}, \mathbf{380}, \mathbf{100})$
Π_{KEM}-768	Classical	$(1021, 620, 181)$	$(881, 570, 166)$	$(\mathbf{586}, \mathbf{555}, \mathbf{162})$	$(776, 555, 162)$
	Quantum	$(1021, 620, 164)$	$(881, 570, 151)$	$(\mathbf{586}, \mathbf{555}, \mathbf{147})$	$(776, 555, 147)$
Π_{KEM}-1024	Classical	$(1531, 810, 237)$	$(981, 810, 239)$	$(906, 805, 236)$	$(\mathbf{1171}, \mathbf{805}, \mathbf{235})$
	Quantum	$(1531, 810, 215)$	$(981, 810, 217)$	$(906, 805, 214)$	$(\mathbf{1171}, \mathbf{805}, \mathbf{213})$

Table 9. The overall security of Π_{KEM}

Parameters	Classical security	Quantum security
Π_{KEM}-512	111	100
Π_{KEM}-768	162	147
Π_{KEM}-1024	235	213

Table 10. Comparison between AMLWE and MLWE under "comparable" parameters

Parameters	$(n, k, q, \eta_1, \eta_2)$	Classical security	Quantum security	$\eta_1 \cdot \eta_2$
Π_{KEM}-512	$(256, 2, 7681, 2, 12)$	111	100	24
MLWE I	$(256, 2, 7681, 5, 5)$	112	102	25
Π_{KEM}-768	$(256, 3, 7681, 1, 4)$	162	147	4
MLWE II	$(256, 3, 7681, 2, 2)$	163	148	4
Π_{KEM}-1024	$(512, 2, 12289, 2, 8)$	235	213	16
MLWE III	$(512, 2, 12289, 4, 4)$	236	214	16

Further, in order to study the complexity relations of asymmetric (M)LWE and standard (M)LWE, we give a comparison in Table 10 between the AMLWE and the corresponding MLWE, in terms of the parameter choices used by Π_{KEM}, which shows that the hardness of AMLWE with Gaussian standard variances

α_1, α_2 is "comparable" to that of MLWE with Gaussian standard variance $\sqrt{\alpha_1 \alpha_2}$. We note that the comparison only focuses on security, and the corresponding MLWE, for the parameters given in Table 10, if ever used to build a KEM, cannot achieve the same efficiency and correctness as our Π_{KEM} does.

5.2   Concrete Security of Π_{SIG}

As before, in order to obtain an overall security estimation of the Π_{SIG} under the three proposed parameter settings against key recovery attacks, we enumerate all possible values of m and b to reach a conservative estimation sec about the computational complexities of primal attacks and dual attacks by using a python script. Tables 11 and 12 estimate the complexities of the three parameter sets of the underlying ALWE problem against primal attacks and dual attacks by taking the minimum of sec over all possible values of (m, b).

Likewise, we enumerate all possible values of m and b to reach a conservative estimation sec about the computational complexities of ℓ_2-norm and ℓ_∞-norm attacks. Tables 13 and 14 estimate the complexities of the three parameter sets of the underlying ASIS problem against ℓ_2-normal and ℓ_∞-normal attacks by taking the minimum of sec over all possible values of (m, b).

In Table 15, we give the overall security of Π_{SIG} under the three parameter settings against key recovery and forgery attacks, which takes account of both AMLWE and AMSIS attacks.

Table 11. The security of Π_{SIG} against AMLWE primal attacks (The last row of the third column has no figures, because the complexity (i.e., sec) of the traditional attack for Π_{SIG}-1536 is too large, and our python script fails to compute it)

Parameters	Attack model	Traditional (m, b, sec)	Variant 1 (m, b, sec)	Variant 2 (m, b, sec)
Π_{SIG}-1024	Classical	$(1021, 555, 162)$	$(671, 345, 100)$	$(\mathbf{741}, \mathbf{340}, \mathbf{99})$
	Quantum	$(1021, 555, 147)$	$(671, 345, 91)$	$(\mathbf{741}, \mathbf{340}, \mathbf{90})$
Π_{SIG}-1280	Classical	$(1276, 1060, 310)$	$(996, 500, 146)$	$(\mathbf{896}, \mathbf{490}, \mathbf{143})$
	Quantum	$(1276, 1060, 281)$	$(996, 500, 132)$	$(\mathbf{896}, \mathbf{490}, \mathbf{129})$
Π_{SIG}-1536	Classical	-	$(1101, 660, 193)$	$(\mathbf{1106}, \mathbf{615}, \mathbf{179})$
	Quantum	-	$(1101, 660, 175)$	$(\mathbf{1106}, \mathbf{615}, \mathbf{163})$

Table 12. The security of Π_{SIG} against AMLWE dual attacks

Parameters	Attack model	Traditional (m, b, sec)	Variant 1 (m, b, sec)	Variant 2 (m, b, sec)	Variant 3 (m, b, sec)
Π_{SIG}-1024	Classical	$(1021, 550, 160)$	$(\mathbf{786}, \mathbf{340}, \mathbf{99})$	$(\mathbf{706}, \mathbf{340}, \mathbf{99})$	$(\mathbf{706}, \mathbf{340}, \mathbf{99})$
	Quantum	$(1021, 550, 145)$	$(\mathbf{786}, \mathbf{340}, \mathbf{90})$	$(\mathbf{706}, \mathbf{340}, \mathbf{90})$	$(\mathbf{706}, \mathbf{340}, \mathbf{90})$
Π_{SIG}-1280	Classical	$(1276, 1050, 307)$	$(1121, 495, 144)$	$(\mathbf{966}, \mathbf{485}, \mathbf{141})$	$(\mathbf{966}, \mathbf{485}, \mathbf{141})$
	Quantum	$(1276, 1050, 278)$	$(1121, 495, 131)$	$(\mathbf{966}, \mathbf{485}, \mathbf{128})$	$(\mathbf{966}, \mathbf{485}, \mathbf{128})$
Π_{SIG}-1536	Classical	$(1535, 1535, 464)$	$(1381, 650, 190)$	$(\mathbf{1031}, \mathbf{615}, \mathbf{179})$	$(\mathbf{1036}, \mathbf{615}, \mathbf{179})$
	Quantum	$(1235, 1535, 422)$	$(1381, 650, 172)$	$(\mathbf{1031}, \mathbf{615}, \mathbf{163})$	$(\mathbf{1036}, \mathbf{615}, \mathbf{163})$

Table 13. The security of Π_{SIG} against two-norm attack (for ASIS problem)

Parameters	Attack model	Traditional (m, b, sec)	Variation 1 (m, b, sec)
Π_{SIG}-1024	Classical	$(2031, 750, 219)$	$\mathbf{(2031, 665, 194)}$
	Quantum	$(2031, 750, 198)$	$\mathbf{(2031, 665, 176)}$
Π_{SIG}-1280	Classical	$(2537, 1100, 321)$	$\mathbf{(2537, 900, 263)}$
	Quantum	$(2537, 1100, 291)$	$\mathbf{(2537, 900, 238)}$
Π_{SIG}-1536	Classical	$(3043, 1395, 408)$	$\mathbf{(3043, 1140, 333)}$
	Quantum	$(3043, 1395, 370)$	$\mathbf{(3043, 1140, 302)}$

Table 14. The security of Π_{SIG} against infinity-norm attack (for ASIS problem)

Parameters	Attack model	Traditional (m, b, sec)	Variant 1 (m, b, sec)	Variant 2 (m, b, sec)
Π_{SIG}-1024	Classical	$(1831, 385, 112)$	$(1781, 385, 112)$	$\mathbf{(1731, 360, 105)}$
	Quantum	$(1831, 385, 102)$	$(1781, 385, 102)$	$\mathbf{(1731, 360, 95)}$
Π_{SIG}-1280	Classical	$(2387, 495, 144)$	$(2387, 545, 159)$	$\mathbf{(2187, 485, 141)}$
	Quantum	$(2387, 495, 131)$	$(2387, 545, 144)$	$\mathbf{(2187, 485, 128)}$
Π_{SIG}-1536	Classical	$(2743, 630, 184)$	$(2793, 690, 201)$	$\mathbf{(2543, 615, 179)}$
	Quantum	$(2743, 630, 167)$	$(2793, 690, 183)$	$\mathbf{(2543, 615, 163)}$

Table 15. The overall security of Π_{SIG}

Parameters	Classical security	Quantum security
Π_{SIG}-1024	99	90
Π_{SIG}-1280	141	128
Π_{SIG}-1536	179	163

Acknowledgments. We thank the anonymous reviewers for their helpful suggestions. Jiang Zhang is supported by the National Natural Science Foundation of China (Grant Nos. 61602046, 61932019), the National Key Research and Development Program of China (Grant Nos. 2017YFB0802005, 2018YFB0804105), the Young Elite Scientists Sponsorship Program by CAST (2016QNRC001), and the Opening Project of Guangdong Provincial Key Laboratory of Data Security and Privacy Protection (2017B030301004). Yu Yu is supported by the National Natural Science Foundation of China (Grant No. 61872236), the National Cryptography Development Fund (Grant No. MMJJ20170209). Shuqin Fan and Zhenfeng Zhang are supported by the National Key Research and Development Program of China (Grant No. 2017YFB0802005).

A   Definitions of Hard Problems

The AMLWE Problem (with Binomial Distributions). The decisional AMLWE problem $\text{AMLWE}_{n,q,k,\ell,\eta_1,\eta_2}$ asks to distinguish $(\mathbf{A}, \mathbf{b} = \mathbf{As} + \mathbf{e})$ and uniform over $R_q^{k \times \ell} \times R_q^k$, where $\mathbf{A} \xleftarrow{\$} R_q^{k \times \ell}, \mathbf{s} \xleftarrow{\$} B_{\eta_1}^\ell, \mathbf{e} \xleftarrow{\$} B_{\eta_2}^k$. Obviously, when $\eta_1 = \eta_2$, the AMLWE problem is the standard MLWE problem.

The AMLWE-R Problem. The AMLWE-R problem $\text{AMLWE-R}_{n,q,p,k,\ell,\eta_1,\eta_2}$ asks to distinguish

$$(\mathbf{A}, \bar{\mathbf{t}} = \lceil \mathbf{t} \rfloor_{q \to p}, \mathbf{A}^T \mathbf{s} + \mathbf{e}, \lceil \bar{\mathbf{t}} \rfloor_{p \to q}^T \mathbf{s} + e)$$

from $(\mathbf{A}', \lceil \mathbf{t}' \rfloor_{q \to p}, \mathbf{u}, v) \in R_q^{\ell \times k} \times R_p^\ell \times R_q^k \times R_q$, where $\mathbf{A}, \mathbf{A}' \xleftarrow{\$} R_q^{\ell \times k}, \mathbf{s} \xleftarrow{\$} B_{\eta_1}^\ell, \mathbf{e} \xleftarrow{\$} \mathbf{B}_{\eta_2}^k, e \xleftarrow{\$} B_{\eta_2}, \mathbf{t}, \mathbf{t}' \xleftarrow{\$} R_q^\ell, \mathbf{u} \xleftarrow{\$} R_q^k, v \xleftarrow{\$} R_q$.

The AMSIS Problem. Given a uniform matrix $\mathbf{A} \in R_q^{k \times (\ell_1 + \ell_2 - k)}$, the (Hermite Normal Form) AMSIS problem $\text{AMSIS}_{n,q,k,\ell_1,\ell_2,\beta_1,\beta_2}^\infty$ over ring R_q asks to find a non-zero vector $\mathbf{x} \in R_q^{\ell_1 + \ell_2} \backslash \{\mathbf{0}\}$ such that $(\mathbf{I}_k \| \mathbf{A})\mathbf{x} = \mathbf{0} \bmod q$, $\|\mathbf{x}_1\|_\infty \leq \beta_1$ and $\|\mathbf{x}_2\|_\infty \leq \beta_2$, where $\mathbf{x} = \begin{pmatrix} \mathbf{x}_1 \\ \mathbf{x}_2 \end{pmatrix} \in R_q^{\ell_1 + \ell_2}, \mathbf{x}_1 \in R_q^{\ell_1}, \mathbf{x}_2 \in R_q^{\ell_2}$.

The AMSIS-R Problem. Given a uniformly random matrix $\mathbf{A} \in R_q^{k \times (\ell_1 + \ell_2 - k)}$ and a uniformly random vector $\mathbf{t} \in R_q^k$, the (Hermite Normal Form) AMSIS-R problem $\text{AMSIS-R}_{n,q,d,k,\ell_1,\ell_2,\beta_1,\beta_2}^\infty$ over ring R_q asks to find a non-zero vector $\mathbf{x} \in R_q^{\ell_1 + \ell_2 + 1} \backslash \{\mathbf{0}\}$ such that $(\mathbf{I}_k \| \mathbf{A} \| \mathbf{t}_1 \cdot 2^d) \mathbf{x} = \mathbf{0} \bmod q$, $\|\mathbf{x}_1\|_\infty \leq \beta_1, \|\mathbf{x}_2\|_\infty \leq \beta_2$ and $\|x_3\|_\infty \leq 2$, where $\mathbf{x} = \begin{pmatrix} \mathbf{x}_1 \\ \mathbf{x}_2 \\ x_3 \end{pmatrix} \in R_q^{\ell_1 + \ell_2 + 1}, \mathbf{x}_1 \in R_q^{\ell_1}, \mathbf{x}_2 \in R_q^{\ell_2}, x_3 \in R_q$ and $(\mathbf{t}_1, \mathbf{t}_0) = \text{Power2Round}_q(\mathbf{t}, d)$.

The SelfTargetAMSIS Problem. Let $\mathsf{H} : \{0,1\}^* \to B_{60}$ is a (quantum) random oracle. Given a uniformly random matrix $\mathbf{A} \in R_q^{k \times (\ell_1 + \ell_2 - k)}$ and a uniform vector $\mathbf{t} \in R_q^k$, the SelfTargetAMSIS problem $\text{SelfTargetAMSIS}_{n,q,k,\ell_1,\ell_2,\beta_1,\beta_2}^\infty$ over ring R_q asks to find a vector $\mathbf{y} = \begin{pmatrix} \mathbf{y}_1 \\ \mathbf{y}_2 \\ c \end{pmatrix}$ and $\mu \in \{0,1\}^*$, such that $\|\mathbf{y}_1\|_\infty \leq \beta_1, \|\mathbf{y}_2\|_\infty \leq \beta_2, \|c\|_\infty \leq 1$ and $\mathsf{H}(\mu, (\mathbf{I}_k \| \mathbf{A} \| \mathbf{t})\mathbf{y}) = c$ holds.

References

1. Ajtai, M.: Generating hard instances of lattice problems (extended abstract). In: Proceedings of the Twenty-Eighth Annual ACM Symposium on Theory of Computing, STOC 1996, pp. 99–108. ACM, New York, NY, USA (1996)
2. Albrecht, M.R., Player, R., Scott, S.: On the concrete hardness of learning with errors. J. Math. Cryptol. **9**, 169–203 (2015)

3. Alkim, E., Ducas, L., Pöppelmann, T., Schwabe, P.: Post-quantum key exchange-a new hope. In: USENIX Security Symposium 2016 (2016)
4. Applebaum, B., Cash, D., Peikert, C., Sahai, A.: Fast cryptographic primitives and circular-secure encryption based on hard learning problems. In: Halevi, S. (ed.) CRYPTO 2009. LNCS, vol. 5677, pp. 595–618. Springer, Heidelberg (2009). https://doi.org/10.1007/978-3-642-03356-8_35
5. Bai, S., Galbraith, S.D.: An improved compression technique for signatures based on learning with errors. In: Benaloh, J. (ed.) CT-RSA 2014. LNCS, vol. 8366, pp. 28–47. Springer, Cham (2014). https://doi.org/10.1007/978-3-319-04852-9_2
6. Bos, J., et al.: CRYSTALS - Kyber: a CCA-secure module-lattice-based KEM. In: 2018 IEEE European Symposium on Security and Privacy (EuroS P), pp. 353–367, April 2018
7. Brakerski, Z., Gentry, C., Vaikuntanathan, V.: Fully homomorphic encryption without bootstrapping. In: Innovations in Theoretical Computer Science, ITCS, pp. 309–325 (2012)
8. Brakerski, Z., Vaikuntanathan, V.: Efficient fully homomorphic encryption from (standard) LWE. In: 2011 IEEE 52nd Annual Symposium on Foundations of Computer Science (FOCS), pp. 97–106, October 2011
9. Brakerski, Z., Langlois, A., Peikert, C., Regev, O., Stehlé, D.: Classical hardness of learning with errors. In: Proceedings of the Forty-fifth Annual ACM Symposium on Theory of Computing, STOC 2013, pp. 575–584. ACM, New York, NY, USA (2013)
10. Brakerski, Z., Vaikuntanathan, V.: Fully homomorphic encryption from ring-LWE and security for key dependent messages. In: Rogaway, P. (ed.) CRYPTO 2011. LNCS, vol. 6841, pp. 505–524. Springer, Heidelberg (2011). https://doi.org/10.1007/978-3-642-22792-9_29
11. Cheon, J.H., Kim, D., Lee, J., Song, Y.: Lizard: cut off the tail! A practical post-quantum public-key encryption from LWE and LWR. In: Catalano, D., De Prisco, R. (eds.) SCN 2018. LNCS, vol. 11035, pp. 160–177. Springer, Cham (2018). https://doi.org/10.1007/978-3-319-98113-0_9
12. Ducas, L., et al.: Crystals-dilithium: a lattice-based digital signature scheme. IACR Trans. Cryptogr. Hardw. Embed. Syst. **2018**(1), 238–268 (2018)
13. Fiat, A., Shamir, A.: How to prove yourself: practical solutions to identification and signature problems. In: Odlyzko, A.M. (ed.) CRYPTO 1986. LNCS, vol. 263, pp. 186–194. Springer, Heidelberg (1987). https://doi.org/10.1007/3-540-47721-7_12
14. Fujisaki, E., Okamoto, T.: Secure integration of asymmetric and symmetric encryption schemes. J. Cryptol. **26**(1), 80–101 (2013)
15. Gentry, C., Peikert, C., Vaikuntanathan, V.: Trapdoors for hard lattices and new cryptographic constructions. In: Proceedings of the 40th Annual ACM Symposium on Theory of Computing, STOC 2008, pp. 197–206. ACM, New York, NY, USA (2008)
16. Goldwasser, S., Kalai, Y., Peikert, C., Vaikuntanathan, V.: Robustness of the learning with errors assumption. In: Proceedings of the Innovations in Computer Science 2010. Tsinghua University Press (2010)
17. Grover, L.K.: A fast quantum mechanical algorithm for database search. In: STOC 1996, pp. 212–219. ACM (1996)
18. Hofheinz, D., Hövelmanns, K., Kiltz, E.: A modular analysis of the Fujisaki-Okamoto transformation. In: Kalai, Y., Reyzin, L. (eds.) TCC 2017. LNCS, vol. 10677, pp. 341–371. Springer, Cham (2017). https://doi.org/10.1007/978-3-319-70500-2_12

19. IBM: IBM unveils world's first integrated quantum computing system for commercial use (2019). https://newsroom.ibm.com/2019-01-08-IBM-Unveils-Worlds-First-Integrated-Quantum-Computing-System-for-Commercial-Use

20. Jiang, H., Zhang, Z., Chen, L., Wang, H., Ma, Z.: IND-CCA-secure key encapsulation mechanism in the quantum random oracle model, revisited. In: Shacham, H., Boldyreva, A. (eds.) CRYPTO 2018. LNCS, vol. 10993, pp. 96–125. Springer, Cham (2018). https://doi.org/10.1007/978-3-319-96878-0_4

21. Knuth, D.: The Art of Computer Programming, vol. 2, 3rd edn. Addison-Wesley, Boston (1997)

22. Lindner, R., Peikert, C.: Better key sizes (and Attacks) for LWE-based encryption. In: Kiayias, A. (ed.) CT-RSA 2011. LNCS, vol. 6558, pp. 319–339. Springer, Heidelberg (2011). https://doi.org/10.1007/978-3-642-19074-2_21

23. Lyubashevsky, V.: Fiat-Shamir with aborts: applications to lattice and factoring-based signatures. In: Matsui, M. (ed.) ASIACRYPT 2009. LNCS, vol. 5912, pp. 598–616. Springer, Heidelberg (2009). https://doi.org/10.1007/978-3-642-10366-7_35

24. Lyubashevsky, V.: Lattice signatures without trapdoors. In: Pointcheval, D., Johansson, T. (eds.) EUROCRYPT 2012. LNCS, vol. 7237, pp. 738–755. Springer, Heidelberg (2012). https://doi.org/10.1007/978-3-642-29011-4_43

25. Lyubashevsky, V., Peikert, C., Regev, O.: On ideal lattices and learning with errors over rings. In: Gilbert, H. (ed.) EUROCRYPT 2010. LNCS, vol. 6110, pp. 1–23. Springer, Heidelberg (2010). https://doi.org/10.1007/978-3-642-13190-5_1

26. Micciancio, D.: On the hardness of learning with errors with binary secrets. Theory Comput. **14**(13), 1–17 (2018)

27. Micciancio, D., Regev, O.: Worst-case to average-case reductions based on gaussian measures. In: Proceedings of the 45th Annual IEEE Symposium on Foundations of Computer Science 2004, pp. 372–381 (2004)

28. NSA National Security Agency. Cryptography today, August 2015. https://www.nsa.gov/ia/programs/suiteb_cryptography/

29. National Institute of Standards and Technology. SHA-3 standard: permutation-based hash and extendable-output functions. FIPS PUB 202 (2015). http://nvlpubs.nist.gov/nistpubs/FIPS/NIST.FIPS.202.pdf

30. Regev, O.: On lattices, learning with errors, random linear codes, and cryptography. In: Proceedings of the Thirty-Seventh Annual ACM Symposium on Theory of Computing, STOC 2005, pp. 84–93. ACM, New York, NY, USA (2005)

31. Shor, P.: Polynomial-time algorithms for prime factorization and discrete logarithms on a quantum computer. SIAM J. Comput. **26**(5), 1484–1509 (1997)

32. Zhang, J., Yu, Y., Fan, S., Zhang, Z., Yang, K.: Tweaking the asymmetry of asymmetric-key cryptography on lattices: KEMs and signatures of smaller sizes. Cryptology ePrint Archive, Report 2019/510 (2019)

MPSign: A Signature from Small-Secret Middle-Product Learning with Errors

Shi Bai[1], Dipayan Das[2], Ryo Hiromasa[3], Miruna Rosca[4,5], Amin Sakzad[6], Damien Stehlé[4,7(✉)], Ron Steinfeld[6], and Zhenfei Zhang[8]

[1] Department of Mathematical Sciences, Florida Atlantic University, Boca Raton, USA
[2] Department of Mathematics, National Institute of Technology, Durgapur, Durgapur, India
[3] Mitsubishi Electric, Kamakura, Japan
[4] Univ. Lyon, EnsL, UCBL, CNRS, Inria, LIP, 69342 Lyon Cedex 07, France
[5] Bitdefender, Bucharest, Romania
[6] Faculty of Information Technology, Monash University, Melbourne, Australia
[7] Institut Universitaire de France, Paris, France
damien.stehle@gmail.com
[8] Algorand, Boston, USA

Abstract. We describe a digital signature scheme MPSign, whose security relies on the conjectured hardness of the Polynomial Learning With Errors problem (PLWE) for at least one defining polynomial within an exponential-size family (as a function of the security parameter). The proposed signature scheme follows the Fiat-Shamir framework and can be viewed as the Learning With Errors counterpart of the signature scheme described by Lyubashevsky at Asiacrypt 2016, whose security relies on the conjectured hardness of the Polynomial Short Integer Solution (PSIS) problem for at least one defining polynomial within an exponential-size family. As opposed to the latter, MPSign enjoys a security proof from PLWE that is tight in the quantum-access random oracle model.

The main ingredient is a reduction from PLWE for an arbitrary defining polynomial among exponentially many, to a variant of the Middle-Product Learning with Errors problem (MPLWE) that allows for secrets that are small compared to the working modulus. We present concrete parameters for MPSign using such small secrets, and show that they lead to significant savings in signature length over Lyubashevsky's Asiacrypt 2016 scheme (which uses larger secrets) at typical security levels. As an additional small contribution, and in contrast to MPSign (or MPLWE), we present an efficient key-recovery attack against Lyubashevsky's scheme (or the inhomogeneous PSIS problem), when it is used with sufficiently small secrets, showing the necessity of a lower bound on secret size for the security of that scheme.

1 Introduction

The Polynomial Short Integer Solution (PSIS) and Polynomial Learning With Errors (PLWE) were introduced as variants of the SIS and LWE problems

© International Association for Cryptologic Research 2020
A. Kiayias et al. (Eds.): PKC 2020, LNCS 12111, pp. 66–93, 2020.
https://doi.org/10.1007/978-3-030-45388-6_3

leading to more efficient cryptographic constructions [LM06,PR06,SSTX09]. Let $n, m, q \geq 2$ and $f \in \mathbb{Z}[x]$ monic of degree n. A $\mathsf{PSIS}_{q,m}^{(f)}$ instance consists in m uniformly chosen elements $a_1, \ldots, a_m \in \mathbb{Z}_q[x]/f$, and the goal is to find $z_1, \ldots, z_m \in \mathbb{Z}[x]/f$ not all zero and with entries of small magnitudes such that $z_1 a_1 + \cdots + z_m a_m = 0 \bmod q$. A $\mathsf{PLWE}_q^{(f)}$ instance consists of oracle access to the uniform distribution over $\mathbb{Z}_q[x]/f \times \mathbb{Z}_q[x]/f$; or to oracle access to the distribution of $(a_i, a_i \cdot s + e_i)$, where a_i is uniform in $\mathbb{Z}_q[x]/f$, $e_i \in \mathbb{Z}[x]/f$ has random coefficients of small magnitudes, and the so-called secret $s \in \mathbb{Z}_q[x]/f$ is uniformly sampled but identical across all oracle calls. The goal is to distinguish between the two types of oracles.

For any fixed f, the hardness of $\mathsf{PSIS}^{(f)}$ and $\mathsf{PLWE}^{(f)}$ has been less investigated than that of SIS and LWE. In particular, it could be that $\mathsf{PSIS}^{(f)}$ and $\mathsf{PLWE}^{(f)}$ are easy, or easier, to solve for some defining polynomials f than for others. To mitigate such a risk, Lyubashevsky [Lyu16] introduced a variant of PSIS that is not parametrized by a specific polynomial f but only a degree n, and is at least as hard as $\mathsf{PSIS}^{(f)}$ for exponentially many polynomials f of degree n. We will let it be denoted by $\mathsf{PSIS}^\emptyset$. Further, Lyubashevsky designed a signature scheme whose security relies on the hardness of this new problem, and hence on the hardness of $\mathsf{PSIS}^{(f)}$ for at least one f among exponentially many. This signature scheme enjoys asymptotic efficiency, similar (up to a constant factor) to those based on $\mathsf{PSIS}^{(f)}$ for a fixed f. Later on, Rosca *et al.* [RSSS17] introduced an LWE counterpart of $\mathsf{PSIS}^\emptyset$: the Middle-Product Learning with Errors problem (MPLWE). Similarly to $\mathsf{PSIS}^\emptyset$, MPLWE is not parametrized by a specific polynomial f but only a degree n, and is at least as hard as $\mathsf{PLWE}^{(f)}$ for exponentially many polynomials f of degree n. To illustrate the cryptographic usefulness of MPLWE, Rosca *et al.* built a public-key encryption scheme whose IND-CPA security relies on the MPLWE hardness assumption. A more efficient encryption scheme and a key encapsulation mechanism [SSZ17,SSZ19] were later proposed as a submission to the NIST standardization process for post-quantum cryptography [NIS].

In [RSSS17], it was observed that several $\mathsf{LWE}/\mathsf{PLWE}^{(f)}$ techniques leading to more cryptographic functionalities do not easily extend to MPLWE, possibly limiting its cryptographic expressiveness. These include a polynomial leftover hash lemma, the construction of trapdoors for MPLWE that allow to recover the secret s, and the "HNF-ization" technique of [ACPS09] which would allow to prove hardness of MPLWE with small-magnitude secrets. The leftover hash lemma and trapdoor sampling questions were recently studied in [LVV19], with an application to identity-based encryption, though only for security against an adversary whose distinguishing advantage is non-negligible (as opposed to exponentially small). On the HNF-ization front, the main result of [RSSS17] was mis-interpreted in [Hir18] (see Theorem 1 within this reference), in that the latter work assumed that the hardness result of [RSSS17] was for secrets whose coefficients were distributed as those of noise terms (and hence of small magnitudes). The main result from [Hir18] was a signature scheme with security relying on MPLWE.

1.1   Contributions

In this work, we give a reduction from $\mathsf{PLWE}^{(f)}$ to a variant of MPLWE in which the secret has small-magnitude coefficients. The reduction works for a family of defining polynomials f that grows with the security parameter.

We then build an identification scheme which follows Schnorr's general framework [Sch89] and which can be upgraded to a signature scheme that is tightly secure in the quantum-access random oracle model (QROM), using [KLS18]. We show that MPSign is unforgeable against chosen message attacks (UF-CMA), which means that no adversary may forge a signature on a message for which it has not seen a signature before. We did not manage to prove that there is no adversary who may forge a new signature on a previously signed message, i.e., that the scheme is strongly unforgeable against chosen message attacks (UF-sCMA). Nevertheless, any UF-CMA secure signature can be upgraded to a UF-sCMA secure signature using a one-time UF-sCMA secure signature [Kat10]. Such a one-time signature can be achieved easily by a universal one-way hash function (by Lamport's one-time signature) [Kat10] or key collision resistant pseudo-random function (by Winternitz one-time signature) [BDE+11].

We provide concrete parameters for MPSign corresponding to level 1 security of the NIST post-quantum standardization process (via the SVP core hardness methodology from [ADPS16]), which take into account our tight QROM security proof with respect to small secret MPLWE (rather than just taking in account the classical ROM security proof as, e.g., in the Dilithium scheme parameter selection [DKL+18]). We also provide parameters that achieve similar security to those from [Lyu16], to allow for a reasonably fair comparison. The MPSign verification key is larger but its signature size is twice smaller.

Our MPSign signature length savings over the scheme of [Lyu16] arise mainly due to our use of much smaller secret key coordinates. Therefore, one could wonder the reducing the size of the secret key coordinates in the scheme of [Lyu16] would also give a secure signature scheme. As an additional small contribution, we show that the answer is negative by presenting a simple efficient key recovery attack on Lyubashevsky's scheme with sufficiently small secret coordinates. Our attack works (heuristically) when the underlying inhomogeneous variant of $\mathsf{PSIS}^{\emptyset}$ has a unique solution, and shows that a lower bound similar to that shown sufficient in the security proof of [Lyu16] is also *necessary* for the security of Lyubashevsky's scheme (and the underlying inhomogeneous $\mathsf{PSIS}^{\emptyset}$ problem) with small secret coordinates.

Finally, we provide a proof-of-concept implementation in Sage, publicly available at https://github.com/pqc-ntrust/middle-product-LWE-signature.

1.2   Comparison with Prior Works

Our signature construction is similar to the one in [Hir18]. However, the proof of the latter is incorrect: in its proof of high min-entropy of commitments (see [Hir18, Lemma 7]), it is assumed that the middle n coefficients of the product between a uniform $a \in \mathbb{Z}_q[x]$ of degree $< n$ and a fixed polynomial y of degree $\leq 2n$, are uniform. In fact, this distribution depends on the rank of a Hankel matrix associated to y and encoding the linear function from a to the considered coefficients of the product. This Hankel matrix can be of low rank and, when it is the case, the resulting distribution is uniform on a very small subset of the range. Interestingly, the distribution of these Hankel matrices (for a uniform y) was recently studied in [BBD+19], in the context of proving hardness of an MPLWE variant with deterministic noise. We do not know how to fix the error from [Hir18]. As a result, we use a different identification scheme to be able to make our proofs go through. Concretely, the identification scheme from [Hir18] used the Bai-Galbraith [BG14] compression technique to decrease the signature size. We circumvent the difficulty by not using the Bai-Galbraith compression technique.

Lyubashevsky's signature from [Lyu16] can also be viewed as secure under the assumption that $\mathsf{PLWE}^{(f)}$ is hard for at least one f among exponentially many defining polynomials f, like ours. Indeed, it was proved secure under the assumption that $\mathsf{PSIS}^{\emptyset}$ is hard, it was proved that $\mathsf{PSIS}^{(f)}$ reduces to $\mathsf{PSIS}^{\emptyset}$ for exponentially many defining polynomials f, and $\mathsf{PLWE}^{(f)}$ (directly) reduces to $\mathsf{PSIS}^{(f)}$. Furthermore, MPLWE (both with small-magnitude secrets and uniform secrets) reduces to $\mathsf{PSIS}^{\emptyset}$, whereas the converse is unknown. Hence it seems that in terms of assumptions, Lyubashevsky's signature outperforms ours. However, the security proof from [Lyu16] only holds in the random oracle model, as opposed to ours which is tight in the quantum-access random oracle model (QROM). Recent techniques on Fiat-Shamir in the QROM [LZ19, DFMS19] might be applicable to [Lyu16], but they are not tight.

We now compare MPSign with LWE-based signature schemes and efficient lattice-based signature schemes such as those at Round 2 of the NIST post-quantum standardization process [NIS]: Dilithium [DKL+18], Falcon [PFH+19] and Tesla [BAA+19]. Compared to LWE-based signatures, our proposal results in much smaller values for the sum of sizes of a signature and a public key, with much stronger security guarantees than the efficient schemes based on polynomial rings. For example, scaling Dilithium with NIST security level 1 parameters to LWE requires multiplying the public key size by the challenge dimension $n = 256$, since for an LWE adaptation of Dilithium, the public key would be a matrix with n columns instead of 1. For NIST security level 1, the public key and signature sizes sum would be above 300 KB for an LWE adaptation of Dilithium, whereas the same quantity is 47 KB for MPSign (see Table 2). Now, compared to the Dilithium, Falcon and Tesla NIST candidates, security guarantees are different. The security of Dilithium and Tesla relies on the module variants of PLWE and PSIS for a fixed polynomial [LS15]. In the case of Dilithium, the known security proof in the QROM is quite loose [LZ19], unless one relies on an ad hoc assumption like SelfTargetMSIS [KLS18]. Moreover, in the case of Dilithium, the SIS instance is in an extreme regime: the maximum infinity norm of the vectors to be found are below $q/2$, but their Euclidean norms may be above q. Currently, no reduction backs the assumption that SIS is intractable in that parameter regime. In Falcon, the public key is assumed pseudo-random, which is an adhoc version of the NTRU hardness assumption [HPS98]. Oppositely, the security of MPSign relies on the assumed PLWE hardness for at least one polynomial among exponentially many. Overall, MPSign is an intermediate risk-performance tradeoff between fixed-ring and LWE-based schemes.

2   Preliminaries

The notations in this paper are almost verbatim from [RSSS17] to maintain consistency and facilitate comparison.

Let $q > 1$ be an integer. We let $\mathbb{Z}_q$ denote the ring of integers modulo q and by $\mathbb{Z}_{\leq q}$ the set $\{-q, \ldots, q\}$ of integers of absolute value less or equal to q. We will write $\mathbb{R}_q$ to denote the group $\mathbb{R}/q\mathbb{Z}$.

Let $n > 0$. For a ring R, we will use the notation $R^{<n}[x]$ to denote the set of all polynomials in $R[x]$ with degree less than n. This notation may be extended to any unstructured set S.

For any vector $a = (a_0, a_1, \ldots, a_{n-1})^T \in \mathbb{Z}^n$, we let $\bar{a}$ denote the reversed vector $(a_{n-1}, a_{n-2}, \ldots, a_0)^T \in \mathbb{Z}^n$ and we write $\|a\|_\infty := \max_i |a_i|$. When there is no ambiguity, we identify a polynomial with its vector of coefficients.

For any matrix $M \in \mathbb{R}^{m \times n}$, we let $\sigma_1(M) \geq \sigma_2(M) \geq \cdots \geq \sigma_n(M)$ denote its singular values. We use the notation $\|M\|$ to denote its largest singular value $\sigma_1(M)$ and we denote by $\mathbf{I}_m$ the $m \times m$ identity matrix.

For a distribution D on a set X, we denote by $x \xleftarrow{\$} D$ the choice of an element x according to D. For simplicity, when D is the uniform distribution on X, we use the notation $a \xleftarrow{\$} X$.

All logarithms used in this paper are in base 2.

2.1   Polynomials and Matrices

For a polynomial $f \in \mathbb{Z}[x]$ of degree $m \geq 1$ and a polynomial $a \in \mathbb{Z}^{<k}[x]$, we make use of the following matrices:

- $\mathsf{Rot}_f^d(a)$: the $d \times m$ matrix whose i-th row is given by the coefficients of the polynomial $x^{i-1} \cdot a \bmod f$;
- M_f: the $m \times m$ matrix whose (i, j)-th element is the constant coefficient of the polynomial $x^{i+j-2} \bmod f$;
- M_f^d: the $d \times m$ matrix obtained by keeping only the first d rows of M_f;
- $\mathsf{Toep}^{d,k}(a)$: the $d \times (k+d-1)$ matrix whose i-th row is given by the coefficients of the polynomial $x^{i-1} \cdot a$.

Note that $\mathsf{Rot}_f^d(a) = \mathsf{Toep}^{d,k}(a) \cdot \mathsf{Rot}_f^{k+d-1}(1)$. Also, for any $a' \in \mathbb{Z}[x]$ such that $a' = a \bmod f$, we have that $\mathsf{Rot}_f^d(a) = \mathsf{Rot}_f^d(a')$.

The expansion factor of a polynomial $f \in \mathbb{Z}[x]$ of degree m is defined as:

$$\mathrm{EF}(f) = \max \left(\frac{\|g \bmod f\|_\infty}{\|g\|_\infty} : g \in \mathbb{Z}^{<2m-1}[x] \setminus \{0\} \right).$$

The following lemma provides bounds on the norms of the matrices M_f and $\mathsf{Rot}_f^d(1)$, in terms of $\mathrm{EF}(f)$. A bound on $\|M_f\|$ was first proved in [RSSS17, Le. 2.8] and improved later in [LVV19, Le. 9]. The bound on $\|\mathsf{Rot}_f^k(1)\|$ can be obtained by noticing that $\mathsf{Rot}_f^k(1)$ contains $\mathbf{I}_{\deg(f)}$ as a submatrix and all its other entries are bounded by $\mathrm{EF}(f)$.

Lemma 1. Let $f \in \mathbb{Z}[x]$ and $k \geq \deg(f) \geq d$. Then

1. $\|M_f^d\| \leq \sqrt{d} \cdot \mathrm{EF}(f)$
2. $\|\mathsf{Rot}_f^k(1)\|^2 \leq \deg(f) + (k - \deg(f)) \cdot \deg(f) \cdot \mathrm{EF}(f)^2$.

We now recall the middle-product of two polynomials and some of its elementary properties. Let us consider a pair of polynomials $(a, b) \in \mathbb{Z}^{<d_a}[x] \times \mathbb{Z}^{<d_b}[x]$. Multiplying the two polynomials, we get a polynomial in $\mathbb{Z}^{<d_a+d_b-1}[x]$. If $d_a + d_b - 1 = d + 2k$ for some integers d and k, then the middle-product of size d of a and b is obtained by multiplying a and b, then deleting the coefficients of x^i for $i \leq k - 1$ and $i \geq k + d$ and dividing the remaining by x^k. Note that the middle-product is an additive homomorphism when either of its inputs is fixed.

Definition 1 (Middle-Product). Let d_a, d_b, d, k be integers such that $d_a + d_b - 1 = d + 2k$. The middle-product $\odot_d$ is the map from $\mathbb{Z}^{<d_a}[x] \times \mathbb{Z}^{<d_b}[x]$ to $\mathbb{Z}^{<d}[x]$ defined as: $(a, b) \rightarrow a \odot_d b = \lfloor \frac{a \cdot b \bmod x^{k+d}}{x^k} \rfloor$.

Lemma 2 ([RSSS17, Le. 3.2]). Let $d, k > 0$. For all $r \in \mathbb{Z}^{<k+1}[x]$, $a \in \mathbb{Z}^{<k+d}[x]$ and $b = r \odot_d a$, we have $\overline{b} = \mathsf{Toep}^{d,k+1}(r) \cdot \overline{a}$.

Lemma 3 ([RSSS17, Le. 3.3]). Let $d, k, n > 0$. For all $r \in \mathbb{Z}^{<k+1}[x]$, $a \in \mathbb{Z}^{<n}[x]$ and $s \in \mathbb{Z}^{<n+d+k-1}[x]$, we have $r \odot_d (a \odot_{d+k} s) = (r \cdot a) \odot_d s$.

2.2 Gaussian Distributions

A symmetric matrix $\Sigma \in \mathbb{R}^{n \times n}$ is positive definite if $x^t \Sigma x > 0$ for every non-zero vector $x \in \mathbb{R}^n$. For any non-singular matrix $B \in \mathbb{R}^{n \times n}$, the matrix $\Sigma = BB^t$ is positive definite and we say that $B = \sqrt{\Sigma}$. Every positive definite matrix Σ has a square root $B = QD$, where $\Sigma = QD^2Q^t$ is the spectral decomposition of Σ. Note that the square root of a positive definite matrix is not unique ($B' = BH$ is also a square root of Σ for every orthogonal matrix $H \in \mathbb{R}^{n \times n}$). If $\Sigma \in \mathbb{R}^{n \times n}$ is a positive definite matrix, its inverse is also positive definite and, moreover, the set of positive definite matrices is closed under addition.

For a positive definite matrix $\Sigma \in \mathbb{R}^{n \times n}$, we define the Gaussian function on $\mathbb{R}^n$ of covariance matrix Σ as $\rho_\Sigma(x) = \exp(-\pi x^t \Sigma^{-1} x)$ for every $x \in \mathbb{R}^n$. The probability distribution whose density is proportional to ρ_Σ is called the Gaussian distribution and is denoted D_Σ. When $\Sigma = s^2 \cdot \mathbf{I}_n$, we use the notations ρ_s and D_s instead of ρ_Σ and D_Σ, respectively.

Given a (full-rank) lattice $\Lambda \subset \mathbb{R}^n$ we define $\rho_\Sigma(\Lambda) := \sum_{x \in \Lambda} \rho_\Sigma(x)$. Using this, we can now define the discrete Gaussian distribution over Λ of covariance parameter Σ as $D_{\Lambda,\Sigma}(x) = \rho_\Sigma(x)/\rho_\Sigma(\Lambda)$ for every $x \in \Lambda$. The dual of a lattice $\Lambda \subset \mathbb{R}^n$ is $\Lambda^* := \{y \in \mathbb{R}^n : \langle y, x \rangle \in \mathbb{Z} \text{ for every } x \in \Lambda\}$. For $\varepsilon > 0$, we define the smoothing parameter $\eta_\varepsilon(\Lambda)$ as the smallest $r > 0$ such that $\rho_{1/r}(\Lambda^* \setminus \{0\}) \leq \varepsilon$. If $\Lambda_1 \subseteq \Lambda_2$ are two lattices, we have that $\eta_\varepsilon(\Lambda_2) \leq \eta_\varepsilon(\Lambda_1)$. We will use the following standard results.

Lemma 4 ([MR04, Le. 3.3]). *For any full-rank lattice $\Lambda \subset \mathbb{R}^n$ and $\varepsilon > 0$, we have $\eta_\varepsilon(\Lambda) \leq \lambda_n(\Lambda) \cdot \sqrt{\ln(2n(1+1/\varepsilon))/\pi}$.*

Lemma 5 ([LPSS14, Le. 5]). *Let $\Sigma_1, \Sigma_2 \in \mathbb{R}^{n \times n}$ two covariance matrices and Λ_1, Λ_2 full-rank lattices in $\mathbb{R}^n$ such that $1 \geq \eta_\varepsilon((\Sigma_1^{-1} + \Sigma_2^{-1})^{1/2} \cdot (\Lambda_1 \cap \Lambda_2))$ for some $\varepsilon \in (0, 1/2)$. If $x_1 \xleftarrow{\$} D_{\Lambda_1,\Sigma_1}$ and $x_2 \xleftarrow{\$} D_{\Lambda_2,\Sigma_2}$, then the statistical distance between the distribution of $x_1 + x_2$ and $D_{\Lambda_1+\Lambda_2,\Sigma_1+\Sigma_2}$ is less than 4ε.*

Lemma 6 ([Ban95, Le. 2.10]). *For any full-rank lattice $\Lambda \subset \mathbb{R}^n$ and $\sigma > 0$, we have $\mathrm{Pr}_{x \leftarrow D_{\Lambda,\sigma}}(\|x\|_\infty > \sigma \cdot t) \leq 2n \cdot \exp(-\pi \cdot t^2)$.*

2.3   Polynomial and Middle-Product Learning with Errors

In this section we recall the formal definitions of PLWE and MPLWE and of the distributions they make use of.

Definition 2 (PLWE distribution). *Let f be a polynomial of degree m and $q \geq 2$. Let χ be a distribution over $\mathbb{Z}[x]/(f)$ and s a fixed element in $\mathbb{Z}_q[x]/(f)$. We define $\mathsf{P}_{q,\chi}(s)$ as the distribution obtained by sampling $a \xleftarrow{\$} \mathbb{Z}_q[x]/(f), e \xleftarrow{\$} \chi$, and returning $(a, b = a \cdot s + e) \in \mathbb{Z}_q[x]/(f) \times \mathbb{Z}_q[x]/(f)$.*

Definition 3 (PLWE). *Let f be a polynomial of degree m and $q \geq 2$. Let χ_1 and χ_2 be distributions over $\mathbb{Z}_q[x]/(f)$. The decision $\mathsf{PLWE}_{q,\chi_1,\chi_2}^{(f)}$ problem consists in distinguishing between arbitrarily many samples from $\mathsf{P}_{q,\chi_1}(s)$ and the same number of uniform samples in $\mathbb{Z}_q[x]/(f) \times \mathbb{Z}_q[x]/(f)$, with non-negligible probability over the choice of $s \xleftarrow{\$} \chi_2$.*

The hardness of PLWE was investigated in [SSTX09, LPR13, PRS17, RSW18], among others. Of particular importance to the present work, it was observed in [LPR13] that the reduction from uniform secret to small secret described in [ACPS09] in the context of LWE also applies to PLWE.

Lemma 7. *Let f be a polynomial of degree m and $q \geq m$ such that the factors of f modulo q are distinct. Let χ_1 and χ_2 be distributions over $\mathbb{Z}_q[x]/(f)$. Then there is a ppt reduction from $\mathsf{PLWE}_{q,\chi_1,\chi_2}^{(f)}$ to $\mathsf{PLWE}_{q,\chi_1,\chi_1}^{(f)}$.*

The condition on q ensures that a uniform element in $\mathbb{Z}_q/(f)$ is invertible with non-negligible probability.

Definition 4 (MPLWE distribution). *Let $n, d > 0$. Let χ be a distribution over $\mathbb{Z}^{<d}[x]$ and $s \in \mathbb{Z}_q^{n+d-1}[x]$. We define $\mathsf{MP}_{q,n,d,\chi}(s)$ as the distribution obtained by sampling $a \xleftarrow{\$} \mathbb{Z}_q^{<n}[x], e \xleftarrow{\$} \chi$, and returning $(a, b = a \odot_d s + e) \in \mathbb{Z}_q^{<n}[x] \times \mathbb{Z}_q^{<d}[x]$.*

Definition 5 (MPLWE). *Let $n, d > 0$. Let χ_1 and χ_2 be distributions over $\mathbb{Z}_q^{<d}[x]$ and $\mathbb{Z}_q^{n+d-1}[x]$, respectively. The decision $\mathsf{MPLWE}_{q,n,d,\chi_1,\chi_2}$ problem consists in distinguishing between arbitrarily many samples from $\mathsf{MP}_{q,n,d,\chi_1}(s)$ and the same number of uniform samples in $\mathbb{Z}_q^{<n}[x] \times \mathbb{Z}_q^{<d}[x]$, with non-negligible probability over the choice of $s \xleftarrow{\$} \chi_2$.*

The PLWE (resp. MPLWE) assumption states that the advantage of any polynomial time algorithm trying to solve the PLWE (resp. MPLWE) problem is negligible. The main result in [RSSS17] is a reduction from a variant of $\mathsf{PLWE}^{(f)}$ (for exponentially many f's with respect to parameter n) for which the noise is drawn from a continuous distribution and the secret is uniformly distributed, to a variant of the MPLWE problem for which the noise distribution is also continuous and the secret is also uniformly distributed. In this work, we will be interested in discrete noise distributions and secret distributions taking small values compared to the modulus q. Compared to [RSSS17], discretizing the noise distribution can be achieved via routine techniques and is more convenient both for our proofs and application. Oppositely, having the secret distribution take small values compared to q requires a new idea.

2.4 Cryptographic Definitions

Pseudorandom Functions. We will use a pseudorandom function to transform an identification scheme to a deterministic signature scheme.

Definition 6. *A pseudorandom function PRF is an efficiently computable map $\mathsf{PRF} : \mathcal{K} \times \{0,1\}^n \to \{0,1\}$ where $\mathcal{K}$ is a finite key space and n, k are integers. For any quantum adversary A trying to distinguish the output of the PRF from a uniform output, we associate the advantage function*

$$\mathrm{Adv}_{\mathsf{PRF}}^{\mathsf{PR}}(A) := |\Pr(A^{\mathsf{PRF}(K,\cdot)} = 1 | K \leftarrow \mathcal{K}) - \Pr(A^{\mathsf{RF}(\cdot)} = 1)|$$

where $\mathsf{RF} : \{0,1\}^n \to \{0,1\}$ is a uniformly sampled function and A has only classical access to the oracles $\mathsf{PRF}(K, \cdot)$ and $\mathsf{RF}(\cdot)$.

Identification Schemes. We recall some basic security properties of particular identification schemes. We closely follow the notations used in [KLS18].

A canonical identification scheme is a protocol between two parties: a prover P and a verifier V. The prover sends a commitment W and the verifier selects a uniform challenge c and sends it to P. Upon receiving c, the prover sends back a response Z to the verifier. After it receives Z, the verifier makes a deterministic decision.

Definition 7 (Canonical identification scheme). *A canonical identification scheme is a tuple of classical ppt algorithms $\mathsf{ID} := (\mathsf{IGen}, \mathsf{P}, \mathsf{V})$.*

- *The key generation algorithm IGen takes as input a security parameter λ (in unary) and returns the public and secret keys (pk, sk). The public key defines the set of challenges ChSet, the set of commitments WSet, and the set of responses ZSet.*

- *The prover algorithm* P *consists of two sub-algorithms:* P_1 *takes as input the secret key* sk *and returns a commitment* $W \in \mathsf{WSet}$ *and a state* St; P_2 *takes as inputs the secret key* sk, *a commitment* W, *a challenge* c, *and a state* St *and returns a response* $Z \in \mathsf{ZSet} \cup \{\bot\}$, *where* $\bot \notin \mathsf{ZSet}$ *is a special symbol indicating failure.*
- *The verifier algorithm* V *takes as inputs the public key* pk *and the conversation transcript* (W, c, Z) *and outputs* 1 *(acceptance) or* 0 *(rejection).*

If $Z = \bot$, then we set $(W, c, Z) = (\bot, \bot, \bot)$. The triple $(W, c, Z) \in \mathsf{WSet} \times \mathsf{ChSet} \times \mathsf{ZSet} \cup \{(\bot, \bot, \bot)\}$ generated in this way is called a *transcript*. Given the public key pk, the transcript is valid if $V(pk, W, c, Z) = 1$.

We say that ID has *correctness error* δ if for all public and secret keys generated by IGen, all possible transcripts in $\mathsf{WSet} \times \mathsf{ChSet} \times \mathsf{ZSet}$ with $Z \neq \bot$ are valid and the probability that a honestly generated transcript is $(\bot, \bot, \bot)$ is less than δ.

We say that the canonical identification scheme ID has α *bits of min-entropy* if

$$\Pr_{(\mathsf{pk},\mathsf{sk}) \leftarrow \mathsf{IGen}(\lambda)} (H_\infty(W|(W, St) \leftarrow P_1(\mathsf{sk})) \geq \alpha) \geq 1 - 2^{-\alpha}.$$

We are interested in the following security properties.

Definition 8 (No-abort honest-verifier zero-knowledge). *A canonical identification scheme* ID *is* ε_{zk}-*perfect no-abort honest-verifier zero-knowledge* (ε_{zk}-*perfect* na-HVZK*) if there exists a ppt algorithm* Sim *which given only the public key* pk *outputs* (W, c, Z) *such that the statistical distance between* $(W, c, Z) \leftarrow \mathsf{Sim}(\mathsf{pk})$ *and* $(W, c, Z) \leftarrow \mathsf{Trans}(\mathsf{pk})$ *is at most* ε_{zk} *and the element* c *from* $(W, c, Z) \leftarrow \mathsf{Sim}(\mathsf{pk})$ *follows a uniform distribution conditioned on* $c \neq \bot$.

Definition 9 (Lossiness). *A canonical identification scheme is lossy (and we call it* LID*) if there exists a lossy key generation algorithm* LossyIGen *that takes as input* λ *and returns a public key* pk_{ls} *and no secret key such that the public keys generated by* IGen *and* LossyIGen *are indistinguishable. In other words, for any quantum adversary* A, *the following quantity is negligible:*

$$\mathrm{Adv}_{\mathsf{ID}}^{loss}(A) := |\Pr(A(\mathsf{pk}_{ls}) = 1|\mathsf{pk}_{ls} \leftarrow \mathsf{LossyIGen}(\lambda)) \\ - \Pr(A(\mathsf{pk}) = 1|(\mathsf{pk}, \mathsf{sk}) \leftarrow \mathsf{IGen}(\lambda))|.$$

Definition 10 (Lossy soundness). *A canonical identification scheme is* ε_{ls}-*lossy-sound if, for every quantum adversary* A, *the following probability that* A *could impersonate the prover is less than* ε_{ls}:

$$\Pr\left[V(\mathsf{pk}_{ls}, W^*, c^*, Z^*) = 1 \; \middle| \; \begin{array}{l} \mathsf{pk}_{ls} \leftarrow \mathsf{LossyIGen}(\lambda); \\ (W^*, St) \leftarrow A(\mathsf{pk}_{ls}); \\ c^* \leftarrow \mathsf{ChSet}; Z^* \leftarrow A(St, c^*) \end{array}\right].$$

Digital Signatures. We recall the definition of a digital signature.

Definition 11 (Digital signature). *A digital signature scheme* SIG *with correctness error* $\delta \geq 0$ *consists of a triple of* ppt *classical algorithms* (G, S, V) *such that for every pair of outputs* (sk, vk) *of* $G(1^\lambda)$ *and any message* M,

$$\Pr[V(vk, M, S(sk, M)) = 0] \leq \delta$$

where the probability is taken over the randomness of algorithms S *and* V.

The algorithm G *is called the key-generation algorithm,* S *is called the signing algorithm,* V *is called is the verification algorithm. The elements* sk *and* vk *are the signing and verification keys.*

Definition 12 (Unforgeability). *A signature scheme* SIG := (G, S, V) *is said to be unforgeable against one-per-message chosen message attack (*UF-CMA$_1$*) in the quantum random oracle model if for every* ppt *quantum forger* $\mathcal{F}$ *having quantum access to the random oracle and classical access to the signing oracle, the probability that after seeing the public key and*

$$\{(M_1, S(sk, M_1)), \ldots, (M_Q, S(sk, M_Q))\}$$

for any Q *(*$Q = \text{poly}(n)$*) adaptively chosen distinct messages* M_i *of its choice, forger* $\mathcal{F}$ *can produce* $M^* \notin \{M_i\}$ *and* σ^* *such that* $V(vk, M^*, \sigma^*) = 1$, *is negligibly small. The probability is taken over the randomness of* G, S, V *and* $\mathcal{F}$, *and is denoted by* $\text{Adv}_{\text{SIG}}^{\text{UF-CMA}_1}(\mathcal{F})$.

One can extend this definition to the scenario where the attacker may have access to more than one signature for any of $\text{poly}(n)$ adaptively chosen messages $\{M_i\}$. In that case, if no quantum adversary $\mathcal{F}$ can produce a valid signature for a message $M^* \notin \{M_i\}$, we say that the signature scheme is unforgeable against chosen message attack (UF-CMA).

In the *strong* corresponding UF-CMA/UF-CMA$_1$ experiments, the adversary may return a forgery for a message which has already been queried to the signing oracle, but with a different signature.

As showed in [BPS16], a UF-CMA$_1$ signature scheme can be combined with a pseudo-random function to obtain a signature scheme that is UF-CMA, and the conversion is tight (further, the upgrade preserves strongness). As observed in [KLS18], this transformation still applies when the attacker is quantum and is given quantum access to the random oracle.

From Identification Schemes to Digital Signatures: Fiat-Shamir. The Fiat-Shamir heuristic is a technique to convert an identification scheme ID := (IGen, P, V) to a digital signature scheme SIG := (G = IGen, S, $\overline{V}$) in the random oracle model (ROM).

The main result in [KLS18] is a security statement of the signature scheme obtained via the Fiat-Shamir transformation in the setup where the adversary has quantum access to the random oracle, but classical access to the signing oracle.

$$\mathsf{S}\,(\mathsf{sk}, M)$$

1: $i = 0$
2: **while** $Z = \perp$ and $i \le k_m$ **do**
3:     $i = i + 1$
4:     $(W, St) := \mathsf{P}_1(\mathsf{sk})$
5:     $c := H(W \| M)$
6:     $Z := \mathsf{P}_2(\mathsf{sk}, W, c, St)$
7: **end while**
8: **if** $Z = \perp$ **then**
9:     $\sigma = \perp$
10: **else**
11:     $\sigma = (W, Z)$
12: **end if**
13: output σ

$$\overline{\mathsf{V}}\,(\mathsf{pk}, M, \sigma)$$

1: $c := H(W \| M)$
2: output $\mathsf{V}(\mathsf{pk}, W, c, Z) \in \{0, 1\}$

Fig. 1. The signature SIG obtained via Fiat-Shamir transform

Theorem 1 ([KLS18, Th. 3.1]). *Consider an identification scheme* ID *which is lossy,* ε_{zk}*-perfect* na-HVZK, *has* α *bits of entropy and is* ε_{ls}*-lossy sound and the signature scheme* SIG *obtained by applying the Fiat-Shamir transform to the identification scheme* ID, *as in Fig. 1.*

For any quantum adversary A *against* UF-CMA$_1$ *security that issues at most* Q_H *quantum queries to the random oracle and* Q_S *classical signing queries, there exists a quantum adversary* B *against* ID *such that*

$$\mathrm{Adv}_{\mathsf{SIG}}^{\mathsf{UF\text{-}CMA}_1}(A) \le \mathrm{Adv}_{\mathsf{ID}}^{loss}(B) + 8(Q_H + 1)^2 \cdot \varepsilon_{ls} + k_m Q_S \cdot \varepsilon_{zk} + 2^{-\alpha+1}.$$

and $Time(B) = Time(A) + k_m Q_H$.

Moreover, if we de-randomize the signature scheme in Fig. 1 by using a pseudo-random function PRF, *then for any quantum adversary* A *against* UF-CMA *security that issues at most* Q_H *quantum queries to the random oracle and* Q_S *classical signing queries, there exists a quantum adversary* B *against* ID *and a quantum adversary* C *against the* PRF *such that*

$$\mathrm{Adv}_{\mathsf{DSIG}}^{\mathsf{UF\text{-}CMA}}(A) \le \mathrm{Adv}_{\mathsf{ID}}^{loss}(B) + 8(Q_H + 1)^2 \cdot \varepsilon_{ls} + k_m Q_S \cdot \varepsilon_{zk} + 2^{-\alpha+1} + \mathrm{Adv}_{\mathsf{PRF}}^{\mathsf{PR}}(C).$$

The de-randomized version of the signature scheme DSIG $:= (\mathsf{IGen}, \mathsf{DS}, \overline{\mathsf{V}})$ obtained from Fiat-Shamir transformation is given in Fig. 2. Here, the PRF key K is also a part of the secret key in the signature scheme.

3   Hardness of Middle-Product LWE with Small Secrets

As mentioned earlier, a main obstacle towards building a signature scheme directly from MPLWE with the Fiat-Shamir with aborts methodology is the need of smaller secrets. In this section, we show that MPLWE remains at least as hard as PLWE for numerous parametrizing polynomials f, when the secret s

$$\mathsf{DS}\left((\mathsf{sk}, K), M\right) \qquad\qquad \overline{\mathsf{V}}\left(\mathsf{pk}, M, \sigma\right)$$

1: $i = 0$
2: **while** $Z = \perp$ and $i \le k_m$ **do**
3:    $i = i + 1$
4:    $(W, St) := \mathsf{P}_1\left(\mathsf{sk}; \mathsf{PRF}_K(0\|i\|M)\right)$
5:    $c := H(W\|M)$
6:    $Z := \mathsf{P}_2\left(\mathsf{sk}, W, c, St; \mathsf{PRF}_K(1\|i\|M)\right)$
7: **end while**
8: **if** $Z = \perp$ **then**
9:    $\sigma = \perp$
10: **else**
11:    $\sigma = (W, Z)$
12: **end if**
13: **output** σ

1: $c := H(W\|M)$
2: output $\mathsf{V}(\mathsf{pk}, W, c, Z) \in \{0, 1\}$

Fig. 2. The de-randomized signature DSIG obtained via Fiat-Shamir transform

is sampled from a specific distribution χ_s that produces small secrets with overwhelming probability.

Let $q \ge 2$, $n \ge d > 0$, $T > 0$ and $k := n + d - 1$. By $J_i \in \mathbb{Z}^{i \times i}$ we denote the matrix with 1's on the anti-diagonal and 0's everywhere else. Let $\mathcal{E}(T, d, n)$ denote the set of all monic polynomials $g(x) \in \mathbb{Z}[x]$ with constant coefficient coprime to q, degree $m \in [d, n]$, and $\sigma_m(M_f) \ge T$.

Theorem 2. *For any polynomial* $f \in \mathcal{E}(T, d, n)$ *and* $1 \ge \alpha \ge \frac{2\sqrt{n}}{qT}$, *there is a ppt reduction from* $\mathsf{PLWE}^{(f)}_{q, D_{\mathbb{Z}^m, \alpha q}, D_{\mathbb{Z}^m, \alpha q}}$ *to* $\mathsf{MPLWE}_{q, n, d, D_{\mathbb{Z}^d, \alpha'' q}, D_{\mathbb{Z}^k, \alpha' q}}$, *where* $\alpha' = \alpha n \sqrt{2n} \cdot \mathrm{EF}(f)^2$ *and* $\alpha'' = \alpha \sqrt{2d} \cdot \mathrm{EF}(f)$.

Proof. We first reduce $\mathsf{PLWE}^{(f)}$ to a variant of MPLWE where the dependence on f lies both in the secret and error distributions. Using the same idea as in [RSSS17, Le. 3.7] except for the fact that now we do not rerandomize the secret to make it uniform, we know that there is a ppt reduction from $\mathsf{PLWE}^{(f)}_{q, \chi_e, \chi_s}$ to $\mathsf{MPLWE}_{q, n, d, \chi'_e, \chi'_s}$ where $\chi'_e = J_d \cdot M^d_f \cdot \chi_e$ and $\chi'_s = J_{n+d-1} \cdot \mathsf{Rot}^{d+n-1}_f(1) \cdot M_f \cdot \chi_s$. We now make the following notations: $B_s := J_k \cdot \mathsf{Rot}^k_f(1) \cdot M_f \cdot \alpha q \mathbf{I}_m$ and $B_e := J_d \cdot M^d_f \cdot \alpha q \mathbf{I}_m$, and $\Sigma_s := B_s \cdot B^t_s \in \mathbb{R}^{k \times k}$ and $\Sigma_e := B_e \cdot B^t_e \in \mathbb{R}^{d \times d}$, respectively. This means that there is a ppt reduction from $\mathsf{PLWE}^{(f)}_{q, D_{\mathbb{Z}^m, \alpha q}, D_{\mathbb{Z}^m, \alpha q}}$ to $\mathsf{MPLWE}_{q, n, d, D_{\mathbb{Z}^d, \Sigma_e}, D_{\mathbb{Z}^k, \Sigma_s}}$. We now have, using Lemma 1, that

$$\begin{aligned}
\|\Sigma_s\| &\le (\alpha q)^2 \cdot \|\mathsf{Rot}^{d+n-1}_f(1)\|^2 \cdot \|M_f\|^2 \\
&\le (\alpha q)^2 \cdot \left(m + (d + n - 1 - m) \cdot m \cdot \mathrm{EF}(f)^2\right) m \cdot \mathrm{EF}(f)^2 \\
&\le (\alpha q)^2 \cdot \left(n + (n - 1) \cdot n \cdot \mathrm{EF}(f)^2\right) n \cdot \mathrm{EF}(f)^2 \\
&\le (\alpha q)^2 \cdot n^3 \cdot \mathrm{EF}(f)^4 < (\alpha' q)^2
\end{aligned}$$

and

$$\|\Sigma_e\| \le (\alpha q)^2 \cdot \|M_f^d\|^2 \le d \cdot (\alpha q \cdot \mathrm{EF}(f))^2 < (\alpha'' q)^2.$$

Since $\|\Sigma_s\| < (\alpha' q)^2$ and $\|\Sigma_e\| < (\alpha'' q)^2$, there exist two symmetric positive definite matrices Σ_s' and Σ_e' such that $\Sigma_s + \Sigma_s' = (\alpha' q)^2 \mathbf{I}_k$ and $\Sigma_e + \Sigma_e' = (\alpha'' q)^2 \mathbf{I}_d$. We now replace the rerandomization to uniform of the reduction of [RSSS17, Le. 3.7] by a rerandomization to a Gaussian distribution. We first sample $t \xleftarrow{\$} D_{\mathbb{Z}^k, \Sigma_s'}$. For any $\mathsf{MPLWE}_{q,n,d,D_{\mathbb{Z}^d,\Sigma_e},D_{\mathbb{Z}^k,\Sigma_s}}$ sample (a_i, b_i), we sample $e' \xleftarrow{\$} D_{\mathbb{Z}^d, \Sigma_e'}$ and output $(a_i', b_i') = (a_i, b_i + a_i \odot_d t + e_i')$. If (a_i, b_i) is uniform, so is (a_i', b_i'). If $b_i = a_i \odot_d s + e_i$, then

$$b_i' = a_i \odot_d s + e_i + a_i \odot_d t + e_i' = a_i \odot_d (s + t) + (e_i + e_i').$$

The matrices $\Sigma_s, \Sigma_s', \Sigma_e$ and Σ_e' are all symmetric, so they are in particular orthogonally diagonalizable. Moreover, since Σ_s and Σ_s' (resp. Σ_e and Σ_e') commute, it means that Σ_s and Σ_s' (resp. Σ_e and Σ_e') are simultaneously diagonalizable. We can hence write $\Sigma_s = U D_s U^t$ and $\Sigma_s' = U D_s' U^t$ for two diagonal matrices D_s and D_s' such that $(\alpha' q)^2 \mathbf{I}_k = D_s + D_s'$ and an orthogonal matrix $U \in \mathbb{R}^{k \times k}$. Similarly, we can write $\Sigma_e = V D_e V^t$ and $\Sigma_e' = V D_e' V^t$, where D_e and D_e' are diagonal, $D_e + D_e' = (\alpha'' q)^2 \mathbf{I}_d$ and $V \in \mathbb{R}^{d \times d}$ is orthogonal. Since the smoothing parameter is invariant to rotations, we can write

$$\eta_{2^{-k}}\left(\sqrt{\Sigma_s^{-1} + \Sigma_s'^{-1}} \cdot \mathbb{Z}^k\right) = \eta_{2^{-k}}\left(\sqrt{U(D_s^{-1} + D_s'^{-1})U^t} \cdot \mathbb{Z}^k\right)$$
$$= \eta_{2^{-k}}\left(U\sqrt{D_s^{-1} + D_s'^{-1}} \cdot \mathbb{Z}^k\right)$$
$$= \eta_{2^{-k}}\left(\sqrt{D_s^{-1} + D_s'^{-1}} \cdot \mathbb{Z}^k\right).$$

Using Lemma 4, we have that

$$\eta_{2^{-k}}\left(\sqrt{D_s^{-1} + D_s'^{-1}} \cdot \mathbb{Z}^k\right) \le \max_i \sqrt{1/\sigma_i(\Sigma_s) + 1/((\alpha' q)^2 - \sigma_i(\Sigma_s))} \cdot \sqrt{k+1}.$$

We showed that $\sigma_1(\Sigma_s) \le (\alpha q)^2 \sigma_1(M_f)^2 \sigma_1(\mathsf{Rot}_f^{d+n-1}(1))^2 \le (\alpha' q)^2/2$, which means that $(\alpha' q)^2 - \sigma_i(\Sigma_s) \ge \sigma_i(\Sigma_s)$ for any $i \le k$ and thus $1/\sigma_i(\Sigma_s) + 1/(\alpha' q)^2 - \sigma_i(\Sigma_s) \le 2/\sigma_i(\Sigma_s) \le 2/\sigma_k(\Sigma_s)$ for any $i \le k$.

Using the bound on the smallest singular value of M_f, we now get that $\sigma_k(\Sigma_s) \ge (\alpha q)^2 \sigma_m(M_f)^2 \sigma_m(\mathsf{Rot}_f^{n+d-1}(1))^2 \ge (\alpha q)^2 \cdot T^2$, which guarantees that

$$\eta_{2^{-k}}\left(\sqrt{D_s^{-1} + D_s'^{-1}} \cdot \mathbb{Z}^k\right) \le \sqrt{\frac{2}{(\alpha q)^2 \cdot T^2}} \cdot \sqrt{k+1} \le 1$$

for $\alpha \ge \frac{2\sqrt{n}}{q \cdot T}$. As a consequence, using Lemma 5, the statistical distance between the distribution of $s + t$ and $D_{\mathbb{Z}^k, \alpha' q}$ is $< 4 \cdot 2^{-d} = 4\varepsilon$ as $k > d$.

Similarly, we have $\eta_{2^{-d}}\left(\sqrt{\Sigma_e^{-1} + \Sigma_e'^{-1}} \cdot \mathbb{Z}^d\right) \le 1$ and the statistical distance between the distribution of $e_i + e_i'$ and $D_{\mathbb{Z}^d, \alpha'' q}$ is also $\le 4\varepsilon$. This completes the proof. $\qquad\square$

We notice that in contrast with the reduction from [RSSS17], the above reduction requires a lower bound on the noise parameter α which is used in order to approximate the distribution of the sum of two random discrete variables as in Lemma 5. The following result provides a concrete exponentially large family of polynomials f for which we manage to bound from below the smallest singular value of the matrix M_f.

Lemma 8. *Let* $f = x^m + P(x) \in \mathbb{Z}[x]$ *with* $m \geq 2$ *and* $\deg(P) \leq m/2$. *Then* $\sigma_m(M_f) \geq \frac{1}{2 + \sqrt{m} \cdot \mathrm{EF}(f)}$.

Proof. By reordering the rows of M_f, the singular values stay the same and we can view M_f as a block of four matrices $D_1 \in \mathbb{Z}^{\lfloor m/2 \rfloor \times \lfloor m/2 \rfloor}$, $D_2 \in \mathbb{Z}^{\lceil m/2 \rceil \times \lceil m/2 \rceil}$, $\mathbf{0} \in \mathbb{Z}^{\lceil m/2 \rceil \times \lfloor m/2 \rfloor}$ and $T \in \mathbb{Z}^{\lfloor m/2 \rfloor \times \lceil m/2 \rceil}$ in the following way:

$$M_f = \left[\begin{array}{c|c} D_1 & T \\ \hline \mathbf{0} & D_2 \end{array} \right].$$

The matrices D_1 and D_2 are diagonal, $\mathbf{0}$ is the all-0 matrix and T is an upper triangular matrix. We now use the definition $\sigma_m(M_f) = \min(\|M_f \cdot y\|_2 : y \in \mathbb{R}^m, \|y\|_2 = 1)$. Let $y \in \mathbb{R}^m$ such that $\sigma_m(M_f) = \|M_f \cdot y\|_2$ and $\|y\|_2 = 1$. The vector y can be written as $y = (y_0^t | y_1^t)^t$, with $y_0 \in \mathbb{R}^{\lfloor m/2 \rfloor}$ and $y_1 \in \mathbb{R}^{\lceil m/2 \rceil}$. On the one hand, we have:

$$\begin{aligned}
\|M_f \cdot y\|_2 &\geq \|D_1 \cdot y_0 + T \cdot y_1\|_2 \geq \|D_1 \cdot y_0\|_2 - \|T \cdot y_1\|_2 \\
&\geq \|y_0\|_2 - \|T\| \cdot \|y_1\|_2 \\
&\geq \|y\|_2 - \|y_1\|_2 - \|M_f\| \cdot \|y_1\|_2 \\
&\geq 1 - (1 + \sqrt{m} \cdot \mathrm{EF}(f)) \cdot \|y_1\|_2,
\end{aligned}$$

where the last inequality is by Lemma 1. On the other hand, we also have

$$\|M_f \cdot y\|_2 \geq \|D_2 \cdot y_1\|_2 \geq \|y_1\|_2.$$

This provides the bound

$$\sigma_m(M_f) \geq \max\left(1 - (1 + \sqrt{m} \cdot \mathrm{EF}(f)) \cdot \|y_1\|_2, \|y_1\|_2\right) \geq \frac{1}{2 + \sqrt{m} \cdot \mathrm{EF}(f)}.$$

$\square$

An elementary computation shows that for any polynomial as in the above Lemma 8, we have $\mathrm{EF}(f) \leq \frac{3}{4} m^2 \|P\|_\infty^2$ (see also [LM06, Se. 3.1] for a similar but more general statement). This implies the following corollary of Theorem 2.

Corollary 1. *Fix* $S > 0$. *For any degree* $m \geq 2$ *polynomial* $f = x^m + P(x) \in \mathbb{Z}[x]$ *with constant coefficient coprime with* q *such that* $\deg(P) \leq m/2$ *and* $\|P\|_\infty^2 \leq 4S/3$ *and any* $1 \geq \alpha \geq 2\sqrt{n} \cdot (2 + \sqrt{n}S)/q$ *there is a* ppt *reduction from* $\mathsf{PLWE}_{q,D_{\mathbb{Z}^m},\alpha q, D_{\mathbb{Z}^m},\alpha q}^{(f)}$ *to* $\mathsf{MPLWE}_{q,n,d,D_{\mathbb{Z}^d},\alpha''q, D_{\mathbb{Z}^k},\alpha'q}$, *where* $\alpha' = \alpha n\sqrt{2n} \cdot S^2$ *and* $\alpha'' = \alpha\sqrt{2d} \cdot S$.

4   An Attack on Inhomogeneous $\mathsf{PSIS}^\emptyset$ with Small Secrets

In contrast to our hardness result for MPLWE with small secret coordinates shown in the previous section, here we show a simple efficient attack on the Inhomogeneous $\mathsf{PSIS}^\emptyset$ problem from [Lyu16] with sufficiently small secret coordinates (such that it has a unique solution). Our algorithm gives a key recovery attack against a small secret variant of the signature scheme of [Lyu16], and shows that a lower bound on the size of the secret key coordinates similar to that in the security proof of [Lyu16] is *necessary* for the security of that signature scheme. MPSign achieves lower signature size than [Lyu16], by using small secret coordinates. The attack presented below shows that a similar improvement in signature size *cannot* be securely achieved in [Lyu16], stressing an MPSign advantage over the approach of [Lyu16].

We recall the definition of the Inhomogeneous $\mathsf{PSIS}^\emptyset$ problem (which we denote by I-$\mathsf{PSIS}^\emptyset$) from [Lyu16]. The hardness of that problem underlies the security of the key generation algorithm in the signature scheme of [Lyu16]. We note that our definition below is the 'exact' case of the 'approximate' definition in [Lyu16] (with the parameters of [Lyu16, Def. 3.3] set as $c = 1$, $s = \beta$ and $d_1 = d_2 = d$). This restriction makes our attack even stronger since a solution to the exact problem is also a solution to the 'approximate' problem.

Definition 13 (I-$\mathsf{PSIS}^\emptyset$). *Let* $n, d > 0$. *An instance of the* I-$\mathsf{PSIS}^\emptyset_{q,n,d,k,\beta}$ *problem consists of* $(a_1, \ldots, a_k, t)$, *where* $a_i \xleftarrow{\$} \mathbb{Z}_q^{<n}[x]$ *for* $i = 1, \ldots, k$ *and* $t = \sum_{i=1}^k a_i \cdot s_i \in \mathbb{Z}_q^{<n+d-1}[x]$, *where* $s_i \xleftarrow{\$} [-\beta, \beta]^{<d}[x]$ *for* $i = 1, \ldots, k$. *A solution to the problem is* k *elements* $(s'_1, \ldots, s'_k)$ *with* $s'_i \in [-\beta, \beta]^{<d}[x]$ *for* $i = 1, \ldots, k$ *such that*

$$\sum_{i=1}^k a_i \cdot s'_i = t.$$

Note that the public key of the signature scheme of [Lyu16] consists of an instance of I-$\mathsf{PSIS}^\emptyset$, and a solution is a valid secret key.

Our attack on I-$\mathsf{PSIS}^\emptyset$ works in the case where $s_1, \ldots, s_k$ is the unique solution, and consists of a simple greedy algorithm that exploits the zero triangles in the Toeplitz matrices associated with the polynomials a_i, to reduce the problem to a sequence of k-dimensional knapsack subproblems: for each $r < d$, we recover the k-tuple of coefficients of x^r in the polynomials $s_i(x)$ for $i = 1, \ldots, k$. When k is small (as is the case for efficient parameter sets), the attack is efficient.

In more detail, let $t(x) = \sum_{i=1}^k a_i(x) \cdot s_i(x) \in \mathbb{Z}_q^{<n+d-1}[x]$ be the target polynomial in an instance of I-$\mathsf{PSIS}^\emptyset$. We denote by t_r, $a_{i,r}$ and $s_{i,r}$ the coefficient of x^r in the polynomials $t(x), a_i(x), s_i(x)$, respectively. We observe that for any $r = 0, \ldots, d-1$, the coefficient t_r depends only on the coefficients of x^j for $j \leq r$ of the s_i's, namely we have

$$t_r = \sum_{i=1}^k \sum_{j=0}^r a_{i,j} \cdot s_{i,r-j} = \sum_{i=1}^k a_{i,0} \cdot s_{i,r} + \sum_{i=1}^k \sum_{j=1}^r a_{i,j} \cdot s_{i,r-j}. \tag{1}$$

Given an instance $(a_1, \ldots, a_k, t)$ of the I-PSIS$^{\emptyset}_{q,n,d,k,\beta}$ problem, our algorithm works as follows:

1. For $r = 0, \ldots, d-1$:
   (a) Find *some* vector $s'_{*,r} := (s'_{1,r}, \ldots, s'_{k,r}) \in [-\beta, \beta]^k$ such that

$$t_r = \sum_{i=1}^{k} a_{i,0} \cdot s'_{i,r} + \sum_{i=1}^{k} \sum_{j=1}^{r} a_{i,j} \cdot s'_{i,r-j}. \tag{2}$$

   (b) If no such vector $s'_{*,r}$ exists, return $\bot$.
2. Return $(s'_1, \ldots s'_k)$, where $s'_i = \sum_{j=0}^{d-1} s'_{i,j} x^j$ for $i = 1, \ldots, k$.

Lemma 9. *Suppose q is prime. With probability $\geq 1 - (4\beta + 1)^k / q$ over the choice of $a_1, \ldots, a_k$, the solution $(s'_1, \ldots, s'_k) = (s_1, \ldots, s_k)$ to the I-PSIS$^{\emptyset}_{q,n,d,k,\beta}$ problem is unique, and the above algorithm returns this solution in time $(2\beta + 1)^k \cdot \mathrm{poly}(n, d, \log q)$.*

Proof. It follows from (1) that the solution $(s'_1, \ldots, s'_k) = (s_1, \ldots, s_k)$ satisfies (2) for each r and hence can be output by the algorithm. Now suppose, towards a contradiction, that the algorithm outputs $\bot$ or a different solution $(s'_1, \ldots, s'_k) \neq (s_1, \ldots, s_k)$. Then let $r^* \geq 0$ denote the *least* iteration r of the algorithm where the solution $s'_{*,r^*} := (s'_{1,r^*}, \ldots, s'_{k,r^*})$ to (2) for $r = r^*$ is not equal to $s_{*,r^*} := (s_{1,r^*}, \ldots, s_{k,r})$. From (2), we have

$$t_{r^*} = \sum_{i=1}^{k} a_{i,0} \cdot s'_{i,r^*} + \sum_{i=1}^{k} \sum_{j=1}^{r} a_{i,j} \cdot s_{i,r^*-j} = \sum_{i=1}^{k} a_{i,0} \cdot s_{i,r^*} + \sum_{i=1}^{k} \sum_{j=1}^{r} a_{i,j} \cdot s_{i,r^*-j},$$

and hence

$$\sum_{i=1}^{k} a_{i,0} \cdot (s_{i,r^*} - s'_{i,r^*}) = 0.$$

As a consequence, the vector $v^* := (s_{1,r^*} - s'_{1,r^*}, \ldots, s_{k,r^*} - s'_{k,r^*}) \neq 0$ satisfies $\sum_{i=1}^{k} a_{i,0} v_i^* = 0$, and $v^* \in [-2\beta, 2\beta]^k$. We claim that such a non-zero vector v^* exists with probability at most $(4\beta + 1)^k / q$ over the uniform choice of the $a_{i,0}$'s. Indeed, since q is prime, the probability that a fixed non-zero vector $v \in [-2\beta, 2\beta]^k$ satisfies $\sum_{i=1}^{k} a_{i,0} v_i = 0$ is $1/q$. A union bound over all $\leq (4\beta + 1)^k$ non-zero vectors in $[-2\beta, 2\beta]^k$ provides the claim. Therefore, the algorithm outputs the unique solution $(s'_1, \ldots, s'_k) = (s_1, \ldots, s_k)$ with probability at least $1 - (4\beta + 1)^k / q$. The run-time follows since Step 1(a) in the algorithm can be implemented by an exhaustive search through all $(2\beta + 1)^k$ possible values for $s'_{*,r}$. $\square$

We observe that the run-time can be reduced to $2^{O(k)} \cdot \mathrm{poly}(n, d, \log q)$ using a lattice closest vector algorithm to solve the k-dimensional knapsack problems.

By Lemma 9, our algorithm for I-PSIS$_{q,n,d,k,\beta}^{\emptyset}$ succeeds with high probability when β is at least slightly smaller than $q^{1/k}/4$, and runs in polynomial time when $k = O(1)$, even for very high degrees n and d. In comparison, the hardness reduction for I-PSIS$_{q,n,d,k,\beta}^{\emptyset}$ in [Lyu16, Le. 3.4] requires the lower bound $\beta > 2^{\lambda/(kd)-1} \cdot q^{1/k \cdot (1+n/d)}$ (where λ denotes the security parameter and is such that the success probability of the I-PSIS$^{\emptyset}$ attacker handled by the reduction is $>2^{-\lambda}$). Our attack gives an efficient key recovery attack against the signature scheme of [Lyu16] with small secrets β. For instance, the recommended parameters of the latter scheme have $k = 6$ and $q \approx 2^{30}$ and $\beta \approx 2^{11.5}$, but $\beta < 2^3$ will suffice for our attack to succeed. Moreover, heuristically, we expect that our algorithm will succeed with even larger β corresponding to a unique solution. The runtime is likely in practice to be in the order of minutes on a typical laptop[1], using LLL lattice reduction for solving the 6-dimensional knapsack instances; even a brute-force search of each knapsack instance would take in the order of only $(2\beta)^k < 2^{30}$ arithmetic operations. For the above parameters, our LLL-based implementation solved 7 out of 10 (resp. 2 out of 10) instances with $\beta = 7$ (resp. $\beta = 8$), taking about 3 min on a 3.1 GHz Intel Core i5 CPU.

5   A Signature Scheme Based on Small Secrets MPLWE

In this section, we build an identification scheme based on the middle-product learning with errors with small secrets assumption. Then, we show that Theorem 1 is applicable to our construction by checking all the theorem assumptions, as in [KLS18]. As a consequence, by the Fiat-Shamir transformation, we obtain a digital signature scheme that is secure under the middle-product learning with errors with small secrets assumption in the quantum random oracle model.

5.1   The Identification Scheme

We first present in Fig. 3 an identification scheme which makes use of the middle-product of polynomials.

We use an extendable output function Sam, i.e., a function on bit strings in which the output can be extended to any required length. If we want the deterministic output y of Sam on input x to be uniformly distributed on the set S, we write $y \xleftarrow{\$} S := Sam(x)$.

The key generation starts by choosing a random string ρ and expanding it into a uniform polynomial $a \in \mathbb{Z}_q^{<n}[x]$ using the function Sam. The public key consists of a sample (a, b) drawn from the MP$_{q,n,d+k,\chi}(s)$ distribution, where both the secret s and the error e follow a Gaussian distribution of parameter $\alpha'q$, respectively $\alpha''q$.

In the first step of the protocol, the prover chooses two polynomials y_1 and y_2 whose coefficients are bounded in absolute value by a', respectively a'', and sends to the verifier the polynomial $w = a \odot_d y_1 + y_2$. The verifier chooses a random challenge from the challenge space

---

[1] https://github.com/pqc-ntrust/middle-product-LWE-signature.

$$D_H := \{c \in \{0, 1, -1\}^{<k+1}[x] \text{ with } \|c\|_1 = \kappa\}$$

and sends it back to the prover. The challenge space consists of polynomials of small norms and the parameter κ is chosen such that the cardinality of the challenge space is large. The prover now applies rejection in order to make sure that his answer doesn't leak information about the secret key. Concretely, the prover computes $z_1 = c \odot_{n+d-1} s + y_1$ and $z_2 = c \odot_d e + y_1$ and checks if $\|z_1\|_\infty \le A'$ and $\|z_2\|_\infty \le A''$. If so, it accepts to send his answer (z_1, z_2) to the verifier. Otherwise, it aborts. We provide concrete parameters with which our scheme can be instantiated in practice in the next section.

IGen	**P_1 (sk)**
1: $\rho \xleftarrow{\$} \{0,1\}^{256}$	1: $y_1 \xleftarrow{\$} \mathbb{Z}_{\le a'}^{<n+d-1}[x]$
2: $a \xleftarrow{\$} \mathbb{Z}_q^{<n}[x] := Sam(\rho)$	2: $y_2 \xleftarrow{\$} \mathbb{Z}_{\le a''}^{<d}[x]$
3: $s \xleftarrow{\$} D_{\mathbb{Z}^{n+d+k-1}, \alpha' q}$	3: $w = a \odot_d y_1 + y_2$
4: $e \xleftarrow{\$} D_{\mathbb{Z}^{d+k}, \alpha'' q}$	4: output $W = w, St = (w, y_1, y_2)$
5: $b = a \odot_{d+k} s + e$	
6: $\mathsf{pk} = (\rho, b)$	**$P_2(\mathsf{sk}, W = w, c, St = (w, y_1, y_2))$**
7: $\mathsf{sk} = (\rho, s, e)$	
8: output $(\mathsf{pk}, \mathsf{sk})$	1: $z_1 = c \odot_{n+d-1} s + y_1$
	2: $z_2 = c \odot_d e + y_2$
	3: **if** $\|z_1\|_\infty > A'$ or $\|z_2\|_\infty > A''$ **then**
	4: $(z_1, z_2) = \perp$
	5: **end if**
	6: output $Z = (z_1, z_2)$

V $(\mathsf{pk}, W = w, c, Z = (z_1, z_2))$

1: $a \xleftarrow{\$} \mathbb{Z}_q^{<n}[x] := Sam(\rho)$
2: **if** $w = a \odot_d z_1 + z_2 - c \odot_d b$, $\|z_1\|_\infty \le A'$ and $\|z_2\|_\infty \le A''$ **then**
3:    output 1
4: **else**
5:    output 0
6: **end if**

Fig. 3. The identification scheme $(\mathsf{IGen}, \mathsf{V}, \mathsf{P} = (\mathsf{P}_1, \mathsf{P}_2))$

Lemma 10. *If $A' + \|c \odot_{n+d-1} s\|_\infty \le a'$ and $A'' + \|c \odot_d e\|_\infty \le a''$, then the identification scheme is perfectly na-HVZK, i.e., its transcripts are publicly simulatable and $\varepsilon_{zk} = 0$.*

Proof. Figure 4 (left) shows how to generate a real transcript using the secret key sk, and Fig. 4 (right) shows how to simulate a transcript using only the public key pk. The identification scheme is perfectly na-HVZK if every pair of polynomials $(z_1, z_2) \in \mathbb{Z}_{\le A'}^{<n+d-1}[x] \times \mathbb{Z}_{\le A''}^{<d}[x]$ has the same probability to be generated in the Trans algorithm as in the Sim algorithm. This is indeed the

case: our choice of parameters guarantees that $z_1 - c \odot_{n+d-1} s \in \mathbb{Z}_{\leq a'}^{<n+d-1}[x]$ and $z_2 - c \odot_d e \in \mathbb{Z}_{\leq a''}^{<d}[x]$ and moreover, for any secret key (s, e) and any pair (z_1, z_2), we have that

$$\Pr(z_1 = c \odot_{n+d-1} s + y_1 | y_1 \xleftarrow{\$} \mathbb{Z}_{\leq a'}^{<n+d-1}[x])$$
$$= \Pr(y_1 = z_1 - c \odot_{n+d-1} s | y_1 \xleftarrow{\$} \mathbb{Z}_{\leq a'}^{<n+d-1}[x])$$

and

$$\Pr(z_2 = c \odot_d e + y_2 | y_2 \xleftarrow{\$} \mathbb{Z}_{\leq a''}^{<d}[x]) = \Pr(y_2 = z_2 - c \odot_d s | y_2 \xleftarrow{\$} \mathbb{Z}_{\leq a''}^{<d}[x]).$$

As a consequence, the probability of producing z_1 and z_2 in Trans such that $\|z_1\|_\infty \leq A'$ and $\|z_2\|_\infty \leq A''$ and not returning $\bot$ is $(\frac{2A'+1}{2a'+1})^{n+d-1}(\frac{2A''+1}{2a''+1})^d$, which means that the outputs of Trans and Sim have the same distribution. $\square$

Trans (sk)

1: $a \xleftarrow{\$} \mathbb{Z}_q^{<n}[x] := Sam(\rho)$
2: $y_1 \xleftarrow{\$} \mathbb{Z}_{\leq a'}^{<n+d-1}[x]$
3: $y_2 \xleftarrow{\$} \mathbb{Z}_{\leq a''}^{<d}[x]$
4: $w = a \odot_d y_1 + y_2$
5: $c \xleftarrow{\$} D_H$
6: $z_1 = c \odot_{n+d-1} s + y_1$
7: $z_2 = c \odot_d e + y_2$
8: **if** $\|z_1\|_\infty > A'$ or $\|z_2\|_\infty > A''$ **then**
9:     output $\bot$
10: **else**
11:     output (z_1, z_2, c)
12: **end if**

Sim (pk)

1: $a \xleftarrow{\$} \mathbb{Z}_q^{<n}[x] := Sam(\rho)$
2: with probability
   $1 - (\frac{2A'+1}{2a'+1})^{n+d-1}(\frac{2A''+1}{2a''+1})^d$
3: output $\bot$
4: $c \xleftarrow{\$} D_H$
5: $z_1 \xleftarrow{\$} \mathbb{Z}_{\leq A'}^{<n+d-1}[x]$
6: $z_2 \xleftarrow{\$} \mathbb{Z}_{\leq A''}^{<d}[x]$
7: output (z_1, z_2, c)

Fig. 4. The transcript Trans and the simulation Sim algorithms

Lemma 11. *The scheme has correctness error* $\delta = 1 - (\frac{2A'+1}{2a'+1})^{n+d-1}(\frac{2A''+1}{2a''+1})^d$.

Proof. First, we show that the verification procedure always accepts a honest transcript if $(z_1, z_2) \neq \bot$. Assume that $(z_1, z_2) \neq \bot$. It means that $\|z_1\|_\infty \leq A'$ and $\|z_2\|_\infty \leq A''$. Now we prove that

$$a \odot_d z_1 + z_2 - c \odot_d b = a \odot_d y_1 + y_2.$$

Because of Lemma 3, we have that

$$a \odot_d z_1 = a \odot_d (c \odot_{n+d-1} s + y_1)$$
$$= a \odot_d (c \odot_{n+d-1} s) + a \odot_d y_1$$
$$= (a \cdot c) \odot_d s + a \odot_d y_1$$

and

$$c \odot_d b = c \odot_d (a \odot_{d+k} s + e)$$
$$= c \odot_d (a \odot_{d+k} s) + c \odot_d e$$
$$= (c \cdot a) \odot_d s + c \odot_d e.$$

Overall, we obtain:

$$a \odot_d z_1 + z_2 - c \odot_d b$$
$$= ((a \cdot c) \odot_d s + a \odot_d y_1) + (c \odot_d e + y_2) - ((c \cdot a) \odot_d s + c \odot_d e)$$
$$= a \odot_d y_1 + y_2.$$

Since Sim outputs $\perp$ with the same probability as Trans, we know that the probability to have $(z_1, z_2) = \perp$ is exactly δ. $\qquad\square$

Lemma 12. *The identification scheme* ID *is lossy.*

Proof. In the lossy key generation algorithm LossyIGen (Fig. 5), we generate the public key (a, b) uniformly. The public keys generated by IGen and LossyIGen are indistinguishable by the MPLWE assumption. Indeed, for any quantum adversary A against ID, there exists an adversary B trying to distinguish MPLWE samples from uniform ones such that the loss advantage $\mathrm{Adv}_{\mathsf{ID}}^{loss}(A)$ is equal to the advantage of B. $\qquad\square$

Lemma 13. *The identification scheme* ID *has* $d \cdot \log(2a'' + 1)$ *bits of min-entropy.*

Proof. Indeed, for every commitment ω, we have that:

$$\Pr_{a, y_1, y_2}(a \odot_d y_1 + y_2 = \omega) \le \max_{a, y_1} \Pr_{y_2}(y_2 = \omega - a \odot_d y_1) \le \frac{1}{(2a'' + 1)^d},$$

where the first probability is taken over the uniform choice of $a \in \mathbb{Z}_q^{<n}[x]$, $y_1 \in \mathbb{Z}_{\le a'}^{<n+d-1}[x]$ and $y_2 \in \mathbb{Z}_{\le a''}^{<d}[x]$. In the second one, the probability is taken over the uniform choice of $y_2 \in \mathbb{Z}_{\le a''}^{<d}[x]$ and the maximum is taken over all $a \in \mathbb{Z}_q^{<n}[x]$ and $y_1 \in \mathbb{Z}_{\le a'}^{<n+d-1}[x]$. $\qquad\square$

Lemma 14. *The identification scheme* ID *is* ε_{ls}-*lossy-sound, where*

$$\varepsilon_{ls} \le \frac{1}{|D_H|} + (4A' + 1)^{n+d-1} \cdot (4A'' + 1)^d \cdot |D_H|^2 \cdot q^{-d}.$$

Proof. We show that relatively to a lossy key pk_{ls} generated by the LossyIGen algorithm in Fig. 5, not even an unbounded quantum adversary can impersonate the prover. This reduces to the computation of the following probability taken over the uniform choice of $a \in \mathbb{Z}_q^{<n}[x]$, $b \in \mathbb{Z}_q^{<d+k}[x]$ and $c \in D_H$:

$$P := \Pr(\exists \, z_1 \in \mathbb{Z}_{\le A'}^{<n+d-1}[x], z_2 \in \mathbb{Z}_{\le A''}^{<d}[x] : a \odot_d z_1 + z_2 - c \odot_d b = w).$$

LossyIGen

1: $\rho \xleftarrow{\$} \{0,1\}^{256}$
2: $a \xleftarrow{\$} \mathbb{Z}_q^{<n}[x] := Sam(\rho)$
3: $b \xleftarrow{\$} \mathbb{Z}_q^{<d+k}[x]$
4: output $\mathsf{pk}_{ls} = (a,b)$

Fig. 5. The LossyIGen algorithm

Let S denote the set of pairs (a,b) such that there exists at most one c for which there exist small z_1, z_2 such that $a \odot_d z_1 + z_2 - c \odot_d b = w$. We can write $P \le P_1 + P_2$, where

$$P_1 = \Pr((a,b) \in S) \cdot \frac{1}{|D_H|} \le \frac{1}{|D_H|}$$

and

$$P_2 \le \Pr((a,b) \notin S) \cdot 1$$
$$\le \Pr(\exists\, c \ne c', z_1, z_2, z_1', z_2' : a \odot_d (z_1 - z_1') + z_2 - z_2' - (c - c') \odot_d b = 0)$$
$$= \Pr(\exists\, e_c \in D_H - D_H \setminus \{0\}, e_1 \in \mathbb{Z}_{\le 2A'}^{<n+d-1}, e_2 \in \mathbb{Z}_{\le 2A''}^{<d} :$$
$$a \odot_d e_1 + e_2 - e_c \odot_d b = 0),$$

where a and b are uniformly sampled in $\mathbb{Z}_q^{<n}[x]$, respectively $\mathbb{Z}_q^{<d+k}[x]$, $c, c' \in D_H$, $z_1, z_1 \in \mathbb{Z}_{\le A'}^{<n+d-1}[x]$, and $z_2, z_2' \in \mathbb{Z}_{\le A''}^{<d}[x]$ and $D_H - D_H$ denotes the set $\{d - d' \mid d, d' \in D_H\}$.

Let us fix $(e_c \ne 0, e_1, e_2)$. The rank of $\mathsf{Toep}(e_c)$ is maximum for $e_c \ne 0$, which means that the function $b \mapsto e_c \odot_d b$ maps an element b from the uniform distribution on $\mathbb{Z}_q^{<d+k}[x]$ to an element b' from the uniform distribution on $\mathbb{Z}_q^{<d}[x]$. We can now write:

$$\Pr(a \odot_d e_1 + e_2 - e_c \odot_d b = 0) = \Pr(b' = a \odot_d e_1 + e_2) = q^{-d},$$

where the first probability is taken over the uniform choice of $a \in \mathbb{Z}_q^{<n}[x]$ and $b \in \mathbb{Z}_q^{<d+k}[x]$ and the second one is taken over the choice of $a \in \mathbb{Z}_q^{<n}[x]$ and $b' \in \mathbb{Z}_q^{<d}[x]$. We conclude that $P_2 \le (4A' + 1)^{n+d-1} \cdot (4A'' + 1)^d \cdot |D_H|^2 \cdot q^{-d}$. $\square$

5.2   The Signature Scheme

In Fig. 6, we present our digital signature scheme which is obtained by the derandomized Fiat-Shamir transform of the identification scheme ID. The correctness of the signature scheme follows (see [KLS18, p. 11]) from the correctness of the underlying identification scheme (Lemma 11). The scheme is UF-CMA secure in the quantum random oracle model, as discussed in Subsect. 2.4.

The signature scheme relies on a hash function $H : \{0,1\}^* \to D_H$, which outputs elements with small norms and will be modelled by a random oracle in the security proof. We refer to [DDLL13] for an efficient method to construct such a hash function.

KeyGen

1: $\rho \xleftarrow{\$} \{0,1\}^{256}$
2: $a \xleftarrow{\$} \mathbb{Z}_q^{<n}[x] := Sam(\rho)$
3: $s \xleftarrow{\$} D_{\mathbb{Z}^{n+d+k-1}, \alpha'q}$
4: $e \xleftarrow{\$} D_{\mathbb{Z}^{d+k}, \alpha''q}$
5: $b = a \odot_{d+k} s + e$
6: $\mathsf{vk} = (b, \rho)$
7: $\mathsf{sk} = (s, e, K, \rho)$
8: output $(\mathsf{sk}, \mathsf{vk})$

Sign $(\mathsf{sk} = (s, e, K, \rho), M)$

1: $a \xleftarrow{\$} \mathbb{Z}_q^{<n}[x] := Sam(\rho)$
2: $i = 0$
3: **while** $(z_1, z_2) = \perp$ and $i \le k_m$ **do**
4: $\quad i = i + 1$
5: $\quad y_1 \xleftarrow{\$} \mathbb{Z}_{<a'}^{<n+d-1}[x] := Sam(K\|M\|i\|0)$
6: $\quad y_2 \xleftarrow{\$} \mathbb{Z}_{<a''}^{<d}[x] := Sam(K\|M\|i\|1)$
7: $\quad w = a \odot_d y_1 + y_2$
8: $\quad c := H(w\|M)$
9: $\quad z_1 = c \odot_{n+d-1} s + y_1$
10: $\quad z_2 = c \odot_d e + y_2$
11: $\quad$ **if** $\|z_1\|_\infty > A'$ or $\|z_2\|_\infty > A''$ **then**
12: $\quad\quad (z_1, z_2) = \perp$
13: $\quad$ **end if**
14: **end while**
15: output (z_1, z_2, c)

Verify $(\mathsf{vk} = (b, \rho), M, (z_1, z_2, c))$

1: $a \xleftarrow{\$} \mathbb{Z}_q^{<n}[x] := Sam(\rho)$
2: $w = a \odot_d z_1 + z_2 - c \odot_d b$
3: **if** $c = H(w\|M)$, $\|z_1\|_\infty \le A'$ and $\|z_2\|_\infty \le A''$ **then**
4: $\quad$ output 1
5: **else**
6: $\quad$ output 0
7: **end if**

Fig. 6. The signature scheme

The key generation algorithm samples $a \xleftarrow{\$} \mathbb{Z}_q^{<n}[x]$ using the extendable function Sam seeded with a 256-bit seed ρ, and then two small secret polynomials $s \xleftarrow{\$} D_{\mathbb{Z}^{n+d+k-1}, \alpha'q}$ and $e \xleftarrow{\$} D_{\mathbb{Z}^{d+k}, \alpha''q}$. It outputs $(b = a \odot_{d+k} s + e, \rho)$ as the verification key vk and (s, e, K, ρ) as the signing key sk, K being a random key for the pseudorandom function $Sam(K\|\cdot)$ used in the signature algorithm.

To sign a message M, we first recompute $a \xleftarrow{\$} \mathbb{Z}_q^{<n}[x] := Sam(\rho)$, generate deterministic masking parameters $y_1 \xleftarrow{\$} \mathbb{Z}_{<a'}^{<n+d-1}[x] := Sam(K\|M\|i\|0)$ and $y_2 \xleftarrow{\$} \mathbb{Z}_{<a''}^{<d}[x] := Sam(K\|M\|i\|1)$, where i is the repetition index and compute $w = a \odot_d y_1 + y_2$. Then we compute $c := H(w\|M)$, $z_1 = c \odot_{n+d-1} s + y_1$ and $z_2 = c \odot_d e + y_2$. A potential signature is now (z_1, z_2, c). In order to make the signature pair (z_1, z_2) independent of the signing key, we perform rejection

sampling on potential signatures before outputting the right one. A potential signature (z_1, z_2, c) is output if both $\|z_1\|_\infty \leq A'$ and $\|z_2\|_\infty \leq A''$.

To check if (z_1, z_2, c) is a valid signature for a message M, we first recompute $a \xleftarrow{\$} \mathbb{Z}_q^{<n}[x] := Sam(\rho)$ and $w = a \odot_d z_1 + z_2 - c \odot_d b$ and we accept if $\|z_1\|_\infty \leq A'$, $\|z_2\|_\infty \leq A''$ and $c := H(w\|M)$.

6   Concrete Parameters

In this section we give sample parameters with which our digital signature scheme can be instantiated. The choice of parameters takes into account the correctness error probability, the security and the efficiency of our scheme.

The signing acceptance probability is set to $p = 1/3$ as in [Lyu16] for a fair comparison.

The security proof of the scheme from [Lyu16] uses the random oracle model, while the security of our scheme, which is based on Theorem 1, holds in the more powerful quantum random oracle model.

In terms of efficiency, we focus on minimizing the size of a signature. Our signature size is $(n + d - 1) \lceil \log(A') \rceil + d \lceil \log(A'') \rceil + \kappa(\lceil \log(k+1) \rceil + 1)$ bits. The optimal value of d/n for minimizing the signature length is close to 0.5. As d/n reduces below 0.5, the signature dimension drops. Due to the lossiness condition, d/n and $\log q$ are inversely proportional, so we have to increase n to maintain security, which means that overall the signature length will increase. If d/n increases towards 1, $\log q$ reduces but the signature dimension increases and we cannot reduce the signature length.

The size of our public key (a, b) is $256 + (d + k)\lceil \log(q) \rceil$. Since for our lossiness property in the security proof we need a much larger q than the one used in [Lyu16], our public key becomes larger than the public key used in [Lyu16]. On the other hand, our scheme has significantly shorter signatures. Our savings in MPSign signature length over the scheme in [Lyu16] arise largely from the smaller secret key coordinates in MPSign. As our attack of Sect. 4 shows, such savings are not possible in the scheme of [Lyu16] due to the insecurity of $\mathsf{PSIS}^\emptyset$ with sufficiently small secret coordinates.

In order to set concrete parameters for our scheme achieving λ bits of security, we need to bound from above the advantage of any adversary trying to attack the UF-CMA security of MPSign in the quantum random oracle model by $2^{-\lambda}$. By Theorem 1 and Lemma 12, it is enough to bound Adv, $\mathrm{Adv}_{\mathsf{PRF}}^{PR}(C)$ and $2^{-d\log(2a'+1)+1}$ by $2^{-\lambda}/5$ and $8(Q_H + 1)^2 \cdot \varepsilon_{ls}$ by $2^{-\lambda+1}/5$, where the notations are those from Sect. 5 and Adv stands for the advantage of an adversary trying to solve the $\mathsf{MPLWE}_{q,n,d+k,\chi_1,\chi_2}$ problem, where both χ_1 and χ_2 are discrete Gaussians of parameters $\alpha''q$, respectively $\alpha'q$. As it is standard in lattice-based cryptography, we further neglect the noise amplification in Theorem 2 and assume that the MPLWE problem with very small secret (with $\|s\|_\infty \approx 1$) is concretely as hard as the $\mathsf{PLWE}^{(f)}$ problem with very small secret. Indeed, there are no known attacks on the MPLWE with small secrets problem that exploit the very small secret when generic algebraic attacks on LWE are protected against (see, e.g., [AG11, ACF+15a, ACF+15b]). Since the discrete Gaussian distributions of the error and secret have small standard deviation, we assume that we can safely replace them by a corresponding centered binomial distribution, as has been done in many practical lattice-based encryption schemes (see [ADPS16, SSZ19, BDK+19], among others).

We use [APS15] in order to estimate both the classical and quantum bit complexities of the primal attack against the $\mathsf{PLWE}^{(f)}$ problem associated to a polynomial f of maximum degree n from the family. The cost models we choose are bkz.sieve for classical security, respectively bkz.qsieve for quantum security.

We present in Table 1 a comparison between the efficiency of MPSign and the scheme described in [Lyu16]. For the same Hermite factor $\delta_0 = 1.005$ (driving the security level), by choosing $n = 2500$, $d = 1300$, $k = 512$ for our scheme, we manage to shorten the size of a signature by a factor of 2.1 and the size of the secret key by a factor of 11 at the cost of doubling the size of the public key.

Table 1. Efficiency of MPSign

	MPSign	[Lyu16]
public key size	19 KB	9.6 KB
secret key size	0.7 KB	8.8 KB
signature size	13 KB	27 KB
q	$\approx 2^{87}$	$\approx 2^{30}$

In the first column of Table 2, we provide concrete parameters for MPSign that satisfy both classical and quantum level 1 NIST requirements. Concretely, they achieve $\lambda \geq 143$ for classical adversaries and $\lambda \geq 130$ for quantum adversaries. The second column contains parameters for $\lambda = 89$ bits of quantum security, corresponding to a Hermite factor $\delta = 1.005$.

7   Implementation

We implemented MPSign in Sage (Python) as a proof-of-concept and the source code is publicly available.[2] For the experiments, we used a MacBook Pro with Intel i7-8559U CPU at 2.7 GHz. Turbo-boost and hyperthreading were both disabled. For a fair comparison, we also implemented the scheme from [Lyu16]. It is expected that both implementations are slower than if they were implemented with a system language (such as C) with an aim for optimization. Nonetheless, since both implementations use the same Gaussian sampler, the same *hash to challenge* function, and the same polynomial multiplication algorithm, we believe that the comparison is relatively fair.

---

[2] https://github.com/pqc-ntrust/middle-product-LWE-signature.

Table 2. Sample parameters for MPSign

	$\lambda = 143$	$\lambda = 89$
n	3800	2500
d	1910	1300
k	512	512
q	$\approx 2^{90.9}$	$\approx 2^{87.3}$
κ	53	53
$|D_H|$	$\approx 2^{294}$	$\approx 2^{294}$
$\log A'$	≈ 21.0	≈ 20.4
$\log A''$	≈ 19.4	≈ 18.9
δ	1.004	1.005
$\alpha' q$	$2\sqrt{\pi}$	$2\sqrt{\pi}$
$\alpha'' q$	$2\sqrt{\pi}$	$2\sqrt{\pi}$
public key size	26.9 KB	19.5 KB
secret key size	1.06 KB	0.74 KB
signature size	20.1 KB	12.8 KB

We instantiate MPSign and the scheme from [Lyu16] with corresponding parameters achieving $\delta = 1.005$. (for MPSign these parameters may be found in Table 2). In both benchmarks we iterated 1000 times, each time with a different seed and a different message to sign. The results of our comparison may be found in Table 3. The data are for the average cost in milliseconds. Our scheme is almost twice faster than the one from [Lyu16] in key generation and verification, and four times faster in signing. This is mainly due to the fact that the scheme from [Lyu16] requires scalar multiplications over vectors of polynomials, while our scheme involves a single middle-product (over a somewhat longer polynomial).

Table 3. Performance comparison, in ms

	[Lyu16]			MPSign		
	min	ave	max	min	ave	max
key generation	22.3	**25.9**	46.7	14.6	**16.3**	27.1
signing	111	**418**	5771	28.3	**99.6**	713
verification	15.0	**30.8**	53.0	16.3	**18.8**	28.6

Acknowledgments. The work of Shi Bai has been supported in part through NIST awards 60NANB18D216 and 60NANB18D217 and through NATO SPS Project G5448. The work of Damien Stehlé has been supported by BPI-France in the context of the national project RISQ (P141580) and by the European Union in the context of the PROMETHEUS project (Horizon 2020 Research and Innovation Program, grant 780701). Part of this work was done while Damien Stehlé was visiting the Simons Institute for the Theory of Computing. The work of Ron Steinfeld was supported in part by ARC Discovery Project grant DP180102199.

References

[ACF+15a] Albrecht, M.R., Cid, C., Faugère, J.-C., Fitzpatrick, R., Perret, L.: Algebraic algorithms for LWE problems. ACM Commun. Comput. Algebra **49**(2), 62 (2015)

[ACF+15b] Albrecht, M.R., Cid, C., Faugère, J.-C., Fitzpatrick, R., Perret, L.: On the complexity of the BKW algorithm on LWE. Des. Codes Crypt. **74**(2), 325–354 (2013). https://doi.org/10.1007/s10623-013-9864-x

[ACPS09] Applebaum, B., Cash, D., Peikert, C., Sahai, A.: Fast cryptographic primitives and circular-secure encryption based on hard learning problems. In: Halevi, S. (ed.) CRYPTO 2009. LNCS, vol. 5677, pp. 595–618. Springer, Heidelberg (2009). https://doi.org/10.1007/978-3-642-03356-8_35

[ADPS16] Alkim, E., Ducas, L., Pöppelmann, T., Schwabe, P.: Post-quantum key exchange - a new hope. In: USENIX, pp. 327–343 (2016)

[AG11] Arora, S., Ge, R.: New algorithms for learning in presence of errors. In: Aceto, L., Henzinger, M., Sgall, J. (eds.) ICALP 2011. LNCS, vol. 6755, pp. 403–415. Springer, Heidelberg (2011). https://doi.org/10.1007/978-3-642-22006-7_34

[APS15] Albrecht, M.R., Player, R., Scott, S.: On the concrete hardness of LWE. J. Math. Cryptol. **9**(3), 169–203 (2015)

[BAA+19] Bindel, N., et al.: qTESLA: algorithm specifications and supporting documentation. NIST PQC round 2 submission document (2019)

[Ban95] Banaszczyk, W.: Inequalities for convex bodies and polar reciprocal lattices in R^n. Discret. Comput. Geom. **13**(2), 217–231 (1995). https://doi.org/10.1007/BF02574039

[BBD+19] Bai, S., Boudgoust, K., Das, D., Roux-Langlois, A., Wen, W., Zhang, Z.: Middle-product learning with rounding problem and its applications. In: Galbraith, S.D., Moriai, S. (eds.) ASIACRYPT 2019. LNCS, vol. 11921, pp. 55–81. Springer, Cham (2019). https://doi.org/10.1007/978-3-030-34578-5_3

[BDE+11] Buchmann, J., Dahmen, E., Ereth, S., Hülsing, A., Rückert, M.: On the security of the Winternitz one-time signature scheme. In: Nitaj, A., Pointcheval, D. (eds.) AFRICACRYPT 2011. LNCS, vol. 6737, pp. 363–378. Springer, Heidelberg (2011). https://doi.org/10.1007/978-3-642-21969-6_23

[BDK+19] Bos, J.W., et al.: CRYSTALS - Kyber: a CCA-secure module-lattice-based KEM. In: Euro S P, pp. 353–367 (2019)

[BG14] Bai, S., Galbraith, S.D.: An improved compression technique for signatures based on learning with errors. In: Benaloh, J. (ed.) CT-RSA 2014. LNCS, vol. 8366, pp. 28–47. Springer, Cham (2014). https://doi.org/10.1007/978-3-319-04852-9_2

[BPS16] Bellare, M., Poettering, B., Stebila, D.: From identification to signatures, tightly: a framework and generic transforms. In: Cheon, J.H., Takagi, T. (eds.) ASIACRYPT 2016. LNCS, vol. 10032, pp. 435–464. Springer, Heidelberg (2016). https://doi.org/10.1007/978-3-662-53890-6_15

[DDLL13] Ducas, L., Durmus, A., Lepoint, T., Lyubashevsky, V.: Lattice signatures and bimodal Gaussians. In: Canetti, R., Garay, J.A. (eds.) CRYPTO 2013. LNCS, vol. 8042, pp. 40–56. Springer, Heidelberg (2013). https://doi.org/10.1007/978-3-642-40041-4_3

[DFMS19] Don, J., Fehr, S., Majenz, C., Schaffner, C.: Security of the Fiat-Shamir transformation in the quantum random-oracle model. In: Boldyreva, A., Micciancio, D. (eds.) CRYPTO 2019. LNCS, vol. 11693, pp. 356–383. Springer, Cham (2019). https://doi.org/10.1007/978-3-030-26951-7_13

[DKL+18] Ducas, L., et al.: CRYSTALS - Dilithium: digital signatures from module lattices. In: CHES, pp. 238–268 (2018)

[Hir18] Hiromasa, R.: Digital signatures from the middle-product LWE. In: Baek, J., Susilo, W., Kim, J. (eds.) ProvSec 2018. LNCS, vol. 11192, pp. 239–257. Springer, Cham (2018). https://doi.org/10.1007/978-3-030-01446-9_14

[HPS98] Hoffstein, J., Pipher, J., Silverman, J.H.: NTRU: a ring-based public key cryptosystem. In: Buhler, J.P. (ed.) ANTS 1998. LNCS, vol. 1423, pp. 267–288. Springer, Heidelberg (1998). https://doi.org/10.1007/BFb0054868

[Kat10] Katz, J.: Digital Signatures. Springer, Boston (2010). https://doi.org/10.1007/978-0-387-27712-7

[KLS18] Kiltz, E., Lyubashevsky, V., Schaffner, C.: A concrete treatment of Fiat-Shamir signatures in the quantum random-oracle model. In: Nielsen, J.B., Rijmen, V. (eds.) EUROCRYPT 2018. LNCS, vol. 10822, pp. 552–586. Springer, Cham (2018). https://doi.org/10.1007/978-3-319-78372-7_18

[LM06] Lyubashevsky, V., Micciancio, D.: Generalized compact knapsacks are collision resistant. In: Bugliesi, M., Preneel, B., Sassone, V., Wegener, I. (eds.) ICALP 2006. LNCS, vol. 4052, pp. 144–155. Springer, Heidelberg (2006). https://doi.org/10.1007/11787006_13

[LPR13] Lyubashevsky, V., Peikert, C., Regev, O.: On ideal lattices and learning with errors over rings. J. ACM **60**(6), 43:1–43:35 (2013)

[LPSS14] Ling, S., Phan, D.H., Stehlé, D., Steinfeld, R.: Hardness of k-LWE and applications in traitor tracing. In: Garay, J.A., Gennaro, R. (eds.) CRYPTO 2014. LNCS, vol. 8616, pp. 315–334. Springer, Heidelberg (2014). https://doi.org/10.1007/978-3-662-44371-2_18

[LS15] Langlois, A., Stehlé, D.: Worst-case to average-case reductions for module lattices. Des. Codes Crypt. **75**(3), 565–599 (2014). https://doi.org/10.1007/s10623-014-9938-4

[LVV19] Lombardi, A., Vaikuntanathan, V., Vuong, T.D.: Lattice trapdoors and IBE from middle-product LWE. In: Hofheinz, D., Rosen, A. (eds.) TCC 2019. LNCS, vol. 11891, pp. 24–54. Springer, Cham (2019). https://doi.org/10.1007/978-3-030-36030-6_2

[Lyu16] Lyubashevsky, V.: Digital signatures based on the hardness of ideal lattice problems in all rings. In: Cheon, J.H., Takagi, T. (eds.) ASIACRYPT 2016. LNCS, vol. 10032, pp. 196–214. Springer, Heidelberg (2016). https://doi.org/10.1007/978-3-662-53890-6_7

[LZ19] Liu, Q., Zhandry, M.: Revisiting post-quantum Fiat-Shamir. In: Boldyreva, A., Micciancio, D. (eds.) CRYPTO 2019. LNCS, vol. 11693, pp. 326–355. Springer, Cham (2019). https://doi.org/10.1007/978-3-030-26951-7_12

[MR04] Micciancio, D., Regev, O.: Worst-case to average-case reductions based on Gaussian measures. In: FOCS, pp. 372–381. IEEE (2004)

[NIS] NIST: Post-quantum cryptography - round 1 submissions. https://csrc.nist.gov/Projects/Post-Quantum-Cryptography/Round-1-Submissions

[PFH+19] Prest, T., et al.: Falcon: algorithm specifications and supporting documentation. NIST PQC round 2 submission document (2019)

[PR06] Peikert, C., Rosen, A.: Efficient collision-resistant hashing from worst-case assumptions on cyclic lattices. In: Halevi, S., Rabin, T. (eds.) TCC 2006. LNCS, vol. 3876, pp. 145–166. Springer, Heidelberg (2006). https://doi.org/10.1007/11681878_8

[PRS17] Peikert, C., Regev, O., Stephens-Davidowitz, N.: Pseudorandomness of ring-LWE for any ring and modulus. In: STOC, pp. 461–473. ACM (2017)

[RSSS17] Roşca, M., Sakzad, A., Stehlé, D., Steinfeld, R.: Middle-product learning with errors. In: Katz, J., Shacham, H. (eds.) CRYPTO 2017. LNCS, vol. 10403, pp. 283–297. Springer, Cham (2017). https://doi.org/10.1007/978-3-319-63697-9_10

[RSW18] Rosca, M., Stehlé, D., Wallet, A.: On the ring-LWE and polynomial-LWE problems. In: Nielsen, J.B., Rijmen, V. (eds.) EUROCRYPT 2018. LNCS, vol. 10820, pp. 146–173. Springer, Cham (2018). https://doi.org/10.1007/978-3-319-78381-9_6

[Sch89] Schnorr, C.P.: Efficient identification and signatures for smart cards. In: Brassard, G. (ed.) CRYPTO 1989. LNCS, vol. 435, pp. 239–252. Springer, New York (1990). https://doi.org/10.1007/0-387-34805-0_22

[SSTX09] Stehlé, D., Steinfeld, R., Tanaka, K., Xagawa, K.: Efficient public key encryption based on ideal lattices. In: Matsui, M. (ed.) ASIACRYPT 2009. LNCS, vol. 5912, pp. 617–635. Springer, Heidelberg (2009). https://doi.org/10.1007/978-3-642-10366-7_36

[SSZ17] Steinfeld, R., Sakzad, A., Zhao, R.K.: Titanium: proposal for a NIST post-quantum public-key encryption and KEM standard (2017)

[SSZ19] Steinfeld, R., Sakzad, A., Zhao, R.K.: Practical MP-LWE-based encryption balancing security-risk versus efficiency. Des. Codes Crypt. **87**(12), 2847–2884 (2019)

Proofs and Arguments II

Witness Indistinguishability for Any Single-Round Argument with Applications to Access Control

Zvika Brakerski[1(✉)] and Yael Kalai[2]

[1] Weizmann Institute of Science, Rehovot, Israel
zvika.brakerski@weizmann.ac.il
[2] Microsoft Research and MIT, Cambridge, USA

Abstract. Consider an access policy for some resource which only allows access to users of the system who own a certain set of attributes. Specifically, we consider the case where such an access structure is defined by some *monotone* function $f : \{0,1\}^N \to \{0,1\}$, belonging to some class of function F (e.g. conjunctions, space bounded computation), where N is the number of possible attributes.

In this work we show that any succinct single-round delegation scheme for the function class F can be converted into a *succinct* single-round *private* access control protocol. That is, a verifier can be convinced that an approved user (i.e. one which holds an approved set of attributes) is accessing the system, without learning any additional information about the user or the set of attributes.

As a main tool of independent interest, we show that assuming a quasi-polynomially secure two-message oblivious transfer scheme with statistical sender privacy (which can be based on quasi-polynomial hardness of the DDH, QR, DCR or LWE assumptions), we can convert *any* single-round protocol into a *witness indistinguishable* one, with similar communication complexity.

1 Introduction

The main goal in the study of *delegation of computation* is to construct a single-round *succinct* argument system for a wide class of functions, in which the communication complexity and verification computational complexity are independent (or at least sublinear) in the computational complexity of deciding the statement, and where the prover (given a witness if needed) can compute a proof efficiently (i.e. with comparable complexity to that of deciding the statement). Delegation schemes for polynomially computable functions under standard assumptions were presented by [GKR08, KRR13, KRR14, KP15, RRR16,

Z. Brakerski—Supported by the Binational Science Foundation (Grant No. 2016726), and by the European Union Horizon 2020 Research and Innovation Program via ERC Project REACT (Grant 756482) and via Project PROMETHEUS (Grant 780701).

A. Kiayias et al. (Eds.): PKC 2020, LNCS 12111, pp. 97–123, 2020.
https://doi.org/10.1007/978-3-030-45388-6_4

BHK17,KPY18]. In this work, we consider delegation for **NP**. Constructing delegation for all of **NP** under standard assumptions is an important open problem, and such schemes are only known in the random oracle model [Mic94], and under knowledge assumptions [DFH12,BCCT13,BCC+14]. However, for restricted classes of **NP** languages, there are delegation schemes from standard assumptions [BHK17,BKK+17].

When delegating an **NP** statement, the prover needs to hold a witness that allows to decide the statement. In such a case a natural question is whether the privacy of the witness is preserved by the delegation scheme. In this work we show a general transformation that translates any delegation scheme into a witness indistinguishable one, without blowing up the communication by much. We then apply this transformation to known delegation schemes based on standard assumptions, and construct an object that we call "succinct access control scheme". These objects allow a master authority to distribute credentials of attributes to parties, in a way that will allow them to provide a succinct proof that the credentials that they hold satisfy a predicate, without revealing the credentials or their identity.

1.1 Our Witness Indistinguishability Transformation

We show a *generic transformation* that converts any single-round (2-message) delegation scheme into one that is also *witness indistinguishable* (WI), *without blowing up the communication complexity*. This transformation relies on the existence of a quasi-poly secure OT scheme, which can be based on the quasi-polynomial hardness of the DDH, QR, Paillier's decisional composite residuosity assumption (DCR) and recently also the Learning with Errors assumption (LWE). The communication complexity and verifier complexity remain unchanged up to $\text{poly}(\lambda)$ factors. This transformation relies on a recent 2-message strong WI protocol in the delayed input setting, proposed by [JKKR17]. (In this work we achieve computational WI, but we believe it may be possible to achieve statistical witness indistinguishability using the results and techniques of [KKS18].) See details in Sects. 1.3 and 2.

It should be noted that the high level approach of executing a delegation scheme homomorphically in order to achieve privacy for the witness can be traced back to prior works, e.g. [BBK+16]. However, our result statement and analysis are different from what is done in prior works.

1.2 Application: Succinct Single-Round Access Control

By applying our WI transformation to a class of succinct single-round argument systems in the literature, that we call "batch **NP** families", we get a succinct single-round witness indistinguishable argument system that allows a user to prove that they contain a set of attributes that satisfies a given monotone access structure. We call this "a succinct access control scheme". We start by explaining what delegation for batch **NP** family is, and proceed with our construction.

Delegation for Batch NP Families. The work of [BHK17] considered a special setting of delegation for **NP** languages. They considered a conjunction (AND function) of a number of "small" **NP** statements, and showed a delegation protocol whose communication complexity scaled with the witness length of a small statement, rather than a concatenation of the witnesses. We can consider an extension of this paradigm, replacing the conjunction with other classes of functions. Note that this only makes sense for monotone functions, since a prover can always claim not to have a witness for a specific small instance.

Formally, our batch **NP** families will be characterized by a family of monotone functions F. The statements to be proven will be characterized by a collection of instances $x_1, \ldots, x_N$ respective to a language L, and a monotone function (i.e. without negation gates) $f : \{0,1\}^N \to \{0,1\}$ in F. The statement $((x_1, \ldots, x_N), f)$ holds if $f(\mathbf{1}_{x_1 \in L}, \ldots, \mathbf{1}_{x_N \in L}) = 1$, where $\mathbf{1}_{x_i \in L} = 1$ if and only if $x_i \in L$. For example, we can consider statements of the form $(((x_1 \in L) \wedge (x_2 \in L)) \vee (x_3 \in L)) \wedge (x_4 \in L)$, and much more. In order to produce an accepting proof, an honest prover needs a set of witnesses for a subset $S \subseteq [N]$ of the x_i's that makes f accept. Namely a set of witnesses $\{w_i\}_{i \in S}$ so that w_i is a witness for x_i and the set S is sufficient for f to accept; i.e., $f(\mathbf{1}_{1 \in S}, \ldots, \mathbf{1}_{N \in S}) = 1$. Since f is monotone, this indeed implies that $f(\mathbf{1}_{x_1 \in L}, \ldots, \mathbf{1}_{x_N \in L}) = 1$ (since S is a subset of the x_i's that are in L).

A delegation scheme for such a family is said to be succinct if the communication complexity is independent of N (most desirably $(m + \text{polylog}(n, N)) \cdot \text{poly}(\lambda)$) and the verifier computational complexity only depends on N to the extent that it is required to read the input and a description of the function f. In particular, if f has a succinct representation, e.g. it can be generated by a Turing machine, then the verification complexity can be lower. Indeed, our results are interesting for families F that consist of functions f that have a succinct description. We also require a *proof-of-knowledge* property, meaning that one can efficiently extract a valid witness $\{w_i\}_{i \in S}$ from any (possibly cheating) prover that convinces the verifier to accept with non-negligible probability.

As mentioned above, if the class F is the class of conjunctions, [BHK17] provide a delegation scheme with the aforementioned properties. We also notice that the work of Badrinarayanan et al. [BKK+17] implies such a delegation scheme for space-bounded non-deterministic computations.

Access Control Schemes. Consider a setting where there are N public keys $\mathsf{pk}_1, \ldots, \mathsf{pk}_N$ (for a very large N), and each user receives for some subset $S \subset [N]$ (corresponding to his credentials) a set of secret keys $\{\mathsf{sk}_i\}_{i \in S}$, where each sk_i corresponds to pk_i. Now suppose a user wishes to prove *anonymously* and *succinctly* that his credentials satisfy some monotone formula $f : \{0,1\}^N \to \{0,1\}$. Namely, he wishes to prove that his set S satisfies $f(\mathbf{1}_{1 \in S}, \ldots, \mathbf{1}_{n \in S}) = 1$. Combining our two main results (monotone **NP** delegation and our WI transformation) we obtain a single-round *succinct* and *anonymous* scheme, where a user can succinctly prove that his set of secret keys satisfies some monotone access structure (formulated as a monotone formula), where the anonymity property is WI and the length of a proof is $|\mathsf{sk}_i| \cdot \text{poly}(\log N, \lambda)$, where $|\mathsf{sk}_i|$ is the length of a *single* secret key, and λ is the security parameter. We call such a scheme a *succinct single-round access control scheme*.

Moreover, we can make our scheme *collusion resilient*. Namely, we can ensure that if two users have credentials corresponding to two sets $S_1, S_2 \subseteq [N]$, then together they cannot get credentials corresponding to $S_1 \cup S_2$, and moreover together they cannot prove more than what each user could have proven individually. This is done by introducing a signature scheme and setting each secret key to be a signature on the attribute concatenated with a random tag that is unique for the user. The random tags will prevent mixing an matching between different users' attributes. We refer to Sect. 3 for the formal definition and the construction.

We note that our notion of access control systems is similar to the notion of *anonymous credentials* [Cha85]. We identify two main differences between the two notions. One is that anonymous credentials require anonymity even against the issuer of the credentials, whereas in our model the issuer is a trusted party. The second is that anonymous credentials are not required to be succinct, in the sense that the proof could depend on the number of attributes, whereas succinctness is a cornerstone in the definition of access control systems. We believe that our techniques may be useful towards the construction of *succinct* anonymous credential schemes under standard assumptions by replacing the signature scheme from our construction in Sect. 3 with *blind signatures* [Cha82].

1.3   Technical Overview of Our WI Transformation

We show how to convert any single-round (2-message) argument system (and in particular, our single-round delegation protocol) with super-polynomial security into a witness indistinguishable one, with minimal (asymptotic) blowup to the communication complexity, albeit witness indistinguishability holds only against polynomial time distinguishers. We note that we can get super-polynomial security by properly strengthening the assumption, namely for any function $T(\lambda) \geq \lambda$ (where λ is the security parameter), if the original scheme was secure against any $\mathrm{poly}(T)$-size adversary then we get witness indistinguishability against all $T^{o(1)}$-size adversaries. Furthermore, if the original protocol is extractable then the transformation would allow to apply the extractor as well.

The basic idea is for the verifier to simply send the first message of the protocol, and for the prover to compute its response according to the protocol, but rather than sending it to the verifier "in the clear", it will send a *statistically binding commitment* to the response. The idea is then for the prover to provide a WI proof (in parallel) that he indeed sent a commitment to an accepting response to the verifier's first message.

This idea runs into several obstacles, let us present the most severe ones. First, the original protocol may not be publicly verifiable (and indeed we would like to apply it to our aforementioned privately verifiable protocol), in which case the prover cannot prove that he is committing to a message that corresponds to an accepting response, since he does not know the verifier's verdict function. Second, we require that the prover commits to the accepting response using a statistically binding commitment, but this means that there is only one accepting witness and WI becomes meaningless. We next explain how to address these obstacles.

To address the first obstacle, we consider the secret state that the verifier keeps and is used to render the verdict of acceptance on the prover's response. In our new protocol, the verifier will send, along with its delegation query, its random tape in an encoded form. This encoded form should allow to apply the functionality of the prover under the encoding and send the encoded result back to the verifier, and at the same time hide the state so that soundness is maintained. To this end, we present an abstraction that we call *private remote evaluation scheme*, which can be thought of as a one-time non compact homomorphic encryption scheme with malicious circuit privacy. We show that this primitive can be constructed using garbled circuits and using an oblivious transfer protocol with security against malicious receivers (the same assumption is required for the WI proof system that we need to use). Given the verifier's random tape encoded in this way, the prover can "homomorphicly" check that indeed applying the verifier's query generation on the encoded random tape results in the query string sent by the verifier, and that the prover's response to this query string will result in the verifier accepting. The prover will perform this operation on the encoded random tape (note that the expected output should always be an encoding of 1) and prove in WI that the resulting encoding was indeed generated using the aforementioned operation. Since our encoding scheme is circuit-private, the verifier will not learn anything from the encoding itself (since it is just an encoding of 1), but the WI proof will guarantee that indeed the prover committed to a message that would have made the verifier of the original protocol accept.

The communication complexity of the generic remote evaluation scheme that we present is proportional to the running time of the verifier in the underlying argument system. This aspect could be improved by using a *succinct* remote evaluation scheme (i.e., a circuit private fully homomorphic encryption scheme), where the communication complexity does not grow with the running time. Such an evaluation scheme requires fully homomorphic encryption and can therefore is currently only known based on the learning with errors assumption (LWE), whereas our generic solution can be based on a variety of assumptions. We chose not to specify the succinct version in this work since we anyway inherit a communication blowup from the WI protocol that we use (see below), which in general can anyway grow with the running time of the verifier. Thus, we chose to avoid introducing a new assumption for this purpose.

Let us now specify the properties of the two message WI protocol that is required for this approach to go through. First of all, we notice that we need a protocol with *adaptive soundness*, i.e. soundness holds even against a prover that chooses the statement to be proven after seeing the verifier's first message. We emphasize that even though we use as a building block a WI protocol with adaptive soundness, our resulting (succinct) WI protocol is not adaptively sound (i.e., soundness holds only against provers that choose the statement to be proven before seeing the verifier's message).

Second, we need to address the aforementioned vacuousness of the standard notion of WI when proving with respect to a committed value. This is resolved by resorting to the notion of *strong WI*, which considers two distributions over instance-witness pairs, and requires that if the instance components of the two distributions are computationally indistinguishable, then the verifier cannot distinguish which instance-witness pair was used to generate the proof. Indeed, the recently proposed protocol of Jain et al. [JKKR17] has the required properties (in the delayed input setting), under the assumption that a quasi-poly secure OT scheme exists (we refer to Sect. 2 for details, and in particular to Theorem 2.5).

Lastly, we require extractability, namely being able to extract the committed response to the delegation protocol in case the WI protocol accepted. However, since the prover only sends a single message, we cannot get extractability under standard assumptions. We therefore rely on complexity leveraging, and extract the prover answer by brute-force breaking the hiding of the commitment scheme. This means that in order for soundness to hold, we need all components other than the commitment scheme to be secure even in the presence of this brute-force extractor, i.e. to have super-polynomial security. This way, we can scale down the hardness of the commitment scheme and allow it to be broken while leaving the other building blocks secure.

2 Witness Indistinguishability for Any Argument System

In this section we present our general transformation for converting any 2-message argument system into a 2-message witness indistinguishable one with only modest increase in communication complexity.

2.1 Preliminaries

Our transformation makes use of several cryptographic building blocks, which we present below.

Garbled Circuits. We rely on a decomposable randomized encoding scheme. For the sake of concreteness we consider garbled circuits.

Definition 2.1 (Garbled Circuits). *A garbling scheme consists of a tuple of three algorithms* (Garble, GCEval, GCSim) *where:*

1. Garble$(1^\lambda, C)$ *is a PPT algorithm that takes as input the security parameter λ (ommitted when clear from the context) and a circuit $C : \{0,1\}^n \to \{0,1\}^m$, and outputs a garbled circuit $\widehat{C}$ along with input labels $(\mathsf{lab}_{i,b})_{i\in[n],b\in\{0,1\}}$ where each label $\mathsf{lab}_{i,b} \in \{0,1\}^\lambda$.*
2. GCEval$(1^\lambda, \widehat{C}, \widehat{\mathsf{lab}})$ *is a deterministic algorithm that takes as input a garbled circuit $\widehat{C}$ along with a set of n labels $\widehat{\mathsf{lab}} = (\mathsf{lab}_i)_{i\in[n]}$, and outputs a string $y \in \{0,1\}^m$.*
3. GCSim$(1^\lambda, 1^{|C|}, 1^n, y)$ *is a PPT algorithm that takes as input the security parameter, the description length of C, an input length n and a string $y \in \{0,1\}^m$, and outputs a simulated garbled circuit $\widetilde{C}$ and labels $\widetilde{\mathsf{lab}}$.*

We often omit the first input to these algorithms (namely, 1^λ) when it is clear from the context. We require that the garbling scheme satisfies two properties:

1. *Correctness: For all circuits C, inputs x, and all $(\widehat{C}, (\mathsf{lab}_{i,b})_{i,b}) \leftarrow \mathsf{Garble}(C)$ and $\widehat{\mathsf{lab}} = (\mathsf{lab}_{i,x_i})_{i\in[n]}$, we have that $\mathsf{GCEval}(\widehat{C}, \widehat{\mathsf{lab}}) = C(x)$.*
2. *Simulation Security: For all circuits $C : \{0,1\}^n \to \{0,1\}^m$ and all inputs $x \in \{0,1\}^n$, the following two distributions are computationally indistinguishable:*

$$\left\{ (\widehat{C}, \widehat{\mathsf{lab}}) : (\widehat{C}, (\mathsf{lab}_{i,b})_{i,b}) \leftarrow \mathsf{Garble}(C), \widehat{\mathsf{lab}} = (\mathsf{lab}_{i,x_i})_{i\in[n]} \right\}$$
$$\overset{c}{\approx} \left\{ (\widetilde{C}, \widetilde{\mathsf{lab}}) : (\widetilde{C}, \widetilde{\mathsf{lab}}) \leftarrow \mathsf{GCSim}(1^\lambda, 1^{|C|}, 1^n, C(x)) \right\}.$$

Oblivious Transfer Secure Against Malicious Receivers. We use a notion of oblivious transfer that has computational security against senders (i.e. receiver privacy) but also (statistical) security against malicious receivers (sender privacy). That is, regardless of the receiver's first message, the sender's response never reveals more than one of its inputs, even to an unbounded adversary.

Definition 2.2 (Two-Message Oblivious Transfer with Statistical Sender Security). *A two-message oblivious transfer is a protocol between two parties, a sender S with messages (m_0, m_1) and receiver $R = (R_1, R_2)$ with a choice bit b, such that R obtains output m_b at the end of the protocol. Specifically, $R_1(b) = R_1(1^\lambda, b)$ outputs (σ, e), where e is the message sent to the receiver and σ is a local state that is kept private. The sender responds with an answer $v = S(1^\lambda, (m_0, m_1), e)$. Finally $R_2(1^\lambda, \sigma, v)$ outputs a message m. We omit the security parameter input to these procedures when it is clear from the context.*

We consider OT that satisfies the following properties:

- **Computational Receiver Security.** *The distributions $R_1(0)$ and $R_1(1)$ are computationally indistinguishable. We sometimes require super-polynomial security, specifically, we say that the OT scheme is T-receiver secure if $T \cdot \mathsf{poly}(\lambda)$-size distinguishers have advantage less than $\frac{\mathsf{negl}(\lambda)}{T}$.*
- **Statistical Sender Security.** *For all λ and for all $e^* \in \{0,1\}^*$ there exists a bit b^* such that the distributions $S(1^\lambda, (m_0, m_1), e^*)$ and $S(1^\lambda, (m_{b^*}, m_{b^*}), e^*)$ are statistically indistinguishable. It would sometimes be convenient to think about b^* as produced by a computationally unbounded procedure Ext so that $b^* = \mathsf{Ext}(1^\lambda, e^*)$ (we sometimes omit 1^λ when it is clear from the context).*

Oblivious transfer protocols satisfying these definitions have been introduced based on assumptions such as DDH, QR, DCR and LWE [NP01, Kal05, HK07, BD18].

Delayed-Input Interactive Protocols and Strong Witness Indistinguishability. A ℓ-message delayed-input interactive protocol (P, V) for deciding an **NP** language L with associated relation R_L proceeds in the following manner:

- At the beginning of the protocol, P and V receive the size of the instance and the security parameter, denoted by n and λ, respectively, and execute the first $\ell - 1$ messages.

– Before sending the last message, P receives as input a pair $(x, w) \in R_L$, where $|x| = n$, and V receives x. Upon receiving the last message from P, V outputs 1 or 0.

An execution of (P, V) with instance x and witness w is denoted as $\langle P, V \rangle(x, w)$. Whenever clear from context, we also use the same notation to denote the output of V.

A ℓ-message delayed-input interactive argument for a language L must satisfy the standard notion of completeness (in the delayed-input setting) as well as *adaptive soundness*, where the soundness requirement holds even against malicious PPT provers who choose the statement adaptively, depending upon the first $\ell - 1$ messages of the protocol.

Definition 2.3 (Delayed-Input Interactive Arguments). *A ℓ-message delayed-input interactive protocol (P, V) for deciding a language L is an interactive argument for L if it satisfies the following properties:*

– **Adaptive Completeness:** *For every $(x, w) \in R_L$ chosen adaptively after $\ell - 1$ rounds of interaction,*

$$\Pr\left[\langle P, V \rangle(x, w) = 1\right] = 1,$$

where the probability is over the random coins of P and V.
– **Adaptive Soundness:** *For every (non-uniform) PPT prover P^* that chooses $n = \text{poly}(\lambda)$ and chooses $x \in \{0, 1\}^n \setminus L$ adaptively, depending upon the first $\ell - 1$ messages,*

$$\Pr\left[\langle P^*, V \rangle(x) = 1\right] = \text{negl}(\lambda),$$

where the probability is over the random coins of V.

Definition 2.4 ((Strong) Witness Indistinguishability). *Let $n = n(\lambda) \leq \text{poly}(\lambda)$. An interactive argument (P, V) for a language L is strong witness indistinguishable (which we denote sWI) if for every pair of distributions over pairs $\{(\mathcal{X}_{1,n(\lambda)}, \mathcal{W}_{1,n(\lambda)})\}_{\lambda \in \mathbb{N}}$ and $\{(\mathcal{X}_{2,n(\lambda)}, \mathcal{W}_{2,n(\lambda)})\}_{\lambda \in \mathbb{N}}$ supported over R_L, for which the distributions $\{\mathcal{X}_{1,n(\lambda)}\}_{\lambda \in \mathbb{N}}$ and $\{\mathcal{X}_{2,n(\lambda)}\}_{\lambda \in \mathbb{N}}$ are computationally indistinguishable, for every PPT verifier V^*, and for every (non-uniform) PPT distinguisher $\mathcal{D}$,*

$$\left| \Pr_{(x,w) \leftarrow (\mathcal{X}_{1,n(\lambda)}, \mathcal{W}_{1,n(\lambda)})}\left[\mathcal{D}(x, \text{View}_{V^*}[\langle P, V^* \rangle(x, w)] = 1\right] \right.$$

$$\left. - \Pr_{(x,w) \leftarrow (\mathcal{X}_{2,n(\lambda)}, \mathcal{W}_{2,n(\lambda)})}\left[\mathcal{D}(x, \text{View}_{V^*}[\langle P, V^* \rangle(x, w)] = 1\right] \right| \leq \text{negl}(\lambda).$$

Standard (as opposed to strong) witness indistinguishability (which we denote simply by WI) only requires that the above holds for singleton distributions, which is equivalent (due to the indistinguishability condition) to defining a deterministic sequence of input and witness pairs

$$\{(x_{n(\lambda)}, w_{1,n(\lambda)}, w_{2,n(\lambda)})\}_{\lambda \in \mathbb{N}}.$$

In delayed input *strong witness indistinguishability, the above is only required to hold with respect to PPT verifiers V^* who obtain the instance together with the last prover message in the protocol (i.e., who generate their messages obliviously of x). Note that this notion is vacuous for standard (non-strong) WI.*

Theorem 2.5 ([JKKR17]). *For any $T = \lambda^{\omega(1)}$, assume the existence of a non-interactive statistically binding commitment scheme, that is hiding against poly-size adversaries, but where the hiding property can be broken by $\text{poly}(T)$ adversaries, and assume the existence of a $\text{poly}(T)$-secure OT scheme as in Definition 2.2. Then there exists a 2-message delayed-input strong WI protocol for every language in* **NP** *such that soundness holds against $\text{poly}(T)$-size adversaries, but (strong) WI property holds only against poly-size cheating verifiers.*

Remark 2.6. The strong WI property can be strengthened to hold against $\text{poly}(T^*)$-size cheating verifiers, for any $T^* = T^{o(1)}$. However, this requires assuming that the underlying commitment scheme that can be broken in time $\text{poly}(T)$, is secure against $\text{poly}(T^*)$ size adversaries.

2.2 Private Remote Evaluation

Our transformation makes use of a primitive that we call a *private remote evaluation scheme*. Loosely speaking, this can be thought of as a *one-time* non-succinct fully homomoprhic encryption scheme with strong malicious circuit privacy [GHV10,OPP14].

Rather than formally defining this primitive, we construct it following the outline of Yao's 2-party 2-round secure function evaluation protocol [Yao82] (using a garbling scheme satisfying Definition 2.1 and using an oblivious transfer protocol satisfying Definition 2.2), and state its properties.

Let $(R = (R_1, R_2), S)$ be an OT scheme that satisfies Definition 2.2 and let $(\mathsf{Garble}, \mathsf{GCEval}, \mathsf{GCSim})$ be a garbling scheme. Our private remote evaluation scheme consists of a tuple of four algorithms $(\mathsf{Enc}, \mathsf{Eval}, \mathsf{Dec}, \mathsf{Sim})$, defined as follows.

- The encoding algorithm Enc takes an input a security parameter 1^λ and a string $x \in \{0,1\}^n$, and outputs an encoded output ψ and a secret state σ. Specifically, for every bit of x, Enc runs $R_1(1^\lambda, x_i)$ to compute the first OT receiver message $\psi^{(i)}$ and the state $\sigma^{(i)}$. It outputs $\psi = \{\psi^{(i)}\}_{i \in [n]}$, $\sigma = \{\sigma^{(i)}\}_{i \in [n]}$. We sometimes denote by Enc_1 the algorithm that computes Enc and only outputs the ψ component, and we often omit the security parameter from the notation.
- The evaluation algorithm Eval takes as input a circuit $C : \{0,1\}^n \to \{0,1\}^m$ and an encoded input $\psi = \{\psi^{(i)}\}_{i \in [n]}$. It runs $\mathsf{Garble}C$ to generate a garbled circuit $\widehat{C}$ for C with labels $\mathsf{lab}_{i,b}$, and computes the sender response for each OT execution $\psi'^{(i)} = S((\mathsf{lab}_{i,0}, \mathsf{lab}_{i,1}), \psi^{(i)})$. It finally outputs $\psi' = (\{\psi'^{(i)}\}_{i \in [n]}, \widehat{C})$.

– The decoding procedure Dec takes as input $\psi' = (\{\psi'^{(i)}\}_{i \in [n]}, \widehat{C})$ and $\sigma = \{\sigma^{(i)}\}_{i \in [n]}$, and applies the OT receiver protocol to obtain $\mathsf{lab}_i = R_2(\sigma^{(i)}, \psi'^{(i)})$. It finally runs $\mathsf{GCEval}(\widehat{C}, \{\mathsf{lab}_i\}_{i \in [n]})$ and outputs the resulting $y \in \{0,1\}^m$.

– For all $1^n, 1^m, 1^c$ representing input, output and circuit size (these inputs are often omitted when they are clear from the context), there exists a simulator

$$\mathsf{Sim} = (\mathsf{Sim}_1, \mathsf{Sim}_2),$$

such that the following holds. Let Ext be the OT extractor from Definition 2.2. The simulator Sim_1 takes as input a (possibly adversarially chosen) sequence $\psi = \{\psi^{(i)}\}_{i \in [n]}$, and runs Ext on each $\psi^{(i)}$ to obtain a bit x_i. Let $x \in \{0,1\}^n$ denote the collection of the extracted bits.

The simulator Sim_2, takes as input (ψ, x) together with a string $y \in \{0,1\}^m$, it runs in probabilistic polynomial time, and does the following:

1. It runs the PPT garbled circuit simulator GCSim, on input y (and input $1^\lambda, 1^{|C|}, 1^n$), to generate simulated circuit $\widetilde{C}$ and labels $\widetilde{\mathsf{lab}}$.
2. It generates simulated sender messages $\{\widetilde{\psi}^{(i)}\} \leftarrow S((\widetilde{\mathsf{lab}}_i, \widetilde{\mathsf{lab}}_i), x_i)$.
3. It outputs $\widetilde{\psi} = (\{\widetilde{\psi}^{(i)}\}, \widetilde{C})$.

Claim 2.7. *For any $\psi = \{\psi^{(i)}\}_{i \in [n]}$ and any circuit $C : \{0,1\}^n \to \{0,1\}^m$, it holds that*

$$\mathsf{Eval}(C, \psi) \stackrel{c}{\approx} \mathsf{Sim}_2(\psi, x, C(x)),$$

where $x \leftarrow \mathsf{Sim}_1(\psi)$.

Proof. By definition,

$$\mathsf{Eval}(C, \psi) = \left(\left\{ S((\mathsf{lab}_{i,0}, \mathsf{lab}_{i,1}), \psi^{(i)}) \right\}_{i \in [n]}, \widehat{C} \right).$$

Since ψ is fixed, then the value $x \leftarrow \mathsf{Sim}_1(\psi)$ is also fixed. It follows from Definition 2.2 that

$$\mathsf{Eval}(C, \psi) \stackrel{s}{\approx} \left(\left\{ S((\mathsf{lab}_{i,x_i}, \mathsf{lab}_{i,x_i}), \psi^{(i)}) \right\}_{i \in [n]}, \widehat{C} \right).$$

Now we use the garbled circuit security to argue that

$$\mathsf{Eval}(C, \psi) \stackrel{c}{\approx} \left(\left\{ S((\widetilde{\mathsf{lab}}_i, \widetilde{\mathsf{lab}}_i), \psi^{(i)}) \right\}_{i \in [n]}, \widetilde{C} \right) = \mathsf{Sim}_2(\psi, x, C(x)),$$

where $\widetilde{\mathsf{lab}}, \widetilde{C}$ are produced by the garbled circuit simulator given $y = C(x)$.

The following claims are immediate from the OT correctness and receiver security.

Claim 2.8 (Correctness). *For every $n = n(\lambda)$ (not necessarily polynomially bounded), every $x \in \{0,1\}^n$, every $C : \{0,1\}^n \to \{0,1\}$, letting $(\psi, \sigma) \leftarrow \mathsf{Enc}(1^\lambda, x)$, $\psi' \leftarrow \mathsf{Eval}(C, \psi)$, $y = \mathsf{Dec}(\sigma, \psi')$, it holds that $y = C(x)$ with probability 1.*

Claim 2.9 (Receiver Privacy). *For every $n = n(\lambda) \leq \mathsf{poly}(\lambda)$ and every sequences of inputs $x, x' \in \{0,1\}^n$ it holds that $\mathsf{Enc}_1(1^\lambda, x) \stackrel{c}{\approx} \mathsf{Enc}_1(1^\lambda, x')$.*

2.3   Making Single-Round Protocols Witness Indistinguishable

We show how to convert any single-round (2-message) protocol (P, V) with super-polynomial security and perfect completeness into a single-round (2-message) *witness indistinguishable* (WI) protocol, such that if the communication complexity of the original protocol (P, V) is $cc(n, \lambda)$ then the communication complexity of the resulting WI protocol $(P_{\mathrm{WI}}, V_{\mathrm{WI}})$ is $cc(n, \lambda) + \mathrm{poly}(v(n, \lambda))$, where $v(n, \lambda)$ is the total runtime of the original verifier V, both in generating the query string to be sent to the prover and in verifying the response received by the prover. We use the term *verdict function* to refer to the second step on V, namely the function that takes as input the communication transcript and an internal secret state of the verifier, and outputs whether the verifier accepts or rejects. Our transformation requires that the original protocol (P, V) is sound against super-polynomial time adversaries (as we intend to use complexity leveraging). Our theorem statement follows.

Theorem 2.10. *For any super-polynomial function $T : \mathbb{N} \to \mathbb{N}$, there is a generic transformation that transforms any (privately or publicly verifiable) single-round argument (P, V) for an* **NP** *language L with perfect completeness and with soundness against $\mathrm{poly}(T)$-size cheating provers, into a privately verifiable witness indistinguishable single-round argument $(P_{\mathrm{WI}}, V_{\mathrm{WI}})$ for L with the following properties:*

- **Succinctness.** *If the communication complexity of (P, V) is $cc(n, \lambda)$, and V has total time complexity $v(n, \lambda)$, then the communication complexity of $(P_{\mathrm{WI}}, V_{\mathrm{WI}})$ is*[1]

$$cc_{\mathrm{WI}}(n, \lambda) \triangleq cc(n, \lambda) + \mathrm{poly}(\lambda, v(n, \lambda)).$$

- **Completeness.** *For every $x \in L$ and any witness w for x, it holds that $(P_{\mathrm{WI}}(x.w), V_{\mathrm{WI}}(x))$ accepts with probability 1.*
- **Soundness.** *$(P_{\mathrm{WI}}, V_{\mathrm{WI}})$ is sound against (non-uniform) cheating provers of size $\mathrm{poly}(T)$.*[2]
- **Witness Indistinguishability.** *$(P_{\mathrm{WI}}, V_{\mathrm{WI}})$ is witness indistinguishable against (non-uniform) PPT cheating verifiers (but not against $\mathrm{poly}(T)$-size cheating verifiers, see also Remark 2.12 below).*

  This transformation requires the following building blocks:

- *A statistically binding non-interactive commitment scheme* Com *that can be broken in time $\mathrm{poly}(T)$ for all sufficiently large value of λ.*

---

[1] This guarantee is of interest only if $v(n, \lambda)$ is significantly smaller than the witness size, which is the case for example the argument systems constructed in [BHK17, BKK+17].

[2] We emphasize that the soundness property (both for the underlying argument (P, V) and the resulting one $(P_{\mathrm{WI}}, V_{\mathrm{WI}})$) is non-adaptive soundness, where soundness is required to hold only against cheating provers that choose the statement to be proven before seeing the verifier's message.

- *The private remote evaluation scheme* (Enc, Dec, Eval, Sim), *as described in Sect. 2.2, where the underlying OT scheme has receiver privacy against* $\text{poly}(T)$*-size adversaries (i.e, Claim 2.9 is satisfied against* $\text{poly}(T)$*-size adversaries).*
- *A delayed-input single-round (2-message) strong WI (sWI) argument system* $(P_{\text{sWI}}, V_{\text{sWI}})$ *for* **NP***, that is sound against* $\text{poly}(T)$ *size cheating provers.*

In fact, we will show that our transformation enjoys an even stronger soundness guarantee as described next. There exist black-box non-rewinding, instance preserving (where applicable) $\text{poly}(T)$*-time reductions* M_1, M_2, M_3*, such that for every (possibly inefficient) cheating prover* P_{WI}^* *it holds that* $M_1^{P_{\text{WI}}^*}$ *is a cheating prover against the sWI proof system,* $M_2^{P_{\text{WI}}^*}$ *is a distinguisher for the remote evaluation scheme, and* $M_3^{P_{\text{WI}}^*}$ *is a cheating prover against the original argument system, and it holds that the sum of advantages of these adversaries in their related game is at least the advantage of* P_{WI}^* *in the compiled protocol (up to negligible terms).*

We note that the resulting WI protocol is only privately verifiable, even if the underlying protocol was publicly verifiable.

Remark 2.11. We note that if we rely on a *succinct* remote evaluation scheme (e.g., a circuit-private fully homomorphic encryption scheme), then the communication complexity would be $\text{poly}(\lambda) \cdot \text{cc}(n, \lambda) + \text{cc}(\text{sWI})$, where $\text{cc}(\text{sWI})$ is the communication complexity of the underlying strong WI protocol, which in general can be as large as $v(n, \lambda)$, but can be smaller if the underlying strong WI protocol is succinct.

Remark 2.12. One can strengthen the above theorem so that WI holds against any $\text{poly}(T^*)$-size adversaries, for any $T^* = T^{o(1)}$, by relying on a quantified version of Theorem 2.5 (see Remark 2.6), with WI against $\text{poly}(T^*)$-size adversaries. This requires assuming that the underlying commitment scheme Com, which can be broken in time $\text{poly}(T)$, is secure against $\text{poly}(T^*)$-adversaries.

Proof. Consider a language L, time complexity bound T, a protocol (P, V), a private remote evaluation scheme (Enc, Dec, Eval, Sim) and a delayed input strong WI argument system $(P_{\text{sWI}}, V_{\text{sWI}})$, all as described in the theorem statement. We denote by (Q, A) the first and second message respectively exchanged in the protocol (P, V).

Let Com be a statistically binding non-interactive commitment scheme that can be broken in time $\text{poly}(T)$, as described in the theorem statement. Such commitment schemes can be constructed from injective one-way functions. We note that for our purposes it is possible to use Naor's two-message commitment scheme from any one-way function [Nao89] since we can allow a message from the receiver to the sender prior to the commitment message, but for the sake of simplicity we will assume that Com is non-interactive. We further assume w.l.o.g that the length of the commitment string is equal to the length of the committed message plus an additive $\text{poly}(\lambda)$ term. This can be achieved generically using "key encapsulation" (committing to a PRG seed and using the PRG output to mask the message).

We show how to convert (P, V) into a 2-message witness indistinguishable argument, denoted by $(P_{\mathrm{WI}}, V_{\mathrm{WI}})$, which preserves the succinctness property of (P, V), as stated in the theorem statement. Since (P, V) is not necessarily publicly verifiable, in order to verify a transcript (Q, A) the verifier may need a private state, which we denote by st. We will assume w.l.o.g that st is simply the random tape of the verifier V. This will allow to check, given some possible query string Q whether Q is the string generated when V starts with random tape st. If this condition holds, we say that st is consistent with Q, we denote this by $\mathsf{st} \models Q$. The resulting protocol $(P_{\mathrm{WI}}, V_{\mathrm{WI}})$ makes use of an underlying (not necessarily succinct) delayed-input strong WI 2-message argument $(P_{\mathrm{sWI}}, V_{\mathrm{sWI}})$ for the **NP** language L', defined as follows:

$$L' = \{(1^\lambda, x, Q, c, \mathsf{st}) : \exists (A, r) \text{ s.t.}$$
$$(\mathsf{st} \not\models Q) \vee (c = \mathsf{Com}(A, r) \wedge V(1^\lambda, x, Q, A, \mathsf{st}) = 1)\}. \tag{1}$$

Note that every instance where Q is *inconsistent* with st is trivially *in the language*. Intuitively, this is to force witness indistinguishability also against verifiers who produce inconsistent transcripts. This condition will never be relevant for honest verifiers.

In the protocol $(P_{\mathrm{WI}}, V_{\mathrm{WI}})$, the prover will send a commitment to his answer A (as opposed to sending it in the clear, which may reveal information), followed by a proof that the committed value is an accepting answer. However, to generate such a proof he needs to know the verdict function, and thus, needs the verifier's secret state. However, he cannot receive this secret state "in the clear", since that may breech soundness. Instead, the verifier will send the prover an encoding of his secret state st using the private remote evaluation scheme.

We are now ready to define the protocol $(P_{\mathrm{WI}}, V_{\mathrm{WI}})$:

1. On input 1^λ and $x \in \{0, 1\}^n$ the verifier does the following:
   (a) Compute $(Q, \mathsf{st}) \leftarrow V(1^\lambda, x)$, where Q is the message to be sent to the prover P, and st is the corresponding secret state of V.
   (b) Compute $(\psi, \sigma) \leftarrow \mathsf{Enc}(\mathsf{st})$.
   (c) Compute $(\mathsf{sWI}_1, \mathsf{st}_{\mathrm{sWI}}) \leftarrow V_{\mathrm{sWI}}(1^\lambda)$.
   Note that the first message sWI_1 is independent of the instance since $(P_{\mathrm{sWI}}, V_{\mathrm{sWI}})$ is a delayed-input 2-message argument (see Definition 2.3). Send $(Q, \mathsf{sWI}_1, \psi)$ to the prover, and store $(\sigma, \mathsf{st}, \mathsf{st}_{\mathrm{sWI}})$ as the secret state for verification.
2. The prover, on input $(1^\lambda, x, w)$, and given the message $(Q, \mathsf{sWI}_1, \psi)$, does the following:
   (a) Compute $A \leftarrow P(1^\lambda, x, w, Q)$
   (b) Choose a random string $r \leftarrow \{0, 1\}^{\mathrm{poly}(\lambda)}$ and compute $c = \mathsf{Com}(A, r)$.
   (c) Define (implicitly since st is not known) $x' = (1^\lambda, x, Q, c, \mathsf{st})$, and $w' = (A, r)$ as its corresponding witness with respect to $R_{L'}$, i.e. $(x', w') \in \mathcal{R}_{L'}$.
   (d) Given ψ, compute $\psi' = \mathsf{Eval}(f, \psi)$ where $f = f_{1^\lambda, x, Q, c, w', \mathsf{sWI}_1}$, is the function that on input st outputs $\mathsf{sWI}_2 \leftarrow P_{\mathrm{sWI}}(1^\lambda, x', w', \mathsf{sWI}_1)$.

Send (c, ψ') to the verifier.
3. Upon receiving a message (c, ψ') from the prover, and given a secret state $(\sigma, \mathsf{st}, \mathsf{st}_{\mathsf{sWI}})$ the verifier does the following:
   (a) Decrypt the ciphertext ψ', by computing $\mathsf{sWI}_2 \leftarrow \mathsf{Dec}(\sigma, \psi')$.
   (b) Accept if and only if $V_{\mathsf{sWI}}(1^\lambda, x', \mathsf{sWI}_1, \mathsf{sWI}_2, \mathsf{st}_{\mathsf{sWI}}) = 1$, where $x' = (1^\lambda, x, Q, c, \mathsf{st})$.

Succinctness. We first argue that $(P_{\mathsf{WI}}, V_{\mathsf{WI}})$ satisfies the succinctness property as in the theorem statement. To do this, we argue that

$$\mathsf{cc}(P_{\mathsf{WI}}, V_{\mathsf{WI}}) = \mathsf{cc}(P, V) + \mathsf{poly}(\lambda) + \mathsf{poly}(\lambda, v(n, \lambda)),$$

which would immediately imply the required succinctness.

The first additive $\mathsf{poly}(\lambda)$ term is due to the overhead of sending a commitment to the answer A rather than sending A itself (as explained above, we can assume additive overhead w.l.o.g). The second $\mathsf{poly}(\lambda, v(n, \lambda))$ term is an upper bound on the length of ψ'. The value ψ' is the output of applying Eval on a function f of size $v(n, \lambda) + \mathsf{poly}(\lambda) \leq \mathsf{poly}(\lambda, v(n, \lambda))$ (an upper bound on the prover complexity of P_{sWI} when proving $(x', w') \in \mathcal{R}_{L'}$). Verifying that $(x', w') \in \mathcal{R}_{L'}$ can be done in time proportional to the total complexity of V since checking whether $\mathsf{st} \models Q$ is proportional to running the first phase of V, and checking the value of the verdict function is proportional to the second phase. Add to that checking the commitment which is polynomial in $(\lambda, |A|)$. Since Eval introduces a fixed polynomial overhead, its output length is at most $\mathsf{poly}(\lambda, v(n, \lambda))$.

It remains to prove that $(P_{\mathsf{WI}}, V_{\mathsf{WI}})$ satisfies the standard completeness and soundness guarantees, and in addition that it is witness indistinguishable.

Completeness. The completeness of $(P_{\mathsf{WI}}, V_{\mathsf{WI}})$ follows immediately from the completeness of (P, V), the delayed-input completeness of $(P_{\mathsf{sWI}}, V_{\mathsf{sWI}})$, and the correctness of the underlying private remote evaluation scheme.

Soundness. Consider a cheating prover P_{WI}^* that for any security parameter 1^λ generates $x \in \{0, 1\}^n \setminus L$, where $n \leq \mathsf{poly}(\lambda)$, such that for some non-negligible function $\alpha = \alpha(\lambda)$

$$\Pr[\mathsf{Output}_{V_{\mathsf{WI}}}(P_{\mathsf{WI}}^*, V_{\mathsf{WI}})(1^\lambda, x) = 1] \geq \alpha. \tag{2}$$

Recall that P_{WI}^*, upon receiving a message $(Q, \mathsf{sWI}_1, \psi)$, where $\psi \leftarrow \mathsf{Enc}_1(\mathsf{st})$, from the verifier, generates a response (c, ψ'). Since Com is a statistically binding commitment scheme that can be broken in $\mathsf{poly}(T)$ time, there exists a $\mathsf{poly}(T)$-time algorithm that given c outputs (A', r') such that $c = \mathsf{Com}(A', r')$.

Define

$$\alpha_1 = \alpha_1(\lambda) \triangleq \Pr[(\mathsf{Output}_{V_{\mathsf{WI}}}(P_{\mathsf{WI}}^*, V_{\mathsf{WI}})(1^\lambda, x) = 1) \wedge (V(1^\lambda, x, Q, A', \mathsf{st}) = 0)]. \tag{3}$$

We consider a cheating prover $P_{\mathsf{sWI}}^* = M_1^{P_{\mathsf{WI}}^*}$ (where M_1 is a non-rewinding reduction) that succeeds in breaking the delayed input soundness of $(P_{\mathsf{sWI}}, V_{\mathsf{sWI}})$ with probability α_1. The reduction M_1, takes as input a message sWI_1 from the verifier V_{sWI}, and does the following:

1. Generate $x \leftarrow P^*_{\mathrm{WI}}(1^\lambda)$ using the P^*_{WI} oracle.
2. Compute $(Q, \mathsf{st}) \leftarrow V(1^\lambda, x)$.
3. Compute $(\psi, \sigma) \leftarrow \mathsf{Enc}(\mathsf{st})$.
4. Send $(Q, \mathrm{sWI}_1, \psi)$ to the P^*_{WI} oracle to obtain $(c, \psi') = P^*_{\mathrm{WI}}(Q, \mathrm{sWI}_1, \psi)$.
   Recall that for an honest P_{WI}, it holds that ψ' decrypts to sWI_2.
5. Let $x' = (1^\lambda, x, Q, c, \mathsf{st})$.
6. Compute $\mathrm{sWI}_2 \leftarrow \mathsf{Dec}(\sigma, \psi')$.
7. Send (x', sWI_2) to the verifier.

Note that it suffices to argue that

$$\Pr[V_{\mathrm{sWI}}(1^\lambda, \mathrm{sWI}_1, (x', \mathrm{sWI}_2), \mathsf{st}_{\mathrm{sWI}}) = 1 \wedge (x' \notin L')] \geq \alpha_1.$$

This follows immediately from Eq. (3), together with the fact that $x' \notin L'$ if and only if $V(1^\lambda, x, Q, A', \mathsf{st}) = 0$, where A' is the value that c commits to, and the fact that

$$V_{\mathrm{WI}}(1^\lambda, x, (Q, \mathrm{sWI}_1, \psi), (c, \psi'), \mathsf{st}) = 1$$

only if

$$V_{\mathrm{sWI}}(1^\lambda, \mathrm{sWI}_1, (x', \mathrm{sWI}_2), \mathsf{st}_{\mathrm{sWI}}) = 1.$$

Note that by Eqs. (2) and (3),

$$\Pr[(\mathsf{Output}_{V_{\mathrm{WI}}}(P^*_{\mathrm{WI}}, V_{\mathrm{WI}})(1^\lambda, x) = 1) \wedge (V(1^\lambda, x, Q, A', \mathsf{st}) = 1)] \geq \alpha - \alpha_1. \quad (4)$$

We now present $\mathrm{poly}(T)$-time straight line reductions M_2, M_3 converting P^*_{WI} into an adversary $\mathcal{A}$ that breaks the indistinguishability property of the encoding scheme (i.e., breaks Claim 2.9 with respect to a $\mathrm{poly}(T)$-size adversary), and into cheating prover P^* for the underlying 2-message argument (P, V), respectively, so that the sum of the advantages of the resulting adversaries, denoted α_2, α_3 respectively is $\alpha_2 + \alpha_3 \geq \alpha - \alpha_1$. Furthermore, M_3 is also input preserving.

The distinguisher $\mathcal{A} = M_2^{P^*_{\mathrm{WI}}}$ runs as follows.

1. Generate $x \leftarrow P^*_{\mathrm{WI}}(1^\lambda)$.
2. Run the verifier $V(1^\lambda, x)$ to generate (Q, st).
3. Send $(\mathsf{st}, 0^{|\mathsf{st}|})$ as the two messages for the distinguishing advantage, and receive a challenge encoding ψ from the encoding scheme challenger.
4. Generate $(\mathrm{sWI}_1, \mathsf{st}_{\mathrm{sWI}}) \leftarrow V_{\mathrm{sWI}}(1^\lambda)$.
5. Send $(Q, \mathrm{sWI}_1, \psi)$ to the P^*_{WI} oracle to obtain $(c, \psi') = P^*_{\mathrm{WI}}(Q, \mathrm{sWI}_1, \psi)$.
6. Run in time $\mathrm{poly}(T)$ to find (A', r') such that $c = \mathsf{Com}(A', r')$.
7. Return $V(1^\lambda, x, Q, A', \mathsf{st})$.

The cheating prover $P^* = M_3^{P^*_{\mathrm{WI}}}$ is as follows.

1. Upon receiving a security parameter 1^λ, generate $x \leftarrow P^*_{\mathrm{WI}}(1^\lambda)$.
2. Upon receiving a message Q from the verifier $V(1^\lambda, x)$, do the following:

(a) compute $(\mathrm{sWI}_1, \mathsf{st}_{s\mathrm{WI}}) \leftarrow V_{s\mathrm{WI}}(1^\lambda)$.
(b) Generate $\psi \leftarrow \mathsf{Enc}_1(0^{|\mathsf{st}|})$ (while st itself is unknown, its length is specified by the protocol, we recall that Enc_1 is the algorithm that executes Enc but only outputs the ψ component, see Sect. 2.2).
(c) Send $(Q, \mathrm{sWI}_1, \psi)$ to the P^*_{WI} oracle to obtain $(c, \psi') = P^*_{\mathrm{WI}}(Q, \mathrm{sWI}_1, \psi)$.
3. Run in time $\mathrm{poly}(T)$ to find (A', r') such that $c = \mathrm{Com}(A', r')$.
4. Send A' to the verifier.

Note that σ is not used at all by our P^* (and of course also not by V which is the distinguisher for the original protocol). Consider an experiment with a prover $\tilde{P}^*$ which is identical to P^* except it uses $\psi = \mathsf{Enc}_1(\mathsf{st})$, where st is the actual secret state corresponding to Q. Then by Eq. (4),

$$\Pr[(\tilde{P}^*, V)(x) = 1] \geq \alpha - \alpha_1.$$

However, by definition of $\tilde{P}^*$, it is identical to P^* except for the use of ψ that encodes st instead of $0^{|\mathsf{st}|}$. If the two behave differently this translates to advantage for the distinguisher $\mathcal{A}$. In other words, the success probability of $\mathcal{A}$ is exactly

$$\alpha_2 = \Pr[(P^*, V)(x) = 1] - \Pr[(\tilde{P}^*, V)(x) = 1].$$

We conclude that $\alpha_1 + \alpha_2 + \alpha_3 \geq \alpha$ as required.

Witness Indistinguishability. It remains to argue that $(P_{\mathrm{WI}}, V_{\mathrm{WI}})$ satisfies the WI criterion. Fix a function $n = n(\lambda) \leq \mathrm{poly}(\lambda)$, and fix any ensemble $\{(x_n, w_{1,n}, w_{2,n})\}_{\lambda \in \mathbb{N}}$, such that $(x_n, w_{1,n}) \in \mathcal{R}_L$ and $(x_n, w_{2,n}) \in \mathcal{R}_L$. Suppose for the sake of contradiction that there exists a (non-uniform) poly-size cheating verifier V^*_{WI}, such that

$$\mathsf{View}_{V^*_{\mathrm{WI}}}(P_{\mathrm{WI}}(1^\lambda, x_n, w_{1,n}), V^*_{\mathrm{WI}}(1^\lambda, x_n)) \not\approx \mathsf{View}_{V^*_{\mathrm{WI}}}(P(1^\lambda, x_n, w_{2,n}), V^*_{\mathrm{WI}}(1^\lambda, x_n)).$$

Assume w.l.o.g that V^*_{WI} is deterministic and denote $V^*_{\mathrm{WI}} = (V^*_{\mathrm{WI},1}, V^*_{\mathrm{WI},2})$ s.t. $(Q, \mathrm{sWI}_1, \psi) = V^*_{\mathrm{WI},1}(1^\lambda, x_n)$ generates the first message of V^*_{WI}, and $V^*_{\mathrm{WI},2}(c, \psi')$ is the distinguisher that takes the message from P_{WI} and outputs a bit. Note that λ determines n and thus also x and $(Q, \mathrm{sWI}_1, \psi)$. Let $\mathsf{st} = \mathsf{Sim}_1(\psi)$, where $\mathsf{Sim}_1(\cdot)$ is the possibly inefficient first part of the simulator for the remote evaluation scheme (see Sect. 2.2). Note that st is uniquely well defined per λ.

We design a cheating non-uniform adversary $V^*_{s\mathrm{WI}}$ for the strongly witness indistinguishable scheme. Note that since the adversary is allowed to be non-uniform, we can hard-code the values $(x_n, w_{1,n}, w_{2,n}, Q, \mathrm{sWI}_1, \psi, \mathsf{st})$ into $V^*_{s\mathrm{WI}}$.

We start by defining the two distributions

$$\{\mathcal{X}'_{1,n(\lambda)}, \mathcal{W}'_{1,n(\lambda)}\}_{\lambda \in \mathbb{N}} \text{ and } \{\mathcal{X}'_{2,n(\lambda)}, \mathcal{W}'_{2,n(\lambda)}\}_{\lambda \in \mathbb{N}},$$

as required by the definition of sWI. The samplers for these distributions can also depend on $(x_n, w_{1,n}, w_{2,n}, Q, \mathrm{sWI}_1, \psi, \mathsf{st})$. Formally, for $b \in \{1, 2\}$, the distribution $(\mathcal{X}'_{b,n(\lambda)}, \mathcal{W}'_{b,n(\lambda)})$ generates pairs $(x'_{b,n}, w'_{b,n}) \in \mathcal{R}_{L'}$ as follows:

1. Emulate the prover $P_{\mathrm{WI}}(1^\lambda, x_n, w_{b,n}, Q, \mathrm{sWI}_1, \psi)$, as follows.
   (a) Compute $A \leftarrow P(1^\lambda, x_n, w_{b,n}, Q)$.
   (b) Compute $c = \mathrm{Com}(A, r)$ with uniformly chosen $r \leftarrow \{0, 1\}^{\mathrm{poly}(\lambda)}$.
2. Set $x'_{b,n} = (1^\lambda, x_n, Q, c, \mathsf{st})$ and $w'_{b,n} = (A, r)$.

The computational hiding property of the commitment scheme implies that indeed

$$\{\mathcal{X}'_{1,n(\lambda)}\}_{\lambda \in \mathbb{N}} \stackrel{c}{\approx} \{\mathcal{X}'_{2,n(\lambda)}\}_{\lambda \in \mathbb{N}}.$$

We still need to prove that $(x'_{b,n}, w'_{b,n}) \in R_{L'}$ for $b \in \{1, 2\}$. If $\mathsf{st} \models Q$ then this follows from the perfect completeness of (P, V). If $\mathsf{st} \not\models Q$ this follows by definition (see Eq. (1)).

For this pair of distributions, the cheating verifier V^*_{sWI} runs as follows.

1. Send the fixed value sWI_1 as the first message.
2. Receive $x' = (1^\lambda, x_n, Q, c, \mathsf{st})$ and message $\mathrm{sWI}_2 = P_{\mathrm{sWI}}(x', w', \mathrm{sWI}_1)$.
3. Generate simulated $\psi' = \mathsf{Sim}_2(\psi, \mathsf{st}, \mathrm{sWI}_2)$, where Sim_2 is the simulator for the remote evaluation scheme (see Sect. 2.2), and output $V^*_{\mathrm{WI},2}(c, \psi', \mathrm{sWI}_2)$.

To prove that V^*_{sWI} indeed distinguishes between the distributions $\{\mathcal{X}'_{b,n(\lambda)}, \mathcal{W}'_{b,n(\lambda)}\}_{\lambda \in \mathbb{N}}$, we consider a hybrid where ψ' is generated as $\mathsf{Eval}(f_{1^\lambda, x, Q, c, w'_{b,n}}, \mathrm{sWI}_1, \psi)$. This hybrid is computationally indistinguishable from the original experiment by Claim 2.7. However, in this hybrid the distribution given to $V^*_{\mathrm{WI},2}$ is identical to the one produced by P_{WI}, and since we assume that V^*_{WI} is a successful adversary against WI, it follows that our V^*_{sWI} successfully distinguishes between the distributions $\{\mathcal{X}'_{b,n(\lambda)}, \mathcal{W}'_{b,n(\lambda)}\}_{\lambda \in \mathbb{N}}$ in contradiction to the strong witness indistinguishability property.

3   Succinct Single-Round Access Control Scheme

In this section we formalize the notion of succinct single-round access control presented in Sect. 1.2. The motivation is to allow authorities to provide users with certificates of owning certain attributes (coming from a very large attribute universe). An authority is specified by a pair of master secret and public keys. After being issued a certificate, the user can succinctly prove in a witness indistinguishable manner that its attributes (issued by a specific authority) satisfy a predicate from a given class of predicates. Note that similarly to the setting of secret sharing, only monotone predicates make sense in this setting, since users can always behave as if they do not have a certain attribute, even if they do. We can now formally define the notion of succinct access control schemes.

Definition 3.1. *A succinct access control scheme with respect to a class of monotone functions F consists of a tuple of PPT algorithms* (Setup, KeyGen, Query, Proof, Verdict), *with the following syntax:*

- Setup *takes as input the security parameter 1^λ and outputs a pair* (mpk, msk) *of master public and secret keys.*

- KeyGen *takes as input a tuple* $(1^\lambda, \mathsf{msk}, N, S, \mathsf{id})$, *where* λ *is the security parameter,* msk *is a master secret key (supposedly generated by* $\mathsf{Setup}(1^\lambda)$), $N \in \mathbb{N}$ *is a parameter such that* $N < 2^\lambda$, $S \subseteq [N]$, *and* id $\in \{0,1\}^\lambda$. *It outputs a secret key* sk.
- Query *takes as input the security parameter* 1^λ *and outputs a pair* $(\mathsf{query}, \mathsf{state})$.
- Proof *takes as input a tuple* $(1^\lambda, f, \mathsf{query}, \mathsf{sk})$, *where* $f : \{0,1\}^N \to \{0,1\}$ *is a predicate from the class* F, query *is supposedly generated by running* $\mathsf{Query}(1^\lambda)$, *and* sk *is supposedly generated by running* KeyGen. *It outputs a succinct proof, denoted by* pf, *of length* $\leq \mathrm{poly}(\lambda)$.
- Verdict *takes as input a tuple* $(1^\lambda, f, \mathsf{query}, \mathsf{state}, \mathsf{mpk}, \mathsf{pf})$ *where* $f : \{0,1\}^N \to \{0,1\}$ *is a predicate from the class* F, $(\mathsf{query}, \mathsf{state})$ *is supposedly generated by* $\mathsf{Query}(1^\lambda)$, mpk *is supposedly generated by* $\mathsf{Setup}(1^\lambda)$, *and outputs* 1 *if and only if* pf *is accepting with respect to* $(1^\lambda, f, \mathsf{query}, \mathsf{state}, \mathsf{mpk})$.

  Moreover, the running time of Verdict *should be sublinear in the complexity of* f, *and only depend polynomially (or preferably quasi-linearly) on the input length and the description length of* f.

In addition, an access control scheme must satisfy the following conditions:

- **Completeness.** *For any* $\lambda \in \mathbb{N}$ *any* $N < 2^\lambda$, *any poly-size* $f : \{0,1\}^N \to \{0,1\}$, *any identity* id $\in \{0,1\}^\lambda$, *and any set* $S \subseteq [N]$ *such that* $f(\mathbf{1}_{1 \in S}, \dots, \mathbf{1}_{N \in S}) = 1$,

$$\Pr[\mathsf{Verdict}(1^\lambda, f, \mathsf{query}, \mathsf{state}, \mathsf{mpk}, \mathsf{pf}) = 1] = 1,$$

  where the probability is over the random coin tosses of Verdict, *over* $(\mathsf{query}, \mathsf{state}) \leftarrow \mathsf{Query}(1^\lambda)$, *over* pf $\leftarrow \mathsf{Proof}(1^\lambda, f, \mathsf{query}, \mathsf{sk})$, *where* sk $\leftarrow \mathsf{KeyGen}(1^\lambda, \mathsf{msk}, N, S, \mathsf{id})$ *and* $(\mathsf{mpk}, \mathsf{msk}) \leftarrow \mathsf{Setup}(1^\lambda)$.
- **Soundness.** *For any* $\lambda \in \mathbb{N}$, *any polynomially-bounded* $N = N(\lambda)$, *any poly-size* $f : \{0,1\}^N \to \{0,1\}$, *we consider an oracle* $\mathcal{O} = \mathcal{O}_{\mathsf{msk}}$, *that on input* (id, S), *outputs* sk $\leftarrow \mathsf{KeyGen}(1^\lambda, \mathsf{msk}, N, S, \mathsf{id})$ *if and only if* id $\in \{0,1\}^\lambda$, $S \subseteq [N]$, *and* $f(\mathbf{1}_{1 \in S}, \dots, \mathbf{1}_{N \in S}) = 0$ *(recall that* f *is monotone); and otherwise output* $\perp$.

  The soundness requirement is that for any PPT adversary $\mathcal{A} = (\mathcal{A}_1, \mathcal{A}_2)$ *it holds that*

$$\Pr[\mathsf{Verdict}(1^\lambda, f, \mathsf{query}, \mathsf{state}, \mathsf{mpk}, \mathsf{pf}^*) = 1] = \mathrm{negl}(\lambda),$$

  where pf* $\leftarrow \mathcal{A}_2(1^\lambda, \mathsf{query}, \mathcal{A}_1^{\mathcal{O}_{\mathsf{msk}}}(1^\lambda, \mathsf{mpk}))$, *and in addition* $(\mathsf{query}, \mathsf{state}) \leftarrow \mathsf{Query}(1^\lambda)$ *and* $(\mathsf{mpk}, \mathsf{msk}) \leftarrow \mathsf{Setup}(1^\lambda)$.

  Note that $\mathcal{A}_2$ *does not take any oracle access, i.e. the adversary is first allowed to interact with the oracle, and only then sees the protocol query. We can hope for a stronger variant where oracle access is allowed after seeing the queries as well, but we cannot currently achieve this stronger notion.*
- **Witness Indistinguishability (WI).** *For any* $\lambda \in \mathbb{N}$, *any polynomially-bounded* $N = N(\lambda)$, *any poly-size* $f : \{0,1\}^N \to \{0,1\}$ *in* F, *any* $\mathsf{id}_0, \mathsf{id}_1 \in$

$\{0,1\}^\lambda$, and any sets $S_0, S_1 \subseteq [N]$ such that $f(\mathbf{1}_{1 \in S_b}, \ldots, \mathbf{1}_{N \in S_b}) = 1$ for both $b = 0$ and $b = 1$, the following holds: For any PPT adversary $\mathcal{A}$ that generates $(\mathsf{query}^*, \mathsf{state}^*) = \mathcal{A}(1^\lambda, \mathsf{msk}, \mathsf{mpk})$,

$$(\mathsf{query}^*, \mathsf{state}^*, \mathsf{msk}, \mathsf{mpk}, \mathsf{pf}_0) \approx (\mathsf{query}^*, \mathsf{state}^*, \mathsf{msk}, \mathsf{mpk}, \mathsf{pf}_1),$$

where
$$\mathsf{pf}_b(\lambda) \leftarrow \mathsf{Proof}(1^\lambda, f, \mathsf{query}^*, \mathsf{sk}_b),$$

where $\mathsf{sk}_b \leftarrow \mathsf{KeyGen}(1^\lambda, \mathsf{msk}, N, S_b, \mathsf{id}_b)$.

Remark 3.2. We note that Definition 3.1 above guarantees that the identity of the prover remains hidden, even if the prover issues many proofs. This is the case since we require the WI property to hold even given msk.

We next define delegation for batch **NP** families, which will be a building block for our construction. The construction and proof will then follow.

3.1 Delegation for Batch-NP Families

In this section we define the notion of a (succinct, single-round) delegation scheme for a subclass of languages in **NP**. While achieving the above for all of **NP** is still out of reach under falsifiable assumptions, many meaningful subclasses of **NP** admit such proof systems with short proof length [BHK17, BKK+17]. We start with a definition, and then proceed to derive corollaries based on known schemes in the literature.

Definition 3.3 (NP-Batching of a Function Family). *Let $F \subseteq \{\{0,1\}^* \to \{0,1\}\}$ be a class of functions. Let $\mathcal{R}$ be an **NP** relation corresponding to an **NP**-language L, with witness length $m = m(n)$ for length n instances. For $x \in \{0,1\}^n$ we let $\mathcal{R}_x : \{0,1\}^m \to \{0,1\}$ denote the function where $\mathcal{R}_x(w) = 1$ if and only if $(x, w) \in \mathcal{R}$. Let N be a polynomial.*

We define the $\mathcal{R}^N$-batching of F, denoted $F^{(\mathcal{R},N)}$ as follows. For all n (recalling that m, N are a function of n), let $F_n = F \cap (\{\{0,1\}^N \to \{0,1\}\})$. For all $f \in F_n$ define $g_f : (\{0,1\}^n)^N \times (\{0,1\}^m)^N \to \{0,1\}$ as

$$g_f((x_1, \ldots, x_N), (w_1, \ldots, w_N)) = f(\mathcal{R}_{x_1}(w_1), \ldots, \mathcal{R}_{x_N}(w_N)). \tag{5}$$

We frequently denote $\mathbf{x} = (x_1, \ldots, x_N)$, $\mathbf{w} = (w_1, \ldots, w_N)$.

Finally, $F^{(\mathcal{R},N)}$ is the class of all such functions g_f, formally:

$$F_n^{(\mathcal{R},N)} = \{g_f : f \in F_n\} \tag{6}$$
$$F^{(\mathcal{R},N)} = \cup_{n \in \mathbb{N}} F_n^{(\mathcal{R},N)}. \tag{7}$$

We omit the superscript where $\mathcal{R}, N$ are clear from the context.

We can now define the notion of a succinct delegation scheme for a batch family.

Definition 3.4 (Delegation for Batch Families). *Let $\mathcal{R}, N, F$ be as in Definition 3.3 and let $F^{(\mathcal{R},N)}$ be the N-batching of $\mathcal{R}$ with respect to F.*

A succinct and doubly efficient delegation scheme (or simply "a delegation scheme" for the purpose of this work) for $F^{(\mathcal{R},N)}$ with communication overhead cov *and verification overhead* vov *(both fixed polynomial functions), is a single-round proof system (P, V) running on inputs $(1^\lambda, \mathbf{x}, M)$, where M is a Turing machine s.t. $M(1^n)$ runs in time $\mathsf{T}(n)$ and outputs a circuit that computes a function $g_n \in F_n^{(\mathcal{R},N)}$.*

with the following guarantees.

- **Efficiency.** *The protocol (P, V), on input $(1^\lambda, \mathbf{x}, M)$, has the following efficiency guarantees, for $\mathbf{x} = (x_1, \ldots, x_N)$ where each $|x_i| = n$, and assuming λ is such that $\mathsf{T}(n) \in [\lambda, 2^\lambda]$:*
  1. *The communication complexity is* $\mathsf{cov}(m, \lambda)$ *(ideally $m \cdot \mathrm{poly}(\lambda)$), where m is the length of a witness corresponding to an instance of length n in $\mathcal{R}_L$.*
  2. *The runtime of V is* $\mathsf{vov}(nN, |M|, m, \lambda)$, *where $|M|$ denotes the size of the non-uniform advice of M.*
  3. *The runtime of P, given a witness $\mathbf{w}$ such that $g_n(\mathbf{x}, \mathbf{w}) = 1$, is* $\mathrm{poly}(\mathsf{T}(n))$.
- **Perfect Completeness.** *For every security parameter λ and any inputs $\mathbf{x} \in (\{0,1\}^n)^N$ and M such that $\mathsf{T}(n) \in [\lambda, 2^\lambda]$, and every satisfying assignment $\mathbf{w} \in (\{0,1\}^m)^N$ such that $g_n(\mathbf{x}, \mathbf{w}) = 1$:*

$$\Pr\left[(P(\mathbf{w}), V)(1^\lambda, \mathbf{x}) = 1\right] = 1,$$

where the probability is over the random coin tosses of V.

- **Soundness.** *For every machine M, for any function $n(\lambda)$ s.t. $\mathsf{T}(n(\lambda)) = \mathrm{poly}(\lambda)$ and for every constant $c \in \mathbb{N}$, there exists a PPT oracle machine $\mathcal{E}_c$ such that if there exists a non-uniform PPT cheating prover P^*, that on input 1^λ generates $\mathbf{x} = \mathbf{x} \in (\{0,1\}^n)^N$, such that for infinitely many $\lambda \in \mathbb{N}$,*

$$\Pr\left[(P^*, V)(1^\lambda, \mathbf{x}, M) = 1\right] \geq \frac{1}{\lambda^c},$$

then for these values of λ,

$$\Pr[\mathcal{E}_c^{P^*}(1^\lambda) = (\mathbf{x}, \mathbf{w}) \ s.t. \ g_n(\mathbf{x}, \mathbf{w}) = 1] = 1 - \mathrm{negl}(\lambda).$$

3.2   Known Batch Delegation Schemes

Starting from the work of [BHK17], delegation schemes are known for a number of function classes F. (Recall a batch delegation scheme for the set of all functions from a standard assumption may be too much to hope for, unless major progress in delegation is made and succinct arguments for all of **NP** are constructed.)

Theorem 3.5 ([BHK17]). *There exists a succinct delegation scheme when the class F is the class of all conjunctions, with quasi-linear verification overhead, under the assumption that computational private-information retrieval (PIR) exists. Furthermore, the delegation scheme is sound even against time T adversaries if the PIR scheme is secure against $\mathrm{poly}(T)$ time adversaries.*

A different result can be achieved based on the construction of [BKK+17].

Corollary 3.6 ([BKK+17]). *For any constant c, there exists a succinct delegation scheme for $F = \mathsf{DSPACE}(n^c)$, with fixed polynomial verification overhead, under the assumption that private-information retrieval (PIR) with sub-exponential security exists. Furthermore, the delegation scheme can be made sound even against sub-exponential time adversaries.*

3.3   Our Scheme

We now formally state the result that is hinted in Sect. 1.2.

Theorem 3.7. *Let F be a class of monotone functions. There exists a succinct single-round access control scheme for F if the following exist for some super-polynomial function $T : \mathbb{N} \to \mathbb{N}$.*

- *A batch delegation scheme for the class F as per Definition 3.4 that is sound against $\mathrm{poly}(T)$-size cheating provers.*
- *A $\mathrm{poly}(T)$-secure 2-message oblivious transfer with statistical sender privacy (as in Definition 2.2 where Claim 2.9 is satisfied w.r.t. $\mathrm{poly}(T)$-size adversaries).*
- *A $\mathrm{poly}(T)$-secure signature scheme.*
- *A statistically-binding commitment scheme that can be broken in time $\mathrm{poly}(T)$.*

The required building blocks can be instantiated from various assumptions. For the delegation scheme, we can rely on the schemes in Theorem 3.5 and Corollary 3.6. Given the new maliciously statistical sender private oblivious transfer and private information retrieval schemes from the DDH, QR, LWE and Decisional Composite Residuosity (DCR, a.k.a Paillier) assumptions [DGI+19], the following corollary follows.

Corollary 3.8. *There exists a succinct single-round access control schemes as follows:*

- *For conjunctions, assuming the quasi-poly hardness of either DDH, QR, LWE, DCR, and assuming the existence of a sub-exponentially secure one-way function.*
- *For monotone space-bounded computation, assuming the sub-exponential hardness of either DDH, QR, LWE, DCR, and assuming the existence of a sub-exponentially secure one-way function.*

The access control scheme uses the following components:

- A batch delegation scheme for the class F as per Definition 3.4 that is sound against $\mathrm{poly}(T)$-size cheating provers The schemes in Theorem 3.5 and Corollary 3.6 are examples for such schemes in the literature. We denote this delegation scheme by (P, V).

– WI compiler w.r.t the super polynomial function $T = T(n)$ (as in Theorem 2.10). This can be constructed assuming the existence of a poly(T)-secure 2-message oblivious transfer with statistical sender privacy (as in Definition 2.2 where Claim 2.9 is satisfied w.r.t. poly(T)-size adversaries), and assuming the existence of a statistically binding commitment scheme Com that can be broken in time poly(T).

– A poly(T)-secure signature scheme SIG (i.e., one that is existentially unforgeable against chosen message attacks by a poly(T)-size adversary), which can be based on any poly(T)-hard to invert one-way function, and does not require additional assumptions.

In what follows, we first present an access control scheme without the WI guarantee. We denote the algorithms in this (non WI) scheme by

$$\mathsf{AccessControl}' = (\mathsf{Setup}, \mathsf{KeyGen}, \mathsf{Query}', \mathsf{Proof}', \mathsf{Verdict}')$$

We then use our WI compiler from Sect. 2 to compile $(\mathsf{Query}', \mathsf{Proof}', \mathsf{Verdict}')$ into a witness indistinguishable protocol $(\mathsf{Query}, \mathsf{Proof}, \mathsf{Verdict})$, thus obtaining our final access control scheme

$$\mathsf{AccessControl} = (\mathsf{Setup}, \mathsf{KeyGen}, \mathsf{Query}, \mathsf{Proof}, \mathsf{Verdict}).$$

– $\mathsf{Setup}(1^\lambda)$ generates a pair of keys $(\mathsf{mpk}, \mathsf{msk})$ by running the key generation algorithm of the signature scheme SIG (with security parameter λ).

– $\mathsf{KeyGen}(1^\lambda, \mathsf{msk}, N, S, \mathsf{id})$ samples a random tag $\mathsf{tag} \in \{0,1\}^\lambda$, it computes a signature $\sigma_{\mathsf{tag},i} = \mathsf{Sign}_{\mathsf{msk}}(\mathsf{tag}\|i)$ for every attribute $i \in S$ and in addition $\sigma_{\mathsf{tag},0} = \mathsf{Sign}_{\mathsf{msk}}(\mathsf{tag}\|0)$. It outputs $(\mathsf{tag}, \{\sigma_{\mathsf{tag},i}\}_{i \in S \cup \{0\}})$.

– $\mathsf{Query}'(1^\lambda)$ generates a pair $(Q, \mathsf{st}) \leftarrow V(1^\lambda)$, where Q is the query string and st is the internal state. Note that we use the property that query string generation in the monotone delegation scheme is independent of the instance to be proven.

– $\mathsf{Proof}'(1^\lambda, f, Q, (\mathsf{tag}, \{\sigma_{\mathsf{tag},i}\}_{i \in S \cup \{0\}}))$ runs the prover P (from the monotone **NP** delegation scheme), respective to $(R, f, \{x_i\}_{i \in [N]})$, where $x_i = \mathsf{mpk}\|\mathsf{tag}\|i$, R is the **NP** relation defined by

$$(\mathsf{mpk}\|\mathsf{tag}\|i, \sigma) \in R \Leftrightarrow \mathsf{Verify}_{\mathsf{mpk}}(\mathsf{tag}\|i, \sigma) = 1,$$

and $f \in F$ is the function corresponding to the access structure. Let A denote the answer generated by P. Then Proof' outputs

$$\mathsf{pf} = (A, \mathsf{tag}, \sigma_{\mathsf{tag},0}).$$

– $\mathsf{Verdict}'(1^\lambda, f, Q, \mathsf{pf}, \mathsf{st}, \mathsf{mpk})$ parses $\mathsf{pf} = (A, \mathsf{tag}, \sigma_{\mathsf{tag},0})$, checks that $\mathsf{Verify}_{\mathsf{mpk}}(\mathsf{tag}\|0, \sigma_{\mathsf{tag},0}) = 1$, and checks that A verifies correctly respective to the **NP** statement $\{x_i\}_{i \in [N]}$, where $x_i = \mathsf{mpk}\|\mathsf{tag}\|i$.

Adding Witness Indistinguishability. We wish to augment the scheme $\mathsf{AccessControl}'$, and specifically the algorithms $(\mathsf{Query}', \mathsf{Proof}', \mathsf{Verdict}')$ with witness indistinguishability properties using the transformation from Sect. 2. The first idea would be to simply replace the NP proof system (Q, P, V) with its WI version as obtained from Theorem 2.10, however this is insufficient since Proof' outputs tag, $\sigma_{\text{tag},0}$ in addition to the response A (note that outputting tag is necessary in order to avoid collusion, the role of the signature will be clarified in the proof). However, we can still consider the proof system defined by (Query', Proof', Verdict') itself, and apply Theorem 2.10 to this proof system in order to obtain witness indistinguishability. We now no longer need to think about batch verification, and simply consider the NP relation that takes (mpk, tag, $\{\sigma_{\text{tag},i}\}_{i \in S}$) as instance, verifies the signatures w.r.t tag and verifies that $\mathcal{F}$ accepts relative to the resulting structure.

The description of the new (Query, Proof, Verdict) thus follows from (Query', Proof', Verdict') above together with Theorem 2.10, which concludes the description of our access control scheme. We now show that the required properties still hold.

3.4   Proof of Theorem 3.7 for Our Construction

We show completeness, soundness and WI of the scheme described above. While completeness will follow straightforwardly based on the correctness of the components, and WI follows via the WI properties guaranteed in Theorem 2.10, soundness is a more serious challenge. The reason is that in the soundness experiment, the adversary has access to the oracle $\mathcal{O}$, which in turn uses msk. We want to show that an adversary that violates soundness can forge signatures, but this will require care with respect to the use of the oracle $\mathcal{O}$. Details follow.

Completeness. The completeness follows immediately from the completeness of (P, V), the completeness of the WI transformation (see Theorem 2.10), and the correctness of the signature scheme.

Soundness. We prove soundness by again referring to the variant without privacy AccessControl', which has a valid syntax for an access control scheme. We show that an adversary that breaks soundness in AccessControl can be used to construct an adversary that breaks soundness in AccessControl', and then proceed with ruling out this option given the properties of the proof system and signature scheme. We start by assuming that there exists $\mathcal{A}$ such that (infinitely often)

$$\Pr[\text{Verdict}(1^\lambda, f, \text{query}, \text{state}, \text{mpk}, \text{pf}^*) = 1] \geq \delta(\lambda),$$

where $\delta(\lambda) \geq 1/\text{poly}(\lambda)$, $\text{pf}^* \leftarrow \mathcal{A}_2(1^\lambda, \text{query}, \mathcal{A}_1^{\mathcal{O}_{\text{msk}}}(1^\lambda, \text{mpk}))$, and where (query, state) $\leftarrow$ Query(1^λ) and (mpk, msk) $\leftarrow$ Setup(1^λ).

To reduce the soundness claim from AccessControl to AccessControl', we use the fact that the reduction from Theorem 2.10 is black-box, non-rewinding and instance preserving. This means that given an adversary that breaks the soundness of the delegation scheme (Query, Proof, Verdict) with access to some oracle, then either there is an adversary with comparable advantage for (Query', Proof', Verdict') with the same instance and with access to the same oracle, or alternatively there is an adversary with the same oracle for the sWI scheme or for the remote evaluation scheme. However, for the latter cases oracle access can easily be simulated given msk, but sWI and the remove evaluation scheme are secure even given msk.

Therefore, an adversary against the soundness of AccessControl implies an adversary against the soundness of AccessControl$'$. That is, we assume that thee exists $\mathcal{A}'$ such that (infinitely often)

$$\Pr[\mathsf{Verdict}'(1^\lambda, f, \mathsf{query}, \mathsf{state}, \mathsf{mpk}, \mathsf{pf}^*) = 1] \geq \delta'(\lambda),$$

where $\delta'(\lambda) \geq 1/\mathrm{poly}(\lambda)$, $\mathsf{pf}^* \leftarrow \mathcal{A}'_2(1^\lambda, \mathsf{query}, \mathcal{A}_1'^{\mathcal{O}_{\mathsf{msk}}}(1^\lambda, \mathsf{mpk}))$, and where $(\mathsf{query}, \mathsf{state}) \leftarrow \mathsf{Query}'(1^\lambda)$ and $(\mathsf{mpk}, \mathsf{msk}) \leftarrow \mathsf{Setup}(1^\lambda)$. The idea now is to use Definition 3.4 to extract a signature out of the AccessControl$'$ adversary and violate the unforgability of SIG, of course taking into account that $\mathcal{A}'$ has access to $\mathcal{O}$ which is capable of producing signatures. Let $\mathsf{pf}^* = (A^*, \mathsf{tag}^*, \sigma^*)$ denote the forged proof generated by $\mathcal{A}'$, let q denote a polynomial upper bound on the number of $\mathcal{O}$ queries made by $\mathcal{A}'$, and let $\mathrm{TAGS} = \{\mathsf{tag}_1, \ldots, \mathsf{tag}_q\}$ be the tags generated and returned by $\mathcal{O}$ on these calls (we recall for the future that tag_i are generated uniformly and independently).

We now consider two cases:

1. In the first case, the adversary $\mathcal{A}'$ forges on a new tag:

$$\Pr[\mathsf{Verdict}'(1^\lambda, f, \mathsf{query}, \mathsf{state}, \mathsf{mpk}, \mathsf{pf}^*) = 1 \wedge \mathsf{tag}^* \notin \mathrm{TAGS}] \geq \delta'(\lambda)/2$$

infinitely often. In this case, we do not need to use the soundness of the argument system (P, V) since pf^* includes σ^* which is a valid signature on $(\mathsf{tag}^*\|0)$. Therefore $\mathcal{O}$ can be simulated using a chosen message oracle for the signature scheme, we are guaranteed that this oracle will never be called on $(\mathsf{tag}^*\|0)$ and therefore we can succeed in the forgery attack.

2. In the second case $\mathcal{A}'$ forges on a tag that was generated by $\mathcal{O}$:

$$\Pr[\mathsf{Verdict}'(1^\lambda, f, \mathsf{query}, \mathsf{state}, \mathsf{mpk}, \mathsf{pf}^*) = 1 \wedge \mathsf{tag}^* \in \mathrm{TAGS}] \geq \delta'(\lambda)/2$$

infinitely often. Note that either this case or the previous one must occur. In this case σ^* is not useful since we queried the chosen message oracle on $(\mathsf{tag}^*\|0)$. We therefore would like to use the extraction property of (P, V) to extract a signature on $(\mathsf{tag}^*\|i)$ for $i \notin S^*$ (the set that corresponds to the query that produced tag^*).

We therefore need to convert $\mathcal{A}'$ into a non-adaptive adversary for (P, V). First, we notice that (P, V) is applied to an **NP** language whose instances are of the form $(\mathsf{mpk}, \mathsf{tag})$ and the values $\{x_i\}$ constitute a possible witness. Since Definition 3.4 only allows to extract from a non-adaptive adversary, we will need to create an adversary that decides on $(\mathsf{mpk}, \mathsf{tag})$ before seeing query. The separation between $\mathcal{A}'_1$ and $\mathcal{A}'_2$ will thus be useful. Consider the following distribution over non-adaptive adversaries against (P, V). More accurately, our distribution will sample pairs of instance

$(\mathsf{mpk}, \mathsf{tag}')$ and algorithm $\mathcal{B}$ s.t. $\mathcal{B}(Q)$ is accepted by V with non-negligible probability, where Q is a sampled according to the V-prescribed distribution. The distribution is generated as follows. Sample $\mathsf{mpk}, \mathsf{msk}$ and a random set TAGS. Set tag' to be a random element from TAGS. Execute $\mathcal{A}_1'^{\mathcal{O}}(1^\lambda, \mathsf{mpk})$ to obtain a value ζ, and set $\mathcal{B}(Q) = \mathcal{A}_2'(1^\lambda, Q, \zeta)$. The expected probability of success of $\mathcal{B}(Q)$ is at least $\delta'(\lambda)/(2q) > 1/\mathrm{poly}(\lambda)$, since with probability $1/q$ the guess tag' hits the correct tag^* (which is an element of TAGS with probability $\delta'(\lambda)/2$). This means with non-negligible probability, we sample $(\mathsf{mpk}, \mathsf{tag}')$ for which $\mathcal{B}$ succeeds with non-negligible probability.

We can thus apply the extractor that is implied by Definition 3.4, to conclude that with non-negligible probability, it is possible to extract a set of signatures on messages $(\mathsf{tag}^*\|i)$ for all $i \in S$ where S satisfies $\mathcal{F}$. However, in the above experiment, the oracle $\mathcal{O}$ can be replaced with access to a chosen message signature oracle. We are guaranteed that this oracle is not queries on any S that satisfies $\mathcal{F}$. Therefore the extractor will allow to produce a signature on a message for which the chosen message oracle was not queried, thus violating the unforgability of the signature scheme with non-negligible probability. This completes the soundness argument.

Witness Indistinguishability. The WI condition follows immediately from the fact that the commitment scheme is (computationally) hiding, and from the strong WI property of $(P_{\mathrm{sWI}}, V_{\mathrm{sWI}})$.

References

[BBK+16] Bitansky, N., Brakerski, Z., Kalai, Y.T., Paneth, O., Vaikuntanathan, V.: 3-message zero knowledge against human ignorance. IACR Cryptology ePrint Archive 2016/213 (2016)

[BCC+14] Bitansky, N., et al.: The hunting of the SNARK. IACR Cryptology ePrint Archive 2014/580 (2014)

[BCCT13] Bitansky, N., Canetti, R., Chiesa, A., Tromer, E.: Recursive composition and bootstrapping for SNARKS and proof-carrying data. In: STOC, pp. 111–120. ACM (2013)

[BD18] Brakerski, Z., Döttling, N.: Two-message statistical sender-private OT from LWE. IACR Cryptology ePrint Archive 2018/530 (2018)

[BHK17] Brakerski, Z., Holmgren, J., Kalai, Y.T.: Non-interactive delegation and batch NP verification from standard computational assumptions. In: Hatami, H., McKenzie, P., King, V. (eds.) Proceedings of the 49th Annual ACM SIGACT Symposium on Theory of Computing, STOC 2017, Montreal, QC, Canada, 19–23 June 2017, pp. 474–482. ACM (2017)

[BKK+17] Badrinarayanan, S., Kalai, Y.T., Khurana, D., Sahai, A., Wichs, D.: Non-interactive delegation for low-space non-deterministic computation. Cryptology ePrint Archive, Report 2017/1250 (2017). To appear in STOC 2018

[Cha82] Chaum, D.: Blind signatures for untraceable payments. In: Chaum, D., Rivest, R.L., Sherman, A.T. (eds.) Advances in Cryptology, pp. 199–203. Springer, Boston, MA (1983). https://doi.org/10.1007/978-1-4757-0602-4_18

[Cha85] Chaum, D.: Security without identification: transaction systems to make big brother obsolete. Commun. ACM **28**(10), 1030–1044 (1985)

[DFH12] Damgård, I., Faust, S., Hazay, C.: Secure two-party computation with low communication. In: Cramer, R. (ed.) TCC 2012. LNCS, vol. 7194, pp. 54–74. Springer, Heidelberg (2012). https://doi.org/10.1007/978-3-642-28914-9_4

[DGI+19] Döttling, N., Garg, S., Ishai, Y., Malavolta, G., Mour, T., Ostrovsky, R.: Trapdoor hash functions and their applications. In: Boldyreva, A., Micciancio, D. (eds.) CRYPTO 2019. LNCS, vol. 11694, pp. 3–32. Springer, Cham (2019). https://doi.org/10.1007/978-3-030-26954-8_1

[GHV10] Gentry, C., Halevi, S., Vaikuntanathan, V.: i-hop homomorphic encryption and rerandomizable yao circuits. In: Rabin, T. (ed.) CRYPTO 2010. LNCS, vol. 6223, pp. 155–172. Springer, Heidelberg (2010). https://doi.org/10.1007/978-3-642-14623-7_9

[GKR08] Goldwasser, S., Kalai, Y.T., Rothblum, G.N.: Delegating computation: interactive proofs for muggles. In: Dwork, C. (ed.) Proceedings of the 40th Annual ACM Symposium on Theory of Computing, Victoria, British Columbia, Canada, 17–20 May 2008, pp. 113–122. ACM (2008). Full version in [GKR15]

[GKR15] Goldwasser, S., Kalai, Y.T., Rothblum, G.N.: Delegating computation: interactive proofs for muggles. J. ACM **62**(4), 27 (2015)

[HK07] Halevi, S., Kalai, Y.T.: Smooth projective hashing and two-message oblivious transfer. IACR Cryptology ePrint Archive 2007/118 (2007)

[JKKR17] Jain, A., Kalai, Y.T., Khurana, D., Rothblum, R.: Distinguisher-dependent simulation in two rounds and its applications. In: Katz, J., Shacham, H. (eds.) CRYPTO 2017. LNCS, vol. 10402, pp. 158–189. Springer, Cham (2017). https://doi.org/10.1007/978-3-319-63715-0_6

[Kal05] Kalai, Y.T.: Smooth projective hashing and two-message oblivious transfer. In: Cramer, R. (ed.) EUROCRYPT 2005. LNCS, vol. 3494, pp. 78–95. Springer, Heidelberg (2005). https://doi.org/10.1007/11426639_5

[KKS18] Kalai, Y.T., Khurana, D., Sahai, A.: Statistical witness indistinguishability (and more) in two messages. IACR Cryptology ePrint Archive 2018/168 (2018)

[KP15] Kalai, Y.T., Paneth, O.: Delegating RAM computations. IACR Cryptology ePrint Archive 2015/957 (2015)

[KPY18] Kalai, Y.T., Paneth, O., Yang, L.: On publicly verifiable delegation from standard assumptions. IACR Cryptology ePrint Archive 2018/776 (2018). To appear in STOC 2019

[KRR13] Kalai, Y.T., Raz, R., Rothblum, R.D.: Delegation for bounded space. In: Boneh, D., Roughgarden, T., Feigenbaum, J. (eds.) Symposium on Theory of Computing Conference, STOC 2013, Palo Alto, CA, USA, 1–4 June 2013, pp. 565–574. ACM (2013)

[KRR14] Kalai, Y.T., Raz, R., Rothblum, R.D.: How to delegate computations: the power of no-signaling proofs. In: STOC, pp. 485–494. ACM (2014)

[Mic94] Micali, S.: CS proofs (extended abstracts). In: 35th Annual Symposium on Foundations of Computer Science, Santa Fe, New Mexico, USA, 20–22 November 1994, pp. 436–453. IEEE Computer Society (1994). Full version in SIAM J. Comput. **30**(4), 1253–1298 (2000)

[Nao89] Naor, M.: Bit commitment using pseudo-randomness. In: Brassard, G. (ed.) CRYPTO 1989. LNCS, vol. 435, pp. 128–136. Springer, New York (1990). https://doi.org/10.1007/0-387-34805-0_13

[NP01]   Naor, M., Pinkas, B.: Efficient oblivious transfer protocols. In: Proceedings of the Twelfth Annual Symposium on Discrete Algorithms, Washington, DC, USA, 7–9 January 2001, pp. 448–457 (2001)

[OPP14]   Ostrovsky, R., Paskin-Cherniavsky, A., Paskin-Cherniavsky, B.: Maliciously circuit-private FHE. In: Garay, J.A., Gennaro, R. (eds.) CRYPTO 2014, Part I. LNCS, vol. 8616, pp. 536–553. Springer, Heidelberg (2014). https://doi.org/10.1007/978-3-662-44371-2_30

[RRR16]   Reingold, O., Rothblum, G.N., Rothblum, R.D.: Constant-round interactive proofs for delegating computation. In: Proceedings of the 48th Annual ACM SIGACT Symposium on Theory of Computing, STOC 2016, Cambridge, MA, USA, 18–21 June 2016, pp. 49–62 (2016)

[Yao82]   Yao, A.C.-C.: Protocols for secure computations (extended abstract). In: 23rd Annual Symposium on Foundations of Computer Science, Chicago, Illinois, USA, 3–5 November 1982, pp. 160–164 (1982)

Boosting Verifiable Computation
on Encrypted Data

Dario Fiore[1]([⊠]), Anca Nitulescu[2]([⊠]), and David Pointcheval[3,4]([⊠])

[1] IMDEA Software Institute, Madrid, Spain
dario.fiore@imdea.org
[2] COSMIAN, Paris, France
anca.nitulescu@cosmian.com
[3] DIENS, École normale supérieure, CNRS, PSL University, Paris, France
david.pointcheval@ens.fr
[4] INRIA, Paris, France

Abstract. We consider the setting in which an untrusted server stores a collection of data and is asked to compute a function over it. In this scenario, we aim for solutions where the untrusted server does not learn information about the data and is prevented from cheating. This problem is addressed by verifiable and private delegation of computation, proposed by Gennaro, Gentry and Parno (CRYPTO'10), a notion that is close to both the active areas of homomorphic encryption and verifiable computation (VC). However, in spite of the efficiency advances in the respective areas, VC protocols that guarantee privacy of the inputs are still expensive. The only exception is a protocol by Fiore, Gennaro and Pastro (CCS'14) that supports arithmetic circuits of degree at most 2. In this paper we propose new efficient protocols for VC on encrypted data that improve over the state of the art solution of Fiore et al. in multiple aspects. First, we can support computations of degree higher than 2. Second, we achieve public delegatability and public verifiability whereas Fiore et al. need the same secret key to encode inputs and verify outputs. Third, we achieve a new property that guarantees that verifiers can be convinced about the correctness of the outputs without learning information on the inputs. The key tool to obtain our new protocols is a new SNARK that can efficiently handle computations over a quotient polynomial ring, such as the one used by Ring-LWE somewhat homomorphic encryption schemes. This SNARK in turn relies on a new commit-and-prove SNARK for proving evaluations on the same point of several committed polynomials. We propose a construction of this scheme under an extractability assumption over bilinear groups in the random oracle model.

1 Introduction

Due to the ubiquity of the Internet and the advent of cloud computing, it is increasingly common for users to exchange and receive information processed

---

A. Nitulescu—Work done while being at 3.

© International Association for Cryptologic Research 2020
A. Kiayias et al. (Eds.): PKC 2020, LNCS 12111, pp. 124–154, 2020.
https://doi.org/10.1007/978-3-030-45388-6_5

on remote machines. Online storage services are already widely available on the Internet, and allow users to store, access and share their data from anywhere and from multiple devices. This phenomenon includes not only storage: it is more and more common to rely on computation performed on third party machines.

While this shift in the computing trend brings several benefits, new security challenges also emerge. These challenges are related to a main question: *what happens if the remote machine is not trusted?* In this work we are particularly concerned with two security problems in this space. First, we would like to ensure that the untrusted machine can perform the computation without learning the private data of the users. Second, we would like to enable the receivers of computation results to efficiently check that such results are correct. Both problems are in the scope of two important research lines in cryptography.

Privacy-Preserving Computation. The first problem is related to fully homomorphic encryption (FHE) [RAD78, Gen09]. While for a long time it was only known how to construct homomorphic encryption schemes supporting a single operation (e.g., only addition [Pai99] or multiplication [ElG84]), Gentry's breakthrough showed the first FHE scheme that enables computing any function on encrypted data. If Gentry's first FHE was mostly a feasibility result, research in this area has progressed significantly giving rise to many new FHE schemes (e.g., [SV10, BV11, BGV12, GSW13, DM15, CGGI16, CGGI17]) that are efficient and see their first practical applications.

Ensuring Correctness of Computation. The second problem is related to verifiable computation (VC) [GGP10] and related notions such as interactive proofs [GMR85], probabilistically checkable proofs [AS92] and succinct arguments [Kil92]. Briefly speaking, these are protocols that enable a powerful prover to convince a verifier that a statement (e.g., correctness of a computation, $y = f(x)$) is true in such a way that the verifier can run with fewer resources, e.g., faster than re-executing the function. Similarly to FHE, also in this research area, results have been confined to theory for long time. However, several recent works have shown a change in this trend, and today we have several VC protocols that are efficient and have been experimented in practical scenarios, see e.g., [GKR08, CMT12, GGPR13, PHGR13, BCG+13, Gro16, ZGK+17, WJB+17, AHIV17, WTs+18, BCG+18, BBC+18, BCR+19, MBKM19, CFQ19, XZZ+19].

1.1 Ensuring Correctness of Privacy-Preserving Computation

In spite of the research mentioned above, the problem of ensuring both the correctness and the privacy of computation performed on untrusted machines has received much less attention in the literature. There are three main works that considered explicitly this problem.

The first one is the seminal paper of Gennaro et al. [GGP10] who introduced the notion of non-interactive verifiable computation. In [GGP10] they indeed show how to combine garbled circuits and FHE in order to build a VC scheme for arbitrary functions that also preserves the privacy of the computation's inputs and outputs against the computing machine.

The second work is that of Goldwasser et al. [GKP+13] that shows how to use their succinct single-key functional encryption scheme in order to build a VC protocol that preserves the privacy of the inputs (but not of the outputs).

Both these two solutions [GGP10, GKP+13] are however not very satisfactory in terms of efficiency. The main issue in the construction of [GGP10] is that they need the full power of FHE to perform homomorphic evaluations of garbled circuits. Some of the efficiency issues in [GKP+13] include the use of several instances of an attribute-based encryption that must support an expressive class of predicates (at NC1 circuits), and an inherent design limitation (due to following the approach of [PRV12]) by which their scheme supports functions with a single bit of output (which in practical scenarios like computing on large integers would require multiple instances of their protocol).

A third work that considered the problem of ensuring correctness of privacy-preserving computation is the one of Fiore et al. [FGP14] who proposed a solution that combines an FHE and a VC scheme. The idea of their generic construction is rather simple and consists into using a VC in order to prove that the homomorphic evaluation on ciphertexts has been done correctly. As discussed in [FGP14], even this solution may encounter efficiency limits. This is due to the fact that the VC scheme must be executed on a computation that, due to the FHE ciphertext expansion, is of much larger representation than the computation that would be executed on plain text. Motivated by this issue, [FGP14] also proposed an efficient solution that, for the case of quadratic functions, can avoid this issue. The efficient construction in [FGP14] overcomes the problem of ciphertext expansion in two ways: (1) they consider homomorphic encryption schemes working in the Ring-LWE setting in which ciphertexts are represented by polynomials in a given polynomial ring; (2) they develop, as the VC building block, an homomorphic MAC scheme especially tailored to handle messages that are polynomials in which the prover execution can be independent of the degree of such polynomials. However, for reasons that we will detail later (see Sect. 3), their technique is inherently bound to computations of multiplicative depth 1. Also, by using an homomorphic MAC as VC, verification requires a secret key, the same secret key used to encode the inputs. This limits the applicability of these solutions to scenarios where users and verifiers are either the same entity or they share a secret key.

1.2 Our Contributions

We propose a new protocol for verifiable computation on encrypted data that improves on the state-of-the-art solution of Fiore et al. [FGP14] in multiple aspects. Notably, we can support HE computations of multiplicative depth larger than 1. Second, we achieve public verifiability whereas [FGP14] is only privately verifiable. Finally, our scheme has an additional property that guarantees that verifiers may be convinced of outputs correctness without learning information on the original inputs. This latter property is particularly relevant in the publicly verifiable setting where the users who encrypt the data and the verifiers are distinct entities. Technically, we achieve this property because our protocol allows for re-randomizing the encrypted results, which was not possible in [FGP14] that only considered deterministic HE evaluations.

Our key tool to obtain this result is a new SNARK that can efficiently handle computations that are arithmetic circuits f over a quotient polynomial ring $\mathbb{R}_q :=$ $\mathbb{Z}_q[X]/\langle R(X)\rangle$ (exactly like the popular choice for many Ring-LWE schemes) in which the prover's costs have a minimal dependence on the degree d of $R(X)$. Specifically, let f be the circuit over $\mathbb{R}_q$ and $\hat{f}$ be the corresponding circuit over $\mathbb{Z}_q$ (i.e., the one that would be computed on plaintexts where additions and multiplications in $\mathbb{R}_q$ are replaced by the corresponding operations in $\mathbb{Z}_q$). Then, whereas a naive application of [FGP14]'s generic solution would incur a cost for proof generation at least $O(d \cdot |\hat{f}|)$ where $|\hat{f}|$ is $\hat{f}$'s circuit size, our scheme lets proof generation be doable in time $O(d \cdot n + |\hat{f}|)$ where n is $\hat{f}$'s input size. We stress that here we are considering the cost of proof generation, after having performed the HE computation; or in other words we consider the cost of generating the proof once the witness is available. To see how this efficiency feature concretely improves, consider for example an $\hat{f}$ that is a multivariate polynomial of degree $c \geqslant 2$ by which $|\hat{f}|$ can be n^c, and consider that for Ring-LWE security the degree d can be a rather large integer (e.g., $d \approx 8000$). Then removing the multiplicative factor $d \cdot |\hat{f}|$ can significantly speed up the prover's costs. Let us also notice that the factor $d \cdot n$ is unavoidable as the prover must read the input.

Our SNARK for arithmetic circuits over polynomial rings is built in a modular way using two building blocks: a commit-and-prove SNARK for arithmetic circuits (AC-Π), and a commit-and-prove SNARK for multiple polynomial evaluations (MUniEv-Π).

To instantiate AC-Π, we can use any commit-and-prove SNARK for arithmetic circuits that supports the same commitment key as our scheme MUniEv-Π. Given the recent result of Campanelli et al. [CFQ19], MUniEv-Π can be instantiated with a variety of schemes including the efficient commit-and-prove variant of Groth16 [Gro16] proposed in [CFQ19].

For scheme MUniEv-Π, we propose a construction based on the Strong Diffie-Hellman and Power Knowledge of Exponent (PKE) assumptions in bilinear groups, in the random oracle model. We believe this scheme can also have other applications. Slightly more in detail, MUniEv-Π allows one to prove the following statement: given a commitment C to ℓ degree-d polynomials $\{P_j(X)\}_j$, a commitment C' to a vector of ℓ $\mathbb{Z}_q$-elements $\{p_j\}_j$, and a public point k, show that $p_j = P_j(k)$ for all $j = 1$ to ℓ. In comparison to using an existing general-purpose commit-and-prove SNARK for arithmetic circuits (e.g., LegoGroth16 from [CFQ19]), our scheme MUniEv-Π has slightly smaller proofs and proving time at least three times faster (cf. Sect. 7.3 for more details).

Finally, we note that our scheme MUniEv-Π is in turn constructed from a SNARK BivPE-Π for the partial evaluation of a committed bivariate polynomial, i.e., given commitments C and C' to $P(X,Y)$ and $Q(Y)$ respectively, prove that $Q(Y) = P(k, Y)$ for some public point k. We construct BivPE-Π by extending the univariate polynomial commitment techniques of Kate et al. [KZG10]. It is worth mentioning that other works [PST13, ZGK+17] extended [KZG10] to support the evaluation of multivariate polynomials, which include bivariate ones. However, the main difference (crucial for our application) is that we can support *partial* evaluations in one variable while keeping the result polynomial also committed.

1.3 Organization

In Sect. 2 we introduce notation and basic cryptographic definitions. Section 3 describes our SNARK for arithmetic computations in quotient polynomial rings. In Sect. 4 we show how to combine our SNARK from Sect. 3 together with Ring-LWE-based HE schemes in order to build a verifiable computation scheme with input and output privacy, and also how to achieve the new property of preserving privacy of the inputs from the verifier. In Sect. 5 we state the computational assumptions needed by our schemes, and we present the BivPoly.Com commitment. In Sect. 6 we build our SNARK BivPE-Π for bivariate polynomials partial evaluation and then in Sect. 7 we show how turn it into an efficient MUniEv-Π for the simultaneous evaluation of many univariate polynomials. In Sect. 8 we prove the security of our scheme BivPE-Π.

2   Notation and Definitions

Notation. An adversary is denoted by $\mathcal{A}$ and is assumed to be probabilistic Turing machines that run in polynomial time, i.e., PPT. For two PPT machines A, B, with the writing $(A\|B)(x)$ we denote the execution of A followed by the execution of B on the same input x and with the same random coins.

2.1 Commitment Schemes

Definition 1 (Non-Interactive Commitment). *A non-interactive commitment scheme is a tuple of algorithms* $Com = (\mathsf{ComGen}, \mathsf{Com}, \mathsf{ComVer}, \mathsf{OpenVer})$:

$\mathsf{ComGen}(1^\lambda) \to \mathsf{ck}$: *Generates a commitment public key* ck. *It specifies a message space* M_{ck}, *a randomness (opening) space* R_{ck}, *and a commitment space* C_{ck}. *This algorithm is run by a trusted or distributed authority;*

$\mathsf{Com}(\mathsf{ck}, m) \to (c, o)$: *Outputs a commitment* c *and an opening* o. *Given a message* $m \in M_{\mathsf{ck}}$, *it samples* $o \in R_{\mathsf{ck}}$ *and computes the commitment* (c, o).

$\mathsf{ComVer}(\mathsf{ck}, c) \to 0/1$: *Checks whether* c *is a well-formed commitment. If so, it outputs 1, otherwise it outputs 0;*

$\mathsf{OpenVer}(\mathsf{ck}, c, m, o) \to 0/1$: *Outputs 1 if the value* $m \in M_{\mathsf{ck}}$ *is the committed message in the commitment* c *and 0 if* (m, o, c) *does not correspond to a valid pair opening-commitment.*

We say $Com = (\mathsf{ComGen}, \mathsf{Com}, \mathsf{ComVer}, \mathsf{OpenVer})$ *is a secure commitment scheme if it satisfies the following properties:*

Correctness. *Let* $\mathsf{ck} \leftarrow \mathsf{ComGen}(1^\lambda)$. *Any commitment of* $m \in M_{\mathsf{ck}}$ *honestly generated* $(c, o) \leftarrow \mathsf{Com}(\mathsf{ck}, m)$ *is successfully verified by* $\mathsf{ComVer}(\mathsf{ck}, c)$ *and by* $\mathsf{OpenVer}(\mathsf{ck}, c, m, o)$.

Hiding. *It is statistically hard, for any adversary $\mathcal{A}$, to generate two messages $m_0, m_1 \in M_{ck}$ such that $\mathcal{A}$ can distinguish between their corresponding commitments c_0 and c_1 where $(c_0, o_0) \leftarrow \mathsf{Com}(ck, m_0)$ and $(c_1, o_1) \leftarrow \mathsf{Com}(ck, m_1)$.*

Binding. *It is computationally hard, for any adversary $\mathcal{A}$, to come up with a collision (c, m_0, o_0, m_1, o_1), such that o_0 and o_1 are valid opening values for two different pre-images $m_0 \neq m_1$ for c. For any adversary $\mathcal{A}$, the following probability is negligible*

$$\Pr\left[\begin{array}{c} \mathsf{OpenVer}(ck, c, m_0, o_0) = 1 \\ \wedge\ \mathsf{OpenVer}(ck, c, m_1, o_1) = 1 \\ \wedge\ m_0 \neq m_1 \end{array} \middle| \begin{array}{c} ck \leftarrow \mathsf{ComGen}(1^\lambda) \\ (c, (m_0, o_0), (m_1, o_1)) \leftarrow \mathcal{A}(ck) \end{array}\right].$$

Knowledge Binding [BL07]. *For every adversary $\mathcal{A}$ that produces a valid commitment c associated to a message that verifies, i.e. such that $\mathsf{ComVer}(ck, c) = 1$, there is an extractor $\mathsf{Ext}_{\mathcal{A}}$ that is able to output a pre-image m and a valid opening o of c, with overwhelming probability:*

$$\Pr\left[\mathsf{OpenVer}(ck, c, m, o) = 1 \middle| \begin{array}{c} ck \leftarrow \mathsf{ComGen}(1^\lambda) \\ (c; (m, o)) \leftarrow (\mathcal{A} \| \mathsf{Ext}_{\mathcal{A}})(ck) \\ \mathsf{ComVer}(ck, c) = 1 \end{array}\right] = 1 - \mathsf{negl}(\lambda).$$

For the sake of simplicity, throughout this work, we will omit the commitment key ck from the input of the algorithms, and with a slight abuse of notation, we will adopt the writing $\mathsf{Com}(m) \to (c, o)$.

2.2   SNARKs – Succinct Non-Interactive Arguments of Knowledge

We recall the definition of (zero-knowledge) succinct non-interactive arguments of knowledge (zk-SNARKs).

Definition 2 (SNARK for NP). *A SNARK is defined by three algorithms,*

$\Pi.\mathsf{Gen}(1^\lambda, \mathcal{R}) \to crs$: *on input a security parameter $\lambda \in \mathbb{N}$ and a NP relation $\mathcal{R}$, the generation algorithm outputs a common reference string crs;*

$\Pi.\mathsf{Prove}(crs, u, w) \to \pi$: *given a prover reference string crs, an instance u and a witness w s.t. $(u, w) \in \mathcal{R}$, this algorithm produces a proof π;*

$\Pi.\mathsf{Ver}(crs, u, \pi) \to b$: *on input a verification state crs, an instance u, and a proof π, the verifier algorithm outputs $b = 0$ (reject) or $b = 1$ (accept);*

satisfying completeness, succinctness, knowledge-soundness *as described below:*

Correctness. *For all valid statement $(u, w) \in \mathcal{R}$,*

$$\Pr\left[\begin{array}{c} \mathsf{Ver}(crs, u, \pi) = 0 \\ \wedge\ (u, w) \in \mathcal{R} \end{array} \middle| \begin{array}{c} crs \leftarrow \Pi.\mathsf{Gen}(1^\lambda, \mathcal{R}) \\ \pi \leftarrow \mathsf{Prove}(crs, u, w) \end{array}\right] = \mathsf{negl}(\lambda);$$

Succintness. *The size of the proof is linear in the security parameter λ, i.e. independent of the size of the computation or the witness;*

Knowledge-Soundness [BG93]. *A non-interactive proof system* Π *is knowledge-sound for the class* $\mathcal{Z}$ *of auxiliary input generators if for any* PPT *adversary* $\mathcal{A}^{\mathsf{KS}}$ *there exists an extractor* $\mathsf{Ext}_\mathcal{A}$ *such that:*

$$\Pr\left[\begin{array}{c}\mathsf{Ver}(\mathsf{crs}, u, \pi) = 1 \\ \wedge\ \mathcal{R}(u, w) = 0\end{array}\ \middle|\ \begin{array}{c}\mathsf{crs} \leftarrow \Pi.\mathsf{Gen}(1^\lambda, \mathcal{R}), \mathsf{aux} \leftarrow \mathcal{Z}(\mathsf{crs}) \\ ((u, \pi); w) \leftarrow (\mathcal{A}^{\mathsf{KS}} \| \mathsf{Ext}_\mathcal{A})(\mathsf{crs}, \mathsf{aux})\end{array}\right] = \mathsf{negl}(\lambda).$$

Zero Knowledge. *A* Π *protocol is a (statistical) zero-knowledge for a relation* $\mathcal{R}$ *if there exists a stateful interactive polynomial-size simulator* $\mathsf{Sim} = (\mathsf{Sim}^{\mathsf{crs}}, \mathsf{Sim}^{\mathsf{Prove}})$ *such that for all stateful interactive distinguishers* $\mathcal{D}$, *for every large enough security parameter* $\lambda \in \mathbb{N}$, *every auxiliary input* aux, *the two probabilities are negligibly close:*

$$\Pr[(u, w) \in \mathcal{R} \wedge \mathcal{D}(\pi) = 1 \,|\, (\mathsf{crs}) \leftarrow \mathsf{Gen}(1^\lambda), (u, w) \leftarrow \mathcal{D}(\mathsf{crs}, \mathsf{aux}),$$
$$\pi \leftarrow \mathsf{Prove}(\mathsf{crs}, u, w)];$$
$$\Pr[(u, w) \in \mathcal{R} \wedge \mathcal{D}(\pi) = 1 \,|\, (\mathsf{crs}, \mathsf{trap}) \leftarrow \mathsf{Sim}^{\mathsf{crs}}(1^\lambda), (u, w) \leftarrow \mathcal{D}(\mathsf{crs}, \mathsf{aux}),$$
$$\pi \leftarrow \mathsf{Sim}^{\mathsf{Prove}}(\mathsf{crs}, \mathsf{trap}, u, \mathsf{aux})].$$

Commit and Prove SNARKs. Let $\mathcal{R}(u, w)$ be an NP relation where $w = (\{x_i\}_i, \omega)$. A commit-and-prove SNARK (CaP-SNARK) for commitment scheme $\mathcal{C}om$ and relation $\mathcal{R}(u, w)$ is a SNARK for the "commit-and-prove relation" $\mathcal{R}^{\mathsf{ck}}(u^*, w^*)$ where $u^* = (u, \{c_i\}_i)$, $w^* = (\{x_i\}_i, \{o_i\}_i, \omega)$ and that holds iff $\mathcal{R}(u, (\{x_i\}_i, \omega))$ holds and $\mathsf{OpenVer}(c_i, m_i, o_i) = 1$ for all i. We adopt the syntax for CaP-SNARK used in [CFQ19]:

$\Pi.\mathsf{Gen}(\mathsf{ck}, \mathcal{R}) \to \mathsf{crs}$: on input a relation-independent commitment key ck and a NP relation $\mathcal{R}$, it generates the crs;

$\Pi.\mathsf{Prove}(\mathsf{crs}, (u, \{c_i\}_i), (\{x_i\}_i, \{o_i\}_i, \omega)) \to \pi$: outputs a proof;

$\Pi.\mathsf{Ver}(\mathsf{crs}, (u, \{c_i\}_i), \pi) \to b$: rejects or accepts the proof.

3 Proof Systems for Arithmetic Function Evaluation over Quotient Polynomial Rings

In this section we describe our commit-and-prove SNARK for arithmetic computations in quotient polynomial rings.

Let $\mathbb{R}$ be the quotient ring $\mathbb{Z}/\langle R(X)\rangle$ for some polynomial $R \in \mathbb{Z}[X]$ of degree d. For a prime $q \gg d$ we define $\mathbb{F} = \mathbb{Z}_q$ a finite field and $\mathbb{R}_q = \mathbb{R}/q\mathbb{R}$. We want to construct a succinct non-interactive zero-knowledge argument system for some relation $\mathcal{R}_f$ of correct evaluation of an arithmetic function $f(\cdot) : \mathbb{R}_q{}^n \to \mathbb{R}_q$ taking $n \in \mathbb{N}$ inputs in the quotient ring $\mathbb{R}_q = \mathbb{R}/q\mathbb{R}$. The function f to be evaluated on polynomials $\{P_j\}_{j=1}^n$ in the quotient ring $\mathbb{R}_q$ is considered to be public.

Let MPoly-$\mathcal{C}om$ = (MPoly.ComGen, MPoly.Com, MPoly.ComVer, MPoly.Open Ver) be a linearly homomorphic commitment scheme for (many) univariate polynomials, i.e., the message space M consists in vectors of $n \leqslant \ell$ polynomials of degree $d \leqslant \nu$, for some integer bounds ℓ, ν chosen in MPoly.ComGen. In Sect. 7 we show an efficient instantiation of such a scheme in bilinear groups.

We describe a Commit-and-Prove SNARK, Rq-Π, for commitment scheme MPoly-Com and for the following relation

$$\mathcal{R}_f^{\mathsf{ck}} := \{(u = (C, P); w = (\{P_j\}_{j=1}^n, \rho, T)) :$$
$$\mathsf{MPoly.OpenVer}(C, \{P_j\}, \rho) = 1 \ \land \ P = f(P_j) - TR\}$$

The relation $\mathcal{R}_f^{\mathsf{ck}}$ implicitly contains two bounds ℓ, ν on, respectively, the number of inputs of f and the degree d_f of f as an arithmetic circuit.

In a nutshell, given a compact commitment C and a public polynomial $P \in \mathbb{R}_q$, our Rq-Π scheme allows to prove that C opens to some polynomials $P_j \in \mathbb{R} \ \forall j = 1 \ldots n$ such that P is the result of evaluating the function f on $\{P_j\}_j$, evaluation done in the polynomial ring $\mathbb{R}_q$.

High-Level Description of our Rq-Π SNARK. We build our Rq-Π scheme as a combination of the following building blocks:

– MUniEv-Π = (MUniEv-Π.Gen, MUniEv-Π.Prove, MUniEv-Π.Ver):
  a CaP-SNARK for the simultaneous evaluation of n univariate polynomials $\{P_j\}_{j=1}^n$ in a point k, where $\{P_j\}$ are committed with MPoly-Com. Proposing efficient constructions of MPoly-Com and MUniEv-Π are key technical contributions of this paper; these are detailed in Sect. 7.
– AC-Π = (AC-Π.Gen, AC-Π.Prove, AC-Π.Ver): a CaP-SNARK for arithmetic circuits over $\mathbb{Z}_q$ where inputs and outputs are committed (as a vector of degree-0 polynomials) with the MPoly-Com scheme.
  Various instantiations of AC-Π compatible with our pairing-based MPoly-Com commitment can be obtained by using for example the compiler recently proposed in [CFQ19];[1] a particularly efficient one is a commit-and-prove variant of [Gro16].

The two building blocks above are used as follows.

The prover, knowing a quotient polynomial $T \in \mathbb{Z}_q[X]$ such that $f((P_j)_j) = P + TR$, starts by computing a commitment C_T to $T \in \mathbb{Z}_q[X]$ (which may have degree higher than that of R).

Next, the key idea is that instead of directly proving that $P = f((P_j)_j) - TR$ for the committed polynomials $\{P_j\}$ and T (that would require to work with a large arithmetic circuits f), we use the homomorphic properties of the polynomial ring $\mathbb{Z}_q[X]$ to "compress the computation". Namely, to prove $P = f((P_j)_j) - TR$, we evaluate all the polynomials in a random point k and then prove the relation on the resulting scalars, using the fact that:

$$\hat{f}(P_j(k)) - R(k)T(k) = (f(P_j) - RT)(k) = P(k).$$

---

[1] In particular, relevant to our work is the compiler that shows that commit-and-prove SNARKs for Pedersen-like commitments can be made compatible with one another.

where $\hat{f} : \mathbb{Z}_q^n \to \mathbb{Z}_q$ is an arithmetic circuit that is the same as f except that every addition (resp. multiplication) in $\mathbb{R}_q$ is replaced by an addition (resp. multiplication) in $\mathbb{Z}_q$.

This idea is similar to the homomorphic hash function defined by Fiore et al. [FGP14]. In [FGP14], they let this idea work by evaluating the polynomials "in the exponent", i.e., they publish a set of group elements g^{k^i}, and then they compute homomorphically over these encodings to get $g^{P(k)}$.

This technique however hits two problems: first, they cannot deal with reductions modulo $R(X)$, and second, to compute homomorphically a multiplication on these encodings, they have to "consume" a pairing, and thus only degree-2 computations can be supported.

In our case, we solve these issues by exploiting the power of the commit and prove paradigm in order to obtain, for every evaluation, a fresh random k. Then, having $k \in \mathbb{Z}_q$ allows us to support higher-degree computations as well as to deal with modular reductions.

To proceed with the protocol, the prover thus needs to get a random point k, not of its choice and independent of the values committed in C_T and C and of the statement P. This is possible by using a random oracle Hash to obtain a value k on which it evaluates the polynomials $\{P_j(k) = p_j\}_{j=1}^n, R(k) = r, P(k) = p$ and $T(k) = t'$.

Next, the prover compactly commits to the respective evaluations $(C', \rho') \leftarrow \mathsf{MPoly.Com}(t', \{p_j\}_{j=1}^n)$. At this point the prover will use:

1. the MUniEv-Π scheme to prove that C' is a commitment to a vector of $n+1$ scalars $(t, \{p_j\}_{j=1}^n)$ that are the results of evaluating in point k a vector of $n+1$ polynomials $(T, \{P_j\}_{j=1}^n)$ that are committed in $C_T \times C$;[2]
2. the AC-Π scheme to prove that $p = P(k) = \hat{f}((p_j)_j) - rt'$, and that $t', \{p_j\}_{j=1}^n$ are openings of C'.

More formally, the algorithms of the protocol are described in Fig. 1. A detailed intuition of the functionalities of each algorithm follows.

3.1   Formal Description of Our Rq-Π Scheme

We construct a commit-and-prove SNARK scheme Rq-$\Pi = (\mathsf{Gen}, \mathsf{Prove}, \mathsf{Ver})$ for any relation $\mathcal{R}_f^{\mathsf{ck}}$ with respect to some bounds ℓ, ν on the cardinality of $\{P_j\}_j$ and on the degree d_f of f.

Relations for MUniEv-Π and AC-Π. We define the intermediate statements $\mathcal{R}_{\mathsf{eval}}, \hat{\mathcal{R}}_f$ to be proven using the two SNARKs, MUniEv-Π and AC-Π:

---

[2] We consider linearly homomorphic commitment schemes MPoly-$\mathcal{C}om$ and we commit in C_T and C to vectors of $n + 1 \leq \ell$ polynomials $(C_T, \tau) \leftarrow \mathsf{MPoly.Com}(T, 0, 0 \ldots 0)$ and $(C, \rho) \leftarrow \mathsf{MPoly.Com}(0, \{P_j\}_{j=1}^n)$ with an appropriate number of 0's, i.e., $(T, \{P_j\}) = (T, \{0\}) + (0, \{P_j\})$, such that computing $C_T \times C$ results in a commitment $(C_T \times C, \tau + \rho) \leftarrow \mathsf{MPoly.Com}(T, \{P_j\}_{j=1}^n)$ to the concatenation of $T, \{P_j\}$.

Rq-Π.Gen(ck, $\mathcal{R}_f^{ck}$) → crs

> 1: crs_C ← MUniEv-Π.Gen(ck, $\mathcal{R}_{eval}$), crs' ← AC-Π.Gen(ck, $\hat{\mathcal{R}}_f$)
> 2: return crs := (crs_C, crs')

Rq-Π.Prove(crs, x, w)

> 1: $(C, P) := x, (\{P_j\}_{j=1}^n, \rho, T) := w$
> 2: (C_T, τ) ← MPoly.Com(T)
> 3: k ← Hash(C, P, C_T)
> 4: $p = P(k), r = R(k)$,
> 5: $t' = T(k), p_j = P_j(k)$
> 6: (C', ρ') ← MPoly.Com($t', \{p_j\}$)
> 7: $u_C := (C_T \times C, C', k)$
> 8: π_C ← MUniEv-Π.Prove(crs_C, u_C, w_C),
> 9: π' ← AC-Π.Prove(crs', $u' = (C', p, r), w'$)
> 10: returns $\pi = (C_T, C', \pi_C, \pi')$

Rq-Π.Ver(crs, $x = (C, P), \pi$)

> 1: $\pi := (C_T, C', \pi_C, \pi')$
> 2: k ← Hash(C, P, C_T)
> 3: $p := P(k), r := R(k)$
> 4: $u_C := (C_T \times C, C', k)$
> 5: $u' := (C', p, r)$
> 6: b_C ← MUniEv-Π.Ver(crs_C, u_C, π_C)
> 7: b' ← AC-Π.Ver(crs', u', π')
> 8: return ($b_C \wedge b'$) = 1.

Fig. 1. Our SNARK Rq-Π for Evaluations over Polynomial Rings

$\mathcal{R}_{eval}$: We first define the relation for simultaneous evaluation of multiple polynomials on a point k, to be supported by MUniEv-Π. The prover has to convince the verifier that for a given point k (that in our case is random, but part of the statement) and two commitments $C_T \times C$ and C', it knows the corresponding opening values $(T, \{P_j\}_j, \tau + \rho)$ and $(t', \{p_j\}_j, \rho')$ such that $P_j(k) = p_j$ for all j, and $T(k) = t'$.

More formally, MUniEv-Π.Prove takes as input a statement $u_C = (C_T \times C, C', k)$, and a witness $w_C = ((T, \{P_j\}), (t', \{p_j\}), \tau + \rho, \rho')$, and $\mathcal{R}_{eval}$ holds for (u_C, w_C) iff:

$$\mathcal{R}_{eval} := \{(u_C, w_C) : \forall j, \ p_j = P_j(k) \wedge t' = T(k) \wedge (C', \rho') = \mathsf{MPoly.Com}(t', \{p_j\})$$
$$\wedge (C_T \times C, \tau + \rho) = \mathsf{MPoly.Com}(T, \{P_j\}_j)\}.$$

$\hat{\mathcal{R}}_f$: We define the relation for correct computation of $\hat{f}$, to be supported by AC-Π. The prover has to convince the verifier that an equality holds for some scalar values $t', \{p_j\}, p, r \in \mathbb{Z}_q$. The inputs p, r are known by the verifier (they are public) and $t', \{p_j\}$ are given implicitly in a committed form $(C', \rho') = \mathsf{MPoly.Com}(t', \{p_j\})$. More formally, given a statement $u' = (C', p, r)$ and a witness $w' = (\rho', t', \{p_j\})$ for the computation $p = \hat{f}(p_j) - rt'$ and for the opening of C', the relation is defined as follows:

$$\hat{\mathcal{R}}_f := \{(u', w') : p = \hat{f}(p_j) + rt' \wedge (C', \rho') = \mathsf{MPoly.Com}(t', \{p_j\})\}.$$

CRS Generation. The setup algorithm Rq-Π.Gen(ck, $\mathcal{R}_f^{ck}$), given a commitment key ck ← MPoly.ComGen(1^λ) that supports commitments up to ℓ different polynomials $P_j \in \mathbb{R}_q$ (all of degrees $\leq d$) and one commitment to a polynomial

$T \in \mathbb{Z}_q[X]$ of higher degree (up to ν)[3] and the NP relation $\mathcal{R}_f^{\mathsf{ck}}$ including the bound parameters ℓ, ν, outputs a crs enabling the proof and verification of a function f of degree $d_f < \nu$ over a set of polynomials $\{P_j\}_{j=1}^n$ of cardinality $n \leq \ell$.

First it runs the generation algorithm for MUniEv-Π and computes a part of the setup, $\mathsf{crs}_C \leftarrow \mathsf{MUniEv\text{-}\Pi.Gen}(\mathsf{ck}, \mathcal{R}_{\mathsf{eval}})$.

Then it generates a common reference string for AC-Π that will be used for proving computations of $\hat{f}$: $\mathsf{crs}' \leftarrow \mathsf{AC\text{-}\Pi.Gen}(\mathsf{ck}, \hat{\mathcal{R}}_f)$. As an observation, AC-$\Pi$ assumes commitments to vectors of scalars; these can be done with MPoly-$\mathcal{Com}$, by seeing them as vectors of degree-0 polynomials.

Prover. Given a reference string crs, statement $u = (C, P)$ and witness $w = (\{P_j\}_{j=1}^n, \rho, T)$ where P is a public polynomial, C is a compact commitment to polynomials $\{P_j\}_{j=1}^n \in \mathbb{R}_q$ with opening ρ, and $T \in \mathbb{Z}_q[X]$ is a quotient polynomial, the prover algorithm produces a proof π that $f((P_j)_j) = P + TR$ as follows:

- The prover commits to $T = \sum_{i=0}^{\nu} T_i X^i$: $(C_T, \tau) \leftarrow \mathsf{MPoly.Com}(T)$.
- The prover then runs $k \leftarrow \mathsf{Hash}(C, P, C_T)$ to obtain a random value k.
- The prover evaluates the polynomials in k : $\{P_j(k) = p_j\}_{j=1}^n, R(k) = r$, $P(k) = p$ and $T(k) = t$.
- The prover commits the respective evaluations $t', \{p_j\}_{j=1}^n$ as $(C', \rho') \leftarrow \mathsf{MPoly.Com}(\mathsf{ck}, t', \{p_j\}_{j=1}^n)$.
- The prover runs the algorithm for MUniEv-Π to prove that the opening values $t', \{p_j\}$ of the commitment C' are evaluation in k of the polynomials $T, \{P_j\}$, committed in $C_T \times C$:

$$\pi_C \leftarrow \mathsf{MUniEv\text{-}\Pi.Prove}(\mathsf{crs}_C, u_C, w_C)$$

  where $u_C = (C_T \times C, C', k)$, $w_C = ((T, \{P_j\}), (t', \{p_j\}), \tau + \rho, \rho')$.

- It then runs the proving algorithm of AC-Π for proving the evaluation of $\hat{f}$ on scalars with a witness w' for the computation $p = \hat{f}(p_j) - rt$ and for the opening of C':

$$\pi' \leftarrow \mathsf{AC\text{-}\Pi}(\mathsf{crs}', u' = (C', p, r), w').$$

- The prover eventually outputs $\pi = (C_T, C', \pi_C, \pi')$.

Verifier. The algorithm Ver on input a statement $u = (C, P)$ and a proof $\pi := (C_T, C', \pi_C, \pi')$ recomputes the randomness k by running $k \leftarrow \mathsf{Hash}(C, P, C_T)$. Then the Verifier has only to evaluate the known polynomials P, R in k obtaining $p := P(k), r := R(k)$. Once it has all the elements to redefine the two statements $u_C := (C_T \times C, C', k)$ and $u' := (C', p, r)$ for the proofs π_C and π' it runs the corresponding verification algorithms of these two SNARKs, MUniEv-Π.Ver and AC-Π.Ver to check the proofs and outputs the conjunction of the two answers.

---

[3] The commitment key ck can have some special property for optimization, for example, it may consist of two keys, one for committing to polynomials $P_j \in \mathbb{R}_q$ of degrees $\leq d$ and another longer key to commit to polynomials $T \in \mathbb{Z}_q[X]$ of degree ν.

3.2   Security Analysis

Theorem 3. *Assuming that* AC-Π *and* MUniEv-Π *are secure commit-and-prove arguments of knowledge, the new construction* Rq-Π *described above satisfies* completeness, succinctness, zero-knowledge *and* knowledge-soundness.

For lack of space, the proof appears in the full version. Here we provide a short intuition. Correctness is rather straightforward, and zero-knowledge follows from the zero-knowledge property of the two SNARKs and the perfect hiding of the commitment scheme. For knowledge soundness, the proof consists of two main steps. First, we rely on the knowledge-soundness of the two SNARKs to show that for any adversary creating an accepting proof there is a knowledge extractor that, with all but negligible probability, returns witnesses that correctly satisfy the two relations $\mathcal{R}_{\mathsf{eval}}, \hat{\mathcal{R}}_f$ mentioned previously. Second, the only remaining possibility is that the polynomial $V = P^* - f(P_j) + TR$ is nonzero. However, $V(k) = 0$ and this holds for a random point k sampled by the random oracle independently of V, which can happen only with probability $\deg(V)/q$ which is negligible.

4   Applications to Computing on Encrypted Data

In this section we detail on how we can use our scheme Rq-Π for computations over polynomial rings to build a VC scheme with input and output privacy.

4.1   Verifiable Computation

Here we recall the notion of *verifiable computation* from [GGP10]. We adapt the definitions to fit the setting (that is in the scope of our construction) where we have public verifiability and public delegatability [PRV12], as well as privacy of the inputs and outputs. A VC scheme $\mathcal{VC} = (\mathsf{KeyGen}, \mathsf{ProbGen}, \mathsf{Compute}, \mathsf{Verify}, \mathsf{Decode})$ consists of the following algorithms:

$\mathsf{KeyGen}(1^\lambda, f) \to (PK_f, SK_f)$: Given the security parameter, the key generation algorithm outputs a public key and a matching secret key for the function f.
$\mathsf{ProbGen}_{PK_f}(\boldsymbol{x}) \to (\sigma_x, \tau_x)$: The problem generation algorithm uses the public key PK_f to encode the input x into a public value σ_x, to be given to the computing party, and a public value τ_x to be given to the verifier.
$\mathsf{Compute}_{PK_f}(\sigma_x) \to \sigma_y$: Given the public key PK_f and the encoded input, the compute algorithm returns an encoded version of the function's output.
$\mathsf{Verify}_{PK_f}(\tau_x, \sigma_y) \to acc$: Given the public key PK_f for function f, and the public verifier information τ_x, the verification algorithm accepts (output $acc = 1$) or rejects (output $acc = 0$) an output encoding σ_y.
$\mathsf{Decode}_{SK_f}(\sigma_y) \to y$: Given the secret key SK_f for function f, and an output encoding σ_y, the decoding algorithm outputs a value y.

The correctness of a VC scheme is the obvious property: if one runs Compute on an honestly generated input encoding of $\boldsymbol{x}$, then the output must verify and its decoding should be $y = f(\boldsymbol{x})$.

For security, intuitively we want to say that an adversary that receives the public parameters for a function f and an encoding of an input $\boldsymbol{x}$ cannot create an encoding that passes verification and decodes to $y' \neq f(\boldsymbol{x})$. More formally, we say that a publicly verifiable computation scheme $\mathcal{VC}$ is *secure* for a function f, if for any PPT adversary $\mathcal{A}$, we have that $\Pr[\mathbf{Exp}_{\mathcal{A}}^{PubVerif}[\mathcal{VC}, f, \lambda] = 1] = \mathsf{negl}(\lambda)$, where the experiment $\mathbf{Exp}^{PubVerif}$ is described below.

The *input privacy* notion intuitively says that no information about the inputs is leaked. This is defined using a typical indistinguishability experiment. Note that input privacy implies also *output privacy*. More formally, we say that a publicly verifiable (and publicly delegatable) VC scheme $\mathcal{VC}$ is *private* for a function f, if for any PPT adversary $\mathcal{A}$, we have that $\Pr[\mathbf{Exp}_{\mathcal{A}}^{Priv}[\mathcal{VC}, f, \lambda] = 1] \leqslant \frac{1}{2} + \mathsf{negl}(\lambda)$, where the experiment $\mathbf{Exp}^{Priv}$ is described below.

Experiment $\mathbf{Exp}_{\mathcal{A}}^{PubVerif}[\mathcal{VC}, f, \lambda]$
$\quad (PK, SK) \leftarrow \mathsf{KeyGen}(1^\lambda, f);$
$\quad \boldsymbol{x} \leftarrow \mathcal{A}(PK_f);$
$\quad (\sigma_x, \tau_x) \leftarrow \mathsf{ProbGen}_{PK_f}(\boldsymbol{x});$
$\quad \hat{\sigma}_y \leftarrow \mathcal{A}(PK_f, \sigma_x, \tau_x);$
$\quad a\hat{c}c \leftarrow \mathsf{Verify}_{PK_f}(\tau_x, \hat{\sigma}_y)$
$\quad \hat{y} \leftarrow \mathsf{Decode}_{SK_f}(\hat{\sigma}_y)$
$\quad$ If $a\hat{c}c = 1$ and $\hat{y} \neq f(\boldsymbol{x})$,
$\quad\quad$ output '1', else '0';

Experiment $\mathbf{Exp}_{\mathcal{A}}^{Priv}[\mathcal{VC}, f, \lambda]$
$\quad b \leftarrow \{0, 1\};$
$\quad (PK_f, SK_f) \leftarrow \mathsf{KeyGen}(1^\lambda, f);$
$\quad (\boldsymbol{x}_0, \boldsymbol{x}_1) \leftarrow \mathcal{A}(PK_f)$
$\quad (\sigma_b, \tau_b) \leftarrow \mathsf{ProbGen}_{PK_f}(\boldsymbol{x}_b);$
$\quad \hat{b} \leftarrow \mathcal{A}(PK_f, \sigma_b)$
$\quad$ If $\hat{b} = b$, output '1', else '0'

4.2   Our VC Scheme

We describe our VC scheme below. The construction is essentially an instantiation of the generic solution of Fiore et al. [FGP14] when using an homomorphic encryption scheme whose homomorphic evaluation algorithm fits our relation $\mathcal{R}_f$. This can be obtained by using HE schemes in the Ring-LWE setting where the ciphertext space works over the same ring $\mathbb{R}_q$ supported by our Rq-Π construction, and where the evaluation algorithm does not involve modulus switches and rounding operations. An example of such a scheme is the one of Brakerski and Vaikunthanatan [BV11].

Let $\mathsf{MPoly}\text{-}\mathcal{Com} = (\mathsf{MPoly}.\mathsf{ComGen}, \mathsf{MPoly}.\mathsf{ComVer}, \mathsf{MPoly}.\mathsf{OpenVer})$ be a polynomial commitment scheme, $\mathsf{Rq}\text{-}\Pi = (\mathsf{Rq}\text{-}\Pi.\mathsf{Gen}, \mathsf{Rq}\text{-}\Pi.\mathsf{Prove}, \mathsf{Rq}\text{-}\Pi.\mathsf{Ver})$ be a CaP zk-SNARK for polynomial rings computation, and let $\mathsf{HE} = (\mathsf{HE}.\mathsf{KeyGen}, \mathsf{HE}.\mathsf{Enc}, \mathsf{HE}.\mathsf{Eval}, \mathsf{HE}.\mathsf{Dec})$ be a homomorphic encryption scheme in the Ring-LWE setting. Then our VC scheme works as follows:

$\mathsf{KeyGen}(1^\lambda, \hat{f}) \rightarrow (PK_f, SK_f)$:
- Run $(\mathsf{pk}, \mathsf{sk}) \leftarrow \mathsf{HE}.\mathsf{KeyGen}(\lambda)$ to generate a key pair for HE.
- Run $\mathsf{crs} \leftarrow \mathsf{Rq}\text{-}\Pi.\mathsf{Gen}(\mathsf{ck}, \mathcal{R}_f^{\mathsf{ck}})$ to generate the common reference string of Rq-Π for the relation $\mathcal{R}_f^{\mathsf{ck}}$.
- Set $PK_f = (\mathsf{pk}, \mathsf{crs}, \hat{f})$ and $SK_f = (\mathsf{sk}, \mathsf{crs})$.

$\mathsf{ProbGen}_{PK_f}(\boldsymbol{x}) \to (\sigma_x, \tau_x)$:
- Parse $\boldsymbol{x} = \{x_i\}_{i=1}^n$ and compute ciphertexts $P_i \leftarrow \mathsf{HE.Enc}(\mathsf{pk}, x_i)$
- Compute the commitment $(C, \rho) = \mathsf{MPoly.Com}(\{P_i\})$ and define $\sigma_x = (C, \{P_i\}, \rho)$ and $\tau_x = C$.

$\mathsf{Compute}_{PK_f}(\sigma_x) \to \sigma_y$:
- Parse $\sigma_x = (C, \{P_i\}, \rho)$;
- Compute the result ciphertext $P \leftarrow \mathsf{HE.Eval}(\mathsf{pk}, \hat{f}, \{P_i\}) = f(\{P_i\})$.
- Run $\pi \leftarrow \mathsf{Rq\text{-}\Pi.Prove}(\mathsf{crs}, (C, P), (\{P_i\}, \rho))$.
- Define $\sigma_y = (P, \pi)$

$\mathsf{Verify}_{PK_f}(\tau_x, \sigma_y) \to acc$: output $b \leftarrow \mathsf{Rq\text{-}\Pi.Ver}(\mathsf{crs}, (C, P), \pi)$.

$\mathsf{Decode}_{SK_f}(\tau_x, \sigma_y) \to y$: Decrypt $y = \mathsf{HE.Dec}(\mathsf{sk}, P)$.

Following the general result in [FGP14], the scheme satisfies correctness, security and privacy. In particular, privacy relies on the semantic security of HE, and security on the soundness of the SNARK.

4.3   Preserving Privacy of the Inputs Against the Verifier

The VC scheme described in the previous section works when the homomorphic computation $P \leftarrow f(\{P_i\})$ on the ciphertexts is deterministic. This can raise the issue that the result ciphertext P may reveal information on the plaintexts $\{x_i\}$ underlying $\{P_i\}$ (e.g., in lattice-based schemes such information may be inferred by looking at the distribution of the noise recovered as P's decryption time).

It would be therefore interesting to capture the setting where one wants to hide information on the x_i's even from the decryptor. Such a property would turn useful in scenarios where the data encryptor and decryptor are different entities. As an example, consider the case of users that store medical data x on a cloud server which computes some query f on behalf of an analyst, who however is not entitled to learn more than $f(x)$.

In this section, we provide a formal definition of this property, that we call context-hiding, and then describe how our scheme from the previous section can be extended to achieve this additional property.

Defining Context-Hiding. Informally, this property says that output encodings σ_y, as well as the input verification tokens τ_x, do not reveal any information on the input $\boldsymbol{x}$. Notably this should hold even against the holders of the secret key SK_f. We formalize this definition in a zero-knowledge style, requiring the existence of simulator algorithms that, without knowing the input, should generate (τ_x, σ_y) that look like the real ones. More precisely, a VC scheme is context-hiding for a function f if there exist simulator algorithms S_1, S_2 such that:

- the keys (PK_f, SK_f) and (PK'_f, SK'_f) are statistically indistinguishable, where $(PK_f, SK_f) \leftarrow \mathsf{KeyGen}(1^\lambda, f)$ and $(PK_f, SK_f, \mathsf{td}) \leftarrow S_1(1^\lambda, f)$;

– for any input $\boldsymbol{x}$, the following distributions are negligibly close

$$(PK_f, SK_f, \sigma_x, \tau_x, \sigma_y) \approx (PK_f, SK_f, \sigma_x, \tau'_x, \sigma'_y)$$

where $(PK_f, SK_f, \mathsf{td}) \leftarrow S_1(1^\lambda, f)$, $(\sigma_x, \tau_x) \leftarrow \mathsf{ProbGen}_{PK_f}(\boldsymbol{x})$, $\sigma_y \leftarrow \mathsf{Compute}_{PK_f}(\sigma_x)$, and $(\sigma'_y, \tau'_x) \leftarrow S_2(\mathsf{td}, SK_f, f(\boldsymbol{x}))$.

Our Context-Hiding Secure VC Scheme. Before describing the scheme in detail, let us provide some intuition.

The first observation is that for the HE scheme this problem can be solved by adding to the result P an encryption of 0, P_0^*, whose noise can statically hide that in P (a so called noise flooding technique). However if we do this change in our VC scheme we have two issues: (1) the computation is not deterministic anymore; (2) the prover may create a bogus encryption of 0, not of the correct distribution, in order to make decryption fail. We can solve these issues by using the fact that, as underlying tool for verifiability, we are using a SNARK that can handle deterministic computations. In particular, we can do the following.

For (2) we add to the public key s honestly generated encryptions of 0 $\{P_i^*\}_{i=1}^s$, and then ask the untrusted party to compute the result as $P' = P + P_0^*$ with $P_0^* = \sum_{i=1}^n b_i \cdot P_i^*$, for uniformly random bits b_i. By choosing appropriately the noise parameters in the P_i^*'s and by taking $s \approx \lambda$, based on the leftover hash lemma, P_0^* can statistically hide the noise in P.

Formally, adding such a randomization at the end of computing a function f guarantees leveled circuit privacy. In a nutshell, a somewhat-FHE HE is leveled circuit private if there exists a simulator algorithm HE.S such that $\mathsf{HE.S}(\mathsf{pk}, d, f(\boldsymbol{x})) \approx \mathsf{HE.Eval}(\mathsf{pk}, f, \mathsf{HE.Enc}(\boldsymbol{x}))$ are statistically close. Here the input d taken by the simulator represents information on the depth of f.

For (1), we simply consider proving a slightly different relation, that is:

$$\mathcal{R}_f^* := \{(u = (C, P', \{P_i^*\}_{i=1}^s); w = (\{P_j\}_{j=1}^n, T, \rho, b_1, \ldots, b_s)) :$$
$$(C, \rho) = \mathsf{MPoly.Com}(\{P_j\}) \ \wedge \ \forall i \in [s] \ b_i \in \{0, 1\} \ \wedge$$
$$P' = f(P_j) + \sum_{i=1}^s b_i P_i^* - TR \}$$

To use our scheme Rq-Π on the above relation, we can do the following. Given a function $f : \mathbb{R}_q^n \to \mathbb{R}_q$, define the function $f' : \mathbb{R}_q^{n+s} \times \mathbb{Z}_q^s \to \mathbb{R}_q$ that takes $n + 2s$ inputs such that

$$\hat{f}'(x_1, \ldots, x_n, o_1, \ldots, o_s, b_1, \ldots, b_s) = \hat{f}(x_1, \ldots, x_n) + \sum_{i=1}^s b_i \cdot o_i.$$

Then we use our Rq-Π on the following relation

$$\mathcal{R}_f' := \{(u = (C', P'); w = (\{P_j\}_{j=1}^n, \{P_i^*\}_{i=1}^s, \{b_i\}_{i=1}^s, T, \rho')) :$$
$$(C', \rho') = \mathsf{MPoly.Com}(\{P_j\}, \{P_i^*\}, \{b_i\}) \ \wedge \ \forall i \in [s] b_i \in \{0, 1\} \ \wedge$$
$$P' = f'(P_j, \{P_i^*\}, \{b_i\}) - TR \}$$

where $C' = C \times C^* \times C_b$ and $\rho' = \rho + \rho^* + \rho_b$. It can be seen that $\mathcal{R}'_f$ matches the format $\mathcal{R}_{f'}$ (for the function f' and a larger set of inputs) of relations supported by our Rq-Π scheme. One change however is that the commitment C' cannot be created directly by ProbGen as it contains elements that depend on a specific computation. We can solve this problem by using the homomorphic property of the commitment scheme: namely we assume that at key generation a commitment $(C^*, \rho^*) = \mathsf{MPoly.Com}(\{P_i^*\})$ is created and made public, and that the prover creates a similar commitment $(C_b, \rho_b) = \mathsf{MPoly.Com}(\{b_i\})$ to the random coefficients. Then C' can be obtained as $C \cdot C^* \cdot C_b$ and its opening is $\rho' = \rho + \rho^* + \rho_b$.

A more precise description of the protocol is given below.

KeyGen$(1^\lambda, \hat{f}) \to (PK_f, SK_f)$:
- Run $(\mathsf{pk}, \mathsf{sk}) \leftarrow \mathsf{HE.KeyGen}(\lambda)$ to generate the key pair for HE.
- Run crs $\leftarrow$ Rq-Π.Gen$(\mathsf{ck}, \mathcal{R}_{f'})$ to generate the Rq-Π crs for the relation $\mathcal{R}_{f'}$.
- For $i = 1$ to s: $P_i^* \leftarrow \mathsf{HE.Enc}(\mathsf{pk}, 0)$ and compute a commitment $(C^*, \rho^*) = \mathsf{MPoly.Com}(\{P_i^*\})$.
- Set $PK_f = (\mathsf{pk}, \{P_i^*\}_{i=1}^s, C^*, \rho^*, \mathsf{crs}, \hat{f})$ and $SK_P = (\mathsf{sk}, \mathsf{crs})$.

ProbGen$_{PK_f}(\boldsymbol{x}) \to (\sigma_x, \tau_x)$: this is the same as in the previous section.

Compute$_{PK_f}(\sigma_x) \to \sigma_y$: parsing $\sigma_x = (C, \{P_i\}, \rho)$, do the following:
- Sample $b_1, \ldots, b_s \leftarrow_\$ \{0, 1\}$ uniformly at random, and compute a commitment $(C_b, \rho_b) = \mathsf{MPoly.Com}(\{b_i\})$ (thinking of each b_i as a degree-0 polynomial).
- Compute the result ciphertext $P' \leftarrow f(\{P_i\}) + \sum_{i=1}^s b_i P_i^*$.
- Run $\pi \leftarrow$ Rq-Π.Prove$(\mathsf{crs}, (C \times C^* \times C_b, P'), (\{P_i\}, \{P_i^*\}, \{b_i\}, \rho, \rho^*, \rho_b))$.
- Define $\sigma_y = (P', C_b, \pi)$.

Verify$_{PK_f}(\tau_x, \sigma_y) \to acc$: output $b \leftarrow$ Rq-Π.Ver$(\mathsf{crs}, (C \times C^* \times C_b, P), \pi)$.

Decode$_{SK_f}(\tau_x, \sigma_y) \to y$: Decrypt $y = \mathsf{HE.Dec}(\mathsf{sk}, P')$.

Theorem 4. *If HE is semantically secure and circuit private, and Rq-Π is knowledge sound and zero-knowledge, then the VC described above is correct, secure, private and context-hiding.*

Proof (Sketch). The proof of the result is rather simple. Below we provide a proof sketch. First, notice that based on the correctness of Rq-Π and that of HE, we obtain correctness of our protocol.

The security follows from the knowledge soundness of the SNARK. The only detail to mention is that we also rely on the correctness of the HE scheme in order to make sure that, for honestly generated ciphertexts $\{P_i\}$ of $\{x_i\}$, and $\{P_i^*\}$ for 0, and for binary coefficients $\{b_i\}$, the ciphertext $P' \leftarrow f(\{P_i\}) + \sum_{i=1}^s b_i P_i^*$ decrypts to $\hat{f}(x)$.

Finally, we can prove context-hiding via a simple hybrid argument based on the privacy property of the HE scheme and the zero-knowledge of our SNARK. We define the $\mathcal{VC}$ simulators as follows. S_1 proceeds exactly as KeyGen except that it runs the SNARK simulator $(\mathsf{crs}, \mathsf{td}) \leftarrow \mathsf{Sim}^{\mathsf{crs}}(\mathcal{R}_{f'}, \lambda)$ instead of Gen, and set its trapdoor to be td. $S_2(\mathsf{td}, SK_f, y)$ first sets $\tau'_x = C$ where C is created as a commitment to some dummy input. Next, it creates C_b as another commitment to a dummy value, and computes P' as an encryption of y using $\mathsf{HE.S}(\mathsf{pk}, d, y)$ (where d is information on the depth of f), and finally it invokes the SNARK simulator $\pi \leftarrow \mathsf{Sim}^{\mathsf{Prove}}(\mathsf{crs}, (C \times C^* \times C_b, P'))$. Then S_2 outputs τ'_x and $\sigma'_y = (P', C_b, \pi)$.

The indistinguishability of the keys is immediate from the zero-knowledge of the SNARK. For the second property, we can define an hybrid simulator S' that, with knowledge of σ_x, runs as S_2 but creates P' as in Compute. It is easy to see that the output of S' is indistinguishable from that of S_2 by the property of HE.Hide, also by the hiding of the commitment and by the zero-knowledge of the SNARK we obtain that the values (τ'_x, σ'_y) generated by S' are indistinguishable from the ones generated using ProbGen and Compute.

5   Bivariate Polynomial Commitment

Our final goal is to build an efficient instantiation of the MUniEv-Π scheme for the evaluation on the same point of *many* univariate polynomials committed with MPoly-$\mathcal{C}om$. This is the key tool for our Rq-Π scheme for computations over polynomial rings presented in Sect. 3.

We construct MPoly-$\mathcal{C}om$ and MUniEv-Π starting from a commitment scheme BivPoly.$\mathcal{C}om$ for bivariate polynomials and a commit-and-prove argument BivPE-Π for the partial evaluation, in one variable, of a committed bivariate polynomial.

In this section we recall bilinear pairings and the computational assumptions needed by our schemes, and then we present the BivPoly.$\mathcal{C}om$ commitment scheme. The construction of the BivPE-Π commit-and-prove SNARK is described in Sect. 6, while their conversion into MPoly-$\mathcal{C}om$ and MUniEv-Π appears in Sect. 7.

5.1   Computational Assumptions

Security of our constructions rely on various computational assumptions. We state here our assumptions over bilinear groups. Some of them are standard q-type assumptions in the frame of DLog-hard groups and others are extractable (non-falsifiable) assumptions, a class of assumptions inherent to the security of SNARKs as shown in [GW11].

Bilinear Groups. Let the generator $\mathcal{G}$ input a security parameter λ and output a description of a bilinear group $\mathsf{gk} := (q, \mathbb{G}, \mathfrak{G}, \mathbb{G}_T, \mathsf{e}) \leftarrow_{\$} \mathcal{G}(1^\lambda)$ such that q is a λ-bit prime; $\mathbb{G}, \mathfrak{G}, \mathbb{G}_T$ are cyclic groups of order q; $\mathsf{e} : \mathbb{G} \times \mathfrak{G} \to \mathbb{G}_T$ is a bilinear asymmetric map (pairing), which means that $\forall a, b \in \mathbb{Z}_q : \mathsf{e}(g^a, \mathfrak{g}^b) = \mathsf{e}(g, \mathfrak{g})^{ab}$; if g and $\mathfrak{g}$ generate $\mathbb{G}$ and $\mathfrak{G}$ respectively, then $\mathsf{e}(g, \mathfrak{g})$ generates $\mathbb{G}_T$; membership in $\mathbb{G}, \mathfrak{G}, \mathbb{G}_T$ can be efficiently decided, group operations and the pairing e are efficiently computable, generators are efficiently sampleable, and the descriptions

$\mathsf{Biv.ComGen}(1^\lambda, d, \ell) \to \mathsf{ck}$

1: $\mathsf{gk} \leftarrow \mathcal{G}(1^\lambda)$, $g, h \leftarrow_\$ \mathbb{G}$, $\mathfrak{g} \leftarrow_\$ \mathfrak{G}$, $\alpha, s, t \leftarrow_\$ \mathbb{Z}_q$
2: $\hat{g} := g^\alpha, \hat{h} := h^\alpha, \hat{\mathfrak{g}} := \mathfrak{g}^\alpha$
3: $g_{ij} := g^{s^i t^j}$, $\hat{g}_{ij} := \hat{g}^{s^i t^j}$ $\forall\ i < d, j < \ell$
4: $\mathfrak{g}_1 := \mathfrak{g}^s, h_1 := h^s$
5: return $\mathsf{ck} = \{\mathsf{gk}, (g_{ij})_{i,j=0}^{d,\ell}, (\hat{g}_{ij})_{i,j=0}^{d,\ell}; (h, \hat{h}); (\mathfrak{g}, \hat{\mathfrak{g}}); (\mathfrak{g}_1, h_1)\}$

$\mathsf{Biv.Com}(\mathsf{ck}, P) \to (C, \rho)$

1: $P := \sum_{i,j=0}^{d,\ell} a_{ij} X^i Y^j$
2: $\rho \leftarrow_\$ \mathbb{Z}_q$
3: $c = h^\rho \prod_{i=0,j=0}^{d,\ell} g_{ij}^{a_{ij}}$
4: $\hat{c} = \hat{h}^\rho \prod_{i=0,j=0}^{d,\ell} \hat{g}_{ij}^{a_{ij}}$
5: $C \leftarrow (c, \hat{c})$
6: return (C, ρ)

$\mathsf{Biv.ComVer}(\mathsf{ck}, C) \to b$

1: $C := (c, \hat{c})$
2: return $b := (\mathsf{e}(c, \hat{\mathfrak{g}}) = \mathsf{e}(\hat{c}, \mathfrak{g}))$

$\mathsf{Biv.OpenVer}(\mathsf{ck}, C, P, \rho) \to P$

1: $C := (c, \hat{c})$, $P = \sum_{i,j=0}^{d,\ell} a_{ij} X^i Y^j$
2: $b_1 \leftarrow \mathsf{ComVer}(\mathsf{ck}, C)$
3: $b_2 \leftarrow (c = h^\rho \prod_{i,j=0}^{d,\ell} g_{ij}^{a_{ij}})$
4: return $(b_1 \wedge b_2)$

Fig. 2. Our BivPoly.*Com* for Bivariate Polynomial

of the groups and group elements each have size $O(\lambda)$ bits.

The d–Strong Diffie-Hellman Assumption (d–SDH). The Strong Diffie-Hellman assumption [BB08] says that given $(g, g^s, \ldots, g^{s^d})$ it is infeasible to compute $y = g^{\frac{1}{s-r}}$ for a chosen $r \in \mathbb{Z}_q$. In our applications, a few more group elements Σ are given as input to the adversary:

Assumption 1 (d–SDH). *The d–Strong Diffie-Hellman assumption holds relative to a bilinear group* gk *if for all* PPT *adversaries* $\mathcal{A}$ *we have, on the probability space* $\mathsf{gk} \leftarrow \mathcal{G}(1^\lambda)$, $\Sigma \leftarrow ((g, g^s, \ldots g^{s^d}); (\mathfrak{g}, \mathfrak{g}^s))$, $g \leftarrow_\$ \mathbb{G}$, $\mathfrak{g} \leftarrow_\$ \mathfrak{G}$, *and* $s \leftarrow_\$ \mathbb{Z}_q$:

$$\mathsf{Adv}_{\mathcal{A}}^{d-\mathsf{sdh}}(\lambda) := \Pr\left[(r, y) \leftarrow \mathcal{A}(\mathsf{gk}, \Sigma) \wedge y = g^{\frac{1}{s-r}}\right] = \mathsf{negl}(\lambda).$$

An adaptation of the proof in Boneh and Boyen [BB08] shows that our variant of the $d - \mathsf{SDH}$ assumption holds in the generic bilinear group model.

Knowledge of Exponent Assumptions. The knowledge of exponent (KEA) assumption introduced by Damgard [Dam92] says that given g, g^α in a group $\mathbb{G}$ it is infeasible to create $c, \hat{c}$ so $\hat{c} = c^\alpha$ without knowing a so $c = g^a$ and $\hat{c} = (g^\alpha)^a$. d-Power Knowledge of Exponent Assumption ($d - \mathsf{PKE}$) is another long-standing extractable assumption. It says that given $\{g, g^s, g^{s^2}, \ldots, g^{s^d}, \hat{g}, \hat{g}^s, \hat{g}^{s^2}, \ldots, \hat{g}^{s^d}\}$ with $\hat{g} = g^\alpha$, it is infeasible to create $c, \hat{c}$ where $\hat{c} = c^\alpha$ without knowing $a_0, a_1, \ldots a_d$ that satisfy $c = \prod_{i=0}^d (g^{s^i})^{a_i}$.

The (d, ℓ)–Bivariate PKE Assumption $((d, \ell) - \mathsf{BPKE})$. We introduce a bivariate power knowledge of exponent assumption that is a simple extension of the popular $d - \mathsf{PKE}$ assumption.

The (d, ℓ)–Bivariate Power Knowledge of Exponent Assumption for a bilinear group gk, noted by $(d, \ell) - \mathsf{BPKE}$ is a hybrid between PKE assumption for d different powers of s and ℓ powers of t and KEA assumption for input $(h, \hat{h} := h^\alpha) \in \mathbb{G}^2$. It takes the two basis $(g, \hat{g} := g^\alpha), (h, \hat{h} := h^\alpha)$ and all the powers $\{g^{s^i t^j}, \hat{g}^{s^i t^j}\}_{i,j=0}^{d,\ell}$ and claims that it is infeasible to create $c, \hat{c}$ such that $\hat{c} = c^\alpha$ without knowing $\delta, \{a_{ij}\}_{i,j=0}^{d,\ell}$, that satisfy $c = h^\delta \prod_{i,j=0}^{d,\ell} (g^{s^i t^j})^{a_{ij}}$. More formally:

Assumption 2 $((d, \ell) - \mathsf{BPKE})$. *The* $(d, \ell) - \mathsf{BPKE}$ *assumption holds relative to a bilinear group* gk *for the class* $\mathcal{Z}$ *of auxiliary input generators if, for every* aux $\in$ $\mathcal{Z}$ *and PPT adversary* $\mathcal{A}$, *there exists a PPT extractor* Ext *such that, on the probability space* gk $\leftarrow \mathcal{G}(1^\lambda)$, $\Sigma \leftarrow (g, \{g^{s^i t^j}\}_{i,j=0}^{d,\ell}, \{\hat{g}^{s^i t^j}\}_{i,j=0}^{d,\ell}; (h, \hat{h}, h^s); (\mathfrak{g}, \hat{\mathfrak{g}}, \mathfrak{g}^s))$, aux $\leftarrow \mathcal{Z}(\mathsf{gk}, \Sigma)$, $g, h \leftarrow_\$ \mathbb{G}$, $\mathfrak{g} \leftarrow_\$ \mathfrak{G}$, $\alpha, s, t \leftarrow_\$ \mathbb{Z}_q$, $\hat{g} := g^\alpha$, $\hat{h} := h^\alpha$, *and* $\hat{\mathfrak{g}} := \mathfrak{g}^\alpha$:

$$\mathsf{Adv}_{\mathcal{A}}^{\mathsf{d-pke}}(\lambda) := \Pr\left[\begin{array}{c} (c, \hat{c}; \delta, \{a_{ij}\}_{i,j=0}^{d,\ell}) \leftarrow (\mathcal{A} \| \mathsf{Ext})(\mathsf{gk}, \Sigma; \mathsf{aux}) \\ \mathsf{e}(\hat{c}, \mathfrak{g}) = \mathsf{e}(c, \mathfrak{g}^\alpha) \ \wedge \ c \neq h^\delta \prod_{i,j=0}^{d,\ell}(g^{s^i t^j})^{a_{ij}} \end{array} \right] = \mathsf{negl}(\lambda).$$

5.2 Knowledge Commitment for Bivariate Polynomials

Based on an efficient construction of a polynomial commitment scheme proposed by [KZG10] we further construct a knowledge commitment scheme for bivariate polynomials that is perfectly hiding and computationally binding. This will later allow us to use commitments in a CaP-SNARK BivPE-Π for polynomial partial evaluation.

The commitment scheme BivPoly.$\mathcal{C}om$ = (Biv.ComGen, Biv.Com, Biv.ComVer, Biv.OpenVer) consists of four algorithms as described in Fig. 2 and it is specialized for (bivariate) polynomials $P \in \mathbb{Z}_q[X, Y]$: the message space M_{ck} is defined by polynomials in $\mathbb{Z}_q[X, Y]$ of degree in X bounded by a value d and degree in Y bounded by some value ℓ.

Remark 5. The Biv.ComGen algorithm computes two extra values $\mathfrak{g}_1 := \mathfrak{g}^s, h_1 := h^s$ to be added to ck (step 4). Although these elements are not used by the commitment scheme, they are useful to construct our Commit and Prove SNARK for partial evaluations of polynomials committed with BivPoly.$\mathcal{C}om$. In other words, used as a stand alone commitment scheme, BivPoly.$\mathcal{C}om$ may have a slightly shorter commitment key ck (by removing step 4 from Biv.ComGen).

Security of the Commitment BivPoly.$\mathcal{C}om$**.** We call BivPoly.$\mathcal{C}om$ a knowledge commitment, since the prover cannot make a valid commitment without "knowing" the committed values. We will rely on the $(d, \ell) - \mathsf{BPKE}$ assumption for extracting the committed polynomials. We can state the following theorem on the security of BivPoly.$\mathcal{C}om$, whose proof can be found in the full version.

Theorem 6. *The commitment scheme* BivPoly.$\mathcal{C}om$ *is perfectly hiding and computationally binding assuming the* $d - \mathsf{SDH}$ *assumption holds in* $\mathbb{G}$. *Moreover, assuming* $(d, \ell) - \mathsf{BPKE}$, *the scheme is knowledge binding.*

6 CaP-SNARK for Bivariate Polynomial Evaluation

In this section we show how to construct a commit-and-prove SNARK BivPE-Π for the partial evaluation in a single variable of bivariate polynomials.

6.1 Relations for Bivariate Polynomial Partial Evaluation

The relation $\mathcal{R}$ for partial evaluation of bivariate polynomials is defined over tuples $(k, P(X,Y), Q(Y)) \in \mathbb{Z}_q \times \mathbb{Z}_q[X,Y] \times \mathbb{Z}_q[Y]$ as follows

$$\mathcal{R} := \{(k, P(X,Y), Q(Y)) : Q(Y) = P(k,Y)\}.$$

The scheme we propose in this section is a Commit-and-Prove (CaP) SNARK for the above $\mathcal{R}$ where $P \in \mathbb{Z}_q[X,Y]$ and $Q \in \mathbb{Z}_q[Y]$ are committed in C and C' respectively using BivPoly.$\mathcal{C}om$.[4]

Namely, following the definition from Sect. 2.2, BivPE-Π is a zk-SNARK for the following commit-and-prove relation

$$\begin{aligned}
\mathcal{R}_{\mathsf{ck}} := \{(u = (C, C', k); w = (P, Q, \rho, \rho')) : \hspace{2cm} (1) \\
(C, \rho) = \mathsf{Biv.Com}(P) \ \wedge \ (C', \rho') = \mathsf{Biv.Com}(Q) \ \wedge \ Q(Y) = P(k,Y)\}.
\end{aligned}$$

6.2 Our BivPE-Π Scheme for Bivariate Polynomial Evaluation

We aim to build an efficient commit-and-prove SNARK, BivPE-Π, dedicated to partial evaluation for bivariate polynomials $P \in \mathbb{Z}_q[X,Y]$ in $X = k \in \mathbb{Z}_q$.

Our scheme is based on an algebraic property of polynomials. We remark that $(X - k)$ perfectly divides the polynomial $P(X,Y) - P(k,Y)$ for $k \in \mathbb{Z}_q$.

BivPE-Π works for an ($\mathcal{R}$-independent) bivariate polynomial commitment scheme BivPoly.$\mathcal{C}om$ = (Biv.ComGen, Biv.Com, Biv.ComVer, Biv.OpenVer), as detailed in Fig. 3, and has to satisfy *completeness*, *succinctness*, *zero-knowledge* and *knowledge-soundness*.

Description of Our BivPE-Π **Protocol.** Let BivPoly.$\mathcal{C}om$ be a bi-variate polynomial knowledge commitment scheme. We construct a zero-knowledge SNARK scheme for any relation $\mathcal{R}_{\mathsf{ck}}$ with respect to some bounds d, ℓ on the degrees in X and in Y of the polynomials $P \in \mathbb{Z}_q[X,Y]$ supported by BivPoly.$\mathcal{C}om$. Our protocol is formally depicted in Fig. 3.

CRS Generation. The setup algorithm outputs a crs enabling the proof and verification of statements for the associated relation $\mathcal{R}_{\mathsf{ck}}$ defined in Eq. (1).

We remark that Gen algorithm is just using the same public information (commitment key) ck from the BivPoly.$\mathcal{C}om$ scheme.

Prover. Given crs, the statement $u = (C, C', k)$ (two commitments C, C' and an evaluation point k) and the witness $w = (P, Q, \rho, \rho')$ (the corresponding polynomials $P \in \mathbb{Z}_q[X,Y], Q \in \mathbb{Z}_q[Y]$ and their randomness ρ, ρ'), the prover proceeds to compute a proof π that $P(k,Y) = Q(Y)$, $(C, \rho) = \mathsf{Biv.Com}(P)$, and $(C', \rho') = \mathsf{Biv.Com}(Q)$ in two steps:

---

[4] Note that, although Q is a uni-variate polynomial in Y, it can also be seen as a bivariate polynomial.

$$\mathsf{BivPE}\text{-}\Pi.\mathsf{Gen}(\mathsf{ck}, \mathcal{R}_{\mathsf{ck}}) \to \mathsf{crs} := \mathsf{ck}$$

$\mathsf{BivPE}\text{-}\Pi.\mathsf{Prove}(\mathsf{crs}, u, w)$	$\mathsf{BivPE}\text{-}\Pi.\mathsf{Ver}(\mathsf{crs}, u, \pi) \to b$
1: $(C, C', k) := u, (P, Q, \rho, \rho') := w$	1: $(C, C', k) := u, (D, e, \sigma, \tau) := \pi$
2: $W := (P - Q)/(X - k)$	2: $(c, \hat{c}) := C, (c', \hat{c}') := C', (d, \hat{d}) := D$
3: $(D, \omega) \leftarrow \mathsf{Biv.Com}(W)$	3: $b_1 \leftarrow \mathsf{Biv.ComVer}(C)$
4: $\tilde{g} := h_1/h^k, \quad x, y \leftarrow_{\$} \mathbb{Z}_q$	4: $b_2 \leftarrow \mathsf{Biv.ComVer}(C')$
5: $\mathbb{U} := \mathsf{e}(h^x \tilde{g}^y, \mathfrak{g})$	5: $b_3 \leftarrow \mathsf{Biv.ComVer}(D)$
6: $e \leftarrow \mathsf{Hash}(u, D, \mathbb{U})$	6: $\mathbb{A} = \mathsf{e}(d, \mathfrak{g}_1/\mathfrak{g}^k) \cdot \mathsf{e}(c/c', \mathfrak{g})^{-1}$
7: $\sigma = x - (\rho' - \rho)e \mod q$	7: $\mathbb{U} := \mathsf{e}(h^\sigma \tilde{g}^\tau, \mathfrak{g})\mathbb{A}^e$, s.t. $\tilde{g} := h_1/h^k$
8: $\tau = y - \omega e \mod q$	8: $b_4 \leftarrow (e = \mathsf{Hash}(u, D, \mathbb{U}))$
9: return $\pi := (D, e, \sigma, \tau)$	9: return $(b_1 \wedge b_2 \wedge b_3 \wedge b_4)$

Fig. 3. Our CaP-SNARK for Bivariate Polynomial Partial Evaluation

Step 1. (From 1 to 3 in the Prove algorithm from Fig. 3.) The prover computes a witness to the correct (partial) evaluation in $k \in \mathbb{Z}_q$ of the polynomial $P \in \mathbb{Z}_q[X, Y]$ as $P(k, Y) = Q \in \mathbb{Z}_q[Y]$. The witness of this evaluation is a polynomial $W \in \mathbb{Z}_q[X, Y]$ defined as the quotient $W := \frac{P(X,Y) - Q(Y)}{X - k}$. This is a well-defined polynomial in $\mathbb{Z}_q[X, Y]$ if and only if $P(k, Y) = Q \in \mathbb{Z}_q[Y]$. The element of the proof π that enables checking this algebraic property over the polynomials P and Q will be a commitment $(D = (d, \hat{d}), \omega)$ to the polynomial W, where $\omega \leftarrow_{\$} \mathbb{Z}_q$ is a fresh randomness.

Remark 7. To this point, the verifier should be convinced that the polynomial Q is the good evaluation in k of P, only by checking the corresponding polynomial equation evaluated in a random hidden point $(s, t) : W(s, t)(s - k) = P(k, t) - Q(t)$. This can be translated in terms of commitments $(C, \rho)(C', \rho'), (D, \omega)$ to P, Q, W as a pairing check: $\mathsf{e}(d, \mathfrak{g}_1/\mathfrak{g}^k) \cdot \mathsf{e}(c/c', \mathfrak{g})^{-1} = \mathsf{e}(h^{(s-t)\omega - (\rho - \rho')}, \mathfrak{g})$ where $C = (c, \hat{c}), C' = (c', \hat{c}'), D = (d, \hat{d})$.

Because of the hiding property, the verifier does not have access to the openings of the commitments, as it does not know the randomness ρ, ρ', ω.

We therefore need the prover to provide something more together with the commitment D. The prover needs to compute an extra proof of knowledge of the randomnesses ω used to create this comitment and of the correct relation to satisfy with respect to the randomness ρ, ρ' of the statement commitments C, C' such that the pairing expression cancels the respective terms $h^{(\rho - \rho')}$ and $h^{(s-t)\omega}$.

This is easily solved by building a Schnorr proof of knowledge of the exponents $\omega, (\rho' - \rho)$ that appear in $\mathbb{A} = \mathsf{e}(h^{(s-k)\omega - (\rho - \rho')}, \mathfrak{g}) = \mathsf{e}(h^{(\rho' - \rho)} h^{(s-k)\omega}, \mathfrak{g})$. If we define $\tilde{g} := h_1/h^k = h^{s-k}$, then this proof is a classical Schnorr proof for the public value $\mathbb{A} = \mathsf{e}(h^{\rho' - \rho} \tilde{g}^\omega, \mathfrak{g}) = \mathsf{e}(h, \mathfrak{g})^{\rho' - \rho} \cdot \mathsf{e}(\tilde{g}, \mathfrak{g})^\omega$ in the target group $\mathfrak{G}$. But we will show we can make it more efficient.

Step 2. (From 4 to 7 in the Prove algorithm from Fig. 3.) This step consists in this non-interactive Schnorr proof associated to the value $\mathbb{A} = \mathsf{e}(h^{\rho' - \rho} \tilde{g}^\omega, \mathfrak{g})$:
  - Choose $x, y \in \mathbb{Z}_q$,

- Define $\mathbb{U} = e(h^x \tilde{g}^y, \mathfrak{g})$, this corresponds to the first round in the interactive Schnorr proof protocol, where the prover sends its commitment.
- Sample the challenge to the Schnorr proof by running the random oracle (hash function) on input the statement to be proven and the commitment $\mathbb{U}$: $e \leftarrow \mathsf{Hash}(u, D, \mathbb{U})$,
- Compute the answers $\sigma = x - (\rho' - \rho)e \bmod q$ and $\tau = y - \omega e \bmod q$.

The values sent as Schnorr proof are three scalars e, σ, τ, where e is the output of the hash function $\mathsf{Hash}(u, D, \mathbb{U})$ and does not depend on the size of $\mathbb{U} \in \mathbb{G}_T$. After the two described steps, the prover algorithm outputs $\pi := (D, e, \sigma, \tau)$.

Verifier. First, the verifier parses the received statement and proof (steps 1 and 2 in the Ver algorithm from Fig. 3), then it makes sure the commitments C, C', D are well-formed (steps 3 to 5 in the Ver algorithm from Fig. 3) by running the Biv.ComVer algorithm. If this is not the case, we discard the proof π. To verify the proof π, one needs the polynomial equation $W(X, Y)(X - k) = P(k, Y) - Q(Y)$ to hold for some secret evaluation points (s, t). We can rewrite this equation in terms of pairings applied to the commitments (C, C', D): $e(d, \mathfrak{g}_1/\mathfrak{g}^k) \cdot e(c/c', \mathfrak{g})^{-1}$. If the polynomials W, P, Q evaluated in the secret points s, t satisfy the equation $W(s, t)(s - k) = P(k, t) - Q(t)$, then all the exponents in base g cancel out in the pairing expression. It is not the case for the exponents in base h which correspond to the randomness used in the commitments. The important remark is that if D is correct, the remaining value $\mathbb{A} = e(d, \mathfrak{g}_1/\mathfrak{g}^k) \cdot e(c/c', \mathfrak{g})^{-1}$ can be written only in terms of the 3 randomness ρ, ρ', ω used to commit to P, Q, W:

$$\mathbb{A} = e(h^{(s-k)\omega} h^{(\rho'-\rho)}, \mathfrak{g}) = e(h^{\rho'-\rho} \tilde{g}^\omega, \mathfrak{g}).$$

This can be checked by the usual verification procedure of the Schnorr proof transmitted in π, *i.e.* the values (e, σ, τ): Compute $\mathbb{A} = e(d, \mathfrak{g}_1/\mathfrak{g}^k) \cdot e(c/c', \mathfrak{g})^{-1}$ and $\mathbb{U} = e(h^\sigma \tilde{g}^\tau, \mathfrak{g}) \cdot \mathbb{A}^e$ then run the Hash function to check whether $e = \mathsf{Hash}(u, D, \mathbb{U})$.

Security of BivPE-Π. The security of our scheme is captured in the following theorem whose proof is elaborated in Sect. 8:

Theorem 8. *Assuming both the $d - \mathsf{SDH}$ and $(d, \ell) - \mathsf{BPKE}$ assumptions hold in the bilinear group* gk, *the protocol* CaP-BivPE-Π *is a zero-knowledge Succinct Non-Interactive Argument of Knowledge in the random oracle model.*

Remark 9. We point out that in the case one is *not* interested in hiding the committed bivariate polynomial P and its partial evaluation Q, then it is possible to define a simplified version of our scheme that does not need the Schnorr-style proof and thus is secure *without* random oracles. This protocol is the same as CaP-BivPE-Π except that one would set $\omega = \rho = \rho' = 0$ (so the commitments are no longer hiding); this way the evaluation proof can be just the commitment D and it can be verified with the pairing check $e(d, \mathfrak{g}_1/\mathfrak{g}^k) = e(c/c', \mathfrak{g})$.

7 CaP-SNARK for Simultaneous Evaluations

In this section we show how we can use our BivPE-Π scheme for the partial evaluation of *one* bivariate polynomial on a point k in order to prove the evaluation of *many* univariate polynomials on the same point k. The resulting scheme MUniEv-Π can be used in the protocol presented in Sect. 4 for verifiable computation using HE on Ring-LWE.

More precisely, we show how to use our BivPoly.$\mathcal{C}om$ and BivPE-Π to define a commitment scheme and a compact proof system dedicated to multi-polynomials evaluation in the same random point k: given a single compact knowledge commitment C for a set of univariate polynomials $\{P_j(X)\}_j \in \mathbb{Z}_q[X]$ and a public evaluation point $k \in \mathbb{Z}_q$, we want to prove that some values $\{p_j\}_j$ committed in C' are indeed evaluations of the committed polynomials in this point k.

7.1 Commitment for Multiple Univariate Polynomials

We describe below, MPoly-$\mathcal{C}om$, our new knowledge commitment for a set of univariate polynomials. It is obtained in a straightforward way from BivPoly.$\mathcal{C}om$. It is defined as follows, where for simplicity we consider $\ell + 1$ committed univariate polynomials $P_j = \sum_{i=0}^{d} p_{ij} X^i$ for all $0 \leqslant j \leqslant \ell, 0 \leqslant i \leqslant d$:

MPoly.ComGen($1^\lambda, d, \ell$) → ck: Given some degree bound d and some maximal bound $\ell + 1$ on the cardinal of the polynomial set to be committed, it runs ck ← Biv.ComGen($1^\lambda, d, \ell$), where d, ℓ are the bounds on the degrees on X and Y of the bivariate polynomials in $\mathbb{Z}_q[X, Y]$.

MPoly.Com(ck, $\{P_j\}_{0 \leqslant j \leqslant \ell}$) → (C, ρ): Given a set $\{P_j\}$ of $\ell + 1$ polynomials in $\mathbb{Z}_q[X]$, with coefficients $\{p_{ij}\}_{i,j=0}^{i \leqslant d, j \leqslant \ell}$ we can define the bivariate polynomial $P = \sum_{i,j=0}^{d,\ell} p_{ij} X^i Y^j$ and run (C, ρ) ← Biv.Com(ck, P);

MPoly.ComVer(ck, $C = (c, \hat{c})$) → 0/1: Runs b ← Biv.ComVer(ck, $C = (c, \hat{c})$);

MPoly.OpenVer(ck, $C, \{P_j\}_{0 \leqslant j \leqslant \ell}, \rho$) → $\{P_j\}_j$: Runs P ← Biv.OpenVer(ck, C, P, ρ) where P is parsed as $\sum_{i,j=0}^{d,\ell} p_{ij} X^i Y^j$. then output 1, else output 0 (reject).

We state the following theorem. Its proof (see the full version) simply follows from the way we encode multiple polynomials into a bivariate one.

Theorem 10. *This commitment scheme MPoly-$\mathcal{C}om$ is perfectly hiding, computationally binding, and knowledge binding assuming the scheme BivPoly.$\mathcal{C}om$ also is so.*

7.2 Succinct Proof of Multiple Evaluations in a Point k

The construction of an efficient MUniEv-Π dedicated to multiple uni-variate polynomial evaluations in some common point k follows as well from the BivPE-Π scheme we built for partial evaluations. More precisely, for some parameters d, ℓ and some given knowledge commitments C, C' for polynomials of maximal degree d, $\{P_j\}_{0 \leqslant j \leqslant \ell} \in \mathbb{Z}_q[X]$ and scalars $\{p_j\}_{0 \leqslant j \leqslant \ell} \in \mathcal{Z}$ and a public evaluation point $k \in \mathbb{Z}_q$, we want to prove that p_j is the evaluation $P_j(k)$ for any $0 \leqslant j \leqslant \ell$.

Description of Our CaP MUniEv-Π Protocol. We now describe our protocol for proving multiple uni-variate polynomial evaluations in some common point k, where the j index is always considered as $0 \leqslant j \leqslant \ell$, and thus for $\ell + 1$ polynomials:

MUniEv-Π.Gen($1^\lambda, \mathcal{R}_{\text{uni}}$) $\rightarrow$ crs: On input a security parameter $\lambda \in \mathbb{N}$ and a NP relation $\mathcal{R}_{\text{uni}} := \{(u = (\{P_j\}_j, k); w = \{p_j\}) : P_j(k) = p_j\}$, define the associated relation $\mathcal{R}_{\text{bi}} := \{(u = (P(X,Y), k); w = Q(Y)) : Q(Y) = P(k, Y)\}$ where $P(X,Y) := \sum_{j=0}^\ell P_j Y^j, Q(Y) := \sum_{j=0}^\ell p_j Y^j$. Output the common reference string by running crs $\leftarrow$ Gen(ck, $\mathcal{R}_{\text{bi}}$);

MUniEv-Π.Prove(crs, $u = (C, C', k), w = (\{P_j\}_j, \{p_j\}_j, \rho, \rho')$): Given crs, the instance u and the witness w, the prover defines new bi-variate polynomials $P(X,Y) := \sum_{j=0}^\ell P_j Y^j, Q(Y) := \sum_{j=0}^\ell p_j Y^j$ and compute the proof π for those: $\pi \leftarrow$ Prove(crs, $u = (C, C', k), w = (P, Q, \rho, \rho')$). Output $\pi := (D, e, \sigma, \tau)$;

MUniEv-Π.Ver(crs, u, π) $\rightarrow b$: Same algorithm as for partial-evaluation BivPE-Π.

Remark 11. The commitment D to the bivariate polynomial $W \in \mathbb{Z}_q[X, Y]$ that appears in the proof can be seen as a commitment to a vector of univariate polynomials $\{W_j\}_j$ using the MPoly-$\mathcal{C}om$ as follows: Write $W_j = \sum_{i=0}^d w_{ij} X^i$, then running MPoly.Com(ck, $\{W_j\}_j$) gives the same output (D, ω) as running Biv.Com(ck, W).

Theorem 12. *Assuming the* BivPE-Π *is a public coin argument of knowledge of openings of C and C' to some polynomials $P \in \mathbb{Z}_q[X, Y], Q \in \mathbb{Z}_q[Y]$ such that $P(k, Y) = Q(Y)$, then* MUniEv-Π *is a public coin argument of knowledge of openings of C and C' to a set of polynomials $\{P_j\}_j \in \mathbb{Z}_q[X]$ and a set of scalars $\{p_j\}_j \in \mathbb{Z}_q$ such that $P_j(k) = p_j \forall 0 \leqslant j < \ell$.*

For lack of space, the proof appears in the full version. It is almost a straightforward reduction to the properties of BivPE-Π.

7.3   Efficiency and Comparison

We summarize the performance of our scheme MUniEv-Π in terms of prover and verification time and proof size. The proof consists of 2 elements from the group $\mathbb{G}$ and 3 elements of $\mathbb{Z}_q$. Generating a proof for ℓ polynomials of degree d requires a total of $2\ell d$ exponentiations in $\mathbb{G}$ in order to compute the commitment D, and $O(\ell d \log d)$ operations in $\mathbb{Z}_q$ in order to compute the polynomial $W(X, Y)$ using polynomial division.[5] Verifying a proof requires 5 pairings, and the following number of exponentiations: 6 in $\mathbb{G}$, 1 in $\mathfrak{G}$ and 1 in $\mathbb{G}_T$. The numbers are obtained by observing that the six pairings for Biv.ComVer can be batched resulting into 2 pairings and 4 exponentiations in $\mathbb{G}$.

---

[5] Note that W can be computed by aggregating the results of ℓ polynomial divisions of degree d.

We compare MUniEv-Π against a solution based on a general-purpose SNARK restricted to proving multiple polynomial evaluations in a commit-and-prove fashion. For the latter, we choose the *LegoGroth16* scheme from [CFQ19], which makes the SNARK of [Gro16] (which is currently among the most efficient SNARKs) to efficiently work with committed inputs, and that achieves the following efficiency. The proof consists of 4 elements of $\mathbb{G}$ and 1 element of $\mathfrak{G}$. Let m and n be the size and degree of the QAP modeling the evaluation of ℓ polynomials of degree d, and note that $m, n \geqslant \ell d$. Proof generation requires $2m + n + \ell d + \ell$ and m exponentiations in $\mathbb{G}$ and $\mathfrak{G}$ respectively, as well as $O(n \log n)$ operations in $\mathbb{Z}_q$ for a polynomial division. Verification requires 7 pairings.

The analysis above shows that our scheme MUniEv-Π has slightly smaller proofs and, more notably, has faster proof generation. Considering that $m, n \geqslant \ell d$ and that $\mathfrak{G}$ operations are at least twice slower than in $\mathbb{G}$, our prover is at least 3 times faster.

8   Security Analysis of Our CaP BivPE-Π

In what follows we prove the main security result of our paper, Theorem 8. We focus on knowledge soundness of our CaP BivPE-Π scheme. We defer the reader to the full version for the proof of correctness and zero-knowledge.

Before going into the technical details of the proof, we provide some intuition about its strategy. The polynomial commitment scheme BivPoly.$\mathcal{C}om$ requires the prover Prove to exhibit two values $(c, \hat{c})$, that are the same encoding of coefficients of a polynomial $P(X, Y)$ in the exponent, but with respect to different bases. The reason that we require the prover to duplicate its effort w.r.t. α is so that the simulator in the security proof can extract representations of $(c, \hat{c})$ as a polynomial $P(X, Y)$, under the $(d, \ell) -$ BPKE assumption.

Suppose an adversary $\mathcal{A}$ manages to forge a SNARK of a false statement that nonetheless passes the verification test. The intuition behind the proof is to use the adversary $\mathcal{A}$ and the fact that the commitment scheme BivPoly.$\mathcal{C}om$ is extractable to be able to solve the $d -$ SDH assumption for $d = \deg(P)$ in X. There is a similar complementary case that allows this adversary to solve the $d -$ SDH assumption for $d = \deg(P)$ in Y (actually ℓ in our notations).

To proceed to proving Theorem 8, we first need two preliminary lemmas:

Lemma 13 (Global Extractor). *Assume that* BivPoly.$\mathcal{C}om$ *is an extractable commitment scheme with perfect hiding and computational binding properties and that* $(d, \ell) -$ BPKE *assumption holds in the bilinear group* gk. *For any PPT adversary* $\mathcal{A}^{\mathsf{KS}}$ *agains the knowledge soundness of* BivPE-Π *that has non-negligible probability of success in breaking the scheme, there exists an extractor* Ext *such that:*

$$\Pr\left[\begin{array}{c} C = \mathsf{Biv.Com}(P, \rho) \\ \wedge\ C' = \mathsf{Biv.Com}(Q, \rho') \\ \wedge\ D = \mathsf{Biv.Com}(W, \omega) \end{array} \middle| \begin{array}{c} \mathsf{crs} \leftarrow \mathsf{BivPE\text{-}\Pi.Gen}(1^\lambda, \mathcal{R}),\ z \leftarrow \mathcal{Z}(\mathsf{crs}) \\ ((u, \pi); \mathsf{wit}) \leftarrow (\mathcal{A}^{\mathsf{KS}} \| \mathsf{Ext}^*)(\mathsf{crs}, z) \\ u := (C, C', k),\ \pi := (D, \mathbb{U}, \sigma, \tau) \\ \mathsf{wit} := (P, \rho, Q, \rho', W, \omega) \\ \mathsf{BivPE\text{-}\Pi.Ver}(\mathsf{crs}, u, \pi) = 1 \end{array}\right]$$

$$= 1 - \mathsf{negl}(\lambda).$$

Proof. We show the existence of an extractor Ext^* that will output the polynomials $P(X,Y)$, $Q(Y)$, $W^*(X,Y)$ and the randomness ρ, ρ', ω corresponding to the commitments C, C', D, with overwhelming probability.

Let $\mathcal{A}^{\mathsf{KS}}$ be an adversary that breaks the KS of the protocol $\mathsf{BivPE\text{-}\Pi}$ with overwhelming probability, meaning it outputs a false proof that passes the verifier checks. Consider now the adversary $\mathcal{B}^{\mathsf{BPKE}}$ that takes as input $\sigma \leftarrow (g, \{g^{s^i t^j}\}_{i,j=0}^{d,\ell}, \{\hat{g}^{s^i t^j}\}_{i,j=0}^{d,\ell}; (h, \hat{h}, h^s); (\mathfrak{g}, \mathfrak{g}^\alpha, \mathfrak{g}^s))$ and runs the adversary $\mathcal{A}^{\mathsf{KS}}$ against the scheme. $\mathcal{B}^{\mathsf{BPKE}}$ can provide a valid CRS to $\mathcal{A}^{\mathsf{KS}}$ by using its inputs:

$$\mathsf{crs} = \{\mathsf{gk}, (g_{ij})_{i,j=0}^{d,\ell}, (\hat{g}_{ij})_{i,j=0}^{d,\ell}; (h, \hat{h}, h_1); (\mathfrak{g}, \mathfrak{g}^\alpha, \mathfrak{g}_1)\}.$$

The statement u, corresponding to $\pi \leftarrow \mathcal{A}^{\mathsf{KS}}(\mathsf{crs})$, contains the values $C := (c, \hat{c})$, $C' := (c', \hat{c}')$ that verify $\mathsf{e}(c, \hat{\mathfrak{g}}) = \mathsf{e}(\hat{c}, \mathfrak{g})$ and $\mathsf{e}(c', \hat{\mathfrak{g}}) = \mathsf{e}(\hat{c}', \mathfrak{g})$. The same holds for the value D provided in the proof $\pi = (D, e, \sigma, \tau)$, i.e. $\mathsf{e}(d, \hat{\mathfrak{g}}) = \mathsf{e}(\hat{d}, \mathfrak{g})$.

Provided that for any adversary $\mathcal{B}^{\mathsf{BPKE}}$ that outputs valid commitment pair $(c, \hat{c})$, there exists an extractor that returns the corresponding witness (the opening). We run the extractor $\mathsf{Ext}_\mathcal{B}$ associated to $\mathcal{B}^{\mathsf{BPKE}}$ for each of the inputs $C = (c, \hat{c}), C' = (c', \hat{c}'), D = (d, \hat{d})$. This returns the description of polynomials $P(X,Y), Q(Y), W^*(X,Y)$ and some scalars ρ, ρ', ω. Note that the existence and efficacy of $\mathsf{Ext}_\mathcal{B}$ is guaranteed by the $(d, \ell) - \mathsf{BPKE}$ assumption. We will then define a *general* extractor Ext^* associated to the adversary $\mathcal{A}^{\mathsf{KS}}$ by running $\mathsf{Ext}_\mathcal{B}$ on the same input. We call this global algorithm composed of the adversary $\mathcal{A}^{\mathsf{KS}}$ and the general extractor Ext^*, machine $M := \mathcal{A}^{\mathsf{KS}} \| \mathsf{Ext}^*$.   □

Lemma 14 (Extended Adversary Machine). *Assume that $(d, \ell) - \mathsf{BPKE}$ assumption holds in the bilinear group gk and that Schnorr proof used in the $\mathsf{BivPE\text{-}\Pi}$ protocol is sound. For any PPT adversary $\mathcal{A}^{\mathsf{KS}}$ against the knowledge soundness of the scheme $\mathsf{BivPE\text{-}\Pi}$ that outputs $u = (C, C', k), \pi = (D, e, \sigma, \tau)$, where C, C', D are well-formed commitments under $\mathsf{BivPoly}.\mathcal{C}om$ and the proof π verifies, i.e. $\mathsf{Ver}(\mathsf{crs}, u, \pi)$, there exists a machine, extended adversary $\mathcal{A}^*$ that outputs the same as $\mathcal{A}^{\mathsf{KS}}$ together with an extended witness $\mathsf{wit} = (P, \rho, Q, \rho', W, \omega, \delta, \gamma)$, where $P, W \in \mathbb{Z}_q[X,Y], Q \in \mathbb{Z}_q[Y]$ are the openings of the commitments (C, C', D) under randomness ρ, ρ', ω and δ, γ are such that $\mathbb{A} = \mathsf{e}(d, \mathfrak{g}_1/\mathfrak{g}^k) \cdot \mathsf{e}(c/c', \mathfrak{g})^{-1} = \mathsf{e}(h^\delta \tilde{g}^\gamma, \mathfrak{g}).$*

Proof. We use the previous defined machine M from Lemma 13 and the rewinding technique [PS00] for proving the soundness of the Schnorr's proof to extract the scalars δ, γ such that $\mathbb{A} = \mathsf{e}(h^\delta \tilde{g}^\gamma, \mathfrak{g})$: Consider the game between the challenger and the machine M against the soundness of the Schnorr's proof. The challenger runs M by fixing the values (C, C', D) and changing the oracle definition to get a fork with $e' \leftarrow \mathsf{Hash}(U, D, \mathbb{U}) \neq e$. The forger M will output two distinct forgeries corresponding to the same random oracle query, but for two distinct answers of the random oracle, e and e'. The Forking Lemma shows that by rewinding the adversary $\mathcal{O}(q_h/\varepsilon)$ times, where q_h is the maximal number of random oracle queries of the machine M and ε its success probability, then one finds two such forgeries $(\sigma, \tau), (\sigma', \tau')$ with constant probability, which enables to compute the values δ, γ such that $\mathbb{A} = \mathsf{e}(h^\delta \tilde{g}^\gamma, \mathfrak{g})$.

Using the existence of Ext^* extractor and of the algorithm that rewinds the machine M in order to obtain the output δ, γ as described before, we can define an aggregate machine $\mathcal{A}^*$ corresponding to the concatenation of both. This machine $\mathcal{A}^*$ takes the same input as $\mathcal{A}^{\mathsf{KS}}$ and outputs the witness corresponding to the commitment openings $(P, \rho), (Q, \rho'), (W, \omega)$ and two scalars δ, γ satisfying $\mathbb{A} = \mathsf{e}(h^\delta \tilde{g}^\gamma, \mathfrak{g})$. □

Knowledge Soundness. We now have all the tools to prove the soundness in two steps.

Step 1. First we show that for every PPT adversary $\mathcal{A}^{\mathsf{KS}}$ against the soundness of the protocol, there exists an extractor $\mathsf{Ext}_\mathcal{A}$ that runs on the same input and random coins as $\mathcal{A}^{\mathsf{KS}}$ and outputs a witness. Defining the extractor $\mathsf{Ext}_\mathcal{A}$ is straightforward from the Lemma 13 by running the Ext^* and keeping just the values (P, ρ, Q, ρ') from its output.

Assuming the existence of an adversary $\mathcal{A}^{\mathsf{KS}}$ and extractor $\mathsf{Ext}_\mathcal{A}$ that has a non-negligible success probability in winning the soundness game against the protocol BivPE-Π, we now show that we can either solve the discrete logarithm problem, or break the $d - \mathsf{SDH}$ assumption.

Step 2. Suppose the machine $\mathcal{A}^*$ associated to $\mathcal{A}^{\mathsf{KS}}$ defined in the Lemma 14 is able to output a cheating pair statement-proof $u = (C, C', k), \pi = (D, e, \sigma, \tau)$ and a witness $\mathsf{wit} = (\rho, \rho', \omega, P, Q^*, W^*, (\delta, \gamma))$ such that it passes verification checks, but the extracted values $P \in \mathbb{Z}_q[X, Y], Q^* \in \mathbb{Z}_q[Y]$ are not satisfying the expected relation $Q^*(Y) = P(k, Y)$.

For simplicity, we will call $\Delta = \rho' - \rho$. Assuming that the commitment scheme is binding, then one of the following scenarios must hold:

1. The polynomials extracted do not satisfy the correct relation not even when evaluated in s: $W^*(s, t) \neq \frac{P(s,t) - Q^*(t)}{s - k}$. This type of forgery can be reduced to the DLog problem for $(g, h) \in \mathbb{G}$, in the case 1 below (see Lemma 15);
2. The polynomial $W^* \in \mathbb{Z}_q[X, Y]$ committed in D does not satisfy the correct relation with respect to the other extracted values P, Q^*, but still evaluated in s, t we have that $W^*(s, t) = \frac{P(s,t) - Q^*(t)}{s - k}$. We reduce the case to the $d - \mathsf{SDH}$ assumption in the case 2 below (see Lemma 16).

Lemma 15 (Case 1). *Consider the adversarial machine $\mathcal{A}^*$ associated to $\mathcal{A}^{\mathsf{KS}}$ defined by the Lemma 14 that outputs some values $u = (k, C, C', D, e, \sigma, \tau)$ and $(\rho, P, \rho', Q^*, \omega, W^*, \delta, \gamma)$, such that $P(k, Y) \neq Q^*(Y)$, where $P, W^* \in \mathbb{Z}_q[X, Y]$, $Q^* \in \mathbb{Z}_q[Y]$ and $(P, \rho), (Q^*, \rho'), (W^*, \omega)$ are the openings of the commitments (C, C', D) and (δ, γ) satisfy $\mathbb{A} := \mathsf{e}(h^\omega g^{W^*(s,t)}, \mathfrak{g}_1 / \mathfrak{g}^k) \cdot \mathsf{e}(h^{-\Delta} g^{P(s,t) - Q^*(t)}, \mathfrak{g})^{-1} = \mathsf{e}(h^\delta \tilde{g}^\gamma, \mathfrak{g})$. Given that the verification check outputs 1 for π, there is a negligible probability that the values k, P, Q^*, W^* are such that $W^*(s, t) \neq \frac{P(s,t) - Q^*(t)}{(s-k)}$ under DLog assumption with respect to the group $\mathbb{G}$.*

Lemma 16 (Case 2). *Consider the adversarial machine $\mathcal{A}^*$ associated to $\mathcal{A}^{\mathsf{KS}}$ defined by the Lemma 14 that outputs some values $u = (k, C, C', D, e, \sigma, \tau)$ and $(\rho, P, \rho', Q^*, \omega, W^*, \delta, \gamma)$, such that $P(k, Y) \neq Q^*(Y)$, where $P, W^* \in \mathbb{Z}_q[X, Y]$, $Q^* \in \mathbb{Z}_q[Y]$ and $(P, \rho), (Q^*, \rho'), (W^*, \omega)$ are the openings of the commitments (C, C', D) and (δ, γ) satisfy $\mathbb{A} := \mathsf{e}(h^\omega g^{W^*(s,t)}, \mathfrak{g}_1/\mathfrak{g}^k) \cdot \mathsf{e}(h^{-\Delta} g^{P(s,t)-Q^*(t)}, \mathfrak{g})^{-1} = \mathsf{e}(h^\delta \tilde{g}^\gamma, \mathfrak{g})$. Given that the verification check outputs 1 for π, there is a negligible probability that the values k, P, Q^*, W^* satisfy $W^*(s, t) = \frac{P(s,t)-Q^*(t)}{(s-k)}$ under $d' - \mathsf{SDH}$ assumption with respect to the bilinear group gk, where $d' = \max\{d, \ell\}$.*

For lack of space, the proofs of the lemmas above is in the full version.

Acknowledgments. This work was supported in part by the European Community's Seventh Framework Programme (FP7/2007-2013 Grant Agreement no. 339563 – CryptoCloud). The first author has been partially supported by the Spanish Government under projects SCUM (ref. RTI2018-102043-B-I00), CRYPTOEPIC (ref. EUR2019-103816), and SECURITAS (ref. RED2018-102321-T), by the Madrid Regional Government under project BLOQUES (ref. S2018/TCS-4339), and by a research gift from Protocol Labs.

References

[AHIV17] Ames, S., Hazay, C., Ishai, Y., Venkitasubramaniam, M.: Ligero: lightweight sublinear arguments without a trusted setup. In: Thuraisingham, B.M., Evans, D., Malkin, T., Xu, D. (eds.) ACM CCS 2017, pp. 2087–2104. ACM Press, October/November 2017

[AS92] Arora, S., Safra, S.: Probabilistic checking of proofs; a new characterization of NP. In: 33rd FOCS, pp. 2–13. IEEE Computer Society Press, October 1992

[BB08] Boneh, D., Boyen, X.: Short signatures without random oracles and the SDH assumption in bilinear groups. J. Cryptol. **21**(2), 149–177 (2008)

[BBC+18] Baum, C., Bootle, J., Cerulli, A., del Pino, R., Groth, J., Lyubashevsky, V.: Sub-linear lattice-based zero-knowledge arguments for arithmetic circuits. In: Shacham, H., Boldyreva, A. (eds.) CRYPTO 2018. LNCS, vol. 10992, pp. 669–699. Springer, Cham (2018). https://doi.org/10.1007/978-3-319-96881-0_23

[BCG+13] Ben-Sasson, E., Chiesa, A., Genkin, D., Tromer, E., Virza, M.: SNARKs for C: verifying program executions succinctly and in zero knowledge. In: Canetti, R., Garay, J.A. (eds.) CRYPTO 2013. LNCS, vol. 8043, pp. 90–108. Springer, Heidelberg (2013). https://doi.org/10.1007/978-3-642-40084-1_6

[BCG+18] Bootle, J., Cerulli, A., Groth, J., Jakobsen, S., Maller, M.: Arya: nearly linear-time zero-knowledge proofs for correct program execution. In: Peyrin, T., Galbraith, S. (eds.) ASIACRYPT 2018. LNCS, vol. 11272, pp. 595–626. Springer, Cham (2018). https://doi.org/10.1007/978-3-030-03326-2_20

[BCR+19] Ben-Sasson, E., Chiesa, A., Riabzev, M., Spooner, N., Virza, M., Ward, N.P.: Aurora: transparent succinct arguments for R1CS. In: Ishai, Y., Rijmen, V. (eds.) EUROCRYPT 2019. LNCS, vol. 11476, pp. 103–128. Springer, Cham (2019). https://doi.org/10.1007/978-3-030-17653-2_4

[BG93]   Bellare, M., Goldreich, O.: On defining proofs of knowledge. In: Brickell, E.F. (ed.) CRYPTO 1992. LNCS, vol. 740, pp. 390–420. Springer, Heidelberg (1993). https://doi.org/10.1007/3-540-48071-4_28

[BGV12]   Brakerski, Z., Gentry, C., Vaikuntanathan, V.: (Leveled) fully homomorphic encryption without bootstrapping. In: Goldwasser, S. (ed.) ITCS 2012, pp. 309–325. ACM, January 2012

[BL07]   Buldas, A., Laur, S.: Knowledge-binding commitments with applications in time-stamping. In: Okamoto, T., Wang, X. (eds.) PKC 2007. LNCS, vol. 4450, pp. 150–165. Springer, Heidelberg (2007). https://doi.org/10.1007/978-3-540-71677-8_11

[BV11]   Brakerski, Z., Vaikuntanathan, V.: Fully homomorphic encryption from ring-lwe and security for key dependent messages. In: Rogaway, P. (ed.) CRYPTO 2011. LNCS, vol. 6841, pp. 505–524. Springer, Heidelberg (2011). https://doi.org/10.1007/978-3-642-22792-9_29

[CFQ19]   Campanelli, M., Fiore, D., Querol, A.: LegoSNARK: modular design and composition of succinct zero-knowledge proofs. In: Cavallaro, L., Kinder, J., Wang, X., Katz, J. (eds) ACM CCS 2019, pp. 2075–2092. ACM Press, November 2019

[CGGI16] Chillotti, I., Gama, N., Georgieva, M., Izabachène, M.: Faster fully homomorphic encryption: bootstrapping in less than 0.1 seconds. In: Cheon, J.H., Takagi, T. (eds.) ASIACRYPT 2016. LNCS, vol. 10031, pp. 3–33. Springer, Heidelberg (2016). https://doi.org/10.1007/978-3-662-53887-6_1

[CGGI17] Chillotti, I., Gama, N., Georgieva, M., Izabachène, M.: Faster packed homomorphic operations and efficient circuit bootstrapping for TFHE. In: Takagi, T., Peyrin, T. (eds.) ASIACRYPT 2017. LNCS, vol. 10624, pp. 377–408. Springer, Cham (2017). https://doi.org/10.1007/978-3-319-70694-8_14

[CMT12]   Cormode, G., Mitzenmacher, M., Thaler, J.: Practical verified computation with streaming interactive proofs. In: Goldwasser, S., (ed.) ITCS 2012, pp. 90–112. ACM, January 2012

[Dam92]   Damgård, I.: Towards practical public key systems secure against chosen ciphertext attacks. In: Feigenbaum, J. (ed.) CRYPTO 1991. LNCS, vol. 576, pp. 445–456. Springer, Heidelberg (1992). https://doi.org/10.1007/3-540-46766-1_36

[DM15]   Ducas, L., Micciancio, D.: FHEW: bootstrapping homomorphic encryption in less than a second. In: Oswald, E., Fischlin, M. (eds.) EUROCRYPT 2015. LNCS, vol. 9056, pp. 617–640. Springer, Heidelberg (2015). https://doi.org/10.1007/978-3-662-46800-5_24

[ElG84]   ElGamal, T.: A public key cryptosystem and a signature scheme based on discrete logarithms. In: Blakley, G.R., Chaum, D. (eds.) CRYPTO 1984. LNCS, vol. 196, pp. 10–18. Springer, Heidelberg (1985). https://doi.org/10.1007/3-540-39568-7_2

[FGP14]   Fiore, D., Gennaro, R., Pastro, V.: Efficiently verifiable computation on encrypted data. In: Ahn, G.-J., Yung, M., Li, N. (eds.) ACM CCS 2014, pp. 844–855. ACM Press, November 2014

[Gen09]   Gentry, C.: Fully homomorphic encryption using ideal lattices. In: Mitzenmacher, M. (ed.) 41st ACM STOC, pp. 169–178. ACM Press, May/June 2009

[GGP10] Gennaro, R., Gentry, C., Parno, B.: Non-interactive verifiable comput-
         ing: outsourcing computation to untrusted workers. In: Rabin, T. (ed.)
         CRYPTO 2010. LNCS, vol. 6223, pp. 465–482. Springer, Heidelberg
         (2010). https://doi.org/10.1007/978-3-642-14623-7_25
[GGPR13] Gennaro, R., Gentry, C., Parno, B., Raykova, M.: Quadratic span programs
         and succinct NIZKs without PCPs. In: Johansson, T., Nguyen, P.Q. (eds.)
         EUROCRYPT 2013. LNCS, vol. 7881, pp. 626–645. Springer, Heidelberg
         (2013). https://doi.org/10.1007/978-3-642-38348-9_37
[GKP+13] Goldwasser, S., Kalai, Y.T., Popa, R.A., Vaikuntanathan, V., Zeldovich,
         N.: How to run turing machines on encrypted data. In: Canetti, R., Garay,
         J.A. (eds.) CRYPTO 2013. LNCS, vol. 8043, pp. 536–553. Springer, Hei-
         delberg (2013). https://doi.org/10.1007/978-3-642-40084-1_30
[GKR08] Goldwasser, S., Kalai, Y.T., Rothblum, G.N.: Delegating computation:
         interactive proofs for muggles. In: Ladner, R.E., Dwork, C. (eds.) 40th
         ACM STOC, pp. 113–122. ACM Press, May 2008
[GMR85] Goldwasser, S., Micali, S., Rackoff, C.: The knowledge complexity of inter-
         active proof-systems (extended abstract). In: 17th ACM STOC, pp. 291–
         304. ACM Press, May 1985
[Gro16] Groth, J.: On the size of pairing-based non-interactive arguments. In: Fis-
         chlin, M., Coron, J.-S. (eds.) EUROCRYPT 2016. LNCS, vol. 9666, pp.
         305–326. Springer, Heidelberg (2016). https://doi.org/10.1007/978-3-662-
         49896-5_11
[GSW13] Gentry, C., Sahai, A., Waters, B.: Homomorphic encryption from learning
         with errors: conceptually-simpler, asymptotically-faster, attribute-based.
         In: Canetti, R., Garay, J.A. (eds.) CRYPTO 2013. LNCS, vol. 8042, pp.
         75–92. Springer, Heidelberg (2013). https://doi.org/10.1007/978-3-642-
         40041-4_5
[GW11]   Gentry, C., Wichs, D.: Separating succinct non-interactive arguments from
         all falsifiable assumptions. In: Fortnow, L., Vadhan, S.P. (eds.) 43rd ACM
         STOC, pp. 99–108. ACM Press, June 2011
[Kil92] Kilian, J.: A note on efficient zero-knowledge proofs and arguments
         (extended abstract). In: 24th ACM STOC, pp. 723–732. ACM Press, May
         1992
[KZG10] Kate, A., Zaverucha, G.M., Goldberg, I.: Constant-size commitments to
         polynomials and their applications. In: Abe, M. (ed.) ASIACRYPT 2010.
         LNCS, vol. 6477, pp. 177–194. Springer, Heidelberg (2010). https://doi.
         org/10.1007/978-3-642-17373-8_11
[MBKM19] Maller, M., Bowe, S., Kohlweiss, M., Meiklejohn, S.: Sonic: zero-knowledge
         SNARKs from linear-size universal and updatable structured reference
         strings. In: Cavallaro, L., Kinder, J., Wang, X., Katz, J. (eds.) ACM CCS
         2019, pp. 2111–2128. ACM Press, November 2019
[Pai99] Paillier, P.: Public-key cryptosystems based on composite degree resid-
         uosity classes. In: Stern, J. (ed.) EUROCRYPT 1999. LNCS, vol. 1592,
         pp. 223–238. Springer, Heidelberg (1999). https://doi.org/10.1007/3-540-
         48910-X_16
[PHGR13] Parno, B., Howell, J., Gentry, C., Raykova, M.: Pinocchio: nearly practical
         verifiable computation. In: 2013 IEEE Symposium on Security and Privacy,
         pp. 238–252. IEEE Computer Society Press, May 2013

[PRV12] Parno, B., Raykova, M., Vaikuntanathan, V.: How to delegate and verify in public: verifiable computation from attribute-based encryption. In: Cramer, R. (ed.) TCC 2012. LNCS, vol. 7194, pp. 422–439. Springer, Heidelberg (2012). https://doi.org/10.1007/978-3-642-28914-9_24

[PS00] Pointcheval, D., Stern, J.: Security arguments for digital signatures and blind signatures. J. Cryptol. **13**(3), 361–396 (2000)

[PST13] Papamanthou, C., Shi, E., Tamassia, R.: Signatures of correct computation. In: Sahai, A. (ed.) TCC 2013. LNCS, vol. 7785, pp. 222–242. Springer, Heidelberg (2013). https://doi.org/10.1007/978-3-642-36594-2_13

[RAD78] Rivest, R., Adleman, L., Dertouzos, M.: On data banks and privacy homomorphisms. Found. Secur. Comput. 4, 169–177 (1978)

[SV10] Smart, N.P., Vercauteren, F.: Fully homomorphic encryption with relatively small key and ciphertext sizes. In: Nguyen, P.Q., Pointcheval, D. (eds.) PKC 2010. LNCS, vol. 6056, pp. 420–443. Springer, Heidelberg (2010). https://doi.org/10.1007/978-3-642-13013-7_25

[WJB+17] Wahby, R.S., et al.: Full accounting for verifiable outsourcing. In: Thuraisingham, B.M., Evans, D., Malkin, T., Xu, D. (eds.) ACM CCS 2017, pp. 2071–2086. ACM Press, October/November 2017

[WTs+18] Wahby, R.S., Tzialla, I., Shelat, A., Thaler, J., Walfish, M.: Doubly-efficient zkSNARKs without trusted setup. In: 2018 IEEE Symposium on Security and Privacy, pp. 926–943. IEEE Computer Society Press, May 2018

[XZZ+19] Xie, T., Zhang, J., Zhang, Y., Papamanthou, C., Song, D.: Libra: succinct zero-knowledge proofs with optimal prover computation. In: Boldyreva, A., Micciancio, D. (eds.) CRYPTO 2019. LNCS, vol. 11694, pp. 733–764. Springer, Cham (2019). https://doi.org/10.1007/978-3-030-26954-8_24

[ZGK+17] Zhang, Y., Genkin, D., Katz, J., Papadopoulos, D., Papamanthou, C.: vSQL: verifying arbitrary SQL queries over dynamic outsourced databases. In: 2017 IEEE Symposium on Security and Privacy, pp. 863–880. IEEE Computer Society Press, May 2017

Isogeny-Based Cryptography

Lossy CSI-FiSh: Efficient Signature Scheme with Tight Reduction to Decisional CSIDH-512

Ali El Kaafarani[1,2], Shuichi Katsumata[3], and Federico Pintore[1(✉)]

[1] Mathematical Institute, University of Oxford, Oxford, UK
`federico.pintore@maths.ox.ac.uk`
[2] PQShield, Oxford, UK
`elkaafarani@pqshield.com`
[3] National Institute of Advanced Industrial Science and Technology (AIST),
Tokyo City, Japan
`shuichi.katsumata@aist.go.jp`

Abstract. Recently, Beullens, Kleinjung, and Vercauteren (Asiacrypt'19) provided the first practical isogeny-based digital signature, obtained from the Fiat-Shamir (FS) paradigm. They worked with the CSIDH-512 parameters and passed through a new record class group computation. However, as with all standard FS signatures, the security proof is highly non-tight and the concrete parameters are set under the heuristic that the only way to attack the scheme is by finding collisions for a hash function.

In this paper, we propose an FS-style signature scheme, called Lossy CSI-FiSh, constructed using the CSIDH-512 parameters and with a security proof based on the "Lossy Keys" technique introduced by Kiltz, Lyubashevsky and Schaffner (Eurocrypt'18). Lossy CSI-FiSh is *provably secure* under the same assumption which underlies the security of the key exchange protocol CSIDH (Castryck et al. (Asiacrypt'18)) and is *almost as efficient* as CSI-FiSh. For instance, aiming for small signature size, our scheme is expected to take around $\approx 800\,\text{ms}$ to sign/verify while producing signatures of size ≈ 280 bytes. This is only twice slower than CSI-FiSh while having similar signature size for the same parameter set. As an additional benefit, our scheme is by construction secure *both* in the classical and quantum random oracle model.

1 Introduction

1.1 Background

Isogeny-based cryptography is one of the promising candidates for post-quantum cryptography. While isogeny problems offer simple and efficient solutions to encryption schemes (or equivalently, key-exchange protocols) [8,25], they turned out to be rather elusive to use for constructing signature schemes.

At the highest level, all isogeny-based signatures we know thus far are based on the Fiat-Shamir paradigm [1,18]: prepare a hard relation $\mathcal{R}$ based on an

© International Association for Cryptologic Research 2020
A. Kiayias et al. (Eds.): PKC 2020, LNCS 12111, pp. 157–186, 2020.
https://doi.org/10.1007/978-3-030-45388-6_6

isogeny problem, construct an identification protocol (or sigma protocol) for $\mathcal{R}$, and use a cryptographic hash function to compile the identification protocol into a signature scheme in the random oracle model (ROM). Both the two central isogeny problems—the computational supersingular isogeny (CSSI) problem [13] and the group action inverse problem (GAIP) [8]—have been the basis for constructing signatures. Those based on CSSI, proposed in [21,42], produce signatures of size at least 12 KB even in the most optimized variant [21]. On the other hand, relying on GAIP and employing the Fiat-Shamir with aborts strategy [31], De Feo and Galbraith introduced a compact isogeny-based signature named SeaSign [12]. Despite the inefficiency in the signature generation and verification, SeaSign provides signatures of a remarkably small size (less than 1 kilobyte at the 128-bit security level).

Very recently, a new record class group computation has allowed Beullens, Kleinjung and Vercauteren [6] to improve SeaSign and obtain the first practical isogeny-based signature scheme, named CSI-FiSh. Their computation has shed light on the structure of the ideal class group determined by a specific set of CSIDH parameters, named CSIDH-512 [8]. This granted a proper uniform sampling from the ideal class group, and canonical representation of its elements, which enabled to overcome the costly remedy made by SeaSign. That is, the adoption of a redundant representation of class group elements and performing rejection sampling. The result is practical efficiency in both signature generation and verification while maintaining the short signature size offered by SeaSign. However, one important remark is that, since CSI-FiSh is specific to the special set of parameters CSIDH-512, it can offer *at most* the same security level provided by a hard problem defined over the CSIDH-512 parameters. Specifically, CSI-FiSh relies on the GAIP problem, which is believed to have 128-bits of classical and (at most) 64-bits of quantum security over the CSIDH-512 parameters [8,34].

Tight Security. Fiat-Shamir (FS) signatures [1,18] admit an intuitive and simple construction in the ROM, however, they are notorious for having a very loose reduction. Since a loose reduction forces for a stronger hardness assumption, and consequently a less efficient scheme, it has been the focus of several works to tighten the reduction loss, e.g., [3,19,22,26,32,33,37].

To give a more precise perception of the security loss, assume we had a FS signature that is secure based on the hardness of a particular hard problem Π. Then, the security proof of FS signatures in the classical ROM dictates that the reduction algorithm can break the underlying problem Π with advantage $Q^{-1} \cdot \epsilon^2$, where Q is the number of hash evaluations an adversary can perform and ϵ is the advantage of an adversary breaking the security of the FS signature. Therefore, if we want to instantiate the FS signature with *provably secure* parameters, we must assume the hardness of the problem Π for a security level that is much higher than expected. For instance, if we aim for 128-bits of security for the FS signature (i.e., $\epsilon = 2^{-128}$), then assuming a modest $Q \approx 2^{40}$, we require at least 296-bits of security for the hard problem Π. Since a hard problem with a higher level of security must necessitate larger parameters, this leads to inefficient schemes.

This undesirable loss in security and efficiency is common to all standard FS signatures and CSI-FiSh is no exception. However, one large difference between CSI-FiSh and other FS signatures is that CSI-FiSh relies on a hard problem defined for a *specific* security level—the GAIP problem over the CSIDH-512 parameters. For the time being, no other parameter sets are known to provide the nice algebraic structure required for CSI-FiSh. This is in sharp contrast with FS signatures based on other hardness assumptions since most hardness assumptions can "absorb" the reduction loss by setting the parameters larger. Since GAIP over the CSIDH-512 parameters only offers 128-bits of classical security, we cannot argue any notion of *provable* security for CSI-FiSh if we aim for 128-bits of security. Concretely, if we plug in $Q \approx 2^{40}$ as above, we can only provably argue 44-bits of security for CSI-FiSh. Moreover, if we aim for quantum security, the situation is worse since the reduction algorithm can break the underlying problem Π with only advantage $Q^{-6} \cdot \epsilon^3$ [16,30]. We note that the currently available resources would probably allow other record computations for bigger parameters for which GAIP is believed to have a much higher security level; however, the benefit of having a higher security level would likely be beaten by the significant slow-down in efficiency.

In practice, this inconvenient reduction loss in FS signatures is usually overlooked or simply ignored, and the parameters are set assuming that the best attack against the FS signature is (roughly) finding a collision in the hash function. In [6], the parameters for CSI-FiSh are set under this simplified assumption as well. Considering this undesirable gap between practice and theory, a natural question which arises is:

Can we design an isogeny-based signature scheme as efficient as CSI-FiSh with provable secure parameters?

1.2 Our Contribution

In this work, we provide a partial answer to the above problem and propose a new signature scheme, Lossy CSI-FiSh, with the following features:

- It is *tightly secure* under a natural hardness assumption over the CSIDH-512 parameters, that is, the *decisional CSIDH* (D-CSIDH) assumption.
  We note D-CSIDH is not a new assumption introduced in this paper, as it was originally defined by Stolbunov in his PhD thesis [39, Problem 2.2] and implicitly underlies the security of the key exchange protocol CSIDH [8].[1]
- It is *almost as efficient* as CSI-FiSh. Compared to CSI-FiSh, the signature size is the same, the public key is only twice as large, and the runtime of the signature generation and verification is estimated to be (at most) twice as slow. For instance, aiming for small signature size, our scheme is expected to take around $\approx 800\,\mathrm{ms}$ to sign/verify while producing signatures of size

---

[1] Roughly, this is parallel to the relation between the Diffie-Hellman (DH) protocol and the decisional DH assumption [15]. For a more formal discussion, we refer to Sect. 3.1.

≈ 280 bytes. This is still 150 times faster and around 3 times smaller than an optimized version of SeaSign for the same parameter set.
- It is secure *both* in the classical and quantum ROM (QROM). In particular, we do not require a separate construction using the Unruh transform [40] to achieve security in the QROM.

We obtain our results by following the line of work that constructs *lossy* identification protocols to obtain tightly secure FS signatures [2,26,27,41]. A lossy identification protocol comes with an additional *lossy statement* generator that produces lossy statements which are computationally indistinguishable from honestly generated statements for the hard relation $\mathcal{R}$ induced by some hardness assumption. Moreover, relative to the lossy statements, the protocol admits statistical soundness. That is, not even a computationally unbounded adversary can successfully impersonate a prover. Using the result of Kiltz, Lyubashevsky, and Schaffner [27] (see Theorem 2.1), a lossy identification protocol directly provides us an FS signature with a *tight reduction* in the *classical and quantum ROM*.

The idea to use a lossy identification protocol to achieve tight security for isogeny-based FS signatures was also considered by De Feo and Galbraith for SeaSign [12, Section 8]. In particular, they proposed to take a very large ideal class group (determined by a big prime p) and then only a small subset as the space of possible private keys (that results in valid public keys being chosen from a set of roughly the same cardinality). The signature generation and verification processes are not altered from the *standard* SeaSign scheme. The result is that the lossy variant inherits the inefficiency of the main scheme, with the increment of the prime p further aggravating the issue. It is evident that the above approach does not extend to the current version of CSI-FiSh, which requires the specific CSIDH-512 parameter set.

The lossy identification protocol proposed in this work—which arises from the observation that the D-CSIDH relation over the CSIDH-512 parameters naturally admits a lossy mode—appears to be much simpler and it smoothly leads to a practical signature scheme. Our identification protocol enjoys the same optimizations used in [12] and [6]. Using D-CSIDH instead of GAIP as the underlying assumption, we encounter an obstacle that stems from the fact that D-CSIDH does not provide natural random self-reducibility properties. However, we discuss that this issue does not have much of a big impact on the concrete choice of parameters.

Related Works. There are only a handful of efficient signature schemes that are tightly and provably secure in the (Q)ROM that we are aware of. The lattice-based Gentry-Peikert-Vaikuntanathan (GPV) signature [23] or its much-optimized successor FALCON [20] have tight security in the (Q)ROM. One notable feature is that the construction natively supports tight security in both classical and quantum ROM *without* incurring any overhead. Dilithium [17], which is a lattice-based FS-type signature, also has tight security in the (Q)ROM [27]. To achieve tight security, they must modify the public key of their non-tightly secure scheme to obtain a lossy mode. Unfortunately, when using a lattice-based hard problem (that is, the learning with errors problem), this comes at the cost of making the public key size at least 5 times larger and the signature size at least 2 times larger, e.g., public key and signature size grows from $(1472, 2701)$ bytes up to $(7712, 5690)$ bytes. As we mentioned above, SeaSign [12] goes through the lossy argument as well. They require to use of a non-standard variant of the GAIP problem and makes it difficult to assess the increase in signature and public key sizes. We like to highlight that although we go through the same paradigm of *lossy* arguments, Lossy CSI-FiSh is based on a standard assumption and does not incur a large blow up in size; the public key is only 2 times larger and the signature size remains the same compared to the non-tight variant CSI-FiSh. Finally, the hash-based signature SPHINCS$^+$ [4] also enjoys tight security in the (Q)ROM under several heuristic assumptions on the underlying cryptographic hash function.

Roadmap. The rest of the paper is organized as follows. In Sect. 2 we give a brief preliminary on identification protocols and class group actions. In Sects. 3 and 4 we introduce the new lossy identification protocol and we adapt it using the optimizations proposed in [6,12] to enlarge the challenge space. In Sect. 5 we describe the signature scheme obtained through the Fiat-Shamir transform, and we compare it to CSI-FiSh in terms of bandwidth and computational complexity. In Sect. 6 we report concluding remarks.

2   Preliminaries

2.1   Identification Protocols

Given two sets X and Y, a subset $\mathcal{R} \subset X \times Y$ is a polynomially computable binary relation on $X \times Y$ if, given $(\mathsf{X}, \mathsf{W}) \in X \times Y$, we can check $(\mathsf{X}, \mathsf{W}) \in \mathcal{R}$ in time $\mathsf{poly}(|\mathsf{X}|)$. The language $\mathcal{L}_{\mathcal{R}}$ corresponding to $\mathcal{R}$ is the set $\{\mathsf{X} \in X \mid \exists \mathsf{W} \in Y : (\mathsf{X}, \mathsf{W}) \in \mathcal{R}\}$, where we call W a witness for the statement $\mathsf{X} \in \mathcal{L}_{\mathcal{R}}$.

An identification protocol ID for a relation $\mathcal{R}$ is a three-move interactive protocol between a prover and a verifier. Informally, a prover holding a statement-witness pair $(\mathsf{X}, \mathsf{W}) \in \mathcal{R}$ can prove to the verifier that they indeed possess a valid witness W without revealing any more than the mere fact that they know W.

Definition 2.1 (Identification Protocol). *An identification protocol* ID *for a relation* $\mathcal{R}$ *consists of four PPT algorithms* $(\mathsf{IGen}, \mathsf{P} = (\mathsf{P}_1, \mathsf{P}_2), \mathsf{V})$, *where* V *is deterministic and we assume* P_1 *and* P_2 *share states. Let* ComSet, ChSet, *and* ResSet *be the commitment space, challenge space, and response space, respectively. Then, an identification protocol is defined in the following way.*

- *The key generation algorithm* IGen *takes the security parameter* 1^{λ} *as input, and outputs a statement-witness pair* $(\mathsf{X}, \mathsf{W}) \in \mathcal{R}$.
- *The prover, on input* (X, W), *first executes* $\mathsf{com} \leftarrow \mathsf{P}_1(\mathsf{X}, \mathsf{W})$, *and then sends the* commitment com *to the verifier.*
- *The verifier chooses a random* challenge $\mathsf{ch} \leftarrow \mathsf{ChSet}$ *and sends* ch *to the prover.*

- *The prover, given* ch, *runs* resp ← $P_2(X, W, com, ch)$ *and returns a* response resp *to the verifier. Finally, the verifier runs* $V(X, com, ch, resp)$ *and outputs 1 if they accept, 0 otherwise.*

The protocol transcript $(com, ch, resp) \in ComSet \times ChSet \times ResSet$ *is said to be valid in case* $V(X, com, ch, resp)$ *outputs 1.*

We require the following properties from an identification protocol ID. Some of them may seem non-standard, however, they are all necessary to argue security of the Fiat-Shamir transform in the (quantum) random oracle model. We note that some of the properties are simplified and stronger than those in [27], e.g. we ignore negligible correctness errors. This is done without loss of generality, since our proposed identification protocol satisfies all the stronger properties.

Correctness. The following holds for all $(X, W) \in \mathcal{R}$:

$$\Pr\left[V(X, com, ch, resp) = 1 \;\middle|\; \begin{array}{l} com \leftarrow P_1(X, W), \\ ch \leftarrow ChSet, \\ resp \leftarrow P_2(X, W, com, ch) \end{array}\right] = 1.$$

(Perfect) Honest-Verifier Zero-Knowledge (HVZK). There exists a PPT simulator algorithm Sim that takes as inputs a statement $X \in \mathcal{L}_{\mathcal{R}}$ and a challenge ch $\in$ ChSet, and outputs a commitment com and a response resp such that $(com, ch, resp)$ is a valid transcript for X. Moreover, the output distribution of Sim on input (X, ch) is equal to the distribution of those outputs generated via an honest execution conditioned on the verifier using ch as the challenge. We note we can consider relaxed variants of HVZK where the distributions are only required to be computationally indistinguishable.

Min-Entropy. The identification protocol ID has α bits of min-entropy if

$$\Pr_{(X,W) \leftarrow IGen(1^\lambda)} \left[\text{min-entropy}(com \mid com \leftarrow P_1(X, W)) \geq \alpha)\right] \geq 1 - 2^{-\alpha}.$$

(Optional) Perfect Unique Response. With overwhelming probability over the random choice of $(X, W) \leftarrow IGen(1^\lambda)$, for any com $\in$ ComSet and ch $\in$ ChSet, there exists a unique response resp $\in$ ResSet that leads to a valid transcript $(com, ch, resp)$. This property is required when aiming for *strong* unforgeability (i.e., su-cma) of the FS signature scheme. As we will see, our identification protocol supports this property by default.

(Optional) Commitment Revocability. With overwhelming probability over the random choice of $(X, W) \leftarrow IGen(1^\lambda)$, for any ch $\in$ ChSet and resp $\in$ ResSet, there exists a unique commitment com $\in$ ComSet that makes $(com, ch, resp)$ a valid transcript. Such a commitment can be publicly computed by means of an algorithm taking $(X, ch, resp)$ as input. This property is unnecessary from a security stand point and only allows for shorter signatures. Again, our identification protocol supports this property by default.

   To achieve a *tight* security proof for Fiat-Shamir signatures (formally defined later), we further require the identification protocol to satisfy some notion of *lossiness* defined below.

Definition 2.2 (Lossy Identification Protocol). *An identification protocol* ID *is called lossy - and denoted by* $\mathsf{ID}_{\mathsf{ls}}$ - *if it admits an extra PPT algorithm* $\mathsf{LossylGen}$, *named lossy key generation algorithm, that on input* 1^λ *outputs* $\mathsf{X}_{\mathsf{ls}} \in X \setminus \mathcal{L}_\mathcal{R}$.

We require a lossy identification protocol $\mathsf{ID}_{\mathsf{ls}}$ to satisfy the following two properties.

Indistinguishability of Lossy Statements. We ask that a statement generated with the lossy key generation algorithm is indistinguishable from a statement generated by the real key generation algorithm. Let us define the following advantage for an adversary $\mathcal{A}$:

$$\mathsf{Adv}_\mathcal{A}^{\mathsf{lossy}}(\lambda) := |\Pr[\mathcal{A}(\mathsf{X}_{\mathsf{ls}}) = 1 \mid \mathsf{X}_{\mathsf{ls}} \leftarrow \mathsf{LossylGen}(1^\lambda)] - \Pr[\mathcal{A}(\mathsf{X}) = 1 \mid (\mathsf{X}, \mathsf{W}) \leftarrow \mathsf{IGen}(1^\lambda)]|$$

We say the lossy identification protocol satisfies indistinguishability of lossy statements if for any PPT (or quantum PT) adversary we have $\mathsf{Adv}_\mathcal{A}^{\mathsf{lossy}}(\lambda) = \mathsf{negl}(\lambda)$.

Statistical Lossy Soundness. The definition of statistical lossy soundness relies on the following game, named *lossy impersonation game*, played by an adversary $\mathcal{A}$ and a challenger.

Setup: The challenger runs $\mathsf{X}_{\mathsf{ls}} \leftarrow \mathsf{LossylGen}(1^\lambda)$ and provides the adversary $\mathcal{A}$ the lossy statement X_{ls}.

Commitment and challenge selection: On input X_{ls} the adversary $\mathcal{A}$ selects a commitment $\mathsf{com} \in \mathsf{ComSet}$ and sends it to the challenger. The challenger responds by returning a random challenge $\mathsf{ch} \in \mathsf{ChSet}$.

Output: $\mathcal{A}$ outputs a response $\mathsf{resp} \in \mathsf{ResSet}$. The adversary $\mathcal{A}$ wins the game if $(\mathsf{com}, \mathsf{ch}, \mathsf{resp})$ is a valid transcript for X_{ls}.

We say $\mathsf{ID}_{\mathsf{ls}}$ is ϵ_{ls}-lossy sound if for any unbounded (possibly quantum) adversary $\mathcal{A}$ the winning probability in the above game is less than ϵ_{ls}.

2.2   Digital Signature Schemes

Here we introduce the definition of standard signature schemes.

Definition 2.3. *A signature scheme* Π_S *consists of three PPT algorithms* $(\mathsf{S.KeyGen}, \mathsf{S.Sign}, \mathsf{S.Vrfy})$ *such that:*

– $\mathsf{S.KeyGen}(1^\lambda) \to (\mathsf{vk}, \mathsf{sk})$: *On input a security parameter* 1^λ, *the key generation algorithm outputs a pair of verification and signing keys* $(\mathsf{vk}, \mathsf{sk})$;
– $\mathsf{S.Sign}(\mathsf{sk}, \mathsf{M}) \to \sigma$: *On input a signing key* sk *and a message* M, *the signing algorithm outputs a signature* σ;
– $\mathsf{S.Vrfy}(\mathsf{vk}, \mathsf{M}, \sigma) \to 1/0$: *On input a verification key* vk, *a message* M *and a signature* σ, *the verification key outputs 1 (accept) or 0 (reject).*

We require a signature scheme Π_S to satisfy the following two properties.

Correctness. For every security parameter 1^λ, with $\lambda \in \mathbb{N}$, and every message M the following holds:

$$\Pr\left[\mathsf{S.Vrfy(vk, M, \sigma)} = 1 \;\middle|\; \begin{array}{c} \mathsf{(vk, sk)} \leftarrow \mathsf{S.KeyGen}(1^\lambda), \\ \sigma \leftarrow \mathsf{S.Sign(sk, M)} \end{array} \right] = 1.$$

Unforgeability. We define the _strong unforgeability under chosen message attack_ su-cma by the following game played by an adversary $\mathcal{A}$ and a challenger.

Setup: The challenger runs $\mathsf{(vk, sk)} \leftarrow \mathsf{S.KeyGen}(1^\lambda)$ and provides the adversary $\mathcal{A}$ the verification key vk. It also prepares an empty set $\mathcal{S} = \emptyset$.
Signing Queries: The adversary $\mathcal{A}$ may adaptively submit messages M to the challenger. The challenger responds by returning $\sigma \leftarrow \mathsf{S.Sign(sk, M)}$ to $\mathcal{A}$. It then updates the set $\mathcal{S} \leftarrow \mathcal{S} \cup \{(\mathsf{M}, \sigma)\}$.
Output: Finally, $\mathcal{A}$ outputs a forgery (M^*, σ^*). We say the adversary $\mathcal{A}$ wins if $(\mathsf{M}^*, \sigma^*) \notin \mathcal{S}$ and $\mathsf{S.Vrfy(vk, M^*, \sigma^*)} = 1$.

We define the advantage of $\mathcal{A}$ as the probability it wins the above game, that is, $\mathsf{Adv}_{\mathcal{A}}^{\mathsf{su\text{-}cma}}(1^\lambda) := \Pr[\mathcal{A} \text{ wins}]$.

Definition 2.4 (Su-cma Security). _We say a signature scheme_ Π_S _is_ su-cma _secure if for all PPT adversaries_ $\mathcal{A}$, _we have_ $\mathsf{Adv}_{\mathcal{A}}^{\mathsf{su\text{-}cma}}(\lambda) = \mathsf{negl}(\lambda)$.

2.3   Pseudorandom Functions

Consider a mapping $\mathsf{PRF} : \mathcal{K} \times \mathcal{X} \to \mathcal{Y}$, where $\mathcal{K}$ is a key space. We say PRF is a _pseudorandom function_ if for all PPT (or quantum) adversaries, their advantage defined below is negligible:

$$\mathsf{Adv}_{\mathcal{A}}^{\mathsf{PRF}}(\lambda) := \left| \Pr[\mathcal{A}^{\mathsf{PRF}(K, \cdot)}(1^\lambda) = 1 \mid K \leftarrow \mathcal{K}] - \Pr[\mathcal{A}^{\mathsf{RF}(\cdot)}(1^\lambda) = 1] \right|,$$

where $\mathsf{RF} : \mathcal{X} \to \mathcal{Y}$ is a perfect random function. In practice, any standard hash function (e.g., SHA-3) is believed to be a (quantumly) secure PRF.

2.4   Fiat-Shamir Transformation

The original Fiat-Shamir transformation [1,18] turns a (not necessarily lossy) identification protocol ID into a digital signature scheme by means of a cryptographic hash function $\mathsf{H} : \{0, 1\}^* \to \mathsf{ChSet}$ modeled as a _classical_ random oracle (RO). For each parallel execution of ID, the challenge is obtained as $\mathsf{H(com, M)}$, where M is the message to sign. Then the resulting digital signature σ is a t-tuple composed by t commitments and the corresponding responses, where t is set in such a way that $|\mathsf{ChSet}|^t$ is exponentially large. Recently, the Fiat-Shamir transformation has been extended to the _quantum_ random oracle model (QROM) as well [16,27,30].

In this work, we will be interested in Fiat-Shamir transformations for a specific type of identification protocol (namely, *lossy* identification protocol) which admits *tight* security proofs. For a general identification protocol, it is well-known that the Fiat-Shamir signature incurs a prohibitively large reduction loss: the advantage of breaking the underlying hard problem degrades as $O(Q^{-1} \cdot \epsilon^2)$ in the classical ROM and as $O(Q^{-6} \cdot \epsilon^3)$ in the quantum ROM, where Q is the number or random oracle queries made by the adversary and ϵ is the advantage against the Fiat-Shamir signature scheme.

The following result is taken from the recent work of Kiltz, Lyubashevsky, and Schaffner [27].

Theorem 2.1. *Assume the identification protocol* ID *is lossy, perfect HVZK, has α bits of min-entropy, has perfect unique response, and is ϵ_{ls}-lossy sound. The Fiat-Shamir transformation provides a signature scheme such that, for any quantum adversary $\mathcal{A}$ against* su-cma *security that issues at most Q_H queries to the quantum random oracle, there exists quantum adversaries $\mathcal{B}$ and $\mathcal{D}$ such that*

$$\mathsf{Adv}_{\mathcal{A}}^{\mathsf{su\text{-}cma}}(\lambda) \leq \mathsf{Adv}_{\mathcal{B}}^{\mathsf{lossy}}(\lambda) + 8(Q_H + 1)^2 \cdot \epsilon_{ls} + 2^{-\alpha+1} + \mathsf{Adv}_{\mathcal{D}}^{\mathsf{PRF}}(\lambda),$$

and $\mathsf{Time}(\mathcal{B}) = \mathsf{Time}(\mathcal{D}) = \mathsf{Time}(\mathcal{A}) + Q_H \approx \mathsf{Time}(\mathcal{A})$.

In the classical setting, the only difference is that the bound depends linearly on Q_H instead of quadratically.

The above theorem is obtained by derandomizing the Fiat-Shamir signature by a pseudorandom function PRF and plugging it in Theorem 3.1 of [27]. We note that some simplification to Theorem 3.1 of [27] is made since our proposed lossy identification protocol achieves *perfect* HVZK and *perfect* unique response.

2.5 Class Group Actions and Hardness Assumption

The action of ideal class groups on elliptic curves was firstly proposed for cryptographic purposes by Couveignes [9], and Rostovtsev and Stolbunov [35,38]. Their approach was then revised by De Feo, Kieffer and Smith [14], who were unable to turn it intro practicality despite the introduction of remarkable mathematically-driven speed-ups. The efficiency issues were overcome by Castryck *et al.* [8], that introduced the CSIDH key-exchange protocol restricting to supersingular elliptic curves. In the following, we will give a brief background on ideal class groups and their action on supersingular curves. For a more detailed overview we suggest the consultation of [8] and Cox's book [10].

Let $\mathbb{F}_p$ denote a prime field, with p being an odd prime. Given two elliptic curves E, E' defined over $\mathbb{F}_p$, an isogeny $\varphi : E \to E'$ is a non-constant morphism mapping 0_E to $0'_E$. Hence each coordinate of $\varphi(x, y)$ can be expressed as a fraction of two polynomials belonging to $\overline{\mathbb{F}}_p[x, y]$. If their coefficients are contained in $\mathbb{F}_p$, then we say that φ is defined over $\mathbb{F}_p$. A separable isogeny (it induces a separable extension of function fields) having $\{0_E\}$ as kernel is an isomorphism; an isogeny having the same domain and range is an endomorphism.

The set of all endomorphisms of an elliptic curve E, together with the zero map, form a ring under pointwise addition and composition. Such a ring is called the *endomorphism ring of* E and it is denoted by $\text{End}(E)$. If $\text{End}(E)$ is abelian, the curve is said to be ordinary, otherwise it is said to be supersingular. The restriction $\text{End}_p(E)$ to the endomorphisms defined over $\mathbb{F}_p$ constitutes a subring, which is isomorphic to an order in the quadratic field $\mathbb{K} = \mathbb{Q}(\sqrt{-p})$. An order is a subring of $\mathbb{Q}(\sqrt{-p})$ which is also a finitely-generated $\mathbb{Z}$-module containing a basis of $\mathbb{K}$ as a $\mathbb{Q}$-vector space. The set $\mathbb{Z}[\sqrt{-p}] = \{m + n\sqrt{-p} \mid m, n \in \mathbb{Z}\}$ satisfies the above three conditions and we will denote it by $\mathcal{O}$. We then consider the set $\mathcal{E}\ell\ell_p(\mathcal{O}, \pi)$ containing all supersingular curves E defined over $\mathbb{F}_p$ - modulo isomorphisms defined over $\mathbb{F}_p$ - such that there exists an isomorphism between $\mathcal{O}$ and $\text{End}_p(E)$ mapping $\sqrt{-p} \in \mathcal{O}$ into the Frobenius endomorphism $(x, y) \mapsto (x^p, y^p)$. As shown in [8], each isomorphism class in $\mathcal{E}\ell\ell_p(\mathcal{O}, \pi)$ can be uniquely represented by a single element of $\mathbb{F}_p$ if $p \geq 5$ is a prime such that $p \equiv 3 \pmod 8$.

A fractional ideal $\mathfrak{a}$ of $\mathcal{O}$ is a finitely generated $\mathcal{O}$-submodule of $\mathbb{K}$. When $\mathfrak{a}$ is contained in $\mathcal{O}$, it is said to be integral; when $\mathfrak{a} = \alpha\mathcal{O}$ for some $\alpha \in \mathbb{K}$, it is said to be principal; when there exists another fractional ideal $\mathfrak{b}$ such that $\mathfrak{a}\mathfrak{b} = \mathcal{O}$, it is called invertible. The invertible fractional ideals of $\mathcal{O}$ form an abelian group. Its quotient by the subgroup composed by principal fractional ideals is a finite group called *ideal class group* of $\mathcal{O}$, usually denoted by $\mathcal{C}\ell(\mathcal{O})$. Its cardinality is the class number of $\mathcal{O}$.

The ideal class group $\mathcal{C}\ell(\mathcal{O})$ acts freely and transitively on the set $\mathcal{E}\ell\ell_p(\mathcal{O}, \pi)$ via the group action $\star$:

$$\star : \mathcal{C}\ell(\mathcal{O}) \times \mathcal{E}\ell\ell_p(\mathcal{O}, \pi) \rightarrow \mathcal{E}\ell\ell_p(\mathcal{O}, \pi)$$
$$(\mathfrak{a}, E) \qquad \mapsto \mathfrak{a} \star E.$$

For simplicity, we will use representatives instead of equivalence classes to denote elements of $\mathcal{C}\ell(\mathcal{O})$ and $\mathcal{E}\ell\ell_p(\mathcal{O}, \pi)$. When p is of the form $4\ell_1\ell_2 \cdots \ell_s - 1$, with $\ell_1, \ldots, \ell_s$ small odd primes, a special integral ideal $\mathfrak{I}_{\ell_i} \subset \mathcal{O}$ corresponds to each prime ℓ_i. These ideals allow an easy computation of the group action. In particular, the action of $\mathfrak{I}_{\ell_i}$ on a curve $E \in \mathcal{E}\ell\ell_p(\mathcal{O}, \pi)$ is determined by an isogeny having as kernel the unique rational ℓ_i-torsion subgroup of E.

The general variant of the CSIDH key-exchange scheme relies on the heuristic that the equivalence classes of the ideals $\mathfrak{I}_{\ell_1}, \ldots, \mathfrak{I}_{\ell_s}$, together with their inverses, generate the entire ideal class group $\mathcal{C}\ell(\mathcal{O})$. In [8], Castryck *et al.* propose different sets of parameters for CSIDH, each of them supposedly achieving a specific quantum security level. For the *smallest*[2] set of parameters, named CSIDH-512 since $p \simeq 2^{512}$, the class group structure of $\mathcal{C}\ell(\mathcal{O})$ has been recently computed by Beullens *et al.* [6]. They showed that $\mathcal{C}\ell(\mathcal{O})$ is a cyclic group of odd order N, where $N \simeq 2^{257.1}$ and $\mathcal{C}\ell(\mathcal{O}) = \langle \mathfrak{I}_3 \rangle$. As a consequence, this group admits a canonical representation (as $\mathbb{Z}_N$) and an efficient uniform sampling of its elements. For simplicity, in the following we will denote by $\mathfrak{g}$ the generator $\mathfrak{I}_3$.

---

[2] The parameter set having the smallest value for the prime p.

Hardness Assumption. The group action inverse problem (GAIP) is the hardness assumption originally introduced by [8], which underlies the security of both SeaSign [12] and CSI-FiSh [6]. Although we will not directly use GAIP in our construction, we provide it as a base point to compare the assumption we introduce.

Definition 2.5 (Group Action Inverse Problem (GAIP)). *Given two supersingular elliptic curves, $E, E_1 \in \mathcal{E}\ell\ell_p(\mathcal{O}, \pi)$, find an element $\mathfrak{a} \in \mathcal{C}\ell(\mathcal{O})$ such that $\mathfrak{a} \star E = E_1$.*

3   Base Lossy Identification Protocol from CSIDH-512

The CSI-FiSh signature is obtained by applying the Fiat-Shamir transformation to an identification protocol originally sketched by Couveignes [9] and Stolbunov [39]. In this section, we introduce our base *lossy* identification protocol for any set of CSIDH parameters for which the ideal class group $\mathcal{C}\ell(\mathcal{O})$ is cyclic, with a known order N and generator $\mathfrak{g}$. We further discuss the corresponding hardness assumption on which its security relies. Such a scheme considers an exponent $a \in \mathbb{Z}_N$, the private key, and two pairs of curves, where the second pair, the public key, is determined by the action of $\mathfrak{g}^a$ on the first pair. For the concrete instantiation in Sect. 5, we use the CSIDH-512 parameters.

3.1   Hardness Assumption: Decisional CSIDH

We construct a lossy identification protocol based on the *decisional* CSIDH (D-CSIDH) problem, originally defined by Stolbunov in his PhD thesis [39, Problem 2.2].

Definition 3.1 (Decisional CSIDH Problem). *Given the set $\mathcal{E}\ell\ell_p(\mathcal{O}, \pi)$ and the ideal class group $\mathcal{C}\ell(\mathcal{O})$, the decisional CSIDH (D-CSIDH) problem asks to distinguish between the following two distributions:*

- *$(E, H, \mathfrak{a} \star E, \mathfrak{a} \star H)$, where the supersingular elliptic curves E and H are sampled uniformly from $\mathcal{E}\ell\ell_p(\mathcal{O}, \pi)$, while $\mathfrak{a}$ is sampled uniformly from $\mathcal{C}\ell(\mathcal{O})$;*
- *(E, H, E', H') where E, H, E', H' are supersingular elliptic curves sampled uniformly from $\mathcal{E}\ell\ell_p(\mathcal{O}, \pi)$.*

We denote by $\mathsf{Adv}_{\mathcal{A}}^{\mathsf{D\text{-}CSIDH}}(\lambda)$ the advantage of an adversary $\mathcal{A}$ distinguishing the two distributions. We say that the D-CSIDH assumption holds if for every PPT (or possibly quantum) adversary $\mathcal{A}$, $\mathsf{Adv}_{\mathcal{A}}^{\mathsf{D\text{-}CSIDH}}(\lambda)$ is negligible.

The D-CSIDH assumption forms the foundation of the security of the key exchange protocol proposed by [8], called CSIDH. However, to be completely accurate, the security of CSIDH *not* always is equivalent to the D-CSIDH problem we defined above. The reason for this is that when the structure of the ideal class group is not known, we cannot properly sample a uniform ideal from $\mathcal{C}\ell(\mathcal{O})$ (and hence a uniform elliptic curve from the set $\mathcal{E}\ell\ell_p(\mathcal{O}, \pi)$). Namely, in that case, a party will sample an ideal that is *heuristically* shown to be close to uniformly random over $\mathcal{C}\ell(\mathcal{O})$. Then, to show security of CSIDH, we must assume the hardness of D-CSIDH for that particular heuristically uniform distribution. Notably, we do not get a reduction from the above D-CSIDH assumption defined for truly uniform samples over $\mathcal{C}\ell(\mathcal{O})$. Hence, for the D-CSIDH assumption to be useful both in a theoretical *and* practical sense, it is desirable to have an *efficient* uniform sampler from the ideal class group $\mathcal{C}\ell(\mathcal{O})$. In this case, the security of CSIDH will indeed be equivalent to the D-CSIDH assumption.

As for the definition of D-CSIDH, we would like to simply keep it agnostic to the existence of an efficient sampler from the ideal class group $\mathcal{C}\ell(\mathcal{O})$. However, throughout the paper, we will always consider a cyclic class group $\mathcal{C}\ell(\mathcal{O})$ with known order and generator (i.e., the one derived from the CSIDH-512 parameters) so as to be able to efficiently sample uniformly over $\mathcal{C}\ell(\mathcal{O})$.

3.2 Construction of Base Lossy Identification Protocol

The base lossy identification protocol we are going to describe requires $\mathcal{C}\ell(\mathcal{O})$ to be efficiently sampleable. As anticipated, we will restrict to the case where $\mathcal{C}\ell(\mathcal{O})$ is cyclic, with a known order N and generator $\mathfrak{g}$. This reduces sampling from $\mathcal{C}\ell(\mathcal{O})$ to uniformly sampling from $\mathbb{Z}_N$, and considering the corresponding power of $\mathfrak{g}$.

Let the set X be composed by pairs $((E_1^{(0)}, E_2^{(0)}), (E_1^{(1)}, E_2^{(1)}))$, where $E_1^{(0)}$, $E_2^{(0)}$, $E_1^{(1)}$, $E_2^{(1)}$ belong to $\mathcal{E}\ell\ell_p(\mathcal{O}, \pi)$. By Y we denote the set of witnesses $\{a \in \mathbb{Z}_N\}$, with N being the cardinality of $\mathcal{C}\ell(\mathcal{O})$. We consider the following binary relation $\mathcal{R}$ on $X \times Y$:

$$\mathcal{R} = \{(((E_1^{(0)}, E_2^{(0)}), (E_1^{(1)}, E_2^{(1)})), a) \mid E_1^{(1)} = \mathfrak{g}^a \star E_1^{(0)}, E_2^{(1)} = \mathfrak{g}^a \star E_2^{(0)}\} \quad (1)$$

We note that the language $\mathcal{L}_\mathcal{R}$ is strictly contained in X, i.e. X contains *lossy* statements. On the other hand, each statement in X is a valid instance of the D-CSIDH problem.

The lossy identification protocol $\mathsf{ID}_{\mathsf{ls}}^{\mathsf{base}}$ deduced from relation $\mathcal{R}$ consists of a challenge set $\mathsf{ChSet} = \{0, 1\}$ and five algorithms $(\mathsf{IGen}, \mathsf{LossyIGen}, \mathsf{P}_1, \mathsf{P}_2, \mathsf{V})$, detailed in the following. We note that $E_0 \in \mathcal{E}\ell\ell_p(\mathcal{O}, \pi)$ is the base curve, specified by the system parameters, and defined by the equation $y^2 = x^3 + x$ over $\mathbb{F}_p$.

- Algorithm IGen uniformly samples $a, b, c \in \mathbb{Z}_N$ and outputs a statement-witness pair $(\mathsf{X}, \mathsf{W}) \in \mathcal{R}$, where $\mathsf{X} = ((E_1^{(0)} = \mathfrak{g}^b \star E_0, E_2^{(0)} = \mathfrak{g}^c \star E_0), (E_1^{(1)} = \mathfrak{g}^a \star E_1^{(0)}, E_2^{(1)} = \mathfrak{g}^a \star E_2^{(0)}))$, and $\mathsf{W} = a$.
- Algorithm $\mathsf{LossyIGen}$ uniformly samples $a, a', b, c \in \mathbb{Z}_N$ and outputs a lossy statement $\mathsf{X}_{\mathsf{ls}} = ((E_1^{(0)} = \mathfrak{g}^b \star E_0, E_2^{(0)} = \mathfrak{g}^c \star E_0), (E_1^{(1)} = \mathfrak{g}^a \star E_1^{(0)}, E_2^{(1)} = \mathfrak{g}^{a'} \star E_2^{(0)}))$.

– On input (X, W), P_1 generates a random integer $r \in \mathbb{Z}_N$ and returns the commitment $\mathsf{com} = (F_1 = \mathfrak{g}^r \star E_1^{(0)}, F_2 = \mathfrak{g}^r \star E_2^{(0)})$.

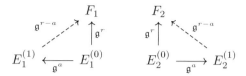

– On input $(X, W, \mathsf{com}, \mathsf{ch})$, where $\mathsf{ch} \in \mathsf{ChSet}$, P_2 outputs the response resp which is r if $\mathsf{ch} = 0$, $r - a$ if $\mathsf{ch} = 1$.
– On input $(X, \mathsf{com}, \mathsf{ch}, \mathsf{resp})$, the verification algorithm V checks that

$$\begin{cases} (\mathfrak{g}^{\mathsf{resp}} \star E_1^{(0)} = F_1, \mathfrak{g}^{\mathsf{resp}} \star E_2^{(0)} = F_2) & \text{if } \mathsf{ch} = 0 \\ (\mathfrak{g}^{\mathsf{resp}} \star E_1^{(1)} = F_1, \mathfrak{g}^{\mathsf{resp}} \star E_2^{(1)} = F_2) & \text{if } \mathsf{ch} = 1 \end{cases} \tag{2}$$

The interaction between a prover and a verifier within the identification protocol is summarised in Fig. 1.

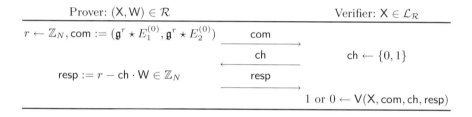

Fig. 1. The base lossy identification protocol and its transcript $(\mathsf{com}, \mathsf{ch}, \mathsf{resp})$.

3.3 Security of Base Lossy Identification Protocol $\mathsf{ID}_{\mathsf{ls}}^{\mathsf{Base}}$

We show that the proposed lossy identification protocol $\mathsf{ID}_{\mathsf{ls}}^{\mathsf{base}}$ satisfies all the desired properties presented in Sect. 2.1. Properties for standard identification protocols - namely, correctness, perfect unique response, and commitment revocability - are straightforward to prove, with the last two verified by noticing that the group action $\star$ is transitive and free. Moreover, for the Honest-Verifier Zero-Knowledge property, consider a simulator Sim defined as follows:

$\mathsf{Sim}(X, \mathsf{ch})$: on input a statement $X = ((E_1^{(0)}, E_2^{(0)}), (E_1^{(1)}, E_2^{(1)})) \in \mathcal{L}_{\mathcal{R}}$ and a challenge bit $\mathsf{ch} \in \{0, 1\}$, the simulator samples a random $u \in \mathbb{Z}_N$ and outputs either of the following tuples, depending on whether $\mathsf{ch} = 0$ or $\mathsf{ch} = 1$:

$$\big((\mathfrak{g}^u \star E_1^{(0)}, \mathfrak{g}^u \star E_2^{(0)}), \mathsf{ch} = 0, u\big), \quad \big((\mathfrak{g}^u \star E_1^{(1)}, \mathfrak{g}^u \star E_2^{(1)}), \mathsf{ch} = 1, u\big).$$

It can be checked that the transcripts output by the simulator Sim are indistinguishable from honest transcripts, since both have uniformly random distributed values as responses. Finally, by construction, we have $\log N$ bits of min-entropy.

The remaining issue is showing that $\mathsf{ID}_{\mathsf{ls}}^{\mathsf{base}}$ satisfies the lossy properties (see Definition 2.2). Specifically, it has indistinguishability of lossy statements and statistical lossy soundness.

Lemma 3.1. *Our lossy identification protocol $\mathsf{ID}_{\mathsf{ls}}^{\mathsf{base}}$ satisfies indistinguishability of lossy statements assuming the hardness of the D-CSIDH problem. Specifically, an adversary $\mathcal{A}$ with advantage $\mathsf{Adv}_{\mathcal{A}}^{\mathsf{lossy}}(\lambda)$ can be turned into an adversary $\mathcal{B}$ against the D-CSIDH problem with advantage $\mathsf{Adv}_{\mathcal{B}}^{\mathsf{D\text{-}CSIDH}}(\lambda) = \mathsf{Adv}_{\mathcal{A}}^{\mathsf{lossy}}(\lambda)$ and the same running time.*

Proof. The statement is an immediate consequence of the D-CSIDH problem. In particular, the distribution induced by IGen corresponds to valid D-CSIDH instances and that of $\mathsf{LossyIGen}$ corresponds to random D-CSIDH instances.

Lemma 3.2. *Our lossy identification protocol $\mathsf{ID}_{\mathsf{ls}}^{\mathsf{base}}$ satisfies statistical ϵ_{ls}-lossy soundness for $\epsilon_{\mathsf{ls}} = 1/2 + 1/2N$, where $N = |\mathcal{C}\ell(\mathcal{O})|$.*

Proof. First of all, a simple calculation shows that the set of valid statements $\mathcal{L}_{\mathcal{R}}$ has size N^3. Therefore, since $\mathsf{LossyIGen}$ outputs a uniformly random image in the set X, which has size N^4, we have $\Pr[\mathsf{X}_{\mathsf{ls}} \leftarrow \mathsf{LossyIGen}(1^\lambda) : \mathsf{X}_{\mathsf{ls}} \in \mathcal{L}_{\mathcal{R}}] = 1/N$. Furthermore, for an adversary $\mathcal{A}$ against the lossy impersonation game, the following holds:

$$\Pr[\mathcal{A} \text{ wins}] = \Pr[\mathcal{A} \text{ wins} \mid \mathsf{X}_{\mathsf{ls}} \notin \mathcal{L}_{\mathcal{R}}] \Pr[\mathsf{X}_{\mathsf{ls}} \notin \mathcal{L}_{\mathcal{R}}] +$$
$$\Pr[\mathcal{A} \text{ wins} \mid \mathsf{X}_{\mathsf{ls}} \in \mathcal{L}_{\mathcal{R}}] \Pr[\mathsf{X}_{\mathsf{ls}} \in \mathcal{L}_{\mathcal{R}}]$$
$$\leq \Pr[\mathcal{A} \text{ wins} \mid \mathsf{X}_{\mathsf{ls}} \notin \mathcal{L}_{\mathcal{R}}] \cdot \left(1 - \frac{1}{N}\right) + \frac{1}{N}.$$

We show that for any statement $\mathsf{X}_{\mathsf{ls}} \notin \mathcal{L}_{\mathcal{R}}$ and commitment $\mathsf{com} \in \mathsf{ComSet}$, there exists at most one challenge $\mathsf{ch} \in \mathsf{ChSet}$ that admits a *valid* response $\mathsf{resp} \in \mathsf{ResSet}$. Since this implies $\Pr[\mathcal{A} \text{ wins} \mid \mathsf{X}_{\mathsf{ls}} \notin \mathcal{L}_{\mathcal{R}}] \leq 1/|\mathsf{ChSet}| = 1/2$, we obtain $(1/2 + 1/2N)$-lossy soundness as desired.

Given a statement $\mathsf{X}_{\mathsf{ls}} = ((E_1^{(0)}, E_2^{(0)}), (E_1^{(1)}, E_2^{(1)})) \notin \mathcal{L}_{\mathcal{R}}$, let us assume there exist two valid transcripts for X_{ls}. Namely, consider $(\mathsf{com}, \mathsf{ch}, \mathsf{resp})$ and $(\mathsf{com}, \mathsf{ch}', \mathsf{resp}')$, with $\mathsf{ch} \neq \mathsf{ch}'$ and $\mathsf{com} = (F_1, F_2)$. Then, it is possible to extract a witness W such that $(\mathsf{X}_{\mathsf{ls}}, \mathsf{W}) \in \mathcal{L}_{\mathcal{R}}$. Indeed, assuming $\mathsf{ch} = 0$, the responses $\mathsf{resp}, \mathsf{resp}'$ must satisfy

$$\begin{cases} \mathfrak{g}^{\mathsf{resp}} \star E_1^{(0)} = F_1, & \mathfrak{g}^{\mathsf{resp}} \star E_2^{(0)} = F_2, \\ \mathfrak{g}^{\mathsf{resp}'} \star E_1^{(1)} = F_1, & \mathfrak{g}^{\mathsf{resp}'} \star E_2^{(1)} = F_2. \end{cases} \tag{3}$$

Therefore, $\mathsf{resp} - \mathsf{resp}'$ is the desired witness, that is, $E_1^{(1)} = \mathfrak{g}^{\mathsf{resp}-\mathsf{resp}'} \star E_1^{(0)}$ and $E_2^{(1)} = \mathfrak{g}^{\mathsf{resp}-\mathsf{resp}'} \star E_2^{(0)}$. However, this is a contradiction to $\mathsf{X}_{\mathsf{ls}} \notin \mathcal{L}_{\mathcal{R}}$. Therefore, there can exist at most one challenge that possesses a valid response. This concludes the proof.

3.4   Lossy Soundness Amplification of $\mathsf{ID}_{\mathsf{ls}}^{\mathsf{Base}}$

As typically done, we use standard parallel repetition of the base lossy identification protocol $\mathsf{ID}_{\mathsf{ls}}^{\mathsf{base}}$ to make the lossy soundness ϵ_{ls} negligibly small, as required when setting the concrete parameters for the relative FS signature according to Theorem 2.1. Specifically, on input (X, W), the prover runs parallel execution of the protocol with the verifier, where the verifier uses independent challenges in each execution.

We make this standard procedure explicit since, unlike sigma-protocols with 2-special soundness, lossy soundness is not closed under parallel repetition. That is, even if we run t parallel instances of our base protocol $\mathsf{ID}_{\mathsf{ls}}^{\mathsf{base}}$, this will not result in a protocol with $(\epsilon_{\mathsf{ls}})^t$-lossy soundness. Namely, we have the following result.

Lemma 3.3. *Consider running t parallel rounds of the base lossy identification protocol* $\mathsf{ID}_{\mathsf{ls}}^{\mathsf{base}}$ *(with the same statement-witness pair). Then it satisfies statistical ϵ_{ls}-lossy soundness for* $\epsilon_{\mathsf{ls}} = 1/2^t \cdot (1 - 1/N) + 1/N$, *where* $N = |\mathcal{C}\ell(\mathcal{O})|$. *In particular, we have* $\epsilon_{\mathsf{ls}} \leq 1/2^t + 1/N$.

Proof. The proof is straightforward. In case $\mathsf{X}_{\mathsf{ls}} \notin \mathcal{L}_{\mathcal{R}}$, we can argue that the adversary has at most $1/2^t$ probability in winning the lossy impersonation game. Recalling that $\mathsf{X}_{\mathsf{ls}} \in \mathcal{L}_{\mathcal{R}}$ happens with probability $1/N$ over the random choice of LossyIGen, we can upper bound the advantage of $\mathcal{A}$ by $\epsilon_{\mathsf{ls}} = 1/2^t(1 - 1/N) + 1/N$. This concludes the proof. ∎

All other properties are closed under parallel repetition and inherited directly from $\mathsf{ID}_{\mathsf{ls}}^{\mathsf{base}}$.

4   Optimized Lossy Identification Protocol from CSIDH-512

We show several methods to optimize our base lossy identification protocol, following closely the work of [6,12]. We first prepare a slight variant of the D-CSIDH assumption, which will form the basis of our optimized schemes.

4.1   Hardness Assumption: Fixed-Curve Multi-decisional CSIDH

We consider a slight variant of D-CSIDH, where we are given many D-CSIDH tuples, with the first two elliptic curves of each tuple being fixed. Formally, we consider the following problem, which is equivalent to D-CSIDH when $S = 1$.

Definition 4.1 (Fixed-Curve Multi-decisional CSIDH Problem). *Let S be a positive integer. Given the ideal class group $\mathcal{C}\ell(\mathcal{O})$ and the set $\mathcal{E}\ell\ell_p(\mathcal{O}, \pi)$, the fixed-curve multi-decisional CSIDH (FCMD-CSIDH) problem with parameter S asks to distinguish between the following two distributions[3]:*

---

[3] With $[S]$ we denote the set $\{1, \dots, S\}$.

- $(E, H, (\mathfrak{a}_i \star E, \mathfrak{a}_i \star H)_{i \in [S]})$, where the supersingular elliptic curves E and H are sampled uniformly from $\mathcal{E}\ell\ell_p(\mathcal{O}, \pi)$, and $\mathfrak{a}_i$ for $i \in [S]$ are sampled uniformly from $\mathcal{C}\ell(\mathcal{O})$;
- $(E, H, (E_i', H_i')_{i \in [S]})$ where E, H, E_i', H_i' for $i \in [S]$ are supersingular elliptic curves sampled uniformly from $\mathcal{E}\ell\ell_p(\mathcal{O}, \pi)$.

We denote by $\mathsf{Adv}_{\mathcal{A},S}^{\mathsf{FCMD\text{-}CSIDH}}(\lambda)$ the advantage of an adversary $\mathcal{A}$ distinguishing the two distributions. We say that the FCMD-CSIDH assumption with parameter S holds if for any PPT (or possibly quantum) adversary $\mathcal{A}$, $\mathsf{Adv}_{\mathcal{A},S}^{\mathsf{FCMD\text{-}CSIDH}}(\lambda)$ is negligible.

A *tight* reduction from the (one-instance) decisional CSIDH problem to the fixed-curve *multi*-decisional CSIDH problem with parameter S would have been desirable, however, this seems to be highly challenging (as long as we view the group action $\star$ as a black box). This is in sharp contrast with the classical decisional DH problem, which admits a nice random self-reducibility property. The main reason why D-CSIDH does not possess this property seems to stem from the fact that the group action only allows to add a known constant to the exponent of $\mathfrak{g}$ when considering a curve $\mathfrak{g}^a * E$. In other words, we do not have an analogous of the mapping $g^a \mapsto (g^a)^r$ exploited in the classical DH setting.

Therefore, we only have a trivial non-tight reduction from the D-CSIDH problem to the FCMD-CSIDH problem with parameter S. This is formally stated in the following lemma.

Lemma 4.1 (D-CSIDH to FCMD-CSIDH). *Let S be a positive integer. Let $\mathcal{C}\ell(\mathcal{O})$ be the ideal class group of an order $\mathcal{O}$ in $\mathbb{Q}(\sqrt{-p})$, with p a prime, and $\mathcal{E}\ell\ell_p(\mathcal{O}, \pi)$ be the corresponding set of supersingular elliptic curves. Then, for any adversary $\mathcal{A}$ for the FCMD-CSIDH problem with parameter S, there exists an adversary $\mathcal{B}$ for the D-CSIDH problem such that*

$$\mathsf{Adv}_{\mathcal{A},S}^{\mathsf{FCMD\text{-}CSIDH}} \leq S \cdot \mathsf{Adv}_{\mathcal{B}}^{\mathsf{D\text{-}CSIDH}},$$

and $\mathsf{Time}(\mathcal{B}) \approx \mathsf{Time}(A)$.

Proof. The proof is elementary. We consider $S+1$ hybrid games where, in the j-th game[4], an adversary is given $(E, H, (E_i', H_i')_{i \in [S]})$, where $(E_i', H_i')_{i \in [j]}$ is random over $\mathcal{E}\ell\ell_p(\mathcal{O}, \pi)^2$ and $(E_i', H_i')_{i \in [S] \setminus [j]}$ is of the form $(\mathfrak{a}_i \star E, \mathfrak{a}_i \star H)$ for a random $\mathfrak{a}_i \in \mathcal{C}\ell(\mathcal{O})$. We then simply show that each game is indistinguishable using the D-CSIDH problem to conclude the proof. However, one thing we remark is that in order for the D-CSIDH adversary $\mathcal{B}$ to simulate the view to the FCMD-CSIDH adversary $\mathcal{A}$, $\mathcal{B}$ must be able to sample uniformly from $\mathcal{C}\ell(\mathcal{O})$. This justifies once more our restriction to cyclic ideal class groups $\mathcal{C}\ell(\mathcal{O})$ having known order and generator.

We leave it as an interesting open problem to achieve a tight reduction. We believe a technique which allows such a reduction will most likely have applications elsewhere.

---

[4] j varies from 0 to S, and with [0] we denote the set $\{0\}$.

Impact on Signature Scheme (and Identification Protocol). Although this loose reduction is not desirable, fortunately, the integer S will not have a tremendous impact on the concrete choice of parameters for our signature scheme (and identification protocol). This is because S is only a parameter chosen at the setup of the scheme, which is in particular *independent* of the adversary. This should be compared to standard non-tight Fiat-Shamir signatures which incurs a reduction loss of $Q^{-1} \cdot \epsilon^2$ in the classical ROM and $Q^{-6} \cdot \epsilon^3$ in the quantum ROM, where Q is an *adversarially dependent* parameter denoting the number of RO queries. In particular, in the original paper of CSI-FiSh [6], S is a constant set between 1 to $2^{18} - 1$. Depending on the value of S, we have a tradeoff between the runtimes of several algorithms and size of public keys and signatures. We refer to Sect. 5 for more details.

4.2 Enlarging Challenge Space of Base Lossy Identification Protocol

We show a variant of our base lossy identification protocol which is obtained adapting the idea from [6,12] to enlarge the challenge space. In particular, we will use the FCMD-CSIDH problem with parameter S instead of the D-CSIDH problem to define the language used in the identification protocol. Formally, the set of (possibly non-valid) statements is:

$$X = \left\{ ((E_1^{(0)}, E_2^{(0)}), (E_1^{(1)}, E_2^{(1)}), \ldots, (E_1^{(S)}, E_2^{(S)})) \mid E_1^{(i)}, E_2^{(i)} \in \mathcal{E}\ell\ell_p(\mathcal{O}) \right\},$$

while the set of witnesses is $Y = \{(a_1, \ldots, a_S) \mid a_1, \ldots, a_S \in \mathbb{Z}_N\}$. We then consider the following binary relation on $X \times Y$:

$$\mathcal{R} = \{(((E_1^{(0)}, E_2^{(0)}), (E_1^{(1)}, E_2^{(1)}), \ldots, (E_1^{(S)}, E_2^{(S)})), (a_1, \ldots, a_S)) \in X \times Y \mid$$

$$\mathfrak{g}^{a_i} \star E_1^{(0)} = E_1^{(i)}, \mathfrak{g}^{a_i} \star E_2^{(0)} = E_2^{(i)} \text{ for } i \in [S]\}.$$

The lossy identification protocol with enlarged challenge space $\mathsf{ID}_{\mathsf{ls}}^{\mathsf{enCh}}$ deduced from the above relation $\mathcal{R}$ is a simple adaptation of the base scheme $\mathsf{ID}_{\mathsf{ls}}^{\mathsf{base}}$. We provide the details below for completeness, where the challenge space is enlarged to $\mathsf{ChSet} = \{0, 1, \cdots, S\}$. Note that S is a parameter chosen by the scheme. Our base scheme is obtained by setting $S = 1$.

- Algorithm IGen uniformly samples $(a_i)_{i \in [S]}, b, c \in \mathbb{Z}_N$ and outputs a statement-witness pair $(\mathsf{X}, \mathsf{W}) \in \mathcal{R}$, where

$$\mathsf{X} = \left((E_1^{(0)} = \mathfrak{g}^b \star E_0, E_2^{(0)} = \mathfrak{g}^c \star E_0), (E_1^{(i)} = \mathfrak{g}^{a_i} \star E_1^{(0)}, E_2^{(i)} = \mathfrak{g}^{a_i} \star E_2^{(0)})_{i \in [S]} \right),$$

and $\mathsf{W} = (a_i)_{i \in [N]}$.
- Algorithm $\mathsf{LossyIGen}$ uniformly samples $(a_i, a_i')_{i \in [S]}, b, c \in \mathbb{Z}_N$ and outputs a lossy statement

$$\mathsf{X} = \left((E_1^{(0)} = \mathfrak{g}^b \star E_0, E_2^{(0)} = \mathfrak{g}^c \star E_0), (E_1^{(i)} = \mathfrak{g}^{a_i} \star E_1^{(0)}, E_2^{(i)} = \mathfrak{g}^{a_i'} \star E_2^{(0)})_{i \in [S]} \right),$$

- On input (X, W), P_1 generates a random integer $r \in \mathbb{Z}_N$ and returns the commitment $com = (F_1 = \mathfrak{g}^r \star E_1^{(0)}, F_2 = \mathfrak{g}^r \star E_2^{(0)})$.
- On input (X, W, com, ch), where $ch \in ChSet$, P_2 outputs the response $resp$ which is r if $ch = 0$, $r - a_{ch}$ if $ch > 0$.
- On input $(X, com, ch, resp)$, the verification algorithm V checks that

$$\mathfrak{g}^{resp} \star E_1^{(ch)} = F_1, \quad \mathfrak{g}^{resp} \star E_2^{(ch)} = F_2$$

Security of Lossy Identification Protocol ID_{ls}^{enCh}. The proposed lossy identification protocol ID_{ls}^{enCh} inherits most of the desired standard properties presented in Sect. 2.1 from the base lossy identification protocol ID_{ls}^{base}. Namely, correctness, min-entropy, perfect unique response, and commitment revocability trivially follow from those of ID_{ls}^{base}. Moreover, the Honest-Verifier Zero-Knowledge property holds similarly as well. Simply consider a simulator Sim which, on input $X \in \mathcal{L}_\mathcal{R}$ and $ch \in \{0, 1, \cdots, S\}$, outputs $((g^u \star E_1^{(ch)}, g^u \star E_2^{(ch)}), ch, u)$, where u is randomly sampled from $\mathbb{Z}_N$.

We next show that ID_{ls}^{enCh} satisfies the lossy properties (see Definition 2.2). Specifically, it has indistinguishability of lossy statements and statistical lossy soundness.

Lemma 4.2. *Our lossy identification protocol ID_{ls}^{enCh} satisfies indistinguishability of lossy statements assuming the hardness of the FCMD-CSIDH problem with parameter S. Specifically, an adversary $\mathcal{A}$ with advantage $Adv_{\mathcal{A}}^{lossy}(\lambda)$ can be turned into an adversary $\mathcal{B}$ against the FCMD-CSIDH problem with advantage $Adv_{\mathcal{B},S}^{FCMD\text{-}CSIDH}(\lambda) = Adv_{\mathcal{A}}^{lossy}(\lambda)$ and same running time.*

Proof. The proof is analogous to that of Lemma 3.1.

Lemma 4.3. *The lossy identification protocol ID_{ls}^{enCh} satisfies statistical ϵ_{ls}-lossy soundness for $\epsilon_{ls} = (1/(S+1)) \prod_{i=1}^{S}((N-i)/N) + (1 - \prod_{i=1}^{S}((N-i)/N))$, where $N = |\mathcal{Cl}(\mathcal{O})|$.*

Proof. The general strategy is similar to that used for proving Lemma 3.3. We separate the set X in such a way that in one of the subsets the adversary $\mathcal{A}$ has exactly $1/(S+1)$ probability in winning the lossy impersonation game. We then argue that $LossyIGen$ outputs a statement belonging to this subset with overwhelming probability. However, unlike the proof in Lemma 3.3, we will not be able to simply use $X \backslash \mathcal{L}_\mathcal{R}$ as such a subset. This is because a computationally unbounded adversary may be able, for some of the instances in $X \backslash \mathcal{L}_\mathcal{R}$, to forge a response for any $ch \in ChSet$.

Recall the set X we consider is of the following form:

$$\left((E_1^{(0)}, E_2^{(0)}), (E_1^{(i)} = \mathfrak{g}^{a_i} \star E_1^{(0)}, E_2^{(i)} = \mathfrak{g}^{a_i'} \star E_2^{(0)})_{i \in [S]} \right),$$

where $(E_1^{(0)}, E_2^{(0)})$ are arbitrary elements in $\mathcal{Ell}_p(\mathcal{O}, \pi)$, and a_i, a_i' are arbitrary elements in $\mathbb{Z}_N$. We define the set X_{BAD} as the subset of X which satisfies the following conditions for all distinct $i, j \in [S]$:

$$\begin{cases} a_i \neq a'_i, \\ a_j - a_i \neq a'_j - a'_i. \end{cases} \qquad (4)$$

Below, we first compute $|X_{\mathsf{BAD}}|$ and then show that $\Pr[\mathcal{A} \text{ wins} \mid \mathsf{X}_{\mathsf{ls}} \in X_{\mathsf{BAD}}]$ is at most $1/(S+1)$.

First, fix arbitrary $(E_1^{(0)}, E_2^{(0)})$. Then, let us consider fixing arbitrary $(a_1, a'_1) \in (\mathbb{Z}_N)^2$, conditioned on conditions (4). Then, there exist at most $N(N-1)$ choices of such pairs. Let us further consider fixing arbitrary $(a_2, a'_2) \in (\mathbb{Z}_N)^2$, conditioned on conditions (4). Then, since we have to also satisfy $a_2 - a_1 \neq a'_2 - a'_1$, there exist at most $N(N-2)$ choices of such pairs. Continuing this procedure, each pair $(a_i, a'_i) \in (\mathbb{Z}_N)^2$, with $i \in [S]$, has exactly $N(N-i)$ freedom. Therefore, we have $|X_{\mathsf{BAD}}| = N^{2+S}(N-1)\cdots(N-S)$ and $\Pr[\mathsf{X}_{\mathsf{ls}} \leftarrow \mathsf{LossylGen} : \mathsf{X}_{\mathsf{ls}} \in X_{\mathsf{BAD}}]$ equal to $(N-1)\cdots(N-S)/N^S$.

Let us now compute $\Pr[\mathcal{A} \text{ wins} \mid \mathsf{X}_{\mathsf{ls}} \in X_{\mathsf{BAD}}]$. Assume there exist two valid transcripts for X_{ls}. Namely, consider $(\mathsf{com}, \mathsf{ch}, \mathsf{resp})$ and $(\mathsf{com}, \mathsf{ch}', \mathsf{resp}')$, with $\mathsf{ch} \neq \mathsf{ch}'$ and $\mathsf{com} = (F_1, F_2)$. Then, we have

$$\begin{cases} \mathfrak{g}^{\mathsf{resp}} \star E_1^{(\mathsf{ch})} = F_1, & \mathfrak{g}^{\mathsf{resp}} \star E_2^{(\mathsf{ch})} = F_2, \\ \mathfrak{g}^{\mathsf{resp}'} \star E_1^{(\mathsf{ch}')} = F_1, & \mathfrak{g}^{\mathsf{resp}'} \star E_2^{(\mathsf{ch}')} = F_2. \end{cases}$$

Therefore, we can deduce

$$\mathfrak{g}^{\mathsf{resp}-\mathsf{resp}'} \star E_1^{(\mathsf{ch})} = E_1^{(\mathsf{ch}')} \quad \text{and} \quad \mathfrak{g}^{\mathsf{resp}-\mathsf{resp}'} \star E_2^{(\mathsf{ch})} = E_2^{(\mathsf{ch}')}.$$

However, this clearly contradicts conditions (4). Therefore, there can exist at most one challenge that admits a valid response in case $\mathsf{X}_{\mathsf{ls}} \in X_{\mathsf{BAD}}$. In particular, this proves $\Pr[\mathcal{A} \text{ wins} \mid \mathsf{X}_{\mathsf{ls}} \in X_{\mathsf{BAD}}] \leq 1/(S+1)$.

Combining everything together, we conclude.

$\Pr[\mathcal{A} \text{ wins}]$
$= \Pr[\mathcal{A} \text{ wins} \mid \mathsf{X}_{\mathsf{ls}} \in X_{\mathsf{BAD}}] \Pr[\mathsf{X}_{\mathsf{ls}} \in X_{\mathsf{BAD}}] + \Pr[\mathcal{A} \text{ wins} \mid \mathsf{X}_{\mathsf{ls}} \notin X_{\mathsf{BAD}}] \Pr[\mathsf{X}_{\mathsf{ls}} \notin X_{\mathsf{BAD}}]$
$\leq \dfrac{1}{S+1} \cdot \dfrac{(N-1)\cdots(N-S)}{N^S} + \left(1 - \dfrac{(N-1)\cdots(N-S)}{N^S}\right).$

4.3 (Almost) Doubling Challenge Space of Lossy Identification Scheme $\mathsf{ID}_{\mathsf{ls}}^{\mathsf{EnCh}}$

Following the work of [6] and their exploitation of quadratic twists, we show a simple method to almost double the challenge space of the previous scheme $\mathsf{ID}_{\mathsf{ls}}^{\mathsf{enCh}}$. The new scheme $\mathsf{ID}_{\mathsf{ls}}^{\mathsf{denCh}}$ (with a doubly-enlarged challenge set) has statement-witness pairs almost identical to those of $\mathsf{ID}_{\mathsf{ls}}^{\mathsf{enCh}}$. The statement remains the same, while the witness contains two extra-coordinates, namely $b, c \in \mathbb{Z}_N$ such that $\mathfrak{g}^b \star E_0 = E_1^{(0)}$, $\mathfrak{g}^c \star E_0 = E_2^{(0)}$. The algorithm IGen is adjusted according to this modification, while the lossy key generation algorithm $\mathsf{LossylGen}$ and prover's first move P_1 are defined exactly the same.

The challenge set ChSet now admits also negative values, in particular it is the set $\{0, \pm 1, \ldots, \pm S\}$. The third move P_2 and the Verification algorithm V are hence converted to deal with these new challenge values:

- On input $(X, W, \mathsf{com}, \mathsf{ch})$, where $\mathsf{ch} \in \mathsf{ChSet}$, P_2 outputs the response resp which is r if $\mathsf{ch} = 0$, $r - a_{\mathsf{ch}}$ if $\mathsf{ch} > 0$ and $r + b + c + a_{|\mathsf{ch}|}$ if $\mathsf{ch} < 0$.
- On input $(X, \mathsf{com}, \mathsf{ch}, \mathsf{resp})$, the verification algorithm V checks that $\mathfrak{g}^{\mathsf{resp}} \star E_1^{(\mathsf{ch})} = F_1$, $\mathfrak{g}^{\mathsf{resp}} \star E_2^{(\mathsf{ch})} = F_2$ if $\mathsf{ch} \geq 0$, and

$$\mathfrak{g}^{\mathsf{resp}} \star E_1^{(|\mathsf{ch}|),\mathsf{tw}} = F_2, \quad \mathfrak{g}^{\mathsf{resp}} \star E_2^{(|\mathsf{ch}|),\mathsf{tw}} = F_1$$

if $\mathsf{ch} < 0$.

We note that the symbols $E_1^{(|\mathsf{ch}|),\mathsf{tw}}$, $E_2^{(|\mathsf{ch}|),\mathsf{tw}}$ denote the quadratic twists of the curve $E_1^{(|\mathsf{ch}|)}$ and $E_2^{(|\mathsf{ch}|)}$, respectively. In particular $E_1^{(|\mathsf{ch}|),\mathsf{tw}} = \mathfrak{g}^{-a_{|\mathsf{ch}|}-b} \star E_0$, and $E_2^{(|\mathsf{ch}|),\mathsf{tw}} = \mathfrak{g}^{-a_{|\mathsf{ch}|}-c} \star E_0$.

Remark 4.1. We exploit the quadratic twist in a slightly different way compared to [6]. This has the effect of allowing us to base security on the FCMD-CSIDH assumption rather than the more restricted FCMD-CSIDH assumption where $E_1^{(0)}$ is fixed to be the special elliptic curve E_0. The variant proposed in [6, Section 2.5] in order to extend the challenge set to negative values relies on the fact that the public key and the commitment are computed starting from the specific elliptic curve E_0. Consequently, the security of their derived sigma protocol requires the GAIP problem to be hard for this specific E_0 as the base point. This is in contrast to all other schemes provided in [6] which only need the standard GAIP problem.

Security of Lossy Identification Scheme $\mathsf{ID}_{\mathsf{ls}}^{\mathsf{denCh}}$. The proposed lossy identification protocol $\mathsf{ID}_{\mathsf{ls}}^{\mathsf{denCh}}$ inherits all the standard properties of a lossy identification protocol (see Definition 2.1) from the previous scheme $\mathsf{ID}_{\mathsf{ls}}^{\mathsf{enCh}}$. Moreover, since the statement output by IGen and $\mathsf{LossyIGen}$ is identical to $\mathsf{ID}_{\mathsf{ls}}^{\mathsf{enCh}}$, the protocol $\mathsf{ID}_{\mathsf{ls}}^{\mathsf{denCh}}$ satisfies indistinguishability of lossy statements assuming the hardness of the FCMD-CSIDH problem.

Finally, the statistical lossy soundness is addressed in the following lemma. As it can be seen, the shape of ϵ_{ls} remains unchanged with respect to Lemma 4.3.

Lemma 4.4. *Our lossy identification protocol $\mathsf{ID}_{\mathsf{ls}}^{\mathsf{denCh}}$ satisfies statistical ϵ_{ls}-lossy soundness for $\epsilon_{\mathsf{ls}} = (1/(2S+1)) \cdot \prod_{i=1}^{S}((N-i)/N) + (1 - \prod_{i=1}^{S}((N-i)/N))$, where $N = |\mathcal{C}\ell(\mathcal{O})|$.*

Proof. The proof is almost identical to that of Lemma 4.3. We consider exactly the same partition X_{BAD}, $X \backslash X_{\mathsf{BAD}}$ for the set of statements X which was introduced in Lemma 4.3. The only difference is that three extra-cases arise from the extension of the challenge space when computing $\Pr[\mathcal{A} \text{ wins} \mid X_{\mathsf{ls}} \in X_{\mathsf{BAD}}]$. Namely, consider $(\mathsf{com}, \mathsf{ch}, \mathsf{resp})$ and $(\mathsf{com}, \mathsf{ch}', \mathsf{resp}')$, with $\mathsf{ch} \neq \mathsf{ch}'$ and $\mathsf{com} = (F_1, F_2)$, as valid transcripts for X_{ls}. If ch and ch' are both negative, we have that $\mathsf{resp} - \mathsf{resp}'$ satisfies

$$\begin{cases} \mathfrak{g}^{\mathsf{resp}-\mathsf{resp}'} \star E_1^{(|\mathsf{ch}|),\mathsf{tw}} = E_1^{(|\mathsf{ch}'|),\mathsf{tw}} \\ \mathfrak{g}^{\mathsf{resp}-\mathsf{resp}'} \star E_2^{(|\mathsf{ch}|),\mathsf{tw}} = E_2^{(|\mathsf{ch}'|),\mathsf{tw}} \end{cases}$$

i.e. $a_{|ch|} - a_{|ch'|} = a'_{|ch|} - a'_{|ch'|}$. When $ch > 0$ and $ch' < 0$, for the value $resp - resp'$ it holds

$$\begin{cases} \mathfrak{g}^{resp-resp'} \star E_1^{(ch)} = E_2^{(|ch'|),tw} \\ \mathfrak{g}^{resp-resp'} \star E_2^{(ch)} = E_1^{(|ch'|),tw} \end{cases}$$

which implies the analogous relation $a_{ch} - a_{|ch'|} = a'_{ch} - a'_{|ch'|}$. The last case to be taken into account has $ch = 0$ and $ch' < 0$, for which we deduce

$$\begin{cases} \mathfrak{g}^{resp-resp'} \star E_1^{(0)} = E_2^{(|ch'|),tw} \\ \mathfrak{g}^{resp-resp'} \star E_2^{(0)} = E_1^{(|ch'|),tw} \end{cases}$$

and then the relation $a_{|ch'|} = a'_{|ch'|}$.

Therefore, combining this with conditions (4) in Lemma 4.3, we conclude that in case $X_{ls} \in X_{BAD}$, there can exist at most one $ch \in \{0, \pm 1, \ldots, \pm S\}$ which leads to a valid response $resp$. This concludes the proof.

4.4 Lossy Soundness Amplification of ID_{ls}^{DenCh}

For completeness, we provide the following lemma.

Lemma 4.5. *Consider running t parallel rounds of the lossy identification protocol ID_{ls}^{denCh} (with the same statement-witness pair). Then it satisfies statistical ϵ_{ls}-lossy soundness for $\epsilon_{ls} = (1/(2S+1)^t) \cdot \prod_{i=1}^{S}((N-i)/N) + (1 - \prod_{i=1}^{S}((N-i)/N))$, where $N = |\mathcal{C}\ell(\mathcal{O})|$.*

Proof. The proof is analogous to Lemma 3.3.

5 Lossy CSI-FiSh: Tightly Secure Signature from CSIDH-512

5.1 Construction of Lossy CSI-FiSh

We depict our Lossy CSI-FiSh signature scheme, whose security is based on the FCMD-CSIDH assumption with parameter S, in Algorithms 1 to 3. It is obtained by applying the Fiat-Shamir transformation on the (soundness-amplified) lossy identification protocol ID_{ls}^{denCh} introduced in Sect. 4.3. We note that we use a (quantumly secure) PRF to derandomize the signature generation, to comply with the hypothesis of Theorem 2.1. In practice, one can simply use any standard hash function (e.g., SHA-3).[5] Moreover, we use the extra property of commitment revocability (see Definition 2.1) of our lossy identification protocol ID_{ls}^{denCh} and let the verifier recover com from $resp$ and ch. This allows us to send t-hash values rather than $2t$-elliptic curves over $\mathcal{E}\ell\ell_p(\mathcal{O}, \pi)$, and greatly reduces the signature size.

---

[5] We note that assuming that a standard cryptographic hash function acts as a PRF does not add to our set of assumptions, since we are already working in the ROM.

The values S and t are parameters of the signature scheme and can be chosen by the user allowing for different tradeoffs between security, efficiency and signature size. Roughly, the only condition which S and t must satisfy is $t \cdot \log_2 S \approx \lambda$ in the classical setting, where λ is the desired security level. In the quantum setting, we will require $t \cdot \log_2 S \approx \lambda + \log_2 Q_H$, where Q_H is the number of hash evaluations an adversary can make. For fixed S and t, the resulting signature size is $t \cdot (\lceil \log_2 N \rceil + \lceil \log_2 S \rceil)$. A selection of candidate parameters is provided in Sect. 5.2.

The following asserts the tight security of Lossy CSI-FiSh based on the FCMD-CSIDH assumption. Observe that the computational advantages appear with a constant factor (one). Moreover, viewing S as a constant parameter, Lossy CSI-FiSh admits tight security based on the D-CSIDH assumption as well.

Theorem 5.1. *Let Lossy CSI-FiSh be the signature scheme depicted in Algorithms 1, 2, and 3. Then, for any quantum adversary $\mathcal{A}$ against su-cma security of Lossy CSI-FiSh that issues at most Q_H queries to the quantum random oracle, there exists a quantum adversary $\mathcal{B}$ against the FCMD-CSIDH problem with parameter S and an quantum adversary $\mathcal{D}$ against the PRF such that*

$$\mathsf{Adv}_{\mathcal{A}}^{\mathsf{su\text{-}cma}}(\lambda) \leq \mathsf{Adv}_{\mathcal{B},S}^{\mathsf{FCMD\text{-}CSIDH}}(\lambda) + \mathsf{Adv}_{\mathcal{D}}^{\mathsf{PRF}}(\lambda) + \frac{2}{N} +$$
$$+ 8(Q_H + 1)^2 \cdot \left(\frac{1}{(2S+1)^t} \cdot \prod_{i \in [S]} \frac{N-i}{N} + \left(1 - \prod_{i \in [S]} \frac{N-i}{N}\right) \right)$$

and $\mathsf{Time}(\mathcal{B}) = \mathsf{Time}(\mathcal{D}) = \mathsf{Time}(\mathcal{A}) + Q_H \approx \mathsf{Time}(\mathcal{A})$. Moreover, we can replace $\mathcal{B}$ by a quantum adversary $\mathcal{B}'$ against the D-CSIDH problem such that

$$\mathsf{Adv}_{\mathcal{B},S}^{\mathsf{FCMD\text{-}CSIDH}}(\lambda) \leq S \cdot \mathsf{Adv}_{\mathcal{B}'}^{\mathsf{D\text{-}CSIDH}}(\lambda)$$

and $\mathsf{Time}(\mathcal{B}) \approx \mathsf{Time}(B')$.

In the classical setting, the only difference is that the above bound depends linearly on Q_H instead of quadratically. That is, we can replace $8(Q_H + 1)^2$ with $Q_H + 1$.[6]

Proof. The theorem is a consequence of Theorem 2.1, Lemmas 4.1, and 4.5, along with the additional security claims made in Sect. 4. Note that the lossy identification protocol $\mathsf{ID}_{\mathsf{ls}}^{\mathsf{denCh}}$ has N bits of min entropy, where N is the cardinality of $\mathcal{Cl}(\mathcal{O})$.

Remark 5.1. **(Shorter Secret Key).** Since the secret key sk is composed of random values, we can use standard tricks to derive them from the PRF key. In particular, we only require one PRF key, e.g., a 16-byte seed for SHA-3, as the secret key. This modification has (almost) no effect on the overall concrete security. In order to simplify the readability, in Algorithm 1 we do not make the use of the PRF explicit while uniformly sampling in $\mathbb{Z}_N$.

---

[6] We can get rid of the constant 8 in the classical setting since it is due to the reduction from the generic *quantum* search problem. See [24,43] for example.

Algorithm 1. KeyGen

Input: E_0, class number $N = |\mathcal{C}\ell(\mathcal{O})|$
Output: (pk, sk)
1: $b \leftarrow \mathbb{Z}_N$, $c \leftarrow \mathbb{Z}_N$
2: $E_1^{(0)} = \mathfrak{g}^b \star E_0$, $E_2^{(0)} = \mathfrak{g}^c \star E_0$
3: **for** $i \in \{1, \ldots, S\}$ **do**
4:     $a_i \leftarrow \mathbb{Z}_N$
5:     $E_1^{(i)} = \mathfrak{g}^{a_i} \star E_1^{(0)}$, $E_2^{(i)} = \mathfrak{g}^{a_i} \star E_2^{(0)}$
6: pk $= [(E_1^{(j)}, E_2^{(j)}) : j \in \{0, \ldots, S\}]$
7: $K \leftarrow \mathcal{K}$ ▷ Sample key for PRF.
8: sk $= [b, c, a_i : i \in \{1, \ldots, S\}, K]$
return: (pk, sk)

Algorithm 2. Sign

Input: (pk, sk, message M)
Output: σ
1: **for** $k \in \{1, \ldots, t\}$ **do**
2:     $r_k \leftarrow \mathbb{Z}_N$ ▷ Derive randomness using PRF(K, M$||k$).
3:     $F_1^{(k)} = \mathfrak{g}^{r_k} \star E_1^{(0)}$, $F_2^{(k)} = \mathfrak{g}^{r_k} \star E_2^{(0)}$
4: $(\mathsf{ch}_1, \ldots, \mathsf{ch}_t) = H(F_1^{(1)} || F_2^{(1)} || \cdots || F_1^{(t)} || F_2^{(t)} || M)$
5: **for** $k \in \{1, \ldots, t\}$ **do**   ▷ Define sign(0) := 0.
6:     $\mathsf{resp}_k = r_k - \mathrm{sign}(\mathsf{ch}_k) a_{|\mathsf{ch}_k|} - \frac{\mathrm{sign}(\mathsf{ch}_k) - |\mathrm{sign}(\mathsf{ch}_k)|}{2}(b + c) \pmod{N}$
7: $\sigma = (\mathsf{resp}_1, \ldots, \mathsf{resp}_t, \mathsf{ch}_1, \ldots, \mathsf{ch}_t)$
return: σ

Algorithm 3. Verify

Input: (pk, signature σ, message M)
Output: Valid / Invalid
1: Parse σ as $(\mathsf{resp}_1, \ldots, \mathsf{resp}_t, \mathsf{ch}_1, \ldots, \mathsf{ch}_t)$
2: **for** $i \in \{1, \ldots, S\}$ **do**
3:     $E_1^{(-i)} = E_1^{(i),\mathsf{tw}}$, $E_2^{(-i)} = E_2^{(i),\mathsf{tw}}$ ▷ Compute quadratic twists.
4: **for** $k \in \{1, \ldots, t\}$ **do**
5:     **if** $\mathsf{ch}_k \geq 0$ **then**
6:         $F_1^{(k)} = \mathfrak{g}^{\mathsf{resp}_k} \star E_1^{(\mathsf{ch}_k)}$, $F_2^{(k)} = \mathfrak{g}^{\mathsf{resp}_k} \star E_2^{(\mathsf{ch}_k)}$
7:     **else**
8:         $F_1^{(k)} = \mathfrak{g}^{\mathsf{resp}_k} \star E_2^{(\mathsf{ch}_k)}$, $F_2^{(k)} = \mathfrak{g}^{\mathsf{resp}_k} \star E_1^{(\mathsf{ch}_k)}$
9: $(\mathsf{ch}_1', \ldots, \mathsf{ch}_t') = H(F_1^{(1)} || F_2^{(1)} || \cdots || F_1^{(t)} || F_2^{(t)} || M)$
10: **if** $(\mathsf{ch}_1, \ldots, \mathsf{ch}_t) == (\mathsf{ch}_1', \ldots, \mathsf{ch}_t')$ **then**
11:     **return:** Valid
12: **else**
13:     **return:** Invalid

5.2 Instantiations and Comparison to CSI-FiSh

In this section, we specialise the Lossy CSI-FiSh to the CSIDH-512 parameters, and we consider distinct possible values for t and S both in the classical and quantum setting. For each choice of (S, t), Theorem 5.1 dictates how many bits of classical/quantum security the scheme guarantees. Clearly, different choices for (S, t) will lead to different bandwidth and computational efficiency.

Here, the term γ-bit of security for a cryptographic scheme is defined as the non-existence of an adversary that breaks the scheme with a success ratio bigger than $2^{-\gamma}$, where the success ratio is the quotient between the adversary's success probability and its running time [3]. In the light of Theorem 5.1, the number of bits of security guaranteed by the signature scheme Lossy CSI-FiSh is upper bounded by the security of the FCMD-CSIDH problem. In line with [8], in the following we assume that the best methodology to solve the D-CSIDH problem (and hence FCMD-CSIDH) is solving one of the corresponding GAIP instances.

Aligning with [6], we consider a hash function that is a factor 2^u slower than a standard hash function (as, for example, SHA3) and vary u to obtain tradeoffs between security and efficiency. Moreover, for the sake of easy comparison, we consider the same values for S and u that are used in [6]. Below, we first provide discussions on the size of the public key and signature size of Lossy CSI-FiSh, both in the classical and quantum setting. We then discuss the efficiency of our scheme with respect to the running times of signature generation and verification. The analysis on runtime will be the same for both the classical and quantum setting.

Classical Setting. The best known classical algorithm to solve the GAIP problem applies the meet-in-the-middle strategy, and hence has a time complexity $O(\sqrt{N})$, where N is the cardinality of $\mathcal{C}\ell(\mathcal{O})$. The class group computation executed in [6] has shown that $N \simeq 2^{257.1}$ for CSIDH-512 parameters. This means that the D-CSIDH problem guarantees at most 128 bits of classical security and then, in turn, the FCMD-CSIDH problem guarantees at most 128-bits when $S = 1$, and at most $128/\log_2 S$ bits when $S > 1$ (see Lemma 4.1).

By Theorem 5.1, for all classical adversaries running in time at most 2^{128} and making at most 2^{128} (random) queries Q_H, it holds:

$$\frac{\mathsf{Adv}_{\mathcal{A}}^{\mathsf{su\text{-}cma}}(\lambda)}{\mathsf{Time}(\mathcal{A})} \leq S \cdot \frac{\mathsf{Adv}_{\mathcal{B}'}^{\mathsf{D\text{-}CSIDH}}(\lambda)}{\mathsf{Time}(\mathcal{B}')} + \frac{\mathsf{Adv}_{\mathcal{D}}^{\mathsf{PRF}}(\lambda)}{\mathsf{Time}(\mathcal{D})} +$$
$$+ 2^{-u} \cdot \left(\frac{1}{(2S+1)^t} \cdot \prod_{i \in [S]} \frac{N-i}{N} + \left(1 - \prod_{i \in [S]} \frac{N-i}{N}\right) \right)$$
$$\simeq S \cdot 2^{-128} + 2^{-256} + 2^{-u} \cdot (2S+1)^{-t},$$

where we ignore the min-entropy since it does not give any significant contribution, being smaller than 2^{256}. Furthermore, $1 - \prod_{i \in [S]}(N-i)/N$ is less than 2^{-242} even for the biggest value of S considered in the following, i.e. $2^{15} - 1$. Hence, the last term can be safely approximated as $2^{-u} \cdot (2S+1)^{-t}$. Now, since each of the values of S is of the form $2^w - 1$, we deduce that $2^{-u} \cdot (2S+1)^{-t}$

must be bounded by 2^{-129} to reach $-128 + w$ bits of security. For a fixed value of u, the smallest value of t for which the above inequality is satisfied is uniquely defined.

In the following Table 1 we report: for each choice of S and u, the minimum value of t for which we obtain the maximal security guaranteed by Lossy CSI-FiSh, the number of bits of such security level, the sizes of signatures and the sizes of public keys for Lossy CSI-FiSh and CSI-FiSh. The column "bits of security" is dismissed for CSI-FiSh as it does not provide provable concrete security. We highlight that for a fixed triple (S, t, u), the signatures produced with our scheme Lossy CSI-FiSh have exactly the same size as those produced with CSI-FiSh. Finally, we note that the values for CSI-FiSh reported in Table 1 slightly differ from those of [6, Table 3], where some approximations were made (e.g., $2S -1$ was approximated with $2S$), while our parameters are chosen without any approximation.

Table 1. Comparison between Lossy CSI-FiSh and CSI-FiSh.

| S | t | u | $\lvert\sigma\rvert$ | Lossy CSI-FiSh | | CSI-FiSh |
				$\lvert pk \rvert$	Bits of security	$\lvert pk \rvert$
1	74	16	2405 B	256 B	127	64 B
3	43	14	1403 B	512 B	126	192 B
7	30	16	983 B	1024 B	125	448 B
15	25	13	822 B	2048 B	124	960 B
$2^6 - 1$	17	16	564 B	8.2 KB	122	4 KB
$2^8 - 1$	14	11	468 B	32.8 KB	120	16.3 KB
$2^{10} - 1$	12	7	404 B	131 KB	118	65.5 KB
$2^{12} - 1$	10	11	339 B	524 KB	116	262 KB
$2^{15} - 1$	8	16	274 B	4 MB	113	2 MB

The differences on the public key sizes between Lossy CSI-FiSh and CSI-FiSh have a double cause:

- in Lossy CSI-FiSh the *starting curves* $E_1^{(0)}, E_2^{(0)}$ are computed by each user and are part of the public key, while in CSI-FiSh the starting curve E_0 is part of the public parameters of the scheme;
- for each coordinate a_i of the private key, with $i \in [S]$, Algorithm 1 computes two curves that will become part of the public key, while in CSI-FiSh only $\mathfrak{g}^{a_i} \star E_0$ is appended to the public key.

Recalling that each curve in $\mathcal{E}\ell\ell_p(\mathcal{O}, \pi)$ can be uniquely represented by an element of $\mathbb{F}_p$, with $p \simeq 2^{512}$, for a given S the size of a CSI-FiSh's public key is $S \cdot 512$ while the size of a public key produced with Lossy CSI-FiSh has length equal to $(S + 2) \cdot 512$, with the increment given by the extra term more visible for small values of S.

Quantum Setting. The best known quantum algorithm for the GAIP problem is Kuperberg's algorithm for the hidden shift problem [28,29], which has a subexponential complexity. The concrete security estimates, however, are still an active area of research [5,7,34]. In the following we will consider 56 bits of quantum security as a conservative choice, and 64 bits as a more optimistic choice for the D-CSIDH problem. Consequently, we consider quantum adversaries running in time at most 2^{56} in the conservative variant, and 2^{64} in the more optimist one. Analogously, we upper bound the number of possible queries Q_H by 2^{56} in the former case, and by 2^{64} in the latter. In both cases, the upper bound on the security of Lossy CSI-FiSh depends quadratically in Q_H.

Considering the optimistic variant, the following inequality holds due to Theorem 5.1:

$$\frac{\mathsf{Adv}_{\mathcal{A}}^{\mathsf{su\text{-}cma}}(\lambda)}{\mathsf{Time}(\mathcal{A})} \leq S \cdot \frac{\mathsf{Adv}_{\mathcal{B}'}^{\mathsf{D\text{-}CSIDH}}(\lambda)}{\mathsf{Time}(\mathcal{B}')} + \frac{\mathsf{Adv}_{\mathcal{D}}^{\mathsf{PRF}}(\lambda)}{\mathsf{Time}(\mathcal{D})}$$
$$+ 8 \cdot (Q_H + 1) \cdot 2^{-u} \cdot \left(\frac{1}{(2S+1)^t} \cdot \prod_{i \in [S]} \frac{N-i}{N} + \left(1 - \prod_{i \in [S]} \frac{N-i}{N}\right) \right)$$
$$\simeq S \cdot 2^{-64} + 2^{-256} + 2^{67-u} \cdot (2S+1)^{-t},$$

where the approximation is validated by the same argument as in the classical setting. We require $2^{67-u} \cdot (2S+1)^{-t}$ to be bounded by 2^{-65} in order to reach $-64 + w$ bits of quantum security, with $S = 2^w - 1$. Analogously, in the conservative variant, we require $2^{59-u} \cdot (2S+1)^{-t}$ to be bounded by 2^{-57} in order to reach $-56 + w$ bits of quantum security, with $S = 2^w - 1$.

In the following Table 2 we differentiate the Conservative and Optimistic variants, reporting the values of t for each choice of S and u, the security levels guaranteed in the two cases, and signatures and public keys sizes. We note that the size of the public key only depends on S, hence it achieves the same size as in the classical setting (see Table 1).

Table 2. Parameters and achieved quantum security level for Lossy CSI-FiSh.

S	u	|pk|	Conservative variant			Optimistic variant		
			t	$\|\sigma\|$	Bits of security	t	$\|\sigma\|$	Bits of security
1	16	256 B	64	2080 B	55	74	2405 B	63
3	14	512 B	37	1208 B	54	43	1403 B	62
7	16	1024 B	26	852 B	53	30	983 B	61
15	13	2048 B	21	691 B	52	25	822 B	60
$2^6 - 1$	16	8.2 KB	15	497 B	50	17	564 B	58
$2^8 - 1$	11	32.8 KB	12	401 B	48	14	468 B	56
$2^{10} - 1$	7	131 KB	10	337 B	46	12	404 B	54
$2^{12} - 1$	11	524 KB	9	305 B	44	10	339 B	52
$2^{15} - 1$	16	4 MB	7	240 B	41	8	274 B	49

Estimated Performance. The costs of key generation, signing and verifying are dominated by the class group actions to be executed in each algorithm. For fixed S and t, the number of actions for each of them is as follows:

- key generation (Algorithm 1) requires $2S + 2$ actions, while S of them are those also computed by the key generation algorithm of CSI-FiSh;
- both signing (Algorithm 2) and verifying (Algorithm 3) need $2t$ actions, exactly twice as many as required by the corresponding algorithms of CSI-FiSh.

As it can be seen, the key generation would be slighter slower than twice the key generation of CSI-FiSh, while the signature generation and verification would be twice that of CSI-FiSh. To provide a concrete benchmark, we estimate the running times using the two triples $(2^{15} - 1, 7, 16)$ and $(2^3 - 1, 28, 16)$ reporting the values of S, t and u for two instances from [6, Table 3]. These two parameter settings are chosen in order to achieve a small signature size and a small sum of signature and public key size, respectively. For the first (resp. second) triple, CSI-FiSh takes the following: 28 m (resp. 400 ms) for key generation, 395 ms (resp. 1.48 s) for signature generation, and 393 ms (resp. 1.48 s) for signature verification[7]. Therefore, we can estimate that for Lossy CSI-FiSh it will take the following for the respective tuples: ~ 56 m (resp. $\sim$920 ms) for key generation, $\sim$800 ms (resp. 3 s) for signature generation and verification. Here for estimating the runtime of key generation, we simply scaled the runtime of CSI-FiSh by a factor $(2S + 2) \cdot S^{-1}$.

Finally, we provide one potential optimization for lowering the computation time required by the signing and verifying algorithms of Lossy CSI-FiSh. We recall that, in order to efficiently compute the action of $\mathfrak{g}^a$ on a given curve, with $a \in \mathbb{Z}_N$, it is necessary to find an equivalent representation of $\mathfrak{g}^a$ as a product of small powers of the special ideals $\mathfrak{I}_{\ell_i}$ (see Sect. 2.5). In [6], an algorithm solving an approximate Closest Vector Problem (CVP) has been proposed to this task. Therefore, the computation of a class group action consists of two steps: finding the equivalent representation and computing the isogenies corresponding to the ideals' powers. Here, we observe that in Lossy CSI-FiSh most of the group actions are pairwise coupled, i.e. they use the same exponent. The result is that the signing and verifying algorithms do not need to execute the finding-equivalent-representation step for each of the class actions. Therefore, this may potentially lead to more efficient algorithms depending on the exact runtime of finding the equivalent representation. We leave it as future work to implement and verify the validity of this observation.

6   Conclusions and Open Problems

In this work, we construct a new signature scheme based on the CSIDH-512 parameters, called Lossy CSI-FiSh. It is *provably secure* and *tightly reduces* to the

---

[7] Their benchmarking experiments were performed on a Dell OptiPlex 3050 machine with Intel Core i5-7500T CPU @ 2.70 GHz.

D-CSIDH (or FCMD-CSIDH) assumption. Lossy CSI-FiSh inherits most of the efficiency of CSI-FiSh and shows that a slight modification to CSI-FiSh allows to set the concrete parameters in a provably secure manner with minimal cost. In particular, the signature size is as small as CSI-FiSh while the signature generation and verification are around a factor of two slower. We hope that further research will allow to improve the efficiency. Optimisations may be specialized for the scheme (like, for example, halving the number of approximate CVP-problems to be solved in the key generation) or, more generally, be designed for CSI-FiSh. Indeed, the latter would likely have an impact also on our scheme.

One of the biggest open problems is to devise a (lossy or non-lossy) identification protocol that allows for the challenge set to be $\mathbb{Z}_N$ rather than the small set $\{-S, \cdots, S\}$, as also mentioned in [6]. This will allow for an analogue of the highly efficient Schnorr signature [36] based on the discrete logarithm problem. Another challenging yet interesting open problem is to show any type of random self-reducibility property for the D-CSIDH problem. We believe such a technique will lend hands to other tightly-secure primitives (e.g., tightly-secure key exchange protocols) and perhaps shed light to Cramer-Shoup-like techniques [11] in the isogeny setting.

Acknowledgement. The second author was supported by JST CREST Grant Number JPMJCR19F6.

References

1. Abdalla, M., An, J.H., Bellare, M., Namprempre, C.: From identification to signatures via the Fiat-Shamir transform: minimizing assumptions for security and forward-security. In: Knudsen, L.R. (ed.) EUROCRYPT 2002. LNCS, vol. 2332, pp. 418–433. Springer, Heidelberg (2002). https://doi.org/10.1007/3-540-46035-7_28
2. Abdalla, M., Fouque, P.-A., Lyubashevsky, V., Tibouchi, M.: Tightly-secure signatures from lossy identification schemes. In: Pointcheval, D., Johansson, T. (eds.) EUROCRYPT 2012. LNCS, vol. 7237, pp. 572–590. Springer, Heidelberg (2012). https://doi.org/10.1007/978-3-642-29011-4_34
3. Bellare, M., Rogaway, P.: The exact security of digital signatures-how to sign with RSA and Rabin. In: Maurer, U. (ed.) EUROCRYPT 1996. LNCS, vol. 1070, pp. 399–416. Springer, Heidelberg (1996). https://doi.org/10.1007/3-540-68339-9_34
4. Bernstein, D.J., Hülsing, A., Kölbl, S., Niederhagen, R., Rijneveld, J., Schwabe, P.: The SPHINCS signature framework. In: ACM-CCS, pp. 17–43 (2019). Submission to the NIST PQC project
5. Bernstein, D.J., Lange, T., Martindale, C., Panny, L.: Quantum circuits for the CSIDH: optimizing quantum evaluation of isogenies. In: Ishai, Y., Rijmen, V. (eds.) EUROCRYPT 2019. LNCS, vol. 11477, pp. 409–441. Springer, Cham (2019). https://doi.org/10.1007/978-3-030-17656-3_15
6. Beullens, W., Kleinjung, T., Vercauteren, F.: CSI-FiSh: efficient isogeny based signatures through class group computations. In: Galbraith, S.D., Moriai, S. (eds.) ASIACRYPT 2019. LNCS, vol. 11921, pp. 227–247. Springer, Cham (2019). https://doi.org/10.1007/978-3-030-34578-5_9
7. Bonnetain, X., Schrottenloher, A.: Quantum security analysis of CSIDH and ordinary isogeny-based schemes. Cryptology ePrint Archive, Report 2018/537 (2018)

8. Castryck, W., Lange, T., Martindale, C., Panny, L., Renes, J.: CSIDH: an efficient post-quantum commutative group action. In: Peyrin, T., Galbraith, S. (eds.) ASIACRYPT 2018. LNCS, vol. 11274, pp. 395–427. Springer, Cham (2018). https://doi.org/10.1007/978-3-030-03332-3_15

9. Couveignes, J.-M.: Hard homogeneous spaces. Cryptology ePrint Archive, Report 2006/291 (2006)

10. Cox, D.A.: Primes of the form $x^2 + ny^2$ (2011)

11. Cramer, R., Shoup, V.: A practical public key cryptosystem provably secure against adaptive chosen ciphertext attack. In: Krawczyk, H. (ed.) CRYPTO 1998. LNCS, vol. 1462, pp. 13–25. Springer, Heidelberg (1998). https://doi.org/10.1007/BFb0055717

12. De Feo, L., Galbraith, S.D.: SeaSign: compact isogeny signatures from class group actions. In: Ishai, Y., Rijmen, V. (eds.) EUROCRYPT 2019. LNCS, vol. 11478, pp. 759–789. Springer, Cham (2019). https://doi.org/10.1007/978-3-030-17659-4_26

13. Jao, D., De Feo, L.: Towards quantum-resistant cryptosystems from supersingular elliptic curve isogenies. In: Yang, B.-Y. (ed.) PQCrypto 2011. LNCS, vol. 7071, pp. 19–34. Springer, Heidelberg (2011). https://doi.org/10.1007/978-3-642-25405-5_2

14. De Feo, L., Kieffer, J., Smith, B.: Towards practical key exchange from ordinary isogeny graphs. In: Peyrin, T., Galbraith, S. (eds.) ASIACRYPT 2018. LNCS, vol. 11274, pp. 365–394. Springer, Cham (2018). https://doi.org/10.1007/978-3-030-03332-3_14

15. Diffie, W., Hellman, M.: New directions in cryptography. IEEE Trans. Inf. Theory **22**(6), 644–654 (1976)

16. Don, J., Fehr, S., Majenz, C., Schaffner, C.: Security of the Fiat-Shamir transformation in the quantum random-Oracle model. In: Boldyreva, A., Micciancio, D. (eds.) CRYPTO 2019. LNCS, vol. 11693, pp. 356–383. Springer, Cham (2019). https://doi.org/10.1007/978-3-030-26951-7_13

17. Ducas, L., et al.: CRYSTALS-Dilithium: a lattice-based digital signature scheme. IACR TCHES **1**, 238–268 (2018)

18. Fiat, A., Shamir, A.: How To prove yourself: practical solutions to identification and signature problems. In: Odlyzko, A.M. (ed.) CRYPTO 1986. LNCS, vol. 263, pp. 186–194. Springer, Heidelberg (1987). https://doi.org/10.1007/3-540-47721-7_12

19. Fleischhacker, N., Jager, T., Schröder, D.: On tight security proofs for Schnorr signatures. In: Sarkar, P., Iwata, T. (eds.) ASIACRYPT 2014. LNCS, vol. 8873, pp. 512–531. Springer, Heidelberg (2014). https://doi.org/10.1007/978-3-662-45611-8_27

20. Fouque, P.-A., et al.: Falcon: Fast-Fourier lattice-based compact signatures over NTRU

21. Galbraith, S.D., Petit, C., Silva, J.: Identification protocols and signature schemes based on supersingular isogeny problems. In: Takagi, T., Peyrin, T. (eds.) ASIACRYPT 2017. LNCS, vol. 10624, pp. 3–33. Springer, Cham (2017). https://doi.org/10.1007/978-3-319-70694-8_1

22. Garg, S., Bhaskar, R., Lokam, S.V.: Improved bounds on security reductions for discrete log based signatures. In: Wagner, D. (ed.) CRYPTO 2008. LNCS, vol. 5157, pp. 93–107. Springer, Heidelberg (2008). https://doi.org/10.1007/978-3-540-85174-5_6

23. Gentry, C., Peikert, C., Vaikuntanathan, V.: Trapdoors for hard lattices and new cryptographic constructions. In: 40th ACM STOC, pp. 197–206 (2008)

24. Hülsing, A., Rijneveld, J., Song, F.: Mitigating multi-target attacks in hash-based signatures. In: Cheng, C.-M., Chung, K.-M., Persiano, G., Yang, B.-Y. (eds.) PKC 2016. LNCS, vol. 9614, pp. 387–416. Springer, Heidelberg (2016). https://doi.org/10.1007/978-3-662-49384-7_15

25. Jao, D., De Feo, L.: Towards quantum-resistant cryptosystems from supersingular elliptic curve isogenies. In: Yang, B.-Y. (ed.) PQCrypto 2011. LNCS, vol. 7071, pp. 19–34. Springer, Heidelberg (2011). https://doi.org/10.1007/978-3-642-25405-5_2

26. Katz, J., Wang, N.: Efficiency improvements for signature schemes with tight security reductions. In: ACM CCS, pp. 155–164 (2003)

27. Kiltz, E., Lyubashevsky, V., Schaffner, C.: A concrete treatment of Fiat-Shamir signatures in the quantum random-Oracle model. In: Nielsen, J.B., Rijmen, V. (eds.) EUROCRYPT 2018. LNCS, vol. 10822, pp. 552–586. Springer, Cham (2018). https://doi.org/10.1007/978-3-319-78372-7_18

28. Kuperberg, G.: Another subexponential-time quantum algorithm for the dihedral hidden subgroup problem. In: TQC, vol. 22, pp. 20–34 (2013)

29. Kuperberg, G.: A subexponential-time quantum algorithm for the dihedral hidden subgroup problem. SIAM J. Comput. **35**(1), 170–188 (2005)

30. Liu, Q., Zhandry, M.: Revisiting post-quantum Fiat-Shamir. In: Boldyreva, A., Micciancio, D. (eds.) CRYPTO 2019. LNCS, vol. 11693, pp. 326–355. Springer, Cham (2019). https://doi.org/10.1007/978-3-030-26951-7_12

31. Lyubashevsky, V.: Fiat-Shamir with aborts: applications to lattice and factoring-based signatures. In: Matsui, M. (ed.) ASIACRYPT 2009. LNCS, vol. 5912, pp. 598–616. Springer, Heidelberg (2009). https://doi.org/10.1007/978-3-642-10366-7_35

32. Micali, S., Reyzin, L.: Improving the exact security of digital signature schemes. J. Cryptol. **15**(1), 1–18 (2002). https://doi.org/10.1007/s00145-001-0005-8

33. Paillier, P., Vergnaud, D.: Discrete-log-based signatures may not be equivalent to discrete log. In: Roy, B. (ed.) ASIACRYPT 2005. LNCS, vol. 3788, pp. 1–20. Springer, Heidelberg (2005). https://doi.org/10.1007/11593447_1

34. Peikert, C.: He gives C-Sieves on the CSIDH. Cryptology ePrint Archive: Report 2019/725 (2019)

35. Rostovtsev, A., Stolbunov, A.: Public-key cryptosystem based on isogenies. Cryptology ePrint Archive: Report 2006/145 (2006)

36. Schnorr, C.P.: Efficient identification and signatures for smart cards. In: Brassard, G. (ed.) CRYPTO 1989. LNCS, vol. 435, pp. 239–252. Springer, New York (1990). https://doi.org/10.1007/0-387-34805-0_22

37. Seurin, Y.: On the exact security of Schnorr-type signatures in the random Oracle model. In: Pointcheval, D., Johansson, T. (eds.) EUROCRYPT 2012. LNCS, vol. 7237, pp. 554–571. Springer, Heidelberg (2012). https://doi.org/10.1007/978-3-642-29011-4_33

38. Stolbunov, A.: Constructing public-key cryptographic schemes based on class group action on a set of isogenous elliptic curves. Adv. Math. Commun. **4**(2), 215–235 (2010)

39. Stolbunov, A.: Cryptographic schemes based on isogenies (2012)

40. Unruh, D.: Non-interactive zero-knowledge proofs in the quantum random Oracle model. In: Oswald, E., Fischlin, M. (eds.) EUROCRYPT 2015. LNCS, vol. 9057, pp. 755–784. Springer, Heidelberg (2015). https://doi.org/10.1007/978-3-662-46803-6_25

41. Unruh, D.: Post-quantum security of Fiat-Shamir. In: Takagi, T., Peyrin, T. (eds.) ASIACRYPT 2017. LNCS, vol. 10624, pp. 65–95. Springer, Cham (2017). https://doi.org/10.1007/978-3-319-70694-8_3

42. Yoo, Y., Azarderakhsh, R., Jalali, A., Jao, D., Soukharev, V.: A post-quantum digital signature scheme based on supersingular isogenies. In: Kiayias, A. (ed.) FC 2017. LNCS, vol. 10322, pp. 163–181. Springer, Cham (2017). https://doi.org/10.1007/978-3-319-70972-7_9

43. Zhandry, M.: How to construct quantum random functions. In: 53rd FOCS, pp. 679–687 (2012)

Threshold Schemes from Isogeny Assumptions

Luca De Feo[1] and Michael Meyer[2,3]($\boxtimes$)

[1] IBM Research Zürich, Zürich, Switzerland
[2] University of Applied Sciences Wiesbaden, Wiesbaden, Germany
michael.meyer@hs-rm.de
[3] University of Würzburg, Würzburg, Germany

Abstract. We initiate the study of threshold schemes based on the Hard Homogeneous Spaces (HHS) framework of Couveignes. Quantum-resistant HHS based on supersingular isogeny graphs have recently become usable thanks to the record class group precomputation performed for the signature scheme CSI-FiSh.

Using the HHS equivalent of the technique of *Shamir's secret sharing in the exponents*, we adapt isogeny based schemes to the threshold setting. In particular we present threshold versions of the CSIDH public key encryption, and the CSI-FiSh signature schemes.

The main highlight is a threshold version of CSI-FiSh which runs almost as fast as the original scheme, for message sizes as low as $1880\,\mathrm{B}$, public key sizes as low as $128\,\mathrm{B}$, and thresholds up to 56; other speed-size-threshold compromises are possible.

Keywords: Threshold cryptography · Hard Homogeneous Spaces · Isogeny-based cryptography · CSIDH · CSI-FiSh

1 Introduction

Threshold cryptography and secret sharing are large areas of interest in the cryptographic community since the late 1970s, when Shamir [51] and Blakley [7] published the first secret sharing schemes. In 1989, Desmedt and Frankel [21] constructed a practical threshold cryptosystem based on Shamir's secret sharing and ElGamal encryption [26].

The goal of a k-out-of-n, or (k, n)-threshold scheme is to split a secret key into multiple shares and distribute them among n parties, each party receiving one share. Then, for a certain threshold $k \leq n$, any k collaborating parties must be able to compute the cryptographic operation, e.g. decrypt or sign, without learning the secret key, while any set of less than k parties must be unable to do so.

After the publication of Desmedt and Frankel's scheme, several other threshold protocols were proposed; among others, a threshold variant of ElGamal signatures

---

M. Meyer—Supported by Elektrobit Automotive, Erlangen, Germany.

A. Kiayias et al. (Eds.): PKC 2020, LNCS 12111, pp. 187–212, 2020.
https://doi.org/10.1007/978-3-030-45388-6_7

by Harn [34], a threshold DSA scheme by Gennaro *et al.* [32], and Desmedt and Frankel's and Shoup's threshold RSA signature schemes [22,53]. More recently, applications of threshold schemes in the context of blockchains and cryptocurrencies led to a renewed interest in threshold ECDSA schemes [24,31].

However, all of these schemes are either based on discrete logarithm or integer factorization problems, and are thus not quantum-resistant, since they fall prey to Shor's algorithm [52]. Only very recently, Cozzo and Smart [15] reviewed the post-quantum signature schemes that entered the second round of the NIST PQC standardization process [43] for threshold variants. Their main observation is that only the multivariate-based schemes LUOV [5] and Rainbow [23] allow for a natural threshold construction.

Another popular family of post-quantum schemes is provided by isogeny-based cryptography [35,36]. While this family is not represented in the NIST PQC track for signatures, isogeny-based signatures have recently attracted much attention [4,17,19]. In this work we introduce the first isogeny-based threshold encryption and signature schemes, based on Shamir's secret sharing.

Our schemes are simple adaptations of Desmedt and Frankel's and related schemes to the *Hard Homogeneous Spaces (HHS)* framework. This framework was introduced by Couveignes [14], to generalize both discrete logarithm and isogeny-based schemes. Encryption schemes for HHS were first proposed by Couveignes [14] and Rostovtsev and Stolbunov [49], then improved by De Feo, Kieffer and Smith [18], eventually lead to the development of CSIDH by Castryck, Lange, Martindale, Panny, and Renes [11].

The possibility of signature schemes based on HHS was first suggested by Couveignes [14] and Stolbunov [55,56], although no instantiation was known until recently, when Beullens, Kleinjung, and Vercauteren introduced CSI-FiSh [4]. Before that, an alternative signature scheme based on a weaker notion of HHS, named SeaSign, was presented by De Feo and Galbraith [17].

Our Contributions. We introduce threshold variants of the Couveignes–Rostovtsev–Stolbunov encryption and signature schemes, based on Shamir's secret sharing. To make the results more easily accessible to non-experts, we first present our schemes in an abstract way, using the language of HHS, and only later we analyze their instantiation using CSIDH/CSI-FiSh.

The encryption scheme is a direct adaptation of [21]; the signature scheme is similar to threshold versions of Schnorr signatures [50]. Both schemes can only be proven secure in a *honest-but-curious* security model [9]; we skip the easy proof for the encryption scheme, and we focus on the more technical one for the signature scheme, which we prove secure in a *static corruptions* model, under a generalization of the Decision Diffie-Hellman Group Action (DDHA) assumption of Stolbunov.

We conclude with an analysis of the instantiations of the schemes based on isogeny graphs, in particular on the supersingular isogeny graphs used in CSIDH and CSI-FiSh.

We view this work as an initial step towards practical threshold schemes based on HHS and isogenies. Several technical improvements, such as better security properties and proofs, are necessary before these protocols can be considered truly practical. We discuss these issues at the end of this work.

Outline. Section 2 recalls basic facts on secret sharing, threshold cryptography, and HHS. Section 3 then introduces threshold encryption and signature schemes based on HHS, and reviews their security features. In Sect. 4, we give details about the instantiation of these threshold schemes using isogeny graphs. We conclude by summarizing open problems towards practical applications of our schemes.

2 Preliminaries

We briefly recall here two fundamental constructions in group-theoretic cryptography. The first, Shamir's secret sharing [51], lets a *dealer* split a secret s into n *shares*, so that any k shares are sufficient to reconstruct s; it is a basic primitive upon which several threshold protocols can be built.

The second, Couveignes' *Hard Homogeneous Spaces* (HHS) [14], is a general framework that abstracts some isogeny protocols, and that eventually inspired CSIDH [11]. Although most popular isogeny-based primitives are not, strictly speaking, instances of HHS, the protocols introduced in this work require an instance of an HHS in the strictest sense, and will thus be presented using that formalism.

2.1 Shamir's Secret Sharing and Threshold Cryptosystems

Shamir's scheme relies on polynomial interpolation to construct a k-out-of-n threshold secret sharing, for any pair of integers $k \leq n$.

Concretely, a prime $q > n$ is chosen, and the secret s is sampled from $\mathbb{Z}/q\mathbb{Z}$. To break the secret into shares, the dealer samples random coefficients $c_1, \ldots, c_{k-1} \in \mathbb{Z}/q\mathbb{Z}$ and forms the polynomial

$$f(x) = s + \sum_{i=1}^{k-1} c_i x^i;$$

then they form the shares $s_1 = f(1), \ldots, s_n = f(n)$ and distribute them to the n participants, denoted by $\mathcal{P}_1, \ldots, \mathcal{P}_n$. We shall call i the *identifier* of a participant $\mathcal{P}_i$, and s_i his *share*.

Any k participants, but no less, can reconstruct f using Lagrange's interpolation formula, and then recover s by evaluating f at 0. Explicitly, a set of participants $\mathcal{P}_i$, with indices taken from a set $S \subset \{1, \ldots, n\}$ of cardinality at least k, can recover the secret s in a single step through the formula

$$s = f(0) = \sum_{i \in S} f(i) \cdot \prod_{\substack{j \in S \\ j \neq i}} \frac{j}{j - i}.$$

Shamir's secret sharing enjoys *perfect* or *information theoretic* security, meaning that less than k shares provide no information on the secret. Indeed, assuming that $k-1$ participants, w.l.o.g. $\mathcal{P}_1, \ldots, \mathcal{P}_{k-1}$, put their shares together, the map

$$(s, c_1, \ldots, c_{k-1}) \mapsto \big(f(0), f(1), \ldots, f(k-1)\big)$$

is, by Lagrange's formula, an isomorphism of $(\mathbb{Z}/q\mathbb{Z})$-vector spaces; hence, each tuple $\big(s = f(0), f(1), \ldots, f(k-1)\big)$ is equally likely to occur.

Threshold Schemes. A major step towards practical threshold schemes based on Shamir's secret sharing was Desmedt and Frankel's threshold variant of ElGamal decryption [21]; a similar approach to design threshold signatures was proposed by Harn [34]. Many other threshold protocols follow a similar pattern, colloquially referred to as *secret sharing in the exponents*, that we are now going to briefly recall.

Let the secret $s \in \mathbb{Z}/q\mathbb{Z}$ and the shares s_i be distributed as above. Let G be a cyclic group of order q, and let g be a generator. Assuming that discrete logarithms are hard in G, the participants' goal is to compute the *shared key* g^s without letting anyone learn the secret s. We can again use Lagrange interpolation, but this time in the exponent:

$$g^s = g^{\sum s_i \prod \frac{j}{j-i}}.$$

To make this idea into a protocol, each party computes g^{s_i} from its share s_i, and sends it to all other parties. Given at least k shares s_i of the key with $i \in S$ and $\#S \geq k$, any party can then compute the shared key as

$$g^s = \prod_{i \in S} (g^{s_i})^{L^S_{0,i}},$$

where the exponents

$$L^S_{l,i} = \prod_{\substack{j \in S \\ j \neq i}} \frac{j-l}{j-i} \quad \mod q \tag{1}$$

can be precomputed from public information.

If broadcasting the shares g^{s_i} to all participants is too expensive, an alternative is to send them to a central *combiner*, who is then in charge of computing g^s and finalizing the protocol. As we shall see later, this flexibility will be lost in our setting.

Secret Sharing in Rings. The proof of perfect security of Shamir's secret sharing scheme fundamentally relies on $\mathbb{Z}/q\mathbb{Z}$ being a field. For reasons that will become apparent later, we shall need to adapt the scheme to non-prime q, and thus to general rings of modular integers. This presents two problems: ensuring that no impossible inversions happen when computing the coefficients $L^S_{l,i}$ in Eq. (1), and proving security in the more general setting. These obstacles are not difficult to overcome, as already highlighted in, e.g., RSA-based threshold schemes [53]; we briefly explain how this is done.

Impossible inversions arise during the reconstruction of the shared secret whenever one of the denominators $(j - i)$ in Lagrange's formula is not coprime to q. If q_1 is the smallest prime factor of q, then there can be at most q_1 distinct values modulo q_1; however, any identifier i congruent to 0 modulo q_1 must be prescribed, since otherwise $f(i) \bmod q_1$ would leak information on $s \bmod q_1$. Hence, at most $q_1 - 1$ participants can take part to Shamir's scheme in $\mathbb{Z}/q\mathbb{Z}$; for example, using $1, 2, \ldots, q_1 - 1$ as identifiers ensures that no difference of two of them shares a common factor with q.

Perfect security of the scheme is also achieved by restricting the identifiers to $1, 2, \ldots, q_1 - 1$, or any other set of integers distinct and non-zero modulo all divisors of q, thus restricting the number of participants to $n < q_1$. We formally prove this below.

Proposition 1. *Let q be an integer with prime factorization $q = \prod q_i^{e_i}$. Assume q_1 is the smallest of the prime factors, let $k \leq n < q_1$, and sample $s, c_1, \ldots, c_{k-1} \in \mathbb{Z}/q\mathbb{Z}$ uniformly at random. Let*

$$f(x) = s + \sum_{i=1}^{k-1} c_i x^i$$

and let $x_1, \ldots x_{k-1} \in \mathbb{Z}/q\mathbb{Z}$ be distinct and non-zero modulo all q_i. Associate a random variable S to s, and random variables Y_i to each $f(x_i)$.

The random variables $S, Y_1, \ldots Y_{k-1}$ are independent; in particular Shamir's (k, n)-secret sharing scheme over $\mathbb{Z}/q\mathbb{Z}$ is perfectly secure, in the sense that, given the shares $f(x_1), \ldots, f(x_{k-1})$, every secret s is equally likely to have originated them.

Proof. Consider the map

$$\rho : (s, c_1, \ldots, c_{k-1}) \mapsto \big(f(0), f(x_1), \ldots, f(x_{k-1})\big);$$

since all $x_i \bmod q_j$ are distinct and non-zero, its reduction modulo q_j is an isomorphism of $\mathbb{Z}/q_j\mathbb{Z}$-vector spaces; thus, by the Chinese Remainder Theorem, ρ is an isomorphism of $\mathbb{Z}/q\mathbb{Z}$-modules.

Introducing random variables Y_0 for $f(0)$ and C_i for the c_i's, we have that

$$P\{Y_0 = f(0), Y_1 = f(x_1), \ldots, Y_{k-1} = f(x_{k-1})\}$$
$$= P\{S = s, C_1 = c_1, \ldots, C_{k-1} = c_{k-1}\} = q^{-k},$$

from which we deduce that $P\{Y_i = f(x_i)\} = q^{-1}$. In particular, since $s = f(0)$,

$$P\{S = s, Y_1 = f(x_1), \ldots, Y_{k-1} = f(x_{k-1})\}$$
$$= P\{S = s\} \cdot P\{Y_1 = f(x_1)\} \cdots P\{Y_{k-1} = f(x_{k-1})\}$$

for any $s, f(x_1), \ldots, f(x_{k-1})$, implying that S and the Y_i's are independent. $\square$

2.2   Hard Homogeneous Spaces

Hard Homogeneous Spaces (HHS) were introduced by Couveignes in [14] as a generalization of Diffie-Hellman schemes. A *principal homogeneous space*, or $\mathcal{G}$-*torsor* is a set $\mathcal{E}$ endowed with a faithful and transitive group action by a group $\mathcal{G}$.[1] In other words, it is defined by a mapping

$$\mathcal{G} \times \mathcal{E} \to \mathcal{E},$$
$$\mathfrak{g} * E = E',$$

satisfying the following properties:

- *Compatibility:* $\mathfrak{g}' * (\mathfrak{g} * E) = (\mathfrak{g}'\mathfrak{g}) * E$ for any $\mathfrak{g}, \mathfrak{g}' \in \mathcal{G}$ and $E \in \mathcal{E}$;
- *Identity:* $\mathfrak{e} * E = E$ if and only if $\mathfrak{e} \in \mathcal{G}$ is the identity element;
- *Transitivity:* for any $E, E' \in \mathcal{E}$ there exists a unique $\mathfrak{g} \in \mathcal{G}$ such that $\mathfrak{g} * E = E'$;

In particular, if $\mathcal{G}$ is finite, these axioms imply that $\#\mathcal{G} = \#\mathcal{E}$.

Couveignes defines a HHS as a finite principal homogeneous space with some additional algorithmic properties. He requires that the following problems can be solved efficiently (e.g., in polynomial time):

- *Group operations:* decide whether a string $\mathfrak{g}$ represents an element of $\mathcal{G}$, decide whether $\mathfrak{g} = \mathfrak{g}'$, compute $\mathfrak{g}^{-1}$ and $\mathfrak{g}\mathfrak{g}'$;
- *Sampling:* sample uniformly random elements from $\mathcal{G}$;
- *Membership:* decide whether a string E represents an element of $\mathcal{E}$, decide whether $E = E'$;
- *Action:* Given $\mathfrak{g}$ and E, compute $\mathfrak{g} * E$.

Furthermore, the following problems should be hard (e.g., not known to be solvable in polynomial time):

- *Vectorization:* Given $E, E' \in \mathcal{E}$, find $\mathfrak{g} \in \mathcal{G}$ such that $\mathfrak{g} * E = E'$;
- *Parallelization:* Given $E, E', F \in \mathcal{E}$, such that $E' = \mathfrak{g} * E$, find $F' = \mathfrak{g} * F$.

As a simple example, let $\mathcal{E}$ be a group of prime order q, then $\mathcal{G} = (\mathbb{Z}/q\mathbb{Z})^{\times}$ acts on $\mathcal{E} \setminus \{1\}$ by $a * g = g^a$. In this case, the Vectorization problem is the discrete logarithm problem in $\mathcal{E}$, and the Parallelization problem is the Computational Diffie–Hellman problem. Hence any discrete logarithm group is also a HHS.

Couveignes' original proposal used as HHS sets of ordinary elliptic curves over finite fields, with complex multiplication by a quadratic imaginary order $\mathcal{O}$; indeed, these are torsors for the class group $\mathrm{cl}(\mathcal{O})$, and the Vectorization and Parallelization problems are not known to be easily solvable. Based on this HHS, he defined key exchange as a straightforward generalization of the Diffie–Hellman protocol, and he also sketched an interactive identification scheme.

---

[1] The reader will excuse our extravagant font choices for set and group elements: our goal is to be consistent with the notation used in Sect. 4 for isogeny-based HHS.

However, Couveignes' proposal presents several difficulties, as neither the group action nor random sampling are known to be easily computable. Independently from Couveignes, Rostovtsev and Stolbunov [49,55] proposed a key-exchange scheme based on the same group action, but with a different representation of elements of $cl(\mathcal{O})$. This proposal had the benefit of making key-exchange feasible, if not practical, and subsequent research [18] eventually led to the development of CSIDH [11], an efficient key exchange scheme based on the action of a quadratic class group on a set of supersingular curves.

Nevertheless, none of these constructions satisfies exactly the axioms of a HHS, since, for example, the cost of evaluating $\mathfrak{g} * E$ in CSIDH is in the worst case exponential in the size of $\mathfrak{g}$. While every group element has an equivalent representation that permits to efficiently evaluate the action, computing such representation is difficult in general. This is not a problem for key-exchange schemes based on CSIDH, but, for example, it makes identification and signature schemes more involved and less efficient than what Couveignes had originally envisioned [17,19].

The roadblock in all these constructions is the fact that the structure of the class group $cl(\mathcal{O})$ is unknown, and it is thus impossible to have a unique representation for its elements. The best algorithm for computing the class group structure runs in sub-exponential time, and is thus neither practical nor scalable; nevertheless the application to isogeny-based signatures motivated Beullens, Kleinjung and Vercauteren [4] to run an intensive computation for the CSIDH-512 parameter set, which allowed them to construct CSI-FiSh, the most efficient isogeny-based signature to date.

Currently, CSI-FiSh is the only known instance of HHS based on isogenies: group elements have unique representation, the group action can be evaluated efficiently, and the Vectorization and Parallelization problems are believed to be hard, both classically and quantumly. Unfortunately, parameter generation requires exponential time in the security parameter, thus CSI-FiSh is a HHS only in a practical sense for a specific security level, but not in the asymptotic sense.

In the next sections we are going to introduce threshold schemes based on HHS; then we will give more details on CSI-FiSh, and look at how the threshold schemes can be instantiated with it.

3   Threshold Schemes from HHS

We now present threshold schemes based on Hard Homogeneous Spaces.

Let a group $\mathcal{G}$ and a set $\mathcal{E}$ be given, such that $\mathcal{G}$ acts faithfully and transitively on $\mathcal{E}$ and the HHS axioms are satisfied. We are going to require an additional property: that an element $\mathfrak{g} \in \mathcal{G}$ of order q is known, and we shall write q_1 for the smallest prime divisor of q. In particular, these hypotheses imply that there is an efficiently computable embedding $\mathbb{Z}/q\mathbb{Z} \hookrightarrow \mathcal{G}$ defined by $a \mapsto \mathfrak{g}^a$, which we are going to exploit to embed Shamir's secret sharing in the HHS.

Notation. From now on we will use capital letters $E, F, \ldots$ to denote elements of the HHS $\mathcal{E}$, and gothic letters $\mathfrak{a}, \mathfrak{b}, \mathfrak{g}, \ldots$ to denote elements of the group $\mathcal{G}$. Following [4], it will be convenient to see $\mathbb{Z}/q\mathbb{Z}$ as acting directly on $\mathcal{E}$: we will write $[a]$ for $\mathfrak{g}^a$, and $[a]E$ for $\mathfrak{g}^a * E$, where $\mathfrak{g}$ is the distinguished element of order q in $\mathcal{G}$.[2] Be wary that under this notation $[a][b]E = [a+b]E$.

Remark 1. The additional hypothesis excludes, in particular, HHS of unknown order, such as CSIDH (outside of the parameter set shared with CSI-FiSh).

Note that, assuming the factorization of q is known, given any element of $\mathcal{G}$ it is easy to test whether it is of order q. Nevertheless, in some instances it may be difficult to decide whether an element $\mathfrak{g}' \in \mathcal{G}$ belongs to $\langle \mathfrak{g} \rangle$; this may happen, for example, if $\mathcal{G} \simeq (\mathbb{Z}/q\mathbb{Z})^2$. This will not impact the protocols we define here, but is an important property to consider when designing threshold protocols in the general HHS setting. At any rate, for instantiations based on CSI-FiSh it is always easy to test membership of $\langle \mathfrak{g} \rangle$.

On the other hand, unless $\mathcal{G} = \langle \mathfrak{g} \rangle$, it is a well known hard problem (exponential in $\log q$) to decide whether given $E, E' \in \mathcal{E}$ there exists $a \in \mathbb{Z}/q\mathbb{Z}$ such that $E' = [a]E$. Indeed, a generic solution to this problem would imply an efficient generic algorithm for solving many instances of discrete logarithms [11].

We now describe a distributed algorithm to compute the group action of $\langle \mathfrak{g} \rangle$ on $\mathcal{E}$ in a threshold manner, and explain how it impacts the communication structure of threshold protocols. Then we present two simple threshold protocols, a KEM and a signature, directly adapted from their non-threshold counterparts.

3.1   Threshold Group Action

Like in Sect. 2, we assume that the participants $\mathcal{P}_1, \mathcal{P}_2, \ldots$ possess shares $s_i = f(i)$ of a secret $s \in \mathbb{Z}/q\mathbb{Z}$; their goal is to evaluate the group action $[s]E_0$ for any given $E_0 \in \mathcal{E}$, without communicating their shares s_i.

Let $S \subset \{1, \ldots, n\}$ be a set of cardinality at least k, and recall the definition of the Lagrange coefficients in Eq. (1):

$$L_{l,i}^S = \prod_{\substack{j \in S \\ j \neq i}} \frac{j-l}{j-i} \quad \bmod q.$$

Then the participants $\mathcal{P}_i$ for $i \in S$ determine the shared secret by $s = \sum_{i \in S} s_i \cdot L_{0,i}^S$. For the sake of simplicity, we will assume that $S = \{1, \ldots, k\}$.

The participants coordinate as follows. First, E_0 is sent to $\mathcal{P}_1$, who starts by computing

$$E_1 = [s_1 \cdot L_{0,1}^S]E_0.$$

The resulting E_1 is passed on to $\mathcal{P}_2$, who continues by computing

$$E_2 = [s_2 \cdot L_{0,2}^S]E_1 = [s_2 \cdot L_{0,2}^S + s_1 \cdot L_{0,1}^S]E_0.$$

---

[2] Note that this action is only transitive if $\mathfrak{g}$ generates $\mathcal{G}$.

This procedure repeats analogously for the parties $\mathcal{P}_3, ..., \mathcal{P}_{k-1}$, and at last $\mathcal{P}_k$ can compute

$$E_k = \left[s_k \cdot L_{0,k}^S \right] E_{k-1} = \left[\sum_{i \in S} s_i \cdot L_{0,i}^S \right] E_0 = [s]E_0.$$

Communication Structure. Comparing the algorithm to classical threshold Diffie-Hellman protocols as in Sect. 2.1, it is obvious that there are differences in their structures. There, each party $\mathcal{P}_i$ computes $g_i = g^{s_i}$ from its secret share s_i and a common generator g. Anyone can then compute $g_i^{L_{0,i}^S}$ for each $i \in S$, and multiply the results to obtain g^s.

In our HHS setting, the situation is different. First, $\left[s_i \cdot L_{0,i}^S \right] E$ cannot be computed from the knowledge of $[s_i]E$ and $L_{0,i}^S$, thus only $\mathcal{P}_i$ can compute it. Consequently, each participant has to know in advance the set S of parties taking part to the computation, in order to apply $L_{0,i}^S$.

Further, it is not possible to introduce a combiner, who could proceed as in the classical case by receiving the different $\left[s_i \cdot L_{0,i}^S \right] E_0$ and combining them to obtain $[s]E_0$, since in general the set $\mathcal{E}$ is not equipped with a compatible group operation $\mathcal{E} \times \mathcal{E} \to \mathcal{E}$. Therefore, it is necessary to adopt a sequential round-robin communication structure:

$$\xrightarrow{E_0,S} \mathcal{P}_1 \xrightarrow{E_1,S} \mathcal{P}_2 \xrightarrow{E_2,S} ... \xrightarrow{E_{k-1},S} \mathcal{P}_k \xrightarrow{[s]E_0} .$$

Note that the order of the $\mathcal{P}_i$ can be changed without affecting the final result.

However, this means that $\mathcal{P}_k$ is the only party who ends up knowing the result of the group action. If a cryptographic protocol needs to handle this element secretly, our algorithm is only suitable for situations where only one participant is required to know the secret result. Algorithm 1 summarizes the described approach in the general case.

Algorithm 1: Threshold variant of the group action computation.

Input : $E_0 \in \mathcal{E}$, set of participants S.
Output: $[s]E_0$.

1 Set $E \leftarrow E_0$.
2 **foreach** $i \in S$ **do**
3   If $E \notin \mathcal{E}$, participant $\mathcal{P}_i$ outputs $\perp$ and the algorithm stops.
4   Participant $\mathcal{P}_i$ outputs $E \leftarrow \left[s_i \cdot L_{0,i}^S \right] E$.
5 **return** E.

In a different setting where all participants are required to secretly know the final result, several modifications are possible. For example, when encrypted channels between the participants exist, the last participant can simply distribute through them the resulting $[s]E_0$.

Alternatively, k parallel executions of Algorithm 1, each arranging the participants in a different order, let all participants know the final result. The cost of this modification is rather high: $O(k^2)$ elements of $\mathcal{E}$ need to be transmitted, and $O(k^2)$ group actions evaluated. This can be improved to $O(k \log k)$ transmitted elements of $\mathcal{E}$ (but still $O(k^2)$ group actions) using a binary splitting strategy.

Remark 2. Algorithm 1 does nothing to prevent corrupted participants from leading to an incorrect output. While threshold schemes based on discrete logarithms can often detect and correct malicious behavior (using, e.g., error correcting codes [32]), this is more difficult for HHS. Indeed, there seems to be no way for a participant to verify the previous participant's output in Algorithm 1, outside of generic zero-knowledge techniques.

3.2   Threshold HHS ElGamal Decryption

The first application we present for our threshold group action is *threshold decryption*, a direct adaptation of [21].

Inspired by the classical ElGamal encryption scheme [26], a PKE protocol in the HHS settings was first introduced by Stolbunov [49,55,56]. We briefly recall it here, using the terminology of KEMs.

Public parameters: A HHS $(\mathcal{E}, \mathcal{G})$, a *starting element* $E_0 \in \mathcal{E}$, and a hash function H from $\mathcal{E}$ to $\{0,1\}^\lambda$.

Keygen: Sample a secret key $\mathfrak{a} \in \mathcal{G}$, output $\mathfrak{a}$ and the public key $E_a = \mathfrak{a} * E_0$.

Encaps: Sample $\mathfrak{b} \in \mathcal{G}$, output $K = H(\mathfrak{b} * E_a)$ and $E_b = \mathfrak{b} * E_0$.

Decaps: Given E_b, if $E_b \in \mathcal{E}$ output $K = H(\mathfrak{a} * E_b)$, otherwise output $\perp$.

The **Decaps** routine is easily adapted into a threshold algorithm requiring k participants to collaborate in order to recover the decryption key K. This also requires modifying **Keygen**, which must now be executed by a trusted dealer and integrate Shamir's secret sharing.

Public parameters: A HHS $(\mathcal{E}, \mathcal{G})$ with a distinguished element $\mathfrak{g} \in \mathcal{G}$ of order q, a *starting element* $E_0 \in \mathcal{E}$, and a hash function H from $\mathcal{E}$ to $\{0,1\}^\lambda$.

Keygen:
  – Sample a secret $s \in \mathbb{Z}/q\mathbb{Z}$ and generate shares $s_i \in \mathbb{Z}/q\mathbb{Z}$ using Shamir's secret sharing;
  – Distribute privately s_i to participant $\mathcal{P}_i$;
  – Output public key $E_a = [s]E_0$.

Encaps: Sample $\mathfrak{b} \in \mathcal{G}$, output $K = H(\mathfrak{b} * E_a)$ and $E_b = \mathfrak{b} * E_0$.

Decaps: Given E_b and a set S of participants, $\#S \geq k$, run Algorithm 1 to compute $E = [s]E_b$; output $\perp$ if the algorithm returns $\perp$, otherwise output $K = H(E)$.

The asymmetry of the scheme will not be lost on the reader: while the shared secret for the threshold group is restricted to be in $\langle \mathfrak{g} \rangle$, there are no restrictions for **Encaps**. Although it would be completely possible (maybe even desirable for practical reasons) to restrict secrets to $\langle \mathfrak{g} \rangle$ also in the encapsulation, we do not do so because there is no known way for decapsulation to test whether E_b has been generated this way.

It is clear that this scheme achieves the stated goal of threshold decryption: upon receiving a ciphertext, at least k participants must agree to decrypt in order to recover the key K; only the last participant in the chain learns K. If less than k participants agree to decrypt, the key K cannot be recovered; however this security property is only guaranteed when all participants behave honestly.

When allowing for corruptions, the scheme immediately becomes broken. Indeed in Algorithm 1, when a participant beyond the first receives an input, they are unable to link it to the ciphertext E_b. This makes it possible to trick an unwilling participant $\mathcal{P}$ into helping decrypt a message: let c be such a message, a group of $k-1$ participants only has to wait for a message c' that $\mathcal{P}$ is willing to decrypt; when $\mathcal{P}$ agrees, they submit to it an intermediate value of a computation for c, which $\mathcal{P}$ is unable to distinguish from one for c'. Contrast this to the original El Gamal threshold decryption of Desmedt and Frankel [21], where each participant performs its computation directly on the input.

Because of this, the security of the protocol can only be proven in a *honest-but-curious* model. We skip the easy security proof, and leave the search for more refined threshold decryption protocols for future work.

3.3   Threshold Signatures

An identification scheme in the HHS framework was first sketched by Couveignes [14]; in his PhD thesis [56] Stolbunov also suggested applying the Fiat-Shamir transform [29] to it to obtain a signature scheme. Nevertheless these schemes stood out of reach until recently, when the class group computation for CSIDH-512 was completed [4]; CSI-FiSh is effectively Stolbunov's scheme, combined with optimizations introduced in SeaSign [17].

CSI-FiSh and its ancestors can be easily adapted into threshold protocols. We start by recalling the basic interactive zero-knowledge identification scheme: a prover Peggy wants to convince a verifier Vic that she knows a secret element $\mathfrak{a} \in \mathcal{G}$ such that $E_a = \mathfrak{a} * E_0$. They proceed as follows:

- Peggy samples a random $\mathfrak{b} \in \mathcal{G}$ and commits to $E_b = \mathfrak{b} * E_0$.
- Vic challenges with a random bit $c \in \{0,1\}$.
- If $c = 0$, Peggy replies with $\mathfrak{z} = \mathfrak{b}$; otherwise she replies with $\mathfrak{z} = \mathfrak{b}\mathfrak{a}^{-1}$.
- If $c = 0$, Vic verifies that $\mathfrak{z} * E_0 = E_b$; otherwise, he verifies that $\mathfrak{z} * E_a = E_b$.

It is immediately seen that the scheme is correct, thanks to the properties of homogeneous spaces, and that it has soundness $1/2$. For the zero-knowledge property, it is crucial that elements in $\mathcal{G}$ can be sampled uniformly, and that they have unique representation. See [4,17,56] for detailed proofs.

We now adapt this scheme into a threshold signature by applying the Fiat-Shamir transform and Shamir's secret sharing as before.

We let again $(\mathcal{E}, \mathcal{G})$ be a HHS with a distinguished element $\mathfrak{g}$ of order q, we fix a starting element $E_0 \in \mathcal{E}$, and a hash function $H : \{0,1\}^* \to \{0,1\}^\lambda$. We assume that a trusted dealer has sampled a random secret $s \in \mathbb{Z}/q\mathbb{Z}$, securely distributed shares s_i to the participants $\mathcal{P}_i$, and published the public key $E_s = [s]E_0$.

Here is a sketch of how participants $\mathcal{P}_1, \dots, \mathcal{P}_k$ can cooperate to sign a message m:

- In the commitment phase, the participants collaborate to produce a random element $[b]E_0$ in a way similar to Algorithm 1, by producing each a random value $b_i \in \mathbb{Z}/q\mathbb{Z}$ and evaluating $E_i = [b_i]E_{i-1}$.
- Once $E_k = [b]E_0$ is computed, the challenge bit c is obtained from the hash $H(E_k, m)$.
- If $c = 0$, each $\mathcal{P}_i$ outputs $z_i = b_i$, else each $\mathcal{P}_i$ outputs $z_i = b_i - s_i \cdot L_{0,i}^S$.
- The signature is $(c, z = \sum z_i)$.

To verify the signature it suffices to check that $H([z]E_0, m) = 0 \ldots$, if $c = 0$, or that $H([z]E_s, m) = 1 \ldots$, if $c = 1$. Of course, this sketch must be repeated λ times, in order to ensure the appropriate level of security.

The complete signing algorithm is summarized in Algorithm 2. As presented there, it is rather inefficient in terms of signature size and signing/verification time. All the key/signature size compromises presented in CSI-FiSh [4] are compatible with our threshold adaptation, and would produce a more efficient signature scheme. The details are left to the reader.

Security Analysis. We conclude with a study of the security of the threshold signature scheme. Like the other schemes presented here, it is only secure against (static) honest-but-curious adversaries; however the security proof is more technical, and we give it in more detail. Since our threshold signature has the same public key and produces the same signatures as the Stolbunov/CSI-FiSh non-threshold scheme, we are able to use Gennaro et al.'s security model [32], with the appropriate modifications to handle a trusted dealer. In a nutshell, security in this model is proven by showing that the transcript of the threshold protocol can be simulated given only the signature, even in presence of up to $k-1$ corrupted participants; then, security follows from the unforgeability of the non-threshold signature scheme. We start with a brief description of the model.

Communication model. We assume the n participants $\mathcal{P}_1, \dots, \mathcal{P}_n$ have access to a broadcast channel they use to exchange messages when executing the signature protocol. On top of that, each participant has access to a private channel with the trusted dealer $\mathcal{T}$, that they use to receive the secret shares.

The adversary. We consider a *static honest-but-curious* adversary, i.e., one that chooses up to $k-1$ players to corrupt at the beginning of the unforgeability game, and then observes all their communications, including the secret shares received from the dealer; other than that, all parties strictly follow the protocol. In the literature, this type of adversary is often also called *semi-honest* or *passive*.

Algorithm 2: Threshold HHS signature.

Input   : Message m, participant set S.
Output: A signature on m.

1 Set $(E_1^0, \ldots, E_\lambda^0) \leftarrow (E_0, \ldots, E_0)$.
2 Let $k \leftarrow 0$.
3 **foreach** $i \in S$ **do**
4 $\quad$ Let $k \leftarrow k + 1$.
5 $\quad$ **foreach** $1 \leq j \leq \lambda$ **do**
6 $\quad\quad$ If $E_j \notin \mathcal{E}$, participant $\mathcal{P}_i$ outputs $\perp$ and aborts the protocol.
7 $\quad\quad$ $\mathcal{P}_i$ samples $b_{i,j} \in \mathbb{Z}/q\mathbb{Z}$ uniformly at random.
8 $\quad\quad$ $\mathcal{P}_i$ outputs $E_j^k \leftarrow [b_{i,j}]E_j^{k-1}$.

9 Let $c_1 \cdots c_\lambda \leftarrow H(E_1^k, \ldots, E_\lambda^k, m)$.
10 **foreach** $i \in S$ **do**
11 $\quad$ **foreach** $1 \leq j \leq \lambda$ **do**
12 $\quad\quad$ **if** $c_j = 0$ **then**
13 $\quad\quad\quad$ $\mathcal{P}_i$ outputs $z_{i,j} = b_{i,j}$.
14 $\quad\quad$ **else**
15 $\quad\quad\quad$ $\mathcal{P}_i$ outputs $z_{i,j} = b_{i,j} - s_i \cdot L_{0,i}^S$.

16 **foreach** $1 \leq j \leq \lambda$ **do**
17 $\quad$ Let $z_j = \sum_{i \in S} z_{i,j}$.
18 **return** the signature $(c_1 \cdots c_\lambda, z_1, \ldots, z_\lambda)$.

The *view* of an adversary is the probability distribution on the transcript of all the information seen by it during the protocol execution: this includes secret shares, the message m to sign, the messages received from other parties, and the resulting signature.

Unforgeability. A threshold signature scheme is *unforgeable* if no polynomial-time adversary $\mathcal{A}$ can produce a signature for a previously unsigned message m, given the view of $\mathcal{A}$ for adaptively chosen messages $m_1, \ldots, m_Q$. This definition is analogous to the usual notion of UF-CMA. In other words, this means that $\mathcal{A}$ does not learn enough information from transcripts of protocol executions to forge a valid signature.

Simulatability. Gennaro et al. proved that a threshold signature scheme is unforgeable if the underlying signature scheme is, and the threshold scheme is *simulatable*. This is defined as there being a polynomial time *simulator* $\mathcal{S}$ that takes as input a message m, the public key E_s, a valid signature on m, and the shares of the corrupted participants, and outputs transcripts that are computationally indistinguishable from the view of the adversary. Intuitively, this means that the adversary gains no more information from seeing the transcript, than from the signature alone.

The trusted dealer. Unlike the threshold scheme of Gennaro et al., our signature does not feature a distributed key generation. We thus adopt a hybrid model, where the generation of the trusted shares is modeled by an ideal functionality $\mathcal{F}_T$, that executes Shamir's secret sharing, publishes the public key, and distributes the secret shares to each participant through the private channel.

In particular, the adversary is not able to tamper with $\mathcal{F}_T$, and the distinguisher has no knowledge of the master secret generated by it.

We will prove simulatability under a new assumption, that we call *Power-DDHA*. This decision version of the *Scalar-HHS* problem of Felderhoff [28] is a generalization of the Decision Diffie–Hellman Group Action (DDHA) introduced by Stolbunov [55], and is related to the *P*-DDH assumption introduced by Kiltz for discrete logarithm groups [38].

Problem 1 (Power-DDHA problem). Let $(\mathcal{E}, \mathcal{G})$ be a HHS. Let $E \in \mathcal{E}$ and $1 < a < \#\mathcal{G}$ an integer; let $\mathfrak{s}$ be a uniformly random element in $\mathcal{G}$. The *a-Power-DDHA problem* is: given $(a, E, \mathfrak{s} * E, F)$, where $F \in \mathcal{E}$ is an element, either sampled from the uniform distribution on $\mathcal{E}$, or $F = \mathfrak{s}^a * E$, decide from which distribution F is drawn.

Remark 3. The special case of (-1)-Power-DDHA where the HHS is instantiated with a graph of $\mathbb{F}_p$-isomorphism classes of supersingular curves, and E is the special curve $E : y^2 = x^3 + x$, is known to be solvable efficiently. Other "special" curves in the graph also enjoy this property, see [12].

This obstacle is easy, but tedious, to circumvent in the proof of the next theorem. We leave the details to the reader.

Felderhoff proved that the search version of Power-DDHA (Scalar-HHS) is equivalent to Parallelization whenever the order of $\mathcal{G}$ is known and odd [28]. We also recall the formal definition of the Vectorization problem, also known as *Group Action Inverse Problem* [55].

Problem 2 (GAIP). Let $(\mathcal{E}, \mathcal{G})$ be a HHS, let E, F be uniformly random elements of $\mathcal{E}$. The *Group Action Inverse Problem* asks to compute $\mathfrak{a} \in \mathcal{G}$ such that $E = \mathfrak{a} * F$.

It is clear that GAIP is harder than Power-DDHA: given a GAIP solver one can simply apply it to $(E, \mathfrak{s} * E)$, and then use the answer to solve Power-DDHA.

Theorem 1. *Under the Power-DDHA assumption, the signature scheme of Algorithm 2 is simulatable.*

Stolbunov's signature scheme is proven secure in the ROM under GAIP (see [4,17,56]); since GAIP is harder than Power-DDHA, we immediately get the following theorem.

Corollary 1. *Under the Power-DDHA assumption, the signature scheme of Algorithm 2 is unforgeable, when the hash function H is modeled as a random oracle.*

Proof of Theorem 1. Observe that the public key $E_s = [s]E_0$ uniquely determines s; but that, together with the $k - 1$ corrupted shares, uniquely determines the polynomial f in Shamir's secret sharing, and thus all other shares. We shall denote by $s_1, \ldots, s_n$ these uniquely determined shares, note however that the simulator only knows the corrupted ones.

Let $(c_1 \cdots c_\lambda, z_1, \ldots, z_\lambda)$ be a signature, and let S be the set of k signers (who signs a given message is decided by the adversary). To simulate a transcript, the simulator draws integers $z_{i_1,j}, \ldots, z_{i_{k-1},j} \in \mathbb{Z}/q\mathbb{Z}$ at random, for any $1 \le j \le \lambda$, and sets $z_{i_k,j} = z_j - z_{i_1,j} - \cdots - z_{i_{k-1},j}$. Since z_j is uniformly distributed, it is clear all $z_{i,j}$ also are. These values make the second part of the transcript (lines 12–15 in Algorithm 2).

To complete the transcript, the simulator now needs to output commitments $E_j^{k_i}$ (line 8), where for each $i \in S$ we denote by $1 \le k_i < k$ the position of i in S. We start with the case where S contains only one uncorrupted participant, which can be simulated perfectly.

If $c_j = 0$ the simulator simply sets

$$E_j^{k_i} = [b_{k_1,j} + b_{k_2,j} + \cdots + b_{k_i,j}]E_0 = [z_{k_1,j} + z_{k_2,j} + \cdots + z_{k_i,j}]E_0,$$

as in Algorithm 2. If $c_j = 1$, define the sequence

$$E_s^0 = E_0,$$
$$E_s^{k_i} = \left[s_i \cdot L_{0,i}^S\right]E_s^{k_i-1},$$

so that $E_s = E_s^k$. The simulator can compute all curves $E_s^{k_i}$ as follows: assume the uncorrupted participant $\mathcal{P}_i$ is in position k_i in S, for any $k' < k_i$ it computes $E_s^{k'}$ *directly*:

$$E_s^{k'} = \left[\sum_{i \in S, k_i \le k'} s_i \cdot L_{0,i}^S\right]E_0,$$

whereas for all $k' \ge k_i$ it computes it *backwards* from E_s:

$$E_s^{k'} = \left[\sum_{i \in S, k_i > k'} -s_i \cdot L_{0,i}^S\right]E_s.$$

Then, the commitments are computed as

$$E_j^{k_i} = [z_{k_1,j} + z_{k_2,j} + \cdots + z_{k_i,j}]E_s^{k_i},$$

which is immediately seen as being the same as in Algorithm 2, thanks to $b_{i,j} = z_{i,j} + s_i \cdot L_{0,i}^S$. An example of this computation where participants $\mathcal{P}_1$ and $\mathcal{P}_3$ are corrupted and participant $\mathcal{P}_2$ is not is pictured in Fig. 1.

Because all the choices are uniquely determined once the values $z_{i,j}$ have been chosen, it is clear that this transcript is perfectly indistinguishable from a real one, even for a computationally unbounded distinguisher.

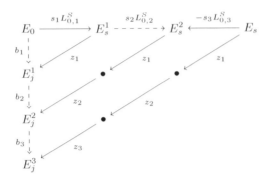

Fig. 1. Recomputation of $E_j^{k_i}$ given $z_{i,j}$.

We are left with the case where the set S contains more than one uncorrupted participant; in this case, we will resort to random sampling. For simplicity, we will assume that sets S are always sorted in increasing order, so that the relative order of the participants' actions does not change from one signature to another.

Like above, we start one *direct* chain from E_0, and one *backwards* from E_s; both chains stop when they encounter an uncorrupted participant $\mathcal{P}_i$. Now, let $E_s^{k_i-1}$ be the last curve in the *direct* chain, we set the next curve $E_s^{k_i} = [r_i]E_0$, where r_i is sampled uniformly from $\mathbb{Z}/q\mathbb{Z}$. We also store r_i in association with S, and keep it for reuse the next time the adversary queries for the set S.

We continue the *direct* chain from $E_s^{k_i}$, either using the knowledge of $s_i \cdot L_{0,i}^S$ for corrupted participants, or sampling a random r_i for uncorrupted ones; we stop when we meet the *backwards* chain. An example of this process is pictured below:

$$E_0 \xrightarrow{\;r_1\;} \mathbf{E_s^1} \xrightarrow{\;s_2 L_{0,2}^S\;} E_s^2 \xrightarrow{\;r_3\;} \mathbf{E_s^3} \dashrightarrow E_s^4 \xrightarrow{\;s_4 L_{0,4}^S\;} E_s$$

we write in bold data that is obtained through random sampling; the value r_4 is implicitly determined by the other four values. After we have determined this data, we compute the $E_j^{k_i}$'s and complete the transcript as before.

Now, this transcript is no longer indistinguishable from the real view of the adversary, however we argue that it still is computationally indistinguishable assuming Power-DDHA. Indeed, when $c_j = 1$, the distinguisher is able to recover $E_s^{k_i}$ from $E_j^{k_i}$ as $E_s^{k_i} = [-z_{k_1,j} - z_{k_2,j} - \cdots - z_{k_i,j}]E_j^{k_i}$. This means that the distinguisher will collect many pairs of the form $\left(E, \left[s_i \cdot L_{0,i}^S\right]E\right)$ (in queries where $\mathcal{P}_i$ is the only uncorrupted participant in S), and many others of the form $(E', [r_i]E')$ (where the expected relation would be $\left(E', \left[s_i \cdot L_{0,i}^{S'}\right]E'\right)$ instead). In general, it will be the case that $E' = [b]E$ for some $b \in \mathbb{Z}/q\mathbb{Z}$ not necessarily known to the distinguisher; however, by subtracting known factors coming from corrupted players, the distinguisher can reduce to a distinguishing problem between $([\sum s_i']E_0, [\sum s_i' a_i]E_0)$ and $([\sum s_i']E_0, [r]E_0)$, where the s_i' are unknowns related to uncorrupted shares s_i, the a_i are known (and possibly 0), and r is random. This is an instance of a problem more general than Power-DDHA, and is thus at least as hard as Power-DDHA.

Hence, assuming Power-DDHA is hard, no polynomial time algorithm can distinguish between the simulated transcript and the real interaction, thus proving that the threshold scheme is simulatable.   □

Remark 4. It is evident from the proof that the security of the (n, n)-threshold signature scheme can be proven without assuming Power-DDHA. The appearance of this surprising assumption seems an artifact related to the limitations of the HHS framework; indeed, the analogous scheme based on discrete logarithms can be proven as hard as standard Schnorr signatures without additional assumptions [54]. We hope that further research will improve the state of security proofs for HHS threshold schemes.

Remark 5. Although our scheme is unforgeable in a (static) honest-but-curious model, it is obviously *non-robust*: any participant can lead to an invalid signature without being detected. Robustness can be added using generic zero-knowledge techniques, however it would be interesting to achieve it in a more efficient bespoke fashion.

Another desirable improvement would be to prove security in a stronger *adaptive* corruptions model, where the adversary can query the signing oracle before choosing which participants to corrupt.

4   Instantiations Based on Isogeny Graphs

We now describe an instantiation of the previous schemes based on a principal homogeneous space of supersingular elliptic curves defined over a finite field $\mathbb{F}_p$.

It was first observed by Delfs and Galbraith [20] that the set of all supersingular curves defined over a prime field $\mathbb{F}_p$ partitions into one or two *levels*, each level being a principal homogeneous space for the class group of an order of the quadratic imaginary field $\mathbb{Q}(\sqrt{-p})$, in a way analogous to the well known theory of *complex multiplication*.

These principal homogeneous spaces were first used for a cryptographic purpose in the key-exchange scheme CSIDH [11], however only the precomputation performed recently by Beullens *et al.* for the signature scheme CSI-FiSh [4] permits to turn one of these into a true HHS.

We now briefly recall some key facts on CSIDH and CSI-FiSh, before turning to the instantiation of our threshold schemes. More details on the mathematical background of isogeny-based cryptography can be found in [16].

4.1   Supersingular Complex Multiplication

From now on we let p be a prime, $\mathbb{F}_p$ the field with p elements, and $\bar{\mathbb{F}}_p$ an algebraic closure. An elliptic curve E defined over $\mathbb{F}_p$ is said to be *supersingular* if and only if $\#E(\mathbb{F}_p) = p + 1$. It is well known that there are approximately

$p/12$ isomorphism classes of supersingular curves, all defined over $\mathbb{F}_{p^2}$; of these, $O(\sqrt{p})$ are defined over $\mathbb{F}_p$.

Let E be a supersingular curve defined over $\mathbb{F}_p$, an *endomorphism* is an isogeny from E to itself, and it is said to be *defined over* $\mathbb{F}_p$ (or $\mathbb{F}_p$-rational) if it commutes with the *Frobenius endomorphism* π. The $\mathbb{F}_p$-rational endomorphisms of E form a ring, denoted by $\mathrm{End}_{\mathbb{F}_p}(E)$, isomorphic to an order[3] of $\mathbb{Q}(\sqrt{-p})$; more precisely, it is isomorphic to either $\mathbb{Z}[\sqrt{-p}]$ or $\mathbb{Z}[(\sqrt{-p}+1)/2]$. Let $\mathcal{O}$ be such an order, the *class group* $\mathrm{cl}(\mathcal{O})$ is the quotient of the group of invertible ideals of $\mathcal{O}$ by the group of its principal ideals; it is a finite abelian group.

The set of all supersingular curves with $\mathrm{End}_{\mathbb{F}_p}(E)$ isomorphic to a given order $\mathcal{O} \subset \mathbb{Q}(\sqrt{-p})$ is called the *horizontal isogeny class* associated to $\mathcal{O}$. A straightforward extension to the theory of complex multiplication states that the horizontal isogeny class of $\mathcal{O}$, up to $\mathbb{F}_p$-isomorphism, is a principal homogeneous space for $\mathrm{cl}(\mathcal{O})$. To make this into a HHS, an efficient (e.g., polynomial in $\log(p)$) algorithm to evaluate the action of $\mathrm{cl}(\mathcal{O})$ is needed. This is where isogenies play an important role. Fix an isomorphism $\mathrm{End}_{\mathbb{F}_p}(E) \simeq \mathcal{O}$, for any invertible ideal $\mathfrak{a}$, the action $\mathfrak{a} * E$ can be computed as follows: first define the $\mathfrak{a}$-*torsion* subgroup of E as

$$E[\mathfrak{a}] = \{P \in E(\bar{\mathbb{F}}_p) \mid \alpha(P) = 0 \text{ for all } \alpha \in \mathfrak{a}\},$$

this is a finite subgroup of E, and it is stabilized by the Frobenius endomorphism π; then the unique isogeny $\phi : E \to E/\langle E[\mathfrak{a}]\rangle$ with kernel $E[\mathfrak{a}]$ is such that $\mathfrak{a} * E = E/\langle E[\mathfrak{a}]\rangle$. It follows that, if $\mathfrak{a}$ and $\mathfrak{b}$ are two ideals in the same class, i.e., such that $\mathfrak{a} = (\alpha) \cdot \mathfrak{b}$ for some element $\alpha \in \mathcal{O}$, then $E/\langle E[\mathfrak{a}]\rangle \simeq E/\langle E[\mathfrak{b}]\rangle$.

The curve $E/\langle E[\mathfrak{a}]\rangle$ can be efficiently computed using an isogeny evaluation algorithm [27,57], however the complexity of this operation is polynomial in the degree of the isogeny, or, equivalently, in the norm $N(\mathfrak{a}) = \#(\mathcal{O}/\mathfrak{a})$. This implies that the action of an element $\mathfrak{a} \in \mathrm{cl}(\mathcal{O})$ can only be efficiently computed when a representative of small norm of $\mathfrak{a}$ is known, or, more generally, when a decomposition

$$\mathfrak{a} = \prod_i \mathfrak{l}_i$$

with all $\mathfrak{l}_i$ of small norm is known.

Now, for any prime ℓ, the ideal $(\ell) \subset \mathcal{O}$ is either prime, or it splits into a product of two (possibly equal) conjugate prime ideals $\mathfrak{l}\bar{\mathfrak{l}} = (\ell)$ of norm ℓ. In the former case, there are no invertible ideals of norm ℓ in $\mathcal{O}$; in the latter, $\mathfrak{l}$ and $\bar{\mathfrak{l}}$ are the only ideals of norm ℓ, and they are the inverse of one another in $\mathrm{cl}(\mathcal{O})$. Asymptotically, about 50% of the primes ℓ split, thus we may hope to form a basis of generators of $\mathrm{cl}(\mathcal{O})$ of norms bounded by polylog(p), such that any element of $\mathrm{cl}(\mathcal{O})$ can be represented as a product of polylog(p) elements of the basis.[4]

This representation for the elements of $\mathrm{cl}(\mathcal{O})$ using a *smooth basis* is at the heart of the Couveignes–Rostovtsev–Stolbunov key exchange scheme, and of

---

[3] In this context, an order is a $\mathbb{Z}$-module isomorphic to $\mathbb{Z} \oplus \omega\mathbb{Z} \simeq \mathbb{Z}[\omega]$ for some $\omega \notin \mathbb{Q}$.

[4] Jao, Miller and Venkatesan [37] showed that it is indeed possible to bound the norms by $O(\log^2(p))$, assuming the Generalized Riemann Hypothesis.

CSIDH. However, having a smooth basis may not be enough: to have a HHS, one still needs to be able to rewrite any element of $cl(\mathcal{O})$ as a compact product of smooth elements. This is the key difference between CSIDH and CSI-FiSh, as we shall see next.

4.2 CSIDH and CSI-FiSh

CSIDH was designed to make evaluating the group action of $cl(\mathcal{O})$ as efficient as possible. To this end, a prime p of the form

$$p + 1 = 4 \prod_{i=1}^{n} \ell_i$$

is selected, where $\ell_1, \ldots, \ell_{n-1}$ are the first $n-1$ odd primes, and ℓ_n is chosen so to make p prime. This choice guarantees several desirable properties:

- The curve $E \; : \; y^2 = x^3 + x$ has $\mathbb{F}_p$-rational endomorphism ring isomorphic to $\mathbb{Z}[\pi]$, where $\pi = \sqrt{-p}$ is the image of the Frobenius endomorphism of E;
- All curves in the horizontal isogeny class of $\mathbb{Z}[\pi]$ can be written in the form $y^2 = x^3 + Ax^2 + x$, and the coefficient A uniquely characterizes the $\mathbb{F}_p$-isomorphism class;
- All ℓ_i split in $\mathbb{Z}[\pi]$ as $(\ell_i) = \mathfrak{l}_i \bar{\mathfrak{l}}_i = \langle \ell_i, \pi - 1 \rangle \cdot \langle \ell_i, \pi + 1 \rangle$;
- For any curve E, the $\mathfrak{l}_i$-torsion subgroup is easily found as $E[\mathfrak{l}_i] = E[\ell_i] \cap E(\mathbb{F}_p)$.

The first two properties ensure that supersingular isomorphism classes are easy to construct and represent uniquely, the third guarantees[5] that a number exponential in n of ideal classes of $\mathbb{Z}[\pi]$ can be efficiently represented and its action evaluated, the fourth enables some important optimizations for computing isogenies of degree ℓ_i.

In CSIDH and optimized variants [13,41,42,44], all ideal classes are implicitly represented as products

$$\mathfrak{a} = \prod_{i=1}^{n} \mathfrak{l}_i^{e_i},$$

with the exponents e_i in some box $[-B_i, B_i]$ (negative exponents are interpreted as powers of $\bar{\mathfrak{l}}_i$). Explicitly, the representation of an ideal class $\mathfrak{a}$ is simply the vector of exponents $(e_1, \ldots, e_n)$. The action of such ideals can be evaluated in time $poly(B_i, e_i, n)$ using isogeny formulas.

In practice, a single parameter set has been fully specified for CSIDH, corresponding to the NIST post-quantum level 1.[6] The set has $n = 74$, $\ell_{73} = 373$, and $\ell_{74} = 587$, yielding a prime p of approximately 512 bits; we shall refer to it as CSIDH-512. Protocols based on CSIDH-512 usually sample exponents in

---

[5] This guarantee is only heuristic: it is possible, although unlikely, that all $\mathfrak{l}_i$ have small order in $cl(\mathbb{Z}[\pi])$, and thus generate a small subgroup.

[6] NIST defines the security of level 1 as being equivalent to AES-128.

a box $[-5, 5]$, which heuristically covers almost all the class group, and which permits to evaluate one class group action in under 30 ms [42].

However, based on this data only, CSIDH is *not* a HHS. Indeed, all axioms of an HHS are satisfied but two: it is not possible to efficiently evaluate the action of *any* element of $cl(\mathbb{Z}[\pi])$, and it is not always possible to test equality of two elements of $cl(\mathbb{Z}[\pi])$. Take for example the exponent vector $(2^{128}, 0, \ldots, 0)$, corresponding to the ideal $\mathfrak{a} = \langle 3, \pi - 1 \rangle^{2^{128}}$; this is a valid element of $cl(\mathbb{Z}[\pi])$, however without further knowledge its action can only be evaluated through 2^{128} isogeny evaluations. Hopefully, $\mathfrak{a}$ has an equivalent representation on the basis $\mathfrak{l}_1, \ldots, \mathfrak{l}_n$ with much smaller exponents, however we have no way to compute it and, even if we were given it, we could not test their equality.

These problems go away once we have computed the group structure of $cl(\mathbb{Z}[\pi])$. More precisely, we need to know the *relation lattice* of $\mathfrak{l}_1, \ldots, \mathfrak{l}_n$, i.e., the lattice

$$\Lambda = \left\{ (e_1, \ldots, e_n) \;\middle|\; \prod_{i=0}^{n} \mathfrak{l}_i^{e_i} = 1 \right\},$$

which yields a representation of the class group as $cl(\mathbb{Z}[\pi]) \simeq \mathbb{Z}^n / \Lambda$. Now, equality of two exponent vectors $\boldsymbol{e}, \boldsymbol{f}$ can be tested by checking that $\boldsymbol{e} - \boldsymbol{f} \in \Lambda$, and any exponent vector $\boldsymbol{e}$ can be evaluated efficiently by finding an (approximate) closest vector $\boldsymbol{f} \in \Lambda$ and evaluating $\boldsymbol{e} - \boldsymbol{f}$ instead.

Neither computing the relation lattice, nor computing a good reduced basis for it are easy tasks: the former requires subexponential time in $\log(p)$, and the latter exponential time in n.[7] Nevertheless, the computation for the CSIDH-512 parameter set happens to be just within reach of contemporary computers, as proven by Beullens *et al.* [4]: they managed to compute the structure of the class group, which happens to be cyclic of order

$$\#cl(\mathbb{Z}[\pi]) = 3 \cdot 37 \cdot 1407181 \cdot 51593604295295867744293584889 \cdot$$
$$31599414504681995853008278745587832204909 \approx 2^{257.136}, \tag{2}$$

and a BKZ-reduced basis for the relation lattice. In particular, they found out that the ideal $\mathfrak{l}_1 = \langle 3, \pi - 1 \rangle$ generates $cl(\mathbb{Z}[\pi])$.

Thanks to CSI-FiSh, we thus dispose of a HHS with quantum security estimated at the NIST-1 security level, although scaling to higher security levels currently looks problematic.

4.3 Instantiation of the Threshold Schemes

Given the CSI-FiSh data, we can now instantiate our threshold schemes. However, it is evident by Eq. (2) that the full group $\langle \mathfrak{l}_1 \rangle = cl(\mathbb{Z}[\pi])$ is not suitable for them, because the smallest prime factor of its order is 3, thus limiting the schemes to just 2 participants. We may instead choose as generator $\mathfrak{l}_1^3$, which

---

[7] Using a quantum computer, the relation lattice can be computed in polynomial time, however lattice reduction still requires exponential time.

limits the schemes to 36 participants, or $\mathfrak{l}_1^{111}$, allowing more than a million participants.[8]

Efficiency. The performance of our schemes can be readily inferred from that of the CSI-FiSh signature scheme.

To evaluate the action of an ideal in $\mathrm{cl}(\mathbb{Z}[\pi])$, CSI-FiSh first solves an approximate closest vector problem using Babai's nearest plane algorithm [1], and an algorithm by Doulgerakis, Laarhoven and de Weger [25]; then uses the isogeny evaluation algorithm of CSIDH. The average cost for one evaluation is reported to be $135.3 \cdot 10^6$ cycles (40–50 ms on a commercial CPU), which is only 15% slower than the original CSIDH evaluation.[9]

In the encryption scheme, each participant computes exactly one class group action. Since the participants must do their computations sequentially, the total time for decryption is multiplied by the number of participants; the time for encryption, on the other hand, is unaffected by the number of participants, indeed the threshold nature of the protocol is transparent to the user.

In the signature scheme, using the optimization described in [4], depending on the choice of parameters each participant computes between 6 and 56 group actions. Since the group action largely dominates the cost of the whole signing algorithm, we can expect to complete a (k, n)-threshold signature in approximately $k \cdot t \cdot 135.3 \cdot 10^6$ cycles, where $6 \leq t \leq 56$. However, the t group actions by a each participant are independent and can be computed in parallel; since the round-robin evaluation in the threshold scheme leaves plenty of idle cycles for participants while they wait for other participants' results, by carefully staggering the threshold group evaluations the k participants can evaluate the t group actions with the same efficiency as the non-threshold scheme, as long as $k \leq t$. According to [4, Tables 3, 4], this would provide, for example, quantum-resistant threshold signatures for up to 16 participants in under 1 s, with public keys of 4 KB and signature size of only 560 B. Another example are 1880 B signatures with public key size of 128 B and k up to 56 in under 3 s; other interesting compromises are possible. These numbers compare favorably to other post-quantum threshold signatures that are expected to run in seconds [15], and may be especially interesting for side-channel protected implementations of CSI-FiSh.

Attacks. The security of the threshold schemes is essentially the same as that of the original single-participant signature and encryption schemes.

---

[8] An alternative way to allow up to 36 participants is to use the action of $\mathrm{cl}(\mathbb{Z}[(\pi + 1)/2])$ on the horizontal isogeny class of $y^2 = x^3 - x$: the class group is 3 times smaller than $\mathrm{cl}(\mathbb{Z}[\pi])$, and still generated by $\langle 3, \pi - 1 \rangle$. Because the two class group actions are compatible, the CSI-FiSh data can easily be repurposed for this variant without additional computations. This approach is detailed in [10].

[9] Benchmarks in [4] are based on the original CSIDH implementation [11]. A speed-up of roughly 30% is to be expected using the techniques in [42].

The fact that secrets are sampled in a subgroup of $cl(\mathbb{Z}[\pi])$ of index 3 or 111 has a minor impact on security, as cryptanalyses can exploit this information to speed-up their searches.

In the classical setting, the best algorithm for both Vectorization and Parallelization is a random-walk approach [20] that finds a path between two supersingular curves in $O(\sqrt{\#cl(\mathbb{Z}[\pi])}) = O(\sqrt[4]{p})$. If, like in our case, we restrict to a vertex set that is x times smaller, the random walk algorithm will find a collision approximately $\sqrt{x}$ times faster. Hence, we expect a loss in classical security of less than 4 bits.[10]

Note that this gain is optimal: if an algorithm could solve the Vectorization problem in a subgroup of size N/x more than $O(\sqrt{x})$ times faster, then by a divide and conquer approach the Vectorization problem in the full group of size N could be solved in less than $O(\sqrt{N})$ operations.

A similar gain can also be obtained in the best quantum algorithm for solving the Vectorization problem [39,40,48]. However, since its complexity is subexponential, the final gain is even less than 4 bits. The exact quantum security of CSIDH and CSI-FiSh is currently debated [3,6,8,11,47], nevertheless whatever the final consensus turns out to be, the quantum security of our threshold schemes will be extremely close to it.

5   Conclusion

We introduced threshold variants of encryption and signature schemes based on Hard Homogeneous Spaces, and efficient quantum-safe instantiations thereof based on isogeny graphs of supersingular curves (CSIDH).

Our schemes are similar to well known Diffie–Hellman-style threshold schemes, however they are sharply different in the communication structure: whereas classical schemes have participants output messages in parallel with little coordination, our schemes impose a strictly sequential round-robin message passing style. Apparently, this limitation trickles down, negatively affecting many aspects: security properties, security proofs, efficiency.

In our ElGamal-style decryption algorithm, only one participant learns the cleartext, and we are only able to prove security in a *honest-but-curious* setting. While the communication structure is slightly less problematic for the signature scheme, its security too can only be proven in a *honest-but-curious* setting with *static corruptions*. Interesting questions for future research are efficient protocols where all participants learn the cleartext, or with stronger security properties, such as the ability to detect malicious participants.

Another topic we did not address in this work are verifiable distributed key generation algorithms, which would allow to run the threshold schemes without resorting to a trusted dealer. As observed by Benaloh [2], Shamir's secret sharing is $(+,+)$-homomorphic: given two secrets s and s' with respective shares s_i

---

[10] In reality, it is well known that the size of the search space can also be reduced by 3 in the original CSIDH, by *walking to the surface*. Thus, the only reduction in security comes from the factor of 37.

and s_i', the sums of shares $s_i + s_i'$ form valid shares of $s + s'$. Based on this observation, Pedersen [45] constructed a DKG scheme without a trusted dealer, by having each party set up its own (k, n)-Shamir secret sharing scheme, and then combining these schemes using the homomorphic property.

While the same homomorphic property also applies to HHS threshold schemes, it seems difficult to achieve verifiability of the DKG like in [30,33,46]. An interesting research question is the construction of a verifiable DKG in the general HHS framework, or for specific isogeny-based instantiations.

Finally, the instantiation of our schemes is limited by the feasibility of parameter generation: to the present date the only available parameter set is the CSIDH-512 HHS, as computed by Beullens *et al.*, with security currently estimated at the NIST-1 level. Higher security levels would require extremely intensive computations that are currently out of reach.

Acknowledgment. We thank Gustavo Banegas, Tanja Lange, Chloe Martindale, and Dustin Moody for raising the topic of threshold cryptography at the Oxford PQC workshop. We thank Bertram Poettering, Patrick Towa Nguenewou for helpful discussions, the anonymous referees and Christophe Petit for helping improve the quality of the manuscript. Finally, we thank Jörn Steuding and the organizers of the summer school "Cryptography meets Graph Theory" in Würzburg for supporting Luca De Feo's visit, and thereby helping to bootstrap this collaboration.

References

1. Babai, L.: On Lovász' lattice reduction and the nearest lattice point problem. Combinatorica **6**(1), 1–13 (1986)

2. Benaloh, J.C.: Secret sharing homomorphisms: keeping shares of a secret secret (extended abstract). In: Odlyzko, A.M. (ed.) CRYPTO 1986. LNCS, vol. 263, pp. 251–260. Springer, Heidelberg (1987). https://doi.org/10.1007/3-540-47721-7_19

3. Bernstein, D.J., Lange, T., Martindale, C., Panny, L.: Quantum circuits for the CSIDH: optimizing quantum evaluation of isogenies. In: Ishai, Y., Rijmen, V. (eds.) EUROCRYPT 2019. LNCS, vol. 11477, pp. 409–441. Springer, Cham (2019). https://doi.org/10.1007/978-3-030-17656-3_15

4. Beullens, W., Kleinjung, T., Vercauteren, F.: CSI-FiSh: efficient isogeny based signatures through class group computations. In: Galbraith, S.D., Moriai, S. (eds.) Advances in Cryptology - ASIACRYPT 2019, pp. 227–247. Springer, Cham (2019). https://doi.org/10.1007/978-3-030-34578-5_9

5. Beullens, W., Preneel, B., Szepieniec, A., Vercauteren, F.: LUOV. Round 2 submission, NIST Post-Quantum Cryptography Standardization (2019). https://www.esat.kuleuven.be/cosic/pqcrypto/luov/

6. Biasse, J.-F., Iezzi, A., Jacobson, M.J.: A note on the security of CSIDH. In: Chakraborty, D., Iwata, T. (eds.) INDOCRYPT 2018. LNCS, vol. 11356, pp. 153–168. Springer, Cham (2018). https://doi.org/10.1007/978-3-030-05378-9_9

7. Blakley, G.R.: Safeguarding cryptographic keys. In: Proceedings of the National Computer Conference, vol. 48 (1979)

8. Bonnetain, X., Schrottenloher, A.: Submerging CSIDH. Cryptology ePrint Archive, Report 2018/537 (2018). https://eprint.iacr.org/2018/537

9. Brandão, L.T.A.N., Mouha, N., Vassilev, A.: Threshold schemes for cryptographic primitives: challenges and opportunities in standardization and validation of threshold cryptography. NISTIR 8214 (2018). https://nvlpubs.nist.gov/nistpubs/ir/2019/NIST.IR.8214.pdf

10. Castryck, W., Decru, T.: CSIDH on the surface. Cryptology ePrint Archive, Report 2019/1404 (2019). https://eprint.iacr.org/2019/1404

11. Castryck, W., Lange, T., Martindale, C., Panny, L., Renes, J.: CSIDH: an efficient post-quantum commutative group action. In: Peyrin, T., Galbraith, S. (eds.) ASIACRYPT 2018. LNCS, vol. 11274, pp. 395–427. Springer, Cham (2018). https://doi.org/10.1007/978-3-030-03332-3_15

12. Castryck, W., Panny, L., Vercauteren, F.: Rational isogenies from irrational endomorphisms. In: Eurocrypt 2020 (2020, to appear). https://eprint.iacr.org/2019/1202

13. Cervantes-Vázquez, D., Chenu, M., Chi-Domínguez, J.J., De Feo, L., Rodríguez-Henríquez, F., Smith, B.: Stronger and faster side-channel protections for CSIDH. To appear at LATINCRYPT 2019 (2019). https://eprint.iacr.org/2019/837

14. Couveignes, J.M.: Hard homogeneous spaces. Cryptology ePrint Archive, Report 2006/291 (2006). https://eprint.iacr.org/2006/291

15. Cozzo, D., Smart, N.P.: Sharing the LUOV: threshold post-quantum signatures. In: Second PQC Standardization Conference (2019). https://csrc.nist.gov/CSRC/media/Events/Second-PQC-Standardization-Conference/documents/accepted-papers/cozzo-luov-paper.pdf

16. De Feo, L.: Mathematics of isogeny based cryptography (2017). http://arxiv.org/abs/1711.04062

17. De Feo, L., Galbraith, S.D.: SeaSign: compact isogeny signatures from class group actions. In: Ishai, Y., Rijmen, V. (eds.) EUROCRYPT 2019. LNCS, vol. 11478, pp. 759–789. Springer, Cham (2019). https://doi.org/10.1007/978-3-030-17659-4_26

18. De Feo, L., Kieffer, J., Smith, B.: Towards practical key exchange from ordinary isogeny graphs. In: Peyrin, T., Galbraith, S. (eds.) ASIACRYPT 2018. LNCS, vol. 11274, pp. 365–394. Springer, Cham (2018). https://doi.org/10.1007/978-3-030-03332-3_14

19. Decru, T., Panny, L., Vercauteren, F.: Faster seasign signatures through improved rejection sampling. In: Ding, J., Steinwandt, R. (eds.) PQCrypto 2019. LNCS, vol. 11505, pp. 271–285. Springer, Cham (2019). https://doi.org/10.1007/978-3-030-25510-7_15

20. Delfs, C., Galbraith, S.D.: Computing isogenies between supersingular elliptic curves over $\mathbb{F}_p$. Des. Codes Crypt. **78**(2), 425–440 (2016). https://doi.org/10.1007/s10623-014-0010-1

21. Desmedt, Y.: Threshold cryptosystems. In: Seberry, J., Zheng, Y. (eds.) AUSCRYPT 1992. LNCS, vol. 718, pp. 1–14. Springer, Heidelberg (1993). https://doi.org/10.1007/3-540-57220-1_47

22. Desmedt, Y., Frankel, Y.: Shared generation of authenticators and signatures. In: Feigenbaum, J. (ed.) CRYPTO 1991. LNCS, vol. 576, pp. 457–469. Springer, Heidelberg (1992). https://doi.org/10.1007/3-540-46766-1_37

23. Ding, J., Chen, M.S., Petzoldt, A., Schmidt, D., Yang, B.Y.: Rainbow. Round 2 submission, NIST Post-Quantum Cryptography Standardization (2019). https://csrc.nist.gov/projects/post-quantum-cryptography/round-2-submissions

24. Doerner, J., Kondi, Y., Lee, E., Shelat, A.: Secure two-party threshold ECDSA from ECDSA assumptions. In: 2018 IEEE Symposium on Security and Privacy (SP), pp. 980–997. IEEE (2018)

25. Doulgerakis, E., Laarhoven, T., de Weger, B.: Finding closest lattice vectors using approximate Voronoi cells. In: Ding, J., Steinwandt, R. (eds.) PQCrypto 2019. LNCS, vol. 11505, pp. 3–22. Springer, Cham (2019). https://doi.org/10.1007/978-3-030-25510-7_1

26. ElGamal, T.: A public key cryptosystem and a signature scheme based on discrete logarithms. IEEE Trans. Inf. Theory **31**(4), 469–472 (1985)

27. Elkies, N.D.: Elliptic and modular curves over finite fields and related computational issues. In: 1995 Computational Perspectives on Number Theory. Studies in Advanced Mathematics, Chicago, IL, vol. 7, pp. 21–76. AMS International Press, Providence (1998)

28. Felderhoff, J.: Hard homogenous spaces and commutative super singular isogeny based Diffie-Hellman. Internship report, Inria, France, August 2019. https://hal.archives-ouvertes.fr/hal-02373179

29. Fiat, A., Shamir, A.: How to prove yourself: practical solutions to identification and signature problems. In: Odlyzko, A.M. (ed.) CRYPTO 1986. LNCS, vol. 263, pp. 186–194. Springer, Heidelberg (1987). https://doi.org/10.1007/3-540-47721-7_12

30. Fouque, P.-A., Stern, J.: One round threshold discrete-log key generation without private channels. In: Kim, K. (ed.) PKC 2001. LNCS, vol. 1992, pp. 300–316. Springer, Heidelberg (2001). https://doi.org/10.1007/3-540-44586-2_22

31. Gennaro, R., Goldfeder, S.: Fast multiparty threshold ECDSA with fast trustless setup. In: Proceedings of the 2018 ACM SIGSAC Conference on Computer and Communications Security, pp. 1179–1194. ACM (2018)

32. Gennaro, R., Jarecki, S., Krawczyk, H., Rabin, T.: Robust threshold DSS signatures. In: Maurer, U. (ed.) EUROCRYPT 1996. LNCS, vol. 1070, pp. 354–371. Springer, Heidelberg (1996). https://doi.org/10.1007/3-540-68339-9_31

33. Gennaro, R., Jarecki, S., Krawczyk, H., Rabin, T.: Secure distributed key generation for discrete-log based cryptosystems. In: Stern, J. (ed.) EUROCRYPT 1999. LNCS, vol. 1592, pp. 295–310. Springer, Heidelberg (1999). https://doi.org/10.1007/3-540-48910-X_21

34. Harn, L.: Group-oriented (t, n) threshold digital signature scheme and digital multisignature. IEEE Proc.-Comput. Digit. Tech. **141**(5), 307–313 (1994)

35. Jao, D., et al.: SIKE. Round 2 submission, NIST Post-Quantum Cryptography Standardization (2019). https://sike.org/

36. Jao, D., De Feo, L.: Towards quantum-resistant cryptosystems from supersingular elliptic curve isogenies. In: Yang, B.-Y. (ed.) PQCrypto 2011. LNCS, vol. 7071, pp. 19–34. Springer, Heidelberg (2011). https://doi.org/10.1007/978-3-642-25405-5_2

37. Jao, D., Miller, S.D., Venkatesan, R.: Expander graphs based on GRH with an application to elliptic curve cryptography. J. Number Theory **129**(6), 1491–1504 (2009). https://doi.org/10.1016/j.jnt.2008.11.006

38. Kiltz, E.: A tool box of cryptographic functions related to the Diffie-Hellman function. In: Rangan, C.P., Ding, C. (eds.) INDOCRYPT 2001. LNCS, vol. 2247, pp. 339–349. Springer, Heidelberg (2001). https://doi.org/10.1007/3-540-45311-3_32

39. Kuperberg, G.: Another sub exponential-time quantum algorithm for the dihedral hidden subgroup problem. In: TQC. LIPIcs, vol. 22, pp. 22–34. Schloss Dagstuhl - Leibniz-Zentrum für Informatik (2013)

40. Kuperberg, G.: A subexponential-time quantum algorithm for the dihedral hidden subgroup problem. SIAM J. Comput. **35**(1), 170–188 (2005)

41. Meyer, M., Campos, F., Reith, S.: On Lions and Elligators: an efficient constant-time implementation of CSIDH. In: Ding, J., Steinwandt, R. (eds.) PQCrypto 2019. LNCS, vol. 11505, pp. 307–325. Springer, Cham (2019). https://doi.org/10.1007/978-3-030-25510-7_17

42. Meyer, M., Reith, S.: A faster way to the CSIDH. In: Chakraborty, D., Iwata, T. (eds.) INDOCRYPT 2018. LNCS, vol. 11356, pp. 137–152. Springer, Cham (2018). https://doi.org/10.1007/978-3-030-05378-9_8

43. National Institute of Standards and Technology (NIST): Post-Quantum Cryptography Standardization (2016). https://csrc.nist.gov/Projects/post-quantum-cryptography/Post-Quantum-Cryptography-Standardization

44. Onuki, H., Aikawa, Y., Yamazaki, T., Takagi, T.: (Short paper) a faster constant-time algorithm of CSIDH keeping two points. In: Attrapadung, N., Yagi, T. (eds.) IWSEC 2019. LNCS, vol. 11689, pp. 23–33. Springer, Cham (2019). https://doi.org/10.1007/978-3-030-26834-3_2

45. Pedersen, T.P.: A threshold cryptosystem without a trusted party. In: Davies, D.W. (ed.) EUROCRYPT 1991. LNCS, vol. 547, pp. 522–526. Springer, Heidelberg (1991). https://doi.org/10.1007/3-540-46416-6_47

46. Pedersen, T.P.: Non-interactive and information-theoretic secure verifiable secret sharing. In: Feigenbaum, J. (ed.) CRYPTO 1991. LNCS, vol. 576, pp. 129–140. Springer, Heidelberg (1992). https://doi.org/10.1007/3-540-46766-1_9

47. Peikert, C.: He gives C-Sieves on the CSIDH. In: Eurocrypt 2020 (2020, to appear). https://eprint.iacr.org/2019/725

48. Regev, O.: A subexponential time algorithm for the dihedral hidden subgroup problem with polynomial space. arXiv preprint quant-ph/0406151 (2004). https://arxiv.org/abs/quant-ph/0406151

49. Rostovtsev, A., Stolbunov, A.: Public-key cryptosystem based on isogenies. Cryptology ePrint Archive, Report 2006/145 (2006). http://eprint.iacr.org/2006/145

50. Schnorr, C.P.: Efficient identification and signatures for smart cards. In: Brassard, G. (ed.) CRYPTO 1989. LNCS, vol. 435, pp. 239–252. Springer, New York (1990). https://doi.org/10.1007/0-387-34805-0_22

51. Shamir, A.: How to share a secret. Commun. ACM **22**(11), 612–613 (1979)

52. Shor, P.W.: Polynomial-time algorithms for prime factorization and discrete logarithms on a quantum computer. SIAM Rev. **41**(2), 303–332 (1999)

53. Shoup, V.: Practical threshold signatures. In: Preneel, B. (ed.) EUROCRYPT 2000. LNCS, vol. 1807, pp. 207–220. Springer, Heidelberg (2000). https://doi.org/10.1007/3-540-45539-6_15

54. Stinson, D.R., Strobl, R.: Provably secure distributed Schnorr signatures and a (t, n) threshold scheme for implicit certificates. In: Varadharajan, V., Mu, Y. (eds.) ACISP 2001. LNCS, vol. 2119, pp. 417–434. Springer, Heidelberg (2001). https://doi.org/10.1007/3-540-47719-5_33

55. Stolbunov, A.: Constructing public-key cryptographic schemes based on class group action on a set of isogenous elliptic curves. Adv. Math. Commun. **4**(2), 215–235 (2010)

56. Stolbunov, A.: Cryptographic schemes based on isogenies. Doctoral thesis, NTNU (2012)

57. Vélu, J.: Isogénies entre courbes elliptiques. C.R. Acad. Sc. Paris, Série A. **271**, 238–241 (1971)

Multiparty Protocols

Topology-Hiding Computation
for Networks with Unknown Delays

Rio LaVigne[1], Chen-Da Liu-Zhang[2], Ueli Maurer[2], Tal Moran[3],
Marta Mularczyk[2(✉)], and Daniel Tschudi[4]

[1] MIT, Cambridge, USA
`rio@mit.edu`
[2] ETH Zurich, Zürich, Switzerland
`{lichen,maurer,mumarta}@inf.ethz.ch`
[3] IDC Herzliya, Herzliya, Israel
`talm@idc.ac.il`
[4] Concordium, Zürich, Switzerland
`dt@concordium.com`

Abstract. Topology-Hiding Computation (THC) allows a set of parties to securely compute a function over an incomplete network without revealing information on the network topology. Since its introduction in TCC'15 by Moran et al., the research on THC has focused on reducing the communication complexity, allowing larger graph classes, and tolerating stronger corruption types.

All of these results consider a fully synchronous model with a known upper bound on the maximal delay of all communication channels. Unfortunately, in any realistic setting this bound has to be extremely large, which makes all fully synchronous protocols inefficient. In the literature on multi-party computation, this is solved by considering the fully asynchronous model. However, THC is unachievable in this model (and even hard to define), leaving even the definition of a meaningful model as an open problem.

The contributions of this paper are threefold. First, we introduce a meaningful model of unknown and random communication delays for which THC is both definable and achievable. The probability distributions of the delays can be arbitrary for each channel, but one needs to make the (necessary) assumption that the delays are independent.

R. LaVigne—This material is based upon work supported by the National Science Foundation Graduate Research Fellowship under Grant No. 1122374. Any opinion, findings, and conclusions or recommendations expressed in this material are those of the authors(s) and do not necessarily reflect the views of the National Science Foundation. Research supported in part by NSF/BSF grant no. 1350619, an MIT-IBM grant, and a DARPA Young Faculty Award.

T. Moran—Supported in part by ISF grant no. 1790/13 and by the Bar-Ilan Cybercenter.

M. Mularczyk—Research supported by the Zurich Information Security and Privacy Center (ZISC).

D. Tschudi—Work was done while author was at Aarhus University, supported by advanced ERC grant MPCPRO.

A. Kiayias et al. (Eds.): PKC 2020, LNCS 12111, pp. 215–245, 2020.
https://doi.org/10.1007/978-3-030-45388-6_8

The existing fully-synchronous THC protocols do not work in this setting and would, in particular, leak information about the topology. Second, in the model with trusted stateless hardware boxes introduced at Eurocrypt'18 by Ball et al., we present a THC protocol that works for any graph class. Third, we explore what is achievable in the standard model without trusted hardware and present a THC protocol for specific graph types (cycles and trees) secure under the DDH assumption. The speed of all protocols scales with the actual (unknown) delay times, in contrast to all previously known THC protocols whose speed is determined by the assumed upper bound on the network delay.

1   Introduction

In the wake of GDPR and other privacy laws, companies need ways to process data in a way such that the trust is distributed among several parties. A fundamental solution to this problem is secure multiparty computation. Here, one commonly assumes that all parties have pairwise communication channels. In contrast, for many real-world scenarios, the communication network is not complete, and parties can only communicate with a subset of other parties. A natural question is whether a set of parties can successfully perform a joint computation over an incomplete communication network while revealing no information about the network topology.

The problem of *topology-hiding computation* (THC) was introduced by Moran et al. [MOR15], who showed that THC is possible in the setting with passive corruptions and graphs with logarithmic diameter. Further solutions improve the communication efficiency [HMTZ16] or allow for larger classes of graphs [AM17, ALM17]. Recent results [BBMM18, LLM+18] even provide THC for fail-stop or semi-malicious adversaries (although at the price of leaking some small amount of information about the topology).

However, all those results consider the *fully synchronous* model, where a protocol proceeds in rounds. This model makes two assumptions: first, the parties have access to synchronized clocks, and second, every message is guaranteed to be delivered within one round. While the first assumption is reasonable in practice, as nowadays computers usually stay synchronized with milliseconds of variation, the second assumption makes protocols inherently impractical. This is because the running time of a protocol is always counted in the number of rounds, and the round length must be chosen based on the most pessimistic bound on the message delivery time. For concreteness, consider a network where most of the time messages are delivered within milliseconds, but one of the connections, once in a while, may slow down to a couple of hours. In this case, a round would have to take a couple of hours.

1.1   Contributions

This motivates the goal of this work, which is to construct THC protocols for more realistic settings, where messages are not guaranteed to be delivered within a fixed time bound.

Model. A natural starting point would be to consider the strongest possible adversary, i.e. one who fully controls message delivery (this is the standard setting considered by asynchronous MPC, e.g. [BOCG93, Can01]). First, note that this standard model is not well suited for our setting, since in order to decide when messages are delivered, the adversary must know the network, which we attempt to hide. The next logical step is to consider a model where the adversary can only interfere with delays between parties he controls, but unfortunately, even this grants the adversary too much power. In fact, we prove in Appendix A that it is impossible to get a topology-hiding broadcast in this model.

This forces us to define a slightly weaker model. We call it the Probabilistic Unknown Delay Model and we formally define it in Sect. 2. In this model the messages are delayed independently of the adversary, but different connections have different, unbounded probabilistic delays. This means that we throw off the assumption that makes the synchronous protocols impractical. Still, parties have access to synchronized clocks.

Protocols. We remark that it is not easy to modify synchronous THC protocols (even those tolerating fail-stop adversaries) to remain secure in the Probabilistic Unknown Delay Model. For example, consider the standard technique of letting each party attach to each message a round number r, and then wait until it receives all round-r messages before proceeding to the next round. This seems to inherently leak the topology, as the time at which a party receives a message for round r reveals information about the neighborhood of the sender (e.g., that it contains an edge with very long delays).

This forces us to develop new techniques, which result in three new protocols, secure in the Probabilistic Unknown Delay Model against any number of passive corruptions. We require a setup, but this setup is independent of the network topology (it only depends on the number of parties), and it can be used to run multiple instances of the protocols, with different communication graphs.

Our first two protocols (Sect. 3) implement topology-hiding broadcast (any functionality can then be realized using standard techniques, by executing a sequence of broadcasts). The protocols are based on standard assumptions, but can only be used in limited classes of graphs (the same ones as in [AM17]): cycles and trees, respectively.[1]

Furthermore, observe that the running time of a protocol could itself leak information about the topology. Indeed, this issue seems very difficult to overcome, since, intuitively, making the running time fully independent of the graph delays conflicts with our goal to design protocols that run as fast as the *actual* network. We deal with this by making the running time of our protocols depend only on the sum of all the delays in the network.

Then, in Sect. 4, we introduce a protocol that implements any functionality, works on arbitrary connected graphs, and its running time corresponds to

---

[1] Our second protocol works for any graphs, as long as we agree to reveal a spanning tree: the parties know which of their edges are on the tree and execute the protocol, ignoring other edges. See also [AM17].

(one sample of) the sum of all delays. On the other hand, we assume stateless secure hardware. Intuitively, a hardware box is a stateless program with an embedded secret key (the same for all parties). This assumption was introduced in [BBMM18] in order to deal with fail-stop adversaries in THC. Similar assumptions have also been considered before, for example, stateless tamper-proof tokens [CGS08, GIS+10, CKS+14][2], or honestly-generated secure hardware [HMQU05, CT10].

While secure hardware is a very strong assumption, the paradigm of constructing protocols with the help of a hardware oracle and then replacing the hardware oracle by more standard assumptions is common in the literature (see for example the secure hardware box assumption for the case of synchronous topology-hiding computation (with known upper bounds on the delays) for fail-stop adversaries [BBMM18], which was later relaxed to standard assumptions [LLM+18], or the Signature Card assumption for proofs-carrying-data schemes [CT10]). We hope that the techniques presented in this paper can be useful to construct protocols in more standard models.

1.2   Related Work

Topology-hiding computation was introduced by Moran et al. in [MOR15]. The authors propose a broadcast protocol tolerating any number of passive corruptions. The construction uses a series of nested multi-party computations, in which each node is emulated by its neighbors. This broadcast protocol can then be used to achieve topology-hiding MPC using standard techniques to transform broadcast channels into secure point-to-point channels. In [HMTZ16], the authors provide a more efficient construction based on the DDH assumption. However, both results are only feasible for graphs with logarithmic diameter. Topology-hiding communication for certain classes of graphs with large diameter was described in [AM17]. This result was finally extended to arbitrary (connected) graphs in [ALM17]. These results were extended to the fail-stop setting in [BBMM18] based on stateless secure hardware, and [LLM+18] based on standard assumptions. All of the results mentioned above are in the cryptographic setting. Moreover, all results are stated in the synchronous communication model with known upper bounds on the delays.

In the information-theoretic setting, the main result is negative [HJ07]: any topology-hiding MPC protocol inherently leaks information about the network graph. This work also shows that if the routing table is leaked, one can construct an MPC protocol which leaks no additional information.

2   The Probabilistic Unknown Delay Model

At a high level, we assume loosely synchronized clocks, which allow the parties to proceed in rounds. However, we do not assume that the messages are always

---

[2] The difference here is that a token typically needs to be passed around during the protocol and the parties can embed their own programs in it, whereas a secure hardware box is used only by one party and is initialized with the correct program.

delivered within one round. Rather, we model channels that have delays drawn from some distributions each time a message is sent along (a different distribution for each channel). These delays are a property of the network. As already mentioned, this allows to achieve a significant speedup, comparable to that of asynchronous protocols and impossible in the fully synchronous model.

2.1   Impossibility of Stronger Models

Common models for asynchronous communication [BOCG93, Can01] consider a worst-case scenario and give the adversary the power to schedule the messages. By scheduling the messages, the adversary automatically learns which parties are communicating. As a consequence, it is unavoidable that the adversary learns the topology of the communication graph, which we want to hide.

A natural definition, then, would be to give to the adversary control over scheduling on channels from his corrupted parties. However, any reasonable model in which the adversary has the ability to delay messages for an unbounded amount of time allows him to learn something about the topology of the graph. In essence, a very long delay from a party behaves almost like an abort, and an adversary can exploit this much like a fail-stop adversary in the impossibility result of [MOR15]. We formally prove this in a very weak adversarial model in Appendix A.

Since delays cannot depend on the adversary without leaking topology, delays are an inherent property of the given network, much like in real life. As stated before, we give each edge a delay distribution, and the delays of messages traveling along that edge are sampled from this distribution. This allows us to model real-life networks where the adversary cannot tamper with the network connections. For example, on the Internet, delays between two directly connected nodes depend on their distance and the reliability of their connection.

2.2   Adversary

We consider an adversary, who statically and passively corrupts any set $\mathcal{Z} \subseteq \mathcal{P} = \{P_1, \ldots, P_n\}$ of parties, with $|\mathcal{Z}| < n$. Static corruptions mean that the set $\mathcal{Z}$ is chosen before the protocol execution. Passively corrupted parties follow the protocol instructions, but the adversary can access their internal states during the execution.

The setting with passive corruptions and secure hardware boxes is somewhat subtle. In particular, the adversary is allowed to input to the box of a corrupted party any messages of his choice, even based on secret states of other corrupted parties; he can even replay messages from honest parties with different corrupted inputs. This will be why we need authenticated encryption, for example. Importantly, in the passive model, the messages actually sent by a corrupted party are produced using the box with valid inputs.

2.3   Communication Network and Clocks

Clocks. Each party has access to a clock that *ticks* at the same rate as every other clock. These ticks are fast; one can think of them as being milliseconds long or even faster (essentially, the smallest measurable unit of time).

We model the clocks by the clock functionality $\mathcal{F}_{\text{CLOCK}}$ of [KMTZ13], which we recall here for completeness. The functionality keeps the absolute time τ, which is just the number of ticks that have passed since the initialization. Every single tick, a party is activated, given the time, and runs a part of the protocol. To ensure that honest parties are activated at least once every clock tick, the absolute time is increased according to "Ready" messages from honest parties.

Functionality $\mathcal{F}_{\text{CLOCK}}$

The clock functionality stores a counter τ, initially set to 0. For each honest party P_i it stores a flag d_i, initialized to 0.

ReadClock: On input (READCLOCK) from party P_i return τ.

Ready: On input (READY) from honest party P_i set $d_i = 1$.

ClockUpdate: On every activation the functionality runs this code before doing anything else.
1: **if** for every honest party P_i it holds $d_i = 1$ **then**
2:     Set $d_i = 0$ for every honest party P_i.
3:     Set $\tau = \tau + 1$.

Because clocks wait for "Ready" messages, computation is instant, happening within a single clock-tick. While this is not exactly what happens in the real world, our protocols do not abuse this property. In particular, they proceed in rounds, where each round takes a number (e.g., one million) clock-ticks. Parties process and send messages only once in a round, and remain passive at other times (in real world, this would be the time they perform the computation).

Network. The (incomplete) network with delays is modeled by the network functionality $\mathcal{F}_{\text{NET}}$. Similar to the synchronous models for THC, the description of the communication graph is inputted before the protocol execution by a special party P_{setting}. In our case, this description also contains a (possibly different) probability distribution for each edge indicating its delay. Each party can ask the functionality for its neighborhood in the communication graph and the delay distributions on the edges to its neighbors.[3] During the protocol execution, at

---

[3] In fact, our hardware-based protocol does not use this information, and our protocols for cycles and trees only need upper bounds on the expected values of the delays. This bound can be easily established, e.g. by probing the connection.

every clock tick, parties can send to each neighbor a message, which is delivered after a delay sampled from a given distribution.

Functionality $\mathcal{F}_{\text{NET}}$

The functionality is connected to a clock functionality $\mathcal{F}_{\text{CLOCK}}$. The functionality stores a communication graph G and, for each edge e, a distribution D_e from which delays are sampled. Initially, G contains no edges. The functionality also stores the current time τ and a set of message tuples `buffer` which initially is empty.

Clock Update: Each time the functionality is activated, it first queries $\mathcal{F}_{\text{CLOCK}}$ for the current time and updates τ accordingly.

Initialization Step: // This is done at most once, before the protocol starts.
The party P_{setting} inputs a communication graph G and, for each edge e, a distribution D_e. The functionality stores G and D_e.

Graph Info: On input (GETINFO) from an honest party P_i, the functionality outputs to P_i its neighborhood $\mathbf{N}_G(P_i)$ and the delay distribution $D_{(i,j)}$ for all $j \in \mathbf{N}_G(P_i)$.

Communication Step:

- On input (SEND, i, j, m) from party P_i, where $P_j \in \mathbf{N}_G(P_i)$, $\mathcal{F}_{\text{NET}}$ samples the delay d_{ij} for the edge (i, j) from $D_{(i,j)}$ and records the tuple $(\tau + d_{ij}, P_i, P_j, m)$ in `buffer`.[a]
- On input (FETCHMESSAGES, i) from P_i, for each message tuple (T, P_k, P_i, m) from `buffer` where $T \leq \tau$, the functionality removes the tuple from `buffer` and outputs (k, m) to P_i.

---

[a] Technically, our model allows to send in one round multiple independent messages. However, our protocols do not exploit this property; we only assume that messages are independent if they are sent in different rounds.

Leakage in the Ideal World. During the protocol execution the adversary can learn local neighborhoods from $\mathcal{F}_{\text{NET}}$. Therefore, any ideal-world adversary should also have access to this information. This is ensured by the ideal-world functionality $\mathcal{F}_{\text{INFO}}^{\mathcal{L}}$, which has the same initialization step and the same graph information as $\mathcal{F}_{\text{NET}}$, but does not allow for actual communication.

Moreover, in any protocol it is unavoidable that the adversary learns the time at which the output is revealed. In previous synchronous THC protocols, this quantity corresponded to a fixed number of rounds (depending on an upper bound on the graph size or its diameter). This can no longer be the case in our model, where the number of rounds it takes to deliver a message is unbounded. Hence, it is necessary to parameterize $\mathcal{F}_{\text{INFO}}^{\mathcal{L}}$ by a leakage function $\mathcal{L}$, that allows the adversary to compute the output time. $\mathcal{L}$ depends on the set $\mathcal{D}$ of all delay distributions in the network, but it does not depend on the communication graph itself. Additionally, we allow the adversary to pass to $\mathcal{L}$ an auxiliary input, that will accommodate any protocol parameters that influence the output time.

For example, in our protocol based on secure hardware, $\mathcal{L}$ will return the distribution of the sum of all network delays, rounded to the next multiple of the round length R (where R is provided as auxiliary input by the adversary).

Functionality $\mathcal{F}_{\mathrm{INFO}}^{\mathcal{L}}$

Initialization Step: // This is done at most once, before the protocol starts.
The party P_{setting} inputs a communication graph G and, for each edge e, a distribution D_e. The functionality stores G and D_e.

Graph Info:
- On input (GETINFO) from an honest party P_i, the functionality outputs to P_i its neighborhood $\mathbf{N}_G(P_i)$ and the delay distribution $D_{(i,j)}$ for all $j \in \mathbf{N}_G(P_i)$.
- On the first input (GETINFO, aux) from the adversary the functionality outputs: the neighborhood of all corrupted parties, the delay distribution of every edge where at least one of the nodes is corrupted, and the leakage $\mathcal{L}(\mathsf{aux}, \mathcal{D})$, where $\mathcal{D}$ is the set of all delay distributions in the network.

2.4   Additional Related Work

Katz et al. [KMTZ13] introduce eventual-delivery and channels with a fixed known upper bound. These functionalities implement communication between two parties, where the adversary can set, for each message, the delay after which it is delivered. For reasons stated at the beginning of this section, such functionalities cannot be used directly to model topology-hiding computation. Instead of point-to-point channels we need to model the whole communication network, and we cannot allow the adversary to set the delays. Intuitively, $\mathcal{F}_{\mathrm{NET}}$ implements a number of bounded-delay channels, each of which is modified so that the delay is chosen once and independently of the adversary. If we did not consider hiding the topology, our modified channels would be a stronger assumption.

Cohen et al. [CCGZ16] define different channels with probabilistic delays, for example point-to-point channels (the SMT functionalities) and an all-to-all channel (parallel SMT, or PSMT). However, their PSMT functionality cannot be easily modified to model THC, since the delivery time is sampled once for all parties. One could modify the SMT functionalities and use their parallel composition, but we find our formulation simpler and much better suited for THC.

3 Protocols for Restricted Classes of Graphs

This section considers protocols that realize topology-hiding broadcast in the Probabilistic Unknown Delay Model under standard assumptions (in particular, we give an instantiation based on DDH), but in the limited setting where graphs are trees or cycles. We stress that we can deal with any graphs if a spanning tree is revealed. In the following, we first recall the known technique to achieve fully-synchronous THC using random walks and so-called PKCR encryption [ALM17]. Then, we extend PKCR by certain additional properties, which allows us to construct a broadcast protocol for cycles in the Probabilistic Unknown Delay Model. Finally, we extend this protocol to trees.

3.1 Synchronous THC from Random Walks

Currently, the most efficient fully-synchronous THC protocols are based on the technique of correlated random walks, introduced in [ALM17]. Intuitively, a PKCR scheme is assumed, which is an enhanced public-key encryption scheme on group elements, where the public keys come with a group operation: we write $\mathrm{pk}_{12} = \mathrm{pk}_1 \circledast \mathrm{pk}_2$. The encryption and decryption algorithms are denoted $\mathsf{PKCR.Enc}(m, \mathrm{pk})$ and $\mathsf{PKCR.Dec}(c, \mathrm{sk})$, respectively. Additionally, a party can add a layer of encryption to a ciphertext c encrypted under pk_1, using the algorithm $\mathsf{PKCR.AddLayer}(c, \mathrm{sk}_2)$, which outputs an encryption c' under the combined key pk_{12}. This operation can be undone with $\mathsf{PKCR.DelLayer}(c', \mathrm{sk}_2)$. We also require that PKCR is homomorphic and rerandomizable (note that the latter is implied).

The goal is to broadcast one bit. However, we instead realize the OR functionality, which can then be used for broadcast (in the semi-honest setting) by having the sender input his bit, and all other parties input 0. The protocol proceeds as follows. A party starts by encrypting 0 if its input bit is 0, and a random group element otherwise, under a fresh key. In the first, so-called aggregate phase, this ciphertext travels along a random walk for a fixed number of rounds R (collecting the input bits of each party until it has traversed the whole graph with high probability). In each round, each party adds a layer of encryption to the received ciphertext (using a freshly generated key) and homomorphically adds its input. After R rounds, the parties start the decrypt phase, in which they send the final ciphertext back through the same walk it traversed in the first phase, and the layers of encryption are removed (using the secret keys stored during the aggregate phase). It is important that the ciphertext is sent via the same walk, to remove exactly the same layers of encryption that were added in the first phase. The parties determine this walk based on how they routed the ciphertext in the corresponding round of the aggregate phase. After another R rounds, each party interprets the group element as a 0-bit (the 0 element) or as a 1-bit (any other element).

This technique breaks down in the Probabilistic Unknown Delay Model. For example, it is not clear how to choose R such that the walk traverses the whole graph since it would depend on an upper bound on the delays. Moreover, in the decrypt phase, parties no longer know how to route a ciphertext back via the same walk it took in the aggregate phase. This is because they do not know the number of steps it already made in the backward walk (this depends on the actual delays). Furthermore, it is not straightforward to modify the random walk technique to deal with this. For instance, the standard method of attaching a round number to every message (to count the number of encryption layers) reveals information about the topology.

3.2   Protocol for Cycles

We assume an enhanced PKCR scheme, denoted PKCR*. The main differences from PKCR are as follows. First, the message space in PKCR* is now the set $\{0, 1\}$, and it is disjoint from the ciphertext space. This allows to distinguish between a layered ciphertext and a plaintext. Moreover, we no longer require explicit homomorphism, but instead use the algorithm PKCR*.ToOne(c) that transforms an encryption of 0 into an encryption of 1 without knowing the public key.[4] We formally define PKCR* and give an instantiation based on the DDH assumption in Appendix B.

Rounds. Although we are striving for a protocol that behaves in a somewhat asynchronous way, we still have a notion of rounds defined by a certain number of clock ticks. Even though each party is activated in every clock tick, each party receives, processes and sends a message only every R clock ticks—this keeps parties in sync despite delays, without clogging the network. Even if no message is received, a message is sent.[5] This means that at time τ, we are on round $r_\tau = \lfloor \tau/R \rfloor$; the τ parameter will be dropped if obvious from context. Moreover, observe that the message complexity increases as R decreases. For reference, R can be thought of as relatively large, say 1,000 or more; this is also so that parties are able to completely process messages every round.

A Protocol with Constant Delays. To better explain our ideas, we first describe our protocol in the setting with constant delays, and then modify it to deal with any delay distributions.

The high-level idea is to execute directly the decrypt phase of the random-walk protocol, where the walk is simply the cycle traversal, and the combined public key corresponding to the ciphertext resulting from the aggregate phase is given as the setup (note that this is independent of the order of parties on the graph). More concretely, we assume that each party P_i holds a secret key sk_i

---

[4] Its functionality does not matter and is left undefined on encryptions of 1.

[5] If the parties do not send at every round, the topology would leak. Intuitively, when a party P_i sends the initial message to its right neighbor P_j, the right neighbor of P_j learns how big the delay from P_i to P_j was. We can extend this to larger neighborhood, eventually revealing information about relative positions of corrupted parties.

and the combined public key $\text{pk} = \text{pk}_1 \circledast \ldots \circledast \text{pk}_n$. Assume for the moment that each party knows who the next clockwise party is in the cycle. At the beginning, a party P_i, every round (i.e., every R clock ticks), starts a new cycle traversal by sending to the next party a fresh encryption of its input $\text{PKCR*.Enc}(b_i, \text{pk})$. Once P_i starts receiving ciphertexts from its neighbor (note that since the delays are fixed, there is at most one ciphertext arriving in a given round), it instead continues the cycle traversals. That is, every time it receives a ciphertext c from the previous neighbor, it deletes the layer of encryption using its secret key: $\text{PKCR*.DelLayer}(c, \text{sk}_i)$. It then rerandomizes the result and sends it to the next party. The sender additionally transforms the ciphertext it receives to a 1-ciphertext in case its bit is 1. After traversing the whole cycle, all layers of encryption are removed and the parties can recognize a plaintext bit. This happens at the same time for every party.

In order to remove the assumption that each party knows who the next clockwise party is, we simply traverse the cycle in both directions.

A Protocol Accounting for Variable Delays. The above approach breaks down with arbitrary delays, where many messages can arrive at the same round. We deal with this by additionally ensuring that every message is received in a predictable timely manner: we will be repeating message sends. As stated in Sect. 2, the delays could be variable, but we make the assumption that if messages are sent at least R clock-ticks from each other, then the delay for each message is independent. We also assume that the median value of the delay along each edge is polynomial, denoted as $\text{Med}[D_e]$. Now, since the protocol will handle messages in rounds, the actual values we need to consider are all in rounds: $\lceil \text{Med}[D_e]/R \rceil$.

Now, if over κ rounds, P_1 sends a message c each round, the probability that none of the copies arrives after $\kappa + \lceil \text{Med}[D_e]/R \rceil$ rounds is negligible in terms of κ, the security parameter (see full version [LLM+19] for the proof). Because we are guaranteed to have the message by that time (and we believe with reasonable network delays, median delay is small), we wait until time $(\kappa + \lceil \text{Med}[D_e]/R \rceil) \cdot R$ has passed from when the original message was sent before processing it.[6]

For the purposes of this sketch, we will just consider sending messages one way around the protocol. We will also focus on P_1 (with neighbors P_n and P_2) since all parties will behave in an identical manner. First, the setup phase gives every party the combined public key $\text{pk} = \text{pk}_1 \circledast \ldots \circledast \text{pk}_n$. At each step, processing a message will involve using the PKCR.DelLayer functionality for their key.

In the first round, P_1 sends its bit (0 if not the source node, b_s if the source node) encrypted under pk to P_2, let's call this message $c_1^{(1)}$. P_1 will wait $\text{w} = \kappa + \lceil \text{Med}[D_e]/R \rceil$ rounds to receive P_n's first message during this time. Now, because P_1 needs to make sure $c_1^{(1)}$ makes it to P_2, for the next κ rounds, P_1 continues to send $c_1^{(1)}$. However, because P_1 also needs to hide w (and thus cannot

---

[6] Note that delays between rounds are independent, but not within the round. This means we need to send copies of the message over multiple rounds for this strategy to work.

reveal when it starts sending its processed message from P_n), P_1 starts sending a new ciphertext encrypting the same message, $c_2^{(1)}$ (again κ times over κ rounds), until it has waited w rounds—so, P_1 is sending $c_1^{(1)}$ and $c_2^{(1)}$ in the second round, $c_1^{(1)}$, $c_2^{(1)}$ and $c_3^{(1)}$ the third round and so forth until it sends $c_1^{(1)}, \ldots c_\kappa^{(1)}$ in round κ. Then it stops sending $c_1^{(1)}$ and starts sending $c_{\kappa+1}^{(1)}$. P_1 will only ever send κ messages at once per round. Once it has waited w rounds, P_1 is guaranteed to have received the message from P_n and can process and forward that message, again sending it κ times over κ rounds. In the next round, P_1 will then be guaranteed to receive the next message from P_n, and so on.

Let $\mathrm{MedRSum}[D] = \sum_{i=1}^{n} \left\lceil \mathrm{Med}[D_{(i,(i+1 \bmod n)+1)}]/R \right\rceil$ denote the median-round-sum of the delays. Because each party waits like this, the protocol has a guaranteed time to end, the same for all parties:

$$R \cdot \sum_{i=1}^{n} \mathsf{w}_i = R\left(n\kappa + \mathrm{MedRSum}[D]\right).$$

This is the only information 'leaked' from the protocol: all parties learn the sum of ceiling'd medians, $\mathrm{MedRSum}[D]$. Additionally, parties all know the (real, not a round-delay) distribution of delays for messages to reach them, and thus can compute $\lceil \mathrm{Med}[D_e]/R \rceil$ for their adjacent edges.

Formally, the protocol CycleProt is described as follows.

Protocol CycleProt

// The common input of all parties is the round length R. Additionally, the sender P_s has the input bit b_s.

Setup: For $i \in \{1, \ldots, n\}$, let $(\mathsf{pk}_i, \mathsf{sk}_i) = \mathsf{PKCR^*.KGen}(1^\kappa)$. Let $\mathsf{pk} = \mathsf{pk}_1 \circledast \ldots \circledast \mathsf{pk}_n$. The setup outputs to each party P_i its secret key sk_i and the product public key pk.

Initialization for each P_i:

- Send (GETINFO) to the functionality $\mathcal{F}_{\text{NET}}$ and assign randomly the labels P^0, P^1 to the two neighbors.
- Let $\mathsf{Rec}^0, \mathsf{Rec}^1$ be lists of received messages from P^0 and P^1 respectively, both initialized to $\perp$. Let Send^0 and Send^1 be sets initialized to $\varnothing$; these are the sets of messages that are ready to be sent.
- For each $\ell \in \{0, 1\}$, $D_{(i,\ell)}$ is the delay distribution on the edge between P_i and P^ℓ, obtained from $\mathcal{F}_{\text{INFO}}$.
- Let $\mathsf{w}^\ell = \kappa + \lceil \mathrm{Med}[D_{(i,\ell)}]/R \rceil$ be the time P_i waits before sending a message from P^ℓ to $P^{1-\ell}$

Execution for each P_i:

1: Send (READCLOCK) to the functionality $\mathcal{F}_{\text{CLOCK}}$ and let τ be the output. If τ mod $R \neq 0$, send (READY) to the functionality $\mathcal{F}_{\text{CLOCK}}$. Otherwise, let $\mathsf{r} = \tau/R$ be the current round number and do the following:

2: *Receive messages:* Send ($\text{FETCHMESSAGES}, i$) to the functionality $\mathcal{F}_{\text{NET}}$. For each message (r_c, c) received from a neighbor P^ℓ, set $\text{Rec}^\ell[r_c + \text{w}^\ell] = c$.

3: *Process if no messages received:* For each neighbor P^ℓ such that $\text{Rec}^\ell[r] = \bot$, start a new cycle traversal in the direction of $P^{1-\ell}$:
   - If P_i is sender (i.e. $i = s$) then add $(\kappa, r, \text{PKCR*.Enc}(b_s, \text{pk}))$ to $\text{Send}^{1-\ell}$.
   - Otherwise, add $(\kappa, r, \text{PKCR*.Enc}(0, \text{pk}))$ to $\text{Send}^{1-\ell}$.

4: *Process received messages:* For each P^ℓ such that $\text{Rec}^\ell[r] \neq \bot$ (we have received a message from P^ℓ), set $\text{d} = \text{PKCR*.DelLayer}(\text{Rec}^\ell[r], \text{sk}_i)$, and do the following:
   - If $\text{d} \in \{0, 1\}$, output d and halt (we have decrypted the source bit).
   - Otherwise, if $i = s$ and $b_s = 1$, then set $\text{d} = \text{PKCR*.ToOne}(\text{d})$. Then, in either case, add $(\kappa, r, \text{PKCR*.Rand}(\text{d}))$ to $\text{Send}^{1-\ell}$.

5: *Send message:* For each $\ell \in \{0, 1\}$, let $\text{Sending}^\ell = \{(k, r_c, c) \in \text{Send}^\ell : k > 0\}$. For each $(k, r_c, c) \in \text{Sending}^\ell$, send (r_c, c) to P^ℓ.

6: *Update* Send *set:* For each $(k, r_c, c) \in \text{Sending}^\ell$, remove (k, r_c, c) from Send^ℓ and insert $(k - 1, r_c, c)$ to Send^ℓ.

7: Send (READY) to the functionality $\mathcal{F}_{\text{CLOCK}}$.

In the full version [LLM+19] we prove the following theorem ($\mathcal{F}_{\text{BC}}$ denotes the broadcast functionality).

Theorem 1. *The protocol* CycleProt *UC-realizes* $(\mathcal{F}_{\text{CLOCK}}, \mathcal{F}_{\text{INFO}}^{\mathcal{L}_{\text{median}}}, \mathcal{F}_{\text{BC}})$ *in the* $(\mathcal{F}_{\text{CLOCK}}, \mathcal{F}_{\text{NET}})$*-hybrid model with an adversary who statically passively corrupts any number of parties, where the leakage function is defined as* $\mathcal{L}_{\text{median}}(R, \mathcal{D}) = \text{MedRSum}[\mathcal{D}]$.[7]

3.3 Protocol for Trees

We show how to modify the cycle protocol presented in the previous section to securely realize the broadcast functionality $\mathcal{F}_{\text{BC}}$ in any tree. As observed in [AM17], given a tree, nodes can locally compute their local views of a cycle-traversal of the tree. However, to apply the cycle protocol to this cycle-traversal, we would need as setup a combined public key that has each secret key sk_i as many times as P_i appears in the cycle-traversal. To handle that, each party simply removes its secret key from the ciphertexts received from the first neighbor, and we can assume the same setup as in the cycle protocol.

In the full version [LLM+19] we give a formal description of the protocol TreeProt. The proof of the following theorem is a straightforward extension of the proof of Theorem 1.

Theorem 2. *The protocol* TreeProt *UC-realizes* $(\mathcal{F}_{\text{CLOCK}}, \mathcal{F}_{\text{INFO}}^{\mathcal{L}_{\text{median}}}, \mathcal{F}_{\text{BC}})$ *in the* $(\mathcal{F}_{\text{CLOCK}}, \mathcal{F}_{\text{NET}})$*-hybrid model with an adversary who statically passively corrupts any number of parties, where the leakage function is defined as* $\mathcal{L}_{\text{median}}(R, \mathcal{D}) = \text{MedRSum}[\mathcal{D}]$.

---

[7] Note that the round length R is a parameter of the protocol, so we allow the adversary to provide it.

4   Protocol for General Graphs

We present a protocol that allows us to securely realize any functionality in any connected communication graph with unknown delay distributions on the edges. For that, we use the same setup as [BBMM18]: we assume that the parties have access to secure hardware boxes, initialized with the same secret key, and executing the same functionality $\mathcal{F}_{\mathrm{HW}}$, independent of the graph and the realized functionality (see [BBMM18] for details of this model).

Our protocol is divided into two sub-protocols: preprocessing and computation. Both sub-protocols do not terminate on their own. Rather, we assume that each party gets a signal when it can finish each sub-protocol.[8] The preprocessing is executed only once, before any input is specified and can be re-used. Intuitively, it outputs, for each party, an encryption of the entire communication graph under the secret key embedded in the hardware boxes. The computation allows to evaluate any function, with the help of the encrypted information outputted by the preprocessing. One output of preprocessing can be used to execute the computation any number of times, each time with different function and different inputs.

In the following, we formally describe both protocols. To make the exposition easier to follow, we postpone the precise definition of the functionality $\mathcal{F}_{\mathrm{HW}}$ executed by the hardware boxes, to Appendix C, and for now only give an informal description of its behavior whenever $\mathcal{F}_{\mathrm{HW}}$ is invoked.

4.1   Preprocessing

The preprocessing is executed without any inputs. The output is a pair (id_i, c), where id_i is a (secret) random string used to identify a party, and c is a ciphertext that contains an encrypted state with the whole graph. This output pair will be inputted to the computation protocol.

At a high level, the protocol floods the network with encrypted partial images of the graph, until the signal to terminate occurs. We assume that the signal occurs late enough for all parties to collect all information. In more detail, throughout the protocol, a party P_i keeps an encrypted state c, containing information about the graph and parties' id's, that it collected up to a given point. Initially, c contains only the local neighborhood and id_i chosen at random by P_i. Then, every round, P_i sends c to all its neighbors. When it receives a state c_j from a neighbor P_j, it uses the functionality $\mathcal{F}_{\mathrm{HW}}$ box to update c with the information from c_j. That is, $\mathcal{F}_{\mathrm{HW}}$ gets as input two encrypted states containing partial images on the graph, respectively, decrypts both states and merges the information into a new state, which is encrypted and output.

---

[8] In practice, this is not an unrealistic assumption. It would be enough, for example, if each party was given a very rough upper bound on the time it takes to flood the network and traverse all edges of the graph (for instance, a constant number proportional to the sum of delays on all edges). This is still faster than assuming worst-case upper bounds on the delays along edges, as one would need to do to adapt a fully synchronous protocol.

Protocol Hw-Preprocessing

// The common input of all parties is the round length R.

Setup: Each party P_i has access to a secure hardware box functionality $\mathcal{F}_{\mathrm{HW}}$.

Initialization for each P_i: Choose an identifier id_i at random and send (GETINFO) to $\mathcal{F}_{\mathrm{NET}}$, to obtain the neighborhood $\mathbf{N}_G(P_i)$. Input $(i, \mathrm{id}_i, \mathbf{N}_G(P_i))$ to $\mathcal{F}_{\mathrm{HW}}$ and store the resulting encrypted state c.

Execution for each P_i at every round (every R clock ticks):

1: Send c to each $P_j \in \mathbf{N}_G(i)$.
2: Send (FETCHMESSAGES, i) to $\mathcal{F}_{\mathrm{NET}}$. For each received message c', input (id_i, c, c') to $\mathcal{F}_{\mathrm{HW}}$ and set the updated state c to the result.

Termination for each P_i: Upon receiving the signal, output (id_i, c).

4.2 Computation

The inputs to the computation protocol are, for every P_i, its input x_i, a description of the function f_i that evaluates P_i's output of the computed function, and the values id_i and c_i, outputted by preprocessing.

The high-level idea is that the hardware box $\mathcal{F}_{\mathrm{HW}}$ gets as part of its input the value c_i, containing, among others, the encrypted communication graph. This allows it to deterministically compute an Eulerian cycle, which visits every edge exactly twice. Then, every party starts a traversal of the Eulerian cycle, in order to collect the inputs from all parties. Once all inputs are collected, the box computes the function and gives the output to the party. Traversing each edge exactly twice allows all parties to learn the output at a time that does not depend on the graph topology but (roughly) on the distribution of the sum of the delays. Of course, all messages are encrypted under the secret key embedded in the hardware boxes.

This means that at any time during the protocol there are n cycle traversals going through the graph (one per a starting party). Each of the traversals visits all edges in the graph twice. So in each round a party P_i processes messages for up to n traversals. To hide the number of actual traversal processed P_i sends n messages to each of its neighbors. This means that each round, P_i receives from each neighbor n messages. It inputs all of them to its hardware box (together with its input to the computed function) and receives back, for each neighbor, a set of n messages that it then sends to him.

A party receives the output once the cycle has been traversed, which takes time proportional to the sum of the rounded delays. Once the parties receive output, they continue executing the protocol until they receive the termination signal, which we assume occurs late enough for *all* parties to get their outputs.

There are still some subtle issues, that the above sketch does not address. First, the adversary could try to tamper with the ciphertexts. For example, in our protocol a message contains a list of id's that identifies the path it already traversed. This is done so that the adversary cannot extend the traversal on behalf of an honest party P_i without knowing its secret id_i. Now the adversary could try to extend this list nevertheless, by copying part of the encrypted state of a corrupted party—recall that this state contains all id_i's. To prevent such situations, we use authenticated encryption.

Second, we need to specify when the parties input the function they are evaluating into the box. Doing this at the very end would allow the adversary to evaluate many functions of her choice, including the identity. So instead, in our protocol the function is inputted once, when the cycle traversal is started, and it is always a part of the message. This way, when the output is computed, the function is taken from a message that has been already processed by all honest parties. Since honest parties only process messages that are actually sent to them, and even corrupted parties only send correctly generated messages, this function must be the correct one. In some sense, when sending the first message to an honest party, the adversary commits herself to the correct function.

A similar problem occurs when the parties input to their boxes the inputs to the computed function. A sequence of corrupted parties at the end of the traversal can emulate the last steps of the protocol many times, with different inputs. To prevent this, we traverse the cycle twice. After the first traversal, the inputs are collected and the function is evaluated. Then, the (still encrypted) output traverses the cycle for the second time, and only then is given to the parties.

Finally, we observe that at the end of the protocol, a graph component of neighboring corrupted parties learns where the traversal enters their component (this can be done by fast-forwarding the protocol). Depending on how the eulerian cycle is computed, this could leak information about the topology. To address this, we introduce in Sect. 4.3 an algorithm for computing the traversal that does not have this issue (formally, the last part of the cycle can be simulated).

Protocol Hw-Computation

// The common input of all parties is the round length R. Additionally, each P_i has input (x_i, f_i, id_i, c_i), where id_i is the identifier chosen in Hw-Preprocessing, and c_i is the encrypted state outputted by Hw-Preprocessing.

Setup: Each party P_i has access to a secure hardware box functionality $\mathcal{F}_{\mathrm{HW}}$.

Initialization for each P_i: For each neighbor P_j, let $E_j = \varnothing$.

Execution for each P_i at every r clock ticks:

1: Send (FETCHMESSAGES) to $\mathcal{F}_{\mathrm{NET}}$ and receive the messages $(E_1, \ldots, E_\nu)$.

2: Choose r at random and input $(i, \mathtt{id}_i, c_i, \bigcup_j E_j, x_i, f_i, r)$ to $\mathcal{F}_{\mathrm{HW}}$. Get the result $(\mathtt{val}, \{(E'_1, \mathtt{next}_1), \ldots, (E'_k, \mathtt{next}_k)\})$. If $\mathtt{val} \neq \perp$, output $\mathtt{val}$, but continue running.
3: For each $(E'_j, \mathtt{next}_j)$, for each $e \in E'_j$, send e to $\mathtt{next}_j$ via $(\mathrm{SEND}, i, \mathtt{next}_j, e)$.[a]

Termination for each P_i: Upon receiving the signal, terminate.

---

[a] We will assume that every message sent in this round is independent. In this case this is equivalent to assuming only independence between rounds—since there is an upper bound n on the number of messages sent at once, one can always make the round longer, partition it into slots separated by a sufficient time interval, and send one message in every slot.

Realizing Reactive Functionalities. Reactive functionalities are those which require explicit interaction between parties, e.g. if the function we realize is very simple but we want to evaluate a complex function, parties may need to run this protocol multiple times in sequence, using previous outputs to generate the next inputs. Our current hardware protocol allows us to realize secure function evaluation. In the synchronous setting, this can be easily extended to reactive functionalities by invoking many function evaluations in sequence. However, in the setting with unknown delays this is no longer clear. For example, if our protocol is composed sequentially in the naive way, then parties start the second execution at different times, which leaks topology.

So, to get reactive functionalities or composition to work for this hardware protocol we can do one of two things. First, we could add a synchronization point before each 'round' of the reactive function. Second, we could employ the same trick as for the cycle/tree protocol in Sect. 3, sending the same message many times so that with high probability it arrives to the next node within some reasonable time interval. With this method, every party ends the protocol at exactly the same time, and so can start the next protocol at the same time, despite the delays.

The running time of the protocol Hardware depends only on the sum of all delays in the network, each rounded to the next multiple of the round length R, which is the only information leaked in the ideal world. In the full version [LLM+19] we prove the following theorem.

Theorem 3. *For any efficiently computable and well-formed[9] functionality $\mathcal{F}$, the protocol Hardware UC-realizes $(\mathcal{F}_{\mathrm{CLOCK}}, \mathcal{F}_{\mathrm{INFO}}^{\mathcal{L}_{\mathsf{sum}}}, \mathcal{F})$ in the $(\mathcal{F}_{\mathrm{CLOCK}}, \mathcal{F}_{\mathrm{NET}}, \mathcal{F}_{\mathrm{HW}})$-hybrid model with an adversary who statically passively corrupts any number of parties, where $\mathcal{L}_{\mathsf{sum}} := R \sum_{D_e \in \mathcal{D}} \lceil D_e / R \rceil$.*

Remark. One can observe that in our protocol the hardware boxes must be able to evaluate a complex function. This can be resolved at the cost of efficiency, by

---

[9] Intuitively, a functionality is well-formed if its code does not depend on the ID's of the corrupted parties. We refer to [CLOS02] for a detailed description.

computing the functionality by many calls to the simple broadcast functionality. Note that even if we require one synchronization point per broadcast, this still seems reasonable, since it is possible to evaluate any function with constant number of broadcasts [DI05, LPSY15].

4.3   Computing the Eulerian Cycle

It turns out that not every algorithm computing an Eulerian cycle can be used in $\mathcal{F}_{\text{HW}}$ to achieve THC. In particular, during the execution of our protocol the adversary learns some information about a part of the cycle, which for some algorithms depends on the graph. More technically, during the simulation, it is necessary to compute the time when the adversary learns the output, and this happens as soon as the Eulerian cycle traversal enters a fragment of consecutive corrupted parties containing the output party. This is because it can "fast-forward" the protocol (without communication). Hence, we need an algorithm for computing such a cycle on a graph with doubled edges, for which the "entry point" to a connected component (of corrupted parties) can be simulated with only the knowledge of the component.

Common algorithms, such as Fleury or Hierholzer [Fle83, Fle91], check a global property of the graph and hence cannot be used without the knowledge of the entire graph topology. Moreover, a distributed algorithm in the local model (where the parties only have knowledge of its neighbors) such as [Mak97] is also not enough, since the algorithm has to be executed until the end in order to know what is the last part of the cycle.

We present the algorithm EulerianCycle, which, if executed from a node u on a connected neighborhood containing u, leads to the same starting path as if it was executed on the whole graph. This property is enough to simulate, since the simulator can compute the last fragment of the Eulerian Cycle in the corrupted neighborhood. We note that the start of the cycle generated by our algorithm can be simulated, however, the simulator needs to compute the end. Hence, the hardware boxes will traverse the path outputted by EulerianCycle from the end.

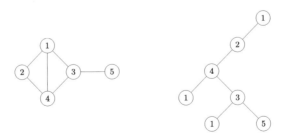

Fig. 1. An example of a graph G (on the left) and the corresponding tree $\mathcal{T}$, computed by EulerianCycle$(1, G)$ (on the right). The eulerian cycle (on the graph with doubled edges) is $(1, 2, 4, 1, 3, 1, 3, 5, 3, 4, 2, 1)$.

The idea is to generate a tree from the graph, in such a way that the generated tree contains exactly the same edges as the graph. To do that, the tree is generated in a DFS-manner from a source u. At every step, a new edge (the one that leads to the smallest id according to a DFS order, and without repeating nodes) is added to the tree. Since the graph is connected, all edges are eventually added. Moreover, each edge is added exactly once, since no repeated nodes are expanded. See Fig. 1 for an example execution.

Algorithm EulerianCycle($u, G = (E, V)$)

// Computes an eulerian cycle on the graph G with the set of nodes V and the set of edges E (where each edge is considered doubled), starting at node $u \in V$. We assume some ordering on V.

1: Let $\mathcal{T}$ be the tree with a single root node u.
2: **while** $E \neq \varnothing$ **do**
3:    **if** there is no $v \in V$ such that $(u, v) \in E$ **then**
4:       Set $u = \mathsf{parent}(\mathcal{T}, u)$
5:    **else**
6:       Pick the smallest v such that $(u, v) \in E$ and append v to the children of u in $\mathcal{T}$.
7:       Set $E = E \setminus \{(u, v)\}$.
8:       If $v \notin \mathsf{nodes}(\mathcal{T})$, then set $u = v$.
9: Output the path corresponding to the in-order traversal of $\mathcal{T}$.

Appendix

A   Adversarially-Controlled Delays Leak Topology

Much like how adversarially-controlled aborts were shown to leak topological information in [MOR15], we can show that adversarially-controlled delays also leak topological information. First, note that if we have bounded delays, we can always use a synchronous protocol, starting the next round after waiting the maximum delay. So, in order for this model to be interesting, we must assume the adversary has unbounded delays. In order to be as general as possible, we prove this with the weakest model we can while still giving the adversary some control over its delays: the adversary can only add delay to messages leaving corrupt nodes.

Our proof will follow the structure of [MOR15], using a similar game-based definition and even using the same adversarially-chosen graphs (see Fig. 2). Our game is straightforward. The adversary gives the challenger two graphs and a set of corrupt nodes so that the corrupt neighborhoods are identical when there is no adversarially added delay. The challenger then chooses one of those graphs at random, runs the protocol, and gives the views of all corrupt nodes to the adversary. The adversary wins if she can tell which graph was used. In [MOR15], the adversary would choose a round to failstop one of its corrupt parties. In our model, the adversary will instead choose a time (clock-tick) to add what we call a long-delay (which is just a very long delay on sending that and all subsequent messages). The adversary will be able to detect the delay based on when the protocol ends: if the delay was early in the protocol, the protocol takes longer to finish for all parties, and if it was late, the protocol will still finish quickly for most parties.

This impossibility result translates to an impossibility in the simulation-based setting since a secure protocol for the simulation-based setting would imply a secure protocol for the game-based setting.

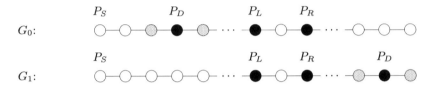

Fig. 2. Graphs used to prove the impossibility of THC with adversarial delays. P_S is the sender. The corrupted parties (black dots) are: P_L and P_R (they delay messages), and the detective P_D. The adversary determines whether P_D (and its two neighbors) are on the left or on the right.

A.1 Adversarially-Controlled Delay Indistinguishability-based Security Definition

Before proving the impossibility result, we first formally define our model. This model is as weak as possible while still assuming delays are somewhat controlled by the adversary. We will assume a minimum delay along edges: it takes at least one clock-tick for a message to get from one party to another.

Delay Algorithms. In order to give the adversary as little power as possible, we define a public (and arbitrary) randomized algorithm that outputs the delays for a graph for protocol Π. Both the adversary and challenger have access to this algorithm and can sample from it.

Definition 1. *A indistinguishability-delay algorithm (IDA) for a protocol Π,* DelayAlgorithm$_\Pi$, *is a probabilistic polynomial-time algorithm that takes as input an arbitrary graph outputs unbounded polynomial delays for every time τ and every edge in the graph. Explicitely, for any graph $G = (V, E)$,* DelayAlgorithm(G) *outputs $\mathcal{T}$ such that for every edge $(i, j) \in E_b$ and time τ, $\mathcal{T}((i, j), \tau) = d_{(i,j),\tau}$ is a delay that is at least one.*

The Indistinguishability Game. This indistinguishability definition is a game between an adversary $\mathcal{A}$ and challenger $\mathcal{C}$ adapted from [MOR15]. Let DelayAlgorithm be an IDA as defined above.

- Setup: Let $\mathcal{G}$ be a class of graphs and Π a topology-hiding broadcast protocol that works on any of the networks described by $\mathcal{G}$ according to our adversarial delay model, and let DelayAlgorithm be a public, fixed IDA algorithm. Without loss of generality, let P_1 have input $x \in \{0,1\}$, the broadcast bit.
- $\mathcal{A}$ chooses two graphs $G_0 = (V_0, E_0)$ and $G_1 = (V_1, E_1)$ from $\mathcal{G}$ and then a subset $\mathcal{Z}$ of the parties to corrupt. $\mathcal{Z}$ must look locally the same in both G_0 and G_1. Formally, $\mathcal{Z} \subset V_0 \cap V_1$ and $\mathbf{N}_{G_0}(\mathcal{Z}) = \mathbf{N}_{G_1}(\mathcal{Z})$. If this doesn't hold, $\mathcal{C}$ wins automatically.
  $\mathcal{A}$ then generates $\mathcal{T}_{\mathcal{Z}}$, a function defining delays for every edge at every time-step controlled by the adversary. That is, $\mathcal{T}_{\mathcal{Z}}((i,j), \tau) = d_{(i,j),\tau}$, and if $P_i \in \mathcal{Z}$, then every message sent from P_i to P_j at time τ is delayed by an extra $d_{(i,j),\tau}$. $\mathcal{A}$ sends $G_0, G_1, \mathcal{Z},$ and $\mathcal{T}_{\mathcal{Z}}$ to $\mathcal{C}$.
- $\mathcal{C}$ chooses a random $b \in \{0,1\}$ and executes Π in G_b with delays according to DelayAlgorithm$(G_b) = \mathcal{T}$ for all messages sent from honest parties. For messages sent from corrupt parties, delay is determined by the time and parties as follows: for time τ a message sent from party $P_i \in \mathcal{Z}$ to P_j has delay $\mathcal{T}((i,j), \tau) + \mathcal{T}_{\mathcal{Z}}((i,j), \tau)$ in reaching P_j. $\mathcal{A}$ receives the view of all parties in $\mathcal{Z}$ during the execution.
- $\mathcal{A}$ then outputs $b' \in \{0,1\}$ and wins if $b' = b$ and loses otherwise.

Notice that in this model, the adversary statically and passively corrupts any set of parties, and statically determines what delays to add to the protocol.

Definition 2. *A protocol Π is* indistinguishable under chosen delay attack (IND-CDA) *over a class of graphs $\mathcal{G}$ if for any PPT adversary $\mathcal{A}$, there exists an IDA* DelayAlgorithm *such that*

$$\Pr[\mathcal{A} \text{ wins}] \leq \frac{1}{2} + negl(n).$$

A.2   Proof that Adversarially-Controlled Delays Leak Topology

First, we will define what we mean when we say a protocol is 'weakly' realized in the adversarial delay model. Intuitively, it is just that the protocol outputs the correct bit to all parties if there is no adversarial delay.

Definition 3. *A protocol Π* weakly realizes the broadcast functionality *if Π is such that when all parties execute honestly with delays determined by any IDA, all parties get the broadcast bit within polynomial time (with all but negligible probability).*

Theorem 4. *There does not exist an IND-CDA secure protocol Π that weakly realizes the broadcast functionality of any class of graphs $\mathcal{G}$ that contains line graphs.*

Throughout the proof and associated claim, we refer to a specific pair of graphs that the adversary has chosen to distinguish between, winning the IND-CDA game. Both graphs will be a line of n vertices: $G = (V, E)$ where $E =$

$\{(P_i, P_{i+1})\}_{i=1,\ldots,n-1}$. We will let Π be a protocol executed on G that weakly realizes broadcast when P_1 is the broadcaster, see Fig. 2.

Our adversary in this model will either add no delay, or will add a very long polynomial delay to every message sent after some time τ.

Notice that $\mathcal{A}$ is given access to DelayAlgorithm at the start of the protocol. One can sample from DelayAlgorithm using G_0, G_1, and $\mathcal{Z}$ to get an upper bound T on the time it takes Π to terminate with all but negligible probability. Since Π weakly realizes broadcast, T is polynomial. So, $\mathcal{A}$ has access to this upper bound T.

Long-Delays. Let a long-delay be a delay that lasts for T clock-ticks. Consider an adversary that will only add long-delays to a protocol, and once an adversary has long-delayed a message, he must continue to long-delay messages along that edge until the end of the protocol. That is, once the adverary decides to delay along some edge, all subsequent messages along that edge cannot arrive for at least T clock-ticks.

Claim. Consider any party P_v whose neighbors do not add any extra delay as described by the long-delay paragraph above. As in [MOR15], let $H_{v,b}$ be the event that P_v outputs the broadcast bit by time T (P_v may still be running the protocol by time T or terminate by guessing a bit by T). Let E_τ be the event that the first long-delay is at time τ. Then either Π is not IND-CDA secure, or there exists a bit b such that

$$|\Pr\left[H_{v,b}|E_{T-1}\right] - \Pr\left[H_{v,b}|E_0\right]| \geq \frac{1}{2} - \mathrm{negl}(n).$$

Proof. If some P_i long-delays at time 0, then the first message it sends is at time T, and so the graph is disconnected until time T. This makes it impossible for parties separated from P_1 to learn about the output bit by time T. So, by that time, these parties must either guess an output bit (and be right with probability at most $1/2$) or output nothing and keep running the protocol (which is still not $H_{v,b}$). If Π is IND-CDA secure, then all honest parties must have the same probability of outputting the output bit by time T, and so there exists a b such that $\Pr[H_{v,b}|E_0] \leq \frac{1}{2} - \mathrm{negl}(n)$ for all honest parties P_v.

However, if P_i long-delays at time $T - 1$, then the only parties possibly affected by P_i are P_{i-1} and P_{i+1}; all other parties will get the output by time T and the information that P_i delayed cannot reach them (recall we assumed a minimum delay of at least one clock-tick in the DelayAlgorithm). So, $\Pr[H_{v,b}|E_0] = \Pr[H_{v,b}|\text{no extra delays}] = 1 - \mathrm{negl}(n)$ for all honest parties without a delaying neighbor by the definition of weakly realizing broadcast.

The claim follows: $|\Pr\left[H_{v,b}|E_{T-1}\right] - \Pr\left[H_{v,b}|E_0\right]| \geq |\frac{1}{2} - \mathrm{negl}(n) - 1| \geq \frac{1}{2} - \mathrm{negl}(n)$. □

Proof (Theorem 4). This just follows from the previous claim. A simple hybrid argument shows that there exists a pair $(\tau^*, b) \in \{0, \ldots, T-1\} \times \{0, 1\}$ such that

$$|\Pr\left[H_{v,b}|E_{\tau^*}\right] - \Pr\left[H_{v,b}|E_{\tau^*+1}\right]| \geq \frac{1}{2T} - \mathrm{negl}(n)$$

for all P_v who do not have a neighbor delaying. Since T is polynomial, this is a non-negligible value. Without loss of generality, assume $\Pr[H_{v,b}|E_{\tau^*}] > \Pr[H_{v,b}|E_{\tau^*+1}]$. Leveraging this difference, we will construct an adversary $\mathcal{A}$ that can win the IND-CDA game with non-negligible probability.

$\mathcal{A}$ chooses two graphs G_0 and G_1. $G = G_0$ and G_1 is G except parties 3, 4, and 5 are exchanged with parties $n-2$, $n-1$, and n respectively. $\mathcal{A}$ corrupts the source part $P_S := P_1$, a left party $P_L := P_{n/2-1}$, a right party $P_R := P_{n/2+1}$, and the detective party $P_D := P_4$. See Fig. 2 for how this looks. The goal of $\mathcal{A}$ will be to determine if P_D is to the left or right side of the network (close to the broadcaster or far).

$\mathcal{A}$ computes the upper bound T using DelayAlgorithm and randomly guesses (τ^*, b) that satisfy the inequality above. At time τ, $\mathcal{A}$ initiates a long-delay at party P_L, and at time $\tau+1$, $\mathcal{A}$ initiates a long-delay at party P_R. So, $\mathcal{A}$ gives the challenger $\mathcal{T}_\mathcal{Z}$ where $\mathcal{T}_\mathcal{Z}((i, j), t) = 0$ for $t < \tau^*$, and for $t \geq \tau^*$: $\mathcal{T}_\mathcal{Z}((L, n/2), t) = \mathcal{T}_\mathcal{Z}((L, n/2 - 2), t)T$ and $\mathcal{T}_\mathcal{Z}((R, n/2), t + 1) = \mathcal{T}_\mathcal{Z}((R, n/2 + 2), t + 1) = T$.

Notice that news of P_L's delay at time τ^* cannot reach P_R or any other party on the right side of the graph by time T. Also note that the time $\mathcal{A}$ gets output for each of its corrupt parties is noted in the transcript.

If $\mathcal{C}$ chooses G_0, then P_D is on the left side of the graph and has probability $\Pr[H_{D,b}|E_{\tau^*}]$ of having the output bit by time T because its view is consistent with P_L delaying at time τ^*. If $\mathcal{C}$ chooses G_1, then P_D is on the right side of the graph, and has a view consistent with the first long delay happening at time $\tau^* + 1$ and therefore has $\Pr[H_{D,b}|E_{\tau^*}]$ of having the output bit by time T. Because there is a noticeable difference in these probabilities, $\mathcal{A}$ can distinguish between these two cases with $\frac{1}{2}$ plus some non-negligible probability.   □

Consequences of this Lower Bound. We note that this is just one model where we prove it is impossible for the adversary to control delays. However, we restrict the adversary a great deal, to the point of saying that regardless of what the natural network delays are, the adversary can learn something about the topology of the graph. The lower bound proved in this model seems to rule out any possible model (simulation or game-based) where the adversary has power over delays.

B   PKCR* Encryption

This section formally defines PKCR*—the extended Privately Key Commutative and Rerandomizable (PKCR) encryption of [AM17].

Let $\mathcal{PK}$, $\mathcal{SK}$ and $\mathcal{C}$ denote the public key, secret key and ciphertext spaces. In contrast to PKCR, the message space is $\{0, 1\}$. Moreover, $\mathcal{C} \cap \{0, 1\} = \varnothing$. As in any public-key encryption scheme, we have the algorithms PKCR*.KGen : $\{0, 1\}^* \rightarrow \mathcal{PK} \times \mathcal{SK}$ and PKCR*.Enc : $\{0, 1\} \times \mathcal{PK} \rightarrow \mathcal{C}$ for key generation and encryption, respectively (decryption can be implemented via deleting layers). Moreover, we require the following properties, where only the first two are provided (with minor differences) by PKCR.

Key-Commutative. $\mathcal{PK}$ forms a commutative group under the operation $\circledast$. In particular, given any $pk_1, pk_2 \in \mathcal{PK}$ and the secret key sk_1 corresponding to pk_1, we can efficiently compute $pk_3 = pk_1 \circledast pk_2 \in \mathcal{PK}$ (note that sk_1 can be replaced by sk_2, since $\mathcal{PK}$ is commutative).

This group must interact well with ciphertexts; there exists a pair of deterministic efficiently computable algorithms PKCR*.AddLayer : $\mathcal{C} \times \mathcal{SK} \to \mathcal{C}$ and PKCR*.DelLayer : $\mathcal{C} \times \mathcal{SK} \to \mathcal{C} \cup \{0,1\}$ such that for every pair of public keys $pk_1, pk_2 \in \mathcal{PK}$ with corresponding secret keys sk_1 and sk_2, for every bit $b \in \{0,1\}$, and every ciphertext $c = $ PKCR*.Enc(b, pk_1), with overwhelming probability it holds that:

- The ciphertext PKCR*.AddLayer(c, sk_2) is an encryption of b under the public key $pk_1 \circledast pk_2$.
- PKCR*.DelLayer(c, sk_2) is an encryption of b under the public key $pk_1 \circledast pk_2^{-1}$.
- PKCR*.DelLayer$(c, sk_1) = b$.

Notice that we need the secret key to perform these operations.[10]

Rerandomizable. There exists an efficient probabilistic algorithm PKCR*.Rand : $\mathcal{C} \to \mathcal{C}$, which re-randomizes a ciphertext.[11] Formally, we require that for every public key $pk \in \mathcal{PK}$, every bit b, and every $c = $ PKCR*.Enc(b, pk), the following distributions are computationally indistinguishable:

$$\{(b, c, pk, \text{PKCR*.Enc}(b, pk))\} \approx \{(b, c, pk, \text{PKCR*.Rand}(c, pk))\}$$

Transforming a 0-ciphertext to a 1-ciphertext. There exists an efficient algorithm PKCR*.ToOne : $\mathcal{C} \to \mathcal{C}$, such that for every $pk \in \mathcal{PK}$ and for every $c = $ PKCR*.Enc$(0, pk)$, the output of PKCR*.ToOne(c) is an encryption of 1 under pk.

Key anonymity. A ciphertext reveals no information about which public key was used in encryption. Formally, we require that PKCR* is key-indistinguishable (or IK-CPA secure), as defined by Bellare et al. [BBDP01].

B.1   Construction of PKCR* Based on DDH

We use a cyclic group $G = \langle g \rangle$. We keep as ciphertext a pair of group elements (c_1, c_2). The first group element contains the message. The second group element contains the secret keys of each layer of encryption. All information is contained in the exponent.

To add a layer of encryption with a secret key sk, one simply raises the second element to sk. Similarly, one can remove layers of encryption. When all layers of encryption are removed, both group elements are either equal $c_1 = c_2$

---

[10] In PKCR of [ALM17], computing $pk_1 \circledast pk_2$ does not require the secret key. Moreover, PKCR requires perfect correctness.

[11] In [ALM17] the rerandomization algorithm is given the public key as input. We also note that they require public keys to be re-randomizable, while we do not need this property.

(the message is 0) or $c_1 = c_2^2$ (the message is 1). To transform an encryption of 0 to an encryption of 1, one simply squares the first group element.

Algorithm PKCR*

We let G be a group of order p, generated by g. These parameters are implicitly passed to all algorithms (formally, they are part of each ciphertext and an input to key generation).

PKCR*.KGen

1: Sample the secret key sk uniform at random from $\mathbb{Z}_p$.
2: Output $(g^{\mathsf{sk}}, \mathsf{sk})$.

PKCR*.Enc(b, y)

1: Sample r at random from $\mathbb{Z}_p$.
2: Output $c = (g^{(b+1)r}, y^r)$.

PKCR*.AddLayer$((c_1, c_2), \mathsf{sk})$

1: Output (c_1, c_2^{sk}).

PKCR*.Rand$((c_1, c_2))$

1: Sample r at random from $\mathbb{Z}_p$.
2: Output (c_1^r, c_2^r).

PKCR*.DelLayer$((c_1, c_2), \mathsf{sk})$

1: Set $c_2' = c_2^{\mathsf{sk}^{-1}}$.
2: **if** $c_1 = c_2'$ **then** Output 0.
3: **else if** $c_1 = c_2'^2$ **then** Output 1.
4: **else** Output (c_1, c_2').

PKCR*.ToOne$((c_1, c_2))$

1: Output (c_1^2, c_2).

The proof of security of our scheme can be found in the full version [LLM+19].

C   The Function Executed by the Hardware Boxes

The functionality $\mathcal{F}_{\mathrm{HW}}$ contains hard-wired the following values: a symmetric encryption key pk, and a key rk for a pseudo-random function prf. Whenever it outputs an encryption, it uses an authenticated encryption scheme AE with key pk, and with encryption randomness computed as $\mathsf{prf}_{rk}(x)$, where x is the whole input of $\mathcal{F}_{\mathrm{HW}}$. $\mathcal{F}_{\mathrm{HW}}$ can receive three types of input, depending on the current stage of the protocol: the initial input and an intermediate input during Hw-Preprocessing, and an intermediate input during Hw-Computation. On any other inputs, $\mathcal{F}_{\mathrm{HW}}$ outputs $\perp$.

Behavior During Preprocessing. During the preprocessing, the first input is a triple $(i, \mathsf{id}_i, \mathbf{N}_G(P_i))$, and next inputs are triples (id, c, c_j), where c and c_j are states of parties, encrypted under pk. In particular, the state of a party P_i consists of the following information:

- i: the index of P_i,
- G: the current image of the graph (stored in an n-by-n matrix),
- $\mathsf{ID} = (\mathsf{id}_1, \ldots, \mathsf{id}_n)$: a vector, containing the currently known identifiers of parties.

On the first input, $\mathcal{F}_{\mathrm{HW}}$ outputs an encryption of the initial state, that is, the state where the graph G contains only the direct neighborhood of P_i, and ID

contains only the value $\mathtt{id}_i$ chosen by P_i. For the inputs of the form $(\mathtt{id}, c, c_j)$, $\mathcal{F}_{\mathrm{HW}}$ decrypts the states c and c_j and merges the information they contain into a new state s, which it then encrypts and outputs.

Behavior During Computation. Recall that the goal of $\mathcal{F}_{\mathrm{HW}}$ at this stage is to compute the next encrypted messages, which a party P_i will send to its neighbors. That is, it takes as input a set of encrypted messages received by P_i and, for each neighbor of P_i, outputs a set of n messages to be sent.

Each encrypted message contains information about which graph traversal it is a part of, about the current progress of the traversal, and about all the inputs collected so far. Moreover, we include the information from the encrypted state: $(i, G, \mathtt{ID})$ and the function f of the party starting the cycle. Intuitively, the reason for including f and the encrypted state is that, since the adversary is passive, the information taken from the message must be correct (for example, now a corrupted party cannot use its box to evaluate any function of its choice). Formally, an encrypted message from another node decrypts to a message m_j containing the following elements:

- j is the party number (the publicly known number between 1 and n, not the party's $\mathtt{id}$)
- $\mathtt{ID}_j$ is the vector of unique random id's. Carrying this in the message allows us to ensure that inputs are all consistent with the same parties.
- G_j is the adjacency matrix of the network graph. It is also used to check consistency.
- $\mathtt{Path}_j = (\mathtt{id}^1, \ldots, \mathtt{id}^{4n^2})$: a vector of length $4n^2$, containing the current set of identifiers of parties visited so far along the graph traversal starting at P_j (recall that the eulerian cycle of length at most $2n^2$ is traversed twice).
- f_j is the function that parties will compute.
- $\vec{x}_j$ is a vector that has a slot for every party to put its input. It starts as being completely empty, but gains an entry when it visits a new node on the graph. We also check this for consistency (a party trying to input a different value from the one they started with will not be able to use the hardware).

At a high level, $\mathcal{F}_{\mathrm{HW}}$ first discards any dummy or repeated messages (a party can receive many messages, but the hardware box needs to continue at most n Eulerian cycles), and then processes each remaining message. If a message has traversed the whole Eulerian cycle, $\mathcal{F}_{\mathrm{HW}}$ computes and reveals the function applied to the inputs. Otherwise, it creates an encryption of a new message with the current party's id added to the current path, and its input added to the list of inputs, and $\mathtt{next}$ contains the id of the destination neighbor. After processing all messages, for each destination neighbor, it adds correctly formated dummy encryptions, so that exactly n encryptions are sent to each neighbor.

The functionality $\mathcal{F}_{\mathrm{HW}}$ is formally described below. It calls the following subroutines:

- **AggregateTours** takes as input a set of messages M. Each of these messages contain information about a Eulerian Cycle, the party that started that Eulerian Cycle, and the path traversed so far. The subroutine selects the (at most

n) messages that start from different parties. It is expected that Eulerian Cycles starting from the same party, are exactly the same message.
- **ContinueTour** takes as input a specific message, a Eulerian Cycle that the message must traverse, and a current party's input and number. If the Eulerian Cycle has not been traversed, it then creates a new message containing a path with the current party's input and id appended to the corresponding variables, and also the id of the party where the message should be sent. Otherwise, it outputs a flag indicating that the Eulerian Cycle has ended and the output must be revealed.
- **EncryptAndFormatOutput** takes as input a set of pairs message-destination, and appends to each possible destination parsable messages until there are n messages. It then encrypts each message and outputs, for each possible destination a set of encryptions and the id of the party where the encryptions must be sent.

Functionality $\mathcal{F}_{\mathrm{HW}}$

Setup: The hardware box is initialized with a symmetric encryption key pk and a PRF key rk.

Initial input during Hw-Preprocessing

    Input: $x = (i, \mathtt{id}_i, \mathbf{N}_G(P_i))$
1: Compute the initial vector ID as a vector of n $\perp$'s except with $\mathtt{id}_i$ in the i-th position.
2: Compute a new adjacency matrix G_i with the only entries being the local neighborhood of P_i.
3: Compute the initial state $s = (i, \mathtt{ID}, G_i)$
    Output: the encrypted initial state $\mathsf{AE.Enc}_{pk}(s; \mathsf{prf}_{rk}(x))$.

Intermediate input during Hw-Preprocessing

    Input: $x = (\mathtt{id}, c, c_j)$, where $\mathtt{id}$ is the identifier of P_i, c is the encrypted state of P_i, and c_j is the state of a neighbor P_j.
1: Compute the states $(i, \mathtt{ID}, G) = \mathsf{AE.Dec}_{pk}(c)$ and $(j, \mathtt{ID}_j, G_j) = \mathsf{AE.Dec}_{pk}(c_j)$.
2: Compute the new state $s = (i, \mathtt{ID}', G')$, where $\mathtt{ID}'$ contains all identifiers which appear in $\mathtt{ID}_j$ or $\mathtt{ID}$, and G' is the union of G and G_j.
    Output: the encrypted state $\mathsf{AE.Enc}_{pk}(s; \mathsf{prf}_{rk}(x))$.

Intermediate input during Hw-Computation

    Input: $x = (i, \mathtt{id}, c, E, x_i, f_i, r)$, where i is the party's index, $\mathtt{id}$ is the identifier of P_i, c is the encrypted state of P_i, E is the set of encrypted messages (freshly gotten from the buffer), x_i is the input, f_i is the evaluated function and r is a fresh random value.
1: Decrypt the messages $M = \{\mathsf{AE.Dec}_{pk}(e) \mid e \in E\}$ (output $\perp$ if any decryption fails).
2: Let $L = \mathrm{AggregateTours}(M)$, and output $\perp$ if AggregateTours outputs $\perp$.

 3: Let $S = \varnothing$, val $= \perp$.
 4: **if** $L = \varnothing$ **then** // Start the traversal.
 5:     Decrypt the state $(i, \text{ID}, G) = \text{AE.Dec}_{pk}(c)$ (output $\perp$ if the decryption fails). // The graph and the ID-vector are taken from the encrypted state.
 6:     Let $\text{Path} = (\text{id}, \perp, \ldots, \perp)$ be a vector of length $4n^2$. Let x be the vector of length n, initialized to $\perp$ and set $\text{x}[i] = x_i$.
 7:     Compute Tour_i as the reverse Euler Cycle for G starting at party P_i.
 8:     Let $m = (i, \text{ID}, G, \text{Path}, f_i, \text{x})$.
 9:     Add $(m, \text{Tour}_i[2])$ to S.
10: **else** // Continue traversals.
11:     **for** $m \in L$ **do**
12:         Parse $m = (j, \text{ID}_j, G_j, \text{Path}_j, f_j, \vec{x}_j)$. // The graph and the ID-vector are taken from the message.
13:         Compute Tour_j as the reverse Euler Cycle for G starting at party P_j.
14:         Parse $\text{Path}_j = (p_1, \ldots, p_{\ell_j}, \perp, \ldots, \perp)$. Output $\perp$ if any of the following conditions holds:
            - $\text{id} \neq \text{ID}_j[i]$
            - $p_{\ell_j} \neq i$
            - for any $l \in [\ell_j]$, $p_l \neq \text{Tour}_j[l \mod 2m]$
15:         Let $(m', \text{next}) = \text{ContinueTour}(m, x_i, i, \text{Tour}_j)$.
16:         **if** $m' = \text{Output}$ **then**
17:             Let val $= f_i(\vec{x}_j)$.
18:         **else**
19:             Add (m', next) to S.
20: **Output :** $(\text{val}, \text{EncryptAndFormatOutput}(i, G, r, S, 0))$

Functionality $\mathcal{F}_{\text{HW}}$-subroutines

AggregateTours (M)

// Takes a set of messages and for each party outputs a message that corresponds to its Euler Cycles.

 1: If any $m \in M$ does not parse properly, return $\perp$.
 2: Let $L = \varnothing$.
 3: **for each** $m \in M$ **do**
 4:     Parse $m = (j, \text{ID}, G, \text{Path}, f, \vec{x})$.
 5:     **if** $\exists m' := (j, *, *, *, *, *) \in L$ and $m' \neq m$ **then**
 6:         Output $\perp$.
 7:     **if** $m \notin L$ **then**
 8:         Add m to L.
 9: **return** L

ContinueTour $(m_j, x_i, i, \text{Tour}_j)$

 1: Parse $m_j = (j, \text{ID}_j, G_j, \text{Path}_j, f_j, \vec{x}_j)$.

2: Parse $\texttt{Path}_j = (p_1, \ldots, p_{\ell_j}, \perp, \ldots, \perp)$.
3: **if** $\ell_j = 4m - 1$ and $\texttt{Tour}_j[(\ell_j + 1) \mod 2m] = i$ **then**
4:    **return** $(\texttt{Output}, 0)$.
5: Set $\texttt{Path}_j = (p_1, \ldots, p_{\ell_j}, \texttt{Tour}_j[(\ell_j + 1) \mod 2m], \perp, \ldots, \perp)$.
6: If $\vec{x}_j[i] = \perp$, then set $\vec{x}_j[i] = x_i$.
7: **return** $(m_j, \texttt{Tour}_j[(\ell_j + 1) \mod 2m])$.

EncryptAndFormatOutput $(i, G, r, S, \texttt{sim})^{\text{a}}$

1: For each $d \in \mathbf{N}_G(i)$, let $M_d = \{m : (m, d) \in S\}$.
2: **for** $d \in \mathbf{N}_G(i)$ **do**
3:    If $|M_d| < n$, pad M_d with fake, but parsable, messages until it is length n (messages that start with the party number being 0).
4: **for** $d \in \mathbf{N}_G(i)$ **do**
5:    Let $k = 0$, $E_d = \varnothing$.
6:    **for** $m \in M_d$ **do**
7:       **if** $\texttt{sim} = 0$ **then**
8:          Add $\mathsf{AE.Enc}_{pk}(m; \mathsf{prf}_{rk}(M_d, k, r))$ to E_d. // Used in protocol
9:       **else**
10:          Add $\mathsf{AE.Enc}_{pk}(m; r)$ to E_d. // Used in simulator
11: **return** $\{(E_d, d) : d \in \mathbf{N}_G(i)\}$

---

[a] The additional input $\texttt{sim} \in \{0, 1\}$ will be used by the simulator and can be ignored at this point.

References

[ALM17] Akavia, A., LaVigne, R., Moran, T.: Topology-hiding computation on all graphs. In: Katz, J., Shacham, H. (eds.) CRYPTO 2017, Part I. LNCS, vol. 10401, pp. 447–467. Springer, Cham (2017). https://doi.org/10.1007/978-3-319-63688-7_15

[AM17] Akavia, A., Moran, T.: Topology-hiding computation beyond logarithmic diameter. In: Coron, J.-S., Nielsen, J.B. (eds.) EUROCRYPT 2017, Part II. LNCS, vol. 10212, pp. 609–637. Springer, Cham (2017). https://doi.org/10.1007/978-3-319-56617-7_21

[BBDP01] Bellare, M., Boldyreva, A., Desai, A., Pointcheval, D.: Key-privacy in public-key encryption. In: Boyd, C. (ed.) ASIACRYPT 2001. LNCS, vol. 2248, pp. 566–582. Springer, Heidelberg (2001). https://doi.org/10.1007/3-540-45682-1_33

[BBMM18] Ball, M., Boyle, E., Malkin, T., Moran, T.: Exploring the boundaries of topology-hiding computation. In: Nielsen, J.B., Rijmen, V. (eds.) EURO-CRYPT 2018. LNCS, vol. 10822, pp. 294–325. Springer, Cham (2018). https://doi.org/10.1007/978-3-319-78372-7_10

[BOCG93] Ben-Or, M., Canetti, R., Goldreich, O.: Asynchronous secure computation. In: 25th ACM STOC, pp. 52–61. ACM Press, May 1993

[Can01] Canetti, R.: Universally composable security: a new paradigm for cryptographic protocols. In: 42nd FOCS, pp. 136–145. IEEE Computer Society Press, October 2001

[CCGZ16] Cohen, R., Coretti, S., Garay, J., Zikas, V.: Probabilistic termination and composability of cryptographic protocols. In: Robshaw, M., Katz, J. (eds.) CRYPTO 2016, Part III. LNCS, vol. 9816, pp. 240–269. Springer, Heidelberg (2016). https://doi.org/10.1007/978-3-662-53015-3_9

[CGS08] Chandran, N., Goyal, V., Sahai, A.: New constructions for UC secure computation using tamper-proof hardware. In: Smart, N. (ed.) EUROCRYPT 2008. LNCS, vol. 4965, pp. 545–562. Springer, Heidelberg (2008). https://doi.org/10.1007/978-3-540-78967-3_31

[CKS+14] Choi, S.G., Katz, J., Schröder, D., Yerukhimovich, A., Zhou, H.-S.: (Efficient) universally composable oblivious transfer using a minimal number of stateless tokens. In: Lindell, Y. (ed.) TCC 2014. LNCS, vol. 8349, pp. 638–662. Springer, Heidelberg (2014). https://doi.org/10.1007/978-3-642-54242-8_27

[CLOS02] Canetti, R., Lindell, Y., Ostrovsky, R., Sahai, A.: Universally composable two-party and multi-party secure computation. In: Proceedings of the Thiry-Fourth Annual ACM Symposium on Theory of Computing, pp. 494–503. ACM (2002)

[CT10] Chiesa, A., Tromer, E.: Proof-carrying data and hearsay arguments from signature cards. In: ICS, vol. 10, pp. 310–331 (2010)

[DI05] Damgård, I., Ishai, Y.: Constant-round multiparty computation using a black-box pseudorandom generator. In: Shoup, V. (ed.) CRYPTO 2005. LNCS, vol. 3621, pp. 378–394. Springer, Heidelberg (2005). https://doi.org/10.1007/11535218_23

[Fle83] Fleury, M.: Deux problèmes de géométrie de situation. J. de mathématiques élémentaires **2**, 257–261 (1883)

[Fle91] Fleischner, H.: X. 1 algorithms for Eulerian trails. Eulerian Graphs Relat. Top. : Part 1 (Ann. Discrete Math.) **2**(50), 1–13 (1991)

[GIS+10] Goyal, V., Ishai, Y., Sahai, A., Venkatesan, R., Wadia, A.: Founding cryptography on tamper-proof hardware tokens. In: Micciancio, D. (ed.) TCC 2010. LNCS, vol. 5978, pp. 308–326. Springer, Heidelberg (2010). https://doi.org/10.1007/978-3-642-11799-2_19

[HJ07] Hinkelmann, M., Jakoby, A.: Communications in unknown networks: preserving the secret of topology. Theor. Comput. Sci. **384**(2–3), 184–200 (2007)

[HMQU05] Hofheinz, D., Müller-Quade, J., Unruh, D.: Universally composable zero-knowledge arguments and commitments from signature cards. In: 5th Central European Conference on Cryptology (2005)

[HMTZ16] Hirt, M., Maurer, U., Tschudi, D., Zikas, V.: Network-hiding communication and applications to multi-party protocols. In: Robshaw, M., Katz, J. (eds.) CRYPTO 2016, Part II. LNCS, vol. 9815, pp. 335–365. Springer, Heidelberg (2016). https://doi.org/10.1007/978-3-662-53008-5_12

[KMTZ13] Katz, J., Maurer, U., Tackmann, B., Zikas, V.: Universally composable synchronous computation. In: Sahai, A. (ed.) TCC 2013. LNCS, vol. 7785, pp. 477–498. Springer, Heidelberg (2013). https://doi.org/10.1007/978-3-642-36594-2_27

[LLM+18] LaVigne, R., Liu-Zhang, C.-D., Maurer, U., Moran, T., Mularczyk, M., Tschudi, D.: Topology-hiding computation beyond semi-honest adversaries. In: Beimel, A., Dziembowski, S. (eds.) TCC 2018. LNCS, vol. 11240, pp. 3–35. Springer, Cham (2018). https://doi.org/10.1007/978-3-030-03810-6_1

[LLM+19] LaVigne, R., Liu-Zhang, C.-D., Maurer, U., Moran, T., Mularczyk, M., Tschudi, D.: Topology-hiding computation for networks with unknown delays. Cryptology ePrint Archive, Report 2019/1211 (2019). https://eprint.iacr.org/2019/1211

[LPSY15] Lindell, Y., Pinkas, B., Smart, N.P., Yanai, A.: Efficient constant round multi-party computation combining BMR and SPDZ. In: Gennaro, R., Robshaw, M. (eds.) CRYPTO 2015. LNCS, vol. 9216, pp. 319–338. Springer, Heidelberg (2015). https://doi.org/10.1007/978-3-662-48000-7_16

[Mak97] Makki, S.A.M.: A distributed algorithm for constructing an Eulerian tour. In: IEEE International Performance, Computing, and Communications Conference, 1997. IPCCC 1997, pp. 94–100. IEEE (1997)

[MOR15] Moran, T., Orlov, I., Richelson, S.: Topology-hiding computation. In: Dodis, Y., Nielsen, J.B. (eds.) TCC 2015, Part I. LNCS, vol. 9014, pp. 159–181. Springer, Heidelberg (2015). https://doi.org/10.1007/978-3-662-46494-6_8

Sublinear-Round Byzantine Agreement Under Corrupt Majority

T.-H. Hubert Chan[1]([✉]), Rafael Pass[2], and Elaine Shi[3]

[1] The University of Hong Kong, Pok Fu Lam, Hong Kong
hubert@cs.hku.hk
[2] Cornell Tech, New York, USA
[3] Cornell University, New York, USA

Abstract. Although Byzantine Agreement (BA) has been studied for three decades, perhaps somewhat surprisingly, there still exist significant gaps in our understanding regarding its round complexity. A long-standing open question is the following: *can we achieve BA with sublinear round complexity under corrupt majority?* Due to the beautiful works by Garay et al. (FOCS'07) and Fitzi and Nielsen (DISC'09), we have partial and affirmative answers to this question albeit for the narrow regime $f = n/2 + o(n)$ where f is the number of corrupt nodes and n is the total number of nodes. So far, no positive result is known about the setting $f > 0.51n$ even for static corruption!

In this paper, we make progress along this somewhat stagnant front. We show that there exists a corrupt-majority BA protocol that terminates in $O(\frac{1}{\epsilon} \log \frac{1}{\delta})$ rounds in the worst case, satisfies consistency with probability at least $1 - \delta$, and tolerates $(1 - \epsilon)$ fraction of corrupt nodes. Our protocol secures against an adversary that can corrupt nodes adaptively during the protocol execution but cannot perform "after-the-fact" removal of honest messages that have already been sent prior to corruption. Our upper bound is optimal up to a logarithmic factor in light of the elegant $\Omega(1/\epsilon)$ lower bound by Garay et al. (FOCS'07).

Keywords: Byzantine agreement · Sublinear round complexity · Corrupt majority

1 Introduction

A central abstraction in distributed systems and cryptography is Byzantine Agreement (BA), where a designated sender aims to communicate a bit to multiple receivers. We require two security properties, *consistency* and *validity*. Consistency requires that all honest nodes output the same bit; and validity requires that they all output the sender's bit if the sender is honest. Since the beginning of distributed computing, a foundational and important question is the *round*

T.-H. Hubert Chan is partially supported by the Hong Kong RGC under the grant 17200418.

A. Kiayias et al. (Eds.): PKC 2020, LNCS 12111, pp. 246–265, 2020.
https://doi.org/10.1007/978-3-030-45388-6_9

complexity of Byzantine Agreement. A line of elegant works have investigated this question. The celebrated work of Dolev and Strong [11] showed that there exists an $(f+1)$-round BA protocol that tolerates up to f Byzantine corruptions for any $f < n$. Further, they showed that $f + 1$ rounds is optimal for *deterministic* protocols. Subsequently, it was shown that *randomized* protocols can overcome this $f + 1$ round complexity lower bound: specifically, a sequence of works [2,12,21], beginning with Feldman and Micali [12]'s ingenious work, showed the existence of *expected constant-round* protocols in the *honest-majority* setting.

Now, an important question is whether we can achieve similar results for the corrupt majority setting, i.e., *can randomized protocols help us overcome the $(f+1)$-round complexity lower bound when the majority of nodes can be corrupt?*

Perhaps somewhat surprisingly, despite decades of research on Byzantine Agreement, our understanding of this fundamental question remains limited. To the best of our knowledge, the only known results prior to our work are restricted to very narrow parameter regimes, that is, when the number of corrupt nodes is just a little more than $1/2$. Specifically, Fitzi and Nielsen [13] showed that if the number of corrupt nodes is $n/2 + k$, then an $O(k)$-round (randomized) BA protocol exists assuming the existence of a PKI and secure signatures (and their work improves the earlier result by Garay et al. [14]). In other words, so far we only know how to construct sublinear-round BA protocols in the corrupt majority setting when the number of corruptions is $n/2 + o(n)$.

1.1 Our Results and Contributions

We make progress along this somewhat stagnant front. We show a positive result in the corrupt majority setting assuming the existence of a public-key infrastructure and standard cryptographic assumptions. For any $0 < \epsilon, \delta < 1$, suppose that the adversary corrupts at most $(1 - \epsilon)n$ nodes and runs in time polynomial in some security parameter κ, then we can construct a BA protocol that reaches agreement in $O(\log(1/\delta)/\epsilon)$ number of rounds with probability $1 - \delta - \mathsf{negl}(\kappa)$ where $\mathsf{negl}(\kappa)$ is a negligibly small function in κ corresponding to the probability that the cryptographic primitives employed are broken.

Remark 1. Typically, one requires that the protocol's (statistical) failure probability δ be a negligible function in some statistical security parameter[1] λ: in this typical case, the reader can think of $\log(1/\delta)$ as being polylogarithmic in λ (and independent of n).

Our result is almost optimal in light of an elegant round-complexity lower bound for randomized Byzantine Agreement (BA) by Garay et al. [14]. Specifically, they show that any randomized BA protocol (allowing up to constant failure probability) must consume $\Omega(n/(n-f))$ rounds—note that for $f = (1-\epsilon)n$, the lower bound becomes $\Omega(1/\epsilon)$. In comparison, our upper bound is optimal up to a $\log(1/\delta)$ factor.

---

[1] Here we use a different parameter λ to distinguish from the security parameter κ that is related to the strength of the cryptographic primitives employed.

Note that our result allows for ϵ to be a function in n. For example, for $\epsilon = O(1)$, we give an $O(\log(1/\delta))$-round protocol; and for $\epsilon = O(1/\sqrt{n})$, we give an $O(\sqrt{n} \cdot \log(1/\delta))$-round protocol. Finally, for any $f \leq n - \omega(\log(1/\delta))$, we achieve sublinear (in n) number of rounds which is asymptotically better than the celebrated Dolev-Strong protocol [11].

Theorem 1 (Nearly round-optimal protocols for corrupt majority). *Assume the existence of a public-key infrastructure (PKI) and standard cryptographic assumptions. For parameters $\epsilon, \delta \in (0,1)$ which are allowed to be functions in n, there exists a protocol that terminates in $O(\log(1/\delta)/\epsilon)$ number of rounds and achieves BA with $1 - \delta - \mathsf{negl}(\kappa)$ probability in the presence of an adversary that adaptively corrupts at most $(1 - \epsilon)n$ nodes and runs in time polynomial in κ.*

We stress that previously, except for the narrow parameter regime $f = 0.5n + o(n)$, no sublinear-round protocol is known for the corrupt majority setting, not even under *static* corruption and making any conceivable assumption including very strong ones such as random oracles and the ability of honest nodes to erase secrets from memory. Importantly, *even under static corruption, the standard random committee election technique that is commonly adopted for an honest-majority setting* [1,3,19,23,24] *fails for corrupt majority* for reasons we will explain later in this section as well as Sect. 3.1! Our protocol works in a model where the adversary may adaptively corrupt nodes in the middle of the execution, as long as the adversary cannot retroactively erase messages that were already sent before the corruption took place [1].

Finally, to aid understanding of Theorem 1, we remark that the existence of a public-key infrastructure is long known to be necessary for achieving BA under corrupt majority—without any setup assumptions, BA is not possible under 1/3 or more corruptions [25].

Technical Highlights. In an *honest majority* setting assuming static corruption, a standard technique [1,3,19,23,24] is to elect a random, polylogarithmically sized committee to run a round-inefficient BA protocol; and non-committee members will decide on a value that is vouched for by the majority of the committee. It is tempting to think that the same technique will work for a corrupt majority setting but this intuition turns out to be wrong because majority voting no longer works here.

Our approach adopts a two-step recipe. First, we describe a new technique that combines the random committee election idea with the well-known Dolev-Strong protocol [11], but in a *non-blackbox* manner to allow non-committee members who do not have voting power to keep committee members informed of their latest local state during the consensus. With this technique, we can construct an $O(\log(1/\delta)/\epsilon)$-round BA protocol secure against $(1-\epsilon)n$ *static corruptions*. Even this static-corruption result is new and advances the state-of-the-art regarding the round complexity of BA under corrupt majority.

Next, we describe a technique to upgrade our protocol to defend against even an adaptive adversary. The challenge here is that if the random committee is elected a priori, an adaptive adversary can simply corrupt the entire committee. To defend against such an adversary, we employ adaptively secure Verifiable Random Functions (VRFs) to secretly elect a committee, such that the committee is not revealed until they need to cast votes in the protocol. Not only so, an important technical subtlety is that the committee election must be *bit-specific*, i.e., the committee that is allowed to vote on 0 is elected independently from the committee that is allowed to vote on 1—otherwise, upon observing some committee members voting for 0, the adaptive adversary can immediately corrupt these nodes and make them vote for 1 too (and it turns out that such an attack can break both consistency and validity). Bit-specific committee election is a new technique that was first described in the very recent works by Abraham et al. [1] (PODC'19) and Chan et al. [5] (Eurocrypt'19) where they focus on constructing adaptively secure, bandwidth-efficient consensus protocols. Interestingly, while existing works [1,5] rely on this technique to improve the *bandwidth consumption* of adaptively secure BA under honest majority, we are the first to use these techniques to achieve a non-trivial *round complexity* result for corrupt majority.

Last but not the least, our techniques for achieving these results are in fact conceptually simpler than those of Fitzi and Nielsen [13] (which is an improvement of Garay et al. [14]); and moreover, our results apply to a broad parameter regime whereas the prior works [13,14] only achieve sublinear-round for the narrow regime $f < n/2 + o(n)$. We view the conceptual simplicity as an advantage of our approach.

Open Questions. Although our work advances the state-of-the-art in a fundamental area that has been somewhat stagnant, we still have not completely closed the gap in our understanding. Some interesting open questions remain.

- For example, can we achieve sublinear-round BA under corrupt majority with a *strongly* adaptive adversary who is even allowed to *remove* messages sent by an honest node in round r by adaptively corrupting the node in the same round? Many earlier works in the BA literature in fact consider such a strongly adaptive adversary [4,11,16,21,23].
- Another interesting question is whether we can weaken the setup assumptions needed to get such a result. Specifically, observe that the setup assumptions we need are slightly stronger than that of Dolev and Strong [11].
- For honest majority, expected constant round BA is known [1,2,12,21]. The protocols in this paper are not expected constant round. Therefore, an interesting direction is whether we can have expected constant round protocols in the corrupt majority setting—note that due to the lower bound by Garay et al. [14], this can only be possible if constant fraction of the nodes are corrupt.

We leave these directions for future work.

Additional Related Work. Several other works [8,20] proved lower bounds on the *worst-case* round complexity of randomized BA; and the online full version of this paper [6] presented complete proofs of these lower bounds. Note that these lower bounds are incomparable to Garay et al.'s lower bound [14]. Cohen et al. [10] prove lower bounds on the round complexity of randomized Byzantine agreement (BA) protocols, bounding the halting probability of such protocols after one and two rounds.

A line of works in the literature [9,15,18] have focused on a simulation-based notion of adaptive security for Byzantine Broadcast, where the concern is that the adversary should not be able to observe what the sender wants to broadcast, and then adaptively corrupt the sender to flip the bit. This notion is stronger than what we consider in this paper, but such a strong notion was only achieved earlier by making stronger assumptions than in our paper [15], i.e., the "atomic message" model: after adaptively corrupting a node i, the adversary not only is unable to erase a message i already sent in this round, but also must wait for at least one maximum network delay before the corrupt i can start sending corrupt messages.

2   Preliminaries

2.1   Protocol Execution Model

We assume a standard protocol execution model with n nodes indexed with $[n] := \{1, 2, \ldots, n\}$. An external party called the environment and denoted $\mathcal{Z}$ provides inputs to honest nodes and receives outputs from the honest nodes. An adversary denoted $\mathcal{A}$ controls a subset of the nodes which are said to be *corrupt*; all other nodes are said to be *honest*. All corrupt nodes are under the control of $\mathcal{A}$, i.e., the messages they receive are forwarded to $\mathcal{A}$, and $\mathcal{A}$ controls what messages they will send once they become corrupt. The adversary $\mathcal{A}$ and the environment $\mathcal{Z}$ are allowed to freely exchange messages any time during the execution. To capture protocols that employ cryptography, we assume that all nodes as well as $\mathcal{A}$ and $\mathcal{Z}$ are Interactive Turing Machines that run in time polynomial in some security parameter κ; further, we assume that κ is known to all nodes as well as $\mathcal{A}$ and $\mathcal{Z}$.

We assume a standard *synchronous* network model. Whenever honest nodes send a message, the message is delivered to honest recipients at the beginning of the next round.

Adaptivity of the Adversary. We shall assume an *adaptive* adversary that can corrupt nodes in the middle of the execution. The adversary can observe all currently honest nodes' messages in round r before deciding which subset of these nodes to corrupt in round r. Suppose an honest node P sends a message in some round r and then becomes corrupt in the same round—in this case we assume that the adversary cannot perform "after-the-fact" removal and a-posteriori delete the message that was sent by P in round r before it became corrupt. However, since P is corrupt, the adversary may now inject additional round-r messages on behalf of P.

For ease of understanding, in our exposition we will first describe a warmup protocol secure against a *static* adversary: such an adversary is required to declare the set of corrupt nodes before the start of the execution.

2.2 Byzantine Agreement

In this section we formally define Byzantine Agreement. Recall that there are n nodes indexed by $\{0, 1, 2, \ldots, n-1\}$. Without loss of generality, we shall assume that node 0 is the designated sender.

Syntax. Before the protocol starts, the sender receives an input $b \in \{0, 1\}$ from the environment $\mathcal{Z}$. At the end of the protocol, every node i (including the sender) outputs a bit b_i to the environment $\mathcal{Z}$.

Security Definition. We say that a protocol (satisfying the above syntax) achieves BA with probability p with respect to $(\mathcal{A}, \mathcal{Z})$, iff with probability at least p over the choice of the randomized execution, the following properties are satisfied:

- *Consistency.* If an honest node outputs b_i and another honest node outputs b_j to $\mathcal{Z}$, then it must hold that $b_i = b_j$.
- *Validity.* If the designated sender remains honest throughout and its input is b, then any honest node's output to $\mathcal{Z}$ must be b.

3 Technical Roadmap: Nearly Round-Optimal BA for Corrupt Majority

In this section, we give a slightly informal presentation of our construction. Later on in Sects. 4 and 5, we present a formal description along with formal proofs.

3.1 Warmup: Any Constant Fraction of Static Corruption

For simplicity, let us first focus on the simpler case when the adversary is constrained to making static corruptions. Let ϵ denote the fraction of honest nodes, where ϵ can potentially be a function of n; however, as a warmup, we assume ϵ to be some arbitrarily small constant in this section. We will later extend our approach to more general choices of ϵ and to the case of adaptive corruptions. We stress, however, that except for the narrow parameter regimes in Garay et al.'s result [14], previously it was unknown how to achieve sublinear-round BA in the corrupt majority setting even assuming static corruptions. We use $\delta > 0$ to denote the failure probability (for consistency).

Flawed Strawman Approach. One tempting but flawed approach is to randomly elect a small committee of $\log(1/\delta)$ nodes—for the time being, imagine that a random leader election oracle exists—and have the committee run a corrupt-majority BA protocol such as Dolev-Strong [11]. For the special case $\epsilon = \Theta(1)$ and static corruption, it is not hard to show that except with $O(\delta)$ probability, the committee consists of at least 1 honest node. Thus all honest nodes within the small committee can reach agreement on a bit b^* in $\log(1/\delta)$ number of rounds. Unfortunately, there does not seem to be any straightforward way to securely convey this bit to the non-committee nodes (note that the common approach of taking a majority vote among the committee fails to work in the corrupt majority setting).

To resolve this challenge, our insight is to combine the random committee election idea and the Dolev-Strong protocol in a non-blackbox manner.

Background: the Dolev-Strong Protocol. We start by reviewing the classical Dolev-Strong protocol [11] that achieves linear round complexity and tolerates any number of corruptions—henceforth the term "multicast" means "send to everyone"[2]:

- Every node i maintains an Extracted$_i$ set that is initialized to be empty. In round 0, the sender signs its input bit b, and multicasts b and the signature.
- For each round $r = 1 \ldots n$: for each bit $b \in \{0, 1\}$, if node i has observed valid signatures on b from at least r distinct nodes including the designated sender and $b \notin$ Extracted$_i$: compute a signature on b; multicast b and all signatures it has observed on b (including its own); include b in Extracted$_i$.
- At the end of the protocol, each node i outputs the bit contained in Extracted$_i$ if $|$Extracted$_i| = 1$; else it outputs a canonical bit 0.

This protocol retains consistency, if the number K of rounds is strictly larger than the number f of (eventually) corrupt nodes. First, if an honest node i first adds a bit b to its Extracted$_i$ set in any round $r < K$, then by the end of round $r + 1$, b must be in every honest node's Extracted set. Further, if a honest node i first adds a bit b to its Extracted$_i$ set in the last round K (which is at least $f + 1$), then at least one out of the $K \geq f + 1$ signatures it has observed in round K must be from an honest node—it holds that this honest node must have added b to its Extracted set in some round $r < K$ before the last round; and thus by the end of the last round K, every honest node will have b in its Extracted set.

Achieving Agreement for Non-committee Members. Recall that the problem with the naïve committee election approach is how to convey the committee's decision to the non-committee members. To this end we will combine the committee election idea with Dolev and Strong's protocol in a non-blackbox manner. Suppose that a leader election oracle exists that helps us elect a committee of $\log(1/\delta)$ nodes after the adversary chooses the corrupt nodes. As argued earlier, except with probability $O(\delta)$, there is at least one honest node in the committee.

---

[2] Since in many consensus works the word broadcast is used to mean "Byzantine Agreement", we use "multicast" rather than "broadcast" to avoid ambiguity.

Henceforth we assume that only the committee members are authorized signers and signatures from any non-committee node will be ignored. Our key insight is to divide each round r of the Dolev-Strong protocol into two mini-rounds:

- Every node i maintains an Extracted$_i$ set that is initialized to be empty. In round 0, the sender signs its input bit b, and multicasts b and the signature.
- For each round $r = 1, 2, \ldots, S + 1$ where $S = \log(1/\delta)$ denotes the committee size,
   1. In the first mini-round, if *any* node i receives a bit $b \notin$ Extracted$_i$ with r signatures from distinct signers, it adds b to Extracted and multicasts b tagged with all signatures observed so far for b.
   2. In the second mini-round, only the committee members perform the actions above and moreover a committee member always appends its own signature for b when multicasting b (and all other seen signatures on b).
- Each node i outputs the bit contained in Extracted$_i$ if $|$Extracted$_i| = 1$; else it outputs a canonical bit 0.

Note that this approach guarantees that if any honest node newly adds a bit b to its Extracted set in round r, then all committee nodes must have signed it by the end of round r (if not earlier) and multicast the corresponding signature. Thus in the first mini-round of round $r + 1$, every honest node will have added b to its Extracted set. At this moment, it is not difficult to see that as long as one committee member is honest, if the above protocol is executed for at least $f + 1$ rounds then we can argue consistency using a similar approach as Dolev-Strong.

3.2 Achieving Adaptive Security and Removing the Leader Election Oracle

The above protocol enables the committee to securely convey its decision to non-committee nodes; unfortunately, the protocol does not defend against adaptive corruptions. Specifically, since the elected committee is small relative to n, an adaptive adversary can simply corrupt all committee members after they are elected. We now present an approach for achieving adaptive security borrowing the "bit-specific committee election" idea that was previously employed in the construction of small-bandwidth honest-majority BA protocols by Abraham et al. [1] and Chan et al. [5]. As a by-product we will have instantiated the leader election oracle that was needed earlier.

Our idea is to *tie the committee election to each individual bit*, i.e., there is a separate committee that are allowed to vote on 0 and 1 respectively (henceforth called the 0-committee and the 1-committee respectively), and the designated sender is in both committees. Specifically, Abraham et al. [1] and Chan et al. [5] describe how to realize bit-specific committee election using a suitable Verifiable Random Function (VRF) with adaptive security. Take $b = 0$ as an example. For a node i to determine if he is on the 0-committee, he checks the following:

$$\text{let } (\rho, \pi) := \mathsf{VRF}_{\mathsf{sk}_i}(0), \text{ and check if } \rho < D_p$$

Here sk_i is his private key, D_p is an appropriate difficulty parameter that determines the success probability (denoted p) of each election attempt, and π is a proof generated by the VRF which will be used below for verification. Concretely, the probability p is chosen such that the expected number of nodes elected into either the 0-committee or 1-committee is $\log(1/\delta)$. To convince others that i is indeed an eligible member of the 0-committee, i reveals both ρ and π, and everyone can now verify, using i's public key, that indeed ρ is the correct outcome of the VRF.

We now explain how to use bit-specific committee election to achieve adaptive security. Suppose a 0-committee member i becomes immediately corrupt after signing 0 and multicasting signatures on 0. However, corrupting node i does not necessarily help voting for the bit 1—in particular, since the two committees are independently selected, node i is *only as good as any other node in terms of its likelihood of being elected into the 1-committee*. Thus, corrupting node i is only as good as corrupting any other node at this point. In the proof of Lemma 2, we will formalize the above intuition.

Putting it Altogether. We say that a tuple (b, i, π) is a valid *vote* on b iff either (1) $i = 1$ is the designated sender and π is a valid signature on b from i; or (2) $i \neq 1$ and π is a valid VRF proof proving i to be in the b-committee. The protocol is described below.

- Every node i initializes $\mathsf{Extracted}_i := \emptyset$. The sender signs its input bit b and multicasts b as well as the signature.
- For round $r = 1, \ldots, \log(1/\delta)$, every node i performs the following:
  1. First mini-round: for every $b \notin \mathsf{Extracted}_i$ such that the node has observed at least r votes from distinct nodes including the sender: add b to $\mathsf{Extracted}_i$; multicast b and all observed votes on b.
  2. Second mini-round: for every $b \notin \mathsf{Extracted}_i$, if node i belongs to the b-committee and moreover the node has observed at least r votes from distinct nodes including the sender: add b to $\mathsf{Extracted}_i$; compute a new vote on b; multicast b and all observed votes on b (including the newly created one).
- Every node i outputs the bit contained in $\mathsf{Extracted}_i$ if $|\mathsf{Extracted}_i| = 1$; else output a canonical bit 0.

3.3 Organization of the Subsequent Formal Sections

The subsequent sections formalize the description contained in this section. Specifically, in Sect. 4, we describe an idealized version of the protocol assuming an ideal eligibility election oracle, and we conduct stochastic analysis of the idealized protocol for more general choices of ϵ. Next, in Sect. 5, we describe how to replace the idealized leader eligibility election oracle with suitable *adaptively secure* cryptographic primitives, and yet retain the security properties of the idealized protocol.

4   Formal Description of $\mathcal{F}_{\mathrm{mine}}$-Hybrid Protocol

In the sections to follow, we will formally present our upper bound for the corrupt majority case. We will first describe our protocol assuming an idealized oracle called $\mathcal{F}_{\mathrm{mine}}$ that is in charge of random eligibility election [3]—this approach allows us to "abstract away" the cryptography and focus on analyzing the stochastic properties of the protocol first. Later in Sect. 5, we will show how to leverage standard techniques to remove the $\mathcal{F}_{\mathrm{mine}}$ assumption and instantiate it with appropriate, adaptively secure cryptography.

Henceforth, to make our description and proofs more precise, we define some additional terminology. At any time in the protocol, nodes that remain honest so far are referred to as *so-far honest* nodes; nodes that remain honest till the end of the protocol are referred to as *forever honest* nodes.

4.1   Ideal Functionality $\mathcal{F}_{\mathrm{mine}}$ for Random Eligibility Determination

The idealized oracle $\mathcal{F}_{\mathrm{mine}}$ provides the following functionality. A node i can query $\mathcal{F}_{\mathrm{mine}}$ to check if it is an eligible member of the b-committee where $b \in \{0, 1\}$. Upon receiving such a query, $\mathcal{F}_{\mathrm{mine}}$ flips a random coin (with appropriate probability) to determine the answer; further $\mathcal{F}_{\mathrm{mine}}$ stores this answer and returns it to any node that queries it henceforth.

More formally, the $\mathcal{F}_{\mathrm{mine}}$ ideal functionality has two activation points:

- Whenever a node i calls $\mathtt{mine}(b)$ for the first time where $b \in \{0, 1\}$, $\mathcal{F}_{\mathrm{mine}}$ flips a random coin (parametrized with an appropriate probability p) to decide if i is a committee member for b.
  Henceforth if a node i calls $\mathcal{F}_{\mathrm{mine}}.\mathtt{mine}(b)$, we also say that i makes a mining attempt for the bit b.
- If node i has called $\mathtt{mine}(b)$ and the attempt is successful, anyone who calls $\mathcal{F}_{\mathrm{mine}}.\mathtt{verify}(b, i)$ will obtain an answer of 1; all other calls to $\mathcal{F}_{\mathrm{mine}}.\mathtt{verify}(b, i)$ will return 0.

Henceforth in the paper, we assume that the choice of the success probability p is a global, public parameter. We will describe how to choose p later.

4.2   Formal Protocol in the $\mathcal{F}_{\mathrm{mine}}$-Hybrid World

We describe how to achieve adaptively secure BA with sublinear round complexity, tolerating $1 - \epsilon$ fraction of corruption for any arbitrarily small positive constant ϵ. Recall that without loss of generality, we assume that node 0 is the designated sender.

Valid Vote. With respect to some moment in time, a *valid vote* for the value b from node i is of the following form:

---

[3] The name $\mathcal{F}_{\mathrm{mine}}$ is making an analogy to Bitcoin mining. Each call to $\mathcal{F}_{\mathrm{mine}}$ is like an attempt to mine a ticket to vote in the protocol.

Byzantine Agreement: Synchronous Network with Corrupt Majority

Parameters: Let ϵ be the fraction of forever honest nodes and δ be the desired failure probability.
$\mathcal{F}_{\mathrm{mine}}$ is instantiated with a probability $p := \min\{1, \frac{1}{\epsilon n} \log \frac{2}{\delta}\}$. Let $R = \lceil \frac{3}{\epsilon} \cdot \ln \frac{2}{\delta} \rceil$ be the total number of stages.

Stage 0: Initialization. No message is multicast in this stage.

- The sender 0 produces a valid 1-batch of vote for its value b_0 by producing a signature $\mathtt{Sig}_0(b_0)$.
- Every node i sets $\mathsf{Extracted}_i \leftarrow \emptyset$.

Stage $r \in [1..R]$. Each such stage consists of 2 rounds.

1. In the first round, every node i performs the following:
   - For each bit b, if node i has seen a valid r-batch of votes for b and $b \notin \mathsf{Extracted}_i$, then it multicasts any such r-batch for b to everyone, and sets $\mathsf{Extracted}_i \leftarrow \mathsf{Extracted}_i \cup \{b\}$.
2. In the second round, each node $i \neq 1$ does the following. For each bit b, if it has seen a valid r-batch of votes for b and node i has never called $\mathcal{F}_{\mathrm{mine}}.\mathtt{mine}(b)$ before, then it calls $\mathcal{F}_{\mathrm{mine}}.\mathtt{mine}(b)$ and executes the following if the result is successful:
   - It sets $\mathsf{Extracted}_i \leftarrow \mathsf{Extracted}_i \cup \{b\}$.
   - It multicasts a valid $(r+1)$-batch of votes for b, possibly by adding its own valid vote (b, i).

Stage $R + 1$: Termination. No message is multicast in this stage. Every node i performs the following:

- For each bit b, if node i has seen a valid $(R+1)$-batch for b, it sets $\mathsf{Extracted}_i \leftarrow \mathsf{Extracted}_i \cup \{b\}$.
- **Output to $\mathcal{Z}$.** If $|\mathsf{Extracted}_i| = 1$, then it outputs the unique $b_i \in \mathsf{Extracted}_i$ to $\mathcal{Z}$; otherwise, outputs the default value 0 to $\mathcal{Z}$.

Fig. 1. Our protocol. The protocol is described in the $\mathcal{F}_{\mathrm{mine}}$-hybrid world. Section 5 will explain how to instantiate $\mathcal{F}_{\mathrm{mine}}$ with cryptographic assumptions.

- If $i = 0$, i.e., i is the sender, then a valid vote is of the form $(b, 0, \mathtt{Sig}_0(b))$, where $\mathtt{Sig}_0(b)$ denotes a valid signature from the sender on the bit b.
- For $i \neq 0$, a valid vote w.r.t. some time t is of the form (b, i) such that $\mathcal{F}_{\mathrm{mine}}.\mathtt{verify}(b, i)$ returns 1 at time t, i.e., by time t, node i must have called $\mathcal{F}_{\mathrm{mine}}.\mathtt{mine}(b)$ and the result must have been successful.

Valid Vote Batch. For $r \geq 1$, a valid r-batch of votes for value b consists of valid votes for value b from r distinct nodes, one of which must be the sender 0. Note that just like the definition of a valid vote, a valid vote batch is also defined w.r.t. to some moment of time (which we sometimes omit writing explicitly if the context is clear).

Since we have explained the intutition behind our protocol earlier, we now give a formal presentation of the protocol in Fig. 1—here "multicast" means sending a message to everyone.

4.3   Analysis in the $\mathcal{F}_{\mathrm{mine}}$-Hybrid World

In this subsection, we shall prove the following theorem for our $\mathcal{F}_{\mathrm{mine}}$-hybrid-world protocol described in Fig. 1.

Theorem 2. *Assume that the signature scheme is secure. For any $0 < \epsilon, \delta < 1$ (that can be functions of n), the $\mathcal{F}_{\mathrm{mine}}$-hybrid Byzantine agreement protocol described in Fig. 1 satisfies consistency (with probability at least $1-\delta$) and validity and terminates in $2 \cdot \lceil \frac{3}{\epsilon} \ln \frac{2}{\delta} \rceil$ rounds (with probability 1) w.r.t. any non-uniform p.p.t. $(\mathcal{A}, \mathcal{Z})$ that corrupts no more than $(1 - \epsilon)n$ nodes.*

Committee. Without loss of generality, we consider a modification to the protocol, where $\mathcal{F}_{\mathrm{mine}}$ flips a coin for each (b, i) pair upfront. When $\mathcal{F}_{\mathrm{mine}}$ receives **mine** queries, it simply retrieves the corresponding coin that has already been flipped earlier. In this world, we can define the notion of *committees* more easily: For each bit b, a node $i \neq 1$ is in the committee Com_b for b, if $\mathsf{Coin}[b, i] = 1$.

Honest and Corrupt Votes. A (valid) vote for a bit b from a node i is said to be honest if the node is so-far honest at the moment the vote is cast, which is the moment when node i calls $\mathcal{F}_{\mathrm{mine}}.\mathsf{mine}(b)$; otherwise, the (valid) vote is said to be corrupt or dishonest.

Handling Signature Failure. Assume that the signature scheme is secure, and that $\mathcal{A}$ and $\mathcal{Z}$ are probabilistic polynomial time, it must hold that except with negligible probability, no so-far honest node should have a forged signature in view. This is formalized in the following fact:

Fact 1 (No signature failure). *Assume that the signature scheme is secure. Then, except with negligible probability, the following holds: if the sender is so-far honest and did not sign the bit $b \in \{0,1\}$, then no so-far honest node has seen a valid signature on b from the sender.*

Proof. By straightforward reduction to signature security.

There are two types of bad events that can cause our protocol's security to fail: (1) signature failure (captured by Fact 1); and (2) other stochastic bad events related to $\mathcal{F}_{\mathrm{mine}}$'s coin flips. In the next subsection, we will bound the probability of the latter type of bad events—and there we will pretend that the signature scheme is "ideal" and there are no signature failures—but we stress that technically, we are actually taking a union bound over signature failure and the stochastic bad events analyzed in the next subsection.

Proofs: Bounding Stochastic Bad Events. The protocol clearly satisfies termination; and validity also follows trivially from Fact 1. Thus the remainder of this section will focus on the consistency proof. Our proofs work for general choices of parameters, including the honest fraction ϵ (which can be a function of n) and the failure probability δ. As a special case, assuming that ϵ is any arbitrarily small positive constant and moreover, the mining difficulty parameter p and the total number of stages R are chosen as in Fig. 1, then the failure probability $\delta = e^{-\omega(\log \kappa)}$ would be a negligible function in the security parameter κ.

To prove consistency, we will prove that there is no *discrepancy* for either bit (except with δ probability), which is formally defined as follows.

Discrepancy for b. A *discrepancy* for $b \in \{0, 1\}$ occurs if at the end of the protocol there exist two honest nodes such that b is in exactly one of the two corresponding extracted sets. We further classify the following two types of discrepancy if, in addition, the following conditions are satisfied.

Type-A. A type-A discrepancy for b occurs when b is first added to some honest node's extracted set in some stage in $[1..R]$.

Type-B. A type-B discrepancy for value b occurs when $R + 1$ is the only stage in which b is added to any honest node's extracted set.

Fact 2. *If an honest vote is cast for value b (at the second round of some stage) during the protocol, then for each forever honest node i, it holds at termination that $b \in$ Extracted$_i$.*

Lemma 1 (Type-A Discrepancy). *Suppose the probability of success for $\mathcal{F}_{\mathrm{mine}}.\mathrm{mine}(\cdot)$ is $p := \min\{1, \frac{1}{\epsilon n} \cdot \log \frac{1}{\delta}\}$. For any value b, a type-A discrepancy for value b happens with probability at most δ.*

Proof. It suffices to prove the claim that if a type-A discrepancy for value b occurs, then there are at least ϵn nodes, each of which has called $\mathcal{F}_{\mathrm{mine}}.\mathrm{mine}(b)$ with unsuccessful result at some moment when it is still so-far honest. For the trivial case $e^{-\epsilon n} \geq \delta$, we have $p = 1$ and every mining attempt must be successful. For the case $e^{-\epsilon n} < \delta$, this event happens with probability at most $(1 - p)^{\epsilon n} \leq \exp(-\epsilon np) \leq \delta$, which implies the result of the lemma.

The rest of the proof establishes the above claim. Observe that a type-A discrepancy implies that at some moment, there is a first time when a so-far honest node adds b to its extracted set in some stage $r \in [1..R]$. If this happened in the **second** round of stage r, then this so-far honest node is in Com$_b$ and would have been able to cast a valid $(r+1)$-batch of votes that can be seen by everyone in stage $r + 1$. Therefore, a type-A discrepancy means that b is first added to a so-far honest node i in the **first** round of stage r, which means node i has seen some valid r-batch of votes.

Since this node i is so-far honest, it will multicast this batch to everyone, and every so-far honest node that has not tried to call $\mathcal{F}_{\mathrm{mine}}.\mathrm{mine}(b)$ before will call $\mathcal{F}_{\mathrm{mine}}.\mathrm{mine}(b)$ in the second round of stage r.

Since a type-A discrepancy occurs, it must be case that all (previous or present) trials of $\mathcal{F}_{\text{mine}}.\text{mine}(b)$ by so-far honest nodes have returned unsuccessful. Since at any moment, the number of so-far honest nodes is at least ϵn, we conclude that the claim is true, and this completes the proof.

Fact 3 (Chernoff Bound). *Suppose X is the sum of independent $\{0,1\}$-random variables. Then, for any $\tau > 0$, the following holds:*

$$\Pr[X \geq (1+\tau)E[X]] \leq \exp(-\frac{\tau \cdot \min\{\tau, 1\} \cdot E[X]}{3})$$

Lemma 2 (Type-B Discrepancy). *Let $p := \min\{1, \frac{1}{\epsilon n} \log \frac{1}{\delta}\}$ as in Lemma 1, and set $R := \lceil \frac{3}{\epsilon} \cdot \ln \frac{1}{\delta} \rceil$. Then, for any value b, a type-B discrepancy for b happens with probability at most δ.*

Proof. A type-B discrepancy for b occurs implies that some honest node i sees a valid $(R+1)$-batch of votes, which are all cast by dishonest nodes. This is because if one of the votes was cast by a so-far honest node (in the second round) of some stage $r \in [1..R]$, then everyone would have seen a valid $(r+1)$-batch in stage $r+1$, in which case a discrepancy would not have occurred.

Observe that a dishonest vote is cast only if a node is corrupted before it calls $\mathcal{F}_{\text{mine}}.\text{mine}(b)$ for the first time. There are at most $(1-\epsilon)n$ dishonest nodes and each of them can call $\mathcal{F}_{\text{mine}}.\text{mine}(b)$ successfully independently with probability p. **Important:** Note that even if nodes are corrupted adaptively (for instance, based on mining results of other values), the success probability of mining value b is still p.

For the trivial case, $\delta \leq e^{-\epsilon n}$, $R \geq 3n$ is not interesting; hence, it suffices to consider $\delta > e^{-\epsilon n}$ and $p < 1$. We next consider two cases.

Case $\epsilon \geq \frac{1}{4}$. Set $\tau := \frac{3\epsilon}{1-\epsilon} \geq 1$. By Chernoff Bound, the probability that there are more than $R = \lceil \frac{3}{\epsilon} \cdot \ln \frac{1}{\delta} \rceil \geq (1+\tau)(1-\epsilon)np$ dishonest votes is at most $\exp(-\frac{\tau(1-\epsilon)np}{3}) = \delta$.

Case $\epsilon < \frac{1}{4}$. Set $\tau = 1$. By Chernoff Bound, the probability that there are more than $R = \lceil \frac{3}{\epsilon} \cdot \ln \frac{1}{\delta} \rceil \geq (1+\tau)(1-\epsilon)np$ dishonest votes is at most $\exp(-\frac{(1-\epsilon)np}{3}) \leq \delta$.

Corollary 1. *Suppose that with probability 1, there are at least ϵ fraction of forever honest nodes and let δ be the desired failure probability. By setting the mining success probability $p := \min\{1, \frac{1}{\epsilon n} \log \frac{2}{\delta}\}$ and $R := \lceil \frac{3}{\epsilon} \cdot \ln \frac{2}{\delta} \rceil$, the protocol satisfies consistency with probability at least $1 - \delta$.*

Proof. For the trivial case $\frac{\delta}{2} \leq e^{-\epsilon n}$, the bound $R \geq 3n$ is not interesting. Hence, it suffices to consider $\frac{\delta}{2} > e^{-\epsilon n}$ and $p < 1$.

To use union bound over type-A and type-B discrepancy for both values of b, we set the failure probability to be $\frac{\delta}{2}$ in Lemmas 1 and 2.

5 Removing the Idealized Functionality $\mathcal{F}_{\mathsf{mine}}$

So far, we have assumed the existence of an $\mathcal{F}_{\mathsf{mine}}$ ideal functionality. In this section, we describe how to instantiate the protocols in the real world. Our techniques follow the approach described by Abraham et al. [1]. Although this part is not a contribution of our paper, for completeness, we describe all the building blocks and the approach in a self-contained manner.

5.1 Preliminary: Adaptively Secure Non-interactive Zero-Knowledge Proofs

We use $f(\kappa) \approx g(\kappa)$ to mean that there exists a negligible function $\nu(\kappa)$ such that $|f(\kappa) - g(\kappa)| < \nu(\kappa)$.

A non-interactive proof system henceforth denoted nizk for an NP language $\mathcal{L}$ consists of the following algorithms.

- crs $\leftarrow$ Gen($1^\kappa, \mathcal{L}$): Takes in a security parameter κ, a description of the language $\mathcal{L}$, and generates a common reference string crs.
- $\pi \leftarrow$ P(crs, stmt, w): Takes in crs, a statement stmt, a witness w such that (stmt, w) $\in \mathcal{L}$, and produces a proof π.
- $b \leftarrow$ V(crs, stmt, π): Takes in a crs, a statement stmt, and a proof π, and outputs 0 (reject) or 1 (accept).

Perfect Completeness. A non-interactive proof system is said to be perfectly complete, if an honest prover with a valid witness can always convince an honest verifier. More formally, for any (stmt, w) $\in \mathcal{L}$, we have that

$$\Pr\left[\mathsf{crs} \leftarrow \mathsf{Gen}(1^\kappa, \mathcal{L}),\ \pi \leftarrow \mathsf{P}(\mathsf{crs}, \mathsf{stmt}, w) : \mathsf{V}(\mathsf{crs}, \mathsf{stmt}, \pi) = 1\right] = 1$$

Non-erasure Computational Zero-Knowledge. Non-erasure zero-knowledge requires that under a simulated CRS, there is a simulated prover that can produce proofs without needing the witness. Further, upon obtaining a valid witness to a statement a-posteriori, the simulated prover can explain the simulated NIZK with the correct witness.

We say that a proof system (Gen, P, V) satisfies non-erasure computational zero-knowledge iff there exists probabilistic polynomial time algorithms (Gen$_0$, P$_0$, Explain) such that

$$\Pr\left[\mathsf{crs} \leftarrow \mathsf{Gen}(1^\kappa), \mathcal{A}^{\mathsf{Real}(\mathsf{crs}, \cdot, \cdot)}(\mathsf{crs}) = 1\right] \approx$$
$$\Pr\left[(\mathsf{crs}_0, \tau_0) \leftarrow \mathsf{Gen}_0(1^\kappa), \mathcal{A}^{\mathsf{Ideal}(\mathsf{crs}_0, \tau_0, \cdot, \cdot)}(\mathsf{crs}_0) = 1\right],$$

where Real(crs, stmt, w) runs the honest prover P(crs, stmt, w) with randomness r and obtains the proof π, it then outputs (π, r); Ideal(crs$_0$, τ_0, stmt, w) runs the simulated prover $\pi \leftarrow$ P$_0$(crs$_0$, τ_0, stmt, ρ) with randomness ρ and without a witness, and then runs $r \leftarrow$ Explain(crs$_0$, τ_0, stmt, w, ρ) and outputs (π, r).

Perfect Knowledge Extraction. We say that a proof system (Gen, P, V) satisfies perfect knowledge extraction, if there exists probabilistic polynomial-time algorithms (Gen$_1$, Extr), such that for all (even unbounded) adversary $\mathcal{A}$,

$$\Pr\left[\text{crs} \leftarrow \text{Gen}(1^\kappa) : \mathcal{A}(\text{crs}) = 1\right] = \Pr\left[(\text{crs}_1, \tau_1) \leftarrow \text{Gen}_1(1^\kappa) : \mathcal{A}(\text{crs}_1) = 1\right],$$

and moreover,

$$\Pr[(\text{crs}_1, \tau_1) \leftarrow \text{Gen}_1(1^\kappa); (\text{stmt}, \pi) \leftarrow \mathcal{A}(\text{crs}_1); w \leftarrow \text{Extr}(\text{crs}_1, \tau_1, \text{stmt}, \pi) :$$
$$\text{V}(\text{crs}_1, \text{stmt}, \pi) = 1, \text{ but } (\text{stmt}, w) \notin \mathcal{L}] = 0$$

5.2 Adaptively Secure Non-interactive Commitment Scheme

An adaptively secure non-interactive commitment scheme consists of the following algorithms:

- crs $\leftarrow$ Gen(1^κ): Takes in a security parameter κ, and generates a common reference string crs.
- $C \leftarrow$ com(crs, v, ρ): Takes in crs, a value v, and a random string ρ, and outputs a committed value C.
- $b \leftarrow$ ver(crs, C, v, ρ): Takes in a crs, a commitment C, a purported opening (v, ρ), and outputs 0 (reject) or 1 (accept).

Computationally Hiding Under Selective Opening. We say that a commitment scheme (Gen, com, ver) is computationally hiding under selective opening, iff there exists a probabilistic polynomial time algorithms (Gen$_0$, com$_0$, Explain) such that

$$\Pr\left[\text{crs} \leftarrow \text{Gen}(1^\kappa), \mathcal{A}^{\text{Real}(\text{crs}, \cdot)}(\text{crs}) = 1\right] \approx$$
$$\Pr\left[(\text{crs}_0, \tau_0) \leftarrow \text{Gen}_0(1^\kappa), \mathcal{A}^{\text{Ideal}(\text{crs}_0, \tau_0, \cdot)}(\text{crs}_0) = 1\right],$$

where Real(crs, v) runs the honest algorithm com(crs, v, r) with randomness r and obtains the commitment C, it then outputs (C, r); Ideal(crs$_0, \tau_0, v$) runs the simulated algorithm $C \leftarrow$ com$_0$(crs$_0, \tau_0, \rho$) with randomness ρ and without v, and then runs $r \leftarrow$ Explain(crs$_0, \tau_0, v, \rho$) and outputs (C, r).

Perfectly Binding. A commitment scheme is said to be perfectly binding iff for every crs in the support of the honest CRS generation algorithm, there does not exist $(v, \rho) \neq (v', \rho')$ such that com(crs, v, ρ) = com(crs, v', ρ').

Theorem 3 (Instantiation of our NIZK and commitment schemes [17]).
Assume standard bilinear group assumptions[4]. Then, there exists a proof system that satisfies perfect completeness, non-erasure computational zero-knowledge, and perfect knowledge extraction. Further, there exist a commitment scheme that is perfectly binding and computationally hiding under selective opening.

---

[4] We need either the subgroup decision assumption or the decisional linear assumption according to Groth et al. [17].

Proof. The existence of such a NIZK scheme was shown by Groth et al. [17] via a building block that they called *homomorphic proof commitment scheme*. This building block can also be used to achieve a commitment scheme with the desired properties.

NP Language Used in Our Construction. In our construction, we will use the following NP language $\mathcal{L}$. A pair $(\mathsf{stmt}, w) \in \mathcal{L}$ iff

- parse $\mathsf{stmt} := (\rho, c, \mathsf{crs}_{\mathrm{comm}}, b)$, parse $w := (\mathsf{sk}, s)$;
- it must hold that $c = \mathsf{comm}(\mathsf{crs}_{\mathrm{comm}}, \mathsf{sk}, s)$, and $\mathsf{PRF}_{\mathsf{sk}}(b) = \rho$.

5.3   Removing $\mathcal{F}_{\mathrm{mine}}$ with Cryptography

Cryptographic Building Blocks. We can remove the $\mathcal{F}_{\mathrm{mine}}$ oracle by leveraging cryptographic building blocks including a pseudorandom function family, a non-interactive zero-knowledge proof system that satisfies computational zero-knowledge and computational soundness, and a perfectly binding and computationally hiding commitment scheme.

Compiler from Ideal-World Protocol to a Real-World Protocol. Essentially, with these primitives we can construct an appropriate VRF with adaptive security. Note that some earlier works [7,22] also achieved such an adaptively secure VRF using unique signatures and random oracles. Here we adopt the approach in Abraham et al. [1], since it removes the random oracle assumption.

We now provide a formal description of how to compile our $\mathcal{F}_{\mathrm{mine}}$-hybrid protocols into real-world protocols using cryptography. The intuition is very simple. Every node commits to a PRF secret key in its public key. This committed secret key is used to evaluate a PRF on $b = 0$ or $b = 1$ to determine whether the node belongs to the b-th committee. The node can then prove to everyone that the eligibility determination is performed correctly by employing a NIZK. Below we give a more formal description of how to rely on this idea to compile the earlier $\mathcal{F}_{\mathrm{mine}}$-hybrid protocol to the real world.

- **PKI setup.** Upfront, a trusted party runs the CRS generation algorithms of the commitment and the NIZK scheme to obtain $\mathsf{crs}_{\mathrm{comm}}$ and $\mathsf{crs}_{\mathrm{nizk}}$. It then chooses a secret PRF key for every node, where the i-th node has key sk_i. It publishes $(\mathsf{crs}_{\mathrm{comm}}, \mathsf{crs}_{\mathrm{nizk}})$ as the public parameters, and each node i's public key denoted pk_i is computed as a commitment of sk_i using a random string s_i. The collection of all users' public keys is published to form the PKI, i.e., the mapping from each node i to its public key pk_i is public information. Further, each node i is given the secret key (sk_i, s_i).
- **Instantiating $\mathcal{F}_{\mathrm{mine}}.\mathsf{mine}$.** Recall that in the ideal-world protocol a node i calls $\mathcal{F}_{\mathrm{mine}}.\mathsf{mine}(b)$ to check if it is in the b-th committee. Now, instead, the node i calls $\rho := \mathsf{PRF}_{\mathsf{sk}_i}(b)$, and computes the NIZK proof

$$\pi := \mathsf{nizk}.\mathsf{P}((\rho, \mathsf{pk}_i, \mathsf{crs}_{\mathrm{comm}}, b), (\mathsf{sk}_i, s_i))$$

where s_i the randomness used in committing sk_i during the trusted setup. Intuitively, this zero-knowledge proof proves that the evaluation outcome ρ is correct w.r.t. the node's public key (which is a commitment of its secret key). The mining attempt for b is considered successful if $\rho < D_p$ where D_p is an appropriate difficulty parameter such that a random string of appropriate length is less than D_p with probability p—the probability p is selected in the same way as the earlier $\mathcal{F}_{\mathrm{mine}}$-hybrid world in Fig. 1.

Recall that earlier in our $\mathcal{F}_{\mathrm{mine}}$-hybrid protocol, every message multicast by a so-far honest node i is a vote of the form (b, i) where node i has successfully called $\mathcal{F}_{\mathrm{mine}}.\mathtt{mine}(b)$. Each such message (b, i) that node i wants to multicast is translated to the real-world protocol as follows: we rewrite (b, i) as (b, i, ρ, π) where the terms ρ and π are those generated by i in place of calling $\mathcal{F}_{\mathrm{mine}}.\mathtt{mine}(b)$ in the real world (as explained above). Note that in our $\mathcal{F}_{\mathrm{mine}}$-hybrid protocols a node $j \neq i$ may also relay a message (b, i) mined by i—in the real world, node j would be relaying (b, i, ρ, π) instead.

- **Instantiating $\mathcal{F}_{\mathrm{mine}}.\mathtt{verify}$.** In the $\mathcal{F}_{\mathrm{mine}}$-hybrid world, a node would call $\mathcal{F}_{\mathrm{mine}}.\mathtt{verify}$ to check the validity of votes upon receiving them, In the real-world protocol, we perform the following instead: upon receiving the vote (b, i, ρ, π), a node can verify the vote's validity by checking:
  1. $\rho < D_p$ where p is an appropriate difficulty parameter parametrized in the same way as Fig. 1 and
  2. π is indeed a valid NIZK for the statement formed by the tuple $(\rho, \mathsf{pk}_i, \mathsf{crs}_{\mathrm{comm}}, b)$. The tuple is discarded unless both checks pass.

Extending the Security Guarantees to the Real-World Protocol. Now using the same proofs as Abraham et al. [1], we can prove that the compiled real-world protocols enjoy the same security properties as the $\mathcal{F}_{\mathrm{mine}}$-hybrid protocols. Since the proofs follow identically, we omit the details and refer the reader to Abraham et al. [1]. In the following theorem we assume that the pseudorandom function family employed is secure, the non-interactive zero-knowledge proof system employed satisfies computational zero-knowledge and computational soundness, and moreover, the commitment scheme is perfectly binding and computationally hiding.

Theorem 4 (Real-world protocol: restatement of Theorem 1). *Assume that the cryptographic primitives employed are secure in the sense mentioned above[5]. For parameters $\epsilon, \delta \in (0, 1)$ which are allowed to be functions in n, the aforementioned real-world protocol terminates in $O(\log(1/\delta)/\epsilon)$ number of rounds and achieves BA with $1 - \delta - \mathsf{negl}(\kappa)$ probability in the presence of an adversary that adaptively corrupts at most $(1 - \epsilon)n$ nodes and runs in time polynomial in κ.*

---

[5] Specifically, see the "Cryptographic building blocks" paragraph above for the required security notions of the cryptographic primitives employed.

Proof. Note our techniques for instantiating $\mathcal{F}_{\text{mine}}$ with actual cryptography are borrowed from Abraham et al. [1]. Their proof for showing that the real-world protocol preserves the security properties proved in the ideal world is immediately applicable to our case.

Acknowledgments. We would like to thank Vassilis Zikas for very helpful discussions, and we gratefully thank the PKC'2020 reviewers for the detailed and thoughtful comments.

References

1. Abraham, I., et al.: Communication complexity of Byzantine agreement, revisited. In: PODC (2019)
2. Abraham, I., Devadas, S., Dolev, D., Nayak, K., Ren, L.: Synchronous Byzantine agreement with optimal resilience, expected $o(n^2)$ communication, and expected $o(1)$ rounds. In: Financial Cryptography and Data Security (FC) (2019)
3. Boyle, E., Chung, K.-M., Pass, R.: Large-scale secure computation: multi-party computation for (parallel) RAM programs. In: Gennaro, R., Robshaw, M. (eds.) CRYPTO 2015. LNCS, vol. 9216, pp. 742–762. Springer, Heidelberg (2015). https://doi.org/10.1007/978-3-662-48000-7_36
4. Braud-Santoni, N., Guerraoui, R., Huc, F.: Fast Byzantine agreement. In: ACM Symposium on Principles of Distributed Computing, PODC 2013, Montreal, QC, Canada, 22–24 July 2013, pp. 57–64 (2013)
5. Hubert Chan, T.-H., Pass, R., Shi, E.: Consensus through herding. In: Ishai, Y., Rijmen, V. (eds.) EUROCRYPT 2019. LNCS, vol. 11476, pp. 720–749. Springer, Cham (2019). https://doi.org/10.1007/978-3-030-17653-2_24
6. Hubert Chan, T.-H., Pass, R., Shi, E.: Sublinear-round Byzantine agreement under corrupt majority (2019). Online full version of this paper. https://eprint.iacr.org/2019/886
7. Chen, J., Micali, S.: ALGORAND: the efficient and democratic ledger (2016). https://arxiv.org/abs/1607.01341
8. Chor, B., Merritt, M., Shmoys, D.B.: Simple constant-time consensus protocols in realistic failure models. J. ACM **36**(3), 591–614 (1989)
9. Cohen, R., Coretti, S., Garay, J., Zikas, V.: Probabilistic termination and composability of cryptographic protocols. In: Robshaw, M., Katz, J. (eds.) CRYPTO 2016. LNCS, vol. 9816, pp. 240–269. Springer, Heidelberg (2016). https://doi.org/10.1007/978-3-662-53015-3_9
10. Cohen, R., Haitner, I., Makriyannis, N., Orland, M., Samorodnitsky, A.: On the round complexity of randomized Byzantine agreement. In: 33rd International Symposium on Distributed Computing, DISC 2019, Budapest, Hungary, 14–18 October 2019, pp. 12:1–12:17 (2019)
11. Dolev, D., Strong, H.R.: Authenticated algorithms for Byzantine agreement. SIAM J. Comput. SIAM COMP **12**(4), 656–666 (1983)
12. Feldman, P., Micali, S.: An optimal probabilistic protocol for synchronous Byzantine agreement. SIAM J. Comput. **26**(4), 873–933 (1997)
13. Fitzi, M., Nielsen, J.B.: On the number of synchronous rounds sufficient for authenticated Byzantine agreement. In: Keidar, I. (ed.) DISC 2009. LNCS, vol. 5805, pp. 449–463. Springer, Heidelberg (2009). https://doi.org/10.1007/978-3-642-04355-0_46

14. Garay, J., Katz, J., Koo, C.-Y., Ostrovsky, R.: Round complexity of authenticated broadcast with a dishonest majority. In: 48th Annual IEEE Symposium on Foundations of Computer Science (FOCS), November 2007

15. Garay, J.A., Katz, J., Kumaresan, R., Zhou, H.-S.: Adaptively secure broadcast, revisited. In: Proceedings of the 30th Annual ACM SIGACT-SIGOPS Symposium on Principles of Distributed Computing, PODC 2011, pp. 179–186. ACM, New York (2011)

16. Goldwasser, S., Pavlov, E., Vaikuntanathan, V.: Fault-tolerant distributed computing in full-information networks. In: Proceedings of the 47th Annual IEEE Symposium on Foundations of Computer Science (FOCS 2006), Berkeley, California, USA, 21–24 October 2006, pp. 15–26 (2006)

17. Groth, J., Ostrovsky, R., Sahai, A.: New techniques for noninteractive zero-knowledge. J. ACM **59**(3), 11:1–11:35 (2012)

18. Hirt, M., Zikas, V.: Adaptively secure broadcast. In: Gilbert, H. (ed.) EURO-CRYPT 2010. LNCS, vol. 6110, pp. 466–485. Springer, Heidelberg (2010). https://doi.org/10.1007/978-3-642-13190-5_24

19. Kapron, B.M., Kempe, D., King, V., Saia, J., Sanwalani, V.: Fast asynchronous Byzantine agreement and leader election with full information. ACM Trans. Algorithms **6**(4), 68:1–68:28 (2010)

20. Karlin, A., Yao, A.C.-C.: Probabilistic lower bounds for byzantine agreement. Manuscript (1986)

21. Katz, J., Koo, C.-Y.: On expected constant-round protocols for Byzantine agreement. J. Comput. Syst. Sci. **75**(2), 91–112 (2009)

22. Kiayias, A., Russell, A., David, B., Oliynykov, R.: Ouroboros: a provably secure proof-of-stake blockchain protocol. In: Katz, J., Shacham, H. (eds.) CRYPTO 2017. LNCS, vol. 10401, pp. 357–388. Springer, Cham (2017). https://doi.org/10.1007/978-3-319-63688-7_12

23. King, V., Saia, J.: Breaking the $O(N^2)$ bit barrier: scalable Byzantine agreement with an adaptive adversary. J. ACM **58**(4), 18:1–18:24 (2011)

24. King, V., Saia, J., Sanwalani, V., Vee, E.: Scalable leader election. In: SODA (2006)

25. Lamport, L., Shostak, R., Pease, M.: The Byzantine generals problem. ACM Trans. Program. Lang. Syst. **4**(3), 382–401 (1982)

Bandwidth-Efficient Threshold EC-DSA

Guilhem Castagnos[1], Dario Catalano[2], Fabien Laguillaumie[3],
Federico Savasta[2,4], and Ida Tucker[3(✉)]

[1] Université de Bordeaux, Inria, CNRS, IMB UMR 5251, 33405 Talence, France
[2] Università di Catania, Catania, Italy
[3] Univ Lyon, EnsL, UCBL, CNRS, Inria, LIP, 69342 Lyon Cedex 07, France
ida.tucker@ens-lyon.fr
[4] Scuola Superiore di Catania, Catania, Italy

Abstract. Threshold Signatures allow n parties to share the power of issuing digital signatures so that any coalition of size at least $t + 1$ can sign, whereas groups of t or less players cannot. Over the last few years many schemes addressed the question of realizing efficient threshold variants for the specific case of EC-DSA signatures. In this paper we present new solutions to the problem that aim at reducing the overall bandwidth consumption. Our main contribution is a new variant of the Gennaro and Goldfeder protocol from ACM CCS 2018 that avoids all the required range proofs, while retaining provable security against malicious adversaries in the dishonest majority setting. Our experiments show that – for all levels of security – our signing protocol reduces the bandwidth consumption of best previously known secure protocols for factors varying between 4.4 and 9, while key generation is consistently two times less expensive. Furthermore compared to these same protocols, our signature generation is faster for 192-bits of security and beyond.

1 Introduction

A threshold signature scheme allows n, mutually mistrusting, users to share the capability of signing documents under a common public key. The threshold $t < n$ typically indicates that any subset of at least $t+1$ users can collaborate in order to issue a valid signature. On the other hand, no coalition of t or less users can do so. Moreover, if an attacker corrupts up to t users this does not leak any information on the underlying secret key. This latter property is very useful in practice as it significantly reduces the loss induced by a security break in. The study of threshold signatures (and more generally of threshold cryptography [Des88, DF90, GJKR96b, SG98, Sho00, Boy86, CH89, MR01]) attracted significant interest from the early 1990s to the early 2000s. Over the last few years, threshold signatures and, in particular, threshold EC-DSA signatures raised renewed interest. This mainly comes from the fact that EC-DSA is the signature scheme adopted in Bitcoin and other cryptocurrencies. Indeed, a secure, flexible and efficient protocol for threshold EC-DSA signatures can be very effective against the theft of Bitcoins. Protecting EC-DSA signing keys is equivalent to securing Bitcoin: instead of storing a signing key in one single location one could share

© International Association for Cryptologic Research 2020
A. Kiayias et al. (Eds.): PKC 2020, LNCS 12111, pp. 266–296, 2020.
https://doi.org/10.1007/978-3-030-45388-6_10

it among several servers so that none of them knows it in full and a quorum is needed to produce new signatures. This also means that an attacker should be able to break in into more than t servers to get anything meaningful.

Notice that, in order for a secure solution to be any useful in the cryptocurrency world, efficiency and flexibility are of fundamental importance. Here flexibility mainly refers to the possibility of arbitrarily setting the threshold. Efficiency, on the other hand, takes into account both the computational costs and the bandwidth consumption induced by the protocol.

Before the advent of cryptocurrencies, known solutions to the problem fell short either in terms of flexibility or in terms of efficiency (or both). The state of the art was the work of Gennaro *et al.* [GJKR96a] where to implement a threshold of t servers one needed to share the key among a total of at least $n = 2t + 1$ servers, thus making n-out-of-n sharings impossible (i.e. sharings where all parties are required to participate to the signing process). This was later addressed by Mackenzie and Reiter [MR01] for the specific two party setting (i.e. where $t = 1$ and $n = 2$) but the proposed protocol heavily relies on inefficient zero knowledge proofs, thus making the resulting protocol of little practical interest.

Over the last few years, improved solutions have been proposed both for the two party [Lin17,DKLs18,CCL+19] and for the more general t-out-of-n case [GGN16,GG18,LN18,DKLs19]. Focusing on the latter case, all these solutions still have drawbacks either in terms of bandwidth costs (e.g. [DKLs19] and [LN18] for their OT implementation), somewhat heavy setup [GGN16] or underlying assumptions [GG18].

Our Contribution. In this paper we present new techniques to realize efficient threshold variants of the EC-DSA signature scheme. Our resulting protocols are particularly efficient in terms of bandwidth consumption and, as several recent works (e.g. [GG18]) allow to consider any threshold t such that $n \geq t + 1$.

Our main contribution is a new variant of the Gennaro and Goldfeder protocol [GG18] that manages to avoid all the required range proofs, while retaining comparable overall (computational) efficiency.

To better explain our contribution let us briefly describe how (basic) EC-DSA works. The public key is an elliptic curve point Q and the signing key is x, where $Q \leftarrow xP$, and P is a generator of the group of points of the elliptic curve of prime order q. To sign a message m one first hashes it using some hash function H and then proceeds as follows. Choose a random $k \in \mathbf{Z}/q\mathbf{Z}$ and compute $R = k^{-1}P$. Letting $r \leftarrow r_x \bmod q$ – where $R = (r_x, r_y)$ – set $s \leftarrow k(H(m) + rx) \bmod q$. The signature is the pair (r, s).

The difficulty when trying to devise a threshold variant of this scheme comes from the fact that one has to compute both $R = k^{-1}P$ and a multiplication of the two secret values k, x. In [GG18] Gennaro and Goldfeder address this as follows. Starting from two secrets $a = a_1 + \cdots + a_n$, $b = b_1 + \cdots + b_n$ additively shared among the parties (i.e. P_i holds a_i and b_i), players compute $ab = \sum_{i,j} a_i b_j$ by computing additive shares of each $a_i b_j$. This can be achieved via a simple two party protocol, originally proposed by Gilboa [Gil99] in the setting of two party RSA key generation, which parties execute in a pairwise way. Slightly more in detail, this latter protocol relies on linearly homomorphic encryption and

Gennaro and Goldfeder implement it using Paillier's cryptosystem as underlying building block. This choice, however, becomes problematic when dealing with malicious adversaries, as Paillier plaintexts live in $(\mathbf{Z}/N\mathbf{Z})$ (for N large composite) whereas EC-DSA signatures live in $\mathbf{Z}/q\mathbf{Z}$ (q prime). To avoid inconsistencies, one then needs to choose N significantly larger than q, so that no wrap arounds occur during the execution of the whole protocol. To prevent malicious behavior, this also induces the need of expensive range proofs, i.e. when sending $\mathsf{Enc}(x_i)$ a player also needs to prove that x_i is small enough.

To fix this, one might be tempted to resort to the hash proof systems based technique recently proposed by Castagnos *et al.* [CCL+19]. This methodology allows an efficient instantiation from class groups of imaginary quadratic fields that, in turn, builds upon the Castagnos and Laguillaumie [CL15] homomorphic encryption scheme. One key feature of this scheme and its variants (CL from now on) is that they allow instantiations where the message space is $\mathbf{Z}/q\mathbf{Z}$ and this q can be the same large prime used in EC-DSA signatures. Unfortunately, however, this feature comes at the cost of loosing surjectivity. More precisely, and differently than Paillier, CL is not surjective in the ciphertext space and the set of valid CL ciphertexts is not even efficiently recognizable. Even worse, known techniques to prove the validity of a CL ciphertext are rather inefficient as they all use binary challenges. This means that to get soundness error 2^{-t} the proof needs to be repeated t times.

Back to our threshold EC-DSA setting, naively switching from Paillier to CL, only means trading inefficient range proofs with inefficient proofs of validity for ciphertexts!

In this paper, we develop new techniques that address exactly this issue. As a first contribution we develop new efficient protocols to prove CL ciphertexts are well formed. This result is quite general and can have useful applications even beyond the specific threshold setting considered in this paper (and indeed can be used to improve the efficiency of the recent two party protocol from [CCL+19]).

Next, we revisit the Gennaro and Goldfeder protocol and propose a new CL-based EC-DSA variant where the aforementioned multiplication step can be done efficiently and without resorting to range proofs.

Our constructions rely on two recently introduced assumptions on class groups. Informally, given a group $\widehat{G}$ the first one states that it is hard to find low order elements in $\widehat{G}$ (low order assumption) while the latter assumes that it is hard to find roots of random elements in $\widehat{G}$ (strong root assumption). Both these assumptions are believed to hold in class groups of imaginary quadratic fields [BH01, DF02, BBHM02, Lip12] and were recently used in, e.g. [BBF18, Pie19, Wes19].

From a technical perspective, resorting to these assumptions allows us to dramatically improve the efficiency of the (zero knowledge) arguments of knowledge needed by our protocols. Informally this can be explained as follows. In the class group setting, the order of the group $\widehat{G}$ is unknown (to all parties, even to those who set up the parameters). This is typically a bad thing when doing arguments of knowledge as, unless one restricts to binary challenges, it is not immediate how to argue the extractability of the witness.

In our proofs, we manage to prove that, no matter how big the challenge space is, either one can extract the witness or one can find a root for some given (random) element of the group, thus violating the strong root assumption. Our argument is actually more convoluted than that as, for technical reasons that won't be discussed here, we still need to make sure that no undetected low order elements are maliciously injected in the protocols (e.g. to extract unauthorized information). This is where the low order assumption comes into play and allows us to avoid hard to handle corner cases in our proofs. Challenges also arise from the fact that in order to reduce to the hardness of finding roots, our reduction should output e^{th} roots where e is not a power of two, since, as observed in concluding remarks of [CCL+19], computing square roots or finding elements of order 2 can be done efficiently in class groups knowing the factorization of the discriminant (which is public in our case).

We also provide in Sect. 5 a zero knowledge proof of knowledge (without computational assumptions) for groups of unknown order in order to improve our setup. That proof can also be of independent interest and actually improves the key generation of [CCL+19] for two party EC-DSA.

Efficiency Comparisons. We compare the speed and communication costs of our protocol to those of the scheme by Gennaro and Goldfeder [GG18] and that of Lindell *et al.* [LN18] for the standard NIST curves P-256, P-384 and P-521, corresponding to levels of security 128, 192 and 256. For the encryption scheme, we start with a 112 bit security, as in their implementations, but also study the case where its level of security matches that of the elliptic curves. Our comparisons show that for all security levels our signing protocol reduces the bandwidth consumption of best previously known secure protocols for factors varying between 4.4 and 9, while key generation is consistently two times less expensive. Moreover, we even outperform (for all security levels) the stripped down implementation of [GG18] where a number of range proofs are omitted. We believe this to be an important aspect of our schemes. Indeed, as Gennaro and Goldfeder themselves point out in [GG18], omitting these proofs leaks information on the shared signing key. While they conjecture that this information is limited enough for the protocol to remain secure, no formal analysis is provided.

In terms of timings, though for standard levels of security (112 and 128) our signing protocol is up to four times slower than that of [LN18], for higher levels of security the trend is inverted, such that for 256-bit security we are twice as fast as all other secure schemes considered[1].

2   Preliminaries

Notations. For a distribution $\mathcal{D}$, we write $d \hookleftarrow \mathcal{D}$ to refer to d being sampled from $\mathcal{D}$ and $b \xleftarrow{\$} B$ if b is sampled uniformly in the set B. In an interactive protocol IP, between parties $P_1, \ldots, P_n$ for some integer $n > 1$, we denote by

---

[1] But still twice as slow as the stripped down [GG18] protocol.

$\mathsf{IP}\langle x_1; \ldots; x_n \rangle \to \langle y_1; \ldots; y_n \rangle$ the joint execution of parties $\{P_i\}_{i \in [n]}$ in the protocol, with respective inputs x_i, and where P_i's private output at the end of the execution is y_i. If all parties receive the same output y we write $\mathsf{IP}\langle x_1; \ldots; x_n \rangle \to \langle y \rangle$. A (P)PT algo stands for an algorithm running in (probabilistic) polynomial time w.r.t. the length of its inputs.

Classical tools that we use (Zero-knowledge proofs, Feldman verifiable secret sharing, Commitments) are described in the full version [CCL+20, Section 2.1].

2.1 The Elliptic Curve Digital Signature Algorithm

Elliptic Curve Digital Signature Algorithm. EC-DSA is the elliptic curve analogue of the Digital Signature Algoritm (DSA). It was put forth by Vanstone [Van92] and accepted as ISO, ANSI, IEEE and FIPS standards. It works in a group $(\mathbb{G}, +)$ of prime order q (of say μ bits) of points of an elliptic curve over a finite field, generated by P and consists of the following algorithms.

$\mathsf{KeyGen}(\mathbb{G}, q, P) \to (x, Q)$ where $x \xleftarrow{\$} \mathbf{Z}/q\mathbf{Z}$ is the secret signing key and $Q := xP$ is the public verification key.
$\mathsf{Sign}(x, m) \to (r, s)$ where r and s are computed as follows:
  1. Compute m': the μ leftmost bits of $\mathsf{SHA256}(m)$ where m is to be signed.
  2. Sample $k \xleftarrow{\$} (\mathbf{Z}/q\mathbf{Z})^*$ and compute $R := k^{-1}P$; denote $R = (r_x, r_y)$ and let $r := r_x \mod q$. If $r = 0$ choose another k.
  3. Compute $s := k \cdot (m' + r \cdot x) \mod q$.
$\mathsf{Verif}(Q, m, (r, s)) \to \{0, 1\}$ indicating whether or not the signature is accepted.

The standard security notion required of digital signature schemes is that of existential unforgeability under chosen message attacks (eu-cma) [GMR88].

Definition 1 (Existential unforgeability [GMR88]). *Consider a digital signature scheme $\mathsf{S} = (\mathsf{KeyGen}, \mathsf{Sign}, \mathsf{Verif})$, and a PPT algorithm $\mathcal{A}$, which is given as input a verification key vk output by $\mathsf{KeyGen}(1^\lambda) \to (\mathsf{sk}, \mathsf{vk})$ and oracle access to the signing algorithm $\mathsf{Sign}(\mathsf{sk}, .)$ to whom it can (adaptively) request signatures on messages of its choice. Let $\mathfrak{M}$ be the set of queried messages. S is existentially unforgeable if for any such $\mathcal{A}$, the probability $\mathsf{Adv}_{\mathsf{S}, \mathcal{A}}^{\mathsf{eu\text{-}cma}}$ that $\mathcal{A}$ produces a valid signature on a message $m \notin \mathfrak{M}$ is a negligible function of λ.*

(t, n)-*threshold EC-DSA.* For a threshold t and a number of parties $n > t$, threshold EC-DSA consists of the following interactive protocols:

$\mathsf{IKeyGen}\langle (\mathbb{G}, q, P); \ldots; (\mathbb{G}, q, P) \rangle \to \langle (x_1, Q); \ldots; (x_n, Q) \rangle$ s.t. $\mathsf{KeyGen}(\mathbb{G}, q, P) \to (x, Q)$ where $x_1, \ldots, x_n$ constitute a (t, n) threshold secret sharing of x.
$\mathsf{ISign}\langle (x_1, m); \ldots; (x_n, m) \rangle \to \langle (r, s) \rangle$ **or** $\langle \bot \rangle$ where $\bot$ is the error output, signifying the parties may abort the protocol, and $\mathsf{Sign}(x, m) \to (r, s)$.

The verification algorithm is non interactive and identical to that of EC-DSA.

Following [GJKR96b], we present a game-based definition of security analogous to eu-cma: threshold unforgeability under chosen message attacks (tu-cma).

Definition 2 (Threshold signature unforgeability [GJKR96b]**).** *Consider a (t, n)-threshold signature scheme* $\mathsf{IS} = (\mathsf{IKeyGen}, \mathsf{ISign}, \mathsf{Verif})$, *and a PPT algorithm $\mathcal{A}$, having corrupted at most t players, and which is given the view of the protocols* $\mathsf{IKeyGen}$ *and* ISign *on input messages of its choice (chosen adaptively) as well as signatures on those messages. Let $\mathcal{M}$ be the set of aforementioned messages.* IS *is unforgeable if for any such $\mathcal{A}$, the probability* $\mathsf{Adv}_{\mathsf{IS},\mathcal{A}}^{\mathsf{tu\text{-}cma}}$ *that $\mathcal{A}$ can produce a signature on a message $m \notin \mathcal{M}$ is a negligible function of λ.*

2.2   Building Blocks from Class Groups

An Instantiation of the CL *Framework.* Castagnos and Laguillaumie introduced the framework of a group with an easy discrete logarithm (Dlog) subgroup in [CL15], which was later enhanced in [CLT18, CCL+19] and gave concrete instantiation from class groups of quadratic fields. Some background on class groups of quadratic fields in cryptography can be found in [BH01] and in [CL15, Appx. B].

We briefly sketch the instantiation given in [CCL+19, Sec. 4.1] and the resulting group generator Gen that we will use in this paper. The interested reader can refer to [CL15, CCL+19] for concrete details.

Given a prime q consider another random prime $\tilde{q}$, the fundamental discriminant $\Delta_K = -q\tilde{q}$ and the associated class group $C(\Delta_K)$. By choosing $\tilde{q}$ s.t. $q\tilde{q} \equiv -1 \pmod 4$ and $(q/\tilde{q}) = -1$, we have that the $2-$Sylow subgroup of $C(\Delta_K)$ has order 2. The size of $\tilde{q}$ is chosen s.t. computing the class number $h(\Delta_K)$ takes time 2^λ. We then consider the suborder of discriminant $\Delta_q = -q^2\Delta_K$. Then, we denote $(\widehat{G}, \cdot)$ the finite abelian subgroup of squares of $C(\Delta_q)$, which corresponds to the odd part. It is possible to check efficiently if an element is in $\widehat{G}$ (cf. [Lag80]). One can exhibit a subgroup F generated by $f \in \widehat{G}$ where f is represented by an ideal of norm q^2. This subgroup has order q and there exists a deterministic PT algorithm for the discrete logarithm (Dlog) problem in F (cf. [CL15, Proposition C – 1]). Then we build deterministically a $q-$th power of $\widehat{G}$ by lifting the class of an ideal of discriminant Δ_K above the smallest splitting prime. In the following, we will denote $\hat{g}_q$ this deterministic generator. We will then consider an element g_q constructed as a random power of $\hat{g}_q$. This slightly changes the construction of [CCL+19], in order to make a reduction to a strong root problem for the soundness of the argument of knowledge of Subsect. 3.1. One can compute an upper bound $\tilde{s}$ for the order of $\hat{g}_q$, using an upper bound of $h(\Delta_K)$. For this, one can use the fact that $h(\Delta_K) < \frac{1}{\pi}\log|\Delta_K|\sqrt{|\Delta_K|}$, or obtain a slightly better bound from the analytic class number formula.

For our application the prime q will have at least 256 bits, in that case q is prime to $h(\Delta_K)$ except with negligible probability. Therefore q will be prime to the order of $\hat{g}_q$ which is a divisor of $h(\Delta_K)$.

Notation. We denote Gen the algorithm that on input a security parameter λ and a prime q, outputs $(\tilde{s}, f, \hat{g}_q, \widehat{G}, F)$ defined as above. We also denote Solve the deterministic PT algorithm that solves the Dlog problem in F. This pair of algorithms is an instance of the framework of a group with an easy Dlog subgroup (cf. [CCL+19, Definition 4]). For a random power g_q of $\hat{g}_q$ we will denote G^q the subgroup generated by g_q, $g = g_q f$ and G the subgroup generated by g.

Hard Subgroup Membership Assumption. We recall the definition of the HSM problem for an output $(\tilde{s}, f, \hat{g}_q, \widehat{G}, F)$ of Gen. For a random power g_q of $\hat{g}_q$ the HSM assumption states it is hard to distinguish the elements of G^q in G. As a result this HSM assumption is closely related to Paillier's DCR assumption, they are essentially the same assumption in different groups, hence there is no direct reduction between them. HSM was first used by [CLT18] within class groups, though cryptography based on class groups is now well established, and is seeing renewed interest (e.g. [CIL17, CLT18, BBBF18, Wes19, CCL+19]).

Definition 3 (HSM assumption). *For* $(\tilde{s}, f, \hat{g}_q, \widehat{G}, F)$ *an output of Gen,* g_q *a random power of* $\hat{g}_q$ *and* $g := g_q f$, *we denote* $\mathcal{D}$ *(resp.* $\mathcal{D}_q$*) a distribution over the integers s.t. the distribution* $\{g^x, x \hookleftarrow \mathcal{D}\}$ *(resp.* $\{\hat{g}_q^x, x \hookleftarrow \mathcal{D}_q\}$*) is at distance less than* $2^{-\lambda}$ *from the uniform distribution in* $\langle g \rangle$ *(resp. in* $\langle \hat{g}_q \rangle$*). Let* $\mathcal{A}$ *be an adversary for the* HSM *problem, its advantage is defined as:*

$$\mathsf{Adv}_{\mathcal{A}}^{\mathsf{HSM}}(\lambda) := \left| 2 \cdot \Pr\left[b = b^\star : (\tilde{s}, f, \hat{g}_q, \widehat{G}, F) \leftarrow \mathsf{Gen}(1^\lambda, q), t \hookleftarrow \mathcal{D}_q, g_q = \hat{g}_q^t, \right. \right.$$

$$x \hookleftarrow \mathcal{D}, x' \hookleftarrow \mathcal{D}_q, b \xleftarrow{\$} \{0,1\}, Z_0 \leftarrow g^x, Z_1 \leftarrow g_q^{x'},$$

$$\left. \left. b^\star \leftarrow \mathcal{A}(q, \tilde{s}, f, \hat{g}_q, g_q, \widehat{G}, F, Z_b, \mathsf{Solve}(.)) \right] - 1 \right|$$

The HSM *problem is said to be hard in* G *if for all probabilistic polynomial time algorithm* $\mathcal{A}$, $\mathsf{Adv}_{\mathcal{A}}^{\mathsf{HSM}}(\lambda)$ *is negligible.*

Remark that compared to previous works, we modify slightly the assumption by considering a random element g_q instead of using the deterministic element $\hat{g}_q$.

Resulting Encryption Scheme. We recall the linearly homomorphic encryption scheme of [CLT18] whose ind-cpa-security relies on the HSM assumption. The scheme somewhat generalises Camenisch and Shoup's approach in [CS03]. This scheme is the basis of the threshold EC-DSA protocol of Sect. 3. We use the output of $\mathsf{Gen}(1^\lambda, q)$ and as in Definition 3, we set $g_q = \hat{g}_q^t$ for $t \hookleftarrow \mathcal{D}_q$. The public parameters of the scheme are $\mathsf{pp} := (\tilde{s}, f, \hat{g}_q, g_q, \widehat{G}, F, q)$. To instantiate $\mathcal{D}_q$, we set $\tilde{A} \geq \tilde{s} \cdot 2^{40}$ s.t. $\{g_q^r, r \hookleftarrow [\tilde{A}]\}$ is at distance less than 2^{-40} from the uniform distribution in G^q. The plaintext space is $\mathbf{Z}/q\mathbf{Z}$. The scheme is depicted in Fig. 1.

Theorem 1 ([CLT18]). *The* CL *scheme described in Fig. 1 is semantically secure under chosen plaintext attacks (*ind-cpa*) under the* HSM *assumption.*

2.3 Algorithmic Assumptions

We here provide further definitions for the algorithmic assumptions on which the security of our protocol relies. As in [CCL+19], we need the HSM assumption

Algo. KeyGen(pp)	**Algo.** Enc(pk, m)	**Algo.** Dec(sk, (c_1, c_2))
1. Pick sk $\hookleftarrow [\tilde{A}]$ and pk $:= g_q^{sk}$	1. Pick $r \hookleftarrow [\tilde{A}]$	1. Compute $M = c_2/c_1^{sk}$
2. Return (pk, sk)	2. Return $(g_q^r, f^m pk^r)$	2. Return Solve(M)

Fig. 1. Description of the CL encryption scheme

guaranteeing the ind-cpa-security of the linearly homomorphic encryption scheme. We also use two additional assumptions: one which states that it is hard to find low order elements in the group $\widehat{G}$, and one which states that it is hard to find roots in $\widehat{G}$ of random elements of the subgroup $\langle \hat{g}_q \rangle$. These assumptions allow us to significantly improve the efficiency of the ZKAoK needed in our protocol. Indeed, as the order of the group we work in is unknown, we cannot (unless challenges are binary as done in [CCL+19]) immediately extract the witness from two answers corresponding to two different challenges of a given statement. However we show in the ZKAoK of Sect. 3.1 that whatever the challenge space, if one cannot extract the witness, then one can break at least one of these two assumptions. Consequently these assumptions allow us to significantly increase the challenge space of our proofs, and reduce the number of rounds in the protocol to achieve a satisfying soundness, which yields an improvement both in terms of bandwidth and of computational complexity.

Using such assumptions in the context of generalized Schnorr Proofs in groups of unknown order is not novel (*cf.* e.g. [DF02,CKY09]). We adapt these techniques for our specific subgroups of a class group of an imaginary quadratic field, and state them with respect to Gen.

Definition 4 (Low order assumption). *Consider a security parameter $\lambda \in \mathbf{N}$, and $\gamma \in \mathbf{N}$. The γ-low order problem (LOP_γ) is $(t(\lambda), \epsilon_{LO}(\lambda))$-secure for Gen if, given the output of Gen, no algorithm $\mathcal{A}$ running in time $\leq t(\lambda)$ can output a γ-low order element in $\widehat{G}$ with probability greater than $\epsilon_{LO}(\lambda)$. More precisely,*

$$\epsilon_{LO}(\lambda) := \Pr[\mu^d = 1, 1 \neq \mu \in \widehat{G}, 1 < d < \gamma :$$
$$(\tilde{s}, f, \hat{g}_q, \widehat{G}, F) \xleftarrow{\$} \text{Gen}(1^\lambda, q); (\mu, d) \xleftarrow{\$} \mathcal{A}(\tilde{s}, f, \hat{g}_q, \widehat{G}, F)].$$

The γ-low order assumption holds if $t = poly(\lambda)$, and ϵ_{LO} is negligible in λ.

We now define a strong root assumption for class groups. This can be seen as a generalisation of the strong RSA assumption adapted to class groups where computing square roots is easy knowing the factorisation of the discriminant, and tailor it to our needs by considering challenges in a subgroup.

Definition 5 (Strong root assumption for Class Groups). *Consider a security parameter $\lambda \in \mathbf{N}$, and let $\mathcal{A}$ be a probabilistic algorithm. We run Gen on input $(1^\lambda, q)$ to get $(\tilde{s}, f, \hat{g}_q, \widehat{G}, F)$ and we give this output and a random $Y \in \langle \hat{g}_q \rangle$ as an input to $\mathcal{A}$. We say that $\mathcal{A}$ solves the strong root problem for class groups (SRP) if $\mathcal{A}$ outputs a positive integer $e \neq 2^k$ for all k and $X \in \widehat{G}$, s.t. $Y = X^e$. In particular, the SRP is $(t(\lambda), \epsilon_{SR}(\lambda))$-secure for Gen if any adversary $\mathcal{A}$, running in time $\leq t(\lambda)$, solves the SRP with probability at most $\epsilon_{SR}(\lambda)$.*

On the Hardness of These Assumptions in Class Groups. For our applications, we will use the strong root assumption and the low order assumption in the context of class groups. These assumptions are not completely novel in this setting: Damgård and Fujisaki [DF02] explicitly consider variants of these assumptions in this context. Then, Lipmaa used a strong root assumption in class groups to build accumulators without trusted setup in [Lip12]. Recently, an interactive variant of the strong root assumption was used, still in the context of class groups, by Wesolowski to build verifiable delay functions without trusted setup. Furthermore, the low order assumption is also used to implement Pietrzak's verifiable delay functions with class groups (see [BBF18, Pie19]). In the following, we advocate the hardness of these assumptions in the context of class groups.

The root problem and its hardness was considered in [BH01, BBHM02] in the context of class groups to design signature schemes. It is similar to the RSA problem: the adversary is not allowed to choose the exponent e. These works compare the hardness of this problem with the problem of computing the group order and conclude that there is no better known method to compute a solution to the root problem than to compute the order of the group.

The strong root assumption is a generalisation of the strong RSA assumption. Again, the best known algorithm to solve this problem is to compute the order of the group to be able to invert exponents. For strong RSA this means factoring the modulus. For the strong root problem in class groups, this means computing the class number, and best known algorithms for this problem have worst complexity than those to factor integers.

Note that we have specialized this assumption for exponents e which are not powers of 2: as mentioned in [CCL+19], one can compute square roots in polynomial time in class groups of quadratic fields, knowing the factorisation of the discriminant (which is public in our setting), cf. [Lag80].

Concerning the low order assumption, we need the $\gamma-$low order problem to be hard in $\widehat{G}$, where γ can be up to 2^{128}. Note that in our instantiation, the discriminant is chosen such that the $2-$Sylow subgroup is isomorphic to $\mathbf{Z}/2\mathbf{Z}$. It is well known that the element of order 2 can be computed from the (known) factorisation of Δ_q. However, we work with the odd part, which is the group of squares in this context, so we do not take this element into account.

Let us see that the proportion of such elements of low order is very low in the odd part. From the Cohen Lenstra heuristics [CL84] the odd part of a class group $C(\Delta)$ of an imaginary quadratic field is cyclic with probability 97.75%. In [HS06], extending these heuristics, it is conjectured that the probability an integer d divides the order $h(\Delta)$ of $C(\Delta)$ is less than $(\frac{1}{d} + \frac{1}{d \log d})$. As a consequence, if the odd part of $C(\Delta)$ is cyclic then the expected number of elements of order less than γ is less than $\sum_{d \leqslant \gamma} \left(\frac{1}{d} + \frac{1}{d \log d} \right) \varphi(d)$, which can be bounded above by 2γ. For 128 bits of security, our class number will have around 913 bits, so the proportion of elements of order less than 2^{128} is less than 2^{-784}.

Moreover, if the odd part of the class group is non cyclic, it is very likely that it is of the form $\mathbf{Z}/n_1\mathbf{Z} \oplus \mathbf{Z}/n_2\mathbf{Z}$ where $n_2|n_1$ and n_2 is very small. Still from the Cohen Lenstra heuristics, the probability that the $p-$rank (the number of cyclic factors in the $p-$Sylow subgroup) of the odd part is equal to r is equal to $\frac{\eta_\infty(p)}{p^{r^2}\eta_r(p)^2}$ where $\eta_r(p) = \prod_{k=1}^r(1 - p^{-k})$. If we have two cyclic factors, and $p|n_2$, then the $p-$rank is 2. If $p > 2^{20}$ the probability of having a $p-$rank equal to 2 is less than 2^{-80}. Similarly, we cannot have many small cyclic components: the $3-$rank is 6 with probability less than 2^{-83}. Actually, we know only 3 class groups of such 3 ranks [Que87].

There have been intense efforts on the construction of families of discriminants such that there exist elements of a given small order p or with a given $p-$rank. However, these families are very sparse and will be reached by our generation algorithm of the discriminant only with negligible probability. The basic idea of these constructions is to build a discriminant Δ in order to obtain solutions of a Diophantine equation that gives m and the representation of a non principal ideal I of norm m such that I^p is principal, and I has order p in $C(\Delta)$ (see eg [Bue76] or [Bel04] for more references).

Solving such a norm equation for a fixed discriminant has been mentioned as a starting point for an attack in [BBF18] combined with the Coppersmith's method, but no concrete advances on the problem have been proposed.

3   Threshold EC-DSA Protocol

We here provide a construction for (t, n)-threshold EC-DSA signing from the CL framework. Security – which does not degrade with the number of signatures queried by the adversary in the tu-cma game (*cf.* Definition 2) – relies on the assumptions and tools introduced in Sect. 2. Throughout the article we consider the group of points of an elliptic curve $\mathbb{G}$ of order q, generated by P.

As in many previous works on multiparty EC-DSA (*e.g.* [MR01, Lin17, GG18]), we use a linearly homomorphic encryption scheme. This enables parties to perform operations collaboratively while keeping their inputs secret. Explicitly a party P_i sends a ciphertext encrypting its secret share (under its own public key) to party P_j, P_j then performs homomorphic operations on this ciphertext (using its own secret share), and sends the resulting ciphertext back to P_i – intuitively P_i should learn nothing more about the operations performed by P_j than that revealed by decrypting the ciphertext it receives. To ensure this, P_i must prove to P_j that the ciphertext it first sent is 'well formed'. To this end in Sect. 3.1, we provide an efficient zero-knowledge argument of knowledge of the plaintext and of the randomness used to compute a CL ciphertext (defined in Sect. 2.3). This ZKAoK is essential to secure our protocol against malicious adversaries. Next, in Sect. 3.2 we explain how parties interactively set up the public parameters of the CL encryption scheme, so that the assumptions underlying the ZKAoK hold. Though – for clarity – we describe this interactive set up as a separate protocol, it can be done in parallel to the IKeyGen protocol of threshold EC-DSA, thereby only increasing by one the number of rounds of the threshold signing protocol. Finally, in Sect. 3.3 we present our (t, n)-threshold EC-DSA signing protocol, whose security will be demonstrated in Sect. 4.

3.1 ZKAoK Ensuring a CL Ciphertext Is Well Formed

Consider a prover P having computed an encryption of $a \in \mathbf{Z}/q\mathbf{Z}$ with randomness $r \overset{\$}{\leftarrow} [\tilde{A}]$, i.e. $\mathbf{c} := (c_1, c_2)$ with $c_1 := g_q^r$, $c_2 := \mathsf{pk}^r f^a$. We present a zero knowledge argument of knowledge for the following relation:

$$\mathsf{R}_{\mathsf{Enc}} := \{(\mathsf{pk}, \mathbf{c}); (a, r) \mid \mathsf{pk} \in \widehat{G}; \ r \in [\tilde{A}C(2^{40} + 2)]; \ a \in \mathbf{Z}/q\mathbf{Z}; \ c_1 = g_q^r \wedge c_2 = \mathsf{pk}^r f^a\}.$$

The interactive protocol is given in Fig. 2. We denote $\mathcal{C}$ the challenge set, and $C := |\mathcal{C}|$. The only constraint on C is that the C-low order assumption holds.

Setup:

1. $(\tilde{s}, f, \hat{g}_q, \widehat{G}, F) \leftarrow \mathsf{Gen}(1^\lambda, q)$.
2. Let $\tilde{A} := \tilde{s} \cdot 2^{40}$, sample $t \overset{\$}{\leftarrow} [\tilde{A}]$ and let $g_q := \hat{g}_q^t$.

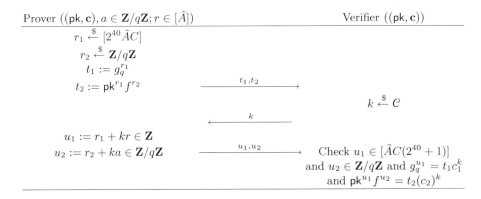

Fig. 2. Zero-knowledge argument of knowledge for $\mathsf{R}_{\mathsf{Enc}}$.

Theorem 2. *If the strong root assumption is $(t'(\lambda), \epsilon_{SR}(\lambda))$-secure for* Gen, *and the C-low order assumption is $(t'(\lambda), \epsilon_{LO}(\lambda))$-secure for* Gen, *denoting $\epsilon := \max(\epsilon_{SR}(\lambda), \epsilon_{LO}(\lambda))$, then the interactive protocol of Fig. 2 is a computationally convincing proof of knowledge for $\mathsf{R}_{\mathsf{Enc}}$ with knowledge error κ, time bound t and failure probability $\nu(\lambda)$, where $\nu(\lambda) = 8\epsilon$, $t(\lambda) < t'(\lambda)/448$ and $\kappa(\lambda) = \max(4/C, 448t(\lambda)/t'(\lambda))$. If $r \in [\tilde{s} \cdot 2^{40}]$ (it is so when the prover is honest), the protocol is honest verifier statistical zero-knowledge.*

Proof. Computational soundness is proven in the full version [CCL+20, Thm. 2].

Completeness. If P knows $r \in [\tilde{A}]$ and $a \in \mathbf{Z}/q\mathbf{Z}$ s.t. $(\mathsf{pk}, \mathbf{c}); (a, r) \in \mathsf{R}_{\mathsf{Enc}}$, and both parties follow the protocol, one has $u_1 \in [\tilde{A}C(2^{40} + 1)]$ and $u_2 \in \mathbf{Z}/q\mathbf{Z}$; $\mathsf{pk}^{u_1} f^{u_2} = \mathsf{pk}^{r_1 + k \cdot r} f^{r_2 + k \cdot a} = \mathsf{pk}^{r_1} f^{r_2} (\mathsf{pk}^r f^a)^k = t_2 c_2^k$; and $g_q^{u_1} = g_q^{r_1 + k \cdot r} = t_1 c_1^k$.

Honest Verifier Zero-Knowledge. Given pk, $\mathbf{c} = (c_1, c_2)$ a simulator can sample $k \overset{\$}{\leftarrow} [C[, u_1 \overset{\$}{\leftarrow} [\tilde{A}C(2^{40} + 1)]$ and $u_2 \overset{\$}{\leftarrow} \mathbf{Z}/q\mathbf{Z}$, compute $t_2 := \mathsf{pk}^{u_1} f^{u_2} c_2^{-k}$ and $t_1 := g_q^{u_1} c_1^{-k}$ such that the transcript $(\mathsf{pk}, \mathbf{c}, t_2, t_1, k, u_1, u_2)$ is indistinguishable from a transcript produced by a real execution of the protocol.

3.2   Interactive Set Up for the CL Encryption Scheme

Generating a Random Generator g_q. In order to use the above ZKAoK it must hold that g_q is a random element of the subgroup $\langle \hat{g}_q \rangle$ where $(\tilde{s}, f, \hat{g}_q, \widehat{G}, F) \leftarrow$ Gen$(1^\lambda, q)$. Precisely if a malicious prover P^* could break the soundness of the ZKAoK, an adversary S trying to break the SRP, given input a random g_q, should be able to feed this input to P^*, and use P^* to solve it's own challenge. Consequently, as the ZKAoK will be used peer-to-peer by all parties in the threshold EC-DSA protocol, they will collaboratively generate – in the interactive IKeyGen – the public parameters $(\tilde{s}, f, \hat{g}_q, \widehat{G}, F)$, and a common g_q which is random to each party. We call this interactive sub-protocol ISetup, since it allows parties to collaboratively set up the public parameters for the CL encryption scheme. All parties then use this g_q to compute their public keys and as a basis for the CL encryption scheme. As explained in Sect. 2.2 the generation of $(\tilde{s}, f, \hat{g}_q, \widehat{G}, F)$ is deterministic from a pair of primes $\tilde{q}$ and q, we overload the notation $(\tilde{s}, f, \hat{g}_q, \widehat{G}, F) \leftarrow$ Gen$(\tilde{q}, q)$ to refer to this deterministic set up. We first define the functionality computed by ISetup, running in two steps.

Definition 6. *For a number of parties n, ISetup consists of the following interactive protocols:*

Step 1. $\langle k; \dots; k \rangle \rightarrow \langle \tilde{q} \rangle$ *or* $\langle \perp \rangle$ *where* $\perp$ *is the error output, signifying the parties may abort the protocol, and $\tilde{q}$ is a random k bit prime.*
Step 2. $\langle (\tilde{q}, q); \dots; (\tilde{q}, q) \rangle \rightarrow \langle (\tilde{s}, f, \hat{g}_q, \widehat{G}, F, g_q, t_1); \dots; (\tilde{s}, f, \hat{g}_q, \widehat{G}, F, g_q, t_n) \rangle$ *or* $\langle \perp \rangle$ *where* $(\tilde{s}, f, \hat{g}_q, \widehat{G}, F) \leftarrow$ Gen$(\tilde{q}, q)$, *and values $t_1, \dots, t_n \in [2^{40}\tilde{s}]$ constitute additive shares of t such that $g_q = \hat{g}_q^t$.*

For n parties to collaboratively run ISetup, they perform the following steps:

Step 1—Generation of random public prime $\tilde{q}$ of bit-size k.

1. Each P_i samples a random $r_i \xleftarrow{\$} \{0,1\}^k$, computes $(c_i, d_i) \leftarrow$ Com(r_i) and broadcasts c_i.
2. After receiving $\{c_j\}_{j \neq i}$, each P_i broadcasts d_i thus revealing r_i.
3. All players compute the common output $\tilde{q} := \text{next-prime}(\bigoplus_{j=1}^n r_j)$.

Step 2—Generation of g_q.

1. From $\tilde{q}$, (and the order of the elliptic curve q) all parties can use the deterministic set up of [CL15, CCL+19] which sets a generator $\hat{g}_q$.
2. Next each player P_i performs the following steps:
   (a) Sample a random $t_i \xleftarrow{\$} [2^{40}\tilde{s}]$; compute $g_i := \hat{g}_q^{t_i}$; $(\tilde{c}_i, \tilde{d}_i) \leftarrow$ Com(g_i), and broadcast $\tilde{c}_i$.
   (b) Receive $\{\tilde{c}_j\}_{j \neq i}$. Broadcast $\tilde{d}_i$ thus revealing g_i.
   (c) Perform a ZKPOK of t_i such that $g_i = \hat{g}_q^{t_i}$.[2] If a proof fails, abort.
3. Each party computes $g_q := \prod_{j=1}^n g_j = \hat{g}_q^{\sum t_j}$, and has output $(\tilde{s}, f, \hat{g}_q, \widehat{G}, F, g_q, t_i)$.

---

[2] This can be done as in [CCL+19] (without relying on the strong root assumption).

Theorem 3 states the security of the interactive protocol described in steps 1 and 2 above. The simulation and proof of indistinguishability are provided in the full version [CCL+20].

Theorem 3. *If the commitment scheme is non-malleable and equivocal; and the proofs π_i are zero knowledge proofs of knowledge of discrete logarithm in $\langle \hat{g}_q \rangle$, then steps 1 and 2 described above securely compute ISetup with abort, in the presence of a malicious adversary corrupting any $t < n$ parties, with point-to-point channels.*

Remark 1. The randomness of $\tilde{q}$ is not crucial to the security of the EC-DSA protocol: conversely to RSA prime factors, here $\tilde{q}$ is public. However traditionally, class group based crypto uses random discriminants; we provide a distributed version of the setup of [CL15] in which the prime $\tilde{q}$ is random. In our ISetup algorithm, the output of next-prime is biased. To patch this, for the same complexity, parties could jointly generate a seed for a prime pseudo-random generator to generate $\tilde{q}$; such a source of randomness would be sufficient in this context.

3.3   Resulting Threshold EC-DSA Protocol

We now describe the overall protocol. Participants run on input $(\mathbb{G}, q, P)$ used by the EC-DSA signature scheme. In Fig. 3, and in phases 1, 3, 4, 5 of Fig. 4, all players perform the same operations (on their respective inputs) w.r.t. all other parties, so we only describe the actions of some party P_i. In particular if P_i broadcasts some value v_i, implicitly P_i receives v_j broadcast by P_j for all $j \in [n]$, $j \neq i$. Broadcasts from P_i to all other players are denoted by double arrows, whereas peer-to-peer communications are denoted by single arrows.

On the other hand, Phase 2 of Fig. 4 is performed by all pairs of players $\{(P_i, P_j)\}_{i \neq j}$. Each player will thus perform $(n-1)$ times the set of instructions on the left (performed by P_i on the figure) and $(n-1)$ times those on the right hand side of the figure (performed by P_j).

Key Generation. We assume that prior to the interactive key generation protocol IKeyGen, all parties run the ISetup protocol of Sect. 3.2 s.t. they output a common random generator g_q. Each party uses this g_q to generate its' CL encryption key pair, and to verify the ZKAoK in the ISign protocol. Although IKeyGen and ISetup are here described as two separate protocols, they can be ran in parallel. Consequently, in practice the number of rounds in IKeyGen increases by 1 broadcast per party if the ZK proofs are made non interactive, and by 2 broadcasts if it is performed interactively between players.

The IKeyGen protocol (also depicted in Fig. 3) proceeds as follows:

1. Each P_i samples a random $u_i \xleftarrow{\$} \mathbf{Z}/q\mathbf{Z}$; computes $[\mathsf{kgc}_i, \mathsf{kgd}_i] \leftarrow \mathsf{Com}(u_i P)$ and generates a pair of keys $(\mathsf{sk}_i, \mathsf{pk}_i)$ for the CL encryption scheme. Each P_i broadcasts $(\mathsf{pk}_i, \mathsf{kgc}_i)$.
2. Each P_i broadcasts kgd_i. Let $Q_i \leftarrow \mathsf{Open}(\mathsf{kgc}_i, \mathsf{kgd}_i)$. Party P_i performs a (t, n) Feldman-VSS of u_i, with Q_i as the free term in the exponent. The EC-DSA public key is set to $Q = \sum_{i=1}^{n} Q_i$. Each player adds the private shares

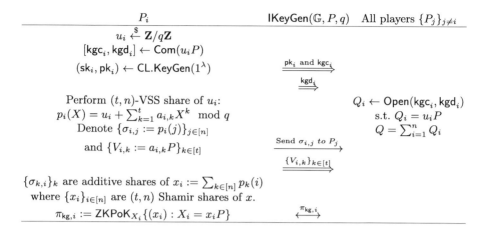

Fig. 3. Threshold key generation

received during the n Feldman VSS protocols. The resulting values x_i are a (t, n) Shamir's secret sharing of the secret signing key x. Observe that all parties know $\{X_i := x_i \cdot P\}_{i \in [n]}$.

3. Each P_i proves in ZK that he knows x_i using Schnorr's protocol [Sch91].

Signing. The signature generation protocol runs on input m and the output of the IKeyGen protocol of Fig. 3. We denote $S \subseteq [n]$ the subset of players which collaborate to sign m. Assuming $|S| = t$ one can convert the (t, n) shares $\{x_i\}_{i \in [n]}$ of x into (t, t) shares $\{w_i\}_{i \in S}$ of x using the appropriate Lagrangian coefficients. Since the $X_i = x_i \cdot P$ and Lagrangian coefficients are public values, all parties can compute $\{W_i := g^{w_i}\}_{i \in S}$. We here describe the steps of the algorithm. A global view of the interactions is also provided in Fig. 4.

Phase 1: Each party P_i samples $k_i, \gamma_i \overset{\$}{\leftarrow} \mathbf{Z}/q\mathbf{Z}$ and $r_i \overset{\$}{\leftarrow} [\tilde{A}]$ uniformly at random. It computes $c_{k_i} \leftarrow \mathsf{Enc}(\mathsf{pk}_i, k_i; r_i)$, a ZKAoK π_i that the ciphertext is well formed, and $[c_i, d_i] \leftarrow \mathsf{Com}(\gamma_i P)$. Each P_i broadcasts (c_i, c_{k_i}, π_i).

Phase 2: *Intuition: denoting $k := \sum_{i \in S} k_i$ and $\gamma := \sum_{i \in S} \gamma_i$ it holds that $k\gamma = \sum_{i,j \in S} k_j \gamma_i$ and $kx = \sum_{i,j \in S} k_j w_i$. The aim of Phase 2 is to convert the multiplicative shares k_j and γ_i of $(k_j \gamma_i)$ (resp. k_j and w_i of $(k_j w_i)$) into additive shares $\alpha_{j,i} + \beta_{j,i} = k_j \gamma_i$ (resp. $\mu_{j,i} + \nu_{j,i} = k_j w_i$). Phase 2 is performed peer-to-peer between each pair $\{(P_i, P_j)\}_{i \neq j}$, s.t. at the end of the phase, P_i knows $\{\alpha_{i,j}, \beta_{j,i}, \mu_{i,j}, \nu_{j,i}\}_{j \in S, j \neq i}$.*

Each peer-to-peer interaction proceeds as follows:

(a) P_i samples $\beta_{j,i}, \nu_{j,i} \overset{\$}{\leftarrow} \mathbf{Z}/q\mathbf{Z}$, and computes $B_{j,i} := \nu_{j,i} \cdot P$. It uses the homomorphic properties of the encryption scheme and the ciphertext c_{k_j} broadcast by P_j in Phase 1 to compute $c_{k_j \gamma_i}$ and $c_{k_j w_i}$: encryptions under pk_j of $k_j \gamma_i - \beta_{j,i}$ and $k_j w_i - \nu_{j,i}$ respectively.

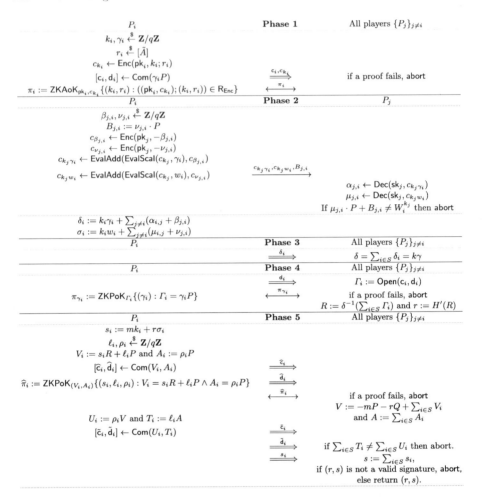

Fig. 4. Threshold signature protocol

(b) P_i sends $(c_{k_j \gamma_i}, c_{k_j w_i}, B_{j,i})$ to P_j, who decrypts both ciphertexts to recover respectively $\alpha_{j,i}$ and $\mu_{j,i}$.

(c) Since W_i is public, P_j verifies that P_i used the same w_i as that used to compute Q by checking $\mu_{j,i} \cdot P + B_{j,i}$. If the check fails, P_j aborts.

P_i computes $\delta_i := k_i \gamma_i + \sum_{j \neq i}(\alpha_{i,j} + \beta_{j,i})$ and $\sigma_i := k_i w_i + \sum_{j \neq i}(\mu_{i,j} + \nu_{j,i})$.

Phase 3: Each P_i broadcasts δ_i. All players compute $\delta := \sum_{i \in S} \delta_i$.

Phase 4: (a) Each P_i broadcasts d_i which decommits to Γ_i.

(b) Each P_i proves knowledge of γ_i s.t. $\Gamma_i = \gamma_i P$. All players compute $R := \delta^{-1}(\sum_{i \in S} \Gamma_i) = k \cdot P$ and $r := H'(R) \in \mathbf{Z}/q\mathbf{Z}$.

Phase 5: (a) Each P_i computes $s_i = k_i m + \sigma_i r$, samples $\ell_i, \rho_i \xleftarrow{\$} \mathbf{Z}/q\mathbf{Z}$ uniformly at random, computes $V_i := s_i R + \ell_i P$; $A_i := \rho_i P$; and $[\widehat{\mathsf{c}}_i, \widehat{\mathsf{d}}_i] \leftarrow \mathsf{Com}(V_i, A_i)$. Each P_i broadcasts $\widehat{\mathsf{c}}_i$.

(b) Each party P_i decommits by broadcasting $\widehat{\mathsf{d}}_i$ along with a NIZKPoK of (s_i, ℓ_i, ρ_i) s.t. $(V_i = s_i R + \ell_i P) \wedge (A_i = \rho_i P)$. It checks all the proofs it gets from other parties. If a proof fails P_i aborts.

(c) All parties compute $V := -mP - rQ + \sum_{i \in S} V_i$, $A := \sum_{i \in S} A_i$. Each party P_i computes $U_i := \rho_i V$, $T_i := \ell_i A$ and the commitment $[\tilde{\mathsf{c}}_i, \tilde{\mathsf{d}}_i] \leftarrow \mathsf{Com}(U_i, T_i)$. It then broadcasts $\tilde{\mathsf{c}}_i$.

(d) Each P_i decommits to (U_i, T_i) by broadcasting $\tilde{\mathsf{d}}_i$.

(e) All players check $\sum_{i \in S} T_i = \sum_{i \in S} A_i$. If the check fails they abort.

(f) Each P_i broadcasts s_i s.t. all players can compute $s := \sum_{i \in S} s_i$. They check that (r, s) is a valid EC-DSA signature, if so, they output (r, s), otherwise they abort the protocol.

4   Security

The security proof is a reduction to the unforgeability of standard EC-DSA. We demonstrate that if there exists a PPT algorithm $\mathcal{A}$ which breaks the threshold EC-DSA protocol of Figs. 3 and 4, then we can construct a forger $\mathcal{F}$ which uses $\mathcal{A}$ to break the unforgeability of standard EC-DSA. To this end $\mathcal{F}$ must simulate the environment of $\mathcal{A}$, so that $\mathcal{A}$'s view of its interactions with $\mathcal{F}$ are indistinguishable from $\mathcal{A}$'s view in a real execution of the protocol. Precisely, we show that if an adversary $\mathcal{A}$ corrupts $\{P_j\}_{j>1}$, one can construct a forger $\mathcal{F}$ simulating P_1 s.t. the output distribution of $\mathcal{F}$ is indistinguishable from $\mathcal{A}$'s view in an interaction with an honest party P_1 (all players play symmetric roles in the protocol so it is sufficient to provide a simulation for P_1). $\mathcal{F}$ gets as input an EC-DSA public key Q, and has access to a signing oracle for messages of its choice. After this query phase, $\mathcal{F}$ must output a forgery, i.e. a signature σ for a message m of its choice, which it did not receive from the oracle.

4.1   Simulating the Key Generation Protocol

On input a public key $Q := x \cdot P$, the forger $\mathcal{F}$ must set up in its simulation with $\mathcal{A}$ this same public key Q (w/o knowing x). This will allow $\mathcal{F}$ to subsequently simulate interactively signing messages with $\mathcal{A}$, using the output of its' (standard) EC-DSA signing oracle.

The main differences with the proof of [GG18] arise from the fact $\mathcal{F}$ knows it's own decryption key sk_1, but does not extract that of other players. Indeed the encryption scheme we use results from hash proof systems, whose security is statistical, thus the fact $\mathcal{F}$ uses its' secret key does not compromise security, and we can still reduce the security of the protocol to the ind-cpa-security of the encryption scheme. However as we do not prove knowledge of secret keys associated to public keys in the key generation protocol, $\mathcal{F}$ can not extract the decryption keys of corrupted players. The simulation is described below.

Simulating. P_1 **in** IKeyGen

1. $\mathcal{F}$ receives a public key Q from it's EC-DSA challenger.

2. Repeat the following steps (by rewinding $\mathcal{A}$) until $\mathcal{A}$ sends correct decommitments for $P_2, \ldots, P_n$ on both iterations.

3. $\mathcal{F}$ selects a random value $u_1 \in \mathbf{Z}/q\mathbf{Z}$, computes $[\mathsf{kgc}_1, \mathsf{kgd}_1] \leftarrow \mathsf{Com}(u_1 P)$ and broadcasts kgc_1. $\mathcal{F}$ receives $\{\mathsf{kgc}_j\}_{j \in [n], j \neq 1}$.

4. $\mathcal{F}$ broadcasts kgd_1 and receives $\{\mathsf{kgd}_j\}_{j \in [n], j \neq 1}$. For $i \in [n]$, let $Q_i \leftarrow \mathsf{Open}(\mathsf{kgc}_i, \mathsf{kgd}_i)$ be the revealed commitment value of each party. Each player performs a (t, n) Feldman-VSS of the value Q_i, with Q_i as the free term in the exponent.

5. $\mathcal{F}$ samples a CL encryption key pair $(\mathsf{pk}_1, \mathsf{sk}_1) \xleftarrow{\$} \mathsf{KeyGen}(1^\lambda)$.

6. $\mathcal{F}$ broadcasts pk_1 and receives the public keys $\{\mathsf{pk}_j\}_{j \in [n], j \neq 1}$.

7. $\mathcal{F}$ rewinds $\mathcal{A}$ to the decommitment step and
   - equivocates P_1's commitment to $\widehat{\mathsf{kgd}}$ so that the committed value revealed is now $\widehat{Q}_1 := Q - \sum_{j=2}^n Q_j$.
   - simulates the Feldman-VSS with free term $\widehat{Q}_1$.

8. $\mathcal{A}$ will broadcast the decommitments $\{\widehat{\mathsf{kgd}}_j\}_{j \in [n], j \neq 1}$. Let $\{\widehat{Q}_j\}_{j=2\ldots n}$ be the committed value revealed by $\mathcal{A}$ at this point ($\perp$ if $\mathcal{A}$ refuses to decommit).

9. All players compute the public signing key $\widehat{Q} := \sum_{i=1}^n \widehat{Q}_i$. If any $Q_i = \perp$ in the previous step, then $\widehat{Q} := \perp$.

10. Each player P_i adds the private shares it received during the n Feldman VSS protocols to obtain x_i (such that the x_i are a (t, n) Shamir's secret sharing of the secret key $x = \sum_i u_i$). Note that due to the free term in the exponent, the values $X_i := x_i \cdot P$ are public.

11. $\mathcal{F}$ simulates the ZKPoK that it knows x_1 corresponding to X_1, and for $j \in [n]$, $j \neq 1$, $\mathcal{F}$ receives from $\mathcal{A}$ a Schnorr ZKPoK of x_j such that $X_j := x_j \cdot P$. $\mathcal{F}$ can extract the values $\{x_j\}_{j \in [n], j \neq 1}$ from these ZKPoK.

4.2 Simulating the Signature Generation

On input m, $\mathcal{F}$ must simulate the interactive signature protocol from $\mathcal{A}$'s view.

We define $\tilde{k}_i := \mathsf{Dec}(\mathsf{sk}_i, c_{k_i})$, which $\mathcal{F}$ can extract from the proofs Π, and $\tilde{k} := \sum_{i \in S} \tilde{k}_i$. Let $k \in \mathbf{Z}/q\mathbf{Z}$ denote the value s.t. $R := k^{-1} \cdot P$ in Phase 4 of the signing protocol. Notice that if any of the players mess up the computation of R by revealing wrong shares δ_i, we may have $k \neq \tilde{k} \mod q$. As in [GG18], we distinguish two types of executions of the protocol: an execution where $\tilde{k} = k \mod q$ is said to be *semi-correct*, whereas an execution where $\tilde{k} \neq k \mod q$ is *non semi-correct*. Both executions will be simulated differently. At the end of Phase 4, when both simulations diverge, $\mathcal{F}$ knows k and $\tilde{k}$, so it can detect if it is in a semi-correct execution or not and chose how to simulate P_1.

We point out that $\mathcal{F}$ does not know the secret share w_1 of x associated with P_1, but it knows the shares $\{w_j\}_{j \in S, j \neq 1}$ of all the other players. Indeed $\mathcal{F}$ can compute these from the values $\{x_j\}_{j \in [n], j \neq 1}$ extracted during key generation. It also knows $W_1 = w_1 \cdot P$ from the key generation protocol. Moreover $\mathcal{F}$ knows the encryption keys $\{\mathsf{pk}_j\}_{j \in S}$ of all players, and it's own decryption key sk_1.

In the following simulation $\mathcal{F}$ aborts whenever $\mathcal{A}$ refuses to decommit any of the committed values, fails a ZK proof, or if the signature (r, s) does not verify.

Simulating. P_1 **in** ISign

Phase 1: As in a real execution, $\mathcal{F}$ samples $k_1, \gamma_1 \xleftarrow{\$} \mathbf{Z}/q\mathbf{Z}$ and $r_1 \xleftarrow{\$} [\tilde{A}]$ uniformly at random. It computes $c_{k_1} \leftarrow \mathsf{Enc}(\mathsf{pk}_1, k_1; r_1)$, the associated ZKAoK Π_1, and $[\mathsf{c}_1, \mathsf{d}_1] \leftarrow \mathsf{Com}(\gamma_1 P)$. It broadcasts $(\mathsf{c}_1, c_{k_1}, \Pi_1)$ before receiving $\{\mathsf{c}_j, c_{k_j}, \Pi_j\}_{j \in S, j \neq 1}$ from $\mathcal{A}$. $\mathcal{F}$ checks the proofs are valid and extracts the encrypted values $\{k_j\}_{j \in S, j \neq 1}$ from which it computes $\tilde{k} := \sum_{i \in S} k_i$.

Phase 2: (a) For $j \in S, j \neq 1$, $\mathcal{F}$ computes $\beta_{j,1}$, $c_{k_j \gamma_1}$ as in a real execution of the protocol, however since it only knows $W_1 = w_1 P$ (but not w_1), it samples a random $\mu_{j,1} \xleftarrow{\$} \mathbf{Z}/q\mathbf{Z}$ and sets $c_{k_j w_1} \leftarrow \mathsf{Enc}(\mathsf{pk}_j, \mu_{j,1})$, and $B_{j,1} := k_j \cdot W_1 - \mu_{j,1} \cdot P$. $\mathcal{F}$ then sends $(c_{k_j \gamma_1}, c_{k_j w_1}, B_{j,1})$ to P_j.

(b) When it receives $(c_{k_1 \gamma_i}, c_{k_1 w_j}, B_{1,j})$ from P_j, it decrypts as in a real execution of the protocol to obtain $\alpha_{1,j}$ and $\mu_{1,j}$.

(c) $\mathcal{F}$ verifies that $\mu_{1,j} P + B_{1,j} = k_1 W_j$. If so, since $\mathcal{F}$ also knows k_1 and w_j, it computes $\nu_{1,j} = k_1 w_j - \mu_{1,j} \mod q$

$\mathcal{F}$ computes $\delta_1 := k_1 \gamma_1 + \sum_{k \neq 1} \alpha_{1,k} + \sum_{k \neq 1} \beta_{k,1}$. However $\mathcal{F}$ cannot compute σ_1 since it does not know w_1, but it can compute

$$\sum_{i>1} \sigma_i = \sum_{i>1}\left(k_i w_i + \sum_{j \neq i} \mu_{i,j} + \nu_{j,i}\right) = \sum_{i>1}\sum_{j \neq i}(\mu_{i,j} + \nu_{j,i}) + \sum_{i>1} k_i w_i$$

$$= \sum_{i>1}(\mu_{i,1} + \nu_{1,i}) + \sum_{i>1; j>1} k_i w_j$$

since it knows all the values $\{k_j\}_{j \in S}$, $\{w_j\}_{j \in S, j \neq 1}$, it chooses the random values $\mu_{i,1}$ and it can compute all of the shares $\nu_{1,j} = k_1 w_j - \mu_{1,j} \mod q$.

Phase 3: $\mathcal{F}$ broadcasts δ_1 and receives all the $\{\delta_j\}_{j \in S, j \neq 1}$ from $\mathcal{A}$. Let $\delta := \sum_{i \in S} \delta_i$.

Phase 4: (a) $\mathcal{F}$ broadcasts d_1 which decommits to Γ_1, and $\mathcal{A}$ reveals $\{\mathsf{d}_j\}_{j \in S, j \neq 1}$ which decommit to $\{\Gamma_j\}_{j \in S, j > 1}$.

(b) $\mathcal{F}$ proves knowledge of γ_1 s.t. $\Gamma_1 = \gamma_1 P$, and for $j \in S, j \neq 1$, receives the PoK of γ_j s.t. $\Gamma_j = \gamma_j P$. $\mathcal{F}$ extracts $\{\gamma_j\}_{j \in S, j \neq 1}$ from which it computes $\gamma := \sum_{i \in S} \gamma_i \mod q$ and $k := \delta \cdot \gamma^{-1} \mod q$.

(c) If $k = \tilde{k} \mod q$ (semi-correct execution), $\mathcal{F}$ proceeds as follows:
   – $\mathcal{F}$ requests a signature (r, s) for m from its EC-DSA signing oracle.
   – $\mathcal{F}$ computes $R := s^{-1}(m \cdot P + r \cdot Q) \in \mathbb{G}$ (note that $r = H'(R) \in \mathbf{Z}/q\mathbf{Z}$).
   – $\mathcal{F}$ rewinds $\mathcal{A}$ to the decommitment step at Phase 4. (a) and equivocates P_1's commitment to open to $\widehat{\Gamma}_1 := \delta \cdot R - \sum_{i>1} \Gamma_i$. It also simulates the proof of knowledge of $\widehat{\gamma}_1$ s.t. $\widehat{\Gamma}_1 = \widehat{\gamma}_1 P$. Note that $\delta^{-1}(\widehat{\Gamma}_1 + \sum_{i>1} \Gamma_i) = R$.

Phase 5: Now $\mathcal{F}$ knows $\sum_{j \in S, j \neq 1} s_j$ held by $\mathcal{A}$ since $s_j = k_j m + \sigma_j r$.
   • $\mathcal{F}$ computes s_1 held by P_1 as $s_1 := s - \sum_{j \in S, j \neq 1} s_j$.
   • $\mathcal{F}$ continues the steps of Phase 5 as in a real execution.

(d) Else $k \neq \tilde{k} \mod q$ (non-semi-correct), and $\mathcal{F}$ proceeds as follows:
   - $\mathcal{F}$ computes $R := \delta^{-1}(\sum_{i \in S} \Gamma_i) = k \cdot P$ and $r := H'(R) \in \mathbf{Z}/q\mathbf{Z}$.
   - Phase 5: $\mathcal{F}$ does the following
     - sample a random $\tilde{s}_1 \xleftarrow{\$} Zq$.
     - sample $\ell_1, \rho_1 \xleftarrow{\$} \mathbf{Z}/q\mathbf{Z}$, compute $V_1 := s_1 R + \ell_1 P$; $A_1 := \rho_1 P$; $[\hat{c}_1, \hat{d}_1] \leftarrow \mathsf{Com}(V_1, A_1)$ and send $\hat{c}_1$ to $\mathcal{A}$.
     - receive $\{\hat{c}_j\}_{j \neq 1}$ and decommit by broadcasting $\hat{d}_1$. Proove knowledge of (s_1, ℓ_1, ρ_1) s.t. $(V_1 = s_1 R + \ell_1 P) \wedge (A_1 = \rho_1 P)$.
     - For $j \in S$, $j \neq 1$, $\mathcal{F}$ receive $\hat{d}_j$ and the ZKPoK of (s_j, ℓ_j, ρ_j) s.t. $V_j = s_j R + \ell_j P \wedge A_j = \rho_j P$.
     - Compute $V := -mP - rQ + \sum_{i \in S} V_i$, $A := \sum_{i \in S} A_1$, $T_1 := \ell_1 A$ and sample a random $U_1 \xleftarrow{\$} \mathbb{G}$.
     - Compute $[\tilde{c}_1, \tilde{d}_1] \leftarrow \mathsf{Com}(U_1, T_1)$ and send $\tilde{c}_1$ to $\mathcal{A}$. Upon receiving $\{\tilde{c}_j\}_{j \neq 1}$ from $\mathcal{A}$, broadcast $\tilde{d}_1$ and receive the $\{\tilde{d}_j\}_{j \neq 1}$.
     - Now since $\sum_{i \in S} T_1 \neq \sum_{i \in S} U_1$ both $\mathcal{A}$ and $\mathcal{F}$ abort.

4.3   The Simulation of a Semi-correct Execution

Lemma 1. *Assuming the strong root assumption and the C-low order assumption hold for* Gen*; the* CL *encryption scheme is* ind-cpa*-secure; and the commitment scheme is non-malleable and equivocable; then on input m the simulation either outputs a valid signature (r, s) or aborts, and is computationally indistinguishable from a semi-correct real execution.*

Proof. The differences between the real and simulated views are the following:

1. $\mathcal{F}$ does not know w_1, so it cannot compute $c_{k_j w_1}$ as in a real execution of the protocol. However under the strong root and C-low order assumption in $\widehat{G}$, $\mathcal{F}$ can extract k_j from the proofs in Phase 1. It then samples a random $\mu_{j,1} \in \mathbf{Z}/q\mathbf{Z}$, computes $B_{j,1} := k_j \cdot W_1 - \mu_{j,1} \cdot P$, and $c_{k_j w_1} \leftarrow \mathsf{Enc}(\mathsf{pk}_j, \mu_{j,1})$. The resulting view of $\mathcal{A}$ is indistinguishable from an honestly generated one since $\mu_{j,1}$ is uniformly distributed in $\mathbf{Z}/q\mathbf{Z}$, both in real and simulated executions; c_{k_j} was proven to be a valid ciphertext, so ciphertexts computed using homomorphic operations over c_{k_j} and fresh ciphertexts computed with pk_j follow identical distributions from $\mathcal{A}$'s view. And finally $B_{j,1}$ follows a uniform distribution in $\mathbb{G}$ both in real and simulated executions, and passes the check $B_{j,1} + \mu_{j,1} \cdot P = k_j \cdot W_1$ performed by $\mathcal{A}$.

2. $\mathcal{F}$ computes $\widehat{\Gamma}_1 := \delta \cdot R - \sum_{i > 1} \Gamma_i$, and equivocates its commitment c_1 s.t. d_1 decommits to $\widehat{\Gamma}_1$. Let us denote $\widehat{\gamma}_1 \in \mathbf{Z}/q\mathbf{Z}$ the value s.t. $\widehat{\Gamma}_1 = \widehat{\gamma}_1 P$, where $\widehat{\gamma}_1$ is unknown to $\mathcal{F}$, but the forger can simulate the ZKPoK of $\widehat{\gamma}_1$. Let us further denote $\widehat{k} \in \mathbf{Z}/q\mathbf{Z}$ the randomness (unknown to $\mathcal{F}$) used by its' signing oracle to produce (r, s). It holds that $\delta = \widehat{k}(\widehat{\gamma}_1 + \sum_{j \in S, j > 1} \gamma_j)$. Finally, let us denote $\widehat{k}_1 := \widehat{k} - \sum_{j \in S, j > 1} k_j$. Since δ was made public in Phase 3, by decommiting to $\widehat{\Gamma}_1 = \widehat{\gamma}_1 P$ instead

of $\Gamma_1 = \gamma_1 P$, $\mathcal{I}$ is implicitly using $\widehat{k}_1 \neq k_1$, even though $\mathcal{A}$ received an encryption of k_1 in Phase 2. However, if $\mathcal{A}$ could tell apart a real and simulated execution based on this difference, one could use $\mathcal{A}$ to break the indistinguishabilty of the encryption scheme. So, under the assumption the CL encryption scheme is ind-cpa-secure, this change is unnoticeable to $\mathcal{A}$.

3. $\mathcal{I}$ does not know σ_1, and thus cannot compute s_1 as in a real execution. Instead it computes $s_1 = s - \sum_{j \in S, j \neq 1} s_j = s - \sum_{j \in S, j \neq 1} (k_j m + \sigma_j r)$ where (implicitly) $s = \widehat{k}(m + rx)$. So $s_1 = \widehat{k}_1 m + r(\widehat{k}x - \sum_{j \in S, j \neq 1} \sigma_j)$, and $\mathcal{I}$ is implicitly setting $\widehat{\sigma}_1 := \widehat{k}x - \sum_{j \in S, j \neq 1} \sigma_j$ s.t. $\widehat{k}x = \widehat{\sigma}_1 + \sum_{j \in S, j \neq 1} \sigma_j$.

   We note that, since the real execution is semi correct, the correct shares of k for the adversary are the k_i that the simulator knows and $R = \widehat{k}P = (\widehat{k}_1 + \sum_{j \in S, j \neq 1} k_j)$. Therefore the value s_1 computed by $\mathcal{I}$ is consistent with a correct share for P_1 for a valid signature (r, s), which makes Phase 5 indistinguishable from the real execution to the adversary.

   In particular, observe that if none of the parties aborted during Phase 2, the output shares are correct. So if $\mathcal{A}$ here uses the values $\{\sigma_j\}_{j \in S, j > 1}$ as computed in a real execution of the protocol, it expects the signature generation protocol to output a valid signature. And indeed with $\mathcal{I}$'s choice of $\widehat{\sigma}_1$ and $\widehat{k}_1$, the protocol will terminate, outputting the valid signature (r, s) it received from its signing oracle. Conversely, if $\mathcal{A}$ attempts to cheat in Phase 5 by using a different set of σ_j's than those prescribed by the protocol, the check $\sum_{i \in S} T_i = \sum_{i \in S} U_i$ will fail, and all parties abort, as in a real execution of the protocol. ∎

4.4   Non Semi-correct Executions

Lemma 2. *Assuming the strong root assumption and the C-low order assumption hold for* Gen; *the* DDH *assumption holds in* $\mathbb{G}$; *and the commitment scheme is non-malleable and equivocable; then the simulation is computationally indistinguishable from a non-semi-correct real execution.*

Proof. We construct three games between the simulator $\mathcal{I}$ (running P_1) and the adversary $\mathcal{A}$ (running all other players). In G_0, $\mathcal{I}$ runs the real protocol. The only change between G_0 and G_1 is that in G_1, $\mathcal{I}$ chooses U_1 as a random group element. In G_2 the simulator $\mathcal{I}$ runs the simulation described in Sect. 4.2.

Indistinguishability of G_0 and G_1. We prove that if there exists an adversary $\mathcal{A}_0$ distinguishing games G_0 and G_1, $\mathcal{A}_0$ can be used to break the DDH assumption in $\widehat{G}$. Let $\tilde{A} = a \cdot P$, $\tilde{B} = b \cdot P$, $\tilde{C} = c \cdot P$ be the DDH challenge where $c = ab$ or c is random in $\mathbb{Z}_q$. The DDH distinguisher $\mathcal{I}_0$ runs $\mathcal{A}_0$, simulating the key generation phase s.t. $Q = \tilde{B}$. It does so by rewinding $\mathcal{A}_0$ in step 7 of the IKeyGen simulation and changing the decommitment of P_1 to $Q_1 := \tilde{B} - \sum_{j \in [n], j \neq 1} Q_j$. $\mathcal{I}_0$ also extracts the values $\{x_j\}_{j \in [n], j \neq 1}$ chosen by $\mathcal{A}_0$ from the ZKPoK of step 11 of the IKeyGen simulation. Note that at this point $Q = \tilde{B}$ and $\mathcal{I}_0$ knows x_i and the decryption key sk_1 matching pk_1, but not b and therefore not x_1.

Next $\mathcal{J}_0$ runs the signature generation protocol for a non-semi-correct execution. Recall that $S \subseteq [n]$ denotes the subset of players collaborating in ISign. Denoting $t := |S|$, the (t, n) shares $\{x_i\}_{i \in'n]}$ are converted into (t, t) shares $\{w_i\}_{i \in S}$ as per the protocol. Thus $b = \sum_{i \in S} w_i$ where $\mathcal{J}_0$ knows $\{w_j\}_{j \in S, j \neq 1}$ but not w_1. We denote $w_A := \sum_{j \in S, j \neq 1} w_j$ (which is known to $\mathcal{J}_0$) s.t. $w_1 = b - w_A$. $\mathcal{J}_0$ runs the protocol normally for Phases $1, 2, 3, 4$. It extracts the values $\{\gamma_j\}_{j \in S, j \neq 1}$ from the proof of knowledge in Phase 4, and knows γ_1 since it ran P_1 normally. Therefore $\mathcal{J}_0$ knows k such that $R = k^{-1} \cdot P$ since $k = (\sum_i \gamma_i)^{-1} \delta \mod q$. It also knows k_1 (chosen normally according to the protocol) and $\{k_j\}_{j \in S, j \neq 1}$ which it can extract from the proofs in Phase 1.

Before moving to the simulation of Phase 5, let's look at Phase 2 of the protocol for the computation of the shares σ_i. We note that since $\mathcal{J}_0$ knows sk_1 it also knows all the shares $\mu_{1,j}$ since it can decrypt the ciphertext $c_{k_1 w_j}$ it receives from P_j. However $\mathcal{J}_0$ does not know w_1 therefore it sends the encryption of a random $\mu_{j,1}$ to P_j and sets (implicitly) $\nu_{j,1} = k_j w_1 - \mu_{j,1}$. At the end the share σ_1 held by P_1 is

$$\sigma_1 = k_1 w_1 + \sum_{j \in S, j \neq 1} (\mu_{1,j} + \nu_{j,1}) = \tilde{k} w_1 + \sum_{j \in S, j \neq 1} (\mu_{1,j} - \mu_{j,1}) \text{ where } \tilde{k} = \sum_{i \in S} k_i.$$

Recall that since this is a non-semi-correct execution $\tilde{k} \neq k$ where $R = k^{-1} \cdot P$. Since $w_1 = b - w_A$ we have $\sigma_1 = \tilde{k} b + \mu_1$ where $\mu_1 = \sum_{j \in S, j \neq 1}(\mu_{1,j} - \mu_{j,1}) - \tilde{k} w_A$ with $\mu_1, \tilde{k}$ known to $\mathcal{J}_0$. This allows $\mathcal{J}_0$ to compute the correct value $\sigma_1 \cdot P = \tilde{k}\tilde{B} + \mu_1 \cdot P$ and therefore the correct value of $s_1 \cdot R$ as:

$$s_1 \cdot R = (k_1 m + r\sigma_1) \cdot R = k^{-1}(k_1 m + r\sigma_1) \cdot P$$
$$= k^{-1}(k_1 m + r\mu_1) \cdot P + k^{-1}(\tilde{k}r) \cdot \tilde{B} = \hat{\mu}_1 \cdot P + \hat{\beta}_1 \cdot \tilde{B}$$

where $\hat{\mu}_1 = k^{-1}(k_1 m + r\mu_1)$ and $\hat{\beta}_1 = k^{-1}\tilde{k}r$ are known to $\mathcal{J}_0$.

In the simulation of Phase 5, $\mathcal{J}_0$ selects a random ℓ_1 and sets $V_1 := s_1 \cdot R + \ell_1 \cdot P$, $A_1 = \rho_1 \cdot P = \tilde{A} = a \cdot P$. It simulates the ZK proof (since it does not know ρ_1 or s_1). It extracts s_i, ℓ_i, ρ_i from $\mathcal{A}_0$'s proofs s.t. $V_i = s_i \cdot R + \ell_i \cdot P = k^{-1} s_i \cdot P + \ell_i \cdot P$ and $A_i = \rho_i \cdot P$. Let $s_A = \sum_{j \in S, j \neq 1} k^{-1} s_j$. Note that, substituting the above relations (and setting $\ell = \sum_{i \in S} \ell_i$), we have: $V = -m \cdot P - r \cdot Q + \sum_{i \in S} V_i = \ell \cdot P + s_1 \cdot R + (s_A - m) \cdot P - r \cdot Q$. Moreover $Q = \tilde{B}$ so $-r \cdot Q = -r \cdot \tilde{B}$, and:

$$V = \ell \cdot P + \hat{\mu}_1 \cdot P + \hat{\beta}_1 \cdot \tilde{B} + (s_A - m) \cdot P - r \cdot \tilde{B} = (\ell + \theta) \cdot P + \kappa \cdot \tilde{B}$$

where $\mathcal{J}_0$ knows $\theta = \hat{\mu}_1 + s_A - m$ and $\kappa = \hat{\beta}_1 - r$. Note that for executions that are not semi-correct $\kappa \neq 0$.

Next $\mathcal{J}_0$ computes $T_1 := \ell_1 \cdot A$ (correctly), but computes U_1 as $U_1 := (\ell + \theta) \cdot \tilde{A} + \kappa \cdot \tilde{C}$, using this U_1 it continues as per the real protocol and aborts on the check $\sum_{i \in S} T_i = \sum_{i \in S} U_i$.

Observe that when $\tilde{C} = ab \cdot P$, by our choice of $a = \rho_1$ and $b = x$, we have that $U_1 = (\ell + \theta)\rho_1 \cdot P + \kappa \cdot \rho_1 \tilde{B} = \rho_1 \cdot V$ as in Game G_0. However when $\tilde{C}$ is a random group element, U_1 is uniformly distributed as in G_1. Therefore under the DDH assumption G_0 and G_1 are indistinguishable.

Indistinguishability of G_1 and G_2. In G_2, $\mathcal{F}$ broadcasts a random $\tilde{V}_1 = \tilde{s}_1 \cdot R + \ell_1 \cdot P$. This is indistinguishable from the correct $V_1 = s_1 \cdot R + \ell_1 \cdot P$ thanks to the mask $\ell_1 \cdot P$ which (under the DDH assumption) is computationally indistinguishable from a random value, since the adversary only knows A_1. To be precise, let $\tilde{A} = (a - \delta) \cdot P, \tilde{B} = b \cdot P$ and $\tilde{C} = ab \cdot P$ be the DDH challenge where δ is either 0 or random in $\mathbb{Z}_q$. The simulator proceeds as in G_0 (i.e. the regular protocol) until Phase 5. In Phase 5 $\mathcal{F}_0$ broadcasts $V_1 = \tilde{s}_1 \cdot R + \tilde{A}$ and $A_1 = \tilde{B}$. It simulates the ZKPoK (it does not know ℓ_1 or ρ_1), and extracts s_i, ℓ_i, ρ_i from the adversary s.t. $V_i = s_i \cdot R + \ell_i \cdot P = k^{-1}s_i \cdot P + \ell_i \cdot P$ and $A_i = \rho_i \cdot P$.

Next $\mathcal{F}_0$ samples a random U_1 and sets $T_1 := \tilde{C} + \sum_{j \in S, j \neq 1} \rho_j \cdot \tilde{A}$ before aborting. Note that when $\tilde{A} = a \cdot P$, we implicitly set $a = \ell_1$ and $b = \rho_1$ and have $V_1 = s_1 \cdot R + \ell_1 \cdot P$ and $T_1 = \ell_1 \cdot A$ as in Game G_1. However when $\tilde{A} = a \cdot P - \delta \cdot P$ with a random δ, then this is equivalent to having $V_1 = \tilde{s}_1 \cdot R + \ell_1 \cdot P$ and $T_1 = \ell_1 \cdot A$ with a randomly distributed $\tilde{s}_1$ as in Game G_2. Therefore under the DDH assumption G_1 and G_2 are indistinguishable.

4.5   Concluding the Proof

As mentioned at the beginning of Sect. 4.2 the forger $\mathcal{F}$ simulating $\mathcal{A}$'s environment can detect whether we are in a semi-correct-execution or not, i.e. whether $\mathcal{A}$ decides to be malicious and terminate the protocol with an invalid signature. Consequently $\mathcal{F}$ always knows how to simulate $\mathcal{A}$'s view and all simulations are indistinguishable of real executions of the protocol. Moreover if $\mathcal{A}$, having corrupted up to t parties in the threshold EC-DSA protocol, outputs a forgery, since $\mathcal{F}$ set up with $\mathcal{A}$ the same public key Q as it received from its' EC-DSA challenger, $\mathcal{F}$ can use this signature as its own forgery, thus breaking the existential unforgeability of standard EC-DSA.

Denoting $\mathsf{Adv}^{\mathsf{tu\text{-}cma}}_{\Pi, \mathcal{A}}$, $\mathcal{A}$'s advantage in breaking the existential unforgeability of our threshold protocol, and $\mathsf{Adv}^{\mathsf{eu\text{-}cma}}_{\mathsf{ecdsa}, \mathcal{F}}$ the forger $\mathcal{F}$'s advantage in breaking the existential unforgeability of standard EC-DSA, from Lemmas 1 and 2 it holds that if the DDH assumption holds in $\mathbb{G}$; the strong root assumption and the C-low order assumption hold for Gen; the CL encryption scheme is ind-cpa-secure; and the commitment scheme is non-malleable and equivocable then: $|\mathsf{Adv}^{\mathsf{eu\text{-}cma}}_{\mathsf{ecdsa}, \mathcal{F}} - \mathsf{Adv}^{\mathsf{tu\text{-}cma}}_{\Pi, \mathcal{A}}| \leq \mathsf{negl}(\lambda)$. Under the security of the EC-DSA signature scheme, $\mathsf{Adv}^{\mathsf{eu\text{-}cma}}_{\mathsf{ecdsa}, \mathcal{F}}$ must be negligible, which implies that $\mathsf{Adv}^{\mathsf{tu\text{-}cma}}_{\Pi, \mathcal{A}}$ should too, thus contradicting the assumption that $\mathcal{A}$ has non-negligible advantage of forging a signature for our protocol. We can thus state the following theorem, which captures the security of the protocol.

Theorem 4. *Assuming standard EC-DSA is existentially unforgeable; the* DDH *assumption holds in* $\mathbb{G}$*; the strong root assumption and the C-low order assumption hold for* Gen*; the* CL *encryption scheme is* ind-cpa-*secure; and the commitment scheme is non-malleable and equivocable, then the (t, n)-threshold EC-DSA protocol of Figs. 3 and 4 is an existentially unforgeable threshold signature scheme.*

5   Further Improvements

5.1   An Improved ZKPoK Which Kills Low Order Elements

We here provide a proof of knowledge of discrete logarithm in a group of unknown order. Traditionally, if one wants to perform such a proof, the challenge set must be binary, which implies expensive protocols as the proof must be repeated many times to achieve a satisfying (non computational) soundness error. Here using what we call the *lowest common multiple* trick, we are able to significantly increase the challenge set, and thereby reduce the number of repetitions required of the proof. We first present the resulting proof, before providing two applications: one for the CL.ISetup protocol of Sect. 3.2, and another for the two party EC-DSA protocol of [CCL+19]. Throughout this subsection we denote $y := \mathrm{lcm}(1, 2, 3, \ldots, 2^{10})$.

The Lowest Common Multiple Trick. For a given statement h, the proof does not actually prove knowledge of the Dlog of h, but rather of h^y. Precisely, the protocol of Fig. 5 is a zero knowledge proof of knowledge for the following relation:

$$\mathsf{R_{lcm-DL}} := \{(h, g_q); z \mid h^y = g_q^z\}.$$

$P(x, h := g_q^x)$	public: g_q	$V(h)$
$r \xleftarrow{\$} [0, \tilde{s} \cdot 2^{90}]$		
$t := g_q^r$	$\xrightarrow{\quad t \quad}$	
		$k \xleftarrow{\$} \{0,1\}^{10}$
	$\xleftarrow{\quad k \quad}$	
$u := r + kx \in \mathbf{Z}$	$\xrightarrow{\quad u \quad}$	
		Check $g_q^u = t \cdot h^k$

Fig. 5. ZKPoK of z s.t. $h^y = g_q^z$ where $y = \mathrm{lcm}(1, 2, 3, \ldots, 2^{10})$

Correctness. If $h = g_q^x$, then $g_q^u = g_q^{r+kx} = g_q^r \cdot (g_q^x)^k = t \cdot h^k$ and V accepts.

Special Soundness. Suppose that for a committed value t, prover P^* can answer correctly for two different challenges k_1 and k_2. We call u_1 and u_2 the two answers. Let $k := k_1 - k_2$ and $u := u_1 - u_2$, then since $g_q^{u_1} = t \cdot h^{k_1}$ and $g_q^{u_2} = t \cdot h^{k_2}$, it holds that $g_q^u = h^k$. By the choice of the challenge set, y/k is an integer and so $(g_q^u)^{y/k} = (h^k)^{y/k} = h^y$. Denoting $z := uy/k$, P^* can compute z such that $g_q^z = h^y$, so if P can convince V for two different challenge values, then P^* can compute a z satisfying the relation.

Zero Knowledge. Given h a simulator can sample $k \xleftarrow{\$} \{0,1\}^{10}$ and $u \xleftarrow{\$} [0, \tilde{s} \cdot (2^{90} + k)]$, compute $t := g_q^u \cdot h^{-k}$, such that distribution of the resulting transcript (h, t, k, u) is statistically close to those produced by a real execution of the protocol (this holds since an honest prover samples x from $[\tilde{s} \cdot 2^{40}]$, the challenge space is of size 2^{10} and r is sampled from a set of size $\tilde{s} \cdot 2^{90}$, which thus statistically hides kx).

Application to the CL *Interactive Set Up.* In the ISetup protocol of Sect. 3.2, in Step 2. 2. (c) each P_i computes $\pi_i := \mathsf{ZKPoK}_{g_i}\{(t_i) : g_i = \widehat{g}_q^{t_i}\}$. In fact it suffices for them to compute $\mathsf{ZKPoK}_{g_i}\{(z_i) : g_i^y = \widehat{g}_q^{z_i}\}$, where $y := \mathrm{lcm}(1, 2, 3, \ldots, 2^{10})$ using the lcm trick. Then in Step 2. 3. all players compute $g_q := (\prod_{j=1}^{n} g_j)^y$. The resulting g_q has the required properties to be plugged into the IKeyGen protocol. We use this modified interactive set up for our efficiency comparisons of Sect. 6.

Application to the [CCL+19] *Interactive Key Generation.* Castagnos et al. recently put forth a generic two party EC-DSA protocol from hash proof systems [CCL+19]. They rely on a ZKPoK for the following relation:

$$\mathsf{R_{CL-DL}} := \{(\mathsf{pk}, (c_1, c_2), Q); (x, r) \mid c_1 = g_q^r \wedge c_2 = f^x \mathsf{pk}^r \wedge Q = xP\}.$$

The interactive proof they provide uses binary challenges, consequently in order to achieve a satisfying soundness error of $2^{-\lambda}$, the proof must be repeated λ times. Using the lcm trick one can divide by 10 this number of rounds, though we obtain a ZKPoK for the following relation:

$$\mathsf{R_{CL-lcm}} := \{(\mathsf{pk}, (c_1, c_2), Q); (x, z) \mid c_1^y = g_q^z \wedge c_2^y = f^{x \cdot y} \mathsf{pk}^z \wedge Q = xP\}.$$

In their protocol this ZKPoK is computed by Alice, who sends this proof to Bob s.t. he is convinced her ciphertext $\mathbf{c} = (c_1, c_2)$ is well formed. Bob then performs some homomorphic operations on $\mathbf{c}$ and sends the result back to Alice. Now since with the proof based on the lcm trick, Bob is only convinced that $\mathbf{c}^y$ is a valid ciphertext, Bob raises $\mathbf{c}$ to the power y before performing his homomorphic operations[3]. When Alice decrypts she multiplies the decrypted value by y^{-1} mod q (this last step is much more efficient than Bob's exponentiation).

Remark 2. The size of the challenge set $\mathcal{C}$ from which k is sampled fixes the number of protocol repetitions required to achieve a reasonable soundness error. It is thus desirable to take $\mathcal{C}$ as large as possible. However, at the end of the protocol, V is only convinced that h^y is well formed, where $y = \mathrm{lcm}(1, \ldots, |\mathcal{C}|)$. So if V wants to perform operations on h which are returned to P, without risking leaking any information to P, V must raise h to the power y before proceeding. When plugged into the [CCL+19] two-party EC-DSA protocol this entails raising a ciphertext to the power y at the end of the key generation phase. So $|\mathcal{C}|$ must be chosen small enough for this exponentiation to take reasonable time. Hence we set $\mathcal{C} := \{0, 1\}^{10}$, and $y = \mathrm{lcm}(1, \ldots, 2^{10})$, which is a 1479 bits integer, so exponentiating to the power y remains efficient. To achieve a soundness error of $2^{-\lambda}$ the protocol must be repeated $\lambda/10$ times.

5.2   Assuming a Standardised Group

If we assume a standardised set up process, which allowed to provide a description of $\widehat{G}$, of the subgroups F and G_q and of a *random* generator g_q of G_q, one could completely omit the interactive set up phase for the CL encryption

---

[3] For correctness Bob also needs to multiply the signed message m' by y mod q, during the signature algorithm.

scheme and have all parties use the output of this standardised process. This significantly improves the IKeyGen protocol, as mentionned in Sect. 6.

Furthermore, assuming such a set up, we can replace the most expensive ZKPoK in [CCL+19] by an argument of knowledge for the same relation using similar techniques to those of Sect. 3.1, and relying on the strong root and low order assumptions in $\widehat{G}$. The resulting ZKAoK and a proof of its security are provided in the full version of this article [CCL+20, Section 5.2].

6   Efficiency Comparisons

In this section, we analyse the theoretical complexity of our protocol by counting the number of exponentiations and communication of group elements. We compare the communication cost of our protocol to that of [GG18,LN18][4] for the standard NIST curves P-256, P-384 and P-521, corresponding to levels of security 128, 192 and 256. For the encryption scheme, we start with a 112 bit security, as in the implementations of [GG18,LN18], but also study the case where its level of security matches the security of the elliptic curves.

The computed comm. cost is for our provably secure protocol as described in Sect. 3. Conversely the implementation which [GG18] provided omits a number of range proofs present in their described protocol. Though this substantially improves the efficiency of their scheme, they themselves note that removing these proofs creates an attack which leaks information on the secret signing key shared among the servers. They conjecture this information is limited enough for the protocol to remain secure, however since no formal analysis is performed, the resulting scheme is not proven secure. For a fair comparison we estimate the comm. cost and timings of both their secure protocol and the stripped down version. In terms of bandwidth we outperform even their stripped down protocol.

In both protocols, when possible zero knowledge proofs are performed non interactively, replacing the challenge by a hash value, whose size depends on the security parameter λ. We note that our interactive set up for the CL encryption scheme uses a ZKPoK where challenges are of size 10bits (using the lcm trick), it must thus be repeated $\lambda/10$ times. We note however that the PoK of integer factorization used in the key generation of [GG18] has similar issues.

For non-malleable equivocable commitments, we use a cryptographic hash function H and define the commitment to x as $h = H(x, r)$, for a uniformly chosen r of length λ and assume that H behaves as a random oracle.

---

[4] These are the best performing protocols using similar construction techniques to us (from homomorphic encryption), and achieving the same functionality, i.e. (t, n)-threshold ECDSA for any t s.t. $n \geq t + 1$. We do not compare to [DKLs18,DKLs19] as they use OT which leads to protocols with a much higher communication cost. Similarly, and as noted in [DKO+19] a direct comparison to [DKO+19,SA19] is difficult as they rely on preprocessing to achieve efficient signing, which is a level of optimisation we have not considered. We don't compare to [GGN16,BGG17] as [GG18] is already faster and cheaper in terms of communication complexity.

The comm. cost comparison is done by counting the number of bits that are both sent and received by a given party throughout the protocol[5]. In terms of timings, we count the number of exponentiations in the class group (for our protocol), the bit size of the exponent, and multiply this by $3/2$ of the cost of a multiplication in the group. We compare this to an equivalent computation for [GG18], where we count exponentiations modulo N and N^2, the bit size of the exponent, and multiply this by $3/2$ of the cost of a multiplication modulo N (resp. N^2). We do not count exponentiations and multiplications over the group of points of the elliptic curve as these are very cheap compared to the aforementioned computations, furthermore both protocols essentially perform identical operations on the curve.

The [LN18] *Protocol with Paillier Encryption.* We use the figures Lindell et al. provide in [LN18, Table 1] to compare our protocol to theirs. We note that – to their advantage – their key generation should include additional costs which are not counted in our figures (e.g. local Paillier key generation, verification of the ZKP of correctness of the Paillier key). The resulting costs are given in Fig. 6a

The [GG18] *Protocol with Paillier Encryption.* The main cost in their key generation protocol is the ZKPoK of integer factorization, which is instantiated using [PS00, Theorem 8]. Precisely each prover commits to K values mod N, the challenge lives mod B, the final opening is an element of size A, where, as prescribed by Poupard and Stern, we take $\log(A) = \log(N)$, $\log(B) = \lambda$ and $K = \frac{\lambda + \log(|N|)}{\log(C)}$ where $C := 2^{60}$ is chosen s.t. Floyd's cycle-finding algorithm is efficient in a space smaller than C. For their signature protocol, the cost of the ZK Proofs used in the MtA protocol are counted using [GG18, Appendix A].

The results are summarized in Fig. 6b. Since the range proofs (omitted in the stripped down version) only occur in the signing protocol, the timings and comm. cost of their interactive key generation is identical in both settings, we thus only provide these figures once. The comm. cost of each protocol is given in Bytes. The columns correspond to the elliptic curve used for EC-DSA, the security parameter λ in bits for the encryption scheme, the corresponding bit size of the modulus N, the timings of one Paillier exponentiation, of the key generation and of the signing phase and the total comm. in bytes for each interactive protocol. Modulus sizes are set according to the NIST recommendations.

Our Protocol with CL *Encryption.* For key generation we take into account the interactive key generation for the CL encryption scheme, which is done in parallel with IKeyGen s.t. the number of rounds of IKeyGen increases by only one broadcast per player. In IKeyGen, each party performs 2 class group exponentiations of $\log(\tilde{s}) + 40$ bits (where $\tilde{s} \approx \sqrt{q \cdot \tilde{q}}$), to compute generators g_i and public keys pk_i, and $\lambda/10 \times n$ exponentiations of $\log(\tilde{s}) + 90$ bits for the proofs and checks in the ISetup sub-protocol.

Note that exponentiations in $\langle f \rangle$ are almost free. Signing uses $2 + 10t$ exponentiations of $\log(\tilde{s}) + 40$ bits (for computing ciphertexts and homomorphic

---

[5] Broadcasting one element is counted as sending one element.

operations), $2(t+1)$ of $\log(\tilde{s}) + 80 + \lambda$ (for the ZKAoK) and $2t$ exponentiations of size q (for homomorphic scalar multiplication of ciphertexts).

The results for our protocols are summarized in Fig. 6c. The columns correspond to the elliptic curve used for EC-DSA, the security parameter λ in bits for the encryption scheme, the corresponding fundamental discriminant $\Delta_K = -q \cdot \tilde{q}$ bit size, the timings of one class group exponentiation (for an exponent of $\lambda + 40$ bits, i.e. that used for encryption), of the key generation and of the signing phase and the total comm. in bytes for IKeyGen and ISign. The discriminant sizes are chosen according to [BJS10].

Rounds. In terms of the number of rounds, we perform identically to [LN18]. Our IKeyGen requires 5 rounds (only 4 assuming a standardised set up), compared to 4 in [GG18]. Our signing protocol requires 8 rounds as opposed to 9 in [GG18].

Curve	λ (bits)	N (bits)	Mult. (ms)	IKeyGen (ms)	ISign (ms)	IKeyGen (Bytes)	ISign (Bytes)
P-256	112	2048	0.0023	$> 52n + 52$	$99t$	$> 6\,336(n-1)$	$16\,064t$
P-256	128	3072	0.0048	$> 162n + 162$	$310t$	$> 9\,152(n-1)$	$22\,208t$
P-384	192	7680	0.0186	$> 1\,571n + 1571$	$3\,000t$	$> 22\,176(n-1)$	$51\,744t$
P-521	256	15360	0.0519	$> 8\,769n + 8\,769$	$16\,741t$	$> 43\,672(n-1)$	$99\,845t$

(a) [LN18]'s secure t out of n protocol.

Curve	λ (bits)	N (bits)	Mult. (ms)	IKeyGen (ms)	Provably secure (with range proofs)			Stripped down	
					ISign (ms)	IKeyGen (Bytes)	ISign (Bytes)	ISign (ms)	ISign (Bytes)
P-256	112	2048	0.0023	$64n + 7$	$140t$	$32(n+t) + 9\,990n - 64$	$23\,308t + 588$	$28t$	$4\,932t + 588$
P-256	128	3072	0.0048	$293n + 22$	$428t$	$32(n+t) + 21\,392n - 64$	$33\,568t + 608$	$88t$	$7\,008t + 608$
P-384	192	7680	0.0186	$7\,017n + 214$	$4\,071t$	$48(n+t) + 128\,088n - 96$	$81\,072t + 912$	$857t$	$16\,656t + 912$
P-521	256	15360	0.0519	$77\,725n + 1196$	$22\,528t$	$65(n+t) + 503\,591n - 130$	$159\,391t + 1\,232$	$4783t$	$32\,470t + 1\,231$

(b) [GG18]'s t out of n protocol.

Curve	λ (bits)	Δ_K (bits)	Mult. (ms)	IKeyGen (ms)	ISign (ms)	IKeyGen (Bytes)	ISign (Bytes)
P-256	112	1348	0.029	$366n + 62$	$430t + 137$	$\mathbf{32(n+t) + 2951n - 64}$	$\mathbf{3\,670t + 1\,747}$
P-256	128	1827	0.038	$744n + 109$	$730t + 237$	$\mathbf{32(n+t) + 4\,297n - 64}$	$\mathbf{4\,455t + 2\,052}$
P-384	192	3598	0.077	$4\,145n + 424$	$\mathbf{2\,780t + 903}$	$\mathbf{48(n+t) + 10\,851n - 96}$	$\mathbf{8\,022t + 3\,560}$
P-521	256	5971	0.137	$16\,432n + 1\,243$	$\mathbf{8\,011t + 2,608}$	$\mathbf{65(n+t) + 22\,942n - 130}$	$\mathbf{12\,576t + 5\,433}$

(c) Our secure t out of n protocol – With an interactive CL setup.

Fig. 6. Comparative sizes (in bits), timings (in ms) & comm. cost (in Bytes)

Comparison. Figure 6 shows that the protocols of [LN18, GG18] are faster for both key generation and signing for standard security levels for the encryption scheme (112 and 128 bits of security) while our solution remains of the same order of magnitude. However our signing protocol is fastest from a 192-bits security level. In terms of communication, our solution outperforms both protocols for all security levels, factors vary according to the number of users n and the threshold t. In terms of rounds, our protocols use the same number of rounds as Lindell's. For key generation we use one more than [GG18], for signing we use one less.

This situation can be explained by the following facts. Firstly with class groups of quadratic fields we can use lower parameters than with $\mathbf{Z}/n\mathbf{Z}$ (the best algorithm against the discrete logarithm problem in class groups has complexity $\mathcal{O}(L[1/2, o(1)])$ compared to an $\mathcal{O}(L[1/3, o(1)])$ for factoring). However, the group law is more complex in class groups, indeed exponentiations in class groups are cheaper than those modulo N^2 from the 192 bits level. So even if removing range proofs allows us to drastically reduce the number of exponentiations, our solution only takes less time from that level (while being of the same order of magnitude below this level).

We note that assuming a standardized set up for CL (as mentioned in Sect. 5.2), one would reduce the bandwidth consumption of IKeyGen by a factor varying from 6 to 16 (for increasing levels of security). Moreover in terms of timings, the only exponentiation in the class group would be each party computing its own ciphertext, and so the only operations linear in the number of users n would be on the curve (or integers modulo q), which are extremely efficient.

Acknowledgements. We thank Rosario Gennaro and Steven Goldfeder for fruitful discussions. We also thank Omer Shlomovits for interesting insight on issues related to the practical implementation of threshold EC-DSA. This work was supported by the French ANR ALAMBIC project (ANR-16-CE39-0006). The research of Dario Catalano was partially supported by the Università degli Studi di Catania, "Piano della Ricerca 2016/2018—Linea di intervento 2".

References

[BBBF18] Boneh, D., Bonneau, J., Bünz, B., Fisch, B.: Verifiable delay functions. In: Shacham, H., Boldyreva, A. (eds.) CRYPTO 2018, Part I. LNCS, vol. 10991, pp. 757–788. Springer, Cham (2018). https://doi.org/10.1007/978-3-319-96884-1_25

[BBF18] Boneh, D., Bünz, B., Fisch, B.: A survey of two verifiable delay functions. Cryptology ePrint Archive, Report 2018/712 (2018)

[BBHM02] Biehl, I., Buchmann, J., Hamdy, S., Meyer, A.: A signature scheme based on the intractability of computing roots. Des. Codes Crypt. **25**(3), 223–236 (2002)

[Bel04] Belabas, K.: On quadratic fields with large 3-rank. Math. Comput. **73**(248), 2061–2074 (2004)

[BGG17] Boneh, D., Gennaro, R., Goldfeder, S.: Using level-1 homomorphic encryption to improve threshold DSA signatures for bitcoin wallet security. In: Lange, T., Dunkelman, O. (eds.) LATINCRYPT 2017. LNCS, vol. 11368, pp. 352–377. Springer, Cham (2019). https://doi.org/10.1007/978-3-030-25283-0_19

[BH01] Buchmann, J., Hamdy, S.: A survey on IQ cryptography. In: Public Key Cryptography and Computational Number Theory. De Gruyter Proceedings in Mathematics (2001)

[BJS10] Biasse, J.-F., Jacobson, M.J., Silvester, A.K.: Security estimates for quadratic field based cryptosystems. In: Steinfeld, R., Hawkes, P. (eds.) ACISP 2010. LNCS, vol. 6168, pp. 233–247. Springer, Heidelberg (2010). https://doi.org/10.1007/978-3-642-14081-5_15

[Boy86] Boyd, C.: Digital multisignature. In: Cryptography and Coding (1986)

[Bue76] Buell, D.A.: Class groups of quadratic fields. Math. Comput. **30**(135), 610–623 (1976)

[CCL+19] Castagnos, G., Catalano, D., Laguillaumie, F., Savasta, F., Tucker, I.: Two-party ECDSA from hash proof systems and efficient instantiations. In: Boldyreva, A., Micciancio, D. (eds.) CRYPTO 2019, Part III. LNCS, vol. 11694, pp. 191–221. Springer, Cham (2019). https://doi.org/10.1007/978-3-030-26954-8_7

[CCL+20] Castagnos, G., Catalano, D., Laguillaumie, F., Savasta, F., Tucker, I.: Bandwidth-efficient threshold EC-DSA. Cryptology ePrint Archive, Report 2020/084 (2020)

[CH89] Croft, R.A., Harris, S.P.: Public-key cryptography and reusable shared secret. In: Cryptography and Coding (1989)

[CIL17] Castagnos, G., Imbert, L., Laguillaumie, F.: Encryption switching protocols revisited: switching modulo p. In: Katz, J., Shacham, H. (eds.) CRYPTO 2017, Part I. LNCS, vol. 10401, pp. 255–287. Springer, Cham (2017). https://doi.org/10.1007/978-3-319-63688-7_9

[CKY09] Camenisch, J., Kiayias, A., Yung, M.: On the portability of generalized Schnorr proofs. In: Joux, A. (ed.) EUROCRYPT 2009. LNCS, vol. 5479, pp. 425–442. Springer, Heidelberg (2009). https://doi.org/10.1007/978-3-642-01001-9_25

[CL84] Cohen, H., Lenstra, H.W.: Heuristics on class groups. In: Chudnovsky, D.V., Chudnovsky, G.V., Cohn, H., Nathanson, M.B. (eds.) Number Theory. LNM, vol. 1052, pp. 26–36. Springer, Heidelberg (1984). https://doi.org/10.1007/BFb0071539

[CL15] Castagnos, G., Laguillaumie, F.: Linearly homomorphic encryption from DDH. In: Nyberg, K. (ed.) CT-RSA 2015. LNCS, vol. 9048, pp. 487–505. Springer, Cham (2015). https://doi.org/10.1007/978-3-319-16715-2_26

[CLT18] Castagnos, G., Laguillaumie, F., Tucker, I.: Practical fully secure unrestricted inner product functional encryption modulo p. In: Peyrin, T., Galbraith, S. (eds.) ASIACRYPT 2018, Part II. LNCS, vol. 11273, pp. 733–764. Springer, Cham (2018). https://doi.org/10.1007/978-3-030-03329-3_25

[CS97] Camenisch, J., Stadler, M.: Efficient group signature schemes for large groups. In: Kaliski, B.S. (ed.) CRYPTO 1997. LNCS, vol. 1294, pp. 410–424. Springer, Heidelberg (1997). https://doi.org/10.1007/BFb0052252

[CS03] Camenisch, J., Shoup, V.: Practical verifiable encryption and decryption of discrete logarithms. In: Boneh, D. (ed.) CRYPTO 2003. LNCS, vol. 2729, pp. 126–144. Springer, Heidelberg (2003). https://doi.org/10.1007/978-3-540-45146-4_8

[DDN00] Dolev, D., Dwork, C., Naor, M.: Nonmalleable cryptography. SIAM J. Comput. **30**(2), 391–437 (2000)

[Des88] Desmedt, Y.: Society and group oriented cryptography: a new concept. In: Pomerance, C. (ed.) CRYPTO 1987. LNCS, vol. 293, pp. 120–127. Springer, Heidelberg (1988). https://doi.org/10.1007/3-540-48184-2_8

[DF90] Desmedt, Y., Frankel, Y.: Threshold cryptosystems. In: Brassard, G. (ed.) CRYPTO 1989. LNCS, vol. 435, pp. 307–315. Springer, New York (1990). https://doi.org/10.1007/0-387-34805-0_28

[DF02] Damgård, I., Fujisaki, E.: A statistically-hiding integer commitment scheme based on groups with hidden order. In: Zheng, Y. (ed.) ASIACRYPT 2002. LNCS, vol. 2501, pp. 125–142. Springer, Heidelberg (2002). https://doi.org/10.1007/3-540-36178-2_8

[DKLs18] Doerner, J., Kondi, Y., Lee, E., Shelat, A.: Secure two-party threshold ECDSA from ECDSA assumptions. In: 2018 IEEE Symposium on Security and Privacy. IEEE Computer Society Press (2018)

[DKLs19] Doerner, J., Kondi, Y., Lee, E., Shelat, A.: Threshold ECDSA from ECDSA assumptions: the multiparty case. In: 2019 IEEE Symposium on Security and Privacy. IEEE Computer Society Press (2019)

[DKO+19] Dalskov, A.P.K., Keller, M., Orlandi, C., Shrishak, K., Shulman, H.: Securing DNSSEC keys via threshold ECDSA from generic MPC. IACR Cryptology ePrint Archive, 2019:889 (2019)

[Fel87] Feldman, P.: A practical scheme for non-interactive verifiable secret sharing. In: Proceedings of FOCS 1987. IEEE Computer Society (1987)

[GG18] Gennaro, R., Goldfeder, S.: Fast multiparty threshold ECDSA with fast trustless setup. In: ACM CCS 2018. ACM Press (2018)

[GGN16] Gennaro, R., Goldfeder, S., Narayanan, A.: Threshold-optimal DSA/ECDSA signatures and an application to bitcoin wallet security. In: Manulis, M., Sadeghi, A.-R., Schneider, S. (eds.) ACNS 2016. LNCS, vol. 9696, pp. 156–174. Springer, Cham (2016). https://doi.org/10.1007/978-3-319-39555-5_9

[Gil99] Gilboa, N.: Two party RSA key generation. In: Wiener, M. (ed.) CRYPTO 1999. LNCS, vol. 1666, pp. 116–129. Springer, Heidelberg (1999). https://doi.org/10.1007/3-540-48405-1_8

[GJKR96a] Gennaro, R., Jarecki, S., Krawczyk, H., Rabin, T.: Robust and efficient sharing of RSA functions. In: Koblitz, N. (ed.) CRYPTO 1996. LNCS, vol. 1109, pp. 157–172. Springer, Heidelberg (1996). https://doi.org/10.1007/3-540-68697-5_13

[GJKR96b] Gennaro, R., Jarecki, S., Krawczyk, H., Rabin, T.: Robust threshold DSS signatures. In: Maurer, U. (ed.) EUROCRYPT 1996. LNCS, vol. 1070, pp. 354–371. Springer, Heidelberg (1996). https://doi.org/10.1007/3-540-68339-9_31

[GMR88] Goldwasser, S., Micali, S., Rivest, R.L.: A digital signature scheme secure against adaptive chosen-message attacks. SIAM J. Comput. 17(2), 281–308 (1988)

[HS06] Hamdy, S., Saidak, F.: Arithmetic properties of class numbers of imaginary quadratic fields. JP J. Algebra Number Theory Appl. 6(1), 129–148 (2006)

[Lag80] Lagarias, J.: Worst-case complexity bounds for algorithms in the theory of integral quadratic forms. J. Algorithms 1(2), 142–186 (1980)

[Lin17] Lindell, Y.: Fast secure two-party ECDSA signing. In: Katz, J., Shacham, H. (eds.) CRYPTO 2017, Part II. LNCS, vol. 10402, pp. 613–644. Springer, Cham (2017). https://doi.org/10.1007/978-3-319-63715-0_21

[Lip12] Lipmaa, H.: Secure accumulators from euclidean rings without trusted setup. In: Bao, F., Samarati, P., Zhou, J. (eds.) ACNS 2012. LNCS, vol. 7341, pp. 224–240. Springer, Heidelberg (2012). https://doi.org/10.1007/978-3-642-31284-7_14

[LN18] Lindell, Y., Nof, A.: Fast secure multiparty ECDSA with practical distributed key generation and applications to cryptocurrency custody. In: ACM CCS 2018. ACM Press (2018)

[MR01] MacKenzie, P.D., Reiter, M.K.: Two-party generation of DSA signatures. In: Kilian, J. (ed.) CRYPTO 2001. LNCS, vol. 2139, pp. 137–154. Springer, Heidelberg (2001). https://doi.org/10.1007/3-540-44647-8_8

[Pie19] Pietrzak, K.: Simple verifiable delay functions. In: ITCS 2019. LIPIcs (2019)

[PR05] Pass, R., Rosen, A.: Concurrent non-malleable commitments. In: 46th FOCS. IEEE Computer Society Press (2005)

[PS00] Poupard, G., Stern, J.: Short proofs of knowledge for factoring. In: Imai, H., Zheng, Y. (eds.) PKC 2000. LNCS, vol. 1751, pp. 147–166. Springer, Heidelberg (2000). https://doi.org/10.1007/978-3-540-46588-1_11

[Que87] Quer, J.: Corps quadratiques de 3-rang 6 et courbes elliptiques de rang 12. C. R. Acad. Sci. Paris Sér. I **305**, 215–218 (1987)

[SA19] Smart, N.P., Alaoui, Y.T.: Distributing any elliptic curve based protocol: with an application to MixNets. IACR Cryptology ePrint Archive 2019:768 (2019)

[Sch91] Schnorr, C.-P.: Efficient signature generation by smart cards. J. Cryptol. **4**(3), 161–174 (1991)

[SG98] Shoup, V., Gennaro, R.: Securing threshold cryptosystems against chosen ciphertext attack. In: Nyberg, K. (ed.) EUROCRYPT 1998. LNCS, vol. 1403, pp. 1–16. Springer, Heidelberg (1998). https://doi.org/10.1007/BFb0054113

[Sha79] Shamir, A.: How to share a secret. Commun. ACM **22**(11), 612–613 (1979)

[Sho00] Shoup, V.: Practical threshold signatures. In: Preneel, B. (ed.) EUROCRYPT 2000. LNCS, vol. 1807, pp. 207–220. Springer, Heidelberg (2000). https://doi.org/10.1007/3-540-45539-6_15

[Van92] Vanstone, S.: Responses to NIST's proposal. Commun. ACM **35**, 41–54 (1992). (communicated by John Anderson)

[Wes19] Wesolowski, B.: Efficient verifiable delay functions. In: Ishai, Y., Rijmen, V. (eds.) EUROCRYPT 2019, Part III. LNCS, vol. 11478, pp. 379–407. Springer, Cham (2019). https://doi.org/10.1007/978-3-030-17659-4_13

Secure Computation and Related Primitives

Blazing Fast OT for Three-Round UC OT Extension

Ran Canetti[1], Pratik Sarkar[1(✉)], and Xiao Wang[2]

[1] Boston University, Boston, USA
{canetti,pratik93}@bu.edu
[2] Northwestern University, Evanston, USA
wangxiao@cs.northwestern.edu

Abstract. Oblivious Transfer (OT) is an important building block for multi-party computation (MPC). Since OT requires expensive public-key operations, efficiency-conscious MPC protocols use an OT extension (OTE) mechanism [Beaver 96, Ishai et al. 03] to provide the functionality of *many independent* OT instances with the same sender and receiver, using only symmetric-key operations plus *few* instances of some *base OT* protocol. Consequently there is significant interest in constructing *OTE friendly* protocols, namely protocols that, when used as base-OT for OTE, result in extended OT that are both round-efficient and cost-efficient. We present the most efficient OTE-friendly protocol to date. Specifically:

- Our base protocol incurs only 3 exponentiations per instance.
- Our base protocol results in a 3 round extended OT protocol.
- The extended protocol is UC secure in the Observable Random Oracle Model (ROM) under the CDH assumption.

For comparison, the state of the art for base OTs that result in 3-round OTE are proven only in the programmable ROM, and require 4 exponentiations under Interactive DDH or 6 exponentiations under DDH [Masney-Rindal 19]. We also implement our protocol and benchmark it against the Simplest OT protocol [Chou and Orlandi, Latincrypt 2015], which is the most efficient and widely used OT protocol but not known to suffice for OTE. The computation cost is roughly the same in both cases. Interestingly, our base OT is also 3 rounds. However, we slightly modify the extension mechanism (which normally adds a round) so as to preserve the number of rounds in our case.

1 Introduction

Oblivious Transfer (OT) is a fundamental primitive for multi-party computation (MPC). It has been shown to be complete [GMW87,Kil88] and has become the most widely used building block in both the two-party setting [Yao86,NNOB12] and the multi-party setting [BLO16,WRK17,HSS17]. However, oblivious transfer is expensive since it requires public key operations [IR89]. This limitation is mitigated by the seminal concept of OT extension [Bea96,IKNP03], which allows the parties to compute $m = \text{poly}(\kappa)$ number of OTs using only κ "base

© International Association for Cryptologic Research 2020
A. Kiayias et al. (Eds.): PKC 2020, LNCS 12111, pp. 299–327, 2020.
https://doi.org/10.1007/978-3-030-45388-6_11

OTs" and $O(m)$ symmetric-key operations, where κ is the computational security parameter. This yields a large number of OTs at the cost of $\mathcal{O}(1)$ symmetric key operations.

The state-of-the-art protocol for malicious OT extension [KOS15] can compute more than ten million OTs per second in a high bandwidth network setting. As such, it appears that the problem of constructing efficient OT extension has been resolved. However, some challenges remain. First, we note that the cost of the base OTs remains a significant consideration when m is only moderately larger than κ and security against all-but-one corruption is needed. For instance, Wang et al. [WRK17] reported that in their implementation of a malicious 128-party computation tolerating 127-party corruption in the WAN setting, it takes about 140 s to securely evaluate an AES circuit, where 80 s (more than 55% of the total cost!) are spent on computing base OTs.

Another challenge is the number of rounds. Ideally, we would like to obtain extended OT with only two rounds. However, here we have only two known solutions: The original OT extension pf Beaver [Bea96] which is highly inefficient due to non-black-box use of the underlying symmetric-key primitives, and the Boyle et al. [BCG+19] two-round OT extension, based on the Learning Parity with Noise (LPN) assumption, whose performance is better than IKNP-like OT extension only when the network bandwidth is low ($\approx$100 Mbps).

The other approach taken in the literature is to apply a black-box OT extension (such as that of [KOS15]) to some base OT. This method, however results in an additional round. In fact, recent result by Garg et al. [GMMM18] shows that this is inevitable, namely $(n + 1)$ rounds for OT extension are necessary if an n-round base OT is used. Thus, this approach seems to result in extended OT protocols with three or more rounds. Furthermore, the state-of-the-art two-round OT protocols are much slower than the best three-round OT protocols. For example, the two-round OT by Peikert et al. [PVW08] requires 11 exponentiations. More recently, [MR19] proposed an OT that requires 6 exponentiations under standard DDH assumption or 4 exponentiations under non-standard IDDH assumption. This means that even three-round extended OT protocols, obtained in this way, are less than optimally efficient.

Another set of challenges revolves around the level of security obtained and the assumptions used. Chou and Orlandi [CO15] proposed a base-OT protocol with malicious security (dubbed as CO-OT). The work of [HL17] proposed a similar protocol. However, it has been shown [BPRS17,GIR17,LM18] that this protocol and [HL17] cannot be proven secure with simulation-based security because a simulator cannot extract a corrupt receiver's choice bit. There have been some works [BPRS17,DKLs18] trying to fix this issue, but all of them require either much more computation or higher round complexity. Masny and Rindal [MR19] recently proposed a UC-secure OT in the programmable random oracle model (ROM). Their performance is slightly worse than CO-OT under non-standard notion of interactive version of the Decisional Diffie Hellman (IDDH) assumption and much worse under Decisional Diffie Hellman (DDH) assumption.

Table 1. Comparison to related protocols. "#Rounds of OT extension" is the round complexity of the best OT extension with selected base OT protocol. IDDH refers to interactive DDH, not known to be reducible to DDH. PRO refers to programmable RO; ORO refers to observable RO.
[a]Do not provide simulation-based security.
[b]Incur a one-time computation cost of one NIZKPoK.

Protocol	#Exponentiations per base OT	#Rounds of OT Extension	Computational Assumption	Trusted Setup
[PVW08]	11	3	DDH	CRS
[CO15][a]	3	4	CDH	PRO
[BPRS17]	11	3	DDH	PRO
[HL17][a]	5	4	CDH	PRO
[DKLs18][b]	3	6	CDH	ORO
[MR19]	4	3	IDDH	PRO
[MR19]	6	3	DDH	PRO
This work	3	3	CDH	ORO

1.1 Our Contributions

In this paper, we construct an OT protocol tailored to be base OT for the [KOS15] OT extension. Our protocol is highly efficient, and results in a 3 round extended OT that is UC secure in the observable ROM assuming only CDH. See Table 1 for comparison with the state of the art.

The key idea underlying our construction is to design a three-round base OT protocol that circumvents the lower bound proved by Garg et al. [GMMM18]. This is achieved by considering a slight modification of the KOS extension, that is specific to our base OT protocol: The parties use the inputs for the base OT protocol to compute the OT extension messages in parallel to the execution of the base-OT computation. This yields a round-preserving three-round OT extension protocol. To preserve efficiency, we only use some specific property of the base OT protocol (and thus non-black-box to base OT), but avoid non-black-box use of any underlying primitives or computational assumptions. We observe that our protocol is compatible with OT extension protocols [ALSZ15, PSS17, OOS17] in the IKNP domain. It also works for state-of-the-art 1-out-of-N OT extension protocols [PSS17, OOS17]. See Sect. 3 for more discussion. Our detailed contributions are listed as follows:

- **Weaker base-OT Functionality.** To securely realize OT extension efficiently, we consider a UC-secure base-OT functionality that allows selective failure attack by a corrupt sender. We further relax the UC-security requirement to only sender-sided simulation-based security; on the receiver-side, we demonstrate that indistinguishability based security suffices for KOS, provided the receiver's input can be extracted.
- **Weaker Assumptions.** Our protocol is secure assuming CDH in the observable random oracle (ORO) model. Our assumptions and trusted setup are

weaker and far more well-studied than other protocols with comparable efficiency. When used in the OT extension, the OT extension protocol becomes UC-secure.

- **Best efficiency.** Our protocol requires three exponentiations per OT and is as efficient as the CO-OT [CO15]. This is also experimentally verified based on implementation. Since CO-OT (which is insecure) is the most efficient among all existing OT protocols, our new OT with provable security is also the most efficient.
- **Round Preserving.** Our OT protocol requires three rounds, one round more than necessary; however, one unique feature of our protocol is that its *last two rounds of messages* can be securely sent in parallel with the OT-extension messages and thus resulting in a three-round OT extension protocol.
- **Empirical Comparison.** Finally, we implement our protocol and demonstrate its high performance. In detail, our protocol is as efficient as the OT by Chou and Orlandi (which cannot be proven UC secure). When used in the OT extension, our protocol results in a even better performance due to reduced round complexity.

We note that the original KOS paper had an interactive coin tossing subprotocol. It resulted in a 5 rounds protocol and it relied on Correlation Robust Function (CRF). The subprotocol was made non-interactive by the work of [DKLs18] using the Fiat-Shamir transform by relying on a non-programmable random oracle. This reduced the round complexity to 3. We consider this round optimized variant of KOS in the RO model since we already require the RO for our OT protocol.

1.2   More Discussion on Related Works

Here we highlight the protocols from prior OT literature that are relevant to our work. A comparison can be found in Table 1.

- The two-round UC-secure OT protocol by [PVW08] is a candidate for the base OTs in KOS. Its optimized variant computes 11 exponentiations and is proven secure in the common reference string model under DDH assumption.
- The Simplest OT (or CO-OT) was proposed by Chou and Orlandi [CO15]. It computes 3 exponentiations in the programmable random oracle (PRO) model assuming CDH. It requires 2 rounds to compute a random OT, but their OT messages cannot be parallelized with the OT extension messages, thus resulting in a 4 round OT extension. It has been shown [LM18] that this protocol cannot be proven secure with simulation-based security because a simulator cannot extract a corrupt receiver's choice bit. For proving UC-security of the OT extension protocol, the inputs of the receiver (of the base OT) has to be extracted.
- The work of [DKLs18] proposed a 5 round OT protocol, with selective failure, for the base OTs in the ORO model. They compute 3 exponentiations per OT and incur a one-time computation of a non-interactive zero-knowledge

proof of knowledge (NIZKPoK) for Discrete Log. The high round complexity of the base OTs leads to a 6 round OT extension since their last OT message cannot be parallelized with the last message of the OT extension.

– A recent work by [MR19] proposed non-interactive OTs from non-interactive Key Exchange. The resulting OT extension would still require 3 rounds. Their optimized variant requires 4 exponentiations under IDDH assumption and their unoptimized variant requires 6 exponentiations in the PRO model. However, IDDH is not known to be reducible to the standard DDH assumption.

– Silent OT extension [BCG+19] does not follow the IKNP-style extension. Instead, it can be viewed as a special case of vector OLE [BCGI18] and requires an LPN assumption. The resulting protocol can be more efficient than KOS under low network bandwidth.

Roadmap. In the next section, we introduce some notations and important concepts used in this paper. In Sect. 3, we present the key intuitions behind our protocols. This is followed by our weakened OT functionality in Sect. 4. Then, we show that our weakened OT functionality suffices to obtain the KOS OT extension in Sect. 5. We instantiate κ instances of our OT functionality in Sect. 6. Finally, we present our implementation details and compare it with the CO-OT in Sect. 7.

2   Preliminaries

Notations. We denote by $a \leftarrow D$ a uniform sampling of an element a from a distribution D. The set of elements $\{1, \ldots, n\}$ is represented by $[n]$. A function $\mathsf{neg}(()\cdot)$ is said to be negligible, if for every polynomial $p(\cdot)$, there exists a constant c, such that for all $n > c$, it holds that $\mathsf{neg}(()n) < \frac{1}{p(n)}$. We denote a probabilistic polynomial time algorithm as PPT. We denote the computational security parameter by κ and statistical security parameter by μ respectively. Let $\mathbb{Z}_q$ denote the field of order q, where $q = \frac{p-1}{2}$ and p are primes. Let $\mathbb{G}$ be the multiplicative group corresponding to $\mathbb{Z}_p^*$ with generator g, where CDH assumption holds. We denote a field of size 2^κ as $\mathbb{F}$. Our security proofs are in the Universal Composability (UC) framework of [Can01]. We refer to the original paper for details. For a bit $b \in \{0, 1\}$, we denote $1 - b$ by $\bar{b}$. We denote a matrix as $\mathbf{M}$ where $\mathbf{M}^i$ refers to the ith column and $\mathbf{M}_j$ as the jth row of $\mathbf{M}$ respectively. Given a field element $x \in \mathbb{F}$ and a bit vector $\mathbf{a} = (a_1, a_2, \ldots, a_\kappa)$ we denote component-wise multiplication as $x \cdot \mathbf{a} = (a_1 \cdot x, a_2 \cdot x, \ldots, a_\kappa \cdot x)$. In our OT extension protocol, the sender is denoted as $\mathsf{S_{Ext}}$ and the receiver is denoted as $\mathsf{R_{Ext}}$ respectively.

Random Oracle Model. A random oracle (RO) functionality is parametrized by a domain and a range and it is as $\mathcal{F}_{\mathsf{RO}}$ in Fig. 2. A random oracle query on message m is denoted by $\mathcal{F}_{\mathsf{RO}}(m)$. The random oracle functionality can be broadly classified [CDG+18] into three categories based on its features- plain RO, observable RO and programmable RO. A plain RO returns a random string, from

---

$$\mathcal{F}_{\mathsf{OT}}$$

$\mathcal{F}_{\mathsf{OT}}$ interacts with a sender S and a receiver R:

- On input (CHOOSE, rec, sid, b) from R where $b \in \{0, 1\}$; if no message of the form (rec, sid, b) has been recorded in the memory, store (rec, sid, b) and send (rec, sid) to S.

- On input (TRANSFER, sen, sid, (a_0, a_1)) from S with $a_0, a_1 \in \{0, 1\}^n$, if no message of the form (sen, sid, (a_0, a_1)) is recorded and a message of the form (rec, sid, b) is stored, send (sent, sid, a_b) to R and (sent, sid) to S. Ignore future messages with the same sid.

Fig. 1. The ideal functionality $\mathcal{F}_{\mathsf{OT}}$ for Oblivious Transfer

its range, upon being queried on a message m, from its domain. An observable RO inherits the properties of the plain RO but in addition it grants the simulator to observe the queries made, to $\mathcal{F}_{\mathsf{RO}}$, by the adversary. Our proofs hold in the global RO (GRO) model of [CJS14] where the observable RO is replaced by the GRO.

Tweakable Correlation Robust Hash. OT extension requires a correlation robust hash function. We adopted the definition proposed by Guo et al. [GKW+19], where a tweak is explicitly included in the hash function too. Given a function $\text{CRF} : \mathcal{T} \times \{0, 1\}^\kappa \to \{0, 1\}^\kappa$, define $\mathcal{O}_\Delta(t, w) \overset{\text{def}}{=} \text{CRF}(t, w \oplus \Delta)$, where $t \in \mathcal{T}$. Let Func denote the set of functions from $\mathcal{T} \times \{0, 1\}^\kappa$ to $\{0, 1\}^\kappa$.

Definition 1. *Given a function* $\text{CRF} : \mathcal{T} \times \{0, 1\}^\kappa \to \{0, 1\}^\kappa$, *a uniform distribution on* $\{0, 1\}^\kappa$ *namely* U_κ, *we say that* CRF *is tweakable correlation robust if for any PPT distinguisher D, if*

$$\left| \Pr_{\Delta \leftarrow U_\kappa} \left[D^{\Delta(\cdot)} = 1 \right] - \Pr_{f \leftarrow \mathsf{Func}} \left[D^{f(\cdot)} = 1 \right] \right| = \mathsf{negli}(\kappa).$$

Note that in our use of tweakable correlation robust hash, $\mathcal{T}$ is a tuple of values, one for sid and one for index i.

Oblivious Transfer. In a 1-out-of-2 OT, we have a sender (S) holding two inputs $a_0, a_1 \in \{0, 1\}^n$ and a receiver (R) holding a choice bit b. The correctness of OT means that R will obtain a_b as the outcome of the protocol. At the same time, S should learn nothing about b, and R should learn nothing about the other input of S, namely $a_{\bar{b}}$. The ideal OT functionality $\mathcal{F}_{\mathsf{OT}}$ is shown in Fig. 1.

3   Technical Overview

In this section we give an overview of our technical contributions. First, we recall the KOS OT extension from a high-level. We argue that the base OTs in KOS

$\mathcal{F}_{\mathsf{RO}}$

$\mathcal{F}_{\mathsf{RO}}$ is parameterized by a domain D and range R and it proceeds as follows, running on security parameter k:

- $\mathcal{F}_{\mathsf{RO}}$ maintains a list L (which is initially empty) of pairs of values $(\hat{m}, \hat{h})$, s.t. $\hat{m} \in D$ and $\hat{h} \in R$.
- Upon receiving a value (sid, m) (where $m \in D$) perform the following: If there is a pair $(m, \hat{h})$, for some $\hat{h} \in R$, in the list L, set $h := \hat{h}$. If there is no such pair, sample $h \leftarrow_R R$ and store the pair (m, h) in L. Once h is set, reply to the activating machine with (sid, h).

Fig. 2. The ideal functionality $\mathcal{F}_{\mathsf{OT}}$ for Random Oracle

do not require UC security. Building on this idea, we propose a weaker OT functionality and then we provide an efficient three-round OT protocol which would yield a three round OT extension.

3.1 Overview of KOS

In the KOS OT extension, the sender $\mathsf{S}_{\mathsf{Ext}}$ and receiver $\mathsf{R}_{\mathsf{Ext}}$ wants to generate m OTs using κ invocations to $\mathcal{F}_{\mathsf{OT}}$ (base OTs) and symmetric key operations. The sender $\mathsf{S}_{\mathsf{Ext}}$ plays the role of a receiver in the base OTs. He samples a random κ bit string $\mathbf{s}$ and invokes ith instance of $\mathcal{F}_{\mathsf{OT}}$ with ith bit of $\mathbf{s}$ for $i \in [\kappa]$. The receiver $\mathsf{R}_{\mathsf{Ext}}$ invokes $\mathcal{F}_{\mathsf{OT}}$ as sender with random pads $(\mathbf{k}_{i,0}, \mathbf{k}_{i,1})$. $\mathsf{S}_{\mathsf{Ext}}$ obtains $\mathbf{k}_{i,s_i}$ from the ith base OT. In addition, $\mathsf{R}_{\mathsf{Ext}}$ also sends a mapping $\mathbf{D}$ from his inputs to the $(\mathbf{k}_{i,0}, \mathbf{k}_{i,1})$ values. Upon obtaining this mapping $\mathbf{D}$ and the base-OT output, the sender computes his mapping $\mathbf{Q}$. He computes correlated pads for the extended OTs using $\mathbf{s}$ and $\mathbf{Q}$ as $\mathrm{CRF}(\mathsf{sid}, j, \mathbf{Q}_j)$ and $\mathrm{CRF}(\mathsf{sid}, j, \mathbf{Q}_j \oplus \mathbf{s})$ for $j \in [m]$, where CRF is a correlation robust function. If the receiver's input bit for j-th extended OT is 0, then he can compute $\mathbf{Q}_j$, else he can compute $\mathbf{Q}_j \oplus \mathbf{s}$. The other value remains hidden due to $\mathbf{s}$ and security of CRF. Using the correlated pads, $\mathsf{S}_{\mathsf{Ext}}$ encrypts his inputs for the extended OTs and sends it to $\mathsf{R}_{\mathsf{Ext}}$.

In addition, $\mathsf{S}_{\mathsf{Ext}}$ also performs a consistency check on matrix $\mathbf{D}$ is correctly formed by $\mathsf{R}_{\mathsf{Ext}}$, else a malformed $\mathbf{D}$ matrix would leak the bits of $\mathbf{s}$ rendering the protocol insecure. The original KOS paper had an interactive check phase. It was made non-interactive by the work of [DKLs18] using the Fiat-Shamir transform by relying on the observable random oracle. Our protocol also uses the same non-interactive check to obtain a 3-round OT extension protocol where the checks are run in the second OT extension message. The base OTs are run for 3 rounds and the last message of the OT extension is sent in parallel to the last message of the base OT. Next, we discuss our proposed relaxations in the base OT functionality.

3.2   Relaxation in the OT Functionality

Firstly, it can be observed that the parties invoke the base OTs in KOS with random OTs. So, one can consider random OT functionality instead of full OT functionality. Next, we can allow selective failure in the base OTs. The work of KOS and [DKLs18] showed that the base OTs do not require full UC-security of an OT functionality. Instead, the functionality can allow a corrupt sender (i.e. R_{Ext} in the OT extension) to launch a selective failure attack on the s bits of the receiver (i.e. S_{Ext} in the OT extension). In such a case, the corrupt R_{Ext}^* will still have a negligible advantage in breaking the security of the extended OTs. We claim that the OT functionality can be further relaxed based on the following observations in the KOS protocol.

1. **Delayed input extraction of receiver:** The inputs of the receiver (S_{Ext}) in the base OTs can be extracted after S_{Ext} sends the last message of the OT Extension protocol. Recall, that the last message of the OT Extension protocol consists of the inputs of S_{Ext} encrypted with the correlated pads. The simulator against a corrupt S_{Ext}^* can simulate the second message of the OT extension without the knowledge of s. Later, it can extract s from the base OTs and then extract S_{Ext}'s inputs from the last message.
2. **Corrupt receiver can abort after base OT:** A corrupt receiver (S_{Ext}) can abort after obtaining the results of base-OT protocol corresponding to s. In such a case, the honest R_{Ext} would just abort the protocol as the base OTs resulted in an abort. For each base OT, one of the input of R_{Ext} remain hidden from S_{Ext} due to the security of the OT; thus hiding R_{Ext}'s inputs.
3. **Batch of κ OT:** The OT extension protocol requires κ base OTs between the parties. So, the base OTs can be computed in a batch of κ OTs instead of κ independent instances of the OT protocol.

Based on the above observations we can consider the following relaxations to the OT functionality for a corrupt receiver.

1. **Indistinguishability based security against corrupt receiver with input extraction:** We can reduce the simulation based security for a corrupt receiver to an indistinguishability based security. We need an extractor algorithm Ext that can extract the input bit b of a corrupt receiver, given blackbox access to it. The corrupt receiver cannot distinguish its real world view from a view constructed with the sender's message corresponding to bit $\bar{b}$ set as 0^κ.
2. **Corrupt receiver can abort without input extraction:** A corrupt receiver can decide to abort in the OT functionality and in such a case the Ext does not need to extract his inputs.
3. **Corrupt receiver cannot compute both sender messages:** A corrupt receiver cannot compute both sender input messages from the OT transcript and his internal randomness, even if he aborts the protocol.

3.3 Usage in KOS OT Extension

The above relaxations in the base-OT functionality are justified since we do not require simulation based security in the OT extension protocol for the base OTs. This is because the base OTs are internal to the protocol; hence the input/output of the honest parties in the base OTs are inaccessible to the environment $\mathcal{Z}$ who tries to distinguish between real and ideal world executions of the OT extension protocol. Indistinguishability based security suffices for a corrupt receiver (i.e. a corrupt $\mathsf{S}_{\mathsf{Ext}}$) in the base OTs, if we are guaranteed that the following conditions hold:

1. If the base OTs succeed then the input $\mathbf{s}$ of the receiver (i.e. $\mathsf{S}_{\mathsf{Ext}}$) can be extracted after obtaining the OT extension last message as that is used by the simulator (for a corrupt $\mathsf{S}^*_{\mathsf{Ext}}$) to extract the input messages of $\mathsf{S}^*_{\mathsf{Ext}}$. This is guaranteed by the correctness of Ext algorithm when the base OT protocol succeeds.
2. In case the base OT aborts, then the Ext does not need to extract the inputs of $\mathsf{S}^*_{\mathsf{Ext}}$ since the OT extension protocol terminates with an abort too.
3. The corrupt $\mathsf{S}^*_{\mathsf{Ext}}$ should not be able to distinguish between the real world interaction with honest $\mathsf{R}_{\mathsf{Ext}}$, and ideal world interaction with the simulator. In the ideal world, the simulator runs with input for the extended OTs as all 0s string. $\mathsf{S}^*_{\mathsf{Ext}}$, playing the role of receiver in the base OT, cannot compute both sender messages of the base OT. Based on this property, we tweak our OT extension protocol by relying on the random oracle. The tweak ensures that one of the sender's messages in the each base OT will be hidden from $\mathsf{S}^*_{\mathsf{Ext}}$. Thus, he cannot distinguish the real world from the ideal world by relying on the security of the original KOS protocol. Our tweak incurs a minimal overhead of 2 RO queries for each base OT.

We also utilize the fact that the base OTs are computed in a batch of κ OTs. This allows us to efficiently implement a batch of κ instances of the above (weakened) OT functionality based on observable random oracle. Next, we discuss our OT protocol which implements a batch of κ instances of weak OT functionality, as discussed above.

3.4 Optimized OT Protocol in the Observable RO Model

We consider an OT protocol in the observable random oracle model where the receiver R generates receiver OT parameter T by invoking a random oracle $\mathcal{F}_{\mathsf{RO1}}$ on a seed. He samples a random $\alpha \leftarrow \mathbb{Z}_q$ and computes his first message based on his input bit b as B, where

$$B = g^\alpha \cdot T^b$$

He sends B and seed to the sender S. The sender computes T from seed and samples a random $r \leftarrow \mathbb{Z}_q$. S computes sender OT parameters- $z = g^r$ and sends z to R. S computes his random pads p_0 and p_1 by invoking a random oracle $\mathcal{F}_{\mathsf{RO2}}$ as follows:

$$p_0 = \mathcal{F}_{RO2}(\mathsf{sid}, B^r)$$

$$p_1 = \mathcal{F}_{RO2}(\mathsf{sid}, (\tfrac{B}{T})^r)$$

Upon obtaining z, R computes his output pad p_b as follows:

$$p_b = \mathcal{F}_{RO2}(\mathsf{sid}, z^\alpha) = \mathcal{F}_{RO2}(\mathsf{sid}, g^{r\alpha})$$

This protocol ensures that a corrupt receiver R^* cannot compute both random pads as that would require invoking $\mathcal{F}_{RO2}$ on B^r and $(\tfrac{B}{T})^r = \tfrac{B^r}{T^r}$. Such a corrupt receiver could be used to break the CDH assumption where $(T, z) = (g^t, g^r)$ is the CDH challenge. The queries made by R^* to $\mathcal{F}_{RO2}$ can be used to obtain T^r which is the answer to the CDH challenge. This OT protocol also perfectly hides the input b of an honest receiver from a corrupt receiver as α and $\alpha - t$ are valid receiver randomness for $b = 0$ and $b = 1$ respectively, where $B = g^\alpha$. However, this protocol doesn't allow extraction of receiver or sender's inputs from the OT messages in the observable RO model.

Adding Receiver Input Extraction. To add receiver's input extraction the sender adds a challenge in the second round of the OT protocol.

$$\mathsf{chall} = \mathcal{F}_{RO3}(\mathsf{sid}, p_0) \oplus \mathcal{F}_{RO3}(\mathsf{sid}, p_1).$$

The receiver has to respond to the challenge by computing his answer Ans.

$$\mathsf{Ans} = \mathcal{F}_{RO3}(\mathsf{sid}, p_b) \oplus (b \cdot \mathsf{chall}) = \mathcal{F}_{RO3}(\mathsf{sid}, p_0).$$

R has to query $\mathcal{F}_{RO3}$ to compute Ans and assists a simulator to extract a corrupt receiver's input. R sends Ans to the sender in a third OT message. This increases the round complexity to 3 but it ensures that the simulator can extract the receiver's input bit from the RO queries of $\mathcal{F}_{RO3}$ if Ans is valid. This is similar to the challenge-response paradigm introduced in the work of [DKLs18]. However, a corrupt sender can compute the challenge in a malicious way such that he can find out the bits of receiver from the response and the receiver fails to identify such an attack. The work of [DKLs18] tackles this issue by making the sender open his randomness (for computing the challenge) to the receiver in a fourth OT message. We ensure correctness of the challenge by making the sender send a proof γ along with the challenge in the second OT message,

$$\gamma = \mathcal{F}_{RO3}(\mathsf{sid}, \mathcal{F}_{RO3}(\mathsf{sid}, p_0)) = \mathcal{F}_{RO3}(\mathsf{sid}, \mathsf{Ans}).$$

After obtaining the second OT message, the receiver can compute Ans and verify the proof γ. If γ is valid then he sends Ans to sender else he aborts. This ensures input extraction of receiver as argued before but it adds selective failure attack by a corrupt sender S^*. S^* can try to guess the bits of receiver and based on that he can maliciously construct the challenge. However, our OT functionality accommodates selective failure attack over a batch of κ OTs and hence this challenge-prove-response paradigm would work in our case. Next, we show that this trick already provides extraction of a corrupt sender's input.

Adding Sender Input Extraction. Our challenge-prove-response paradigm allows us to construct a protocol where the sender's inputs can be extracted if a batch of $\ell > \mu$ OTs are run together. In KOS, κ OTs are run where $\kappa > \mu$. Now, we will explain the reason behind our assumption of $\ell > \mu$. In a batch of ℓ OTs, every OT uses the same T and $z = g^r$, i.e. the ith OT pad is of the form:

$$p_{i,0} = \mathcal{F}_{\mathsf{RO2}}(\mathsf{sid}, B_i^r),$$

$$p_{i,1} = \mathcal{F}_{\mathsf{RO2}}(\mathsf{sid}, (\tfrac{B_i}{T})^r),$$

where B_i is chosen by R based on his randomness α_i and input bit b_i for the i-th OT. In such a case, the sender sends a unique challenge chall_i for each OT as follows:

$$\mathsf{chall}_i = \mathcal{F}_{\mathsf{RO3}}(\mathsf{sid}, p_{i,0}) \oplus \mathcal{F}_{\mathsf{RO3}}(\mathsf{sid}, p_{i,1}).$$

Now, the receiver computes the answer resp to the challenge as:

$$\mathsf{resp}_i = \mathcal{F}_{\mathsf{RO3}}(\mathsf{sid}, p_b) \oplus (b \cdot \mathsf{chall}) = \mathcal{F}_{\mathsf{RO3}}(\mathsf{sid}, p_0).$$

The answer to the challenge is optimized to sending one string for the whole batch instead of κ strings, as follows:

$$\mathsf{Ans} = \mathcal{F}_{\mathsf{RO4}}(\mathsf{sid}, \mathcal{F}_{\mathsf{RO3}}(\mathsf{sid}, \mathsf{resp}_1), \mathcal{F}_{\mathsf{RO3}}(\mathsf{sid}, \mathsf{resp}_2), \ldots \mathcal{F}_{\mathsf{RO3}}(\mathsf{sid}, \mathsf{resp}_\kappa))$$

$$= \mathcal{F}_{\mathsf{RO4}}(\mathsf{sid}, \mathcal{F}_{\mathsf{RO3}}(\mathsf{sid}, p_{1,0}), \mathcal{F}_{\mathsf{RO3}}(\mathsf{sid}, p_{2,0}), \ldots \mathcal{F}_{\mathsf{RO3}}(\mathsf{sid}, p_{\kappa,0})).$$

The proof sent by the sender is also modified accordingly as:

$$\gamma = \mathcal{F}_{\mathsf{RO3}}(\mathsf{sid}, \mathcal{F}_{\mathsf{RO4}}(\mathsf{sid}, \mathcal{F}_{\mathsf{RO3}}(\mathsf{sid}, p_{1,0}), \mathcal{F}_{\mathsf{RO3}}(\mathsf{sid}, p_{2,0}), \ldots \mathcal{F}_{\mathsf{RO3}}(\mathsf{sid}, p_{\kappa,0})))$$

$$= \mathcal{F}_{\mathsf{RO3}}(\mathsf{sid}, \mathsf{Ans}).$$

The receiver can check his computed answer with the proof and then respond with Ans. This tweak allows us to extract a corrupt sender's input for $\ell > \mu$ OTs. The simulator can extract T^r by observing the queries- B_i^r and $(\tfrac{B_i}{T})^r$ made by S to $\mathcal{F}_{\mathsf{RO2}}$. Sender needs to query $\mathcal{F}_{\mathsf{RO2}}$ for computing $p_{i,0}$ and $p_{i,1}$ values, which are in turn used to compute the challenge and proof for $\ell > \mu$ OTs. Sender can avoid querying $\mathcal{F}_{\mathsf{RO2}}$ with both- B_i^r and $(\tfrac{B_i}{T})^r$. In that case, he has to either guess the corresponding RO query results, i.e. $p_{i,0}$ or $p_{i,1}$, or he launches a selective failure attack for every OT and he has to correctly guess receiver's input bit for every OT. This is because, the receiver's input is random and he will compute the Ans and it will not match with the γ sent by the sender, except with $2^{-\mu}$ probability, since γ and chall_i were computed without correctly computing the $p_{i,0}$ or $p_{i,1}$ values, for every $i \in [\ell]$. Thus, the simulator can observe $\mathcal{F}_{\mathsf{RO2}}$, compute the candidate $p_{i,0}, p_{i,1}$, match with chall_i values and γ and extract the correct T^r. Using T^r, he can extract the sender's input messages.

3.5   Circumventing the Impossibility Result of [GMMM18]

We circumvent the impossibility result of [GMMM18] by allowing the OT extension receiver $\mathsf{R}_{\mathsf{Ext}}$, i.e. base OT sender, to use the base OT output messages to send his mapping $\mathbf{D}$ in the second round of the OT extension protocol. If the base OT receiver fails to answer the base OT challenge then R_{Ext} aborts else he computes his OT extension output message. The base OT security ensures that a corrupt base OT receiver (i.e. S_{Ext}^*) cannot compute both messages of the base OT sender (i.e. R_{Ext}). This hides the input of R_{Ext} in $\mathbf{D}$ even though we use the base OT messages before it has terminated. Such non-blackbox usage of the 3 round base-OT protocol allows us to obtain a 3 round OT extension protocol.

4   Weakening the Oblivious Transfer Functionality

In this section, we discuss the type of security that we require from the base OT protocols of the KOS OT extension. We demonstrate that by gradually relaxing the $\mathcal{F}_{OT}$ functionality, where the parties choose their own input, to a random OT where the functionality provides random inputs to the parties. Next, we allow selective failure attack by a sender on receiver's inputs and define it as $\mathcal{F}_{SF\text{-}rOT}$. We also allow a corrupt receiver to abort the protocol. We relax the UC-security of this protocol to one-sided simulation. Finally, we formally define our notion of weakened OT which provides simulation based security for a corrupt sender and indistinguishability security against a corrupt receiver.

Random Oblivious Transfer. The OT functionality can be relaxed to consider random inputs, i.e. $\mathcal{F}_{rOT}$. In this case, the inputs of an honest sender and an honest receiver are chosen randomly by the functionality. However, a malicious sender (also a malicious receiver) can choose his own inputs. The ideal random OT functionality has been presented in Fig. 3.

Random Oblivious Transfer with Selective Failure and Explicit Abort. We can further weaken the $\mathcal{F}_{rOT}$ functionality to allow selective failure attacks by a corrupt sender. Here, the corrupt sender S^* can try to guess the random input of the receiver by setting its message, corresponding to bit 0 as $\perp$, whereas the message corresponding to bit 1 is set correctly. An honest receiver would abort if his input bit b is 0, else he continues with the protocol. This would leak b to S^*. We also allow a corrupt receiver R^* to explicitly abort the protocol after it obtains its input message a_b. In such a case, the functionality notifies the sender regarding the abort. Our $\mathcal{F}_{SF\text{-}rOT}$ functionality has been modeled in Fig. 4.

Oblivious Transfer for KOS. It was shown in the work of KOS and [DKLs18] that κ instances of $\mathcal{F}_{SF\text{-}rOT}$ (without the ABORT option) suffices to instantiate the κ base OTs in the KOS OT extension protocol. However, this requires simulation based security against a corrupt R^*, where the simulator needs to extract the input of R^* and simulate the sender's message s.t. they open to the correct message, i.e. a_b, even if R^* aborts the protocol. However, such a strong requirement from $\mathcal{F}_{SF\text{-}rOT}$ is an overkill for instantiating the base-OT protocols. We demonstrate that the security against a corrupt receiver can be reduced to indistinguishability based security and his input need not be extracted when he aborts. More precisely:

$$\mathcal{F}_{\text{rOT}}$$

$\mathcal{F}_{\text{OT}}$ interacts with a sender S and a receiver R:

- On input (CHOOSE, rec, sid) from R; if no message of the form (rec, sid, b) has been recorded in the memory, sample $b \leftarrow \{0, 1\}$, store (rec, sid, b) and send (rec, sid) to S and (b, sid) to R.

- On input (CHOOSE*, rec, sid, b) from R* where $b \in \{0, 1\}$; if no message of the form (rec, sid, b) has been recorded in the memory, store (rec, sid, b) and send (rec, sid) to S and (b, sid) to R.

- On input (TRANSFER, sen, sid) from S, if no message of the form (sen, sid, (a_0, a_1)) is recorded and a message of the form (rec, sid, b) is stored, sample $a_0, a_1 \leftarrow \{0, 1\}^n$, store (sen, sid, (a_0, a_1)) in memory and send (sent, sid, (b, a_b)) to R and (sent, sid, (a_0, a_1)) to S. Ignore future messages with the same sid.

- On input (TRANSFER*, sen, sid, (a_0, a_1)) from S* with $a_0, a_1 \in \{0, 1\}^n$, if no message of the form (sen, sid, (a_0, a_1)) is recorded and a message of the form (rec, sid, b) is stored, send (sent, sid, (b, a_b)) to R and (sent, sid, (a_0, a_1)) to S. Ignore future messages with the same sid.

Fig. 3. The ideal functionality $\mathcal{F}_{\text{rOT}}$ for random Oblivious Transfer

- **Indistinguishability against a Malicious R*:** In the KOS OT extension, the invocations to the base OT functionality is internal to the OT extension protocol. The environment $\mathcal{Z}$ does not have access to it; hence it cannot choose inputs for the honest parties in the base OT functionality. This permits us to use an efficient OT protocol to emulate the functionality, s.t. it provides simulation based security against a corrupt S* whereas for a corrupt R*, it provides indistinguishability based security. Such a relaxation allows us to use observable random oracle instead of a programmable one in 3 rounds. Previous protocols, like [DKLs18] used observable RO but they required 5 rounds for the base OTs, where the last 2 rounds where spent in simulating the honest sender's messages, i.e. providing simulation based security against corrupt R*. The work of [MR19] obtain a two-round OT but they require twice the amount of exponentiation as ours by extracting the receiver's input from the first OT message.

- **Input of R* need not be extracted during Abort:** When the sender S_{Ext}^* of the OT extension protocol (acting as the receiver R* of the base OTs) misbehaves and causes an abort, the OT extension protocol leads to an abort. In such a case, the input messages (in the extended OTs) of S_{Ext}^* need not be extracted. Hence, it is not necessary to extract the inputs of S_{Ext}^*(or R*) in the base OTs. This allows us to push the extraction of the R* input until the last round of the base OT (in our case also the last round of OT extension), where it can be extracted when he computes the base OTs correctly. In case he aborts then it is guaranteed that he cannot compute both sender messages. This allows us to save on the number of exponentiations.

$\mathcal{F}_{\mathsf{SF\text{-}rOT}}$

$\mathcal{F}_{\mathsf{SF\text{-}rOT}}$ interacts with a sender S and receiver R :

- On input (CHOOSE, rec, sid) from R; if no message of the form (rec, sid, b) has been recorded in the memory, sample $b \leftarrow \{0, 1\}$, store (rec, sid, b) and send (rec, sid) to S and (b, sid) to R. If a message of the form (sen, sid, (a_0, a_1)) is stored, send (sent, sid, (b, a_b)) to R and (sent, sid, (a_0, a_1)) to S and ignore future messages with the same sid.

- On input (CHOOSE*, rec, sid, b) from R* where $b \in \{0, 1\}$; if no message of the form (rec, sid, b) has been recorded in the memory, store (rec, sid, b) and send (rec, sid) to S and (b, sid) to R. If a message of the form (sen, sid, (a_0, a_1)) is stored, send (sent, sid, (b, a_b)) to R and (sent, sid, (a_0, a_1)) to S and ignore future messages with the same sid.

- On input (GUESS*, sen, sid, b') from S*, if (rec, sid, b) exists in memory, $b' \in \{0, 1, \perp\}$ and there does not exist (sen, sid, (GUESS, ·)) in memory then store (sen, sid, (GUESS, b')) in memory and perform the following:
  - If $b' = \perp$, do nothing.
  - If $b' = \top$, send (CHEAT-DETECTED, S) to R and (CHEAT-DETECTED) to S.
  - If $b' = b$, send (CHEAT-UNDETECTED) to S.
  - If $b' \neq b$, send (CHEAT-DETECTED, S) to R and (CHEAT-DETECTED) to S.

- On input (TRANSFER, sen, sid) from S, if no message of the form (sen, sid, (a_0, a_1)) is stored; sample $a_0, a_1 \leftarrow \{0, 1\}^\kappa$, store (sen, sid, ($a_0, a_1$)) in memory and send (RECEIVED, sid) to R and S. If a message of the form (rec, sid, b) is stored, send (sent, sid, (b, a_b)) to R and (sent, sid, (a_0, a_1)) to S and ignore future messages with the same sid.

- On input (TRANSFER*, sen, sid, (a_0, a_1)) from S*, if no message of the form (sen, sid, (a_0, a_1)) is stored then store (sen, sid, (a_0, a_1)) in memory and send (RECEIVED, sid) to R and S. If a message of the form (rec, sid, b) is stored, then send (sent, sid, (b, a_b)) to R and (sent, sid, (a_0, a_1)) to S and ignore future messages with the same sid.

- On input (ABORT, rec, b, sid) from R*, if messages of the form - (sen, sid, (a_0, a_1)) is stored; send (sent, sid, (b, a_b)) to R and (ABORT, sid, (a_0, a_1)) to S. Ignore future messages with the same sid.

Fig. 4. The ideal functionality $\mathcal{F}_{\mathsf{SF\text{-}rOT}}$ for Random Oblivious Transfer with Selective Failure

- **Batch of $\kappa > \mu$ OTs:** We consider a batch of $\kappa > \mu$ invocations of OT protocol for the base OTs. This is necessary since a corrupt receiver of OT extension $\mathsf{R}^*_{\mathsf{Ext}}$ can launch a selective failure attack on the inputs of $\mathsf{S}_{\mathsf{Ext}}$ to the base OT. Since the inputs are random, $\mathsf{R}^*_{\mathsf{Ext}}$ can at most determine μ inputs bits of $\mathsf{S}_{\mathsf{Ext}}$'s randomness. However, that gives him a negligible advantage in breaking the security of the OT extension protocol due to the security of the underlying OT extension protocol.

We also assume there exists a PPT algorithm Ext that can extract the input of a malicious R*, if he does not abort the protocol. We formally define our sender-simulatable $\mathcal{F}_{\text{SF-rOT}}$ with the following security properties required against a corrupt receiver:

Definition 2. *Let $\mathcal{F}_{\text{SF-rOT}}$ be the Oblivious Transfer functionality as shown in Fig. 4. We say that a protocol π_{OT} securely computes $\mathcal{F}_{\text{SF-rOT}}$ with sender-sided simulation with input extractability of receiver if the following holds:*

1. *For every non-uniform PPT adversary S^* controlling the sender in the real model, there exists a non-uniform PPT adversary* Sim *for the ideal model, such that for any environment $\mathcal{Z}$,*

$$\text{IDEAL}_{\mathcal{F}_{\text{SF-rOT}},\text{Sim},\mathcal{Z}}((a_0,a_1),b,z)_{z\in\{0,1\}^*} \approx \text{REAL}_{\pi_{OT},S^*,\mathcal{Z}}((a_0,a_1),b,z)_{z\in\{0,1\}^*}.$$

2. *For every non-uniform PPT adversary $\mathcal{A}$ controlling the receiver R^*, the following holds:*
   – *Property 1: If the sender did not abort, then there exists a PPT extractor algorithm Ext such that the following holds:*

$$\Pr\left[(a_0,a_1) \leftarrow S^{\mathcal{F}_{\text{SF-rOT}}}, (b,a_b) \leftarrow \mathcal{A}^{\mathcal{F}_{\text{SF-rOT}}}, b' \leftarrow \text{Ext}^{\mathcal{A}} \right.$$
$$\left. : (b \neq b') \wedge (a_0 \neq \perp) \wedge (a_1 \neq \perp)\right] \leq \text{negli}(\kappa)$$

   – *Property 2: If the sender did not abort, then the view of R^* is independent of $a_{\bar{b}}$. More formally the following condition holds:*

$$\mathcal{V}^S_{\pi_{OT},R^*(z)}((a_0,a_1),b,z)_{z\in\{0,1\}^*} \approx \mathcal{V}^S_{\pi_{OT},R^*(z)}((\widetilde{a}_0,\widetilde{a}_1),b,z)_{z\in\{0,1\}^*},$$

   where Ext outputs b on interacting with R^*. $\mathcal{V}^S_{\pi_{OT},R^*(z)}$ denotes the view of adversarial R^* after a real execution of protocol π_{OT} with the honest sender S, with random sender inputs (a_0,a_1), and $(\widetilde{a}_0,\widetilde{a}_1)$ where $\widetilde{a}_b \leftarrow \{0,1\}^\kappa$ and $\widetilde{a}_{\bar{b}} = 0^\kappa$ respectively.
   – *Property 3: R^* cannot compute both sender messages except with negligible probability. More formally the following condition holds:*

$$\Pr\left[(a_0,a_1) \leftarrow S^{\mathcal{F}_{\text{SF-rOT}}}, (a'_0,a'_1) \leftarrow \mathcal{A}^{\mathcal{F}_{\text{SF-rOT}}} : (a_0 = a'_0) \wedge (a_1 = a'_1)\right] \leq \text{negli}(\kappa)$$

5   Oblivious Transfer Extension Using π^κ_{OT}

In this section we show that the base OTs (a.k.a seed OTs) in the KOS OT extension can be instantiated using κ invocations to the modified (according to Definition 2) $\mathcal{F}_{\text{SF-rOT}}$. This results in an efficient seed OT phase, where each base OT requires 3 exponentiations. We assume that there exists a protocol π^κ_{OT} which implements(according to Definition 2) κ instances of $\mathcal{F}_{\text{SF-rOT}}$. Then we use π^κ_{OT} to implement the base OTs. Our protocol has been presented in Fig. 5.

$$\pi_{\mathsf{KOS}}$$

- **Public Inputs:** Group $\mathbb{G}$, fields $\mathbb{Z}_q$ and $\mathbb{F}$, and generator g of group $\mathbb{G}$.
- **Private Inputs:** S has m pairs $\{a_{j,0}, a_{j,1}\}_{j \in [m]}$ of κ bit strings. R has m selection bit vector $\mathbf{r} = (r_1, \cdots, r_m)$ such that each $r_j \in \{0, 1\}$.
- **Functionalities:** $\mathsf{PRG} : \{0,1\}^\kappa \to \{0,1\}^{m+\kappa}$, $\mathcal{F}_{\mathsf{RO1}} : \{0,1\}^* \times \{0,1\}^\kappa \to \{0,1\}^\kappa$, $\mathcal{F}_{\mathsf{RO2}} : \{0,1\}^* \times \{0,1\}^{(m+\kappa) \times \kappa} \to \mathbb{F}^{m+\kappa}$ and $\mathsf{CRF} : \{0,1\}^* \times [m] \times \{0,1\}^\kappa \to \{0,1\}^\kappa$.
- **Notations:** π_{OT}^κ implements κ instances of $\mathcal{F}_{\mathsf{SF\text{-}rOT}}$ (according to Def. 2).

Seed OT Phase I:

1. For $i \in [\kappa]$, S invokes the ith instance of π_{OT}^κ with message $(\textsc{Choose}, \mathsf{rec}, \mathsf{sid})$ to obtain s_i. He forms $\mathbf{s} = \{s_1, s_2, \ldots, s_\kappa\} \in \{0,1\}^\kappa$.
2. For $i \in [\kappa]$, R invokes the ith instance of π_{OT}^κ with message $(\textsc{Transfer}, \mathsf{sen}, \mathsf{sid})$ to obtain $\mathbf{k}_{i,0}, \mathbf{k}_{i,1} \in \{0,1\}^\kappa$.

OT Extension Phase I:

1. R forms three $(m + \kappa) \times \kappa$ matrices $\mathbf{M}$, $\mathbf{R}$ and $\mathbf{D}$ in the following way and sends $\mathbf{D}$ to S:
   - Sets $\mathbf{M}^i = \mathsf{PRG}(\mathcal{F}_{\mathsf{RO1}}(\mathsf{sid}, \mathbf{k}_{i,0}))$.
   - Samples $\tau \leftarrow \{0,1\}^\kappa$ and sets $\mathbf{r}' = \mathbf{r} \| \tau$.
   - Sets $\mathbf{R}_j = (r'_j, \ldots, r'_j)$. Clearly, $\mathbf{R}^i = \mathbf{r}'$.
   - Set $\mathbf{D}^i = \mathbf{M}^i \oplus \mathsf{PRG}(\mathcal{F}_{\mathsf{RO1}}(\mathsf{sid}, \mathbf{k}_{i,1})) \oplus \mathbf{R}^i$.

Consistency Check Phase I :

1. R computes challenge $\chi = \{\chi_1, \ldots, \chi_{m+\kappa}\}$ of consistency check as follows: $\widetilde{\chi} = \{\chi_1, \ldots, \chi_{m+\kappa}\} = \mathcal{F}_{\mathsf{RO2}}(\mathsf{sid}, \mathbf{D})$.
2. R computes $\mathbf{u} = \bigoplus_{j \in (m+\kappa)} (\chi_j \cdot \mathbf{M}_j)$ and $\mathbf{v} = \bigoplus_{j \in (m+\kappa)} (\chi_j \cdot \mathbf{R}_j)$. R sends $\mathbf{u}$ and $\mathbf{v}$ to S.

Seed OT Phase II:

1. If S receives a $\textsc{Cheat-Detected}$ message from π_{OT}^κ then he aborts.
2. S receives $\mathbf{k}_{i,\mathbf{s}_i}$ from the ith instance of π_{OT}^κ for $i \in [\kappa]$.

Consistency Check Phase II :

1. On receiving $\mathbf{D}$, S forms $(m + \kappa) \times \kappa$ matrix $\mathbf{Q}$ with the jth column of $\mathbf{Q}$ set as $\mathbf{Q}^i = (s_i \odot \mathbf{D}^i) \oplus \mathsf{PRG}(\mathcal{F}_{\mathsf{RO1}}(\mathsf{sid}, \mathbf{k}_{i,s_i}))$. Clearly, (i) $\mathbf{Q}^i = (\mathbf{M}^i \oplus (s_i \odot \mathbf{R}^i))$ and (ii) $\mathbf{Q}_j = (\mathbf{M}_j \oplus (\mathbf{s} \odot \mathbf{R}_j)) = (\mathbf{M}_j \oplus (\mathbf{s} \odot r_j))$.
2. S obtains $\widetilde{\chi}$ values from $\mathbf{D}$ and computes $\mathbf{w} = \bigoplus_{j \in (m+\kappa)} (\chi_j \cdot \mathbf{Q}_j)$. S checks that $\mathbf{w} = \mathbf{u} \oplus \mathbf{s} \cdot \mathbf{v}$.

OT Extension Phase II:

1. For every $j \in [m]$, S computes $\mathbf{y}_{j,0} = a_{j,0} \oplus \mathsf{CRF}(\mathsf{sid}, j, \mathbf{Q}_j)$ and $\mathbf{y}_{j,1} = a_{j,1} \oplus \mathsf{CRF}(\mathsf{sid}, j, \mathbf{Q}_j \oplus \mathbf{s})$. S sends $\{\mathbf{y}_{j,0}, \mathbf{y}_{j,1}\}_{j \in [m]}$ to R.
2. If R obtains $\textsc{Abort}$ message from π_{OT}^κ, then he aborts.
3. For every $j \in [m]$, R recovers $a'_j = \mathbf{y}_{j,r_j} \oplus \mathsf{CRF}(\mathsf{sid}, j, \mathbf{M}_j)$. R outputs $\{a'_j\}_{j \in [m]}$.

Fig. 5. KOS OT Extension using π_{OT}^κ

5.1   Security Proof

We prove UC-security of our OT extension protocol π_{KOS} by relying on the security properties of $\pi_{\mathsf{OT}}^{\kappa}$, correlation robust function, PRG and RO. More precisely, we prove Theorem 1.

Theorem 1. *Assuming PRG is a secure pseudorandom generator, CRF is a tweakable correlation robust function, $\mathcal{F}_{RO2}$ is an observable random oracle and $\pi_{\mathsf{OT}}^{\kappa}$ implements (according to Definition 2) κ instances of $\mathcal{F}_{SF\text{-}rOT}$, then π_{KOS} UC-securely implements $m = \mathrm{poly}(\kappa)$ instances of $\mathcal{F}_{OT}$ functionality.*

Proof. We will first argue security for a corrupt sender and then for a corrupt receiver. In both cases, we give a simulator algorithm and provide an indistinguishability argument.

The simulator for a statically corrupt S^* constructs the $\mathbf{M}, \mathbf{R}$ and $\mathbf{D}$ matrices using $\mathbf{r} = 0^m$ by following the honest receiver algorithm. S^* cannot obtain both $\mathbf{k}_{i,0}$ and $\mathbf{k}_{i,1}$ (due to the security of $\pi_{\mathsf{OT}}^{\kappa}$ against a corrupt receiver). Hence, $\mathbf{R}$ remains hidden due to the PRG security. The simulator will invoke the Ext algorithm of $\pi_{\mathsf{OT}}^{\kappa}$ to obtain the randomness of S^*, i.e. $\mathbf{s}$. Using $\mathbf{s}$, the simulator can compute back the sender's messages. Our simulator has been provided in Fig. 6. We argue indistinguishability between real and ideal world by providing hybrids and proving indistinguishability between each pair of consecutive hybrids as follows:

- **HYB$_0$:** Real world.
- **HYB$_1$:** Same as HYB$_0$, except the reduction constructs $\mathbf{M}, \mathbf{D}$ and $\mathbf{R}$ using $\mathbf{r} = 0^m$. Indistinguishability follows since the corrupt sender cannot compute both messages in the base OTs due to security of $\pi_{\mathsf{OT}}^{\kappa}$. Then one of $\mathcal{F}_{\mathsf{RO1}}(\mathsf{sid}, \mathbf{k}_{i,0})$ and $\mathcal{F}_{\mathsf{RO1}}(\mathsf{sid}, \mathbf{k}_{i,1})$ remains hidden for every $i \in [\kappa]$ due to the RO assumption of $\mathcal{F}_{\mathsf{RO1}}$.
- **HYB$_2$:** Same as HYB$_1$, except the reduction extracts $\mathbf{s}$ by invoking Ext algorithm of $\pi_{\mathsf{OT}}^{\kappa}$. Indistinguishability follows due to the correctness of Ext algorithm, which is guaranteed by the security of $\pi_{\mathsf{OT}}^{\kappa}$ when the OT extension sender does not abort.
- **HYB$_3$:** Same as HYB$_2$, except the reduction successfully extracts sender's input messages using $\mathbf{M}$ and $\mathbf{s}$. This HYB$_3$ is identical to HYB$_2$ due to correctness of the OT extension protocol.

Next, we discuss the simulation for a corrupt R^*. The simulator will extract the $(\mathbf{k}_{i,0}, \mathbf{k}_{i,1})$ values by invoking the simulator(for corrupt sender) of $\pi_{\mathsf{OT}}^{\kappa}$. A corrupt R^* can perform selective failure attack on the base OTs but the KOS protocol is resilient to such attacks. R^* can also construct the $\mathbf{R}$ matrix in such a way that it is not monochrome, i.e. some of the rows of $\mathbf{M}$ does not contain all 0s or all 1s. In such a case the consistency checks detect it with high probability and the sender aborts. If the checks pass, then R^* infers limited knowledge about the bits of $\mathbf{s}$. We refer to the original KOS [KOS15] paper for more details. Our simulator algorithm has been presented in Fig. 7. Next, we present our hybrids and indistinguishability argument:

- **Functionalities:** $\text{PRG} : \{0,1\}^\kappa \to \{0,1\}^{m+\mu}$, $\mathcal{F}_{\text{RO1}} : \{0,1\}^\kappa \times \{0,1\}^\kappa \to \{0,1\}^\kappa$, $\mathcal{F}_{\text{RO2}} : \{0,1\}^\kappa \times \{0,1\}^{(m+\kappa)\times\kappa} \to \mathbb{F}^{m+\kappa}$ and $\text{CRF} : \{0,1\}^\kappa \times [m] \times \{0,1\}^\kappa \to \{0,1\}^\kappa$.

Seed OT Phase I:

1. Sim invokes the ith instance of π_{OT}^κ with message $(\textsc{Transfer}, \text{sen}, \text{sid})$ to obtain $\mathbf{k}_{i,0}, \mathbf{k}_{i,1} \in \{0,1\}^\kappa$ for $i \in [\kappa]$.

OT Extension Phase I:

- Sim forms matrices $\mathbf{M}$, $\mathbf{R}$ and $\mathbf{D}$, following the honest receiver algorithm using $\mathbf{r} = 0^m$.
- Sim sends $\mathbf{D}^i = \mathbf{M}^i \oplus \text{PRG}(\mathcal{F}_{\text{RO1}}(\text{sid}, \mathbf{k}_{i,1})) \oplus \mathbf{R}^i$.

Consistency Check Phase I :

Sim computes $\mathbf{u}$ and $\mathbf{v}$ using the honest receiver algorithm and sends it to S^*.

Seed OT Phase II:

S^* performs his own adversarial algorithm.

Consistency Check Phase II :

S^* performs his own adversarial algorithm.

OT Extension Phase II:

1. For every $j \in [m]$, S^* sends $\{\mathbf{y}_{j,0}, \mathbf{y}_{j,1}\}_{j\in[m]}$ to Sim.
2. If Sim obtains $\textsc{Abort}$ message from π_{OT}^κ, then he aborts.
3. Else, Sim invokes Ext algorithm to obtain $\mathbf{s}$.
4. For every $j \in [m]$, Sim recovers $a'_{j,0} = \mathbf{y}_{j,0} \oplus \text{CRF}(\text{sid}, j, \mathbf{M}_j)$ and $a'_{j,1} = \mathbf{y}_{j,1} \oplus \text{CRF}(\text{sid}, j, \mathbf{M}_j \oplus \mathbf{s})$.
5. For $j \in [m]$, Sim invokes jth instance of $\mathcal{F}_{\text{OT}}$ with input $(a'_{j,0}, a'_{j,1})$.

Fig. 6. Simulation against a statically corrupt S^*

- **HYB$_0$:** Real world.
- **HYB$_1$:** Same as HYB_0, except the reduction invokes the simulator (for corrupt sender) of $\mathcal{F}_{\text{SF-rOT}}$ to obtain $(\mathbf{k}_{i,0}, \mathbf{k}_{i,1})$.
- **HYB$_2$:** Same as HYB_1, except the reduction aborts if $\mathbf{M}$ has more than μ non-monochromatic rows. The real world sender would abort due to the correctness of the consistency checks, which follow from the RO assumption. Thus, indistinguishability follows from the RO assumption.
- **HYB$_3$:** Same as HYB_2, except the simulator extracts R^* input and simulates the $\mathbf{y}_{j,0}$ and $\mathbf{y}_{j,1}$ according to the simulation algorithm. Indistinguishability follows due to the CRF assumption. □

5.2 Efficiency

Our instantiation of the KOS protocol has a minimal overhead of two random oracle, per base OT, on top of the modified KOS protocol of [DKLs18]. The original communication complexity remains preserved. Using Fiat-Shamir like

---

- **Functionalities:** PRG : $\{0,1\}^\kappa \to \{0,1\}^{m+\mu}$, $\mathcal{F}_{\mathsf{RO1}} : \{0,1\}^\kappa \times \{0,1\}^\kappa \to \{0,1\}^\kappa$, $\mathcal{F}_{\mathsf{RO2}} : \{0,1\}^\kappa \times \{0,1\}^{(m+\kappa)\times\kappa} \to \mathbb{F}^{m+\kappa}$ and CRF : $\{0,1\}^\kappa \times [m] \times \{0,1\}^\kappa \to \{0,1\}^\kappa$.

Seed OT Phase I:

For $i \in [\kappa]$, Sim invokes the ith instance of π_{OT}^κ with message (CHOOSE, rec, sid) to obtain s_i. He forms $\mathbf{s} = \{s_1, s_2, \ldots, s_\kappa\} \in \{0,1\}^\kappa$.

OT Extension Phase I:

R^* sends $\mathbf{D}$ to Sim.

Consistency Check Phase I :

R^* sends $\mathbf{u}$ and $\mathbf{v}$ to Sim.

Seed OT Phase II:

1. If Sim receives a CHEAT-DETECTED message from π_{OT}^κ then he aborts.
2. Sim invokes the simulator (for corrupt sender) of $\mathcal{F}_{\mathsf{SF\text{-}rOT}}$ to obtain $(\mathbf{k}_{i,0}, \mathbf{k}_{i,1})$ values for $i \in [\kappa]$.

Consistency Check Phase II :

1. Sim computes $\mathbf{Q}$ matrix following the honest sender algorithm.
2. Sim computes $\mathbf{R}^i = \mathbf{D}^i \oplus \mathsf{PRG}(\mathcal{F}_{\mathsf{RO1}}(\mathsf{sid}, \mathbf{k}_{i,0})) \oplus \mathsf{PRG}(\mathcal{F}_{\mathsf{RO1}}(\mathsf{sid}, \mathbf{k}_{i,1}))$ for $i \in [\kappa]$.
3. Sim verifies $\mathbf{u}$ and $\mathbf{v}$ by following the honest sender algorithm and aborts if check fails.
4. Sim aborts if $\mathbf{M}$ has at least μ non-monochromatic rows.

OT Extension Phase II:

1. For every $j \in [m]$, Sim invokes jth instance of $\mathcal{F}_{\mathsf{OT}}$ with input r_j to obtain a_j.
2. For every $j \in [m]$, Sim sets $\mathbf{y}_{j,r_j} = a_j \oplus \mathsf{CRF}(\mathsf{sid}, j, \mathbf{Q}_j \oplus r_j \cdot \mathbf{s})$ and $\mathbf{y}_{j,\bar{r}_j} \leftarrow \{0,1\}^\kappa$.

Fig. 7. Simulation against a statically corrupt R^*

transform of [DKLs18] the consistency checks have become non-interactive. In the original KOS protocol, the consistency checks required 2 extra rounds for coin-tossing protocol between the parties. In the next section we will provide an efficient protocol for π_{OT}^κ using 3 rounds. The base-OT messages can be sent in parallel to the OT extension messages. Thus, it would be round preserving and it will circumvent the impossibility result of [GMMM18] since we consider non-blackbox usage of the base-OT protocol.

6 Implementing κ Instances of $\mathcal{F}_{\mathsf{SF\text{-}rOT}}$

In this section we present our protocol π_{OT}^ℓ which implements (according to Definition 2) $\ell = \kappa$ instances of $\mathcal{F}_{\mathsf{SF\text{-}rOT}}$ assuming Observable Random Oracle, where $\kappa > \mu$. We refer to Sect. 3 for a detailed overview. Our protocol has been presented in Fig. 8.

$$\pi_{\mathsf{OT}}^{\ell}$$

- **Public Inputs:** Group $\mathbb{G}$, field $\mathbb{Z}_q$ and generator g of group $\mathbb{G}$.
- **Private Inputs:** Sender S and receiver R do not possess any private inputs.
- **Random Oracles:** $\mathcal{F}_{\mathsf{RO1}} : \{0,1\}^{2\kappa} \to \mathbb{G}$, $\mathcal{F}_{\mathsf{RO2}} : \{0,1\}^{\kappa} \times \mathbb{G} \to \{0,1\}^{\kappa}$, $\mathcal{F}_{\mathsf{RO3}} :$ $\{0,1\}^{2\kappa} \to \{0,1\}^{\kappa}$, $\mathcal{F}_{\mathsf{RO4}} : \{0,1\}^{(\ell+1)\kappa} \to \{0,1\}^{\kappa}$.

Choose:

- *Receiver Parameters:* R samples seed $\leftarrow \{0,1\}^{\kappa}$ and computes $T \leftarrow$ $\mathcal{F}_{\mathsf{RO1}}(\mathsf{sid}, \mathsf{seed})$. R sends seed as OT receiver parameters.

- *Receiver Message:* For $i \in [\ell]$, R computes its message for ith OT as follows :
  - R samples b_i as its random input for ith OT.
  - R samples $\alpha_i \leftarrow \mathbb{Z}_q$ and sets $B_i = g^{\alpha_i} T^{b_i}$
  - R sends B_i as ith OT message.

Transfer:

- *Sender Parameters:* S computes $T \leftarrow \mathcal{F}_{\mathsf{RO1}}(\mathsf{sid}, \mathsf{seed})$. S samples $r \leftarrow \mathbb{Z}_q$ and computes $z = g^r$. S sends z to R as OT sender parameters.

- *Sender Message:* For $i \in [\ell]$, S computes its message for ith OT as follows :
  - S computes $p_{i,0} = \mathcal{F}_{\mathsf{RO2}}\left(\mathsf{sid}, B_i^r\right)$ and $p_{i,1} = \mathcal{F}_{\mathsf{RO2}}\left(\mathsf{sid}, \left(\frac{B_i}{T}\right)^r\right)$.
  - S sets $(p_{i,0}, p_{i,1})$ as its random inputs messages for ith OT.

- *Challenge Computation:* S computes the challenge for ith OT as $\mathsf{chall}_i = \mathcal{F}_{\mathsf{RO3}}(\mathsf{sid}, p_{i,0}) \oplus \mathcal{F}_{\mathsf{RO3}}(\mathsf{sid}, p_{i,1})$ for $i \in [\ell]$. S sends $\mathsf{Chall} = (\mathsf{chall}_1, \mathsf{chall}_2, \ldots, \mathsf{chall}_\ell)$ to R.

- *Proof Computation:* S computes the answer to the challenge as follows :
$$\mathsf{Ans} = \mathcal{F}_{\mathsf{RO4}}(\mathsf{sid}, \mathcal{F}_{\mathsf{RO3}}(\mathsf{sid}, p_{1,0}), \mathcal{F}_{\mathsf{RO3}}(\mathsf{sid}, p_{2,0}), \ldots, \mathcal{F}_{\mathsf{RO3}}(\mathsf{sid}, p_{\ell,0})).$$
S computes the validity proof of challenge as $\gamma = \mathcal{F}_{\mathsf{RO3}}(\mathsf{sid}, \mathsf{Ans})$. S sends the proof γ to R.

Response:

- *Message Decryption:* For $i \in [\ell]$, R computes $p_{i,b_i} = \mathcal{F}_{\mathsf{RO2}}(\mathsf{sid}, z^{\alpha_i})$.

- *Response Computation:* For $i \in [\ell]$, R computes $\mathsf{resp}_i = \mathcal{F}_{\mathsf{RO3}}(\mathsf{sid}, p_{i,b_i}) \oplus (b \cdot \mathsf{chall}_i)$. R computes response as $\mathsf{Ans}' = \mathcal{F}_{\mathsf{RO4}}(\mathsf{sid}, \mathsf{resp}_1, \mathsf{resp}_2, \ldots, \mathsf{resp}_\ell)$.

- *Challenge Verification:* R aborts if $\mathcal{F}_{\mathsf{RO3}}(\mathsf{sid}, \mathsf{Ans}') \neq \gamma$. Else, he sends Ans' to S and outputs $\{(b_i, p_{b_i})\}_{i \in [\ell]}$.

Verification:

- S aborts if $\mathsf{Ans} \neq \mathsf{Ans}'$. Else, he outputs $(p_{i,0}, p_{i,1})$ as his output for ith OT.

Fig. 8. Protocol computing ℓ instances of $\mathcal{F}_{\mathsf{SF\text{-}rOT}}$ according to Definition 2

6.1 Security Proof

We prove security of our protocol π_{OT} by proving Theorem 2. In Sect. 5, we will show that such a relaxation in security suffices for KOS OT extension.

Theorem 2. *Assuming the Decisional Diffie-Hellman holds in group $\mathbb{G}$, then $\pi_{\mathsf{OT}}^{\kappa}$ (Fig. 8) UC-securely implements $\ell(> \mu)$ instances of $\mathcal{F}_{\mathsf{SF\text{-}rOT}}$ functionality (according to Definition 2) in the observable random oracle model with sender-sided simulation.*

Proof. We will first argue security for a corrupt sender and then for a corrupt receiver. In the first case we provide a simulator and in the latter part we provide an indistinguishability argument.

The simulator for a statically corrupt sender S^* will use the observability of the ROs to extract the sender's input, since he cannot program $\mathcal{F}_{\mathsf{RO1}}$ on seed. He will compute the receiver message with random input bits. He can compute either $g^{\alpha_i r}$ by following the receiver algorithm and extract one of the sender's input message for ith OT. In order to extract the other sender's input message, he needs to find out T^r. Assume for sake of simplicity, that the simulator's input bit for all OTs are $b_i = 0$ and he can compute $p_{i,0}$ and $a_{i,0}$, for all $i \in [\kappa]$. He tries to compute $p_{i,1}$ values as follows:

1. Observe the queries made by S^* to $\mathcal{F}_{\mathsf{RO3}}$ for computing chall_i using $p_{i,1}$ for every $i \in [\kappa]$. Extract candidate $p_{i,1}$ values s.t. chall is well-formed using $p_{i,0}$ and $p_{i,1}$. It is guaranteed that from every chall_i, Sim can get at most one candidate $p_{i,1}$ value.
2. After obtaining candidate $p_{i,1}$ values for each ith OT, the simulator observes the queries made to $\mathcal{F}_{\mathsf{RO2}}$ to obtain $p_{i,1}$. If there aren't any such query, then the simulator sets adversary's guess for ith OT as 0 in the selective failure attack. Else, simulator will obtain an unique (guaranteed by RO assumption) query $\rho_{i,1}$, s.t. $\mathcal{F}_{\mathsf{RO2}}(\mathsf{sid}, \rho_{i,1}) = p_{i,1}$.
3. Simulator obtains all the candidate values of T^r from $\rho_{i,0}$(which he can compute locally) and $\rho_{i,1}$. Let $\mathbf{A} = \{A_1, A_2, \ldots, A_\ell\}$ denote the list of values obtained as $A_i = \frac{\rho_{i,0}}{\rho_{i,1}}$ for $i \in [\kappa]$ for $i \in [\kappa]$. Let A be the value which has been obtained the maximum number of times from the OTs. The simulator sets A as the supposed T^r value. If there are more than μ OTs whose A_i values are different from A, then simulator sends $(\textsc{Guess}, \mathsf{Sim}, \top, \mathsf{sid})$ to $\mathcal{F}_{\mathsf{SF\text{-}rOT}}$ and aborts. In such a case, S^* can distinguish the real and ideal world, only if the honest receiver does not abort. To ensure that, S^* must correctly guess the random input bits of the honest R. Thus, S^* can distinguish with $2^{-\mu}$ probability if he miscomputed more than μ OTs. Otherwise, the simulator can extract $T^r = A$ value correctly.
4. Given the correct T^r value, simulator computes the correct $p_{i,1}$ values whose corresponding A_j values were different from A.

Next, the simulator needs to simulate the selective OT failure attacks. Sim simulates the selective failure attack by checking whether chall_i is correctly formed or not, i.e. if $\text{chall}_i = \mathcal{F}_{\text{RO3}}(\text{sid}, p_{i,0}) \oplus \mathcal{F}_{\text{RO3}}(\text{sid}, p_{i,1})$ then $\mathcal{A}$ is not performing a selective failure attack. Else, he has performed a selective failure attack on the receiver's input. Simulator needs to find out the bit b' which adversary has guessed and invoke $\mathcal{F}_{\text{SF-rOT}}$ with $(\text{GUESS}, \text{Sim}, \text{sid}, \top)$. Sim performs this by observing the queries made by $\mathcal{A}$ to $\mathcal{F}_{\text{RO4}}$ and $\mathcal{F}_{\text{RO3}}$.

1. Sim observes the queries made to $\mathcal{F}_{\text{RO3}}$ and compares it with γ. If γ was formed without querying $\mathcal{F}_{\text{RO3}}$, then Sim aborts as the real world sender would also abort irrespective of input, due to RO assumption. There can be only one such candidate query β s.t. $\mathcal{F}_{\text{RO3}}(\text{sid}, \beta) = \gamma$, due to RO assumption. β is the candidate for Ans that S must have obtained while computing γ.
2. Next, Sim searches for $y = (y_1 y_2 \ldots y_\ell)$, s.t. $\mathcal{F}_{\text{RO4}}(\text{sid}, y) = \beta$, due to RO assumption.
3. Upon finding such a y tuple, it individually checks for y_i' values s.t. $y_i = \mathcal{F}_{\text{RO3}}(\text{sid}, y_i')$.
4. These y_i' values are then individually matched with the pads $(p_{i,0}, p_{i,1})$ and chall_i. If $p_{i,0} = y_i'$, then chall_i is correctly formed for $b' = 0$ and so Sim sets $b' = 0$. If $\mathcal{F}_{\text{RO3}}(\text{sid}, p_{i,1}) \oplus \text{chall}_i = y_i'$ then chall_i is correctly formed for $b' = 0$ and so Sim sets $b' = 1$. Else, the challenge is malformed for both $b' = 0$ and $b' = 1$; hence the simulator aborts as the honest sender would also abort.

If there are more than μ OTs where the $\mathcal{A}$ has launched a selective failure attack then the simulator aborts and sends $(\text{GUESS}, \text{Sim}, \text{sid}, \top)$ to $\mathcal{F}_{\text{SF-rOT}}$. Finally, the simulator invokes $\mathcal{F}_{\text{SF-rOT}}$ with input $(\text{GUESS}, \text{Sim}, b', \text{sid})$. It should be noted that the input bit b_i remains perfectly hidden in $B_i = g^{\alpha_i}$ since α_i and $\alpha_i - t$ are valid randomness for $b_i = 0$ and $b_i = 1$ respectively. The real and ideal world are statistically indistinguishable except with $2^{-\mu}$ probability. The simulation algorithm has been provided in Fig. 9 and the formal hybrids and indistinguishability argument are as follows:

– **HYB$_0$**: Real world.
– **HYB$_1$**: Same as HYB$_0$, except the reduction except the reduction computes $(p_{i,0}, p_{i,1})$ by following the simulation strategy and computes $A = T^r$, or aborts if necessary. Indistinguishability follows due to RO assumption as discussed previously.
– **HYB$_2$**: Same as HYB$_1$, except the reduction invokes $\mathcal{F}_{\text{SF-rOT}}$ with input $p_{i,0} = p_{i,1} = \bot$ and aborts if there are 0 or 2 (and more) candidate values for β. Indistinguishability follows from RO assumption.
– **HYB$_3$**: Same as HYB$_2$, except the reduction invokes $\mathcal{F}_{\text{SF-rOT}}$ with input $p_{i,0} = p_{i,1} = \bot$ and aborts if there are 0 or 2 (and more) candidate values for y. Indistinguishability follows from RO assumption.
– **HYB$_4$**: Same as HYB$_3$, except the reduction invokes $\mathcal{F}_{\text{SF-rOT}}$ with input $p_{i,0} = p_{i,1} = \bot$ and aborts if there are 0 or 2 (and more) candidate values for y_i' for each $i \in [\ell]$. Indistinguishability follows from RO assumption.
– **HYB$_5$**: Same as HYB$_4$, except the reduction aborts if there are $¿\mu$ OTs where the sender has launched a selective failure attack. Indistinguishability follows statistically since the inputs of the honest sender are identically distributed

to the inputs of the reduction, and both are random. The probability that the reduction aborts and the sender doesn't abort in the real world is $2^{-\mu}$.

- **HYB$_6$:** Same as HYB$_5$, except the reduction simulates the selective failure attack following the simulation algorithm. Indistinguishability follows due to the RO assumption.
- **HYB$_7$:** Same as HYB$_6$, except Sim computes $(p_{i,0}, p_{i,1})$ following the simulation strategy and invokes $\mathcal{F}_{\mathsf{SF\text{-}rOT}}$ with it. This hybrid is identical to the previous hybrid.

This completes the security proof for a corrupt sender. Next, we discuss the case for a corrupt receiver. In this case, the simulator either extracts the input bit of a corrupt receiver or it aborts. In the real world, the honest sender would also abort. However, in both cases the receiver can obtain the message corresponding to his bit after the OT protocol results in an abort by the sender. More formally, the simulator for a corrupt receiver R^* will set $(c_{i,0}, c_{i,1})$ values randomly. Later, upon obtaining the second OT second message, the receiver can follow either of the two tactics:

- **Resp is valid:** The receiver can query $\mathcal{F}_{\mathsf{RO2}}$ to compute p_{i,b_i}, corresponding to his input bit b_i for ith OT. Then he can correctly compute the response to the challenge by running the honest receiver algorithm. This would result in the sender accepting the response to the challenge. The simulator can observe the queries made to the random oracles to extract b_i and invoke $\mathcal{F}_{\mathsf{SF\text{-}rOT}}$ with input b_i.
- **Resp is invalid:** On the other hand, the receiver can send a random response to the challenge and force the sender to abort. However, the receiver can decrypt the message corresponding to his input bit b_i after the protocol ends by running the honest receiver's algorithm. This would hamper simulation as the simulator cannot extract b_i during the protocol since R^* did not query the random oracles. Hence, the message decrypted (after the protocol aborted) by R^* in the simulated world will be distinguishable from the message decrypted (after the protocol aborted) by R^* in the simulated world. Based on a_{b_i}, the view of R^* can be distinguished by the environment $\mathcal{Z}$; hence simulation would fail.

Next, we show indistinguishability based security for a corrupt receiver. We demonstrate that there exists a PPT algorithm Ext who can extract the input choice bit of R^* if Ext has blackbox access to R^* for the protocol session. If R^* decides to forcefully abort the protocol, then it is guaranteed that he cannot compute both sender input messages as that would require solving the CDH problem. We present our Ext algorithm in Fig. 10 and we modularly discuss the details of our proof by arguing that each property in Definition 2 holds for our protocol.

- **Correctness of Ext algorithm:** The corrupt receiver has to compute a correct answer to the challenge. To do that, he has to query either B_i^r or $(B_i \cdot T^{-1})^r$ to $\mathcal{F}_{\mathsf{RO2}}$, to obtain $p_{i,0}$ or $p_{i,1}$ and construct the correct response

- **Functionalities:** Random Oracles $\mathcal{F}_{RO1} : \{0,1\}^{\kappa} \times \{0,1\}^{\kappa} \to \mathbb{G}$, $\mathcal{F}_{RO2} : \{0,1\}^{\kappa} \times \mathbb{G} \to \{0,1\}^{\kappa}$, $\mathcal{F}_{RO3} : \{0,1\}^{\kappa} \times \{0,1\}^{\kappa} \to \{0,1\}^{\kappa}$, $\mathcal{F}_{RO4} : \{0,1\}^{\kappa} \times \{0,1\}^{\ell\kappa} \to \{0,1\}^{\kappa}$.

Choose:

- *Receiver Parameters:* Sim runs the honest receiver algorithm.

- *Receiver Message:* Sim runs the honest receiver algorithm.

Transfer:

- S^* sends $(z, \texttt{Chall}, \gamma)$.

Response:

- *Message Decryption:* Sim extracts and sender's messages as follows:
  - Sim computes $p_{i,b_i} = \mathcal{F}_{RO2}(\mathsf{sid}, z_i^{\alpha})$.
  - Sim extracts candidate $p_{i,\bar{b}_i}$ values for each $i \in [\kappa]$ by observing the queries made to $\mathcal{F}_{RO3}$ for computing $\mathsf{chall}_i = \mathcal{F}_{RO3}(\mathsf{sid}, p_{i,0}) \oplus \mathcal{F}_{RO3}(\mathsf{sid}, p_{i,1})$.
  - Sim extracts $\rho_{i,\bar{b}_i}$ from the query list of $\mathcal{F}_{RO2}$, s.t. $\mathcal{F}_{RO2}(\mathsf{sid}, \rho_{i,\bar{b}_i}) = p_{i,\bar{b}_i}$.
  - Sim computes $\mathbf{A} = \{A_i\}_{i \in [\kappa]} = \frac{\rho_{i,0}}{\rho_{i,1}}$. Sets A as the most frequent A_i value in $\mathbf{A}$. If there are at least μ A_i values s.t. $A_i \neq A$, then invoke $\mathcal{F}_{SF\text{-}rOT}$ with message (GUESS, Sim, sid, $\top$) and abort. Else, consider $T^{\tau} = A$.
  - Sim computes the correct value of $p_{i,\bar{b}_i} = \mathcal{F}_{RO2}(\mathsf{sid}, z^{\alpha_i} \cdot A^{-1})$.

- *Challenge Verification and Response Computation:* Sim extracts values by observing RO queries as follows:
  - Sim extracts β s.t. $\mathcal{F}_{RO3}(\mathsf{sid}, \beta) = \gamma$. Set $\texttt{Ans} = \beta$ by observing $\mathcal{F}_{RO3}$. Sim observes $\mathcal{F}_{RO4}$ to extract $y = (y_1, y_2, \ldots, y_\ell)$, s.t. $\mathcal{F}_{RO4}(\mathsf{sid}, y) = \texttt{Ans}$.
  - For $i \in [\ell]$, Sim extracts y_i' s.t. $\mathcal{F}_{RO3}(\mathsf{sid}, y_i') = y_i$ for each $i \in [\ell]$.
  If Sim either finds two or more matching queries, or he finds no matching query then he invokes $\mathcal{F}_{SF\text{-}rOT}$ with input messages $p_{i,0} = p_{i,1} = \bot$ and aborts. For $i \in [\ell]$, Sim computes $\mathsf{chall}_i' = \mathcal{F}_{RO3}(p_{i,0}) \oplus \mathcal{F}_{RO3}(p_{i,1})$ and performs the following:
  - If $\mathsf{chall}_i = \mathsf{chall}_i'$: If $y_i' = p_{i,0}$ and $p_{i,1}$ was queried to $\mathcal{F}_{RO3}$, then invoke $\mathcal{F}_{SF\text{-}rOT}$ with input (GUESS, Sim, sid, $\bot$) else abort.
  - If $\mathsf{chall}_i \neq \mathsf{chall}_i'$: If $y_i' = p_{i,0}$ then set $b_i' = 0$ else if $\mathcal{F}_{RO3}(\mathsf{sid}, p_{i,0}) \oplus \mathsf{chall}_i = y_i'$ then set $b_i' = 1$. Invoke $\mathcal{F}_{SF\text{-}rOT}$ with input (GUESS, Sim, sid, b_i').
  - Else, Sim aborts in the simulated execution.
- If Sim receives (CHEAT-DETECTED) from any $\mathcal{F}_{SF\text{-}rOT}$ instance then he aborts.
- For $i \in [\ell]$, Sim computes $\texttt{Ans}'$ following honest receiver algorithm using input $\{b_i\}_{i \in [\ell]}$. Sends $\texttt{Ans}'$ to S^* or he aborts.
- Sim invokes ith instance of $\mathcal{F}_{SF\text{-}rOT}$ with input (TRANSFER*, sen, sid, $(p_{i,0}, p_{i,1})$) for $i \in [\ell]$.

Fig. 9. Simulation against a statically corrupt S^*

using $\mathcal{F}_{RO3}(\mathsf{sid}, p_{i,0})$ or $\mathcal{F}_{RO3}(\mathsf{sid}, p_{i,1})$. He can bypass querying the RO if he can correctly guess $p_{i,0}$ or $p_{i,1}$ or $\mathcal{F}_{RO3}(\mathsf{sid}, p_{i,0})$ or $\mathcal{F}_{RO3}(\mathsf{sid}, p_{i,1})$. However, that occurs with negligible probability. Thus, the Ext algorithm succeeds if

---

- **Functionalities:** Random Oracles $\mathcal{F}_{RO1} : \{0,1\}^\kappa \times \{0,1\}^\kappa \to \mathbb{G}$, $\mathcal{F}_{RO2} : \{0,1\}^\kappa \times \mathbb{G} \to \{0,1\}^\kappa$, $\mathcal{F}_{RO3} : \{0,1\}^\kappa \times \{0,1\}^\kappa \to \{0,1\}^\kappa$, $\mathcal{F}_{RO4} : \{0,1\}^\kappa \times \{0,1\}^{\ell\kappa} \to \{0,1\}^\kappa$.

Choose:
- *Receiver Parameters:* R* sends seed as OT receiver parameters.
- *Receiver Message:* For $i \in [\ell]$, R* sends B_i as ith OT message.

Transfer:
Ext follows honest sender algorithm.

Response:
R* sends Ans$'$.

Verification:
- If Ans$'$ is not valid then set $b_i = \bot$ for $i \in [\ell]$ and abort.
- For $i \in [\ell]$, Ext extracts b_i as follows and performs the following -
  - If R* queried both B_i^r and $(B_i \cdot T^{-1})^r$ to $\mathcal{F}_{RO3}$ then set $b_i = \bot$.
  - If R* queried $\rho_{i,b_i'} = (B_i \cdot T^{-b_i'})^r$ to $\mathcal{F}_{RO3}$ to obtain $p_{i,b_i'}$ then set $b_i = b_i'$ else set $b_i = \bot$.
  - Output b_i.

Fig. 10. Extractor Algorithm Ext

R* correctly responds to the challenge. In such a case, R* queries $\mathcal{F}_{RO2}$; hence Ext can correctly extract b_i.

- **R* cannot compute both $p_{i,0}$ and $p_{i,1}$:** It can be observed that if R* obtains both $p_{i,0}$ and $p_{i,1}$ by querying $\mathcal{F}_{RO2}$ on $\rho_{i,0}$ and $\rho_{i,1}$ respectively, then he can be used to solve the CDH problem where the CDH challenge instance is $T = g^t$ and $z = g^r$. The solution to the CDH challenge would be $T^r = \frac{\rho_{i,0}}{\rho_{i,1}}$. Here, we can assume that the reduction programs $\mathcal{F}_{RO1}$ on seed s.t. it returns the CDH challenge T. This is a reasonable assumption to make since we are programming the RO in the reduction. Such programming instances can be found out in the work of [DKLs18].

- **Indistinguishability of R* views:** The real world view of the corrupt receiver R* $- \mathcal{V}^S_{\pi_{OT}, R^*(z)}((p_{i,0}, p_{i,1}), b, z)_{z \in \{0,1\}^*}$, after executing an OT protocol with S using random inputs is indistinguishable from the ideal world view of R* $- \mathcal{V}^S_{\pi_{OT}, R^*(z)}((\widetilde{p_{i,0}}, \widetilde{p_{i,1}}), b, z)_{z \in \{0,1\}^*}$, after executing an OT protocol with sender since the sender only sends z. This is because R* cannot query $\rho_{i,\tilde{b}_i}$ to $\mathcal{F}_{RO2}$ (due to CDH assumption) and hence $p_{i,\bar{b}_i}$ and $\widetilde{p_{i,\bar{b}_i}} = 0^\kappa$ would look indistinguishable due to the RO assumption.

This completes our proof of Theorem 2.   □

Table 2. Comparing the performance to compute $\kappa = 128$ base OTs using our protocol and CO-OT.

RTT	< 0.1 ms	50 ms	100 ms	200 ms
CO-OT [CO15]	21 ms	67 ms	117 ms	217 ms
This work	21 ms	67 ms	117 ms	217 ms

6.2 Efficiency

Overall the complexity of our protocol is similar to the CO-OT protocol. Our protocol requires the receiver to compute 2 exponentiations and the sender to compute 1 exponentiation for each OT. The sender needs to compute 5 RO queries and the receiver need to query the RO for 4 times, for each OT. The receiver needs to communicate one group element and one κ bit string for each OT. The sender needs to send 4κ bit strings for each OT.

In addition, the sender has a one-time computation of 1 exponentiation, one RO query and communication of one group element, which can be reused. The receiver has a one-time communication of κ bit string and one-time computation of one RO query.

7   Implementation and Evaluation

We will study the concrete performance of our OT protocol in this section. As we have analyzed in previous sections, our OT protocol is expected to be as fast as the CO-OT protocol by Chou and Orlandi [CO15], which is the most efficient OT protocol but not provably UC-secure and does not provide input extraction of a corrupt receiver. Since all state-of-the-art OT protocols are slower than CO-OT, the above is sufficient to demonstrate the efficiency of our protocol against all other alternatives [MR19, DKLs18].

We implement CO-OT and our protocol using relic-toolkit [AG] and test them on a machine with a 3 GHz Intel Xeon CPU. No multi-thread or assembly-level optimization is used. We throttle the network bandwidth to be 1 Gbps but with different network round-trip time (RTT, measured by `ping`). The performance is summarized in Table 2, where we can see that the performance of our protocol is identical to the CO-OT protocol for different network latency values. This is expected as both protocols have the same number of exponentiation operations. Note that prior works [CO15, MR19] reported performance of CO-OT with low-level hardware-dependent accelerations. Our protocol can benefit from them too, resulting in even higher performance. We further applied both protocols as the base OT to compute OT extension. We can see that due to the reduce round complexity of our protocol, we are to obtain a better efficiency with the overall running time improved by one RTT (Table 3).

Table 3. Comparing the performance to compute 10^7 random OTs using KOS with base OT as our protocol and CO-OT.

RTT	< 0.1 ms	50 ms	100 ms	200 ms
CO-OT [CO15]+KOS	1300 ms	1388 ms	1496 ms	1679 ms
This work +KOS	1300 ms	1327 ms	1391 ms	1485 ms

Acknowledgements. This work was supported by the IARPA ACHILLES project, the NSF MACS project and NSF grant CNS-1422965. The first author also thanks the Check Point Institute for Information Security.

References

[AG] Aranha, D.F., Gouvêa, C.P.L.: RELIC is an Efficient LIbrary for Cryptography. https://github.com/relic-toolkit/relic

[ALSZ15] Asharov, G., Lindell, Y., Schneider, T., Zohner, M.: More efficient oblivious transfer extensions with security for malicious adversaries. In: Oswald, E., Fischlin, M. (eds.) EUROCRYPT 2015. LNCS, vol. 9056, pp. 673–701. Springer, Heidelberg (2015). https://doi.org/10.1007/978-3-662-46800-5_26

[BCG+19] Boyle, E., et al.: Efficient two-round OT extension and silent non-interactive secure computation. In: Cavallaro, L., Kinder, J., Wang, X., Katz, J. (eds.) ACM CCS 2019: 26th Conference on Computer and Communications Security, pp. 291–308. ACM Press, November 2019

[BCGI18] Boyle, E., Couteau, G., Gilboa, N., Ishai, Y.: Compressing vector OLE. In: Lie, D., Mannan, M., Backes, M., Wang, X. (eds.) ACM CCS 2018: 25th Conference on Computer and Communications Security, pp. 896–912. ACM Press, October 2018

[Bea96] Beaver, D.: Correlated pseudorandomness and the complexity of private computations. In: 28th Annual ACM Symposium on Theory of Computing, pp. 479–488. ACM Press, May 1996

[BLO16] Ben-Efraim, A., Lindell, Y., Omri, E.: Optimizing semi-honest secure multiparty computation for the internet. In: Weippl, E.R., Katzenbeisser, S., Kruegel, C., Myers, A.C., Halevi, S. (eds.) ACM CCS 2016: 23rd Conference on Computer and Communications Security, pp. 578–590. ACM Press, October 2016

[BPRS17] Byali, M., Patra, A., Ravi, D., Sarkar, P.: Fast and universally-composable oblivious transfer and commitment scheme with adaptive security. Cryptology ePrint Archive, Report 2017/1165 (2017). https://eprint.iacr.org/2017/1165

[Can01] Canetti, R.: Universally composable security: a new paradigm for cryptographic protocols. In: 42nd Annual Symposium on Foundations of Computer Science, pp. 136–145. IEEE Computer Society Press, October 2001

[CDG+18] Camenisch, J., Drijvers, M., Gagliardoni, T., Lehmann, A., Neven, G.: The wonderful world of global random oracles. In: Nielsen, J.B., Rijmen, V. (eds.) EUROCRYPT 2018. LNCS, vol. 10820, pp. 280–312. Springer, Cham (2018). https://doi.org/10.1007/978-3-319-78381-9_11

[CJS14]   Canetti, R., Jain, A., Scafuro, A.: Practical UC security with a global random oracle. In: Ahn, G.-J., Yung, M., Li, N. (eds.) ACM CCS 2014: 21st Conference on Computer and Communications Security, pp. 597–608. ACM Press, November 2014

[CO15]   Chou, T., Orlandi, C.: The simplest protocol for oblivious transfer. In: Lauter, K., Rodríguez-Henríquez, F. (eds.) LATINCRYPT 2015. LNCS, vol. 9230, pp. 40–58. Springer, Cham (2015). https://doi.org/10.1007/978-3-319-22174-8_3

[DKLs18]   Doerner, J., Kondi, Y., Lee, E., Shelat, A.: Secure two-party threshold ECDSA from ECDSA assumptions. In: 2018 IEEE Symposium on Security and Privacy, pp. 980–997. IEEE Computer Society Press, May 2018

[GIR17]   Genç, Z.A., Iovino, V., Rial, A.: "The simplest protocol for oblivious transfer" revisited. Cryptology ePrint Archive, Report 2017/370 (2017). http://eprint.iacr.org/2017/370

[GKW+19]   Guo, C., Katz, J., Wang, X., Weng, C., Yu, Y.: Better concrete security for half-gates garbling (in the multi-instance setting). Cryptology ePrint Archive, Report 2019/1168 (2019). https://eprint.iacr.org/2019/1168

[GMMM18]   Garg, S., Mahmoody, M., Masny, D., Meckler, I.: On the round complexity of OT extension. In: Shacham, H., Boldyreva, A. (eds.) CRYPTO 2018. LNCS, vol. 10993, pp. 545–574. Springer, Cham (2018). https://doi.org/10.1007/978-3-319-96878-0_19

[GMW87]   Goldreich, O., Micali, S., Wigderson, A.: How to play any mental game or a completeness theorem for protocols with honest majority. In: Aho, A. (ed.) 19th Annual ACM Symposium on Theory of Computing, pp. 218–229. ACM Press, May 1987

[HL17]   Hauck, E., Loss, J.: Efficient and universally composable protocols for oblivious transfer from the CDH assumption. Cryptology ePrint Archive, Report 2017/1011 (2017). http://eprint.iacr.org/2017/1011

[HSS17]   Hazay, C., Scholl, P., Soria-Vazquez, E.: Low cost constant round MPC combining BMR and oblivious transfer. In: Takagi, T., Peyrin, T. (eds.) ASIACRYPT 2017. LNCS, vol. 10624, pp. 598–628. Springer, Cham (2017). https://doi.org/10.1007/978-3-319-70694-8_21

[IKNP03]   Ishai, Y., Kilian, J., Nissim, K., Petrank, E.: Extending oblivious transfers efficiently. In: Boneh, D. (ed.) CRYPTO 2003. LNCS, vol. 2729, pp. 145–161. Springer, Heidelberg (2003). https://doi.org/10.1007/978-3-540-45146-4_9

[IR89]   Impagliazzo, R., Rudich, S.: Limits on the provable consequences of one-way permutations. In: Proceedings of the 21st Annual ACM Symposium on Theory of Computing, Seattle, Washington, USA, 14–17 May 1989, pp. 44–61 (1989)

[Kil88]   Kilian, J.: Zero-knowledge with log-space verifiers. In: 29th Annual Symposium on Foundations of Computer Science, pp. 25–35. IEEE Computer Society Press, October 1988

[KOS15]   Keller, M., Orsini, E., Scholl, P.: Actively secure OT extension with optimal overhead. In: Gennaro, R., Robshaw, M. (eds.) CRYPTO 2015. LNCS, vol. 9215, pp. 724–741. Springer, Heidelberg (2015). https://doi.org/10.1007/978-3-662-47989-6_35

[LM18]   Li, B., Micciancio, D.: Equational security proofs of oblivious transfer protocols. In: Abdalla, M., Dahab, R. (eds.) PKC 2018. LNCS, vol. 10769, pp. 527–553. Springer, Cham (2018). https://doi.org/10.1007/978-3-319-76578-5_18

[MR19] Masny, D., Rindal, P.: Endemic oblivious transfer. In: Cavallaro, L.,
          Kinder, J., Wang, X., Katz, J. (eds.) ACM CCS 2019: 26th Conference
          on Computer and Communications Security, pp. 309–326. ACM Press,
          November 2019
[NNOB12] Nielsen, J.B., Nordholt, P.S., Orlandi, C., Burra, S.S.: A new approach
          to practical active-secure two-party computation. In: Safavi-Naini, R.,
          Canetti, R. (eds.) CRYPTO 2012. LNCS, vol. 7417, pp. 681–700. Springer,
          Heidelberg (2012). https://doi.org/10.1007/978-3-642-32009-5_40
[OOS17] Orrù, M., Orsini, E., Scholl, P.: Actively secure 1-out-of-N OT exten-
          sion with application to private set intersection. In: Handschuh, H. (ed.)
          CT-RSA 2017. LNCS, vol. 10159, pp. 381–396. Springer, Cham (2017).
          https://doi.org/10.1007/978-3-319-52153-4_22
[PSS17] Patra, A., Sarkar, P., Suresh, A.: Fast actively secure OT extension for
          short secrets. In: 24th Annual Network and Distributed System Secu-
          rity Symposium, NDSS 2017, San Diego, California, USA, 26 February–1
          March 2017 (2017)
[PVW08] Peikert, C., Vaikuntanathan, V., Waters, B.: A framework for efficient
          and composable oblivious transfer. In: Wagner, D. (ed.) CRYPTO 2008.
          LNCS, vol. 5157, pp. 554–571. Springer, Heidelberg (2008). https://doi.
          org/10.1007/978-3-540-85174-5_31
[WRK17] Wang, X., Ranellucci, S., Katz, J.: Global-scale secure multiparty compu-
          tation. In: Thuraisingham, B.M., Evans, D., Malkin, T., Xu, D. (eds.)
          ACM CCS 2017: 24th Conference on Computer and Communications
          Security, pp. 39–56. ACM Press, October/November 2017
[Yao86] Yao, A.C.-C.: How to generate and exchange secrets (extended abstract).
          In: 27th Annual Symposium on Foundations of Computer Science, pp.
          162–167. IEEE Computer Society Press, October 1986

Going Beyond Dual Execution:
MPC for Functions with Efficient Verification

Carmit Hazay[1]([⊠]), Abhi Shelat[2]([⊠]),

and Muthuramakrishnan Venkitasubramaniam[3]([⊠])

[1] Bar-Ilan University, Ramat Gan, Israel
carmit.hazay@biu.ac.il
[2] Northeastern University, Boston, USA
abhi@neu.edu
[3] University of Rochester, Rochester, USA
muthuv@cs.rochester.edu

Abstract. The *dual execution* paradigm of Mohassel and Franklin (PKC'06) and Huang, Katz and Evans (IEEE '12) shows how to achieve the notion of *1-bit leakage* security at roughly twice the cost of semi-honest security for the special case of *two-party secure computation*. To date, there are no multi-party computation (MPC) protocols that offer such a strong trade-off between security and semi-honest performance.

Our main result is to address this shortcoming by designing 1-bit leakage protocols for the multi-party setting, albeit for a special class of functions. We say that function $f(x, y)$ is *efficiently verifiable by g* if the running time of g is always smaller than f and $g(x, y, z) = 1$ if and only if $f(x, y) = z$.

In the two-party setting, we first improve *dual execution* by observing that the "second execution" can be an evaluation of g instead of f, and that by definition, the evaluation of g is asymptotically more efficient.

Our main MPC result is to construct a 1-bit leakage protocol for such functions from any passive protocol for f that is *secure up to additive errors* and any active protocol for g. An important result by Genkin et al. (STOC '14) shows how the classic protocols by Goldreich et al. (STOC '87) and Ben-Or et al. (STOC '88) naturally support this property, which allows to instantiate our compiler with two-party and multi-party protocols.

A key technical result we prove is that the passive protocol for distributed garbling due to Beaver et al. (STOC '90) is in fact *secure up to additive errors* against malicious adversaries, thereby, yielding another powerful instantiation of our paradigm in the constant-round multi-party setting.

As another concrete example of instantiating our approach, we present a novel protocol for computing *perfect matching* that is secure in the 1-bit leakage model and whose communication complexity is less than the honest-but-curious implementations of textbook algorithms for perfect matching.

Keywords: Secure computation · Semi-honest security · Dual execution · Greedy algorithms

ⓒ International Association for Cryptologic Research 2020
A. Kiayias et al. (Eds.): PKC 2020, LNCS 12111, pp. 328–356, 2020.
https://doi.org/10.1007/978-3-030-45388-6_12

1   Introduction

Current approaches for designing secure two-party (2PC) and multi-party (MPC) protocols follow a generic *compiler* pattern that transforms the function f into either a Boolean circuit or a RAM program and then applies a method to securely evaluate each gate or RAM operation in the program. This approach has been successful at evaluating many interesting functions such as the AES function [MOR03, MNPS04, BNP08, LP12, NO09, NNOB12, KSS12, RHH14], edit distance [HEKM11], textbook RSA operations [KSMB13] and graph algorithms [LHS+14, KS14].

The main result in this paper is to introduce a new method for constructing secure computation protocols that exploits the properties of the function of interest f. Our resulting protocols are secure in the one-bit leakage security model[1] and are asymptotically more efficient than using generic compiler-based techniques. In particular, we study secure computation protocols for a natural class of functions f which have *efficient verifiers*, i.e., given x, y, z, it is more efficient to verify $f(x, y) = z$ than to compute $f(x, y)$.

Notable examples in this class include: (a) Frievald [Fre77]'s celebrated technique verifies a matrix multiplication in time $O(\ell^2)$ whereas the schoolbook algorithms for matrix multiplication require $O(\ell^3)$ operations, (b) although it takes $O(E^2 V)$ or $O(V^3)$ to compute a maxflow for a graph $G = (V, E)$, given the flow f, one can verify its min-cut in time $O(E + V)$, (c) a minimum spanning tree can be verified in linear time [Kin95], (d) after solving any linear program, slack variables can be used to verify the optimal against the input constraints. Another interesting class includes sampling from complex distributions via rejection sampling. Here the procedure is to sample uniformly and apply a predicate to the result until the sample passes. Verification of the sample, on the other hand, requires only 1 application of the predicate, and can thus be asymptotically faster. Moreover, in a secure computation context, the parties' inputs are simply their random coins. Thus, 1-bit leakage can have essentially no security implication since the adversary can easily guess. One such example is sampling from the set of RSA moduli (product of two primes, as required for threshold RSA crypto systems). The best methods to (securely) sample [FLOP18] require roughly $O(\log^2(n))$ attempts to chose an $O(n)$-bit prime and then perform a multiplication and apply a bi-primality test, whereas verifying takes 1 multiplication and 1 bi-primality test.

On the other hand, we remark that there are some situations where leaking even 1 but could be harmful. For instance, in case of functions with one input bit, the adversary can leak the entire input of the honest party. Another example is when the secure computation is involved with medical or financial data where the attacker can extract a high order bit of information, such as whether an employee earns more than a certain amount of money or whether the DNA string includes a certain gene that causes a particular disease.

In the 1-bit leakage model, where the adversary is allowed to learn at most 1-bit of the honest party's input, the dual execution paradigm of Mohassel and Franklin [MF06] is the most efficient black-box protocol to date, incurring twice the cost of the passive

---

[1] Where the security definition allows the adversary to submit an arbitrary leakage predicate such that the honest party learns its output condition on whether the predicate is true when applied on the parties' inputs.

Yao protocol. Even though protocols for full security [WRK17a, WRK17b, KRRW18] have improved significantly over the recent past, dual execution offers much better concrete efficiency at low overhead without significantly compromising security [HKE12]. Security with 1-bit leakage is arguably sufficient in many cases, as the leakage legitimately allowed by the ideal functionality is often more significant than the very limited type of leakage in this model. For instance, secure computation with one bit of leakage has been adopted by Calctopia [cal] to perform secure computation on data stored in local private spreadsheets of the parties. In this paper, for the special class of functions with efficient verifiers, we are able to show an overhead that is *less than twice* the cost of passive protocol.

1-bit Leakage for 2-party. To introduce the power of efficiently verifiable f, our first result is a black-box two-party protocol that securely computes a function f in the *1-bit leakage model* with communication complexity roughly $p(|f|, \kappa) + p(|g|, \kappa) + poly(\kappa)$ where p represents the cost of Yao's *garbled encoding* of a function [Yao86], κ is a security parameter and $|f|$ and $|g|$ represent the size of the circuits that compute those functions respectively. Prior work requires $2p(|f|, \kappa) + poly(\kappa)$, and thus, our methods offer improvement (up to a factor of 2) for functions with asymptotically faster verification (e.g., matrix multiplication). Our main insight is to modify the *dual execution* technique introduced by Mohassel and Franklin [MF06] and refined by Huang, Katz and Evans [HKE12] to exploit the efficient verifier. Our analysis also shows that the secure equality test that is used at the end of both prior protocols is not necessary. While this result is purely a concrete improvement for a special class of functions, it introduces the insight needed for our main results in this paper. Importantly, we stress that the verification circuit g is never more complex than f, as in the worst case it can be instantiated with f. Our protocol takes advantage of the case when *the (multiplicative) complexity of g is smaller than f* where checking is often easier than computing.

1-bit Leakage Beyond 2-party Boolean Computations via Dual Execution. Our main result is to show how to extend the dual execution technique to multi-party protocols such as [GMW87] and [BMR90]. These are the first general class of black-box protocols in the multi-party setting to achieve security against 1-bit leakage *where the cost of the protocol is $(1 + \epsilon)$ times the passive counterparts*. Our insight here is that while prior work on dual execution required "one-sided security" in the analysis (where one-sided security implies active security for one party and passive security for the other), we can instead rely on the weaker property of *additive independent errors*—a useful notion introduced by Genkin et al. in [GIP+14]. We remark that prior work on the paradigm of dual execution explicitly applies to boolean computation via garbled circuits and *only* for the two-party setting.

In the multi-party setting, the recent maliciously secure protocol of Wang et al. [WRK17b] relies on cut-and-choose mechanism and incurs $\Omega(s/\log|C|)$ overhead for a statistical parameter s and circuit C. A crucial idea in this family of works toward achieving active security is to generate authenticated triples. Our paradigm can be used to improve their overheads (at the price of 1-bit leakage and verifiable functions) by requiring fewer triples that are authenticated. Our computation requires (unauthenticated) triples (secure up to additive attacks) for computing the function and authenticated triples for verifying the result. If we relax the black-box requirement, the work of [KPR18] achieves malicious security using tailor-made zero-knowledge proofs, but, still incurs a significant overhead over the passive protocol.

While the maliciously secure MPC protocols of [IPS08, IPS09, CGH+18] have constant communication overhead, their computational overhead is *super-constant* in the circuit size. Meanwhile, the work of [HSS17] introduces an asymptotically good protocol that achieves constant communication overhead over a passive protocol, but only for a constant number of parties due to the restrictions imposed by the IPS compiler. Our work (similar to the dual-execution paradigm) achieves both *constant computation and communication overheads* theoretically and concretely in the most general setting, albeit for a restricted class of functionalities, but in both honest and dishonest majority settings.

Finally, Hazay et al. [HIV17] demonstrate a non-interactive two-party protocol with leakage for arbitrary functions with communication overhead that is strictly greater than $1 + s/k$ where s and k are the statistical and computational security parameters. In contrast, our work can achieve overheads $1 + 1/n$ if verification is $O(1/n)$ simpler than computing (which is the case for many of our examples). Secondly, the computational overhead of our approach is also close to 1 while the work of [HIV17] is $O(log n)$ due to Shamir Sharing.

The Additive Security of [BMR90]**-Style Garbling.** The work of [GIP+14] allows us to instantiate our protocol with the [GMW87] protocol in the OT and OLE hybrids for Boolean and arithmetic functionalities. However, these protocols require more than a constant number of rounds. As a third contribution, we show that we can instantiate our framework with the distributed garbling (BMR) protocol due to Beaver, Micali and Rogaway [BMR90]. Specifically, a key technical lemma we prove is that the BMR protocol is secure up to additive independent errors on the internal wires of the circuit. We remark that this is the first constant-round protocol for which such a result has been established. Furthermore, this result is of independent interest as it can enable communication efficient multi-party protocols in the full security (i.e., no leakage) setting assuming the exitance of efficient Binary AMD circuit transformations.

Additive Security of Perfect Matching. As a case study for practitioners of our technique, we present a protocol for the problem of computing a *perfect matching* in a graph. This considers a scenario where the edges of a graph are distributed between the participants. Secure perfect matching and its generalization maximum matching are useful for assigned drivers to passengers in ridesharing services and more generally resource allocation. We show how this protocol satisfies the property that an adversary is limited to forcing additive, input-independent errors, and thus, we can apply our technique. Our protocol is iterative and requires secure computation of smaller independent tasks, most notably, matrix multiplication and matrix inversion for which we use Beaver triples techniques similar to Mohossel and Zhang [MZ17]. The communication complexity of our protocol is $O(V^2 \log V)$ which is *asymptotically more efficient than even using passive generic MPC* on the best algorithm to compute perfect matching [Har06], which would result in communication $O(V^\omega)$ where ω is the matrix-multiplication exponent (3 in the case of schoolbook algorithm). Passive generic MPC techniques applied to other algorithms for computing matchings (e.g., flow-based algorithms) would require ORAM data structures and would be even less efficient than $O(V^\omega)$.

Constant-Overhead Cryptography. A fundamental goal in cryptography is to obtain constant-overhead in computation (and consequently communication as well) over their "insecure" analogues. The recent work of Appelbaum et al. [ADI+17] provided the first construction of a passively secure protocol for evaluating an arithmetic circuit over a finite field $\mathbb{F}$ in the setting of secure two-party computation where the computational overhead is constant over naively computing via an insecure protocol. We are interested in a related fundamental problem of achieving constant-overhead in computation for constructing an actively secure protocol over the best passive analogue. To frame the question more precisely (and eliminate inefficient constructions based on stronger primitives), we can restrict to constructions in the OT - hybrid for boolean computations (resp., OLE-hybrid for arithmetic computations). Recent works [GIP+14, HIV17] have shown constant communication (as opposed to computation) overhead passive-to-active compilation. However, achieving constant computation overhead has largely remained an open problem. The dual execution framework provides the first construction of a constant computational overhead compilation boolean circuits in the two-party setting at the price of 1-bit leakage, where the constant, in fact, is 2. Our work can be seen as making significant progress in answering this fundamental questions, where, at the same price of 1-bit leakage, we demonstrate a $1 + o(1)$ computational overhead passive-to-active compilation for securely computing boolean and arithmetic computations in two party and multi-party settings where the computations are "easily" verifiable.

We now discuss our key insights for each of the above contributions.

1.1   Results in the 1-bit Leakage Model

Brief Summary of Dual Execution. In the dual execution technique introduced by Mohassel and Franklin in [MF06], the parties run Yao's 2-party protocol first with Alice as the *generator* and Bob as the *evaluator*, and a second time with the roles reversed. Thus, Alice and Bob have putative outputs from the protocol instance in which they act as evaluator. However, if one party constructs an incorrect circuit, then the other holds an incorrect result. To ensure correctness, Alice and Bob perform a maliciously secure protocol to check equality of their outputs. If this check passes, they both output their respective strings. Mohassel and Franklin further provided a definition of a k-leakage model. Intuitively, when $k = 1$, the adversary can learn "1-bit" of the counter party's input from the equality test. (See Sect. 2.2 for a formal definition.) In a followup, Huang, Katz and Evans [HKE12] used the same approach, providing a security proof for this notion. They also specified a custom-designed equality test in the random oracle model that relies on an additively homomorphic encryption scheme. Note that even if the final equality test passes, the adversary may still learn a bit about the honest party's input due *selective failure* attacks. For example, an adversary corrupting Alice may produce a garbled circuit that produces the correct answer if the first bit of Bob's input is 1. Then, in the case that Bob's input begins with 1, the protocol execution is indistinguishable from an honest execution, and yet, Alice concludes that Bob's input begins with 1. This 1 bit of leakage seems unavoidable when the adversary fully controls one of the garbled circuits.

Our Contribution. As noted above, prior work requires two copies of the garbled circuit for the function f and then run a maliciously secure equality test between outputs.[2] Our first observation is that after the first execution, one of the parties has a putative answer, $z = f(x, y)$, which *can be used* in the next protocol execution. In particular, for functions whose outputs can be efficiently verified in less time than it takes to compute the output, we show that it is unnecessary to compute f again. Rather, it suffices for the second party to run the verification algorithm $g(x, y, z)$ instead. Despite the simplicity of the concept, we encountered a number of subtle issues before settling on the following high-level approach for the 2-party setting. We present a novel protocol that make black-box usage of its underlying primitives.

In the first execution, Bob, as the evaluator, learns wire labels w_z for the output z but it is important that Bob does not have the decoding information for w_z. Instead, Alice provides a commitment to the decoding information for these wire labels. In the second execution, Bob acts as the generator of the checking circuit and commits to the 2 output labels for the single-bit of its output. In this circuit, Alice inputs x and the decoding information whereas Bob inputs the wire labels w_z. The checking circuit verifies the correctness of the former, performs the decoding of w_z and runs the efficient verification $g(x, y, z)$. The output of this circuit is a single bit denoting whether the verification succeeded. Alice evaluates the garbled circuit and commits to the single output wire label $\tilde{v}$. Bob sends the decoding information, and if the verification passes (i.e., the output decodes to 1), then Alice decommits to $\tilde{v}$ and Bob decommits to w_z.

Notice that the above requires Alice to commit to decoding for wire labels w_z, and for the check circuit to decode the labels. One approach to implement our commitment scheme is using verifiable secret-sharing (VSS), which allows the verification circuit to be "non-cryptographic" (and in fact information theoretic) so that our overall protocol is black-box in the underlying cryptographic primitives.[3] In particular, Alice uses a k-out-of-n VSS scheme to commit to the decoding information for these wire labels, and Alice and Bob use OT so that Bob can recover k such shares (and thus needs 1 more share to decode). In the second execution, Alice inputs x and the n VSS decoding shares whereas Bob inputs the wire labels w_z and his k decoding shares. Finally, the checking circuit verifies that Bob's k shares appear in the set of Alice's n shares.

Let us now argue correctness (omitting subtle issues that are handled in the simulation argument in the proof of Theorem 3). In essence, our protocol guarantees two properties. First, if an answer is revealed to Bob, then there must be a valid input x' for Alice such that the result is the computation of $f(x', y)$. Second, the leakage to Alice is whether an arbitrary pre-determined predicate chosen by Alice over Bob's input is equal to the value of the function under specific inputs for Alice and Bob. This leakage is morally similar to the leakage introduced in the Mohassel-Franklin dual execution approach. As we mentioned above, selective failure attacks still apply and thus, the best

---

[2] [HKE12] observed that their protocol need not achieve fully malicious security, but does satisfy a notion that is stronger than honest-but-curious security.

[3] One could instead use commitments for the translation table, but this would require the check circuit to implement the cryptographic verification procedure of the decommitments. In some circumstances AES-based commitments (or other methods) might be concretely better than decoding the VSS.

security we can guarantee against a malicious Alice is 1-bit leakage. We claim, however, a slightly stronger version of security than [HKE12], where the adversary learns the output of the function *only if* the 1-bit leakage predicate evaluates to 1.[4]

When Bob is malicious, then Bob holds one set of wire labels that is correct as the garbled circuit is correct. However, Bob could produce a malicious program checker. The basic guarantee of the protocol w.r.t Alice is that the only output that can be revealed to Alice is through the wire labels obtained by Bob in the first phase; since Alice is honest, this is a valid output of the function under some specific inputs of Alice and Bob. Bob can force Alice to reveal the decoding information, but with very high probability, Alice either outputs abort (because Bob denies Alice the output), or Alice outputs the correct output. In both cases, we can construct a simulator for Bob.

Our protocol does not need a maliciously secure equality test as per [MF06, HKE12]. While our protocol achieves less overall *communication and computation*, for some very small circuits our protocol may not achieve a faster *wall-clock*. However, for large functions, the factor of 2 savings in communication and computational can overcome this penalty.

1.2   Extending Dual Execution to Other Protocols

The dual execution technique has so far only applied to Yao's garbled circuit protocols because Yao's protocol offers a one-sided correctness property. Namely, the honest garbler can ensure that the counter-party computes a correct output. The main result in this paper is to answer the natural question of whether other secure computation protocols that do not offer one-sided correctness can be efficiently transformed into ones that offer 1-bit leakage security at a cost that is much less than fully malicious security. A second question is whether we can go beyond the two-party setting. It is not clear apriori how 1-bit leakage in the dual execution paradigm is possible in the multi-party setting where there is not a natural notion of "running the protocol in the other direction".

We answer these questions affirmatively for efficiently verifiable functions by showing how to construct novel 1-bit leakage protocols from classic secure computation protocols such as [GMW87] and [BGW88], extending the dual execution paradigm in the two domains. Our technique leverages the work of Genkin et al. [GIP+14] who shows that slight modifications of these protocols already offer security *up to additive errors*. Specifically, they show that for slight variants of the passive protocols, the attack space of a malicious adversary is limited to adding an input-independent value to any wire of the circuit. Whereas Genkin et al. then refine such protocols to be fully malicious, we present a lightweight alternative that achieves 1-bit leakage. Namely, after evaluating f modulo such additive errors, the parties perform a maliciously secure evaluation of $g(x, y, z)$, and determine the output based on the result of that computation. In contrast, the work of Genkin et al. [GIP+14] shows how to transform the function to another function that is immune to additive attacks. While this work and follow up works [GIP+14, GIP15, GIW16] demonstrate compilers with constant overhead for arithmetic circuits over a large field, for the case of Boolean circuits, the best

---

[4] While this notion is suggested heuristically in [HKE12], we achieve it formally. This notion is similar to the 2^{-s}-CovIDA notion presented by Mohassel and Riva [MR13].

compilation due to [GIW16] incurs a polylogarithmic overhead. Moreover, the previous works have worked only for non-constant round protocols, specifically those whose complexity is proportional to the depth of the circuit.

In this work, we make two important contributions. Our simple compiler offers lightweight malicious protocols for efficiently verifiable f for a wide variety of protocols both in the two-party and multi-party settings. The computation and communication complexities of our protocols are less than twice the cost of the passive counterparts (in the OT or OLE-hybrid models). Second, we provide a key technical lemma that shows the first constant-round protocol that fits the [GIP+14] paradigm. More precisely, we show that a variant of the distributed garbling protocol (BMR) due to Beaver et al. [BMR90] offers security *up to additive errors*. This result allows us to instantiate our paradigm with the multi-party BMR protocol as well.

Unlike in our Yao-based protocol, we here *require* a malicious evaluation of g. It would be preferable to use a simpler, additive error secure protocol for g, but we currently do not know how to securely combine the outputs of f and g if *both* have additive errors. Nonetheless, even the malicious evaluation of g can be substantially more efficient than the *honest-but-curious* evaluation of f. For example, when f grows as ℓ^3 and g grows as ℓ^2, as soon as ℓ exceeds the security parameter κ (i.e., for moderate input sizes), the overall communication for a malicious evaluation of g can be less than that of f. Second, our approach extends to the multi-party setting. Examples of such functions include max-flow, perfect-matching, linear program. Thus our technique offers an advantage for an interesting class of functions. We remark that the input-independent additive security property was crucially used when (sequentially) composing a protocol for f with a protocol g. Specifically, an attempt to weaken this security property requires the simulator to precisely obtain the "attack" from the adversary.

Finally, we highlight an interesting theoretical consequence of our result regarding the additive resilience of the BMR protocol. As mentioned before, for the case of Boolean circuits, the best AMD compilation is due to [GIW16] and incurs a polylogarithmic overhead. If this result [GIW16] can be improved from polylogarithmic overhead to a constant, then combined with our protocol will yield the *first* constant-round multi-party protocol for Boolean computations whose communication and computation complexity is a constant overhead over the passive counterpart, where previous protocols have incurred $\Omega(s)$ overhead for a statistical parameter s.

Beyond Additively Secure Protocols. In all our instantiations (of the second result), we rely on an "additive security" property of the protocol implementing f. It is tempting to ask if our framework can work for other weaker variants. It is conceivable that the only demand one would need from the protocol for f is privacy against active adversaries, however, to formally prove 1-bit leakage, one needs to precisely capture the attack caused by an active adversary on the protocol in order to extract the leakage function. In this respect, additive security is one formulation that facilitates this. We leave it as future work to generalize this approach for other types of attacks.

On Randomized Functionalities. In this work, we prove our theorems for deterministic f and g. However, the techniques extend to some cases when f and g are randomized. For example, Harvey's perfect matching algorithm is a randomized algorithm and it works in our framework because it has a unique output. We believe our framework will generalize to randomized f and g if the algorithm admits "unique" outputs. While we do not formalize "uniqueness" for algorithms, the reason our compilers require the output to be unique is because the "weaker" protocol we rely on for f could allow an active adversary to adaptively choose one of the solutions if more than one exist. Such an adversary will not be caught in our framework as g might return accept for all solutions and it is unclear how to simulate or how to formalize this attack via an ideal functionality. That being said, we believe that in some cases we can extend our framework beyond deterministic functionalities and leave it for future work.

2   Preliminaries

2.1   Verifiable Secret Sharing (VSS)

A verifiable secret sharing (VSS) [CGMA85] scheme is a two-stage secret sharing protocol for implementing the following functionality. In the first stage, denoted by Share(s), a special player referred to as dealer, shares a secret s among n players, in the presence of at most t corrupted players. In the second stage, denoted by Recon, players exchange their views of the share stage, and reconstruct the value s. We use notation Recon($S_1, \ldots, S_n$) to refer to this procedure. The functionality ensures that when the dealer is honest, before the second stage begins, the t corrupted players have no information about the secret. Moreover, when the dealer is dishonest, at the end of the share phase the honest players would have realized it through an accusation mechanism that disqualifies the dealer. A VSS scheme can tolerate errors on malicious dealer and players on distributing inconsistent or incorrect shares, indeed the critical property is that even in case the dealer is dishonest but has not been disqualified, still the second stage always reconstructs the same string among the honest players. In this paper, we use a (n, t)-perfectly secure VSS scheme with a deterministic reconstruction procedure [GIKR01].

Definition 1 (VSS Scheme). *An $(n + 1, t)$-perfectly secure VSS scheme consists of a pair of protocols* VSS $= \langle$Share, Recon$\rangle$ *that implement respectively the sharing and reconstruction phases as follows.*

Share(s). *Player P_{n+1} referred to as dealer runs on input a secret s and randomness r_{n+1}, while any other player P_i, $1 \leq i \leq n$, runs on input a randomness r_i. During this phase players can send (both private and broadcast) messages in multiple rounds.*

Recon($S_1, \ldots, S_n$). *Each shareholder sends its view v_i of the sharing phase to each other player, and on input the views of all players (that can include bad or empty views) each player outputs a reconstruction of the secret s.*

All computations performed by honest players are efficient. The computationally unbounded adversary can corrupt up to t players that can deviate from the above procedures. The following security properties hold.

- **Commitment:** *if the dealer is dishonest then one of the following two cases happen: (1) during the sharing phase honest players disqualify the dealer, therefore they output a special value $\perp$ and will refuse to play the reconstruction phase; (2) during the sharing phase honest players do not disqualify the dealer, therefore such a phase* *determines a unique value* s^* *that belongs to the set of possible legal values that does not include* $\perp$, *which will be reconstructed by the honest players during the reconstruction phase.*

- **Secrecy:** *if the dealer is honest then the adversary obtains no information about the shared secret before running the protocol* Recon.
- **Correctness:** *if the dealer is honest throughout the protocols then each honest player will output the shared secret* s *at the end of protocol* Recon.

We are interested in a deterministic reconstruction procedure, therefore we adopt the scheme of [GIKR01] that implements an $(n+1, \lfloor n/4 \rfloor)$-perfectly secure VSS scheme.

2.2 Secure Computation with 1-bit Leakage

In this section, we present a security definition that incorporates the notion of 1-bit leakage. For simplicity, we provide it for the two-party setting. It can easily be extended to multiparty setting. We consider static corruptions by malicious adversaries who may deviate from the protocol in an arbitrary manner. Our notion will follow the standard Goldreich's formalization of an Ideal and Real executions [Gol04] with the appropriate weakening from [HKE12] in which the adversary is allowed to submit a leakage predicate. However, our notion will be stronger than the definition in [HKE12] because the adversary learns the output in the optimistic case. These experiments will capture the idea of correctness and input independence: the honest party's output still corresponds to $f(x, y)$ and the adversary's input is independent of the honest party's input.

Real Execution. A two-party protocol Π is executed by Alice and Bob. The adversary A receives the inputs of the corrupted party and arbitrary auxiliary input z and sends all messages on behalf of the corrupted party. The honest party follows the instructions in Π. We define the random variable $\mathbf{View}_{\Pi, A(z)}(x, y, \kappa)$ to denote the entire view of adversary A in the execution of Π where Alice holds input x, Bob holds input y and the security parameter is 1^κ. We define the random variable $\mathsf{out}_{\Pi, A(z)}(x, y, \kappa)$ to denote the output of the honest party after the execution of the protocol. Finally, define the tuple

$$\mathrm{REAL}_{\Pi, A(z)}(x, y, z) \equiv \left(\mathbf{View}_{\Pi, A(z)}(x, y, \kappa), \mathsf{out}_{\Pi, A(z)}(x, y, \kappa) \right)$$

Ideal Execution. In the ideal execution, parties Alice and Bob interact with an ideal functionality; as before, the adversary has corrupted one of the parties, Alice holds input x, Bob holds input y and both hold the security parameter 1^κ. The adversary receives the input of the corrupted party and has an arbitrary auxiliary input string z. The honest party sends its input to the trusted party. The corrupted party controlled by A may send an arbitrary input $\tilde{y}$ to the trusted party. Denote the pair of inputs sent to the trusted party as $(\tilde{x}, \tilde{y})$. The adversary also sends an arbitrary Boolean function g to the trusted party. The trusted party computes the predicate $g(\tilde{x}, \tilde{y})$. If the predicate evaluates to 0, the trusted party sends "abort" to both parties. If the predicate evaluates to 1, the trusted party evaluates $f(\tilde{x}, \tilde{y})$ and and gives both values to the adversary. If the adversary sends the message "stop" to the trusted third party, then the honest party is given $\perp$. Otherwise, the honest party is given $f(\tilde{x}, \tilde{y})$. (This models the inherent lack of complete fairness.) The honest party outputs the message given by the trusted third party. The adversary can output an arbitrary string of its view. We define the random variable $\text{out}^A_{f,A(z)}(x,y,\kappa)$ to denote the output of the adversary A and $\text{out}^h_{f,A(z)}(x,y,\kappa)$ to denote the output of the honest party. Finally, define the tuple $\text{IDEAL}_{f,A(z)}(x,y,\kappa) \equiv (\text{out}^A_{f,A(z)}(x,y,\kappa), \text{out}^h_{f,A(z)}(x,y,\kappa))$.

Definition 1. *A protocol Π for the function f is said to securely compute f with 1-bit leakage if for every p.p.t. adversary A, there exists a p.p.t. simulator S in the ideal model such that*

$$\left\{\text{REAL}_{\Pi,A(z)}(x,y,\kappa)\right\}_{x,y,z\in\{0,1\}^*,\kappa\in\mathbb{N}} \approx_c \left\{\text{IDEAL}_{f,S(z)}(x,y,\kappa)\right\}_{x,y,z\in\{0,1\}^*,\kappa\in\mathbb{N}}$$

Remark. We mention the security notion of ϵ-CovIDA introduced by Mohassel and Riva [MR13] which implies our notion for the correct parameters. Essentially, this notion requires that if a player is trying to cheat, the other players can catch it with probability $1 - \epsilon$, but even if it is not caught (i.e., with probability ϵ) the cheater can only learn a single bit of extra information about the other players' inputs, and the correctness of the output is still guaranteed.

Extending to Multiparty Protocols. Similarly to the two-party case, we define the random variable $\text{View}_{\Pi,A(z),\mathcal{I}}(x_1,\ldots,x_m,n)$ to denote the entire view of adversary A in the execution of Π where party P_i holds input x_i, the adversary corrupts the parties in $\mathcal{I}$, and the security parameter is 1^n. We define the random variable $\text{out}_{\Pi,A(z),\mathcal{I}}(x_1,\ldots,x_m,n)$ to denote the output of the honest party $j \in [m]/\mathcal{I}$ after the execution of the protocol. Finally, define the tuple

$$\begin{aligned}&\text{REAL}_{\Pi,A(z),\mathcal{I}}(x_1,\ldots,x_m,n)\\ &\equiv (\text{View}_{\Pi,A(z),\mathcal{I}}(x_1,\ldots,x_m,n), \text{out}_{\Pi,A(z),\mathcal{I}}(x_1,\ldots,x_m,n))\end{aligned}$$

Analogously, in the ideal world, we allow the adversary to submit a leakage function g to the ideal functionality. We define $\text{out}^A_{f,A(z),\mathcal{I}}(x_1,\ldots,x_m,n)$ to denote the output of the adversary A and $\text{out}^h_{f,A(z),\mathcal{I}}(x_1,\ldots,x_m,n)$ to denote the output of the honest party. Finally, define the tuple

$$\begin{aligned}&\text{IDEAL}_{f,A(z)}(x_1,\ldots,x_m,n)\\ &\equiv (\text{out}^A_{f,A(z),\mathcal{I}}(x_1,\ldots,x_m,n), \text{out}^h_{f,A(z),\mathcal{I}}(x_1,\ldots,x_m,n))\end{aligned}$$

Finally, security is defined by requiring indistinguishability of **REAL** and **IDEAL**.

Remark 1. To achieve stand-alone (full) security our proofs only rely on sequential composition, which in turn requires the sub-protocols to only satisfy stand-alone security. Nevertheless, we note that our proofs can further achieve UC security if the underlying sub-protocols achieve UC security.

2.3   Garbled Circuits

Definition 2 (Garbling scheme). *A garbling scheme* Garb $=$ (Grb, Enc, Eval, Dec) *consists of four polynomial-time algorithms that work as follows:*

- $(\widetilde{C}, \mathbf{dk}, \mathsf{sk}) \leftarrow \mathsf{Grb}(1^\kappa, C)$: *is a probabilistic algorithm that takes as input a circuit* C *with* $2n$ *input wires and* n *output wires and returns a garbled circuit* $\widetilde{C}$, *a set of decoding keys* $\mathbf{dk} = (\mathsf{dk}_1, \ldots, \mathsf{dk}_n)$ *and a secret key* sk.
- $\widetilde{\mathbf{x}} := \mathsf{Enc}(\mathsf{sk}, \mathbf{x})$ *is a deterministic algorithm that takes an input a secret key* sk, *an input* $\mathbf{x}$ *and returns an encoded input* $\widetilde{\mathbf{x}}$. *We denote this algorithm by* $\widetilde{\mathbf{x}} := \mathsf{Enc}(\mathsf{sk}, \widetilde{\mathbf{x}})$. *In this work we consider* decomposable *garbled schemes. Namely, the algorithm takes multiple input bits* $\mathbf{x} = (x_1, \ldots, x_n)$, *runs* $\mathsf{Enc}(\mathsf{sk}, \cdot)$ *on each* x_i *and returns the garbled inputs* $\widetilde{x}_1$ *through* $\widetilde{x}_n$, *denoted by input labels.*
- $\widetilde{\mathbf{y}} := \mathsf{Eval}(\widetilde{C}, \widetilde{\mathbf{x}})$: *is a deterministic algorithm that takes as input a garbled circuit* $\widetilde{C}$ *and encoded inputs* $\widetilde{\mathbf{x}}$ *and returns encoded outputs* $\widetilde{\mathbf{y}}$.
- $\{\perp, y_i\} := \mathsf{Dec}(\mathsf{dk}_i, \widetilde{y}_i)$: *is a deterministic algorithm that takes as input a decoding key* dk_i *and an encoded output* $\widetilde{y}_i$ *and returns either the failure symbol* $\perp$ *or an output* y_i. *We write* $\{\perp, \mathbf{y}\} := \mathsf{Dec}(\mathbf{dk}, \widetilde{\mathbf{y}})$ *to denote the algorithm that takes multiple garbled outputs* $\widetilde{\mathbf{y}} = (\widetilde{y}_1 \ldots \widetilde{y}_n)$, *runs* $\mathsf{Dec}(\mathsf{dk}_i, \cdot)$ *on each* $\widetilde{y}_i$ *and returns the outputs* y_1 *through* y_n.

We remark that we only require that our garbling scheme maintains the privacy property, rather than stronger properties such as authenticity or obliviousness.

Correctness. We say that Garb is correct if for all $n \in \mathbb{N}$, for any polynomial-size circuit C, for all inputs $\mathbf{x}$ in the domain of C, for all $(\widetilde{C}, \mathbf{dk}, \mathsf{sk})$ output by $\mathsf{Grb}(1^\kappa, C)$, for $\widetilde{\mathbf{x}} := \mathsf{Enc}(\mathsf{sk}, \mathbf{x})$ and $\widetilde{\mathbf{y}} := \mathsf{Eval}(\widetilde{C}, \widetilde{\mathbf{x}})$ and for all $i \in [n]$, $y_i := \mathsf{Dec}(\mathsf{dk}_i, \widetilde{y}_i)$, where $(y_1, \ldots, y_n) = C(\mathbf{x})$.

Privacy. We say that a garbling scheme Garb is secure if there exists a PPT algorithm SimGC such that for any family of polynomial-size circuits C_κ and sequence of inputs $\{\mathbf{x}_\kappa\}_\kappa$,

$$\{(\widetilde{C}, \mathbf{dk}, \mathsf{sk}) \leftarrow \mathsf{Grb}(1^\kappa, C_\kappa); \widetilde{\mathbf{x}} := \mathsf{Enc}(\mathsf{sk}, \mathbf{x}_\kappa) : (\widetilde{C}, \widetilde{\mathbf{x}}, \mathbf{dk})\}_\kappa \stackrel{c}{\approx}$$
$$\{\mathbf{y} = C(\mathbf{x}_\kappa) : \mathsf{SimGC}\,(1^\kappa, C_\kappa, \mathbf{y})\}_\kappa.$$

2.4   The [BMR90] Garbling

An extension of Yao garbled circuits approach [Yao86] for any number of parties n introduced by Beaver, Micali and Rogaway in [BMR90] leading to the first constant-round protocol. This protocol has an offline phase in which the garbled circuit is created, and an online phase in which the garbled circuit is evaluated. The [BMR90] garbling technique involves garbling each gate separately using pseudorandom generators (or pseudorandom functions) while ensuring consistency between the wires. This method was recently improved by Lindell et al. in [LPSY15] which introduced an NC^0 functionality for this task, while demonstrating that the PRF values submitted by each party need not be checked for consistency (or computed by the functionality), as inconsistency would imply an abort by at least one honest party. Moreover, an abort event is independent of the honest parties' inputs due to the way each gate is garbled. In more details, the garbling functionality used in [LPSY15] is a modification of the garbling functionality introduced in [BMR90] and is applicable for any number of parties n. Namely, let C denote the circuit computed by the parties. Then for every wire w, party P_i inputs to the functionality two keys $k_{w,0}^i, k_{w,1}^i$ and the PRF computations based on these keys, as well as a masking bit share λ_w^i. The functionality creates the garbling for each gate which includes four rows such that each row is combined of n ciphertexts.

We will now describe the technical details of the BMR garbling. Without loss of generality, we assume that C is a Boolean circuit comprising of fan-in two AND and XOR gates, a total number of W wires and G gates. Then for every AND gate $g \in G$ with input wires $1 \le a, b \le W$ and output wire c, the garbled row $r_1, r_2 \in \{0,1\}$ in gate g is expressed as the concatenation of $\mathbf{R}_{g,r_1,r_2} = \{R_{g,r_1,r_2}^j\}_{j=1}^n$, where

$$R_{r_1 r_2}^{g,j} = \underbrace{\bigoplus_{i=1}^n \left(\mathsf{PRF}_{k_{a,r_1}^i}(g,j,r_1,r_2) \oplus \mathsf{PRF}_{k_{b,r_2}^i}(g,j,r_1,r_2) \right)}_{\text{Ciphertext Padding}}$$

$$\underbrace{\oplus\, k_{c,0}^j \oplus \left(\underbrace{\chi_{r_1,r_2}}_{\text{Perm. Bit}} \cdot \underbrace{(k_{c,1}^j \oplus k_{c,0}^j)}_{\text{Wire's } \Delta} \right)}_{\text{Plaintext}}$$

and PRF is a PRF, $k_{a,0}^i, k_{a,1}^i$ and $k_{b,0}^i, k_{b,1}^i$ are the respective input keys of party P_i, whereas $k_{c,0}^i, k_{c,1}^i$ are its output keys. Furthermore, for every a, b and r_1, r_2 as above the permutation bit χ_{r_1,r_2}, that "chooses" the output key to be encrypted, is defined by

$$\chi_{r_1,r_2} = ((\lambda_a \oplus r_1) \cdot (\lambda_b \oplus r_2)) \oplus \lambda_c$$

As specified above, the inputs to the [LPSY15]-style functionality may be inconsistent, implying an incorrect computation. We next describe their functionality for a general circuit C with n inputs $x_1, \ldots, x_n$ where x_i represents the value input by party P_i. Let $F = \{\mathsf{PRF}_k : \{0,1\}^\kappa \to \{0,1\}^\kappa\}_{k\in\{0,1\}^*,\kappa\in\mathbb{N}}$ be a family of PRFs. Then the encoding procedure takes the inputs $x_1, \ldots, x_n$ and additional random inputs $R_1, \ldots, R_n$ where each R_j is comprised of PRF keys $\{k_{w,0}^j, k_{w,1}^j\}_w$, masking bits shares $\{\lambda_w^j\}_w$ and PRF evaluations

$$\{F_{w,0,0}^{g,j}, F_{w,0,1}^{g,j}, F_{w,1,0}^{g,j}, F_{w,1,1}^{g,j}\}_{w\in W, g\in G}$$

that allegedly correspond to

$$\{\mathsf{PRF}_{k_{w,0}^j}(g,j,0,0), \mathsf{PRF}_{k_{w,0}^j}(g,j,0,1), \mathsf{PRF}_{k_{w,1}^j}(g,j,1,0), \mathsf{PRF}_{k_{w,1}^j}(g,j,1,1)\}_{w\in W, g\in G}$$

The encoding procedure BMR.Encode on input $((x_1, R_1), ..., (x_n, R_n))$ outputs

$$\underbrace{(R_{00}^{g,j}, R_{01}^{g,j}, R_{10}^{g,j}, R_{11}^{g,j})_{g\in G, j\in[n]}}_{\text{Garbled Tables}} \quad \underbrace{(\Lambda_w, k_{w,\Lambda_w}^1, \ldots, k_{w,\Lambda_w}^n)_{w\in\mathsf{Inp}}}_{\text{keys and masks for input wires}} \quad \underbrace{(\lambda_w)_{w\in\mathsf{Out}}}_{\text{Output translation table}}$$

where

$$R_{r_1,r_2}^{g,j} = \left(\bigoplus_{i=1}^{n} F_{a,r_1,r_2}^{g,i} \right) \oplus \left(\bigoplus_{i=1}^{n} F_{b,r_1,r_2}^{g,i} \right) \oplus S_{r_1,r_2}^{g,j}$$

$$S_{r_1,r_2}^{g,j} = k_{c,0}^{j} \oplus \chi_{r_1,r_2} \cdot (k_{c,1}^{j} \oplus k_{c,0}^{j})$$

$$\chi_{r_1,r_2} = \mathsf{AND}(\lambda_a \oplus r_1, \lambda_b \oplus r_2) \oplus \lambda_c = [(\lambda_a \oplus r_1) \cdot (\lambda_b \oplus r_2)] \oplus \lambda_c$$

$$\lambda_w = \begin{cases} \lambda_w^{j_w} & \text{if } w \in \mathsf{Inp} \quad\quad // \text{ input wire} \\ \lambda_w^1 \oplus \cdots \oplus \lambda_w^n & \text{if } w \in W/\mathsf{Inp} \;\; // \text{ internal wire} \end{cases}$$

$$\Lambda_w = \lambda_w \oplus x_w \text{ for all } w \in \mathsf{Inp} \quad\quad\quad\quad // \text{ masked input bit}$$

and wires a, b and $c \in W$ denote the input and output wires respectively for gate $g \in G$. $\mathsf{Inp} \subseteq W$ denotes the set of input wires to the circuit, $j_w \in [n]$ denotes the party whose input flows the wire w and x_w the corresponding input. $\mathsf{Out} \subseteq W$ denotes the set of output wires.

The decoding procedure basically corresponds to the evaluation of the garbled circuit. More formally, the decoding procedure BMR.Decode is defined iteratively gate by gate according to some standard (arbitrary) topological ordering of the gates. In particular, given an encoding information k_{w,Λ_w}^{j} for every input wire w and $j \in [n]$, of some input x, then for each gate g with input wires a and b and output wire c compute

$$k_c^j = R_{r_1,r_2}^{g,j} \oplus \bigoplus_{i=1}^{n} \left(\mathsf{PRF}_{k_{a,\Lambda_a}^{i}}(g,j,\Lambda_a,\Lambda_b) \oplus \mathsf{PRF}_{k_{b,\Lambda_b}^{i}}(g,j,\Lambda_a,\Lambda_b) \right)$$

Finally given Λ_w for every output wire w, compute the output carried in wire w as $\Lambda_w \oplus \left(\bigoplus_{j=1}^{n} \lambda_w^j \right)$.

Our proof makes use of the active key terminology originated from [LP09] which refers to a PRF key that is revealed to the adversary during the garbled circuit evaluation. Similarly, an inactive key refers to a wire key that is not revealed to the adversary during the evaluation. Each wire in the circuit is always associated with one active key and one inactive key (otherwise privacy would be violated). Developing this notion, an active path refers to the entire path visited throughout the evaluation. In the BMR-style garbling, the active path is chosen at random based on the masking bits that hide the actual wire value.

3 Dual Execution with Efficient Verification

In this section, we present a secure computation protocol for functions that have efficient verification that achieves security against active adversaries with 1-bit leakage. The protocol follows the spirit of the dual-execution [MF06]. However, we achieve greater efficiency as we do not require to garble the same circuit twice and our protocols do not require an extra secure equality test. Note, our technique can also be applied to functions that do not have efficient verification: namely, the predicate g can simply recompute f in addition to performing its other checks. In this sense, our framework subsumes prior dual-execution techniques for achieving 1-bit leakage.

Definition 2. *We say that function* $f : \{0,1\}^* \times \{0,1\}^* \rightarrow \{0,1\}^*$ *can be verified with predicate* g*, if* $f(x_A, x_B) = z \Leftrightarrow g(x_A, x_B, z) = 1$

Our protocol is described in the $(\mathcal{F}_{\text{COM}}, \mathcal{F}_{\text{OT}})$-hybrid where $\mathcal{F}_{\text{COM}}$ is the *ideal* commitment functionality and $\mathcal{F}_{\text{OT}}$ is the *ideal* 1-out-of-2 oblivious transfer functionality. We require a garbling scheme $\text{Garb} = (\text{Grb}, \text{Enc}, \text{Eval}, \text{Dec})$ as per Definition 2 in our protocol. Let f be an arbitrary two-party functionality that can be verified with predicate g. Let P_x describe the circuit that on input y computes $f(x, y)$. Let $P_{y,\widetilde{\mathbf{w}},\bar{\mathbf{t}},S}$ describe the circuit that on input $(x, \bar{\mathbf{s}})$ outputs 1 if and only if

1. $\bar{\mathbf{t}}$ and $\bar{\mathbf{s}}$ are consistent on the set $S \subset [n]$, and
2. $g(x, y, w) = 1$ where $w = \text{Dec}(\mathbf{dk}, \widetilde{\mathbf{w}})$ and $\mathbf{dk}$ is the reconstruction of $\bar{\mathbf{s}}$, and
3. $w \neq \perp$.

and otherwise outputs $\perp$.

Theorem 3. *Assuming the existence of a garbling scheme, protocol* $\Pi^f_{1-\text{LEAK}}$ *described in Fig. 1 securely realizes* $\mathcal{F}^f_{1-\text{LEAK}}$ *in the* $(\mathcal{F}_{\text{COM}}, \mathcal{F}_{\text{OT}})$-*hybrid with communication complexity* $p(|f|) + p(|g| + O(\kappa)) + poly(\kappa)$.

Remark 2. Note that when $|g| = o(|f|)$, then our protocol achieves complexity that is $(1 + o(1))|f|$, whereas prior work requires $2|f|$ communication. In practice, this factor of 2 in complexity can be substantial.

Proof: We first describe simulators for Alice and Bob and then prove correctness of simulation.

Simulating Alice. In the ideal world, the simulator $\mathcal{S}^A$ internally simulates $\mathcal{F}_{\text{COM}}$ and $\mathcal{F}_{\text{OT}}$ for Alice.

In Phase 1, Bob does not send any message directly to Alice. Bob only provides inputs to the $\mathcal{F}_{\text{OT}}$. The calls made to the $\mathcal{F}_{\text{OT}}$ functionality are internally simulated by $\mathcal{S}^A$ where it collects all the sender's message to the functionality. At the end of Phase 1, $\mathcal{S}^A$ obtains sk, $\bar{\mathbf{s}}$ from adversary Alice via the OT calls. Using $\bar{\mathbf{s}}$ it reconstructs $\mathbf{dk}$. It chooses a random t subset S of $[n]$ and sets $\bar{\mathbf{t}} = \{s_i\}_{i \in S}$.

In Phase 2, recall that Bob garbles the circuit $P_{y,\widetilde{\mathbf{w}},\bar{\mathbf{t}},S}$ where y is Bob's input, $\bar{\mathbf{t}}$ is the set of shares of $\mathbf{dk}$ obtained by Bob on set S, and $\widetilde{\mathbf{w}}$ is the output of the garbled circuit evaluation in Phase 1. It first obtains Alice's input $x, \mathbf{s}'$ from its message to the $\mathcal{F}_{\text{OT}}$ functionality in the second step of Phase 2. In the third message, the simulator has to send a garbling to Alice. If $\mathbf{s}'$ fails to agree with $\bar{\mathbf{s}}$ on the set of indices S or does not reconstruct to $\mathbf{dk}$, then $\mathcal{S}^A$ generates a Garbled Circuit that outputs 0 on all inputs. Otherwise, $\mathcal{S}^A$ computes the leakage function g^A as follows:

Function g^A: Input y, Parameters: $\widetilde{C}, \mathbf{dk}, \text{sk}, x$.

- Compute $\widetilde{\mathbf{y}} := \text{Enc}(\text{sk}, y)$, evaluate $\widetilde{\mathbf{w}} := \text{Eval}(\widetilde{C}, \widetilde{\mathbf{y}})$ and obtain $w = \text{Dec}(\mathbf{dk}, \widetilde{\mathbf{w}})$.
- Then compute $g(x, y, w)$ and output the result.

Protocol $\Pi^f_{1-\text{LEAK}}$.

Phase 1:

1. Alice with input x, computes $(\widetilde{C}, \mathbf{dk}, \mathsf{sk}) \leftarrow \mathsf{Grb}(1^\kappa, C_x)$.

2. Alice and Bob engage in n parallel executions of the $\mathcal{F}_{\text{OT}}$-functionality where Alice sends (k_i^0, k_i^1) to $\mathcal{F}_{\text{OT}}$ in the ith parallel instance and Bob sends y_i where $\mathsf{sk} = (k_1^0, k_1^1, \ldots, k_n^0, k_n^1)$ and Bob's inputs is $y = y_1 \cdots y_n$. Let $\widetilde{\mathbf{y}}$ be the concatenation of the outputs received from the n oblivious-transfer executions.

3. Next, Alice sends $\widetilde{C}$ to Bob. Bob evaluates the garbled circuit by computing $\widetilde{\mathbf{w}} := \mathsf{Eval}(\widetilde{C}, \widetilde{\mathbf{y}})$.

4. Alice encodes $\mathbf{dk}$ into $\bar{\mathbf{s}} = (s_1, \ldots, s_n)$ using a t-out-of-n VSS scheme. Then Alice and Bob engage in a k-out-of-n oblivious transfer, where Bob as the receiver picks k indices of n, say set, $S \subset [n]$ and the sender uses the VSS shares as its input. Let $\bar{\mathbf{t}} = \{s_i\}_{i \in S}$ the set of shares received by Bob.

5. Bob then commits to $\widetilde{\mathbf{w}}$ using $\mathcal{F}_{\text{COM}}$.

Phase 2:

1. Bob then computes garbling $(\widetilde{P}, \mathbf{dk}_P, \mathsf{sk}_P) \leftarrow \mathsf{Grb}(1^\kappa, P_{y, \widetilde{\mathbf{w}}, \bar{\mathbf{t}}})$.

2. Alice and Bob engage in n parallel executions of $\mathcal{F}_{\text{OT}}$ where Bob sends $(\widetilde{k}_i^0, \widetilde{k}_i^1)$ to $\mathcal{F}_{\text{OT}}$ in the ith parallel instance and Alice sends the ith bit of $(x, \bar{\mathbf{s}})$ where $\mathsf{sk}_P = (\widetilde{k}_1^0, \widetilde{k}_1^1, \ldots, \widetilde{k}_m^0, \widetilde{k}_m^1)$. Let $\widetilde{\mathbf{x}}$ be the concatenation of the outputs received from the m oblivious-transfer executions.

3. Next, Bob sends $\widetilde{P}$ to Alice. Alice evaluates the garbled circuit by computing $\widetilde{\mathbf{v}} := \mathsf{Eval}(\widetilde{P}, \widetilde{\mathbf{y}})$.

4. Alice commits to $\widetilde{\mathbf{v}}$ using $\mathcal{F}_{\text{COM}}$.

5. Bob sends $\mathbf{dk}_P$ to Alice. Using $\mathbf{dk}_P$, Alice computes the answer $v \leftarrow \mathsf{Dec}(\mathbf{dk}_P, \widetilde{\mathbf{v}})$.

6. If $v \neq 1$, Alice aborts. Otherwise it decommits $\widetilde{\mathbf{v}}$ and sends $(s_1, \ldots, s_n)$ to Bob.

7. If $\bar{\mathbf{t}}$ is not consistent with $\bar{\mathbf{s}}$, then Bob aborts. Otherwise it reconstructs $\mathbf{dk}$ from $\bar{\mathbf{s}}$ and computes $w \leftarrow \mathsf{Dec}(\mathbf{dk}, \widetilde{\mathbf{w}})$. Then it decommits its commitment to $\widetilde{\mathbf{w}}$ from Step 5, Phase 1 to Alice.

8. Alice computes w from $\widetilde{\mathbf{w}}$ and both parties output w.

Fig. 1. $\Pi^f_{1-\text{LEAK}}$: A 1-LEAK protocol for f

The simulator submits this leakage function g^A along with Alice's input x. Recall that the ideal functionality w.r.t Alice will return $f(x, y)$ if and only if $g(y) = 1$. If $g(y) = 1$ and the simulator obtains $w = f(x, y)$ then it will simulate a garbled circuit that outputs 1.

If Alice fails to send the result of the evaluation or sends inconsistent shares of $\mathbf{dk}$, the simulator does not allow the output to be delivered to Bob. Otherwise, it completes the execution with Alice and outputs its view by first computing $\widetilde{\mathbf{w}}$ such that $w = \mathsf{Dec}(\mathbf{dk}, \widetilde{\mathbf{w}})$ where w was received from the ideal functionality and faking the decommitment to $\widetilde{\mathbf{w}}$ in the end of Phase 2. If the protocol completes, then the Simulator lets the output to be delivered to Bob.

Correctness of Simulation: It follows from the description of the simulator $\mathcal{S}^A$ that the only messages that the simulator fakes in the ideal world include the garbled circuit

Bob generates in Phase 2 and the decommitment to $\widetilde{\mathbf{w}}$ in step 7. Indistinguishability will essentially follow from the fact that the simulator uses the correct output for the simulated garbled circuit in Phase 2 and the security of the garbling scheme.

More precisely, we consider an intermediate hybrid H and a simulator S_1 that receives Bob's input y. The simulation proceeds identically to the real world in Phase 1 with the exception that all the $\mathcal{F}_{OT}$ and $\mathcal{F}_{COM}$ calls are simulated by S_1 where it obtains all the messages between Alice and these functionalities. In the second phase, the garbled circuit is constructed according to the real simulator S where g is computed locally by S_1 as it has Bob's input. If in the computation by g, the value obtained for $\widetilde{\mathbf{w}}$ is inconsistent with what was decoded by Bob in Phase 1, then the simulator aborts.

Hybrid H_1. Indistinguishability of H_1 from the real world can be reduced to the security of the garbling scheme if we show that (1) the probability that the simulator aborts is negligible, and (2) the output used by the simulator S_1 to simulate the garbled circuit in the Phase 2 is indistinguishable distributed to the output obtained by Alice in the real world while evaluating the garbled circuit. There are two cases:

Case 1: Output is 0 because $\overline{\mathbf{s}^I}$ is inconsistent with $\overline{\mathbf{t}}$: The probability that this event occurs is identical in the real and simulation (an in particular in this hybrid experiment).

Case 2: $\overline{\mathbf{s}^I}$ is consistent with $\overline{\mathbf{t}}$: By a standard analysis, we can claim that except with negligible probability $\overline{\mathbf{s}^I}$ is reconstructed correctly to $\mathbf{dk}$ in evaluation of program garbled program P in the real world, where $\mathbf{dk}$ is the reconstruction of $\overline{\mathbf{s}}$. Next, we observe that the first step in the computation of g^A proceeds identically to the actions of Bob in Phase 1. Therefore, the $\widetilde{\mathbf{w}}$ obtained in the computation by g^A will be indistinguishable distributed to $\widetilde{\mathbf{w}}$ seen in the protocol in Phase 1 in this hybrid. Conditioned on this, the second step of the computation of g^A follows identical to the evaluation of P because the w obtained by computing $\mathrm{Dec}(\mathbf{dk}, \widetilde{\mathbf{w}})$ will result in the same value and the other values x and y are the same by construction.

This means that, except with negligible probability, the output of g conditioned on $\overline{\mathbf{s}^I}$ being consistent with $\overline{\mathbf{t}}$ is identical to the evaluation of the program P in the real world. Therefore, we can conclude the view of the adversary in the real world and H_1 are computationally indistinguishable.

Next, we compare H_1 and the ideal world. The only difference between these two experiments is in Step 7 of Phase 2 where the message $\widetilde{\mathbf{w}}$ is decommitted to by Bob to Alice. In H_1 this is done according to the real world and in the ideal world, S computes $\widetilde{\mathbf{w}}$ from $\mathbf{dk}$ and w. To argue indistinguishability, we first remark that conditioned on $\overline{\mathbf{s}^I}$ being consistent with $\overline{\mathbf{t}}$, then except with negligible probability, if g^A returns a 1, it holds that the value obtained by Bob in the first Phase must have been $\widetilde{\mathbf{w}}$ and that $f(x, y) = w$ by the correctness of the function g. This means when $\overline{\mathbf{s}^I}$ is consistent with $\overline{\mathbf{t}}$ the simulation is identically distributed and the output received by Bob in the ideal world is correct. On the other hand, when $\overline{\mathbf{s}^I}$ is inconsistent with $\overline{\mathbf{t}}$, the view of Alice in H_1 and the ideal world are identically distributed. This concludes the proof of indistinguishability and the correctness of the simulation.

Simulating Bob. To simulate a malicious Bob in Phase 1, $\mathcal{S}^B$ obtains Bob's input y from the $\mathcal{F}_{OT}$ calls. Next, it samples wire labels $\widetilde{\mathbf{w}}$ and creates a simulated garbled circuit that evaluates to set of wire labels $\widetilde{\mathbf{w}}$. Next Bob tries to retrieve a subset of the VSS shares of $\mathbf{dk}$. Let S be the set of indices. $\mathcal{S}^B$ creates t shares $\bar{\mathbf{t}}$ and provides that as the output to Bob in Step 4. Finally, it collects the message committed to by Bob in the last step of Phase 1.

In Phase 2, the simulator obtains $\mathsf{sk}_P, \mathbf{dk}_P$ from Bob and the garbling $\widetilde{\mathsf{P}}$. It constructs the following leakage function g^B.

Function g^B: Input x, Parameters: $\widetilde{\mathsf{P}}, \mathbf{dk}_P, \mathsf{sk}_P, y, \mathbf{dk}$.

– Compute $w = f(x, y)$ and extends the shares $\bar{\mathbf{t}}$ to set of shares $\bar{\mathbf{s}} = (s_1, \ldots, s_n)$ such that $\bar{\mathbf{s}}$ agrees with $\bar{\mathbf{t}}$ on set S and $\bar{\mathbf{s}}$ reconstructs to $\mathbf{dk}$ such that $\mathsf{Dec}(\mathbf{dk}, \widetilde{\mathbf{w}}) = w$.
– Compute $\widetilde{\mathbf{x}} := \mathsf{Enc}(\mathsf{sk}_P, (x, \bar{\mathbf{s}}))$, evaluate $\widetilde{\mathbf{v}} := \mathsf{Eval}(\widetilde{\mathsf{P}}, \widetilde{\mathbf{x}})$ and obtain $v = \mathsf{Dec}(\mathbf{dk}_P, \widetilde{\mathbf{v}})$ and return v as the result.

$\mathcal{S}^B$ submits the leakage function to the ideal functionality. If the result is 0, then $\mathcal{S}^B$ makes Alice abort. If the result of the leakage function is 1, it obtains $w = f(x, y)$ from the ideal functionality. Alice sends $\widetilde{\mathbf{v}}$ to Bob such that $1 = \mathsf{Dec}(\mathbf{dk}_P, \widetilde{\mathbf{v}})$ (computed using $\mathbf{dk}_P$) and set of shares $(s_1, \ldots, s_n)$ such that $w = \mathsf{Dec}(\mathbf{dk}, \widetilde{\mathbf{w}})$ and $(s_1, \ldots, s_n)$ reconstructs to $\mathbf{dk}$ and agrees with $\bar{\mathbf{t}}$ on the set S.

Correctness of Simulation: Briefly, we follow a similar approach as with the simulation of Alice. In other words, we argue that the leakage function g^B mimics the evaluation by Alice in Phase 2 on the right inputs. We consider intermediate hybrid experiments to argue indistinguishability.

Hybrid H_1: In this hybrid, we consider a simulator that receives Alice's input. The hybrid experiment proceeds identically to the real world with the exception that the simulator picks a translation table $\mathbf{dk}$ computes $\widetilde{\mathbf{w}}$ such that $w = \mathsf{Dec}(\mathbf{dk}, \widetilde{\mathbf{w}})$ where $w = f(x, y)$. Recall that the simulator can extract y from Bob in Step 2 from the OT call. Next, it simulates a garbled circuit on behalf of Alice such that the evaluation by Bob results in $\widetilde{\mathbf{w}}$. The rest of the protocol follows identically to the real world. Indistinguishability of H_1 and the real world follows from the simulation of the garbling scheme.

Hybrid H_2: In this hybrid, we consider a simulator that only chooses $\widetilde{\mathbf{w}}$ to create a simulated garbled circuit. Then it samples only VSS shares received by Bob. Namely, it simulates t shares for the indexes received by Bob. Then it follows the algorithm g^B and extends the shares $\bar{\mathbf{t}}$ to set of shares $\bar{\mathbf{s}} = (s_1, \ldots, s_n)$ such that $\bar{\mathbf{s}}$ agrees with $\bar{\mathbf{t}}$ on set S and $\bar{\mathbf{s}}$ reconstructs to $\mathbf{dk}$ such that $\mathsf{Dec}(\mathbf{dk}, \widetilde{\mathbf{w}}) = w$. The rest of the execution proceeds identically to H_1. Indistinguishability of H_2 and H_1 follows from the perfect security of the VSS scheme and the fact the distribution of $\mathbf{dk}$ is identically distributed in H_1 and H_2 conditioned on the event $\mathsf{Dec}(\mathbf{dk}, \widetilde{\mathbf{w}}) = w$.

Finally, we argue that Hybrid H_2 and the real simulation are identically distributed as the computation performed by g^B follows exactly the simulation in H_2. This completes the security proof. ∎

4   Additively Secure Protocols with Program Checkers

In this section, we show how to obtain security with one-bit leakage against malicious adversaries for a wide class of functionalities both in the two-party and the multi-party settings. On a high-level, we combine (1) an additively secure protocol for f, that is, a protocol that is secure against active adversaries up to additive attacks (cf. Definition 7) and, (2) a protocol for the verification algorithm g that is secure against malicious adversaries. We can rely on any malicious protocol for g.

To instantiate the additively secure protocol, we rely on a core lemma proving by Genkin et al. in [GIP+14], a work which introduced the notion of *additively secure circuits*. This lemma considers the malicious security of classic passively secure protocols, such as [GMW87, Bea91, BGW88], when executed in the presence of malicious adversaries. Informally speaking, Genkin et al. showed that for most classic honest-but-curious secure computation protocols for circuit evaluation, the effect of any active adversary corresponds precisely to an additive attack on the original circuit's wires where the additive attack is independent of the honest party's inputs. In particular, such protocols provide a mechanism to simulate adversaries where in addition to extracting an input from the adversary also extracts an additive attack to be supplied to the ideal functionality. Genkin et al. showed that slight variations of the passively secure protocols by Goldreich, Micali and Wigderson [GMW87] (Construction 5.8 [GIP+14]), Ben-Or, Goldwasser and Wigderson [BGW88] (Construction 5.5 [GIP+14]) and several others, are secure up to additive attacks.

Our contributions in this section are two fold:

1. In Sect. 4.2, we show that the distributed garbling protocol of Beaver et al. [BMR90] is in fact additively secure when the "offline" part of the protocol is executed using any additively secure protocol. This is the first constant-round protocol that has shown to be additively secure in the OT-hybrid. All previous works [GIP+14, GIP15, GIW16] considered protocols whose round complexity is proportional to the depth of the circuit or worked in the OLE-hybrid for large fields.
2. In Sect. 4.3, we provide a compiler that takes any additively secure protocol for f and combines it with a maliciously secure protocol for the "leaner" g to obtain a maliciously protocol for f that is secure against malicious adversaries up to 1-bit leakage. Roughly speaking the idea is that in an additively secure protocol, the adversary can only affect the computation in an input-independent and private manner. Therefore, a checking step can prevent an incorrect answer from being revealed.

4.1   Additive Attacks and AMD Circuits

In what follows we borrow the terminology and definitions verbatim from [GIP+14, GIW16]. We note that in this work we work with binary fields $\mathbb{F}_2$.

Definition 4 (AMD code [CDF+08]). *An (n, k, ε)-AMD code is a pair of circuits* (Encode, Decode) *where* Encode $: \mathbb{F}^n \to \mathbb{F}^k$ *is randomized and* Decode $: \mathbb{F}^k \to \mathbb{F}^{n+1}$ *is deterministic such that the following properties hold:*

– Perfect completeness. *For all* $\mathbf{x} \in \mathbb{F}^n$,

$$\Pr[\mathsf{Decode}(\mathsf{Encode}(\mathbf{x})) = (0, \mathbf{x})] = 1.$$

– Additive robustness. *For any* $\mathbf{a} \in \mathbb{F}^k$, $\mathbf{a} \neq 0$, *and for any* $\mathbf{x} \in \mathbb{F}^n$ *it holds that*

$$\Pr[\mathsf{Decode}(\mathsf{Encode}(\mathbf{x}) + \mathbf{a}) \notin \mathsf{ERROR}] \leq \varepsilon.$$

Definition 5 (Additive attack). *An additive attack* $\mathbf{A}$ *on a circuit* C *is a fixed vector of field elements which is independent from the inputs and internal values of* C. $\mathbf{A}$ *contains an entry for every wire of* C, *and has the following effect on the evaluation of the circuit. For every wire* ω *connecting gates* a *and* b *in* C, *the entry of* $\mathbf{A}$ *that corresponds to* ω *is added to the output of* a, *and the computation of the gate* b *uses the derived value. Similarly, for every output gate* o, *the entry of* $\mathbf{A}$ *that corresponds to the wire in the output of* o *is added to the value of this output.*

Definition 6 (Additively corruptible version of a circuit). *Let* $\mathrm{C} : \mathbb{F}^{I_1} \times \ldots \times \mathbb{F}^{I_n} \to \mathbb{F}^{O_1} \times \ldots \times \mathbb{F}^{O_n}$ *be an n-party circuit containing W wires. We define the additively corruptible version of* C *to be the n-party functionality* $\tilde{f} : \mathbb{F}^{I_1} \times \ldots \times \mathbb{F}^{I_n} \times \mathbb{F}^W \to \mathbb{F}^{O_1} \times \ldots \times \mathbb{F}^{O_n}$ *that takes an additional input from the adversary which indicates an additive error for every wire of* C. *For all* $(\mathbf{x}, \mathbf{A})$, $\tilde{f}(\mathbf{x}, \mathbf{A})$ *outputs the result of the additively corrupted* C, *denoted by* $\mathrm{C}^{\mathbf{A}}$, *as specified by the additive attack* $\mathbf{A}$ ($\mathbf{A}$ *is the simulator's attack on* C) *when invoked on the inputs* $\mathbf{x}$.

Definition 7 (Additively secure implementation). *Let* $\varepsilon > 0$. *We say that a randomized circuit* $\widehat{\mathrm{C}} : \mathbb{F}^n \to \mathbb{F}^t \times \mathbb{F}^k$ *is an* ε-*additively-secure implementation of a function* $f : \mathbb{F}^n \to \mathbb{F}^k$ *if the following holds.*

– Completeness. *For every* $\mathbf{x} \in \mathbb{F}^n$, $\Pr[\widehat{\mathrm{C}}(\mathbf{x}) = f(\mathbf{x})] = 1$.
– Additive attack security. *For any additive attack* $\mathbf{A}$ *there exist* $a^{in} \in \mathbb{F}^n$, *and a distribution* $\mathbf{A}^{out}$ *over* $\mathbb{F}^k$, *such that for every* $\mathbf{x} \in \mathbb{F}^n$,

$$SD(\mathrm{C}^{\mathbf{A}}(\mathbf{x}), f(\mathbf{x} + a^{in}) + \mathbf{A}^{out}) \leq \varepsilon$$

where SD denotes statistical distance between two distributions.

Towards introducing our transformations, we conclude with definition of a *protocol compiler* to be a function Γ that takes as input the description of a functionality $\mathcal{F}$ and parameter param and gives a protocol specification $\Pi_{\mathcal{F}} = \Gamma(\mathsf{param}, \mathcal{F})$. Furthermore,

Definition 8. *Let* κ *be the security parameter. A protocol compiler* Γ *is said to be* secure up to additive attacks *if for any functionality* $\mathcal{F}$, $\Gamma(\mathcal{F}, \kappa)$ *realizes* $\widetilde{\mathcal{F}}$ *with security against active adversaries, where* $\widetilde{\mathcal{F}}$ *is defined to be the functionality that is identical to* $\mathcal{F}$ *with the exception that it additionally receives an additive attack* $\mathbf{A}$ *from the adversary, to be applied to each wire of the circuit.*

4.2 Additive Security of BMR Distributed Garbling

In this section we will prove that the BMR encoding is resilient to additive attacks. Recall that in the standard passive BMR protocol for the function f, the parties first jointly compute garbled tables in an offline phase for the circuit C that computes f. Then in an online phase, each party P_i reveals their masked input bits followed by the parties revealing their input key labels corresponding to the input bits. Upon receiving the values, the parties evaluate the garbled circuit and output the result of the evaluation. Now, we prove that if we replace the passive protocol to compute the garbled tables with an additively secure protocol then we obtain an additively secure protocol for the underlying function f. More formally, let $\pi_1 = \Gamma(C_{\text{BMR}}, \kappa)$ be the additively secure protocol that computes the shares of the garbled tables in the distributed BMR garbling functionality C_{BMR} specified in Sect. 2.4 and let π_2 be the protocol obtained by replacing the offline phase of the passive BMR protocol with π_1. For example, one can instantiate this protocol with the GMW protocol. We prove the following theorem,

Theorem 9. *For an arbitrary n-party function f, let π_2 be as defined above. Then for any malicious adversary $\mathcal{A}$, there exists a simulator $\mathcal{S}$ that can simulate $\mathcal{A}$'s view in the $\tilde{f}_C(x_1, \ldots, x_n, \mathbf{A})$-hybrid where $\tilde{f}_C$ outputs the result of the additively corrupted C as specified by the additive attack $\mathbf{A}$.*

Before we proceed to the proof of Theorem 9, we illustrate an interesting application of our theorem. One of the main applications to additive resilient circuits was compiling secure computation protocols from passive to active security with low overhead. While the works [GIP+14, GIP15] resolve the question for arithmetic computations over large fields, the question remains open for Boolean computations. The work of Genkin et al. [GIW16] provides a passive to active compilation for Boolean circuits with polylogarithmic overhead. However, all the protocols that have been considered in previous work belong to the class of non-constant round protocols (protocols whose complexity depends on the depth of the circuit). We are the first to demonstrate this property for a constant-round protocol. Moreover, if optimal compilation of binary AMD circuits is achievable, then our result will imply communication optimal multi-party protocols for Boolean computations in constant-round. All previous works, incur at least an $\Omega(s/log|C|)$ overhead of compiling passive to active in the OT-hybrid in the multi-party setting.[5]

We next provide a high-level overview of the additive security against malicious adversaries of the BMR protocol in the (non-leaky) full security setting. Consider the BMR distributed garbling functionality C_{BMR} that outputs shares of the garbled tables. We need to translate an additive attack to the offline functionality to a corresponding attack on the wires of the original circuit C. Towards this, we first recall how a garbled row in the distributed garbling of BMR looks like. Recall that each party P_i contributes a pair of keys $(k_{w,0}^i, k_{w,1}^i)$ for every wire w and mask λ_w^i. The combined mask (or color bit) of a gate is defined as $\lambda_w = \oplus_i \lambda_w^i$. Then the $(r_1, r_2)^{th}$ row for $r_1, r_2 \in \{0, 1\}$ of the garbled gate g can be expressed as follows:

---

[5] In the two-party setting, the work of [HIV17] provides a constant overhead passive to active compiler for garbled circuits.

$$R_{r_1 r_2}^{g,j} = \bigoplus_{i=1}^{n} \left(\underbrace{\mathsf{PRF}_{k_{a,r_1}^i}(g,j,r_1,r_2) \oplus \mathsf{PRF}_{k_{b,r_2}^i}(g,j,r_1,r_2)}_{\text{Ciphertext Padding}} \right)$$

$$\oplus\, k_{c,0}^j \oplus \underbrace{\left(\underbrace{\chi_{r_1,r_2}}_{\text{Perm. Bit}} \cdot \underbrace{(k_{c,1}^j \oplus k_{c,0}^j)}_{\text{Wire's } \Delta} \right)}_{\text{Plaintext}}$$

where $\chi_{r_1,r_2} = ((\lambda_a \oplus r_1) \cdot (\lambda_b \oplus r_2)) \oplus \lambda_c$.

Next, we analyze an additive attack on the protocol computing the distributed garbling. We break this into two main parts: additive errors on the PRF values and additive errors on the plaintext part (containing the target keys). It was already shown in prior work [HSS17] that additive errors on the PRF values cannot affect the correctness of the computation if the plaintext is computed correctly. On a high-level, this is because for the computation at a gate to change, the adversary will have to guess the difference of the two keys of the honest party for the output wire. We next analyze an additive attack on the plaintext. The formula for computing the plaintext is:

$$\left(\chi_{r_1,r_2} \cdot (k_{c,1}^j \oplus k_{c,0}^j) \right)$$
$$= \left[\left(\underbrace{\bigoplus_{j\in[n]} \lambda_a^j \oplus r_1}_{\oplus\, e_1} \right) \cdot \left(\underbrace{\bigoplus_{j\in[n]} \lambda_b^j \oplus r_2}_{\oplus\, e_2} \right) \oplus \left(\underbrace{\bigoplus_{j\in[n]} \lambda_c^j}_{\oplus\, e_3} \right) \right] \cdot \underbrace{(k_{c,1}^j \oplus k_{c,0}^j)}_{\oplus\, e_4}.$$

The high-level goal here is that given an additive attack $\mathbf{A}_{\mathsf{BMR}}^{g}$ on the garbling of gate g, we need to extract a corresponding additive attack on the wires of the original computed circuit C. We can define additive errors e_1, e_2, e_3 and e_4 and express any generic additive attack on this part as follows:

$$\left[\left(\bigoplus_{j\in[n]} \lambda_a^j \oplus r_1 \oplus e_1 \right) \cdot \left(\bigoplus_{j\in[n]} \lambda_b^j \oplus r_2 \oplus e_2 \right) \oplus \left(\bigoplus_{j\in[n]} \lambda_c^j \oplus e_3 \right) \right]$$
$$\cdot \left(k_{c,1}^j \oplus k_{c,0}^j \oplus e_4 \right)$$

To argue that the additive error e_4 cannot render an incorrect computation, we observe that, this error can, at best, mess with the key being encrypted, but cannot change the value unless the adversary can guess the key chosen by the honest party. Therefore, this will not cause any additive error in the computation of the circuit wires. The remaining errors seem to correspond directly to corresponding wires of the circuit. While this is the basic intuition, formally arguing that given any additive attack on the computation of the distributed garbling, extracting a corresponding attack on the actual circuit (being garbled) turns out to be subtle and technical. We now proceed to the formal proof of security.

Proof: We will start with a protocol that is secure up to additive attacks for realizing the distributed garbling functionality. For example, we can rely on the passive [GMW87] protocol instantiated with a malicious OT protocol. Therefore, given any active adversary that attacks this protocol, we can consider an equivalent adversary in the C_{BMR}^{A}-hybrid that provides its inputs and an attack vector for the distributed garbling functionality.

Description of the Simulator. The simulator S begins a real execution with adversary A. First, it extracts the adversary's inputs and an additive attack vector $\mathbf{A}_{BMR}$ for functionality C_{BMR}. Next, the simulator determines the active path. The inactive rows for the garbled tables will then be replaced with random values. To determine the active path, it defines Λ_w values for all wires. For the input wires carrying honest party inputs, it will choose them at random. For the internal wires, it will proceed in a topological ordering of the gates, determining the Λ_w values for the output of the gates along this ordering. Towards this, it picks an honest party P_j. Let g be a gate in this ordering. Inductively, on the topological ordering, we will ensure that a Λ_w value has already been chosen for the output wires of gates $1, \ldots, (g-1)$. Let a and b denote the input wires of gate g. Then the simulator proceeds as follows. From the attack vector $\mathbf{A}_{BMR}$, the simulator identifies the additive errors $e_1, e_2, e_3^j, e_4^j, e_5^j$ such that row number (Λ_a, Λ_b) in the garbled table for g can be written as:

$$
\bigoplus_{i=1}^{n} \left(\mathsf{PRF}_{k_{a,r_1}^i}(g, j, r_1, r_2) \oplus \mathsf{PRF}_{k_{b,r_2}^i}(g, j, \Lambda_a, \Lambda_b) \right)
$$

$$
\oplus \left[\left(\bigoplus_{j \in [n]} \lambda_a^j \oplus \Lambda_a \oplus e_1 \right) \cdot \left(\bigoplus_{j \in [n]} \lambda_b^j \oplus \Lambda_b \oplus e_2 \right) \oplus \left(\bigoplus_{j \in [n]} \lambda_c^j \oplus e_3^j \right) \right]
$$

$$
\cdot \left(k_{c,1}^j \oplus k_{c,0}^j \oplus e_4^j \right) \oplus k_{c,0}^j \oplus e_5^j
$$

Next, it defines

$$
\Lambda_c = \left(\bigoplus_{j \in [n]} \lambda_a^j \oplus \Lambda_a \oplus e_1 \right) \cdot \left(\bigoplus_{j \in [n]} \lambda_b^j \oplus \Lambda_b \oplus e_2 \right) \oplus \left(\bigoplus_{j \in [n]} \lambda_c^j \oplus e_3^j \right)
$$

Recall that the simulator needs to extract an additive attack vector $\mathbf{A}_C$ on the underlying circuit. The simulator includes the additive errors e_1, e_2, e_3^j respectively to the wires a, b and c in this vector.

Note that the set of Λ_w values for all wires specifies the active rows for all gates. Namely, the row (Λ_a, Λ_b) is the active row for gate g with input wires a, b. In simulating the inactive rows, the simulator sets the honest party's shares to be uniformly random. For the active rows, the simulator first picks one key k_c^j for the honest party P_j and sets the active row as follows:

- $\bigoplus_{i=1}^{n} \left(\mathsf{PRF}_{k_a^i}(g, j, \Lambda_a, \Lambda_b) \oplus \mathsf{PRF}_{k_b^i}(g, j, \Lambda_a, \Lambda_b) \right) \oplus k_c^j \oplus e_5^j$ if $\Lambda_c = 0$.
- $\bigoplus_{i=1}^{n} \left(\mathsf{PRF}_{k_a^i}(g, j, \Lambda_a, \Lambda_b) \oplus \mathsf{PRF}_{k_b^i}(g, j, \Lambda_a, \Lambda_b) \right) \oplus k_c^j \oplus e_4 \oplus e_5^j$ else.

Based on this garbled table, the shares are revealed for the honest party. Finally, for the output translation table the simulator submits the attack vector $\mathbf{A}_C$ to the ideal functionality and receives the output. The simulator fixes λ_w^j so that $\Lambda_w \oplus (\oplus_{j=1}^n \lambda_w^j)$ is equal to the output received from the functionality.

The complete proof is provided in the full version. ∎

4.3 Compiling Additively Secure Protocols

We now present a compiler that takes an additively secure protocol for $\mathcal{F}$ and a malicious protocol for the leaner verifier functionality and produces a protocol that is secure against active adversaries with 1-bit leakage for functionalities that have efficient verifiability.

Theorem 10. *Let Γ_1 be a protocol compiler that is secure up to additive attacks against static, active adversaries, Γ_2 a protocol compiler that is fully secure against corruption by static, active adversaries. Then, there exists a protocol compiler Γ to securely compute with abort a deterministic functionality $\mathcal{F} : \{0,1\}^n \times \{0,1\}^n \to \{0,1\}^m$ verifiable with predicate $\mathcal{G}$ against static, active adversaries up to 1-bit leakage for the same corruption model. Furthermore, the computational and communication complexity of $\Gamma(\mathcal{F}, \kappa)$ is proportional to sum of the respective measures of $\Gamma_1(\mathcal{F}^*, \kappa)$ and $\Gamma_2(\mathcal{G}^*, \kappa)$ where $|\mathcal{F}^*| = O(|\mathcal{F}|) + \text{poly}(n, m, \kappa)$ and $|\mathcal{G}^*| = O(|\mathcal{G}|) + \text{poly}(m, n, \kappa)$.*

Proof: Unlike our protocol for garbled circuits from Sect. 3, where a protocol with one-sided security suffices, here we require a fully-secure protocol for $\mathcal{G}$. Nonetheless, as we show in Sect. 5 that such a protocol can still lead to efficiency improvements over other techniques. The functionality $\mathcal{F}^*$ is a slight variant of $\mathcal{F}$, which outputs additive shares of the output to the parties instead of the output itself. Similarly, the functionality $\mathcal{G}^*$ is a slight variant of $\mathcal{G}$, that takes as input the additive shares of the output and applies the function on the reconstructed value. Our protocol compiler proceeds in the following steps given a security parameter κ and n-party functionality $\mathcal{F}$ that takes n inputs $x_1, \ldots, x_n$ and gives shares of the m-bit to all parties. Consider an arbitrary functionality $\mathcal{F}$ verifiable with predicate $\mathcal{G}$.

- Construct functionality $\mathcal{F}^*$ that takes input x_i from P_i ($i \in [n]$) and outputs $(s_1, \ldots, s_n)$ where party P_i receives output s_i such that $\sum_i s_i = f(x_1, \ldots, x_n)$.
- Let $\mathcal{G}^*$ be the function that takes as input (x_i, s_i) from party P_i ($i \in [n]$) and computes $s = \sum_i s_i$ and b$=\mathcal{G}(x_1, \ldots, x_n, s)$. Finally, It outputs s if and only if $b = 1$.

The protocol now proceeds as follows:

1. In the first step, the parties execute protocol $\Pi_1 = \Gamma_1(\mathcal{F}^*, \kappa)$ where P_i uses input x_i and receives s_i as the output.
2. The parties next engage in the protocol $\Pi_2 = \Gamma_2(\mathcal{G}^*, \kappa)$ where Alice uses (x_i, s_i) as its input. Their final output is their output from protocol Π_2.

We show that this protocol achieves security against active adversaries with 1-bit leakage. For simplicity, we consider a hybrid protocol Π^* in the $(\widetilde{\mathcal{F}}^*, \mathcal{G}^*)$-hybrid where

$\widetilde{\mathcal{F}}^*$ is the functionality that besides the inputs for $\mathcal{F}^*$ also gets an additive attack $\mathbf{A}$ from the adversary. Note that we only need to rely on a sequential composition, which holds even in the simple stand-alone setting. The protocol proceeds in two steps. Honest parties provide inputs to $\widetilde{\mathcal{F}}^*$ as specified in Step 1 of the above protocol, receive their answer, and following that send their inputs to $\mathcal{G}^*$ as specified in Step 2 and receive their answers. We construct a simulator $\mathcal{S}$ for an arbitrary adversary $\mathcal{A}$ in this modified protocol Π^*. We remark that to consider the protocol in this hybrid, we crucially rely on the fact that both protocols admit standard security in the presence of active adversaries. In particular, both protocols provide a mechanism to extract the corrupted parties' inputs (and possibly other auxiliary information).

Let $\mathcal{A}$ be an adversary that corrupts the set of parties $\mathcal{I}$. The simulator begins an execution and receives from the adversary the inputs set $\{x_i\}_{i\in\mathcal{I}}$ as well as an additive attack vector $\mathbf{A}$. It provides as output random values $\{s_i\}_{i\in\mathcal{I}}$. Next it receives as input $\{(x_i^*, s_i^*)\}_{i\in\mathcal{I}}$ and computes the following leakage predicate described in Fig. 2.

FUNCTION $g^B(x)$

Parameters: $\mathbf{A}, \{x_i, s_i, x_i^*, s_i^*\}_{i\in\mathcal{I}}$

Input: $\{x_i\}_{i\in[n]/\mathcal{I}}$.

Output: The functionality proceeds as follows:

Let $\hat{y} = \widetilde{\mathcal{F}}^*(x_1, \ldots, x_n, \mathbf{A})$.

Output $\mathcal{G}(\hat{x}_1, \ldots, \hat{x}_n, \hat{y} + \sum_{i\in\mathcal{I}}(s_i^* - s_i))$ where $\hat{x}_i = x_i^*$ for $i \in \mathcal{I}$ and $\hat{x}_i = x_i$ for $i \in [n]/\mathcal{I}$.

Fig. 2. Leakage function for $\mathcal{A}$.

The simulator submits $\{x_i^*\}_{i\in\mathcal{I}}$ and g^B to the ideal functionality and receives y which it feeds internally to $\mathcal{A}$. Recall that the functionality returns an answer if and only if the leakage predicate returns 1. We remark that even if $\mathcal{G}$ can be realized with a protocol that has guaranteed output delivery, the resulting protocol will only achieve security with abort as the adversary can make the computation fail by making the first part of the protocol output an incorrect answer.

Proof of Correctness. As the leakage function simulates what happens in the real protocol and the additive sharing of the output information theoretically hides the output, our simulation is perfect. We only need to argue that if an output is received by an honest party then it corresponds to the right output. In other words, we need to argue that $\hat{y} = y$. This follows directly from the definition of efficiently verifiable functions and the fact that $\mathcal{F}$ is deterministic.   ∎

5 Perfect Matching Protocol Secure up to Additive Attacks

A perfect matching of a graph is a matching in which every vertex of the graph is incident to exactly one edge of the matching. Algorithms for perfect matchings are well-studied. For instance, the classic Ford-Fulkerson algorithm for maxflow can be used to find a matching in $O(VE)$ for the specific case of bipartite graphs. However, when this algorithm is transformed into a secure protocol, each execution of breadth-first requires the use of special ORAM data structures.

In the general case, finding a perfect matching in G reduces to solving a system of V linear equations in E variables. Applying such general methods from prior work to construct a secure computation protocol results in a communication complexity of at least $O(VE)$ which for dense graphs could be $O(V^3)$. An alternative approach would be to construct a protocol from one of the many standard algorithms for solving perfect matching. The textbook algorithm for perfect matching due to Edmond runs in time $O(V^2E)$ and the Micali-Vazirani algorithm requires $O(E\sqrt{V})$. However, both these algorithms require complicated input-dependent memory accesses which when translated to a secure protocol incurs heavy communication and computational overhead. Rabin and Vazirani [RV89] gave a randomized algorithm with runtime $O(V^{\omega+1})$ where ω is the matrix multiplication exponent. Mucha and Sankowski [MS04] improve this approach to $O(V^\omega)$. In contrast, the algorithm that we present below in the matrix multiplication hybrid model runs in *local* time $O(V^\omega)$ where ω is the (best) matrix multiplication exponent and requires communication $O(V^2 \log V)$.

Our starting point is the work of Harvey [Har06] who showed an $O(V^\omega)$ algorithm to compute the perfect matching. Our first insight is that an oblivious algorithm can be extracted from this work and adapted to a secure computation protocol in a hybrid model where the parties have access to a matrix-multiplication and matrix-inverse functionalities that work on shared inputs. While Harvey's algorithm runs in time $O(V^\omega)$, our communication complexity is better because a secure computation protocol for matrix multiplication requires $O(n^2)$ communication using (additively) homomorphic encryption while locally computing it requires $O(n^\omega)$ time. Next, we show that by instantiating the above functionalities using a maliciously secure protocol, the passive version of the protocol is secure against active adversaries up to additive attacks, analogous to [GMW87] additive security in the OT-hybrid from [GIP+14].

Finally, to obtain a protocol with 1-bit leakage, we note that it is easy to verify a perfect matching. It suffices to ensure that each vertex appears at most once in the matching, the size of the matching is $V/2$ and the edges were present in E. In fact, it can be done in time $O(V + E)$ but it suffices for our application that the verification be done in $O(V^2)$. We can achieve this obliviously by scanning element by element in the adjacency matrix of the graph and verifying the above conditions. We conclude with the following theorem proven in the full version.

Theorem 11. *For a graph $G = (V, E)$, there exists a data-oblivious algorithm that verifies that a putative matching M for G is perfect in time $O(V^2)$.*

Acknowledgements. We thank the anonymous PKC 2020 reviewers for their valuable feedback. The first author is supported by the BIU Center for Research in Applied Cryptography and Cyber Security in conjunction with the Israel National Cyber Bureau in the Prime Minister's Office, and by ISF grant 1316/18. The second author is supported by NSF Awards 1664445 and 1646671. The third author is supported by Google Faculty Research Grant and NSF Award CNS-1618884. The views expressed are those of the authors and do not reflect the official policy or position of Google, the Department of Defense, the National Science Foundation, or the U.S. Government.

References

[ADI+17] Applebaum, B., Damgård, I., Ishai, Y., Nielsen, M., Zichron, L.: Secure arithmetic computation with constant computational overhead. In: Katz, J., Shacham, H. (eds.) CRYPTO 2017. LNCS, vol. 10401, pp. 223–254. Springer, Cham (2017). https://doi.org/10.1007/978-3-319-63688-7_8

[Bea91] Beaver, D.: Efficient multiparty protocols using circuit randomization. In: Feigenbaum, J. (ed.) CRYPTO 1991. LNCS, vol. 576, pp. 420–432. Springer, Heidelberg (1992). https://doi.org/10.1007/3-540-46766-1_34

[BGW88] Ben-Or, M., Goldwasser, S., Wigderson, A.: Completeness theorems for non-cryptographic fault-tolerant distributed computation (extended abstract). In: STOC, pp. 1–10 (1988)

[BMR90] Beaver, D., Micali, S., Rogaway, P.: The round complexity of secure protocols (extended abstract). In: STOC, pp. 503–513 (1990)

[BNP08] Ben-David, A., Nisan, N., Pinkas, B.: FairplayMP: a system for secure multi-party computation. In: CCS, pp. 257–266 (2008)

[cal] http://www.calctopia.com

[CDF+08] Cramer, R., Dodis, Y., Fehr, S., Padró, C., Wichs, D.: Detection of algebraic manipulation with applications to robust secret sharing and fuzzy extractors. In: Smart, N. (ed.) EUROCRYPT 2008. LNCS, vol. 4965, pp. 471–488. Springer, Heidelberg (2008). https://doi.org/10.1007/978-3-540-78967-3_27

[CGH+18] Chida, K., et al.: Fast large-scale honest-majority MPC for malicious adversaries. In: Shacham, H., Boldyreva, A. (eds.) CRYPTO 2018. LNCS, vol. 10993, pp. 34–64. Springer, Cham (2018). https://doi.org/10.1007/978-3-319-96878-0_2

[CGMA85] Chor, B., Goldwasser, S., Micali, S., Awerbuch, B.: Verifiable secret sharing and achieving simultaneity in the presence of faults (extended abstract). In: FOCS, pp. 383–395 (1985)

[FLOP18] Frederiksen, T.K., Lindell, Y., Osheter, V., Pinkas, B.: Fast distributed RSA key generation for semi-honest and malicious adversaries. In: Shacham, H., Boldyreva, A. (eds.) CRYPTO 2018. LNCS, vol. 10992, pp. 331–361. Springer, Cham (2018). https://doi.org/10.1007/978-3-319-96881-0_12

[Fre77] Freivalds, F.: Probabilistic machines can use less running time. In: IFIP Congress, pp. 839–842 (1977)

[GIKR01] Gennaro, R., Ishai, Y., Kushilevitz, E., Rabin, T.: The round complexity of verifiable secret sharing and secure multicast. In: STOC, pp. 580–589 (2001)

[GIP+14] Genkin, D., Ishai, Y., Prabhakaran, M., Sahai, A., Tromer, E.: Circuits resilient to additive attacks with applications to secure computation. In: STOC, pp. 495–504 (2014)

[GIP15] Genkin, D., Ishai, Y., Polychroniadou, A.: Efficient multi-party computation: from passive to active security via secure SIMD circuits. In: Gennaro, R., Robshaw, M. (eds.) CRYPTO 2015. LNCS, vol. 9216, pp. 721–741. Springer, Heidelberg (2015). https://doi.org/10.1007/978-3-662-48000-7_35

[GIW16] Genkin, D., Ishai, Y., Weiss, M.: Binary AMD circuits from secure multiparty computation. In: Hirt, M., Smith, A. (eds.) TCC 2016. LNCS, vol. 9985, pp. 336–366. Springer, Heidelberg (2016). https://doi.org/10.1007/978-3-662-53641-4_14

[GMW87] Goldreich, O., Micali, S., Wigderson, A.: How to play any mental game or a completeness theorem for protocols with honest majority. In: STOC, pp. 218–229 (1987)

[Gol04] Goldreich, O.: The Foundations of Cryptography - Volume 2, Basic Applications. Cambridge University Press, Cambridge (2004)

[Har06]   Harvey, N.J.A.: Algebraic structures and algorithms for matching and matroid problems. In: FOCS, pp. 531–542 (2006)

[HEKM11] Huang, Y., Evans, D., Katz, J., Malka, L.: Faster secure two-party computation using garbled circuits. In: USENIX (2011)

[HIV17]   Hazay, C., Ishai, Y., Venkitasubramaniam, M.: Actively secure garbled circuits with constant communication overhead in the plain model. In: Kalai, Y., Reyzin, L. (eds.) TCC 2017. LNCS, vol. 10678, pp. 3–39. Springer, Cham (2017). https://doi.org/10.1007/978-3-319-70503-3_1

[HKE12]   Huang, Y., Katz, J., Evans, D.: Quid-pro-quo-tocols: strengthening semi-honest protocols with dual execution. In: IEEE Symposium on Security and Privacy, pp. 272–284 (2012)

[HSS17]   Hazay, C., Scholl, P., Soria-Vazquez, E.: Low cost constant round MPC combining BMR and oblivious transfer. In: Takagi, T., Peyrin, T. (eds.) ASIACRYPT 2017. LNCS, vol. 10624, pp. 598–628. Springer, Cham (2017). https://doi.org/10.1007/978-3-319-70694-8_21

[IPS08]   Ishai, Y., Prabhakaran, M., Sahai, A.: Founding cryptography on oblivious transfer – efficiently. In: Wagner, D. (ed.) CRYPTO 2008. LNCS, vol. 5157, pp. 572–591. Springer, Heidelberg (2008). https://doi.org/10.1007/978-3-540-85174-5_32

[IPS09]   Ishai, Y., Prabhakaran, M., Sahai, A.: Secure arithmetic computation with no honest majority. In: Reingold, O. (ed.) TCC 2009. LNCS, vol. 5444, pp. 294–314. Springer, Heidelberg (2009). https://doi.org/10.1007/978-3-642-00457-5_18

[Kin95]   King, V.: A simpler minimum spanning tree verification algorithm. In: Akl, S.G., Dehne, F., Sack, J.-R., Santoro, N. (eds.) WADS 1995. LNCS, vol. 955, pp. 440–448. Springer, Heidelberg (1995). https://doi.org/10.1007/3-540-60220-8_83

[KPR18]   Keller, M., Pastro, V., Rotaru, D.: Overdrive: making SPDZ great again. In: Nielsen, J.B., Rijmen, V. (eds.) EUROCRYPT 2018. LNCS, vol. 10822, pp. 158–189. Springer, Cham (2018). https://doi.org/10.1007/978-3-319-78372-7_6

[KRRW18] Katz, J., Ranellucci, S., Rosulek, M., Wang, X.: Optimizing authenticated garbling for faster secure two-party computation. In: Shacham, H., Boldyreva, A. (eds.) CRYPTO 2018. LNCS, vol. 10993, pp. 365–391. Springer, Cham (2018). https://doi.org/10.1007/978-3-319-96878-0_13

[KS14]   Keller, M., Scholl, P.: Efficient, oblivious data structures for MPC. In: Sarkar, P., Iwata, T. (eds.) ASIACRYPT 2014. LNCS, vol. 8874, pp. 506–525. Springer, Heidelberg (2014). https://doi.org/10.1007/978-3-662-45608-8_27

[KSMB13] Kreuter, B., Shelat, A., Mood, B., Butler, K.R.B.: PCF: a portable circuit format for scalable two-party secure computation. In: USENIX, pp. 321–336 (2013)

[KSS12]   Kreuter, B., Shelat, A., Shen, C.-H.: Billion-gate secure computation with malicious adversaries. In: USENIX, pp. 285–300 (2012)

[LHS+14] Liu, C., Huang, Y., Shi, E., Katz, J., Hicks, M.W.: Automating efficient RAM-model secure computation. In: IEEE Symposium on Security and Privacy, pp. 623–638 (2014)

[LP09]   Lindell, Y., Pinkas, B.: A proof of security of Yao's protocol for two-party computation. J. Cryptol. 22(2), 161–188 (2009). https://doi.org/10.1007/s00145-008-9036-8

[LP12]   Lindell, Y., Pinkas, B.: Secure two-party computation via cut-and-choose oblivious transfer. J. Cryptol. 25(4), 680–722 (2012). https://doi.org/10.1007/s00145-011-9107-0

[LPSY15] Lindell, Y., Pinkas, B., Smart, N.P., Yanai, A.: Efficient constant round multi-party computation combining BMR and SPDZ. In: Gennaro, R., Robshaw, M. (eds.) CRYPTO 2015. LNCS, vol. 9216, pp. 319–338. Springer, Heidelberg (2015). https://doi.org/10.1007/978-3-662-48000-7_16

[MF06] Mohassel, P., Franklin, M.: Efficiency tradeoffs for malicious two-party computation. In: Yung, M., Dodis, Y., Kiayias, A., Malkin, T. (eds.) PKC 2006. LNCS, vol. 3958, pp. 458–473. Springer, Heidelberg (2006). https://doi.org/10.1007/11745853_30

[MNPS04] Malkhi, D., Nisan, N., Pinkas, B., Sella, Y.: Fairplay - secure two-party computation system. In: USENIX, pp. 287–302 (2004)

[MOR03] MacKenzie, P.D., Oprea, A., Reiter, M.K.: Automatic generation of two-party computations. In: CCS, pp. 210–219 (2003)

[MR13] Mohassel, P., Riva, B.: Garbled circuits checking garbled circuits: more efficient and secure two-party computation. In: Canetti, R., Garay, J.A. (eds.) CRYPTO 2013. LNCS, vol. 8043, pp. 36–53. Springer, Heidelberg (2013). https://doi.org/10.1007/978-3-642-40084-1_3

[MS04] Mucha, M., Sankowski, P.: Maximum matchings via Gaussian elimination. In: FOCS, pp.248–255 (2004)

[MZ17] Mohassel, P., Zhang, Y.: SecureML: a system for scalable privacy-preserving machine learning. In: IEEE SP 2017 (2017)

[NNOB12] Nielsen, J.B., Nordholt, P.S., Orlandi, C., Burra, S.S.: A new approach to practical active-secure two-party computation. In: Safavi-Naini, R., Canetti, R. (eds.) CRYPTO 2012. LNCS, vol. 7417, pp. 681–700. Springer, Heidelberg (2012). https://doi.org/10.1007/978-3-642-32009-5_40

[NO09] Nielsen, J.B., Orlandi, C.: LEGO for two-party secure computation. In: Reingold, O. (ed.) TCC 2009. LNCS, vol. 5444, pp. 368–386. Springer, Heidelberg (2009). https://doi.org/10.1007/978-3-642-00457-5_22

[RHH14] Rastogi, A., Hammer, M.A., Hicks, M.: Wysteria: a programming language for generic, mixed-mode multiparty computations. In: IEEE Symposium on Security and Privacy, pp. 655–670 (2014)

[RV89] Rabin, M.O., Vazirani, V.V.: Maximum matchings in general graphs through randomization. J. Algorithms **10**(4), 557–567 (1989)

[WRK17a] Wang, X., Ranellucci, S., Katz, J.: Authenticated garbling and efficient maliciously secure two-party computation. In: CCS, pp. 21–37 (2017)

[WRK17b] Wang, X., Ranellucci, S., Katz, J.: Global-scale secure multiparty computation. In: CCS, pp. 39–56 (2017)

[Yao86] Yao, A.C.-C.: How to generate and exchange secrets (extended abstract). In: FOCS, pp. 162–167 (1986)

MonZ$_{2^k}$a: Fast Maliciously Secure Two Party Computation on Z$_{2^k}$

Dario Catalano[1], Mario Di Raimondo[1(✉)], Dario Fiore[2], and Irene Giacomelli[3]

[1] Dipartimento di Matematica e Informatica, Università di Catania, Catania, Italy
diraimondo@dmi.unict.it
[2] IMDEA Software Institute, Madrid, Spain
[3] Protocol Labs, San Francisco, USA

Abstract. In this paper we present a new 2-party protocol for secure computation over rings of the form $\mathbb{Z}_{2^k}$. As many recent efficient MPC protocols supporting dishonest majority, our protocol consists of a heavier (input-independent) pre-processing phase and a very efficient online stage. Our offline phase is similar to BeDOZa (Bendlin *et al.* Eurocrypt 2011) but employs Joye-Libert (JL, Eurocrypt 2013) as underlying homomorphic cryptosystem and, notably, it can be proven secure without resorting to the expensive sacrifice step. JL turns out to be particularly well suited for the ring setting as it naturally supports $\mathbb{Z}_{2^k}$ as underlying message space. Moreover, it enjoys several additional properties (such as valid ciphertext-verifiability and efficiency) that make it a very good fit for MPC in general. As a main technical contribution we show how to take advantage of all these properties (and of more properties that we introduce in this work, such as a ZK proof of correct multiplication) in order to design a two-party protocol that is efficient, fast and easy to implement in practice.

Our solution is particularly well suited for relatively large choices of k (*e.g.* $k = 128$), but compares favorably with the state of the art solution of SPDZ$_{2^k}$ (Cramer *et al.* Crypto 2018) already for the practically very relevant case of $\mathbb{Z}_{2^{64}}$.

1 Introduction

Secure Multi-Party Computation (MPC) allows a set of mutually mistrusting parties to jointly compute a function f of their inputs $x_1, \ldots x_n$ in such a way that correctness and security are guaranteed. Correctness means that at the end of the protocol the parties have computed $f(x_1, \ldots, x_n)$. Security means that, at the end of the interaction, party P_i, holding x_i, learns only (the i-th component of) the output $f(x_1, \ldots, x_n)$ and nothing else. The interesting feature of MPC is that security should be preserved even when there is an adversary $\mathcal{A}$ that controls some of the participants and, for the case of malicious security, takes full control of the corrupted parties, influencing their behaviors in arbitrary ways. The security model for MPC (*e.g.*, the Universal Composability framework [7]) formalizes this by stating that a protocol should be considered secure if its

© International Association for Cryptologic Research 2020
A. Kiayias et al. (Eds.): PKC 2020, LNCS 12111, pp. 357–386, 2020.
https://doi.org/10.1007/978-3-030-45388-6_13

execution is essentially equivalent to an ideal protocol where the computation is performed by a fully trusted third party.

In terms of applications, a particularly relevant case is the two party setting or, more in general, the case where the adversary (maliciously) controls half or more users. This scenario is notoriously hard to handle efficiently. Indeed, it is well-known that fast information theoretic solutions are not possible and expensive public key cryptography needs to be employed to achieve security.

In recent years, several works (e.g. [4, 13]) noticed that one can improve efficiency by dividing the computation in two stages: an expensive *offline* stage where public key cryptography is used in order to perform a pre-computation independent of the inputs, and an *online* stage in which, once the inputs become available, one performs the actual computation in a fast way, using only information theoretic techniques. More in detail, in these works pre-computation essentially consists in creating random triples of the form (a, b, ab). There are two main approaches to create these triples: using fast, but bandwidth inefficient, oblivious transfer extensions (e.g. [18]), or using more compact, but less computationally efficient, homomorphic encryption schemes.

When it comes to achieve security against malicious adversaries, the main technique used by these protocols are unconditionally secure MACs. For instance, in the celebrated SPDZ protocol [11, 13] a MAC key is shared and used to authenticate the random triples generated in the offline phase; this prevents players from cheating when using this same material in the on-line phase. Since information theoretically secure MACs are typically constructed over finite fields, most existing solutions for dishonest majority MPC assume that the computation takes the form of an arithmetic circuit over a finite field (such as $\mathbb{Z}_p$ for prime p). An exception is the recent work of Cramer *et al.* [9] (SPDZ$_{2^k}$) that proposes an efficient protocol that supports operations modulo 2^k. This choice comes particularly handy in practice: for instance, working modulo 2^k (and specifically 2^{64}) closely matches modern CPU computations and allows protocol designers to directly apply optimizations and tricks that are possible there and that are often expensive to emulate modulo p. In order to handle operations in $\mathbb{Z}_{2^k}$, the key technical contribution of the Cramer *et al.* solution is a new information theoretic MAC that allows to authenticate messages in this ring. In a nutshell, they achieve this by choosing a random secret key in a sufficiently large space $\mathbb{Z}_{2^s}$ and by performing all the computations in the larger ring $\mathbb{Z}_{2^{k+s}}$ so as to be able to bound with 2^{-s} the probability that an information theoretic adversary can forge a valid MAC. The new MAC is then used to construct an online protocol a-la SPDZ where computation is done in the ring $\mathbb{Z}_{2^{k+s}}$ (*i.e.* the values and the MACs are additively secret-shared in $\mathbb{Z}_{2^{k+s}}$). The preprocessing stage, on the other hand, is implemented via a MASCOT-like [18] protocol, whose communication costs are roughly twice those of the original MASCOT.

Our Contribution. In this paper we propose MonZa[1], a fast, two-party protocol for secure computation over the ring $\mathbb{Z}_{2^k}$. Our solution uses the authen-

---

[1] The name MonZa is inspired by the famous race track hosting the Formula One Italian Grand Prix.

tication mechanism of [9], but we generate random triples using homomorphic encryption. Specifically, we use the Joye-Libert [5,17] additively homomorphic cryptosystem (JL from now on), that turns out to be very well suited for our setting as it naturally supports $\mathbb{Z}_{2^n}$ (for flexible choices of n) as underlying message space. This scheme is efficient both in terms of encryption/decryption costs and in terms of bandwidth consumption (much more efficient than Paillier, for instance). More crucially, the JL cryptosystem has three additional properties that make it a perfect fit for multiparty computation. First, in JL all valid ciphertexts are publicly and efficiently recognizable. Second, JL has circuit privacy (for linear functionalities) in a very natural way. Third, one can generate different instances of JL that share the same plaintext space. The first two properties are particularly useful as they allow us to *avoid the use of expensive zero-knowledge proofs* for proving ciphertexts validity; this is in contrast to solutions based on lattice-based schemes where ciphertexts validity and circuit privacy require cumbersome techniques (related to preventing the injection of "bad noise" by a dishonest party). Moreover, since the scheme naturally works over $\mathbb{Z}_{2^n}$ we also do not need zero-knowledge proofs to show that a plaintext lies in a certain range (this would be needed if using Paillier, for instance).

In this paper we show how to take advantage of all the aforementioned properties of the JL cryptosystem (and even more properties that we add in this work – see slightly below) in order to design an efficient 2PC protocol for computations over the ring $\mathbb{Z}_{2^k}$.

We fully implemented MonZa's off-line phase[2] and performed a collection of experiments in order to evaluate, in terms of both bandwidth and computation, the efficiency of our solution. Details are given in Sect. 5. Notably, our bandwidth analysis shows that MonZa is particularly convenient for relatively large choices of k (*e.g.* $k = 64$ or 128) in which case it compares favorably with the state of the art solution of SPD$\mathbb{Z}_{2^k}$ [9]. The benchmarks confirm the practical efficiency of our protocol.

An Overview of Our Techniques. In order to design an efficient (preprocessing) 2PC protocol based on JL we cannot simply plug it as "yet another additively-homomorphic encryption" in existing approaches.

If we consider SPDZ [13], one could in principle enhance JL to support one homomorphic multiplication using the transformation of [8]; SPDZ however requires parties to threshold-decrypt ciphertexts at the end of preprocessing, and one drawback of JL is that it misses an efficient threshold decryption protocol[3].

Another option is to plug JL into a BeDOZa-style protocol [4]. In addition to the fact that BeDOZa works over a finite field while in our case we work in a ring with non-invertible elements, a major challenge is that in BeDOZa each party must execute a ZK protocol for correct multiplication, and such a protocol is *not* available for JL. Moreover, due to the fact that not all elements of the ring are invertible, one cannot use classical Sigma-protocol techniques to get it.

---

[2] We only focuses on the preprocessing stage since the online one is identical to [9].

[3] Also, coming up with an efficient, constant-round, protocol for a threshold JL decryption seems far from trivial due to the bit-by-bit extraction technique in the algorithm.

Finally, if one is concerned with avoiding proofs of correct multiplication, the recent Overdrive protocol [19] (still working over finite fields) showed how to avoid them if the linearly homomorphic encryption scheme satisfies a stronger security notion called *enhanced CPA*. Very informally, this property states that non-linear operations on ciphertexts are not possible. Somewhat surprisingly, this route turns out to not be viable in the setting of $\mathbb{Z}_{2^n}$. We formally prove that no encryption scheme that is linearly homomorphic over plaintext space $\mathbb{Z}_{2^n}$ can achieve enhanced CPA security. This essentially tells us that, in the $\mathbb{Z}_{2^n}$ setting, proofs of correct multiplication are sort of unavoidable.

Our (preprocessing) protocol shares some similarities with both BeDOZa [4] and Overdrive [19] in the sense that it employs an asymmetric Gilboa-like [15] multiplication protocol: P_1 has a key pair (sk, pk) and P_2 has the public key pk. To multiply their shares a_1 and b_2 the parties perform the following simple protocol. P_1 sends $\mathsf{Enc}_{\mathsf{pk}}(a_1)$ to P_2. P_2 chooses a random $r \in \mathbb{Z}_{2^n}$ and sends $C = \mathsf{Enc}_{\mathsf{pk}}(a_1)^{b_2}\mathsf{Enc}_{\mathsf{pk}}(-r) = \mathsf{Enc}_{\mathsf{pk}}(a_1 b_2 - r)$ back to P_1. P_1 decrypts the received plaintext and sets it as its share of the product $a_1 b_2$. P_2's share is just r. Notice that both BeDoZa and Overdrive use this protocol in a symmetric way: each player has a different key pair and to compute the shares of the product of secret-shared values in the two-party setting the protocol is executed two times (once for each mixed product). On the other hand, the design of the offline phase of our MonZa protocol is *asymmetric*: we require only one key pair and one party computes the intermediate ciphertexts of the form of C for both mixed products, while the other party decrypts. Since generating a ciphertext C is much less expensive than decrypting it (in JL), our MonZa protocol is well-suited for applications in the server-client model, where one party has less computational power than the other one.

Making the basic multiplication protocol described before secure against malicious adversaries requires more work though. Intuitively, P_2 has to show that he performed the above operation correctly. In principle this can be done with a ZK proof protocol where P_2 sends a commitment $\mathsf{Com}(a_2)$ and convinces P_1 that C satisfies the multiplicative relation $C = \mathsf{Enc}_{\mathsf{pk}}(a_1)^{a_2}\mathsf{Enc}_{\mathsf{pk}}(-r)$. A difficulty arises from the fact that doing this with JL is tricky. Solving these challenges is one of the main technical contributions of this paper.

To illustrate the problem let us consider the simpler case of proving knowledge of a JL plaintext. Informally, JL can be seen as a generalization of the well known Goldwasser-Micali cryptosystem [16]. The message space is $\mathcal{M} = \mathbb{Z}_{2^n}$, and the public key is N, g, where $N = pq$ is the product of two primes $p = 2^n p' + 1$ and $q = 2q' + 1$ such that p', q' are also primes[4], and g is an element of maximal order in $\mathbb{Z}_N^*$ and whose Jacobi symbol is 1. To encrypt $m \in \mathcal{M}$ one chooses a random $x \in \mathbb{Z}_N^*$ and sets $C = g^m x^{2^n} \bmod N$. To prove knowledge of m one would be tempted to use (an adapted version of) a standard, Schnorr-like, three move protocol. Very roughly this would go as follows. The prover starts by sending the encryption R of a random message r and, upon receiving a challenge $e \in \{0,1\}^n$,

---

[4] We remark that the original scheme from [17] allows more flexibility in the choice of p and q. For the sake of this discussion the choices above are good enough.

it sends z, y such that $g^z y^{2^n} = RC^e \mod N$. Completeness and (honest) verifier ZK are easy to argue, but the problems are in proving (special) soundness. Indeed two accepting transcripts (for the same R) lead to an equation of the form $g^{z_1 - z_2} \hat{y}^{2^n} = C^{e_1 - e_2} \mod N$ from which we *cannot* always extract the message since $e_1 - e_2$ might well be non invertible in $\mathbb{Z}_{2^n}$.

We overcome this issue by defining a slightly different protocol and by doing a careful analysis which shows that one can actually extract the least $n - s$ significant bits of the plaintext encrypted in C. More importantly, we extend this technique to work in the more involved case of proving a multiplication relation. Precisely, we propose an HVZK sigma-protocol for proving knowledge of $b, r \mod 2^{n-s}$ such that $C = A^b \mathsf{Enc}_{\mathsf{pk}_1}(r)$ and $B = \mathsf{Enc}_{\mathsf{pk}_2}(b)$, where $\mathsf{pk}_1 \; \mathsf{pk}_2$ are public keys of two different JL instances with the same message space $\mathbb{Z}_{2^n}$. Our protocol for correct multiplication is quite efficient – the prover sends 7 elements of $\mathbb{Z}_N^*$ and 2 values of n bits each – and this is partly due to the fact that JL allows to naturally create two instantiations with the same message space (this is for example not possible with Paillier's encryption scheme). In order to cope with the limitation of extracting fewer bits in our applications, we show that we can instantiate JL with a larger message space $\mathbb{Z}_{2^{k+2s}}$ while keeping the shares of our triples over $\mathbb{Z}_{2^{k+s}}$.

As additional remark, we point out that our MonZa protocol departs from previous work [4,13] also in the fact that it does not resort to the expensive sacrifice step to guarantee security. Informally, many existing protocols check the validity of each produced triple by "sacrificing" another triple where the same multiplication relation is expected to hold. This techniques makes the resulting protocols less efficient than one would like them to be as one needs to generate twice as many triples than needed. By exploiting both the algebraic properties of JL and the fact that our protocol is specifically tailored to the two party setting, we manage to replace the sacrifice step with a simplified (and more efficient) version of the HVZK sigma-protocol discussed above.

Other Related Work. There are several works about MPC protocol based on secret-sharing, however only few of these focus on computation over the rings [10]. For the ring $\mathbb{Z}_{2^k}$ besides the SPD$\mathbb{Z}_{2^k}$ protocol mentioned above, Sharemind [6] is a well-known and efficient protocol based on replicated secret-sharing. Sharemind works in the 3-party setting with honest-majority and it is passively secure only. Recently, Araki et al. [2] improved the efficiency of Sharemind, while [1,14] extended it to the case of active corruption. However, all these works are restricted to the case of honest majority. Damgaard et al. [12] present a compiler for achieving active security starting from a passively-secure MPC protocol that can be used for ring-MPC protocols too. The compiler is perfectly secure, however the active security comes at the price of reducing the corruption threshold (from t corrupted players to approximately $\sqrt{t}$).

In a concurrent and independent work, Orsini et al. [20] proposed a protocol, Overdrive2k, to perform secure MPC over $\mathbb{Z}_{2^k}$ from somewhat homomorphic encryption. Similarly to ours, their solution improves SPD$\mathbb{Z}_{2^k}$ in terms of bandwidth consumption. In terms of techniques, Overdrive2k and MonZa are rather different. At the heart of Overdrive2k is a new packing technique for the BGV cryptosystem that works for $\mathbb{Z}_{2^k}$; also their protocol works in the general multi-party setting (*i.e.*, the number of participants is ≥ 2). Our solution, on the other hand, is tailored to the two-party setting and builds on new zero-knowledge techniques for the JL cryptosystem, and the overall protocol is arguably mathematically simpler.

Road Map. We start describing the notation, the cryptography primitives and the security model used in this paper in Sect. 2. In particular, Sect. 2.5 recalls the information theoretic MAC defined in SPD$\mathbb{Z}_{2^k}$ and also used by MonZa. Then, our MPC protocol is described in the following two sections: Sect. 3 describes the new offline phase that we design for MonZa (protocol Π_{Offline}), while the online phase, which follows the SPD$\mathbb{Z}_{2^k}$ blueprint, is described in the full version of this paper. Sect. 4 recalls the JL encryption scheme and presents the new proof of correct multiplication for this encryption scheme (protocol Π_{ZKPoCM}). Finally, we conclude with an analysis of the efficiency of Π_{Offline} and Π_{ZKPoCM} in Sect. 5.

2   Preliminaries

2.1   Notation

Given a finite set D, sampling a uniformly random element from D is denoted by $r \leftarrow D$. We denote by $\mathbb{Z}_M$ the ring of the integers modulo M (where $M \geq 2$). We say that a function ϵ is negligible in n if for every positive polynomial p there exists a constant c such that $\epsilon(n) < \frac{1}{p(n)}$ when $n > c$. Two families $X = \{X_n\}_{n \in \mathbb{N}}$ and $Y = \{Y_n\}_{n \in \mathbb{N}}$ of random variables are said to be *statistically indistinguishable*, denoted by $X \approx_s Y$, if it holds that $\sum_a |\Pr[X_n = a] - \Pr[Y_n = a]|$ is negligible in n. Two ensembles are said to be *computationally indistinguishable*, denoted by $X \approx_c Y$, if it holds that for any computationally bounded (non-uniform probabilistic polynomial-time (PPT)) distinguisher $D \mid \Pr[D(X_n) = 1] - \Pr[D(Y_n) = 1]|$ is negligible in n.

2.2   Linearly-Homomorphic Encryption for Messages in $\mathbb{Z}_{2^n}$

To design our protocols, we use a public-key encryption scheme whose message space is the ring $\mathbb{Z}_{2^n}$ and it has a linear homomorphic property. More precisely, we assume that there exists a triple of algorithms (Gen, Enc, Dec) with the following property:

Algorithms: $\text{Gen}(1^\lambda, n)$ is a randomized procedure that takes as input the security parameter λ and the message bit-length n, and outputs a matching pair of secret and public keys (sk, pk). The public key defines a ciphertext space $\mathcal{C}$. Enc is a randomized algorithm keyed by pk that takes as input values in $\mathbb{Z}_{2^n}$. We write $\text{Enc}_{\text{pk}}(m, r)$ when we want to explicitly indicate that r is the random value used in the procedure, otherwise we write $\text{Enc}_{\text{pk}}(m)$.

Dec is a deterministic function keyed by sk. It holds that for any $m \in \mathbb{Z}_{2^n}$, $\Pr[\mathsf{Dec}_{\mathsf{sk}}(\mathsf{Enc}_{\mathsf{pk}}(m)) = m] = 1$ (the probability is taken over the random coins of Gen and Enc).

Additive property: Let $\mathcal{C}$ be the set of all possible ciphertexts, then there exists an operation $\odot$ on $\mathcal{C}$ such that for any a-tuple of ciphertexts $c_1 \leftarrow \mathsf{Enc}_{\mathsf{pk}}(m_1), \ldots, c_a \leftarrow \mathsf{Enc}_{\mathsf{pk}}(m_a)$ (a positive integer), it holds that $\Pr[\mathsf{Dec}_{\mathsf{sk}} (c_1 \odot \cdots \odot c_a) = m_1 + \cdots + m_a \mod 2^n] = 1$. We will use the notation $c^{\odot a} = c \odot \cdots \odot c$ (a times).

Lossy keys[5]: We also require the existence of a modified key generation algorithm, $\widetilde{\mathsf{Gen}}$, that on the same input λ, n generates a public key $\widetilde{\mathsf{pk}}$ with the following property. For any $m \in \mathbb{Z}_{2^n}$, $\{\mathsf{Enc}_{\widetilde{\mathsf{pk}}}(m)\}_\lambda \approx_s \{\mathsf{Enc}_{\widetilde{\mathsf{pk}}}(0)\}_\lambda$ (*i.e.*, $\mathsf{Enc}_{\widetilde{\mathsf{pk}}}(m)$ is statistically indistinguishable from an encryption of zero). Moreover, public keys produced by $\widetilde{\mathsf{Gen}}$ (called *lossy keys*) are computationally indistinguishable from those produced by the standard key generation algorithm.

Notice that *semantic security* follows from the indistinguishability of keys and the indistinguishability of encryption under the lossy keys.

Circuit privacy for linear functions: Informally, this property states that ciphertexts obtained through homomorphic evaluations are statistically indistinguishable from fresh encryptions of the resulting message. For simplicity, in our work we assume that homomorphic operations (i.e., $\odot$) are deterministic, and we state circuit privacy slightly differently: for any $a, b \in \mathbb{Z}_{2^n}$ and any ciphertext $A \in \mathsf{Enc}_{\mathsf{pk}}(a), B \in \mathsf{Enc}_{\mathsf{pk}}(b)$ we have that $A \odot B \odot \mathsf{Enc}_{\mathsf{pk}}(0) \approx_s \mathsf{Enc}_{\mathsf{pk}}(a+b)$. An implication of this property (that we use in our protocols) is that for any plaintexts $\alpha, \beta, \gamma \in \mathbb{Z}_{2^n}$ and any $C \in \mathsf{Enc}_{\mathsf{pk}}(\gamma)$, it holds $C^{\odot \alpha} \odot \mathsf{Enc}_{\mathsf{pk}}(\beta) \approx_s \mathsf{Enc}_{\mathsf{pk}}(\alpha\gamma + \beta)$.

Publicly Checkable Ciphertexts: we require that membership of a ciphertext in the ciphertext space, *i.e.*, $C \in \mathcal{C}$, can be efficiently and publicly tested given only the public key.

2.3 Commitments

Another building block we use in our constructions is an extractable commitment scheme for messages in $\mathbb{Z}_{2^n}$. That is, in the following we assume that there exists a tuple of algorithms (cGen, Com) with the following properties:

Algorithms: The procedure $\mathsf{cGen}(1^\lambda, n)$ takes as input the security parameter λ and the message bit-length n. The output is the commitment key ck and the extraction trapdoor information t_X.

Com is a randomized algorithm keyed by ck that takes as input values in $\mathbb{Z}_{2^n}$. We write $\mathsf{Com}_{\mathsf{ck}}(m, r)$ when we want to explicitly indicate that r is the random value used in the procedure, otherwise we write $\mathsf{Com}_{\mathsf{ck}}(m)$.

---

[5] For a CPA-secure additive encryption scheme this property always holds: include $C = \mathsf{Enc}_{\mathsf{pk}}(b)$ in the public key with $b = 0$ for Gen and $b = 1$ for $\widetilde{\mathsf{Gen}}$, and redefine encryption as $\mathsf{Enc}_{\mathsf{pk}}(m) = C^{\odot m} \odot \mathsf{Enc}_{\mathsf{pk}}(0)$.

Computationally hiding and unconditionally binding: We require that (1) for any $m, m' \in \mathbb{Z}_{2^n}$, $\mathsf{Com}_{\mathsf{ck}}(m) \approx_c \mathsf{Com}_{\mathsf{ck}}(m')$, and (2) for any C in the commitment space there exists at most one pair (m, r) such that it holds that $C = \mathsf{Com}_{\mathsf{ck}}(m, r)$.

Extractability: Finally, we require the existence of a PPT algorithm that allows to compute m from a commitment $C = \mathsf{Com}_{\mathsf{ck}}(m, r)$ and the trapdoor t_X.

Finally, we also require the existence of lossy keys for the commitment scheme too. That is, there exists a modified key-generation algorithm $\widetilde{\mathsf{cGen}}$ that generates lossy commitment keys (*i.e.*, any $\mathsf{Com}_{\widetilde{\mathsf{ck}}}(m)$, where $\widetilde{\mathsf{ck}} \leftarrow \widetilde{\mathsf{cGen}}$, is statistically indistinguishable from a commitment to zero) that are computationally indistinguishable from those produced by the standard key generation algorithm. From the above description it is rather clear that such a commitment scheme can be instantiated using a public key encryption scheme with the lossy key property. Indeed, in Sect. 4 we show that the Joye-Libert encryption scheme [5,17] satisfies the definition of additive encryption scheme given in Sect. 2.2 and can be used to instantiate the commitment scheme with the properties required here.

In the following we will use the notation $\mathsf{Enc}_{\mathsf{pk}}(m)$ (or $\mathsf{Com}_{\mathsf{ck}}(m)$) for a message $m \in \mathbb{Z}_{2^{n'}}$ also when the encryption (or commitment) scheme has message space $\mathbb{Z}_{2^n}$ (with $n \geq n'$). Indeed, we can think $\mathbb{Z}_{2^{n'}}$ as a subset of $\mathbb{Z}_{2^n}$.

2.4   Security Model

The protocols presented in this paper are for two parties, P_1 and P_2, and they are proven secure in the Universal Composability (UC) model [7]. In particular, our protocols will be proven secure against a malicious static adversary. In other words, the adversary may deviate from the protocol in any arbitrary way and can only corrupt parties before the protocol execution starts. Since it is not possible to construct an UC-secure MPC protocol with dishonest majority without a set-up assumption, in this paper we rely on the registered public-key model [3]. In particular, we assume that there is a functionality $\mathcal{F}_{\mathsf{KeyGen}}$ (described in Fig. 1) that generates correct keys for both the additive encryption scheme and the mixed commitment scheme.

Finally, for the sake of simpler protocol description, we will use a standard coin tossing functionality $\mathcal{F}_{\mathsf{Rand}}$ to generate public randomness. When activated from all the parties with input (rand, u), the functionality $\mathcal{F}_{\mathsf{Rand}}$ samples $r \leftarrow \{0, 1\}^u$ and return it to all parties. $\mathcal{F}_{\mathsf{Rand}}$ can be implemented using commitments of random values in the random oracle model or additive encryption in the key-register model.

2.5   Value-Representation in SPD$\mathbb{Z}_{2^k}$

The SPD$\mathbb{Z}_{2^k}$ protocol [9] is an n-party MPC protocol in the preprocessing model for computation over a ring. The backbone of this protocol is the representation of values: each element is authenticated via an information-theoretic MAC and both the value and the MAC are secret-shared among the parties. In this section

---

Functionality $\mathcal{F}_{\mathsf{KeyGen}}$

Let $(\mathsf{Gen}, \mathsf{Enc}, \mathsf{Dec})$ be additive encryption scheme and $(\mathsf{cGen}, \mathsf{Com})$ an extractable commitment scheme. $\mathcal{F}_{\mathsf{KeyGen}}$ interacts with the parties P_1 and P_2 and the simulator $\mathcal{S}$, which can abort any time, and proceeds as follows.

- When activated on input $(\mathsf{EncKeys}, sid, \lambda, n)$ from both parties: if P_1 is honest, $\mathcal{F}_{\mathsf{KeyGen}}$ runs $\mathsf{Gen}(1^\lambda, n)$ and generates a key-pair $(\mathsf{sk}, \mathsf{pk})$; if P_1 is corrupted the functionality gets r^* from $\mathcal{S}$ and it runs $\mathsf{Gen}(1^\lambda, n)$ using r^* as random tape. The functionality sends $(\mathsf{sk}, \mathsf{pk})$ to P_1 and pk to P_2.

- When activated on input $(\mathsf{ComKey}, sid, \lambda, n)$ from both parties: if P_2 is honest, $\mathcal{F}_{\mathsf{KeyGen}}$ runs $\mathsf{cGen}(1^\lambda, n)$ and generates a commitment key ck; if P_2 is corrupted the functionality gets r' from $\mathcal{S}$ and it runs $\mathsf{cGen}(1^\lambda, n)$ using r' as random tape. The functionality sends ck to both parties.

Fig. 1. Functionality for the keys generation.

we recall the details of the SPDZ$_{2^k}$ value-representation because our 2-party protocol will use it.

The MAC scheme has two parameter: k, where $\mathbb{Z}_{2^k}$ is the ring in which the inputs lie, and the security parameter s. The MAC key[6] α is sampled uniformly at random from $\mathbb{Z}_{2^{k+s}}$ and the MAC of a value $x \in \mathbb{Z}_{2^k}$ is defined as

$$m(x) = \alpha \cdot \tilde{x} \mod 2^{k+s}$$

where $\tilde{x} \in \mathbb{Z}_{2^{k+s}}$ such that $x = \tilde{x} \mod 2^k$. Then the values $\tilde{x}$ and $m(x)$ are additively secret-shared among the parties. The key α is fixed and also additively shared (*i.e.* $\alpha = \sum_{i=1}^{n} \alpha^{(i)} \mod 2^{k+s}$ and $\alpha^{(i)} \in \mathbb{Z}_{2^{k+s}}$ held by player P_i). In other words, the $[\cdot]$-representation of a value $x \in \mathbb{Z}_{2^k}$ is given by:

$$[x] = \{(x^{(i)}, m^{(i)}(x))\}_{i=1,\dots,n} \text{ and } \sum_{i=1}^{n} m^{(i)}(x) = (\sum_{i=1}^{n} x^{(i)}) \cdot (\sum_{i=1}^{n} \alpha^{(i)}) \mod 2^{k+s}$$

where $(x^{(i)}, m^{(i)}(x)) \in (\mathbb{Z}_{2^{k+s}})^2$ is known by player P_i.

Linear operations on shared and authenticated values are possible. In particular, we recall here the procedure `AffineComb` of [9]: the parties have u values $[x_1], \dots, [x_u]$, to compute the representation of $y = c + \sum_{i=1}^{u} c_i \cdot x_i \mod 2^k$, where $c, c_1, \dots, c_u$ are public values, the parties proceed as follow:

1. Party P_1 sets $y^{(1)} = c + \sum_{i=1}^{u} c_i \cdot x_i^{(1)} \mod 2^{k+s}$;
2. Each party P_j with $j \neq 1$ sets $y^{(j)} = \sum_{i=1}^{u} c_i \cdot x_i^{(j)} \mod 2^{k+s}$;
3. Each party P_j sets $m^{(j)}(y) = \alpha^{(j)} \cdot c + \sum_{i=1}^{u} c_i \cdot m^{(j)}(x_i) \mod 2^{k+s}$;

---

[6] The last (most significant) k bits of the MAC key are not actually required to be random, since the security of the MPC protocol follows from $\alpha \mod 2^s$ being random. However, sampling α from $\mathbb{Z}_{2^{k+s}}$ simplifies the description of the protocols.

In the following, we will say that parties compute $[y] = c + \sum_{i=1}^{u} c_i \cdot [x_i]$ to indicate that this procedure is executed.

3   Offline Phase

Our 2-party MPC protocol is divided in two phases: an offline phase, which is independent of both the input and the function, and an online phase, where the actual computation takes place. In the offline phase, the parties generate correlated randomness in the form of *singles* and *triples*. Then, in the on-line phase, as in the SPDZ$_{2^k}$ protocol, these values are consumed to create representation of the inputs, and to multiply shared and authenticated values and to verify the MACs (more details in the full version of this paper).

The exact functionality $\mathcal{F}_{\text{Offline}}$ that is implemented in the offline phase is described in Fig. 2. The correlated randomness generated by $\mathcal{F}_{\text{Offline}}$ for honest players has three forms: (1) authenticated single[7] $(j, [r])$, where r is sampled uniformly at random from $\mathbb{Z}_{2^{k+s}}$, and r is expressed in the $[\cdot]$-representation using a trivial sharing: $r^{(j)} = r$ and the other share is zero (*i.e.*, r is known by P_j only), (2) shared and authenticated single $[r]$, where again r is sampled uniformly at random from $\mathbb{Z}_{2^{k+s}}$ and expressed using the $[\cdot]$-representation, but no party knows the value, and (3) shared and authenticated triple $[a], [b], [c]$. Here, a, b, c are all shared and authenticated singles over $\mathbb{Z}_{2^{k+s}}$ such that it holds $c = a \cdot b \mod 2^k$.

The idea behind the specification of the corruption is that the environment is allowed to specify the share of a single for P_i corrupted ($i = 1$ or $i = 2$), and the share of c in a triple and the share of the MACs for P_2 corrupted. Then, the data for the honest party is chosen consistently with the values given by the environment to guarantee correctness of the MAC and the multiplication. Notice that the environment has no power to choose some of the shares of a corrupted P_1 (*i.e.*, the share of c and of the MACs); this is to reflect the different roles that the two parties have in our offline protocol and, in particular in the multiplication sub-protocol (more detail in the following).

The basic building block we use to generate both a single and a triple is a 2-party multiplication protocol (*i.e.*, a protocol to compute an additive sharing of the product of two secret values). Indeed in the 2-party case, and due to the nature of the MACs used in the $[\cdot]$-representation, such multiplication protocol is sufficient for computing both the product of secret-shared values and to authenticate a secret-shared value. Similarly to other MPC protocols like BeDOZa [4] and Overdrive [19], in order to implement the 2-party multiplication protocol we use an additive encryption scheme (Gen, Enc, Dec) as defined in Sect. 2.2. The high-level idea is simple: assume that party P_1 has a pair (pk, sk) and input $x^{(1)}$, while party P_2 knows only the public key pk and has input $x^{(2)}$. To compute an additive sharing of $x^{(1)} \cdot x^{(2)}$, P_1 sends $C_1 = \text{Enc}_{\text{pk}}(x^{(1)})$

---

[7] The $[\cdot]$-representation for a value x of $k + s$ bits means that we additively share in $\mathbb{Z}_{2^{k+s}}$ the value x and its MAC $x \cdot \alpha \mod 2^{k+s}$. However, only the first k bits of x are authenticated.

Functionality $\mathcal{F}_{\mathsf{Offline}}$

$\mathcal{F}_{\mathsf{Offline}}$ interacts with the parties P_1 and P_2 and the simulator $\mathcal{S}$, which can abort any time, and proceeds as follows.

For the sake of brevity, the description of functionality uses the following macro (*i.e.*, internal subroutine) that is executed to compute an additive secret-sharing of the MAC of secret-shared values respect to a given global key α.

$\mathsf{Auth}(x^{(1)}, x^{(2)})$:

1. Let $x = x^{(1)} + x^{(2)} \bmod 2^{k+s}$ and $m(x) = \alpha \cdot x \bmod 2^{k+s}$;
   If P_2 is corrupted, wait for $m_2 \in \mathbb{Z}_{2^{k+s}}$ from $\mathcal{S}$, otherwise sample $m_2 \leftarrow \mathbb{Z}_{2^{k+s}}$ at random. Define $m_1 = m(x) - m_2 \bmod 2^{k+s}$.
2. Send m_1 to P_1, and send m_2 to P_2 if P_2 honest.

Initialize: When activated on the first time on input $(\mathsf{Init}, sid, k, s)$ from all the parties, the functionality stores k and s. Then, for $j = 1, 2$, $\mathcal{F}_{\mathsf{Offline}}$ waits for $\mathcal{S}$ to send $\alpha^{(j)} \in \mathbb{Z}_{2^{k+s}}$ if P_j is corrupted, otherwise $\mathcal{F}_{\mathsf{Offline}}$ samples $\alpha^{(j)} \leftarrow \mathbb{Z}_{2^{k+s}}$ and forwards it to P_j. The functionality stores $\alpha = \alpha^{(1)} + \alpha^{(2)} \bmod 2^{k+s}$.

In each other activation,

Single: On input $(\mathsf{Single}, P_j, sid, ssid)$ from all parties, the functionality does the following.

1. $\mathcal{F}_{\mathsf{Offline}}$ waits for $\mathcal{S}$ to send $r \in \mathbb{Z}_{2^{k+s}}$ if P_j is corrupted, otherwise it samples $r \leftarrow \mathbb{Z}_{2^{k+s}}$ and forwards it to P_j.
2. $\mathcal{F}_{\mathsf{Offline}}$ executes $\mathsf{Auth}(r, 0)$: P_1 gets $m^{(1)}(r)$ and P_2 gets $m^{(2)}(r)$. The values $(ssid, r, m^{(j)}(r))$ and $(ssid, 0, m^{(i)}(r))$ are stored as local share of $(j, [r])$ by P_j and the other player P_i.

On input $(\mathsf{Single}, sid, ssid)$ from all parties, the functionality does the following.
1. For $j = 1, 2$, $\mathcal{F}_{\mathsf{Offline}}$ waits for $\mathcal{S}$ to send $r^{(j)} \in \mathbb{Z}_{2^{k+s}}$ if P_j is corrupted; otherwise it samples $r^{(j)} \leftarrow \mathbb{Z}_{2^{k+s}}$ and forwards it to P_j.
2. $\mathcal{F}_{\mathsf{Offline}}$ executes $\mathsf{Auth}(r^{(1)}, r^{(2)})$: for $j = 1, 2$, P_j gets $m^{(j)}(r)$ and stores $(ssid, r^{(j)}, m^{(j)}(r))$ as its local share of $[r]$.

Triple: On input $(\mathsf{Triple}, sid, ssid)$ from all parties, the functionality does the following.

1. For $j = 1, 2$, $\mathcal{F}_{\mathsf{Offline}}$ waits for $\mathcal{S}$ to send $a^{(j)}, b^{(j)} \in \mathbb{Z}_{2^{k+s}}$ if P_j is corrupted, otherwise $\mathcal{F}_{\mathsf{Offline}}$ samples $a^{(j)}, b^{(j)} \leftarrow \mathbb{Z}_{2^{k+s}}$ and forwards these to P_j. Let $a = a^{(1)} + a^{(2)} \bmod 2^{k+s}$, $b = b^{(1)} + b^{(2)} \bmod 2^{k+s}$ and $c \in \mathbb{Z}_{2^{k+s}}$ such that $c = a \cdot b \bmod 2^k$.
2. If P_2 is corrupted, wait for $c^{(2)} \in \mathbb{Z}_{2^{k+s}}$ from $\mathcal{S}$, otherwise sample $c^{(2)} \leftarrow \mathbb{Z}_{2^{k+s}}$ at random. Define $c^{(1)} = c - c^{(2)} \bmod 2^{k+s}$. The functionality sends $c^{(1)}$ to P_1, and sends $c^{(2)}$ to P_2 if P_2 honest.
3. $\mathcal{F}_{\mathsf{Offline}}$ executes $\mathsf{Auth}(a^{(1)}, a^{(2)})$, $\mathsf{Auth}(b^{(1)}, b^{(2)})$ and $\mathsf{Auth}(c^{(1)}, c^{(2)})$: for $j = 1, 2$, P_j gets $m^{(j)}(a)$, $m^{(j)}(b)$ and $m^{(j)}(c)$; party P_j stores $(ssid_i, a^{(j)}, m^{(j)}(a))$, $(ssid_i, b^{(j)}, m^{(j)}(b))$ and $(ssid_i, c^{(j)}, m^{(j)}(c))$ as its share of $([a], [b], [c])$.

Fig. 2. Functionality for the offline phase (preprocessing). It generates the shares of the global MAC key, and it produces singles and triples.

to P_2, who samples $y^{(2)}$ uniformly at random from the message space and computes $C = C_1^{\odot x^{(2)}} \odot \mathsf{Enc}_{\mathsf{pk}}(y^{(2)})$. Now, P_2 sends C to P_1, who decrypts and get $y^{(1)} = x^{(1)} \cdot x^{(2)} + y^{(2)}$. Passive security follows easily from the properties of the underlying encryption scheme. To achieve active security, we need to assure that P_1 sends an actual encryption and that P_2 computes C following the instruction in the protocol. The first property is easy to guarantee because we assume that the underlying encryption scheme has a publicly checkable ciphertext space. For the other task, we use a Zero-Knowledge (ZK) proof.

More precisely in the description of protocol Π_{Offline}, we assume the existence of the sub-protocol Π_{ZKPoCM}. This is a 3-move standard Σ-protocol where the functionality $\mathcal{F}_{\mathsf{Rand}}$ (Sect. 2.4) generates the challenge sent in the second messages for both players. We assume that the keys for an additive encryption scheme and an extractable commitment scheme have been generated correctly by an invocation to $\mathcal{F}_{\mathsf{KeyGen}}$. Both schemes have the same message space $\mathbb{Z}_{2^{k+2s}}$. The prover wants to convince the verifier that a given ciphertext C satisfy a precise relation among a value it knows and another public ciphertext C_1. That is, the common input is two ciphertexts, C and C_1, and a commitment C_2, the private input of the prover is $m, r \in \mathbb{Z}_{2^{k+s}}$ such that $C_2 = \mathsf{Com}_{\mathsf{ck}}(\tilde{m})$ and $C = C_1^{\odot m} \odot \mathsf{Enc}_{\mathsf{pk}}(\tilde{r})$ where $\tilde{m}$ and $\tilde{r}$ are values in the (larger) message space such that $m = \tilde{m} \bmod 2^{k+s}$ and $r = \tilde{r} \bmod 2^{k+s}$. We give more details on this and an instantiation of this sub-protocol in Sect. 4.1.

Protocol Π_{Offline} is described in Figs. 3 and 4. For the sake of brevity, we use the sub-protocol Mult that captures the actively secure multiplication protocol described before (assuming that the ciphertext C_1 and the commitment C_2 were sent previously). Mult is used to compute both the MAC of a given value and the product of shared values. For example, to implement (Single, P_1) (*i.e.*, to authenticate a value r known by P_1), the parties need to compute the shares of the product $r \cdot \alpha^{(2)} \bmod 2^{k+s}$ (where $\alpha^{(2)}$ is P_2's share of the global MAC key). This is done by running the 2-party multiplication protocol Mult where C_1 is an encryption of r done by P_1 and C_2 is a commitment to $\alpha^{(2)}$ (Fig. 3).

Analogously, to compute the mixed products for generating a triple (*e.g.*, $a^{(1)} \cdot b^{(2)} \bmod 2^{k+s}$ where $a^{(i)}$, $b^{(j)}$ are shares of singles) the parties execute Mult two times (in the example, C_1 is an encryption of $a^{(1)}$ and C_2 is a commitment to $b^{(2)}$). Finally, the Mult sub-protocol is used again to authenticate the product c (Fig. 4). Notice that the sub-protocol Mult does not commit a party to its output, therefore for the triple generation we need to add an extra check. This guarantees that a party uses the correct value (*i.e.* its output from the multiplication step) in the authentication step. Without this check a corrupted party could authenticate a wrong share $\tilde{c}^{(i)}$ and this would create an insecure triple (*i.e.*, a triple where $c = a \cdot b + \Delta \bmod 2^{k+s}$ and $\Delta \neq 0 \bmod 2^k$ known by the corrupted party). We implement the check using again a ZK proof for encrypted/committed values[8].

---

[8] In order to use the same ZK-proof for both players we need to assume that the commitment scheme has the same homomorphic property as the encryption scheme. If the commitment scheme is instantiated using the encryption as observed in Sect. 2.3, the homomorphic property clearly holds.

Protocol Π_{Offline}

The protocol is run by parties P_1 and P_2. (Gen, Enc, Dec) is an additive encryption scheme and (cGen, Com) is an extractable commitment scheme as defined in Section 2. For both these schemes, the message space is in $\mathbb{Z}_{2^{k+2s}}$.

In the steps of Π_{Offline} described in the following, we will use multiple times the sub-protocol Mult described below.

Mult($x^{(1)}, C_1, x^{(2)}, C_2$):

Common input: the commitment $C_2 = \text{Com}_{\text{ck}}(x^{(2)})$ and the ciphertext $C_1 = \text{Enc}_{\text{pk}}(x^{(1)})$; Input for P_1: $x^{(1)} \in \mathbb{Z}_{2^{k+s}}$; Input for P_2: $x^{(2)} \in \mathbb{Z}_{2^{k+s}}$.

1. P_2 samples $\tilde{r} \leftarrow \mathbb{Z}_{2^{k+2s}}$, sends $D = C_1^{\odot x^{(2)}} \odot \text{Enc}_{\text{pk}}(\tilde{r})$ to P_1 and invokes Π_{ZKPoCM} playing the role of the prover with private input $(x^{(2)}, \tilde{r} \bmod 2^{k+s})$ and public input (C_1, D, C_2);
2. If Π_{ZKPoCM} doesn't abort, P_1 computes $\tilde{y}^{(1)} = \text{Dec}_{\text{sk}}(D)$

Output: for P_1 the value $y^{(1)} = \tilde{y}^{(1)} \bmod 2^{k+s}$, for P_2 the value $y^{(2)} = -\tilde{r} \bmod 2^{k+s}$. Notice that $y^{(1)} + y^{(2)} = x^{(1)} \cdot x^{(2)} \bmod 2^{k+s}$.

Initialize:

1. For $i = 1, 2$, when activated on the first time on input (Init, sid, k, s), P_i sends (EncKeys, $sid, \lambda, k + 2s$) and (ComKey, $sid, \lambda, k + 2s$) to $\mathcal{F}_{\text{KeyGen}}$; P_1 gets sk, pk, ck and P_2 gets pk, ck.
2. P_1 samples $\alpha^{(1)} \leftarrow \mathbb{Z}_{2^{k+s}}$ and sends $\Delta_1 = \text{Enc}_{\text{pk}}(\alpha^{(1)})$ to P_2;
3. P_2 samples $\alpha^{(2)} \leftarrow \mathbb{Z}_{2^{k+s}}$ and sends $\Delta_2 = \text{Com}_{\text{ck}}(\alpha^{(2)})$ to P_1.

In each other activation,

Single:

On input (Single, $P_1, sid, ssid$), the parties do the following.

1. P_1 samples $r \leftarrow \mathbb{Z}_{2^{k+s}}$, sends $R = \text{Enc}_{\text{pk}}(r)$ to P_2;
2. P_2 invokes Mult($r, R, \alpha^{(2)}, \Delta_2$), P_1 gets $y^{(1)}$ and P_2 gets $y^{(2)}$;
3. P_1 sets $m^{(1)}(r) = \alpha^{(1)} \cdot r + y^{(1)} \bmod 2^{k+s}$ and stores $(ssid, r, m^{(1)}(r))$ as its share of $(1, [r])$, P_2 stores $(ssid, 0, y^{(2)})$ as its share of $(1, [r])$.

On input (Single, $P_2, sid, ssid$), the parties do the following.

1. P_2 samples $r \leftarrow \mathbb{Z}_{2^{k+s}}$ and sends $R = \text{Com}_{\text{ck}}(r)$ to P_1;
2. P_1 invokes Mult($\alpha^{(1)}, \Delta_1, r, R$), P_1 gets $y^{(1)}$ and P_2 gets $y^{(2)}$;
3. P_2 sets $m^{(2)}(r) = \alpha^{(2)} \cdot r + y^{(2)} \bmod 2^{k+s}$ and stores $(ssid, r, m^{(2)}(r))$ as its share of $(2, [r])$, P_1 stores $(ssid, 0, y^{(1)})$ as its share of $(2, [r])$.

On input (Single, $sid, ssid$), the parties do the following.

1. Run (Singles, P_1) and (Singles, P_2) and generate $(1, [r^{(1)}])$ and $(2, [r^{(2)}])$, respectively;
2. Compute $[r] = [r^{(1)}] + [r^{(2)}]$ and store it with index $ssid$.

Fig. 3. Protocol for preprocessing.

In particular, we use a modified (simpler) version of Π_{ZKPoCM}. This version, which we call Π_{ZKPoMCV}, allows the prover to convince the verifier that, given three ciphertexts (or commitments) $A, B, \tilde{C}$, the prover knows b such that $\tilde{C} = A^{\odot b}$. We give more details on this and an instantiation of this ZK proof in Sect. 4.2.

Protocol Π_{Offline} (continued)

Triple: On input $(\mathsf{Triple}, sid, ssid)$, the parties do the following.

1. The parties run two times the Single command and get their shares of $[a]$ and $[b]$ (let $A^{(1)} = \mathsf{Enc}_{\mathsf{pk}}(a^{(1)})$, $A^{(2)} = \mathsf{Com}_{\mathsf{ck}}(a^{(2)})$ and $B^{(1)} = \mathsf{Enc}_{\mathsf{pk}}(b^{(1)})$, $B^{(2)} = \mathsf{Com}_{\mathsf{ck}}(b^{(2)})$ be the intermediate values computed during the execution of the Single steps);
2. *Multiplication:*
   - P_2 invokes $\mathsf{Mult}(a^{(1)}, A^{(1)}, b^{(2)}, B^{(2)})$, P_i gets $y^{(i)}$ for $i = 1, 2$;
     (let $D = (A^{(1)})^{\odot b^{(2)}} \odot \mathsf{Enc}_{\mathsf{pk}}(-y^{(2)})$ be the ciphertext computed and sent by P_2 in this Mult and let $R = \mathsf{Com}_{\mathsf{ck}}(-y^{(2)})$ be the commitment computed and send by P_2 during the corresponding Π_{ZKPoCM}, see Section 4.1)
   - P_2 invokes $\mathsf{Mult}(b^{(1)}, B^{(1)}, a^{(2)}, A^{(2)})$, P_i gets $z^{(i)}$ for $i = 1, 2$;
     (let $D' = (B^{(1)})^{\odot a^{(2)}} \odot \mathsf{Enc}_{\mathsf{pk}}(-z^{(2)})$ be the ciphertext computed and sent by P_2 in this Mult and let $R' = \mathsf{Com}_{\mathsf{ck}}(-z^{(2)})$ be the commitment computed and send by P_2 during the corresponding Π_{ZKPoCM}, see Section 4.1)
   - For $j = 1, 2$, P_j sets $c^{(j)} = a^{(j)} \cdot b^{(j)} + y^{(j)} + z^{(j)} \mod 2^{k+s}$.
3. *Authentication:*
   - P_1 computes $\tilde{C}^{(1)} = \mathsf{Enc}_{\mathsf{pk}}(a^{(1)}b^{(1)})$ and P_2 computes $\tilde{C}^{(2)} = \mathsf{Com}_{\mathsf{ck}}(a^{(2)}b^{(2)})$; for $j = 1, 2$, P_j sends $\tilde{C}^{(j)}$ to the other party and invokes Π_{ZKPoMCV} playing the role of the prover with public input $(A^{(j)}, B^{(j)}, \tilde{C}^{(j)})$. If the ZK proofs do not abort, P_2 computes $C^{(1)} = \tilde{C}^{(1)} \odot D \odot D'$ and P_1 computes $C^{(2)} = \tilde{C}^{(2)} \odot^{-1} R \odot^{-1} R'$;
   - P_2 invokes $\mathsf{Mult}(c^{(1)}, C^{(1)}, \alpha^{(2)}, \Delta_2)$, P_i gets $y^{(i)}$ for $i = 1, 2$;
   - P_2 invokes $\mathsf{Mult}(\alpha^{(1)}, \Delta_1, c^{(2)}, C^{(2)})$, P_i gets $z^{(i)}$ for $i = 1, 2$;
   - For $j = 1, 2$, P_j sets $m^{(j)}(c) = c^{(j)} \cdot \alpha^{(j)} + y^{(j)} + z^{(j)} \mod 2^{k+s}$ and store $(c^{(j)}, m^{(j)}(c))$ as its share of $[c]$ $(c = a \cdot b \mod 2^{k+s})$;

Fig. 4. Triple generation in the preprocessing.

Theorem 1. *Assume that the underlying encryption scheme and commitment scheme satisfy the definitions in Sect. 2. Then, protocol Π_{Offline} implements $\mathcal{F}_{\mathsf{Offline}}$ with computational security against any static active adversary in the $(\mathcal{F}_{\mathsf{KeyGen}}, \mathcal{F}_{\mathsf{Rand}})$-hybrid model.*

Proof. We use the variant of the UC model where the environment $\mathcal{Z}$ plays the role of both the distinguisher and the adversary. The environment always chooses the input for the honest player and gets its output when the execution is done. Moreover, in the protocol execution $\mathcal{Z}$ corrupts P_i ($i = 1$ or $i = 2$) and takes control of its actions (*i.e.* $\mathcal{Z}$ decides the messages sent by P_i and reads the message received by this party). We argue about UC security, defining a simulator $\mathcal{S}_i$ that interacts with $\mathcal{Z}$ and the functionality $\mathcal{F}_{\mathsf{Offline}}$ and simulates the view of $\mathcal{Z}$ when attacking the protocol execution. The simulator $\mathcal{S}_i$ has the power of choosing the input that P_i sends to $\mathcal{F}_{\mathsf{Offline}}$ and getting its output. In Figs. 5 and 6 we define $\mathcal{S}_1$ and $\mathcal{S}_2$, respectively. The simulator $\mathcal{S}_i$ behaves as an honest party P_{3-i} running the protocol with the environment $\mathcal{Z}$ controlling the corrupted party. Here we show that a poly-time environment $\mathcal{Z}$ can not distinguish between the real view (*i.e.*, the view in the execution of the protocol) and an ideal view (*i.e.* the view in the interaction with the simulator).

Case $i = 1$ (P_1 is corrupted). We will argue now that the existence of a poly-time environment $\mathcal{Z}$ that distinguishes a real-view from an ideal one contradicts the key-indistinguishability property of the underlying commitment scheme. More in details, assume that there exists a $\mathcal{Z}$ that can distinguish between a real view and an ideal one with significant probability ϵ. We construct a distinguisher D that given a commitment key ck^* produces a *view* of the same form as what $\mathcal{Z}$ sees and with the following property: D uniformly chooses a bit b, if ck^* is a standard key, then *view* is an ideal-view when $b = 1$ and *view* is an real-view when $b = 0$; if ck^* is lossy, then *view* generated when $b = 0$ and *view* generated when $b = 1$ are statistically indistinguishable. The *view* produced by D is given to $\mathcal{Z}$ that outputs a bit b' (*i.e.*, $b' = 0$ means protocol execution and $b' = 1$ means simulated execution); if $b' = b$, D outputs "standard key", otherwise it outputs "lossy key". It is easy to see that D wins with probability close to $\epsilon/2$. We define D as follow.

On input ck^*, D generates $(\mathsf{sk}, \mathsf{pk})$ using Gen, initializes a local copy of $\mathcal{Z}$, sends ck^* and $(\mathsf{sk}, \mathsf{pk})$ to $\mathcal{Z}$ and starts executing the protocol Π_{Offline} where $\mathcal{Z}$ controls party P_1 and D plays P_2. The distinguisher D samples a bit $b \leftarrow \{0,1\}$. If $b = 1$, D plays P_2 running the same instruction written for the simulator $\mathcal{S}_1$. D completes *view* choosing the outputs for P_2 as $\mathcal{F}_{\mathsf{Offline}}$ would do. If $b = 0$, D follows the instructions for an honest P_2 in the protocol Π_{Offline} and P_2's outputs in *view* are the values used in this execution. By construction, if ck^* is a standard key, then the view produced by D corresponds to a real-view if $b = 0$, and to an ideal-view if $b = 1$. On the other hand, if ck^* is a lossy key, then in any view each commitment is statistically indistinguishable from a commitment to zero and the messages produced as prover in Π_{ZKPoCM} are statistically indistinguishable because they can be simulated by the ZK simulator (unconditional zero-knowledge property, special case of Theorem 3). The same holds for Π_{ZKPoMCV} (the messages produced as prover in Π_{ZKPoMCV} are statistically indistinguishable because of the unconditional zero-knowledge property, refer to Sect. 4.2). Moreover, in any view each ciphertext of the form $C = C_1^{\odot b} \odot \mathsf{Enc}_{\mathsf{pk}}(r)$ is statistically indistinguishable to a fresh encryption of a random message (circuit privacy). Therefore the view produced by D when $b = 0$ is statistically close to the one produced when $b = 1$.

The simulator $\mathcal{S}_1$ is defined by the following instructions:

- Simulating the initialize command:
  1. Simulation of the call to $\mathcal{F}_{\mathsf{KeyGen}}$: $\mathcal{S}_1$ runs $\mathsf{Gen}(1^\lambda, k + 2s)$, $\mathsf{cGen}(1^\lambda, k + 2s)$ and gets $(\mathsf{sk}, \mathsf{pk})$ and ck. $\mathcal{S}_1$ sends $\mathsf{pk}, \mathsf{sk}, \mathsf{ck}$ to $\mathcal{Z}$.
  2. $\mathcal{S}_1$ receives Δ'_1 from $\mathcal{Z}$, computes $\alpha'^{(1)} = \mathsf{Dec}_{\mathsf{sk}}(\Delta'_1)$ and sends $(\mathsf{Init}, \alpha'^{(1)})$ to $\mathcal{F}_{\mathsf{Offline}}$.
  3. The simulator behaves as an honest P_2 in the protocol Π_{Offline}: $\mathcal{S}_1$ samples $\alpha'^{(2)} \leftarrow \mathbb{Z}_{2^{k+s}}$ and sends $\Delta'_2 = \mathsf{Com}_{\mathsf{ck}}(\alpha'^{(2)})$ to $\mathcal{Z}$.

- Simulating the (Single, P_1) command:
  1. $\mathcal{S}_1$ receives $R' \in \mathcal{C}$ from $\mathcal{Z}$ and computes $r' = \mathsf{Dec}_{\mathsf{sk}}(R')$.
  2. The simulator behaves as an honest P_2 in the sub-protocol $\mathsf{Mult}(r', R', \alpha'^{(2)}, \Delta'_2)$: $\mathcal{S}_1$ samples $\tilde{r}' \leftarrow \mathbb{Z}_{2^{k+2s}}$, computes $C' = R'^{\odot \alpha'^{(2)}} \odot \mathsf{Enc}_{\mathsf{pk}}(\tilde{r}')$ and sends C' to $\mathcal{Z}$. Then the simulator behaves as an honest prover in the protocol Π_{ZKPoCM} with private input $(\alpha'^{(2)}, \tilde{r}' \bmod 2^{k+s})$ and common input C', R', Δ'_2 (the simulator also simulates $\mathcal{F}_{\mathsf{Rand}}$). If there is no abort, the simulator sends r' to $\mathcal{F}_{\mathsf{Offline}}$.

- Simulating the (Single, P_2) command:
  1. The simulator behaves as an honest P_2 in the protocol Π_{Offline}: $\mathcal{S}_1$ samples $r' \leftarrow \mathbb{Z}_{2^{k+s}}$ and sends $R' = \mathsf{Com}_{\mathsf{ck}}(r')$ to $\mathcal{Z}$.
  2. The simulator behaves as an honest P_2 in the sub-protocol $\mathsf{Mult}(\alpha'^{(1)}, \Delta'_1, r', R')$: $\mathcal{S}_1$ samples $\tilde{r}' \leftarrow \mathbb{Z}_{2^{k+2s}}$, computes $C' = \Delta_1'^{\odot r'} \odot \mathsf{Enc}_{\mathsf{pk}}(\tilde{r}')$ and sends C' to $\mathcal{Z}$. Then the simulator behaves as an honest prover in the protocol Π_{ZKPoCM} with private input $(r', \tilde{r}' \bmod 2^{k+s})$ and common input C', R', Δ'_1.

- Simulating the Single command:
  1. The same as before in (Single, P_1) to extract $(1, r'^{(1)})$ and emulating an honest P_2 in (Single, P_2) to generate $(2, r'^{(2)})$.

- Simulating the Triple command:
  1. The same as in Single to extract $a'^{(1)}$ and $b'^{(1)}$, and emulating an honest P_2 to generate $a'^{(2)}$ and $b'^{(2)}$.
  2. In any invocation of the sub-protocols Mult and Π_{ZKPoMCV}, the simulator behaves as an honest P_2.
  3. If the ZK-proofs do not fail, $\mathcal{S}_1$ sends $a'^{(1)}$ and $b'^{(1)}$ to $\mathcal{F}_{\mathsf{Offline}}$.

Fig. 5. Simulator for a corrupted P_1 in the Π_{Offline} protocol.

Case $i = 2$ (P_2 is corrupted). The rationale is the same as in the previous case: we show that a poly-time environment $\mathcal{Z}$ that distinguishes a real view from an ideal one can be used to construct a distinguisher D that contradicts the key-indistinguishability property of the underlying encryption scheme. We define D as follow.

The simulator $\mathcal{S}_2$ is defined by the following instructions:

- Simulating the initialize command:
    1. Simulation of the call to $\mathcal{F}_{\mathsf{KeyGen}}$: $\mathcal{S}_2$ runs $\mathsf{Gen}(1^\lambda, k + 2s)$, $\mathsf{cGen}(1^\lambda, k + 2s)$ and it gets $(\mathsf{sk}, \mathsf{pk})$ and (ck, t_X). $\mathcal{S}_2$ sends pk, ck to $\mathcal{Z}$ and stores the trapdoor t_X.
    2. The simulator behaves as an honest P_1 in the protocol Π_{Offline}: $\mathcal{S}_2$ samples $\alpha'^{(1)} \leftarrow \mathbb{Z}_{2^{k+s}}$, sends $\Delta'_1 = \mathsf{Enc}_{\mathsf{pk}}(\alpha'^{(1)})$ to $\mathcal{Z}$.
    3. $\mathcal{S}_2$ receives Δ'_2 from $\mathcal{Z}$, extracts $\alpha'^{(2)}$ from Δ'_2 using t_X and sends $(\mathsf{Init}, \alpha'^{(2)})$ to $\mathcal{F}_{\mathsf{Offline}}$.

- Simulating the (Single, P_1) command:
    1. The simulator behaves as an honest P_1 in the protocol Π_{Offline}: $\mathcal{S}_2$ samples $r' \leftarrow \mathbb{Z}_{2^{k+s}}$, sends $R' = \mathsf{Enc}_{\mathsf{pk}}(r')$ to $\mathcal{Z}$.
    2. Simulation of the sub-protocol $\mathsf{Mult}(r', R', \alpha'^{(2)}, \Delta'_2)$: $\mathcal{S}_2$ receives C' and behaves as an honest verifier in the protocol Π_{ZKPoCM} on public input (R', Δ'_2, C') ($\mathcal{S}_2$ simulates $\mathcal{F}_{\mathsf{Rand}}$ too). If the proof is accepted, the simulator computes $y'^{(2)} = r' \cdot \alpha'^{(2)} - \mathsf{Dec}_{\mathsf{sk}}(C') \bmod 2^{k+s}$ and sends $(\mathsf{Single}, P_2, y'^{(2)})$ to $\mathcal{F}_{\mathsf{Offline}}$.

- Simulating the (Single, P_2) command:
    1. $\mathcal{S}_2$ receives R' from $\mathcal{Z}$ and extracts r' from R' using t_X;
    2. Simulation of the sub-protocol $\mathsf{Mult}(\alpha'^{(1)}, \Delta'_1, r, R')$: $\mathcal{S}_2$ receives C' and behaves as an honest verifier in the protocol Π_{ZKPoCM} on common input (Δ'_1, R', C'). If the proof is accepted, $\mathcal{S}_2$ computes $y'^{(2)} = r' \cdot \alpha'^{(1)} - \mathsf{Dec}_{\mathsf{sk}}(C') \bmod 2^{k+s}$ and sends $(\mathsf{Single}, P_2, r', y'^{(2)})$ to $\mathcal{F}_{\mathsf{Offline}}$.

- Simulating the Single command:
    1. The same as before in (Single, P_1) and (Single, P_2) to extract $(2, r'^{(2)}, m^{(2)}(r'))$.

- Simulating the Triple command:
    1. The same as in Single to extract $(a'^{(2)}, m^{(2)}(a'))$ and $(b'^{(2)}, m^{(2)}(b'))$. In a similar way, the simulator extracts the environment's shares $(c'^{(2)}, m^{(2)}(c'))$ from the ciphertexts received in the multiplication and the authentication step.
    2. In any invocation of the sub-protocol Π_{ZKPoMCV}, the simulator behaves as an honest P_1.
    3. If the ZK-proofs do not fail, $\mathcal{S}_2$ sends the extracted values to $\mathcal{F}_{\mathsf{Offline}}$.

Fig. 6. Simulator for a corrupted P_2 in the Π_{Offline} protocol.

On input pk^*, D generates (ck, t_X) using cGen, initializes a copy of $\mathcal{Z}$, sends pk^* and ck to $\mathcal{Z}$ and starts executing the protocol Π_{Offline} where $\mathcal{Z}$ controls party P_2 and D plays P_1. The distinguisher D samples a bit $b \leftarrow \{0, 1\}$. If $b = 1$, D plays P_1 running the same instruction written for the simulator $\mathcal{S}_2$ and completes *view* choosing the outputs for P_1 as $\mathcal{F}_{\mathsf{Offline}}$ would do. If $b = 0$, D follows the instructions for an honest P_1 in the protocol. However, in the Mult sub-protocol, when D receives the ciphertext C, it can not decrypt because it does not have the secret key. On the other hand, D is allowed to rewind its copy of $\mathcal{Z}$ and therefore it can use the knowledge extractor of protocol Π_{ZKPoCM} (Theorem 4). For example, if the proof Π_{ZKPoCM} is run to check $C = \mathsf{Enc}_{\mathsf{pk}}(a)^{\odot \tilde{b}} \odot \mathsf{Enc}_{\mathsf{pk}}(-\tilde{r})$, D gets from the knowledge extractor $b = \tilde{b} \bmod 2^{k+s}$ and $r = \tilde{r} \bmod 2^{k+s}$ and it can compute its share as $y = a \cdot b - r \bmod 2^{k+s}$, and then continues the protocol as if it had decrypted. Again, by construction, if pk^* is a standard key, then the view produced by D corresponds (statistically) to a real-view if $b = 0$, and to an ideal-view if $b = 1$. On the other hand, if pk^* is a lossy key, the ciphertexts contained in the two views are statistically indistinguishable by definition of lossy key. And, as in case $i = 1$, the messages produced as prover in Π_{ZKPoMCV} (and contained in the two views) are statistically indistinguishable because of the unconditional zero-knowledge property.

3.1 On the Impossibility of Enhanced-CPA Security in $\mathbb{Z}_{2^n}$: Comparing with Overdrive Offline Phase

Recently Keller et al. [19] constructed an n-party MPC protocol in the preprocessing model, where the online phase goes as the one in the SPDZ protocol, while the offline is base on a 2-party multiplication protocol similar to the one used in our paper. However, in [19] the ZK proof of correct multiplication is replaced by a postponed check to verify the correctness of the output (similar to the "SPDZ sacrifice"). The possibility of a selective failure attack that this approach introduces is avoided assuming that the underlying encryption scheme satisfies a stronger notion of security called *enhanced CPA*. This notion is recalled in the full version of this paper. Here we prove that, somewhat surprisingly, this notion cannot be achieved by encryption schemes that are linearly homomorphic over rings of the form $\mathbb{Z}_{2^n}$. More precisely, we show that any encryption scheme that is both linearly homomorphic and whose message space is $\mathbb{Z}_{2^n}$ cannot satisfy enhanced CPA security.

Theorem 2. *Let* $(\mathsf{Gen}, \mathsf{Enc}, \mathsf{Dec})$ *be an additive encryption scheme whose message space is* $\mathbb{Z}_{2^n}$ *(see Sect. 2.2), then the scheme cannot achieve enhanced CPA security (see the full version of this paper for further details).*

Proof. We prove the theorem by showing an efficient adversary $\mathcal{A}$ that successfully wins in the enhanced CPA-security game, with non negligible advantage. $\mathcal{A}$ works as follows. It receives from the challenger both the public key pk and the encryption $C = \mathsf{Enc}_{\mathsf{pk}}(m)$ of a random message $m \in \mathbb{Z}_{2^n}$. Using the homomorphic properties of the scheme, $\mathcal{A}$ computes a new ciphertext C' that encrypts the original message "shifted" by $n - 1$ positions to the left. Notice that this only amounts at (homomorphically) multiplying the plaintext by the constant 2^{n-1} (*i.e.*, $C' = C^{\odot 2^{n-1}} = \mathsf{Enc}_{\mathsf{pk}}(2^{n-1} \cdot m)$). $\mathcal{A}$ proceeds by querying the oracle on input C': if the answer is yes $\mathcal{A}$ learns that the least significant bit (lsb) of m is 0; otherwise it learns that it is 1. Now, when the challenger sends out the test message m', $\mathcal{A}$ checks if $\mathsf{lsb}(m') \neq \mathsf{lsb}(m)$ and outputs 1 if this is the case (and 0 otherwise). It is easy to check that such an adversary manages to guess the secret bit chosen by the challenger much better than at random (*i.e.* the winning probability for $\mathcal{A}$ is $1/4$).

4   Joye-Libert Cryptosystem and Companion Protocols

In this section we recall the Joye-Libert (JL) cryptosystem [5,17], we refer to the original papers for details missing here.

$\mathsf{Gen}(1^\lambda, n)$: The algorithm starts by choosing two random λ-bit primes p, q, satisfying the following constraints $p \equiv 1 \bmod 2^n$ and $q \equiv 3 \bmod 4$. For simplicity, we let $p = 2^n p' + 1$ and $q = 2q' + 1$ where both p' and q' are primes.[9] Let g be a random generator of both $\mathbb{Z}_p^*$ and $\mathbb{Z}_q^*$, $N = pq$, and $\mu = p'$. The public key is $\mathsf{pk} = (g, n, N)$ and the secret key is $\mathsf{sk} = \mu$.

The message space is $\mathcal{M} = \{0,1\}^n$ while the ciphertext space $\mathcal{C}$ is the subset of $\mathbb{Z}_N^*$ with Jacobi symbol 1. We note that membership in $\mathcal{C}$ can be efficiently and publicly checked by computing the Jacobi symbol $\left(\frac{C}{N}\right)$ of a purposed ciphertext C.

$\mathsf{Enc}_{\mathsf{pk}}(m)$: Choose a random $x \in \mathbb{Z}_N^*$ and output $C = g^m x^{2^n} \bmod N$. With a slight abuse of notation we write $\mathsf{Enc}_{\mathsf{pk}}(m; x)$ to specify the randomness used.

$\mathsf{Dec}_{\mathsf{sk}}(C)$: First, compute $d = C^\mu \bmod p$ and then retrieve m bit by bit, as follows. Notice that $d = (g^\mu)^m \bmod p$ where g^μ is an element of order 2^n in $\mathbb{Z}_p^*$. One can compute the least significant bit m_0 of $m = m_{n-1}...m_0$ by computing $d^{2^{n-1}} \bmod p$. Indeed, this is 1 if and only if $m_0 = 0$. Knowing $m_{i-1}...m_0$ one computes m_i as follows: set $m_i = 0$ if and only if

$$\left(d/(g^{\mu(m_{i-1}...m_0)})\right)^{2^{n-i-1}} = 1 \bmod p$$

If one is interested in retrieving only the lowest $n' < n$ bits of the message, the above mechanism can simply stop at the n'-th step. We can use this optimization in our application where $n = k + 2s$ and one is supposed to decrypt and then take the result mod 2^{k+s}. It is worthy to note that the decryption cost is linear in the message bit-size: for the considered settings it can be even faster than a Paillier cryptosystem as confirmed by experiments in Sect. 5. As shown in [5,17], the scheme is linearly homomorphic over $\mathbb{Z}_{2^n}$.

Security. As shown in [5,17], the JL scheme is semantically secure under the n-quadratic residuosity (n-QR) assumption (that is like the standard quadratic residuosity for a $p \equiv 1 \bmod 2^n$). Moreover, the security analysis shows that the scheme has the nice property of lossy public keys that we require in our applications (see Sect. 2.2). The "lossy" key generation algorithm Gen consists into sampling g as a 2^n-residue, i.e., $g \leftarrow h^{2^n}$ for a random $h \in \mathbb{Z}_N^*$. Indistinguishability of lossy keys from real ones is proven in [5,17]. Finally, observe

---

[9] It is not strictly necessary that p' and q' are both primes: nevertheless for security each of them should contain a big enough prime factor.

that for JL circuit privacy holds whenever one adds a fresh encryption of 0 after an homomorphic computation (or equivalently, as used in our applications, the homomorphic computation involves an addition of a freshly generated cipher-text).

JL as a Commitment Scheme. It is straightforward to see that the JL cryptosystem is a perfectly binding and computationally hiding commitment scheme for messages in $\mathbb{Z}_{2^n}$: opening simply consists into revealing the randomness used to generate a ciphertext. Such commitments are extractable using an X-trapdoor that is the decryption key. Moreover, the lossy keys property immediately yields that JL is also a "mixed" commitment. Indeed, when generating the public key in lossy mode, commitments become computationally binding and perfectly hiding.

Here we show that in lossy mode, the commitment is also equivocable. This result is of independent interest since we do not use equivocation in our protocols.

First, recall that a key in equivocation mode is a $g = h^{2^n}$ for a random $h \in \mathbb{Z}_N^*$ that is stored as the equivocation trapdoor. Given h one can equivocate a commitment to m with randomness r to an arbitrary m' as follows. Let $C = g^m r^{2^n} \bmod N = (h^m r)^{2^n} \bmod N$ and let $m' = m + \alpha$ over integers; we can rewrite the previous equation as $(h^{m+\alpha-\alpha} r)^{2^n} \bmod N = g^{m'} (h^{-\alpha} r)^{2^n} \bmod N$ and thus setting $r' = h^{-\alpha} r \bmod N$ does the job.

Companion Protocols. In the next section we propose an HVZK protocol for proving correct multiplication relations. Then we show a protocol for proving (partial) knowledge of plaintexts of JL ciphertexts. This is not used in our 2PC protocol but is of independent interest and is given in the full version of this paper.

4.1   Zero-Knowledge Proof of Correct Multiplication

Here we propose an instantiation of the protocol Π_{ZKPoCM}. For $i = 1, 2$, let $\mathsf{pk}_i = (g_i, n, N_i)$ be a JL public key (both working with the same message space) and let $\mathcal{C}_i$ be the respective ciphertext spaces. In Fig. 7 we describe a Σ-protocol for the NP relation $\mathcal{R}' \subseteq (\mathbb{Z}_{2^{n-s}})^2 \times \mathcal{C}_1^2 \times \mathcal{C}_2$:

$$\mathcal{R}' = \{((b,r),(A,C,B)) \mid \exists (\tilde{b},\tilde{r}) \in (\mathbb{Z}_{2^n})^2, (x_r,x_b) \in \mathbb{Z}_{N_1}^* \times \mathbb{Z}_{N_2}^* \text{ s.t.}$$
$$B = \mathsf{Enc}_{\mathsf{pk}_2}(\tilde{b}, x_b), \ C = A^{\odot \tilde{b}} \odot \mathsf{Enc}_{\mathsf{pk}_1}(\tilde{r}, x_r), \ b = \tilde{b} \bmod 2^{n-s}, \ r = \tilde{r} \bmod 2^{n-s}\}.$$

This proof system allows one to prove knowledge of the least $n - s$ significant bits of the messages $\tilde{b}, \tilde{r}$ used to define the ciphertext C.

Intuitively, the reason why we do not prove knowledge of the entire messages is that, for technical reasons related to the fact that not all messages are invertible, this is actually not possible. Interestingly enough, however, if we set challenges to be integers of s bits, then we can recover all but the s most significant bits. This means that if one carefully encrypts messages that are small enough (e.g., all the s most significant bits are zero), then one can actually recover the full message.

In what follows we prove that the protocol Π_{ZKPoCM} guarantees correctness, (honest verifier) zero knowledge and special soundness.

Completeness. This can be seen by inspection of the protocol.

Protocol Π_{ZKPoCM}

Common input for prover and verifier: two JL public keys $\mathsf{pk}_i = (g_i, n, N_i)$, for $i = 1, 2$, and JL ciphertexts $A, C \in \mathcal{C}_1$ and $B \in \mathcal{C}_2$.
Private input for the prover: $\tilde{b}, \tilde{r} \in \mathbb{Z}_{2^n}$ and $(x_r, x_b) \in \mathbb{Z}_{N_1}^* \times \mathbb{Z}_{N_2}^*$ such that $B = \mathsf{Enc}_{\mathsf{pk}_2}(\tilde{b}, x_b)$ and $C = A^{\odot \tilde{b}} \odot \mathsf{Enc}_{\mathsf{pk}_1}(\tilde{r}, x_r)$.

1. P samples $\beta \in \mathbb{Z}_{N_2}^*$ and computes $R = \mathsf{Enc}_{\mathsf{pk}_2}(\tilde{r}, \beta) = g_2^{\tilde{r}} \beta^{2^n} \bmod N_2$. Also it samples $x, y \leftarrow \mathbb{Z}_{2^n}$ and $v \leftarrow \mathbb{Z}_{N_1}^*, \gamma_x, \gamma_y \leftarrow \mathbb{Z}_{N_2}^*$ and computes: $D = A^x g_1^y v^{2^n} \bmod N_1$, $X = g_2^x \gamma_x^{2^n} \bmod N_2$, $Y = g_2^y \gamma_y^{2^n} \bmod N_2$. It sends R, D, X, Y to the verifier.
2. The verifier sends back[a] $e \leftarrow \mathbb{Z}_{2^s}$.
3. The prover computes $z_b = x + e\tilde{b} \bmod 2^n$, $z_r = y + e\tilde{r} \bmod 2^n$ and q_b, q_r such that $q_b 2^n = x + e\tilde{b} - z_b$ and $q_r 2^n = y + e\tilde{r} - z_r$, computes $\delta_b = \gamma_x x_b^e g_2^{q_b} \bmod N_2, \delta_r = \gamma_y \beta^e g_2^{q_r} \bmod N_2, \omega = A^{q_b} x_r^e g_1^{q_r} v \bmod N_1$, and sends to the verifier $z_b, z_r, \delta_b, \delta_r, \omega$.
4. The verifier accepts if and only if all the following checks pass
   (a) $DC^e = A^{z_b} \mathsf{Enc}_{\mathsf{pk}_1}(z_r, \omega)$
   (b) $XB^e = g_2^{z_b} \delta_b^{2^n} \bmod N_2 = \mathsf{Enc}_{\mathsf{pk}_2}(z_b, \delta_b)$
   (c) $YR^e = g_2^{z_r} \delta_r^{2^n} \bmod N_2 = \mathsf{Enc}_{\mathsf{pk}_2}(z_r, \delta_r)$
   and if $A, C, D \in \mathcal{C}_1$ and $B, R, X, Y \in \mathcal{C}_2$ hold.

---

[a] For the sake of simplicity, $\mathcal{F}_{\mathsf{Rand}}$ is used to generate the challenge e when Π_{ZKPoCM} is used as sub-protocol of Π_{Offline}.

Fig. 7. Proof of correct multiplication for JL-encryptions

Theorem 3 (Honest-Verifier Zero-Knowledge). *If JL is a semantically secure public key encryption, then the protocol in Fig. 7 is honest-verifier zero-knowledge. Furthermore, if in the protocol the public key pk_2 is generated in lossy mode, then honest-verifier zero-knowledge holds unconditionally.*

Proof. First, we describe a simulator that works as follows. Given a challenge e and JL ciphertexts A, B, C: sample $z_b, z_r \leftarrow \mathbb{Z}_{2^n}$, $R \leftarrow \mathcal{C}_2$, $\delta_b, \delta_r \leftarrow \mathbb{Z}_{N_2}^*$, $\omega \leftarrow \mathbb{Z}_{N_1}^*$, and set $D = A^{z_b} g_1^{z_r} \omega^{2^n} C^{-e} \bmod N_1$, $X = g_2^{z_b} \delta_b^{2^n} B^{-e} \bmod N_2$ and $Y = g_2^{z_r} \delta_r^{2^n} R^{-e} \bmod N_2$.

We claim that the simulated proof is computationally indistinguishable from the real one under the assumption that JL is semantically secure. The only (information-theoretic) difference between the real proof and the simulated one is that in the simulation R is the encryption of a random message, not the same $\tilde{r}$ known by the honest prover. This however is not noticeable to a computationally-bounded distinguisher. More formally, this can be argued by defining an hybrid simulator that takes as input $\tilde{r}$ and computes the proof as the simulator above with the only difference that R is a fresh encryption of $\tilde{r}$. The proofs created by this hybrid simulator are computationally indistinguishable from the ones created by the ZK simulator under the assumption that JL (over public key pk_2) is semantic secure. As a next step, one must argue that the proofs created by this hybrid simulator and the ones of the honest prover are distributed identically. This can be verified by inspection.

Finally, when pk_2 is lossy, then we can skip the computational step of the proof since, even if R is sampled randomly, by the lossy property is distributed identically to a lossy encryption of $\tilde{r}$.

Theorem 4 (Special Soundness). *The protocol in Fig. 7 has special soundness.*

Proof. We prove that a prover cannot succeed in proving a wrong statement unless with negligible probability. We prove this as follows.

Assume that, for the same values used in steps 1 and 2 of the protocol, a prover manages to successfully answer for a non negligible fraction of challenges e. This means that there exist e_1, e_2, $e_1 \neq e_2$ (and wlog $e_1 > e_2$) such that

1. $C^{\Delta e = e_1 - e_2} = A^{\Delta z_b = z_{b1} - z_{b2}} \mathsf{Enc}(\Delta z_r = z_{r1} - z_{r2}, \omega/\omega')$
2. $B^{\Delta e} = g_2^{\Delta z_b} (\delta_b/\delta_b')^{2^n} \bmod N_2$
3. $R^{\Delta e} = g_2^{\Delta z_r} (\delta_r/\delta_r')^{2^n} \bmod N_2$

We distinguish between 2 cases, depending on whether $\gcd(\Delta e, 2^n) = 1$ or not.

Case $\gcd(\Delta e, 2^n) = 1$. In this case one can easily extract a full $\tilde{b} \in \mathbb{Z}_{2^n}$ as $\tilde{b} = \Delta z_b/\Delta e \bmod 2^n$ and $\tilde{r} \in \mathbb{Z}_{2^n}$ as $\tilde{r} = \Delta z_r/\Delta e \bmod 2^n$.

Case $\gcd(\Delta e, 2^n) \neq 1$. In this case let $\gcd(\Delta e, 2^n) = 2^t$ for some $t \leq s$ (the latter holds because $e_1, e_2 \in \mathbb{Z}_{2^s}$). We can rewrite the three equations above as follows

  1. $C^{2^t e'} = A^{\Delta z_b} \mathsf{Enc}(\Delta z_r, \omega/\omega')$
  2. $B^{2^t e'} = g_2^{\Delta z_b} (\delta_b/\delta_b')^{2^n} \bmod N_2$
  3. $R^{2^t e'} = g_2^{\Delta z_r} (\delta_r/\delta_r')^{2^n} \bmod N_2$

From now on let us focus on the second equation above (the same argument will trivially hold for the third equation). First let d be the inverse of $e' \bmod 2^n$. Exponentiating both sides of the equation to d leads to the following $B^{2^t} = g_2^{d \Delta z_b} \left((\delta_b/\delta_b')^d \right)^{2^n} \bmod N_2$. Notice that since g_2 is *not* a quadratic residue, the integer $d\Delta z_b$ must be even. Let t' be the largest integer such that $2^{t'}$ divides

$d\Delta z_b$, i.e., $d\Delta z_b = 2^{t'} d'$ for some odd number d'. Clearly $t' \leq n$. We can rewrite the equation as

$$B^{2^t} = g_2^{2^{t'} d'} \left((\delta_b/\delta_b')^d \right)^{2^n} \mod N_2 \tag{1}$$

We distinguish two cases: (a) $t > t'$ and (b) $t \leq t'$.

Case (a) $t > t'$: If (1) holds and $B^{2^{t-t'}} / (g_2^{d'} \left((\delta_b/\delta_b')^d \right)^{2^{n-t'}}) \mod N_2 \notin \{-1, 1\}$, then we can immediately factor N_2 since we found a nontrivial root of unity. Given the factorization of N_2 extracting $\tilde{b}$ from B is possible using decryption. Otherwise, we have that

$$B^{2^{t-t'}} = u \cdot g_2^{d'} \left((\delta_b/\delta_b')^d \right)^{2^{n-t'}} \mod N_2 \tag{2}$$

for $u = 1$ or $u = -1$. We show that neither of the cases can occur. If $u = 1$, the equality (2) is not possible because d' is odd and g_2 is not a quadratic residue by construction. If $u = -1$, (2) is not possible because in this group setting ($p \equiv 1 \mod 2^n$ and $q \equiv 3 \mod 4$) -1 has Jabobi symbol -1 in $\mathbb{Z}_{N_2}^*$ (see [5, Theorem 1]) whereas all the other terms of the equation have Jacobi symbol 1. This concludes case (a).

Case (b) $t \leq t'$: Let $\tilde{b} \in \mathbb{Z}_{2^n}$ be the integer encrypted in B. By the homomorphic property of JL we have that B^{2^t} is a ciphertext that encrypts $2^t \tilde{b} \mod 2^n = 2^t (\tilde{b} \mod 2^{n-t}) = 2^t b_t$.

From Eq. (1), we can write B^{2^t} as an encryption of $2^{t'} d'$. Combined with the previous observation we have $2^t (\tilde{b} \mod 2^{n-t}) = 2^{t'} d'$ and using the fact that $t \leq t'$ we obtain that $b_t = \tilde{b} \mod 2^{n-t} = 2^{t'-t} d' = d\Delta z_b 2^{-t}$. This shows that $d\Delta z_b 2^{-t} \in \mathbb{Z}_{2^{n-t}}$ is the $(n-t)$-bit portion of the message encrypted in B. Finally, since $t \leq s$ we can set $b = (d\Delta z_b 2^{-t}) \mod 2^{n-s}$. This concludes the proof about extractability of b.

By applying exactly the same argument above to R and the third verification equation, we can extract $r \in \mathbb{Z}_{2^{n-s}}$ as $r = (d\Delta z_r 2^{-t}) \mod 2^{n-s}$.

Towards concluding the proof, let us recall that the relation requires

$$B = \mathsf{Enc}_{\mathsf{pk}_2}(\tilde{b}, x_b), \ C = A^{\odot \tilde{b}} \odot \mathsf{Enc}_{\mathsf{pk}_1}(\tilde{r}, x_r), \ b = \tilde{b} \mod 2^{n-s}, \ r = \tilde{r} \mod 2^{n-s}$$

We have already extracted b and r; in what follows we need to argue that they satisfy the relation above. The check about B is already satisfied. So let us focus on the remaining checks.

Let $\tilde{a}$ be the integer encrypted in A, namely let us write $A = g_1^{\tilde{a}} x_a^{2^n}$. Similarly, let $\tilde{c} \in \mathbb{Z}_{2^n}$ be the integer encrypted in C. Then showing that the extracted values satisfy the relation means to show that $\tilde{c} = \tilde{a}\tilde{b} + \tilde{r} \mod 2^n$ such that the least $n - s$ significant bits of $\tilde{b}, \tilde{r}$ are b and r respectively. More formally, this means to show that there is some q_s such that $\tilde{c}$ can be written as $a_s b + r + q_s 2^{n-s}$, for $a_s = \tilde{a} \mod 2^{n-s}$. In other words, $c_s = \tilde{c} \mod 2^{n-s} = a_s b + r \mod 2^{n-s}$.

Now let us consider the first equation. By the homomorphic property we have that C^{2^t} is a ciphertext that encrypts $c' = 2^t \tilde{c} \bmod 2^n = 2^t (\tilde{c} \bmod 2^{n-t}) = 2^t c_t$.

From the first verification equation, exponentiating both sides of the equation by $d = e'^{-1} \bmod 2^n$, we get $C^{2^t} = A^{d\Delta z_b} g_1^{d\Delta z_r} \left((\omega/\omega')^d \right)^{2^n} \bmod N_1$ and using the expression of A, we can rewrite the equation as

$$C^{2^t} = g_1^{d(\tilde{a}\Delta z_b + \Delta z_r)} \left(x_a^{d\Delta z_b} (\omega/\omega')^d \right)^{2^n} \bmod N_1$$
$$= g_1^{\tilde{a}(d\Delta z_b) + (d\Delta z_r)} \left(x_a^{d\Delta z_b} (\omega/\omega')^d \right)^{2^n} \bmod N_1$$
$$= g_1^{\tilde{\alpha}} \left(g_1^{q_\alpha} x_a^{d\Delta z_b} (\omega/\omega')^d \right)^{2^n} \bmod N_1$$

where in the last equation we used $\tilde{a}d\Delta z_b + d\Delta z_r = \tilde{\alpha} + q_\alpha 2^n$.

Thus we have that $c' = \alpha$. Notice that 2^t divides both $d\Delta z_b$ and $d\Delta z_r$ (this follows from the arguments used in the extractability of b and r), and thus by definition of $\tilde{\alpha}$, $2^t \mid \tilde{\alpha}$. In particular, $\tilde{\alpha}2^{-t} = \tilde{a}d\Delta z_b 2^{-t} + d\Delta z_r 2^{-t} - q_\alpha 2^{n-t}$.

Therefore, $c_t = c'2^{-t} = \tilde{\alpha}2^{-t} = \tilde{a}d\Delta z_b 2^{-t} + d\Delta z_r 2^{-t} - q_\alpha 2^{n-t} = \tilde{a}b_t + r_t - q_\alpha 2^{n-t} = a_t b_t + r_t + q2^{n-t}$.

If we take both sides mod 2^{n-s} (recall that $t \leq s$), we have that $c_s = \tilde{c} \bmod 2^{n-s} = a_s b + r \bmod 2^{n-s}$ as it was to be proven.

4.2 Zero-Knowledge Proof of Correct Multiplication of Two Committed (or Encrypted) Values

Here we propose an instantiation of the protocol Π_{ZKPoMCV} that allows a prover to show that she correctly performed multiplication of two committed (or encrypted) values. The protocol is given in Fig. 8. Essentially, it considers a special case of the relation supported by the protocol in the previous section in which $r = 0$ and the ciphertexts are under the same public key. This specialization allows us to simplify and optimize the resulting protocol. Let $\mathsf{pk} = (g, n, N)$ be a JL public key and $\mathcal{C}$ its corresponding ciphertext space[10]. Specifically, we give a Σ-protocol for the NP relation $\mathcal{R} \subseteq (\mathbb{Z}_{2^{n-s}}) \times \mathcal{C}^3$:

$$\mathcal{R} = \{ (b, (A, C, B)) \mid \exists \tilde{b} \in \mathbb{Z}_{2^n}, (x_r, x_b) \in (\mathbb{Z}_N^*)^2 \text{ s.t.}$$
$$B = \mathsf{Enc}_{\mathsf{pk}}(\tilde{b}, x_b), \ C = A^{\odot \tilde{b}} \odot \mathsf{Enc}_{\mathsf{pk}}(0, x_r), \ b = \tilde{b} \bmod 2^{n-s} \}.$$

As in previous protocols in this paper, this proof system allows one to prove knowledge of the least $n - s$ significant bits of the message $\tilde{b}$ used to define the ciphertext C.

Notice that correctness of the protocol Π_{ZKPoCM} can be easily inferred by inspection. Special soundness follows as a special case of Theorem 4 (when ignoring the third equation and setting $r = 0$). Honest verifier zero-knowledge also

---

[10] When Π_{ZKPoMCV} is used in the offline phase of $\mathsf{MonZ}_{2^k}\mathsf{a}$, we have $\mathsf{pk} = \mathsf{pk}_1$ if the P_1 is the prover or $\mathsf{pk} = \mathsf{pk}_2$ if P_2 is the prover ($\mathsf{pk}_1, \mathsf{pk}_2$ are the keys used in Π_{ZKPoCM}).

follows as a special case of Theorem 3. Interestingly, however, in this protocol Π_{ZKPoMCV} the zero knowledge property holds unconditionally. Recall that in the proof of Theorem 3 the only reason we needed to resort to the semantic security of JL was because of the possible difference between the ciphertext R used by the prover and the one sampled by the simulator. Since in our case there is no such a difference, there is also no difference between the real proof and the simulated one.

Protocol Π_{ZKPoMCV}

Common input for prover and verifier: A JL public key $\mathsf{pk} = (g, n, N)$, and JL commitments (ciphertexts) $A, B, C \in \mathcal{C}$.
Private input for the prover: $\tilde{b} \in \mathbb{Z}_{2^n}$ and $x_b, x_r \in \mathbb{Z}_N^*$ such that $B = \mathsf{Enc}_{\mathsf{pk}}(\tilde{b}, x_b)$ and $C = A^{\odot \tilde{b}} \odot \mathsf{Enc}_{\mathsf{pk}}(0, x_r)$.

1. P samples $x \leftarrow \mathbb{Z}_{2^n}$ and $v, \gamma_x \leftarrow \mathbb{Z}_N^*$ and computes: $D = A^x v^{2^n} \bmod N$, $X = g^x \gamma_x^{2^n} \bmod N$. It sends D, X to the verifier.
2. The verifier sends back[a] $e \leftarrow \mathbb{Z}_{2^s}$.
3. The prover computes $z_b = x + e\tilde{b} \bmod 2^n$ and q_b such that $q_b 2^n = x + e\tilde{b} - z_b$, computes
   $\delta_b = \gamma_x x_b^e g^{q_b} \bmod N$, $\omega = A^{q_b} v x_r^e \bmod N$, and sends to the verifier z_b, δ_b, ω.
4. The verifier accepts if and only if all the following checks pass
   (a) $DC^e = A^{z_b} \mathsf{Enc}_{\mathsf{pk}}(0, \omega)$
   (b) $XB^e = g^{z_b} \delta_b^{2^n} \bmod N = \mathsf{Enc}_{\mathsf{pk}}(z_b, \delta_b)$
   and if $A, B, C, D, X \in \mathcal{C}$ holds.

---

[a] Again, for the sake of simplicity, $\mathcal{F}_{\mathsf{Rand}}$ is used to generate the challenge e when Π_{ZKPoMCV} is used as sub-protocol of Π_{Offline}.

Fig. 8. Modified (simpler) version of Π_{ZKPoCM}.

5 Efficiency Analysis

Here we turn to estimate the efficiency of our preprocessing protocol with respect to SPDZ$_{2^k}$ in [9]; the online phase is essentially the same. Before entering into the details of the evaluation, in the next section we discuss a variant of our offline protocol that significantly reduces the overall bandwidth consumption at the cost of (1) explicitly requiring the random oracle heuristic, and (2) increasing the computational overhead of both players. Next, we analyze the efficiency of both the base and optimized versions.

Optimization Using Random Oracles. First, assume that P_1 knows the secret key corresponding to the encryption scheme (Gen, Enc, Dec) (as it already holds), and that P_2 is given the extraction trapdoor for the (extractable) commitment (cGen, Com). Since valid JL ciphertexts – and commitments – are both easy to recognize and easy to sample, the holder of the secret decryption key (resp. extraction trapdoor) has an alternative way to generate a couple $(m, \mathsf{Enc}(m))$ (resp. $(m, \mathsf{Com}(m))$ with m random: it first samples a random ciphertext $\mathsf{Enc}(m)$ (resp. commitment $\mathsf{Com}(m)$), and then extracts m using the secret key[11]. It is straightforward to see that these two sampling procedures (i.e., via encryption or decryption) generate the same distribution.

The related security proofs would require minor changes to the simulators $\mathcal{S}_1, \mathcal{S}_2$: for example, $\mathcal{S}_1$ in (Single, P_1) would get R' from $\mathcal{F}_{\mathsf{Rand}}$, instead of from $\mathcal{Z}$, and in (Single, P_2) it would compute r' from R' (again received from $\mathcal{F}_{\mathsf{Rand}}$) using the extraction trapdoor of the commitment, as the honest P_2 would do.

This simple idea can be used to gain in communication complexity as follows. In protocol Π_{Offline} on input (Single, $P_1, sid, ssid$), the parties can get a common $R = \mathsf{Enc}_{\mathsf{pk}}(r)$, without any communication, by simply setting $R \leftarrow H_1(\omega_1, sid, ssid)$ where ω_1 is some common auxiliary information and H_1 is a random oracle mapping into the ciphertext space of $\mathsf{Enc}_{\mathsf{pk}}$. Similarly, on input (Single, $P_2, sid, ssid$), the parties can get a common $R = \mathsf{Com}_{\mathsf{ck}}(r)$ by setting $R \leftarrow H_2(\omega_2, sid, ssid)$ (where, again, ω_2 is some common auxiliary information and H_2 is a random oracle mapping into the commitment space of $\mathsf{Com}_{\mathsf{ck}}$).

Similarly, the communication complexity of Π_{ZKPoCM} (see Sect. 4.1) can be reduced by generating X and Y using the random oracle in exactly the same way. Moreover the resulting protocols remain secure with these modifications as, all the quantities retain the same original distribution and, as proved in Sect. 4.1, the (special) soundness of Π_{ZKPoCM} holds unconditionally. The same holds for Π_{ZKPoMCV} (see Sect. 4.2): the transmission of X (an encryption of random value x) can be avoided.

Bandwidth Usage. The bandwidth of our sub-protocols depends on few parameters: the size of the generic modulus used in the JL encryption/commitment schemes denoted as $|N|$, the message bit-length k, the statistical security parameter s and the internal parameter $n = k + 2s$.

We analyze the elements exchanged between the parties. The sub-protocol Π_{ZKPoCM} in Fig. 7 sends a total of 7 elements of size $|N|$ and two of n bits. The sub-protocol Π_{ZKPoMCV} in Fig. 8 sends four elements of size $|N|$ and one of n bits. The multiplication sub-protocol Mult in Fig. 3 sends an element of size $|N|$ before an invocation of Π_{ZKPoCM}. The sub-protocols (Single, P_i) in Fig. 3 send an encryption/commitment (size $|N|$) followed by an instance of Mult; the variant Single, used to generate a shared random value unknown to all parties, runs (Single, P_1) and (Single, P_2). Finally, in Triple one invokes two times Single, four times Mult, two times Π_{ZKPoCM} and sends four encryptions/commitments

---

[11] More precisely, in order for the above idea to be any useful in our protocols, we also need to extract the randomness associated to the encryption/commitment. Luckily, this happens to be the case when using JL as underlying building block.

Table 1. Bandwidth analysis of our sub-protocols

	Π_{ZKPoCM}	Π_{ZKPoMCV}	Mult	(Single, P_i)	Single	Triple
Mon$\mathbb{Z}_{2^k}$a base	$7|N| + 2n$	$4|N| + n$	$8|N| + 2n$	$9|N| + 2n$	$18|N| + 4n$	$78|N| + 18n$
Mon$\mathbb{Z}_{2^k}$a optim.	$5|N| + 2n$	$3|N| + n$	$6|N| + 2n$	$6|N| + 2n$	$12|N| + 4n$	$56|N| + 18n$

with size $|N|$ bits[12]. In the summary on Table 1 we also consider the optimized version of our protocol discussed in Sect. 5.

For a concrete comparison we consider some significant settings, varying the available parameters, and comparing the results with data on SPD$\mathbb{Z}_{2^k}$ in [9]. For each considered computational security level $S \in \{80, 112, 128\}$, we select a proper statistical security parameter s according to the message bit-length $k \in \{32, 64, 128\}$. The size of the modulus N is selected according to recent NIST recommendations[13]. The extended comparison is reported in Table 2 with bold remarks on the best values per triple and single generation[14]. The global costs to generate a triple and a single (input sharing) in SPD$\mathbb{Z}_{2^k}$ are computed according to the formulas $2(k + 2s)(9s + 4k)$ and $(s + 1)(k + 2s)$ reported in Section 7 of [9]. For the input sharing step of our protocols we consider the cost of (Single, P_i) as a random shared value known to P_i is later used to share a secret input belonging to him .

Implementation and Computational Benchmark. We implemented the off-line phase of the base version of Mon$\mathbb{Z}_{2^k}$a[15]: it produces triples and singles that could be used in the on-line phase of SPD$\mathbb{Z}_{2^k}$. Our implementation is written in language C and uses the GNU Multiprecision Library[16] (GMP) for the MPI operations. We used two servers equipped with an Intel Xeon 8124M CPU running at 3.0 GHz: each server hosts a single thread running one of the two parties. We simulated three typical deploying scenarios: two servers connected by a common 1 Gigabit Ethernet LAN with an average latency (intended as Round Trip Time—RTT) of 0.5 ms and two servers hosted by two different data-centers connected by a fast WAN with 17 ms of latency[17] or by a very-limited WAN with 100 ms of latency and a bandwidth of 50 Mb/s.

---

[12] Similarly to the analysis in [9], we ignore the negligible costs of $\mathcal{F}_{\mathsf{Rand}}$ and of the check of the openings in Triple as it can be performed in a batch when producing many triples at once.

[13] https://keylength.com.

[14] For sake of completeness, in the border case with $S = 80$, $s = 40$ and $k = 128$, we considered a slightly larger modulus $|N| = 1160$ in order to satisfy the security constraint $k + 2s < \frac{1}{4}\log_2(N) - S$ on JL scheme from [5].

[15] The source code of our project is publicly available at: https://github.com/crypto-unict/monza-mpc.

[16] https://gmplib.org.

[17] We considered the actual ping delay between Amazon and Google data-centers.

Table 2. Bandwidth comparison with SPDZ$_{2^k}$ (costs in kbit)

S	$|N|$	k	s	SPDZ$_{2^k}$		MonZ$_{2^k}$a base		MonZ$_{2^k}$a optim.	
				triple	input	triple	input	triple	input
80	1024	32	32	79.87	**3.17**	81.60	9.41	**59.07**	6.34
		64	40	177.41	**5.90**	82.46	9.50	**59.94**	6.43
		128	40	362.75	8.53	94.22	10.86	**68.70**	**7.38**
112	2048	32	32	**79.87**	**3.17**	161.47	18.62	116.42	12.48
		64	56	267.52	**10.03**	162.91	18.78	**117.86**	12.64
		128	56	487.68	13.68	164.06	18.91	**119.01**	**12.77**
128	3072	32	32	**79.87**	**3.17**	241.34	27.84	173.76	18.62
		64	64	319.49	**12.48**	243.07	28.03	**175.49**	18.82
		128	64	557.06	**16.64**	244.22	28.16	**176.64**	18.94

(S: comp. sec. level; N: JL-schemes modulus; k: message bit-length; s: stat. sec. level)

The underlying JL encryption scheme has been implemented following the specifications in [5] with few adjustments: adaptation of the decryption algorithm to support the partial extraction of the plaintext[18] (as described in Sect. 4), usage of some precomputed values derived by some components of the public and secret keys (as described in Section 5.2 in [5]) and a faster encryption exploiting some fixed base exponentiations.

For each protocol we measured the effective (wall clock) time required to get the final output but also the CPU usage (in percent): indeed in a real implementation the CPU can become idle waiting for incoming values delayed by network latency. Even a medium latency can degrade the final performance of an interactive protocol: in order to overcome this limit, we engineered the possibility to run on a single CPU thread a batch of interlaced runs in order to piggyback the passing network messages. As shown by our tests, this allows to get even on a very slow WAN connection almost the same throughput rate of a LAN.

The experiments used the following parameters: message bit-length $k = 64$, computational security level $S = 112$, statistical security level $s = 56$ and JL modulus size $|N| = 2048$ bit. The benchmarks reported in Table 3 are obtained as average on a batch of several runs with low standard deviation (1%). The value in the column "average time" is intended as the average cost of a single item of the batch.

---

[18] JL decryption can be surprisingly fast for small messages; as reference a Paillier decryption, with identical parameters/machine/setting used in Table 3, has a cost that range from 7864 μs to 4323 μs (if CRT is exploited). JL requires only 4054 μs.

Table 3. Benchmarks on Mon$\mathbb{Z}_{2^k}$a off-line protocol

latency (ms)	batch (items)	triple				input			
		av. time (ms)	CPU P_1 (%)	CPU P_2 (%)	throug. (item/s)	av. time (ms)	CPU P_1 (%)	CPU P_2 (%)	throug. (item/s)
0.5 (LAN)	1	56.65	80%	32%	17.65	7.99	70%	24%	125.16
	100	**52.24**	86%	35%	**19.14**	**7.41**	74%	26%	**134.95**
	1000	52.36	85%	35%	19.10	7.43	74%	26%	134.59
17.0 (WAN)	1	253.68	18%	7%	3.94	40.37	14%	5%	24.77
	1000	53.05	84%	34%	18.85	7.52	74%	25%	132.99
	2000	**52.34**	85%	34%	**19.11**	**7.42**	74%	26%	**134.77**
100.0 (WAN)	1	1252.53	4%	2%	206.85	40.37	3%	1%	4.83
	1000	58.34	77%	31%	17.14	8.25	67%	23%	121.21
	4000	**55.44**	81%	33%	**18.03**	**7.95**	70%	24%	**125.79**

Acknowledgements. The research of Dario Catalano and Mario Di Raimondo has been partially supported by the Università degli Studi di Catania, "Piano della Ricerca 2016/2018—Linea di intervento 2".

The research of Dario Fiore has been partially supported by the Spanish Government under projects SCUM (ref. RTI2018-102043-B-I00), CRYPTOEPIC (ref. EUR2019-103816), and SECURITAS (ref. RED2018-102321-T), and by the Madrid Regional Government under project BLOQUES (ref. S2018/TCS-4339).

References

1. Araki, T., et al.: Optimized honest-majority MPC for malicious adversaries - breaking the 1 billion-gate per second barrier. In: 2017 IEEE Symposium on Security and Privacy, pp. 843–862. IEEE Computer Society Press, May 2017
2. Araki, T., Furukawa, J., Lindell, Y., Nof, A., Ohara, K.: High-throughput semi-honest secure three-party computation with an honest majority. In: Weippl, E.R., Katzenbeisser, S., Kruegel, C., Myers, A.C., Halevi, S. (eds.), ACM CCS 2016, pp. 805–817. ACM Press, October 2016
3. Barak, B., Canetti, R., Nielsen, J.B., Pass, R.: Universally composable protocols with relaxed set-up assumptions. In: 45th FOCS, pp. 186–195. IEEE Computer Society Press, October 2004
4. Bendlin, R., Damgård, I., Orlandi, C., Zakarias, S.: Semi-homomorphic encryption and multiparty computation. In: Paterson, K.G. (ed.) EUROCRYPT 2011. LNCS, vol. 6632, pp. 169–188. Springer, Heidelberg (2011). https://doi.org/10.1007/978-3-642-20465-4_11
5. Benhamouda, F., Herranz, J., Joye, M., Libert, B.: Efficient cryptosystems from 2^k-th power residue symbols. J. Cryptol. **30**(2), 519–549 (2017). https://doi.org/10.1007/s00145-016-9229-5
6. Bogdanov, D., Laur, S., Willemson, J.: Sharemind: a framework for fast privacy-preserving computations. In: Jajodia, S., Lopez, J. (eds.) ESORICS 2008. LNCS, vol. 5283, pp. 192–206. Springer, Heidelberg (2008). https://doi.org/10.1007/978-3-540-88313-5_13

7. Canetti, R.: Universally composable security: a new paradigm for cryptographic protocols. In: 42nd FOCS, pp. 136–145. IEEE Computer Society Press, October 2001

8. Catalano, D., Fiore, D.: Using linearly-homomorphic encryption to evaluate degree-2 functions on encrypted data. In: Ray, I., Li, N., Kruegel, C. (eds.) ACM CCS 2015, pp. 1518–1529. ACM Press, October 2015

9. Cramer, R., Damgård, I., Escudero, D., Scholl, P., Xing, C.: SPDZ$_{2^k}$: efficient MPC mod 2^k for dishonest majority. In: Shacham, H., Boldyreva, A. (eds.) CRYPTO 2018, Part II. LNCS, vol. 10992, pp. 769–798. Springer, Heidelberg (2018). https://doi.org/10.1007/978-3-319-96881-0_26

10. Cramer, R., Fehr, S., Ishai, Y., Kushilevitz, E.: Efficient multi-party computation over rings. In: Biham, E. (ed.) EUROCRYPT 2003. LNCS, vol. 2656, pp. 596–613. Springer, Heidelberg (2003). https://doi.org/10.1007/3-540-39200-9_37

11. Damgård, I., Keller, M., Larraia, E., Pastro, V., Scholl, P., Smart, N.P.: Practical covertly secure MPC for dishonest majority – or: breaking the SPDZ limits. In: Crampton, J., Jajodia, S., Mayes, K. (eds.) ESORICS 2013. LNCS, vol. 8134, pp. 1–18. Springer, Heidelberg (2013). https://doi.org/10.1007/978-3-642-40203-6_1

12. Damgård, I., Orlandi, C., Simkin, M.: Yet another compiler for active security or: efficient MPC over arbitrary rings. In: Shacham, H., Boldyreva, A. (eds.) CRYPTO 2018, Part II. LNCS, vol. 10992, pp. 799–829. Springer, Cham (2018). https://doi.org/10.1007/978-3-319-96881-0_27

13. Damgård, I., Pastro, V., Smart, N.P., Zakarias, S.: Multiparty computation from somewhat homomorphic encryption. In: Safavi-Naini, R., Canetti, R. (eds.) CRYPTO 2012. LNCS, vol. 7417, pp. 643–662. Springer, Heidelberg (2012). https://doi.org/10.1007/978-3-642-32009-5_38

14. Furukawa, J., Lindell, Y., Nof, A., Weinstein, O.: High-throughput secure three-party computation for malicious adversaries and an honest majority. In: Coron, J.-S., Nielsen, J.B. (eds.) EUROCRYPT 2017, Part II. LNCS, vol. 10211, pp. 225–255. Springer, Cham (2017). https://doi.org/10.1007/978-3-319-56614-6_8

15. Gilboa, N.: Two party RSA key generation. In: Wiener, M. (ed.) CRYPTO 1999. LNCS, vol. 1666, pp. 116–129. Springer, Heidelberg (1999). https://doi.org/10.1007/3-540-48405-1_8

16. Goldwasser, S., Micali, S.: Probabilistic encryption and how to play mental poker keeping secret all partial information. In: 14th ACM STOC, pp. 365–377. ACM Press, May 1982

17. Joye, M., Libert, B.: Efficient cryptosystems from 2^k-th power residue symbols. In: Johansson, T., Nguyen, P.Q. (eds.) EUROCRYPT 2013. LNCS, vol. 7881, pp. 76–92. Springer, Heidelberg (2013). https://doi.org/10.1007/978-3-642-38348-9_5

18. Keller, M., Orsini, E., Scholl, P.: MASCOT: faster malicious arithmetic secure computation with oblivious transfer. In: Weippl, E.R., Katzenbeisser, S., Kruegel, C., Myers, A.C., Halevi, S. (eds.) ACM CCS 2016, pp. 830–842. ACM Press, October 2016

19. Keller, M., Pastro, V., Rotaru, D.: Overdrive: making SPDZ great again. In: Nielsen, J.B., Rijmen, V. (eds.) EUROCRYPT 2018, Part III. LNCS, vol. 10822, pp. 158–189. Springer, Cham (2018). https://doi.org/10.1007/978-3-319-78372-7_6

20. Orsini, E., Smart, N.P., Vercauteren, F.: Overdrive2k: efficient secure MPC over z_{2^k} from somewhat homomorphic encryption. Cryptology ePrint Archive, Report 2019/153 (2019)

Post-Quantum Primitives

Generic Authenticated Key Exchange in the Quantum Random Oracle Model

Kathrin Hövelmanns[1(✉)], Eike Kiltz[1], Sven Schäge[1], and Dominique Unruh[2]

[1] Ruhr-Universität Bochum, Bochum, Germany
{kathrin.Hoevelmanns,eike.kiltz,sven.schaege}@rub.de
[2] University of Tartu, Tartu, Estonia
unruh@ut.ee

Abstract. We propose $\mathsf{FO_{AKE}}$, a generic construction of two-message authenticated key exchange (AKE) from any passively secure public key encryption (PKE) in the quantum random oracle model (QROM). Whereas previous AKE constructions relied on a Diffie-Hellman key exchange or required the underlying PKE scheme to be perfectly correct, our transformation allows arbitrary PKE schemes with non-perfect correctness. Dealing with imperfect schemes is one of the major difficulties in a setting involving active attacks. Our direct construction, when applied to schemes such as the submissions to the recent NIST post-quantum competition, is more natural than previous AKE transformations. Furthermore, we avoid the use of (quantum-secure) digital signature schemes which are considerably less efficient than their PKE counterparts. As a consequence, we can instantiate our AKE transformation with any of the submissions to the recent NIST competition, e.g., ones based on codes and lattices.

$\mathsf{FO_{AKE}}$ can be seen as a generalisation of the well known Fujisaki-Okamoto transformation (for building actively secure PKE from passively secure PKE) to the AKE setting. As a helper result, we also provide a security proof for the Fujisaki-Okamoto transformation in the QROM for PKE with non-perfect correctness which is tighter and tolerates a larger correctness error than previous proofs.

Keywords: Authenticated key exchange · Quantum random oracle model · NIST · Fujisaki-Okamoto

1 Introduction

AUTHENTICATED KEY EXCHANGE. Besides public key encryption (PKE) and digital signatures, authenticated key exchange (AKE) is arguably one of the most important cryptographic building blocks in modern security systems. In the last two decades, research on AKE protocols has made tremendous progress in developing more solid theoretical foundations [10,19,31,38] as well as increasingly efficient designs of AKE protocols [37,44,47]. Most AKE protocols rely on constructions based on an ad-hoc Diffie-Hellman key exchange that is authenticated either via digital signatures, non-interactive key exchange

© International Association for Cryptologic Research 2020
A. Kiayias et al. (Eds.): PKC 2020, LNCS 12111, pp. 389–422, 2020.
https://doi.org/10.1007/978-3-030-45388-6_14

(usually a Diffie-Hellman key exchange performed on long-term Diffie-Hellman keys), or public key encryption. While in the literature one can find many protocols that use one of the two former building blocks, results for PKE-based authentication are rather rare [8,17]. Even rarer are constructions that only rely on PKE, discarding Diffie-Hellman key exchanges entirely. Notable recent exceptions are [23,24] and the protocol in [2], the latter of which has been criticised for having a flawed security proof and a weak security model [39,46].

THE NIST POST-QUANTUM COMPETITION. Recently, some of the above mentioned designs have gathered renewed interest in the quest of finding AKE protocols that are secure against quantum adversaries, i.e., adversaries equipped with a quantum computer. In particular, the National Institute of Standards and Technology (NIST) announced a competition with the goal to standardise new PKE and signature algorithms [41] with security against quantum adversaries. With the understanding that an AKE protocol can be constructed from low level primitives such as quantum-secure PKE and signature schemes, the NIST did not require the submissions to describe a concrete AKE protocol. Many PKE and signature candidates base their security on the hardness of certain problems over lattices and codes, which are generally believed to resist quantum adversaries.

THE QUANTUM ROM. Quantum computers may execute all "offline primitives" such as hash functions on arbitrary superpositions, which motivated the introduction of the quantum (accessible) random oracle model (QROM) [14]. While the adversary's capability to issue quantum queries to the random oracle renders many proof strategies significantly more complicated, it is nowadays generally believed that only proofs in the QROM imply provable security guarantees against quantum adversaries.

AKE AND QUANTUM-SECURE SIGNATURES. Digital signatures are useful for the "authentication" part in AKE, but unfortunately all known quantum-secure constructions would add a considerable overhead to the AKE protocol. Therefore, if at all possible, we prefer to build AKE protocols only from PKE schemes, without using signatures.[1] Our ultimate goal is to build a system that remains secure in the presence of quantum computers, meaning that even currently employed (very fast) signatures schemes based on elliptic curves are not an option.

CENTRAL RESEARCH QUESTION FOR QUANTUM-SECURE AKE. In summary, motivated by post-quantum secure cryptography and the NIST competition, we are interested in the following question:

How to build an actively secure AKE protocol from any passively secure PKE in the quantum random oracle model, without using signatures?

(The terms "actively secure AKE" and "passively secure PKE" will be made more precise later.) Surprisingly, one of the main technical difficulties is that

---

[1] Clearly, PKE requires a working public-key infrastructure (PKI) which in turn requires signatures to certify the public-key. However, a user only has to verify a given certificate once and for all, which means the overhead of a quantum-secure signature can be neglected.

the underlying PKE scheme might come with a small probability of decryption failure, i.e., first encrypting and then decrypting does not yield the original message. This property is called non-perfect correctness, and it is common for quantum-secure schemes from lattices and codes, rendering them useless for all previous constructions that relied on perfect correctness.[2]

PREVIOUS CONSTRUCTIONS OF AKE FROM PUBLIC-KEY PRIMITIVES. The generic AKE protocol of Fujioka et al. [23] (itself based on [17]) transforms a passively secure PKE scheme PKE and an actively (i.e., IND-CCA) secure PKE scheme PKE_{cca} into an AKE protocol. We will refer to this transformation as $FSXY[PKE, PKE_{cca}]$. Since the FSXY transformation is in the standard model, it is likely to be secure with the same proof in the post-quantum setting and thus also in the QROM. The standard way to obtain actively secure encryption from passively secure ones is the Fujisaki-Okamoto transformation $PKE_{cca} = FO[PKE, G, H]$ [25, 26]. In its "implicit rejection" variant [28], it comes with a recently discovered security proof [43] that models the hash functions G and H as quantum random oracles. Indeed, the *combined AKE transformation* $FSXY[PKE, FO[PKE, G, H]]$ transforms passively secure encryption into AKE that is very likely to be secure in the QROM, without using digital signatures, hence giving a first answer to our above question. It has, however, two main drawbacks.

- **Perfect correctness requirement.** Transformation FSXY is not known to have a security proof if the underlying scheme does not satisfy perfect correctness. Likewise, the relatively tight QROM proof for FO that was given in [43] requires the underlying scheme to be perfectly correct, and a generalisation of the proof for schemes with non-perfect correctness is not straightforward. Hence, it is unclear whether $FSXY[PKE, FO[PKE, G, H]]$ can be instantiated with lattice- or code-based encryption schemes.
- **Lack of simplicity.** The Fujisaki-Okamoto transformation already involves hashing the key using hash function H, and FSXY involves even more (potentially redundant) hashing of the (already hashed) session key. Overall, the combined transformation seems overly complicated and hence impractical.

In [24], a transformation was given that started from oneway-secure KEMs, but its security proof was given in the ROM, and its generalisation to the QROM was explicitly left as an open problem. Furthermore, it involves more hashing, similar to transformation FSXY.

Hence, it seems desirable to provide a simplified transformation that gets rid of unnecessary hashing steps, and that can be proven secure in the QROM even

---

[2] There exist generic transformations that can immunise against decryption errors (e.g., [22]). Even though they are quite efficient in theory, the induced overhead is still not acceptable for practical purposes. While lattice schemes could be rendered perfectly correct by putting a limit on the noise, and setting the modulus of the LWE instance large enough (see, e.g., [12, 29]), the security level cannot be maintained without increasing the problem's dimension, accordingly. Since this modification would lead to increased public-key and ciphertext length, many NIST submissions deliberately made the design choice of having imperfect correctness.

if the underlying scheme does not satisfy perfect correctness. As a motivating example, note that the Kyber AKE protocol [16] can be seen as a result of applying such a simplified transformation to the Kyber PKE scheme, although coming without a formal security proof.

1.1   Our Contributions

Our main contribution is a transformation, $\mathsf{FO_{AKE}[PKE, G, H]}$ ("Fujisaki-Okamoto for AKE") that converts any passively secure encryption scheme into an actively secure AKE protocol, with provable security in the quantum random oracle model. It can deal with non-perfect correctness and does not use digital signatures. Our transformation $\mathsf{FO_{AKE}}$ can be viewed as a modification of the transformation given in [24]. Furthermore, we provide a precise game-based security definition for two-message AKE protocols. As a side result, we also give a security proof for the Fujisaki-Okamoto transformation in the QROM in Sect. 3 that deals with correctness errors. It can be seen as the KEM analogue of our main result, the AKE proof. Our proof strategy differs from and improves on the bounds of a previously published proof of the Fujisaki-Okamoto transformation for KEMs in the QROM [32].

FO Transformation for KEMs. To simplify the presentation of $\mathsf{FO_{AKE}}$, we first give some background on the Fujisaki-Okamoto transformation for KEMs. In its original form [25,26], FO yields an encryption scheme that is IND-CCA secure in the random oracle model [9] from combining any One-Way secure asymmetric encryption scheme with any one-time secure symmetric encryption scheme. In "A Designer's Guide to KEMs", Dent [21] provided FO-like IND-CCA secure KEMs. (Recall that any IND-CCA secure Key Encapsulation Mechanism can be combined with any (one-time) chosen-ciphertext secure symmetric encryption scheme to obtain a IND-CCA secure PKE scheme [20].) Since all of the transformations mentioned above required the underlying PKE scheme to be perfectly correct, and due to the increased popularity of lattice-based schemes with non-perfect correctness, [28] gave several modularisations of FO-like transformations and proved them robust against correctness errors. The key observation was that FO-like transformations essentially consists of two separate steps and can be dissected into two transformations, as sketched in the introduction of [28]:

- Transformation T: "Derandomise" and "re-encrypt". Starting from an encryption scheme PKE and a hash function G, encryption of $\mathsf{PKE'} = \mathsf{T[PKE, G]}$ is defined by

$$\mathsf{Enc'}(pk, m) := \mathsf{Enc}(pk, m; \mathsf{G}(m)),$$

where $\mathsf{G}(m)$ is used as the random coins for Enc, rendering $\mathsf{Enc'}$ deterministic. $\mathsf{Dec'}(sk, c)$ first decrypts c into m' and rejects if $\mathsf{Enc}(pk, m'; \mathsf{G}(m')) \neq c$ ("re-encryption").

- Transformation $\mathsf{U}_m^{\not\perp}$: "Hashing". Starting from an encryption scheme PKE' and a hash function H, key encapsulation mechanism $\mathsf{KEM}_m^{\not\perp} = \mathsf{U}_m^{\not\perp}[\mathsf{PKE', H}]$ with "implicit rejection" is defined by

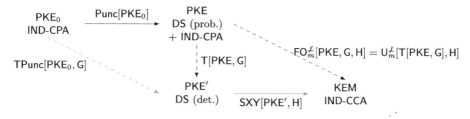

Fig. 1. Comparison of [43]'s modular transformation (green) with ours. Solid arrows indicate tight reductions, dashed arrows indicate non-tight reductions. (Color figure online)

$$\mathsf{Encaps}(pk) := (c \leftarrow \mathsf{Enc}'(pk, m), K := \mathsf{H}(m)), \tag{1}$$

where m is picked at random from the message space, and

$$\mathsf{Decaps}(sk, c) = \begin{cases} \mathsf{H}(m) & m \neq \perp \\ \mathsf{H}(s, c) & m = \perp \end{cases},$$

where $m := \mathsf{Dec}(sk, c)$ and s is a random seed which is contained in sk. In the context of the FO transformation, implicit rejection was first introduced by Persichetti [42, Sec. 5.3].

Transformation T was proven secure both in the (classical) ROM and the QROM, and $\mathsf{U}_m^{\not\perp}$ was proven secure in the ROM. To achieve QROM security, [28] gave a modification of $\mathsf{U}_m^{\not\perp}$, called $\mathsf{QU}_m^{\not\perp}$, but its security proof in the QROM suffered from a quartic[3] loss in tightness, and furthermore, most real-world proposals are designed such that they fit the framework of $\mathsf{FO}_m^{\not\perp} = \mathsf{U}_m^{\not\perp} \circ \mathsf{T}$, not $\mathsf{QU}_m^{\not\perp} \circ \mathsf{T}$.

A slightly different modularisation was introduced in [43]: they gave transformations TPunc ("Puncturing and Encrypt-with-Hash") and SXY ("Hashing with implicit reject and reencryption"). SXY differs from $\mathsf{U}_m^{\not\perp}$ in that it reencrypts during decryption. Hence, it can only be applied to deterministic schemes. Even in the QROM, its CCA security tightly reduces to an intermediate notion called Disjoint Simulatability (DS) of ciphertexts. Intuitively, disjoint simulatability means that we can efficiently sample "fake ciphertexts" that are computationally indistinguishable from real PKE ciphertexts ("simulatability"), while the set of possible fake ciphertexts is required to be (almost) disjoint from the set of real ciphertexts. DS is naturally satisfied by many code/lattice-based encryption schemes. Additionally, it can be achieved using transformation Punc, i.e., by puncturing the underlying schemes' message space at one point and using this message to sample fake encryptions. Deterministic DS can be achieved by using transformation TPunc, albeit non-tightly: the reduction suffers from quadratic loss in security and an additional factor of q, the number of the adversary's hash queries.

---

[3] Not just quadratic, but indeed quartic.

However, the reduction that is given in [43] requires the underlying encryption scheme to be perfectly correct. Later, [32] gave non-modular security proofs for the transformations $\mathsf{FO}_m^{\not\perp}$ and $\mathsf{FO}^{\not\perp}$ as well as a security proof for SXY[4] for schemes with correctness errors, which still suffered from quadratic loss in security and an additional factor of q, the latter of which this work improves to $\sqrt{q}$.

Our transformation $\mathsf{FO}_m^{\not\perp}$ can be applied to any PKE scheme that is both IND-CPA and DS secure. The reduction is tighter than the one that results from combining those of TPunc and SXY in [43], and also than the reduction given in [33]. This is due to our use of the improved Oneway-to-Hiding lemma [3, Thm. 1: "Semi-classical O2H"]. Furthermore, we achieve a better correctness bound (the square of the bound given in [33]) due to a better bound for the generic distinguishing problem. In cases where PKE is not already DS, this requirement can be waived with negligible loss of efficiency: To rely on IND-CPA alone, all that has to be done is to plug in transformation Punc. A visualisation is given in Fig. 1.

Security Model for Two-Message Authenticated Key Exchange. We introduce a simple game-based security model for (non-parallel) two-message AKE protocols, i.e., protocols where the responder sends his message only after having received the initiator's message. Technically, in our model, and similar to previous literature, we define several oracles that the attacker has access to. However, in contrast to most other security models, the inner workings of these oracles and their management via the challenger are precisely defined with pseudo-code.

DETAILS ON OUR MODELS. We define two security notions for two-message AKEs: key indistinguishability against active attacks (IND-AA) and the weaker notion of indistinguishability against active attacks without state reveal in the test session (IND-StAA). IND-AA captures the classical notion of key indistinguishability (as introduced by Bellare and Rogaway [10]) as well as security against reflection attacks, key compromise impersonation (KCI) attacks, and weak forward secrecy (wFS) [37]. It is based on the Canetti-Krawczyk (CK) model and allows the attacker to reveal (all) secret state information as compared to only ephemeral keys. As already pointed out by [17], this makes our model incomparable to the eCK model [38] but strictly stronger than the CK model. Essentially, the IND-AA model states that the session key remains indistinguishable from a random one even if

1. the attacker knows either the long-term secret key or the secret state information (but not both) of both parties involved in the test session, as long as it did not modify the message received by the test session,
2. and also if the attacker modified the message received by the test session, as long as it did not obtain the long-term secret key of the test session's peer.

---

[4] Note that nomenclature of [33] is a bit misleading: while the respective KEM is called $\mathsf{U}_m^{\not\perp}$, it is actually transformation SXY (it reencrypts during decryption, which $\mathsf{U}_m^{\not\perp}$ does not).

We also consider the slightly weaker model IND-StAA (in which we will prove the security of our AKE protocols), where 2. is substituted by

2'. and also if the attacker modified the message received by the test session, as long as it did neither obtain the long-term secret key of the test session's peer **nor the test session's state**. The latter strategy, we will call a *state attack*.

We remark that IND-StAA security is essentially the same notion that was achieved by the FSXY transformation [23].[5] In the full version we provide a more general perspective on how our model compares to existing ones.

Our Authenticated Key-Exchange Protocol. Our transformation FO_{AKE} transforms any passively secure PKE (with potential non-perfect correctness) into an IND-StAA secure AKE. FO_{AKE} is a simplification of the transformation FSXY[PKE, FO[PKE, G, H]] mentioned above, where the derivation of the session key K uses only one single hash function H. FO_{AKE} can be regarded as the AKE analogue of the Fujisaki-Okamoto transformation.

Transformation $FO_{AKE}[PKE, G, H]$ is described in Fig. 2 and uses transform $PKE' = T[PKE, G]$ as a building block. (The full construction is given in Fig. 15, see Sect. 5.) Our main security result (Theorem 3) states that $FO_{AKE}[PKE, G, H]$ is an IND-StAA-secure AKE if the underlying probabilistic PKE is DS as well as IND-CPA secure and has negligible correctness error, and furthermore G and H are modeled as quantum random oracles.

The proof essentially is the AKE analogue to the security proof of $FO_m^{\not\perp}$ we give in Sect. 3.2: By definition of our security model, it always holds that at least one of the messages m_i, m_j and $\tilde{m}$ is hidden from the adversary (unless it loses trivially) since it may not reveal a party's secret key and its session state at the same time. Adapting the simulation technique in [43], we can simulate the session keys even if we do not know the corresponding secret key sk_i (sk_j, $\tilde{sk}$). Assuming that PKE is DS, we can replace the corresponding ciphertext c_i (c_j, $\tilde{c}$) of the test session with a fake ciphertext, rendering the test session's key completely random from the adversary's view due to PKE's disjointness.

Let us add two remarks. Firstly, we cannot prove the security of $FO_{AKE}[PKE, G, H]$ in the stronger sense of IND-AA and actually, it is not secure against state attacks. Secondly, note that our security statement involves the probabilistic scheme PKE rather than PKE'. Unfortunately, we were not able to provide a modular proof of AKE solely based on reasonable security properties of $PKE' = T[PKE, G]$. The reason for this is indeed the non-perfect correctness of PKE. This difficulty corresponds to the difficulty to generalise [43]'s result for deterministic encryption schemes with correctness errors discussed above.

---

[5] The difference is that the model from [23] furthermore allows a "partial reveal" of the test session's state. For simplicity and due to their little practical relevance, we decided not to include such partial session reveal queries in our model. We remark that, however, our protocol could be proven secure in this slightly stronger model.

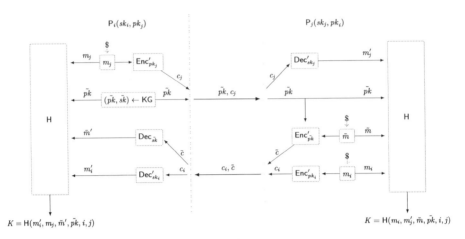

Fig. 2. A visualisation of our authenticated key-exchange protocol $\mathsf{FO}_{\mathsf{AKE}}$. We make the convention that, in case any of the Dec' algorithms returns $\bot$, the session key K is derived deterministically and pseudorandomly from the player's state ("implicit rejection").

CONCRETE APPLICATIONS. Our transformation can be applied to any scheme that is IND-CPA secure with post-quantum security, e.g., Frodo [40], Kyber [16], and Lizard [5]. Recall that the additional requirement of DS can be achieved with negligible loss of efficiency. However, in many applications even this negligible loss is inexistent since most of the aforementioned schemes can already be proven DS under the same assumption that their IND-CPA security is based upon.

Subsequent Work. Since this paper was published on eprint, there has been more work on CCA security of FO in the QROM ([13,35]), essentially achieving the same level of tightness as this work. [13] achieves more modularity, and covers a class of schemes that is both less and more restrictive at the same time: They only require schemes to be oneway-secure (instead of CPA, as required in this work), but the schemes have to meet an additional injectivity requirement (specified below).

TIGHTNESS FOR FO. Reductions from CCA security to CPA security in the QROM usually suffer from tightness loss in two separate ways: The best known bounds for probabilistic schemes to this date are essentially of the form $\sqrt{q}\sqrt{\epsilon}$, where q is the number of the adversary's hash queries, and ϵ is the reduction's CPA advantage. Hence, the loss consists of both a loss regarding q (q-nontightness), and worse, a quadratic loss regarding the level of CPA security (root-nontightness). For the general setting where one starts from a probabilistic scheme, there have not been tightness improvements since this work:

Essentially, [35] is an update of [32] that makes use of the improved Oneway-to-Hiding bounds given in [3], thereby improving [32]'s bound $q\sqrt{\epsilon}$ to $\sqrt{q}\sqrt{\epsilon}$, with the security requirement switching from onewayness to IND-CPA. The result seems to differ from this work solely in its (nonmodular) proof structure.

In [13], a new modular proof for FO was given by starting from probabilistic onewayness and choosing deterministic oneway-security as their intermediate[6] notion, opposed to our (strictly stronger) intermediate notion of deterministic DS. This approach matches the observation that if one can start from a scheme that already is deterministically oneway-secure (like [12]), derandomisation step T is superfluous. In this case, only transformation U has to be applied, which is proven secure q-tightly. The weaker intermediate notion, however, shifts the root-nontightness to second transformation U. Therefore, the result still is heavily non-tight, even if derandomising via T is skipped. Furthermore, no tightness improvements whatsoever are achieved if the underlying scheme is not already deterministic, and thus has to be derandomised using T first.

MODULARITY. The modular proof of [13] is achieved by introducing an additional notion for the intermediate scheme that deals with correctness errors. Unfortunately, the possibility of correctness errors complicate modular attempts on analysing FO: For underlying probabilistic schemes, [13] requires more than this work since its approach only is applicable if the "intermediate" scheme is injective with overwhelming probability. It is very likely that the modular approach of [13] could be generalised to an AKE proof that similarly is modular and hence, conceptually nicer. But this gain in modularity would come at a cost: The approach only is applicable if the derandomised scheme is essentially injective. We would, therefore, add an unnecessary restriction on the class of schemes that AKE can be based upon.

Open Problems. In the literature, one can find several Diffie-Hellman based protocols that achieve IND-AA security, for example HMQV [37]. However, none of them provides security against quantum computers. We leave as an interesting open problem to design a generic and efficient two-message AKE protocol in our stronger IND-AA model, preferably with a security proof in the QROM to guarantee its security even in the presence of quantum adversaries.

While [13] gave a proof of CCA security that is conceptually cleaner, it still is heavily non-tight due to its root-nontightness, with the root-nontightness stemming from its usage of a standard Oneway-to-Hiding strategy. Recent work [34] proved that for reductions using this standard approach, suffering from quadratic security loss is inevitable. We would like to point out, however, that we do not view this result as an impossibility result[7]. It rather proves impossibility of root-tightness *for a certain type of reduction*, and thereby informs us how to adapt possible future proof strategies: A root-tight proof of CCA security still might

---

[6] By "intermediate", we mean the deterministic scheme that is to be plugged into one of the U-transforms. In most cases, it is derived by starting from a probabilistic scheme and first applying derandomisation transformation T.

[7] A strict impossibility result would have to consist of a concrete scheme as well as a concrete attack, with the latter matching the given upper bound.

be achievable, but the respective reduction would have to be more sophisticated than extracting oneway solutions for the underlying scheme by simply applying Oneway-to-Hiding.

2   Preliminaries

For $n \in \mathbb{N}$, let $[n] := \{1, \ldots, n\}$. For a set S, $|S|$ denotes the cardinality of S. For a finite set S, we denote the sampling of a uniform random element x by $x \leftarrow_\$ S$, while we denote the sampling according to some distribution $\mathfrak{D}$ by $x \leftarrow \mathfrak{D}$. By $[\![B]\!]$ we denote the bit that is 1 if the boolean Statement B is true, and otherwise 0.

ALGORITHMS. We denote deterministic computation of an algorithm A on input x by $y := A(x)$. We denote algorithms with access to an oracle O by A^O. Unless stated otherwise, we assume all our algorithms to be probabilistic and denote the computation by $y \leftarrow A(x)$.

GAMES. Following [11,45], we use code-based games. We implicitly assume boolean flags to be initialised to false, numerical types to 0, sets to $\varnothing$, and strings to the empty string ϵ. We make the convention that a procedure terminates once it has returned an output.

2.1   Public-Key Encryption

SYNTAX. A public-key encryption scheme $\mathsf{PKE} = (\mathsf{KG}, \mathsf{Enc}, \mathsf{Dec})$ consists of three algorithms, and a finite message space $\mathcal{M}$ which we assume to be efficiently recognisable. The key generation algorithm KG outputs a key pair (pk, sk), where pk also defines a finite randomness space $\mathcal{R} = \mathcal{R}(pk)$ as well as a ciphertext space $\mathcal{C}$. The encryption algorithm Enc, on input pk and a message $m \in \mathcal{M}$, outputs an encryption $c \leftarrow \mathsf{Enc}(pk, m)$ of m under the public key pk. If necessary, we make the used randomness of encryption explicit by writing $c := \mathsf{Enc}(pk, m; r)$, where $r \leftarrow_\$ \mathcal{R}$. The decryption algorithm Dec, on input sk and a ciphertext c, outputs either a message $m = \mathsf{Dec}(sk, c) \in \mathcal{M}$ or a special symbol $\perp \notin \mathcal{M}$ to indicate that c is not a valid ciphertext.

Definition 1 (Collision probability of key generation). *We define*

$$\mu(\mathsf{KG}) := \Pr[(pk, sk) \leftarrow \mathsf{KG}, (pk', sk') \leftarrow \mathsf{KG} : pk = pk'].$$

Definition 2 (Collision probability of ciphertexts). *We define*

$$\mu(\mathsf{Enc}) := \Pr[(pk, sk) \leftarrow \mathsf{KG}, m, m' \leftarrow_\$ \mathcal{M}, c \leftarrow \mathsf{Enc}(pk, m), c' \leftarrow \mathsf{Enc}(pk, m') : c = c'].$$

Definition 3 (γ-Spreadness). [25] *We say that* PKE *is* γ-spread *iff for all key pairs* $(pk, sk) \in \mathrm{supp}(\mathsf{KG})$ *and all messages* $m \in \mathcal{M}$ *it holds that*

$$\max_{c \in \mathcal{C}} \Pr[r \leftarrow_\$ \mathcal{R} : \mathsf{Enc}(pk, m; r) = c] \leq 2^{-\gamma}.$$

GAME IND-CPA$_b$	**GAME** IND-CCA	DECAPS($c \neq c^*$)
01 $(pk, sk) \leftarrow$ KG	06 $(pk, sk) \leftarrow$ KG	12 $K :=$ Decaps(sk, c)
02 $(m_0^*, m_1^*, \text{st}) \leftarrow A_1(pk)$	07 $b \leftarrow_\$ \mathbb{F}_2$	13 **return** K
03 $c^* \leftarrow$ Enc(pk, m_b^*)	08 $(K_0^*, c^*) \leftarrow$ Encaps(pk)	
04 $b' \leftarrow A_2(pk, c^*, \text{st})$	09 $K_1^* \leftarrow_\$ \mathcal{K}$	
05 **return** b'	10 $b' \leftarrow A^{\text{DECAPS}}(pk, c^*, K_b^*)$	
	11 **return** $[\![b' = b]\!]$	

Fig. 3. Games IND-CPA$_b$ for PKE ($b \in \mathbb{F}_2$) and game IND-CCA for KEM.

Definition 4 (Correctness). [28] *We define* $\delta := \mathbf{E}[\max_{m \in \mathcal{M}} \Pr[c \leftarrow \text{Enc}(pk, m) : \text{Dec}(sk, c) \neq m]]$, *where the expectation is taken over* $(pk, sk) \leftarrow$ KG.

SECURITY. We now define the notion of Indistinguishability under Chosen Plaintext Attacks (IND-CPA) for public-key encryption.

Definition 5 (IND-CPA). *Let* PKE $= ($KG, Enc, Dec$)$ *be a public-key encryption scheme. We define game* IND-CPA *game as in Fig. 3, and the* IND-CPA *advantage function of a quantum adversary* $A = (A_1, A_2)$ *against* PKE *(such that* A_2 *has binary output) as*

$$\text{Adv}_{\text{PKE}}^{\text{IND-CPA}}(A) := |\Pr[\text{IND-CPA}_1^A \Rightarrow 1] - \Pr[\text{IND-CPA}_0^A \Rightarrow 1]|.$$

We also define IND-CPA *security in the random oracle model model, where* PKE *and adversary* A *are given access to a random oracle.*

DISJOINT SIMULATABILITY. Following [43], we consider PKE where it is possible to efficiently sample fake ciphertexts that are indistinguishable from proper encryptions, while the probability that the sampling algorithm hits a proper encryption is small.

Definition 6. *(DS) Let* PKE $= ($KG, Enc, Dec$)$ *be a PKE scheme with message space* $\mathcal{M}$ *and ciphertext space* $\mathcal{C}$, *coming with an additional PPT algorithm* $\overline{\text{Enc}}$. *For quantum adversaries* A, *we define the advantage against* PKE*'s disjoint simulatability as*

$$\text{Adv}_{\text{PKE}, \overline{\text{Enc}}}^{\text{DS}}(A) := |\Pr[pk \leftarrow \text{KG}, m \leftarrow_\$ \mathcal{M}, c \leftarrow \text{Enc}(pk, m) : 1 \leftarrow A(pk, c)]$$

$$- \Pr[pk \leftarrow \text{KG}, c \leftarrow \overline{\text{Enc}}(pk) : 1 \leftarrow A(pk, c)]|.$$

When there is no chance of confusion, we will drop $\overline{\text{Enc}}$ *from the advantage's subscript for convenience.*

We call PKE ϵ_{dis}-*disjoint if for all* $pk \in \text{supp}(\text{KG})$, $\Pr[c \leftarrow \overline{\text{Enc}}(pk) : c \in \text{Enc}(pk, \mathcal{M}; \mathcal{R})] \leq \epsilon_{dis}$.

2.2   Key Encapsulation

SYNTAX. A key encapsulation mechanism KEM = (KG, Encaps, Decaps) consists of three algorithms. The key generation algorithm KG outputs a key pair (pk, sk), where pk also defines a finite key space $\mathcal{K}$. The encapsulation algorithm Encaps, on input pk, outputs a tuple (K, c) where c is said to be an encapsulation of the key K which is contained in key space $\mathcal{K}$. The deterministic decapsulation algorithm Decaps, on input sk and an encapsulation c, outputs either a key $K := \mathsf{Decaps}(sk, c) \in \mathcal{K}$ or a special symbol $\perp \notin \mathcal{K}$ to indicate that c is not a valid encapsulation.

We call KEM δ-correct if

$$\Pr\left[\mathsf{Decaps}(sk, c) \neq K \mid (pk, sk) \leftarrow \mathsf{KG}; (K, c) \leftarrow \mathsf{Encaps}(pk)\right] \leq \delta.$$

Note that the above definition also makes sense in the random oracle model since KEM ciphertexts do not depend on messages.

SECURITY. We now define a security notion for key encapsulation: Indistinguishbility under Chosen Ciphertext Attacks (IND-CCA).

Definition 7 (IND-CCA). *We define the* IND-CCA *game as in Fig. 3 and the* IND-CCA *advantage function of an adversary* A *(with binary output) against* KEM *as*

$$\mathrm{Adv}^{\mathsf{IND\text{-}CCA}}_{\mathsf{KEM}}(\mathsf{A}) := |\Pr[\mathsf{IND\text{-}CCA}^{\mathsf{A}} \Rightarrow 1] - 1/2|.$$

2.3   Quantum Computation

QUBITS. For simplicity, we will treat a *qubit* as a vector $|\varphi\rangle \in \mathbb{C}^2$, i.e., a linear combination $|\varphi\rangle = \alpha \cdot |0\rangle + \beta \cdot |1\rangle$ of the two *basis states* (vectors) $|0\rangle$ and $|1\rangle$ with the additional requirement to the probability amplitudes $\alpha, \beta \in \mathbb{C}$ that $|\alpha|^2 + |\beta|^2 = 1$. The basis $\{|0\rangle, |1\rangle\}$ is called *standard orthonormal computational basis*. The qubit $|\varphi\rangle$ is said to be *in superposition*. Classical bits can be interpreted as quantum bits via the mapping $(b \mapsto 1 \cdot |b\rangle + 0 \cdot |1 - b\rangle)$.

QUANTUM REGISTERS. We will treat a quantum register as a collection of multiple qubits, i.e. a linear combination $|\varphi\rangle := \sum_{x \in \mathbb{F}_2^n} \alpha_x \cdot |x\rangle$, where $\alpha_x \in \mathbb{C}$, with the additional restriction that $\sum_{x \in \mathbb{F}_2^n} |\alpha_x|^2 = 1$. As in the one-dimensional case, we call the basis $\{|x\rangle\}_{x \in \mathbb{F}_2^n}$ the *standard orthonormal computational basis*. We say that $|\varphi\rangle = \sum_{x \in \mathbb{F}_2^n} \alpha_x \cdot |x\rangle$ *contains the classical query* x if $\alpha_x \neq 0$.

MEASUREMENTS. Qubits can be measured with respect to a basis. In this paper, we will only consider measurements in the standard orthonormal computational basis, and denote this measurement by MEASURE($\cdot$), where the outcome of MEASURE($|\varphi\rangle$) for a single qubit $|\varphi\rangle = \alpha \cdot |0\rangle + \beta \cdot |1\rangle$ will be 0 with probability $|\alpha|^2$ and 1 with probability $|\beta|^2$, and the outcome of measuring a qubit register $|\varphi\rangle = \sum_{x \in \mathbb{F}_2^n} \alpha_x \cdot |x\rangle$ will be x with probability $|\alpha_x|^2$. Note that the amplitudes *collapse* during a measurement, this means that by measuring $\alpha \cdot |0\rangle + \beta \cdot |1\rangle$, α

and β are switched to one of the combinations in $\{\pm(1,0), \pm(0,1)\}$. Likewise, in the n-dimensional case, all amplitudes are switched to 0 except for the one that belongs to the measurement outcome and which will be switched to 1.

QUANTUM ORACLES AND QUANTUM ADVERSARIES. Following [6,14], we view a quantum oracle $|\mathsf{O}\rangle$ as a mapping

$$|x\rangle|y\rangle \mapsto |x\rangle|y \oplus \mathsf{O}(x)\rangle,$$

where $\mathsf{O} : \mathbb{F}_2^n \to \mathbb{F}_2^m$, and model quantum adversaries A with access to O by a sequence $U_1, |\mathsf{O}\rangle, U_2, \cdots, |\mathsf{O}\rangle, U_N$ of unitary transformations. We write $\mathsf{A}^{|\mathsf{O}\rangle}$ to indicate that the oracles are quantum-accessible (contrary to oracles which can only process classical bits).

QUANTUM RANDOM ORACLE MODEL. We consider security games in the quantum random oracle model (QROM) as their counterparts in the classical random oracle model, with the difference that we consider quantum adversaries that are given **quantum** access to the (offline) random oracles involved, and **classical** access to all other (online) oracles. For example, in the IND-CPA game, the adversary only obtains a classical encryption, like in [18], and unlike in [15]. In the IND-CCA game, the adversary only has access to a classical decryption oracle, unlike in [27] and [1].

Zhandry [48] proved that no quantum algorithm $\mathsf{A}^{|\mathsf{O}\rangle}$, issuing at most q quantum queries to $|\mathsf{O}\rangle$, can distinguish between a random function $\mathsf{O} : \mathbb{F}_2^m \to \mathbb{F}_2^n$ and a $2q$-wise independent function f_{2q}. For concreteness, we view $f_{2q} : \mathbb{F}_2^m \to \mathbb{F}_2^n$ as a random polynomial of degree $2q$ over the finite field $\mathbb{F}_{2^n}$. The running time to evaluate f_{2q} is linear in q. In this article, we will use this observation in the context of security reductions, where quantum adversary B simulates quantum adversary $\mathsf{A}^{|\mathsf{O}\rangle}$ issuing at most q queries to $|\mathsf{O}\rangle$. Hence, the running time of B is $\mathrm{Time}(\mathsf{B}) = \mathrm{Time}(\mathsf{A}) + q \cdot \mathrm{Time}(\mathsf{O})$, where $\mathrm{Time}(\mathsf{O})$ denotes the time it takes to simulate $|\mathsf{O}\rangle$. Using the observation above, B can use a $2q$-wise independent function in order to (information-theoretically) simulate $|\mathsf{O}\rangle$, and we obtain that the running time of B is $\mathrm{Time}(\mathsf{B}) = \mathrm{Time}(\mathsf{A}) + q \cdot \mathrm{Time}(f_{2q})$, and the time $\mathrm{Time}(f_{2q})$ to evaluate f_{2q} is linear in q. Following [43] and [36], we make use of the fact that the second term of this running time (quadratic in q) can be further reduced to linear in q in the quantum random-oracle model where B can simply use another random oracle to simulate $|\mathsf{O}\rangle$. Assuming evaluating the random oracle takes one time unit, we write $\mathrm{Time}(\mathsf{B}) = \mathrm{Time}(\mathsf{A}) + q$, which is approximately $\mathrm{Time}(\mathsf{A})$.

ONEWAY TO HIDING WITH SEMI-CLASSICAL ORACLES. In [3], Ambainis et al. defined semi-classical oracles that return a state that was measured with respect to one of the input registers. In particular, to any subset $S \subset X$, they associated the following semi-classical oracle $\mathsf{O}_S^{\mathsf{SC}}$: Algorithm $\mathsf{O}_S^{\mathsf{SC}}$, when queried on $|\psi, 0\rangle$, measures with respect to the projectors M_1 and M_0, where $M_1 := \sum_{x \in S} |x\rangle\langle x|$ and $M_0 := \sum_{x \notin S} |x\rangle\langle x|$. The oracle then initialises the second register to $|b\rangle$ for the measured bit b. This means that $|\psi, 0\rangle$ collapses to either a state $|\psi', 0\rangle$ such that $|\psi'\rangle$ only contains elements of $X \setminus S$ or to a state $|\psi', 1\rangle$ such that $|\psi'\rangle$ only contains elements of S. Let $FIND$ denote the event that the latter ever is the case, i.e., that O_S^{SC} ever answers with $|\psi', 1\rangle$ for some ψ'. To a quantum-accessible oracle G and a subset $S \subset X$, Ambainis et al. associate the following punctured oracle $G \setminus S$ that removes S from the domain of G unless $FIND$ occurs (Fig. 4).

$$
\begin{array}{l}
\hline
\mathsf{G} \setminus \mathsf{S}|\psi, \phi\rangle \\
\hline
01\ \ |\psi', b\rangle := \mathsf{O}_\mathsf{S}^{\mathsf{SC}}|\psi, 0\rangle \\
02\ \ \textbf{return}\ U_\mathsf{G}|\psi', \phi\rangle \\
\hline
\end{array}
$$

Fig. 4. Punctured oracle G\S for O2H.

The following theorem is a simplification of statement (2) given in [3, Thm. 1: "Semi-classical O2H"], and of [3, Cor. 1]. It differs in the following way: While [3] consider adversaries that might execute parallel oracle invocations and therefore differentiate between query depth d and number of queries q, we use the upper bound $q \geq d$ for simplicity.

Theorem 1. *Let $S \subset X$ be random. Let $G, H \in Y^X$ be random functions such that $G_{|X\setminus S} = H_{|X\setminus S}$, and let z be a random bitstring. (S, G, H, and z may have an arbitrary joint distribution.) Then, for all quantum algorithms A issuing at most q queries that, on input z, output either 0 or 1,*

$$
|\Pr[1 \leftarrow \mathsf{A}^{|\mathsf{G}\rangle}(z)] - \Pr[1 \leftarrow \mathsf{A}^{|\mathsf{H}\rangle}(z)]| \leq 2 \cdot \sqrt{q \Pr[b \leftarrow \mathsf{A}^{|\mathsf{G}\setminus\mathsf{S}\rangle}(z) : FIND]}.
$$

If furthermore $S := \{x\}$ for $x \leftarrow_\$ X$, and x and z are independent,

$$
\Pr[b \leftarrow \mathsf{A}^{|\mathsf{G}\setminus\mathsf{S}\rangle}(z) : FIND] \leq \frac{4q}{|X|}.
$$

GENERIC QUANTUM DISTINGUISHING PROBLEM WITH BOUNDED PROBABILITIES. For $\lambda \in [0,1]$, let B_λ be the Bernoulli distribution, i.e., $\Pr[b = 1] = \lambda$ for the bit $b \leftarrow B_\lambda$. Let X be some finite set. The generic quantum distinguishing problem ([4, Lemma 37], [30, Lem. 3]) is to distinguish quantum access to an oracle $F : X \rightarrow \mathbb{F}_2$, such that for each $x \in X$, $F(x)$ is distributed according to B_λ, from quantum access to the zero function. We will need the following slight variation. The Gequantum Distinguishing Problem with Bounded probabilities GDPB is like the quantum distinguishing problem with the difference that the Bernoulli parameter λ_x may depend on x, but still is upper bounded by a global λ. The upper bound we give is the same as in [30, Lem. 3]. It is proven in the full version.

Lemma 1 (Generic Distinguishing Problem with Bounded Probabilities). *[Generic Distinguishing Problem with Bounded Probabilities] Let X be a* *finite set, and let* $\lambda \in [0,1]$. *Then, for any (unbounded, quantum) algorithm* A *issuing at most* q *quantum queries,*

$$|\Pr[\mathsf{GDPB}_{\lambda,0}^{\mathsf{A}} \Rightarrow 1] - \Pr[\mathsf{GDPB}_{\lambda,1}^{\mathsf{A}} \Rightarrow 1]| \leq 8(q+1)^2 \cdot \lambda,$$

where games $\mathsf{GDPB}_{\lambda,b}^{\mathsf{A}}$ *(for bit* $b \in \mathbb{F}_2$) *are defined as follows:*

GAME $\mathsf{GDPB}_{\lambda,b}$
01 $(\lambda_x)_{x \in X} \leftarrow \mathsf{A}_1$
02 **if** $\exists x \in X$ s.t. $\lambda_x > \lambda$ **return** 0
03 **if** $b = 0$
04     $F := 0$
05 **else for** all $x \in X$
06     $F(x) \leftarrow B_{\lambda_x}$
07 $b' \leftarrow \mathsf{A}_2^{|F\rangle}$
08 **return** b'

3 The FO Transformation: QROM Security with Correctness Errors

In Sect. 3.1, we modularise transformation TPunc that was given in [43] and that turns any public key encryption scheme that is IND-CPA secure into a deterministic one that is DS. Transformation TPunc essentially consists of first puncturing the message space at one point (transformation Punc, to achieve probabilistic DS), and then applying transformation T. Next, in Sect. 3.2, we show that transformation $\mathsf{U}_m^{\not\perp}$, when applied to T, transforms any encryption scheme that is DS as well as IND-CPA into a KEM that is IND-CCA secure. We believe that many lattice-based schemes fulfill DS in a natural way,[8] but for the sake of completeness, we will show in the full version how transformation Punc can be used to waive the requirement of DS with negligible loss of efficiency.

3.1 Modularisation of TPunc

We modularise transformation TPunc ("Puncturing and Encrypt-with-Hash") that was given in [43], and that turns any IND-CPA secure PKE scheme into a deterministic one that is DS. Note that apart from reencryption, $\mathsf{TPunc}[\mathsf{PKE}_0, \mathsf{G}]$ given in [43] and our modularisation $\mathsf{T}[\mathsf{Punc}[\mathsf{PKE}_0], \mathsf{G}]$ are equal. We first give transformation Punc that turns any IND-CPA secure scheme into a scheme that

---

[8] Fake encryptions could be sampled uniformly random. DS would follow from the LWE assumption, and since LWE samples are relatively sparse, uniform sampling should be disjoint.

Enc$(pk, m \in \mathcal{M})$	$\overline{\mathsf{Enc}}(pk)$
01 $c \leftarrow \mathsf{Enc}_0(pk, m)$	03 $c \leftarrow \mathsf{Enc}_0(pk, \hat{m})$
02 **return** c	04 **return** c

Fig. 5. Encryption and fake encryption sampling of $\mathsf{PKE} = \mathsf{Punc}[\mathsf{PKE}_0]$.

is both DS and IND-CPA. We show that transformation T turns any scheme that is DS as well as IND-CPA secure into a deterministic scheme that is DS.

Transformation Punc: From IND-CPA to probabilistic DS security Transformation Punc turns any IND-CPA secure public-key encryption scheme into a DS secure one by puncturing the message space at one message and sampling encryptions of this message as fake encryptions.

THE CONSTRUCTION. To a public-key encryption scheme $\mathsf{PKE}_0 = (\mathsf{KG}_0, \mathsf{Enc}_0, \mathsf{Dec}_0)$ with message space $\mathcal{M}_0$, we associate $\mathsf{PKE} := \mathsf{Punc}[\mathsf{PKE}_0, \hat{m}] := (\mathsf{KG} := \mathsf{KG}_0, \mathsf{Enc}, \mathsf{Dec} := \mathsf{Dec}_0)$ with message space $\mathcal{M} := \mathcal{M}_0 \setminus \{\hat{m}\}$ for some message $\hat{m} \in \mathcal{M}$. Encryption and fake encryption sampling of PKE are defined in Fig. 5. Note that transformation Punc will only be used as a helper transformation to achieve DS, generically. We prove that Punc achieves DS from IND-CPA security in the full version.

Transformation T: From probabilistic to deterministic DS security Transformation T [7] turns any probabilistic public-key encryption scheme into a deterministic one. The transformed scheme is DS, given that PKE is DS as well as IND-CPA secure. Our security proof is tighter than the proof given for TPunc (see [43, Theorem 3.3]) due to our use of the semi-classical O2H theorem.

THE CONSTRUCTION. Take an encryption scheme $\mathsf{PKE} = (\mathsf{KG}, \mathsf{Enc}, \mathsf{Dec})$ with message space $\mathcal{M}$ and randomness space $\mathcal{R}$. Assume PKE to be additionally endowed with a sampling algorithm $\overline{\mathsf{Enc}}$ (see Definition 6). To PKE and random oracle $\mathsf{G} : \mathcal{M} \to \mathcal{R}$, we associate $\mathsf{PKE}' = \mathsf{T}[\mathsf{PKE}, \mathsf{G}]$, where the algorithms of $\mathsf{PKE}' = (\mathsf{KG}' := \mathsf{KG}, \mathsf{Enc}', \mathsf{Dec}', \overline{\mathsf{Enc}}' := \overline{\mathsf{Enc}})$ are defined in Fig. 6. Note that Enc$'$ deterministically computes the ciphertext as $c := \mathsf{Enc}(pk, m; \mathsf{G}(m))$.

Enc$'(pk, m)$	Dec$'(sk, c)$
01 $c := \mathsf{Enc}(pk, m; \mathsf{G}(m))$	03 $m' := \mathsf{Dec}(sk, c)$.
02 **return** c	04 **if** $m' = \perp$ **or** $\mathsf{Enc}(pk, m'; \mathsf{G}(m')) \neq c$
	05 **return** $\perp$
	06 **else return** m'

Fig. 6. Deterministic encryption scheme $\mathsf{PKE}' = \mathsf{T}[\mathsf{PKE}, \mathsf{G}]$.

The following lemma states that combined IND-CPA and DS security of PKE imply the DS security of PKE'.

Games G_0-G_3		Game G_4-G_5		$G \setminus \{m^*\}|\psi, \phi\rangle$
01 $pk \leftarrow$ KG		10 FIND := **false**		18 $|\psi', b\rangle := O^{\text{SC}}_{\{m^*\}}|\psi, 0\rangle$
02 $m^* \leftarrow_\$ \mathcal{M}$		11 $pk \leftarrow$ KG		19 **if** $b = 1$
03 $c^* \leftarrow \overline{\text{Enc}}(pk)$	$/\!/ G_0$	12 $m^* \leftarrow_\$ \mathcal{M}$		20 FIND := **true**
04 $r^* := G(m^*)$	$/\!/ G_1$	13 $r^* \leftarrow_\$ \mathcal{R}$		21 **return** $U_G|\psi', \phi\rangle$
05 $r^* \leftarrow_\$ \mathcal{R}$	$/\!/ G_2$-G_3	14 $c^* := \text{Enc}(pk, m^*; r^*)$	$/\!/ G_4$	
06 $c^* := \text{Enc}(pk, m^*; r^*)$	$/\!/ G_1$-G_3	15 $c^* := \text{Enc}(pk, 0; r^*)$	$/\!/ G_5$	
07 $b' \leftarrow A^{|G\rangle}(pk, c^*)$	$/\!/ G_0$-G_1, G_3	16 $b' \leftarrow A^{|G\setminus\{m^*\}\rangle}(pk, c^*)$		
08 $b' \leftarrow A^{|H\rangle}(pk, c^*)$	$/\!/ G_2$	17 **return** FIND		
09 **return** b'				

Fig. 7. Games G_0 - G_5 for the proof of Lemma 2.

Lemma 2 (DS security of PKE′). *If* PKE *is* ϵ-*disjoint, so is* PKE′. *For all adversaries* A *issuing at most* q_G *(quantum) queries to* G, *there exist an adversary* B_{IND} *and an adversary* B_{DS} *such that*

$$\text{Adv}^{\text{DS}}_{\text{PKE}'}(A) \leq \text{Adv}^{\text{DS}}_{\text{PKE}}(B_{\text{DS}}) + 2 \cdot \sqrt{q_G \cdot \text{Adv}^{\text{IND-CPA}}_{\text{PKE}}(B_{\text{IND}}) + \frac{4q_G^2}{|\mathcal{M}|}}$$

$$\leq \text{Adv}^{\text{DS}}_{\text{PKE}}(B_{\text{DS}}) + 2 \cdot \sqrt{q_G \cdot \text{Adv}^{\text{IND-CPA}}_{\text{PKE}}(B_{\text{IND}})} + \frac{4q_G}{\sqrt{|\mathcal{M}|}},$$

and the running time of each adversary is about that of B.

Proof. It is straightforward to prove disjointness since $\text{Enc}'(pk, \mathcal{M})$ is subset of $\text{Enc}(pk, \mathcal{M}; \mathcal{R})$. Let A be a DS adversary against PKE′. Consider the sequence of games given in Fig. 7. Per definition,

$$\text{Adv}^{\text{DS}}_{\text{PKE}'}(A) = |\Pr[G_0^A \Rightarrow 1] - \Pr[G_1^A \Rightarrow 1]|$$
$$\leq |\Pr[G_0^A \Rightarrow 1] - \Pr[G_3^A \Rightarrow 1]| + |\Pr[G_1^A \Rightarrow 1] - \Pr[G_3^A \Rightarrow 1]|.$$

To upper bound $|\Pr[G_0^A \Rightarrow 1] - \Pr[G_3^A \Rightarrow 1]|$, consider adversary B_{DS} against the disjoint simulatability of the underlying scheme PKE, given in Fig. 8. B_{DS} runs in the time that is required to run A and to simulate G for q_G queries. Since B_{DS} perfectly simulates game G_0 if run with a fake ciphertext as input, and game G_3 if run with a random encryption $c \leftarrow \text{Enc}(pk, m^*)$,

$$|\Pr[G_0^A \Rightarrow 1] - \Pr[G_3^A \Rightarrow 1]| = \text{Adv}^{\text{DS}}_{\text{PKE}}(B_{\text{DS}}).$$

It remains to upper bound $|\Pr[G_1^A \Rightarrow 1] - \Pr[G_3^A \Rightarrow 1]|$. We claim that there exists an adversary B_{IND} such that

$$|\Pr[G_1^A \Rightarrow 1] - \Pr[G_3^A \Rightarrow 1]| \leq 2\sqrt{q_G \cdot \text{Adv}^{\text{IND-CPA}}_{\text{PKE}}(B_{\text{IND}}) + \frac{4q_G^2}{|\mathcal{M}|}}.$$

$$
\begin{array}{lll}
\underline{\mathsf{B}_{\mathsf{DS}}(pk, c)} & \underline{\mathsf{B}_{\mathsf{IND},1}(pk)} & \underline{\mathsf{G} \setminus \{\mathsf{m}^*\}|\psi, \phi\rangle} \\
01 \ \ b' \leftarrow \mathsf{A}^{|G\rangle}(pk, c) & 03 \ \ m^* \leftarrow_{\$} \mathcal{M} & 08 \ \ |\psi', b\rangle := \mathsf{O}^{\mathsf{SC}}_{\{\mathsf{m}^*\}}|\psi, 0\rangle \\
02 \ \ \mathbf{return} \ b' & 04 \ \ \mathbf{return} \ (0, m^*, \mathrm{st} := m^*) & 09 \ \ \mathbf{if} \ b = 1 \\
& & 10 \qquad \mathrm{FIND} := \mathbf{true} \\
& \underline{\mathsf{B}_{\mathsf{IND},2}(pk, c^*, \mathrm{st} := m^*)} & 11 \ \ \mathbf{return} \ U_{\mathsf{G}}|\psi', \phi\rangle \\
& 05 \ \ \mathrm{FIND} := \mathbf{false} & \\
& 06 \ \ b' \leftarrow \mathsf{A}^{|G\setminus\{\mathsf{m}^*\}\rangle}(pk, c^*) & \\
& 07 \ \ \mathbf{return} \ \mathrm{FIND} &
\end{array}
$$

Fig. 8. Adversaries B_{DS} and $\mathsf{B}_{\mathsf{IND}}$ for the proof of Lemma 2.

GAME G_2. In game G_2, we replace oracle access to G with oracle acces to H in line 08, where H is defined as follows: we pick a uniformly random r^* in line 08 and let $\mathsf{H}(m) := \mathsf{G}(m)$ for all $m \neq m^*$, and $\mathsf{H}(m^*) := r^*$. Note that this change also affects the challenge ciphertext c^* since it is now defined relative to this new r^*, i.e., we now have $c^* = \mathsf{Enc}(pk, m^*; \mathsf{H}(m^*))$. Since r^* is uniformly random and G is a random oracle, so is H, and since we kept c^* consistent, this change is purely conceptual and

$$
\Pr[G_1^{\mathsf{A}} \Rightarrow 1] = \Pr[G_2^{\mathsf{A}} \Rightarrow 1].
$$

GAME G_3. In game G_3, we switch back to oracle access to G, but keep c^* unaffected by this change. We now are ready to use Oneway to Hiding with semiclassical oracles. Intuitively, the first part of O2H states that if oracles G and H only differ on point m^*, the probability of an adversary being able to tell G and H apart is directly related to m^* being detectable in its random oracle queries. Detecting m^* is formalised by game G_4, in which each of the random oracle queries of A is measured with respect to projector $|m^*\rangle\langle m^*|$, thereby collapsing the query to either m^* (and switching flag FIND to **true**) or a superposition that does not contain m^* at all. Following the notation of [3], we denote this process by a call to oracle $\mathsf{O}^{\mathsf{SC}}_{\{\mathsf{m}^*\}}$, see line 08. Applying the first statement of Theorem 1 for $S := \{m^*\}$, and $z := (pk, c^* := \mathsf{Enc}(pk, m^*; r^*))$, we obtain

$$
|\Pr[G_2^{\mathsf{A}} \Rightarrow 1] - \Pr[G_3^{\mathsf{A}} \Rightarrow 1]| \leq 2 \cdot \sqrt{q_{\mathsf{G}} \cdot \Pr[G_4^{\mathsf{A}} \Rightarrow 1]}.
$$

GAME G_5. In game G_5, $c^* \leftarrow \mathsf{Enc}(pk, m^*)$ is replaced with an encryption of 0. Since in game G_5, (pk, c^*) is independent of m^*, we can apply the second statement of O2H that upper bounds the probability of finding an independent point m^*, relative to the number of queries and the size of the search space $\mathcal{M}$. We obtain

$$
\Pr[G_5^{\mathsf{A}} \Rightarrow 1] \leq \frac{4q_{\mathsf{G}}}{|\mathcal{M}|}.
$$

To upper bound $|\Pr[G_4^{\mathsf{A}} \Rightarrow 1] - \Pr[G_5^{\mathsf{A}} \Rightarrow 1]|$, consider adversary $\mathsf{B}_{\mathsf{IND}}$ against the IND-CPA security of PKE, also given in Fig. 8. $\mathsf{B}_{\mathsf{IND}}$ runs in the time that is required to run A and to simulate the measured version of oracle G for q_{G}

Encaps(pk)	Decaps(sk, c)
01 $m \leftarrow_\$ \mathcal{M}$	05 $m' := \mathsf{Dec}(sk, c)$
02 $c := \mathsf{Enc}(pk, m; \mathsf{G}(m))$	06 **if** $m' = \bot$ **or** $\mathsf{Enc}(pk, m'; \mathsf{G}(m')) \neq c$
03 $K := \mathsf{H}(m)$	07 **return** $K := \mathsf{H_r}(c)$
04 **return** (K, c)	08 **else return** $K := \mathsf{H}(m')$

Fig. 9. Key encapsulation mechanism $\mathsf{KEM} = \mathsf{FO}_m^{\not\perp}[\mathsf{PKE}, \mathsf{G}, \mathsf{H}] = \mathsf{U}_m^{\not\perp}[\mathsf{T}[\mathsf{PKE}, \mathsf{G}], \mathsf{H}]$. Oracle $\mathsf{H_r}$ is used to generate random values whenever reencryption fails. This strategy is called implicit reject. Amongst others, it is used in [28,43], and [32]. For simplicity of the proof, $\mathsf{H_r}$ is modelled as an internal random oracle that cannot be accessed directly. For implementation, it would be sufficient to use a PRF.

queries. $\mathsf{B_{IND}}$ perfectly simulates game G_4 if run in game $\mathsf{IND\text{-}CPA}_0$ and game G_5 if run in game $\mathsf{IND\text{-}CPA}_1$, therefore,

$$|\Pr[G_4^A \Rightarrow 1] - \Pr[G_5^A \Rightarrow 1]| = \mathrm{Adv}_{\mathsf{PKE}}^{\mathsf{IND\text{-}CPA}}(\mathsf{B_{IND}}).$$

Collecting the probabilities yields

$$\Pr[G_4^A \Rightarrow 1] \leq \mathrm{Adv}_{\mathsf{PKE}}^{\mathsf{IND\text{-}CPA}}(\mathsf{B_{IND}}) + \frac{4q_\mathsf{G}}{|\mathcal{M}|}.$$

$\square$

3.2 Transformation $\mathsf{FO}_m^{\not\perp}$ and Correctness Errors

Transformation SXY [43] got rid of the additional hash (sometimes called key confirmation) that was included in [28]'s quantum transformation $\mathsf{QU}_m^{\not\perp}$. SXY is essentially the (classical) transformation $\mathsf{U}_m^{\not\perp}$ that was also given in [28], and apart from doing without the additional hash, it comes with a tight security reduction in the QROM. SXY differs from the (classical) transformation $\mathsf{U}_m^{\not\perp}$ only in the regard that it reencrypts during decapsulation. (In [28], reencryption is done during decryption of T.)

The security proof given in [43] requires the underlying encryption scheme to be perfectly correct, and it turned out that their analysis cannot be trivially adapted to take possible decryption failures into account in a generic setting. A discussion of this matter is given in the full version. What we show instead is that the combined transformation $\mathsf{FO}_m^{\not\perp} = \mathsf{U}_m^{\not\perp}[\mathsf{T}[-, \mathsf{G}], \mathsf{H}]$ turns any encryption scheme that is DS as well as IND-CPA into a KEM that is IND-CCA secure in the QROM, even if the underlying encryption scheme comes with a small probability of decryption failure. Our reduction is tighter as the (combined) reduction in [43] due to our tighter security proof for T.

THE CONSTRUCTION. To $\mathsf{PKE} = (\mathsf{KG}, \mathsf{Enc}, \mathsf{Dec})$ with message space $\mathcal{M}$ and randomness space $\mathcal{R}$, and random oracles $\mathsf{H} : \mathcal{M} \to \mathcal{K}$, $\mathsf{G} : \mathcal{M} \to \mathcal{R}$, and an additional internal random oracle $\mathsf{H_r} : \mathcal{C} \to \mathcal{K}$ that can not be directly accessed, we associate $\mathsf{KEM} = \mathsf{FO}_m^{\not\perp}[\mathsf{PKE}, \mathsf{G}, \mathsf{H}] := \mathsf{U}_m^{\not\perp}[\mathsf{T}[\mathsf{PKE}, \mathsf{G}], \mathsf{H}]$, where the algorithms of $\mathsf{KEM} = (\mathsf{KG}, \mathsf{Encaps}, \mathsf{Decaps})$ are given in Fig. 9.

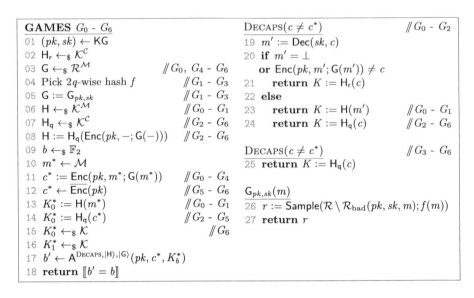

Fig. 10. Games $G_0 - G_6$ for the proof of Lemma 2. f (lines 04 and 26) is an internal $2q$-wise independent hash function, where $q := q_G + q_H + 2 \cdot q_D + 1$, that cannot be accessed by A. Sample(Y) is a probabilistic algorithm that returns a uniformly distributed $y \leftarrow_\$ Y$. Sample($Y; f(m)$) denotes the deterministic execution of Sample(Y) using explicitly given randomness $f(m)$.

SECURITY OF KEM. The following theorem (whose proof is essentially the same as in [43] except for the consideration of possible decryption failure) establishes that IND-CCA security of KEM reduces to DS and IND-CPA security of PKE, in the quantum random oracle model.

Theorem 2 (PKE DS + IND-CPA $\overset{\mathrm{QROM}}{\Rightarrow}$ KEM IND-CCA). *Assume* PKE *to be δ-correct, and to come with a fake sampling algorithm* $\overline{\mathsf{Enc}}$ *such that* PKE *is ϵ_{dis}-disjoint. Then, for any (quantum)* IND-CCA *adversary* A *issuing at most q_D (classical) queries to the decapsulation oracle* DECAPS, *at most q_H quantum queries to* H, *and at most q_G quantum queries to* G, *there exist (quantum) adversaries* B_{DS} *and* B_{IND} *such that*

$$\mathrm{Adv}_{\mathsf{KEM}}^{\mathsf{IND\text{-}CCA}}(A) \leq 8 \cdot (2 \cdot q_G + q_H + q_D + 4)^2 \cdot \delta + \mathrm{Adv}_{\mathsf{PKE}}^{\mathsf{DS}}(B_{DS})$$

$$+ 2 \cdot \sqrt{(q_G + q_H) \cdot \mathrm{Adv}_{\mathsf{PKE}}^{\mathsf{IND\text{-}CPA}}(B_{IND}) + \frac{4(q_G + q_H)^2}{|\mathcal{M}|}} + \epsilon_{dis},$$

and the running time of B_{DS} *and* B_{IND} *is about that of* A.

Proof. Let A be an adversary against the IND-CCA security of KEM, issuing at most q_D queries to DECAPS, at most q_H queries to the quantum random oracle H, and at most q_G queries to the quantum random oracle G. Consider the sequence of games given in Fig. 10.

GAME G_0. Since game G_0 is the original IND-CCA game,

$$\mathrm{Adv}_{\mathsf{KEM}}^{\mathsf{IND\text{-}CCA}}(\mathsf{A}) = |\Pr[G_0^{\mathsf{A}} \Rightarrow 1] - 1/2|.$$

GAME G_1. In game G_1, we enforce that no decryption failure will occur: For fixed (pk, sk) and message $m \in \mathcal{M}$, let

$$\mathcal{R}_{\mathrm{bad}}(pk, sk, m) := \{r \in \mathcal{R} \mid \mathsf{Dec}(sk, \mathsf{Enc}(pk, m; r)) \neq m\}$$

denote the set of "bad" randomness. We replace random oracle G in line 05 with $\mathsf{G}_{pk,sk}$ that only samples from good randomness. Further, define

$$\delta(pk, sk, m) := |\mathcal{R}_{\mathrm{bad}}(pk,sk,m)|/|\mathcal{R}| \tag{2}$$

as the fraction of bad randomness, and $\delta(pk, sk) := \max_{m \in \mathcal{M}} \delta(pk, sk, m)$. With this notation, $\delta = \mathbf{E}[\max_{m \in \mathcal{M}} \delta(pk, sk, m)]$, where the expectation is taken over $(pk, sk) \leftarrow \mathsf{KG}$.

To upper bound $|\Pr[G_0^{\mathsf{A}} = 1] - \Pr[G_1^{\mathsf{A}} = 1]|$, we construct an (unbounded, quantum) adversary B against the generic distinguishing problem with bounded probabilities GDPB (see Lemma 1) in Fig. 11, issuing $q_{\mathsf{G}} + q_D + 1$ queries to F. B draws a key pair $(pk, sk) \leftarrow \mathsf{KG}$ and computes the parameters $\lambda(m)$ of the generic distinguishing problem as $\lambda(m) := \delta(pk, sk, m)$, which are bounded by $\lambda := \delta(pk, sk)$. To analyze B, we first fix (pk, sk). For each $m \in \mathcal{M}$, by the definition of game $\mathsf{GDPB}_{\lambda,1}$, the random variable $\mathsf{F}(m)$ is bernoulli-distributed according to $B_{\lambda(m)} = B_{\delta(pk,sk,m)}$. By construction, the random variable $\mathsf{G}(m)$ defined in line 28 if $\mathsf{F}(m) = 0$ and in line 30 if $\mathsf{F}(m) = 1$ is uniformly distributed in $\mathcal{R}$. Therefore, G is a (quantum-accessible) random oracle, and $\mathsf{B}^{|\mathsf{F}\rangle}$ perfectly simulates game G_0 if executed in game $\mathsf{GDPB}_{\lambda,1}$. Since $\mathsf{B}^{|\mathsf{F}\rangle}$ also perfectly simulates game G_1 if executed in game $\mathsf{GDPB}_{\lambda,0}$,

$$|\Pr[G_0^{\mathsf{A}} = 1] - \Pr[G_1^{\mathsf{A}} = 1]| = |\Pr[\mathsf{GDPB}_{\lambda,1}^{\mathsf{B}} = 1] - \Pr[\mathsf{GDPB}_{\lambda,0}^{\mathsf{B}} = 1]|,$$

and according to Lemma 1,

$$|\Pr[\mathsf{GDPB}_{\lambda,1}^{\mathsf{B}} = 1] - \Pr[\mathsf{GDPB}_{\lambda,0}^{\mathsf{B}} = 1]| \leq 8 \cdot (q_{\mathsf{G}} + q_D + 2)^2 \cdot \delta.$$

GAME G_2. In game G_2, we prepare getting rid of the secret key by plugging in encryption into random oracle H: Instead of drawing $\mathsf{H} \leftarrow_\$ \mathcal{K}^{\mathcal{M}}$, we draw $\mathsf{H}_{\mathsf{q}} \leftarrow_\$ \mathcal{K}^{\mathcal{C}}$ in line 07 and define $\mathsf{H} := \mathsf{H}_{\mathsf{q}}(\mathsf{Enc}(pk, -; \mathsf{G}(-)))$ in line 08. For consistency, we also change key K_0^* in line 14 from letting $K_0^* := \mathsf{H}(m^*)$ to letting $K_0^* := \mathsf{H}_{\mathsf{q}}(c^*)$, which is a purely conceptual change since $c^* = \mathsf{Enc}(pk, m^*; \mathsf{G}(m^*))$. Additionally, we make the change of H explicit in oracle DECAPS, i.e., we change oracle DECAPS in line 14 such that it returns $K := \mathsf{H}_{\mathsf{q}}(c)$ whenever $\mathsf{Enc}(pk, m'; \mathsf{G}(m')) = c$. Since G only samples from good randomness, encryption is rendered perfectly correct and hence, injective. Since encryption is injective, H still is uniformly random. Furthermore, since we only change DECAPS for ciphertexts

```
B₁ = B′₁                                    DECAPS(c ≠ c*)                    // Adversary B
01  (pk, sk) ← KG                           22  m′ := Dec′(sk, c)
02  for m ∈ M                               23  if m′ = ⊥
03     λ(m) := δ(pk, sk, m)                     or Enc(pk, m′; G(m′)) ≠ c
04  return (λ(m))ₘ∈M                         24     return K := Hᵣ(c)
                                            25  else return K := H(m′)
B₂^{|Hᵣ⟩,|H⟩,|F⟩}
05  Pick 2q-wise hash f                      DECAPS(c ≠ c*)                   // Adversary B′
06  b ←$ F₂                                  26  return K := Hq(c)
07  m* ← M
08  c* := Enc(pk, m*; G(m*))                 G(m)
09  K₀* := H(m*)                             27  if F(m) = 0
10  K₁* ←$ K                                 28     G(m) := Sample(R \ R_bad(pk, sk, m); f(m))
11  b′ ← A^{DECAPS,|H⟩,|G⟩}(pk, c*, K_b*)     29  else
12  return ⟦b′ = b⟧                          30     G(m) := Sample(R_bad(pk, sk, m); f(m))
                                            31  return G(m)
B′₂^{|Hᵣ⟩,|Hq⟩,|F⟩}
13  Pick 2q-wise hash f
14  H := Hq(Enc(pk, −; G(−)))
15  b ←$ F₂
16  m* ← M
17  c* := Enc(pk, m*; G(m*))
18  K₀* := Hq(c*)
19  K₁* ←$ K
20  b′ ← A^{DECAPS,|H⟩,|G⟩}(pk, c*, K_b*)
21  return ⟦b′ = b⟧
```

Fig. 11. Adversaries B and B′ executed in game $\mathsf{GDPB}_{\delta(pk,sk)}$ with access to F (and additional oracles $\mathsf{H_r}$ and H or $\mathsf{H_q}$, respectively) for the proof of Theorem 2. Parameters $\delta(pk, sk, m)$ are defined in Eq. (2). Function f (lines 28 and 30) is an internal $2q$-wise independent hash function, where $q := q_G + q_D + 1$ for B, and $q_G + q_H + 1$ for B′, that cannot be accessed by A.

c where $c = \mathsf{Enc}(pk, m'; \mathsf{G}(m'))$, we maintain consistency of H and DECAPS. In conclusion, A's view is identical in both games and

$$\Pr[G_1^A = 1] = \Pr[G_2^A = 1].$$

GAME G_3. In game G_3, we change oracle DECAPS such that it always returns $K := \mathsf{H_q}(c)$, as opposed to returning $K := \mathsf{H_r}(c)$ as in game G_2 whenever decryption or reencryption fails (see line 21). We argue that this change does not affect A's view: If there exists no message m such that $c = \mathsf{Enc}(pk, m; \mathsf{G}(m))$, oracle DECAPS($c$) returns a random value (that can not possibly correlate to any random oracle query to H) in both games, therefore DECAPS(c) is a random value independent of all other input to A in both games. And if there exists some message m such that $c = \mathsf{Enc}(pk, m; \mathsf{G}(m))$, DECAPS($c$) would have returned $\mathsf{H_q}(c)$ in both games, anyway: Since $\mathsf{G}(m) \in \mathcal{R} \backslash \mathcal{R}_{\mathrm{bad}}(pk, sk, m)$ for all messages

m, it holds that $m' := \mathsf{Dec}(sk, c) = m \neq \bot$ and that $\mathsf{Enc}(pk, m'; \mathsf{G}(m')) = c$. Hence, A's view is identical in both games and

$$\Pr[G_2^A = 1] = \Pr[G_3^A = 1].$$

GAME G_4. In game G_4, we switch back to using $\mathsf{G} \leftarrow_\$ \mathcal{R}^{\mathcal{M}}$ instead of $\mathsf{G}_{pk,sk}$. With the same reasoning as for the gamehop from game G_0 to G_1,

$$|\Pr[G_3^A = 1] - \Pr[G_4^A = 1]| = |\Pr[\mathsf{GDPB}_{\lambda,1}^{B'} = 1] - \Pr[\mathsf{GDPB}_{\lambda,0}^{B'} = 1]|$$
$$\leq 8 \cdot (q_\mathsf{G} + q_\mathsf{H} + 2)^2 \cdot \delta,$$

where adversary B' (that issues at most issuing $q_\mathsf{G} + q_\mathsf{H} + 1$ queries to F) is also given in Fig. 11.

So far, we established

$$\mathsf{Adv}_{\mathsf{KEM}}^{\mathsf{IND\text{-}CCA}}(A) \leq |\Pr[G_4^A \Rightarrow 1] - 1/2| + 8 \cdot (2 \cdot q_\mathsf{G} + q_\mathsf{H} + q_D + 4)^2 \cdot \delta.$$

The rest of the proof proceeds similar to the proof in [43], aside from the fact that we consider the particular scheme $\mathsf{T}[\mathsf{PKE}, \mathsf{G}]$ instead of a generic encryption scheme that is deterministically DS.

GAME G_5. In game G_5, the challenge ciphertext c^* gets decoupled from message m^* by sampling $c^* \leftarrow \overline{\mathsf{Enc}}(pk)$ in line 12 instead of letting $c^* := \mathsf{Enc}(pk, m^*; \mathsf{G}(m^*))$. Consider the adversary $\mathsf{C_{DS}}$ against the disjoint simulatability of $\mathsf{T}[\mathsf{PKE}, \mathsf{G}]$ given in Fig. 12. Since $\mathsf{C_{DS}}$ perfectly simulates game G_4 if run with deterministic encryption $c^* := \mathsf{Enc}(pk, m^*; \mathsf{G}(m^*))$ of a random message m^*, and game G_5 if run with a fake ciphertext,

$$|\Pr[G_4^A = 1] - \Pr[G_5^A = 1]| = \mathsf{Adv}_{\mathsf{T}[\mathsf{PKE},\mathsf{G}]}^{\mathsf{DS}}(\mathsf{C_{DS}}),$$

and according to Lemma 2, there exist an adversary $\mathsf{B_{DS}}$ and an adversary $\mathsf{B_{IND}}$ with roughly the same running time such that

$$\mathsf{Adv}_{\mathsf{T}[\mathsf{PKE},\mathsf{G}]}^{\mathsf{DS}}(\mathsf{C_{DS}}) \leq \mathsf{Adv}_{\mathsf{PKE}}^{\mathsf{DS}}(\mathsf{B_{DS}}) + 2 \cdot \sqrt{(q_\mathsf{G} + q_\mathsf{H}) \cdot \mathsf{Adv}_{\mathsf{PKE}}^{\mathsf{IND\text{-}CPA}}(\mathsf{B_{IND}}) + \frac{4(q_\mathsf{G} + q_\mathsf{H})^2}{|\mathcal{M}|}}.$$

GAME G_6. In game G_6, the game is changed in line 15 such that it always uses a randomly picked challenge key. Since both K_0^* and K_1^* are independent of all other input to A in game G_6,

$$\Pr[G_6^A \Rightarrow 1] = 1/2.$$

It remains to upper bound $|\Pr[G_5^A = 1] - \Pr[G_6^A = 1]|$. To this end, it is sufficient to upper bound the probability that any of the queries to $\mathsf{H_q}$ could possibly contain c^*. Each query to $\mathsf{H_q}$ is either a classical query, triggered by A querying DECAPS on some ciphertext c, or a query in superposition, triggered by A querying H. Since queries to DECAPS on c^* are explicitly forbidden, the only possibility would be one of A's queries to H. A's queries to H trigger queries

$\mathsf{C}_{\mathsf{DS}}^{|\mathsf{G}\rangle, |\mathsf{H}_r\rangle |\mathsf{H}_q\rangle}(pk, c^*)$	$\mathrm{DECAPS}(c \neq c^*)$
01 $b \leftarrow_\$ \mathbb{F}_2$	06 **return** $K := \mathsf{H}_q(c)$
02 $K_0^* := \mathsf{H}_q(c^*)$	
03 $K_1^* \leftarrow_\$ \mathcal{K}$	
04 $b' \leftarrow \mathsf{A}^{\mathrm{DECAPS}, |\mathsf{H}\rangle, |\mathsf{G}\rangle}(pk, c^*, K_b^*)$	
05 **return** $[\![b' = b]\!]$	

Fig. 12. Adversary C_{DS} (with access to additional oracles H_r and H_q) against the disjoint simulatability of $\mathsf{T}[\mathsf{PKE}, \mathsf{G}]$ for the proof of Theorem 2.

to H_q that are of the form $\sum_m \alpha_m |\mathsf{Enc}(pk, m; \mathsf{G}(m))\rangle$. They cannot contain c^* unless there exists some message m such that $\mathsf{Enc}(pk, m; \mathsf{G}(m)) = c^*$. Since we assume PKE to be ϵ_{dis}-disjoint,

$$|\Pr[G_5^A = 1] - \Pr[G_6^A = 1]| \leq \epsilon_{\mathrm{dis}}.$$

3.3 CCA Security Without Disjoint Simulatability

In the full version we show that transformation Punc can be used to waive the requirement of DS: Plugging in transformation Punc (before using $\mathsf{FO}_m^{\not\perp}$) achieves IND-CCA security from IND-CPA security alone, as long as PKE is γ-spread (see Definition 3).

4 Two-Message Authenticated Key Exchange

A two-message key exchange protocol $\mathsf{AKE} = (\mathsf{KG}, \mathsf{Init}, \mathsf{Der}_{\mathsf{init}}, \mathsf{Der}_{\mathsf{resp}})$ consists of four algorithms. Given the security parameter, the key generation algorithm KG outputs a key pair (pk, sk). The initialisation algorithm Init, on input sk and pk', outputs a message M and a state st. The responder's derivation algorithm $\mathsf{Der}_{\mathsf{resp}}$, on input sk', pk and M, outputs a key K, and also a message M'. The initiator's derivation algorithm $\mathsf{Der}_{\mathsf{init}}$, on input sk, pk', M' and st, outputs a key K.

RUNNING A KEY EXCHANGE PROTOCOL BETWEEN TWO PARTIES. To run a two-message key exchange protocol, the algorithms $\mathsf{KG}, \mathsf{Init}, \mathsf{Der}_{\mathsf{init}}$, and $\mathsf{Der}_{\mathsf{resp}}$ are executed in an interactive manner between two parties P_i and P_j with key pairs $(sk_i, pk_i), (sk_j, pk_j) \leftarrow \mathsf{KG}$. To execute the protocol, the parties call the algorithms in the following way:

1. P_i computes $(M, \mathsf{st}) \leftarrow \mathsf{Init}(sk_i, pk_j)$ and sends M to P_j.
2. P_j computes $(M', K') \leftarrow \mathsf{Der}_{\mathsf{resp}}(sk_j, pk_i, M)$ and sends M' to P_i.
3. P_i computes $K := \mathsf{Der}_{\mathsf{init}}(sk_i, pk_j, M', \mathsf{st})$.

Note that in contrast to the holder P_i, the peer P_j will not be required to save any (secret) state information besides the key K'.

OUR SECURITY MODEL. We consider N parties $P_1, \ldots, P_N$, each holding a key pair (sk_i, pk_i), and possibly having several sessions at once. The sessions run the protocol with access to the party's long-term key material, while also having their own set of (session-specific) local variables. The local variables of each session, identified by the integer sID, are the following:

$$
\begin{array}{ll}
\underline{\text{Party } P_i\ (pk_i, sk_i)} & \underline{\text{Party } P_j\ (pk_j, sk_j)} \\[4pt]
(M, \text{st}) \leftarrow \text{Init}(sk_i, pk_j) \quad \xrightarrow{\quad M \quad} & \\
& (M', K') \leftarrow \text{Der}_{\text{resp}}(sk_j, pk_i, M) \\
K := \text{Der}_{\text{init}}(sk_i, pk_j, M', \text{st}) \quad \xleftarrow{\quad M' \quad} &
\end{array}
$$

1. An integer **holder** $\in [N]$ that points to the party running the session.
2. An integer **peer** $\in [N]$ that points to the party the session is communicating with.
3. A string **sent** that holds the message sent by the session.
4. A string **received** that holds the message received by the session.
5. A string **st** that holds (secret) internal state values and intermediary results required by the session.
6. A string **role** that holds the information whether the session's key was derived by Der_{init} or Der_{resp}.
7. The session key K.

In our security model, the adversary A is given black-box access to the set of processes Init, Der_{resp} and Der_{init} that execute the AKE algorithms. To model the attacker's control of the network, we allow A to establish new sessions via EST, to call either INIT and DER_{init} or DER_{resp}, each at most once per session (see Fig. 13, page 23). Since both derivation processes can be called on arbitrary input, A may relay their input faithfully as well as modify the data on transit. Moreover, the attacker is additionally granted queries to reveal both secret process data, namely using oracles REVEAL, REV-STATE and CORRUPT (see Fig. 14, page 24). Oracles REVEAL and REV-STATE both can be queried on an arbitrary session ID, with oracle REVEAL revealing the respective session's key (if already defined), and oracle REV-STATE revealing the respective session's internal state. Oracle CORRUPT can be queried on an arbitrary number $i \in [N]$ to reveal the respective party's long-term key material. Usage of this oracle allows the attacker to corrupt the test session's holder, the oracle therefore models the possibility of KCI attacks. Combined usage of oracles REV-STATE and CORRUPT allows the attacker to obtain the state as well as the long-term secret key on both sides of the session, the oracles therefore model the possibility of MEX attacks. After choosing a test session, either the session's key or

GAME IND-AA$_b$		**GAME** IND-StAA$_b$	
01 cnt := 0	//session counter	23 cnt := 0	//session counter
02 sID* := 0	//test session's id	24 sID* := 0	//test session's id
03 **for** $n \in [N]$		25 **for** $n \in [N]$	
04 $(pk_n, sk_n) \leftarrow$ KG		26 $(pk_n, sk_n) \leftarrow$ KG	
05 $b' \leftarrow A^O(pk_1, \cdots, pk_N)$		27 $b' \leftarrow A^O(pk_1, \cdots, pk_N)$	
06 **if** Trivial(sID*)		28 **if** ATTACK(sID*)	
07 **return** 0		29 **return** 0	
08 **return** b'		30 **return** b'	
$\underline{\text{EST}((i,j) \in [N]^2)}$		$\underline{\text{INIT}(\text{sID})}$	
09 cnt ++		31 **if** holder[sID] = $\perp$	
10 holder[cnt] := i		32 **return** $\perp$	//Session not established
11 peer[cnt] := j		33 **if** sent[sID] $\neq \perp$ **return** $\perp$	//no re-use
12 **return** cnt		34 role[sID] := "initiator"	
		35 $(i,j) :=$ (holder[sID], peer[sID])	
$\underline{\text{DER}_{\text{resp}}(\text{sID}, M)}$		36 $(M, \text{st}) \leftarrow \text{Init}(sk_i, pk_j)$	
13 **if** holder[sID] = $\perp$		37 (sent[sID], state[sID]) := (M, st)	
14 **return** $\perp$	//Session not established	38 **return** M	
15 **if** sKey[sID] $\neq \perp$ **return** $\perp$	//no re-use		
16 **if** role[sID] = "initiator" **return** $\perp$		$\underline{\text{DER}_{\text{init}}(\text{sID}, M')}$	
17 role[sID] := "responder"		39 **if** holder[sID] = $\perp$ **or** state[sID] = $\perp$	
18 $(j,i) :=$ (holder[sID], peer[sID])		40 **return** $\perp$	//Session not initalised
19 $(M', K') \leftarrow \text{Der}_{\text{resp}}(sk_j, pk_i, M)$		41 **if** sKey[sID] $\neq \perp$ **return** $\perp$	//no re-use
20 sKey[sID] := K'		42 $(i,j) :=$ (holder[sID], peer[sID])	
21 (received[sID], sent[sID]) := (M, M')		43 st := state[sID]	
22 **return** M'		44 sKey[sID] := $\text{Der}_{\text{init}}(sk_i, pk_j, M', \text{st})$	
		45 received[sID] := M'	

Fig. 13. Games IND-AA$_b$ and IND-StAA$_b$ for AKE, where $b \in \mathbb{F}_2$. The collection of oracles O used in lines 05 and 27 is defined by O := {EST, INIT, DER$_{\text{resp}}$, DER$_{\text{init}}$, REVEAL, REV-STATE, CORRUPT, TEST}. Oracles REVEAL, REV-STATE, CORRUPT, and TEST are given in Fig. 14. Game IND-StAA$_b$ only differs from IND-AA$_b$ in ruling out one more kind of attack: A's bit b' does not count in games IND-AA$_b$ if helper procedure Trivial returns **true**, see line 06. In games IND-StAA$_b$, A's bit b' does not count already if procedure ATTACK (that includes Trivial and additionally checks for state-attacks on the test session) returns **true**, see line 28.

a uniformly random key is returned. The attacker's task is to distinguish these two cases, to this end it outputs a bit.

Definition 8 (Key Indistinguishability of AKE). *We define games* IND-AA$_b$ *and* IND-StAA$_b$ *for* $b \in \mathbb{F}_2$ *as in Figs. 13 and 14.*

We define the IND-AA *advantage function of an adversary* A *against* AKE *as*

$$\text{Adv}_{\text{AKE}}^{\text{IND-AA}}(A) := |\Pr[\text{IND-AA}_1^A \Rightarrow 1] - \Pr[\text{IND-AA}_0^A \Rightarrow 1]|,$$

and the IND-StAA *advantage function of an adversary* A *against* AKE *excluding test-state-attacks as*

$$\text{Adv}_{\text{AKE}}^{\text{IND-StAA}}(A) := |\Pr[\text{IND-StAA}_1^A \Rightarrow 1] - \Pr[\text{IND-StAA}_0^A \Rightarrow 1]|.$$

```
Trivial(sID*)                                    //helper procedure to exclude trivial attacks
46  if sKey[sID*] = ⊥ return true                //test session was never completed
47  v := false
48  (i, j) := (holder[sID*], peer[sID*])
49  if revealed[sID*] return true                //A trivially learned the test session's key
50  if corrupted[i] and revState[sID*]
51     return true                 //A may simply compute Der(sk_i, pk_j, received[sID*], state[sID*])
52  𝔐(sID*) := ∅                                  //create list of matching sessions
53  for 1 ≤ ptr ≤ cnt
54     if (sent[ptr], received[ptr]) = (received[sID*], sent[sID*])
          and (holder[ptr], peer[ptr]) = (j, i) and role[ptr] ≠ role[sID*]
55        𝔐(sID*) := 𝔐(sID*) ∪ {ptr}             //session matches
56     if revealed[ptr] v := true  //A trivially learned the test session's key via matching session
57     if corrupted[j] and revState[ptr]
58        v := true                 //A may simply compute Der(sk_j, pk_i, received[ptr], state[ptr])
59  if |𝔐(sID*)| > 1 return false   //reward for adversary - protocol was not appropr. random.
60  if v = true return true
61  if 𝔐(sID*) = ∅ and corrupted[j] return true  //A tampered with test session, knowing sk_j
62  return false


ATTACK(sID*)              //helper procedure to exclude trivial attacks as well as state-attacks
63  if Trivial(sID*)  return true                           //trivial attack
64  if 𝔐(sID*) = ∅ and revState[sID*] return true           //state-attack
65  return false
```

```
REVEAL(sID)                    REV-STATE(sID)              TEST(sID)    //only one query
66  if sKey[sID] = ⊥ return ⊥  72  if state[sID] = ⊥ return ⊥   75  sID* := sID
67  revealed[sID] := true      73  revState[sID] := true         76  if sKey[sID*] = ⊥
68  return sKey[sID]           74  return state[sID]             77     return ⊥
                                                             78  K_0* := sKey[sID*]
CORRUPT(i ∈ [N])                                            79  K_1* ←_$ 𝒦
69  if corrupted[i] return ⊥                                80  return K_b*
70  corrupted[i] := true
71  return sk_i
```

Fig. 14. Helper procedures Trivial and ATTACK and oracles REVEAL, REV-STATE, CORRUPT, and TEST of games IND-AA and IND-StAA defined in Fig. 13.

We call a session *completed* iff $sKey[sID] \neq \perp$, which implies that either $\mathrm{DER_{resp}}(sID, m)$ or $\mathrm{DER_{init}}(sID, m)$ was queried for some message m. We say that a completed session sID *was recreated* iff there exists a session $sID' \neq sID$ such that $(holder[sID], peer[sID]) = (holder[sID'], peer[sID'])$, $role[sID] = role[sID']$, $sent[sID] = sent[sID']$, $received[sID] = received[sID']$ and $state[sID] = state[sID']$. We say that two completed sessions sID_1 and sID_2 *match* iff $(holder[sID_1], peer[sID_1]) = (peer[sID_2], holder[sID_2])$, $(sent[sID_1], received[sID_1]) = (received[sID_2], sent[sID_2])$, and $role[sID_1] \neq role[sID_2]$. We say that A *tampered with the test session* sID^* if at the end of the security game, there exists no matching session for sID^* Nonexistence of a matching session implies that A must have called the derivation process on a message of its own choosing.

Helper procedure Trivial (Fig. 14) is used in all games to exclude the possibility of trivial attacks, and helper procedure ATTACK (also Fig. 14) is defined in games IND-StAA$_b$ to exclude the possibility of trivial attacks as well as one non-trivial attack that we will discuss below. During execution of Trivial, the game creates list $\mathfrak{M}(\text{sID}^*)$ of all matching sessions that were executed throughout the game (see line 55), and A's output bit b' counts in games IND-AA$_b$ only if Trivial returns false, i.e., if test session sID* was completed and all of the following conditions hold:

1. A did not obtain the key of sID* by querying REVEAL on sID* or any matching session, see lines 49 and 56.
2. A did not obtain both the holder i's secret key sk_i and the test session's internal state, see line 51. We enforce that $\neg$corrupted$[i]$ or $\neg$revState$[\text{sID}^*]$ since otherwise, A is allowed to obtain all information required to trivially compute Der$(sk_i, pk_j, \text{received}[\text{sID}^*], \text{state}[\text{sID}^*])$.
3. A did not obtain both the peer's secret key sk_j and the internal state of any matching session, see line 58. We enforce that $\neg$corrupted$[j]$ or $\neg$revState$[\text{sID}]$ for all sID s. th. sID $\in \mathfrak{M}(\text{sID}^*)$ for the same reason as discussed in 2: A could trivially compute Der$(sk_j, pk_i, \text{received}[\text{sID}], \text{state}[\text{sID}])$ for some matching session sID.
4. A did not both tamper with the test session and obtain the peer j's secret key sk_j, see line 61. We enforce that $\mathfrak{M}(\text{sID}^*) \neq \varnothing$ or $\neg$corrupted$[j]$ to exclude the following trivial attack: A could learn the peer's secret key sk_j via query CORRUPT$[j]$ and either
   - receive a message M by querying INIT on sID*, compute $(M', K') \leftarrow$ Der$_{\text{resp}}(sk_j, pk_i, M)$ without having to call DER$_{\text{resp}}$, and then call DER$_{\text{init}}(\text{sID}^*, M')$, thereby ensuring that sKey$[\text{sID}^*] = K'$,
   - or compute $(M, \text{st}) \leftarrow \text{Init}(sk_j, pk_i)$ without having to call INIT, receive a message M' by querying DER$_{\text{resp}}(\text{sID}^*, M)$, and trivially compute Der$_{\text{init}}(sk_j, pk_i, M', \text{st})$.

A's output bit b' only counts in games IND-StAA$_b$ if ATTACK returns false, i.e., if both of the following conditions hold:

1. Trivial returns **false**
2. A did not both tamper with the test session and obtain its internal state, see line 64. We enforce that $\mathfrak{M}(\text{sID}^*) \neq \varnothing$ or $\neg$revState$[\text{sID}^*]$ in game IND-StAA for the following reason: In an active attack, given that the test session's internal state got leaked, it is possible for some protocols to choose a message M' such that the result of algorithm Der$_{\text{init}}(sk_i, pk_j, M', \text{st})$ can be computed without knowledge of any of the long-term keys sk_i or sk_j. In this setting, an adversary might query INIT on sID*, learn the internal state st by querying REV-STATE on sID*, choose its own message M' without a call to DER$_{\text{resp}}$ and finally call DER$_{\text{init}}(\text{sID}^*, M')$, thereby being enabled to anticipate the resulting key.

Init(sk_i, pk_j):	Der$_{\mathsf{resp}}(sk_j, pk_i, M)$:	Der$_{\mathsf{init}}(sk_i, pk_j, M', \mathsf{st})$:
01 $m_j \leftarrow_\$ \mathcal{M}$	07 Parse $(\bar{pk}, c_j) := M$	18 Parse $(c_i, \bar{c}) := M'$
02 $c_j := \mathsf{Enc}(pk_j, m_j; \mathsf{G}(m_j))$	08 $m_i, \bar{m} \leftarrow_\$ \mathcal{M}$	19 Parse $(\bar{sk}, m_j, M := (\bar{pk}, c_j)) := \mathsf{st}$
03 $(\bar{sk}, \bar{pk}) \leftarrow \mathsf{KG}$	09 $c_i := \mathsf{Enc}(pk_i, m_i; \mathsf{G}(m_i))$	20 $m'_i := \mathsf{Dec}(sk_i, c_i)$
04 $M := (\bar{pk}, c_j)$	10 $\bar{c} := \mathsf{Enc}(\bar{pk}, \bar{m}; \mathsf{G}(\bar{m}))$	21 $\bar{m}' := \mathsf{Dec}(\bar{sk}, \bar{c})$
05 $\mathsf{st} := (\bar{sk}, m_j, M)$	11 $M' := (c_i, \bar{c})$	22 if $m'_i = \bot$
06 return (M, st)	12 $m'_j := \mathsf{Dec}(sk_j, c_j)$	or $c_i \neq \mathsf{Enc}(pk_i, m'_i; \mathsf{G}(m'_i))$
	13 if $m'_j = \bot$	23 if $\bar{m}' = \bot$
	or $c_j \neq \mathsf{Enc}(pk_j, m'_j; \mathsf{G}(m'_j))$	24 $K := \mathsf{H}'_{\mathsf{L}1}(c_i, m_j, \bar{c}, i, j, M, M')$
	14 $K' := \mathsf{H}'_{\mathsf{R}}(m_i, c_j, \bar{m}, i, j, M, M')$	25 else
	15 else	26 $K := \mathsf{H}'_{\mathsf{L}2}(c_i, m_j, \bar{m}', i, j, M, M')$
	16 $K' := \mathsf{H}(m_i, m'_j, \bar{m}, i, j, M, M')$	27 else if $\bar{m}' = \bot$
	17 return (M', K')	28 $K := \mathsf{H}'_{\mathsf{L}3}(m'_i, m_j, \bar{c}, i, j, M, M')$
		29 else $K := \mathsf{H}(m'_i, m_j, \bar{m}', i, j, M, M')$
		30 return K

Fig. 15. IND-StAA secure AKE protocol $\mathsf{AKE} = \mathsf{FO}_{\mathsf{AKE}}[\mathsf{PKE}, \mathsf{G}, \mathsf{H}]$. Oracles H'_R and $\mathsf{H}'_{\mathsf{L}1}$, $\mathsf{H}'_{\mathsf{L}2}$ and $\mathsf{H}'_{\mathsf{L}3}$ are used to generate random values whenever reencryption fails. (For encryption, this strategy is called *implicit reject* Amongst others, it is used in [28], [43] and [32].) For simplicity of the proof, H'_R and $\mathsf{H}'_{\mathsf{L}1}$, $\mathsf{H}'_{\mathsf{L}2}$ and $\mathsf{H}'_{\mathsf{L}3}$ are internal random oracles that cannot be accessed directly. For implementation, it would be sufficient to use a PRF.

5 Transformation from PKE to AKE

Transformation $\mathsf{FO}_{\mathsf{AKE}}$ constructs a IND-StAA-secure AKE protocol from a PKE scheme that is both DS and IND-CPA secure. If we plug in transformation Punc before applying $\mathsf{FO}_{\mathsf{AKE}}$, we achieve IND-StAA-security from CPA security alone.

THE CONSTRUCTION. To a PKE scheme $\mathsf{PKE} = (\mathsf{KG}, \mathsf{Enc}, \mathsf{Dec})$ with message space $\mathcal{M}$, and random oracles G and H, we associate

$$\mathsf{AKE} = \mathsf{FO}_{\mathsf{AKE}}[\mathsf{PKE}, \mathsf{G}, \mathsf{H}] = (\mathsf{KG}, \mathsf{Init}, \mathsf{Der}_{\mathsf{resp}}, \mathsf{Der}_{\mathsf{init}}).$$

The algorithms of AKE are defined in Fig. 15.

IND-StAA SECURITY OF $\mathsf{FO}_{\mathsf{AKE}}$. The following theorem establishes that IND-StAA security of AKE reduces to DS and IND-CPA security of PKE (see Definition 6).

Theorem 3 (PKE DS + IND-CPA $\Rightarrow$ AKE IND-StAA). *Assume PKE to be δ-correct, and to come with a sampling algorithm $\overline{\mathsf{Enc}}$ such that it is ϵ-disjoint. Then, for any IND-StAA adversary B that establishes S sessions and issues at most q_R (classical) queries to* REVEAL, *at most q_G (quantum) queries to random oracle G and at most q_H (quantum) queries to random oracle H, there exists an adversary A_{DS} against the disjoint simulatability of $\mathsf{T}[\mathsf{PKE}, \mathsf{G}]$ issuing at most $q_\mathsf{G} + 2q_\mathsf{H} + 3S$ queries to G such that*

$$\mathsf{Adv}^{\mathsf{IND\text{-}StAA}}_{\mathsf{AKE}}(\mathsf{B}) \leq 2 \cdot S \cdot (S + 3 \cdot N) \cdot \mathsf{Adv}^{\mathsf{DS}}_{\mathsf{T}[\mathsf{PKE}, \mathsf{G}]}(\mathsf{A}_{\mathsf{DS}}) + 32 \cdot (S + 3 \cdot N) \cdot (q_\mathsf{G} + 2q_\mathsf{H} + 4S)^2 \cdot \delta$$

$$+ 4 \cdot S \cdot (S + N) \cdot \epsilon_{dis} + S^2 \cdot (N + 1) \cdot \mu(\mathsf{KG}) \cdot \mu(\mathsf{Enc}) + 2 \cdot S^2 \cdot \mu(\mathsf{KG}),$$

and the running time of A_{DS} *is about that of* B. *Due to Lemma* 2, *there exist adversaries* C_{DS} *and* C_{IND} *against* PKE *such that*

$$\mathrm{Adv}_{AKE}^{IND\text{-}StAA}(B) \leq 2 \cdot S \cdot (S + 3 \cdot N) \cdot \mathrm{Adv}_{PKE}^{DS}(C_{DS})$$

$$+ 4 \cdot S \cdot (S + 3 \cdot N) \cdot \sqrt{(q_G + 2q_H + 3S) \cdot \mathrm{Adv}_{PKE}^{IND\text{-}CPA}(C_{IND}) + \frac{4(q_G + 2q_H + 3S)^2}{|\mathcal{M}|}}$$

$$+ 32 \cdot (S + 3 \cdot N) \cdot (q_G + 2q_H + 3S)^2 \cdot \delta + 4 \cdot S \cdot (S + N) \cdot \epsilon_{dis}$$

$$+ S^2 \cdot (N + 1) \cdot \mu(KG) \cdot \mu(Enc) + 2 \cdot S^2 \cdot \mu(KG),$$

and the running times of C_{DS} *and* C_{IND} *is about that of* B.

PROOF SKETCH. To prove IND-StAA security of $FO_{AKE}[PKE, G, H]$, we consider an adversary B with black-box access to the protocols' algorithms and to oracles that reveal keys of completed sessions, internal states, and long-term secret keys of participating parties as specified in game IND-StAA (see Fig. 13). Intuitively, B will always be able to obtain all-but-one of the three secret messages m_i, m_j and $\tilde{m}$ that are picked during execution of the test session between P_i and P_j:

1. We first consider the case that B executed the test session honestly. Note that on the right-hand side of the protocol there exists no state. We assume that B has learned the secret key of party P_j and hence knows m_j. Additionally, B could either learn the secret key of party P_i and thereby, compute m_i, or the state on the left-hand side of the protocol including $\tilde{sk}$, and thereby, compute $\tilde{m}$, but not both.

2. In the case that B did not execute the test session honestly, B is not only forbidden to obtain the long-term secret key of the test session's peer, but also to obtain the test session's state due to our restriction in game IND-StAA. Given that B modified the exchanged messages, the test session's side is decoupled from the other side. If the test session is on the right-hand side, messages m_j and $\tilde{m}$ can be obtained, but message m_i can not because we forbid to learn peer i's secret key. If the test session is on the left-hand side, messages m_i and $\tilde{m}$ can be obtained, but message m_j can not because we forbid both to learn the test session's state and to learn peer j's secret key.

In every possible scenario of game IND-StAA, at least one message can not be obtained trivially and is still protected by PKE's IND-CPA security, and the respective ciphertext can be replaced with fake encryptions due to PKE's disjoint simulatability. Consequently, the session key K is pseudorandom. A detailed, game-based proof is given in the full version.

So far we have ignored the fact that B has access to an oracle that reveals the keys of completed sessions. This implicitly provides B a decryption oracle with respect to the secret keys sk_i and sk_j. In our proof, we want to make use of the technique from [43] to simulate the decryption oracles by patching encryption into the random oracle H. In order to extend their technique to PKE schemes with non-perfect correctness, during the security proof we also need to patch random oracle G in a way that (Enc', Dec') (relative to the patched G) provides perfect correctness. This strategy is the AKE analogue to the technique used in our analysis of the Fujisaki-Okamoto transformation given in Sect. 3, in particular, during our proof of Theorem 2. The latter also explains why our transformation does not work with any deterministic encryption scheme, but only with the ones that are derived by using transformation T. For more details on this issue, we also refer to the full version.

5.1 IND-StAA Security Without Disjoint Simulatability

In the full version we show that transformation Punc can be used to waive the requirement of DS: Plugging in transformation Punc before using $\mathsf{FO_{AKE}}$ achieves IND-StAA security from IND-CPA security alone, as long as PKE is γ-spread.

Acknowledgments. We would like to thank the anonymous reviewers of Eurocrypt 2018, Crypto 2019 and Asiacrypt 2019 for their helpful comments and suggestions. This work was supported by the European Union PROMETHEUS project (Horizon 2020 Research and Innovation Program, grant 780701), the Deutsche Forschungsgemeinschaft (DFG, German Research Foundation) under Germany's Excellence Strategy (EXC 2092 CASA, 390781972), ERC Project ERCC (FP7/615074), the German Federal Ministry of Education and Research (BMBF) Project DigiSeal (16KIS0695), the United States Air Force Office of Scientific Research (AFOSR) via AOARD Grant "Verification of Quantum Cryptography" (FA2386-17-1-4022), the project "Research and preparation of an ERC grant application on Certified Quantum Security" (MOBERC12), the ERC Consolidator grant "Certified Quantum Security" (819317), the Estonian Centre of Excellence in IT (EXCITE) funded by the ERDF, and by the institutional research funding IUT2-1 of the Estonian Ministry of Education and Research.

References

1. Alagic, G., Jeffery, S., Ozols, M., Poremba, A.: On non-adaptive quantum chosen-ciphertext attacks and learning with errors. CoRR abs/1808.09655 (2018)
2. Alawatugoda, J., Boyd, C., Stebila, D.: Continuous after-the-fact leakage-resilient key exchange. In: Susilo, W., Mu, Y. (eds.) ACISP 2014. LNCS, vol. 8544, pp. 258–273. Springer, Cham (2014). https://doi.org/10.1007/978-3-319-08344-5_17
3. Ambainis, A., Hamburg, M., Unruh, D.: Quantum security proofs using semi-classical oracles. Cryptology ePrint Archive, Report 2018/904 (2018). http://eprint.iacr.org/2018/904
4. Ambainis, A., Rosmanis, A., Unruh, D.: Quantum attacks on classical proof systems: the hardness of quantum rewinding. In: 55th Annual Symposium on Foundations of Computer Science, 18–21 October 2014, pp. 474–483. IEEE Computer Society Press, Philadelphia (2014)
5. Banik, S., Isobe, T.: Some cryptanalytic results on lizard. Cryptology ePrint Archive, Report 2017/346 (2017). http://eprint.iacr.org/2017/346
6. Beals, R., Buhrman, H., Cleve, R., Mosca, M., Wolf, R.: Quantum lower bounds by polynomials. In: 39th Annual Symposium on Foundations of Computer Science, 8–11 November 1998, pp. 352–361. IEEE Computer Society Press, Palo Alto (1998)
7. Bellare, M., Boldyreva, A., O'Neill, A.: Deterministic and efficiently searchable encryption. In: Menezes, A. (ed.) CRYPTO 2007. LNCS, vol. 4622, pp. 535–552. Springer, Heidelberg (2007). https://doi.org/10.1007/978-3-540-74143-5_30

8. Bellare, M., Canetti, R., Krawczyk, H.: A modular approach to the design and analysis of authentication and key exchange protocols (extended abstract). In: 30th Annual ACM Symposium on Theory of Computing, 23–26 May 1998, pp. 419–428. ACM Press, Dallas (1998)

9. Bellare, M., Rogaway, P.: Random oracles are practical: a paradigm for designing efficient protocols. In: Denning, D.E., Pyle, R., Ganesan, R., Sandhu, R.S., Ashby, V. (eds.) ACM CCS 93: 1st Conference on Computer and Communications Security, 3–5 November 1993, pp. 62–73. ACM Press, Fairfax (1993)

10. Bellare, M., Rogaway, P.: Entity authentication and key distribution. In: Stinson, D.R. (ed.) CRYPTO 1993. LNCS, vol. 773, pp. 232–249. Springer, Heidelberg (1994). https://doi.org/10.1007/3-540-48329-2_21

11. Bellare, M., Rogaway, P.: The security of triple encryption and a framework for code-based game-playing proofs. In: Vaudenay, S. (ed.) EUROCRYPT 2006. LNCS, vol. 4004, pp. 409–426. Springer, Heidelberg (2006). https://doi.org/10.1007/11761679_25

12. Bernstein, D.J., Chuengsatiansup, C., Lange, T., van Vredendaal, C.: NTRU prime. Cryptology ePrint Archive, Report 2016/461 (2016). http://eprint.iacr.org/2016/461

13. Bindel, N., Hamburg, M., Hövelmanns, K., Hülsing, A., Persichetti, E.: Tighter proofs of CCA security in the quantum random oracle model. Cryptology ePrint Archive, Report 2019/590 (2019). https://eprint.iacr.org/2019/590

14. Boneh, D., Dagdelen, Ö., Fischlin, M., Lehmann, A., Schaffner, C., Zhandry, M.: Random oracles in a quantum world. In: Lee, D.H., Wang, X. (eds.) ASIACRYPT 2011. LNCS, vol. 7073, pp. 41–69. Springer, Heidelberg (2011). https://doi.org/10.1007/978-3-642-25385-0_3

15. Boneh, D., Zhandry, M.: Secure signatures and chosen ciphertext security in a quantum computing world. In: Canetti, R., Garay, J.A. (eds.) CRYPTO 2013. LNCS, vol. 8043, pp. 361–379. Springer, Heidelberg (2013). https://doi.org/10.1007/978-3-642-40084-1_21

16. Bos, J., et al.: CRYSTALS - Kyber: a CCA-secure module-lattice-based KEM. Cryptology ePrint Archive, Report 2017/634 (2017). http://eprint.iacr.org/2017/634

17. Boyd, C., Cliff, Y., Gonzalez Nieto, J., Paterson, K.G.: Efficient one-round key exchange in the standard model. In: Mu, Y., Susilo, W., Seberry, J. (eds.) ACISP 2008. LNCS, vol. 5107, pp. 69–83. Springer, Heidelberg (2008). https://doi.org/10.1007/978-3-540-70500-0_6

18. Broadbent, A., Jeffery, S.: Quantum homomorphic encryption for circuits of low T-gate complexity. In: Gennaro, R., Robshaw, M. (eds.) CRYPTO 2015. LNCS, vol. 9216, pp. 609–629. Springer, Heidelberg (2015). https://doi.org/10.1007/978-3-662-48000-7_30

19. Canetti, R., Krawczyk, H.: Analysis of key-exchange protocols and their use for building secure channels. In: Pfitzmann, B. (ed.) EUROCRYPT 2001. LNCS, vol. 2045, pp. 453–474. Springer, Heidelberg (2001). https://doi.org/10.1007/3-540-44987-6_28

20. Cramer, R., Shoup, V.: Design and analysis of practical public-key encryption schemes secure against adaptive chosen ciphertext attack. SIAM J. Comput. **33**(1), 167–226 (2003)

21. Dent, A.W.: A designer's guide to KEMs. In: Paterson, K.G. (ed.) Cryptography and Coding 2003. LNCS, vol. 2898, pp. 133–151. Springer, Heidelberg (2003). https://doi.org/10.1007/978-3-540-40974-8_12

22. Dwork, C., Naor, M., Reingold, O.: Immunizing encryption schemes from decryption errors. In: Cachin, C., Camenisch, J.L. (eds.) EUROCRYPT 2004. LNCS, vol. 3027, pp. 342–360. Springer, Heidelberg (2004). https://doi.org/10.1007/978-3-540-24676-3_21

23. Fujioka, A., Suzuki, K., Xagawa, K., Yoneyama, K.: Strongly secure authenticated key exchange from factoring, codes, and lattices. In: Fischlin, M., Buchmann, J., Manulis, M. (eds.) PKC 2012. LNCS, vol. 7293, pp. 467–484. Springer, Heidelberg (2012). https://doi.org/10.1007/978-3-642-30057-8_28

24. Fujioka, A., Suzuki, K., Xagawa, K., Yoneyama, K.: Practical and post-quantum authenticated key exchange from one-way secure key encapsulation mechanism. In: Chen, K., Xie, Q., Qiu, W., Li, N., Tzeng, W.G. (eds.) ASIACCS 13: 8th ACM Symposium on Information, Computer and Communications Security, 8–10 May 2013, pp. 83–94. ACM Press, Hangzhou (2013)

25. Fujisaki, E., Okamoto, T.: Secure integration of asymmetric and symmetric encryption schemes. In: Wiener, M. (ed.) CRYPTO 1999. LNCS, vol. 1666, pp. 537–554. Springer, Heidelberg (1999). https://doi.org/10.1007/3-540-48405-1_34

26. Fujisaki, E., Okamoto, T.: Secure integration of asymmetric and symmetric encryption schemes. J. Cryptol. **26**(1), 80–101 (2013)

27. Gagliardoni, T., Hülsing, A., Schaffner, C.: Semantic security and indistinguishability in the quantum world. In: Robshaw, M., Katz, J. (eds.) CRYPTO 2016. LNCS, vol. 9816, pp. 60–89. Springer, Heidelberg (2016). https://doi.org/10.1007/978-3-662-53015-3_3

28. Hofheinz, D., Hövelmanns, K., Kiltz, E.: A modular analysis of the Fujisaki-Okamoto transformation. In: Kalai, Y., Reyzin, L. (eds.) TCC 2017. LNCS, vol. 10677, pp. 341–371. Springer, Cham (2017). https://doi.org/10.1007/978-3-319-70500-2_12

29. Howgrave-Graham, N., Silverman, J.H., Whyte, W.: Choosing parameter sets for NTRUEncrypt with NAEP and SVES-3. In: Menezes, A. (ed.) CT-RSA 2005. LNCS, vol. 3376, pp. 118–135. Springer, Heidelberg (2005). https://doi.org/10.1007/978-3-540-30574-3_10

30. Hülsing, A., Rijneveld, J., Song, F.: Mitigating multi-target attacks in hash-based signatures. In: Cheng, C.-M., Chung, K.-M., Persiano, G., Yang, B.-Y. (eds.) PKC 2016. LNCS, vol. 9614, pp. 387–416. Springer, Heidelberg (2016). https://doi.org/10.1007/978-3-662-49384-7_15

31. Jager, T., Kohlar, F., Schäge, S., Schwenk, J.: On the security of TLS-DHE in the standard model. In: Safavi-Naini, R., Canetti, R. (eds.) CRYPTO 2012. LNCS, vol. 7417, pp. 273–293. Springer, Heidelberg (2012). https://doi.org/10.1007/978-3-642-32009-5_17

32. Jiang, H., Zhang, Z., Chen, L., Wang, H., Ma, Z.: IND-CCA-secure key encapsulation mechanism in the quantum random oracle model, revisited. In: Shacham, H., Boldyreva, A. (eds.) CRYPTO 2018. LNCS, vol. 10993, pp. 96–125. Springer, Cham (2018). https://doi.org/10.1007/978-3-319-96878-0_4

33. Jiang, H., Zhang, Z., Chen, L., Wang, H., Ma, Z.: IND-CCA-secure key encapsulation mechanism in the quantum random oracle model, revisited. Cryptology ePrint Archive, Report 2017/1096, July 2018. https://eprint.iacr.org/2017/1096/

34. Jiang, H., Zhang, Z., Ma, Z.: On the non-tightness of measurement-based reductions for key encapsulation mechanism in the quantum random oracle model. Cryptology ePrint Archive, Report 2019/494 (2019). https://eprint.iacr.org/2019/494

35. Jiang, H., Zhang, Z., Ma, Z.: Tighter security proofs for generic key encapsulation mechanism in the quantum random oracle model. Cryptology ePrint Archive, Report 2019/134 (2019). https://eprint.iacr.org/2019/134

36. Kiltz, E., Lyubashevsky, V., Schaffner, C.: A concrete treatment of Fiat-Shamir signatures in the quantum random-oracle model. In: Nielsen, J.B., Rijmen, V. (eds.) EUROCRYPT 2018. LNCS, vol. 10822, pp. 552–586. Springer, Cham (2018). https://doi.org/10.1007/978-3-319-78372-7_18

37. Krawczyk, H.: HMQV: a high-performance secure Diffie-Hellman protocol. In: Shoup, V. (ed.) CRYPTO 2005. LNCS, vol. 3621, pp. 546–566. Springer, Heidelberg (2005). https://doi.org/10.1007/11535218_33

38. LaMacchia, B., Lauter, K., Mityagin, A.: Stronger security of authenticated key exchange. In: Susilo, W., Liu, J.K., Mu, Y. (eds.) ProvSec 2007. LNCS, vol. 4784, pp. 1–16. Springer, Heidelberg (2007). https://doi.org/10.1007/978-3-540-75670-5_1

39. Li, Y., Schäge, S.: No-match attacks and robust partnering definitions: defining trivial attacks for security protocols is not trivial. In: Thuraisingham, B.M., Evans, D., Malkin, T., Xu, D. (eds.) ACM CCS 2017: 24th Conference on Computer and Communications Security, 31 October–2 November 2017, pp. 1343–1360. ACM Press, Dallas (2017)

40. Naehrig, M., et al.: FrodoKEM. Technical report, National Institute of Standards and Technology (2017). https://csrc.nist.gov/projects/post-quantum-cryptography/round-1-submissions

41. NIST: National institute for standards and technology. Postquantum crypto project (2017). http://csrc.nist.gov/groups/ST/post-quantum-crypto/

42. Persichetti, E.: Improving the efficiency of code-based cryptography. Ph.D. thesis (2012). http://persichetti.webs.com/Thesis%20Final.pdf

43. Saito, T., Xagawa, K., Yamakawa, T.: Tightly-secure key-encapsulation mechanism in the quantum random oracle model. In: Nielsen, J.B., Rijmen, V. (eds.) EURO-CRYPT 2018. LNCS, vol. 10822, pp. 520–551. Springer, Cham (2018). https://doi.org/10.1007/978-3-319-78372-7_17

44. Schäge, S.: TOPAS: 2-pass key exchange with full perfect forward secrecy and optimal communication complexity. In: Ray, I., Li, N., Kruegel, C. (eds.) ACM CCS 2015: 22nd Conference on Computer and Communications Security, 12–16 October 2015, pp. 1224–1235. ACM Press, Denver (2015)

45. Shoup, V.: Sequences of games: a tool for taming complexity in security proofs. Cryptology ePrint Archive, Report 2004/332 (2004). http://eprint.iacr.org/2004/332

46. Toorani, M.: On continuous after-the-fact leakage-resilient key exchange. In: Proceedings of the Second Workshop on Cryptography and Security in Computing Systems. CS2 2015, pp. 31:31–31:34. ACM, New York (2015). http://doi.acm.org/10.1145/2694805.2694811

47. Yao, A.C.C., Zhao, Y.: OAKE: a new family of implicitly authenticated Diffie-Hellman protocols. In: Sadeghi, A.R., Gligor, V.D., Yung, M. (eds.) ACM CCS 2013: 20th Conference on Computer and Communications Security, 4–8 November 2013, pp. 1113–1128. ACM Press, Berlin (2013)

48. Zhandry, M.: Secure identity-based encryption in the quantum random oracle model. In: Safavi-Naini, R., Canetti, R. (eds.) CRYPTO 2012. LNCS, vol. 7417, pp. 758–775. Springer, Heidelberg (2012). https://doi.org/10.1007/978-3-642-32009-5_44

Threshold Ring Signatures: New Definitions and Post-quantum Security

Abida Haque$^{(\boxtimes)}$ and Alessandra Scafuro

North Carolina State University, Raleigh, USA
{ahaque3,ascafur}@ncsu.edu

Abstract. A t-out-of-N threshold ring signature allows t parties to jointly and anonymously compute a signature on behalf on N public keys, selected in an arbitrary manner among the set of all public keys registered in the system.

Existing definitions for t-out-of-N threshold ring signatures guarantee security only when the public keys are honestly generated, and many even restrict the ability of the adversary to actively participate in the computation of the signatures. Such definitions do not capture the open settings envisioned for threshold ring signatures, where parties can independently add themselves to the system, and join other parties for the computation of the signature.

Furthermore, known constructions of threshold ring signatures are not provably secure in the post-quantum setting, either because they are based on non-post quantum secure problems (e.g. Discrete Log, RSA), or because they rely on transformations such as Fiat-Shamir, that are not always secure in the quantum random oracle model (QROM).

In this paper, we provide the first definition of t-out-of-N threshold ring signatures against *active* adversaries who can participate in the system and arbitrarily deviate from the prescribed procedures. Second, we present a post-quantum secure realization based on *any* (post-quantum secure) trapdoor commitment, which we prove secure in the QROM. Our construction is black-box and it can be instantiated with any trapdoor commitment, thus allowing the use of a variety of hardness assumptions.

Keywords: Threshold ring signatures · QROM · PQ-Security

1 Introduction

A *threshold* cryptographic scheme enforces that a certain cryptographic action is performed only if a quorum of users agree to proceed. For instance, in a threshold signature scheme, a signature for a message msg should be accepted only if at least t signers within a larger group of N signers used their secret keys to compute it. One benefit of a threshold scheme is the tolerance to failures: even

A. Haque and A. Scafuro—Research Supported by NSF grants #1012798, #1764025, Cisco Research Program Award CG#1194107.

if an adversary learns some (less than t) keys of compromised machines, she still will not be able to generate valid signatures. A threshold scheme is also tolerant to benign misbehavior of users: if a set of nodes is off-line, signatures can still be produced, as long as at least t users are active. Due to these additional robustness properties of threshold signatures, there is interest from real applications (e.g., multi-signatures in Bitcoin). Threshold signatures are also target of the latest NIST standardization effort [28].

In this paper, we describe a threshold *ring* signature scheme, where in addition to a quorum of t-out-of-N secret keys, one requires that: (1) the identity of the t signers remains private (from anyone who did not participate in the signing process) within the N public keys of the ring and (2) the set of N public keys is established in an ad-hoc manner among the set of all available public keys in the system (which can be more than N). There is no group manager, nor a centralized join procedure: parties join the system freely with keys of their choice, hence the name *ring* instead of group[1].

Threshold ring signatures [10] suit decentralized settings where parties dynamically join and leave the system, the number of active parties at any point is not known, and there is an interest in protecting the identity of the parties that endorse a certain statement. For example, in a trust blockchain, one could impose that certain transactions are added to the blockchain only if at least t trustees approved the operation, without revealing their identity. Threshold ring signatures can be applied to any scenario where a statement must be endorsed by a quorum, but parties need to protect their identities.

We want two security properties in a threshold ring signature: unforgeability and anonymity. Unforgeability requires that fewer than t users together cannot compute a signature on behalf of any ring. Anonymity requires that if a signature is associated to a ring R of N users, then any possible subset of t users is equally likely to be the set of signers. This can be modeled as: given a signature over a ring R, any either of the two subsets S_0 and S_1 of R are equally likely to be the set of keys used for computing the signature. We call S_0 (S_1) the signing set.

Since ring signatures target open settings where keys are generated independently by each party, when evaluating the security of the scheme one should take into account that some keys can be generated maliciously and possibly adaptively on the public keys already present in the system and the signatures already produced. For example, an adversary could try to join a system with a key that is generated adaptively based on the other keys generated so far, with the purpose of being able to sign a message even if she controls less than t signers, or she can craft her public keys in such a way that if it is included in a ring R by set of signers S, she will be able to learn some information about the signing set S. This observation was already made by Bender, Katz and Morselli in [4] for the case of 1-out-N ring signatures. Note that in the threshold setting, t people must collaborate to obtain the signature, thus the adversary has the additional capabilities of interacting with the honest parties when computing a signature.

---

[1] In group signatures [14], a group manager computes the keys for the users, and possesses the trapdoors to violate the anonymity of a signer.

1.1   Limitations of Previous Work

Security Definitions Capture only Passive Adversaries. Several threshold ring signature schemes have been provided in literature but, somewhat surprisingly, most consider adversaries with the following restrictions. First, the adversary cannot create keys maliciously, that is, an adversary can only obtain honestly generated keys, and in some cases, cannot even choose to receive more (honest) keys, since all public keys are created once and for all and given to her (e.g., [5,31]). Second, the adversary cannot corrupt parties (e.g. [5,30,31]), or, if corruption is allowed, the adversary never participates in the signing process as a member of the signing set. Only Abe et al. [1,2] consider the possibility of an adversary who can add their own keys to the ring, but only for the unforgeability property. Anonymity still relies on all keys being generated honestly.

In the real world, the above restrictions mean that no anonymity (and in most work no unforgeability) guarantee is provided when the adversary is able to observe honest parties' keys (or signatures) before generating her public key, and can be involved in the computation of some of the signatures.

Bender, Katz and Morselli observed in [4] that such restrictions on the adversary do not reflect the setting for which 1-out-N ring signatures were devised in the first place, which is a decentralized open systems where parties can join dynamically. In the case of *threshold* ring signatures where t parties need to *collaborate* to produce a signature, definitions that precisely capture the capability of an active adversary are crucial. Specifically, while it is true that anonymity of a signature σ^* for a ring R can be guaranteed only as long as the adversary did not participate in computing σ^*, one should take into account that the adversary can still participate in the computation of *other* signatures $\sigma_1, \sigma_2, \ldots$, with some of the *same* signers that computed σ^*, and can use this knowledge to infer information about the signers who compute σ^*. To the best of our knowledge there seem to be no definition in literature that captures all of the above adversarial (and realistic) capabilities.

No Provable Post-quantum Security. Existing threshold ring signature schemes do not present a provably post-quantum secure analysis. They are either based on hard problems that are not post-quantum resistant [10,25,30,34,41] (e.g., Discrete Log, RSA, bilinear maps), or, when based on post-quantum resistant hardness assumptions [5,11,27,31] (e.g., lattices, multivariate code) they use the Fiat-Shamir transform [18], the security of which is not known to hold in general in the *quantum* random oracle model (QROM) [3,7]. Exciting recent work [17,26] show that for Sigma-protocols with special properties the Fiat-Shamir transform is secure even in the QROM, however it is not known whether this result can be applied to the existing threshold signatures. We note that it is possible that Abe et al.'s [2] scheme could be instantiated using post-quantum Sigma-protocols (and thus be post-quantum secure), but it is not clear whether this is the case. We discuss previous signatures in more detail in Sect. 2.

1.2   Our Contribution

Our contributions are security definitions and provable post-quantum security. We elaborate on each contribution below.

Security Definitions in Presence of Active Adversaries. We provide the first definitions for threshold ring signatures that capture realistic adversarial capabilities. The adversary may deviate arbitrarily from any of the signature procedures (i.e., key generation and signature generation). This is in contrast with previous work that considered passive adversaries who follow the prescribed procedures.

Provably Post-quantum Secure Threshold Ring Signature in QROM. We provide a general construction of threshold ring signatures in the QROM based on any post-quantum secure trapdoor commitment scheme. The trapdoor commitment scheme is treated as a black-box and therefore can be instantiated with various hardness assumptions. Our construction is an abstraction and generalization of previous approaches. Post-quantum security in the QROM is achieved by applying the Unruh's transform [36]. For completeness, we also discuss an implementation of post-quantum secure trapdoor commitment from any (post-quantum secure) one-way function using the circuit of the one-way-function and a folklore transformation from Sigma-protocols to trapdoor commitments.

Security Definitions in Presence of Active Adversaries. We define new security games for capturing anonymity and unforgeability for threshold ring signatures in presence of adversaries that are actively participating in the system. In our anonymity definition, our adversary can actively participate by adding keys that she maliciously crafted, and by participating in the signing process. More specifically, in the anonymity game, the adversary is given access to oracles that allow her to generate new public keys (on behalf of honest parties), corrupt a party by learning her secret key, and compute signatures for rings R and signings sets S of her choice that can contain arbitrarily malicious keys, added on the fly in the system. The adversary can use these oracles to train by participating in many joint signature computation with other honest parties.

In the challenge phase, the adversary chooses a ring R that can contain malicious or corrupted keys, and two candidate signing sets S_0, S_1. These signing sets must contain only honest keys. She queries the signing oracle with R, S_0, S_1 and a message msg and obtains a signature σ^*, computed using signing set S_b, and she wins the game if she guesses b.

The main difference with existing definitions is that in previous work the adversary could only query the signing oracle with keys honestly generated (via the key generation oracle) and could not participate with malicious keys in the signing process. Such definitions only anonymity guarantee security against an *external observer* who does not actively interact with the system. Our definitions are inspired by Bender et al. [4] but they are not a straightforward extensions of theirs. They are provided in Sect. 3.

Post-quantum Threshold Ring-Signature from any Trapdoor Commitment. A well known paradigm to construct a t-out-of-N threshold signature schemes is to use a t-out-of-N threshold Secret Sharing scheme (e.g. Shamir [33] secret sharing scheme[2]) and leverage the unpredictability properties of a random oracle $\mathcal{H}$ to force t parties to use their secret keys to "adjust" their shares so that they match the output of $\mathcal{H}$.

We follow such a paradigm and use trapdoor commitments to allow signers to adjust the t shares. More specifically, recall that a trapdoor commitment scheme is defined by some public key pk that anyone can use to compute a commitment c of a message y i.e., $c \leftarrow \mathsf{Com}_{pk}(y)$ such that c is hiding, that is, it reveals nothing about y; and binding, that is, later c can only be opened as y. However, if one knows a secret trapdoor sk associated to the parameters pk, she can compute a "fake" commitment $c \leftarrow \mathsf{TCom}_{pk}(sk)$ that can be later opened as any message y' using the trapdoor.

At a high level, our threshold ring signature works as follows: the public key of a signer corresponds to the public key pk of a trapdoor commitment $\mathcal{TC}$ (as well as a field element α used for Shamir's secret sharing); the signing key is the trapdoor sk. When t parties want to jointly sign a message msg, they choose $N - t$ other keys $(pk^{s_1}, pk^{s_2}, \ldots, pk^{s_{N-t}})$ from the set of all keys published so far [3]; they then choose $N - t$ points $(y^{s_1}, y^{s_2}, \ldots, y^{s_{N-t}})$ and use the non-signer public keys to commit to each point, thus obtaining $N - t$ commitments. For the remaining t commitments, each signer pk^s will prepare his own fake commitment. The result of this step is a vector of N commitments $(c^1, \ldots, c^N)$ of which t are trapdoor (and thus can be equivocated later), and $N - t$ are binding.

Next, the random oracle is evaluated on the vector of all N commitments to obtain another point $(0, z)$ where $z = \mathcal{H}(\mathsf{msg}, c^1, \ldots, c^N)$. Now, the signers have $(N - t + 1)$ points that uniquely identify a polynomial P of degree $N - t$. Once P is defined, each signer pk^s can compute $y^s = P(\alpha^s)$ and use the trapdoor sk^s to equivocate commitment c^s so that it opens to y^s. The final signature simply consists of the N commitments and openings. The verifier will simply check that the openings are valid and lead to points $(\alpha^1, y^1), \ldots, (\alpha^N, y^N), (0, z)$ that lie on the same $N - t$-degree polynomial P. The verifier will also check that $z = \mathcal{H}(\mathsf{msg}, c^1, \ldots, c^N)$.

For unforgeability, due to the unpredictability of $\mathcal{H}$, the value z is known to an adversary only *after* the points have been committed in $(c^1, \ldots, c^N)$. If the adversary controls less than t signers—and thus knows less than t trapdoors—she cannot adjust t points, unless she is breaking the (post-quantum[4]) binding property of the underlying commitments. For anonymity, recall that the difference

---

[2] In (t, N)- Shamir Secret Sharing, to share a secret s, a dealer compute a random polynomial P of degree $t - 1$ with constant term s. The i-th share of the secret is computed as $y^i = P(\alpha^i)$, for some field element α^i. Given t shares the secret can be reconstructed using polynomial interpolation.

[3] In practice we will have a leader choosing such points. We stress that the leader does not have to be trusted.

[4] In Sect. 6.1 we discuss in more detail why the issue of binding in presence of quantum adversaries, discussed in [3], does not affect our construction.

between a signature computed by signers in set S_0 versus S_1 is in the positions of the trapdoor commitments. Thus, an adversary winning the anonymity game is able to distinguish which commitments are computed using the trapdoor, therefore violating the (post-quantum) trapdoor property of the commitment.

These security arguments are straightforward at a high level. However, in the formal proof via hybrid arguments one has to switch from the case where the trapdoors are used (and signers and non-signers behave differently) to the case where no trapdoor is used, and thus the adversary has no advantage in breaking anonymity. This is possible by leveraging the programmability of the random oracle $\mathcal{H}$ that would allow the reductions to know the point $(0, z)$ of the polynomial *before* computing the commitments (thus, such commitments do not need to be equivocated). Similarly, when reducing unforgeability to the binding of the underlying trapdoor commitment, we need the reduction to simulate the signing oracle without knowing the trapdoor (otherwise, it would not possible to break binding). In particular, to break binding the reduction needs to know two openings of at least one commitment. In the classical case, this can be done by rewinding the adversary and adaptively programming the random oracle. However, this proof technique is not directly applicable when the adversary has quantum access to the random oracle. As shown by Unruh in [36], rewinding a quantum-capable adversary and programming the random oracle impacts the state of the adversary, and does not guarantee extraction.

In our construction, we obtain *on-line* extractability by applying the Unruh transform [36]. The main idea of this transform is not to extract by rewinding the adversary. Rather, all the outputs that are needed are contained in the signature. In the proof, we replace $\mathcal{H}$ with a $2q$-wise independent function (where q is the maximum number of oracle queries), which is indistinguishable from the random oracle. Thus, the extractor can invert the function and find two openings.

The signature is modified so the same vector of commitments $(c^1, \ldots, c^N)$ is associated to multiple points $z_1, \ldots, z_m$ and therefore will require m different openings. The signers will then encrypt, using a random permutation G, modeled as a random oracle, m *multiple openings* of the *same* commitments c^s. Namely, for a commitment c^s, the signer additionally sends m encryptions $(g_1^s, \ldots, g_m^s)$ where $g_j = \mathcal{G}(y_j^s \| op_j^s \| r_j^s)$ and where y_j^s, op_j^s is the j-th opening of c^s and r_j^s is a random key used for encryption. Here m is the statistical security parameter. Among the m encryptions, each signers will only provide the decryption of one opening (y_j^s, op_j^s) for a single $j \in [m]$ (chosen via a random oracle). Note that for the non-signers, the openings will all be the same value. This technique allow the reduction, who sees all encryptions, to "invert" the values random permutation G and obtain at least two openings $(y_j^s, op_j^s), (\tilde{y}_j^s, \tilde{op}_j^s)$ for the same commitment c^s.

To amplify the probability of inverting and extracting enough openings, this is repeated n times, using cut-and-choose techniques. To sum up, the value n is the number of commitments (of a single ring member) and m is the number of openings a signer makes for each. For each of the n commitments and their m possible openings, in the signature, one will see only one "line" of openings. For programmability, we also use a indistinguishability lemma shown in Unruh [36].

While the secret sharing and Random Oracle paradigm is common to construct ring and threshold ring signatures, our construction presents two novel benefits. First, it is black-box in *any* trapdoor commitment, and thus it can be instantiated under any assumption that allows one to construct trapdoor commitments (e.g., lattice-based or hash-based trapdoor commitments) and it generalizes previous constructions [1]. In particular, this allows parties to potentially use *different* trapdoor commitment schemes, as long as they publish the corresponding public key and the procedure to commit. This does not violate security, since the security of honest parties should not depend on the quality of the other's parties key. Indeed, in the security game, anonymity is guaranteed as long as there are two subsets S_0 and S_1 containing all honest keys, while unforgeability is guaranteed as long as $\leq t$ keys are corrupted. In the other cases, security cannot be guaranteed. Second, our construction is the first to be analyzed in the quantum random oracle model, and therefore provides provably post-quantum security guarantees.

Trapdoor Commitment from Post-quantum Secure One-Way Function. For completeness, we informally discuss a possible implementation of post-quantum secure trapdoor commitment (details are provided in Sect. 6). It is folklore that trapdoor commitment schemes can be constructed from any honest-verifier zero-knowledge (HVZK) Sigma-protocol [16], for a language L. Let f be a post-quantum secure one-way function (e.g., SHA-3), let C_f be the associated arithmetic of boolean circuit. Let $(\Sigma.P_1, \Sigma.V, \Sigma.P_2)$ be the 3 moves of a (post-quantum secure) Sigma protocol, with a transcript (c, e, z) and let $\Sigma.\text{SIM}$ be the HVZK simulator associated to Σ. Let $X \in L$ if there exists an W such that $X = C_f(W)$. The public key of a party is X. The trapdoor key is W. To commit to a message msg honestly, a party simply runs $\text{SIM}(X, \text{msg})$ and obtain c, z where c is the commitment and z, msg will be the opening. To create a trapdoor commitment, a party computes $c \leftarrow \Sigma.P_1(X, W)$ and then to open to a message m^* she will simply run $\Sigma.P_2(X, Y, c, \text{msg}^*)$ and obtain the opening z. A post-quantum secure Σ protocol can be based for example on Blum's protocol for Graph Hamiltonicity instantiated with a statistically binding commitment. ZkBoo [21] is another example of post-quantum secure Sigma-protocol.

Discussion on Our Contribution and Previous Work. A natural question is whether previous constructions of threshold ring signatures also satisfy our stronger security definition – at least classically.

As most previous constructions assume only honest participants, at the very least they lack the appropriate consistency checks. It may be the case that if these schemes are modified to check for malicious participants, they would preserve their security in the presence of active adversaries.

However, we stress that this should not suggest that previous security definitions are sufficient. Indeed, one could devise a threshold ring signature scheme that satisfies all of the security properties in the presence of passive adversaries but that are completely insecure in the presence of active adversaries.

2   Related Work

In this section, we review previous work. We first describe (threshold) ring signatures, pointing out the definitions of security as well as whether their work considered post-quantum security. We summarize the schemes in Table 1. The purpose of the table is not to argue efficiency of our construction, but to highlight the stronger security guarantees that we provide, while achieving asymptotically comparable efficiency. Next, we describe thresholdization techniques, finally, and how to ensure post-quantum security.

(Threshold) Ring Signatures. Threshold ring signatures were introduced by Bresson, Stern and Szydlo (BSS) in [10] as an extension of the ring signatures introduced by Rivest, Shamir and Tauman (RST) [32] to the t-out-of-N case. Schemes such as BSS, Liu et al., Okamoto et al., and Yuen et al. [10,24,29,41] are based on hard problems that are not post-quantum secure. Moreover, their security definitions do not allow adversarially chosen keys.

More recently Bettaieb and Schrek [5] (improving on Aguilar et al. [27]) showed a lattice-based threshold signature. However, the security game they consider is weak: the adversary cannot create nor corrupt keys before choosing the signing sets and the ring for the challenge phase. Furthermore, the security of their scheme is not formally analyzed in the post-quantum setting. Katz, Kolesnikov, and Wang [23] showed a method for building efficient ring signatures using symmetric-key primitives only, it is an interesting question how to extend it to the threshold case, while preserving the efficiency.

Thresholdizing. The concept of trapdoor commitments comes from Brassard et al. [9], and is used by Jakobsson et al. [22] for designated verifier signatures. It is possible to thresholdize their scheme using the ideas of Cramer et al. [15]. Cramer et al. show how to build a threshold scheme in which the prover shows he knows at least t out of N solutions without revealing which t solutions are involved. This concept has obvious parallels with the techniques in our scheme, although it uses different terminology. Many threshold schemes use the same techniques as set forth by Cramer et al.

The basic concept is the use of a secret sharing scheme, in which a secret is distributed among the N parties so that any t of them can recreate the secret. In the first ring signature scheme RST [32], the authors suggested the idea of using [15] to thresholdize their scheme, which was later done by BSS [10].

Related to our work are Boldyreva [6], which discusses threshold and multi-signature schemes though does not focus on anonymity, and the "thresholdizers" shown by Boneh et al. in [8]. However, both works focus on systems that have a centralized setup and group managers; moreover, the work of [6] is based on non-post-quantum secure assumptions such as DDH and RSA.

Post-quantum Security. The Fiat-Shamir transformation [18] is a method to turn a Sigma-protocol into a non-interactive signature. Many of the threshold ring signatures described above utilize Fiat-Shamir. However, as Ambainis et al. [3] showed, the Fiat-Shamir construction is not secure against quantum adversaries in general.

Table 1. Comparison of other threshold ring signature schemes. Other schemes may not use post-quantum secure problems. t, N are the threshold and ring size.

Work	Hardness Assumption/ PQ-Secure?	QROM	Adv. Keys	Signature Size
Our work	**Trapdoor Commitment** ✓	**Yes**	**Yes**	$3Nn + Nmn$ †
Abe et al. [2]	Trapdoor OWPs, Σ-Prot ⋆	No	Yes	$(N - t) + N$
Aguilar et al. [27]	Syndrome Decoding ✓	No (FS)	No	Nk †
Bettaieb et al. [5]	Lattice ✓	No (FS)	No	$1 + 3t + Nt$
Bresson et al. [10]	RSA ✗	No	No	$1^{O(t)} \lceil \log_1(N) \rceil (t + N)$
Chang et al. [12]	T-OWP; Σ-Prot ⋆	No	No	$1(N - t) + N$, cf. [2]
Liu et al. [25]	Bilinear Maps ✗	No	No	$N - t + N$
Okamoto [30]	Discrete Log ✗	No	No	$O(kN)$
Petzoldt [31]	Quadratic MQ Problem ✓	No (FS)	No	$O(N)$
Wong et al. [40]	Trapdoor OWPs ⋆	No	No	$N + 1N$ cf. [10]
Yuen et al. [41]	CDH, subgroup ✗	No	No	$1N+1$

✓ Post-quantum secure problem
✗ Not post-quantum secure
⋆ Shows instances where the generic hardness assumption Trapdoor One-Way Permutations (T-OWP) could be post-quantum secure, although no candidate of PQ-secure T-OWP currently exists. They instantiated their scheme with a discrete logarithm/RSA type of function.
† n, m and k *statistical* security parameters.

To show the security of a scheme using the Fiat-Shamir transformation, one typically uses rewinding. This means that a simulation measures the output from an adversary, rewinds him, and then runs another execution from some save point onwards. However, a quantum adversary may notice that a simulation has measured his output, and this changes his quantum state.

Another possible transformation is Fischlin [20], but Ambainis et al. [3] also showed that Fischlins's scheme is insecure in general. The transformation does not require rewinding, but has a concept of saving the list of all query inputs. In the quantum setting, this list is not well-defined. Furthermore, Fischlin's transformation has the condition that the Sigma-protocols must have "unique responses", which means that it cannot transform all Sigma-protocols. On the other hand, Fiat-Shamir can transform arbitrary Sigma-protocols.

Applying the quantum rewinding technique introduced by Watrous [39] to Sigma-protocols with a "strict soundness" property, Unruh [35] was able to create quantum proofs of knowledge. Requiring strict soundness is stringent, and yields inefficient schemes. Recently, Don et al. [17] and Zhandry/Liu [26] proved some less restrictive settings. Both works find methods that allow reprogramming of the QROM by using "collapsing" Sigma-protocols. The notion of collapsing comes from Unruh [38]. The idea is that it is not possible to tell whether a superposition of responses in a Sigma-protocol were measured or not. While it may be possible to pick settings such that Fiat-Shamir (or Fischlin) remains secure even in the post-quantum setting, the Unruh transformation [36] is a generic quantum-secure construction and can be applied to any Sigma-protocol.

Chase et al. [13] also proposed post-quantum digital signature schemes, in which they showed two variants of a signature scheme. The first, named Fish, was created using the Fiat-Shamir transformation, whereas the second, Picnic, used the Unruh transformation.

3 Preliminaries

In the following, we describe the basic notation. Then we describe the concepts needed to create our threshold ring signature scheme.

Notation. When not explicitly stated, we assume that the algorithms are parameterized by a security parameter λ. We write $[N] = \{1, \ldots, N\}$, and $(a_i)_{i \in [N]}$ to indicate a sequence of values indexed by i. A negligible function $\mathsf{negl}(n) : \mathbb{N} \to \mathbb{R}$ is a function such that for every positive polynomial $\mathsf{poly}(n)$ there exists an N such that for all $n > N$, $\mathsf{negl}(n)(n) < \frac{1}{\mathsf{poly}(n)}$. Most algorithms we describe are classical and probabilistic polynomial time (PPT). Other algorithms are quantum polynomial time (QPT), which is a quantum algorithm that runs in polynomial time. In this paper, a QPT adversary is one who can locally run quantum computation and may have quantum access to the random oracle. We use the notation $s \leftarrow_{\$} S$ to say that s is randomly chosen from a set S. We use the notation $y \leftarrow f(x)$ to show that f is a randomized algorithm. For deterministic algorithms we use $y := f(x)$. We may make randomness explicit and write $y := f(x; r)$. Finally, a family of functions F is k-wise-independent if for any distinct $x_1, \ldots, x_k$, it is the case that for any $f \leftarrow_{\$} F$, $f(x_1), \ldots, f(x_k)$ are independent and uniform random values. Random polynomials of degree $k - 1$ are a $k-$wise-independent family.

Trapdoor Commitment Scheme. A commitment scheme involves two parties, a sender and a receiver. A sender sends some *commitment* of a message to the receiver. The commitment is *hiding*, meaning the receiver cannot discover what the message is. Later, the sender may open their commitment by sending the message and some auxiliary opening information, which acts as evidence. The commitment is *binding*, meaning that the sender cannot change what the original message is.

Trapdoor commitment schemes are commitment schemes [19] where if the user knows some *trapdoor*, then he can open a commitment to any message he wishes. In contrast, without a trapdoor, a user can only open the original message he committed to.

A trapdoor commitment scheme has four security properties: completeness, hiding, binding, and trapdoor indistinguishability. Completeness demands that the receiver always accepts any honest execution of the commitment and opening phase. That is, for any message, the receiver is convinced by any correctly computed commitment and opening. Hiding is the same as for a commitment scheme, and binding is the same for users without access to the trapdoor (thus we omit more detailed description). Finally, trapdoor indistinguishability (or trapdoor for short) means that, upon opening, it should be infeasible for the receiver to distinguish whether the original commitment was honest or a counterfeit. We formalize this property in Experiment 1.

Definition 1 (Trapdoor Commitment Scheme). *A trapdoor commitment scheme is a tuple of PPT algorithms* TC = (Setup, KGen, Com, TCom, TOpen, VerifyOpen) *for a messages space* $\mathcal{M}$ *where:*

- *$pp \leftarrow$ Setup(1^λ). On input the security parameter λ, Setup returns public parameters pp. In some commitment schemes this algorithm may not be needed.*
- *$(pk, \mathsf{trap}) \leftarrow$ KGen($1^\lambda, pp$). On input the security parameter λ and (possibly empty) public parameters pp, outputs a public key pk and a trapdoor trap.*
- *$(c, op) \leftarrow$ Com$_{pk}(m)$: On input a public key pk and a message m, Com returns a commitment c to message m and opening information op.*
- *$(state, c) \leftarrow$ TCom$_{pk}(\mathsf{trap})$. On input a public key pk, a trapdoor trap, TCom returns a counterfeit commitment c, and a state state.*
- *$op \leftarrow$ TOpen($\mathsf{trap}, state, c, m$). On input a trapdoor trap, state, a commitment c, and a message m, TOpen returns an opening op.*
- *$b :=$ VerifyOpen$_{pk}(c, op, m)$. Given a commitment c, a public key pk, auxiliary opening information op, and a message m, outputs a bit b.*
- *$b :=$ Valid(pp, pk): On input public parameters pp and a public key pk, returns whether pk is well-formed.*

Experiment 1 (Trapdoor Indistinguishability Trap$_{\mathcal{A}}^{TC}(\lambda)$). *We define an oracle TrapReal^b which on input m_i, outputs a commitment and opening for m_i. If $b = 0$, TrapReal^0 computes $(c_i, op_i) \leftarrow$ Com$_{pk}(m_i)$. If $b = 1$, then TrapReal^1 computes $(state, c_i) \leftarrow$ TCom$_{pk}(\mathsf{trap})$ and $op_i \leftarrow$ TOpen($\mathsf{trap}, state, c, m_i$).*

Let $\mathcal{A}$ be a QPT with classical access to the challenger.

Training Phase

1. *The challenger runs $pp \leftarrow$ Setup(1^λ) and $(pk, \mathsf{trap}) \leftarrow$ KGen($1^\lambda, pp$) and gives pp and pk to $\mathcal{A}$.*
2. *A uniform bit $b \in \{0, 1\}$ is chosen.*
3. *$\mathcal{A}$ can (classically) query TrapReal^b on input messages m_i and obtain c_i, op_i for polynomially many i.*

Challenge Phase

1. *Finally, $\mathcal{A}$ outputs b'.*
2. *If $b = b'$, then the output of the experiment 1 (and we say $\mathcal{A}$ wins the game). Else, output 0.*

Definition 2 (Trapdoor Indistinguishability). *A trapdoor commitment scheme TC satisfies post-quantum secure trapdoor indistinguishability if for all QPT adversaries $\mathcal{A}$, there exists a negligible function negl such that:*

$$Pr[\mathsf{Trap}_{\mathcal{A}}^{TC}(\lambda) = 1] \leq \frac{1}{2} + \mathsf{negl}(\lambda)$$

3.1   Threshold Ring Signatures in Presence of Active Adversaries

We provide our new definition of a t-out-of-N ring signature scheme which considers active (and thus more realistic) adversaries. We denote the set of all public keys which are added to the system as $P = (vk^1, vk^2, vk^3, \dots)$. We call P a *ring*. The notation R denotes the indices of the keys chosen from P, which we call a *subring*, where $|R| = N$. A *signer* s is represented by their public-private key pair (vk^s, sk^s). We always enumerate the members of R as $1, \dots, N$. The signers are represented by the subset $S \subseteq R$, while the non-signers are denoted as $NS \subseteq R$. We have $S \sqcup NS = R$, where $\sqcup$ represents the disjoint union. We use T to represent the secret keys of the signers, that is: $T = \{sk^s | s \in S\}$.

Definition 3 $((t, N)$-Threshold Ring Signature Scheme). *A (t, N)-threshold ring signature scheme is a 4-tuple of algorithms* (Setup, KGen, ThSign, Vfy). *A set of signers $S \subset P$ signs the message* msg *with respect to a subring $R \subset P$ with $|S| \geq t$.*

- *$pp \leftarrow$ Setup(1^λ). On input the security parameter, generates public parameters pp.*
- *$(vk^s, sk^s) \leftarrow$ KGen$(pp, 1^\lambda)$: On input the security parameter λ and the public parameters pp generates a public-private keypair for ring member s.*
- *$\sigma \leftarrow$ ThSign$_{pp}$(msg, T, R). This is a possibly interactive procedure. The players owning the secret keys in set T interact in order to jointly produce a ring signature σ on a message m and subring $P \subseteq P$, where $|T| \geq t$.*
- *$b :=$ Vfy$_{pp}$(msg, R, σ). Verifier checks that σ is a correct threshold signature on message* msg *with respect to R. If the signature is valid, then $b = 1$, otherwise $b = 0$.*

A threshold ring signature scheme satisfies completeness, t-unforgeability, and t-anonymity. Completeness means that if the signers follow the ThSign algorithm correctly, an honest verifier should accept their proof. Formally:

Definition 4 (Perfect completeness.   (Setup, KGen, ThSign, Vfy) *is complete if for QPT $\mathcal{A}$ it holds:*

$$Pr \left[\begin{array}{l} pp \leftarrow \text{Setup}(1^\lambda) \\ \{(vk^s, sk^s) \leftarrow \text{KGen}(pp)\}_{s \in P} \\ (\text{msg}, S, R) \leftarrow \mathcal{A}(pp, \{(vk_s, sk_s)\}_{s \in P}) \\ \sigma \leftarrow \text{ThSign}_{pp}(\text{msg}, T(S), R) \end{array} : \begin{array}{l} S \subseteq P \implies \\ \text{Vfy}(\text{msg}, R, \sigma) = 1 \end{array} \right] = 1$$

Classical Oracles. For the security properties of unforgeability and anonymity, we give the adversary the ability to (classically) query three different types of oracles in arbitrary interleaf during training. The only difference between an adversary to anonymity and to unforgeability is in the challenge phase.

- OKGen(s): The oracle produces (vk^s, sk^s) for player s using KGen and returns vk^s to $\mathcal{A}$. The set of honestly generated keys is updated by $P = P \cup \{vk^s\}$.

- OSign(msg, S, R): $\mathcal{A}$ requests a signature on message msg with signers S with respect to a ring R, where $|R| = N$ and $R \subset P$. S could contain both honestly generated keys or adversarially generated keys, hence, $S = S_{corr} \sqcup S_{hon}$ (the disjoint union of corrupted and honest members), where S_{corr} denotes the set of corrupted members and S_{hon} is the set of honest members. T is the set of private keys of signers in S_{hon}. The oracle follows the algorithm for OSign with the secret keys that he controls. R and S may include adversarially chosen keys or keys of corrupted parties. To produce a signature, $\mathcal{A}$ must cooperate with the oracle and participate in the signing procedure. Then the oracle outputs $\sigma \leftarrow \mathsf{ThSign}(\mathsf{msg}, T, R)$.
- Corrupt(s): Let P_{corr} be the set of corrupted keys. If $vk^s \notin P_{corr}$ then return the secret key sk^s to $\mathcal{A}$. Update $P_{corr} = P_{corr} \cup \{vk^s\}$.
- ORegister(s, vk): On input a signer s and a public key vk, if $vk \in P$, return $\perp$. Otherwise, the oracle adds $vk^s = vk$ to P and P_{corr}.

Experiment 2 (t-Unforgeability Game $\mathsf{SigForge}_{\mathcal{F}}^{\mathsf{TRS}}(t, \lambda)$). *On a (t, N)-threshold ring signature scheme* $\mathsf{TRS} = (\mathsf{Setup}, \mathsf{KGen}, \mathsf{ThSign}, \mathsf{Vfy})$ *we define a game for a QPT adversary $\mathcal{A}$ and security parameter is λ.*

Training Phase

1. *The challenger runs $pp \leftarrow \mathsf{Setup}(1^\lambda)$ and forwards pp to $\mathcal{A}$.*
2. *Initially, the ring $P = \emptyset$ and the set of corrupted users is $P_{corr} = \emptyset$.*
3. *The adversary $\mathcal{F}$ is given (classical) access to a key generation oracle OKGen, a signing oracle OSign, and a corruption oracle $\mathsf{Corrupt}$, and may add keys using $\mathsf{ORegister}$.*

Challenge Phase $\mathcal{F}$ produces σ^*, msg^* and R^*. $\mathcal{F}$ wins the game if

1. $|R^*| \geq t$
2. $|P_{corr} \cap R^*| < t$
3. (msg^*, R^*) *is new*
4. $\mathsf{Vfy}(\mathsf{msg}^*, R^*, \sigma^*) = 1$

Definition 5 (t-Unforgeability wrt Insider Corruption). *A (t, N)- threshold ring signature scheme* TRS *satisfies t-Unforgeability wrt Insider Corruption if for all QPT adversaries $\mathcal{F}$, there exists a negligible function negl such that:*

$$Pr[\mathsf{SigForge}_{\mathcal{F}}^{\mathsf{TRS}}(t, \lambda) \to 1] \leq \mathsf{negl}(\lambda)$$

Experiment 3 (t-Anonymity wrt adversarial keys). *On a (t, N)-threshold ring signature scheme* TRS, *we define the t-anonymity game* $\mathsf{AnonKey}_{\mathcal{A}}^{\mathsf{TRS}}(\mathsf{t}, \lambda)$ *for a QPT adversary $\mathcal{A}$.*

Training Phase

1. *The challenger runs $pp \leftarrow \mathsf{Setup}(1^\lambda)$ and forwards pp to $\mathcal{A}$.*
2. *Initially, the ring $P = \emptyset$ and the set of corrupted users is $P_{corr} = \emptyset$.*
3. *The adversary $\mathcal{A}$ is given (classical) access to a key generation oracle OKGen, a signing oracle OSign, and a corruption oracle $\mathsf{Corrupt}$, and may add keys using $\mathsf{ORegister}$.*

Challenge Phase

1. *$\mathcal{A}$ requests a signature on message* msg^* *from one of two signing sets* S_0, S_1 *with respect to a ring* R, *where* $|S_0| = |S_1| = t$ *and* $S_0 \cup S_1 \cap P_{corr} = \emptyset$ *(i.e., signing sets do not contain corrupted parties). However, the remaining keys in* R *may contain corrupted parties.*
2. *The challenger returns* $\sigma^* \leftarrow \mathsf{ThSign}(\mathsf{msg}^*, T_b, R)$, *for a random bit* b. *Here* T_b *represents the secret keys corresponding to* S_b.
3. *$\mathcal{A}$ returns the bit* b'. *$\mathcal{A}$ is said to win the game if* $b' = b$.

Definition 6 (Anonymity wrt adversarial Keys). *A (t, N)-threshold ring signature scheme* TRS *satisfies t-Anonymity wrt Adversarial Keys if for all QPT adversaries $\mathcal{A}$, there exists a negligible function* negl *such that:*

$$Pr[\mathsf{AnonKey}_{\mathcal{A}}^{\mathsf{TRS}}(\mathsf{t}, \lambda) \to 1] \leq \frac{1}{2} + \mathsf{negl}(\lambda)$$

4   Post-quantum Secure Threshold Ring Signatures

We describe our (t, N)-threshold ring signature scheme TRS. For reference, all notation in the protocol is in Table 2. We call an ordered list of public keys a *ring* P, where $P = (vk^1, vk^2, \ldots)$. We denote a *subring* of P as R. We always enumerate the R as $1, \ldots, N$. This allows us to avoid more cumbersome notation such as vk^{i_s}. Finally, we reference a signer by their index s, so that he is the s-th public key in R. A ring member $s \in [N]$ is represented by their public-private key pair (vk^s, sk^s). In TRS each ring member s has their public key as $vk^s = (pk^s, \alpha^s)$, where pk^s is the public key for $\mathcal{TC}$ and $\alpha^s \in \mathbb{F}$ is a random element of $\mathbb{F}$. Their private key sk^s is their trapdoor for $\mathcal{TC}$. To simplify the indexing in the construction and proof we denote the set S as a set of indices, that is $S \subseteq [N]$.

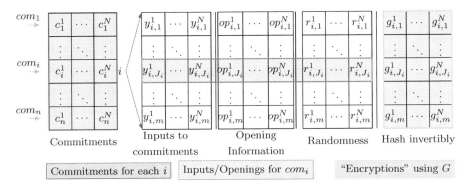

Fig. 1. Graphical representation of a signature.

Our building blocks are a post-quantum secure trapdoor commitment scheme $\mathcal{TC}$, a (t, N) Shamir secret sharing scheme, a random oracle $H = (H_1, H_2)$ and a random permutation G. The index 1 or 2 for H informs the random oracle which type of query is being made. H and G are fixed in the Setup phase.

Suppose that a set of t parties, which we call signers, would like to sign a message msg on behalf of a subring $R \subseteq P$. Let S be the set of indices denoting the signers. Let the remaining members of the subring be denoted as $NS = R \backslash S$.

At a high level, a signature for message msg will consist of N commitments $(c^1, \ldots, c^N)$ – one for each public key pk^i in the ring R – to N points $y^1, \ldots, y^N$ that interpolate to $(N - t)$-degree random polynomial rpoly with constant term z (i.e., such that $\mathsf{rpoly}(0) = z$). The value z is chosen as $H_1(\mathsf{msg}, c^1, \ldots, c^N)$. The commitments are computed as follows. Among the signers there is one distinguished member known as the leader, who is chosen by some arbitrary process. Each of the signers creates a trapdoor commitment, under they public key pk^s, which they can later open to any message. For each of the non-signers in NS the leader creates an honest commitment to a random point y. Using the $N - t$ points committed in the non-signer's commitment and the output of the random oracle z, the leader has $N - t + 1$ points to interpolate a polynomial rpoly using Lagrange interpolation (that we denote by Lagrange). Then each signer uses rpoly to compute the point $y^s := \mathsf{rpoly}(\alpha^s)$. Finally, they use their trapdoor sk^s to equivocate their commitment c^s to y^s.

Table 2. Notation.

Sym	Meaning
t	Threshold
N	Number of members of the ring
P	Ordered list of public keys $P = (vk^1, vk^2, \ldots)$
R	Subring $R \subseteq P$
S	Set of indices identifying the signers in R
T	Secret keys to signers in S, $T = \{sk^s\}_{s \in S}$
NS	Set of indices denoting non-signers where $NS \subseteq [N]$
n	Number of commitments each signer will make
i	Indexing over n
m	Number of openings each signer will make
j	Indexing over m
Lagrange	Lagrange interpolation
$\mathcal{M}$	Message space over field $\mathbb{F}$
$\mathcal{C}$	Commitment space over some field $\mathbb{F}$
G	$G \leftarrow_\$ \mathsf{RO}$. $G : \mathcal{M} \times \mathbb{F} \times \mathbb{F} \to \mathcal{M} \times \mathbb{F} \times \mathbb{F}$
H	$H = (H_1, H_2)$ where $H \leftarrow_\$ \mathsf{RO}$
H_1	$H_1 : \mathcal{M} \times \mathcal{C}^N \times [m] \to \mathbb{F}$
H_2	$H_2 : \mathcal{M} \times \mathcal{C}^N \times (ran(G))^{N \times m} \to [m]$
$\mathcal{TC}$	Trapdoor commitment scheme
$\lambda \in \mathbb{N}$	Security parameter

The signature will consist of all commitments $(c^1, \ldots, c^N)$ and openings $(y^1, \ldots, y^N)$ for polynomial rpoly. Since for the security proof we need to extract two openings (and thus violate binding), we must force the signers to generate many openings for the same trapdoor commitment. This is where we use the Unruh transformation [36]. This is done by having m points $z_1, \ldots, z_m$ and thus m distinct polynomials that should be interpolated using the same set of points committed in $com = (c^1, \ldots, c^N)$. The signers therefore prepare m set of openings, one for each polynomial $\mathsf{rpoly}_1, \ldots, \mathsf{rpoly}_m$. All these openings are "encrypted" using the one-way permutation G (which is invertible by the reduction during the proof), producing the line $(g_i^1, \ldots, g_i^N)$ for each point z_i. Only one set of openings, denoted by J, is eventually revealed to the verifier. J is chosen using another random oracle H_2, computed by (com, g_i^s) for all $i \in [n]$. To amplify the probability of extraction, the above process is repeated n times in parallel. The values n and m are statistical security parameters. The leader and signer procedures are in Figs. 3 and 4. The remaining algorithms (for setup, key generation, and verify) are described in Fig. 2.

To sum up our (t, N) ring signature σ consists of the following elements. n "lines" of commitments com_i where $com_i = (c_i^s)_{s \in [N]}$. For each line we have m rows that represent possible "openings" of the same commitments: $\sigma_i = (\{(c_i^s, y_{i,J_i}^s, op_{i,J_i}^s, r_{i,J_i}^s)\}_{s=1}^N, \{g_{i,j}^s\}_{s=1,j=1}^{N,m})$. We will only reveal one of these m rows. See Fig. 1 for a pictorial representation of the final signature.

5   Post-quantum Security of TRS

Theorem 1. *If* $TC := $ (Setup, Com, TCom, TOpen, VerifyOpen) *is a post-quantum secure Trapdoor Commitment Scheme, and* H_1, H_2, G *are modeled as quantum-accessible random oracles then TRS achieves perfect completeness (per Definition 4), t-Anonymity wrt to Adversially Chosen Keys (per Definition 3) and t-Unforgeability w.r.t to Insider Corruption (per Definition 2) in the quantum random oracle model in presence of QPT adversaries.*

Our threshold ring signature scheme has the properties of completeness, signer anonymity, and unforgeability for a threshold t-out-of-N. The anonymity and unforgeability proofs are similar. The difference is in the challenge phase. For unforgeability, the adversary produces a threshold ring signature; in anonymity, the adversary chooses between two signing sets. Anonymity is proven via reduction to trapdoor indistinguishability, while unforgeability is proven via reduction to binding of the underlying trapdoor commitment scheme.

In both proofs, the QPT adversary has quantum access to the random oracles H_1, H_2, G, to the underlying trapdoor commitment procedure, and classical access to the oracles OSign, Corrupt, and OKGen. This captures the fact that honest parties run classically.

(t, N)- THRESHOLD RING SIGNATURE TRS

Setup: Setup(1^λ). Chooses $G \leftarrow_\$ \mathsf{Perm}$ and $H \leftarrow_\$ \mathsf{RO}$, where H is diversified as H_1, H_2. Returns $pp = (H, G)$.

Key Generation: KGen(pp). For the $s - th$ member joining the ring, running the key generation yields $(pk^s, sk^s) \leftarrow TC.\mathsf{Setup}$ and $\alpha_s \leftarrow_\$ \mathbb{F}$. Set $vk^s = (pk^s, \alpha^s)$.

Threshold Signing Procedure: ThSign$_{pp}$(msg, T, R)

This is an interactive procedure run among the parties in the set S to jointly sign a message msg on behalf of the ring R, with $|R| = N$ and $|S| \geq t$. The non-signers are indexed as NS, so that $R = S \sqcup NS$. Before starting the protocol, all participants check whether the other keys in the chosen ring are valid using Valid. The procedure starts with one party in S (chosen arbitrarily) running the **Leader** procedure (Fig. 3). Every party in S runs the **Signer** procedure (Fig. 4). The two algorithms **Leader** and **Signer** run in parallel.

Verification: Vfy(msg, R, σ) Calculate for each σ_i, $i = 1, \ldots, n$:

$$b \stackrel{?}{=} \mathsf{Valid}(pk^s) \forall s \in R$$

$$1 \stackrel{?}{=} \mathsf{VerifyOpen}_{pk_s}(c_i^s, op_{i,J_i}^s, y_{i,J_i}^s) \forall s \in R$$

$$com_i = \{c_i^s\}_{s \in [N]}$$

$$J_i := H_2(\mathsf{msg}, com_i, \{g_{sij}\}_{s=1,j=1}^{N,m})$$

$$z_{i,J_i} := H_1(\mathsf{msg}, com_i, J_i)$$

$$g_{i,J_i}^s \stackrel{?}{=} G(y_{i,J_i}^s || op_{i,J_i}^s || r_{i,J_i}^s) \forall s \in R$$

$$\mathsf{rpoly}(\cdot) = \mathsf{Lagrange}(\{(\alpha^s, y_{i,J_i}^s) | s \in R\} \cup (0, z_{i,J_i}))$$

$$\deg(\mathsf{rpoly}) \stackrel{?}{\leq} N - t$$

$$\mathsf{rpoly}_{i,J_i}(\alpha^s) \stackrel{?}{=} y_{i,J_i}^s \text{ for all } s \in R$$

If the values match on all checks, then the verifier outputs 1. Otherwise, 0.

Fig. 2. The (t, N) - Threshold Ring Signature scheme TRS

5.1 Proofs

Completeness. Completeness is the idea that honest signers produce a signature which is accepted by an honest verifier, and is proven using the guarantees of Shamir's secret sharing and the commitment scheme. Completeness demands that any t honest parties can compute an accepting signature on any message msg with respect to a subring $R \subseteq P$ ($|R| = N$) of which they are members. We assume that the public keys of the underlying trapdoor commitment scheme TC

$\mathsf{ThSign}_{pp}(\mathsf{msg}, T, R)$

<table>
<tr><td>

Leader

for $i = 1$ to n **do**
  for $q \in NS$ **do**
    $y_i^q \leftarrow_\$ \mathbb{F}$
    $(c_i^q, op_i^q) \leftarrow \mathsf{Com}_{pk^q}(y^q)$
    MULTICAST: Send c_i^q, y_i^q, op_i^q to all $s \in S$.
  for $s \in S$ **do**
    WAIT: Get c_i^s from $s \in S$.
  $com_i := (c_i^s)_{s=1}^N$
  for $j = 1$ to m **do**
    $z_{i,j} := H_1(\mathsf{msg}, com_i, j)$
    $\mathsf{rpoly}_{i,j}(\cdot) := \mathsf{Lagrange}(\{(\alpha^q, y_i^q) | q \in NS\} \cup (0, z_{i,j}))$
    for $s \in S$ **do**
      WAIT: Get $g_{i,j}^s$ $\forall s \in S$.
      for $q \in NS$ **do**
        $r_{i,j}^q \leftarrow_\$ \mathbb{F}$
        $g_{i,j}^q := G(y_i^q \| op_i^q \| r_{i,j}^q)$
      MULTICAST: Sends $g_{i,j}^q$, $r_{i,j}^q$ for $q \in NS$.
  $J_i = H_2(\mathsf{msg}, com_i, (g_{ij}^s)_{s=1, j=1}^{N, m})$
  WAIT: Get openings on index J_i from $\forall s \in S$.
  if $\mathsf{VerifyOpen}_{pk^s}(c_i^s, op_{i,J_i}^s, y_{i,J_i}^s) \overset{?}{=} 1$ $\forall s \in S$ **then**
    $\sigma_i = (\{(c_i^s, y_{i,J_i}^s, op_{i,J_i}^s, r_{i,J_i}^s)\}_{s=1}^N, \{g_{i,j}^s\}_{s=1, j=1}^{N, m})$
  else
    ABORT ▷ Aborts if a signer does not give correct opening.
Return $\sigma = ((\sigma_i)_{i=1}^n, R)$

</td><td>

Signer

for $i = 1$ to n **do**
  $state_i^s, c_i^s \leftarrow \mathsf{TCom}(sk^s)$.
  WAIT: Get y_i^q, c_i^q, op_i^q of $q \in NS$ from Leader, then verify.
  for $q \in NS$ **do**
    $1 \overset{?}{=} \mathsf{VerifyOpen}_{pk^s}(c_i^q, op_i^q)$
  MULTICAST: Send c_i^s to $\forall s \in S$
  WAIT: Get c_i^s $\forall s \in S$
  $com_i = (c_i^s)_{s=1}^N$
  for $j = 1$ to m **do**
    $z_{i,j} := H_1(\mathsf{msg}, com_i, j)$
    $\mathsf{rpoly}_{i,j}(\cdot) := \mathsf{Lagrange}(\{(\alpha^q, y_i^q) | q \in NS\} \cup (0, z_{i,j}))$
    $y_{ij}'^s := \mathsf{rpoly}_{ij}(\alpha^s)$
    $op_{i,j}^s \leftarrow \mathsf{TOpen}(sk^s, state^s, c_i^s, y_{i,j}'^s)$.
    $r_{i,j}^s \leftarrow_\$ \mathbb{F}$
    $g_{i,j}^s := G(y_{i,j}'^s \| op_{i,j}^s \| r_{i,j}^s)$
    MULTICAST: Send g_{ij}^s.
    WAIT: Get $g_{i,j}^s$ for all $s \in S$.
    WAIT: Get from leader $\forall q \in NS$ $g_{i,j}^s$ and $r_{i,j}^s$.
  $J_i = H_2(\mathsf{msg}, com_i, (g_{i,j}^s)_{s=1, j=1}^{N, m})$
  Check $g_{i,J_i}^q \overset{?}{=} G(y_{i,J_i}^q \| op_{i,J_i}^q \| r_{i,J_i}^q)$ for $q \in NS$
Return $(c_{i,J_i}^s, y_{i,J_i}^s op_{i,J_i}^s, r_{i,J_i}^s)_{i=1}^n$

</td></tr>
</table>

Fig. 3. The Leader is chosen arbitrarily from among the signers.

Fig. 4. The Signer algorithm works in parallel with the Leader algorithm.

have the correct format and can be used by anyone to compute valid commitments and openings; the signers may check this using Valid on all public keys of the chosen subring. The t signers can compute valid commitments for the $N - t$ non-signers as well as themselves.

For the ring members from $s = 1, \ldots, N$, consider the vector of commitments com_i and the associated The inputs and openings for com_i at J_i:

$$\left[c_{i,j}^1 \cdots c_{i,j}^t \; c_{i,j}^{t+1} \cdots c_{i,j}^N \right]$$

$$\left[(y_{i,1}^1, op_{i,1}^1) \cdots (y_{i,1}^t, op_{i,1}^t) \; (y_{i,1}^{t+1}, op_{i,1}^{t+1}) \cdots (y_{i,1}^N, op_{i,1}^N) \right]$$

For the inputs $(y_{i,J_i}^s)_{s=1,i=1}^{N,n}$, the Leader picks and commits to random points $(y_{i,J_i}^q)_{q \in NS}$. With up to $N - t$ non-signers, there are $N - t + 1$ points $\{(\alpha^q, y_{i,J_i}^q) | q \in NS\} \cup (0, z_{i,J_i})$. Lagrange interpolation on these points yields a polynomial rpoly_{i,J_i} such that $\deg(\mathsf{rpoly}_{i,J_i}) \leq N - t$. Using rpoly_{i,J_i}, the $s \in S$ use their trapdoors to find points y_{i,J_i}^s that fit on rpoly_{i,J_i}. The commitments computed with both non-signers and signers are valid, so all the openings provided as part of the signature will correctly verify.

Because rpoly_{i,J_i} is the unique polynomial that fits on all points $(y_{i,J_i}^s)_{s=1}^N$, it does not matter which points the verifier uses to recalculate rpoly_{i,J_i}. The verifier will see that $\deg(\mathsf{rpoly}_{i,J_i}) \leq N - t$ and $\mathsf{rpoly}_{iJ_i}(\alpha_s) = y_{i,J_i}^s$ for all i and for all s and for any J_i.

Hybrids (Common for Both Anonymity and Unforgeability). We recall that in the t-Anonymity 3 and t-Unforgeability Experiment 2, the adversary has access to the same oracles in the training phase. It is only in the challenge phase that the experiments differ: an adversary $\mathcal{A}_{anon}$ to anonymity produces two signing sets and must distinguish between them, and a forger $\mathcal{F}$ must produce a t-out-of-N threshold ring signature (knowing only $t - 1$ secret keys).

For both proofs, we replace each trapdoor commitment with an honest commitment over a sequence of arguments. Each step is computationally indistinguishable from the previous step due to trapdoor indistinguishability. To show this formally, we use a hybrid argument where we move from hybrid H_0 where honest signers use their trapdoor to compute their commitments, to hybrid H_{N+5} where all commitments are computed honestly.

In the last hybrid H_{N+5} no honest keys involved in the signatures use the trapdoor. We change how the OSign oracle behaves in order to remove usage of trapdoors in an indistinguishable manner. We denote as $\mathsf{OSign}_{\mathsf{H}_\ell}$ as the modified OSign algorithm in the hybrid sequence.

The proof is divided into two stages. In the first stage, we show a sequence of hybrids to program the output of the random oracles $\mathcal{H}_1$ and $\mathcal{H}_2$. In particular, we program the values J_i and $z_{i,j}$ ahead of time so that for the unopened rows, we no longer use valid openings. Once we have the possibility of not having to use trapdoors anywhere (since we need to provide only one opening, that we know ahead of time), we move to the second stage of hybrids, where we replace trapdoor commitments with honest commitments.

In order to do this, the random oracle $\mathcal{H}$ must be *programmed* such that $\mathcal{H}(x) = z$ for a particular x and z, so long as the values still look random for the adversary. By knowing the point z ahead of time, an oracle can produce a valid signature using only honest commitments.

We define $\mathsf{H}_{\ell+5}$ for $\ell \in [N]$ so that on a signature request, ring members $s \in [\ell]$ are always calculated using an honest commitment, regardless of whether

vk^s is in the signing set. We use the OSign described in H_{N+5} in both proofs of unforgeability and anonymity. We describe the list of hybrids below, changing the OSign oracle.

H_0: The original game with OSign (and H) as defined in Sect. 3.1.

H_1: Instead of getting J_i, $i \in [n]$ from the random oracle, the challenger chooses J_i at random and programs the random oracle H to return the values for J_i. This allows the challenger to know ahead of time which of the lines he needs to open. To show H_0 and H_1 are computationally indistinguishable in presence of a QPT adversary who makes q-queries to the QRO, we use a result by Unruh (see Sect. 3 of [36]).

H_2: (Bridging step). Because J_i is known ahead of time now, we add an if-statement to note when the iteration $j = J_i$ occurs and continue. The challenger is going through the same steps for the inner loop, so this makes no difference.

H_3: The challenger replaces the intercept value z_{i,J_i} with a randomly chosen value and programs H to return z_{i,J_i} on query $H_1(\mathsf{msg}, com_i, J_i)$. Since H_1 is chosen from RO, it is indistinguishable from random by a QPT algorithm. Programming H to return z_{i,J_i} is indistinguishable to a QPT algorithm. We use the fact that com_i has superlogarithmic entropy.

H_4: As z_{i,J_i} is picked before commitments are created, when the challenger knows the openings for the non-signers, he can calculate the polynomial rpoly_{i,J_i}. If the leader is honest, the challenger can simply pick the inputs for the commitments (the y_{i,J_i}^s). Even if the adversary controls the leader and selects inputs in an adversarial way, the use of z_{i,J_i} ensures that the polynomial is random. For corrupted parties, the challenger waits for the adversary to give the inputs. In both H_3 and H_4, Lagrange gives a random polynomial. We only change the order of when the polynomial is calculated. Now that z_{i,J_i} is chosen even before commitments are created.

H_5: Since the values for $j \neq J_i$ of $y_{i,j}^s, op_{i,j}^s, r_{i,j}^s$ are never to be opened, instead of calculating these points using the normal system, the challenger simply picks the inputs and other values at random for all $s \in [N]$. G is hiding, so it is not feasible for any QPT adversary to learn anything more about the pre-image to G. Even when the adversary knows what the openings to the commitments are, G is salted with a random value.

$H_{\ell+5}$: For $\ell = 1, \ldots, N$. For hybrid $H_{\ell+5}$, on a signature query, ring members $s = 1, \ldots, \ell$ are always calculated using an honest commitment, whether s is in the signing set or not. To show $H_{(\ell+1)+5}$ is indistinguishable from $H_{\ell+5}$: On a signing query, in $H_{(\ell+1)+5}$, the commitment for signer $\ell+1$ is calculated using an honest commitment. In $H_{\ell+5}$, the commitment for ring member $\ell+1$ is calculated by using a trapdoor commitment. These two cases are computationally indistinguishable if trapdoor commitments and honest commitments are computationally indistinguishable. We see that for all $\ell = 1, \ldots, N+5$ where $|R| = N$, the probability of distinguishing between H_ℓ and $H_{(\ell-1)}$ is negligible.

Anonymity. Following Fig. 1, a signature σ parses into n lines: com_i (where $com_i = (c_i^s)_{s \in [N]}$) and for each line there are m associated rows. The difference between the signers and non-signers is in the columns. A non-signer column contains the same openings across all m rows; a signer column instead will have a different opening on each row. We note that $\mathcal{A}_{anon}$ is given only one row (among the m) of openings. For other rows he is only given $g_{i,j}^s$, which is calculated as $g_{i,j}^s := G(y_{i,j}^s || op_i^s || r_{i,j}^s)$. If $\mathcal{A}_{anon}$ can distinguish between the signing sets simply observing the openings that were made available, then either it is possible to (1) learn something about the pre-image of $g_{i,j}^s$ or (2) to distinguish between trapdoor and honest commitments. Such an $\mathcal{A}_{anon}$ is therefore either violating the hiding properties of G or the trapdoor indistinguishability of $\mathcal{TC}$. Note that following hybrids $\mathsf{H}_{\ell+5}$ for $\ell = 1, \ldots, N$, an adversary who could distinguish between the signing sets could also distinguish between trapdoor and honest commitments. In H_5, we use the hiding properties of G.

In the t-Anonymity Experiment 3, the QPT adversary $\mathcal{A}_{anon}$ submits a message msg and two signing sets S_0, S_1 from a subring R. S_0 and S_1 must not be corrupted, but R may contain malicious keys. The challenger flips a bit $b \in \{0,1\}$ and computes the signature σ on msg with the keys of S_b. Then $\mathcal{A}_{anon}$ will guess which of S_0, S_1 was used.

Suppose that an adversary in H_0 wins with advantage ν. We change OSign via the hybrids as described before. In H_{N+5}, all honest keys involved in the signature no longer use a trapdoor. This means that regardless of which sets S_0 and S_1 $\mathcal{A}_{anon}$ picks, the signature will be calculated in exactly the same way. Thus the probability of $\mathcal{A}_{anon}$ winning the anonymity game in H_{N+5} must be $\frac{1}{2}$. We conclude that the probability of $\mathcal{A}_{anon}$ winning in H_0 must be at most $\frac{1}{2} + \nu(\lambda)$. Using the fact that each hybrid is computationally indistinguishable from the previous one, we can conclude that no adversary can win the original t-Anonymity game in H_0 except with negligible advantage $\nu(\lambda)$.

To be more specific, here we show the reduction for each step in hybrids $\mathsf{H}_{\ell+5}$ for $\ell = 1, \ldots, N + 5$. Let $\mathcal{A}_{anon}$ be playing in $\mathsf{H}_{\ell+5}$ such that on on each request for OSign, the challenger will return $\mathsf{OSign}_{\mathsf{H}_{\ell+5}}$. Suppose that $\mathcal{A}_{anon}$ wins $\mathsf{H}_{\ell+5}$ with probability $p_\ell(\lambda)$ for all $\ell \in [N]$, i.e.,

$$|Pr[\mathcal{A}_{anon}(\sigma) = 1 | \sigma \leftarrow \mathsf{ThSign}(\mathsf{msg}^*, S_0, R)] -$$
$$Pr[\mathcal{A}_{anon}(\sigma) = 1 | \sigma \leftarrow \mathsf{ThSign}(\mathsf{msg}^*, S_1, R)]| = p_\ell(\lambda).$$

We write the difference between the probability of $\mathcal{A}_{anon}$ winning when playing in $\mathsf{H}_{\ell+5}$ and in $\mathsf{H}_{(\ell+1)+5}$ as $|p_{\ell+1} - p_\ell|$. Assume that $|p_{\ell+1} - p_\ell|$ is non-negligible. Next, we construct an adversary to trapdoor $\mathcal{A}_{tr}$ who uses $\mathcal{A}_{anon}$.

Reduction 1: $\underline{\mathcal{A}_{tr}}$

1. $\mathcal{A}_{tr}$ is given a public parameter pk from his challenger.
2. $\mathcal{A}_{tr}$ picks a random index $\ell \in [N]$ and sets $pk^\ell := pk$.
3. $\mathcal{A}_{tr}$ activates $\mathcal{A}_{anon}$. Then on each query:

- OKGen(s): if $\ell \neq s$, $\mathcal{A}_{tr}$ generates (pk^s, sk^s) and $\alpha^s \leftarrow_\$ \mathbb{F}$. He forwards $vk^s = (pk^s, \alpha^s)$ to $\mathcal{A}_{anon}$. For $s = \ell$, $\mathcal{A}_{tr}$ forwards $pk^\ell := pk$ and some $\alpha^\ell \leftarrow_\$ \mathbb{F}$.
- Corrupt(s): $\mathcal{A}_{anon}$ requests sk^s, which $\mathcal{A}_{tr}$ sends. If $s = \ell$, $\mathcal{A}_{tr}$ will ABORT.
- OSign(msg, S, R), $\mathcal{A}_{tr}$ will follow $\text{OSign}_{\mathsf{H}_{(\ell-1)+5}}(\text{msg}, S, R)$, except for signer ℓ. If ℓ is in the signing set, then $\mathcal{A}_{tr}$ will query his challenger y_ℓ and receive (c^ℓ, op^ℓ) in return. Otherwise, he calculates $(c^\ell, op^\ell) \leftarrow \text{Com}(y^\ell)$.

4. When $\mathcal{A}_{anon}$ requests two signing sets, S_0 and S_1, $\mathcal{A}_{tr}$ picks a bit b and signs with respect to S_b. $\mathcal{A}_{tr}$ follows his same strategy as in the training phase, sending a request out to his challenger if $\ell \in S_b$.
5. $\mathcal{A}_{anon}$ responds with b.
6. When D outputs b, $\mathcal{A}_{tr}$ outputs the same.

Probability Analysis **Case 1.** $\mathcal{A}_{tr}$ is playing with the trapdoor oracle, O_t.

Then for each y^ℓ requested from O_t, $\mathcal{A}_{tr}$ receives c^ℓ and op^ℓ back, where $state^\ell, c^\ell \leftarrow \text{TCom}(sk_i)$ and $op^\ell \leftarrow \text{TOpen}(sk_\ell, state^\ell, c^\ell, y^\ell)$. Then c^ℓ is a trapdoor if $vk^\ell \in S$. Thus to D, the view looks exactly the same as the game for $\mathsf{H}_{\ell+5}$, i.e.,

$$Pr[\mathcal{A}_{anon} \text{ wins } | \mathsf{H}_{\ell+5}] = Pr[\mathcal{A}_{tr}^{O_t} = 1]$$

Case 2. $\mathcal{A}_{tr}$ is playing with the commitment oracle, O_c. For each request y^ℓ, $\mathcal{A}_{tr}$ receives $(c^\ell, op^\ell) \leftarrow \text{Com}_{pk^\ell}(y^\ell)$ back. Then c^ℓ is always an honest commitment regardless of whether $vk^\ell \in S$. Thus to $\mathcal{A}_{anon}$, the view looks exactly the same as the game with a challenger for $\mathsf{H}_{(\ell+1)+5}$, i.e.,

$$Pr[\mathcal{A}_{anon} \text{ wins } | \mathsf{H}_{\ell+1+5}] = Pr[\mathcal{A}_{tr}^{O_c} = 1] \implies$$
$$|Pr[\mathcal{A}_{anon} \text{ wins } | \mathsf{H}_{\ell+5}] - Pr[\mathcal{A}_{anon} \text{ wins } | \mathsf{H}_{\ell+1+5}]| =$$
$$|Pr[\mathcal{A}_{tr}^{O_c} = 1] - Pr[\mathcal{A}_{tr}^{O_t} = 1]| = |p_{\ell+1} - p_\ell|$$

Then $\mathcal{A}_{tr}$ can win the trapdoor indistinguishability game with non-negligible probability, a contradiction. We see that $\mathcal{A}_{anon}$ cannot win $\mathsf{H}_{\ell+5}$ and $\mathsf{H}_{(\ell+1)+5}$ with non-negligible differences for $\ell = 1$ to N.

Unforgeability. A successful forgery verifies for t signers, but the adversary has knowledge of only up to $t-1$ secret keys. As in the anonymity proof, we swap each trapdoor commitment out with an honest commitment over a sequence of arguments. In the final step, the forger receives only honest commitments for all signing queries. The commitments $com = c^1, \ldots, c^N$ must be produced before learning the value z, which is necessary to produce the unique polynomial rpoly of degree $N - t$. In a valid signature, all the openings must somehow fall onto rpoly. As H is unpredictable, the forger cannot guess what z is ahead of time, so she also cannot guess the inputs such that they all fall on rpoly. This means the forger must be able to open the commitments to a different value after learning z. Thus, if the forger is able to produce a valid signature, then with high probability she must have broken the binding of an honest commitment.

In the t-Unforgeability Experiment 2, the adversary has access to the same oracles as in the Anonymity game in the training phase. To win the game she needs to provide a valid signature σ^*, computed on a ring of her choice, and the only restriction is that the ring contains at most $t-1$ corrupted keys. If the adversary provides a valid signature where fewer than t keys were corrupted, then at least one commitment was created using an uncorrupted key (the adversary was not given the corresponding trapdoor). Two openings of that commitment can be extracted using the permutation G.

In addition to the hybrids described above, we write a hybrid in which G is replaced by a uniformly random polynomial of degree $2q_O - 1$. Such a polynomial is a $2q_O$ independent function, and is indistinguishable from G (per Zhandry [42]) in presence of a quantum adversary making at most q_O queries to the G. On a successful forgery, the simulation can invert the values using G and obtain many openings (y_j^s, op_j^s), $(\tilde{y}_j^s, \tilde{o}p_j^s)$ for the same commitment c^s. With high probability, at least one commitment must have two valid openings. As all commitments are honest now, the two valid openings for the same commitment break binding.

In the reduction 2, we show $\mathcal{B}$ that uses a successful forgery by $\mathcal{F}$ to break the binding property of $\mathcal{TC}$. Recall that in the binding experiment, an adversary is given public parameters pk, and their goal is to compute a commitment under pk and two different openings msg, op and msg', op' where $\mathsf{msg} \neq \mathsf{msg}'$. The idea is that $\mathcal{B}$ will place the public pk as the answer of the idx-th query to the key generation oracle.

$\mathcal{B}$ will simulate all the oracles to $\mathcal{F}$. $\mathcal{B}$ will abort only when $\mathcal{F}$ asks to corrupt key pk. When $\mathcal{F}$ provides a forgery σ^* for a ring containing pk, $\mathcal{B}$ checks if pk was chosen by $\mathcal{F}$ as as one of the signers in the forgery. Then $\mathcal{B}$ will try to extract the openings for the commitments computed under key pk by inverting G.

Reduction 2: $\mathcal{B}(1^\lambda, pk)$

1. $\mathcal{B}$ picks an index $idx \in [q_{KG}]$ at random.
2. $\mathcal{B}$ picks G to be a random polynomial of degree $2q_O - 1$, and gets $H \leftarrow_\$ \mathsf{RO}$. Then $pp = (H, G)$.
3. $\mathcal{B}$ activates $\mathcal{F}$. $\mathcal{B}$ forwards pp to $\mathcal{F}$. $\mathcal{F}$ has (quantum) access to H and G. $\mathcal{B}$ emulates the oracles to $\mathcal{F}$ as follows:
   (a) On each $\mathsf{OKGen}(s)$ request from $\mathcal{F}$, $\mathcal{B}$ calculates $(vk^s, sk^s) \leftarrow \mathsf{KGen}(pp)$ and forwards vk^s to $\mathcal{F}$. On the $idx - th$ query, $\mathcal{B}$ will send the pk she received along with some $\alpha^{idx} \leftarrow_\$ \mathbb{F}$.
   (b) On each $\mathsf{Corrupt}(s)$ query, $\mathcal{B}$ returns sk^s. If $\mathcal{F}$ requests $\mathsf{Corrupt}(idx)$, ABORT.
   (c) For $\mathsf{OSign}_{\mathsf{H}_{N+6}}(\mathsf{msg}, S, R)$: $\mathcal{B}$ returns $\sigma \leftarrow \mathsf{OSign}_{\mathsf{H}_{N+6}}(\mathsf{msg}, S, R)$ (i.e., using all honest commitments). Note that if $\mathcal{F}$ does not cooperate, then $\mathcal{B}$ must ABORT.
4. $\mathcal{F}$ has to query H and G for its forgery. For queries to H, $\mathcal{B}$ will answer as H would (except where H has been reprogrammed). $\mathcal{B}$ will calculate answers for G herself.

5. Finally, $\mathcal{F}$ will output a forgery $(\sigma^*, \mathsf{msg}^*, R^*)$. The forged signature contains for $i = 1, \ldots, n$:

$$\sigma_i = (\{(c_i^s, y_{i,J_i}^s, op_{i,J_i}^s, r_{i,J_i}^s)\}_{s=1}^N, \{g_{i,j}^s\}_{s=1,j=1}^{N,m})$$

6. If $\mathcal{F}$ has a successful forgery, and $idx \in R^*$, $\mathcal{B}$ will for $i = 1, \ldots, n$, take σ_i and for $j = 1, \ldots, m$ calculate

$$y_{i,j}^{idx}||op_{i,j}^{idx}||r_{i,j}^{idx} = G^{-1}(g_{i,j}^{idx}).$$

For all j, $\mathcal{B}$ will scan $(y_{ij}^{idx}, op_{ij}^{idx})$. If there exist j, j' $(j \neq j')$ such that:

$$(y_{i,j}^{idx}, op_{i,j}^{idx}) \neq (y_{i,j'}^{idx}, op_{i,j'}^{idx})$$
$$1 = \mathsf{VerifyOpen}_{pk}(c_i^{idx}, op_{i,j}^{idx}, y_{i,j}^{idx})$$
$$1 = \mathsf{VerifyOpen}_{pk}(c_i^{idx}, op_{i,j'}^{idx}, y_{i,j'}^{idx})$$

Then $\mathcal{B}$ will output $(y_{i,j}^{idx}, op_{i,j}^{idx})$, $(y_{i,j'}^{idx}, op_{i,j'}^{idx})$, c_i^{idx}.

Suppose $\mathcal{F}$ makes $q_{\mathsf{KG}}(\lambda)$ queries to KGen, $q_S(\lambda)$ queries to OSign, and $q_O(\lambda)$ to the random oracle H and G. For shorthand, we will write $q_{\mathsf{KG}}, q_S, q_O$ without the security parameter. Consider the following cases where $\mathcal{F}$ has a forgery

$$\sigma^* = \{\sigma_i = (\{(c_i^s, y_{i,J_i}^s, op_{i,J_i}^s, r_{i,J_i}^s)\}_{s=1}^N, \{g_{i,j}^s\}_{s=1,j=1}^{N,m})\}_{i \in [N]}.$$

Since $\mathcal{B}$ is capable of inverting all of G, $\mathcal{B}$ can see all the openings for every commitment for each ring member.

Probability Analysis. $\mathcal{B}$ will for $i = 1, \ldots, n$ take σ_i and for $j = 1, \ldots, m$ calculate

$$y_{i,j}^{idx}||op_{i,j}^{idx}||r_{ij}^{idx} = G^{-1}(g_{i,j}^{idx}).$$

For all j, $\mathcal{B}$ will scan $(y_{ij}^{idx}, op_{ij}^{idx})$. We note that $\mathcal{B}$ wins if there exists an i for which idx has two valid openings on c_i^{idx}. $\mathcal{B}$ does not win if for all i, idx has one or fewer valid openings. We can describe these outcomes as one of the three following cases:

1. (Good: idx is in the signing set and openings are correct) For some i, idx has two valid openings to the commitment c_i^{idx} which are given by $(y_{ij}^{idx}, op_{ij}^{idx})$ and $(y_{ij'}^{idx}, op_{ij'}^{idx})$. We call idx a *signer* in this case.
2. (Bad: idx is non-signer.) If for all i, $(y_{i,j}^s, op_{i,j}^s)$, $j \in [m]$ are all equal, or we have that $idx \notin R^*$. In this case we call idx a *non-signer*. Then $\mathcal{B}$ fails.
3. (Bad: idx has invalid openings) The signature verifies, but $\forall j \neq J_i$, if $(y_{i,j}^{idx}, op_{i,j}^{idx}) \neq (y_{i,J_i}^{idx}, op_{i,J_i}^{idx})$, then it is not true that

$$1 = \mathsf{VerifyOpen}_{pk_{idx}}(c_i^{idx}, op_{i,j}^{idx}, y_{i,j}^{idx}).$$

Case 2: There is a threshold requirement that there must be at least t distinct signers. There are at most q_{KG} ring members. $\mathcal{B}$ picks index idx at random from

$[q_{\mathsf{KG}}]$. That means $\mathcal{B}$ picked an index inside $\mathcal{F}$'s eventual signing set for his ring signature with probability $\frac{t}{q_{\mathsf{KG}}}$. The probability of not being a signer covers both the case of idx being in the ring but not a signer, as well as idx not being in the ring at all. This means $\mathcal{B}$ fails to pick a member of the signing set with probability $1 - \frac{t}{q_{\mathsf{KG}}} = \frac{q_{\mathsf{KG}} - t}{q_{\mathsf{KG}}}$.

Case 3: The signature verifies, but for all $j \neq J_i$, if $(y_{i,j}^{idx}, op_{i,j}^{idx}) \neq (y_{i,J_i}^{idx}, op_{i,J_i}^{idx})$, then $1 \neq \mathsf{VerifyOpen}_{pk^{idx}}(c_i^{idx}, op_{i,j}^{idx}, y_{i,j}^{idx})$. This means $\mathcal{F}$ picked the point y_{i,J_i}^{idx} to commit to such that $(\alpha^{idx}, y_{i,J_i}^{idx})$ would be on a polynomial rpoly_{i,J_i}. Recall that rpoly_{i,J_i} has the point $(0, z_{iJ_i})$, where $z_{i,J_i} = H_1(\mathsf{msg}, com_i, J_i)$. Furthermore, z_{i,J_i} completely determines the polynomial. Even knowing every other coefficient of rpoly_{i,J_i}, $\mathcal{F}$ cannot determine any points on the polynomial.

As z_{i,J_i} is random, $\mathcal{F}$ can determine the correct value of $(\alpha^{idx}, y_{i,J_i}^{idx})$ with probability no better than $\frac{1}{\mathbb{F}}$. Also, $\mathcal{F}$ would also have to know the point J_i where the commitments would be opened. The value of J_i comes from H_2, which is a random oracle. $\mathcal{F}$ would have to have guessed J_i in advance and his probability of doing so is $\frac{1}{m}$. Finally, $\mathcal{F}$ must guess J_i for all $i \in [n]$. Uniformly choosing a correct random J_i and a point $(\alpha^{idx}, y_{i,J_i}^{idx})$ for $i \in [n]$ occurs with probability $\frac{1}{mn}\frac{1}{\mathbb{F}}$.

The bad cases occur with probability: $\frac{q_{\mathsf{KG}} - t}{q_{\mathsf{KG}}} + \frac{1}{mn} \cdot \frac{1}{\mathbb{F}} \leq \frac{q_{\mathsf{KG}} - t}{q_{\mathsf{KG}}} + \mathsf{negl}(\lambda))$.

If $\mathcal{F}$ forges with probability $p(\lambda)$, $\mathcal{B}$ breaks binding with probability

$$p(\lambda) \cdot \left(\frac{t}{q_{\mathsf{KG}}} - \mathsf{negl}(\lambda) \right).$$

This means that if $p(\lambda)$ is non-negligible, then $\mathcal{B}$ is able to break binding with non-negligible probability. We conclude that no adversary $\mathcal{F}$ can produce a successful forgery except with negligible probability.

6   Trapdoor Commitments from OWFs

In this section, we discuss a possible instantiation of a post-quantum secure trapdoor commitment from any post-quantum secure one-way function (OWF). The idea is to leverage a folklore transformation of Σ-protocol into a trapdoor commitment. We start by describing a Σ-protocol and then show how to create a trapdoor commitment scheme from a Σ-protocol. Second, we show how to use any OWF to create an efficiently decidable language L. Finally, we show that how to construct post-quantum Σ-protocols on the language of L.

Description of Σ-protocol. Let L be an NP language, with a witness relation $\mathcal{R}_L$. For our purposes, relation $\mathcal{R}_L$ is *hard*, meaning that for any $(x, y) \in \mathcal{R}_L$, given only the *statement* x it is hard to find the *witness* y. A Σ-protocol [16] for a language L is a three-message proof system between two interactive algorithms, a prover $\mathcal{P}$ and a verifier $\mathcal{V}$. $\mathcal{P}$ knows (x, y) which is a statement and witness where $(x, y) \in \mathcal{R}_L$. $\mathcal{V}$ is given x. The interaction for a Σ-protocol goes as follows:

1. $\Sigma.P_1$: $\mathcal{P}$ starts the interaction by sending a commitment c to the verifier.

2. $\Sigma.V$: Upon receipt of c, V sends a challenge e.
3. $\Sigma.P_2$: P calculates the response z and sends z to V.

V uses the transcript (c, e, z) and statement $x \in L$ and outputs a bit to either accept or reject.

A Σ-protocol for a relation $\mathcal{R}_L$ has three security properties: *completeness*, *special soundness*, and *special honest verifier zero-knowledge* (SHVZK). The completeness property of a Σ-protocol guarantees that if the prover knows a witness y for $x \in L$, then for a commitment c, he is able to answer to any challenge e in the challenge space with z such that the transcript (c, e, z) and $x \in L$ is accepting. Secondly, special soundness guarantees that from any two transcripts for $x \in L$ with the same commitment, i.e., (c, e, z) and (c, e', z') one can extract the witness y. Finally, the SHVZK property guarantees that, if the challenge e is given in advance (that is, before computing c), then a simulator can compute an accepting transcript (c, e, z) in polynomial time *without knowing the witness*. The transcript computed by the simulator has the same distribution as that of a transcript produced by an interaction between the prover and verifier. We denote the simulator by $\text{SIM}(x, e)$ which outputs (c, z).

Let Σ be a Σ-protocol associated with the language L with prover and verifier $(\mathcal{P}, \mathcal{V})$. Let SIM be a SHVZK simulator for Σ. Let $\mathcal{M}$ be the challenge space for Σ. Then $\Sigma = (\Sigma.P_1, \Sigma.V, \Sigma.P_2)$. $\Sigma.P_1$ is the first step where $\mathcal{P}$ sends a commitment c, $\Sigma.V$ has $\mathcal{V}$ send a challenge, and $\Sigma.P_2$ is the response from $\mathcal{P}$.

At a high level, the challenge of the Σ-protocol will correspond to the message that a committer wants to commit to. A committer who knows the witness can answer any challenge, meaning he can open to any message he wants. A committer without knowledge of the witness can still create a transcript using SIM, using their desired input as the challenge. Then we define a trapdoor commitment scheme $\mathcal{TC}$ which is parameterized by a language L and $(\Sigma.P_1, \Sigma.P_2, \Sigma.V)$ for L, simulator SIM.

$\underline{\mathcal{TC}[\Sigma]}$

- $pp \leftarrow \mathsf{Setup}(1^\lambda)$. On input the security parameter λ, generates public parameters: the NP language L for instances of size $\mathsf{poly}(\lambda)$ and the associated proof system $(\Sigma.P_1, \Sigma.P_2, \Sigma.V, \Sigma.\text{SIM})$.
- $(pk, \mathsf{trap}) \leftarrow \mathsf{KGen}(1^\lambda, pp)$. Generates an instance $(x, y) \in \mathcal{R}$ and sets $pk = x$ and $\mathsf{trap} = y$.
- $(c, op) \leftarrow \mathsf{Com}_{pk}(m)$: To commit to a message m, run $(c, op) \leftarrow \text{SIM}(pk, m)$. Output commitment c. The opening op is the response.
- $(state, c) \leftarrow \mathsf{TCom}_x(\mathsf{trap})$. Output $(c, state)$ from $\Sigma.P_1(x, y)$ where $state$ is the internal randomness used by $\Sigma.P_1$.
- $op \leftarrow \mathsf{TOpen}(\mathsf{trap}, state, c, m')$. On a message and commitment m', c output $op = \Sigma.P_2(x, c, m', y, state)$.
- $b := \mathsf{VerifyOpen}_x(c, m, op)$. Output $\mathcal{V}(x, c, m, op)$.

Theorem 2. *If Σ is a Σ-protocol over a hard relation $\mathcal{R}$, then $\mathcal{TC}[\Sigma]$ is hiding, binding, and trapdoor indistinguishable.*

Proof (Sketch).
Binding. Binding follows from special soundness, since one commitment and two openings, i.e., (c, m, op) and (c, m', op') allows one to extract the witness.
Trapdoor and Hiding. Hiding follows from trapdoor indistinguishability. Informally, trapdoor indistinguishability follows from the SHVZK property that guarantees that the simulated transcript (honest commitment) is indistinguishable from the prover's transcript (trapdoor commitment).

How to Instantiate a Post-quantum Secure Relation. Let f be a post-quantum secure OWF. An hard relationship $\mathcal{R}$ can be instantiated with f as follows: $(x, w) \in \mathcal{R}$ if $x = f(w)$. Statement-witness pairs can be generated as follows: let $f : \{0,1\}^{poly(\lambda)} \to \{0,1\}^{poly(\lambda)}$ be an OWF. Pick a random $w \in \{0,1\}^{poly(\lambda)}$ and compute $x = f(w)$. Concretely, one can instantiate f with a collision-resistant hash function such as SHA-3, which is currently considered post-quantum secure.

Post-quantum Secure Σ-Protocol. A post-quantum secure Σ-Protocol must maintain special soundness and HVZK in presence of quantum adversaries. A possible instantiation of such a Σ-Protocol is from the Blum protocol for Hamiltonian Graph (which is NP-complete) when the first round is computed using a statistically binding commitment and the hiding of which is preserved in presence of quantum adversaries. As we discussed in Sect. 6.1, while in the quantum case, the definition of binding does not protect the case in which the adversary might not be actually committed to the message until the actual opening, this does not affect the 2-special soundness property, which simply states that *if* two transcripts (and thus two openings) are provided, *then* a witness can be extracted.

6.1 On the Notion of Binding in Presence of Quantum Adversaries

In order to allow signers to be able to change their inputs to the commitments, we use a computationally binding commitment scheme. Computational binding (classical style) intuitively covers the idea that an adversary cannot change his mind on what the input message is. It is hard to find c, where (m, op) and (m', op') are valid openings for c but $m \neq m'$. Unruh posits [37] that this definition is no good in the quantum realm because of the following attack:

1. $\mathcal{A}$ creates c, a commitment.
2. $\mathcal{A}$ receives a random m from his challenger.
3. $\mathcal{A}$ produces the op s.t. (m, op) is a valid opening to c.

This breaks the intuitive idea that $\mathcal{A}$ can't "change his mind". Is a trapdoor commitment-based ring signature scheme in fact secure against quantum adversaries? Because of the way the ThSign algorithm is constructed, if a trapdoor commit scheme has only the property of classical binding, the threshold ring signature is secure against quantum adversaries.

The Leader is required to come up with inputs and commitments for the non-signers. If the underlying TCom is susceptible to the attack, the Leader could create c_i^q for some non-signer q. However, then he must somehow produce y_i^q, op_i^q that opens c_i^q. As only up to $t - 1$ other signers are corrupt, at least one of the other signers will not accept c_i^q unless he also sees some valid message and opening for it. Thus, the attack of producing any new message and opening (m', op') happens only after the corrupted signer has produced (m, op) as some valid message and opening ahead of time. Producing the original (m, op) collapses the quantum state. We conclude that a commitment scheme which is computationally binding against quantum polynomial time adversaries is sufficient for the security of our threshold ring signature scheme.

References

1. Abe, M., Ohkubo, M., Suzuki, K.: 1-out-of-n signatures from a variety of keys. In: Zheng, Y. (ed.) ASIACRYPT 2002. LNCS, vol. 2501, pp. 415–432. Springer, Heidelberg (2002). https://doi.org/10.1007/3-540-36178-2_26

2. Abe, M., Ohkubo, M., Suzuki, K.: Efficient threshold signer-ambiguous signatures from variety of keys. IEICE Trans. Fundam. Electron. Commun. Comput. Sci. **87**(2), 471–479 (2004)

3. Ambainis, A., Rosmanis, A., Unruh, D.: Quantum attacks on classical proof systems: the hardness of quantum rewinding. In: 2014 IEEE 55th Annual Symposium on Foundations of Computer Science (FOCS), pp. 474–483. IEEE (2014)

4. Bender, A., Katz, J., Morselli, R.: Ring signatures: stronger definitions, and constructions without random oracles. In: Halevi, S., Rabin, T. (eds.) TCC 2006. LNCS, vol. 3876, pp. 60–79. Springer, Heidelberg (2006). https://doi.org/10.1007/11681878_4

5. Bettaieb, S., Schrek, J.: Improved lattice-based threshold ring signature scheme. In: Gaborit, P. (ed.) PQCrypto 2013. LNCS, vol. 7932, pp. 34–51. Springer, Heidelberg (2013). https://doi.org/10.1007/978-3-642-38616-9_3

6. Boldyreva, A.: Threshold signatures, multisignatures and blind signatures based on the gap-Diffie-Hellman-group signature scheme. In: Desmedt, Y.G. (ed.) PKC 2003. LNCS, vol. 2567, pp. 31–46. Springer, Heidelberg (2003). https://doi.org/10.1007/3-540-36288-6_3

7. Boneh, D., Dagdelen, Ö., Fischlin, M., Lehmann, A., Schaffner, C., Zhandry, M.: Random oracles in a quantum world. In: Lee, D.H., Wang, X. (eds.) ASIACRYPT 2011. LNCS, vol. 7073, pp. 41–69. Springer, Heidelberg (2011). https://doi.org/10.1007/978-3-642-25385-0_3

8. Boneh, D., et al.: Threshold cryptosystems from threshold fully homomorphic encryption. In: Shacham, H., Boldyreva, A. (eds.) CRYPTO 2018. LNCS, vol. 10991, pp. 565–596. Springer, Cham (2018). https://doi.org/10.1007/978-3-319-96884-1_19

9. Brassard, G., Chaum, D., Crépeau, C.: Minimum disclosure proofs of knowledge. J. Comput. Syst. Sci. **37**(2), 156–189 (1988)

10. Bresson, E., Stern, J., Szydlo, M.: Threshold ring signatures and applications to ad-hoc groups. In: Yung, M. (ed.) CRYPTO 2002. LNCS, vol. 2442, pp. 465–480. Springer, Heidelberg (2002). https://doi.org/10.1007/3-540-45708-9_30

11. Cayrel, P.-L., Lindner, R., Rückert, M., Silva, R.: A lattice-based threshold ring signature scheme. In: Abdalla, M., Barreto, P.S.L.M. (eds.) LATINCRYPT 2010. LNCS, vol. 6212, pp. 255–272. Springer, Heidelberg (2010). https://doi.org/10.1007/978-3-642-14712-8_16
12. Chang, Y.F., Chang, C.C., Lin, P.Y.: A concealed t-out-of-n signer ambiguous signature scheme with variety of keys. Informatica **18**(4), 535–546 (2007)
13. Chase, M., et al.: Post-quantum zero-knowledge and signatures from symmetric-key primitives. In: Proceedings of the 2017 ACM SIGSAC Conference on Computer and Communications Security, pp. 1825–1842. ACM (2017)
14. Chaum, D., van Heyst, E.: Group signatures. In: Davies, D.W. (ed.) EUROCRYPT 1991. LNCS, vol. 547, pp. 257–265. Springer, Heidelberg (1991). https://doi.org/10.1007/3-540-46416-6_22
15. Cramer, R., Damgård, I., Schoenmakers, B.: Proofs of partial knowledge and simplified design of witness hiding protocols. In: Desmedt, Y.G. (ed.) CRYPTO 1994. LNCS, vol. 839, pp. 174–187. Springer, Heidelberg (1994). https://doi.org/10.1007/3-540-48658-5_19
16. Damgaard, I.: On σ-protocols
17. Don, J., Fehr, S., Majenz, C., Schaffner, C.: Security of the Fiat-Shamir transformation in the quantum random-oracle model. Cryptology ePrint Archive, Report 2019/190 (2019). https://eprint.iacr.org/2019/190
18. Fiat, A., Shamir, A.: How to prove yourself: practical solutions to identification and signature problems. In: Odlyzko, A.M. (ed.) CRYPTO 1986. LNCS, vol. 263, pp. 186–194. Springer, Heidelberg (1987). https://doi.org/10.1007/3-540-47721-7_12
19. Fischlin, M.: Trapdoor commitment schemes and their applications (2001)
20. Fischlin, M.: Communication-efficient non-interactive proofs of knowledge with online extractors. In: Shoup, V. (ed.) CRYPTO 2005. LNCS, vol. 3621, pp. 152–168. Springer, Heidelberg (2005). https://doi.org/10.1007/11535218_10
21. Giacomelli, I., Madsen, J., Orlandi, C.: ZKBoo: faster zero-knowledge for Boolean circuits. In: 25th {USENIX} Security Symposium ({USENIX} Security 16), pp. 1069–1083 (2016)
22. Jakobsson, M., Sako, K., Impagliazzo, R.: Designated verifier proofs and their applications. In: Maurer, U. (ed.) EUROCRYPT 1996. LNCS, vol. 1070, pp. 143–154. Springer, Heidelberg (1996). https://doi.org/10.1007/3-540-68339-9_13
23. Katz, J., Kolesnikov, V., Wang, X.: Improved non-interactive zero knowledge with applications to post-quantum signatures. In: Proceedings of the 2018 ACM SIGSAC Conference on Computer and Communications Security, CCS 2018, Toronto, ON, Canada, 15–19 October 2018, pp. 525–537 (2018). https://doi.org/10.1145/3243734.3243805
24. Liu, J.K., Wei, V.K., Wong, D.S.: A Separable Threshold Ring Signature Scheme. In: Lim, J.-I., Lee, D.-H. (eds.) ICISC 2003. LNCS, vol. 2971, pp. 12–26. Springer, Heidelberg (2004). https://doi.org/10.1007/978-3-540-24691-6_2
25. Liu, J.K., Wong, D.S.: On the security models of (threshold) ring signature schemes. In: Park, C., Chee, S. (eds.) ICISC 2004. LNCS, vol. 3506, pp. 204–217. Springer, Heidelberg (2005). https://doi.org/10.1007/11496618_16
26. Liu, Q., Zhandry, M.: Revisiting post-quantum Fiat-Shamir. Cryptology ePrint Archive, Report 2019/262 (2019). https://eprint.iacr.org/2019/262
27. Melchor, C.A., Cayrel, P.L., Gaborit, P., Laguillaumie, F.: A new efficient threshold ring signature scheme based on coding theory. IEEE Trans. Inf. Theory **57**(7), 4833–4842 (2011)
28. NIST: Threshold schemes for cryptographic primitives. https://csrc.nist.gov/News/2019/threshold-schemes-for-crypto-primitives-nistir8214

29. Okamoto, T., Tso, R., Yamaguchi, M., Okamoto, E.: A k-out-of-n ring signature with flexible participation for signers

30. Okamoto, T., Tso, R., Yamaguchi, M., Okamoto, E.: A k-out-of-n ring signature with flexible participation for signers. IACR Cryptology ePrint Archive 2018, 728 (2018). https://eprint.iacr.org/2018/728

31. Petzoldt, A., Bulygin, S., Buchmann, J.: A multivariate based threshold ring signature scheme. Appl. Algebra Eng. Commun. Comput. **24**(3–4), 255–275 (2013)

32. Rivest, R.L., Shamir, A., Tauman, Y.: How to leak a secret. In: Boyd, C. (ed.) ASIACRYPT 2001. LNCS, vol. 2248, pp. 552–565. Springer, Heidelberg (2001). https://doi.org/10.1007/3-540-45682-1_32

33. Shamir, A.: How to share a secret. Commun. ACM **22**(11), 612–613 (1979)

34. Tsang, P.P., Wei, V.K., Chan, T.K., Au, M.H., Liu, J.K., Wong, D.S.: Separable linkable threshold ring signatures. In: Canteaut, A., Viswanathan, K. (eds.) INDOCRYPT 2004. LNCS, vol. 3348, pp. 384–398. Springer, Heidelberg (2004). https://doi.org/10.1007/978-3-540-30556-9_30

35. Unruh, D.: Quantum proofs of knowledge. In: Pointcheval, D., Johansson, T. (eds.) EUROCRYPT 2012. LNCS, vol. 7237, pp. 135–152. Springer, Heidelberg (2012). https://doi.org/10.1007/978-3-642-29011-4_10

36. Unruh, D.: Non-interactive zero-knowledge proofs in the quantum random oracle model. In: Oswald, E., Fischlin, M. (eds.) EUROCRYPT 2015. LNCS, vol. 9057, pp. 755–784. Springer, Heidelberg (2015). https://doi.org/10.1007/978-3-662-46803-6_25

37. Unruh, D.: Collapse-binding quantum commitments without random oracles. In: Cheon, J.H., Takagi, T. (eds.) ASIACRYPT 2016. LNCS, vol. 10032, pp. 166–195. Springer, Heidelberg (2016). https://doi.org/10.1007/978-3-662-53890-6_6

38. Unruh, D.: Post-quantum security of Fiat-Shamir. Cryptology ePrint Archive, Report 2017/398 (2017). https://eprint.iacr.org/2017/398

39. Watrous, J.: Zero-knowledge against quantum attacks. SIAM J. Comput. **39**(1), 25–58 (2009)

40. Wong, D.S., Fung, K., Liu, J.K., Wei, V.K.: On the RS-code construction of ring signature schemes and a threshold setting of RST. In: Qing, S., Gollmann, D., Zhou, J. (eds.) ICICS 2003. LNCS, vol. 2836, pp. 34–46. Springer, Heidelberg (2003). https://doi.org/10.1007/978-3-540-39927-8_4

41. Yuen, T.H., Liu, J.K., Au, M.H., Susilo, W., Zhou, J.: Threshold ring signature without random oracles. In: Proceedings of the 6th ACM Symposium on Information, Computer and Communications Security. ASIACCS 2011, pp. 261–267. ACM, New York (2011). https://doi.org/10.1145/1966913.1966947

42. Zhandry, M.: Secure identity-based encryption in the quantum random oracle model. Int. J. Quant. Inf. **13**(04), 1550014 (2015)

Tight and Optimal Reductions for Signatures Based on Average Trapdoor Preimage Sampleable Functions and Applications to Code-Based Signatures

André Chailloux[1] and Thomas Debris-Alazard[1,2(✉)]

[1] Inria de Paris, EPI COSMIQ, Paris, France
andre.chailloux@inria.fr
[2] Information Security Group, Royal Holloway, University of London, Egham, UK
thomas.debris@rhul.ac.uk

Abstract. The GPV construction [GPV08] presents a generic construction of signature schemes in the Hash and Sign paradigm and is used in some lattice based signatures. This construction requires a family $\mathcal{F}$ of trapdoor preimage sampleable functions (TPSF). In this work we extend this notion to the weaker Average TPSF (ATPSF) and show that the GPV construction also holds for ATPSF in the Random Oracle Model (ROM). We also introduce the problem of finding a Claw with a random function (Claw(RF)) and present a tight security reduction to the Claw(RF) problem. Our reduction is also optimal meaning that an algorithm that solves the Claw(RF) problem breaks the scheme. We extend these results to the quantum setting and prove this same tight and optimal reduction in the QROM. Finally, we apply these results to code-based signatures, notably the Wave signature scheme and prove security for it in the ROM and the QROM, improving and extending the original analysis of [DST19a].

1 Introduction

Signature schemes are an important element of many cryptographic applications and are one of the schemes standardized by the post-quantum NIST competition [Nis17]. Assessing the exact security (and hence the efficiency) of these schemes is therefore a very important task, both against classical and quantum computers. The GPV construction [GPV08] presents a generic construction of signature schemes in the Hash and Sign paradigm. This construction requires a family $\mathcal{F}$ of trapdoor preimage sampleable functions (TPSF), which informally is a collection of functions that are hard to invert but which can be easily inverted with some trapdoor. There are two specific properties of their construction:

1. The inversion algorithm that uses the trapdoor should have good repartition properties for each image y. This means that for each image y, the inversion algorithm should output a preimage x according to a certain distribution D.

A. Kiayias et al. (Eds.): PKC 2020, LNCS 12111, pp. 453–479, 2020.
https://doi.org/10.1007/978-3-030-45388-6_16

2. The security of the resulting signature scheme is tightly based on the collision resistance of the family $\mathcal{F}$ and not on the one-wayness.

These properties were tailored for lattice based schemes where these two properties hold. For example, the lattice-based FALCON signature scheme [FHK+17] is based on the GPV construction. Notice that it is also possible to base the security on one-wayness instead of collision resistance. However, in the generic setting, this can lead to non tight reductions similarly as for Full Domain Hash signatures [BR93, Cor00].

In this paper, we extend the notion of TPSF where the property (1) above should hold only on average for y, defining the notion of Average TPSF (ATPSF). A direct use of the leftover hash lemma shows that we can go from an ATPSF to a TPSF with a quadratic loss in the security of $\mathcal{F}$[1]. What we show is the following:

- We show that this quadratic loss is not necessary and that we can use ATPSF instead of TPSF without any loss.
- Applying the GPV construction of signature schemes from a family $\mathcal{F}$ of ATPSF, we show that the security of the signature scheme ie equivalent to solving the Claw with Random Function (Claw(RF)) problem for $\mathcal{F}$. Informally, in the Claw(RF) problem, we are given a random function $\mathcal{H}$ and a random f from $\mathcal{F}$ and we want to find (x, y) such that $f(x) = \mathcal{H}(y)$.
- We extend this to the quantum setting and show that our tight and optimal results also hold in the QROM.
- We apply these results to the Wave signature scheme [DST19a] and show more formally its classical and quantum security.

Recently, Chen, Genise and Mukherjee [CGM19] relaxed the GPV construction and use approximate trapdoor functions. They use their results to construct more efficient lattice-based signature schemes. They relax the constraint they put on their preimage. On the other hand, we still require exact preimages but we only require that the inversion algorithm gives a preimage close to the target distribution D only on average on the images. Our results can therefore be seen as another application of relaxing the GPV construction, but for applications beyond lattices.

One of the implications of our results is that:

$$\text{Collision} \preccurlyeq \underset{\text{Signature}}{\overset{\text{Claw(RF)}}{\updownarrow}} \preccurlyeq \text{One way.}$$

This means that the collision problem is easier than the Claw(RF) problem which itself is easier than the preimage problem. Moreover, attacking the signature scheme is equivalently hard to solving the Claw(RF) problem in the ROM. In the case of lattices, we have:[2,3]

---

[1] What we mean by this is explicited by Proposition 3 of this paper.

[2] SIS: Short Integer Solution problem commonly used in lattice-based cryptography.

[3] ISIS: Inhomogeneous Short Integer Solution.

$$Collision \approx \text{SIS} \preccurlyeq \text{ Signature } \preccurlyeq \text{One way} = \text{ISIS} \approx \text{SIS}.$$

From the above diagram, we can see that the GPV construction gives for lattices a tight and optimal reduction to the hardness of inversion. This is because this problem is essentially as hard as finding collisions (SIS $\approx$ ISIS). In the context of code-based cryptography, things are very different. In many regimes used for signatures, the collision problem is actually easy to solve. Therefore, we can only use the non-tight reduction to one wayness. From there, there are two possibilities: (1) lose the factor associated to non-tightness and have a big loss in parameters or (2) ignore the non-tightness and assume it won't have a practical impact. Solution (2) is of course very risky as the security proof of the actual scheme becomes incomplete. On the other hand, those that decide on (1) have a loss in parameters which could be unnecessary. The importance of tightness for security reductions is well shown in the survey paper [KM19]. There has been for example a recent attack [KZ19] on the MQDSS scheme [CHR+16], exploiting non-tightness of the security reduction which wasn't taken into account.

What we also advocate through our result is that if we want to study the concrete security of these signature schemes in the ROM, the Claw(RF) problem is the actual problem we should be looking at. Others that would want to construct a family of ATPSF for which the collision problem is easier than the preimage problem can use our results to study the real security of their schemes. Because we also prove this optimal security in the quantum ROM, our result is especially adapted for post-quantum cryptography.

In order to prove our results, we use fairly standard techniques in the ROM based on reprogramming the hashing and signing oracles. In order to do this formally, we need to keep track of the internal memory of the reprogrammed oracles - which is often a problem that is discarded in game based reductions - and not only look at their output distributions. We take the approach of constructing more explicitly an algorithm for the Claw(RF) problem from an attacker that attacks the signature scheme instead of using the game formalism, even though we strongly inspire ourselves from this formalism. An interesting aspect of our proof is that we manage to reprogram only the signing oracle, and not the hashing oracle, which reduces the requirement on the family of ATPSF functions.

For the quantum case, our proofs mainly use a result by Zhandry [Zha12] on the indistinguishability of close quantum oracles. Here, we need to reprogram the hash function as well since we cannot work on the internal memory of the quantum oracles. Our proof has some similarities with the one in [BDF+11] where the security of the GPV construction is proven in the asymptotic setting. Our contributions here was to extend this proof to ATPSF, to perform practical security claims and to show a tight reduction to the Claw(RF) problem.

2   Preliminaries

Probabilistic Notation. Let $\mathcal{D}$ be a distribution, and X be a random variable. The notation $X \overset{\$}{\leftarrow} \mathcal{D}$ denotes that X is distributed according to $\mathcal{D}$. Furthermore, for a set S, we will denote by $\mathcal{U}(S)$ the uniform distribution over S. We use the same notations for picking elements: $y \xleftarrow{\$} \mathcal{D}$ means that y is picked according to $\mathcal{D}$ while $y \xleftarrow{\$} S$ denotes that y is uniformly distributed over S.

Sometimes when we wish to emphasize on which probability space the probabilities or the expectations are taken, we note on the right of a symbol ":" the random variable specifying the associated probability space over which the probabilities or expectations are taken. For instance the probability $\mathbb{P}(\mathcal{E} : X)$ of the event $\mathcal{E}$ is taken over the random variable X.

The statistical distance between two discrete probability distributions $\mathcal{D}_1, \mathcal{D}_2$ over a same space $\mathcal{E}$ is defined as:

$$\Delta(\mathcal{D}_0, \mathcal{D}_1) \stackrel{\triangle}{=} \frac{1}{2} \sum_{x \in \mathcal{E}} |\mathcal{D}_0(x) - \mathcal{D}_1(x)|.$$

The statistical distance Δ satisfies the triangle inequality.

A function $f(\lambda)$ is said to be negligible, and we denote this by $f \in \text{negl}(\lambda)$, if for all polynomials $p(\lambda)$, $|f(\lambda)| < p(\lambda)^{-1}$ for all sufficiently large λ.

For any two sets D, R, we denote by $\mathfrak{F}_R^D$ the set of functions from D to R.

Query Algorithms and Oracles. For any algorithm $\mathcal{A}$, we denote by $|\mathcal{A}|$ it's total running time. We will also consider query algorithms $\mathcal{A}^{\mathcal{O}}$ that will make a certain amount of calls to an oracle $\mathcal{O}$. For us, an oracle $\mathcal{O}$ will be a deterministic or probabilistic function for which we have only a black box access. When we write $\mathcal{A}^{\mathcal{O}}$, it will mean that the oracle is non specified and we can replace $\mathcal{O}$ with any oracle.

For a query algorithm $\mathcal{A}^{\mathcal{O}}$, we write $|\mathcal{A}^{\mathcal{O}}| = (t, q)$ indicating that its running time is t and that it performs q queries to $\mathcal{O}$. Unless specified otherwise, the running time of the oracle $\mathcal{O}$ is 1. An algorithm can also query different oracles, which we indicate as $\mathcal{A}^{\mathcal{O}_1, \mathcal{O}_2}$ and $|\mathcal{A}^{\mathcal{O}_1, \mathcal{O}_2}| = (t, q_1, q_2)$ indicates that it runs in time t and it performs q_1 queries to $\mathcal{O}_1$ and q_2 queries to $\mathcal{O}_2$.

For any (deterministic or probabilistic) function f, we denote by $\mathcal{O}_f$ its associated oracle, and we will write it:

$$\boxed{\begin{array}{l} \mathcal{O}_f(x) \\ \hline \texttt{return } f(x). \end{array}}$$

An important concept in this paper will be the oracles with internal memory. We will denote by $\mathcal{O}(x; \mathcal{L})$ a query x to oracle $\mathcal{O}$ which has internal memory $\mathcal{L}$. If the result to this query is y and the internal memory is changed to $\mathcal{L}'$, we will write $\texttt{return } (y; \mathcal{L}')$. This internal memory is private and is not part of the public output of the oracle.

One oracle of interest will be the random oracle. It mimics a uniformly chosen random function from $\mathfrak{F}_R^D$. We will denote this oracle $\mathcal{O}_{\text{RO}}$ (the sets D and R are implicit).

$$\boxed{\begin{array}{l} \mathcal{O}_{\text{RO}}(x; \mathcal{L}) \\ \hline \texttt{if } \exists! y : (x, y) \in \mathcal{L}, \texttt{ return } (y; \mathcal{L}) \\ \texttt{otherwise, pick } y \xleftarrow{\$} R_\lambda, \texttt{ return } (y; \mathcal{L} \cup \{(x, y)\}) \end{array}}$$

This oracle mimics a call to a random function. Each time x is queried, a random image y is constructed. If the same x is called afterwards, the same output y should be given. Therefore, we have a list $\mathcal{L}$ that stores values (x, y) already specified by the function. If $\mathcal{L}$ is initialized with $\emptyset$, we should never have $x, y, y' \neq y$ such that $(x, y) \in \mathcal{L}$ and $(x, y') \in \mathcal{L}$. For any algorithm $\mathcal{A}^{\mathcal{O}}$, we have:

$$\mathbb{P}\left(\mathcal{A}^{\mathcal{O}_g} \text{ outputs } 0 \mid g \stackrel{\$}{\leftarrow} \mathfrak{F}_R^D\right) = \mathbb{P}\left(\mathcal{A}^{\mathcal{O}_{\text{RO}}} \text{ outputs } 0 \mid \mathcal{O}_{\text{RO}} \text{ is initialized with } \mathcal{L} = \emptyset\right).$$

Another important aspect of query algorithms is that if we consider an algorithm $\mathcal{A}^{\mathcal{O}}$ and two close oracles $\mathcal{O}_1, \mathcal{O}_2$, then $\mathcal{A}_{\mathcal{O}_1}$ and $\mathcal{A}_{\mathcal{O}_2}$ will be close. This is at the core of the game formalism presented for instance in [Sho04]. More formally,

Proposition 1. *Let $\mathcal{A}^{\mathcal{O}}$ be a query algorithm with $|\mathcal{A}^{\mathcal{O}}| = (t, q)$. Let $\mathcal{O}_1, \mathcal{O}_2$ be two oracles such that:*

$$\forall x, \mathcal{L}, \quad \Delta(\mathcal{O}_1(x; \mathcal{L}), \mathcal{O}_2(x; \mathcal{L})) \leq \delta.$$

Then we have:

$$\left|\mathbb{P}\left(\mathcal{A}^{\mathcal{O}_1} \text{ outputs } 0\right) - \mathbb{P}\left(\mathcal{A}^{\mathcal{O}_2} \text{ outputs } 0\right)\right| \leq q\delta.$$

3   Digital Signatures and EUF-CMA Security Model in a Classical/Quantum Setting

A signature scheme S consists of three algorithms (S.KEYGEN, S.SIGN, S.VERIFY):

- S.KEYGEN$(1^\lambda) \rightarrow (\text{pk}, \text{sk})$ is the generation of the public key pk and the secret key sk from the security parameter λ.
- S.SIGN$(m, \text{pk}, \text{sk}) \rightarrow \sigma_m$: generates the signature σ_m of a message m from m, pk, sk.
- S.VERIFY$(m, \sigma, \text{pk}) \rightarrow \{0, 1\}$ verifies that σ is a valid signature of m using m, σ, pk. The output 1 corresponds to a valid signature.

Correctness. A signature scheme is defined as correct if when we sample $(\text{pk}, \text{sk}) \leftarrow$ S.KEYGEN(1^λ), we have for each m:

$$\text{S.VERIFY}(m, \text{S.SIGN}(m, \text{pk}, \text{sk}), \text{pk}) = 1.$$

Security Definitions. We consider the EUF-CMA (Existential Universal Forgery for Chosen Message Attack) security for signature schemes. A key pair $(\text{pk}, \text{sk}) \leftarrow$ S.KEYGEN(1^λ) is generated. The goal of the adversary $\mathcal{A}$ is, knowing only pk, to construct a pair (m, σ_m) such that σ_m is a valid signature for m but we give him some additional power. He can query a signing oracle $\mathcal{O}_{\text{Sign}}$, that does the following:

$$
\boxed{
\begin{array}{l}
\texttt{proc } \mathsf{Sign}(m) \\
\sigma_m \leftarrow \mathrm{S.SIGN}(m, \mathrm{pk}, \mathrm{sk}) \\
\texttt{return } \sigma_m
\end{array}
}
$$

Notice here that the signing oracle has access to pk and sk. The goal of the adversary is then in this case to output a valid signature σ_{m^*} for a message m^* *that has not been queried* to the signing oracle.

Definition 1. *Let $\mathcal{A}^{\mathcal{O}}$ be a query algorithm, we define*

$$
Adv_{\mathcal{S}}^{\mathrm{EUF\text{-}CMA}}(\mathcal{A}^{\mathcal{O}}) = \mathbb{P}\Big(\mathrm{S.VERIFY}(m^*, \sigma^*, \mathrm{pk}) = 1 \ \textsc{and} \ m^* \ has \ not
$$

$$
been \ queried \ in \ \mathcal{O}_{\mathsf{Sign}} : (\mathrm{pk}, \mathrm{sk}) \leftarrow \mathrm{S.KEYGEN}(1^{\lambda}), (m^*, \sigma^*) \leftarrow \mathcal{A}^{\mathcal{O}_{\mathsf{Sign}}}(\mathrm{pk})\Big).
$$

For any time t and number of queries q_{sign}, we define:

$$
Adv_{\mathcal{S}}^{\mathrm{EUF\text{-}CMA}}(t, q_{sign}) = \max_{\mathcal{A}^{\mathcal{O}} : |\mathcal{A}^{\mathcal{O}}| = (t, q_{sign})} Adv_{\mathcal{S}}^{\mathrm{EUF\text{-}CMA}}(\mathcal{A}^{\mathcal{O}}).
$$

For a quantum adversary, we define similarly the quantum EUF-CMA advantage as:

$$
QAdv_{\mathcal{S}}^{\mathrm{EUF\text{-}CMA}}(t, q_{sign}) = \max_{\mathcal{A}^{\mathcal{O}} : |\mathcal{A}^{\mathcal{O}}| = (t, q_{sign})} Adv_{\mathcal{S}}^{\mathrm{EUF\text{-}CMA}}(\mathcal{A}^{\mathcal{O}}).
$$

where the maximum is over quantum query algorithms that perform classical queries to $\mathcal{O}_{\mathsf{Sign}}$.

It is actually standard, even if the algorithm is quantum, to consider classical queries to the signing oracle. This is because in the real life scenario that motivates this security definition, signing queries are done to an external party that can force you to perform classical queries. In the post-quantum standardization process, the NIST indeed requires only security against classical queries to the signing oracle.

4   Family of ATPSF

In this work we will use the Full Domain Hash (FDH) paradigm of signature schemes [BR96, Cor02]. The key ingredient of this kind of constructions is a trapdoor one-way function $f : D \to R$ and a cryptographic hash function $\mathcal{H}$. The corresponding FDH scheme to sign a message m uses the trapdoor to choose a signature $x \in f^{-1}(\mathcal{H}(m))$. The verification step simply consists in computing $\mathcal{H}(m)$ and $f(x)$ to ensure that $f(x) = \mathcal{H}(m)$. The difficulty for designing such primitives is the fact that each time a message is signed, the signature is made public while the secret trapdoor has been used to produce it. Therefore, we must ensure that no information of the trapdoor leaks after the inversion. However, in the nice case where f is a permutation this does not matter. Indeed, the hash of the message $\mathcal{H}(m)$ is classically considered as random and thus the inverse $x = f^{-1}(\mathcal{H}(m))$ will be random too and in this way distributed independently of the trapdoor. This is typically the case for signatures schemes like RSA. Nevertheless, building one-way permutations in the post-quantum world like in code/lattice-based cryptography is a hard condition to meet. Usually [GPV08,DST19b] functions are many-to-one and then it is non-trivial to build trapdoor candidates with an inversion algorithm which is oblivious to the used trapdoor. Building a secure FDH signature in this situation can be achieved by imposing additional properties [GPV08] to the one-way function. This is mostly captured by the notion of Trapdoor Preimage Sampleable Functions (TPSF) [GPV08, Definition 5.3.1]. We express below this concept in a slightly relaxed way dropping the domain sampleability condition and only assuming that the preimage sampleable property holds *on average* and not for any possible element in the function range. This will be sufficient for proving the security of the associated FDH scheme.

Definition 2. *An ε-ATPSF (for Average Trapdoor Preimage Sampleable Functions (or Function Family)) is an efficient triplet of probabilistic algorithms (*TRAPGEN, SAMPDOM, SAMPPRE*) where:*

- TRAPGEN$(1^\lambda) \rightarrow (f, \tau)$. *Takes the security parameter λ and outputs $f : D_\lambda \rightarrow R_\lambda$, an efficiently computable function with an efficient description, and τ, the trapdoor that will allow to invert f.*
- SAMPDOM$(f) \rightarrow x$. *Takes a function $f : D_\lambda \rightarrow R_\lambda$ (with an efficient description) as an input and outputs some $x \in D_\lambda$.*
- SAMPPRE$(f, \tau, y) \rightarrow x$. *Takes a function f with associated trapdoor τ, an element $y \in R_\lambda$ and outputs $x \in D_\lambda$ s.t. $f(x) = y$.*

We define:

$$\varepsilon_{f,\tau} \stackrel{\triangle}{=} \Delta\Big(\text{SAMPDOM}(f), \text{SAMPPRE}(f, \tau, U(R_\lambda))\Big),$$

where SAMPPRE$(f, \tau, U(R_\lambda))$ *is sampled as follows: pick $y \stackrel{\$}{\leftarrow} R_\lambda$, return* SAMPPRE$(f, \tau, y)$. *We require that our triplet of algorithms satisfies*

$$\mathbb{E}_{(f,\tau) \leftarrow \text{TRAPGEN}(1^\lambda)} (\varepsilon_{f,\tau}) \leq \varepsilon. \tag{1}$$

The main difference with the definition of TPSF as defined [GPV08, Definition 5.3.1] is that we consider an average $y \stackrel{\$}{\leftarrow} R_\lambda$ instead of wanting the property for almost all y. Furthermore, it is also asked for TPSF to verify that $\mathbb{E}_{(f,t) \leftarrow \text{TRAPGEN}(1^\lambda)} (\Delta(f(\text{SAMPDOM}(f)), U(R_\lambda))) \leq \varepsilon'$ (domain sampleability condition) for some ε' whereas we, a priori, don't request anything of this kind for ATPSF. We show now that ε-ATPSF family verifies the domain sampleability condition of [GPV08].

Proposition 2. *Let $\mathcal{F} = ($TRAPGEN, SAMPDOM, SAMPPRE*) be a collection of ε-ATPSF. We have for any f, τ*

$$\Delta(f(\text{SAMPDOM}(f)), U(R_\lambda)) \leq \varepsilon_{f,\tau} \tag{2}$$

where for a fixed f, $f(\text{SAMPDOM}(f))$ is the distribution which is sampled as follows: $x \leftarrow \text{SAMPDOM}(f)$, return $f(x)$. Furthermore,

$$\mathbb{E}_{(f,\tau)\leftarrow\text{TRAPGEN}(1^\lambda)}\left[\Delta(f(\text{SAMPDOM}(f)), U(R_\lambda))\right] \leq \varepsilon \tag{3}$$

Proof. We write

$$
\begin{aligned}
\varepsilon_{f,\tau} &= \Delta\Big(\text{SAMPDOM}(f), \text{SAMPPRE}(f, \tau, U(R_\lambda))\Big) \\
&\geq \Delta\Big(f(\text{SAMPDOM}(f)), f(\text{SAMPPRE}(f, \tau, U(R_\lambda)))\Big) \\
&= \Delta(f(\text{SAMPDOM}(f)), U(R_\lambda))
\end{aligned}
$$

where the first inequality uses the fact that for any deterministic function f and random variables X and Y (see [GM02] for a proof), $\Delta(f(X), f(Y)) \leq \Delta(X, Y)$. This proves Eq. (2). We conclude the proof by taking the expectation over $(f, t) \leftarrow \text{TRAPGEN}(1^\lambda)$. □

We now also show that we can replace the average property of the ATPSF with one that works for almost all y, but with a root loss in the sampleability error ε.

Proposition 3 ([S19]). *Let $\mathcal{F} = (\text{TRAPGEN}, \text{SAMPDOM}, \text{SAMPPRE})$ be an ε-ATPSF and for (f, τ) output by $\text{TRAPGEN}(1^\lambda)$. We have*

$$\frac{1}{|R_\lambda|} \cdot \#\left\{ y \in R_\lambda \ : \ \Delta(\text{SAMPPRE}(f, y), X_y) > \sqrt{\varepsilon_{f,\tau}} \right\} \leq 2\sqrt{\varepsilon_{f,\tau}},$$

where X_y denotes the distribution of $X_y \overset{\$}{\leftarrow} \text{SAMPDOM}(f)$ given $f(X_y) = y$, meaning

$$\forall x \in D_\lambda, \quad \mathbb{P}(X_y = x) \overset{\triangle}{=} \mathbb{P}(\text{SAMPDOM}(f) = x \mid f(\text{SAMPDOM}(f)) = y). \tag{4}$$

Proof. The first part of the proof is to prove the following equation:

$$2\varepsilon_{f,\tau} \geq \frac{1}{|R_\lambda|} \sum_{y \in R_\lambda} \Delta(\text{SAMPPRE}(f, y), X_y) \tag{5}$$

Let us denote for all $y \in R_\lambda$,

$$p_y \overset{\triangle}{=} \mathbb{P}(\text{SAMPDOM}(f) = x \mid f(\text{SAMPDOM}(f)) = y).$$

We have the following computation,

$$
\begin{aligned}
\varepsilon_{f,\tau} &= \Delta(\text{SAMPPRE}(f, t, U(R_\lambda)), \text{SAMPDOM}(f)) \\
&= \frac{1}{2} \sum_y \sum_{x \in f^{-1}(y)} \left| \mathbb{P}(\text{SAMPDOM}(f) = x) - \frac{1}{|R_\lambda|}\mathbb{P}(\text{SAMPPRE}(f, \tau, y) = x) \right| \\
&= \frac{1}{2} \sum_y \sum_{x \in f^{-1}(y)} \left| \mathbb{P}(\text{SAMPDOM}(f) = x) - \frac{p_y}{|R_\lambda|} + \frac{p_y}{|R_\lambda|} - \frac{1}{|R_\lambda|}\mathbb{P}(\text{SAMPPRE}(f, \tau, y) = x) \right| \\
&\geq \frac{1}{2} \sum_y \frac{1}{|R_\lambda|} \sum_{x \in f^{-1}(y)} |p_y - \mathbb{P}(\text{SAMPPRE}(f, \tau, y) = x)| - \frac{1}{2} \sum_y \sum_{x \in f^{-1}(y)} p_y \left| \frac{\mathbb{P}(\text{SAMPDOM}(f) = x)}{p_y} - \frac{1}{|R_\lambda|} \right| \\
&= \sum_{y \in R_\lambda} \frac{1}{|R_\lambda|} \Delta(\text{SAMPPRE}(f, \tau, y), X_y) - \frac{1}{2} \sum_y \sum_{x \in f^{-1}(y)} p_y \left| \frac{\mathbb{P}(\text{SAMPDOM}(f) = x)}{p_y} - \frac{1}{|R_\lambda|} \right| \tag{6}
\end{aligned}
$$

Now we have for all $x \in f^{-1}(y)$ and by definition of p_y,

$$
\begin{aligned}
\frac{\mathbb{P}\left(\text{SampDom}(f) = x\right)}{p_y} &= \frac{\mathbb{P}\left(\text{SampDom}(f) = x\right)}{\mathbb{P}\left(\text{SampDom}(f) = x \mid f(\text{SampDom}(f)) = y\right)} \\
&= \frac{\mathbb{P}\left(\text{SampDom}(f) = x\right)}{\mathbb{P}\left(f(\text{SampDom}(f)) = y \mid \text{SampDom}(f) = x\right) \frac{\mathbb{P}(\text{SampDom}(f) = x)}{\mathbb{P}(f(\text{SampDom}(f)) = y)}} \\
&= \frac{\mathbb{P}(f(\text{SampDom}(f)) = y)}{\mathbb{P}\left(f(\text{SampDom}(f)) = y \mid \text{SampDom}(f) = x\right)} \\
&= \mathbb{P}(f(\text{SampDom}(f)) = y) \qquad (7)
\end{aligned}
$$

where in the last line we used the fact that $f(x) = y$. Therefore, by putting (7) in (6) and using that $\sum_{x \in f^{-1}(y)} p_y = 1$ we get,

$$
\begin{aligned}
\varepsilon_{f,\tau} &\geq \sum_{y \in R_\lambda} \frac{1}{|R_\lambda|} \Delta\left(\text{SampPre}(f, \tau, y), X_y\right) - \Delta(f(\text{SampDom}(f)), \mathcal{U}(R_\lambda)) \\
&\geq \sum_{y \in R_\lambda} \frac{1}{|R_\lambda|} \Delta\left(\text{SampPre}(f, \tau, y), X_y\right) - \varepsilon_{f,\tau}.
\end{aligned}
$$

where the last inequality comes from Proposition 2. This proves Eq. (5). In order to conclude, we write

$$
\sum_{y \in R_\lambda} \frac{1}{|R_\lambda|} \Delta\left(\text{SampPre}(f, \tau, y), X_y\right) \geq \frac{\sqrt{\varepsilon_{f,\tau}}}{|R_\lambda|} \cdot \#\left\{y \in R_\lambda \; : \; \Delta\left(\text{SampPre}(f, y), X_y\right) > \sqrt{\varepsilon_{f,\tau}}\right\}.
$$

Plugging this into Eq. 5, we get the desired result. □

4.1 Constructing a Signature Scheme from ATPSF

As pointed out in [S19], the fact that a collection of ATPSF verifies the preimage property for almost all inputs is enough to build a signature scheme as in [GPV08] and to use the security reduction given in [GPV08, Proposition 6.1]. Nevertheless, by doing this we loose a square factor. We propose here to generalize the construction of [GPV08] by adding a random salt in the signing algorithm. More precisely, given a collection an ATPSF $\mathcal{F} = (\text{TrapGen}, \text{SampDom}, \text{SampPre})$ we define the following Full Domain Hash signature scheme $S^{\mathcal{F}}$: select a cryptographic hash function $\mathcal{H} : \{0,1\}^* \rightarrow R_\lambda$ and a random salt r of size λ_0 (λ_0 will be precised later). Consider the following three algorithms of the signature $S^{\mathcal{F}}$:

$S^{\mathcal{F}}.\text{keygen}(1^\lambda)$	$S^{\mathcal{F}}.\text{sign}(m, \text{pk}, \text{sk})$	$S^{\mathcal{F}}.\text{verify}(m, (x,r), \text{pk})$
$(f, \tau) \leftarrow \text{TrapGen}(1^\lambda)$	$r \xleftarrow{\$} \{0,1\}^{\lambda_0}$	$y \leftarrow \mathcal{H}(m, r)$
return $(\text{pk}, \text{sk}) = (f, \tau)$	$y \leftarrow \mathcal{H}(m, r)$	if $f(x) = y$ return 1
	$x \leftarrow \text{SampPre}(y, \text{sk})$	else return 0
	return(x, r)	

Our aim in what follows is to give a tight security reduction of this scheme using directly the average property of ATPS. In order to do so, we must first define different computational problems to reduce and in particular we introduce our Claw(RF) problem. This is the aim of the following section.

The Random Oracle Model (ROM) in This Construction. In the random oracle model, we replace the function $\mathcal{H}$ with a random function $h : \{0,1\}^* \times \{0,1\}^{\lambda_0} \to R_\lambda$ to which we only give black box access. Recall the EUF-CMA advantage of $\mathrm{S}^{\mathcal{F}}$:

$$Adv_{\mathrm{S}^{\mathcal{F}}}^{\mathrm{EUF\text{-}CMA}}(\mathcal{A}^{\mathcal{O}_{\mathsf{Sign}}}) = \mathbb{P}\Big(\mathcal{H}(m^*, r^*) = f(x^*) \text{ AND } m^* \text{ has not been}$$

$$\text{queried in } \mathcal{O}_{\mathsf{Sign}} : (\mathrm{pk}, \mathrm{sk}) \leftarrow \mathrm{S.KEYGEN}(1^\lambda), (m^*, r^*, x^*) \leftarrow \mathcal{A}^{\mathcal{O}_{\mathsf{Sign}}}(\mathrm{pk})\Big)$$

where $\mathcal{O}_{\mathsf{Sign}}$ is the oracle defined in Sect. 3. The ROM assumption says that any algorithm can only use $\mathcal{H}$ in a black box fashion and that it behaves as a random function. This translates to the fact that $\mathcal{A}$ can be seen as query algorithm not only to the signing oracle but also to the $\mathcal{H}$ function and that the EUF-CMA advantage is equal to the following one:

$$\mathbb{P}\Big(h(m^*, r^*) = f(x^*) \text{ AND } m^* \text{ has not been queried in } \mathcal{O}_{\mathsf{Sign}} : h \xleftarrow{\$} \mathfrak{F}_{R_\lambda}^{\{0,1\}^* \times \{0,1\}^{\lambda_0}}$$

$$(\mathrm{pk}, \mathrm{sk}) \leftarrow \mathrm{S.KEYGEN}(1^\lambda), (m^*, r^*, x^*) \leftarrow \mathcal{A}^{\mathcal{O}_{\mathsf{Sign}}, \mathcal{O}_h}(\mathrm{pk})\Big).$$

5 One-Wayness, Collision Resistance and the Claw with Random Function Problem

The interest in using trapdoor functions for signatures is that these functions should be hard to invert without the trapdoor τ. Ideally, we want to reduce the security of the signature scheme to the hardness of inverting the function. However, this is not always possible and we have to reduce the security to other problems.

5.1 Definitions

We first present the notion of advantage related to one-wayness and collision finding. We then define our Claw(RF) problem and the associated advantage.

Definition 3. *Let $\mathcal{F} = (\mathrm{TRAPGEN}, \mathrm{SAMPDOM}, \mathrm{SAMPPRE})$ be an ATPSF. For any algorithm $\mathcal{A}$, we define:*

$$Adv_{\mathcal{F}}^{OW}(\mathcal{A}) \triangleq \mathbb{P}\Big(f(x) = y : (f, \tau) \leftarrow \mathrm{TRAPGEN}(1^\lambda), \ y \xleftarrow{\$} R_\lambda, \ x \leftarrow \mathcal{A}(f, y)\Big),$$

$$Adv_{\mathcal{F}}^{Coll}(\mathcal{A}) \triangleq \mathbb{P}\Big(f(x_1) = f(x_2) \wedge x_1 \neq x_2 : (f, \tau) \leftarrow \mathrm{TRAPGEN}(1^\lambda), \ (x_1, x_2) \leftarrow \mathcal{A}(f)\Big).$$

For any time t, we also define

$$Adv_{\mathcal{F}}^{OW}(t) \stackrel{\triangle}{=} \max_{\mathcal{A}:|\mathcal{A}|=t} Adv_{\mathcal{F}}^{OW}(\mathcal{A}),$$

$$Adv_{\mathcal{F}}^{Coll}(t) \stackrel{\triangle}{=} \max_{\mathcal{A}:|\mathcal{A}|=t} Adv_{\mathcal{F}}^{Coll}(\mathcal{A}).$$

Now, we define the Claw(RF) problem.

Problem 1 (Claw with Random Function - Claw(RF)).

- Instance: a function f and a random function h to which we only have black box access.
- Goal: find x, y such that $f(x) = h(y)$.

From there, we define the Claw(RF) advantage for any query algorithm $\mathcal{A}^{\mathcal{O}}$.

Definition 4. *Let $\mathcal{F} = (\text{TrapGen}, \text{SampDom}, \text{SampPre})$ be an ATPRF.*

$$Adv_{\mathcal{F}}^{Claw(RF)}(\mathcal{A}^{\mathcal{O}}) \stackrel{\triangle}{=} \mathbb{P}\left(f(x) = h(y) : h \stackrel{\$}{\leftarrow} \mathfrak{F}_R^D, \ (f, \tau) \leftarrow \text{TrapGen}(1^\lambda), \ (x, y) \leftarrow \mathcal{A}^{\mathcal{O}_h}(f) \right)$$

$$= \mathbb{P}\left(f(x) = \mathcal{O}_{RO}(y) : (f, \tau) \leftarrow \text{TrapGen}(1^\lambda), \ (x, y) \leftarrow \mathcal{A}^{\mathcal{O}_{RO}}(f) \right)$$

For any time t and any number of queries q, we also define

$$Adv_{\mathcal{F}}^{Claw(RF)}(t, q) \stackrel{\triangle}{=} \max_{\mathcal{A}^{\mathcal{O}}:|\mathcal{A}^{\mathcal{O}}|=(t,q)} Adv_{\mathcal{F}}^{Claw(RF)}(\mathcal{A}^{\mathcal{O}}).$$

Similarly, if we consider quantum algorithms, we can define the quantum advantages $QAdv_{\mathcal{F}}^{OW}(t), QAdv_{\mathcal{F}}^{Coll}(t)$ and $QAdv_{\mathcal{F}}^{Claw(RF)}(t, q)$ where we maximize over quantum query algorithms. In the case of $QAdv_{\mathcal{F}}^{Claw(RF)}(t, q)$, we allow *quantum queries* to $\mathcal{O}_h$.

5.2   Relating These Different Advantages

In this section, we present the relationship between the different advantages.

Proposition 4. *Let $\mathcal{F}$ be an ε-ATPRF For any time t, we have*

$$Adv_{\mathcal{F}}^{OW}(t) \leq Adv_{\mathcal{F}}^{Claw(RF)}(t, 1)$$

$$Adv_{\mathcal{F}}^{Claw(RF)}(t, q) \leq q \cdot Adv_{\mathcal{F}}^{OW}(t)$$

$$Adv_{\mathcal{F}}^{Claw(RF)}(t, q) \leq Adv_{\mathcal{F}}^{Coll}(t + \tilde{O}(q)) + q\varepsilon + \mathbb{E}_{(f,t) \leftarrow \text{TrapGen}}\left(\frac{1}{\text{MNP}(f)} \right)$$

where for $(f, \tau) \leftarrow \text{TrapGen}(1^\lambda)$, the minimal number of preimages $\text{MNP}(f)$ is

$$\text{MNP}(f) \stackrel{\triangle}{=} \min_y \left(|\{x : f(x) = y|\} \right).$$

Proof. We prove each inequality separately.

1. $Adv_{\mathcal{F}}^{OW}(t) \leq Adv_{\mathcal{F}}^{Claw(RF)}(t, 1)$.

Let $\mathcal{A}$ be an algorithm running in time t with one-way advantage $Adv_{\mathcal{F}}^{OW}(t)$. We consider the following algorithm

$$\mathcal{B}^{\mathcal{O}_g}(f): x_2 \xleftarrow{\$} D, \; y \overset{\triangle}{=} g(x_2), \; x_1 \leftarrow \mathcal{A}(f, y), \; \text{return } (x_1, x_2).$$

For a random g whose inputs are in D, y is a uniform element in R_λ. Moreover, since $f(x_1) = g(x_2)$ is equivalent to $f(x_1) = y$, we have $Adv_{\mathcal{F}}^{OW}(\mathcal{A}) \leq Adv_{\mathcal{F}}^{Claw(RF)}(\mathcal{B}^{\mathcal{O}_g})$. Finally notice that $\mathcal{B}^{\mathcal{O}_g}$ makes a single call to g and runs in the same time as $\mathcal{A}$, which concludes the proof. $\qquad\square$

2. $Adv_{\mathcal{F}}^{Claw(RF)}(t, q) \leq q \cdot Adv_{\mathcal{F}}^{OW}(t)$.

Let $\mathcal{A}^{\mathcal{O}}$ be a query algorithm running in time t, performing q queries to $\mathcal{O}$ with Claw(RF) advantage $Adv_{\mathcal{F}}^{Claw(RF)}(t, q)$. Let $\mathcal{O}_{RO}(x; \mathcal{L})$ be the random oracle. We construct a new procedure $\mathcal{O}''_{j,y_0}$ which is equivalent to $\mathcal{O}_{RO}$ except the jth call that outputs y_0. In the internal memory of $\mathcal{O}''_{j,y_0}$, we will keep track in a index i that corresponds to the number of times the oracle was queried $+1$.

```
proc O''_{j,y_0}(x; L, i)
if ∃!y : (x,y) ∈ L, return (y; L, (i+1))
otherwise if i = j return (y_0; L ∪ {(x, y_0)}, (i+1)
else take y ←$ R_λ, return (y; L ∪ {(x,y)}, (i+1))
```

Notice that if j and y_0 are chosen at random then this doesn't change the behavior of the oracle. We consider the following algorithm

$$\mathcal{B}(f, y_0): j \xleftarrow{\$} \{1, \ldots, q\}, \; (x_1, x_2) \leftarrow \mathcal{A}^{\mathcal{O}''_{j,y_0}}, \; \text{return } x_1$$

Notice that we have replaced in $\mathcal{A}$ calls to $\mathcal{O}_{RO}$ with calls to $\mathcal{O}''_{j,y_0}$. We write

$$Adv_{\mathcal{F}}^{Claw(RF)}(\mathcal{A}^{\mathcal{O}})$$
$$= \mathbb{P}\left(f(x_1) = \mathcal{O}_{RO}(x_2) : (f, \tau) \leftarrow \text{TrapGen}(1^\lambda), \; (x_1, x_2) \leftarrow \mathcal{A}^{\mathcal{O}_{RO}}(f)\right)$$
$$= \mathbb{P}\left[f(x_1) = \mathcal{O}''_{j,y}(x_2) : (f, \tau) \leftarrow \text{TrapGen}(1^\lambda), j \xleftarrow{\$} \{1, \ldots, q\}, \; y \xleftarrow{\$} R_\lambda, \; (x_1, x_2) \leftarrow \mathcal{A}^{\mathcal{O}''_{j,y}}(f)\right]$$
$$\geq \frac{1}{q} \mathbb{P}\left[f(x_1) = y : (f, \tau) \leftarrow \text{TrapGen}(1^\lambda), \; j \xleftarrow{\$} \{1, \ldots, q\}, \; y \xleftarrow{\$} R_\lambda, \; (x_1, x_2) \leftarrow \mathcal{A}^{\mathcal{O}''_{j,y}}(f)\right]$$
$$= \frac{1}{q} \mathbb{P}\left[f(x_1) = y : (f, \tau) \leftarrow \text{TrapGen}(1^\lambda), \; y \xleftarrow{\$} R_\lambda, \; x_1 \leftarrow \mathcal{B}(f, y)\right]$$

where the inequality comes from the fact that when x_2 is queried in $\mathcal{O}''_{j,y}(x_2)$, there is a probability of $\frac{1}{q}$ that this corresponds to the jth query on average on j which corresponds to $\mathcal{O}''_{j,y}(x_2) = y$. $\qquad\square$

3. $Adv_{\mathcal{F}}^{Claw(RF)}(t, q) \leq Adv_{\mathcal{F}}^{Coll}(t + \widetilde{O}(q)) + q\varepsilon + \mathbb{E}_{(f,t) \leftarrow \text{TrapGen}}\left(\frac{1}{\text{MNP}(f)}\right)$.

Let $\mathcal{A}^{\mathcal{O}}$ be a query algorithm running in time t, performing q queries to $\mathcal{O}$ with Claw(RF) advantage $Adv_{\mathcal{F}}^{Claw(RF)}(t, q)$. We use the random oracle $\mathcal{O}_{RO}$ and write

$$Adv_{\mathcal{F}}^{Claw(RF)}(\mathcal{A}^{\mathcal{O}}) = \mathbb{P}\Big(f(x_1) = \mathcal{O}_{RO}(x_2) : (f, \tau) \leftarrow \text{TRAPGEN}(1^{\lambda}),\ (x_1, x_2) \leftarrow \mathcal{A}^{\mathcal{O}_{RO}}(f)\Big) \quad (8)$$

We now define another procedure $\mathcal{O}'_f$ that is similar to $\mathcal{O}_{RO}$ but we change the way y is sampled.

---

proc $\mathcal{O}'_f(x; \mathcal{L})$

if $\exists y : (x, y) \in \mathcal{L}$, **return** $(y; \mathcal{L})$

otherwise compute $z \leftarrow \text{SAMPDOM}(f)$, $y \stackrel{\triangle}{=} f(z)$, **return** $(y; \mathcal{L} \cup \{(x, y)\})$

Therefore we have:

$$\forall x, \mathcal{L}, \quad \Delta\big(\mathcal{O}_{RO}(x; \mathcal{L}), \mathcal{O}'_f(x; \mathcal{L})\big) \leq \varepsilon \quad (9)$$

from Proposition 2.

We now consider the following (queryless) algorithm $\mathcal{B}$: run $\mathcal{A}^{\mathcal{O}}$. Each time $\mathcal{O}$ is called, run $\mathcal{O}'_f$ and keep track efficiently of the internal memory $\mathcal{L}$, with a sorted list. Initialize $\mathcal{L} = \emptyset$. The list $\mathcal{L}$ is of size at most q so each membership query to $\mathcal{L}$ can be done in time at most $O(\log(q))$, so $\mathcal{B}$ runs in time $t + \widetilde{O}(q)$. Moreover, since $\mathcal{O}'_f$ is called q times, using Eqs. (8), (9) and Proposition 1, we have

$$Adv_{\mathcal{F}}^{Claw(RF)}(\mathcal{A}^{\mathcal{O}}) \leq \mathbb{P}\Big(f(x_1) = \mathcal{O}'_f(x_2) : (f, \tau) \leftarrow \text{TRAPGEN}(1^{\lambda}),\ (x_1, x_2) \leftarrow \mathcal{B}(f)\Big) + q\varepsilon.$$

Now, we construct the following algorithm $\mathcal{C}$: run $\mathcal{B}$. Each time $\mathcal{O}'_f(x; \mathcal{L})$ is called, keep track of the value z such that $f(z) = \mathcal{O}'_f(x)$. Let x_1, x_2 be the output of $\mathcal{B}(f)$. Let z such that $\mathcal{O}'_f(x_2) = f(z)$. Output (x_1, z). Again, $\mathcal{C}$ runs in time $t + \widetilde{O}(q)$. We have

$$Adv_{\mathcal{F}}^{Claw(RF)}(\mathcal{A}^{\mathcal{O}}) \leq \mathbb{P}\Big(f(x_1) = f(z) : (f, \tau) \leftarrow \text{TRAPGEN}(1^{\lambda}),\ (x_1, z) \leftarrow \mathcal{C}(f)\Big) + q\varepsilon.$$

In order to relate this to the collision advantage, we just need to find the probability that $x_1 \neq z$ in the above. From the construction of $\mathcal{C}$ and $\mathcal{O}_{f'}$, we have that z is a random preimage of $f(x_1)$. Therefore, $x_1 \neq z$ with probability at least $1 - \frac{1}{MNP(f)}$[4]. From there, we can conclude

$$Adv_{\mathcal{F}}^{Claw(RF)}(\mathcal{A}^{\mathcal{O}}) \leq Adv_{\mathcal{F}}^{Coll}(\mathcal{C}) + q\varepsilon + \mathbb{E}_{(f,t) \leftarrow \text{TRAPGEN}}\left(\frac{1}{MNP(f)}\right).$$

$\square$

---

[4] A similar argument was already implicitly used in [GPV08].

6   Tight Reduction to the Claw Problem, with ATPSF

6.1   Proof of Our Main Theorem

Theorem 1. *Let* $\mathcal{F} = (\mathrm{TRAPGEN}, \mathrm{SAMPDOM}, \mathrm{SAMPPRE})$ *be a collection of* ε-*ATPSF with security parameter* λ. *Let* $S^{\mathcal{F}}$ *be the associated Hash and Sign signature scheme with salt size* λ_0. *For any* t, q_{hash}, q_{sign}, *we have*

$$Adv_{S^{\mathcal{F}}}^{\mathrm{EUF\text{-}CMA}}(t, q_{hash}, q_{sign}) \leq Adv_{\mathcal{F}}^{Claw(RF)}(\widetilde{O}(t), q_{hash}) + q_{sign}\left(\varepsilon + \frac{(q_{sign} + q_{hash})}{2^{\lambda_0}}\right)$$

and by taking $\lambda_0 = \lambda + 2\log(q_{sign}) + \log(q_{hash})$, *we have*

$$Adv_{S^{\mathcal{F}}}^{\mathrm{EUF\text{-}CMA}}(t, q_{hash}, q_{sign}) \leq Adv_{\mathcal{F}}^{Claw(RF)}(\widetilde{O}(t), q_{hash}) + q_{sign}\varepsilon + \frac{1}{2^{\lambda}}.$$

Proof. Let $\mathcal{A}^{\mathcal{O}_{\mathsf{Hash}}, \mathcal{O}_{\mathsf{Sign}}}$ be an attacker with $|\mathcal{A}^{\mathcal{O}_{\mathsf{Hash}}, \mathcal{O}_{\mathsf{Sign}}}| = (t, q_{hash}, q_{sign})$ such that $Adv_{S^{\mathcal{F}}}^{\mathrm{EUF\text{-}CMA}}(t, q_{hash}, q_{sign}) = Adv_{S^{\mathcal{F}}}^{\mathrm{EUF\text{-}CMA}}(\mathcal{A}^{\mathcal{O}_{\mathsf{Hash}}, \mathcal{O}_{\mathsf{Sign}}})$. We show how to construct a query algorithm $\mathcal{C}^{\mathcal{O}}$ to attack the claw with random function property of $\mathcal{F}$. In the signature scheme $S^{\mathcal{F}}$, we have the following hash and sign procedures, where the Hash procedure is the Random Oracle.

proc Hash$(x; \mathcal{L})$
if $\exists! y : (x, y) \in \mathcal{L}$, return $(y; \mathcal{L})$
otherwise, pick $y \xleftarrow{\$} R_\lambda$, return $(y; \mathcal{L} \cup \{(x, y)\})$

proc Sign$(m; \mathcal{L})$
$r \xleftarrow{\$} \{0, 1\}^{\lambda_0}$
$(y; \mathcal{L}') \leftarrow$ Hash$(m\|r; \mathcal{L})$
$x \leftarrow$ SAMPPRE(f, τ, y)
return $(x, r; \mathcal{L}')$

Recall that $\mathcal{L}$ corresponds to the list of input/output pairs already queried to the Hash function. Here, both procedures use the same $\mathcal{L}$ and each time is it updated, this update happens for both procedures at the same time. We first rewrite the Sign procedure by replacing the Hash procedure inside it with its explicit code:

proc Sign$(m; \mathcal{L})$
$r \xleftarrow{\$} \{0, 1\}^{\lambda_0}$
$(y; \mathcal{L}') \leftarrow$ Hash$(m\|r; \mathcal{L})$
$x \leftarrow$ SAMPPRE(f, τ, y)
return $(x, r; \mathcal{L}')$

$=$

proc Sign$(m; \mathcal{L})$
$r \xleftarrow{\$} \{0, 1\}^{\lambda_0}$
if $\exists! y : (m\|r, y) \in \mathcal{L}$
then
$x \xleftarrow{\$}$ SAMPPRE(f, τ, y)
return $(x, r; \mathcal{L})$
else
$y \xleftarrow{\$} R_\lambda$
$x \xleftarrow{\$}$ SAMPPRE(f, τ, y)
$\mathcal{L}' \triangleq \mathcal{L} \cup \{(m\|r, y)\}$
return $(x, r; \mathcal{L}')$

Now, we present a new signature procedure Sign', that will be close to Sign but doesn't use τ.

```
proc Sign'(m; L)
r ←$ {0,1}^{λ_0}
if ∃!y : (m||r, y) ∈ L
then
return ⊥
else
x ←$ SAMPDOM(f)
y ≜ f(x)
L' ≜ L ∪ {(m||r, y)}
return (x, r; L')
```

We made two changes from Sign to Sign'. In the case where $\exists! y_0, : (m||r, y_0) \in \mathcal{L}$, Sign' outputs $\perp$. In the other case, Sign' also has a different way of sampling x and y. We show that these two changes do not change a lot the output distribution of the sign procedure:

Lemma 1. *For any f, τ as well as m and $\mathcal{L}$, we have $\Delta\big(\mathsf{Sign}(m; \mathcal{L}), \mathsf{Sign}' (m; \mathcal{L})\big) \leq \varepsilon_{f,\tau} + \frac{|\mathcal{L}|}{2^{\lambda_0}}$.*

Proof. We consider the following intermediate procedure Sign_{int}

```
proc Sign_int(m; L)
r ←$ {0,1}^{λ_0}
if ∃!y_0 : (m||r, y_0) ∈ L
then
return ⊥
else
y ←$ R_λ
x ←$ SAMPPRE(f, τ, y)
L' ≜ L ∪ {(m||r, y)}
return (x, r; L')
```

$\mathsf{Sign}(m; \mathcal{L})$ and $\mathsf{Sign}_{int}(m; \mathcal{L})$ only differ when for the random choice $r \xleftarrow{\$} \{0,1\}^{\lambda_0}$, $\exists! y_0 : (m||r, y_0) \in \mathcal{L}$. This event happens with probability at most $\frac{|\mathcal{L}|}{2^{\lambda_0}}$ hence $\Delta(\mathsf{Sign}(m; \mathcal{L}), \mathsf{Sign}_{int}(m; \mathcal{L})) \leq \frac{|\mathcal{L}|}{2^{\lambda_0}}$.

Now, let's look at the distance between $\mathsf{Sign}_{int}(m; \mathcal{L})$ and $\mathsf{Sign}'(m; \mathcal{L})$. The only difference in those distributions comes from the way x and y are sampled. Since both in Sign_{int} and Sign', we have $y = f(x)$ (and f is deterministic), the only difference comes from the way x is sampled. Therefore,

$$\Delta\left(\mathsf{Sign}_{int}(m; \mathcal{L}), \mathsf{Sign}'(m; \mathcal{L})\right) = \Delta\left(\mathrm{SAMPPRE}(f, \tau, U(R_\lambda)), \mathrm{SAMPDOM}(f)\right) = \varepsilon_{f,\tau}$$

and we can therefore conclude the proof using the triangle inequality. □

We are now ready to finish the proof of Theorem 1. From an adversary $\mathcal{A}^{\mathcal{O}_{\mathsf{Hash}}, \mathcal{O}_{\mathsf{Sign}}}(f)$, we construct an algorithm $\mathcal{B}^{\mathcal{O}_{\mathsf{Hash}}, \mathcal{O}_{\mathsf{Sign}'}}(f)$ which corresponds to running $\mathcal{A}^{\mathcal{O}_{\mathsf{Hash}}, \mathcal{O}_{\mathsf{Sign}}}$ but calls to $\mathcal{O}_{\mathsf{Sign}}$ are replaced with calls to $\mathcal{O}_{\mathsf{Sign}'}$. We also ask $\mathcal{B}$ to emulate by himself the oracles $\mathcal{O}_{\mathsf{Hash}}, \mathcal{O}'_{\mathsf{Sign}}$. To do this, it initializes $\mathcal{L} = \emptyset$ and runs these algorithms by himself by updating $\mathcal{L}$ efficiently via a sorted list. Notice that this was not possible with $\mathcal{O}_{\mathsf{Sign}}$ because it required τ that $\mathcal{B}$ does not have access to. Let us define $Adv'(\cdot)$ as:

$$Adv'(\mathcal{B}^{\mathcal{O}_{\mathsf{Hash}}, \mathcal{O}_{\mathsf{Sign}'}}) \stackrel{\triangle}{=} \mathbb{P}\Big(f(x^*) = \mathsf{Hash}(m^*||r^*) \;\wedge\; (m^*, e^*, r^*) \text{ wasn't answered}$$

$$\text{by } \mathcal{O}_{\mathsf{Sign}'} \text{ in } \mathcal{B} : (f, \tau) \leftarrow \mathrm{TRAPGEN}(1^\lambda), (m^*, r^*, x^*) \leftarrow \mathcal{B}^{\mathcal{O}_{\mathsf{Hash}}, \mathcal{O}_{\mathsf{Sign}'}}(f)\Big).$$

On average on f, the outputs of $\mathcal{B}^{\mathcal{O}_{\mathsf{Hash}}, \mathcal{O}_{\mathsf{Sign}'}}$ differ from those of $\mathcal{A}^{\mathcal{O}_{\mathsf{Hash}}, \mathcal{O}_{\mathsf{Sign}}}(f)$ only because we replaced calls to $\mathcal{O}_{\mathsf{Sign}}$ with calls to $\mathcal{O}_{\mathsf{Sign}'}$. There are q_{sign} such calls and using Lemma 1, we have:

$$Adv_{\mathrm{S}\mathcal{F}}^{\mathrm{EUF\text{-}CMA}}(\mathcal{A}^{\mathcal{O}_{\mathsf{Hash}}, \mathcal{O}_{\mathsf{Sign}}}) \leq Adv'(\mathcal{B}^{\mathcal{O}_{\mathsf{Hash}}, \mathcal{O}_{\mathsf{Sign}'}}) + q_{sign}\left(\varepsilon + \frac{(q_{sign} + q_{hash})}{2^{\lambda_0}}\right)$$

where we here also averaged over $(f, \tau) \leftarrow \mathrm{TRAPGEN}(1^\lambda)$.

When we first discussed the random oracle model, we showed how when calling an oracle $\mathcal{O}_g$ for a random g, we could "internalize" the random function into each call of $\mathcal{O}_{\mathrm{RO}}$. In order to reach the quantity $Adv_{\mathcal{F}}^{Claw(RF)}$, we have to undo this step and externalize the random function, but we want to keep the internal memory $\mathcal{L}$ since it can also be modified by $\mathcal{O}_{\mathsf{Sign}'}$. More precisely, for any function g, we define

```
proc Hash_g(x; L)
if ∃!y : (x, y) ∈ L, return (y; L)
otherwise, return (g(x); L ∪ {(x, g(x))})
```

When, we run Hash, each time a fresh x is queried - meaning $\forall y, (x, y) \notin \mathcal{L}$ - we pick a random value y as its output. Equivalently, we can compute all those possible values y at the beginning, characterized by values $g(x)$ for a random function g. Therefore, we have

$$Adv'(\mathcal{B}^{\mathcal{O}_{\mathsf{Hash}}, \mathcal{O}_{\mathsf{Sign}'}}) = \mathbb{P}\Big(\mathsf{Hash}_g(m^*||r^*) = f(x^*) \;\wedge\; m^* \text{ wasn't queried to}$$

$$\mathcal{O}_{\mathsf{Sign}'} \text{ in } \mathcal{B} : g \stackrel{\$}{\leftarrow} \mathcal{RF}, (f, \tau) \leftarrow \mathrm{TRAPGEN}(1^\lambda), (m^*, r^*, x^*) \leftarrow \mathcal{B}^{\mathcal{O}_{\mathsf{Hash}_g}, \mathcal{O}_{\mathsf{Sign}'}}(f)\Big).$$

Now, for a fixed g, let's try to characterize $\mathsf{Hash}_g(m||r)$ for any m, r. If $\forall y, (m||r, y) \notin \mathcal{L}$ then $\mathsf{Hash}_g(m||r) = g(m||r)$. Otherwise, let y such that $(m||r, y) \in \mathcal{L}$ and we distinguish 2 cases:

1. $(m||r, y)$ was put in $\mathcal{L}$ after a call to Hash, then $\mathsf{Hash}_g(m||r) = g(m||r)$.
2. $(m||r, y)$ was put in $\mathcal{L}$ after a call to Sign', then m was queried to $\mathcal{O}_{\mathsf{Sign}'}$.

Therefore, for any triplet $(m^*, r^*, x^*) \leftarrow \mathcal{B}^{\mathcal{O}_{\mathsf{Hash}_g}, \mathcal{O}_{\mathsf{Sign}'}}$, we have:

m^* is not queried to $\mathcal{O}_{\mathsf{Sign}'}$ or m^* is queried and (x^*, r^*) is not answered by $\mathcal{O}_{\mathsf{Sign}'}$
$$\Leftrightarrow \mathsf{Hash}_g(m^*||r^*) = g(m^*||r^*).$$

From there, we have:

$$Adv'(\mathcal{B}^{\mathcal{O}_{\mathsf{Hash}}, \mathcal{O}_{\mathsf{Sign}'}}) = \mathbb{P}\Big(g(m^*||r^*) = f(x^*) : g \leftarrow \mathfrak{F}_{R_\lambda}^{\{0,1\}^* \times \{0,1\}^{\lambda_0}},$$
$$(f, \tau) \leftarrow \mathrm{TRAPGEN}(1^\lambda), (m^*, r^*, x^*) \leftarrow \mathcal{B}^{\mathcal{O}_{\mathsf{Hash}}, \mathcal{O}_{\mathsf{Sign}'}}(f)\Big).$$

In order to conclude, notice that the algorithm $\mathcal{B}^{\mathcal{O}_{\mathsf{Hash}_g}, \mathcal{O}_{\mathsf{Sign}'}}$ can be seen as an algorithm $\mathcal{C}^{\mathcal{O}_g}$ that runs in time $\widetilde{O}(t)$ and performs q_{hash} queries to O_g, so

$$Adv'(\mathcal{B}^{\mathcal{O}_{\mathsf{Hash}}, \mathcal{O}_{\mathsf{Sign}'}}) = \mathbb{P}\Big(g(m^*||r^*) = f(x^*) : g \leftarrow \mathfrak{F}_{R_\lambda}^{\{0,1\}^* \times \{0,1\}^{\lambda_0}},$$
$$(f, \tau) \leftarrow \mathrm{TRAPGEN}(1^\lambda), (m^*, r^*, x^*) \leftarrow \mathcal{C}^{\mathcal{O}_g}(f)\Big)$$
$$= Adv_{\mathcal{F}}^{Claw(RF)}(\mathcal{C}^{\mathcal{O}_g})$$

Putting everything together, we get $Adv_{\mathcal{F}}^{Claw(RF)}(\mathcal{C}^{\mathcal{O}_g}) = Adv'(\mathcal{B}^{\mathcal{O}_{\mathsf{Hash}}, \mathcal{O}_{\mathsf{Sign}'}})$ and

$$Adv_{\mathsf{S}^{\mathcal{F}}}^{\mathrm{EUF\text{-}CMA}}(\mathcal{A}^{\mathcal{O}_{\mathsf{Hash}}, \mathcal{O}_{\mathsf{Sign}}}) \le Adv_{\mathcal{F}}^{Claw(RF)}(\mathcal{C}^{\mathcal{O}_g}) + q_{sign}\left(\varepsilon + \frac{(q_{sign} + q_{hash})}{2^{\lambda_0}}\right)$$

which concludes the proof. $\qquad\square$

7 Quantum Security Proof in the QROM

In this section, we will prove that in the quantum setting, we can also prove the security of $\mathsf{S}^{\mathcal{F}}$ for a collection $\mathcal{F}$ of ATPSF. We first present the quantum random oracle model.

7.1 The Quantum Random Oracle Model

The Quantum Random Oracle Model (QROM) is a model where we model a certain function with a random function $\mathcal{H}$ but since we are in the quantum setting, we have a black box access to $\mathcal{H}$ and thus also to the unitary $\mathcal{O}_{\mathcal{H}}(|x\rangle|y\rangle) = |x\rangle|\mathcal{H}(x) + y\rangle$. Unlike the classical setting, when calling $\mathcal{O}_{\mathcal{H}}$ for a randomly chosen $\mathcal{H}$, we will not be able to generate values $\mathcal{H}(x)$ on the fly as we did classically since a quantum query potentially queries all values $\mathcal{H}(x)$ at the same time[5]. Hopefully we will still have tools to reprogram the QROM.

---

[5] It is actually possible to do this via the quantum lazy sampling routine [CMSZ19] but we will use simpler tools here.

When a function h is drawn uniformly from the set of functions $\mathfrak{F}^D_{\{0,1\}^m}$, we can equivalently, for each input $x \in D$, draw $h(x) \xleftarrow{\$} \{0,1\}^m$, which fully specified the function h. For each distribution $\mathcal{T}$ on $\{0,1\}^m$, let us consider the distribution of functions $\mathsf{Fun}_{\mathcal{T}}$ where $h \leftarrow \mathsf{Fun}_{\mathcal{T}}$ means that for each x, $h(x) \xleftarrow{\$} \mathcal{T}$. In [Zha12], Zhandry showed the following relation.

Proposition 5. *Let $\mathcal{A}^{\mathcal{O}}$ be a quantum query algorithm running in time t and making q queries to the oracle $\mathcal{O}$. Let $\mathcal{T}$ be a probability distribution on $\{0,1\}^m$ such that $\Delta(\mathcal{T}, \mathcal{U}(\{0,1\}^m)) \leq \varepsilon$. We have*

$$\left| \mathbb{P}\left(\mathcal{A}^{\mathcal{O}_h} \text{ outputs } 1 : h \leftarrow \mathfrak{F}^D_{\{0,1\}^m} \right) - \mathbb{P}\left(\mathcal{A}^{\mathcal{O}_g} \text{ outputs } 1 : g \leftarrow \mathsf{Fun}_{\mathcal{T}} \right) \right| \leq \frac{8\pi}{\sqrt{3}} q^{3/2} \sqrt{\varepsilon}.$$

One can compare this to the classical case, which follows directly from Proposition 1.

Proposition 6. *Let $\mathcal{A}^{\mathcal{O}}$ be a classical query algorithm running in time t and making q queries to the oracle $\mathcal{O}$. Let $\mathcal{T}$ be a probability distribution on $\{0,1\}^m$ such that $\Delta(\mathcal{T}, \mathcal{U}(\{0,1\}^m)) \leq \varepsilon$. We have*

$$\left| \mathbb{P}\left(\mathcal{A}^{\mathcal{O}_h} \text{ outputs } 1 : h \leftarrow \mathfrak{F}^D_{\{0,1\}^m} \right) - \mathbb{P}\left(\mathcal{A}^{\mathcal{O}_g} \text{ outputs } 1 : g \leftarrow \mathsf{Fun}_{\mathcal{T}} \right) \right| \leq q\varepsilon.$$

With Proposition 5, we will be able to prove the quantum security of $\mathrm{S}^{\mathcal{F}}$.

7.2   Tight Quantum Security of $\mathrm{S}^{\mathcal{F}}$

The goal of this section is to prove the following theorem

Theorem 2. *Let $\mathcal{F} = (\text{TrapGen}, \text{SampDom}, \text{SampPre})$ be an ε-ATPSF. Let $\mathrm{S}^{\mathcal{F}}$ be the associated Hash and Sign signature scheme. Let $q = q_{\mathsf{Hash}} + q_{\mathsf{Sign}}$, we have*

$$QADV^{\text{EUF-CMA}}_{\mathrm{S}^{\mathcal{F}}}(t, q_{hash}, q_{sign}) \leq \frac{1}{2}\left(QADV^{Claw(RF)}(\tilde{O}(t), q_{hash}) + \frac{8\pi}{\sqrt{6}} q^{3/2}\sqrt{\varepsilon} + q_{sign}\left(\varepsilon + \frac{q_{sign}}{2^{\lambda_0}} \right) \right).$$

By taking $\lambda_0 = \lambda + 2\log(q_{sign})$, this gives

$$QADV^{\text{EUF-CMA}}_{\mathrm{S}^{\mathcal{F}}}(t, q_{hash}, q_{sign}) \leq \frac{1}{2}\left(QADV^{Claw(RF)}(\tilde{O}(t), q_{hash}) + \frac{8\pi}{\sqrt{6}} q^{3/2}\sqrt{\varepsilon} + q_{sign}\varepsilon + \frac{1}{2^{\lambda}} \right).$$

Before proving this statement, we need to add another definition. Let $\mathcal{F} = (\text{TrapGen}, \text{SampDom}, \text{SampPre})$ be an ε-ATPSF. We said that $\text{SampDom}(f)$ was an efficient probabilistic algorithm. Here, we need to explicit this randomness and work with a deterministic algorithm. Let $\text{SampDom}_{det}(f, K)$ be the algorithm which corresponds to running $\text{SampDom}(f)$ with randomness $K \in \{0,1\}^k$. What this means is that running $\text{SampDom}(f)$ is done by choosing $K \xleftarrow{\$} \{0,1\}^k$ and running $\text{SampDom}_{det}(f, K)$. With this new definition, we can go and prove our theorem.

Proof (of Theorem 2). Fix $\mathcal{F}, S^{\mathcal{F}}$ and let $\mathcal{A}^{\mathcal{O}_{\mathsf{Hash}}, \mathcal{O}_{\mathsf{Sign}}}$ an adversary in the quantum EUF-CMA model with $|\mathcal{A}^{\mathcal{O}_{\mathsf{Hash}}, \mathcal{O}_{\mathsf{Sign}}}| = (t, q_{\mathsf{Hash}}, q_{\mathsf{Sign}})$ running in time t. In all our discussion, we fix a pair (f, τ) and we consider the Hash and Sign procedures of $S^{\mathcal{F}}$ for this fixed pair. We write $QADV_{S^{\mathcal{F}}}^{\mathrm{EUF\text{-}CMA}}(\mathcal{A}^{\mathcal{O}_{\mathsf{Hash}}, \mathcal{O}_{\mathsf{Sign}}}|(f, \tau))$ the advantage for this pair (f, τ) and we have

$$QADV_{S^{\mathcal{F}}}^{\mathrm{EUF\text{-}CMA}}(\mathcal{A}^{\mathcal{O}_{\mathsf{Hash}}, \mathcal{O}_{\mathsf{Sign}}}) = \mathbb{E}_{(f,\tau) \leftarrow \mathrm{TrapGen}(1^\lambda)} QADV_{S^{\mathcal{F}}}^{\mathrm{EUF\text{-}CMA}}(\mathcal{A}^{\mathcal{O}_{\mathsf{Hash}}, \mathcal{O}_{\mathsf{Sign}}}|(f, \tau)).$$

We consider 2 quantum accessible pseudo-random functions $\mathcal{O}_1 : \{0,1\}^{\lambda_0} \to \{0,1\}$ and $\mathcal{O}_2 : \{0,1\}^* \times \{0,1\}^{\lambda_0} \to \{0,1\}^k$, modeled as random function in the QROM. Using these functions, we construct the following function $\mathsf{Hash}' : \{0,1\}^* \times \{0,1\}^{\lambda_0} \to R_\lambda$ as follows:

---

proc $\mathsf{Hash}'(m, r)$

$b \overset{\triangle}{=} \mathcal{O}_1(r)$.
If $b = 0$, return $\mathsf{Hash}(m, r)$.
if $b = 1$, return $f(\mathrm{SampDom}_{det}(f, \mathcal{O}_2(m, r)))$.

First note that we can easily construct an efficient quantum circuit for $\mathcal{O}_{\mathsf{Hash}'}$ using $\mathcal{O}_{\mathsf{Hash}}$ and $\mathcal{O}_1, \mathcal{O}_2$. Also, since $\mathsf{Hash}, \mathcal{O}_1$ and $\mathcal{O}_2$ are random functions, $\mathsf{Hash}'(m, r)$ follows a distribution which is at most $\frac{\varepsilon_{f,\tau}}{2}$-close to the uniform distribution for each m, r. Indeed, $\mathsf{Hash}'(m, r)$ follows the uniform distribution with probability $\frac{1}{2}$ and the distribution $\mathrm{SampDom}(f)$ with probability $\frac{1}{2}$. But these two distributions are at most at distance $\varepsilon_{f,\tau}$ from Proposition 2. This means that

$$\forall (m, r), \ \Delta(\mathsf{Hash}(m, r), \mathsf{Hash}'(m, r)) \leq \frac{\varepsilon_{f,\tau}}{2}.$$

We also call Sign' the procedure Sign where we replaced Hash with Hash'. From the above, we have

$$\forall m, \ \Delta(\mathsf{Sign}(m), \mathsf{Sign}'(m)) \leq \frac{\varepsilon_{f,\tau}}{2}.$$

Using Proposition 5, we get

$$QADV_{S^{\mathcal{F}}}^{\mathrm{EUF\text{-}CMA}}(\mathcal{A}^{\mathcal{O}_{\mathsf{Hash}}, \mathcal{O}_{\mathsf{Sign}}}|(f, \tau)) \leq QADV_{S^{\mathcal{F}}}^{\mathrm{EUF\text{-}CMA}}(\mathcal{A}^{\mathcal{O}_{\mathsf{Hash}'}, \mathcal{O}_{\mathsf{Sign}'}}|(f, \tau)) + \frac{8\pi}{\sqrt{6}} q^{3/2} \sqrt{\varepsilon_{f,\tau}}.$$

We now change Sign' into Sign'' that doesn't use the trapdoor and can be emulated with only the public key.

---

proc $\mathsf{Sign}'(m)$

$r \overset{\$}{\leftarrow} \{0,1\}^{\lambda_0}$
$y \leftarrow \mathsf{Hash}'(m, r)$
$x \leftarrow \mathrm{SampPre}(f, \tau, y)$
return (x, r)

$\rightarrow$

proc $\mathsf{Sign}''(m)$

$r \overset{\$}{\leftarrow} \{0,1\}^{\lambda_0}$
$b \overset{\triangle}{=} \mathcal{O}_1(r)$. If $b = 0$, go back to step above.
If $b = 1$, $x \overset{\triangle}{=} \mathrm{SampDom}_{det}(f, \mathcal{O}_2(m, r))$
return (x, r).

When calling $\mathsf{Sign}''(m)$, the r chosen part of the output is a random value in $\{0,1\}^{\lambda_0}$ such that $\mathcal{O}_1(m,r) = 1$. The probability that this r wasn't returned by a previous Sign'' query is therefore at least $1 - \frac{q_{\mathsf{Sign}}}{2^{(\lambda_0-1)}}$. When this is the case, the distance between a call to Sign' and Sign'' is equal to $\varepsilon_{f,\tau}$, since K is uniformly random (using Proposition 2). Therefore, we have for each m

$$\Delta(\mathsf{Sign}'(m), \mathsf{Sign}''(m)) \leq \frac{2q_{\mathsf{Sign}}}{2^{\lambda}_0} + \varepsilon_{f,\tau}.$$

Using Proposition 5, we get

$$QADV^{\mathrm{EUF\text{-}CMA}}_{\mathsf{S}\mathcal{F}}(\mathcal{A}^{\mathcal{O}_{\mathsf{Hash}'},\mathcal{O}_{\mathsf{Sign}'}}|(f,\tau)) \leq QADV^{\mathrm{EUF\text{-}CMA}}_{\mathsf{S}\mathcal{F}}(\mathcal{A}^{\mathcal{O}_{\mathsf{Hash}'},\mathcal{O}_{\mathsf{Sign}''}}|(f,\tau)) + q_{\mathrm{sign}}\Big(\frac{2q_{\mathsf{Sign}}}{2^{\lambda}_0} + \varepsilon_{f,\tau}\Big).$$

Putting everything together, we get

$$QADV^{\mathrm{EUF\text{-}CMA}}_{\mathsf{S}\mathcal{F}}(\mathcal{A}^{\mathcal{O}_{\mathsf{Hash}}\cdot\mathcal{O}_{\mathsf{Sign}}}|(f,\tau)) \leq QADV^{\mathrm{EUF\text{-}CMA}}_{\mathsf{S}\mathcal{F}}(\mathcal{A}^{\mathcal{O}_{\mathsf{Hash}'}\cdot\mathcal{O}_{\mathsf{Sign}''}}|(f,\tau)) + \frac{8\pi}{\sqrt{6}}q^{3/2}\sqrt{\varepsilon_{f,\tau}}$$

$$+ q_{\mathrm{sign}}\Big(\frac{2q_{\mathsf{Sign}}}{2^{\lambda}_0} + \varepsilon_{f,\tau}\Big),$$

and by taking the expectation over $(f,\tau) \leftarrow \mathrm{TRAPGEN}(1^{\lambda})$, we get

$$QADV^{\mathrm{EUF\text{-}CMA}}_{\mathsf{S}\mathcal{F}}(\mathcal{A}^{\mathcal{O}_{\mathsf{Hash}},\mathcal{O}_{\mathsf{Sign}}}) \leq QADV^{\mathrm{EUF\text{-}CMA}}_{\mathsf{S}\mathcal{F}}(\mathcal{A}^{\mathcal{O}_{\mathsf{Hash}'},\mathcal{O}_{\mathsf{Sign}''}}) + \frac{8\pi}{\sqrt{6}}q^{3/2}\sqrt{\varepsilon} + q_{\mathrm{sign}}\Big(\frac{2q_{\mathsf{Sign}}}{2^{\lambda}_0} + \varepsilon\Big).$$

where we used the concavity of the root function and Jensen's inequality. In order to conclude, let's write

$$QADV^{\mathrm{EUF\text{-}CMA}}_{\mathsf{S}\mathcal{F}}(\mathcal{A}^{\mathcal{O}_{\mathsf{Hash}'}\cdot\mathcal{O}_{\mathsf{Sign}''}}) = \mathbb{P}\Big(\mathsf{Hash}'(m^*,r^*) = f(x^*) \text{ AND } m^* \text{ has not been queried in } \mathcal{O}_{\mathsf{Sign}''} :$$

$$(f,\tau) \leftarrow \mathrm{TRAPGEN}, (m^*,x^*,r^*) \leftarrow \mathcal{A}^{\mathcal{O}_{\mathsf{Hash}'},\mathcal{O}_{\mathsf{Sign}''}}(f)\Big)$$

$$= \frac{1}{2}\mathbb{P}\Big(\mathsf{Hash}(m^*,r^*) = f(x^*) :$$

$$(f,\tau) \leftarrow \mathrm{TRAPGEN}, (m^*,x^*,r^*) \leftarrow \mathcal{A}^{\mathcal{O}_{\mathsf{Hash}'},\mathcal{O}_{\mathsf{Sign}''}}(f)\Big)$$

$$= \frac{1}{2}QADV^{Claw(RF)}(\mathcal{A}^{\mathcal{O}_{\mathsf{Hash}'},\mathcal{O}_{\mathsf{Sign}''}}).$$

Here, we used the fact that if m^* is not queried in Sign'', the value of $\mathcal{O}_1(m^*,r^*)$ is random and is equal to 0 with probability $\frac{1}{2}$. When this occurs, we have $\mathsf{Hash}'(m,r) = \mathsf{Hash}(m,r)$. Finally, notice that $\mathcal{A}^{\mathcal{O}_{\mathsf{Hash}'},\mathcal{O}''_{\mathsf{Sign}}}$ can be performed locally with the public key and oracle calls to $\mathcal{O}_{\mathsf{Hash}}$ so we can write $\mathcal{A}^{\mathcal{O}_{\mathsf{Hash}'},\mathcal{O}''_{\mathsf{Sign}}} = \mathcal{B}^{\mathcal{O}_{\mathsf{Hash}}}$ for some algorithm $\mathcal{B}$. We have therefore

$$QADV^{\mathrm{EUF\text{-}CMA}}_{\mathsf{S}\mathcal{F}}(\mathcal{A}^{\mathcal{O}_{\mathsf{Hash}},\mathcal{O}_{\mathsf{Sign}}}) \leq \frac{1}{2}\Big(QADV^{Claw(RF)}(\mathcal{B}^{\mathcal{O}_{\mathsf{Hash}}}) + \frac{8\pi}{\sqrt{6}}q^{3/2}\sqrt{\varepsilon} + q_{\mathrm{sign}}\Big(\varepsilon + \frac{q_{\mathrm{sign}}}{2^{\lambda_0}}\Big)\Big).$$

Notice finally that $\mathcal{B}$ makes as much queries to Hash as $\mathcal{A}$ and runs in essentially the same time $(\widetilde{O}(t))$, which concludes the proof. $\square$

8 Applying the Result to Code-Based Signatures Based on ATPSF

In this Section, we present a general analysis of code-based signatures based on ATPSF families. We will show that using the tightness to the $Claw(RF)$ problem gives better results than using the standard inversion or collision problem. This section is motivated by the WAVE signature scheme [DST19a], that constructs a code-based ATPSF family, but is relevant for any such construction.

8.1 Canonical Construction of Code-Based ATPSF

We present here the definition of a canonical code-based ATPSF, adapting Definition 2, that we call CBATPSF.

Here the notation $|\cdot|$ denotes the Hamming weight, *i.e:* the number of non zero component of a vector. Furthermore, vectors will be written with bold letters (such as $\mathbf{e}$) and uppercase bold letters are used to denote matrices (such as $\mathbf{H}$). Vectors will be in row notation.

Definition 5. *An ε-CBATPSF (for Code Based Average Trapdoor Preimage Sampleable Functions (or Function Family)) is an efficient triplet of probabilistic algorithms (*TRAPGEN, SAMPDOM, SAMPPRE*) with parameters n, k, q, w (that can depend on the security parameter λ) where:*

- TRAPGEN$(1^\lambda) \to (\mathbf{H}, \tau)$. *Takes the security parameter λ and outputs $\mathbf{H} \in \mathbb{F}_q^{(n-k)\times n}$, and a trapdoor τ. We also define $D_\lambda = \{\mathbf{e} \in \mathbb{F}_q^n : |\mathbf{e}| = w\}$ and $R_\lambda = \mathbb{F}_q^{n-k}$. The trapdoor function maps then any $\mathbf{e} \in D_\lambda$ to $\mathbf{eH} \in R_\lambda$.*
- SAMPDOM$(\mathbf{H}) \to \mathbf{e}$. *Takes a matrix $\mathbf{H} \in \mathbb{F}_q^{(n-k)\times n}$ and outputs a vector $\mathbf{e} \in D_\lambda$.*
- SAMPPRE$(\mathbf{H}, \tau, \mathbf{s}) \to \mathbf{e}$. *Takes a matrix $\mathbf{H} \in \mathbb{F}_q^{(n-k)\times n}$ with associated trapdoor τ, an element $\mathbf{s} \in R_\lambda$ and outputs $\mathbf{e} \in D_\lambda$ s.t. $\mathbf{eH} = \mathbf{s}$.*

For this definition, the one-wayness, collision and Claw(RF) problems become the following, for a fixed algorithm $\mathcal{A}$ that outputs elements $\mathbf{e}$ in D_λ, meaning that $\mathbf{e} \in \mathbb{F}_q^n$ and $|\mathbf{e}| = w$:

$$Adv_{\mathcal{F}}^{OW}(\mathcal{A}) = \mathbb{P}\left(\mathbf{eH}^\mathsf{T} = \mathbf{s} : (\mathbf{H}, \tau) \leftarrow \text{TRAPGEN}(1^\lambda),\ \mathbf{s} \xleftarrow{\$} \mathbb{F}_2^{n-k},\ \mathbf{e} \leftarrow \mathcal{A}(\mathbf{H}, s)\right),$$

$$Adv_{\mathcal{F}}^{Coll}(\mathcal{A}) = \mathbb{P}\left(\mathbf{e}_1\mathbf{H}^\mathsf{T} = \mathbf{e}_2\mathbf{H}^\mathsf{T} \wedge \mathbf{e}_1 \neq \mathbf{e}_2 : (\mathbf{H}, \tau) \leftarrow \text{TRAPGEN}(1^\lambda),\ (\mathbf{e}_1, \mathbf{e}_2) \leftarrow \mathcal{A}(\mathbf{H})\right),$$

$$Adv_{\mathcal{F}}^{Claw(RF)}(\mathcal{A}^{\mathcal{O}}) = \mathbb{P}\left(\mathbf{e}_1\mathbf{H}^\mathsf{T} = \mathbf{e}_2\mathbf{H}^\mathsf{T} : h \xleftarrow{\$} \mathfrak{F}_{R_\lambda}^{D_\lambda},\ (\mathbf{H}, \tau) \leftarrow \text{TRAPGEN}(1^\lambda),\ (\mathbf{e}_1, \mathbf{e}_2) \leftarrow \mathcal{A}^{\mathcal{O}_h}(\mathbf{H})\right).$$

These problems are directly related to standard problems used in code-based cryptography as we will see in the next section. These problem are believed to be hard when the matrix $\mathbf{H}$ is chosen uniformly at random from the set of full rank matrices. However, in the CBATPSF construction, this matrix is generated from TRAPGEN so it needn't be uniform. We therefore have to argue that these problems remains hard for matrices $\mathbf{H}$ generated from TRAPGEN. A way to do this is to argue that these matrices are computationally indistinguishable from uniformly random matrices of full rank.

Let $\mathrm{FR}_q^{k,n} \triangleq \{\mathbf{H} \in \mathbb{F}_q^{k \times n} : \mathbf{H} \text{ has full rank}\}$. We define the advantage $Adv_{\mathcal{F}}^{TvsU}(\mathcal{A})$ of distinguishing matrices generated from TRAPGEN(1^λ) with uniformly chosen matrices of full rank, for any algorithm $\mathcal{A}$:

$$Adv_{\mathcal{F}}^{TvsU}(\mathcal{A}) \triangleq \left| \mathbb{P}\left(\mathcal{A}(\mathbf{H}) \text{ outputs } 1 : (\mathbf{H}, \tau) \leftarrow \text{TRAPGEN}(1^\lambda)\right) - \mathbb{P}\left(\mathcal{A}(\mathbf{H}) \text{ outputs } 1 : \mathbf{H} \xleftarrow{\$} \mathrm{FR}_q^{k,n}\right) \right|.$$

We also define, for any time t: $Adv_{\mathcal{F}}^{TvsU}(t) = \max_{\mathcal{A}:|\mathcal{A}|=t} Adv_{\mathcal{F}}^{TvsU}(\mathcal{A})$.

8.2 Relating Hardness of Breaking the CBATPSF with the Hardness of Breaking Standard Code-Based Problems

In this section, we will relate the different advantages (for one-wayness, collision and Claw(RF)) with known problems in code-based cryptography. This will show that using our tight reduction to the Claw(RF) will give better results than using one-wayness or collision finding.

One-Wayness vs. Syndrome Decoding. The syndrome decoding problem is the most studied problem in code-based cryptography.

Problem 2 (Syndrome Decoding - SD(n, q, k, w)).

- Instance: a parity-check matrix $\mathbf{H} \in \mathbb{F}_q^{(n-k) \times n}$ of rank $n - k$, a syndrome $\mathbf{s} \in \mathbb{F}_q^{n-k}$,
- Output: $\mathbf{e} \in \mathbb{F}_q^n$ of Hamming weight w such that $\mathbf{eH}^\intercal = \mathbf{s}$

This problem is believed to be hard when the matrix $\mathbf{H}$ is chosen randomly from $\mathrm{FR}_q^{k,n}$ and the syndrome $\mathbf{s}$ is chosen at random. This setting has been extensively studied in [Pra62, Ste88, Dum91, Bar97, FS09, MMT11, BJMM12, CS15, MO15, DT17, BM18, BCDL19]. It is also known to be NP-complete in the worst case [BMvT78] and there is a search to decision reduction (see for instance [FS96]). For any algorithm $\mathcal{A}$, we define the (average case) syndrome decoding advantage as

Definition 6 (SD-advantage(n, q, k, w)). *For any algorithm $\mathcal{A}$, we define*

$$Adv_{(n,q,k,w)}^{SD}(\mathcal{A}) \triangleq \mathbb{P}\left(\mathbf{eH}^\intercal = \mathbf{s} \text{ and } |\mathbf{e}| = w : \mathbf{H} \xleftarrow{\$} FR_q^{k,n}, \ \mathbf{s} \xleftarrow{\$} \mathbb{F}_q^{n-k}, \ \mathbf{e} \leftarrow \mathcal{A}(\mathbf{H}, \mathbf{s})\right),$$

and for any time t, we also define, $Adv_{(n,q,k,w)}^{SD}(t) \triangleq \max_{\mathcal{A}:|\mathcal{A}|=t} Adv_{(n,q,k,w)}^{SD}(\mathcal{A})$.

Notice that this is exactly the one-wayness advantage of the CBATPSF , except that $\mathbf{H}$ is chosen uniformly and not from TRAPGEN. Therefore, we immediately have for any t

$$Adv_{\mathcal{F}}^{OW}(t) \leq Adv_{(n,q,R,\omega)}^{SD}(t) + Adv_{\mathcal{F}}^{TvsU}(t). \tag{10}$$

Now consider the signature scheme $S^{\mathcal{F}}$ based on a CBATPSF $\mathcal{F}$ as defined in Definition 5. By combining Theorem 1, Proposition 4, and Eq. (10), we immediately get the following proposition.

Proposition 7. *Let $\mathcal{F}$ be an ε-CBATPSF as defined in Definition 5 and let $S^{\mathcal{F}}$ be the corresponding signature scheme. We have:*

$$Adv_{S\mathcal{F}}^{\text{EUF-CMA}}(t, q_{hash}, q_{sign}) \leq q_{hash}\left(Adv_{(n,q,k,w)}^{SD}(\widetilde{O}(t)) + Adv_{\mathcal{F}}^{TvsU}(t)\right) + q_{sign}\left(\varepsilon + \frac{(q_{sign} + q_{hash})}{2^{\lambda_0}}\right).$$

Notice here that there is a q_{hash} factor in front of $Adv_{(n,q,k,w)}^{SD}(\widetilde{O}(t))$ which implies a significant loss in the security reduction.

Claw(RF) vs. DOOM Problem. Decode One Out of Many is a multitarget generalization of the syndrome decoding problem. Instead of giving one syndrome s as input, we give several random syndromes and we have to solve the syndrome decoding problem for one of these syndromes. The way we model having access to these syndromes is by giving a black box access to a random function h that outputs these syndromes.

Problem 3 (Decoding One Out of Many - DOOM(n, q, k, w)).

- Instance: a parity-check matrix $\mathbf{H} \in \mathbb{F}_q^{(n-k)\times n}$ of rank $n - k$ and a function $h : D \to \mathbb{F}_q^n$ for some domain D, to which we only have a black box access.
- Output: $\mathbf{e} \in \mathbb{F}_q^n$ of Hamming weight w and $i \in D$ such that $\mathbf{eH}^\intercal = h(i)$

This is problem is sometimes defined when we get as an input N random syndromes $s_1, \ldots, s_N$. This can be reformulated in our problem by first computing $h(i)$ for $i \in \{1, \ldots, N\}$ and setting $s_i = h(i)$. This problem has been studied in quite a few papers [JJ02, Sen11, DST17, BCDL19]. It is easier than the syndrome decoding problem and sometimes quite significantly. We define the DOOM advantage as follows, for any query algorithm $\mathcal{A}^{\mathcal{O}}$.

Definition 7 (DOOM-advantage(n, q, k, w)). *For any algorithm $\mathcal{A}$, we define*

$$Adv_{(n,q,k,w)}^{DOOM}(\mathcal{A}^{\mathcal{O}}) \triangleq \mathbb{P}\left(\mathbf{eH}^\intercal = h(i) \text{ and } |\mathbf{e}| = w : \mathbf{H} \xleftarrow{\$} FR_q^{k,n}, h \xleftarrow{\$} \mathfrak{F}_{R_\lambda}^{D_\lambda}, (\mathbf{e}, i) \leftarrow \mathcal{A}^{\mathcal{O}_h}(\mathbf{H})\right),$$

and for any time t, we also define $Adv_{(n,q,k,w)}^{DOOM}(t, q) \triangleq \max_{\mathcal{A}^{\mathcal{O}} : |\mathcal{A}^{\mathcal{O}}| = (t,q)} Adv_{(n,q,k,w)}^{DOOM}(\mathcal{A}^{\mathcal{O}})$.

Again, this is exactly the $Claw(RF)$ advantage up to the distribution of the input matrix $\mathbf{H}$. This means we have

$$Adv_{\mathcal{F}}^{Claw(RF)}(t, q) \leq Adv_{(n,q,k,w)}^{DOOM}(t, q) + Adv_{\mathcal{F}}^{TvsU}(t). \tag{11}$$

By combining Theorem 1 and Eq. (11), we immediately get:

Proposition 8. *Let $\mathcal{F}$ be an ε-CBATPSF as defined in Definition 5 and let $S^{\mathcal{F}}$ be the corresponding signature scheme. We have*

$$Adv_{S^{\mathcal{F}}}^{\text{EUF-CMA}}(t, q_{hash}, q_{sign}) \leq Adv_{(n,q,k,w)}^{DOOM}(t) + Adv_{\mathcal{F}}^{TvsU}(t) + q_{sign}\left(\varepsilon + \frac{(q_{sign} + q_{hash})}{2^{\lambda_0}}\right).$$

Here, we have the reduction to the DOOM problem. Even though it is simpler than syndrome decoding, the reduction is tight so it will overall give much better results.

Using the Collision Problem. One could also, as in [GPV08], replace the Claw(RF) problem with the collision problem. However, in the case of codes, this problem is much simpler. Actually, there is a large range of parameters for which the problem can be solved in polynomial time while the syndrome decoding or DOOM problems are solved in exponential time.

8.3   Wave Instantiation

In this context authors, of [DST19a] constructed a signature scheme called Wave, based on an CBATPSF family. As far as we know, this is the first post-quantum signature scheme based on this paradigm that doesn't use lattice based assumptions. To accomplish this they introduced a family of codes which forms their trapdoor, namely the permuted generalized $(U, U + V)$-codes. The presentation of this trapdoor is out of the scope of this paper. Wave constructs an ε-CBATPSF family with the following parameters:

$$n = 66.34\lambda, \quad w = 0.9396n, \quad q = 3, \quad k = 0.66n.$$

With this choice of parameters, ε and $Adv_{\mathcal{F}}^{TvsU}(t)$ are small enough to have 128 bits of security. The interested reader can read the long version of Wave [DST19b], in particular [DST19b, Theorem 3, p39] and [DST19b, Proposition 14, page 31] to have more details. Notice also that the public key has $\log_2(3)n^2$ bits.

Here, we are in a parameter range where the collision problem is simple, so we can't use the original tight GPV bound. However, as studied in [BCDL19], the best classical algorithms for DOOM have essentially the same complexity than those for Syndrome Decoding. This means that in order to derive the security of Wave, if Proposition 7 was used instead of Proposition 8, we would have to double the value of n and hence increase the public key size (already quite large) by a factor of 4. This shows on a concrete example the importance of our results.

9   Conclusion

In this paper, we extended the GPV construction of signature schemes by allowing the use of ATPSF instead of TPSF. We also presented a security reduction of these signature schemes to the Claw(RF) which is not only tight but also optimal, meaning that an algorithm that solves the Claw(RF) also breaks the underlying signature scheme.

Our results allow to extend the GPV construction to non-lattice based schemes. In particular, for code-based cryptography, it is often easy to find collisions for the underlying trapdoor function. What we showed is that with this construction, we cannot have a tight reduction to Syndrome Decoding so we cannot ignore the non-tightness to SD. On the other side, losing a q factor (the number of queries) in the security reduction is greatly overkill. The good approach is to consider the Claw(RF) problem which in the code-based setting is the DOOM problem. Because of our optimality results, the Claw(RF) should always be the studied problem in GPV-like construction in order to correctly assess the security of the signature scheme.

More generally, we advocate that all Hash and Sign signatures should follow similar guidelines. This was implicitly done for lattices because SIS and $ISIS$ are considered of same difficulty and the associated Claw(RF) problem lies between them.

Acknowledgments. The work of Debris-Alazard was supported by the grant EPSRC EP/S02087X/1.

References

[Bar97] Barg, A.: Minimun distance decoding algorithms for linear codes. In: Mora, T., Mattson, H. (eds.) AAECC 1997. LNCS, vol. 1255, pp. 1–14. Springer, Heidelberg (1997). https://doi.org/10.1007/3-540-63163-1_1

[BCDL19] Bricout, R., Chailloux, A., Debris-Alazard, T., Lequesne, M.: Ternary syndrome decoding with large weights. preprint, February 2019. arXiv:1903.07464. To appear in the proceedings of SAC 2019

[BDF+11] Boneh, D., Dagdelen, Ö., Fischlin, M., Lehmann, A., Schaffner, C., Zhandry, M.: Random oracles in a quantum world. In: Lee, D.H., Wang, X. (eds.) ASIACRYPT 2011. LNCS, vol. 7073, pp. 41–69. Springer, Heidelberg (2011). https://doi.org/10.1007/978-3-642-25385-0_3

[BJMM12] Becker, A., Joux, A., May, A., Meurer, A.: Decoding random binary linear codes in $2^{n/20}$: how $1 + 1 = 0$ improves information set decoding. In: Pointcheval, D., Johansson, T. (eds.) EUROCRYPT 2012. LNCS, vol. 7237, pp. 520–536. Springer, Heidelberg (2012). https://doi.org/10.1007/978-3-642-29011-4_31

[BM18] Both, L., May, A.: Decoding linear codes with high error rate and its impact for LPN security. In: Lange, T., Steinwandt, R. (eds.) PQCrypto 2018. LNCS, vol. 10786, pp. 25–46. Springer, Cham (2018). https://doi.org/10.1007/978-3-319-79063-3_2

[BMvT78] Berlekamp, E., McEliece, R., van Tilborg, H.: On the inherent intractability of certain coding problems. IEEE Trans. Inf. Theory **24**(3), 384–386 (1978)

[BR93] Bellare, M., Rogaway, P.: Random oracles are practical: a paradigm for designing efficient protocols. In: CCS 1993, Proceedings of the 1st ACM Conference on Computer and Communications Security, Fairfax, Virginia, USA, 3–5 November 1993, pp. 62–73 (1993)

[BR96]   Bellare, M., Rogaway, P.: The exact security of digital signatures-how to sign with RSA and Rabin. In: Maurer, U. (ed.) EUROCRYPT 1996. LNCS, vol. 1070, pp. 399–416. Springer, Heidelberg (1996). https://doi.org/10.1007/3-540-68339-9_34

[CGM19]   Chen, Y., Genise, N., Mukherjee, P.: Approximate trapdoors for lattices and smaller hash-and-sign signatures. In: Galbraith, S.D., Moriai, S. (eds.) ASIACRYPT 2019. LNCS, vol. 11923, pp. 3–32. Springer, Cham (2019). https://doi.org/10.1007/978-3-030-34618-8_1

[CHR+16] Chen, M.-S., Hülsing, A., Rijneveld, J., Samardjiska, S., Schwabe, P.: From 5-pass $\mathcal{MQ}$-based identification to $\mathcal{MQ}$-based signatures. In: Cheon, J.H., Takagi, T. (eds.) ASIACRYPT 2016. LNCS, vol. 10032, pp. 135–165. Springer, Heidelberg (2016). https://doi.org/10.1007/978-3-662-53890-6_5

[CMSZ19] Czajkowski, J., Majenz, C., Schaffner, C., Zur, S.: Quantum lazy sampling and game-playing proofs for quantum indifferentiability. Cryptology ePrint Archive, Report 2019/428 (2019). https://eprint.iacr.org/2019/428

[Cor00]   Coron, J.-S.: On the exact security of full domain hash. In: Bellare, M. (ed.) CRYPTO 2000. LNCS, vol. 1880, pp. 229–235. Springer, Heidelberg (2000). https://doi.org/10.1007/3-540-44598-6_14

[Cor02]   Coron, J.-S.: Optimal security proofs for PSS and other signature schemes. In: Knudsen, L.R. (ed.) EUROCRYPT 2002. LNCS, vol. 2332, pp. 272–287. Springer, Heidelberg (2002). https://doi.org/10.1007/3-540-46035-7_18

[CS15]   Canto-Torres, R., Sendrier, N.: Analysis of information set decoding for a sub-linear error weight (2015). Preprint

[DST17]   Debris-Alazard, T., Sendrier, N., Tillich, J.-P.: SURF: a new code-based signature scheme. Preprint, September 2017. arXiv:1706.08065v3

[DST19a] Debris-Alazard, T., Sendrier, N., Tillich, J.-P.: Wave: a new family of trapdoor one-way preimage sampleable functions based on codes. In: Galbraith, S.D., Moriai, S. (eds.) ASIACRYPT 2019. LNCS, vol. 11921, pp. 21–51. Springer, Cham (2019). https://doi.org/10.1007/978-3-030-34578-5_2

[DST19b] Debris-Alazard, T., Sendrier, N., Tillich, J.-P.: Wave: a new family of trapdoor one-way preimage sampleable functions based on codes. Cryptology ePrint Archive, Report 2018/996, March 2019. https://eprint.iacr.org/2018/996

[DT17]   Debris-Alazard, T., Tillich, J.-P.: Statistical decoding. preprint, January 2017. arXiv:1701.07416

[Dum91]   Dumer, I.: On minimum distance decoding of linear codes. In: Proceedings of the 5th Joint Soviet-Swedish International Workshop Information Theory, Moscow, pp. 50–52 (1991)

[FHK+17] Fouque, P.-A., et al.: Falcon: fast-Fourier lattice-based compact signatures over NTRU. First round submission to the NIST post-quantum cryptography call, November 2017

[FS96]   Fischer, J.-B., Stern, J.: An efficient pseudo-random generator provably as secure as syndrome decoding. In: Maurer, U. (ed.) EUROCRYPT 1996. LNCS, vol. 1070, pp. 245–255. Springer, Heidelberg (1996). https://doi.org/10.1007/3-540-68339-9_22

[FS09]   Finiasz, M., Sendrier, N.: Security bounds for the design of code-based cryptosystems. In: Matsui, M. (ed.) ASIACRYPT 2009. LNCS, vol. 5912, pp. 88–105. Springer, Heidelberg (2009). https://doi.org/10.1007/978-3-642-10366-7_6

[GM02]   Goldwasser, S., Micciancio, D.: Complexity of Lattice Problems: A Crypto-graphic Perspective. Kluwer International Series in Engineering and Computer Science, vol. 671. Kluwer Academic Publishers, Heidelberg (2002)

[GPV08] Gentry, C., Peikert, C., Vaikuntanathan, V.: Trapdoors for hard lattices and new cryptographic constructions. In: Proceedings of the Fortieth Annual ACM Symposium on Theory of Computing, pp. 197–206. ACM (2008)

[JJ02]   Johansson, T., Jönsson, F.: On the complexity of some cryptographic problems based on the general decoding problem. IEEE Trans. Inf. Theory **48**(10), 2669–2678 (2002)

[KM19]   Koblitz, N., Menezes, A.: Critical perspectives on provable security: fifteen years of "another look" papers. Adv. Math. Commun. **13**, 517–558 (2019)

[KZ19]   Kales, D., Zaverucha, G.: NIST round-2 official comment (2019). https://csrc.nist.gov/csrc/media/projects/post-quantum-cryptography/documents/round-2/official-comments/mqdss-round2-official-comment.pdf

[MMT11] May, A., Meurer, A., Thomae, E.: Decoding random linear codes in $\tilde{\mathcal{O}}(2^{0.054n})$. In: Lee, D.H., Wang, X. (eds.) ASIACRYPT 2011. LNCS, vol. 7073, pp. 107–124. Springer, Heidelberg (2011). https://doi.org/10.1007/978-3-642-25385-0_6

[MO15]   May, A., Ozerov, I.: On computing nearest neighbors with applications to decoding of binary linear codes. In: Oswald, E., Fischlin, M. (eds.) EUROCRYPT 2015. LNCS, vol. 9056, pp. 203–228. Springer, Heidelberg (2015). https://doi.org/10.1007/978-3-662-46800-5_9

[Nis17] NIST: Post-quantum cryptography standardization (2017). https://csrc.nist.gov/projects/post-quantum-cryptography

[Pra62] Prange, E.: The use of information sets in decoding cyclic codes. IRE Trans. Inf. Theory **8**(5), 5–9 (1962)

[S19]   Personal communication with Damien Stehlé

[Sen11] Sendrier, N.: Decoding one out of many. In: Yang, B.-Y. (ed.) PQCrypto 2011. LNCS, vol. 7071, pp. 51–67. Springer, Heidelberg (2011). https://doi.org/10.1007/978-3-642-25405-5_4

[Sho04] Shoup, V.: Sequences of games: a tool for taming complexity in security proofs. IACR Cryptology ePrint Archive, 2004:332 (2004)

[Ste88] Stern, J.: A method for finding codewords of small weight. In: Cohen, G., Wolfmann, J. (eds.) Coding Theory 1988. LNCS, vol. 388, pp. 106–113. Springer, Heidelberg (1989). https://doi.org/10.1007/BFb0019850

[Zha12] Zhandry, M.: How to construct quantum random functions. In: Proceedings of the 2012 IEEE 53rd Annual Symposium on Foundations of Computer Science. FOCS 2012, pp. 679–687. IEEE Computer Society, Washington, DC (2012)

Cryptanalysis and Concrete Security

Faster Cofactorization with ECM Using Mixed Representations

Cyril Bouvier and Laurent Imbert$^{(\boxtimes)}$

LIRMM, CNRS, Univ. Montpellier, Montpellier, France
{cyril.bouvier,laurent.imbert}@lirmm.fr

Abstract. This paper introduces a novel implementation of the elliptic curve factoring method specifically designed for medium-size integers such as those arising by billions in the cofactorization step of the Number Field Sieve. In this context, our algorithm requires fewer modular multiplications than any other publicly available implementation. The main ingredients are: the use of batches of primes, fast point tripling, optimal double-base decompositions and Lucas chains, and a good mix of Edwards and Montgomery representations.

Keywords: Elliptic curve method · Cofactorization · Double-base representation · Twisted Edwards curve · Montgomery curve · CADO-NFS

1 Introduction

The Elliptic Curve Method (ECM) invented by H. W. Lenstra Jr. in 1985 [18] is probably the most versatile algorithm for integer factorization. It remains the asymptotically fastest known method for finding medium-size prime factors of large integers. The 50 largest factors found with ECM have 68 to 83 digits; they are recorded in [26]. ECM is also a core ingredient of the Number Field Sieve (NFS) [17], the most efficient general purpose algorithm for factoring "hard" composite integers of the form $N = pq$ with $p, q \approx \sqrt{N}$. ECM is equally essential in all NFS variants for computing discrete logarithms over finite fields. In NFS and its variants, ECM is used as a subroutine of the sieving phase. It is also employed in the descent phase for discrete logarithms computations. Together with other factoring algorithms such as the Quadratic Sieve, $p - 1$ or $p + 1$, it is extensively used in the so-called cofactorization step. This important step consists of breaking into primes billions of composite integers of a hundred-ish bits that are known to have no small prime factor. The time spent in ECM for these medium-size, yet hard to factor integers is therefore substantial. For example, with CADO-NFS [24], the cofactorization time for a 200-digit RSA number represents between 15% and 22% of the sieving phase. According to [9], cofactorization represented roughly one third of the sieving phase and 5% to 20% of the total wall-clock time in the current world-record factorization of a 768-bit RSA number [16]. For larger factorization or discrete logarithm computations,

© International Association for Cryptologic Research 2020
A. Kiayias et al. (Eds.): PKC 2020, LNCS 12111, pp. 483–504, 2020.
https://doi.org/10.1007/978-3-030-45388-6_17

Bos and Kleinjung anticipate that the time spent in cofactorization, notably ECM, becomes more and more important [9].

Since its invention, ECM has been the subject of many improvements [27]. It has been shown that the choice of "good" elliptic curve representations and parameters plays an important role in both the efficiency of ECM and its probability of success. Historically, Lenstra considered short Weierstrass curves together with Jacobian coordinates. Then, Montgomery introduced a new model for elliptic curves together with a system of coordinates perfectly suited to ECM [22]. Montgomery curves have been the best option for about twenty five years. This setting is used in GMP-ECM [28], a state-of-the-art implementation of ECM. More than twenty five years later, building over the works of Edwards [13], Bernstein et al. proposed an efficient implementation of ECM using twisted Edwards curves [4]. Yet, there is no clear general answer to the question of which curve model is best suited to ECM.

In this work, we propose an algorithm specifically designed for the medium-size integers that occur in the cofactorization step of NFS. We extend ideas from Dixon and Lenstra [12] and from Bos and Kleinjung [9] by processing the scalar of the first stage of ECM by batches of primes. Unlike [9] and [15] which only consider NAF decompositions for these batches, we take advantage of the fastest known tripling formula on twisted Edwards curves [6] together with optimal double-base decompositions. Finally, we also use Lucas chains by exploiting the birational equivalence between twisted Edwards curves and Montgomery curves and by switching from one model to the other when appropriate. Our algorithm performs fewer modular multiplications than any other publicly available implementation. Our results are implemented in the CADO-NFS software [24]. Updates and more detailed data are available online at http://eco.lirmm.net/double-base_ECM/.

2   Preliminaries

In this section, we present the basics of ECM. Then we recall the definitions of Montgomery curves and twisted Edwards curves together with the associated point representations and arithmetic operations.

In order to compare the cost of the different elliptic operations and scalar multiplication algorithms, we count the number of modular multiplications ($\mathbf{M}$) and squarings ($\mathbf{S}$). To ease the comparisons, we assume that both operations take the same time (i.e. $1\mathbf{S} = 1\mathbf{M}$) as in other ECM implementation papers [4,9,15].[1]

2.1   The Elliptic Curve Method

Lenstra's elliptic curve method [18] is often viewed as a generalization of Pollard's $p-1$ algorithm in the sense that it exploits the possible smoothness of the order

---

[1] This claim is also supported by our experiments with CADO-NFS modular arithmetic functions for 64-bit, 96-bit and 128-bit integers.

of an elliptic curve defined over an unknown prime divisor of a given composite integer N.

ECM starts by choosing an elliptic curve E over $\mathbb{Z}/N\mathbb{Z}$ and a point P on E. In practice, one usually selects a "random" curve $E_{\mathbb{Q}} : y^2 = x^3 + ax + b$ over $\mathbb{Q}$ together with a nontorsion point P' on $E_{\mathbb{Q}}$, and then reduces the curve parameters a, b and the coordinates of P' modulo N to get E and P. Unlike elliptic curves defined over finite fields, the set of points $E(\mathbb{Z}/N\mathbb{Z})$ contains non-affine points that are different from the point at infinity, i.e., projective points $(X : Y : Z)$ with $Z \neq 0$ and Z not invertible modulo N. For these "special" points, $\gcd(N, Z)$ gives a factor of N. The purpose of ECM is thus to produce these "special" points with a reasonably high probability and at reasonably low cost.

Let p be an unknown prime dividing N, and let E_p be the curve defined over $\mathbb{F}_p$ by reducing the equation of E modulo p. The goal of ECM is to produce (virtually) the point at infinity on E_p while carrying-out all the computations on E. ECM does so by computing $Q = [k]P \in E$ for a fixed scalar k. It achieves its goal whenever $\#E_p$ divides k. To that end, k is chosen such that, $\#E_p \mid k$ whenever $\#E_p$ is B_1-powersmooth for a carefully chosen bound B_1. (An integer is B-powersmooth if none of the prime powers dividing that integer is greater than B.) Most current implementations use $k = \mathrm{lcm}(2, 3, 4, \ldots, B_1)$ as it offers an excellent balance between efficiency and probability of success. For $B_1 \in \mathbb{N}$, we have:

$$k = \mathrm{lcm}(2, 3, 4, \ldots, B_1) = \prod_{p \text{ prime } \leq B_1} p^{\lfloor \log_p(B_1) \rfloor} \tag{1}$$

In the following, the multiset composed of all primes p less than or equal to B_1, each occurring exactly $\lfloor \log_p(B_1) \rfloor$ times, is denoted $\mathcal{M}_{B_1}$.

The approach described so far is often referred to as "stage 1". There is a "stage 2" continuation for ECM which takes as input an integer bound $B_2 \geq B_1$ and succeeds if the order $\#E_p$ is B_1-powersmooth except for one prime factor which may lie between B_1 and B_2.

In this article, we focus on the use of ECM as a subroutine of the NFS algorithm. In this case, the values of B_1 and B_2 are relatively small and usually hardcoded. For example, in CADO-NFS [24], the ECM computations are done with a predefined set of values for B_1 and B_2 (some possible values for B_1 are 105, 601 and 3517). In this context, it may be worthwhile to perform some precomputations on the hardcoded values.

2.2 Montgomery Curves

Historically, the elliptic curve method was implemented using short Weierstrass curves. Montgomery curves were described in [22] to improve the efficiency of ECM by reducing the cost of elliptic operations. Montgomery curves are used in many implementations of ECM, for example in GMP-ECM [28], the most-widely used ECM implementation.

Definition 1 (Montgomery curve). *Let K be a field and $A, B \in K$ such that $B(A^2 - 4) \neq 0$. A Montgomery curve, denoted $E_{A,B}^M$, is an elliptic curve whose affine points are all $(x, y) \in K^2$ such that*

$$By^2 = x^3 + Ax^2 + x. \tag{2}$$

In practice, projective coordinates $(X : Y : Z)$ are used to avoid field inversions. Montgomery proposed to drop the Y coordinate, performing the computations on X and Z only. In the so-called XZ coordinate system, a point is denoted $(X : : Z)$. An immediate consequence is that one cannot distinguish between a point and its opposite. This implies that, given two distinct points on the curve, one can compute their sum, only if one knows their difference. This new operation is called a *differential addition*.

As seen in Table 1, XZ coordinates on Montgomery curves allow for very fast point doubling and differential addition. However, the condition imposed by the use of a differential addition forces to use specific scalar multiplication algorithms (see Sect. 3.3).

Note that the doubling formula is often accounted for $2\mathbf{M} + 2\mathbf{S}$ plus one multiplication by a small constant. Yet, this operation count is relevant only when the curve coefficient A is chosen such that $(A+2)/4$ is small. In Table 1 we report a cost of $5\mathbf{M}$ for dDBL because our choice of parameterization prevents us from assigning any particular value to $(A + 2)/4$. We give more details in Sect. 2.5.

Table 1. Arithmetic cost of elliptic operations for Montgomery curves in XZ coordinates under the assumption $1\mathbf{S} = 1\mathbf{M}$

Elliptic Operation	Notation	Input	$\rightarrow$	Output	Cost
Differential Addition	dADD	XZ	$\rightarrow$	XZ	$4\mathbf{M} + 2\mathbf{S} = 6\mathbf{M}$
Doubling	dDBL	XZ	$\rightarrow$	XZ	$3\mathbf{M} + 2\mathbf{S} = 5\mathbf{M}$

2.3   Twisted Edwards Curves

In [13] Edwards introduced a new normal form for elliptic curves which, among other advantages, benefit from fast elliptic operations. These curves have been generalized by Bernstein et al. [2]. A new coordinate system with a faster group law was introduced in [14], and their usage in ECM was considered in [3,4].

Definition 2 (Twisted Edwards curve). *Let K be a field and let $a, d \in K$ such that $ad(a - d) \neq 0$. A twisted Edwards curve, denoted $E_{a,d}^E$, is an elliptic curve whose affine points are all $(x, y) \in K^2$ such that*

$$ax^2 + y^2 = 1 + dx^2y^2. \tag{3}$$

In practice, the fastest formulas are obtained using a combination of three coordinates systems denoted projective, completed and extended. Input and output points are always represented in extended or projective coordinates, whereas completed coordinates are mainly used as an internal format. In the following, we shall use the best known formula from [14] for point doubling and point addition on twisted Edwards curves. Besides, an important feature of twisted Edwards curves is the existence of an efficient formula for point tripling [6].

In this article, we only consider twisted Edwards curves with $a = -1$. These curves allow for faster arithmetic and enjoy good torsion properties with regard to their use in ECM [1]. (See Sect. 2.5 for more details.) The input and output formats as well as the costs of the different elliptic operations that will be considered in the following are summarized in Table 2.

Table 2. Arithmetic cost of elliptic operations for twisted Edwards curves with $a = -1$ under the assumption $1S = 1M$

Elliptic Operation	Notation	Input	$\rightarrow$	Output	Cost
Addition	ADD_{comp}	ext.	$\rightarrow$	comp.	$4M$
	ADD	ext.	$\rightarrow$	proj.	$7M$
	ADD_ε	ext.	$\rightarrow$	ext.	$8M$
Doubling	DBL	ext. or proj.	$\rightarrow$	proj.	$3M + 4S = 7M$
	DBL_ε	ext. or proj.	$\rightarrow$	ext.	$4M + 4S = 8M$
Tripling	TPL	ext. or proj.	$\rightarrow$	proj.	$9M + 3S = 12M$
	TPL_ε	ext. or proj.	$\rightarrow$	ext.	$11M + 3S = 14M$

Contrary to Montgomery curves, twisted Edwards curves have a true elliptic addition. Hence the scalar multiplication can be computed using every generic algorithm available.

2.4   The Best of Both Worlds

The best choice between Montgomery and Edwards curves for implementing the first stage of ECM depends on many parameters on top of which are the size of k (which depends on B_1), the memory available to store precomputed values, and the scalar multiplication algorithm used to compute $[k]P$. In this article, we exploit the best of both worlds by mixing twisted Edwards and Montgomery representations. We exploit a result from [2] which states that every twisted Edwards curve is birationally equivalent over its base field to a Montgomery curve. To the best of our knowledge, mixing Edwards and Montgomery representations was first suggested in [10] to speed-up arithmetic on elliptic curves in the x-coordinate-only setting. More recently, the idea has also been employed in the SIDH context [19].

Let K be a field with $\text{char}(K) \neq 2$. According to [2, Theorem 3.2], every twisted Edwards curve $E_{a,d}^E$ defined over K is birationally equivalent over K to the Montgomery curve $E_{A,B}^M$, where $A = 2(a+d)(a-d)$ and $B = 4/(a-d)$. The map

$$(x, y) \mapsto ((1+y)/(1-y), (1+y)/(1-y)x) \tag{4}$$

is a birational equivalence from $E_{a,d}^E$ to $E_{A,B}^M$. (see [2, page 4] for a proof.) Using this map, we define a partial addition formula, denoted ADD_M, which takes two points in extended coordinates on a twisted Edwards curve and computes their sum in XZ coordinates on the equivalent Montgomery curve. We express ADD_M as the composition of the group law on the completed twisted Edwards curve $\overline{E}_{a,d}^E$ and a partial conversion map, where

$$\overline{E}_{a,d}^E = \{((X:Z),(Y:T)) \in \mathbf{P}^1 \times \mathbf{P}^1 : aX^2T^2 + Y^2Z^2 = Z^2T^2 + dX^2Y^2\}.$$

(See [8] for more details on completed twisted Edwards curves and [3] for their usage in the ECM context.)

Given two points in extended coordinates on a twisted Edwards curve, the elliptic operation denoted ADD_{comp} computes their sum in completed coordinates $((X:Z),(Y:T))$ in $4\mathbf{M}$. Then, given that point in completed coordinates, one gets a representative in extended coordinates in another $4\mathbf{M}$ using the map

$$((X:Z),(Y:T)) \mapsto (XT:YZ:ZT:XY). \tag{5}$$

If only projective coordinates are needed, one simply omits the product XY. Observe that in the addition formulas on twisted Edwards curves introduced in [14] and recorded in Bernstein and Lange's Explicit Formula Database [7], the completed coordinates of the sum correspond to the four intermediate values $((E:G),(H:F))$.

For $X \neq 0$, the composition of the maps (4) and (5) is well defined. The map

$$((X:Z),(Y:T)) \longmapsto (T+Y:Z(T+Y)/X:T-Y) \tag{6}$$

sends points on a completed twisted Edwards curve with $X \neq 0$ to projective points on the equivalent Montgomery curve. For XZ coordinates, one simply omits the second coordinate:

$$((X:Z),(Y:T)) \longmapsto (T+Y::T-Y). \tag{7}$$

Therefore, when defined, the operation ADD_M, which takes as input two points of a twisted Edwards curves in extended coordinates and computes their sum on the equivalent Montgomery curves in XZ coordinates, costs only $4\mathbf{M}$ (see Table 3).

Let us now focus on the points for which (6) is not defined. The completed points with $X = 0$ correspond on $E_{a,d}^E$ to $(0, -1)$, the affine point of order 2, or $(0, 1)$ the point at infinity. Using (7), the completed point $((0:1),(-1,1))$ of order 2 is mapped to the point $(0::1)$ of order 2 on the Montgomery curve. In this case, the mapping to XZ coordinates is thus well defined.

However, the map (7) sends the completed point at infinity $((0 : 1), (1 : 1))$ to the point $(2 : : 0)$ on the Montgomery curve, which is different from $(0 : 1 : 0)$, the point at infinity on $E_{A,B}^M$. Nevertheless, in our context, using the point $(2 : : 0)$ in place of the point at infinity $(0 : : 0)$ is sufficient. Indeed, for all prime p dividing N, if the computations on the Edwards curve produce the point at infinity modulo p, what is important is that the map (7) returns a point on the equivalent Montgomery curve with $Z \equiv 0 \pmod{p}$. From the formulas for dDBL and dADD, it is easy to see that the remaining computations on the Montgomery curve also produce a point with $Z \equiv 0 \pmod{p}$. We have thus preserved the fact that p should divide the greatest common divisor between N and the Z-coordinate of the final point.

Table 3. New elliptic operation to switch from twisted Edwards curves to Montgomery curves

Elliptic Operation	Notation	Input $\rightarrow$ Output	Cost
Add & Switch	$\mathrm{ADD_M}$	Twisted Edwards ext. $\rightarrow$ Montgomery XZ	**4M**

Note that after an $\mathrm{ADD_M}$, moving back to the twisted Edwards curve is not possible since the map (7) is not invertible, as the Y coordinate on the Montgomery curve is "lost". Nevertheless, as will be explained in Sect. 3, we easily circumvent this obstacle by processing all the computations on the twisted Edwards curve before moving to the equivalent Montgomery curve for finalizing the scalar multiplication. Therefore, we never need to convert a point from XZ Montgomery back to the equivalent twisted Edwards curve.

2.5 Parameterization

In order to improve the probability of success of the ECM algorithm, we need to be able to generate curves with good torsion properties. Infinite families of curves with a rational or elliptic parametrization are used in the context of ECM to generate many different curves. Many of the best families for twisted Edwards curves have $a = -1$. So, restricting ourselves to twisted Edwards curves with $a = -1$ not only improves the arithmetic cost but also allows us to use curves with good torsion properties [1].

In practice, we use the parameterization from [3, Theorem 5.4] to generate a twisted Edwards curve with $a = -1$. We only need to compute the coefficients of the starting point in extended coordinates as the curve parameter d is never used in the formulæ. For the equivalent Montgomery curve, we solely compute the curve coefficient A since B is never used in the formulæ.

Using the parametrization from [3, Theorem 5.4] prevents us from choosing the curve coefficient A of the associated Montgomery curve. By choosing A such that $(A + 2)/4$ is small, we could have replaced, in the doubling formula, a multiplication by a multiplication by a small constant. In our context, i.e., using medium-size integers, the arithmetic gain is not significant. Thus, we favored better torsion properties over a slightly lower theoretical arithmetic cost.

3   Scalar Multiplication

After choosing a smoothness bound B_1 and a point P on an elliptic curve E, the core of the first stage of ECM consists of multiplying P by the scalar

$$k = \mathrm{lcm}(2, 3, 4, \ldots, B_1) = \prod_{p \text{ prime } \leq B_1} p^{\lfloor \log_p(B_1) \rfloor}$$

An elementary algorithm for computing $[k]P$ thus consists of performing, for each prime $p \leq B_1$, exactly $\lfloor \log_p(B_1) \rfloor$ scalar multiplications by p. These scalar multiplications may be computed using any addition chain compatible with the chosen curve E. If one uses the traditional binary addition chain, the number of point doublings depends on the bitlength of p, whereas the number of point additions is determined by its Hamming weight $w(p)$. Reducing the number of point additions by lowering the density of non-zero digits in the representation of the scalar is the core of many efficient scalar multiplication algorithms.

In the ECM context, the scalar k is entirely determined by the smoothness bound B_1. We may therefore derive much more efficient algorithms for computing $[k]P$. For example, instead of considering the primes p_i one at a time, one may multiply some of them together such that the weight of the product $w(\prod_i p_i)$ is lower than the sum of the individual weights $\sum_i w(p_i)$. This idea was first proposed by Dixon and Lenstra [12]. As an example, they give three primes $p_1 = 1028107$, $p_2 = 1030639$, $p_3 = 1097101$, of respective Hamming weights 10, 16 and 11, such that their product has Hamming weight 8. Beyond this example, the idea is advantageous only if one can find "good" recombinations for all the prime factors of k. Dixon and Lenstra used a greedy approach to find combination of primes by triples and managed to divide the overall number of point additions by roughly three. At that time, finding such a partition of the multiset $\mathcal{M}_{B_1}$ by triples was the best they could hope for. Surprisingly, they did not consider signed-digit representations to further reduce the overall cost. Clearly, their approach becomes unpractical for larger B_1 values and/or more general prime recombinations. Twenty years after Dixon and Lenstra's paper, Bos and Kleinjung managed to generalize the idea to arbitrary recombinations of primes and to extend its applicability to much larger B_1 values [9]. Considering all possible partitions of $\mathcal{M}_{B_1}$ being totally out of reach, they opted for the opposite strategy. A huge quantity of integers with very low density of non-zero digits in NAF form was first tested for smoothness. Then, among those integers that were B_1-powersmooth, a greedy algorithm was used to find a partition of $\mathcal{M}_{B_1}$ such that the cost of the resulting sequence of operations was minimal. For $B_1 = 256$, the best chain found led to a scalar multiplication algorithm which require 361 doublings and only 38 additions. The decomposition of $k = \mathrm{lcm}(2, \ldots, 256)$ into 15 batches of prime-products and their NAF expansions[2] are given in Table 4.

---

[2] You may have observed that two of the given expansions do not satisfy the non-adjacent form, with two consecutive ones in their most significant positions. This is simply because evaluating $3P$ as $4P - P$ is more expensive than $2P + P$.

Table 4. An example of the best chain found for $B_1 = 256$ (see [9])

Batches of prime-products	NAF expansion	Cost
$23 \cdot 89$	$2^{11} - 2^0$	86M
$83 \cdot 197$	$2^{14} - 2^5 - 2^0$	115M
$191 \cdot 193$	$2^{15} + 2^{12} - 2^0$	122M
$13 \cdot 19 \cdot 199$	$2^{15} + 2^{14} + 2^0$	122M
$5 \cdot 13 \cdot 37 \cdot 109$	$2^{18} + 2^0$	135M
$3^2 \cdot 7 \cdot 53 \cdot 157$	$2^{19} - 2^6 - 2^0$	150M
$103 \cdot 137 \cdot 223$	$2^{21} + 2^{20} + 2^{10} + 2^0$	172M
$5 \cdot 61 \cdot 149 \cdot 179$	$2^{23} - 2^{18} + 2^{13} - 2^0$	186M
$3 \cdot 5 \cdot 29 \cdot 43 \cdot 113 \cdot 127$	$2^{28} - 2^0$	205M
$3 \cdot 7 \cdot 11 \cdot 167 \cdot 173 \cdot 181$	$2^{30} + 2^{27} + 2^{11} + 2^0$	235M
$3 \cdot 47 \cdot 59 \cdot 67 \cdot 73 \cdot 211$	$2^{33} - 2^{22} - 2^{19} + 2^8 + 2^6 - 2^0$	272M
$11 \cdot 31 \cdot 79 \cdot 101 \cdot 131 \cdot 241$	$2^{36} + 2^{34} + 2^{18} + 2^2 + 2^0$	285M
$17 \cdot 107 \cdot 139 \cdot 163 \cdot 229 \cdot 233$	$2^{41} - 2^{24} - 2^{13} - 2^9 - 2^0$	320M
$41 \cdot 71 \cdot 97 \cdot 151 \cdot 227 \cdot 239 \cdot 251$	$2^{49} + 2^{44} + 2^{36} + 2^{32} - 2^3 - 2^0$	383M
2^8	2^8	56M
Total		2844M

In the following, we shall use the term "block" to denote a batch of prime-products such as those given in Table 4. For each block, Dixon and Lenstra simply used addition chains, whereas Bos and Kleinjung took advantage of addition-subtraction chains through NAF decompositions. In this work, we consider more general decompositions in order to further reduce the overall cost. More precisely, we use three types of representations: double-base expansions, double-base chains (which contain NAF) and a subset of Lucas addition chains.

As an example, let us consider the primes $p_1 = 100003$, $p_2 = 100019$ and $p_3 = 109831$. Using the NAF decomposition, computing $[p_1]P$ requires 9 DBL, 7 DBL_ε, 6 ADD and 1 ADD_ε, resulting in 169**M**. Similarly, $[p_2]P$ and $[p_3]P$ require 169**M** and 168**M** respectively. The NAF representation of their product only requires 447**M**, i.e. 59 fewer multiplications than the cost of considering p_1, p_2 and p_3 independently.

Let us now consider the following double-base representations of the same three primes. We have:

$$100003 = 2^{15}3^1 + 2^9 3^1 + 2^6 3^1 - 2^3 3^1 - 2^2 - 1 \tag{8}$$

$$100019 = 2^{15}3^1 + 2^9 3^1 + 2^6 3^1 - 2^2 3^1 - 1 \tag{9}$$

$$109831 = 2^{12}3^3 - 2^8 3^1 + 2^3 - 1 \tag{10}$$

Using (8), one may thus compute $[p_1]P$ with 10 DBL, 5 DBL_ε, 1 TPL, 4 ADD and 1 ADD_ε for a total cost of 158 **M**. Using (9) and (10), $[p_2]P$ and $[p_3]P$

requires 150**M** and 145**M** respectively. On twisted Edwards curves, the usage of triplings is thus already advantageous. Yet, the following double-base chain for their product

$$(((((2^2 3^1 + 1)2^6 3^1 - 1)2^{14} 3^3 - 1)2^4 3^1 - 1)2^4 3^3 - 1)2^4 3^1 - 1, \qquad (11)$$

leads to a chain for computing $[p_1 p_2 p_3]P$ with 28 DBL, 6 DBL$_\varepsilon$, 10 TPL, 6 ADD and 1 ADD$_\varepsilon$, for a total cost of 407**M**. This represents an extra 40**M** saving compared to the NAF-based approach.

In the next sections, we detail the generation of double-base expansions and double-base chains (which includes NAF) that are both compatible with twisted Edwards curves. We also present our strategy for generating a subset of Lucas chains for use with Montgomery curves.

3.1 Generation of Double-Base Expansions

Let n be a positive integer, and let α, β be two pairwise integers. A double-base expansion of n can be seen as a partition of n into distinct parts of the form $\alpha^a \beta^b$. In this work, we solely consider the special case $(\alpha, \beta) = (2, 3)$ and we extend the usual notion of partition by allowing the parts to be either positive or negative, such that

$$n = \sum_{i=0}^{m} \pm 2^{d_i} 3^{t_i}, \qquad (12)$$

where $(d_i, t_i) \neq (d_j, t_j)$ for every $0 \leq i < j \leq m$. Following the usual convention for integer partitions, we assume that the parts form a non-increasing[3] sequence so that $|2^{d_i} 3^{t_i}| > |2^{d_j} 3^{t_j}|$ for all $0 \leq i < j \leq m$. The length of a double-base expansion is equal to the number of parts in (12). Examples of double-base expansions of lengths 6, 5 and 4 respectively are given in (8), (9) and (10).

Given a double-base expansion for n as in (12), one can compute $[n]P$ with $D = \max_i d_i$ doublings, $T = \max_i t_i$ triplings and at most m additions using an algorithm by Meloni and Hasan [23]. Their algorithm is inspired by Yao's method [25] and requires the evaluation and storage of at most m elliptic curve points.

In order to limit the amount of additional storage in the resulting algorithms, we generated double-base expansions with at most 4 terms, i.e. for m varying from 1 to 3. In practice, the memory requirements for the resulting algorithms are very low (see Sect. 5) and comparable to Bos and Kleinjung's low storage setting.

In fact, setting such a low value for the maximal length of double-base expansions was necessary to reduce computational workload. Indeed, without any restrictions, the total number of double-base chains with $m + 1$ terms and such that $D \leq D_{\max}$ and $T \leq T_{\max}$ is equal to

---

[3] In this case a decreasing sequence since the parts are distincts.

$$2^{m+1}\binom{(D_{\max} + 1)(T_{\max} + 1)}{m + 1}.$$

In our context, it was clearly more appropriate to let D and T cover larger ranges than to increase m. In Table 5, we give the parameters for m, D and T that we considered.

A few observations can be made to avoid generating the same double-base expansion more than once. First, notice that a double-base expansion for n immediately provides a double-base expansion for $-n$ by switching the sign of all the parts in (12). Hence, by imposing the sign of one of the terms, we generated only double-base expansions for positive integers; hence dividing the work effort by a factor two. We also noticed that a double-base expansion for n is easily converted into a double-base expansion for any integer of the form $n \times 2^a 3^b$, by adding a (resp. b) to each d_i (resp. t_i). Therefore, we only generated double-base expansions whose terms have no common factors. Given $D > 0$ and $T > 0$, the number of double-base expansions of length $m + 1$ satisfying the above conditions can be computed exactly using a classical inclusion-exclusion principle. For completeness, we give the exact formula in Appendix A. In Table 5, we give the total number of double-base expansions that we generated for $m = 1, 2, 3$ and different intervals for D and T. For each double-base expansion, we tested the corresponding integer for 2^{13}-powersmoothness. We then evaluated the cost of Meloni and Hasan's scalar multiplication algorithm for those remaining double-base expansions. Unlike NAF decompositions, the double-base number system is highly redundant. For each value of m, we removed duplicates by keeping only double-base expansions of minimal cost. Yet, there might still exist duplicates for different values of m. Finally, we observed that it is always faster to process the powers of 2 after switching to Montgomery XZ coordinates. Thus, in order to reduce memory and speed-up the combination step (see Sect. 4), we filtered out all blocks corresponding to even integers. In Table 5, the column #db-exp gives the numbers of different double-base expansions that we generated for each value of m, the column #pow.smooth is the number of those expansions which corresponded to B_1-powersmooth integers, and the column #uniq (odd) accounts only for expansions of minimal costs corresponding to odd integers.

As seen in Table 5, for $m = 3$, we had to drastically reduce the upper bounds on D and T. Indeed, allowing D and T to span the intervals of values used for $m < 3$ would have required the generation of around $1.84 \cdot 10^{14}$ expansions. Nonetheless, in order to generate more integers of potential interest, we considered a subset of double-base expansions, namely double-base chains.

Table 5. Data on generated double-base expansions for $B_1 = 2^{13}$

m	D	T	#db-exp	#pow.smooth	#uniq (odd)	CPU time
1	$0 - 255$	$0 - 127$	$1.30 \cdot 10^5$	$1.15 \cdot 10^3$	$1.06 \cdot 10^3$	0 h
2	$0 - 255$	$0 - 127$	$6.37 \cdot 10^9$	$4.09 \cdot 10^5$	$2.97 \cdot 10^5$	3 h
3	$0 - 128$	$0 - 64$	$3.04 \cdot 10^{12}$	$1.64 \cdot 10^8$	$9.04 \cdot 10^7$	1048 h
Total			$3.04 \cdot 10^{12}$	$1.64 \cdot 10^8$		1051 h

3.2 Generation of Double-Base Chains

A double-base chain for n is a double-base expansion as in (12) with divisibility conditions on the parts. More precisely, we impose that $2^{d_i}3^{t_i} \succeq 2^{d_{i+1}}3^{t_{i+1}}$ for $i \geq 0$, where $\succeq$ denotes the divisibility order, i.e. $x \succeq y \iff y|x$. All the double-base expansions given in the previous example are in fact double-base chains. The use of double-base chains for elliptic curve scalar multiplication was first introduced by Dimitrov et al. [11].

Given a double-base chain for n, one can compute $[n]P$ with m additions, $D = d_0$ doublings and $T = t_0$ triplings using a natural decomposition à la Horner as in (11). Unlike double-base expansions, the subsequent scalar multiplication algorithm does not require any additional storage.

The divisibility condition on the parts allows us to generate double-base chains for much larger values for m, D and T. As for double-base expansions, we only generated double-base chains for positive integers by fixing the sign of the first part $2^{d_0}3^{t_0}$. We also restricted our generation to double-base chains whose terms have no common factors, i.e. such that the smallest part $2^{d_m}3^{t_m} = \pm 1$. Under these conditions, the number of double-base chains with exactly D doublings, T triplings and m additions is given by:

$$2^m \sum_{i=0}^{m-1} (-1)^{m-i+1} \binom{m}{i+1} \binom{D+i}{D} \binom{T+i}{T}.$$

In Table 6 we give the number of double-base chains that we generated for different set of parameters m, D and T. Observe that double-base chains with $T = 0$ correspond to NAF expansions. In total, we generated more than $2.57 \cdot 10^{13}$ double-base chains, among which $2.29 \cdot 10^{10}$ corresponded to B_1-powersmooth integers, in approximately 9000 CPU hours.

3.3 Generation of Lucas Chains

As seen in Sect. 2.2, Montgomery curves only admit a differential addition. Therefore the previous constructions (double-base expansions and chains) cannot be used to perform scalar multiplication. Instead, one uses Lucas chains.

Let n be a positive integer. A Lucas chain of length ℓ for n is a sequence of integers $(c_0, c_1, \ldots, c_\ell)$ such that $c_0 = 1$, $c_\ell = n$, and for every $1 \leq i \leq \ell$, either

Table 6. Data on generated double-base chains with smoothness bound 2^{13}

m	D	T	#db-chains	#pow.smooth	#uniq (odd)	CPU time
1	$0-255$	$0-127$	$6.55 \cdot 10^4$	$4.35 \cdot 10^2$	$3.93 \cdot 10^2$	0 h
2	$0-255$	$0-127$	$1.09 \cdot 10^9$	$3.82 \cdot 10^4$	$2.82 \cdot 10^4$	1 h
3	$0-220$	$0-110$	$3.41 \cdot 10^{12}$	$2.67 \cdot 10^6$	$1.54 \cdot 10^6$	1653 h
3	$221-255$	0	$7.84 \cdot 10^6$	0	0	0 h
4	$0-75$	$0-40$	$3.20 \cdot 10^{12}$	$1.43 \cdot 10^8$	$5.99 \cdot 10^7$	1013 h
4	$76-255$	0	$2.73 \cdot 10^9$	$5.46 \cdot 10^2$	$3.12 \cdot 10^2$	1 h
5	$0-50$	$0-10$	$2.86 \cdot 10^{11}$	$1.86 \cdot 10^9$	$4.25 \cdot 10^8$	68 h
5	$51-255$	0	$2.76 \cdot 10^{11}$	$2.98 \cdot 10^5$	$2.06 \cdot 10^5$	121 h
6	$0-25$	$0-10$	$2.35 \cdot 10^{11}$	$1.68 \cdot 10^{10}$	$9.04 \cdot 10^8$	171 h
6	$26-200$	0	$5.27 \cdot 10^{12}$	$3.01 \cdot 10^7$	$1.33 \cdot 10^7$	2204 h
7	$0-115$	0	$5.61 \cdot 10^{12}$	$3.68 \cdot 10^8$	$1.19 \cdot 10^8$	1596 h
8	$0-80$	0	$7.42 \cdot 10^{12}$	$3.66 \cdot 10^9$	$9.09 \cdot 10^8$	2240 h
Total			$2.57 \cdot 10^{13}$	$2.29 \cdot 10^{10}$		9068 h

it exists $j < i$ such that $c_i = 2c_j$ (doubling step), or there exist $j_0, j_1, j_d < i$ such that $c_i = c_{j_0} + c_{j_1}$ and $c_{j_d} = \pm(c_{j_0} - c_{j_1})$ (addition step).

Using a Lucas chain for n, $[n]P$ can be obtained by computing $[c_i]P$, for $1 \le i \le \ell$. When an addition step is encountered, the definition ensures that the difference of the two operands is already available. In general, Lucas chains are longer than binary, NAF, or double-base chains. Nevertheless, they sometimes lead to fast scalar multiplication algorithms since the cost of a differential addition is smaller than that of a plain addition.

The PRAC algorithm proposed by Montgomery [21] provides an efficient way to generate Lucas chains for any given integer n. It works by applying rules to a set of 3 points A, B and C, starting with $A = [2]P$, $B = C = P$. The rule to apply is chosen from a set of 9 rules based on two auxiliary integers d and e, starting with $d = n - \lfloor n/\phi \rfloor$ and $e = 2\lfloor n/\phi \rfloor - n$, where ϕ is the golden ratio. The two following invariants are maintained throughout the algorithm: $\pm C = A - B$ and $[n]P = [d]A + [e]B$.

We produced Lucas chains by generating all possible combinations using up to 13 PRAC rules. Observe that the nine rules from PRAC are not uniform regarding the type and number of curve operations they gather. For example, rule #2 consists of 2 doublings and 2 additions, whereas rule #4 only performs 1 addition. Consequently, the exhaustive generation of PRAC chains of length up to 13 allowed us to generate integers of size up to 26 bits. As there was lots of duplicates, we only kept the best Lucas chains for all odd integers before testing for smoothness. Data on the Lucas chains that we generated is given in Table 7.

Table 7. Data on generated Lucas chains for $B_1 = 2^{13}$. Only Lucas chains correspond-ing to odd integers were considered

#PRAC rules	#Lucas chains	#uniq	#pow.smooth	CPU time
13	$2.08 \cdot 10^{19}$	$1.25 \cdot 10^7$	$4.63 \cdot 10^6$	741 h

4   Combination of Blocks for ECM Stage 1

Let $\mathcal{B}$ be the set of all blocks generated with one of the method described in the previous section. For each block $b \in \mathcal{B}$, we define $n(b)$ as the integer associated to b, and $\mathcal{M}_b$ as the multiset composed of the prime factors (counted with multiplicity) of $n(b)$. We also define the arithmetic cost of b, denoted $\mathrm{cost}(b)$, as the sum of the costs of the elliptic operations used to compute the scalar multiplication by $n(b)$ using the algorithm associated to b. The arithmetic cost per bit, denoted $\mathrm{acpb}(b)$, is defined as $\mathrm{cost}(b)/\log_2(n(b))$.

By extension, we use the same notations for a set of blocks. Let $\mathcal{A} \subset \mathcal{B}$. Then $n(\mathcal{A}) = \prod_{b \in \mathcal{A}} n(b)$, $\mathcal{M}_{\mathcal{A}} = \bigcup_{b \in \mathcal{A}} \mathcal{M}_b$, $\mathrm{acpb}(\mathcal{A}) = \mathrm{cost}(\mathcal{A})/\log_2(n(\mathcal{A}))$. For the arithmetic cost, we need to take into account the switch from the twisted Edwards curve to the Montgomery curve, if necessary. Thus

$$\mathrm{cost}(\mathcal{A}) = \sum_{b \in \mathcal{A}} \mathrm{cost}(b) + \delta(\mathcal{A}) \underbrace{(\mathrm{cost}(\mathrm{ADD_M}) - \mathrm{cost}(\mathrm{ADD}_\varepsilon))}_{-4\mathbf{M}},$$

where

$$\delta(\mathcal{A}) = \begin{cases} 1 \text{ if } \mathcal{A} \text{ contains at least 1 PRAC block} \\ 0 \text{ otherwise} \end{cases}$$

In practice, it is always cheaper to process the $\lfloor \log_2 B_1 \rfloor$ occurrences of the prime 2 in $\mathcal{M}_{B_1}$ using PRAC blocks. Therefore, we always switch from a twisted Edwards curve to the equivalent Montgomery curve at some point. Yet, the computations performed on the Montgomery curve are not restricted to the powers of 2. The PRAC blocks used in our best combinations often contains a few primes greater than 2 (see Table 8 and the data recorded at http://eco.lirmm.net/double-base_ECM/).

Let $B_1 > 0$ be the smoothness bound for ECM stage 1. The combination algorithms presented in the next sections consist of finding a subset $\mathcal{S}$ of $\mathcal{B}$ such that $\bigcup_{b \in \mathcal{S}} \mathcal{M}_b = \mathcal{M}_{B_1}$, or equivalently $\prod_{b \in \mathcal{S}} n(b) = k$, which minimizes $\mathrm{cost}(\mathcal{S})$.

4.1   Bos–Kleinjung Algorithm

In 2012, Bos and Kleinjung describe a fast algorithm to compute a non-optimal solution (see [9, Algorithm 1]). The algorithm can be sketched as follow: start with $\mathcal{M} = \mathcal{M}_{B_1}$ and $\mathcal{S} = \emptyset$. Then, while $\mathcal{M} \neq \emptyset$: pick the "best" block $b \in \mathcal{B}$ such that $\mathcal{M}_b \subseteq \mathcal{M}$ and the ratio $\mathrm{dbl}(b)/\mathrm{add}(b)$ is large enough (where $\mathrm{dbl}(b)$ and $\mathrm{add}(b)$ denote the number of doublings and additions in the NAF chain used to represent $n(b)$). Then, add b in $\mathcal{S}$ and subtract $\mathcal{M}_b$ from $\mathcal{M}$. Once the loop is exited, the algorithm returns $\mathcal{S}$. The bound on $\mathrm{dbl}(b)/\mathrm{add}(b)$ can be decreased during the algorithm if no block satisfies both conditions.

At each iteration, the "best" block is chosen with the help of a score function. This function is defined to favor blocks whose multisets share many large factors with the current multiset $\mathcal{M}$ of remaining factors. For a multiset $\mathcal{M}$ and a block b such that $\mathcal{M}_b \neq \emptyset$ and $\mathcal{M}_b \subseteq \mathcal{M}$, the score function is defined by[4]:

$$\mathrm{score}(b, \mathcal{M}) = \sum_{\substack{\ell=1 \\ a_\ell(\mathcal{M})\neq 0}}^{\lceil \log_2(\max(\mathcal{M})) \rceil} \frac{a_\ell(\mathcal{M}_b)}{a_\ell(\mathcal{M})}, \tag{13}$$

where

$$a_\ell(\mathcal{M}) = \frac{\#\{p \in \mathcal{M} \mid \lceil \log_2(p) \rceil = \ell\}}{\#\mathcal{M}}.$$

By default, the "best" block is the one which minimizes the score function.

In [9], a randomized version of the algorithm is also presented. The randomization is used to generate lots of different sets of solution and, hopefully, to improve the cost of the best one. Given an integer $0 < x < 1$, the randomized version selects the block with the smallest score with probability x or, with probability $1 - x$, skip it and repeat this procedure for the block with the second smallest score and so on.

4.2   Our Algorithm

In a recent work, the authors of [15] replaced the ratio $\mathrm{dbl}(b)/\mathrm{add}(b)$ from Bos and Kleinjung's algorithm by the function

$$\kappa(b) = \frac{\log_2(n(b))}{\mathrm{dbl}(b) + 8/7\,\mathrm{add}(b) - \log_2(n(b))},$$

in order to take into account the bitlength of $n(b)$. This function κ produces slightly better results than Bos and Kleinjung's algorithm (see Table 9 in the "no storage" context). Yet, it is not readily adapted to our setting since it makes it difficult to take into account the costs of triplings and the fact that we use both twisted Edwards and Montgomery curves. For our combination algorithm, we consider a more generic function based on the arithmetic cost per bit of a block (acpb) as defined at the beginning of Sect. 4. Notice that on twisted Edwards curves, the function κ used by the authors of [15] is closely related to the arithmetic cost per bits of a NAF block. Indeed, we have $\mathrm{acpb}(b) \simeq (7\,\mathrm{dbl}(b) + 8\,\mathrm{add}(b))/\log_2(n(b)) = 7/\kappa(b) + 7$.

For our combination algorithm, we decided not to use the score function from Bos and Kleinjung's algorithm as we observed that it does not always achieve its goal to favor blocks with many large factors. For example, let us

---

[4] There is a small mistake in the definition given in [9] which we were able to correct thanks to the examples following the definition.

consider $B_1 = 256$ and two blocks b_1 and b_2 such that $\mathcal{M}_{b_1} = \{233, 193, 163\}$ and $\mathcal{M}_{b_2} = \{233, 193, 179, 109, 103, 73\}$. We would like the score function to favor the block b_2 since it contains more factors of sizes similar to the size of the elements of b_1. Yet, using (13), one gets $\text{score}(b_1, \mathcal{M}_{B_1}) = 3.043$ and $\text{score}(b_2, \mathcal{M}_{B_1}) = 4.214$, which means that the algorithm would select b_1 instead of b_2. Moreover, if b_3 is the best block that we could imagine with $\mathcal{M}_{b_3} = \mathcal{M}_{B_1}$, then its score would be worse than the two previous one, with $\text{score}(b_3, \mathcal{M}_{B_1}) = 8$.

We observed that using an algorithm similar the Bos and Kleinjung's algorithm where we always choose the block with the smallest arithmetic cost per bit did not yield better results than [9] or [15]. Thus, we tried a more exhaustive approach. A complete exhaustive search was totally out of reach, even for not-so-large values of B_1. However, the information provided by the previous results allowed us to envisage a somewhat exhaustive strategy.

Recall that our goal is to construct a subset $\mathcal{S}$ of $\mathcal{B}$ which minimizes $\text{cost}(\mathcal{S})$ and satisfies $\bigcup_{b \in \mathcal{S}} \mathcal{M}_b = \mathcal{M}_{B_1}$.

In order to reduce the enumeration depth, our first heuristic was to bound the number of blocks in the solution set $\mathcal{S}$. This constraint is rather natural as we want to favor blocks with many factors.

To further speed up our combination algorithm, we try to reduce the width of each step in the enumeration. First, notice that we can very easily obtain an upper bound on the arithmetic cost of the best solution set, for example by running the algorithms from Bos and Kleinjung [9] or from Ishii et al. [15] using our set of blocks $\mathcal{B}$. Then, we can use the following observation. Let C be an upper bound on the arithmetic cost of the best solution set and let $\mathcal{S}_0 \subseteq \mathcal{B}$ be a partial solution, i.e., such that $\bigcup_{b \in \mathcal{S}_0} \mathcal{M}_b \subsetneq \mathcal{M}_{B_1}$. Then a solution set $\mathcal{S}$ containing $\mathcal{S}_0$ satisfies $\text{cost}(\mathcal{S}) < C$, only if $\mathcal{S} \setminus \mathcal{S}_0$ contains at least one block whose arithmetic cost per bit is not greater than

$$\text{acpb}_{\max} = \frac{C - (\text{cost}(\mathcal{S}_0) + (1 - \delta(\mathcal{S}_0))(\text{cost}(\text{ADD}_M) - \text{cost}(\text{ADD}_\varepsilon)))}{\log_2(n(\mathcal{M}_{B_1})) - \log_2(n(\mathcal{S}_0))}. \quad (14)$$

If we build our solution sets by adding blocks by increasing value of their arithmetic cost per bit, Equation (14) provides an upper bound for the arithmetic cost per bit of the next block that can be added to a partial solution set. A pseudo-code version of our combination algorithm is described in Algorithm 1 and an implementation in C is available at http://eco.lirmm.net/double-base_ECM/.

In Table 8, we give the best combination produced with Algorithm 1 for $B_1 = 256$. The resulting scalar multiplication algorithm requires 96 fewer multiplications than the best result from Bos and Kleinjung (see Table 4).

5   Results and Comparison

In this section, we compare the cost of our implementation of ECM with the following implementations:

Algorithm 1 combine

Input: a set of blocks $\mathcal{B}$, a positive integer B_1, a bound ℓ on the length and an upper
bound C on the arithmetic cost

Output: the solution set $\mathcal{S}$ with minimal cost such that $\#\mathcal{S} \leq \ell$, $\mathrm{cost}(\mathcal{S}) < C$ and
$\mathcal{M}_{\mathcal{S}} = \mathcal{M}_{B_1}$; or FAILURE if not such set exists

1: **function** ENUM_REC($\mathcal{S}_0$, $\mathcal{M}_{\mathrm{rem}}$, $\mathcal{B}_{\mathrm{rem}}$)
2:     $\mathcal{S} \leftarrow$ FAILURE   ▷ by convention, we define $\mathrm{cost}($FAILURE$)$ to be C
3:     $\mathcal{B}_{\mathrm{new}} \leftarrow \mathcal{B}_{\mathrm{rem}}$
4:     $\mathrm{acpb}_{\mathrm{max}} \leftarrow$ value obtained using Equation (14) with $\mathcal{S}_0$, $\mathcal{M}_{B_1}$ and C
5:     **for all** $b \in \mathcal{B}_{\mathrm{rem}}$ **do**
6:         **if** $\mathrm{acpb}(b) > \mathrm{acpb}_{\mathrm{max}}$ **then**
7:             break from the for loop
8:         **else if** $\mathcal{M}_b \subseteq \mathcal{M}_{\mathrm{rem}}$ **then**
9:             $\mathcal{S}_{\mathrm{new}} \leftarrow \mathcal{S}_0 \cup \{b\}$
10:             $\mathcal{M}_{\mathrm{new}} \leftarrow \mathcal{M}_{\mathrm{rem}} \setminus \mathcal{M}_b$
11:             **if** $\mathcal{M}_{\mathrm{new}} = \emptyset$ and $\mathrm{cost}(\mathcal{S}_{\mathrm{new}}) < \mathrm{cost}(\mathcal{S})$ **then**
12:                 $\mathcal{S} \leftarrow \mathcal{S}_{\mathrm{new}}$
13:             **else if** $\mathcal{M}_{\mathrm{new}} \neq \emptyset$ and $\#\mathcal{S}_{\mathrm{new}} < \ell$ **then**
14:                 $\mathcal{S}_{\mathrm{rec}} \leftarrow$ ENUM_REC($\mathcal{S}_{\mathrm{new}}$, $\mathcal{M}_{\mathrm{new}}$, $\mathcal{B}_{\mathrm{new}}$)
15:                 **if** $\mathrm{cost}(\mathcal{S}_{\mathrm{rec}}) < \mathrm{cost}(\mathcal{S})$ **then**
16:                     $\mathcal{S} \leftarrow \mathcal{S}_{\mathrm{rec}}$
17:             $\mathcal{B}_{\mathrm{new}} \leftarrow \mathcal{B}_{\mathrm{new}} \setminus \{b\}$
18:     **return** $\mathcal{S}$

19: Sort $\mathcal{B}$ by increasing value of acpb
20: **return** ENUM_REC($\emptyset$, $\mathcal{M}_{B_1}$, $\mathcal{B}$)

- the ECM code inside CADO-NFS [24] (version 2.3),
- the software EECM-MPFQ [5],
- the article "ECM at Work" [9],
- the article [15], referenced as "ECM on Kalray" in the following.

The ECM code inside CADO-NFS is the only implementation that uses
Montgomery curves. The other three use twisted Edwards curves with $a = -1$.
For "ECM at work", we consider the two settings called no storage and low
storage as presented in the article. The cost comparison for the stage 1 of ECM
is given in Table 9. In Fig. 1, we compare the arithmetic cost per bit of these
various implementations for more values of B_1.

For curves with the same torsion as the ones we use (see Sect. 2.5), the stage
1 of GMP-ECM is implemented with Montgomery curves and uses the same
algorithms as CADO-NFS. Thus, for theses curves, the stage 1 of GMP-ECM
and CADO-NFS have the same cost.

Regarding storage requirements, our implementation is also competitive. For
the blocks using Lucas chains on Montgomery curves, we only need three extra
points in XZ coordinates, in addition to the input and output points. For double-
base chains, we do not need any extra point and for double-base expansions, as

Table 8. The best set of blocks computed with our algorithm for $B_1 = 256$. Type c corresponds to double-base chains, type e to double-base expansions and type m to blocks processed on the Mongomery model.

Blocks	Type		Cost
$193 \cdot 127 \cdot 109 \cdot 107 \cdot 61 \cdot 13 \cdot 7$	c	$2^{12} \cdot 3^{18} - 1$	309M
$151 \cdot 31 \cdot 7$	c	$2^{15} - 1$	114M
$227 \cdot 73 \cdot 67 \cdot 17$	c	$2^{21} \cdot 3^2 + 1$	180M
$167 \cdot 149 \cdot 5$	c	$2^9 \cdot 3^5 - 1$	132M
$251 \cdot 43 \cdot 41$	c	$2^{14} \cdot 3^3 + 2^4 \cdot 3^2 + 1$	151M
$241 \cdot 229 \cdot 19$	c	$2^{20} + 2^4 - 1$	157M
$211 \cdot 139 \cdot 13 \cdot 11$	c	$2^{22} - 2^8 - 1$	171M
$233 \cdot 191 \cdot 173 \cdot 157$	c	$2^{27} \cdot 3^2 + 2^{18} \cdot 3 - 1$	230M
$223 \cdot 137 \cdot 103 \cdot 83 \cdot 37$	c	$2^{30} \cdot 3^2 + 2^{11} - 1$	251M
$179 \cdot 101 \cdot 97 \cdot 47 \cdot 29 \cdot 23 \cdot 5$	c	$2^{38} - 2^3 - 1$	283M
$181 \cdot 131 \cdot 89 \cdot 59 \cdot 11$	c	$2^{24} \cdot 3^4 + 2^{17} \cdot 3^4 - 2^8 - 1$	241M
$239 \cdot 199 \cdot 197 \cdot 163 \cdot 113 \cdot 79 \cdot 71 \cdot 53$	e	$2^{46} \cdot 3^6 + 2^{42} + 2^{14} + 3^3$	421M
Switch to Montgomery. Last addition in the above block is an ADD_M			−4M
$5 \cdot 3^5$	m		72M
2^8	m		40M
Total			2748M

Table 9. Number of modular multiplication (**M**) for various implementations of ECM (stage 1) and some commonly used smoothness bounds B_1 assuming $1\mathbf{S} = 1\mathbf{M}$

$B_1 =$	256	512	1024	8192
CADO-NFS [24]	3091	6410	12916	104428
EECM-MPFQ [5]	3074	6135	12036	93040
ECM at Work (no storage) [9]	2844	5806	11508	91074
ECM on Kalray [15]	2843	5786	11468	90730
ECM at Work (low storage) [9]	2831	5740	11375	89991
this work	2748	5667	11257	89572

we only generated expansions with at most 4 terms, we need at most 4 additional points in extended coordinates. So our storage requirements are similar to the low storage setting of [9] and much lower than the hundred of points required by EECM-MPFQ.

We note that the fact that the output of stage 1 is a point in XZ coordinates on a Montgomery curve is not a burden for the stage 2 of the ECM algorithm. The stage 2 from [9,15] is computed using a baby-step giant-step algorithm. A complete description in the case of twisted Edwards curves is given in [20, Sect. 3.2]. In CADO-NFS, the stage 2 also uses a baby-step giant-step algorithm,

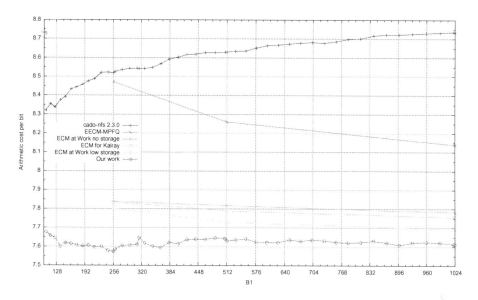

Fig. 1. Arithmetic cost per bit for the scalar multiplication of ECM stage 1 of ECM assuming $1\mathbf{S} = 1\mathbf{M}$.

Table 10. Number of modular multiplications ($\mathbf{M}$) for ECM stage 2 assuming $1\mathbf{S} = 1\mathbf{M}$

	$B_1 =$	256	512	1024	8192
	$B_2 =$	2^{14}	$3 \cdot 2^{14}$	$7 \cdot 2^{14}$	$80 \cdot 2^{14}$
CADO-NFS [24]		2387	6120	13264	134761
ECM on Kalray [15] (based on [20])		2538	5812	11410	91122
this work		2227	5160	10273	89866

but on Montgomery curves. Using the same approach, we managed to greatly reduce the cost of stage 2 thanks to using finer parameters adjustments. More precisely, the baby-step giant-step method for stage 2 of ECM is parameterized by a value called ω, which in CADO-NFS was set to a constant value. We observed that adjusting ω according to the values of B_1 and B_2 yields significant speed-ups for large values of B_1 and B_2. The costs of the stage 2 for these different implementations are given in Table 10.

In order to evaluate the practical impact of our approach, we implemented our new algorithms for scalar multiplications in CADO-NFS. To assess the efficiency for large composite numbers, we run a small part of the sieving phase for RSA-200 and RSA-220 with the default parameters and observed that the cofactorization time decreased by 5% to 10%, in accordance with our theoretical estimates.

6   Conclusion

In the context of NFS cofactorization, ECM is used to break billions of medium-size integers into primes. In practice, only a few B_1-values are used, making it possible to precompute almost optimal algorithms for these customary B_1-values. Following the works from Dixon and Lenstra and Bos and Kleinjung, we generated over 10^{19} chains of various types and combined them using a quasi exhaustive approach. Our implementation uses both twisted Edwards curves, through efficient double-base decompositions, and Montgomery curves. For switching from one model to the other, we introduced a partial addition-and-switch operation which computes the sum in Montgomery XZ coordinates of two points given on an equivalent Edwards curve.

For $B_1 \leq 8192$, our implementation requires fewer modular multiplications than any other publicly available implementation of ECM. It requires significantly less memory than EECM-MPFQ. The arithmetic cost per bit of our implementation is relatively stable, around $7.6\mathbf{M}$. Extending the current approach based on prime batches and recombination, for example by considering extended double-base expansions and chains, is possible. Yet, significant speed-ups seems difficult to prefigure. For larger B_1-values, our combination algorithm is likely to become unpractical. However, it can be used iteratively to extend any current best combination results.

A   Counting Double-Base Expansions

Number of double-base expansions of the form $n = 2^{d_0}3^{t_0} + \sum_{i=1}^{m} \pm 2^{d_i}3^{t_i}$ with $\max_i d_i = D$, $\max_i t_i = T$ and whose terms have no common factors:

$$
2^m \left[\binom{(D+1)(T+1)}{m+1} - 2\binom{(D+1)T}{m+1} - 2\binom{(T+1)D}{m+1} \right.
$$
$$
+ 4\binom{DT}{m+1} + \binom{(D+1)(T-1)}{m+1} + \binom{(T+1)(D-1)}{m+1}
$$
$$
\left. -2\binom{(D-1)T}{m+1} - 2\binom{(T-1)D}{m+1} + \binom{(D-1)(T-1)}{m+1} \right]
$$

The proof is omitted. It follows a classical inclusion-exclusion principle.

References

1. Barbulescu, R., Bos, J.W., Bouvier, C., Kleinjung, T., Montgomery, P.: Finding ECM-friendly curves through a study of Galois properties. In: ANTS X: Proceedings of the Tenth Algorithmic Number Theory Symposium. Open Book Series, vol. 1, pp. 63–86 (2013). https://doi.org/10.2140/obs.2013.1.63
2. Bernstein, D.J., Birkner, P., Joye, M., Lange, T., Peters, C.: Twisted edwards curves. In: Vaudenay, S. (ed.) AFRICACRYPT 2008. LNCS, vol. 5023, pp. 389–405. Springer, Heidelberg (2008). https://doi.org/10.1007/978-3-540-68164-9_26

3. Bernstein, D.J., Birkner, P., Lange, T.: Starfish on strike. In: Abdalla, M., Barreto, P.S.L.M. (eds.) LATINCRYPT 2010. LNCS, vol. 6212, pp. 61–80. Springer, Heidelberg (2010). https://doi.org/10.1007/978-3-642-14712-8_4

4. Bernstein, D.J., Birkner, P., Lange, T., Peters, C.: ECM using Edwards curves. Math. Comput. **82**, 1139–1179 (2013)

5. Bernstein, D.J., Birkner, P., Lange, T., Peters, C., et al.: EECM-MPFQ: ECM using Edwards curves. http://eecm.cr.yp.to/index.html

6. Bernstein, D.J., Chuengsatiansup, C., Lange, T.: Double-base scalar multiplication revisited. Cryptology ePrint Archive, Report 2017/037 (2017). https://eprint.iacr.org/2017/037

7. Bernstein, D.J., Lange, T.: Explicit-formulas database. http://www.hyperelliptic.org/EFD/. joint work by Daniel J. Bernstein and Tanja Lange, building on work by many authors

8. Bernstein, D.J., Lange, T.: A complete set of addition laws for incomplete Edwards curves. Cryptology ePrint Archive, Report 2009/580 (2009). https://eprint.iacr.org/2009/580

9. Bos, J.W., Kleinjung, T.: ECM at work. In: Wang, X., Sako, K. (eds.) ASIACRYPT 2012. LNCS, vol. 7658, pp. 467–484. Springer, Heidelberg (2012). https://doi.org/10.1007/978-3-642-34961-4_29

10. Castryck, W., Galbraith, S., Farashahi, R.R.: Efficient arithmetic on elliptic curves using a mixed Edwards-Montgomery representation. Cryptology ePrint Archive, Report 2008/218 (2008). https://eprint.iacr.org/2008/218

11. Dimitrov, V., Imbert, L., Mishra, P.K.: Efficient and secure elliptic curve point multiplication using double-base chains. In: Roy, B. (ed.) ASIACRYPT 2005. LNCS, vol. 3788, pp. 59–78. Springer, Heidelberg (2005). https://doi.org/10.1007/11593447_4

12. Dixon, B., Lenstra, A.K.: Massively parallel elliptic curve factoring. In: Rueppel, R.A. (ed.) EUROCRYPT 1992. LNCS, vol. 658, pp. 183–193. Springer, Heidelberg (1993). https://doi.org/10.1007/3-540-47555-9_16

13. Edwards, H.M.: A normal form for elliptic curves. Bull. Am. Math. Soc. **44**, 393–422 (2007)

14. Hisil, H., Wong, K.K.-H., Carter, G., Dawson, E.: Twisted edwards curves revisited. In: Pieprzyk, J. (ed.) ASIACRYPT 2008. LNCS, vol. 5350, pp. 326–343. Springer, Heidelberg (2008). https://doi.org/10.1007/978-3-540-89255-7_20

15. Ishii, M., Detrey, J., Gaudry, P., Inomata, A., Fujikawa, K.: Fast modular arithmetic on the Kalray MPPA-256 processor for an energy-efficient implementation of ECM. IEEE Transactions on Computers **66**(12), 2019–2030 (2017). https://doi.org/10.1109/TC.2017.2704082, https://hal.inria.fr/hal-01299697

16. Kleinjung, T., et al.: Factorization of a 768-Bit RSA modulus. In: Rabin, T. (ed.) CRYPTO 2010. LNCS, vol. 6223, pp. 333–350. Springer, Heidelberg (2010). https://doi.org/10.1007/978-3-642-14623-7_18

17. Lenstra, A.K., Lenstra, H.W. (eds.): The Development of the Number Field Sieve. Lecture Notes in Mathematics, vol. 1554. Springer, Heidelberg (1993). https://doi.org/10.1007/BFb0091534

18. Lenstra, H.W.: Factoring integers with elliptic curves. Ann. Math. **126**(3), 649–673 (1987)

19. Meyer, M., Reith, S., Campos, F.: On hybrid SIDH schemes using Edwards and Montgomery curve arithmetic. Cryptology ePrint Archive, Report 2017/1213 (2017). https://eprint.iacr.org/2017/1213

20. Miele, A.: On the analysis of public-key cryptologic algorithms. Ph.D. thesis, EPFL (2015)

21. Montgomery, P.L.: Evaluating recurrences of form $X_{m+n} = f(X_m, X_n, X_{m-n})$ via Lucas chains (1983, unpublished)
22. Montgomery, P.L.: Speeding the Pollard and elliptic curve methods of factorization. Math. Comput. **48**(177), 243–264 (1987)
23. Méloni, N., Hasan, M.A.: Elliptic curve scalar multiplication combining Yao's algorithm and double bases. In: Clavier, C., Gaj, K. (eds.) CHES 2009. LNCS, vol. 5747, pp. 304–316. Springer, Heidelberg (2009). https://doi.org/10.1007/978-3-642-04138-9_22
24. The CADO-NFS Development Team: CADO-NFS, an implementation of the number field Sieve algorithm (2017). http://cado-nfs.gforge.inria.fr/. release 2.3.0
25. Yao, A.C.C.: On the evaluation of powers. SIAM J. Comput. **5**(1), 100–103 (1976)
26. Zimmermann, P.: 50 largest factors found by ECM. https://members.loria.fr/PZimmermann/records/top50.html
27. Zimmermann, P., Dodson, B.: 20 Years of ECM. In: Hess, F., Pauli, S., Pohst, M. (eds.) ANTS 2006. LNCS, vol. 4076, pp. 525–542. Springer, Heidelberg (2006). https://doi.org/10.1007/11792086_37
28. Zimmermann, P., et al.: GMP-ECM (elliptic curve method for integer factorization). https://gforge.inria.fr/projects/ecm/

Improved Classical Cryptanalysis of SIKE in Practice

Craig Costello[1], Patrick Longa[1], Michael Naehrig[1(✉)], Joost Renes[2], and Fernando Virdia[3(✉)]

[1] Microsoft Research, Redmond, WA, USA
{craigco,plonga,mnaehrig}@microsoft.com
[2] Digital Security Group, Radboud University, Nijmegen, The Netherlands
j.renes@cs.ru.nl
[3] Information Security Group, Royal Holloway, University of London, Egham, UK
fernando.virdia.2016@rhul.ac.uk

Abstract. The main contribution of this work is an optimized implementation of the van Oorschot-Wiener (vOW) parallel collision finding algorithm. As is typical for cryptanalysis against conjectured hard problems (e.g. factoring or discrete logarithms), challenges can arise in the implementation that are not captured in the theory, making the performance of the algorithm in practice a crucial element of estimating security. We present a number of novel improvements, both to generic instantiations of the vOW algorithm finding collisions in arbitrary functions, and to its instantiation in the context of the supersingular isogeny key encapsulation (SIKE) protocol, that culminate in an improved classical cryptanalysis of the computational supersingular isogeny (CSSI) problem. In particular, we present a scalable implementation that can be applied to the Round-2 parameter sets of SIKE that can be used to give confidence in their security levels.

Keywords: Post-quantum cryptography · Supersingular elliptic curves · Isogenies · SIDH · SIKE · Parallel collision search · van Oorschot-Wiener algorithm

1 Introduction

The supersingular isogeny key encapsulation (SIKE) proposal [7] – the actively secure version of Jao and De Feo's SIDH key exchange [8] – is one of 17 second

J. Renes—Partially supported by the Technology Foundation STW (project 13499 – TYPHOON & ASPASIA), from the Dutch government. Part of this work was done while Joost was an intern at Microsoft Research.
F. Virdia—Partially supported by the EPSRC and the UK government as part of the Centre for Doctoral Training in Cyber Security at Royal Holloway, University of London (EP/P009301/1). Part of this work was done while Fernando was an intern at Microsoft Research.

© International Association for Cryptologic Research 2020
A. Kiayias et al. (Eds.): PKC 2020, LNCS 12111, pp. 505–534, 2020.
https://doi.org/10.1007/978-3-030-45388-6_18

round candidate public key encryption or key establishment proposals submitted to the post-quantum cryptography standardization process initiated by the U.S. National Institute of Standards and Technology (NIST). It is the only proposal whose security is based on the computational supersingular isogeny (CSSI) problem. Currently, the best known classical and quantum attacks on the CSSI problem are generic *claw finding attacks*: given two functions $f\colon A \to C$ and $g\colon B \to C$ with domains of equal size, the *claw finding problem* is to find a pair (a,b) such that $f(a) = g(b)$. The original security analysis by Jao and De Feo [8, §5.2] estimates the complexity of the CSSI problem by assuming the optimal black-box *asymptotic* complexities for the claw finding problem: classically, it can be solved in $O(|A|+|B|)$ time using $O(|A|)$ space. On a quantum computer, Tani's algorithm [22] relies on a generalization of Grover's search algorithm by Szegedy [21] and uses quantum walks on Johnson graphs to solve the claw finding problem in $O(\sqrt[3]{|A||B|})$ time. Following Jao and De Feo, the SIKE team used these asymptotics to specify three Round-1 parametrizations that were intended to meet the requirements for the NIST security categories 1, 3 and 5 defined in terms of resources needed for AES key search [14, p. 18].

Prior to 2018, the literature on SIDH (starting with Jao and De Feo's original paper [8]) has consistently cited a meet-in-the-middle algorithm for claw finding as the best known classical algorithm for solving the CSSI problem. In 2018, Adj, Cervantes-Vázquez, Chi-Domínguez, Menezes and Rodríguez-Henríquez [1] made a significant step towards a better understanding of the problem's concrete classical complexity. They show that, while the meet-in-the-middle algorithm has the lowest known classical runtime, its storage requirements are so large (for instances of cryptographic size) that its application is not meaningful in any reasonable model of cryptanalytic computation. Indeed, the best classical AES key search algorithms only require a modest amount of storage, so a fair and correct analysis must take into account the available time/memory trade-offs. Consequently, Adj *et al.* fix a conservative upper bound on storage capacity that is considered "prohibitively costly for the foreseeable future" [1, §5], i.e., 2^{80} *units* of storage, and analyze the runtime of relevant algorithms subject to this capacity. They conclude that despite its higher running time, the van Oorschot-Wiener (vOW) parallel collision finding algorithm [23] has significantly lower space requirements and is the best classical algorithm for the CSSI problem. Thus, its concrete complexity should instead be used to assess the security of SIDH/SIKE against (known) classical attacks. Their analysis ultimately shows that the SIKE team used rather conservative classical security estimates and that significantly smaller parameters can be used to achieve the requisite level of classical security.

Jaques and Schanck [9] provide an in-depth analysis of quantum algorithms for claw finding applied to the CSSI problem. In particular, they analyse the complexity of implementing and querying quantum memory, which is needed in Tani's algorithm and which previously had not been taken into account in the quantum security estimates for SIDH/SIKE. Along with Tani's algorithm, they also consider a direct application of Grover search [5] to claw finding. Similar to the classical analysis of Adj *et al.*, they conclude that the SIKE proposal's quantum security estimates were too conservative. In fact, Jaques and Schank's analysis shows that the best known quantum algorithms do not achieve a significant advantage over the classical vOW algorithm. In some attack scenarios, it is the classical security that is the limiting factor for achieving a specified security level. While quantum algorithms promise to be more efficient for attackers with limited memory, classical vOW outperforms quantum algorithms for attackers with limited time. Thus, the precise, real-world complexity of the vOW parallel collision search algorithm is paramount in the discussion of (current and future) parameters for SIDH/SIKE.

Based on the above cryptanalytic results, the parameter sets in the SIKE specification were adjusted in Round 2 of the NIST standardization process. The specification now contains the parameter sets SIKEp434, SIKEp503, SIKEp610 and SIKEp751 targeting the NIST security categories 1, 2, 3 and 5, respectively.

Contributions. We present an implementation of the van Oorschot-Wiener algorithm that is intended to be a step towards a real-world, large-scale cryptanalytic effort. Our work extends that of Adj *et al.* by introducing novel improvements to implementations of the generic vOW collision finding algorithm and improving the instantiations specific to the contexts of SIDH and SIKE. Besides significantly optimizing the efficiency of the underlying finite-field and elliptic-curve arithmetic by incorporating the state-of-the-art formulas, we present several optimizations related to the structure of the isogeny graph.

The source code will be released under a free license. Beyond being able to reproduce our results, we hope that our C/C++ implementations can function as the basis for further experiments to assess the security of isogeny-based cryptography, and that they can be used for other applications of the collision finding algorithm. In fact, we provide two implementations: an optimized C code base for both generic collision finding as well as solving the CSSI problem, and a C++ version designed for modularity, and to allow easy porting to alternative collision finding settings at little cost to efficiency (e. g. for the hybrid attack on lattice-based schemes [6], symmetric cryptography, or highly distributed setups).

Our extensions and improvements to the vOW implementation and analysis in [1] include:

- *Faster collision checking.* One of the main steps in the vOW algorithm is to check whether a given collision is the *golden collision* (see Sect. 2). Experimentally, our optimized version of generic vOW found that it constitutes close to 20% of the entire algorithm (aligning with van Oorschot and Wiener's analysis [23, §4.2]). We give a novel, much more efficient method, which is based on a cycle-finding technique by Sedgewick, Szymanski and Yao [18]. It temporarily uses a small amount of local storage (which can be input dynamically as a parameter) during the random walks to accelerate collision checking – see Sect. 3.4.
- *SIKE-specific optimizations.* Although the best algorithm for the general CSSI problem is generic (i.e. there are no better known algorithms that exploit its underlying mathematical structure), we take advantage of multiple optimizations that apply to the concrete instantiations in the SIKE specification [7].

Firstly, we show how to exploit the choice of the starting curve as a subfield curve, by defining random walks on (conjugate) classes of j-invariants; such a modified walk is analogous to the walk that exploits the negation map in Pollard's rho algorithm for the ECDLP [27] – see Sect. 3.1. Secondly, we show how to exploit that, in SIKE, the isomorphism class of the output curve is not randomized (this possibility was already pointed out by De Feo, Jao and Plût [3]), by using the leakage of the dual of the final isogeny – see Sect. 3.1. We quantify the precise security loss suffered by these choices.

- *Precomputation.* Generic collision finding algorithms like vOW are often implemented to target high-speed symmetric primitives. In contrast to those applications, for the CSSI problem, the computation of large-degree isogenies is the overwhelming bottle-neck of the random walks. Therefore, speeding up the isogeny computations translates directly to a similar speedup of the entire collision finding process. We show how to exhaust any available local memory to achieve such speedups via the precomputation of parts of the isogeny tree – see Sect. 3.3.

- *Experimental results.* For all of the improvements mentioned above, we demonstrate their feasibility by analyzing the runtime of the implementation. In doing so, we re-confirm the analyses of van Oorschot and Wiener [23] and Adj *et al.* [1] in the context of SIDH (with a factor 2 improvement) and extend them to SIKE – see Table 1. Furthermore, we go beyond the setting of small parameters and propose an alternative way of predicting the vOW runtime for actual Round 2 parameters, in particular SIKEp434, giving an *upper* bound on their security level – see Sect. 5.1.

2   Preliminaries: van Oorschot-Wiener's Collision Search

After defining the CSSI problem in Sect. 2.1, we describe the classical meet-in-the-middle claw finding algorithm in Sect. 2.2. It is both simpler than, and helps motivate, the description of the vOW parallel collision finding algorithm in Sect. 2.3. The complexity analysis of the generic vOW algorithm is given in Sect. 2.4.

2.1   The CSSI Problem

Herein, we restrict to the popular scenario whereby an instance of SIDH/SIKE is parameterized by a prime $p = 2^{e_2} 3^{e_3} - 1$ with $2^{e_2} \approx 3^{e_3}$ and $e_3 \gg 1$; all known implementations, including those in the SIKE submission, specify a prime of this form. Since $p \equiv 3 \bmod 4$, we fix $\mathbb{F}_{p^2} = \mathbb{F}_p(i)$ with $i^2 + 1 = 0$ throughout. We work with the set of isomorphism classes of supersingular elliptic curves in characteristic p. There are roughly $p/12$ such classes, and these are identified by their $\mathbb{F}_{p^2}$-rational j-invariants [20, p. 146]. Each supersingular j-invariant belongs to the same isogeny class [11].

In this paper, isogenies are non-constant rational maps between two elliptic curves that are also group homomorphisms. We work only with *separable* isogenies, meaning that the degree of any given isogeny is equal to the size of its kernel. Any subgroup $G \subset E$ determines a unique isogeny (up to isomorphism) whose kernel is G; this isogeny can be computed using Vélu's formulas [25].

For a prime $\ell \neq p$, there are precisely $\ell + 1$ isogenies of degree ℓ that emanate from a given supersingular curve. This induces a graph $\mathcal{G}_\ell$ – called a supersingular isogeny graph – whose nodes are the supersingular isomorphism classes and whose vertices are the degree-ℓ isogenies (up to isomorphism) between them. The graph $\mathcal{G}_\ell$ is connected and, with the exception of the nodes corresponding to j-invariants 0 and 1728, an $(\ell + 1)$-regular multigraph which satisfies the Ramanujan expansion property (see [3, §2.1]). Since every isogeny $\phi : E \to E'$ has a unique (up to isomorphism) *dual* isogeny $\hat{\phi} : E' \to E$, we can view $\mathcal{G}_\ell$ as an undirected graph (excluding $j = 0, 1728$). We discuss the special node with j-invariant 1728 in Sect. 3.1.

For any n with $p \nmid n$, the set of n-torsion points, $E[n] = \{P \in E(\bar{\mathbb{F}}_p) : [n]P = 0_E\}$, satisfies $E[n] \cong \mathbb{Z}_n \oplus \mathbb{Z}_n$. Let $(\ell, e) \in \{(2, e_2), (3, e_3)\}$. Following [3, Problem 5.2] (see also [1, §2.4]), we define a simplified version of the CSSI problem that underlies the SIDH and SIKE protocols within the above context as follows.

Definition 1 (CSSI). *Given two supersingular elliptic curves E and E/G defined over $\mathbb{F}_{p^2}$ such that up to isomorphism there exists a unique isogeny $\phi : E \to E/G$ of degree ℓ^e with (cyclic) kernel $\ker \phi = G$, the computational supersingular isogeny (CSSI) problem is to compute ϕ or, equivalently, to determine a generator for G.*

2.2 The Meet-in-the-middle Claw Finding Algorithm

The most naive approach to solving CSSI is to perform a brute force search for G. Since the number of cyclic subgroups of order ℓ^e in $E(\mathbb{F}_{p^2})$ is $(\ell + 1)\ell^{e-1}$, this takes $O(\ell^e)$ time. The claw finding algorithm uses the fact that we can view $\mathcal{G}_\ell$ as an undirected graph, so that we can instead *meet in the middle*. Following [8] (and assuming for simplicity that e is even), we can build two trees of curves: the leaves of the first determine the set of all isomorphism classes $\ell^{e/2}$-isogenous to that of E, those of the second the set of all classes $\ell^{e/2}$-isogenous to that of E/G. While there are $(\ell + 1)\ell^{e/2 - 1}$ classes in each set, with overwhelmingly high probability there is only one class that lies in both sets [8, §5.1]. It corresponds to the node in the middle of the path from E to E/G, and once it is found, the CSSI problem is solved by composing the $\ell^{e/2}$-isogeny emanating from E with the dual of that emanating from E/G. Assuming that all $(\ell + 1)\ell^{e/2 - 1}$ classes emanating from one of the sides can be computed and stored, solving the CSSI problem this way takes $O(\ell^{e/2})$ time.

It was not until the work of Adj *et al.* [1] that the classical complexity of this claw finding algorithm in the context of CSSI analysis was scrutinized. Given that $\ell^{e/2} \approx p^{1/4}$, and that the smallest prime p used to instantiate SIDH/SIKE prior to [1] was larger than 2^{500}, Adj *et al.* argue that the $O(p^{1/4})$ storage required to solve the problem as described above is infeasible. Instead, they fix 2^{80} as an upper bound on the number of *units* that can be stored, and analyze the runtime of the claw finding algorithm subject to this storage capacity. At any given time, an attacker can now only afford to store a small fraction of the $O(\ell^{e/2})$ nodes emanating from one side, try all nodes from the other side, and repeat this process until the CSSI problem is solved. Adj *et al.* therefore conclude that, for CSSI instances of cryptographic relevance, the meet-in-the-middle algorithm is more costly than the vOW algorithm described in the sequel.

2.3 Solving CSSI with van Oorschot-Wiener

Let $S = \{0,1\} \times \{0,\ldots,(\ell+1)\ell^{e/2-1} - 1\}$, $E_0 = E$ and $E_1 = E/G$. Each $(i,y) \in S$ represents a kernel subgroup on the elliptic curve E_i. For example, for $\ell = 2$, Adj *et al.* [1, §4.4] define a correspondence between $(i,y) = (i,(b,k)) \in \{0,1\} \times (\{0,1,2\} \times \{0,\ldots,2^{e/2-1} - 1\})$ and the cyclic subgroup $\langle R_i \rangle \subset E_i$ with

$$R_i = \begin{cases} P_i + \left[b2^{e/2-1} + k \right] Q_i & \text{if } b = 0,1 \,, \\ [2k] P_i + Q_i & \text{if } b = 2 \,, \end{cases} \text{, where } \langle P_i, Q_i \rangle = E_i[2^{e/2-1}].$$

Let $h : S \rightarrow E_0(\mathbb{F}_{p^2}) \cup E_1(\mathbb{F}_{p^2}), (i,y) \mapsto R_i$ and let $f : S \rightarrow S$ be the function that, on input of (i,y), computes the isogeny of degree $\ell^{e/2}$ with kernel subgroup $\langle R_i \rangle$ emanating from E_i, evaluates the j-invariant $j(E_i/\langle R_i \rangle)$, and maps it back to S using a function g. In order to make f behave like a (pseudo-)random function on S, the function $g : \mathbb{F}_{p^2} \rightarrow S$ is chosen to be (pseudo-)random.

A collision for f is a pair $x, x' \in S$ with $f(x) = f(x')$ and $x \neq x'$. If f is modeled as a random function, the expected number of collisions (over the set of random functions) is around $|S|/2$ [23, §4.2]. For SIDH, we rely on the function h described above, while for SIKE, h is defined in Sect. 3.2 (in both cases for $\ell = 2$). Note that necessarily there exists one special collision, namely the one between the two subgroups (one on E and one on E/G) that map to the same j-invariant and solve the CSSI problem. Since this is the only useful collision, we follow convention [1,23] and refer to it as the *golden collision*. For the remainder of this section we abstract away from the setting of isogenies, since it is not necessary to understand the van Oorschot-Wiener algorithm. That is, we assume that f is a truly random function on S for which we aim to find a single golden collision.

The vOW algorithm requires a proportion θ of the points in $|S|$ to be *distinguished points*. Whether or not a point is distinguished can be decided by any efficiently computable function $S \rightarrow \{0,1\}$, so long as it ensures that close to $\theta \cdot |S|$ of the $|S|$ points are deemed distinguished. The algorithm searches for collisions of f by performing many iterative walks in parallel as follows. Each walk starts at a random point $x_0 \in S$ and produces a trail of points $x_i = f(x_{i-1})$ for $i = 1,2,\ldots$ until a *distinguished point* x_d is reached. The triple (x_0, x_d, d) is then added to a single common list and the processor chooses a new starting point at random to produce a new trail.[1]

---

[1] In our scenario, many collisions are encountered before the golden collision is found. Starting new trails (rather than continuing on from distinguished points) avoids falling into cycles and repeatedly detecting the same collisions [23, p. 6, Footnote 5].

Let w denote the number of triples of the form (x_0, x_d, d) that can be stored in the list. To simplify memory access, van Oorschot and Wiener suggest making the memory address for a given triple a function of its distinguished point. Optimized parametrizations geared towards real-world CSSI instantiations will have $w \ll \theta \cdot |S|$, i.e. one cannot store enough triples to account for all of the distinguished points. This gives rise to three scenarios when we attempt to store a given triple in memory. The first is that the memory at the given address is empty, in which case we write the triple there and continue; the second is that the memory is occupied by a triple with a different distinguished point, in which case we overwrite it with the new triple and continue; the third scenario is that the two triples contain the same distinguished point, in which case we have a collision and we must now check whether or not it is the golden collision. Let these two triples be (x_0, x_d, d) and $(x_0', x_{d'}', d')$ with $x_d = x_{d'}'$, and assume $d' > d$. To check the collision, we walk x_0' forward by iterating $(x_0', d') \leftarrow (f(x_0'), d' - 1)$ until $d' = d$, so that both walks are the same number of steps from the distinguished point. We then step both walks forward in unison iterating $(x_0, x_0') \leftarrow (f(x_0), f(x_0'))$ until we find $x_0 \neq x_0'$ such that $f(x_0) = f(x_0')$. If this is the golden collision, we are done. Otherwise, we replace the old triple with the new triple and continue. Note that the expected value of d, i.e. the expected length of the trails, is geometrically distributed with mean $1/\theta$.

Van Oorschot and Wiener note that two undesirable occurrences can arise during their algorithm. First, a trail can collide with the starting point of another trail, which is called a *Robin Hood*. In practice, they note that θ is small enough that this occurs rarely. If it does, we replace the triple in memory by the triple found last. Second, a walk can enter into a cycle that does not contain a distinguished point. In [23], the suggested workaround is to set a maximum trail length (e.g. $20/\theta$), and to abandon trails beyond this point.

Perhaps the most subtle aspect of the algorithm is that we are essentially forced to restart the above process many times, for many different instantiations of the random function f. As explained in [23, §4.2], there exist roughly $|S|/2$ collisions for f, and on average we have to find this many collisions before we encounter the golden collision. However, not all collisions occur equally likely; for any given f, the golden collision may have a very low probability of detection. For example, one or both of the two points that constitute the golden collision could have very few trails leading into them, or in the extreme case, none at all; if so we would have to be extremely lucky to find the collision, i.e. by randomly choosing the two points as starting points. Thus, van Oorschot and Wiener explain that the best average runtime is achieved by trying a function f until a requisite number of distinguished points have been found (how many will be discussed in the next subsection), and then restarting with a new function until the golden collision is found. Henceforth, we use f_n with $n \in \mathbb{Z}$ instead of f, where the subscript indicates the different function versions.

2.4   Complexity Analysis of van Oorschot-Wiener

Van Oorschot and Wiener give a complexity analysis for finding a golden collision [23, §4.2], but note that their complexity analysis is "flawed", giving multiple reasons as to why a precise closed formula for the runtime is difficult to achieve. Instead, after obtaining a general form for the runtime formula, they choose to determine several of the constants experimentally. We reproduce this *flawed* analysis, since we refer back to it throughout.

Recall that w triples (x_0, x_d, d) can be stored in memory. Whenever the memory is full, the average number of points on trails leading to those w distinguished points is w/θ. Writing $N = |S|$ and given any element of S, (uniformly) randomly generated as output of the random function f_n, the probability of it being on the pre-existing trails is therefore $w/(N\theta)$. Thus, on average we compute $N\theta/w$ points per collision. Checking a collision using the method described above requires $2/\theta$ steps on average, which gives the total average cost per collision as $N\theta/w + 2/\theta$. Taking $\theta = \sqrt{2w/N}$ minimizes this cost to $\sqrt{8N/w}$. As $N/2$ collisions are required (on average) to find the golden collision, we require (on average) $\sqrt{2N^3/w}$ function iterations to solve the CSSI problem.

Let m be the number of processors run in parallel and t the time taken to evaluate the function f_n. Since the algorithm parallelizes perfectly [23, §3] (in theory), the total runtime T required to find the golden collision is

$$T = \frac{2.5}{m}\sqrt{N^3/w} \cdot t, \tag{1}$$

where 2.5 is one of the constants determined experimentally in [23]. Some adjustments need to be made to the parameters because the phase where the memory is being filled with distinguished points is not accurately captured in the analysis. To describe the true performance of the algorithm, the fraction of distinguished points is set to $\theta = \alpha\sqrt{w/N}$ and the optimal constant α is determined experimentally. The heuristic analysis by van Oorschot and Wiener suggests $\alpha = 2.25$, which is verified by Adj *et al.* for SIDH.

Equation (1) shows that the memory size of w distinguished points has a crucial influence on the runtime of the vOW algorithm. It is therefore important to store distinguished points as compactly as possible. If the property for a point to be distinguished is a number of leading or trailing zeroes in its bit representation, these zeroes do not have to be stored, shortening the bit length of x_d in the triple (x_0, x_d, d). Given a distinguished point rate θ, the number of zeroes would be $\lfloor -\log\theta \rfloor$. The counter d must be large enough to store the number of steps in the longest trail, for example d must have $\lceil \log(20/\theta) \rceil$ bits. A distinguished point can thus be stored with about $2\log N + \log 20$ bits as most of the counter can be stored in the space of the omitted zero bits.

This deduction of the total runtime assumes that f_n behaves like an average random function. The average behavior can be achieved by using a number of different function versions f_n as explained above. To decide how long one such function f_n should be run before moving on, van Oorschot and Wiener introduce the constant β. The function version needs to be changed and distinguished points in memory discarded after $\beta \cdot w$ distinguished points have been produced. This constant is determined heuristically, analogously to the determination of α. For that purpose, a single n is fixed and run until $\beta \cdot w$ distinguished points are produced. In the meantime, the number of function iterations (i) and distinct collisions (c) are counted. The number of function versions can then be approximated as $n/(2c)$, while the expected runtime can be estimated as $in/(2c)$. It is concluded that the latter is minimal for $\beta = 10$.

We note that this experiment is extremely useful. Namely, it provides a very close estimate on the runtime without having to complete the full algorithm. For that reason, we run the same experiment to estimate the impact of improved collision checking (see Fig. 3 in Sect. 3.4).

3   Parallel Collision Search for Supersingular Isogenies

In this section we describe optimizations that we employ when specializing the van Oorschot-Wiener algorithm to SIKE. We discuss improvements based on the SIKE design in Sect. 3.1 and explain the specific instantiation of the vOW algorithm in Sect. 3.2. Finally, we show how to use local memory for precomputation in Sect. 3.3 and to improve collision locating in Sect. 3.4.

3.1   Solving SIKE Instances

Although the problem underlying SIKE is closely related to the original SIDH problem, there are slight differences. In this section, we discuss their impact on the vOW algorithm and show how to reduce the search space from size $3 \cdot 2^{e_2-1}$ (resp. $4 \cdot 3^{e_3-1}$) to 2^{e_2-4} (resp. 3^{e_3-1}).

As usual, let $\{\ell, m\} = \{2,3\}$ and let $\phi : E \to E_A$ be an isogeny of degree ℓ^{e_ℓ} for which the goal is to retrieve the (cyclic) kernel $\ker \phi$. We opt to represent curves in Montgomery form [13] $E_A : y^2 = x^3 + Ax^2 + x$ with constant $A \in \mathbb{F}_{p^2}$. The Montgomery form allows for very efficient arithmetic, which is why it has been used in the SIKE proposal. Further note that, if $\{U, V\}$ is a basis of $E[m^{e_m}]$, then the points $\phi(U), \phi(V)$ are given as well. But as we do not use these points on E_A and assume the simplified version of the CSSI problem as presented in Definition 1, we simply think of a challenge as being given by the curve E_A.

Since isogenies of degree ℓ^{e_ℓ} are determined by cyclic subgroups of size ℓ^{e_ℓ}, there are exactly $(\ell + 1)\ell^{e_\ell - 1}$ of them. This forms the basis for the general algorithm specified for SIDH by Adj *et al.* [1], essentially defining a random function on the set of cyclic subgroups.

Moving to SIKE, we observe that an important public parameter of its specification is the starting curve E_0. Since $p = 2^{e_2} \cdot 3^{e_3} - 1$ is congruent to 3 modulo 4 for $e_2 > 1$, the curve $y^2 = x^3 + x$ is supersingular for any choice of (large) e_2 and e_3, and this curve was chosen as the starting curve in the Round-1 SIKE specification. In Round 2, the starting curve has been changed to $y^2 = x^3 + 6x^2 + x$.

Choice of Secret Keys. Any point R of order ℓ^{e_ℓ} on E_0 satisfies $R = [s]P + [r]Q$ for $r, s \in \mathbb{Z}_{\ell^{e_\ell}}$, where both s and r do not vanish modulo ℓ. The SIKE specification [7, §1.3.8] assumes s to be invertible and simply sets $s = 1$. This choice simplifies implementations by making the secret key a sequence of random bits that is easy to sample. When $\ell = 2$, an appropriate choice of P, Q allows to avoid exceptional cases in the isogeny arithmetic [17, Lemma 2]. The main consequence of this is that the key space has size ℓ^{e_ℓ} as opposed to $(\ell + 1)\ell^{e_\ell - 1}$.

The Initial Step. Our first observation is that although nodes in the isogeny graph generally have in-degree $\ell + 1$, this is not true for vertices adjacent or equal to $j = 0$ or $j = 1728$. In particular, the curve $E_0 : y^2 = x^3 + x$ has j-invariant $j = 1728$ which in the case of $\ell = 2$ has in-degree 2, while its (only) adjacent node has in-degree 4. This is shown in Fig. 1a. For $\ell = 3$ the curve has in-degree 2, while its adjacent nodes have in-degree 5; see Fig. 1b. This illustrates that although the number of distinct kernels is ℓ^{e_ℓ}, the number of distinct walks (say, as a sequence of j-invariants) in the isogeny graph is only $2^{e_2 - 1}$ (resp. $2 \cdot 3^{e_3 - 1}$) for $\ell = 2$ (resp. $\ell = 3$). We align the two (without loss of precision) by starting our walks from the curve $E_6 : y^2 = x^3 + 6x^2 + x$ when $\ell = 2$. If $\ell = 3$, we can define the kernel on a curve in the class of the left or right adjacent node to $j = 1728$ (the choice indicated by a single bit).

The reason for this behavior is that E_0 has a non-trivial automorphism group containing the distortion map ψ that maps $(x, y) \mapsto (-x, iy)$ (with inverse $-\psi$). For any kernel $\langle R \rangle$ of size ℓ^{e_ℓ} we have $E_0/\langle R \rangle \cong E_0/\langle \psi(R) \rangle$ while $\langle R \rangle \neq \langle \psi(R) \rangle$, essentially collapsing the two kernels into a single walk in the graph.

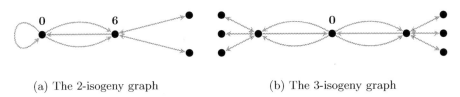

(a) The 2-isogeny graph   (b) The 3-isogeny graph

Fig. 1. Isogeny graphs starting from curves $y^2 = x^3 + Ax^2 + x$ where nodes are labeled by their A-coefficient.

Remark 1. The presence of the distortion map on the node with $j = 1728$ thus leads to loops and double edges in the graph, which reduces the entropy of the private and public keys. This security reduction for SIDH or SIKE can be easily circumvented by moving the starting node from E_0 to E_6 (with $j(E_6) = 287496$), which avoids the loop and double edge for $\ell = 2$. More concretely, setting up a torsion basis $\{P, Q\}$ of $E_6[2^e]$ such that $[2^{e-1}]Q = (0, 0)$ and choosing private keys $r \in \mathbb{Z}_{\ell^e}$ corresponding to kernels $\langle P + [r]Q \rangle$ implies this result. This suggestion has indeed been included in the Round-2 update to the SIKE specification. Note that the Round-1 SIKE specification set up Q as a point of order 2^e defined over $\mathbb{F}_p$ [7, §1.3.3]. Such a point does not exist on E_6, as

$E_6[2^e](\mathbb{F}_p) \cong \mathbb{Z}_{2^{e-1}} \times \mathbb{Z}_2$. This only implies that the description of Q is longer as it lies in $E_6(\mathbb{F}_{p^2}) \setminus E_6(\mathbb{F}_p)$.

It is not obvious how the nodes of E_6 and E_0 are connected in the 3-isogeny graph, there is no reason to believe they are close. Therefore, we believe moving to E_6 alleviates issues with double edges in the 3-isogeny graph as well.

The Final Step. Recall that our elliptic curves are represented in Montgomery form and that isogenies of degree 2^{e_2} are computed as a sequence of 4-isogenies. As already noted in [3, §4.3.2], the choice of arithmetic in SIKE implies that the points $(1, \pm\sqrt{A+2}) \in E_A$ lie in the kernel of the dual of the secret isogeny. Hence, the final step can be immediately recomputed from the public key. Consequently, $E_A/\langle(1, \pm\sqrt{A+2})\rangle$ is isogenous to E_0 by an isogeny of degree 2^{e_2-2}, and to E_6 by an isogeny of degree 2^{e_2-3}. Therefore, replacing E_A by $E_A/\langle(1, \pm\sqrt{A+2})\rangle$ reduces the number of distinct walks to 2^{e_2-3} for $\ell = 2$.

For $\ell = 3$, the representative E_A of its isomorphism class can be obtained as the co-domain curve of a 3-isogeny starting from any of its adjacent nodes. As far as we know, this does not leak any information about the final 3-isogeny.

Remark 2. To address the issue of leaking the final kernel, we notice that for any $\bar{A} \in \mathbb{F}_{p^2}$ with $j(E_{\bar{A}}) = j(E_A)$ we have

$$\bar{A} \in \left\{ \pm A, \pm(3x_2 + A)/\sqrt{x_2^2 - 1}, \pm(3z_2 + A)/\sqrt{z_2^2 - 1} \right\}, \qquad (2)$$

where $x_2, z_2 \in \mathbb{F}_{p^2}$ are chosen such that $x^3 + Ax^2 + x = x(x - x_2)(x - z_2)$. That is, the isomorphism class contains exactly six Montgomery curves. One can show that each of the 6 distinct 4-isogenies emanating from $j(E_A)$ can be computed by selecting $\bar{A}$ as above and using a kernel point (of order 4) with x-coordinate 1. Therefore, randomly choosing $\bar{A}$ from any of the options in (2) is equivalent to randomizing the kernel of the final isogeny. Unfortunately, selecting $\bar{A}$ to be anything other than $\pm A$ seems to require an expensive square root. For this reason, we do not suggest full randomization, but emphasize that the random selection of one of $\pm A$ leads to a single bit of randomization at essentially no computational effort. As a result, one would only leak the kernel of the final 2-isogeny (with kernel $(0,0)$) instead of the last 4-isogeny.

The Frobenius Endomorphism. Every isomorphism class can be represented by an elliptic curve E defined over $\mathbb{F}_{p^2}$ and has an associated Frobenius map $\pi : E \to E^{(p)}, (x, y) \mapsto (x^p, y^p)$. For any kernel $\langle R \rangle \subset E$, we have

$$j(E/\langle R \rangle)^p = j(E^{(p)}/\langle \pi(R) \rangle).$$

As a result, it suffices to search for a path to a curve with j-invariant equal to $j(E_A)$ or $j(E_A)^p$. In other words, we define an equivalence relation on the set of j-invariants by $j_0 \sim j_1$ if and only if $j_1 \in \{j_0, j_0^p\}$. Finding a path to E_A reduces to finding a path to any representative of the class $[j(E_A)]$. In Fig. 2 we show how the classes propagate through the 2-isogeny graph starting at E_6. A very similar structure appears in the 3-isogeny graph. Note that we assume that isogeny degree is approximately $\sqrt{p}$, making it unlikely for endomorphisms of that degree to exist. As such, the leaves of trees such as in Fig. 2 most probably are all distinct.

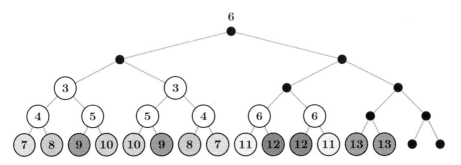

Fig. 2. Part of the 2-isogeny graph for any large $p = 2^{e_2} \cdot 3^{e_3} - 1$ starting at E_6 : $y^2 = x^3 + 6x^2 + x$. Black dots represent curves defined over $\mathbb{F}_p$, j-invariants in the same equivalence class are denoted by equal numbers. All edges represent 2-isogenies. In particular, there are exactly $2^3 + 1 = 9$ classes at distance 4 from E_6.

Although the number of classes is approximately half the number of j-invariants, it is perhaps not obvious how to translate this into a computational advantage. First assume that $\ell = 2$, and that the optimizations specified above are taken into consideration. That is, we start on the curve E_6 and look for an isogeny of degree 2^{e_2-3} to the curve E_A. As usual, kernels are of the form $P + [r]Q$ for some basis $\{P, Q\}$. Note that there is no reason to choose P and Q exactly as (multiples of) those in the SIKE specification, so we expand on a particularly simple choice here.

Recall first that $\#E_6(\mathbb{F}_p) = 2^{e_2} \cdot 3^{e_3}$ [20, Exercise V.5.10]. Since the $\mathbb{F}_p$-rational endomorphism ring of E_6 is isomorphic to one of $\mathbb{Z}[\pi]$ or $\mathbb{Z}[(1+\pi)/2]$ [4, Proposition 2.4], a result by Lenstra [10, Theorem 1(a)] tells us that

$$E_6(\mathbb{F}_p) \cong \begin{cases} \mathbb{Z}_{3^{e_3}} \times \mathbb{Z}_{2^{e_2}} & \text{if } \mathrm{End}_{\mathbb{F}_p}(E) \cong \mathbb{Z}[\pi], \\ \mathbb{Z}_{3^{e_3}} \times \mathbb{Z}_{2^{e_2}-1} \times \mathbb{Z}_2 & \text{if } \mathrm{End}_{\mathbb{F}_p}(E) \cong \mathbb{Z}[\frac{1+\pi}{2}]. \end{cases}$$

Consequently, there exists an $\mathbb{F}_p$-rational point of order 2^{e_2-3} and we can choose Q to be this element. Moreover, $p \equiv 7 \mod 8$ implies that $\sqrt{2} \in \mathbb{F}_p$, and therefore that $E_6[2] \subset E_6(\mathbb{F}_p)$. In other words, π acts trivially on points of order 2. Since π fixes Q and has eigenvalues ± 1, for any other element P such that $\langle P, Q \rangle = E_6[2^{e_2-3}]$, the action of Frobenius is given by

$$\pi|_{\langle P,Q \rangle} = \begin{pmatrix} -1 & 0 \\ \mu & 1 \end{pmatrix}, \quad \text{for some } \mu \in \mathbb{Z}_{2^{e_2-3}}.$$

Note that $[2^{e_2-2}]P$ has order 2 and therefore is fixed under π. As a result, μ is even. Replacing P by $P - \frac{\mu}{2}Q$ leads to a basis $\{P, Q\}$ such that $\pi(P) = -P$ and $\pi(Q) = Q$. Note that the value of μ can be easily found (e. g. by using the Pohlig-Hellman algorithm [19]) since the group order is extremely smooth.

Given such a basis $\{P, Q\}$, the conjugate of the j-invariant determined by $\langle R = P + [r]Q \rangle$ is given by the isogeny with kernel $\langle -\pi(R) = P + [2^{e_2-3} - r]Q \rangle$. As a result, every class $\{j, j^p\}$ can be uniquely represented by $r \in \{0, 1, \ldots, 2^{e_2-4}\}$. If we start the algorithm by separately testing $r = 2^{e_2-4}$, the remainder can be reduced to searching for kernels $\langle P + [r]Q \rangle$ where $r \in \{0, 1, \ldots, 2^{e_2-4} - 1\}$. This reduces the search space to size 2^{e_2-4}.

By a completely analogous (and even simpler) argument, we can fix a basis of $E[3^{e_3-1}]$ on any of the two adjacent nodes of E_0 in the 3-isogeny graph such that the action of π on this basis is described by a diagonal matrix with eigenvalues ± 1. Similar to the case of $\ell = 2$, this allows a reduction of the search space from $2 \cdot 3^{e_3-1}$ to (approximately) 3^{e_3-1}.

Overall, the presence of the Frobenius endomorphism on the node with $j = 1728$ reduces the number of equivalence classes that are at a given distance from j. While the Round-2 SIKE specification has moved away from $j = 1728$, the curve E_6 still has a Frobenius endomorphism. Indeed, in that case it is not helpful to differentiate between j-invariants in the same equivalence class. As (almost) every equivalence class contains 2 representatives at a certain depth, one less bit of randomness is needed to compute an isogeny of the same degree (see e. g. Fig. 2, where the final step could always move to the left node). These issues can be avoided by moving to a curve where the Frobenius map is not an endomorphism. While this prevents the Frobenius trick, it is a subtle issue (see Remark 3).

Remark 3. The curve $E_0 : y^2 = x^3 + x$ has a known endomorphism ring [20, III.4.4], which is helpful in certain attack scenarios [16]. Although one would prefer to start on a *random* node in the graph, there is no known way of randomly selecting one other than choosing a random walk in the isogeny graph. However, the walk itself cannot be public and it is unclear how to verifiably achieve this.

3.2   Applying van Oorschot-Wiener to SIKE

In this section, we fix $\ell = 2$ and describe in detail how to implement the van Oorschot-Wiener algorithm (with parameters defined as in Sects. 2.3–2.4). We point out a subtle mistake in the algorithm (appearing already in the original paper [23] and also used in the work of Adj *et al.* [1]) and show how to overcome it. The solution involves using a different notion of distinguishedness, and it allows us to achieve the average vOW runtime for a *fixed instance*. This allows us to focus on one particular instance, where we are then able to use precomputation in order to analyze the algorithm's behavior (when applied to SIKE) at a much larger scale.

Again, we assume to be given a challenge curve E_A that is isogenous of degree 2^{e_2-3} to E_6 and aim to find the isogeny. We write $e = e_2/2$ and let

$S = \{0, 1, \ldots, 2^{e-1} - 1\}$. Fix points $P, Q \in E_6$ and $U, V \in E_A$ such that $E_6[2^{e-1}] = \langle P, Q \rangle$ and $E_A[2^{e-2}] = \langle U, V \rangle$, where $\pi(P) = -P$ and $\pi(Q) = Q$.

The Step Function. We begin by describing the function family f_n. As f_n maps through classes (of size 1 or 2) in $\mathbb{F}_{p^2}$, we first define a canonical representative of the class. Since the conjugate of $j = a + b \cdot i \in \mathbb{F}_{p^2}$ is $\bar{j} = a - b \cdot i$, we say that j is *even* whenever $\text{lsb}(b) = 0$. Using $>>$ to denote the rightshift operator, we define the function h from S to the set of supersingular j-invariants by

$$h : r \mapsto \begin{cases} j & \text{if } j \text{ is even} \\ \bar{j} & \text{otherwise} \end{cases}, \text{ for } j = \begin{cases} j(E_6/\langle P + [r >> 1]Q \rangle) & \text{if } \text{lsb}(r) = 0 \\ j(E_A/\langle U + [r >> 1]V \rangle) & \text{if } \text{lsb}(r) = 1 \end{cases}.$$

In other words, the least significant bit of r determines whether we compute an isogeny starting from E_6 or E_A, while we always ensure to end up on an even j-invariant. Finally, we define $f_n : S \to S$ by $f_n(r) = g_n(h(r))$, where g_n is a hash function indexed by n that maps $h(r)$ back into S. More concretely, we let g_n be the extended output function (XOF) based on AES in CBC mode using the AES-NI instruction set (see Sect. 4), with the initialization vector and plaintext set to 0 and the key determined by n.

Note that the Frobenius map π is an endomorphism on E_6, but not (necessarily) on E_A. Given $r \in \{0, 1, \ldots 2^{e-2} - 1\}$, kernels of the form $P + [r]Q$ determine isogenies of degree 2^{e-1} starting from E_6, yet it follows from Sect. 3.1 that they correspond to exactly 2^{e-2} (distinct) equivalence classes of j-invariants. Kernels of the form $U + [r]V$ determine 2^{e-2}-isogenies from E_A, all of which lead to distinct, non-conjugate j-invariants. So h maps bijectively into a set of size $2^{e-1} - 1$, with only a single collision given by the isogeny from E_6 to E_A.

Distinguished Points and Memory. Assume the memory to have size w a power of 2. This is not technically necessary, but simplifies both the arguments and the implementation. Elements of S are represented by exactly $e - 1$ bits and we assume that $\log w \ll e - 1$.

Adj et al. [1, §4.4] determine the memory position of a triple (r_0, r_d, d) using the $\log w$ least significant bits of $\text{MD5}(3, r_d)$. Moreover, the value r_d is distinguished if and only if $\text{MD5}(2, r_d) \le 2^{32}\theta \mod 2^{32}$ (viewing the output of MD5 as an integer). Although the algorithm will run, it has several complications.

1. Calling a hash function at every step to check for distinguishedness causes overhead. Similarly, requiring a hash function computation for every read and write operation to memory causes unnecessary overhead.
2. The algorithm (typically) requires the use of several functions f_n for distinct n. Since the memory location of elements is independent of n, distinguished points (r_0, r_d, d) found by f_n and (s_0, s_e, e) found by f_{n+1} (say), with $s_e = r_d$, will be classified as a valid collision, triggering the backtracking subroutine. This will fail since f_n and f_{n+1} give rise to different random functions, leading to work going to waste. To counteract this, one could keep track of n in memory. As this is costly, the approach of Adj et al. is to zero out the memory

when the maximum number of distinguished points for a given n is reached. This can get expensive as well, especially in the case of large distributed memory.

3. The distinguishedness property is independent of n. Although the runtime of the algorithm is estimated to be $2.5\sqrt{|S|^3/w}$ by van Oorschot and Wiener [23, §4.2], this is only true if one takes the average over all collisions. However, for SIKE (and whenever one wants to find a specific collision), its input values are fixed. That is, if the golden collision of the function f is determined by values $r, s \in S$ such that $f(r) = f(s)$, then the golden collision of f_n (for all n) also occurs for r and s. The runtime will be above average if one or both of r and s are distinguished. This is because the algorithm samples a new starting value every time it reaches r or s, only computing $f_n(r)$ or $f_n(s)$ when they are sampled as initial values. Since distinguishedness is independent of n, this behavior propagates throughout all the f_n.

We give a solution to all of these problems. First, we note that elements of S are uniform bit strings of length $e - 1$. Since the value r_d of the triple is always the output of the (random) step function, we simply let the $\log w$ least significant bits determine the memory location. More precisely, the triple (r_0, r_d, d) is stored in the memory location indexed by $(r_d + n) \mod w$. Notice that we choose the location to be dependent on n. Therefore, if two triples (r_0, r_d, d) and (s_0, s_e, e) with $s_e = r_d$ are distinguished under functions f_n and f_m respectively (with $n \neq m$), they will be stored at different locations $(r_d + n) \mod w \neq (s_e + m) \mod w$, sparing us the backtracking. Moreover, any other value (t_0, t_c, c) that is stored during function version f_m at the address of (r_0, r_d, d) will have $t_c \neq r_d$, and will not be a collision, sparing us the backtracking. Of course, a memory address could be written to during both f_n and f_{n+w} and never in between. But for reasonable values of n and w this is highly unlikely, and it would only incur in the (relatively small) cost of checking for an invalid collision when it happens.

Secondly, we define a better distinguishedness property. Since it should be independent of the memory location, we use the value of $r_d \gg \log w$. As usual, using all of the remaining $e - 1 - \log w$ independent bits of r_d, we define an integer bound by $B = \theta \cdot 2^{e-1-\log w}$. We then define r_d to be distinguished if and only if

$$(r_d \gg \log w) + n \cdot B \leq B \mod 2^{e-1-\log w} .$$

With that, every element of S is distinguished for approximately one in every B functions f_n. Although we do not prove that this reduces every instance to the average case, it holds true heuristically.

We observe that the most significant bits $r_d \gg \log w$ of a distinguished element r_d are not always zero. This would be preferable since it reduces the memory requirement, not needing to store the top bits that are zero [23, §6]. Instead we can simply write the value $(r_d \gg \log w) + n \cdot B \mod 2^{e-1-\log w}$ to memory, which by definition is at most B. Adding and subtracting $n \cdot B$ modulo $2^{e-1-\log w}$ when writing to and reading from memory has negligible overhead.

We note that making distinguishedness depend on the function version also causes a triple $(-, r_d, -)$ to be unlikely to be distinguished often (where time is measured in function versions), giving time to the algorithm to overwrite a stored triple (r_0, r_d, d) with a different triple (s_0, s_e, e) with $s_e \neq r_d$, reducing the change of invalid collisions. Since both f_n-dependent memory location and distinguishedness are cheap to realise, we keep both.

Remark 4. The problems we address appear for SIDH, while the above description solves them for SIKE. An analogous solution works for SIDH, but one should be careful that the values of S are *not* uniform bit strings. They are elements $(i, b, k) \in \{1, 2\} \times \{0, 1, 2\} \times \{0, \ldots, 2^{e_2/2} - 1\}$ [1, §4.4] which are represented as $(3 + e_2/2)$-bit strings where the least significant bit determines i and the two next lower order bits determine b. Instead, we define the memory location by the value $((r_d \gg 3) + n) \bmod w$ and the distinguishedness property by

$$(r_d \gg (\log w + 3)) + n \cdot B \leq B \bmod 2^{e-1-\log w}, \quad B = \theta \cdot 2^{e-4-\log w}.$$

Here, one should be even more careful not to lose too much precision for θ, but again the assumption that $e - 1 \gg \log w$ should alleviate this. In all of our instances this is not a concern.

Precomputing the Step Function and Experiments. The main upside to the above modifications is that every problem instance will have a guaranteed average runtime of (approximately) $2.5\sqrt{|S|^3/w}$. As such, we do not have to worry about running into an unlucky instance.

However, there is a second useful consequence: to analyze the behavior of our modifications, it is sufficient to analyze a single instance. Now observe that any function f_n is of the form $f_n = g_n \circ h$, where h is fixed across the different n and by far the most expensive part of the evaluation of f_n. For testing any instance for which $h(S)$ fits into our memory, we can therefore simply precompute $h(r)$ for all $r \in S$ and store them in a table indexed by r. The evaluation of the step function $f_n(r)$ then simply looks up $h(r)$ in the table, and evaluates it under g_n (which is comparatively fast). This improves the speed of our benchmarks significantly, while not affecting any outcomes regarding a precise analysis of the vOW algorithm.[2]

We summarize the results so far in Table 1, comparing the results of our implementation to the expected theoretical outcome as well as the results of Adj *et al.* [1]. Note that our results are close to optimal, and showcase the expected speedup of a factor $\sqrt{6^3} \approx 15\times$ in the number of steps when moving from SIDH to SIKE. Moreover, we note that our software solves the SIDH instances using less than half the number of steps that were taken for the same instances in [1]. The primes used in Table 1 are

$$23 \cdot 2^{32} \cdot 3^{20} - 1, \quad 31 \cdot 2^{36} \cdot 3^{22} - 1, \quad 71 \cdot 2^{40} \cdot 3^{25} - 1, \quad 37 \cdot 2^{44} \cdot 3^{27} - 1,$$
$$13 \cdot 2^{48} \cdot 3^{30} - 1, \quad 2^{52} \cdot 3^{33} - 1, 57 \cdot 2^{56} \cdot 3^{35} - 1.$$

---

[2] Of course, this strategy is not useful for a distributed attack on an actual cryptographically sized problem instance. It only aids the efficiency of small-sized experiments in order to get a better understanding of the algorithm.

Table 1. The average number of function versions n and evaluations of f_n used for finding an isogeny of degree 2^{e_2}. The expected value (Exp.) for the number of function versions resp. steps is reported as $0.45 \cdot |S|/w$ resp. $\log\left(2.5 \cdot \sqrt{|S|^3/w}\right)$, for set size $|S| = 3 \cdot 2^{e_2/2}$ resp. $|S| = 2^{e_2/2-1}$ for SIDH resp. SIKE. The numbers are averaged over 1000 iterations and use 20 cores.

		Function versions					Steps				
		Exp.		[1]	This		Exp.		[1]	This	
e_2	$\log w$	SIDH	SIKE	SIDH	SIDH	SIKE	SIDH	SIKE	SIDH	SIDH	SIKE
32	9	173	29	319	177	28	23.20	19.32	24.38	23.29	19.58
36	10	346	58	838	342	54	25.70	21.82	27.25	25.74	21.89
40	11	691	115	1015	677	103	28.20	24.32	29.01	28.33	24.40
44	13	691	115	942	704	107	30.20	26.32	30.91	30.37	26.42
48	13	2765	461	–	–	434	33.20	29.32	–	–	29.38
52	15	2765	461	–	–	422	35.20	31.32	–	–	31.34
56	17	2765	461	–	–	424	37.20	33.32	–	–	33.38

3.3 Partial Isogeny Precomputation

Computationally, the most expensive part of the vOW step function is the (repeated) evaluation of isogenies of degree $\ell^{e_\ell/2-1}$. To alleviate this burden, one can partially precompute the isogeny tree by computing all possible isogenies of a fixed degree Δ and storing a table of the image curves together with some torsion points (that help to complete the isogenies from these intermediate curves). Such precomputation presents a trade-off between memory and computation time for the step function). We elaborate on the method in detail. As it applies to the general case of SIDH, we discuss that first and then specialize to SIKE instances with $\ell = 2$.[3]

Let E be a supersingular curve and $P, Q \in E$ be such that $\langle P, Q \rangle = E[\ell^d]$, for some $d > 0$ (typically $d \approx e_\ell/2$). Let $R = [s]P + [r]Q$ be a point of order ℓ^d, and $\phi : E \to E/\langle R \rangle$ an isogeny of degree ℓ^d with kernel $\langle R \rangle$. Recall that ℓ does not divide both r and s. We split the isogeny ϕ into two isogenies in the usual way, with the first having degree ℓ^Δ for some $0 < \Delta < d$ as follows.

Write $s = s_0 + s_1 \ell^\Delta$ and $r = r_0 + r_1 \ell^\Delta$ for $s_0, r_0 \in \mathbb{Z}_{\ell^\Delta}$ and $s_1, r_1 \in \mathbb{Z}_{\ell^{d-\Delta}}$. Then $R = [s_0]P + [r_0]Q + [\ell^\Delta]([s_1]P + [r_1]Q)$, while the point $R_\Delta = [\ell^{d-\Delta}]R = [s_0]([\ell^{d-\Delta}]P) + [r_0]([\ell^{d-\Delta}]Q)$ generates the kernel of the isogeny $\phi_\Delta : E \to E/\langle R_\Delta \rangle$ of degree ℓ^Δ. The point $\phi_\Delta(R)$ on $E/\langle R_\Delta \rangle$ has order $\ell^{d-\Delta}$ and determines an isogeny $\psi_\Delta : E/\langle R_\Delta \rangle \to E/\langle R \rangle$ of degree $\ell^{\Delta-d}$ such that $\phi = \psi_\Delta \circ \phi_\Delta$. Crucially, the first pair of partial scalars ($s_0 = s$ mod ℓ^Δ, $r_0 = r$ mod ℓ^Δ) determines ϕ_Δ and the points $\phi_\Delta([s_0]P + [r_0]Q)$, $\phi_\Delta([\ell^\Delta]P)$ and $\phi_\Delta([\ell^\Delta]Q)$ on $E/\langle R_\Delta \rangle$. Given this curve and these points,

---

[3] The extreme case, when the full isogeny tree from one side is precomputed, corresponds to the meet-in-the-middle algorithm as described by Adj *et al.* [1].

the second pair of partial scalars ($s_1 = \lfloor s/\ell^\Delta \rfloor, r_1 = \lfloor r/\ell^\Delta \rfloor$) determines $\ker \psi_\Delta = (\phi_\Delta([s_0]P + [r_0]Q)) + [s_1]\phi_\Delta([\ell^\Delta]P) + [r_1]\phi_\Delta([\ell^\Delta]Q)$ and allows to complete the isogeny ϕ. Therefore, precomputation consists of computing a table with entries

$$\left[E/\langle R_\Delta \rangle, \phi_\Delta([s_0]P + [r_0]Q), \phi_\Delta([\ell^\Delta]P), \phi_\Delta([\ell^\Delta]Q) \right],$$

for all $(s_0, r_0) \in \mathbb{Z}_{\ell^\Delta}^2$ such that ℓ does not divide both s_0 and r_0. Such a table entry can then be used to compute any full degree isogeny of degree ℓ^d with kernel point $R = [s]P + [r]Q$ such that $s \equiv s_0 \mod \ell^\Delta$ and $r \equiv r_0 \mod \ell^\Delta$ and any (s_1, r_1).

However, it suffices to store only two points on $E/\langle R_\Delta \rangle$. If $\ell \nmid s$, we can assume that $s = 1$ and $R = P + [r]Q$ for $r \in \mathbb{Z}_{\ell^d}$. Then $R_\Delta = [\ell^{d-\Delta}]P + [r_0 \cdot \ell^{d-\Delta}]Q$ and the precomputed table only needs to contain entries of the form

$$[E/\langle R_\Delta \rangle, P_\Delta = \phi_\Delta(P + [r_0]Q), Q_\Delta = \phi_\Delta([\ell^\Delta]Q)] \tag{3}$$

for all $r_0 \in \mathbb{Z}_{\ell^\Delta}$. The kernel of ψ_Δ (for completing ϕ) can be computed as $\phi_\Delta(R) = P_\Delta + [r_1]Q_\Delta$ for any r with $r \equiv r_0 \mod \ell^\Delta$. If $\ell \mid s$, then $\ell \nmid r$ and $R = [\ell t]P + Q$ for some $t \in \mathbb{Z}_{\ell^{d-1}}$ such that $s = \ell t$. In that case table entries are of the form

$$[E/\langle R_\Delta \rangle, P_\Delta = \phi_\Delta([\ell^\Delta]P), Q_\Delta = \phi_\Delta([\ell t_0]P + Q)]$$

for all $t_0 \in \mathbb{Z}_{\ell^{\Delta-1}}$, while $\ker \psi_\Delta = [t_1]P_\Delta + Q_\Delta$. Altogether, the table contains $\ell^\Delta + \ell^{\Delta-1} = (\ell + 1) \cdot \ell^{\Delta-1}$ entries and reduces the cost of any isogeny of degree ℓ^d from $d \log d$ to $(d - \Delta) \log(d - \Delta)$ [3, §4.2.2].

Now we move on to SIKE and fix $\ell = 2$. That is, we assume $s = 1$ and every table entry to be of the form (3). Recall that the function h takes as input a value $r \in \mathbb{Z}_{\ell^{e-1}}$ (where $e = e_2/2$) and computes an isogeny with kernel $\langle P + [r \gg 1]Q \rangle$ on E_6 if $\text{lsb}(r) = 0$, and an isogeny with kernel $\langle U + [r \gg 1]V \rangle$ on E_A otherwise. The latter reflects the case above with $d = e - 2$ perfectly, leading to a precomputed table of size 2^Δ from E_A while reducing the cost of the isogeny from $(e - 2) \log(e - 2)$ to $(e - 2 - \Delta) \log(e - 2 - \Delta)$. The case of the curve E_6 is slightly different due to the presence of the Frobenius endomorphism. Although there are 2^{e-2} distinct equivalence classes of j-invariants, the degree of the corresponding isogenies is 2^{e-1}. As such, we compute a table of size 2^Δ comprising of the equivalence classes of j-invariants at depth $\Delta + 1$ away from E_6.[4] As a result, all isogenies used throughout the whole implementation have fixed degree $e - 2 - \Delta$. The isogeny cost reduces from $(e - 1) \log(e - 1)$ to $(e - 2 - \Delta) \log(e - 2 - \Delta)$ and choosing Δ such that $e - 2 - \Delta \equiv 0 \mod 2$ allows the use of 4-isogenies as in SIKE. Table 2 demonstrates the effect of precomputation on the SIKE step function.

---

[4] This slightly changes how an element $r_0 + r_1 2^\Delta \in \mathbb{Z}_{2^{e-2}}$, for $r_0 \in \mathbb{Z}_{2^\Delta}$ and $r_1 \in \mathbb{Z}_{2^{e-2-\Delta}}$, corresponds to an isogeny. Instead of kernel $\langle P + [r_0 + r_1 2^\Delta]Q \rangle$, it now gives rise to the kernel $\langle P + [r_0 + r_1 2^{\Delta+1}]Q \rangle$. This has no impact on the algorithm.

Table 2. Effect of precomputation on the running time of the SIKE step function. Numbers represent the cumulative running time in seconds of 1000000 calls to the step function, for the corresponding modulus and precomputation depth Δ. All experiments were run on Atomkohle.

e_2	0	2	4	6	8	10	12	14	16	18	20	22	24	26	28
32	20.51	17.96	15.47	13.09	10.91	8.84	7.17	4.92	—	—	—	—	—	—	—
36	23.50	20.46	17.91	15.45	13.08	10.85	8.82	7.18	4.84	—	—	—	—	—	—
40	26.79	23.60	20.97	18.45	15.96	13.60	11.42	9.35	7.62	5.00	—	—	—	—	—
44	29.37	26.34	23.58	21.01	18.44	15.96	13.60	11.38	9.32	7.70	4.89	—	—	—	—
48	32.48	29.57	26.88	24.21	21.33	18.80	16.25	13.83	11.57	9.41	7.70	4.87	—	—	—
52	36.38	32.93	29.92	27.13	24.15	21.53	18.85	16.36	13.93	11.64	9.48	7.76	4.87	—	—
56	40.05	35.48	33.29	29.67	26.80	25.60	21.46	18.94	16.43	14.60	11.83	9.73	8.03	4.89	—
60	41.56	38.54	35.72	32.73	29.91	27.09	24.38	21.69	19.17	16.68	14.26	12.03	9.95	8.26	4.96

Computing an Isogeny Tree. To obtain the lookup table, one computes image curves and torsion points for all isogenies of degree 2^Δ (resp. $2^{\Delta+1}$) and stores them indexed by their kernel representation. Adj *et al.* [1, Section 3.2] describe a depth-first-search approach to compute the required curves as the leaves of a full 2-isogeny tree of depth $e_2/2$ for the meet-in-the-middle algorithm (c. f. [1, Fig. 1]). This method is much more efficient than the naive way of computing full $2^{e_2/2}$-isogenies for all possible kernel points. Obviously, it can be applied for partial trees to compute isogenies of degree 2^Δ (resp. $2^{\Delta+1}$) and an analogous version can utilize a 4-isogeny tree.

Using Memory for Precomputation. Depending on the specific problem instances and communication properties of the network, the memory required for precomputation could alternatively be used as part of the main memory that stores distinguished points. In other words, precomputed tables might take away a certain amount of memory from the distinguished point storage space.

Assume that due to latency and communication constraints, each of the m parallel processors needs its own table of size $\tau(\Delta)$, and for simplicity that every processor precomputes the same depth tree. For example, for the SIDH case of Adj *et al.* [1] we would assume each processor to have precomputed a table of size $\tau(\Delta) = 2 \cdot (2^\Delta + 2^{\Delta-1}) = 3 \cdot 2^\Delta$. For SIKE, this size is $\tau(\Delta) = 2 \cdot 2^\Delta = 2^{\Delta+1}$.

As shown in Sect. 2.4, each distinguished point is represented with roughly e_2 bits (i. e. about $\frac{1}{2} \log p$ bits) since $\log |S| = e_2/2 - 1$. This takes into account that the $\lfloor - \log \theta \rfloor$ leading zeros in a distinguished point are omitted in memory. Every entry in the precomputed table can be represented by three $\mathbb{F}_{p^2}$ elements (i. e. about $6 \log p$ bits). Therefore, each such table element uses memory that could store about 12 distinguished points instead. For precomputation depth Δ, the table entries thus use space for $12 \cdot \tau(\Delta)$ distinguished points. This means that the vOW main memory is reduced from w to $w - 12 \cdot \tau(\Delta) \cdot m$ points (when each of the m processors stores its own table). Thus, the number of function iterations increases by a factor $1/\sqrt{1 - 12 \cdot \tau(\Delta) \cdot m/w}$. Note that this is well-defined since $12 \cdot \tau(\Delta) \cdot m$ cannot exceed the maximum available memory w.

While taking away memory increases the expected number of function iterations, precomputation reduces the step function cost by a factor $\sigma(\Delta, e)$. We have $\sigma(\Delta, e) = (e - \Delta) \log(e - \Delta)/(e \log e)$ for SIDH (given e_2 is even), while for SIKE (separating the two equally likely cases where we start from E_6 resp. E_A)

$$\sigma(\Delta, e) = \frac{1}{2} \left(\frac{(e - 2 - \Delta) \log(e - 2 - \Delta)}{(e - 2) \log(e - 2)} + \frac{(e - 2 - \Delta) \log(e - 2 - \Delta)}{(e - 1) \log(e - 1)} \right). \quad (4)$$

The total runtime of the van Oorschot-Wiener algorithm decreases if

$$\frac{\sigma(\Delta, e)}{\sqrt{1 - 12 \cdot \tau(\Delta) \cdot m/w}} < 1.$$

Remark 5. In an actual distributed implementation, the situation might be different and favor precomputation more. For example, it is reasonable to assume that several processors in a multi-core machine are able to share a precomputed table. Furthermore, depending on the design of the main memory, each machine may have memory available that cannot contribute to it and might as well be used to store a table for a limited amount of precomputation. In such situations, using memory for lookup tables might not have any negative effect on the overall runtime. Example 1 shows that speed-ups for cryptographic parameters can be obtained with very small tables, making this scenario more realistic.

Example 1. Let $p = 2^{216} \cdot 3^{137} - 1$ and $(e, m, w) = (108, 2^{64}, 2^{80})$, following the setup of [1, Remark 6]. For both SIKE and SIDH, the (near) optimal precomputation depth is $\Delta = 6$ and each processor pre-computes a local table that takes up space for $12 \cdot \tau(\Delta)$ distinguished elements; this requires around 41 resp. 62 kilobytes of memory per processor (totalling 2.34% resp. 3.52% of the full memory w). In both cases, the step function cost is reduced by a factor $\sigma(\Delta, e) \approx 0.93$. For SIKE, we decrease the runtime of the full algorithm by a factor approximately 0.94, for SIDH, by about 0.95.

However, a more realistic example assumes that many processors can share the precomputation table. In our setup, a machine of 40 cores can share a single table. In that case, the optimal depth is found at $\Delta = 12$. For SIKE, we use a table of about 2.7 megabytes per processor (totalling approximately 3.75% of the total memory w). The cost of the algorithm is reduced by a factor 0.88. For SIDH we obtain a table of size 4.0 megabytes (5.63% of the total memory). The runtime is decreased by a factor 0.89.

3.4   Fast Collision Checking

As discussed in Remark 5, in a distributed implementation processors are likely to have local memory that cannot contribute to the main memory (that which is used for storing distinguished point triples). We now describe another way to use such memory to significantly improve the overall runtime of van Oorschot-Wiener. Analogous to Sect. 3.3, even if memory is consumed that could otherwise be used to store distinguished points, we argue that dedicating a moderate amount of storage to this faster collision checking reduces the overall runtime.

Recall from Sect. 2.3 that a single walk in the vOW algorithm starts at a point $x_0 \in S$ and produces a trail of points $x_i = f(x_{i-1})$ for $i = 1, 2, \ldots$, until it reaches a distinguished point x_d. Assume that the triple (x_0, x_d, d) collides with a triple, say (y_0, y_e, e), previously stored in main memory and that it is not a mere memory collision. To check if we have found the golden collision, we need to locate the indices $i < d$ and $j < e$ for which $x_i \neq y_j$ and $f(x_i) = f(y_j)$. Van Oorschot and Wiener note that, since d and e have expected value $1/\theta$, retracing the two paths from their starting points to the colliding point requires $2/\theta$ total steps on average [23, p. 9]. Our goal is to lower the overall runtime by reducing the number of function iterations for retracing.

Saving Intermediate Values. Suppose that apart from the global memory for keeping distinguished points, a processor has access to enough local memory to store $t - 1$ additional points intermittently (more on what this means in a moment). On a walk from x_0 to x_d, it now stores $t + 1$ points in total. These points $(x_{d_0} = x_0, x_{d_1}, \ldots, x_{d_t} = x_d)$, where $0 = d_0 < d_1 < \cdots < d_t$, can now be used together with (y_0, y_e), to locate the collision more efficiently.

We start by copying y_0 to y', e to e' and iterate steps $y' \leftarrow f(y'), e' \leftarrow e' - 1$. When y' is the same distance away from the distinguished point as the closest of the saved points, say x_{d_j} (i.e. j is minimal with $e' = d_t - d_j$), we check whether $y' = x_{d_j}$. If not, we set $y_0 \leftarrow y'$ and step y' forward $d_{j+1} - d_j$ steps and compare again. This is repeated until y' collides with one of the saved points, say x_{d_k}. Note that equality checks only occur with the x_{d_i} and not at every step as in the original collision checking function. Once the minimal index k with $y' = x_{d_k}$ is detected, we know that the collision must take place between $x_{d_{k-1}}$ and x_{d_k}. At this point, the original collision checking function without saving intermediate points can be called on the triples $(x_{d_{k-1}}, x_{d_k}, d_k - d_{k-1})$ and $(y_0, y', d_k - d_{k-1})$. Note that if the collision occurs at x_{d_0}, we have a Robin Hood and return `false`.

What have we gained? First of all, the trail with stored points is not retraced at all, only in the final call to the original collision checking, on a single subinterval of length $d_k - d_{k-1}$, which in general is much shorter than the original trail length d_t. The trail starting at y_0 is fully retraced to the collision, where additional steps are taken that cover the colliding interval. The savings are larger when intervals are shorter and thus when more intermediate points are saved. This approach is implemented in our software.

Figure 3 shows how the number of function steps for checking and locating collisions is reduced when running vOW on an AES-based function with a set of size 2^{30} and memory of size 2^{15}. With $\alpha = 2.25$, the average walk length is $1/\theta \approx 80$. There is an immediate gain for even allowing a small number of intermediate points. However, additional gains become smaller when increasing this number because, when the maximal number of intermediate points approaches the average trail length, almost every point can be stored and adding more memory does not add more intermediate points, nor influence the distance between them.

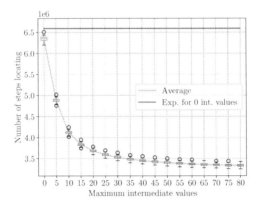

Fig. 3. Number of steps used for locating a collision as a function of maximum amount of intermediate values allowed for the AES-based random function with $\log |S| = 30$, $\log w = 15$. Averaged over 64 function versions, using 28 cores and run on Atomkohle.

Remark 6. There is potential for further improvement by allowing storage for $2t - 2$ points. As above, the $t - 1$ points $(x_{d_0}, \ldots, x_{d_{k-2}}, x_{d_{k+1}}, x_{d_t})$ are stored while walking the trail. But during collision checking against (y_0, y_e, e), $t-1$ additional intermediate points are stored when retracing the trail from y_0. When the collision is encountered, the latter points take the place of the x_{d_i} and $(y_0, y_e) \leftarrow (x_{d_{k-1}}, x_{d_k})$. Storage for the $t - 1$ elements $(x_{d_0}, \ldots, x_{d_{k-2}}, x_{d_{k+1}}, x_{d_t})$ can be reused for keeping intermittent points when retracing the trail from the new y_0. Repeating this procedure, we recurse until $y_e = f(y_0)$, at which point we check for the golden collision. Note that splitting the space for $2t - 2$ points in half eases the exposition, but might be suboptimal. The optimal allocation of memory to the different trails should be determined for a large scale cryptanalytic effort based on how much memory is available.

How to Save Points Intermittently. It remains to describe how the $t-1$ intermediate points are stored. Given the expected trail length of $1/\theta$, one could store points at regular intervals of length $1/(t\theta)$. However, walks much longer than $1/\theta$ would lead to a much larger distance between the final intermediate point and the distinguished point; walks much shorter than $1/\theta$ would lead to unused memory that could have decreased the average gap between intermediate points. In the ideal scenario, a full set of $(t - 1)$ additional points is stored and they are as close to being equally spaced as possible when the distinguished point is reached. Since trails randomly vary in length, the best approach involves overwriting previously placed points in such a way that the distances between points grow with the trail length.

We modify an algorithm for finding cycles in random walks by Sedgewick, Szymanski and Yao [18]. In the first t steps of the trail, the allocated memory is exhausted by storing a point at every step, so that $(d_0, d_1, \ldots, d_{t-1}, d_t) = (0, 1, \ldots, t-1, t)$, and the points are all at distance 1 from one another. At any stage of the procedure, define $\delta = \min_{j>0}\{d_j - d_{j-1}\}$. From hereon, every δ steps, we simply look for the smallest value of j where $d_j - d_{j-1} = \delta$, remove the point x_{d_j} from the list, and add the current point to the list. At some point, the last point that is δ steps away from another point will be deleted and replaced by a point that is twice as far away from the last; by definition, δ is simultaneously doubled and all of the points in the list are δ away from each other.

4   Implementation

We produced two implementations of the van Oorschot-Wiener algorithm, one in C, optimized for efficiency, and a more modular one in C++. The C implementation makes use of the Microsoft SIDH library [12] for field and curve arithmetic when running the attack against SIDH and SIKE instances. We have modified their code to support smaller primes, and added non-constant time operations if beneficial (e.g. finite field inversions). For parallel computations we use the gcc implementation of OpenMP 4.5 [15]. For simplifying batch experiments we wrote Python wrappers to our code using SWIG [2].

The experiments are run on two different machines. The first, referred to as Atomkohle, contains two Intel(R) Xeon(R) E5-2690 v4 CPUs running at 2.60 GHz that both have 14 physical cores (so 28 in total). The second, referred to as Solardiesel, contains two Intel(R) Xeon(R) Gold 6138 CPUs at 2.00 GHz that have 20 cores each (40 in total). Unless specified otherwise, all measurements and statistics reported in this paper have been produced using the C implementation and are compiled with gcc version 6.3.0.

Optimized Implementation. The C software contains three step functions to run experiments. The first is a generic, fast random function, and the other two are those arising from random walks in the 2-isogeny graph as determined by the SIDH (see Sect. 2.3) and SIKE (see Sect. 3.2) specifications. This allows the use of a fast random function to verify that our implementation matches the expected asymptotic values (confirming the original vOW analysis [23]) and linear speed-up on larger sets, while also displaying our improvements in the SIDH and SIKE settings (e.g. as shown in Table 1).

Modular Implementation. While for all SIDH and SIKE experiments we used our C implementation on individual multi-core machines, it would be interesting to deploy the van Oorschot-Wiener algorithm in alternative settings. For example, running attacks with more cores distributed over the internet could change the balance between the cost of a step function evaluation and the cost of memory access, and would certainly present memory topology and core synchronization challenges. Furthermore, collision-finding techniques play a role in the cryptanalysis of other encryption schemes, e.g. NTRU [6,24], where memory constrained

Table 3. Reproduction of Table 3 from [1], using our C++ implementation, using an AES-based generic random function on Atomkohle. Experiments are run using 20 cores. $\#f_n$ is the number of different random functions used per instance.

			Expected		Average		
$\log|S|$	$\log w$	#runs	$\#f_n$	$\log\sqrt{|S|^3/w}$	$\#f_n$	$\log\sqrt{|S|^3/w}$	cycles
18	9	1000	230.40	23.82	204.74	23.83	30.23
20	10	1000	460.80	26.32	420.01	26.27	30.57
22	11	1000	921.60	28.82	898.79	28.86	33.05
24	13	1000	921.60	30.82	850.49	30.74	34.89

cryptanalytic experiments could be useful. Since it could be tricky to adapt our C code to such varied settings, we also produced a C++ implementation with the goal of obtaining a more modular, developer-friendly, code base. Test results on a fast, generic, random function showing that it matches the expected asymptotics can be found in Table 3. Ideally, it should not be too difficult to write "drivers" for access to different forms of memory (say, storage over the internet rather than local RAM), or different sets S and step functions f_n.

Selecting a XOF and PRNG. One goal of actually implementing vOW is to verify the runtime against the asymptotic theoretical values, using a fast random function. Adj *et al.* [1] chose to use an MD5-based random function for this purpose. We have instead opted for a custom XOF based on AES-CBC mode using AES-NI instructions. This provides much better performance on modern hardware, while guaranteeing cryptographic properties of the function. Regarding our PRNG, we use AES-CTR mode with AES-NI instructions.

In Table 4 we reproduce [23, Table 1] which computes the $O(\cdot)$ constant in front of the expected number of steps for the optimal choice of θ and is used to determine the constant α, to demonstrate the validity of our pseudo-random step function.

5   Analysis of SIKE Round-2 Parameters

In the Round 2 of the NIST standardization effort, the analyses of Adj *et al.* [1] and Jaques and Schanck [9] have prompted the introduction of two new parameter sets to the SIKE submission, SIKEp434 and SIKEp610, as well as a security reassessment of the parameter sets SIKEp503 and SIKEp751. The four sets are based on the primes p434 $= 2^{216}3^{137} - 1$, p503 $= 2^{250}3^{159} - 1$, p610 $= 2^{305}3^{192} - 1$ and p751 $= 2^{372}3^{239} - 1$, and target security categories 1, 2, 3 and 5, respectively.

This section provides concrete classical security estimates for these parameter sets, in two different ways; the first follows an approach similar to the one by van Oorschot and Wiener and Adj *et al.* We count the average number of oracle calls to run the vOW algorithm and multiply them by the complexity of the oracle

Table 4. Reproduction of [23, Table 1], using the AES-based XOF on Solardiesel, i.e. the number of function steps required to find the golden collision divided by $|S|^{3/2}/w^{1/2}$. The experiments are averaged over 1000 function versions and run with 20 cores.

				$\log w$				
$\log |S|$	2	4	6	8	10	12	14	16
20	3.90	2.87	2.62	2.52	2.48	2.45	2.40	2.28
24	3.99	2.89	2.60	2.51	2.48	2.48	2.47	2.45
28	3.95	2.92	2.59	2.51	2.49	2.48	2.48	2.47
32	4.07	2.90	2.61	2.51	2.49	2.48	2.48	2.48
36	4.22	2.94	2.60	2.52	2.49	2.48	2.48	2.48

itself, measured in x64 instructions. This leads to a more informed estimate than provided by Adj *et al.* and Jaques and Schanck, but the final result remains the same – see Sect. 5.1. A downside of this approach is that although it captures much of the algorithm's cost, it ignores some potentially significant parts. In particular, it does not account for the cost of memory access (assumed free) or the practical difficulty of scaling across different cores (assumed linear), see [1, §5, Remark 6]. We present an alternative method in Sect. 5.2.

5.1 Concrete Security of SIKE Round-2 Parameters

In Table 5 we use the Round-2 SIKE implementation to estimate the number of x64 instructions necessary to compute *half-size* isogenies. More specifically, we provide estimations for $2^{\lfloor e_2/2 \rfloor - 2}$-isogenies in Table 5a and for $3^{\lfloor e_3/2 \rfloor}$-isogenies in Table 5b. These instruction counts are intended to be lower bounds on the number of classical gates required to mount vOW, and we argue that these estimates are still conservative with respect to the true gate count. A lower bound on the runtime of the vOW algorithm can now simply be obtained by multiplying the costs of the above isogeny oracles with the number of times they are called, which we summarize in Table 6. Our analysis concludes that the number of classical gates required for (i) vOW on SIKEp434 is at least 2^{143}, (ii) vOW on SIKEp503 is at least 2^{170}, (iii) vOW on SIKEp610 is at least 2^{210}, and (iv) vOW on SIKEp751 is at least 2^{262}. Note that the counts for (i) and (iii) closely agree with classical gate counts by Jaques and Schanck, who are also rather conservative in their costing of the isogeny functions – see [9, §7.1].

5.2 Concrete Security of SIKEp434

Finally, we focus our attention on arguably the most interesting cryptanalytic target, namely the SIKE Round-2 category-1 parameter set SIKEp434 with claimed (classical) security comparable to AES-128. Although the analysis in

Table 5. Isogeny costs in terms of the total number of x64 instructions i_{sum}, broken down into multiplication instructions i_{mul}, addition, subtraction and logical instructions i_{asl} and move instructions i_{mov}; **M** denotes multiplication, **S** squaring, **add** addition and **sub** subtraction in $\mathbb{F}_{p^2}$.

	DBL	4-iso	**M**	**S**	**add**	**sub**	i_{mul}	i_{asl}	i_{mov}	$\log(i_{sum})$
SIKEp434	282	166	2124	1560	1726	1228	595476	2099108	1534760	22.01
SIKEp503	362	189	2582	1858	2047	1480	905376	3332506	2099672	22.60
SIKEp610	434	255	3266	2398	2653	1888	1638294	5433856	3553530	23.34
SIKEp751	548	334	4196	3100	3434	2432	3254832	9365124	9863656	24.42

(a) Costs for a $2^{\lfloor e_2/2 \rfloor - 2}$-isogeny (omitting single 2-isogenies for odd exponent) using an optimal strategy composed of quadrupling and 4-isogeny steps; DBL denotes a point doubling, 4-iso a 4-isogeny computation, and the cost for DBL is assumed to be $4M + 2S + 2add + 2sub$ and for 4-iso it is $6M + 6S + 7add + 4sub$.

	TPL	3-iso	**M**	**S**	**add**	**sub**	i_{mul}	i_{asl}	i_{mov}	$\log(i_{sum})$
SIKEp434	199	217	2695	2080	3635	2478	769445	2826741	2067722	22.43
SIKEp503	229	275	3253	2520	4537	2978	1172192	4479442	2875831	23.02
SIKEp610	290	350	4130	3200	5770	3780	2112930	7266720	4861220	23.76
SIKEp751	395	429	5339	4120	7191	4910	4208868	12471749	13228173	24.83

(b) Costs for a $3^{\lfloor e_3/2 \rfloor}$-isogeny (omitting single 3-isogenies for odd exponent) using an optimal strategy composed of point tripling and 3-isogeny steps; TPL denotes a point tripling, 3-iso a 3-isogeny computation and the cost for TPL is assumed to be $7M + 5S + 3add + 7sub$ and for 3-iso it is $6M + 5S + 14add + 5sub$.

Table 6. Average number of x64 instructions to run vOW on the 2- and 3-torsion for the Round-2 SIKE parameters with memory size $w = 2^{80}$, set size $N = |S| = 2^{e_2/2-1}$ for the 2-torsion and $N = |S| = 3^{(e_3-1)/2}$ for the 3-torsion – see Sect. 3. Numbers are shown as the floor of their base-2 logarithms. The number of isogeny computations, #isog, is computed by setting $m = t = 1$ in Eq. (1), and the numbers i_{sum} of instructions for each isogeny are taken from Tables 5a and 5b. The total number of instructions, **vOW**, is the product of #isog and i_{sum} and is intended to act as a lower bound on the number of gates required to solve the CSSI problem with the vOW algorithm.

	2-torsion				3-torsion			
	N	#isog	i_{sum}	**vOW**	N	#isog	i_{sum}	**vOW**
SIKEp434	107	121	22	**143**	107	122	22	**144**
SIKEp503	124	147	23	**170**	125	149	23	**172**
SIKEp610	151	187	23	**210**	150	187	23	**210**
SIKEp751	185	238	24	**262**	188	244	24	**268**

the previous section shows agreement between our estimates and those in the literature, all approaches so far have one thing in common: communication and memory access costs are not taken into account. As these become non-negligible when the memory and the number of cores grow — already mentioned in the context of SIDH/SIKE by Adj. *et al.* [1, Remark 6] — one can wonder how significant they are. Since such costs are often difficult to capture in theoretical models, we take a more practical approach.

We start by noticing that the current complexity estimates are measured in *average number of oracle calls*, where an oracle call corresponds to an isogeny computation (e. g. of degree 2^{106} or 3^{68} for SIKEp434). Given the fact that we now have an optimized implementation of the algorithm itself, a simple alternative is to measure the complexity in *average number of cycles* instead. Much of the heuristic approach of van Oorschot and Wiener [23, §4.2] remains the same; we run a single function version and measure the number of distinct collisions it generates, from which we approximate the runtime of the full algorithm. That is, we assume that each function version behaves approximately the same with respect to the number of distinct collisions it generates, which van Oorschot and Wiener heuristically show to be true for $w \geq 2^{16}$ (the results for different function versions are within 1% of one another). Thus, writing N for the set size and c for the number of distinct collisions generated per function version, every function version has (independent) probability $2c/N$ to find the golden collision and completing the vOW algorithm requires on average $N/(2c)$ versions. If each one requires t cycles to complete, the average total runtime is therefore $tN/(2c)$.

Equivalently, on average we need t/c cycles per generated collision, of which there are $N/2$ in total, leading to the above average runtime. Therefore, one may want to simplify the analysis by generating only very few collisions and approximating the runtime from that. However, we note that t/c is very large in the beginning of the algorithm as the memory starts out being empty, while the distribution of distinguished points in memory becomes biased towards those with lower probability of producing a collision – see [23, §4.2]. It may be possible to run less than a full function version to get a close approximation of t/c, but we consider this out of scope for this work and stick with completing a function version for our estimations.

Looking at the conjectured setup proposed by Adj *et al.* (i. e. memory $w = 2^{80}$, $m = 2^{64}$ cores), when used against SIKEp434 the number of oracle calls grows linearly with $\sqrt{Nw}/m$, where $N = 2^{107}$, while each oracle call takes on the order of 2^{22} x64 instructions (see Table 5a). In the theoretical model where memory accesses are free and the algorithm parallelizes perfectly, the function version can be run with approximately $2^{51.5}$ x64 instructions per core (and to run the full algorithm we need approximately 2^{27} function versions, agreeing with the estimates in Table 6). If each x64 instruction were a single cycle on a machine running at 1 GHz, such a computation would finish in about 37 days. Although it should be noted that such a setup is not realistic, other combinations of resources allow for (theoretically) running a single function version within a reasonable amount of time (say, a year). It is not clear that these runtimes will hold true in practice, as for example distributing the experiment across different machines can cause significant overhead. We consider exploring this overhead, e. g. by analyzing how different network topologies affect the results, a very worthwhile research direction.

In a more constrained environment, i. e. when running experiments on Atom-kohle for which we choose $w \in \{2^{16}, 2^{18}, 2^{20}\}$ and $m = 28$, running a single SIKEp434 function version requires millions of years. Instead, we decrease the degree e of the isogeny we try to reconstruct, but do not change the finite field, to a point where experiments run in a few hours. Crucially, if the theoretical analysis of van Oorschot and Wiener holds up for these resources, then the run-time of a function version grows linearly with $\sqrt{N}$ and we can extrapolate the runtime of a single function version for the actual SIKEp434 parameters on such a setup by drawing a line through the data points. Interestingly, the difference between this approximation of the security of SIKEp434 when compared to the theory can be seen as an error measure for the theoretical analysis of vOW (the better the fit, the closer the theory to reality).

More concretely, we choose $e = 28, 30, \ldots, 42$ and measure the cycle counts to complete one function version and the number of distinct collisions that they generate. We use precomputation depth $\Delta = 16$ and to account for the differ-ence of the cost of the oracle (a 2^e-isogeny) we normalize the cycle count by a factor $\sigma(\Delta, e) \cdot \zeta(e)$, with $\zeta(e) = (1/2) \cdot ((e-2)\log(e-2) + (e-1)\log(e-1))$ the estimated average cost of the oracle and $\sigma(\Delta, e)$ given as in Eq. (4). Hence, we have a measure for the average number t/c of cycles required to generate a single collision, which we summarize in Table 7.

For a fixed w, we then extrapolate, using the least squares method, the function that maps $\sqrt{2^{e-1}}$ to the corresponding value in the table. This leads to the three approximation functions

$$z_{16}(e) = \sigma(\Delta, e) \cdot \zeta(e) \cdot (3.44.. \cdot \sqrt{2^{e-1}} + 19247.78..),$$

$$z_{18}(e) = \sigma(\Delta, e) \cdot \zeta(e) \cdot (1.72.. \cdot \sqrt{2^{e-1}} + 6151.88..),$$

$$z_{20}(e) = \sigma(\Delta, e) \cdot \zeta(e) \cdot (0.87.. \cdot \sqrt{2^{e-1}} - 928.81..),$$

where the factor $\sigma(\Delta, e) \cdot \zeta(e)$ is only there to undo the normalization factor. For any w, the runtime of a single function version for SIKEp434 is then $z_{\log(w)}(e)$ cycles, while the full algorithm has total runtime $2^{e-2} \cdot z_{\log(w)}(e)$ cycles, since $|N| = 2^{e-1}$. Thus, setting $e = 108$, we expect vOW on SIKEp434 to have a runtime of $2^{170.47..}$, $2^{169.47..}$ and $2^{168.50..}$ cycles for $w = 2^{16}$, $w = 2^{18}$ and $w = 2^{20}$ respectively. For comparison, using Eq. (1) combined with the approximation of the cost of the isogeny oracle of Table 5a, we expect runtimes $2^{170.71..}$, $2^{169.71..}$ and $2^{168.71..}$ x64 instructions respectively. We observe that these approximations match very closely, confirming that the theoretical estimates lie very close to the practical runtimes for these values of w and m. Indeed, this is no surprise, as such small values should not cause significant overhead.

However, we emphasize that this is the first time a theoretical estimate on the security of SIKEp434 is met with serious practical consideration (i. e. without

Table 7. Number of cycles (measured in thousands and rounded to the nearest multiple of 10^3) to generate a single collision, for different memory sizes w and isogeny instances of degree 2^{e_2}, where $e = e_2/2$. All numbers are scaled by a factor $\sigma(\Delta, e) \cdot \zeta(e)$.

w	e							
	28	30	32	34	36	38	40	42
2^{16}	69	113	177	391	726	1 331	2 257	5 261
2^{18}	–	57	90	196	362	659	1 122	2 642
2^{20}	–	–	46	99	182	331	557	1 340

ignoring memory access times and issues with parallelism). If our setup with $w = 2^{20}$ was run on an instance with $e = 108$ it would require (on average) $2^{168.50..}$ cycles to complete. We believe this value could therefore be viewed as an *upper* bound on the security level of SIKEp434. On the other hand, the analyses of Adj *et al.* [1] and Jaques and Schanck [9], assuming $w = 2^{80}$ and $m = 2^{64}$, provide a *lower* bound on the security level. This gap could be closed by computing $z_{\log(w)}$ for larger values of w and m and showing that they agree with the theoretical estimations, which is a valuable effort that should be seriously considered to understand the security of SIKEp434. It is of course not clear that the gap between the upper and lower bound will vanish completely; scaling the setup to large memory and distributed systems will cause significant overhead, which is also noticeable in cryptanalytic efforts in other domains [26].

Acknowledgements. We thank Greg Zaverucha and Christian Konig for helpful discussions and their input to this paper, and Martin Albrecht for providing access to two of his machines for running our experiments.

References

1. Adj, G., Cervantes-Vázquez, D., Chi-Domínguez, J.-J., Menezes, A., Rodríguez-Henríquez, F.: On the cost of computing isogenies between supersingular elliptic curves. In: Cid, C., Jacobson Jr., M. (eds.) SAC 2018. LNCS, pp. 322–343. Springer, Heidelberg (2019). https://doi.org/10.1007/978-3-030-10970-7_15
2. Beazley, D.M.: SWIG: an easy to use tool for integrating scripting languages with C and C++. In: USENIX Tcl/Tk Workshop. USENIX Association (1996)
3. De Feo, L., Jao, D., Plût, J.: Towards quantum-resistant cryptosystems from supersingular elliptic curve isogenies. J. Math. Cryptol. **8**(3), 209–247 (2014)
4. Delfs, C., Galbraith, S.D.: Computing isogenies between supersingular elliptic curves over $\mathbb{F}_p$. Des. Codes Crypt. **78**(2), 425–440 (2016)
5. Grover, L.K.: A fast quantum mechanical algorithm for database search. In: STOC 1996. ACM (1996)
6. Howgrave-Graham, N.: A hybrid lattice-reduction and meet-in-the-middle attack against NTRU. In: Menezes, A. (ed.) CRYPTO 2007. LNCS, vol. 4622, pp. 150–169. Springer, Heidelberg (2007). https://doi.org/10.1007/978-3-540-74143-5_9
7. Jao, D., et al.: SIKE: Supersingular isogeny key encapsulation (2017). Manuscript available at sike.org/

8. Jao, D., De Feo, L.: Towards quantum-resistant cryptosystems from supersingular elliptic curve isogenies. In: Yang, B.-Y. (ed.) PQCrypto 2011. LNCS, vol. 7071, pp. 19–34. Springer, Heidelberg (2011). https://doi.org/10.1007/978-3-642-25405-5_2

9. Jaques, S., Schanck, J.M.: Quantum cryptanalysis in the RAM model: claw-finding attacks on SIKE. In: Boldyreva, A., Micciancio, D. (eds.) CRYPTO 2019. LNCS, vol. 11692, pp. 32–61. Springer, Cham (2019). https://doi.org/10.1007/978-3-030-26948-7_2

10. Lenstra Jr., H.W.: Complex multiplication structure of elliptic curves. J. Number Theory **56**(2), 227–241 (1996)

11. Mestre, J.-F.: La méthode des graphes. Exemples et applications. In: Proceedings of the International Conference on Class Numbers and Fundamental Units of Algebraic Number Fields (Katata), pp. 217–242 (1986)

12. Microsoft. SIDH Library v3.0 (2015–2019). https://github.com/Microsoft/PQCrypto-SIDH

13. Montgomery, P.L.: Speeding the Pollard and elliptic curve methods of factorization. Math. Comput. **48**(177), 243–264 (1987)

14. National Institute of Standards and Technology. Post-quantum cryptography standardization, December 2016. https://csrc.nist.gov/Projects/Post-Quantum-Cryptography/Post-Quantum-Cryptography-Standardization

15. OpenMP Architecture Review Board. OpenMP Application Program Interface Version 4.5, November 2015

16. Petit, C.: Faster algorithms for isogeny problems using torsion point images. In: Takagi, T., Peyrin, T. (eds.) ASIACRYPT 2017. LNCS, vol. 10625, pp. 330–353. Springer, Cham (2017). https://doi.org/10.1007/978-3-319-70697-9_12

17. Renes, J.: Computing isogenies between montgomery curves using the action of (0, 0). In: Lange, T., Steinwandt, R. (eds.) PQCrypto 2018. LNCS, vol. 10786, pp. 229–247. Springer, Cham (2018). https://doi.org/10.1007/978-3-319-79063-3_11

18. Sedgewick, R., Szymanski, T.G., Yao, A.C.: The complexity of finding cycles in periodic functions. SIAM J. Comput. **11**(2), 376–390 (1982)

19. Shanks, D.: Class number, a theory of factorization, and genera. In: Proceedings of Symposium Pure Math, vol. 20, pp. 415–440 (1971)

20. Silverman, J.H.: The Arithmetic of Elliptic Curves, vol. 106. Springer, New York (2009). https://doi.org/10.1007/978-0-387-09494-6

21. Szegedy, M.: Quantum speed-up of Markov chain based algorithms. In: FOCS 2004, pp. 32–41. IEEE (2004)

22. Tani, S.: Claw finding algorithms using quantum walk. Theor. Comput. Sci. **410**(50), 5285–5297 (2009)

23. van Oorschot, P.C., Wiener, M.J.: Parallel collision search with cryptanalytic applications. J. Cryptol. **12**(1), 1–28 (1999). https://doi.org/10.1007/PL00003816

24. van Vredendaal, C.: Reduced memory meet-in-the-middle attack against the NTRU private key. LMS J. Comput. Math. **19**(A), 43–57 (2016)

25. Vélu, J.: Isogénies entre courbes elliptiques. Comptes Rendus de l'Académie des Sciences des Paris **273**, 238–241 (1971)

26. Wiener, M.J.: The full cost of cryptanalytic attacks. J. Cryptol. **17**(2), 105–124 (2004). https://doi.org/10.1007/s00145-003-0213-5

27. Wiener, M.J., Zuccherato, R.J.: Faster attacks on elliptic curve cryptosystems. In: Tavares, S., Meijer, H. (eds.) SAC 1998. LNCS, vol. 1556, pp. 190–200. Springer, Heidelberg (1999). https://doi.org/10.1007/3-540-48892-8_15

A Short-List of Pairing-Friendly Curves Resistant to Special TNFS at the 128-Bit Security Level

Aurore Guillevic[(✉)]

Université de Lorraine, CNRS, Inria, LORIA, Nancy, France
aurore.guillevic@inria.fr

Abstract. There have been notable improvements in discrete logarithm computations in finite fields since 2015 and the introduction of the Tower Number Field Sieve algorithm (TNFS) for extension fields. The *Special* TNFS is very efficient in finite fields that are target groups of pairings on elliptic curves, where the characteristic is special (e.g. sparse). The key sizes for pairings should be increased, and alternative pairing-friendly curves can be considered. We revisit the Special variant of TNFS for pairing-friendly curves. In this case the characteristic is given by a polynomial of moderate degree (between 4 and 38) and tiny coefficients, evaluated at an integer (a seed). We present a polynomial selection with a new practical trade-off between degree and coefficient size. As a consequence, the security of curves computed by Barbulescu, El Mrabet and Ghammam in 2019 should be revised: we obtain a smaller estimated cost of STNFS for all curves except BLS12 and BN. To obtain TNFS-secure curves, we reconsider the Brezing–Weng generic construction of families of pairing-friendly curves and estimate the cost of our new Special TNFS algorithm for these curves. This improves on the work of Fotiadis and Konstantinou, Fotiadis and Martindale, and Barbulescu, El Mrabet and Ghammam. We obtain a short-list of interesting families of curves that are resistant to the Special TNFS algorithm, of embedding degrees 10 to 16 for the 128-bit security level. We conclude that at the 128-bit security level, BLS-12 and Fotiadis–Konstantinou–Martindale curves with $k = 12$ over a 440 to 448-bit prime field seem to be the best choice for pairing efficiency. We also give hints at the 192-bit security level.

1 Introduction

A cryptographic pairing is a bilinear non-degenerate map from two groups $\mathbb{G}_1$ and $\mathbb{G}_2$ to a target group $\mathbb{G}_T$, where the three groups share a common prime order r. The first two groups are distinct subgroups of the group of points $E(\mathbb{F}_{p^k})$ of an elliptic curve E defined over a prime field $\mathbb{F}_p$, and the third group is a multiplicative subgroup of order r of a finite field $\mathbb{F}_{p^k}$, where k is the minimal integer such that $r \mid p^k - 1$, and is called the embedding degree. Pairing-friendly curves such that k is small (between 1 and 20 for example) should be designed on purpose, as the embedding degree is usually very large, of the magnitude of r.

© International Association for Cryptologic Research 2020
A. Kiayias et al. (Eds.): PKC 2020, LNCS 12111, pp. 535–564, 2020.
https://doi.org/10.1007/978-3-030-45388-6_19

Freeman, Scott and Teske presented a taxonomy of pairing-friendly curves in [20]. Until 2015, the size of the target finite field $\mathbb{F}_{p^k}$ was chosen to be the same as a prime field $\mathbb{F}_q$ offering the desired security, that is, a 3072-bit (or 3200-bit) finite field for a 128-bit security level. The size of $\mathbb{F}_q$ is deduced from the asymptotic complexity of the Number Field Sieve $L_p(1/3, c) = \exp((c + o(1))(\ln p)^{1/3}(\ln \ln p)^{2/3})$, where $c = (64/9)^{1/3} \approx 1.923$ for general prime fields and $c = (32/9)^{1/3} \approx 1.526$ for special primes having a very sparse representation. Barreto–Naehrig (BN) curves became very popular. A BN curve defined over a prime field has prime order and embedding degree 12, hence choosing p and r of 256 bits gives 128 bits of security on the curve, and p^k is about 3072-bit long, as desired to match the 128-bit security level in $\mathbb{F}_{p^k}$. But it turned out that prime fields and extension fields of the same total size q and p^k do not offer the same security. The state of affairs for extension fields is complicated, with many different cases.

In 2015 and 2016, Barbulescu, Gaudry and Kleinjung, followed by Kim and Barbulescu and Kim and Jeong [5,26,27] revisited Schirokauer's Tower Number Field Sieve algorithm (TNFS) and applied this new setting to finite fields of composite extension degrees. The asymptotic complexity of this new algorithm decreased significantly, from $L_Q(1/3, 2.201)$ to $L_Q(1/3, 1.526)$ and in particular, below the complexity of a generic DL computation in a prime field, in $L_Q(1/3, 1.923)$. This makes mandatory to revisit the sizes and choices of pairing-friendly curves.

Fotiadis and Konstantinou [17] revisited the Brezing–Weng method to generate families of pairing-friendly curves and identified a list of interesting choices of moderate embedding degrees to match the 128-bit security level. However, they considered the asymptotic complexity of STNFS to deduce the security offered by the curves. It gives a first hint on the sizes of finite fields to choose but is not precise enough. Later Menezes, Sarkar and Singh [29], then Barbulescu and Duquesne [3] and in 2019 Guillevic and Singh [23] refined the analysis of STNFS to obtain more precise sizes of finite fields to match a given security level. Fotiadis and Martindale [18] focused on composite embedding degrees $k \in \{8, 9, 10, 12\}$ for the 128-bit security level, Guillevic, Masson and Thomé [22] considered a modification of the Cocks–Pinch method for $k \in \{5, 6, 7, 8\}$, and Barbulescu, El Mrabet and Ghammam spanned embedding degrees from 9 to 53.

This is an active topic: the standardisation of pairings is under discussions at IETF [32] and at ISO for updating the standard on pairing-friendly curves [24]. Particular pairing-friendly curves (e.g. cycles of curves [12]) are also needed in zero-knowledge proofs and blockchains (ZCash uses a BLS12-381 curve [7,35], Ethereum a BN-256 curve [15], and Zexe a BLS12-377 curve and a Cocks–Pinch curve of embedding degree 6 [8, Fig. 8]).

Our Contributions

We introduce a practical variant of special polynomial selection for STNFS that applies to target finite fields of pairing-friendly curves. It does not change the asymptotic complexity of STNFS but it changes the estimated cost of STNFS as computed by Barbulescu and Duquesne.

We extend the work of Fotiadis and Konstantinou [17], and identify another criterion to be resistant to STNFS: the polynomial $p(x)$ defining the field characteristic should have no automorphism. Then we build on the work of Guillevic and Singh [23] to estimate finely the cost of a discrete logarithm computation with STNFS. We write a SageMath script to automatically and systematically compare many polynomial selections, and in particular, change of variables on $p(x)$. We consider embedding degrees from 9 to 17 at the 128-bit security level. This is a complement to the work of Fotiadis and Martindale [18], where embedding degrees 8, 9, 10 and 12 are considered at this security level. We also identify non-optimal parameter choices in the recent preprint of Barbulescu, El Mrabet and Ghammam [4], resulting in over-estimated cost of STNFS and under-estimated finite field size. We conclude with a short-list of STNFS-secure pairing-friendly curves of embedding degrees from 10 to 16. The source code of this work is available in Python/SageMath at

https://gitlab.inria.fr/tnfs-alpha/alpha/tree/master/sage

The work in [22] showed that a pairing-friendly curve over a non-special prime, and with a prime embedding degree $k = 5, 7$ gives a slow pairing computation, about three times slower than the best candidate: a BLS12-curve over a 446-bit prime field. Here we estimate that a curve of prime embedding degree $k = 11, 13$ with a special prime will not provide a competitive pairing computation, despite a smaller prime p, of 333 bits for $k = 11$ and 310 bits for $k = 13$, compared to a 446-bit prime p for BLS12 curves, but may provide a faster arithmetic in $\mathbb{G}_1$ (elliptic curve scalar multiplication over $\mathbb{F}_p$) thanks to a smaller finite field.

Organisation of the Paper. In Sect. 2 we recall briefly the special tower number field sieve algorithm and the approximation of running-time made in [23]. We present our variant of special polynomial selection for pairing-friendly curves. In Sect. 3 we recall the Brezing–Weng construction for pairing-friendly curves, then we list the possible curves for the 128-bit security level, and we present the results of simulation of STNFS for each curve. We select a short-list of nine secure curves. In Sect. 4 we roughly estimate the cost of the Miller loop for an optimal ate pairing computation on the curves of the short-list that do not appear in previous works. In Sect. 5 we estimate the cost of STNFS for curves at the 192-bit security level for $k \in \{14, 15, 20, 21, 27, 28\}$. This is more complex than the 128-bit security level. We conclude in Sect. 6.

2   The Special Tower Number Field Sieve

In this section, we sketch the TNFS algorithm. We refer to [5,23,26,27] for an extended description of TNFS. The TNFS algorithm falls in the broader Number Field Sieve algorithms. To compute a discrete logarithm in a finite field, one first computes a large amount of precomputed data. A first important ingredient is the *factor base*. A finite field $\mathbb{F}_{p^k}$ has no factorisation of elements into irreducible elements or prime elements. However a number field has a ring of integers, and factorisation of ideals in prime ideals. Equipped with a map from a (sub)ring of integers of a number field to a finite field, one can factor ideals in prime ideals, then map each prime factor to the finite field to obtain a factorisation in $\mathbb{F}_{p^k}$. (There are now well-defined and cheap procedures to handle non-principal ideals and non-torsion units). The factor base is made of the prime ideals (usually of degree one) of small norm, bounded by the *smoothness bound* B. The first step of the algorithm is defining two non-isomorphic number fields with two irreducible polynomials f and g, sharing a common irreducible factor ψ of degree k modulo p (a common root if one targets a prime field $\mathbb{F}_p$), so that one has two maps from the ring of integers of number fields defined by f and g, to the same finite field $\mathbb{F}_{p^k} = \mathbb{F}_p[x]/(\psi(x))$.

The next step is collecting a large number of relations involving the primes of the factor base. We will say that an algebraic integer is B-smooth if it factors in prime ideals of degree one and norm bounded by B (B is an integer). Once enough relations are collected, taking the logarithm of the multiplicative relations, one obtains a large set of linear equations whose unknowns are the discrete logarithms of the prime ideals of the factor base. Solving the system, one obtains the discrete logarithms of the factor base elements. Finally, to compute the discrete logarithm of a given target in the finite field, one lifts the target in the number field, and tries to find a smooth decomposition of this target over the prime ideals whose logarithms are known.

In the Number Field Sieve setting, two distinct number fields are needed, so that their ring of integers can be mapped to the finite field $\mathbb{F}_{p^k}$. In the Tower NFS setting, one consider two extensions of a same number field. Let k be the extension degree, and $k = \eta\kappa$ where η, κ are integers ($\eta = k$ and $\kappa = 1$ if k is prime). One chooses an irreducible monic polynomial $h(Y) \in \mathbb{Z}[Y]$, irreducible modulo p, of degree η and small coefficients. Define the number field $K_h = \mathbb{Q}[Y]/(h(Y))$, and let y denotes a root of h in K_h. Let $\mathcal{O}_h$ denotes the ring of integers of K_h, and let $\mathbb{Z}_y$ be a subring of $\mathcal{O}_h$ (we take the same notations as [23]). Let $\mathfrak{p} = (p, h(Y))$ be the unique prime ideal of $\mathcal{O}_h$ above p. One selects a pair of polynomials $f_y(X), g_y(X)$ so that reduced modulo $(p, h(Y))$, they share a common irreducible factor $\psi_y(X)$ of degree κ. Let $K_{y,f}$ and $K_{y,g}$ be the number fields defined above K_h by $f_y(X)$ and $g_y(X)$ respectively, and $\mathcal{O}_{y,f}, \mathcal{O}_{y,g}$ their ring of algebraic integers. Let $x_{y,f}$ be a root of $f_y(X)$ in $K_{y,f}$ and $x_{y,g}$ a root of $g_y(X)$ in $K_{y,g}$. We have the following setting (Fig. 1) and commutative diagram (Fig. 2).

In the relation collection step, one enumerates all $a(Y) = a_0 + a_1 Y + \ldots + a_{\eta-1}Y^{\eta-1}$, $b(Y) = b_0 + b_1 Y + \ldots + b_{\eta-1}Y^{\eta-1} \in \mathbb{Z}[Y]$ such that integers $|a_i|, |b_i|$ are bounded by the *relation collection bound* A. The aim is to compute the norms of $a(y) + b(y)x_{y,f}$ in $K_{y,f}$ and $a(y) + b(y)x_{y,g}$ in $K_{y,g}$ and store the pairs (a, b) whose norms are B-smooth. Assuming $h(Y), f_Y(X)$ are monic, the norm is

$$N_f = \mathrm{Norm}_{K_{y,f}/\mathbb{Q}}(a(y) + b(y)x) = \mathrm{Res}_Y(\mathrm{Res}_X(a(Y) + b(Y)X, f_Y(X)), h(Y))$$

and for a non-monic $g_y(X)$ of leading coefficient $\mathrm{lc}(g_y)$,

$$N_g = \mathrm{Norm}_{K_{y,g}/\mathbb{Q}}(a(y) + b(y)x_{y,f})|\,\mathrm{lc}(g_y)|^n \tag{1}$$

$$= \mathrm{Res}_Y(\mathrm{Res}_X(a(Y) + b(Y)X, g_Y(X)), h(Y)). \tag{2}$$

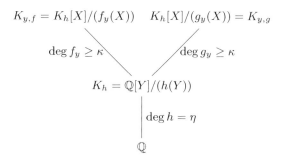

Fig. 1. Extensions of number field for TNFS

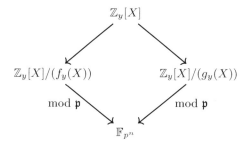

Fig. 2. Commutative diagram for TNFS.

The schedule of TNFS can be summarised in four important steps.

1. Polynomial selection: choosing $h(Y), f_y(X), g_y(X)$ so as to minimise the integers N_f and N_g;
2. Relation collection: obtaining many $a(y) + b(y)X$ whose absolute norms in $K_{y,f}$ and $K_{y,g}$ w.r.t. $\mathbb{Q}$ are B-smooth. The coefficients a_i, b_i have absolute value bounded by A, where $a(y) = a_0 + a_1 y + \ldots + a_i y^{\eta-1}$, $b(y) = b_0 + b_1 y + \ldots + b_i y^{\eta-1}$;
3. Linear algebra: each relation encodes a row of a large sparse matrix. After a filtering step (preprocessing of the matrix to remove the singletons and small cliques) the right kernel is computed with the Block–Wiedemann algorithm;
4. Individual discrete logarithm computation: obtain the database of discrete logarithms of the prime ideals of factor base. Then given a target in $\mathbb{F}_{p^n}$, lift in one of the number fields, $K_{y,f}$ or $K_{y,g}$, and obtain a smooth decomposition. Sum the discrete logarithms of the factor base involved in the smooth decomposition to obtain the logarithm of the target.

2.1 Estimation of TNFS Cost

This is an important concern to know the finite field size needed to match a security level such as 128 bits. Lenstra and Verheul designed an approach to extrapolate prime field sizes from the asymptotic complexity of NFS [28].

This complexity is $L_p(1/3, (64/9)^{1/3})$. First the unknown $o(1)$ in the formula is removed, in other words, it is set to zero. Then one considers a recent record computation, for example the 768-bit DL computation in 2017 for a prime p_{768} required the equivalent of 5300 core-years on Intel Xeon E5-2660 at 2.2 GHz, i.e. about 2^{76} clock-cycles. Then one finds a factor δ s.t. $\delta \exp((64/9)^{1/3} (\log p_{768})^{1/3} (\log \log p_{768})^{2/3}) = 2^{76}$: this is $\delta \approx 8.2$. Finally, one extrapolates and finds b s.t. $\delta \exp((64/9)^{1/3} (\log 2^b)^{1/3} (\log \log 2^b)^{2/3}) = 2^{128}$, this is $b = 2940$. It means that a 2940-bit prime field $\mathbb{F}_p$ would offer 128 bits of security. In practice, a 3072-bit prime field is considered safe for the 128-bit security level.

Unfortunately, this extrapolation trick, which is already debatable for prime fields, cannot be applied straightforwardly for extension fields, as shown in [29]. There is no record computation available for scaling the formula, of the form $L_{p^k}(1/3, c)$, with c a constant for the variant of NFS. Moreover the best asymptotic complexities are met for very specific properties of η, κ (Fig. 1) in terms of p^n and this is [26, Table 4]. For Conjugation-TNFS to obtain $c = (48/9)^{1/3}$, one reads $\kappa = (\ln p^n/(12 \ln \ln p^n))^{1/3}$ for instance. For STNFS to obtain $c = (32/9)^{1/3}$, one needs p to be d-SNFS, that is $p = P(u)$ and P is a polynomial of degree d and very small coefficients, with $d = ((2/3)^{1/3} + o(1))(\ln p^n/(\ln \ln p^n))^{1/3}/\kappa$. But in practice, n is fixed to a small integer, for example $n = 12$, and p^n ranges (roughly) from 3072 to 6144 bits. In other words, the optimal case for the parameters n, η, κ, p^n is not necessarily met for a given p^n in practice.

The asymptotic formula for c, κ, η, p is obtained as follows. One chooses a polynomial selection method. The degree of h is η, its coefficient size is negligible, the degrees of f, g depend on κ and the coefficient sizes of f, g depend on η, κ, p^n. With the Conjugation method, we have $(\deg f, \deg g) = (2\kappa, \kappa)$ and $\|f\|_\infty = O(1)$, $\|g\|_\infty = O(\sqrt{p})$. The integers (resultants) of step 2 are bounded by a formula based on Eq. (1) in $\eta, \kappa, \|f\|_\infty, \|g\|_\infty, \|h\|_\infty$. The Canfield–Erdős–Pomerance theorem states the proportion of B-smooth integers up to a bound N. Multiplying the proportion of B-smooth integers of Step 2 by the number of valid pairs $(a(y), b(y))$, in other words the volume of the relation collection (this is $\approx A^{2\kappa}$), one gets the expected total number of relations, at a cost dominated by the total number of pairs to proceed $(A^{2\kappa})$. One wants as many relations as possible, at a minimal cost. There are $\approx B/\log B$ primes up to B, and prime ideals of norm up to B. The square matrix has $\approx 2B/\log B$ columns, this is the number of prime ideals in the two factor bases. The linear algebra costs roughly B^2 operations. Then one balances the costs of Step 2 and Step 3 by setting them equal. Then one minimises the cost, obtaining a formula for the parameters A, B in terms of the inputs η, κ, p^n, and this is [26, Tab. 4].

Menezes, Sarkar and Singh observed that the bound on the size of the norms is not tight [29]. There are combinatorial factors in $\eta, \kappa, \|h\|_\infty$ that are removed in the asymptotic estimate as they disappear in the $o(1)$, and the size of coefficients of h are assumed to tend to 1, but in practice this is not the case. To circumvent this theoretical limitation, Menezes, Sarkar and Singh reconsidered the steps of the algorithm. They bounded the size of norms for a given input (denote the bound N), and optimised the parameters A, B, but for fixed n, η, κ. They used the first-order term of the Canfield–Erdös–Pomerance asymptotic formula to estimate the proportion of B-smooth integers of size up to N, that is, u^{-u} where $u = \log N / \log B$. Later in [3] Barbulescu and Duquesne averaged the size of norms over a sample of about 26000 random inputs (a, b). They replaced the Canfield–Erdös–Pomerance asymptotic formula by the Dickman-ρ function to compute the B-smoothness probability of random integers of bounded size. Then Guillevic and Singh [23] computed the smoothness bias of the resultants with respect to integers of the same size (α value of polynomials), simulated the relation collection of TNFS, and averaged the smoothness probability over random samples, as a TNFS variant of the Murphy E function. This estimate should be done for each set of parameters $(p(x), u, A, B)$. Theory meets practice at this edge: the Murphy-E function was first designed to rank the yield of pairs of polynomials for a given prime p, smoothness bound B and sieving area A^2, and is based on the Dickman-ρ function. It runs as a brute-force search of promising pairs of polynomials in Step 1, for record computations.

We build on these two previous works [3,23]. In particular, we model the relation collection cost as [23, Eq. 6.3] and the linear algebra cost as [23, Eq. 6.5].

$$\text{Cost of relation collection} = \frac{(2A+1)^{2\cdot\eta} \cdot \log(\log(B))}{2 \cdot (\#\operatorname{aut}(h)\gcd(\deg(f), \deg(g)))} \quad (3)$$

where A is the bound on the coefficients a_i, b_i in the relation collection. The $a(y) = a_0 + a_1 y + \ldots + a_{\eta-1} y^{\eta-1}$ and $b(y) = b_0 + \ldots + b_{\eta-1} y^{\eta-1}$ have coefficients a_i, b_i in $[-A, A]$, and $b_{\eta-1} \geq 0$. There are $(2A+1)^{2\eta}/2$ such pairs $(a(y), b(y))$. For each pair, one computes the norms N_f, N_g and test for B-smoothness, this is estimated as costing $\log\log B$. The process can be faster for specific choices of h, f_y, g_y where automorphisms are available, hence the denominator. We also model

$$\text{Cost of Linear Algebra} = \texttt{cnst} \cdot \texttt{wt} \cdot (\#\mathcal{B} \div \texttt{flt})^2 \quad (4)$$

where $\texttt{cnst}$ is a constant representing the cost of a multiplication modulo ℓ, $\texttt{wt}$ is the weight per row (number of non-zero entries), $\#\mathcal{B}$ is the total size of the factor base (f-side and g-side), and $\texttt{flt}$ is the reducing factor of the filtering step. Following [23], $\texttt{cnst} = \lfloor \ell/64 \rfloor$ is the machine-word size of ℓ, $\texttt{wt} = 200$ and $\texttt{flt} = 20$.

Remark 1. The arbitrary choice $\texttt{wt} = 200$ and $\texttt{flt} = 20$ is not satisfying, in particular for high security levels. The two parameters would need to increase slowly with the size of inputs. Barbulescu and Duquesne set an upper bound $\texttt{flt} = \log_2 B$ [3, Conjecture 1], but compared to recent record computations made with $\texttt{cado-nfs}$, it is a bit too much. More work is needed to solve this issue.

For each pairing-friendly curve parameters $(p(x), u)$ we run Algorithm 2.1 from [23, Alg. 6.1] to estimate the number of relations obtained for given inputs A, B. The Dickman-ρ function is denoted by D_ρ. We write a SageMath code to automatically adjust the parameters A, B so that enough relations are obtained and the cost of linear algebra and relation collection are finely balanced, in order to minimise the total estimated cost of TNFS.

Algorithm 2.1: Monte-Carlo approximation of Murphy's E for TNFS [23, Alg. 6.1] (computes an estimation of the number of relations)

Input: Polynomials $f_y, g_y, h, \alpha_f, \alpha_g$, parameter $A \in \mathbb{N}$, smoothness bound B, $N \approx 10^5$
Output: Yield estimate (number of relations)

1 $P_{fg} \leftarrow 0$
2 **for** $n := 1$ *to* N **do**
3 $\quad (a_0, \ldots, a_{\eta-1}) \leftarrow$ random tuple in $\{-A, A\}^{2 \deg h}$
4 $\quad (b_0, \ldots, b_{\eta-1}) \leftarrow$ random tuple in $\{-A, A\}^{2 \deg h - 1} \times \{0, A\}$
5 $\quad$ **if** $\gcd(a_0, \ldots, a_{\eta-1}, b_0, \ldots, b_{\eta-1}) \neq 1$ **then**
6 $\quad\quad$ continue
7 $\quad a(Y) \leftarrow \sum_{i=0}^{\eta-1} a_i Y^i$; $\mathfrak{a} \leftarrow a(y)\mathcal{O}_h$; $b(Y) \leftarrow \sum_{i=0}^{\eta-1} b_i Y^i$; $\mathfrak{b} \leftarrow b(y)\mathcal{O}_h$
8 $\quad$ **if** *the ideals* $\mathfrak{a}, \mathfrak{b}$ *are not coprime* $(\mathfrak{a} + \mathfrak{b} \neq 1)$ **then**
9 $\quad\quad$ continue
10 $\quad N_f \leftarrow |\mathrm{Res}(h, \mathrm{Res}(f_y, a(Y) - b(Y)X))|$
11 $\quad N_g \leftarrow |\mathrm{Res}(h, \mathrm{Res}(g_y, a(Y) - b(Y)X))|$
12 $\quad u_f \leftarrow (\ln N_f + \alpha_f)/\ln B$; $p_f \leftarrow D_\rho(u_f) + (1 - \gamma)D_\rho(u - 1)/\ln N_f$
13 $\quad u_g \leftarrow (\ln N_g + \alpha_g)/\ln B$; $p_g \leftarrow D_\rho(u_g) + (1 - \gamma)D_\rho(u - 1)/\ln N_g$
14 $\quad P_{fg} \leftarrow P_{fg} + p_f p_g$
15 $P_{fg} \leftarrow P_{fg}/N$
16 $w \leftarrow$ index of group of torsion units of $\mathcal{O}_h$
17 $V \leftarrow (2A + 1)^{2 \deg h}/(2w\zeta_{K_h}(2))$
18 **return** $V \times P_{fg}$

2.2 Special Polynomial Selection

We refine the special polynomial selection introduced in [5] and present a variant particularly suited for certain families of pairing-friendly curves that appear in the recent preprint [4].

Pairing-friendly curves have a special characteristic p, given by a polynomial $p(x)$ of small degree evaluated at an integer u. For BLS12 curves, we have $p(x) = (x^6 - 2x^5 + 2x^3 + x + 1)/3$, and for a 381-bit prime p, $u = -(2^{63} + 2^{62} + 2^{60} + 2^{57} + 2^{48} + 2^{16})$ [7]. Joux and Pierrot introduced a dedicated polynomial selection that takes advantage of the polynomial form $p = p(u)$ [25]. The adaptation to the Tower setting is the following.

Joux–Pierrot Polynomial Selection for TNFS. Assume there exists an integer $u \approx p^{1/d}$ and a polynomial $P(U)$ of degree d and small coefficients $\|P(U)\|_\infty = O(1)$, such that $P(u) = 0 \bmod p$. Select a monic polynomial $S_y(X)$ of degree κ and small coefficients $\|S_y(X)\|_\infty = O(1)$, such that $g_y(X) = S_y(X) - u$ and $f_y(X) = P(S_y(X))$ are irreducible. Finally select a monic irreducible $h(Y)$. Then $(h(Y), f_y(X), g_y(X))$ are STNFS polynomials.

Joux–Pierrot Polynomial Selection for TNFS with Automorphism.
We recall a variant of the Joux–Pierrot method to obtain a pair of polynomials (f_y, g_y) admitting an automorphism, when k is not prime. First select an auxiliary polynomial with automorphism, for example from the list in [16].

- $\kappa = 2$: $c_t(X) = X^2 - tX + 1$, $\sigma : X \mapsto 1/X$; $c_t(X) = X^2 + t$, $\sigma : X \mapsto -X$;
- $\kappa = 3$: $c_t(X) = X^3 - tX^2 - (t+3)X - 1$, $\sigma : X \mapsto -(X+1)/X$;
- $\kappa = 4$: $c_t(X) = X^4 - tX^3 - 6X^2 + tX + 1$, $\sigma : X \mapsto -(X+1)/(X-1)$;
- $\kappa = 6$: $c_t(X) = X^6 - 2tX^5 - (5t+15)X^4 - 20X^3 + 5tX^2 + (2t+6)X + 1$, $\sigma : X \mapsto -(2X+1)/(X-1)$.

If $\gcd(\kappa, \eta) = 1$, define $f_y(X) = \mathrm{Res}_U(c_U(X), P(U))$ and $g_y(X) = c_u(X)$. If $\gcd(\kappa, \eta) > 1$, define $f_y(X) = \mathrm{Res}_U(c_{Uy}(X), P(U))$ and $g_y(X) = c_{uy}(X)$, or alternatively, $f_y(X) = \mathrm{Res}_U(c_{U+y}(X), P(U))$ and $g_y(X) = c_{u+y}(X)$. If f_y, g_y are irreducible, select a monic irreducible $h(Y)$. Then $(h(Y), f_y(X), g_y(X))$ are STNFS polynomials.

Example 1 ([23, Table 7]). To minimise the size of norms and the total estimated cost of STNFS for BLS12-381 curves, one chooses h of degree 6, and f_y, g_y share a common irreducible factor of degree 2 modulo $(p, h(Y))$. The prime p of BLS12 curves satisfies $p = P(u)/3$, where $P(x) = x^6 - 2x^5 + 2x^3 + x + 1$. The polynomials selected in [23, Table 7] are $h = Y^6 - Y^2 + 1$, $f_y = \mathrm{Res}_U(P(U), X^2 - UY) = X^{12} - 2yX^{10} + 2y^3X^6 + y^5X^2 + y^2 - 1 \bmod h(Y)$ and $g_y = X^2 - uy = X^2 + 15132376222941642752y$.

Improvements on the Joux–Pierrot Method. The pairing-friendly curves of Sect. 3 are defined over prime fields whose characteristic has a polynomial form $p = p(u)$ for an integer seed u, where $p(x)$ has very small coefficients and degree from 4 (BN curves) to 46 (Construction 6.7 for $k = 9$, Table 2). We observed that when the degree of $p(x)$ is larger than 12, the average size of norms obtained with Algorithm 2.1 is not satisfying. In other words, for a same size of finite field $\mathbb{F}_{p^k}$ but different families of curves with $p(x)$ of very different degrees, one obtain very different estimated costs of STNFS. We explain in the following our method to obtain a lower estimated cost of STNFS when the degree of $p(x)$ is too large and the Joux–Pierrot method does not give good enough results.

In [5, §5.2] and in the SageMath script provided with [4], one observes that when it is possible, the degree of the polynomial P is divided by two without increasing the size of the coefficients. We name it Variant 1.

Variant 1 (Even polynomial $p(x)$). *When $p(x)$ is an even polynomial (that is, with only even degree monomials, and one has $p(x) = p(-x)$), then one defines $P(x)$ such that $P(x^2) = p(x)$, and P has degree $\deg(p(x))/2$. The pair of polynomials (for TNFS) $(P(x), x - u^2)$ satisfies $\mathrm{Res}_x(P(x), x - u^2) = P(u^2) = p(u) = p$ as desired.*

We adapt this technique to palindrome polynomials (also mentioned in [5, §5.2]).

Variant 2 (Palindrome polynomial $p(x)$**).** *When* $p(x) = p(1/x)x^{\deg p(x)}$, *then we define* $P(x)$ *to be the minimal polynomial of* $\alpha + 1/\alpha$ *in the number field defined by* $p(x)$, $K = \mathbb{Q}[x]/(p(x)) = \mathbb{Q}(\alpha)$. *Then* $P(x)$ *has degree* $\deg(p(x))/2$ *and small coefficients (as long as* $p(x)$ *has small coefficients). The pair of polynomials (for TNFS) is* $(P(x), ux - (u^2 + 1))$, *and* $Res_x(P(x), ux - (u^2 + 1)) = u^{\deg P}P(u + 1/u) \equiv 0 \bmod p(u)$ *as desired.*

Variant 3 (Polynomial $p(x)$ **with automorphism).** *More generally when there is an automorphism available for* $p(x)$, *say* σ, *of order two i.e.* $\sigma^2(a) = a$, *then we define* $P(x)$ *to be the minimal polynomial of* $a + \sigma(a)$ *(the trace of the automorphism is invariant). Then* $P(x)$ *has degree* $\deg(p(x))/2$ *and small coefficients (as long as* $p(x)$ *has small coefficients). The second polynomial for TNFS is* $x - (u + \sigma(u))$. *If* $a + \sigma(a)$ *does not have a good expression (a fraction of linear polynomials in* a), *then one computes a half-extended GCD of* $p(x)$ *and* $x + \sigma(x)$ *to obtain* $x + \sigma(x) = s_1(x)/s_2(x)$. *If the degrees of* s_1 *and* s_2 *are small, one can define* $s_2(u)x - s_1(x)$ *as the second polynomial for NFS. We have* $Res_x(P(x), s_2(u)x - s_1(u)) = s_2^{\deg P}(u)P(u + \sigma(u)) \equiv 0 \bmod p(u)$.

These three variants already allow more possibility of trade-off between f and g in terms of degrees and coefficient size: one divides the degree of f by two and increases the coefficient size of g by a factor two ($\|g_y\|_\infty \approx u^2$ instead of u).

Variant 4. *When* $p(x)$ *has tiny coefficients and a high degree, it might be worth doing the following transformation, knowing the seed* u. *Write* $p(x) = \sum_{i=0}^d p_i x^i$ *where* $d = \deg p(x)$ *and* p_i *are tiny integer coefficients. Then for an integer* l *in the range* $2 \leq l \leq d/2$, *define*

$$P(x) = \sum_{i=0}^d p_i u^{i \bmod l} x^{\lfloor i/l \rfloor}.$$

Then $P(x)$ *has degree* $\lfloor d/l \rfloor$ *(the floor integer of the number* d/l*) and coefficients at most* u^{l-1}, *and* $P(u^l) = p(u)$. *The pair of polynomials (for TNFS) is* $(P(x), x - u^l)$, *and* $Res_x(P(x), x - u^l) = P(u^l) \equiv 0 \bmod p(u)$ *as desired.*

This is possible to combine Variant 4 with one of Variants 1, 2 or 3. With these alternative pairs of polynomials, we can have more balanced size of norms, hence a higher smoothness probability, and a lower DL cost estimation. Our results are given in the right-most column of Table 3 page 18. It has direct impact on many curves of embedding degrees 9, 10, 11, 13, 14, 17, in particular, the curves whose polynomial $p(x)$ has a high degree.

Example 2. Let us consider a curve of embedding degree $k = 13$, discriminant $D = 3$, following Construction 6.6. The polynomial defining the characteristic is $p(x) = (x^{28} + x^{27} + x^{26} + x^{15} - 2x^{14} + x^{13} + x^2 - 2x + 1)/3$. It has no automorphism. We define $P(x) = (u + 1)x^9 + u^2 x^8 + x^5 + u(1 - 2u)x^4 + u^2 - 2u + 1$ such that $P(u^3) = 3p(u)$, and u is a seed for a particular curve. A degree 13 irreducible polynomial $h(Y)$ and the pair $(f, g) = (P(x), x - u^3)$ can be used for polynomial selection with STNFS.

Example 3. Consider a curve of embedding degree 17, named Construction 6.6 in Sect. 3. It has $p(x) = (x^{36} + x^{35} + x^{34} + x^{19} + 4x^{18} + x^{17} + x^2 + x + 1)/3$ and automorphism $\sigma : x \mapsto 1/x$. Variant 2 gives $P(x) = x^{18} + x^{17} - 17x^{16} - 17x^{15} + 119x^{14} + 119x^{13} - 442x^{12} - 442x^{11} + 935x^{10} + 935x^9 - 1122x^8 - 1122x^7 + 714x^6 + 714x^5 - 204x^4 - 204x^3 + 17x^2 + 18x + 4$ such that $P(x+1/x)x^{18} = 3p(x)$. Applying Variant 4, we obtain $P(x) = u(x^9 + (v-17)x^8 - (17v-119)x^7 + (119v - 442)x^6 - (442v - 935)x^5 + (935v - 1122)x^4 - (1122v - 714)x^3 + (714v - 204)x^2 - (204v - 17)x + 18v + 4)$, where $v = (u + 1/u) = (u^2 + 1)/u$ (we multiply by u to get integer coefficients). The pair $(P(x), u^2x - (u^2 + 1)^2)$ can be used for STNFS. Since $\deg p(x) = 36$, the seed u will be very small, and the coefficients of P in u^2 are small.

3   Complete Families of Pairing-Friendly Curves

We will apply our new special polynomial selection to paring-friendly curves whose parameters are given by polynomials, such as BN and BLS12 curves. We recall the generic Brezing–Weng construction of families of pairing-friendly curves. A family will be encoded by three parameters: the embedding degree k, the discriminant D, and a choice e_0 to compute the trace. It allows to capture all cyclotomic constructions of pairing-friendly curves with three parameters. The BN curves, KSS curves [20, §6.2] and Fotiadis–Konstantinou and Fotiadis–Martindale curves [17,18] do not fall in the cyclotomic framework because $r(x)$ is not a cyclotomic polynomial.

3.1   Brezing–Weng Constructions of Pairing-Friendly Curves

A set of the complete families presented in the Freeman, Scott and Teske paper [20] are special instances of the generic Brezing–Weng construction [9] that we recall in Algorithm 3.1. In this framework, $r(x)$ is chosen to be a cyclotomic polynomial, and we name it a cyclotomic construction. For BN curves, $r(x)$ is one factor of an Aurifeuillean factorisation of a cyclotomic polynomial. For KSS curves, $r(x)$ is a minimal polynomial of an algebraic element of a cyclotomic field. Freeman, Scott and Teske [20] obtain complete families that correspond to specific choices of trace in Algorithm 3.1. We recall the BLS construction [6], with $D = 3$ in Table 1. The construction is generalised in [20] as Construction 6.6, and gives polynomial families for any k such that $18 \nmid k$, and $D = 3$. Constructions 6.6 and BLS give the same polynomials for $k = 24$, for other embedding degrees, only the ρ-value is the same. The BLS construction gives a very simple Miller loop of ate pairing, of length $x = t - 1$ (without extra Frobenius and line computation), which is optimal. Constructions 6.2, 6.3 and 6.4 in [20] are polynomial families with $D = 1$ and $k = 1 \bmod 2$, $k = 2 \bmod 4$ and $k = 4 \bmod 8$ respectively. We report the construction number from [20] in Table 2.

Unfortunately, [4] does not consider cyclotomic methods with small discriminants other than 1, 2 and 3. In [9, p. 137], Brezing and Weng give alternatives such as $D = 5$ for $k = 10$. Recently, Fotiadis and Konstantinou used the

---

Algorithm 3.1: CYCLO(k, D, e_0) – Cyclotomic construction of pairing-friendly curves

1   **if** $D = 1$ **then** $m \leftarrow 4/\gcd(4, k)$
2   **else if** $D = 2$ **then** $m \leftarrow 8/\gcd(8, k)$
3   **else if** $D = 3$ **then** $m \leftarrow 3/\gcd(3, k)$
4   **else** $m \leftarrow 1$
5   $r_x \leftarrow \Phi_{km}(x)$; $K \leftarrow \mathbb{Q}[x]/(r(x))$; $\zeta_{km} \leftarrow$ a root of r_x in K
6   **if** $-D$ *is not a square mod* r_x **then return** $\bot$
7   **if** $\gcd(e_0, k) \neq 1$ **then return** $\bot$
8   $t_x \leftarrow x^{me_0} + 1 \bmod r_x$
9   $y_x \leftarrow$ a polynomial in x mapping to $((t_x(\zeta_{km}) - 2)\sqrt{-D}/D)$ in K
10   $p_x \leftarrow (t_x^2 + Dy_x^2)/4$
11   **if** p_x *is not irreducible* **then return** $\bot$
12   **if** p_x *does not represent primes* **then return** $\bot$
13   **return** (p_x, r_x, t_x, y_x, D)

Brezing–Weng method with small discriminants D to generate other pairing-friendly curves whose ρ-value is slightly larger but that are more resistant to TNFS [17]. For $k = 10$, Fotiadis and Konstantinou list alternatives with $D = 5$ and $D = 15$, for $k = 11$, with $D = 11$, for $k = 13$, with $D = 13$. For smaller embedding degrees, between 5 and 8, the ρ value is larger than 2. We refer to [22] for TNFS-resistant curves in this case with a modification of the Cocks–Pinch method.

3.2   Reducing the Possibilities

For BLS12 and BN curves, the finite field size identified as secure for 128 bits of security is about $12 \times 448 = 5376$. The arithmetic on these curves is already very well optimised. Hence we decided to reduce the investigation of other families of curves to those where p^k is smaller than 5376 bits.

The minimum size of r is 256 bits to ensure the security on the curve, and the size of p is given by the ρ-value defined as the ratio between the degree of $p(x)$ and $r(x)$. We choose the sharp constraint (at the 128-bit security level)

$$3072 \leq 256\rho k \leq 5376 \tag{5}$$

to reduce the number of families to consider. If $\rho = 1$ we obtain the upper bound $k \leq 21$, and if $\rho = 2$ then we obtain the lower bound $k \geq 6$. We obtain candidates with $9 \leq k \leq 17$, in Table 2 page 15.

Small Embedding Degrees up to 8. Embedding degree 1 is considered in [10]. Embedding degrees 2 and 3 are obtained with supersingular curves [21, § IX.13 p. 204]. Embedding degrees 3, 4, and 6 are obtained with MNT curves. Embedding degrees 5 to 8 were compared in [22]. We focus on embedding degrees 9 to 17 for the 128-bit security level.

Table 1. Polynomials of the BLS families for $k = 3^i$ and $k = 2^i \cdot 3$ (for example $k \in \{6, 9, 12, 24, 27, 48\}$). In practice, it is very popular for $k = 12$.

$$k = 3^i$$
$$r(x) = \Phi_{3^i}(x)/3 = (x^{2 \cdot 3^{i-1}} + x^{3^{i-1}} + 1)/3$$
$$t(x) = x + 1$$
$$c(x) = (x - 1)^2$$
$$y(x) = (x - 1)(2x^{3^{i-1}} + 1)/3$$
$$p(x) = (t^2(x) + 3y^2(x))/4 = (x^2 + x + 1 + (x - 1)^2 x^{3^{i-1}}(x^{3^{i-1}} + 1))/3$$

$$k = 2^i \cdot 3$$
$$r(x) = \Phi_{2^i \cdot 3}(x) = (x^{2^i} - x^{2^{i-1}} + 1)$$
$$t(x) = x + 1$$
$$c(x) = (x - 1)^2/3$$
$$y(x) = (x - 1)(2x^{2^{i-1}} - 1)/3$$
$$p(x) = (t^2(x) + 3y^2(x))/4 = (x^2 + x + 1 + (x - 1)^2 x^{2^{i-1}}(x^{2^{i-1}} - 1))/3$$

Embedding Degree 9. There are three families of pairing-friendly curves of embedding degree $k = 9$, discriminant $D = 3$ and $\rho = 4/3$. We focus on $D = 3$ to have a twist of order three since $3 \mid k$. Alternatives are $D = 1$ and $\rho = 11/6$, $D = 2$ and $\rho = 23/12$. Another family with $D = 3$ is given in [33, §4.4] from the Aurifeuillean factorisation of $\Phi_9(-3x^2)$.

Embedding Degree 10. We will consider three additional families for $k = 10$: with $D = 1$ and trace $t = x^{18} + 1 \bmod r(x)$ (in [9, p. 137] and [20, Construction 6.5]), with $D = 5, r(x) = \Phi_{20}(x)$ and $t = x^{18} + 1 \bmod r(x)$ ([17, Table 2 and Example 5]), and with $D = 15$, $r(x) = \Phi_{30}(x)$ and $t(x) = x^3 + 1$ [17, Table 2]. With $D = 3$, no cyclotomic construction is valid, we consider the $\rho = 2$ option in [4]. With $D = 2$, the construction is not interesting: the polynomial $p(x)$ has degree 30 and the choices of seeds u are very limited. There were no choice of u to get a pair of primes (p, r) such that r is 256-bit long or more, and p is at most 512-bit long.

Embedding Degree 11. With $D = 1$, $r(x) = \Phi_{44}(x)$ and $t(x) = x^{24} + 1 \bmod r(x)$, the family has $\rho = 1.3$, this is Construction 6.2 in [4]. The other possibilities of $t(x) = x^{4e_0} + 1 \bmod r(x)$ are $e_0 \in \{1, 2, 7\}$. We discard $e_0 = 2$ since no seed u was found so that $p^k \leq 5376$. With $D = 3$, $e_0 = 4$ is Construction 6.6, and $e_0 \in \{8, 1\}$ gives two other valid families of curves. With $D = 11$, we obtain two families of curves with $e_0 \in \{4, 8\}$ ($e_0 = 8$ appears in [17, Table 4]).

Embedding Degree 12. For embedding degree 12, we concentrate on $D = 3$ to maximise the twist. The BLS12 and BN curves are the most popular curves of embedding degree 12, and recently Fotiadis and Martindale highlighted a competitive Fotiadis–Konstantinou (FK) curve of embedding degree 12 and discriminant $D = 3$ [17, 18]. Curves of discriminant $D = 1$ have a twist of degree

4. Construction 6.4 from [20] produces a family with $\rho = 2$, the size of p is not suited. Applying the Brezing–Weng method, we do not obtain other families ($p(x)$ does not produce primes). With $D = 2$ there is one family of curves and $\rho = 7/4$. Note that in this case, only a quadratic twist is available, the pairing computation will be slower compared to BLS12 curves with $D = 3$ and sextic twists.

Embedding Degree 13. Since -13 is not a square in $\mathbb{Q}(\zeta_{13})$, we concentrate on $D = 1$ with $r(x) = \Phi_{4 \times 13}(x)$ and $D = 3$ with $r(x) = \Phi_{3 \times 13}(x)$. For $D = 1$, the trace is $x^{4e_0} + 1$ where $e_0 \in \{1, 7\}$ give valid families of curves, and $e_0 = 7$ corresponds to Construction 6.2. For $D = 3$, the trace is $t(x) = x^{3e_0} + 1$ and $e_0 = 9$ corresponds to Construction 6.6. We also consider $e_0 \in \{1, 2, 10\}$.

Embedding Degree 14. We concentrate on Construction 6.3 and 6.6. The other choices of e_0 in the Brezing–Weng construction do not produce families of curves satisfying the bounds on the size of p^k. In particular, $D = -7$ produces an alternative family whose ρ-value is too large.

Embedding Degree 17. In addition to Construction 6.2 and 6.6, we consider $D = 3$ and trace $t(x) = x^{3 \times 12} + 1 \mod r(x)$ where $r(x) = \Phi_{3 \times 17}$. Actually because of the very large degree of $p(x)$ (36 and 38), it was not possible to find a seed u so that p^k is smaller than 5376 bits. However for a comparison to [4], we include the three families of curves in our security estimate.

Other Embedding Degrees. For embedding degree 16 we take the KSS-16 curves, these are (6.11) in [20]. Embedding degrees 15 and above 17 do not satisfy the conditions (5), however we include $k = 15$ to compare to [4].

For $9 \leq k \leq 17$, we list in Table 2 the available families satisfying Eq. (5). Moreover we will later restrict to $D = 3$ when $3 \mid k$ and $D = 1$ when $4 \mid k$ to ensure the higher degree of twist.

3.3   Security Estimate for the Finite Field

The next step is to determine the size of the finite field $\mathbb{F}_{p^k}$ to ensure the required security w.r.t. a DL computation with any variant of the NFS algorithm.

Refinement of Barbulescu–El Mrabet–Ghammam Results. In the preprint [4], Barbulescu, El Mrabet and Ghammam presented a consequent list of pairing-friendly curves of embedding degrees 6 to 53 for the three common security levels of 128, 192 and 256 bits. There were about 150 distinct curves. We compare the curves of [4] that are listed in Table 2.

We obtain lower DL cost estimates in the embedding field of these curves, except for $k = 9$ construction LZZW (that we set in the BLS framework). Sometimes the cost for STNFS is not given in [4], we give our estimate. We investigated these differences by running the scripts provided with [4] and developing a second implementation based on the SageMath code available with [22,23]. We develop the following improvements.

Table 2. Pairing-friendly Constructions for $9 \le k \le 17$ such that $3072 \le 256\rho k \le 5376$. Parameters m and e_0 match Algorithm 3.1. The value 256ρ is an approximation of the minimal bit-size of p required to ensure r to be of 256 bits, so that the curve $E(\mathbb{F}_p)$ offers 128 bits of security. We include $k = 12$ Construction 6.4, and $k = 15$ although $256\rho k$ is too large, for they are refereed in Tables 3 and 4.

k	Construction	D	m	e_0	ρ	deg $p(x)$	$\sigma_p(x)$	$\lceil 256\rho \rceil$	$\lceil 256\rho k \rceil$
9	Cyclo (BLS)	3	1	1	$1.33 = 4/3$	8	$\frac{x^4-x^3-1}{x^2+x}$	342	3072
9	Cyclo	3	1	4	$1.33 = 4/3$	8	$1/x$	342	3072
9	Cyclo (6.6)	3	1	7	$1.33 = 4/3$	8	$\frac{x^4+x^3+x^2+x-1}{1-x^2}$	342	3072
9	Cyclo (6.2)	1	4	5	$1.83 = 11/6$	22	$-x$	470	4224
9	Cyclo (6.7)	2	8	1	$1.92 = 23/12$	46	$-x$	491	4416
9	Cyclo (FM10)	3	1	5	$2.00 = 2$	12	Id	512	4608
10	Cyclo (6.5)	1	2	9	$1.50 = 3/2$	12	$-x$	384	3840
10	Cyclo (6.3) (FM13)	1	2	1	$1.75 = 7/4$	14	$-x$	448	4480
10	Cyclo (FM16)	2	4	9	$1.88 = 15/8$	30	$-x$	480	4800
10	(Cyclo) 6.6	3	3	1	$2.00 = 2$	16	Id	512	5120
10	Cyclo (FM14)	5	2	9	$1.75 = 7/4$	14	$-x$	448	4480
10	Cyclo (FM15)	15	3	1	$1.75 = 7/4$	14	Id	448	4480
11	Cyclo (6.2)	1	4	6	$1.30 = 13/10$	26	$-x$	333	3661
11	Cyclo	1	4	1	$1.50 = 3/2$	30	$-x$	384	4224
11	Cyclo	1	4	7	$1.70 = 17/10$	34	$-x$	436	4788
11	Cyclo (6.6)	3	3	4	$1.20 = 6/5$	24	$1/x$	308	3380
11	Cyclo	3	3	8	$1.30 = 13/10$	26	Id	333	3661
11	Cyclo	3	3	1	$1.40 = 7/5$	28	Id	359	3943
11	Cyclo	11	1	4	$1.60 = 8/5$	16	Id	410	4506
11	Cyclo	11	1	8	$1.60 = 8/5$	16	$1/x$	410	4506
12	BN (6.8)	3	1	1	$1.00 = 1$	4	$1/(6x)$	256	3072
12	Cyclo (BLS)	3	1	1	$1.50 = 3/2$	6	Id	384	4608
12	FK12 (FM17)	3	1	–	$1.50 = 3/2$	6	Id	384	4608
12	FM19	3	1	–	$1.50 = 3/2$	6	Id	384	4608
12	FM20	3	1	–	$1.50 = 3/2$	6	Id	384	4608
12	Cyclo (6.7) (FM18)	2	2	1	$1.75 = 7/4$	14	$-x$	448	5376
12	(Cyclo) 6.4	1	1	1	$2.00 = 2$	8	$-1/x$	512	*6144*
13	Cyclo (6.2)	1	4	7	$1.25 = 5/4$	30	$-x$	320	4160
13	Cyclo	1	4	1	$1.42 = 17/12$	34	$-x$	363	4715
13	Cyclo (6.6)	3	3	9	$1.17 = 7/6$	28	Id	299	3883
13	Cyclo	3	3	1	$1.33 = 4/3$	32	Id	342	4438
13	Cyclo	3	3	10	$1.42 = 17/12$	34	Id	363	4715
13	Cyclo	3	3	2	$1.58 = 19/12$	38	Id	406	5270
14	Cyclo (6.3)	1	2	1	$1.50 = 3/2$	18	$-x$	384	5376
14	Cyclo (6.6)	3	3	5	$1.33 = 4/3$	16	Id	342	4779
15	Cyclo (BLS)	3	1	1	$1.50 = 3/2$	12	Id	384	*5760*
15	Cyclo (6.6)	3	1	11	$1.50 = 3/2$	12	Id	384	*5760*
16	KSS16 (6.11)	1	–	–	$1.25 = 5/4$	10	Id	320	5120
17	Cyclo (6.2)	1	4	9	$1.18 = 19/16$	38	$-x$	304	5168
17	Cyclo (6.6)	3	3	6	$1.12 = 9/8$	36	$1/x$	288	4896
17	Cyclo	3	3	12	$1.19 = 19/16$	38	Id	304	5168

1. Given p^k as input, for each possible integer factorisation $k = \eta\kappa$ with $\eta > 1$, we generate many irreducible polynomials h of degree η and pairs of polynomials (f_y, g_y).
2. For each set of polynomials (h, f_y, g_y), the code iterates and adjusts automatically the parameters A, B (sieving bound, smoothness bound) in order to find the best combination that balances the costs of relation collection and linear algebra, so that the total cost is minimised. When plugging these values into the former scripts and adding a tiny offset if needed, one obtains the new results.
3. We implement the improvements of the Special setting described in the Variants 1–4: automorphisms and changes of variables on $p(x)$ to minimise the average size of norms.
4. We compute the joint average size of norms and smoothness probabilities for $K_{y,f}$ and $K_{y,g}$ simultaneously. This allows to compute the ratio of non-coprime ideals $a(y)\mathcal{O}, b(y)\mathcal{O}$ and validates the formula $1/\zeta_{K_h}(2)$.

We obtain the results of Tables 3, 4 and 5. In Table 3, we reproduce the results of Barbulescu, El Mrabet and Ghammam [4, §3.4]. We hereafter make the following remarks.

Remark 2.

- We do not consider even embedding degrees k with Construction 6.2. As explained in [20], 6.2 is valid for odd embedding degrees, 6.3 is for $k = 2 \bmod 4$, and 6.4 for $k = 4 \bmod 8$. Hence we do not report even k with 6.2 in Table 3.
- For $k = 10$ and construction 6.3, we obtained a lower DL cost with $\eta = 10$ instead of $\eta = 5$. We obtained 2^{122} instead of 2^{134}.
- For all curves but BN and BLS12, we obtain a lower estimated cost with optimised parameters A, B and Sect. 2.1.
- When the degree of $p(x)$ is large, we apply one of the variants using automorphisms 1, 2 or 3 if applicable, so that $\deg P = \deg p(x)/2$. We compared without the polynomial variants and observed a lower DL cost estimate with Variants 1 or 2 when the degree of $p(x)$ is more than 12. Note that the Variant 2 is commented in the Python script of [4] for $k = 17(6.6)$.
- We observed that when the degree of P is more than 12 (after applying Variants 1, 2 or 3 if applicable), applying our improvement 4 reduces further the estimated complexity of STNFS. We obtained the smallest cost with P of degree between 4 and 12. This case is reported in the right-most column of Tables 3 and 4. The curves involved with this improvement are $k = 9(6.7)$, $k = 10(6.6)$, $k = 11(6.2)$, $k = 13(6.2)$ and $k = 13(6.6)$, $k = 14(6.6)$ and $k = 17(6.2)$, $k = 17(6.6)$.

Moreover, we applied our work to the parameter seeds of [4]. The previous remarks apply: we do not consider the seeds of even k with Construction 6.2 ([4, Table 10]). We identified five seeds that produce insecure curves because the STNFS estimated cost in $\mathbb{F}_{p^k}$ is below 2^{128}: these are $k = 9$ BLS (denoted LZZW in [4, Table 23]), $k = 9$ (6.2), $k = 10$ (6.3), $k = 11$ (6.2) and $k = 11$ (6.6). Our DL security estimate is given in bold coloured font in Table 4.

For $k = 10$ (6.3), the size of u is smaller than the minimum size recommended in [4, §3.4] ($p(u)$ is 433-bit long instead of 446, and $r(u)$ is 249-bit long, smaller than 256 bits). For $k13$(6.2), the minimum size recommended in [4, §3.4] is $p(u)$ of 329 bits, but the seed produces a 599-bit prime p. The security is much larger than 2^{128}. These two cases are reported in italic coloured font in Table 4.

Our Results. In Table 5 we present our estimations of STNFS security. For each curve family in Table 2, we first generate seeds and parameters so that r is at least a 256-bit prime. Then we run our estimation of STNFS, trying many combinations of degrees of $h(Y)$ and of $P(x)$. When the cost is smaller than 2^{128}, we increase the size of the seed u and generate larger parameters $r(u)$ and $p(u)$. We report the minimum size of p so that r is at least 256-bit long, and the security in $\mathbb{F}_{p^k}$ is at least 2^{128}.

For each embedding degree k, we highlight in coloured background the family that has no automorphism available in $p(x)$ so that the Variants 1, 2 and 3 do not apply, and so that $p(u)$ has minimal possible size. We eliminate the embedding degree $k = 17$. Since $p(x)$ has large degree of 36 or 38, it was not possible to find a seed u so that $p(u)$ and $r(u)$ are prime, and $p^k(u)$ is less than 5376 bits (constrain of Eq. (5)). We eliminate embedding degree $k = 9$: the curves whose $p(x)$ has no automorphism do not satisfy $p^k(u) \leq 5376$.

There are eleven highlighted families in Table 5. The families of Fotiadis and Martindale [18] with $k = 12$ and $D = 3$ (denoted FM17, FM19 and FM20) have very similar properties and like in [18], we only include FM17 in our final short list (for the same bitsize of $p(u)$, FM17 produces $r(u)$ one bit larger than FM19 and four bits larger than FM20).

We are left with a final short-list of nine STNFS-secure pairing-friendly curves that we summarise in Table 6. We give the polynomials $p(x), r(x), t(x)$ as Curves 1, 2, 3, 4, 5. We add the modified Cocks–Pinch curve with $k = 8$ from [22] as it looks quite promising in terms of pairing efficiency [1].

Remark 3. The curves listed below all admit a fast endomorphism from the complex multiplication, because their discriminant $-D$ is small. For curves with $-D = -4$ and j-invariant 1728, the endomorphism is $(x, y) \mapsto (-x, iy)$, where $i^2 = -1$ (in short Weierstrass representation). The curves are ordinary, $p \equiv 1 \bmod 4$, and there exists $i \in \mathbb{F}_p$ such that $i^2 = -1 \bmod p$. More precisely, we can easily precompute i. The characteristic p has form $p = (t^2 + y^2)/4$ where t is the trace, and $t^2 - 4p = -y^2$. Then $\sqrt{-1} \equiv t/y \bmod p$. The endomorphism has characteristic polynomial $x^2 + 1$, and eigenvalue $\sqrt{-1} \bmod r$, where $r \mid p + 1 - t$ and r is prime. Writing $p + 1 - t = ((t-2)^2 + y^2)/4$, one has $\sqrt{-1} \equiv (t-2)/y \bmod r$. This is explained in details in [34]. When the cofactor c of the elliptic curve such that $r \cdot c = p + 1 - t$ is larger (not just 1 or 2 for example), and the curve has parameters of polynomial form, one can reduce the lattice spanned by the rows $(r(x), 0)$ and $(y(x), t(x) - 2)$ to obtain a short basis. The Magma language for example allows lattice reduction over polynomials.

For curves with $-D = -3$, the endomorphism is $(x, y) \mapsto (\omega x, y)$, where $\omega \in \mathbb{F}_p$ is a third root of unity, such that $\omega^2 + \omega + 1 = 0$. The endomorphism has

Table 3. Pairing-friendly Constructions for $9 \leq k \leq 17$ from Table 2 and their security estimate in [4], with $\eta = \deg h$, $n = \eta\kappa$ (see Fig. 2). In several cases the data in [4] was missing or unexpected (it seems that the parameters A, B were not enough optimised). The polynomial $P(x^i)$ equals $3p(x)$ for $D = 3$, $4p(x)$ for $D = 1$, $8p(x)$ for $D = 2$, $p(x)$ for BN, and $P(x + 1) = 980p(x)$ for KSS16.

k	Construction	D, m, e₀	deg p(x)	p bits	p^k bits	r	η	poly P	deg P	DL cost [4]	DL cost Section 2.1	new params	deg P	DL cost
9	Cyclo (BLS)	3, 1, 1	8	591	5314	443	9	$P(x)$	8	128	128			
9	Cyclo (6.6)	3, 1, 7	8	535	4810	401	9	$P(x)$	8	129	122			
9	Cyclo (6.2)	1, 4, 5	22	484	4356	266	9	$P(x^2)$	11	134	116			
9	Cyclo (6.7)	2, 8, 1	46	520	4672	273	9	$P(x^2)$	23	266	220	$P(u^4)$	11	140
10	Cyclo (6.3)	1, 2, 1	14	446	4460	256	5	$P(x^2)$	7	134	133	$\eta = 10$	7	121
10	(Cyclo) 6.6	3, 3, 1	16	511	5104	256	10	$P(x)$	16	166	152	$P(u^2)$	8	150
11	Cyclo (6.2)	1, 4, 6	26	337	3698	189	11	$P(x^2)$	13	173	118			
11	Cyclo (6.6)	3, 3, 4	24	311	3421	78	11	$P(x)$	24	$\emptyset$	232	$P(x + 1/x)$	12	114
12	BN (6.8)	3, –, –	4	462	5534	462	6	$P(x)$	4	128	135			
12	Cyclo (BLS)	3, 1, 1	6	461	5525	308	6	$P(x)$	6	128	135			
12	Cyclo (6.7)	2, 2, 1	14	445	5340	256	12	$P(x^2)$	7	148	134			
12	(Cyclo) 6.4	1, 1, 1	8	510	6120	256	12	$P(x)$	8	$\emptyset$	138			
13	Cyclo (6.2)	1, 4, 7	30	329	4265	218	13	$P(x^2)$	15	325	143	$P(u^4)$	7	140
13	Cyclo (6.6)	3, 3, 9	28	309	4009	218	13	$P(x)$	28	$\emptyset$	288	$P(u^3)$	9	140
14	Cyclo (6.3)	1, 2, 1	18	394	5516	264	14	$P(x^2)$	9	148	132			
14	Cyclo (6.6)	3, 3, 5	16	351	4906	264	14	$P(x)$	16	175	151	$P(u^2)$	8	151
15	Cyclo (BLS)	3, 1, 1	12	383	5745	257	15	$P(x)$	12	286	138			
15	Cyclo (6.6)	3, 1, 11	12	383	5736	256	15	$P(x)$	12	175	138			
16	KSS16 (6.11)	1, –, –	10	331	5281	135	16	$P(x + 1)$	10	154	140			
17	Cyclo (6.2)	1, 4, 9	38	304	5153	135	17	$P(x^2)$	19	254	189	$P(u^4)$	9	153
17	Cyclo (6.6)	3, 3, 6	36	348	5914	249	17	$P(x + 1/x)$	18	$\emptyset$	186	$P((u + 1/u)^2)$	9	168

characteristic polynomial $x^2 + x + 1$ and eigenvalue λ mod r such that $\lambda^2 + \lambda + 1 = 0$ mod r. We can easily precompute ω and λ. Since $p = (t^2 + 3y^2)/4$, then $\sqrt{-3} \equiv t/y$ mod p, and $\omega \equiv (-1 + \sqrt{-3})/2 \equiv (-y + t)/(2y)$ mod p. We also have $\sqrt{-3} \equiv (t - 2)/y$ mod r. The eigenvalue is $\lambda \equiv (-1 + \sqrt{-3})/2 \equiv (-y + t - 2)/(2y)$ mod r. Since the square roots are given up to sign, in practice one obtains equality up to sign ($[\pm\lambda](x_P, y_P) = (\omega x_P, y_P)$ or $[\pm\lambda](x_P, y_P) = (\omega^2 x_P, y_P)$), that is, a practical adjustment is required.

We give a polynomial form of low degree for $\beta = \sqrt{-D}$ mod p and $\lambda = \sqrt{-D}$ mod r for the curves below.

Curve 1. A pairing-friendly curve $y^2 = x^3 + ax + b$ with the Brezing–Weng method, $k = 10$, $D = 15$, $m = 3$, $e_0 = 1$, $\rho = 7/4 = 1.75$ ([17, Table 2]).
$r = \Phi_{30}(x) = x^8 + x^7 - x^5 - x^4 - x^3 + x + 1$
$p = (4x^{14} + 4x^{13} + x^{12} - 12x^{11} - 12x^{10} - 7x^9 + 11x^8$
$\qquad + 17x^7 + 15x^6 - 3x^5 - 11x^4 + x^3 - 2x^2 + 3x + 6)/15$
$t = x^3 + 1 \qquad\qquad ; y = (x - 1)(4x^6 + 6x^5 + 6x^4 - 3x^2 - 5x - 3)/15$
$u = 1, 3, 6, 13$ mod 15 ; $c = (x - 1)(2x^2 + x + 2)(2x^2 + 3x + 3)/15$
The Hilbert class polynomial is $H(-15) = x^2 + 191025x - 121287375$ of discriminant $5(3^3 \cdot 5 \cdot 7^2 \cdot 13)^2$. For a root $j_0 = 135(-1415 \pm 637\sqrt{5})/2$ of

Table 4. Seeds provided in [3,4,19]. No seed is given for $k = 9$, $k = 10$ with 6.6, $k = 17$. The seeds for $k = 12, 16$ are from [3].

k	curve	ref	seed u	$p(u)$ bits	$p^k(u)$ bits	$r(u)$ bits	η, special poly	DL cost
9	BLS	[4, T.23]	$2^{74} + 2^{35} - 2^{22} + 2$	591	5314	443	9 $P(x)$	128
9	BLS	[19, §8.1]	$2^{70} + 2^{59} + 2^{46} + 2^{41} + 1$	559	5026	419	9 $P(x)$	125
9	6.2	[4, T.6]	$-1 + 2^3 + 2^4 + 2^5 + 2^9 + 2^{10} + 2^{22}$	483	4339	265	9 $P(x^2)$	116
9	6.7	[4, T.19]	$-1 - 2^4 + 2^6 + 2^9 + 2^{11} = \texttt{0xa2f}$	520	4672	273	9 $P(u^4)$	140
10	6.3	[4, T.7]	$1 + 2^3 - 2^5 + 2^{10} + 2^{13} + 2^{31}$	433	4321	249	10 $P(x^2)$	120
11	6.2	[4, T.6]	$-1 + 2^8 + 2^{14}$	363	3993	281	11 $P(x^2)$	122
11	6.6	[4, T.16]	$2^4 + 2^6 + 2^7 + 2^9 + 2^{10} + 2^{14}$	338	3718	283	11 $P(x + 1/x)$	118
12	BN	[3]	$2^{114} + 2^{101} - 2^{14} - 1$	462	5535	462	6 $P(x)$	135
12	BLS	[3]	$-2^{77} + 2^{50} + 2^{33}$	461	5525	308	6 $P(x)$	134
12	6.7	[4, T.18]	$1 + 2^{14} + 2^{17} + 2^{32}$	446	5341	257	12 $P(x^2)$	134
12	6.4	[4, T.8]	$1 + 2 + 2^3 + 2^8 + 2^9 + 2^{11} + 2^{64}$	511	6121	257	12 $P(x)$	138
13	6.2	[4, T.6]	$1 + 2 + 2^3 + 2^4 + 2^8 + 2^{10} + 2^{14} + 2^{20}$	599	7784	481	13 $P(x^2)$	162
13	6.6	[4, T.16]	$2^4 + 2^7 + 2^{10} + 2^{11} + 2^{13} = \texttt{0x2c90}$	376	4886	324	13 $P(u^3)$	152
14	6.3	[4, T.7]	$1 - 2^2 + 2^6 + 2^9 - 2^{12} - 2^{15} - 2^{19} + 2^{22}$	391	5464	262	14 $P(x^2)$	131
14	6.6	[4, T.15]	$-1 + 2^6 + 2^7 + 2^9 + 2^{10} + 2^{13} + 2^{17} + 2^{22}$	352	4917	265	14 $P(u^4)$	150
15	BLS	[19, §8.1]	$2^2 + 2^5 + 2^{19} + 2^{31}$	371	5557	249	15 $P(x)$	137
15	BLS	[4, T.23]	$2 + 2^{10} + 2^{16} + 2^{19} + 2^{32}$	383	5737	257	15 $P(x)$	138
15	6.6	[4, T.14]	$1 + 2^2 + 2^{12} + 2^{16} + 2^{32}$	383	5737	257	15 $P(x)$	138
16	KSS	[3]	$-2^{34} + 2^{27} - 2^{23} + 2^{20} - 2^{11} + 1$	330	5280	257	16 $P(x + 1)$	140

$H(-15)$ modulo p, one has $a = -3j_0/(j_0 - 1728)$, $b = 2j_0/(j_0 - 1728)$. A simplified pair is $(a, b) = (-3(245 \pm 416\sqrt{5}), 154(\pm 416 + 49\sqrt{5}))$. Moreover if $\omega = j_0/(j_0 - 1728) = 5^2/11^2 \pm 2^5 \cdot 5 \cdot 13\sqrt{5}/(7^2 11^2)$ is a square modulo p, one can have $a' = -3$, $b' = b/\omega^{3/2}$. If the curve $y^2 = x^3 + ax + b$ is the quadratic twist (of order $p + 1 + t$ instead of $p + 1 - t$), then $y^2 = x^3 + a\nu^2 x + b\nu^3$ is the curve we want, where ν is a non-square modulo p.

The short eigenvalue of the endomorphism for GLV (see [34]) is $\lambda = \sqrt{-15} \equiv 2x^7 - 2x^5 - 4x^4 - 2x^3 - 2x^2 + 4x + 3 \equiv (2x^4 + x^3 - 4x^2 + x + 2)/(x^3 - x) \bmod r(x)$. Note that the square root is defined up to sign. We also have $\sqrt{-15} \equiv (-64x^{13} - 24x^{12} + 8x^{11} + 250x^{10} + 92x^9 + 32x^8 - 448x^7 - 226x^6 - 146x^5 + 398x^4 + 222x^3 + 32x^2 - 42x - 159)/45 \bmod p(x)$. The endomorphism can be obtained from a 3-isogeny and a 5-isogeny. There are two 3-isogenies and two 5-isogenies, one combination gives an endomorphism (we were able to check it on a numerical example in Magma, and obtained the eigenvalue $-\lambda(u)$).

Curve 2. A pairing-friendly curve $y^2 = x^3 + b$ with the Brezing–Weng method, $k = 11$, $D = 3$, $m = 3$, $e_0 = 8$, $\rho = 13/10 = 1.30$. Since $D = 3$, $a = 0$.
$r = \Phi_{33}(x) = x^{20} - x^{19} + x^{17} - x^{16} + x^{14} - x^{13} + x^{11} - x^{10} + x^9 - x^7 + x^6$
$\quad - x^4 + x^3 - x + 1$
$p = (x^{26} + x^{24} + x^{22} + x^{15} - 2x^{13} + x^{11} + x^4 - 2x^2 + 1)/3$
$t = x^{3 \times 8} + 1 \bmod r = -x^{13} - x^2 + 1$; $y = (x^{13} + 2x^{11} - x^2 + 1)/3$
$u = 1, 2 \bmod 3$ $\qquad\qquad$; $c = (x^2 - x + 1)(x^2 + x + 1)^2/3$

Table 5. Pairing-friendly Constructions for $9 \le k \le 17$ from Table 2 and our new security estimate. For $k = 17$, r is a prime divisor of $r(u)$ but $r(u)$ itself is not prime, there is a cofactor (mark *). For many families with $k = 11$ and $k = 13$, it was not possible to find a seed u such that r is 256-bit long ($^+$) because $r(x)$ has a high degree.

k	Construction	D, m, e_0	deg $p(x)$	p bits	p^k bits	rbits	η	Sect-ion 2.2	deg P	$\|P\|$	P	DL cost
9	Cyclo (BLS)	3, 1, 1	8	608	_5472_	456	9		8	1	$P(x) = 3p(x)$	130
9	Cyclo (6.6)	3, 1, 7	8	608	_5472_	456	9		8	1	$P(x) = 3p(x)$	130
9	Cyclo (6.2)	1, 4, 5	22	640	_5752_	350	9	(1)	11	1	$P(x^2) = 4p(x)$	130
9	Cyclo (6.7)	2, 8, 1	46	520	_4672_	273$^+$	9	(1+4)	11	u^2	$P(u^4) = 8p(u)$	140
9	Cyclo (FM10)	3, 1, 5	12	608	_5472_	304	9		12	1	$P(x) = 3p(x)$	133
10	Cyclo (6.5)	1, 2, 9	12	480	_4800_	322	5	(1)	6	1	$P(x^2) = 3p(x)$	128
10	Cyclo (6.3, FM13)	1, 2, 1	14	512	_5120_	294	10	(1)	7	1	$P(x^2) = 4p(x)$	129
10	Cyclo (FM16)	2, 4, 9	30	488	_4871_	262$^+$	10	(1)	15	1	$P(x^2) = 8p(x)$	141
10	(Cyclo) 6.6	3, 3, 1	16	511	_5104_	256	10	(4)	8	u	$P(u^2) = 3p(u)$	145
10	Cyclo (FM14)	5, 2, 9	14	480	_4800_	276	10	(1)	7	1	$P(x^2) = 20p(x)$	128
10	**Cyclo (FM15)**	**15, 3, 1**	**14**	**446**	**_4460_**	**256**	**10**		**14**	**1**	**$P(x) = 15p(x)$**	**133**
11	Cyclo (6.2)	1,4,6	26	414	_4554_	320	11	(1)	13	1	$P(x^2) = 4p(x)$	130
11	Cyclo	1, 4, 1	30	391	_4297_	262$^+$	11	(1+4)	7	u^2	$P(u^4) = 4p(u)$	136
11	Cyclo	1, 4, 7	34	444	_4876_	262$^+$	11	(1+4)	8	u^2	$P(u^4) = 4p(u)$	146
11	Cyclo (6.6)	3, 3, 4	24	446	_4899_	373	11	(2)	12	1	$x^{12}P(x + 1/x) = 3p(x)$	128
11	**Cyclo**	**3, 3, 8**	**26**	**333**	**_3663_**	**258$^+$**	**11**	**(4)**	**8**	**u^2**	**$P(u^3) = 3p(u)$**	**131**
11	Cyclo	3, 3, 1	28	355	_3901_	255$^+$	11	(4)	9	u^2	$P(u^3) = 3p(u)$	135
11	Cyclo	3, 3, 1	28	373	_4101_	268$^+$	11	(4)	9	u^2	$P(u^3) = 3p(u)$	139
11	**Cyclo**	**11, 1, 4**	**16**	**411**	**_4521_**	**256**	**11**	**(4)**	**8**	**u**	**$P(u^2) = 11p(u)$**	**145**
11	Cyclo	11, 1, 8	16	480	_5280_	298	11	(2)	8	1	$x^8P(x + 1/x) = 11p(x)$	130
12	**BN (6.8)**	**3, –, –**	**4**	**446**	**_5376_**	**446**	**6**		**4**	**1**	**$P(x) = p(x)$**	**132**
12	**Cyclo (BLS)**	**3, 1, 1**	**6**	**446**	**_5376_**	**299**	**6**		**6**	**1**	**$P(x) = 3p(x)$**	**132**
12	FK12 (FM17)	3, –, –	6	446	_5352_	296	6		6	1	$P(6x + 2) = 108p(x)$	136
12	FM19	3, –, –	6	446	_5352_	295	6		6	1	$P(x) = 225p(x)$	135
12	FM20	3, –, –	6	446	_5352_	292	6		6	1	$P(x + 3) = 1425p(x)$	137
12	Cyclo (6.7, FM18)	2, 2, 1	14	445	_5329_	256	12	(1)	7	1	$P(x^2) = 8p(x)$	134
12	(Cyclo) 6.4	1, 1, 1	8	509	_6097_	256	12		8	1	$P(x) = 4p(x)$	138
13	Cyclo (6.2)	1, 4, 7	30	339	_4396_	256$^+$	13	(1+4)	7	u^2	$P(u^4) = 4p(u)$	142
13	Cyclo	1, 4, 1	34	380	_4931_	270$^+$	13	(1+4)	8	u^2	$P(u^4) = 4p(u)$	141
13	**Cyclo (6.6)**	**3, 3, 9**	**28**	**310**	**_4027_**	**267$^+$**	**13**	**(4)**	**9**	**u^2**	**$P(u^3) = 3p(u)$**	**140**
13	Cyclo	3, 3, 1	32	348	_4512_	262$^+$	13	(4)	10	u^2	$P(u^3) = 3p(u)$	139
13	Cyclo	3, 3, 10	34	388	_5037_	275$^+$	13	(4)	8	u^2	$P(u^4) = 3p(u)$	144
13	Cyclo	3, 3, 2	38	403	_5233_	256	13	(4)	6	u^2	$P(u^6) = 3p(u)$	150
14	Cyclo (6.3)	1, 2, 1	18	382	_5376_	256	14	(1)	9	1	$P(x^2) = 4p(x)$	130
14	**Cyclo (6.6)**	**3, 3, 5**	**16**	**340**	**_4755_**	**256**	**14**	**(4)**	**8**	**u**	**$P(u^2) = 3p(u)$**	**148**
15	**Cyclo (BLS)**	**3, 1, 1**	**12**	**381**	**_5715_**	**256**	**15**		**12**	**1**	**$P(x) = 3p(x)$**	**137**
15	Cyclo (6.6)	3, 1, 11	12	381	_5715_	256	15		12	1	$P(x) = 3p(x)$	137
16	**KSS16 (6.11)**	**1, –, –**	**10**	**330**	**_5280_**	**256**	**16**		**10**	**1**	**$P(x) = 980p(x - 1)$**	**140**
17	Cyclo (6.2)	1, 4, 9	38	382	_6494_	262*	17	(1+4)	9	u^2	$P(u^4) = 4p(u)$	167
17	Cyclo (6.2)	1, 4, 9	38	359	_6087_	254*	17	(1+4)	9	u^2	$P(u^4) = 4p(u)$	164
17	Cyclo (6.6)	3, 3, 6	36	374	_6358_	281*	17	(2+4)	9	u^2	$P((u + 1/u)^2)u^{36} = 3p(u)$	172
17	Cyclo	3, 3, 12	38	337	_5718_	255*	17	(4)	9	u^3	$P(u^4) = 3p(u)$	165

Table 6. Our short-list of pairing-friendly curves at the 128-bit security level.

k	Construction	D, m, e_0	deg $p(x)$	seed u	p bits	p^k bits	r bits	DL cost in $\mathbb{F}_{p^k}$
6	Cocks–Pinch	3, –, –	4	$2^{128} - 2^{124} - 2^{69}$ [22]	672	4028	256	128 [22]
8	Cocks–Pinch	1, –, –	8	$2^{64} - 2^{54} + 2^{37} + 2^{32} - 4$[22]	544	4349	256	131 [22]
10	Cyclo(FM15)	15, 3, 1	14	$2^{32} - 2^{26} - 2^{17} + 2^{10} - 1$, $a = -3$	446	4460	256	133
11	Cyclo	3, 3, 8	26	$-2^{13} + 2^{10} - 2^8 - 2^5 - 2^3 - 2 = -$0x1d2a, $b = 13$	333	3663	258+	131
11	Cyclo	11, 1, 4	16	$-2^{26} + 2^{21} + 2^{19} - 2^{11} - 2^9 - 1$, $a = 2$	412	4522	256	145
12	BN (6.8)	3, –, –	4	$2^{110} + 2^{36} + 1$, $b = 257$ [31]	446	5376	446	132 [23]
12	Cyclo (BLS)	3, 1, 1	6	$-(2^{74} + 2^{73} + 2^{63} + 2^{57} + 2^{50} + 2^{17} + 1)$, $b = 1$ [22,23]	446	5376	299	132 [23]
12	FK12 (FM17)	3, –, –	6	$-2^{72} - 2^{71} - 2^{36}$, $b = -2$ [18, §4(b)]	446	5352	296	136
13	Cyclo (6.6)	3, 3, 9	28	$2^{11} + 2^8 - 2^6 - 2^4 = $ 0x8b0, $b = -17$	310	4027	267+	140
14	Cyclo (6.6)	3, 3, 5	16	$2^{21} + 2^{19} + 2^{10} - 2^6$, $b = -4$	340	4755	256	148
16	KSS16 (6.11)	1, –, –	10	$-2^{34} + 2^{27} - 2^{23} + 2^{20} - 2^{11} + 1$, $a = 1$ [3]	330	5280	257	140 [23]
16	KSS16 (6.11)	1, –, –	10	$2^{34} - 2^{30} + 2^{26} + 2^{23} + 2^{14} - 2^5 + 1$, $a = 1$	330	5268	256	140

The eigenvalue of the endomorphism $(x, y) \mapsto (\omega x, y)$ is $\lambda \equiv (-1 + \sqrt{-3})/2 \equiv x^{11} \equiv (x^{10} - x^9 + x^7 - x^6 + x^4 - x^3 + x - 1)/(x^9 - x^8 + x^6 - x^5 + x^3 - x^2 + 1) \bmod r(x)$, and $\omega \equiv (-1 + \sqrt{-3})/2 \equiv (2x^{25} - x^{24} + 5x^{23} + 7x^{21} - x^{20} + 8x^{19} + x^{18} + 7x^{17} - x^{16} + 8x^{15} + 3x^{14} + 6x^{13} - 2x^{12} + 6x^{11} - x^{10} - 2x^9 + x^8 + 2x^7 - x^6 - 2x^5 + x^4 + 4x^3 - 2x^2 - 3x - 1)/5$.

Curve 3. A pairing-friendly curve $y^2 = x^3 + ax + b$ with the Brezing–Weng method, $k = 11$, $D = 11$, $m = 1$, $e_0 = 4$, $\rho = 8/5 = 1.6$.
$r = \Phi_{11}(x) = x^{10} + x^9 + x^8 + x^7 + x^6 + x^5 + x^4 + x^3 + x^2 + x + 1$
$p = (x^{16} + 2x^{15} + x^{14} - x^{12} - 3x^{11} - x^5 + 9x^4 - x^3 + x + 3)/11$
$t = x^4 + 1$; $y = (2x^8 + 2x^7 - x^4 - 2x^3 + 2x^2 - 2x - 1)/11$
$u = 1 \bmod 11$; $c = (x - 1)^2(x^4 + 3x^3 + 4x^2 + 4x + 3)$
The j-invariant of a curve of discriminant -11 is $-32768 = -2^{15}$, and $(a, b) = (-264, 1694)$. Moreover if 22 is a square modulo p, one can define $(a', b') = (-3, 7\sqrt{22}/2^4)$. The endomorphism can be obtained from a 11-isogeny. The eigenvalue is $\lambda \equiv \sqrt{-11} \equiv 2x^9 + 2x^5 + 2x^4 + 2x^3 + 2x + 1 \equiv (2x^5 + x^4 - 2x^3 + 2x^2 - x - 2)/(x^4 + x) \bmod r(x)$.

Curve 4. A pairing-friendly curve $y^2 = x^3 + b$ with the Brezing–Weng method, $k = 13$, $D = 3$, $m = 3$, $e_0 = 9$ (this is (6.6)), $\rho = 7/6 = 1.17$. Since $D = 3$, $a = 0$.
$r = \Phi_{39}(x) = x^{24} - x^{23} + x^{21} - x^{20} + x^{18} - x^{17} + x^{15} - x^{14} + x^{12} - x^{10} + x^9 - x^7 + x^6 - x^4 + x^3 - x + 1$
$p = (x^{28} + x^{27} + x^{26} + x^{15} - 2x^{14} + x^{13} + x^2 - 2x + 1)/3$
$t = (x^{3 \times 9} + 1) \bmod r = -x^{14} - x + 1$; $y = (x^{14} + 2x^{13} - x + 1)/3$
$u = 1 \bmod 3$; $c = (x^2 + x + 1)^2/3$
The endomorphism is $(x, y) \mapsto (\omega x, y)$ where $\omega \equiv (-1 + \sqrt{-3})/2 \equiv x^{26} + x^{25} + 2x^{24} + x^{23} + 2x^{22} + x^{21} + 2x^{20} + x^{19} + 2x^{18} + x^{17} + 2x^{16} + x^{15} + 2x^{14} + x^{13} -$

$x^{12} + x^{11} - x^{10} + x^9 - x^8 + x^7 - x^6 + x^5 - x^4 + x^3 - x^2 + x - 1 \bmod p(x)$. The eigenvalue is $\lambda \equiv (-1 + \sqrt{-3})/2 \equiv x^{13} \equiv (x^{11} - x^{10} + x^8 - x^7 + x^5 - x^4 + x^2 - x)/(x^{12} - x^{11} + x^9 - x^8 + x^6 - x^5 + x^3 - x^2 + 1) \bmod r(x)$.

Curve 5. A pairing-friendly curve $y^2 = x^3 + b$ with the Brezing–Weng method, $k = 14$, $D = 3$, $m = 3$, $e_0 = 5$ (this is (6.6)), $\rho = 4/3 = 1.33$. Since $D = 3$, $a = 0$.

$r = \Phi_{42}(x) = x^{12} + x^{11} - x^9 - x^8 + x^6 - x^4 - x^3 + x + 1$
$p = (x^{16} + x^{15} + x^{14} - x^9 + 2x^8 - x^7 + x^2 - 2x + 1)/3$
$t = (x^{3 \times 5} + 1) \bmod r = x^8 - x + 1$; $y = (x^8 + 2x^7 + x - 1)/3$
$u = 1 \mod 3$; $c = (x^2 - x + 1)(x^2 + x + 1)/3$

The endomorphism is $(x, y) \mapsto (\omega x, y)$ where $\omega \equiv (-1 + \sqrt{-3})/2 \equiv (2x^{15} + 3x^{14} + 5x^{13} + 4x^{12} + 5x^{11} + 4x^{10} + 5x^9 + 2x^8 + 5x^7 - x^6 + x^5 - x^4 + x^3 - x^2 + 3x - 4)/3 \mod p(x)$. The eigenvalue is $\lambda \equiv (-1 + \sqrt{-3})/2 \equiv x^{13} \equiv (x^5 + x^4 - x^2 - x)/(x^6 - x^4 - x^3 + x + 1) \bmod r(x)$.

4   Optimal Ate Pairing Computation: Miller Loop

We leave to future work the final exponentiation and we focus on the Miller loop, sketched in Algorithm 4.1. We compare the curves of Table 6 to [22, Table 8] and summarise the costs in Table 8. Let $\mathbf{m}_k$ denotes a multiplication in $\mathbb{F}_{p^k}$, $\mathbf{m}$ a multiplication in $\mathbb{F}_p$, $\mathbf{s}_k$ a square in $\mathbb{F}_{p^k}$ and $\mathbf{s}$ a square in $\mathbb{F}_p$. For curves $y^2 = x^3 + b$ with j-invariant 0 ($a = 0$), we give the counts from [13]. For prime embedding degrees ($k = 11, 13$), we apply the formulas from [22, Table 5].

Algorithm 4.1: MILLERFUNCTION(u, P, Q)

   Input: $E, \mathbb{F}_p, \mathbb{F}_{p^k}, P \in E(\mathbb{F}_p)[r], Q \in E(\mathbb{F}_{p^k})[r]$ in affine coord., $\pi_p(Q) = [p]Q$,
       $u \in \mathbb{N}$.
   Result: $f = f_{u,Q}(P)$

1 $f \leftarrow 1; R \leftarrow Q;$
2 **for** b *from the second most significant bit of* u *to the least* **do**
3     $\ell \leftarrow \ell_{R,R}(P); R \leftarrow [2]R$;   DOUBLELINE
4     $v \leftarrow v_{[2]R}(P)$;   VERTICALLINE
5     $f \leftarrow f^2 \cdot \ell/v;$ UPDATE1
6   **if** $b = 1$ **then**
7        $\ell \leftarrow \ell_{R,Q}(P); R \leftarrow R + Q$;   ADDLINE
8        $v \leftarrow v_{R+Q}(P)$;   VERTICALLINE
9        $f \leftarrow f \cdot \ell/v$;   UPDATE2
10 **return** f;

The cost of a Miller function $f_{u,Q}(P)$ for optimal ate pairing computation is given by Eq. (6), where nbits is the bitlength and $\text{HW}_{2\text{-NAF}}$ is the Hamming weight in 2-non-adjacent form, and $\mathbf{i}_k$ an inversion in $\mathbb{F}_{p^k}$ (Table 7).

Table 7. Miller loop cost in Weierstrass model from [11, 13, 22].

k	curve	DoubleLine AddLine	VerticalLine	Update1 Update2	reference
any k	$y^2 = x^3 + ax + b$	$5\mathbf{m}_k + 6\mathbf{s}_k + 2k\mathbf{m}$ $10\mathbf{m}_k + 3\mathbf{s}_k$	$k\mathbf{m}$	$4\mathbf{m}_k + 2\mathbf{s}_k$ $4\mathbf{m}_k$	[22, Alg. 3,4,5]
any k	$y^2 = x^3 + b$	$5\mathbf{m}_k + 5\mathbf{s}_k + 2k\mathbf{m}$ $10\mathbf{m}_k + 3\mathbf{s}_k$	$k\mathbf{m}$	$4\mathbf{m}_k + 2\mathbf{s}_k$ $4\mathbf{m}_k$	[22, Alg. 3,4,5]
$2 \mid k$	$y^2 = x^3 + b$ quadratic twist	$2\mathbf{m}_{k/2} + 7\mathbf{s}_{k/2} + k\mathbf{m}$ $10\mathbf{m}_{k/2} + 2\mathbf{s}_{k/2} + k\mathbf{m}$	0	$\mathbf{m}_k + \mathbf{s}_k$ $\mathbf{m}_k$	[13, §5, Tab. 3]
$2 \mid k$	$y^2 = x^3 - 3x + b$ quadratic twist	$6\mathbf{m}_{k/2} + 4\mathbf{s}_{k/2} + k\mathbf{m}$ $10\mathbf{m}_{k/2} + 3\mathbf{s}_{k/2} + k\mathbf{m}$	0	$\mathbf{m}_k + \mathbf{s}_k$ $\mathbf{m}_k$	[11]

$$
\begin{aligned}
\mathrm{Cost}_{\mathrm{MillerFunction}} = {} & (\mathrm{nbits}(2\text{-NAF}(u)) - 1)\left(\mathrm{Cost}_{\mathrm{DoubleLine}} + \mathrm{Cost}_{\mathrm{VerticalLine}}\right) \\
& + (\mathrm{nbits}(2\text{-NAF}(u)) - 2)\mathrm{Cost}_{\mathrm{Update1}} \\
& + (\mathrm{HW}_{2\text{-NAF}}(u) - 1)(\mathrm{Cost}_{\mathrm{AddLine}} + \mathrm{Cost}_{\mathrm{VerticalLine}} + \mathrm{Cost}_{\mathrm{Update2}}) \\
& + (\text{if there is no twist})\mathbf{i}_k.
\end{aligned}
\tag{6}
$$

The Miller loop is a product of Miller functions $f_{m,Q}(P)$, lines $\ell_{R,S}(P)$ and verticals $v_R(P)$. In all our cases the Miller loop has length of the form $up^i + u^2 p^j + p^l$ with i, j, l positive integers and is computed as

$$
f_{u,Q}^{p^i}(P) f_{u^2,Q}^{p^j}(P) \ell_{\pi_p^i(uQ), \pi_p^j(u^2Q)}(P) / v_{\pi_p^i(uQ) + \pi_p^j(u^2Q)}(P) \ell_{\pi_p^i(uQ) + \pi_p^j(u^2Q), \pi_p^l(Q)}(P).
$$

The vertical $v_{\pi_p^i(uQ) + \pi_p^j(u^2Q) + \pi_p^l(Q)}(P)$ can be removed as the point is at infinity. We can optimise with $f_{u^2,Q}(P) = f_{u,Q}^u(P) f_{u,uQ}(P)$. We first compute $f_{u,Q}(P)$, then we start a second Miller iteration over u from $f = f_{u,Q}(P)$ instead of $f = 1$ and with the point uQ instead of Q. Computing uQ in affine coordinates from Jacobian coordinates costs $\mathbf{i}_k + \mathbf{s}_k + 3\mathbf{m}_k$. The exponentiation $f_{u,Q}^u$ is almost free: the squares are shared with the computation of $f_{u,uQ}(P)$. It costs one more multiplication $\mathbf{m}_k$ in addition steps. The computations $\pi_p^i(uQ), \pi_p^l(Q)$ cost $2\mathbf{f}_k$ because uQ is in affine coordinates, while $\pi_p^j(u^2Q)$ costs $3\mathbf{f}_k$, with u^2Q in projective coordinates. A general formula is

$$
\begin{aligned}
\mathrm{Cost}_{\mathrm{MillerLoop}} = {} & (\mathrm{nbits}(2\text{-NAF}(u)) - 1)(\mathrm{Cost}_{\mathrm{DoubleLine}} + \mathrm{Cost}_{\mathrm{VerticalLine}}) \\
& + (\mathrm{nbits}(2\text{-NAF}(u)) - 2)\mathrm{Cost}_{\mathrm{Update1}} \\
& + (\mathrm{HW}_{2\text{-NAF}}(u) - 1)(\mathrm{Cost}_{\mathrm{AddLine}} + \mathrm{Cost}_{\mathrm{VerticalLine}} + \mathrm{Cost}_{\mathrm{Update2}}) \\
& + \mathbf{i}_k + \mathbf{s}_k + 3\mathbf{m}_k \ (\text{we computed } f_{u,Q}(P) \text{ and } [u]Q \text{ in affine coordinates}) \\
& + (\mathrm{nbits}(u) - 1)(\mathrm{Cost}_{\mathrm{DoubleLine}} + \mathrm{Cost}_{\mathrm{VerticalLine}} + \mathrm{Cost}_{\mathrm{Update1}}) \\
& + (\mathrm{HW}(u) - 1)(\mathrm{Cost}_{\mathrm{AddLine}} + \mathrm{Cost}_{\mathrm{VerticalLine}} + \mathrm{Cost}_{\mathrm{Update2}} + \mathbf{m}_k) \\
& + (1 \text{ or } 2)\mathbf{f}_k + \mathbf{m}_k \ (\text{we computed } f_{u,Q}^{p^i}(P) f_{u^2,Q}^{p^j}(P) \text{ and } [u^2]Q) \\
& + (4 \text{ or } 5)\mathbf{f}_k + 2(\mathrm{Cost}_{\mathrm{AddLine}} + \mathrm{Cost}_{\mathrm{Update2}}) + \mathrm{Cost}_{\mathrm{VerticalLine}} + \mathbf{i}_k
\end{aligned}
\tag{7}
$$

If $HW_{2\text{-NAF}}(u) \ll HW(u)$ then one can replace u by the form $2\text{-NAF}(u)$ and $HW(u)$ by $HW_{2\text{-NAF}}(u)$ in the second Miller loop to save addition steps, at a cost of one extra inversion $\mathbf{i}_k$.

A Tate pairing has Miller loop $f_{r,P}(Q)$. The curve arithmetic is in the base field $\mathbb{F}_p$ instead of $\mathbb{F}_{p^k}$, but the Miller loop has length $\log_2 r$ bits, this is at least 256 bits. The estimated cost has the same formula given in Eq. (6) but with $2\text{-NAF}(r)$ instead of u.

4.1   Prime Embedding Degrees 11 and 13

Curve 2 ($k = 11$, $D = 3$, $a = 0$, p of 333 bits, $u = $ -0x1d2a). The optimal ate Miller loop has length $u + u^2 p^5 + p^6$. The formula is

$$f_{u,Q}(P) f_{u^2,Q}^{p^5}(P) \ell_{uQ,\pi_p^5(u^2Q)} / v_{uQ+\pi_p^5(u^2Q)} \ell_{uQ+\pi_p^5(u^2Q),\pi_p^6(Q)}$$

(we omit $v_{uQ+\pi_p^5(u^2Q)+\pi_p^6(Q)}(P)$ because $uQ + \pi_p^5(u^2Q) + \pi_p^6(Q) = \mathcal{O}$). The seed $u = $ -0x1d2a is 13-bit long and has Hamming weight 7, and $2\text{-NAF}(u)$ is 14-bit long and has Hamming weight 6. Since $D = 3$, we have $a = 0$. No twist is available. From Eq. (7) with $(1+5)\mathbf{f}_k$ for Frobenius, we obtain $87k\mathbf{m} + 413\mathbf{m}_k + 213\mathbf{s}_k + 6\mathbf{f}_k + 2\mathbf{i}_k$. A schoolbook implementation of multiplication and squaring would give $\mathbf{m}_k = k^2\mathbf{m} = 121\mathbf{m}$ and $\mathbf{s}_k = k(k-1)\mathbf{m} = 110\mathbf{m}$. A Frobenius power in $\mathbb{F}_{p^{11}}$ costs $10\mathbf{m}$, assuming $p = 1 \bmod 11$ and some precomputations. We obtain the upper bound $74420\mathbf{m} + 2\mathbf{i}_k$. An optimised Karatsuba multiplication in $\mathbb{F}_{p^k}$ would require at least $k^{\log_2 3}\mathbf{m}$, that is, $45\mathbf{m}$. Assuming that $\mathbf{s}_k \approx \mathbf{m}_k \approx 45\mathbf{m}$, we obtain the lower bound $29187\mathbf{m} + 2\mathbf{i}_k$.

For the Tate pairing, from Eq. (6) with $r = \Phi_{33}(u)$, $2\text{-NAF}(r)$ of 258 bits and Hamming weight 86, we obtain $1026k\mathbf{m} + 1364\mathbf{m}_k + 512\mathbf{s}_k + 2477\mathbf{m} + 1540\mathbf{s} + \mathbf{i}_k$, it is roughly $235127\mathbf{m} + 1540\mathbf{s} + \mathbf{i}_k$ with schoolbook $\mathbf{m}_k, \mathbf{s}_k$, and $98183\mathbf{m} + 1540\mathbf{s} + \mathbf{i}_k$ with optimised Karatsuba-like $\mathbf{m}_k, \mathbf{s}_k$.

Curve 3 ($k = 11$, $D = 11$, $a = 2$, p of 412 bits, $u = $ -0x3d80a01). The optimal ate Miller loop has length $u - p^3$. The formula is

$$f_{u,Q}(P) \ell_{uQ,-\pi_p^3(Q)}(P)$$

(we omit $v_{uQ-\pi_p^3(Q)}(P)$ because $uQ - \pi_p^3(Q) = \mathcal{O}$). We have u of 26 bits and Hamming weight 9, $2\text{-NAF}(u)$ of 27 bits and $HW_{2\text{-NAF}}(u) = 6$, and $a = 2$. No twist is available. We obtain from Eq. (6) with in addition $2\mathbf{f}_k + \text{Cost}_{\text{ADDLINE}} + \text{Cost}_{\text{UPDATE2}}$, the cost $83k\mathbf{m} + 314\mathbf{m}_k + 224\mathbf{s}_k + 3\mathbf{f}_k + \mathbf{i}_k$. With the upper bound $\mathbf{m}_k = k^2\mathbf{m}$ and $\mathbf{s}_k = k(k-1)\mathbf{m}$, the count is $63577\mathbf{m} + \mathbf{i}_k$. With the lower bound $\mathbf{m}_{11} = \mathbf{s}_{11} = 45\mathbf{m}$, the count is $25153\mathbf{m} + \mathbf{i}_k$.

A Tate pairing would cost more than the previous curve since $a = 2$ instead of $a = 0$, with this time $r = \Phi_{11}(u)/11$ of 256 bits, $2\text{-NAF}(r)$ of 257 bits, and $HW_{2\text{-NAF}}(r) = 87$. The estimated cost is $1026k\mathbf{m} + 1364\mathbf{m}_k + 510\mathbf{s}_k + 2738\mathbf{m} + 1794\mathbf{s} + \mathbf{i}_k$, upper bound $235168\mathbf{m} + 1794\mathbf{s} + \mathbf{i}_k$, lower bound $98354\mathbf{m} + 1794\mathbf{s} + \mathbf{i}_k$.

Curve 4 ($k = 13$, $D = 3$, (6.6), $a = 0$, p of 310 bits, $u =$ 0x8b0). The optimal ate Miller loop has length $u^2 + up + p^2$, giving

$$f_{u^2,Q}(P)f_{u,Q}^p(P)\ell_{u^2Q,\pi(uQ)}(P)/v_{u^2Q+\pi(uQ)}\ell_{u^2Q+\pi_p(uQ),\pi_p^2(Q)}$$

(we omit $v_{u^2Q+\pi_p(uQ)+\pi_p^2(Q)}(P)$). We have u and 2-NAF(u) of 12 bits and Hamming weight 4, and $a = 0$, but no twist is available. From Eq. 7 with $(1 + 4)\mathbf{f}_k$, we obtain $73k\mathbf{m} + 313\mathbf{m}_k + 177\mathbf{s}_k + 5\mathbf{f}_k + 2\mathbf{i}_k$. With the schoolbook upper bound $\mathbf{m}_{13} = k^2\mathbf{m} = 169\mathbf{m}$ and $\mathbf{s}_{13} = k(k-1)\mathbf{m} = 156\mathbf{m}$, the count is $81518\mathbf{m} + 2\mathbf{i}_k$. With the Karatsuba-like lower bound $\mathbf{m}_{13} = \mathbf{s}_{13} = 13^{\log_2 3}\mathbf{m} = 59\mathbf{m}$, the count is $29919\mathbf{m} + \mathbf{i}_k$. For Tate from Eq. 6 with 2-NAF(r) of 268 bits and Hamming weight 90, the cost is $1068k\mathbf{m} + 1420\mathbf{m}_k + 532\mathbf{s}_k + 2581\mathbf{m} + 1602\mathbf{s} + \mathbf{i}_k$, upper bound $339437\mathbf{m} + 1602\mathbf{s} + \mathbf{i}_k$ and lower bound $131633\mathbf{m} + 1602\mathbf{s} + \mathbf{i}_k$.

4.2 Even Embedding Degrees 10 and 14

The vertical lines can be removed, thanks to the quadratic twist, because the x-coordinates are in a proper subfield $\mathbb{F}_{p^{k/2}}$. The optimisation of line and tangent computation focused on curves with twists of degrees 3, 4 and 6 in [13]. We refer to the former papers [2,11] for pairing formulas on curves with quadratic twists only. The count is

$$\begin{aligned}
\text{Cost}_{\text{MillerLoop}} = {} & (\text{nbits}(u) - 1)\text{Cost}_{\text{DoubleLine}} + (\text{nbits}(u) - 2)\text{Cost}_{\text{Update1}} \\
& + (\text{HW}(u) - 1)(\text{Cost}_{\text{AddLine}} + \text{Cost}_{\text{Update2}}) \\
& + \mathbf{i}_{k/2} + \mathbf{s}_{k/2} + 3\mathbf{m}_{k/2} \text{ (we computed } f_{u,Q}(P) \text{ and } [u]Q \text{ in affine coord.)} \\
& + (\text{nbits}(u) - 1)(\text{Cost}_{\text{DoubleLine}} + \text{Cost}_{\text{Update1}}) \\
& + (\text{HW}(u) - 1)(\text{Cost}_{\text{AddLine}} + \text{Cost}_{\text{Update2}} + \mathbf{m}_k) \\
& + (1 \text{ or } 2)\mathbf{f}_k + \mathbf{m}_k \text{ (we computed } (f_{u,Q}^{p^i}(P)f_{u^2,Q}^{p^j}(P)) \text{ and } [u^2]Q) \\
& + (2 \text{ or } 3)\mathbf{f}_{k/2} + \text{Cost}_{\text{AddLine}} + \text{Cost}_{\text{Update2}}
\end{aligned} \tag{8}$$

Curve 1 ($k = 10$, $D = 15$, $a = -3$, p of 446 bits, $u =$ 0xfbfe03ff). The optimal ate Miller loop has length $u - p^2 + u^2p^3$. The formula is

$$f_{u,Q}(P)f_{u^2,Q}^{p^3}(P)\ell_{uQ,\pi_p^3(u^2Q)}(P)$$

and we removed the line $\ell_{uQ+\pi_p^3(u^2Q),\pi_p^2(Q)}(P)$ as it is a vertical. Computing $\pi_p^3(u^2Q)$ costs $3\mathbf{f}_{k/2}$. We have u of 32 bits, $\text{HW}(u) = 24$, 2-NAF(u) of 33 bits, $\text{HW}_{\text{2-NAF}}(u) = 5$, $a = -3$, and a quadratic twist is available. We write u in 2-NAF form for both Miller functions, it costs one extra inversion $\mathbf{i}_k$ and allows to save 27 addition steps in the second Miller function, and obtain $72k\mathbf{m} + 76\mathbf{m}_k + 62\mathbf{s}_k + \mathbf{f}_k + 525\mathbf{m}_{k/2} + 280\mathbf{s}_{k/2} + 3\mathbf{f}_{k/2} + \mathbf{i}_k + \mathbf{i}_{k/2}$. We have $\mathbf{m}_{k/2} = \mathbf{m}_5$, a schoolbook implementation of a multiplication in $\mathbb{F}_{p^5}$ would need $\mathbf{m}_5 = k^2\mathbf{m} = 25\mathbf{m}$, and a square $\mathbf{s}_5 = k(k-1)\mathbf{m} = 20\mathbf{m}$, then with a quadratic extension, $\mathbb{F}_{p^{10}}$ would have $\mathbf{m}_{10} = 3\mathbf{m}_5 = 75\mathbf{m}$ (with Karatsuba) and $\mathbf{s}_{10} = 2\mathbf{m}_5 = 50\mathbf{m}$. The total count would be $32648\mathbf{m} + \mathbf{i}_k + \mathbf{i}_{k/2}$. With optimised Karatsuba-like formulas [30], we would have the lower bound $\mathbf{m}_5 = \mathbf{s}_5 = 13\mathbf{m}$, and $\mathbf{m}_{10} = 39\mathbf{m}$, $\mathbf{s}_{10} = 26\mathbf{m}$, and the final count would be $15784\mathbf{m} + \mathbf{i}_k + \mathbf{i}_{k/2}$.

Curve 5 ($k = 14$, $D = 3$, (6.6), $a = 0$, p of 340 bits, $u = $ 0x2803c0). The optimal ate Miller loop has length $u^2 + up + p^2$. The Miller loop formula is

$$f_{u^2,Q}(P)f_{u,Q}^p(P)\ell_{u^2Q,\pi_p(uQ)}(P)$$

We removed the line $\ell_{u^2Q+\pi_p(uQ),\pi_p^2(Q)}$ as it is a vertical. We have u of 22 bits, $\mathrm{HW}(u) = 6$, 2-NAF(u) of 22 bits, $\mathrm{HW}_{2\text{-NAF}}(u) = 4$, $a = 0$, and a quadratic twist is available. Computing $\pi_p(uQ)$ costs $2\mathbf{f}_{k/2}$. We obtain from Eq. (8) $51k\mathbf{m} + 56\mathbf{m}_k + 41\mathbf{s}_k + \mathbf{f}_k + 177\mathbf{m}_{k/2} + 313\mathbf{s}_{k/2} + 2\mathbf{f}_{k/2} + \mathbf{i}_{k/2}$. From [30], we consider the lower (Karatsuba) bound $\mathbf{m}_7 = \mathbf{s}_7 = 22\mathbf{m}$, and $\mathbf{m}_{14} = 3\mathbf{m}_7 = 66\mathbf{m}$, $\mathbf{s}_{14} = 2\mathbf{m}_7 = 44\mathbf{m}$. We obtain $17020\mathbf{m} + \mathbf{i}_7$, where $\mathbf{m}$ is a multiplication in $\mathbb{F}_p$ of 340 bits. With 2-NAF(u) for the second Miller function, the cost is $49k\mathbf{m} + 52\mathbf{m}_k + 41\mathbf{s}_k + \mathbf{f}_k + 157\mathbf{m}_{k/2} + 309\mathbf{s}_{k/2} + 2\mathbf{f}_{k/2} + \mathbf{i}_k + \mathbf{i}_{k/2}$, upper bound $39037\mathbf{m} + \mathbf{i}_k + \mathbf{i}_{k/2}$, lower bound $16200\mathbf{m} + \mathbf{i}_k + \mathbf{i}_{k/2}$.

4.3   Comparison

The five curves of Sects. 4.1 and 4.2 are compared to BN, BLS12, FK12 and KSS16 curves, and modified Cocks-Pinch curves in Table 8. The curves of even embedding degrees $k = 10, 14$ are not competitive by a factor two compared to KSS16 curves (over a 339-bit field, Miller loop in $7691\mathbf{m}$) and BLS12, FK12 curves (over a 446-bit field, Miller loop in $7805\mathbf{m}$ and $7853\mathbf{m}$ resp.), because they have only a quadratic twist, whereas KSS16 curves have a quartic twist and BLS12, FK12 curves have a sextic twist. The curves of prime embedding degrees $k = 11, 13$ are not competitive by a factor four compared to the same curves, because no twist is available.

5   Overview of the 192-Bit Security Level

At the 192-bit security level, we would like to set the constrain

$$7168 \leq 384\rho k \leq 14336. \tag{9}$$

With $\rho = 1$ we obtain $k \leq 37$, and with $\rho = 2$ we obtain $k \geq 10$. Curves like Fotiadis–Konstantinou with exactly $\rho = 2$ satisfy (9) for $10 \leq k \leq 18$. No cyclotomic family of embedding degree above 32 satisfying (9) was found. For BN, BLS12, BLS24, KSS16, KSS18, we reproduce in Table 9 the results of Guillevic and Singh [23]: BN with a 1022-bit p, BLS12 with a 1150-bit p, KSS16 with a 766-bit prime p, KSS18 with a 638-bit prime p, BLS24 with a 509-bit prime p. We list in Table 10 seed ranges for $k \in \{14, 15, 20, 21, 27, 28\}$. We also refer to [18] for alternative curves with $\rho = 2$. We leave to future work a complete study of pairing-friendly curves at the 192-bit security level.

Table 8. Count for Miller loop cost from [22] for Cocks–Pinch and BN, BLS12, KSS16, and from [18] for FK12 (a.k.a. FM17).

Curve	bits p	Miller loop	final exp.	total
Cocks–Pinch $k = 6$	672	4601m	3871m	8472m
Cocks–Pinch $k = 8$	544	4502m	7056m	11558m
BN	446	11620m	5349m	16969m
BLS12	446	7805m	7723m	15528m
FK12 (FM17)	446	7853m	8002m	15855m
KSS16	339	7691m	18235m	25926m
$k = 11, D = 3, a = 0$	333	$29187m + 2i_{11}$		
$k = 11, D = 11, a = 2$	412	$25153m + i_{11}$		
$k = 13, D = 3, a = 0$	310	$29919m + 2i_{13}$		
$k = 10, D = 15, a = -3$	446	$15784m + i_{10} + i_5$		
$k = 14, D = 3, a = 0$	340	$16200m + i_{14} + i_7$		

Table 9. Seeds at the 192-bit security level from [23].

k	curve	r bits	p bits	p^k bits	seed u	DL cost
12	BN	1022	1022	12255	$-2^{254} + 2^{33} + 2^6$	191
12	BLS12	768	1150	13799	$-2^{192} + 2^{188} - 2^{115} - 2^{110} - 2^{44} - 1$	193
16	KSS16	605	766	12255	$2^{78} - 2^{76} - 2^{28} + 2^{14} + 2^7 + 1$	194
18	KSS18	474	638	11477	$2^{80} + 2^{77} + 2^{76} - 2^{61} - 2^{53} - 2^{14}$	193
24	BLS24	409	509	12202	$-2^{51} - 2^{28} + 2^{11} - 1$ [14]	193

Table 10. Seeds at the 192-bit security level for $k \in \{14, 15, 20, 21, 27, 28\}$. For $k = 14, 15$ the range of u is such that p is 928-bit long (a smaller p of 920 to 928 bits is possible). For $k = 20$, u is s.t. r is 448-bit long. For $k = 21, 27, 28$, u is s.t. r is 384-bit long.

k	curve D, m, e_0	r bits	p bits	p^k bits	seed u	DL cost
14	Cyclo 1, 2, 1 (6.3)	620	928	12979–12992	$u \geq$ 0xc382fe8f05eaf $u \leq$ 0xcb2ff529e85b5	194
15	Cyclo 3, 1, 1 (BLS-15)	620	928	13906–13920	$u \leq$ -0x29b3f997f573d609c26f $u \geq$ -0x2c2ecd2df12c9d54ec07 $u \geq$ 0x29b3f997f573d6097e04 $u \leq$ 0x2c2ecd2df12c9d52b8c9	193
20	Cyclo 1, 1, 1 (6.4)	448	669–670	13371–13400	$u \geq$ 0xeac0c6e7dd29e3 $u \leq$ 0xffffffffffffd1ed	192
21	Cyclo 3, 1, 1 (BLS-21)	384	510–511	10691–10719	-0xf1a1c083 $\geq u \geq$ -0xffff6fd1 0xf1a1ddd7 $\leq u \leq$ 0xffffccc1	195
27	Cyclo 3, 1, 1 (BLS-27)	384	426–427	11496–11524	-0x29487b $\geq u \geq$ -0x2ac5ea 0x2955f1 $\leq u \leq$ 0x2ac66d	212
28	Cyclo 1, 1, 1 (6.2)	384	510	14243–14280	0xf1a202f1 $\leq u \leq$ 0xffffd341	208

6   Conclusion

Because of the Special Tower Number Field Sieve algorithm, the security of pairing-friendly curves should be reconsidered. We presented a new variant of STNFS for pairing-friendly curves constructed with the Brezing–Weng method, where the characteristic has a polynomial form. It does not apply to the modified Cocks–Pinch curves of [22]. We refine the analysis of Barbulescu, El Mrabet and Ghammam and present an updated short-list of secure pairing-friendly curves at the 128-bit security level. For embedding degrees from 10 to 16, we obtain curves so that the size of p^k is at least 3663 bits ($k = 11$) and at most 5376 bits (for BLS12 curves). The estimated cost of a DL computation with STNFS for these finite fields is between 2^{128} and 2^{148}. The fastest pairings are obtained with a BLS12 curve or a Fotiadis–Konstantinou–Martindale curve of embedding degree 12, discriminant 3 and twist of degree 6 over a 446-bit prime. The additional curves of this paper have embedding degrees 10, 11, 13 and 14 and a twist of degree 2 for even embedding degrees. It was not sure by how much a prime embedding degree k allows to reduce the total size of p^k: for $k = 11$ the smallest possible p is 333 bit long, and for $k = 13$ p is 310 bit long. Although p is smaller than 446 bits, no twist is available with a prime embedding degree. For this reason, the efficiency of pairings on prime embedding degree curves is not competitive compared to BLS12 and FK12 curves.

References

1. Aranha, D.F., Gouvêa, C.P.L.: RELIC is an Efficient LIbrary for Cryptography. https://github.com/relic-toolkit/relic
2. Arène, C., Lange, T., Naehrig, M., Ritzenthaler, C.: Faster computation of the Tate pairing. J. Number Theory **131**(5, Elliptic Curve Cryptography), 842–857 (2011). https://doi.org/10.1016/j.jnt.2010.05.013. http://cryptojedi.org/papers/#edpair
3. Barbulescu, R., Duquesne, S.: Updating key size estimations for pairings. J. Cryptol. **32**(4), 1298–1336 (2019). https://doi.org/10.1007/s00145-018-9280-5. https://ia.cr/2017/334
4. Barbulescu, R., El Mrabet, N., Ghammam, L.: A taxonomy of pairings, their security, their complexity. ePrint 2019/485, 24 September 2019. https://ia.cr/2019/485
5. Barbulescu, R., Gaudry, P., Kleinjung, T.: The tower number field sieve. In: Iwata, T., Cheon, J.H. (eds.) ASIACRYPT 2015. LNCS, vol. 9453, pp. 31–55. Springer, Heidelberg (2015). https://doi.org/10.1007/978-3-662-48800-3_2. https://ia.cr/2015/505
6. Barreto, P.S.L.M., Lynn, B., Scott, M.: Constructing elliptic curves with prescribed embedding degrees. In: Cimato, S., Persiano, G., Galdi, C. (eds.) SCN 2002. LNCS, vol. 2576, pp. 257–267. Springer, Heidelberg (2003). https://doi.org/10.1007/3-540-36413-7_19
7. Bowe, S.: BLS12-381: New zk-SNARK elliptic curve construction. Zcash blog, 11 March 2017. https://blog.z.cash/new-snark-curve/

8. Bowe, S., Chiesa, A., Green, M., Miers, I., Mishra, P., Wu, H.: ZEXE: enabling decentralized private computation. In: 2020 IEEE Symposium on Security and Privacy (SP), pp. 1114–1131. IEEE Computer Society, Los Alamitos (2020). https://www.computer.org/csdl/proceedings-article/sp/2020/349700b114/1iqVRI2nNra. https://ia.cr/2018/962

9. Brezing, F., Weng, A.: Elliptic curves suitable for pairing based cryptography. Des. Codes Cryptogr. **37**(1), 133–141 (2005). https://doi.org/10.1007/s10623-004-3808-4. https://ia.cr/2003/143

10. Chatterjee, S., Menezes, A., Rodríguez-Henríquez, F.: On instantiating pairing-based protocols with elliptic curves of embedding degree one. IEEE Trans. Comput. **66**(6), 1061–1070 (2017). https://doi.org/10.1109/TC.2016.2633340. https://ia.cr/2016/403

11. Chatterjee, S., Sarkar, P., Barua, R.: Efficient computation of Tate pairing in projective coordinate over general characteristic fields. In: Park, C., Chee, S. (eds.) ICISC 2004. LNCS, vol. 3506, pp. 168–181. Springer, Heidelberg (2005). https://doi.org/10.1007/11496618_13

12. Chiesa, A., Chua, L., Weidner, M.: On cycles of pairing-friendly elliptic curves. SIAM J. Appl. Algebr. Geom. **3**(2), 175–192 (2019). https://doi.org/10.1137/18M1173708

13. Costello, C., Lange, T., Naehrig, M.: Faster pairing computations on curves with high-degree twists. In: Nguyen, P.Q., Pointcheval, D. (eds.) PKC 2010. LNCS, vol. 6056, pp. 224–242. Springer, Heidelberg (2010). https://doi.org/10.1007/978-3-642-13013-7_14. https://ia.cr/2009/615

14. Costello, C., Lauter, K., Naehrig, M.: Attractive subfamilies of BLS curves for implementing high-security pairings. In: Bernstein, D.J., Chatterjee, S. (eds.) INDOCRYPT 2011. LNCS, vol. 7107, pp. 320–342. Springer, Heidelberg (2011). https://doi.org/10.1007/978-3-642-25578-6_23. https://ia.cr/2011/465

15. Euthereum, Go implementation. https://github.com/ethereum/go-ethereum/tree/master/crypto/bn256

16. Foster, K.: HT90 and "simplest" number fields. Illinois J. Math. **55**(4), 1621–1655 (2011). http://arxiv.org/abs/1207.6099

17. Fotiadis, G., Konstantinou, E.: TNFS resistant families of pairing-friendly elliptic curves. Theor. Comput. Sci. **800**, 73–89 (2019). https://doi.org/10.1016/j.tcs.2019.10.017. https://ia.cr/2018/1017

18. Fotiadis, G., Martindale, C.: Optimal TNFS-secure pairings on elliptic curves with composite embedding degree. ePrint 2019/555 (2019). https://ia.cr/2019/555

19. Fouotsa, E., El Mrabet, N., Pecha, A.: Computing optimal ate pairings on elliptic curves with embedding degree 9, 15 and 27. ePrint 2016/1187 (2016). https://ia.cr/2016/1187

20. Freeman, D., Scott, M., Teske, E.: A taxonomy of pairing-friendly elliptic curves. J. Cryptol. **23**(2), 224–280 (2010). https://doi.org/10.1007/s00145-009-9048-z. https://ia.cr/2006/372

21. Galbraith, S.: Pairings. In: Blake, I.F., Seroussi, G., Smart, N.P. (eds.) Advances in Elliptic Curve Cryptography. London Mathematical Society Lecture Note Series, pp. 183–214. Cambridge University Press, Cambridge (2005). https://doi.org/10.1017/CBO9780511546570.011

22. Guillevic, A., Masson, S., Thomé, E.: Cocks–Pinch curves of embedding degrees five to eight and optimal ate pairing computation. Des. Codes Cryptogr. 1–35 (2020). https://doi.org/10.1007/s10623-020-00727-w. https://hal.inria.fr/hal-02305051

23. Guillevic, A., Singh, S.: On the alpha value of polynomials in the tower number field sieve algorithm. ePrint 2019/885 (2019). https://ia.cr/2019/885

24. ISO: ISO/IEC 15946-5:2017 Information technology - Security techniques - Cryptographic techniques based on elliptic curves - Part 5: Elliptic curve generation, 2 edn., August 2017. https://www.iso.org/standard/69726.html

25. Joux, A., Pierrot, C.: The special number field sieve in $\mathbb{F}_{p^n}$ - application to pairing-friendly constructions. In: Cao, Z., Zhang, F. (eds.) Pairing 2013. LNCS, vol. 8365, pp. 45–61. Springer, Cham (2014). https://doi.org/10.1007/978-3-319-04873-4_3. https://ia.cr/2013/582

26. Kim, T., Barbulescu, R.: Extended tower number field sieve: a new complexity for the medium prime case. In: Robshaw, M., Katz, J. (eds.) CRYPTO 2016. LNCS, vol. 9814, pp. 543–571. Springer, Heidelberg (2016). https://doi.org/10.1007/978-3-662-53018-4_20. https://ia.cr/2015/1027

27. Kim, T., Jeong, J.: Extended tower number field sieve with application to finite fields of arbitrary composite extension degree. In: Fehr, S. (ed.) PKC 2017. LNCS, vol. 10174, pp. 388–408. Springer, Heidelberg (2017). https://doi.org/10.1007/978-3-662-54365-8_16. https://ia.cr/2016/526

28. Lenstra, A.K., Verheul, E.R.: Selecting cryptographic key sizes. J. Cryptol. **14**(4), 255–293 (2001). https://doi.org/10.1007/s00145-001-0009-4

29. Menezes, A., Sarkar, P., Singh, S.: Challenges with assessing the impact of NFS advances on the security of pairing-based cryptography. In: Phan, R.C.-W., Yung, M. (eds.) Mycrypt 2016. LNCS, vol. 10311, pp. 83–108. Springer, Cham (2017). https://doi.org/10.1007/978-3-319-61273-7_5. https://ia.cr/2016/1102

30. Montgomery, P.L.: Five, six, and seven-term Karatsuba-like formulae. IEEE Trans. Comput. **54**, 362–369 (2005). https://doi.org/10.1109/TC.2005.49

31. Pereira, G.C., Simplício, M.A., Naehrig, M., Barreto, P.S.: A family of implementation-friendly BN elliptic curves. J. Syst. Softw. **84**(8), 1319–1326 (2011). https://doi.org/10.1016/j.jss.2011.03.083. https://ia.cr/2010/429

32. Sakemi, Y., Kobayashi, T., Saito, T.: Pairing-friendly curves. IETF draft, November 2019. https://tools.ietf.org/html/draft-irtf-cfrg-pairing-friendly-curves-00

33. Scott, M., Guillevic, A.: A new family of pairing-friendly elliptic curves. In: Budaghyan, L., Rodríguez-Henríquez, F. (eds.) WAIFI 2018. LNCS, vol. 11321, pp. 43–57. Springer, Cham (2018). https://doi.org/10.1007/978-3-030-05153-2_2. https://ia.cr/2018/193

34. Smith, B.: Easy scalar decompositions for efficient scalar multiplication on elliptic curves and genus 2 Jacobians. Contemp. Math. **637**, 15 (2015). https://hal.inria.fr/hal-00874925

35. Wahby, R.S., Boneh, D.: Fast and simple constant-time hashing to the BLS12-381 elliptic curve. IACR TCHES **2019**(4), 154–179 (2019). https://doi.org/10.13154/tches.v2019.i4.154-179

Privacy-Preserving Schemes

Privacy-Preserving Authenticated Key Exchange and the Case of IKEv2

Sven Schäge$^{(\boxtimes)}$, Jörg Schwenk, and Sebastian Lauer

Ruhr-Universität Bochum, Bochum, Germany
{sven.schaege,joerg.schwenk,sebastian.lauer}@rub.de

Abstract. In this paper, we present a strong, formal, and general-purpose cryptographic model for privacy-preserving authenticated key exchange (PPAKE) protocols. PPAKE protocols are secure in the traditional AKE sense but additionally guarantee the confidentiality of the identities used in communication sessions. Our model has several useful and novel features, among others: it is a proper extension of classical AKE models, guarantees in a strong sense that the confidentiality of session keys is independent from the secrecy of the used identities, and it is the first to support what we call dynamic modes, where the responsibility of selecting the identities of the communication partners may vary over several protocol runs. We show the validity of our model by applying it to the cryptographic core of IPsec IKEv2 with signature-based authentication where the need for dynamic modes is practically well-motivated. In our analysis, we not only show that this protocol provides strong classical AKE security guarantees but also that the identities that are used by the parties remain hidden in successful protocol runs. Historically, the Internet Key Exchange (IKE) protocol was the first real-world AKE to incorporate privacy-preserving techniques. However, lately privacy-preserving techniques have gained renewed interest in the design process of important protocols like TLS 1.3 (with encrypted SNI) and NOISE. We believe that our new model can be a solid foundation to analyze these and other practical protocols with respect to their privacy guarantees, in particular, in the now so wide-spread scenario where multiple virtual servers are hosted on a single machine.

Keywords: Privacy · Authenticated key exchange · IKE · IPsec · PPAKE · Modes

1 Introduction

1.1 Privacy in AKE Protocols

Privacy in authenticated key exchange (AKE) protocols has a chequered history. In some variants of the early Station-to-Station protocol [16], digital signatures are

S. Schäge—Supported by the German Federal Ministry of Education and Research (BMBF) Project DigiSeal (16KIS0695).

J. Schwenk—Supported by the German Research Foundation under Germany's Excellence Strategy - EXC 2092 CASA - 390781972 and the Cisco University Research Program Fund through the Silicon Valley Community Foundation.

S. Lauer—Supported by the German Research Foundation under Germany's Excellence Strategy - EXC 2092 CASA - 390781972.

A. Kiayias et al. (Eds.): PKC 2020, LNCS 12111, pp. 567–596, 2020.
https://doi.org/10.1007/978-3-030-45388-6_20

encrypted with an Diffie-Hellman (DHKE) key to hide the identity, and in SKEME [28], identities were only sent in encrypted form. Both protocols influenced the development of the Internet Key Exchange (IKEv1) protocol, where identities are protected in 5 out of 6 public key based authentication modes. The main idea was to use keys derived from an unauthenticated DHKE to encrypt those messages (displayed in light grey in Fig. 1) which contain identity information. This approach was adopted for IKEv2, and for novel protocols like QUIC and TLS 1.3.

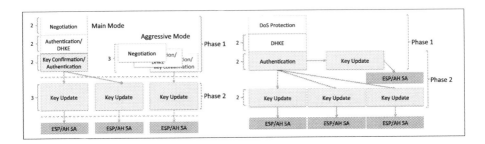

Fig. 1. Overview on the phase structure of IPsec IKEv1 (left) and IKEv2 (right).

The most important AKE protocol, TLS, is up to Version 1.2 not privacy-preserving: Certificates and digital signatures are sent in the clear, so identities of parties can be revealed even by a passive eavesdropper. To describe the situation somewhat dramatically: if someone would use TLS 1.2 in mutual authentication mode over TOR [17], the identity of both client and server would immediately be revealed at the TOR exit node.

With the development of novel protocols and protocol families like QUIC [19], TLS 1.3 [18], NOISE [38], or SIGNAL [9], interest in privacy was revived. "Enhancing privacy" was formulated as a goal for all of these protocols, but the term "privacy" was never formally defined in the context of AKE protocols.

1.2   A New Security Model

We close this gap by presenting a formal model called *privacy-preserving* AKE (PPAKE) that allows us to precisely describe the privacy guarantees offered by protocols like QUIC, TLS 1.3 (with ESNIs), NOISE, and IPsec IKE. Essentially, our model formalizes that in a PPAKE the identities used by the communication partners remain confidential in successful protocol runs.

We stress that our model is a proper extension of classical security models like [7, 32]. Let us provide a brief overview on the features of our model. As one of our main changes to classical models we provide every party with *two* possible identities (key pairs) that this party might use to authenticate messages with. In general, a protocol run may now be executed with either of these keys. Our new notion of privacy formalizes that it should be infeasible in a privacy-preserving AKE protocol, to distinguish which identity is actually used. (We note that, if we set one of these keys to a constant and only use the other, we easily obtain the classical security definition that is formalized in many previous works like [7,32].) The choice of which of the two identities will be used can be independent in each protocol run. (To this end we extend the set of local variables of oracles.)

As one of our main novelties, we also introduce two distinct ways to select which of these identities should actually be used. The first way is for each party to decide on the identity on its own. This models P2P-like protocols. The second way is to *make the communication partner decide on the identity* to be used. This approach of selecting identities, from now on referred to as the *classical* mode, models situations where for example a client would like to choose among the set of identities hosted by a single server machine like in a multi-hosted webserver setting. In such a scenario a single computer may host several (virtual) servers, among which there is one that may provide security-critical information or services (for example information on political opposition groups). We remark that, in such a privacy-preserving protocol, the to-be-used identity needs to be the transferred to the communication partner. For privacy reasons, this cannot happen in the clear what makes such protocols more challenging to build than protocols in classical modes. In the following, and slightly jumping ahead, we generally refer to a particular set of responsibilities that encode who decides on the identities used by initiator and responder as *mode*.

Our new security model formalizes very strong guarantees: we grant the attacker the ability to query the used identities of arbitrary communication partners. For security, we then require that it remains infeasible to decide which identity has actually been used in a successful protocol run. In our analysis we allow each party to use the same long-term keys in all supported modes, possibly differing over several protocol runs.

To illustrate the validity of our approach, we have chosen Internet Key Exchange Version 2 (IKEv2) for several reasons: (1) IKEv2 is fully standardized. (2) IKEv2 is being widely deployed, so we can justify our model with details on how to actually instantiate the protocol in a privacy-preserving way. (3) IKEv2 is interesting in its own right – no reduction-based security analysis of its privacy guarantees has been published up to now, and it is a prime example of an important real-world protocol with somewhat confusing details resulting from the standardization process. We believe that our model can also be deployed on protocols like QUIC or NOISE that also implement mechanisms to protect identities.

1.3   Comparison with TOR and Practical Motivation

A short discussion about TOR [17] is necessary, since TOR is still the benchmark in privacy protection on the Internet.

THE TOR NETWORK. Our model is not suitable for the TOR network, which guarantees privacy even in a Byzantine networking environment, i.e. against an adversary who controls large parts (but not all) of the Internet, and parts of the TOR network itself. Our assumptions on the network are stronger, and our adversary is weaker than a TOR adversary – we assume an active man-in-the-middle attacker that controls a large, but well-defined part of the Internet, such that we can get rid of identifiers like IP or MAC addresses by placing simple, trustworthy TCP proxies at the entry points of the adversary controlled network.

THE TOR PROTOCOL. The cryptographic protocol behind the TOR network is something different. Roughly, it can be compared to three nested executions of a server-only authenticated TLS handshake, the servers being the TOR nodes. In each of these executions, encryption keys from the previous execution are used to protect the handshake messages, and the next TOR node authenticates itself to the TOR client. Our model fits to any of these three executions analyzed separately, but not for the nested case.

REAL-WORLD USEFULNESS OF PRIVACY-PRESERVING KEY EXCHANGE: THE CASE OF SNI-BASED CENSORSHIP IN SOUTH KOREA. To show that PPAKE is nevertheless practically well motivated, recall that when using TLS-secured connections, Server Name Indicators (SNIs) are used by clients to specify which virtual server exactly a clients wants to address when connecting to a public machine that realizes domain-based virtual hosting. Traditionally, SNIs are sent in the clear. In a recent effort to improve the privacy of TLS 1.3, Encrypted Server Name Indicators (ESNI) were introduced that can hide the SNI field from outsiders such that the exact destination a clients wants to communicate with remains secret [39]. In spirit, this implements a privacy-preserving key exchange protocol (though for a final assessment a formal analysis is required – a pressing open problem for future work).

Recently, the South Korean government (i.e. the so-called Korea Communications Standards Commission (KCSC) responsible for censorship) has, in a widely criticized move[1], started to implement a system that denies access to more than 800 pre-selected foreign websites to its citizens[2]. When secured with TLS, this system uses SNI fields to identify destination sites to block the traffic. However, when ESNIs are used, this filtering technique fails. This has prompted the South Korean government to stop ESNI-based traffic entirely. To us, this shows that PPAKE protocols significantly increase the technical difficulties to filter websites. Moreover when PPAKE protocols are widely adopted, this or similar approaches to mass censorship cannot work efficiently anymore without sacrificing the availability of major parts of the Internet infrastructure to their citizens – a move that would likely lead to strong political repercussions.

1.4   IPsec IKEv2 Is PPAKE

The *Internet Key Exchange (IKE)* protocol is the "handshake" protocol for negotiating IPsec keys and algorithms. It currently exists in two versions, IKEv1 [21] and IKEv2 [24, 25]. Both consist of two phases, which are depicted in Fig. 1. Both contain an unauthenticated Diffie-Hellman Key Exchange (DHKE) in Phase 1, where the resulting keys are used to protect privacy-related data in later messages.

IKEv2, which will be explained in detail in Sect. 4, is a 2-stage authenticated key exchange protocol (cf. Fig. 1). Stage/Phase 1 is only executed once, to establish a set of authenticated symmetric keys. This set of keys is the basis of multiple executions of Phase 2, each of which results in freshly derived keys that are used to protect certain IP connections. Jumping ahead, our security analysis will show that these keys

---

[1] https://www.koreatimes.co.kr/www/nation/2019/02/119_264003.html.

[2] Official announcement in Korean, retrieved 05-14-2019: https://kcc.go.kr/user.do?mode= view\&page=A05030000\&dc=K05030000\&boardId=1113\&cp=1\&boardSeq=46820.

are indistinguishable from random. What makes IKEv2 also privacy-preserving is that some related keys are used to encrypt all identity-related data exchanged between the communication partners.

1.5   On the Challenge of Constructing PPAKE

We caution that, although it might appear so, many natural approaches for protecting identities cannot be applied in the setting of PPAKE. This makes the design of new PPAKE protocols a non-trivial task. In particular, standard anonymity preserving primitives like ring or group signatures [3,5,40] cannot be applied in a straight-forward way to implement PPAKE, in contrast to for example recent constructions of deniable key exchange [41]. To explain this, let us consider the following example. Consider a multi-homed server, where each of its virtual servers is associated with a dedicated key pair. Also assume the availability of a basic security protocol that for each virtual server authenticates messages via digital signatures using its corresponding key pair. To construct a privacy-preserving protocol, a naïve approach would advocate the use of ring signatures [40] that are computed using all the public keys of the hosted virtual servers. Intuitively, the ring signature hides which application exactly signed a given message. While this solution indeed provides high anonymity guarantees for the sender, it critically fails in terms of authentication. The problem is that once a single secret key is corrupted, the attacker can easily impersonate any other virtual server to the client with it using the ring signature scheme. We stress that it is not despite the use of a ring signature scheme that this attack is possible but rather because of it: it is the very purpose and core functionality of ring signatures to enable users to craft messages on behalf of other users. A single (unnoticed) corruption would thus threaten all other uncorrupted virtual servers.[3] We believe that these security guarantees are too weak in practice and therefore opt to formalize a much stronger security notion. Importantly, in our model, if a secret key is corrupted, this should have no influence on the security of the remaining virtual servers. This should not only hold for the derived session keys but also for the confidentiality of the identities. Our high requirements in terms of security will likely come at the cost of more complicated designs for provably secure PPAKE protocols as compared to generic constructions that rely on standard building blocks like privacy-preserving signatures.

1.6   Contributions

We make the following contributions:

- We motivate and present a new formal model that allows to describe very precisely the privacy features of real-world key exchange protocols. Our model properly extends existing key exchange models and guarantees that protocols have strong

---

[3] The situation gets worse in case secret keys are used on several server machines, for example in load-balancing solutions. Corrupting a single key would threaten all virtual servers on machines where this key is deployed.

security properties. In particular, and in contrast to previous works, it guarantees that the confidentiality of keys and identities are independent of each other.[4]

- We provide a rigorous and comprehensive reduction-based security analysis of the IKEv2 protocol with signature-based authentication, one of the most important real-world cryptographic protocols. To model a protocol option we exploit our novel mode concept. This results in a proof that covers two modes, the classical mode and one in which the initiator decides on the identity used by the responder. This is the first formal proof of the privacy properties guaranteed by an IKEv2 protocol.

Let us provide some intuition for some of the conceptually novel features of our model:

DYNAMIC MODES. First, we stress that none of the existing works considers what we call dynamic modes. Our model allows that a single party may not only have several key pairs but also behave differently over the course of several protocol runs with regard to its responsibility for selecting the actually used identity. More concretely, in some protocol runs the party may decide on its own which of its identities it will use and sometimes it will be the communication partner who decides this. Likewise the responsibility for choosing the communication partner's key material may vary. We stress that in some situations these protocol runs cannot be examined separately since they all rely on the same long-term key material. Running the protocol in distinct modes may help the attacker considerably to violate the protocol's security.[5] In the full version, we provide a sketch of a protocol that serves as a separation result between security models with static and dynamic modes. Moreover, as mentioned before, we stress that our proof of IPsec will apply the mode concept to model that either the initiator or the responder may decide on the responder's identity.

PUBLIC MODES. Another striking feature of our model is that we allow the attacker to obtain information on the mode of oracles *before* using them. On the one hand, this allows her to adaptively specify in which modes the protocol should be run in by the honest parties. She can thus freely follow an arbitrary learning strategy that relies on a series of clever choices of modes for the respective protocol runs. On the other hand, it also allows for attacks that aim at making oracles communicate with each other that do not have fitting modes, i.e. where there is no common agreement on who is supposed to decide on some identity used by one of the parties. In particular, the attacker may exploit settings where none of the parties or even both of the parties try to specify a certain identity. We technically implement this by using oracles with pre-specified modes among which the attacker may choose. Moreover, the mode is public information and thus also known to the attacker before the execution. Such a modeling is practically well motivated by the fact that protocol implementations often use distinct network interfaces

---

[4] Via this, the model for example covers scenarios well where privacy breaches are generally more probable than attacks on the session key. Even if by some error privacy is violated, the session keys still remain secure. Protocols proven secure in our model are thus well suited in these scenarios.

[5] A rough analogy is that in modern AKE models parties may serve as initiators and responders with the same key material. A corresponding proof should then guarantee that sessions where a party runs the protocol as initiator do not help to break key indistinguishability even when the party also runs the protocol as responder. The security model only covers this, if parties may assume both roles.

(e.g. TCP ports) for different protocol variants (or even just for different communication directions): a user machine may expect incoming connection attempts on a network interface that is distinct from the one used for outgoing connection attempts. In particular, our way of modeling reflects attacks in which the attacker relays messages between oracles that otherwise would not result in a correct protocol execution.

1.7 Related Works

There are several related papers that cover privacy issues in key exchange protocols. Let us describe how our work differs.

SEPARATED SECURITY DEFINITIONS. First of all, we stress that our new security definition is stronger than one in which key indistinguishability and privacy are treated separately *and not all the attacking queries are available in both security experiments*, like [2,20]. We observe that in general such an approach may have the benefit that it can be very simple to re-use existing results: one simply could take a protocol with a proof of key indistinguishability and add the proof of privacy (while even introducing new privacy-related attacking queries). However, we opt for a much stronger model. Our new model requires that classical key indistinguishability of some protocol holds *even* in the presence of attacks that adaptively unmask identities – and vice versa: we require confidentiality of identities even in the presence of queries that let the attacker reveal session keys. Only such an approach formally guarantees that the two security properties are indeed independent in a protocol, i.e. that revealing identities does not violate key indistinguishability and revealing keys does not violate privacy. Moreover, it is clearly stronger than the classical approach, because even in the key indistinguishability game, the attacker is provided more generous attack queries.

SYMMETRIC SETTING. Some of the previous works [20,33] focus on settings with symmetric long-term keys that are used for authentication. However, a closer inspection reveals that technically, the asymmetric AKE setting is much more challenging. This is because in the crucial security experiment of the symmetric setting (involving the Test-oracle), the attacker may not be given the common secret key of the communicating parties since it could then easily impersonate the peer. In contrast, in (strong variants of) the classical AKE model the attacker only may not be given the secret key of the peer (until the peer's oracle accepts): the attacker may always be given the public key of the peer and when modeling key compromise impersonation attacks (KCI) [30] it may also be given the holder's secret key. The holder's keys and the peer's public key may be valuable additional information for the attacker to break the privacy guarantees of the protocol. An analogous attacking resource is not available for symmetric key based key exchange protocols.

ASYMMETRIC SETTING. There are three other works that also introduce security models in the asymmetric setting based on the indistinguishability of identities which we briefly would like to outline here. In [12], the authors focus on an analysis of the OPACITY protocol suite and their model aims to capture the properties provided by that protocol. As a striking feature of their security model they only consider protocol runs where at most a single party has more than one identity. As a consequence they require that the peer of the Test-oracle in general needs to be uncorrupted when defining successful attacks. Our notion is considerably more fine-grained and covers more application scenarios. First, we allow both, the holder of the Test-oracle and its peer to have more than one identity. Next, we allow that all the public keys of some party may be corrupted (at some point in time) which allows modeling of KCI attacks and perfect forward secrecy in the first place. In practice this is an important asset. In multi-homed webservers, it captures, for example, situations where the attacker may obtain the key material of one of the hosted servers. In these cases, the security of other servers that are hosted on the same machine should remain untouched. Moreover, we stress that the model of [12] does not consider dynamic modes. The model rather focuses on a single configuration where in the security game only a client (called card in the context of OPACITY) holds more than one identity. The work probably closest to ours is that of Zhao [43] which also relies on the indistinguishability of identities. However, there are several important differences. Next, and most importantly, we observe that in comparison to our model the one in [43] has considerably weaker security guarantees. In a nutshell, Zhao only introduces a single random bit in the Test-session that at the same time specifies both, (i) which identity will be used in the Test-oracle, and (ii) whether the session key is random or real. As a consequence, the Zhao model may deem protocols secure where (i) we cannot reveal the used identity without compromising the indistinguishability of the session key from random or (ii) we cannot reveal the real session key without compromising the privacy of the used identity. (This is also made explicit in the winning condition in [43].) Essentially this amounts to the fact that the secrecy of the session key and of the used identities may not be independent of each other – although a protocol is provably secure. To us, this seems rather unnatural and we opt for a much stronger notion. Moreover the lack of independence guarantees between keys and identities makes it much harder to argue that Zhao's model (and that of [2]) is a proper extension of classical AKE models since (new) queries – that only reveal used identities – may theoretically violate the security of session keys. What is also technically striking is that in the Zhao model, there is only a single but rather unnatural mechanism to specifically reveal the identity used by some party in the protocol. More concretely, if the attacker would like to reveal the identity used by some oracle it has to *query its partnered oracle* for it. Finally, and similar to the papers mentioned so far, [43] does not provide the same freedom to the attacker as given in our model via the concept of dynamic and public modes. It is thus not clear what security guarantees a protocol has when the identity used by some party is sometimes decided on by itself and sometimes by its communication partner (independent of the current role assumed). Similarly, [43] does not provide a mechanism for the attacker to make two oracles communicate with each other that have distinct expectations on who has to choose the used identities (non-fitting modes). Finally, the most recent work [2] focuses on the unilateral privacy of TLS. The proposed model seems very weak as it treats privacy only. As emphasized before, treating privacy and key indistinguishability separately is generally problematic, as such a definition can, for example, not provide insights on the secrecy of session keys when identities are revealed. Moreover, [2] does not allow for corruptions on parties on the tested machine and so does not model any form of PFS or KCI security. In addition, the work does also not cover what our dynamic modes achieve.

IKE. In, Canetti and Krawczyk use the cryptographic analysis of so-called SIGMA-protocols [8,29] to examine the security of IKE. We note that the variant actually implemented in IPsec [24,25] is considerably more complicated than the IKE description in [8]. In their paper they also argue about the identity concealment of identities but their analysis remains informal. In particular, it is not explicit what exactly constitutes trivial attacks or if the attacker is granted adaptive access to the identity information of other sessions. Moreover, their analysis does not cover some subtle details present in the IPsec standard that may leak crucial information. For example, they do not consider the length of signatures although distinct signature length can help the attacker to easily identify the source of a message.

Finally, in the literature one can also find several other academic proposals for "privacy preserving" protocols that use concepts of "privacy" that are considerably different from what aim to achieve.

DENIABILITY. Intuitively, deniability of a security protocol executed between Alice and Bob means that the transcript of a protocol execution cannot be used to convince any third party Carol that Alice or Bob has actually participated in the protocol run. Stronger forms of deniability [15] also require that Bob should not be able to convince Carol even when Bob reveals to Carol his secret long-term key and all secret session-specific information like his ephemeral secret keys, intermediate values and the final session key. Yao et al. describe a family of deniable Internet key exchange protocols [42]. Deniability is a very strong notion of security. However, it can usually not be fulfilled (except for some very weak, relaxed versions of the definition) by security protocols where the parties authenticate via classical digital signatures [15]. This is simply because Bob can always use Alice's digital signature over some session specific information to prove that Alice actually was involved in that session.

The security property that we try to model is unrelated to the notion of deniability although security mechanism that achieve deniability may also be used to enforce our notion of privacy and vice versa. In particular, the protocol that we will analyse does rely on digital signatures.

1.8   Building Blocks

In our proof, we rely on standard security definitions of digital signature schemes $\mathsf{SIG} = (\mathsf{SIG.Gen}, \mathsf{SIG.Sign}, \mathsf{SIG.Vfy})$, pseudorandom functions (PRFs) $\mathsf{PRF}_k(x) := \mathsf{PRF}(k, x)$, a weak variant of the PRF-ODH assumption and authenticated encryption schemes $\mathsf{AE} = (\mathsf{Enc}, \mathsf{Dec})$.

2   PPAKE in Practice: Generic Construction, Comparison and Limitations

Let us examine in more detail how existing protocols try to protect the identity of the involved parties. To this end we isolate an instructive common design that can be found in several widespread protocols.

WIDESPREAD CONSTRUCTION IN REAL-WORLD AKE PROTOCOLS. Figure 2 depicts the generic construction that is used in TLS 1.3, QUIC, IPsec IKE, SSH and certain patterns of NOISE to protect protocol messages that contain identity-related data such as identities, public keys or digital signatures. This construction consists of an anonymous DH handshake, from which keying material k is derived. This keying material k is then used to encrypt all subsequent messages. There are modifications of this design, e.g. in TLS 1.3 and QUIC the order of messages m_3 and m_4 is reversed, but its main security properties remain identical.

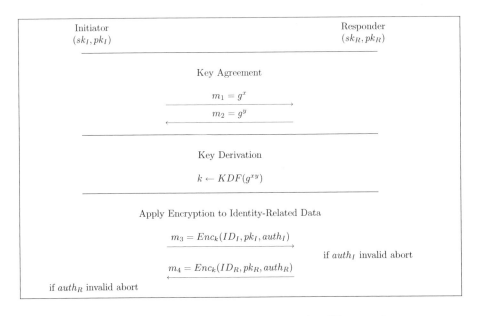

Fig. 2. Generic construction to protect privacy in AKE protocols.

The goal of this construction is to hide the identity of the communicating partners in the presence of a network adversary on the application level, by first establishing anonymous keying material and then using this material to encrypt identity-related data. This construction does of course not hide network-level identity data like IP addresses, so other privacy mechanisms like TCP proxies or the TOR network may be used to hide them when necessary.

Other constructions are possible, but rarely used or critical to privacy. For example, in the NOISE pattern used by WhatsApp, the long-lived public key of the WhatsApp server is known to all clients, and thus there is no need to transmit the server's identity data at the application level – however, this is only possible because the server's identity is public and need not be hidden.

GENERIC WEAKNESS. All protocols following the design pattern from Fig. 2 share the same weakness when it comes to privacy protection – an active attacker can always reveal the identity of the first party which uses the anonymous DH keying material, at the cost of causing a fatal error in the handshake. To do so, she simply establishes herself as a man-in-the-middle for the anonymous DH handshake and is therefore able to derive the (different) keying material used by both parties. She is then able to decrypt the first subsequent protocol message that she receives. In the plaintexts of these messages the parties finally authenticate themselves and the previously exchanged data in some verifiable way. This fact has already been mentioned in [29]. In practice, for protocols like TLS and QUIC, the server identity can always be revealed with this attack. For IPsec IKE, it is the initiator's identity that is vulnerable, and for NOISE this depends on the pattern which is used.

We clarify, however, that this strategy is *not an attack* in the sense of our formal security definition on the privacy properties since the parties will recognize the modifications of the messages and abort the handshake. Our model presented in Sect. 3 (and all previous models as well) rather guarantee that if a party accepts, the used identities remain confidential. On a technical level, this is not different from the classical key-indistinguishability notion of AKE security where we only consider the security of keys computed by partners that accept. However, we caution that conceptually session keys are simply random values that are used to protect meaningful messages later, whereas identities should already be regarded as meaningful messages that are sent in the early key exchange phase. Thus revealing identities is, in a sense, more problematic than revealing session keys, in particular if the initiator's choice of identities cannot be regarded as independent among distinct sessions. It is interesting future work to rigorously formalize and generalize the above generic attack and to provide formal impossibility results for a broader class of protocol designs.

We remark that for the responder, which authenticates second, the above attack seems not applicable. It is therefore conceivable to formalize a stronger property for the secrecy of identities selected by the responder which does not rely on session acceptance. However, this would require a precise formalization of who authenticates second, and it is unclear what this would mean for implicitly authenticated protocols that do not provide authentication in the sense of [4]. Moreover, the practical relevance for such a definition is also not clear.

To avoid the attack in practice one can envisage extra means, like running the protocol (several times[6]) with a randomly chosen identity before the actual communication session. The identities obtained in the pre-runs are then worthless for the attacker. Moreover, frequent aborts in this stage may point to a present active adversary and prompt other actions like for example changing the communication network.

SELECTION OF IDENTITIES. Existing real-world protocols use different approaches on how to select identities. In client-server protocols like TLS 1.3 and QUIC, the client chooses which identity he wants to communicate with (e.g. by selecting the hostname of a virtual webserver in a multi-homed server scenario), and which identity he wants to use (e.g. by selecting one of the client certificates stored in the webbrowser). In classical P2P-protocols, in contrast, identities are traditionally chosen by the holder of that identity itself. A typical example is a party that uses distinct certified key pairs

---

[6] To make it hard for the attacker to decide when the real communication attempt is started one could randomly choose the number of steps.

to access more than one network resource. The IPsec protocol that we analyse allows either the initiator or the responder to decide on the identity used by the responder.

3   Security Model for PPAKE

In the following, we will present our new security model. It is designed as a proper extension to classical AKE models [7,32], a conceptually highly desirable feature in key exchange that helps to prevent the introduction of new models which are incomparable to established ones. In classical models, *indistinguishability of session keys* is used as a primary criterion of the security of the protocols. This is usually checked via a so called Test-query, which, based on a random bit b, either returns the real session key, or a random value. The goal of the adversary is to compute this bit b.

We extend this model by introducing a criterion for *indistinguishability of identities* used in the protocol handshake. To this end, we equip each party (client/initiator and server/responder) with two different identities. Next, we introduce two local variables, the selector bits d and f: d models which identity is used to authenticate data with, while f indicates the identity used by the communication partner.

We emphasize that d, f point to the identities that *are* actually used. However, this is not enough to model the sketched application scenarios comprehensively. Therefore, we also introduce the so-called mode mode $= (u, v)$ that contains a pair of public variables. Essentially, the mode determines *who* is supposed to set the bits d and f in a protocol run. The intuition is that either the used identity d of one party may be determined by the party itself – or its communication partner. In our multi-host server example, the server machine may decide on its own on the actually used virtual server – or let the client choose it. We emphasize that in our security model the mode is our leverage to let the attacker specify who is responsible for choosing selector bits – and create ambiguities about that by relaying messages between oracles with non-fitting modes.

To model security, the adversary may now request two different challenges from the challenger with an extended Test-query:

– By asking Test(π_i^s, KEY), he requests the classical key indistinguishability challenge.
– By asking Test(π_i^s, (ID, 0/1)), he requests an identity indistinguishability challenge, for one of the two pairs of identities.

In the following we provide a formal exposition of the model.

MODES AS PUBLIC VARIABLES. We stress that we deliberately model the mode to be public. The decision to introduce *public* session-specific variables models practice realistically. If a client for example connects to a multi-hosted server, it is well aware of the requirement to select the virtual server precisely (among the set of all hosted virtual servers present). The server, on the other hand, expects the client to choose one of its virtual servers in the protocol run. It does not aim to determine the virtual server on its own.[7] In situations where the communication partners have common expectations

---

[7] An alternative approach is to have each party prepare and manage several *types* of oracles. Each of these types would represent one possible mode and the party will somehow have to choose the correct type for each protocol run.

on who is supposed to determine the two identities we say that their *modes fit* (a formal definition follows). We also stress that our choice is also crucial to cover dynamic modes. Essentially, making the mode session-specific allows modes to differ among the sessions of a single party in the first place. Otherwise, the responsibility of who is allowed to choose identities would be associated to parties (and fixed for each oracle). This is, however not realistic, as in practice the same long-term key material will often be used in several modes because of costs for certification of public keys or simpler key management. As stated before, in our protocol analysis, we also have to consider two modes.

3.1   Computational Model for Key Exchange

Following [4,6,7,11,22,32], we model the execution environment in terms of PPTs. Our notation closely follows [22].

EXECUTION ENVIRONMENT. Let $\mathcal{P} = \{P_1, \ldots, P_n\}$ denote the *parties* involved in the cryptographic protocol Π. Each party P_i holds two identities ID_i^0 and ID_i^1. Moreover, each of these identities is associated with a long-lived key pair (sk_i^b, pk_i^b) for $b \in \{0, 1\}$. Each party P_i may fork off processes $\{\pi_i^s : s \in \{1, ..., l\}\}$ called *oracles* in the following. We use subscripts and superscripts to denote that oracle π_i^s is the s-th oracle of party P_i. P_i is also often called the *holder* of π_i^s. Furthermore, we use the same subscripts and superscripts to denote the variables of π_i^s. If π_i^s sends the first protocol message, we also refer to it as *initiator*, otherwise it is called *responder*.

LOCAL AND GLOBAL VARIABLES. Each oracle π_i^s shares the global variables of party P_i, and may use the secret keys of P_i for decryption or signature generation. It stores the following local variables in its own process memory.

- A session key $k = k_i^s$.
- The *identity selector bit* $d = d_i^s \in \{0, 1\}$. It determines that identity ID_i^d (and sk_i^d) is used in the protocol run.
- A variable Partner $= (j, f)$ that indicates its *intended partner*. It contains a pointer $j \in [1; n]$ to a party $P_j \in \{P_1, \ldots, P_n\}$, often called the *peer* of π, and a *partner selector bit* $f \in \{0, 1\}$. The values stored in Partner$_i^s$ indicate that the public key pk_j^f is used by oracle π_i^s to check if the received data has been authenticated.
- Finally, each oracle π_i^s holds a publicly accessible *mode* mode$_i^s = (u_i^s, v_i^s) \in \{0, 1\}^2$. It is used to indicate how the identity bits of the oracles are chosen in the protocol run. Generally, a 0-entry denotes that variables are chosen by π_i^s, a 1 means that variables are chosen by the communication partner.

All local variables are initially set to some special symbol $\perp$ that is not in the domains of any of these variables. Throughout the protocol execution, each oracle may read and write its variables according to the protocol definition. An oracle π_i^s performs actions as described in the protocol specification, and may either *accept* or *reject* in the end. The final goal of a PPAKE protocol is to establish a session key k. The *adversary* $\mathcal{A} \notin \{P_1, ..., P_n\}$ is a special party that may interact with all process oracles by issuing different types of queries.

FITTING MODES. The bit u_i^s determines if a process oracle π_i^s chooses its own identity (or not) whereas the bit v_i^s determines if π_i^s chooses the identity of its intended partner (or not). More precisely: either d_i^s is simply computed by π_i^s (this is indicated via $u_i^s = 0$), or the communication partner π_j^t of π_i^s is supposed to choose f_j^t and the protocol will make π_i^s set $d_i^s = f_j^t$ at some point (indicated by setting $u_i^s = 1$). Similarly, f_i^s may either simply be computed by π_i^s (indicated by $v_i^s = 0$) or the communication partner π_j^t of π_i^s selects d_j^t and the protocol makes π_i^s set $f_i^s = d_j^t$ (indicated by $v_i^s = 1$). Modes of two communicating oracles π_i^s and π_j^t must *fit* in the absence of an attacker. Intuitively this guarantees that any identity or partner selector bit is set exactly once, i.e. each selector bit is determined by exactly one oracle. More formally:

Definition 1. *We say that (identity) selector bit u_i^s and (partner) selector bit v_j^t fit if $u_i^s + v_j^t = 1$. Moreover, we say that the modes of two oracles π_i^s and π_j^t fit if $u_i^s + v_j^t = 1$ and $v_i^s + u_j^t = 1$.*

Throughout the paper we may sometimes also refer to the mode of some protocol. By that we mean the possible modes an initiator oracle may be in.

3.2 Adversarial Model for Key Exchange

ADVERSARIAL CAPABILITIES. The attacker model defines the capabilities that the attacker is granted. In addition to standard queries we introduce the novel query Unmask that allows the adversary to learn each of the two identity bits used by an oracle. We also extend the classical Test-query to not only provide candidate keys but also candidate selector bits. We stress that if the attacker does not call Unmask at all, restricts itself to only query candidate *keys* via Test (and not identity information), and if for each party the two keys pairs and identities are equal and always corrupted at the same time, we immediately obtain the classical attacker model of authenticated key exchange. Thus our model is a proper extension of the classical AKE model.

- Send(π_i^s, m): The *active* adversary can use this query to send any message m of his own choice to oracle π_i^s. The oracle will respond according to the protocol specification. If $m = (\emptyset, P_j)$, where $\emptyset$ denotes the special string that is not included in the alphabet of the messages, π_i^s is *activated*, i.e. π_i^s will respond with the first protocol message of a protocol run with intended partner P_j.
- Reveal(π_i^s): The adversary may learn the session key k_i^s computed by process π_i^s by asking this query. We require that $k_i^s \neq \bot$ iff π_i^s has accepted.
- Corrupt(P_i, w): For $w \in \{0, 1\}$, the adversary can send this query to any of the oracles π_i^s. The oracle will answer with the long-lived key pairs (sk_i^w, pk_i^w) of party P_i. The pair P_i, w and the corresponding key pair (sk_i^w, pk_i^w) are then marked as *corrupted*. Keys that are not corrupted are called *uncorrupted*.
- Unmask(π_i^s, z): If the bit $z \in \{0, 1\}$ is such that $z = 0$, the adversary is given the identity selector bit d_i^s computed by process π_i^s. In case $z = 1$, the adversary may learn the partner selector bit f_i^s of π_i^s. If π_i^s has not accepted, $\bot$ is output. We require that $d_i^s, f_i^s \neq \bot$ iff π_i^s has accepted.

- $\mathsf{Test}(\pi_i^s, m)$: This query can only be asked once and after this, we often refer to π_i^s as the so-called *Test-oracle*. If process π_i^s has not (yet) accepted, the failure symbol $\perp$ is returned. Otherwise the oracle flips a fair coin b and proceeds as follows:

  $m = \mathsf{KEY}$: If $b = 0$ then the actual session key $k_0 = k$ computed by process π_i^s is returned. If $b = 1$, a uniformly random element k_1 from the keyspace is returned. If $m = \mathsf{KEY}$, the output of the Test-oracle is called the *candidate key*.

  $m = (\mathsf{ID}, z)$: If the bit $z \in \{0, 1\}$ equals 0, the adversary is given $d_i^s \oplus b$. In case $z = 1$, the adversary obtains $f_i^s \oplus b$. If $m = (\mathsf{ID}, z)$, we call the final output of the Test-oracle *candidate (identity or partner) selector bit*.

RATIONALE AND IMPLICATIONS. Essentially our model aims at introducing a new way for the attacker to win the security game besides the classical approach of guessing the session key. Our extension, the computations for case $m = (\mathsf{ID}, z)$, captures that the attacker is given either the real selector bit of the Test-oracle – or its negation. When calling the Test-query the adversary uses z to distinguish between identity selector bit and partner selector bit in case $m = (\mathsf{ID}, z)$. Please note that the role of b is consistent in each of the choices for m. Essentially b determines if the attacker is given the *real* state variable stored by π_i^s ($b = 0$) or *not* ($b = 1$). When formalizing security we will require the attacker to distinguish these two cases.

Observe that the security-critical selector bits, like session keys, are by definition shared among two oracles if no attacker is present: $k_i^s = k_j^t$, $d_i^s = f_j^t$, and $f_i^s = d_j^t$. So intuitively, by allowing to also disclose the partner selector bit our model captures realistic scenarios where an adversary attempts to deduce the used identity of some party via attacking that party itself *or* its communication partner, in contrast to [43]. In this way, a security proof of a protocol in our model provides strong guarantees on the confidentiality of the used identities. Essentially, a proof states that the confidentiality of the session key or selector bits of one oracle does not depend on the security (or insecurity) of the secret information of other, 'unrelated' oracles. It is clear that the definition of 'unrelated' is highly critical in this context and in the following we will devote some effort to motivate our formalization. Also note that even though we introduce multiple identities to each party this does not increase the susceptibility to unknown-key share attacks, where at least one of the communication partners is tricked into believing it shares the session key with some other communication partner. The reason why our model is not more susceptible is that (i) communication endpoints are still fully specified in the security model via combinations of party and identity identifiers and (ii) communication endpoints are still associated with cryptographic key material that is used to authenticate messages with in the protocol run. However, we note that it is not sufficient in the protocol run to specify communication partners solely via their party identifier as is common in classical models where parties are associated with cryptographic keys. Leaving the used identity unspecified, parties could be tricked into believing they share a key with some identity of some peer although they actually share it with another identity of that same peer.

3.3 Original Key Partnering

To exclude trivial attacks in the security model, a variety of definitions exist in the literature, starting with the classical definitions of *matching conversations* [4] and *ses-*

sion identifiers [7], up to the more sophisticated distinction between *contributive* and *matching* session identifiers introduced in [19]. Recently, at CCS'17 the authors of [34] showed that matching conversation based security notions are often vulnerable to so-called no-match attacks. We therefore choose their conceptually novel partnering definition, called original key partnering, that is independent of the exchanged messages of the protocol. We remark that as sketched in [34] it leads to conceptually more simple security proofs since only a subset of active attacks need to be considered. We note, however, that the specification of our model is not bound to one partnering definition. The concrete choice of partnering is rather orthogonal to our contribution. It is only in the security proof for IKEv2 that we will formally rely on original key partnering.

Definition 2 (Original Key). *The original key of a pair of communicating π_i^s and π_j^t oracles is the session key that is computed by each of the oracles in a protocol run with an entirely passive attacker. We use $ok(\pi_i^s, \pi_j^t)$ to denote the original key if π_i^s is the initiator of the protocol run and π_j^t the responder.*

Definition 3 (Original Key Partnering). *Two oracles π_i^s and π_j^t are said to be partnered if both of them have computed their original key $ok(\pi_i^s, \pi_j^t)$.*

In the following we may use M_i^s to denote the set of all oracles partnered with π_i^s.

3.4 Security and Privacy Model

SECURITY GAME. We define protocol security via a game. We call the protocol insecure if an efficient (PPT) adversary can win the game with non-negligible advantage.

Definition 4 (Security Game). *Consider the following security game played between a challenger C and an adversary A.*

1. *The challenger simulates n parties $P_i, i \in \{1, ..., n\}$. For each party P_i, he computes identities ID_i^0, ID_i^1 and randomly generates key pairs (sk_i^0, pk_i^0), (sk_i^1, pk_i^1). All public keys are given to the attacker.*
2. *The adversary may ask arbitrary queries* Send, Reveal, Unmask, Corrupt, *and* Test *to any process π_i^s with $i \in \{1, ..., n\}$, $s \in \{1, ..., \ell\}$. Queries can be made adaptively. For each process π_i^s the challenger chooses random selector bits if the mode requires so: if $u_i^s = 0$, d_i^s is chosen uniformly at random; in case $v_i^s = 0$, f_i^s is chosen uniformly at random. The* Test-query *can only be asked once.*
3. *Finally, the adversary outputs bit $b' \in \{0, 1\}$, its guess for b.*

Definition 5 (Secure PPAKE). *Let A be a PPT adversary, interacting with challenger C in the security game described above. Assume the attacker calls* Test(π_i^s, m) *that internally computes bit b. Let d be π_i^s's identity selector bit, let* Partner$_i^s = (P_j, f)$ *be its intended partner with partner selector bit f, and let b' be the output of A. We say the adversary wins the game, if $b = b'$ and at least one of the following holds*

1. *$m =$ KEY, then we require that (i) no query* Reveal(π_i^s) *has been asked, (ii) no query* Reveal(π_j^t) *has been asked to any oracle π_j^t such that π_i^s is partnered with π_j^t, and (iii)* Partner$_i^s = (P_j, f)$ *has not been corrupted while $M_i^s = \emptyset$ (there is no partner oracle).*

2. $m = (\mathsf{ID}, 0)$, *then we require that (i) no query* $\mathsf{Unmask}(\pi_s^i, 0)$ *has been asked, (ii) no* $\mathsf{Unmask}(\pi_j^t, 1)$ *query has been asked to any oracle* π_i^t *such that* π_i^s *is partnered with* π_j^t, *and (iii)* $\mathsf{Partner}_i^s = (P_j, f)$ *has not been corrupted while* $M_i^s = \emptyset$.

3. $m = (\mathsf{ID}, 1)$, *then we require that (i) no query* $\mathsf{Unmask}(\pi_s^i, 1)$ *has been asked, (ii) no* $\mathsf{Unmask}(\pi_j^t)$ *query has been asked to any oracle* π_j^t *such that* π_i^s *is partnered with* π_j^t, *and (iii)* $\mathsf{Partner}_i^s = (P_j, f)$ *has not been corrupted while* $M_i^s = \emptyset$.

We say that an authenticated key exchange protocol Π *is* $\epsilon_{\mathsf{PP\text{-}AKE}}$-*secure if any PPT adversary* $\mathcal{A}$ *has at most an advantage of* $\epsilon_{\mathsf{PP\text{-}AKE}}$ *i.e.*

$$|\Pr\left[b = b'\right] - 1/2| \leq \epsilon_{\mathsf{PP\text{-}AKE}}.$$

Observe that if we focus on key indistinguishability only, i.e. ignoring the Unmask query and the identity options for the Test query, our model provides all attack queries that are present in the original Bellare-Rogaway model [4]. Moreover, our model captures several important attack variants that involve the corruption of secret keys. To model key compromise impersonation (KCI) attacks [30] we allow the attacker to always corrupt the holder of the Test-oracle. Moreover, we also allow the corruption of long-term keys given in Π_i^s (while carefully ruling out trivial attacks via 1.(iii)). This models (full) perfect forward secrecy. Finally, since there is no restriction on the relation of the key material of initiator or responder our model considers reflection attacks [30], where parties communicate with themselves (e.g. between two devices that use the same long-term secret).

REMARKS. Let us consider a variant of a no-match attack [34] that does the following: (1) it modifies the messages exchanged between two oracles such that the two oracles are not partnered anymore. However, assume further, that the attacker's modifications do not influence the computations of the selector bits of the two oracles. Since the two oracles are not partnered anymore, the attacker may (2) disclose the selector bits of one oracle while answering the Test-query for the other. However, since the computations of the selector bits have not been influenced at all, the attacker may now trivially answer the Test-query for $m = (\mathsf{ID}, z)$. This theoretical attack has major implications for the protocol design. What it amounts to – from a constructionist perspective – is that active modifications that change the partnering status of two oracles should always make their selector bits independent of each other – from the attacker's point of view. At the same time, our model requires a considerable amount of independence between the secrecy of the selector bits and the confidentiality of the session key. To see this observe that our model provides strong guarantees for the secrecy of the selector bits even if the session keys of two partnered oracles are exposed. (Observe that in 1. of Definition 5, there is no restriction on the use of the Reveal query.) In the opposite direction, our model provides strong guarantees for the confidentiality of the session key even if the selector bits of two partnered oracles are exposed using the Unmask query. (We notice that in 2. and 3. of Definition 5 there is no restriction on the use of the Unmask query.)

3.5 Additional Considerations

EXPLICIT AUTHENTICATION. We stress that there is no obstacle to adding classical explicit authentication [4] or its generalizations [34] and variants [31] to the set of security guarantees captured by our model. Technically, all we have to do is to add another winning condition which essentially states that for each accepting oracle, there is exists another oracle that is partnered.

PRIVACY-PRESERVING AUTHENTICATED AND CONFIDENTIAL CHANNEL ESTABLISHMENT (PPACCE). Our modifications to the classical model can be transferred to the ACCE model [22] and its derivatives. In a nutshell, the main difference to AKE protocols is that the security analysis focuses on the security of the transferred messages and not on the secrecy of the derived keys. Recall that in these models, the Test query was replaced by the two queries Encrypt and Decrypt to model the security properties of the established channel.

Exactly as before we may equip oracles with selector bits and modes, and as before we may add two additional winning conditions that revolve around the secrecy of the selector bits. We reintroduce the Test-query for $m = (\mathsf{ID}, z)$ but do not require any changes to the encryption or decryption queries: for better modularity and cleaner security arguments we may consider protocols where only the session key computation depends on the used identity. Once this key is established the symmetric encryption layer is independent of any further reference to identities.

UNILATERAL AUTHENTICATION. Our model is defined with respect to mutual authentication, where both communication partners have long-term keys. However, it can easily be used to analyse protocols with unilateral authentication where only servers have long-term key material to authenticate themselves with. As before, clients or servers may determine which identity the server should use. However, there are no selector bits for the client identity. To obtain a model for unilateral authentication we simply require that the Test-query can only challenge the single identity bit that specifies the used server identity.

4   Internet Protocol Security (IPsec)

IPSEC ARCHITECTURE. IPsec functionality is integrated in virtually all operating systems, and in most network devices. It is the basis for industry-level Virtual Private Networks (VPN), e.g. to connect the automotive industry with their suppliers. Thus its practical importance is comparable to TLS, and the IPsec protocol suite is at least as complex.

In contrast to TLS, the "Record Layer" of IPsec is packet-based, not stream based, and consists of the two data formats *Authentication Header (AH)* [26] and *Encapsulating Security Payload (ESP)* [27]. Both data formats can either be used in *Transport mode*, where the original IP header is used in ESP and AH, and *Tunnel mode*, where a new IP header is prepended to the packet. The security of this packet-based encryption layer is quite well understood today [13,14,37].

IPsec can be used in different scenarios. The end-to-end encryption scenario is called host-to-host (H2H), and this is the only scenario in which Transport mode can be used. Other scenarios involve IPsec gateways as encryption endpoints, which enforces the use of Tunnel mode – host-to-gateway (H2G) to enable remote access to a company network, and gateway-to-gateway (G2G) to connect separate local area networks (LAN) over the Internet.

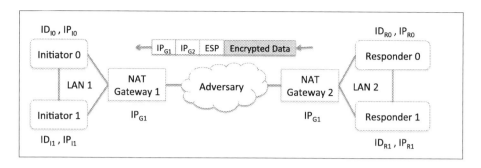

Fig. 3. Host-to-host IPsec connection through two NAT gateways.

To illustrate the applicability of our formal model, consider the typical H2H IPsec scenario depicted in Fig. 3: We have two LANs, which are connected via Network Address Translation (NAT). These gateways do hide all network-level identity information like IP addresses or UDP/TCP port numbers, both in IPsec "Record Layer" communications and in the IKE handshake (Fig. 4), by substituting the private IP addresses used by the different hosts to a single valid IPv4 address. Now a host A in LAN 1 (the *Initiator*) wants to set up an IPsec connection with a host B (the *Responder*) in LAN 2. A therefore performs an IKE handshake with B, which the adversary can observe and manipulate only after network-based identity information has been removed by the NAT gateways – he thus only observes network traffic between LAN 1 and LAN 2.

His goal is to determine the private IP addresses of the hosts A and B which communicate, and this information has been removed from the IP packets. However, before two hosts can communicate via IPsec ESP, they have to perform an IKE handshake which is only partly encrypted, and may leak information about the host's identities $ID_{I0}, ID_{I1}, ID_{R0}$ or ID_{R1}. Our goal is to show that this is *not* the case, under some well-defined assumptions given by our model.

INTERNET KEY EXCHANGE (IKE). The IPsec "handshake", which is called *Internet Key Exchange (IKE)*, is used in two major versions, IKEv1 [21] and IKEv2 [24,25]. Although IKEv1 is declared to be deprecated, it is still active in most codebases.

IKE consists of two phases (cf. Fig. 1): In Phase 1, which is executed only once, DHKE is combined with variety of authentication mechanisms (four in IKEv1, two in IKEv2) to establish a set of authenticated symmetric keys. Phase 2, which can be executed several times, derives fresh symmetric keys to be used in AH or ESP from this set of keys, by exchanging fresh nonces and optionally performing another DHKE.

While the cryptographic core of IPsec has been analyzed quite early [29], the sheer complexity of IPsec made it difficult to provide a reduction-based security proof. A symbolic security analysis, updating [35], has been performed in [10], but due to the high level of abstraction the automated tool (Scyther) required, some small but important details of the protocols had to be simplified. For example, the reflection attack against IKEv2 Phase 2 described in [10] works for the given abstraction, but not against any implementation, because different handshake keys are used in both directions. We note that our abstraction of IPsec also considers distinct keys for the two communication directions.

IKEv2. The target of our security and privacy proof is IKEv2, the current version of IKE. IKEv2 is a complex protocol consisting of two phases. Phase 1 is a complete, public key based authenticated key exchange protocol (comparable to the full TLS handshake), and comprises messages m_1 through m_4 in Fig. 4. With the first two messages, initiator and responder negotiate cryptographic algorithms and parameters (SA and SA), exchange 4 nonces (SPI_I, SPI_R, n_I, n_R), and perform a DHKE. Any active adversary may interfere with these two messages.

Authenticity of the keys derived after this first exchange is only established later, through two digital signatures over partial protocol transcripts. The partial transcript includes all data sent by the signing party in the first exchange, plus the nonce n_X sent by the other party, plus a MAC on the sender's identity.

Phase 1 is however chained and interleaved with Phase 2 (comparable to TLS session resumption) through a key derivation key k_d which is used in both phases. This key is derived after the first message exchange, authenticated in the second exchange, and applied for the first AH/ESP key derivation immediately after the second exchange, in which also a second cryptographic parameter negotiation (SA_2, SA_2) takes place. This second negotiation and the second key derivation are part of Phase 2, and the first instance of Phase 2 is thus interleaved with Phase 1.

The protocol can be configured in two ways: either the initiator or the responder may decide on the responder identity. Technically this is signaled in message m_3 by sending or not sending ID_R. To formally capture this we will use our novel mode concept. We stress that it is not realistic to provide separate proofs for each mode since both use the same long-term keys. Such an approach could not exclude attackers that dynamically switch between modes.

5   IKEv2 Is a Secure PPAKE Protocol

In this section we state the PPAKE security of IKEv2 Phase 1. In our corresponding proof we first show that IKEv2 Phase 1 fulfills the security properties of key indistinguishability as described in Definition 5 (1). Then we prove the privacy properties in the sense of Definition 5 (2) and (3). In our proofs we consider two modes in which the identity of the responder can be either chosen by itself or by the initiator.

RELYING ON THE PRF-ODH ASSUMPTION. In IKEv2 Phase 1 the first two messages are used to exchange ephemeral Diffie-Hellman (DH) shares g^x and g^y. Since both messages are unauthenticated, any adversary could possibly exchange one of the values with its own DH values $g^{x'}$ or $g^{y'}$. For successful simulation, the challenger thus should always be able to answer all queries that involve only one of the values g^x or g^y. However, to argue that the keys $k_{ai}|k_{ar}|k_{ei}|k_{er}$ are secure, the value derived from g^{xy} should still be indistinguishable from random. We therefore deploy the PRF-ODH assumption in the proof: to deal with modified values $g^{x'}$ or $g^{y'}$ the reduction can query the ODH (resp. ODHv) oracle for the correct output of the pseudorandom function.

$$\text{Initiator} \qquad\qquad\qquad\qquad \text{Responder}$$
$$(sk_I, pk_I) \qquad\qquad\qquad\qquad\quad (sk_R, pk_R)$$

IKE_SA_INIT

$$x \overset{\$}{\leftarrow} \mathbb{Z}_q, X \leftarrow g^x,$$
$$n_I \overset{\$}{\leftarrow} \{0,1\}^\mu,$$
$$m_1 := (\vec{SA}, X, n_I)$$

$$\xrightarrow{\quad SPI_I, 0, m_1 \quad}$$

$$y \overset{\$}{\leftarrow} \mathbb{Z}_q, Y \leftarrow g^y$$
$$n_R \overset{\$}{\leftarrow} \{0,1\}^\mu,$$
$$m_2 := (SA, Y, n_R, [CREQ])$$

$$\xleftarrow{\quad SPI_I, SPI_R, m_2 \quad}$$

$$s \leftarrow PRF_1(g^{xy}, n_I | n_R),$$
$$k_d | k_{ai} | k_{ar} | k_{ei} | k_{er} | k_{pi} | k_{pr} \leftarrow PRF_2(s, n_I | n_R | SPI_I | SPI_R)$$

IKE_AUTH

Messages Encrypted-then-MACed with (k_{ei}, k_{ai}), (k_{er}, k_{ar})
parties abort on decryption failure

$$t_i \leftarrow PRF_3(k_{pi}, ID_I)$$
$$\sigma_i \leftarrow$$
$$Sign_{sk_I}(SPI_I | SPI_R | 0 | m_1 | n_R | t_i)$$
$$m_3 :=$$
$$(ID_I, [CERT], [CREQ], [ID_R], \sigma_i, \vec{SA}_2, aux_i)$$

$$\xrightarrow{\quad SPI_I, SPI_R, m_3 \quad}$$

$$\text{if } \sigma_i \text{ invalid abort}$$
$$t_r \leftarrow PRF_3(k_{pr}, ID_R)$$
$$\sigma_r \leftarrow$$
$$Sign_{sk_R}(SPI_I | SPI_R | m_2 | n_I | t_r)$$
$$m_4 :=$$
$$(ID_R, [CERT], \sigma_r, SA_2, aux_r)$$

$$\xleftarrow{\quad SPI_I, SPI_R, m_4 \quad}$$

if σ_r invalid abort

$$k'_{ei} | k'_{ai} | k'_{er} | k'_{ar} \leftarrow PRF_2(k_d, n_I | n_R)$$

Fig. 4. IPsec IKEv2 Phase 1 with digital signature based authentication. Brackets $[\cdot]$ denote optional values. In our security proof we will consider two modes, one where ID_R is decided on by the initiator oracle by indeed sending it in message m_3 and one where ID_R is decided on by the responder oracle. Thus the protocol modes are mode $= (0, 0)$ and mode' $= (0, 1)$. We assume that the responder oracle aborts in case their modes do not fit. (Either the responder oracle does receive ID_R in m_3 although it would like to decide it on its own, or it does not receive ID_R although it expects it.) The common session key is $k'_{ei} | k'_{ai} | k'_{er} | k'_{ar}$.

ON THE (IR)RELEVANCE OF t_i AND t_r FOR SECURITY. In the third and fourth message both parties compute a tag t by using PRF_3 with input ID_I (resp. ID_R). Surprisingly, this value has little influence on the PPAKE security properties of the protocol. To see the reason for this intuitively and jumping ahead, observe that as long as the output of the first evaluation of PRF_2 is indistinguishable from random, the protocol remains secure even if the attacker obtains the keys k_{pi} and k_{pr}. First, key indistinguishability still holds since k_{pi} and k_{pr} are independent from the session key to any PPT attacker. Moreover, the AE keys are independent from these values. However, this means that the AE encryption does not provide any information on the sent plaintexts. Therefore the attacker does not obtain t_i or t_r, and thus no check value to test one of the keys k_{pi}, k_{pr} against. Our security proof will give formal evidence for this, as it indeed does not rely on the security of PRF_3. We find this property striking.

One reason for the introduction of PRF_3 may be that, in the absence of authenticated encryption of message m_3 and m_4, it helps to mitigate attacks where initiator and responder each establish an authenticated connection with the adversary, but the adversary simply forwards the first two messages between them, thus in effect establishing an authenticated channel directly between these two. This constitutes an unknown key share attack. A similar attack was described for TLS Renegotiation [1].

Theorem 1. *Let μ be the length of the nonces and q be the prime-order group $\mathbb{G}$ generated by g. Let n be the number of parties and t be the number of sessions per party. Assume the signature is ϵ_{SIG}-secure and length-preserving, the pseudorandom function PRF_2 is ϵ_{PRF}-secure, the PRF-ODH-problem is $\epsilon_{PRF\text{-}ODH}$-secure with respect to $\mathbb{G}$ and PRF_1. Then, for any PPT ϵ-adversary that breaks the IKEv2 Phase1 protocol as depicted in Fig. 4 (with modes $\mathsf{mode} = (0,0)$ and $\mathsf{mode}' = (0,1)$), we have*

$$\epsilon \leq 2 \cdot \left((nt)^2 \left(4\epsilon_{PRF} + 3\epsilon_{PRF\text{-}ODH} + 3\epsilon_{AE} + \frac{3}{2^\mu} + \frac{3}{q} \right) + 3n^2 t\epsilon_{SIG} \right)$$

We consider different types of adversaries:

1. The Initiator-Adversary, which succeeds by guessing the output of $\mathsf{Test}(\pi_i^s, m)$ correctly where π_i^s is **initiator**
2. The Responder-Adversary which succeeds by guessing the output of $\mathsf{Test}(\pi_i^s, m)$ correctly where π_i^s is **responder**

We prove Theorem 1 by proving two lemmas, the second of which can be found in the full version for space reasons. Lemma 1 bounds the probability that Initiator-adversaries succeed. It remains to show a lemma that bounds the probability that Responder-adversaries succeed. The overall strategy is to first show that all derived keys are indistinguishable from random. This follows from the security of the anonymous key exchange which is authenticated via signatures. Next the security of keys is used to argue that no identity-related information is revealed from the ciphertexts by reducing to the security of the authenticated encryption system. In the following we will provide two lemmas that help to establish a proof for Lemma 1.

5.1 Proof for Initiator-Adversaries

First, we show the security of the protocol in the sense of Definition 5 for Initiator-adversaries with modes mode $= (0,0)$ and mode$' = (0,1)$. We have to distinguish between three different cases for the $\mathsf{Test}(pi_i^s, m)$-query:

1. $m = \mathsf{KEY}$
2. $m = (\mathsf{ID}, z)$ with $z = 0$ ($\mathsf{ID0} - \mathsf{Initiator}$)
3. $m = (\mathsf{ID}, z)$ with $z = 1$ ($\mathsf{ID1} - \mathsf{Initiator}$)

Lemma 1. *For any PPT $\epsilon_{\mathsf{Initiator}}$-adversary that breaks the IKEv2 Phase1 protocol as specified in Fig. 4, we have*

$$\epsilon_{\mathsf{Initiator}} \leq \epsilon_{\mathsf{KEY-Initiator}} + \epsilon_{\mathsf{ID0-Initiator}} + \epsilon_{\mathsf{ID1-Initiator}}.$$

To show the correctness of Lemma 1 we will prove the following lemmas.

Lemma 2. *For any PPT adversary $\mathcal{A}_{\mathsf{KEY-Initiator}}$, the probability that $\mathcal{A}_{\mathsf{KEY-Initiator}}$ answers the $\mathsf{Test}(*, \mathsf{KEY})$-challenge correctly is at most $\frac{1}{2} + \epsilon_{\mathsf{KEY-Initiator}}$ with*

$$\epsilon_{\mathsf{KEY-Initiator}} \leq (nt)^2 \left(2\epsilon_{\mathsf{PRF}} + \epsilon_{\mathsf{PRF-ODH}} + \frac{1}{2^\mu} + \frac{1}{q} \right) + n^2 t \epsilon_{\mathsf{SIG}}.$$

Proof. In the following let $Adv_\delta := |\Pr[b' = b] - \frac{1}{2}|$ be the advantage of $\mathcal{A}$ in Game δ.

Game 0. Game 0 is the original security game PP-AKE and therefore it holds

$$\Pr[b = b'] = \frac{1}{2} + \epsilon_{\mathsf{KEY-Initiator}} = \frac{1}{2} + Adv_0.$$

Game 1. In Game 1 we raise event coll if (i) a nonce collision occurs or (ii) a collision among the ephemeral keys X, Y occurs. In this case the challenger aborts the game and chooses a random bit. We know that at most $n \cdot t$ nonces n_I and n_R with length μ are chosen. Moreover we know that at most $n \cdot t$ ephemeral secret keys are chosen, each from $\mathbb{Z}_q$. We can bound the probability of event coll by $\frac{(nt)^2}{2^\mu} + \frac{(nt)^2}{q}$. We have

$$Adv_0 \leq Adv_1 + \frac{(nt)^2}{2^\mu} + \frac{(nt)^2}{q}.$$

Game 2. We now want to guess the initiator oracle π_i^s and its intended peer which will be tested by the adversary. For this, the challenger chooses random indices $(i^*, s^*, j^*) \xleftarrow{\$} [n] \times [t] \times [n]$. If the attacker issues $\mathsf{Test}(\pi_i^s, \mathsf{KEY})$ with $(i, s) \neq (i^*, s^*)$, $\pi_{i^*}^{s^*}$ is not initiator, or $\mathsf{Partner}_i^s = (j, f)$ with $j \neq j^*$ the challenger aborts the game and chooses b' at random, thus

$$Adv_1 \leq n^2 t \cdot Adv_2.$$

Game 3. In the protocol both parties compute a signature over the exchanged DH shares and nonces. If π_i^s receives a message with a valid signature σ^* while interacting with intended partner j^*, but there exists no oracle $\pi_{j^*}^t$ which has computed the signature, we raise event sigForge. We claim

$$Adv_2 \leq Adv_3 + \Pr[\mathsf{sigForge}].$$

The probability of event sigForge is estimated as follows. Since the signature contains both random nonces, and we have excluded nonce collisions, the attacker cannot replay a previous signature. Now we use this information to build an attacker $\mathcal{B}$ against the security of the signature scheme as follows. $\mathcal{B}$ receives a public key pk^* as input. Since π_i^s has an intended partner oracle π_j^t, the challenger sets $pk_j = pk^*$. Then $\mathcal{B}$ generates all secret and public keys for parties $i \neq j$ honestly. $\mathcal{B}$ simulates the PP-AKE game for $\mathcal{A}_{\mathsf{KEY-Initiator}}$ and can use the SIG challenger to create signatures under pk_j. If $\mathcal{A}_{\mathsf{KEY-Initiator}}$ outputs a message with a valid signature under pk_j, then $\mathcal{B}$ can use the signature to break security. Therefore,

$$Adv_2 \leq Adv_3 + \epsilon_{\mathsf{SIG}}.$$

Thus from now on, we may assume that no signature forgeries occur. Moreover by assumption P_{j^*} is uncorrupted. This means that the signature must indeed have been computed by the responder oracle. Moreover, since $\pi_{i^*}^s$ accepts and because the responder oracle also signs the received nonce n_I, the attacker cannot modify n_I on transit. However, the initiator ephemeral key X is not protected in this way. Observe that the SPI_I and SPI_R are also protected by each signature.

Game 4. In this game we guess $\pi_{j^*}^{t^*}$ the oracle of P_{j^*} that created the signature σ_r received by $\pi_{i^*}^{s^*}$. It holds that

$$Adv_3 \leq t \cdot Adv_4.$$

Game 5. Let g^{x^*} be the Diffie-Hellman share chosen by $\pi_{i^*}^{s^*}$ and g^{y^*} be the Diffie-Hellman share chosen by $\pi_{j^*}^{t^*}$. Both session oracles need to compute $g^{x^*y^*}$ to generate the ephemeral secret $s \leftarrow \mathsf{PRF}_1(g^{x^*y^*}, n_I|n_R)$. In this game we replace the secret s that is computed by the initiator with a random value $\hat{s}$. (Recall that the initiator is indeed guaranteed to compute this value, since the responder's public key is protected against modifications by the signature schemes.) All other values are computed as before. We claim that

$$Adv_4 \leq Adv_5 + \epsilon_{\mathsf{PRF\text{-}ODH}}.$$

Suppose an attacker $\mathcal{A}$ that can distinguish between Games 5 and 4. We use $\mathcal{A}$ to build an attacker $\mathcal{B}$ to solve the PRF-ODH problem. $\mathcal{B}$ plays the PRF-ODH experiment and is first given $g^{x^*} := g^u, g^{y^*} := g^v, n_I|n_R$. $\mathcal{B}$ uses the Diffie-Hellman shares g^{x^*} and g^{y^*} as the first two messages of the oracles $\pi_{i^*}^{s^*}$ and $\pi_{j^*}^{t^*}$ together with the nonces $(n_I)_{i^*}^{s^*} := n_I$ and $(n_R)_{j^*}^{t^*} := n_R$. The initiator will now use z as the output of the PRF. Moreover, if the initiator's ephemeral public key (which is not protected by the responder's signature) is not modified on the way to the responder, the responder will also use z as the output of the PRF. However, if g^{x^*} is modified to $g^{x'} \neq g^{x^*}$, $\mathcal{B}$ can use the oracle of the PRF-ODH assumption ODH to compute the corresponding responder's output s' of the PRF. We note that in this case, s is independent from s'. $\mathcal{B}$ can now use knowledge of s' to simulate the rest of the computations in $\pi_{j^*}^{t^*}$ honestly. If z is the real output of the pseudorandom function we are in Game 4 and if z is a random value we simulate perfectly Game 5, and every attacker that can distinguish both games can be used to solve the PRF-ODH assumption.

Game 6. The next step is to replace the output $u = \mathsf{PRF}_2(s, n_I|n_R|SPI_I|SPI_R)$ by a random value u^*. Thus all the keys derived at this stage, and in particular k_d are also truly random. Only if, $\pi_{i^*}^{s^*}$ and $\pi_{j^*}^{t^*}$ have up to now computed the same value s we will also substitute the output of $\pi_{j^*}^{t^*}$ to u^*. Distinguishing Games 6 and 5 implies an attacker which breaks the security of the pseudorandom function, thus we have

$$Adv_5 \leq Adv_6 + \epsilon_{\mathsf{PRF}}.$$

Game 7. In the last step of the protocol the session keys are computed via $v = \mathsf{PRF}_2(k_d, n_I|n_R)$. In our last game we replace this value by a truly random function. Only if $\pi_{j^*}^{t^*}$ has computed the same value k_d we will also replace its output as well. Every adversary which can distinguish between Games 7 and 6 implies an attacker which can be used to break the security of the pseudorandom function. Moreover, in Game 7 the attacker always receives a random key after sending the Test query, which implies $Adv_7 = 0$ and

$$Adv_6 \leq 0 + \epsilon_{\mathsf{PRF}} = \epsilon_{\mathsf{PRF}}.$$

Summing up all probabilities above we can conclude

$$\epsilon_{\mathsf{KEY-Initiator}} \leq n^2 t \left(t(2\epsilon_{\mathsf{PRF}} + \epsilon_{\mathsf{PRF\text{-}ODH}}) + \epsilon_{\mathsf{SIG}}\right) + \frac{(nt)^2}{2^\mu} + \frac{(nt)^2}{q}.$$

Observe that so far all arguments are independent of the mode actually used. Next, we will prove that the protocol is privacy preserving. We recall that the adversary is allowed to ask Reveal-queries to the Test-oracle and its partner.

Lemma 3. *For any PPT adversary* $\mathcal{A}_{\mathsf{ID0-Initiator}}$, *the probability that* $\mathcal{A}_{\mathsf{ID0-Initiator}}$ *answers the* $\mathsf{Test}(*, (\mathsf{ID}, 0))$-*challenge correctly is at most* $\frac{1}{2} + \epsilon_{\mathsf{ID0-Initiator}}$ *with*

$$\epsilon_{\mathsf{ID0-Initiator}} \leq (nt)^2 \left(\epsilon_{\mathsf{AE}} + \epsilon_{\mathsf{PRF}} + \epsilon_{\mathsf{PRF\text{-}ODH}} + \frac{1}{2^\mu} + \frac{1}{q}\right) + n^2 t \epsilon_{\mathsf{SIG}}.$$

Game 0. In this and the following proofs we extend Game 6 in the proof of Lemma 2 and we have

$$Adv_0 \leq n^2 t \left(t(\mathsf{Adv}_1 + \epsilon_{\mathsf{PRF}} + \epsilon_{\mathsf{PRF\text{-}ODH}}) + \epsilon_{\mathsf{SIG}}\right) + \frac{(nt)^2}{2^\mu} + \frac{(nt)^2}{q}.$$

After *Game* 0 the encryption keys (k_{ei}, k_{er}) and authentication keys (k_{ai}, k_{ar}) are now chosen at uniformly random by the Test-oracle $\pi_{i^*}^{s^*}$.

Game 1. We now substitute $d := d_{i^*}^{s^*}$ by $d' := d_{i^*}^{s^*} \oplus 1$ thus effectively switching from ID_d to $ID_{d'}$. At the same time we substitute the signature generated by the initiator that was constructed using $sk_{i^*}^{(d)}$ by a signature that uses the other secret key $sk_{i^*}^{(d')}$. In case the oracle $\pi_{j^*}^{t^*}$ has computed the same encryption and authentication keys, we will also substitute $f := f_{j^*}^{t^*}$ by $f' := f_{j^*}^{t^*} \oplus 1$. We construct an attacker $\mathcal{B}$ that uses a successful attacker $\mathcal{A}$ against the privacy property of the protocol to break the security of the underlying authenticated encryption scheme as follows. To encrypt $(\mathsf{SPI_I}, \mathsf{SPI_R}, m_3)$ $\mathcal{B}$ uses the ENC oracle of the authenticated encryption scheme and sets M_0 as $\text{SPI}_\text{I}, \text{SPI}_\text{R}, m_3$ with $ID=ID_d$ and M_1 as $(\text{SPI}_\text{I}, \text{SPI}_\text{R}, m_3)$ with $ID=ID_{d'}$. The so generated ciphertext c_d is sent to the responder oracle. After the $w \leftarrow \text{Test}(\pi_i^s, (\text{ID}, 0))$ message for $w = d_{i^*}^{s^*} \oplus b$, $\mathcal{B}$ outputs a random bit b to $\mathcal{A}$ which in turn responds with guess b'. $\mathcal{B}$ can now use b' to break the security of the authenticated encryption scheme by outputting $w \oplus b'$. Therefore,

$$Adv_1 \leq Adv_2 + \epsilon_{\text{AE}}.$$

Game 2. Since we have entirely switched the used identity in the last game, in this game the attacker has advantage 0 to win the security game.

$$Adv_2 = 0.$$

Summing up all probabilities above we can conclude

$$\epsilon_{\text{ID0}-\text{Initiator}} \leq n^2 t \left(t(\epsilon_{\text{AE}} + \epsilon_{\text{PRF}} + \epsilon_{\text{PRF-ODH}}) + \epsilon_{\text{SIG}} \right) + \frac{(nt)^2}{2^\mu} + \frac{(nt)^2}{q}.$$

Again all arguments are independent of the mode as we have shown privacy of the identity used by the initiator. This identity will always be specified by the initiator. Note that we require that signatures have to be length preserving. Else the attacker could trivially break the privacy property by comparing the length of message m_3 under different identities. An other approach would be to employ a length-hiding authenticated encryption scheme.

Lemma 4. *For any PPT adversary* $\mathcal{A}_{\text{ID1}-\text{Initiator}}$, *the probability that* $\mathcal{A}_{\text{ID1}-\text{Initiator}}$ *answers the* $\text{Test}(*, (\text{ID}, 1))$-*challenge of some oracle with* $\text{mode} = (0, 0)$ *or* $\text{mode}' = (0, 1)$ *correctly is at most* $\frac{1}{2} + \epsilon_{\text{ID}-\text{Initiator}}$ *with*

$$\epsilon_{\text{ID1}-\text{Initiator}} \leq (nt)^2 \left(2\epsilon_{\text{AE}} + \epsilon_{\text{PRF}} + \epsilon_{\text{PRF-ODH}} + \frac{1}{2^\mu} + \frac{1}{q} \right) + n^2 t \epsilon_{\text{SIG}}.$$

The proof for Lemma 4 is similar to the previous one and can be found in the full version.

5.2 Additional Considerations

MODELING SIGNATURES AS LENGTH-PRESERVING IN THE SECURITY PROOF. What we expect is that parties use the same signature scheme when dealing with multiple identities on one machine. If this is not the case, or if signatures for the two identities differ in length, the adversary may be able to distinguish identities based on the length of the exchanged ciphertexts. In case signatures have the same length, no matter which identity is used, we may use the classical form of security notions for authenticated encryption. However, we stress that it is very easy to extend the security proof to signature schemes which are not length preserving or where the key pairs key entirely different signature schemes, e.g. an RSA-based scheme for the first identity and an DH-based scheme for the second identity. In this case, we need still to ensure in the security proof for $m = (\mathsf{ID}, z)$ that the adversary cannot notice if we substitute one signature for another, even if the signature lengths may vary. At this point we would need to rely on the security properties of length hiding authenticated encryption as introduced by [36].

PRACTICAL INSTANTIATIONS AND LIMITATIONS. Our security result holds for the protocol specified in Fig. 4 which models IPsec IKEv2 using signature schemes. The standard [24,25] points to various concrete instantiations for the signature scheme, the PRFs, and the authenticated encryption scheme via widespread and well-known cryptographic primitives like AES or HMAC. Our proof clearly only holds if IKEv2 is instantiated with secure variants of these primitives. We stress that, as in previous analyses of real world protocols, our model does not cover all practical attacks. In this sense, we stress that the confidentiality of identities is, of course, only preserved if practical implementations do not reveal them in other messages. Moreover, our model does not cover cross-ciphersuite, cross-protocol, key reuse attacks (e.g. [23]), or physical attacks on devices like side channel analysis. Nevertheless, our result acts as an important source of confidence in the security of IKEv2, provides new insights into the design of the protocol, and may give hints to implementors.

6   Summary and Future Work

In this paper we have proposed a general-purpose key exchange model that formalizes privacy in a very strong way. Our model is a proper extension of classical AKE models. We have applied our model to the analysis of IPsec IKEv2 with authentication based on signature schemes. To formally take full account of both protocol options we have exploited the new features of our novel security model. Our work shows that this protocol is a secure privacy-preserving AKE protocol.

We believe that our model is of independent interest and may serve as a tool to analyse other protocols that aim to guarantee the confidentiality of identities, like TLS 1.3 client identities and certain modes of the NOISE protocol. Our result on IPsec IKEv2 is just a first stepping stone and there are many open questions regarding the security properties of the remaining modes of the protocol that may be subject of future research efforts.

References

1. Alvestrand, H., Housley, R.: IESG Procedures for Handling of Independent and IRTF Stream Submissions. RFC 5742 (Best Current Practice), December 2009
2. Arfaoui, G., Bultel, X., Fouque, P.-A., Nedelcu, A., Onete, C.: The privacy of the TLS 1.3 protocol. In: PoPETs, vol. 2019, no. 4, pp. 190–210 (2019)
3. Bellare, M., Micciancio, D., Warinschi, B.: Foundations of group signatures: formal definitions, simplified requirements, and a construction based on general assumptions. In: Biham, E. (ed.) EUROCRYPT 2003. LNCS, vol. 2656, pp. 614–629. Springer, Heidelberg (2003). https://doi.org/10.1007/3-540-39200-9_38
4. Bellare, M., Rogaway, P.: Entity authentication and key distribution. In: Stinson, D.R. (ed.) CRYPTO 1993. LNCS, vol. 773, pp. 232–249. Springer, Heidelberg (1994). https://doi.org/10.1007/3-540-48329-2_21

5. Bellare, M., Shi, H., Zhang, C.: Foundations of group signatures: the case of dynamic groups. In: Menezes, A. (ed.) CT-RSA 2005. LNCS, vol. 3376, pp. 136–153. Springer, Heidelberg (2005). https://doi.org/10.1007/978-3-540-30574-3_11

6. Blake-Wilson, S., Menezes, A.: Unknown key-share attacks on the station-to-station (STS) protocol. In: Imai, H., Zheng, Y. (eds.) PKC 1999. LNCS, vol. 1560, pp. 154–170. Springer, Heidelberg (1999). https://doi.org/10.1007/3-540-49162-7_12

7. Canetti, R., Krawczyk, H.: Analysis of key-exchange protocols and their use for building secure channels. In: Pfitzmann, B. (ed.) EUROCRYPT 2001. LNCS, vol. 2045, pp. 453–474. Springer, Heidelberg (2001). https://doi.org/10.1007/3-540-44987-6_28

8. Canetti, R., Krawczyk, H.: Security analysis of IKE's signature-based key-exchange protocol. In: Yung, M. (ed.) CRYPTO 2002. LNCS, vol. 2442, pp. 143–161. Springer, Heidelberg (2002). https://doi.org/10.1007/3-540-45708-9_10

9. Cohn-Gordon, K., Cremers, C., Dowling, B., Garratt, L., Stebila, D.: A formal security analysis of the signal messaging protocol. In: 2017 IEEE European Symposium on Security and Privacy (EuroS&P), pp. 451–466. IEEE (2017)

10. Cremers, C.J.F.: Key exchange in IPsec revisited: formal analysis of IKEv1 and IKEv2. In: Atluri, V., Diaz, C. (eds.) ESORICS 2011. LNCS, vol. 6879, pp. 315–334. Springer, Heidelberg (2011). https://doi.org/10.1007/978-3-642-23822-2_18

11. Cremers, C.J.F., Feltz, M.: Beyond eCK: perfect forward secrecy under actor compromise and ephemeral-key reveal. In: Foresti, S., Yung, M., Martinelli, F. (eds.) ESORICS 2012. LNCS, vol. 7459, pp. 734–751. Springer, Heidelberg (2012). https://doi.org/10.1007/978-3-642-33167-1_42

12. Dagdelen, Ö., Fischlin, M., Gagliardoni, T., Marson, G.A., Mittelbach, A., Onete, C.: A cryptographic analysis of OPACITY. In: Crampton, J., Jajodia, S., Mayes, K. (eds.) ESORICS 2013. LNCS, vol. 8134, pp. 345–362. Springer, Heidelberg (2013). https://doi.org/10.1007/978-3-642-40203-6_20

13. Degabriele, J.P., Paterson, K.G.: Attacking the IPsec standards in encryption-only configurations. In: 2007 IEEE Symposium on Security and Privacy, Oakland, CA, USA, 20–23 May 2007, pp. 335–349. IEEE Computer Society Press (2007)

14. Degabriele, J.P., Paterson, K.G.: On the (in)security of IPsec in MAC-then-encrypt configurations. In: Al-Shaer, E., Keromytis, A.D., Shmatikov, V. (eds.) ACM CCS 2010, Chicago, Illinois, USA, 4–8 October 2010, pp. 493–504. ACM Press (2010)

15. Di Raimondo, M., Gennaro, R., Krawczyk, H.: Deniable authentication and key exchange. In: Juels, A., Wright, R.N., De Capitani di Vimercati, S. (eds.) ACM CCS 2006, Alexandria, Virginia, USA, 30 October–3 November 2006, pp. 400–409. ACM Press (2006)

16. Diffie, W., van Oorschot, P.C., Wiener, M.J.: Authentication and authenticated key exchanges. Des. Codes Cryptogr. 2(2), 107–125 (1992). https://doi.org/10.1007/BF00124891

17. Dingledine, R., Mathewson, N., Syverson, P.: Tor: the second-generation onion router. Technical report, Naval Research Lab Washington DC (2004)

18. Dowling, B., Fischlin, M., Günther, F., Stebila, D.: A cryptographic analysis of the TLS 1.3 handshake protocol candidates. In: Ray, I., Li, N., Kruegel, C. (eds.) ACM CCS 2015, Denver, CO, USA, 12–16 October 2015, pp. 1197–1210. ACM Press (2015)

19. Fischlin, M., Günther, F.: Multi-stage key exchange and the case of Google's QUIC protocol. In: Ahn, G.-J., Yung, M., Li, N. (eds.) ACM CCS 2014, Scottsdale, AZ, USA, 3–7 November 2014, pp. 1193–1204. ACM Press (2014)

20. Fouque, P.-A., Onete, C., Richard, B.: Achieving better privacy for the 3GPP AKA protocol. In: PoPETs, vol. 2016, no. 4, pp. 255–275 (2016)

21. Harkins, D., Carrel, D.: The Internet Key Exchange (IKE). RFC 2409 (Proposed Standard), November 1998. Obsoleted by RFC 4306, updated by RFC 4109

22. Jager, T., Kohlar, F., Schäge, S., Schwenk, J.: On the security of TLS-DHE in the standard model. In: Safavi-Naini, R., Canetti, R. (eds.) CRYPTO 2012. LNCS, vol. 7417, pp. 273–293. Springer, Heidelberg (2012). https://doi.org/10.1007/978-3-642-32009-5_17
23. Jager, T., Schwenk, J., Somorovsky, J.: On the security of TLS 1.3 and QUIC against weaknesses in PKCS#1 v1.5 encryption. In: Ray, I., Li, N., Kruegel, C. (eds.) ACM CCS 2015, Denver, CO, USA, 12–16 October 2015, pp. 1185–1196. ACM Press (2015)
24. Kaufman, C., Hoffman, P., Nir, Y., Eronen, P.: Internet Key Exchange Protocol Version 2 (IKEv2). RFC 5996 (Proposed Standard), September 2010. Obsoleted by RFC 7296, updated by RFCs 5998, 6989
25. Kaufman, C. (ed.): Internet Key Exchange (IKEv2) Protocol. RFC 4306 (Proposed Standard), December 2005. Obsoleted by RFC 5996, updated by RFC 5282
26. Kent, S.: IP Authentication Header. RFC 4302 (Proposed Standard), December 2005
27. Kent, S.: IP Encapsulating Security Payload (ESP). RFC 4303 (Proposed Standard), December 2005
28. Krawczyk, H.: SKEME: a versatile secure key exchange mechanism for internet. In: Proceedings of Internet Society Symposium on Network and Distributed Systems Security, pp. 114–127, February 1996
29. Krawczyk, H.: SIGMA: the 'SIGn-and-MAc' approach to authenticated Diffie-Hellman and its use in the IKE protocols. In: Boneh, D. (ed.) CRYPTO 2003. LNCS, vol. 2729, pp. 400–425. Springer, Heidelberg (2003). https://doi.org/10.1007/978-3-540-45146-4_24
30. Krawczyk, H.: HMQV: a high-performance secure Diffie-Hellman protocol. In: Shoup, V. (ed.) CRYPTO 2005. LNCS, vol. 3621, pp. 546–566. Springer, Heidelberg (2005). https://doi.org/10.1007/11535218_33
31. Krawczyk, H.: A unilateral-to-mutual authentication compiler for key exchange (with applications to client authentication in TLS 1.3). In: Weippl, E.R., Katzenbeisser, S., Kruegel, C., Myers, A.C., Halevi, S. (eds.) ACM CCS 2016, Vienna, Austria, 24–28 October 2016, pp. 1438–1450. ACM Press (2016)
32. LaMacchia, B., Lauter, K., Mityagin, A.: Stronger security of authenticated key exchange. In: Susilo, W., Liu, J.K., Mu, Y. (eds.) ProvSec 2007. LNCS, vol. 4784, pp. 1–16. Springer, Heidelberg (2007). https://doi.org/10.1007/978-3-540-75670-5_1
33. Lee, M.-F., Smart, N.P., Warinschi, B., Watson, G.J.: Anonymity guarantees of the UMTS/LTE authentication and connection protocol. Int. J. Inf. Secur. 13(6), 513–527 (2014). https://doi.org/10.1007/s10207-014-0231-3
34. Li, Y., Schäge, S.: No-match attacks and robust partnering definitions: defining trivial attacks for security protocols is not trivial. In: Thuraisingham, B.M., Evans, D., Malkin, T., Xu, D. (eds.), ACM CCS 2017, Dallas, TX, USA, 31 October–2 November 2017, pp. 1343–1360. ACM Press (2017)
35. Meadows, C.:. Analysis of the internet key exchange protocol using the NRL protocol analyzer. In: 1999 IEEE Symposium on Security and Privacy, Oakland, CA, USA, May 1999, pp. 216–231. IEEE Computer Society Press (1999)
36. Paterson, K.G., Ristenpart, T., Shrimpton, T.: Tag size does matter: attacks and proofs for the TLS record protocol. In: Lee, D.H., Wang, X. (eds.) ASIACRYPT 2011. LNCS, vol. 7073, pp. 372–389. Springer, Heidelberg (2011). https://doi.org/10.1007/978-3-642-25385-0_20
37. Paterson, K.G., Yau, A.K.L.: Cryptography in theory and practice: the case of encryption in IPsec. In: Vaudenay, S. (ed.) EUROCRYPT 2006. LNCS, vol. 4004, pp. 12–29. Springer, Heidelberg (2006). https://doi.org/10.1007/11761679_2
38. Perrin, T.: The noise protocol framework, October 2007. http://noiseprotocol.org/noise.pdf. Revision 33
39. Rescorla, E., Oku, K., Sullivan, N., Wood, C.A.: Encrypted server name indication for TLS 1.3. Internet-Draft draft-ietf-tls-esni-03, Internet Engineering Task Force, March 2019. Work in Progress

40. Rivest, R.L., Shamir, A., Tauman, Y.: How to leak a secret. In: Boyd, C. (ed.) ASIACRYPT 2001. LNCS, vol. 2248, pp. 552–565. Springer, Heidelberg (2001). https://doi.org/10.1007/3-540-45682-1_32

41. Unger, N., Goldberg, I.: Deniable key exchanges for secure messaging. In: Ray, I., Li, N., Kruegel, C. (eds.) ACM CCS 2015, Denver, CO, USA, 12–16 October 2015, pp. 1211–1223. ACM Press (2015)

42. Yao, A.C.-C., Zhao, Y.: Privacy-preserving authenticated key-exchange over internet. IEEE Trans. Inf. Forensics Secur. **9**(1), 125–140 (2014)

43. Zhao, Y.: Identity-concealed authenticated encryption and key exchange. In: Weippl, E.R., Katzenbeisser, S., Kruegel, C., Myers, A.C., Halevi, S. (eds.) ACM CCS 2016, Vienna, Austria, 24–28 October 2016, pp. 1464–1479. ACM Press (2016)

Linearly-Homomorphic Signatures and Scalable Mix-Nets

Chloé Hébant[1,2]([✉]), Duong Hieu Phan[3], and David Pointcheval[1,2]

[1] DIENS, École normale supérieure, CNRS, PSL University, Paris, France
chloe.hebant@ens.fr
[2] Inria, Paris, France
[3] Université de Limoges, Limoges, France

Abstract. Anonymity is a primary ingredient for our digital life. Several tools have been designed to address it such as, for authentication, blind signatures, group signatures or anonymous credentials and, for confidentiality, randomizable encryption or mix-nets. When it comes to complex electronic voting schemes, random shuffling of authenticated ciphertexts with mix-nets is the only known tool. However, it requires huge and complex zero-knowledge proofs to guarantee the actual permutation of the initial ciphertexts in a privacy-preserving way.

In this paper, we propose a new approach for proving correct shuffling of signed ElGamal ciphertexts: the mix-servers can simply randomize individual ballots, which means the ciphertexts, the signatures, and the verification keys, with an additional global proof of constant size, and the output will be publicly verifiable. The security proof is in the generic bilinear group model. The computational complexity for the each mix-server is linear in the number of ballots. Verification is also linear in the number of ballots, but independent of the number of rounds of mixing. This leads to a new highly scalable technique. Our construction makes use of linearly-homomorphic signatures, with new features, that are of independent interest.

Keywords: Anonymity · Random shuffling · Linearly-homomorphic signatures

1 Introduction

A shuffle of ciphertexts is a set of ciphertexts of the same plaintexts but in a permuted order such that it is not possible to trace back the senders after decryption. It can be used as a building block to anonymously send messages: if several servers perform a shuffle successively, nobody can trace the messages. More precisely, one honest mix-server suffices to mask the order of the ciphertexts even if all the other ones are dishonest. Moreover increasing the number of mix-servers leads to a safer protocol but also increases its cost. The succession of shuffles constitutes the notion of a mix-net protocol introduced by Chaum [14], with applications to anonymous emails, anonymous routing, but also e-voting.

© International Association for Cryptologic Research 2020
A. Kiayias et al. (Eds.): PKC 2020, LNCS 12111, pp. 597–627, 2020.
https://doi.org/10.1007/978-3-030-45388-6_21

1.1 State of the Art

Usually, a shuffle of ciphertexts is a permutation applied to randomized ciphertexts. Randomization of the ciphertexts provides the privacy guarantee, but one additionally needs to prove the permutation property. This last step requires huge and complex zero-knowledge proofs. In the main two techniques, Furukawa and Sako [21] make proofs of permutation matrices and Neff [31] considers polynomials which remain identical with a permutation of the roots. While the latter approach produces the most efficient schemes, they need to be interactive. Groth and Ishai [23] exploited this interactive approach and proposed the first zero-knowledge argument for the correctness of a shuffle with sub-linear communication complexity, but computational complexity is super-linear which was then improved by Bayer and Groth [3]. As this is a public random coin interactive Zero-Knowledge protocol, the Fiat-Shamir heuristic [18] can be applied to make it non-interactive in the random oracle model. However, with multiple mixing steps, which are required if one wants to guarantee anonymity even if some mix-servers are malicious, the final proof is linear in this number of steps, and the verification cost becomes prohibitive.

The former approach with proof of permutation matrix is more classical, with many candidates. Groth and Lu [24] proposed the first non-interactive zero-knowledge (NIZK) proof of shuffle without random oracles, using Groth-Sahai proofs with pairings [25], but under non-standard computational assumptions that hold in the generic bilinear group model. Even with that, computations are still very expansive because the overhead proof is linear in Nn, where n is the number of ciphertexts and N the number of mixing rounds. In addition, they needed a Common Reference String (CRS) linear in n. More recently, Fauzi *et al.* [17] proposed a new pairing-based NIZK shuffle argument to improve the computation for both the prover and the verifier, and improved the soundness of the protocol. But they still had a CRS linear in the number of ciphertexts, and the soundness holds in the generic bilinear group model.

We propose a totally new approach that handles each ciphertext in an independent way, with just a constant-size overhead in the final proof. The overhead after each shuffle can indeed be updated to keep it constant-size. From our knowledge, this is the most scalable solution. It relies on Groth-Sahai proofs with pairings [25] and a new computational assumption that holds in the generic bilinear group model. As a consequence, assumptions are quite similar to [24], but we have a constant-size CRS and a constant-size overhead proof.

Compared to the most efficient schemes to date, namely the Fauzi *et al.*'s scheme [17], our scheme is also proven in the generic bilinear group model, but the CRS is shorter: just 8 group elements in contrast to a CRS with a number of group elements linear in the number of ballots. Moreover, in our scheme, the proof is constant-size, independently of the number of mixing rounds, while the proof of Fauzi *et al.*'s scheme grows linearly in the number of rounds. Hence, from 2 rounds, our scheme has a better verifier's computation cost and for 3 rounds the proof sizes are almost the same with the two schemes. With more rounds, our construction gets much better compared to the Fauzi *et al.*'s scheme, and the input ballots already contain signatures by their senders, which makes it quite attractive for electronic voting.

1.2 Our Approach

In our shuffle, each ciphertext C_i (encrypted vote in the ballot, in the context of electronic voting) is signed by its sender and the mix-server randomizes the ciphertexts $\{C_i\}$ and permutes them into the set $\{C_i'\}$ in a provable way. The goal of the proof is to show the existence of a permutation Π from $\{C_i\}$ to $\{C_i'\}$ such that for every i, $C_{\Pi(i)}'$ is a randomization of C_i. Then, the output ciphertexts can be mixed again by another mix-server.

Our approach avoids the proof of an explicit permutation Π on all the ciphertexts (per mixing step) but still guarantees the appropriate properties deeply using the linearly-homomorphic signature schemes:

- each user is associated to a signing/verification key-pair for a linearly-homomorphic signature scheme [8], and uses it to sign his ciphertext and a way to randomize it. This guarantees that the mix-server will only be able to generate new signatures on randomized ciphertexts, which are unlinkable to the original ciphertexts, due to the new random coins. However, unchanged verification keys would still allow linkability;
- each verification key of the users is thus also certified with a linearly-homomorphic signature scheme, that allows randomization too as well as adaptation of the above signature on the ciphertext, and provides unlinkability.

When talking about linearly-homomorphic signature schemes, we consider signatures that are malleable and that allow to sign any linear combination of the already signed vectors [8]. In order to be able to use this property on the latter scheme that signs the verification keys of the former scheme, it will additionally require some homomorphic property on the keys.

However, whereas ciphertexts are signed under different keys, which excludes combinations, the verification keys are all signed under the authority's key. Furthermore, a linearly-homomorphic signature scheme not only allows multiplication by a constant, but also linear combinations, which would allow combinations of keys and thus, possibly, of ballots. In order to avoid such combinations, we require a tag-based signature, that allows only linear combinations between signatures using the same tag. As such signatures allow to derive a signature of any message in the sub-vector space spanned by the initially signed messages, when there is no tag, only one sub-vector space can be considered, whereas tags allow to deal with multiple sub-vector space. In the latter case, one thus talks about *Linearly-Homomorphic Signature* (LH-Sign), whereas the former case is named *One-Time Linearly-Homomorphic Signature* (OT-LH-Sign).

In the full version [27], we provide a generic conversion from OT-LH-Sign to LH-Sign, using Square Diffie-Hellman tuples $(g, g^{w_i}, g^{w_i^2})$ for the tags. So, starting from an efficient OT-LH-Sign, one can derive all the tools needed for our mix-net application. However, in the body of the paper, we also provide a more efficient LH-Sign version, and we thus focus on it in the following.

Unforgeability of the signature schemes will essentially provide the soundness of the proof of correct mixing: only permutations of ballots are possible. Eventually, unlinkability (a.k.a. zero-knowledge property) will be satisfied thanks to the randomizations that are indistinguishable for various users, under some DDH-like assumptions, and the final random permutation of all the ciphertexts. With the above linear homomorphisms of the signatures, we can indeed guarantee that the output C'_j is a randomization of an input C_i, and the verification keys are unlinkable.

More precisely, the signature unforgeability will guarantee that all the ballots in the output ballot-box come from legitimate signers: we will also have to make sure that there is no duplicates, nor new ballots, and the same numbers of ballots in the input ballot-box and output ballot-box for the formal proof of permutation.

This technique of randomizing ciphertexts and verification keys, and adapting signatures, can be seen as an extension of signatures on randomizable ciphertexts [5] which however did not allow updates of the verification keys. This previous approach excluded anonymity because of the invariant verification keys. Our new approach can find more applications where anonymity and privacy are crucial properties.

1.3   Organization

In the next section, we recall some usual assumptions in pairing-based groups, and we introduce a new *unlinkability assumption* that will be one of the core assumptions of our applications. Note that it holds in the generic bilinear group model. In Sect. 3, we recall the notion of linearly-homomorphic signatures, with a construction of a one-time linearly-homomorphic signature scheme and its security analysis in the generic bilinear group model. Then we extend it to handle multiple sub-vector spaces. We then apply these constructions to mix-networks in Sect. 4, followed by a detailed security analysis in Sect. 5. Eventually, we conclude with some applications in Sect. 6.

2   Computational Assumptions

In this section, we will first recall some classical computational assumptions and introduce a new one, of independent interest, as it can find many use cases for privacy-preserving protocols.

2.1   Classical Assumptions

All our assumptions will be in the Diffie-Hellman vein, in the pairing setting. We will thus consider an algorithm that, on a security parameter κ, generates $\mathsf{param} = (\mathbb{G}_1, \mathbb{G}_2, \mathbb{G}_T, p, g, \mathfrak{g}, e) \leftarrow \mathcal{G}(\kappa)$, an asymmetric pairing setting, with three groups $\mathbb{G}_1, \mathbb{G}_2, \mathbb{G}_T$ of prime order p (with 2κ bit-length), g is a generator of $\mathbb{G}_1$ and $\mathfrak{g}$ is a generator of $\mathbb{G}_2$. In addition, the application $e : \mathbb{G}_1 \times \mathbb{G}_2 \to \mathbb{G}_T$

is a non-degenerated bilinear map, hence $e(g, \mathfrak{g})$ is also a generator of $\mathbb{G}_T$. For the sake of clarity, in all the paper, elements of $\mathbb{G}_2$ will be in Fraktur font.

Definition 1 (Discrete Logarithm (DL) Assumption). *In a group $\mathbb{G}$ of prime order p, it states that for any generator g, given $y = g^x$, it is computationally hard to recover x.*

Definition 2 (Symmetric External Discrete Logarithm (SEDL) Assumption). *In groups $\mathbb{G}_1$ and $\mathbb{G}_2$ of prime order p, it states that for any generators g and $\mathfrak{g}$ of $\mathbb{G}_1$ and $\mathbb{G}_2$ respectively, given $f = g^x$ and $\mathfrak{f} = \mathfrak{g}^x$, it is computationally hard to recover x.*

Definition 3 (Decisional Diffie-Hellman (DDH) Assumption). *In a group $\mathbb{G}$ of prime order p, it states that for any generator g, the two following distributions are computationally indistinguishable:*

$$\mathcal{D}_{\mathsf{dh}}(g) = \{(g, g^x, h, h^x); h \xleftarrow{\$} \mathbb{G}, x, \xleftarrow{\$} \mathbb{Z}_p\}$$
$$\mathcal{D}_{\$}^4(g) = \{(g, g^x, h, h^y); h \xleftarrow{\$} \mathbb{G}, x, y, \xleftarrow{\$} \mathbb{Z}_p\}.$$

This is well-know, using an hybrid argument, or the random-self-reducibility, that this assumption implies the Decisional Multi Diffie-Hellman (DMDH) Assumption, which claims the indistinguishability, for any constant $n \in \mathbb{N}$, of the distributions:

$$\mathcal{D}_{\mathsf{mdh}}^n(g) = \{(g, (g^{x_i})_i, h, (h^{x_i})_i); h \xleftarrow{\$} \mathbb{G}, (x_i)_i \xleftarrow{\$} \mathbb{Z}_p^n\}$$
$$\mathcal{D}_{\$}^{2n+2}(g) = \{(g, (g^{x_i})_i, h, (h^{y_i})_i); h \xleftarrow{\$} \mathbb{G}, (x_i)_i, (y_i)_i \xleftarrow{\$} \mathbb{Z}_p^n\}.$$

2.2 Unlinkability Assumption

For anonymity properties, we will use some kind of credential, that can be defined as follows for a scalar u and a basis $g \in \mathbb{G}_1$, with $\mathfrak{g} \in \mathbb{G}_2$, $r, t \in \mathbb{Z}_p$:

$$\mathsf{Cred}(u, g; \mathfrak{g}, r, t) = \left(g, g^t, g^r, g^{tr+u}, \mathfrak{g}, \mathfrak{g}^t, \mathfrak{g}^u\right)$$

Definition 4 (Unlinkability Assumption). *In groups $\mathbb{G}_1$ and $\mathbb{G}_2$ of prime order p, for any $g \in \mathbb{G}_1$ and $\mathfrak{g} \in \mathbb{G}_2$, with the definition below, it states that the distributions $\mathcal{D}_{g,\mathfrak{g}}(u, u)$ and $\mathcal{D}_{g,\mathfrak{g}}(u, v)$ are computationally indistinguishable, for any $u, v \in \mathbb{Z}_p$:*

$$\mathcal{D}_{g,\mathfrak{g}}(u, v) = \left\{ (\mathsf{Cred}(u, g; \mathfrak{g}, r, t), \mathsf{Cred}(v, g; \mathfrak{g}', r', t')); \begin{array}{l} \mathfrak{g}' \xleftarrow{\$} \mathbb{G}_2, \\ r, t, r', t' \xleftarrow{\$} \mathbb{Z}_p \end{array} \right\}$$

Intuitively, as we can write the credential as, where $\times$ stands for the element-wise product,

$$\mathsf{Cred}(u, g; \mathfrak{g}, r, t) = \left(\begin{pmatrix} g \\ \mathfrak{g} \end{pmatrix}, \begin{pmatrix} g \\ \mathfrak{g} \end{pmatrix}^t, \begin{pmatrix} g \\ g^t \end{pmatrix}^r \times \begin{pmatrix} 1 \\ g^u \end{pmatrix}, \mathfrak{g}^u \right)$$

the third component is an ElGamal ciphertext of the g^u, which hides it, and makes indistinguishable another encryption g^u from an encryption of g^v while, given $(\mathfrak{g}, \mathfrak{g}^u)$ and $(\mathfrak{g}', \mathfrak{g}'^v)$, one cannot guess whether $u = v$, under the DDH assumption in $\mathbb{G}_2$. However the pairing relation allows to check consistency:

$$e(g^{rt+u}, \mathfrak{g}) = e(g^r, \mathfrak{g}^t) \cdot e(g, \mathfrak{g}^u) = e(g^r, \mathfrak{g}^t) \cdot e(g, \mathfrak{g})^u$$
$$e(g^{r't'+v}, \mathfrak{g}') = e(g^{r'}, \mathfrak{g}'^{t'}) \cdot e(g, \mathfrak{g}'^v) = e(g^{r'}, \mathfrak{g}'^{t'}) \cdot e(g, \mathfrak{g}')^v$$

Because of the independent group elements $\mathfrak{g}$ and $\mathfrak{g}' = \mathfrak{g}^s$ in the two credentials, this assumption clearly holds in the generic bilinear group model, as one would either need to compare $u = v$ or equivalently $rt = r't'$, whereas combinations only lead to $e(g, \mathfrak{g})$ to the relevant powers rt, $sr't'$, as well as u and sv, for an unknown s.

Thanks to this unlinkability assumption, and the randomizability of the above credential, proving knowledge of u can lead to anonymous credentials. However, our main application will be for our anonymous shuffles presented in Sect. 4.

3 Linearly-Homomorphic Signatures

The notion of homomorphic signatures dates back to [29], with notions in [2], but the linearly-homomorphic signatures, that allow to sign vector sub-spaces, were introduced in [8], with several follow-up by Boneh and Freeman [9,10] and formal security definitions in [19]. In another direction, Abe et al. [1] proposed the notion of structure-preserving signature, where keys, messages and signatures all belong in the same group. Later Libert et al. [30] combined both notions and proposed a linearly-homomorphic signature scheme, that is furthermore structure-preserving. Our work is inspired from this construction, but in the asymmetric-pairing setting, and keys do not belong to the same group as the message and signatures. The *structure-preserving* property is then relaxed but fits our needs, as we will use two layers of linearly-homomorphic signature schemes, with swapped groups for the keys and the messages.

3.1 Definition and Security

In this first part, we begin with the formal definition of linearly-homomorphic signature scheme, and the security requirement, the so-called *unforgeability* in case of signatures. Then, we will introduce a new property for linearly-homomorphic signature scheme: the randomizable tag. It will be the key element to obtain the privacy in our mix-net. Our definition is inspired from [30], but with a possible private key associated to a tag.

Definition 5 (Linearly-Homomorphic Signature Scheme (LH-Sign)). *A linearly-homomorphic signature scheme with messages in $\mathcal{M} \in \mathbb{G}^n$, for a cyclic group $(\mathbb{G}, \times)$ of prime order p, some $n \in \mathsf{poly}(\kappa)$, and some tag set $\mathcal{T}$, consists of the seven algorithms* (Setup, Keygen, NewTag, VerifTag, Sign, DerivSign, Verif)*:*

Setup(1^κ): *Given a security parameter κ, it outputs the global parameter* param, *which includes the tag space $\mathcal{T}$;*

Keygen(param, n): *Given a public parameter* param *and an integer n, it outputs a key pair* (sk, vk). *We will assume that* vk *implicitly contains* param *and* sk *implicitly contains* vk;

NewTag(sk): *Given a signing key* sk, *it outputs a tag τ and its associated secret key $\tilde{\tau}$;*

VerifTag(vk, τ): *Given a verification key* vk *and a tag τ, it outputs 1 if the tag is valid and 0 otherwise;*

Sign(sk, $\tilde{\tau}$, $\boldsymbol{M}$): *Given a signing key, a secret key tag $\tilde{\tau}$ and a vector-message $\boldsymbol{M} = (M_i)_i \in \mathbb{G}^n$, it outputs the signature σ under the tag τ;*

DerivSign(vk, τ, $(\omega_i, \boldsymbol{M}_i, \sigma_i)_{i=1}^{\ell}$): *Given a public key* vk, *a tag τ and ℓ tuples of weights $\omega_i \in \mathbb{Z}_p$ and signed messages $\boldsymbol{M}_i$ in σ_i, it outputs a signature σ on the vector $\boldsymbol{M} = \prod_{i=1}^{\ell} \boldsymbol{M}_i^{\omega_i}$ under the tag τ;*

Verif(vk, τ, $\boldsymbol{M}$, σ): *Given a verification key* vk, *a tag τ, a vector-message $\boldsymbol{M}$ and a signature σ, it outputs 1 if* VerifTag(vk, τ) $= 1$ *and σ is also valid relative to* vk *and τ, and 0 otherwise.*

The tag in DerivSign allows linear combinations of signatures under the same tag but excludes any operation between signatures under different tags. The latter exclusion will be formalized by the unforgeability. However, the former property is the correctness: for any keys (sk, vk) $\leftarrow$ Keygen(param, n), for any tags $(\tau, \tilde{\tau}) \leftarrow$ NewTag(sk), if $\sigma_i = $ Sign(sk, $\tilde{\tau}$, $\boldsymbol{M}_i$) are valid signatures for $i = 1, \ldots, \ell$ and $\sigma = $ DerivSign(vk, τ, $\{\omega_i, \boldsymbol{M}_i, \sigma_i\}_{i=1}^{\ell}$) from some scalars ω_i, then both

$$\text{VerifTag(vk}, \tau) = 1 \qquad\qquad \text{Verif(vk}, \tau, \boldsymbol{M}, \sigma) = 1.$$

Our definition includes, but is more relaxed than, [30] as we allow a secret key associated to the tag, hence the NewTag algorithm: in such a case, the signer can only sign a message on a tag he generated himself. When there is no secret associated to the tag, actually one can consider that $\tilde{\tau} = \tau$ is enough to generate the signature (in addition to sk). Whereas the DerivSign algorithm generates a signature under the same tag, we do not enforce to keep the same tag in the unforgeability notion below, this will allow our tag randomizability. However, we expect only signatures on linear combinations of messages already signed under a same tag, as we formalize in the following security notion.

Unforgeability. Whereas linear combinations are possible under the same tag, other combinations (non-linear or under different tags) should not be possible. This is the unforgeability notion (note that we talk about linear combinations component-wise in the exponents, as we consider a multiplicative group $\mathbb{G}$).

Definition 6 (Unforgeability for LH-Sign). *For a LH-Sign scheme with messages in $\mathbb{G}^n$, for any adversary $\mathcal{A}$ that, given tags and signatures on messages $(\boldsymbol{M}_i)_i$ under tags $(\tau_i)_i$ both of its choice (for Chosen-Message Attacks), outputs a valid tuple (vk, τ, $\boldsymbol{M}$, σ) with $\tau \in \mathcal{T}$, there must exist $(\omega_i)_{i \in I_{\tau'}}$, where $I_{\tau'}$ is the set of messages already signed under some tag $\tau' \in \{\tau_i\}_i$, such that $\boldsymbol{M} = \prod_{i \in I_{\tau'}} \boldsymbol{M}_i^{\omega_i}$ with overwhelming probability.*

Again, because of our relaxed version compared to [30], we do not exclude the adversary to be able to generate valid signatures under new tags. The linear-homomorphism for signatures, also known as signatures on vector-spaces, requires that the adversary cannot generate a valid signature on a message outside the vector spaces spanned by the already signed messages. Tags are just a way to keep together vectors that define vector spaces. The adversary can rename a vector space with another tag, this is not a security issue. On the opposite, we will exploit this feature for unlinkability with the additional randomizability property on tags (see below).

However, as in [30], we will also consider a weaker notion of linearly-homomorphic signature: a one-time linearly-homomorphic signature (OT-LH-Sign), where the set of tags is a singleton $\mathcal{T} = \{\epsilon\}$. Then we can drop the algorithms NewTag and VerifTag, as well as the τ and $\tilde{\tau}$.

3.2 Our One-Time Linearly-Homomorphic Signature

Libert *et al.* [30] proposed a construction whose security relies on the Simultaneous Double Pairing assumption, which is implied by the linear assumption in the symmetric case. In our use case we will need two LH-Sign schemes. While the first one can simply be one-time and thus possibly in the standard model, the second one needs randomizable tags and we do not know how to build it in the standard model. Thus, we will consider a variant of Libert *et al.* [30] that can only be proven in the generic bilinear group model [6,11,32].

Setup(1^κ): Given a security parameter κ, let $(\mathbb{G}_1, \mathbb{G}_2, \mathbb{G}_T, p, g, \mathfrak{g}, e)$ be an asymmetric bilinear setting, where g and $\mathfrak{g}$ are random generators of $\mathbb{G}_1$ and $\mathbb{G}_2$ respectively. We set param $= (\mathbb{G}_1, \mathbb{G}_2, \mathbb{G}_T, p, g, \mathfrak{g}, e)$;

Keygen(param, n): Given the public parameters param, one randomly chooses $\mathsf{sk}_i = s_i \xleftarrow{\$} \mathbb{Z}_p$, for $i = 1, \ldots, n$, which defines the signing key $\mathsf{sk} = (\mathsf{sk}_i)_{i=1}^n$, and the verification key $\mathsf{vk} = (\mathfrak{g}_i)_{i=0}^n$ for $\mathfrak{g}_i = \mathfrak{g}^{s_i}$ and $\mathfrak{g}_0 = \mathfrak{g}$;

Sign(sk, $\boldsymbol{M} = (M_i)_i$): Given a signing key $\mathsf{sk} = (s_i)_i$ and a vector-message $\boldsymbol{M} = (M_i)_i \in \mathbb{G}_1^n$, one sets $\sigma = \prod_{i=1}^n M_i^{s_i} \in \mathbb{G}_1$;

DerivSign(vk, $(\omega_i, \boldsymbol{M}_i, \sigma_i)_{i=1}^\ell$): Given a verification key and ℓ tuples of weights $\omega_i \in \mathbb{Z}_p$ and signed messages $\boldsymbol{M}_i$ in σ_i, it outputs $\sigma = \prod \sigma_i^{\omega_i}$;

Verif(vk, $\boldsymbol{M} = (M_i)_i, \sigma$): Given a verification key vk, a vector-message $\boldsymbol{M}$, and a signature σ, one checks whether the equality $e(\sigma, \mathfrak{g}_0) = \prod_{i=1}^n e(M_i, \mathfrak{g}_i)$ holds or not.

From this description, the derivation of signatures is trivial as the signature of the product of messages is the product of the signatures. But we also have additional properties with the keys:

Property 7 (Message Homomorphism). Given several vector-messages with their signatures, it is possible to generate the signature of any linear combination of the vector-messages, applying the operation on the signatures.

When the messages are the same, one can ask for similar property on the key:

Property 8 (Key Homomorphism). Given a vector-message with signatures under several keys, it is possible to generate the signature of this vector-message under any linear combination of the keys.

DerivSignKey(M, $(\omega_i, \mathsf{vk}_i, \sigma_i)_{i=1}^{\ell}$): Given a message M and ℓ tuples of weights $\omega_i \in \mathbb{Z}_p$ and signatures σ_i of M under vk_i, it outputs a signature σ of M under the verification key $\mathsf{vk} = \prod_{i=1}^{\ell} \mathsf{vk}_i^{\omega_i}$.

In our case, if a message-signature is valid for a verification key vk, then it is also valid for the verification key $\mathsf{vk}' = \mathsf{vk}^{\alpha}$, for any α, as $e(\sigma, \mathfrak{g}_0) = \prod_{i=1}^{n} e(M_i, \mathfrak{g}_i)$ implies $e(\sigma, \mathfrak{g}_0^{\alpha}) = \prod_{i=1}^{n} e(M_i, \mathfrak{g}_i^{\alpha})$. However, for two different verification keys vk and vk', and signatures σ and σ' of M: $\prod_{i=1}^{n} e(M_i, \mathfrak{g}_i^{\alpha} \cdot \mathfrak{g}_i'^{\beta}) = \prod_{i=1}^{n} e(M_i, \mathfrak{g}_i)^{\alpha} \cdot e(M_i, \mathfrak{g}_i')^{\beta} = e(\sigma, \mathfrak{g}_0^{\alpha}) \cdot e(\sigma', \mathfrak{g}_0'^{\beta})$, so $\sigma'' = \sigma^{\alpha}\sigma'^{\beta}$ is a valid signature of M under $\mathsf{vk}'' = \mathsf{vk}^{\alpha}\mathsf{vk}'^{\beta}$ if $\mathfrak{g}_0' = \mathfrak{g}_0$.

Property 9 (Weak Key Homomorphism). Given a vector-message with signatures under several keys (with a specific restriction, as a common $\mathfrak{g}_0$ in our case), it is possible to generate the signature of this vector-message under any linear combination of the keys.

Eventually, one needs to prove the unforgeability:

Theorem 10 (Unforgeability). *Let us consider an adversary $\mathcal{A}$ in the generic bilinear group model. Given valid pairs $(M_j, \sigma_j)_j$ under a verification key vk (M_i's possibly of adversary's choice, for Chosen-Message Attacks), when $\mathcal{A}$ produces a new valid pair (M, σ) under the same verification key vk, there exist $(\alpha_j)_j$ such that $M = \prod_j M_j^{\alpha_j}$.*

Proof. The adversary $\mathcal{A}$ is given $(M_j = (M_{j,i})_i, \sigma_j)_j$ which contains group elements in $\mathbb{G}_1$, as well as the verification key $\mathsf{vk} = (\mathfrak{g}_k)_k$ in $\mathbb{G}_2$. Note that in the generic bilinear group model, programmability of the encoding allows to simulate the signatures for chosen messages, which provides the security against Chosen-Message Attacks.

For any combination query, the simulator will consider the input elements as independent variables $X_{j,i}$, V_j, and $\mathfrak{S}_k$ to formally represent the discrete logarithms of $M_{j,i}$ and σ_i in basis g, and $\mathfrak{g}_k$ in basis $\mathfrak{g}_0 = \mathfrak{g}$. As usual, any new element can be seen as a multivariate polynomial in these variables, of degree maximal 2 (when there is a mix between $\mathbb{G}_1$ and $\mathbb{G}_2$ group elements). If two elements correspond to the same polynomial, they are definitely equal, and the simulator will provide the same representation. If two elements correspond to different polynomials, the simulator will provide random independent representations. The view of the adversary remains unchanged unless the actual instantiations would make the representations equal: they would be equal with probability at most $2/p$, when the variables are set to random values. After N combination queries, we have at most $N^2/2$ pairs of different polynomials that might lead to a collision for a random setting with probability less than N^2/p. Excluding such collisions, we can thus consider the polynomial representations only, denoted $\sim$. Then, for the output $(\boldsymbol{M} = (M_k)_k, \sigma)$, one knows $\alpha_{k,j,i}, \beta_{k,j}, \gamma_{i,j}, \delta_j$, such that:

$$M_k \sim \sum_{j,i} \alpha_{k,j,i} X_{j,i} + \sum_j \beta_{k,j} V_j \qquad \sigma \sim \sum_{j,i} \gamma_{j,i} X_{j,i} + \sum_j \delta_j V_j.$$

As $((M_{j,i})_i, \sigma_j)_j$ and $((M_k)_k, \sigma)$, are valid input and output pairs, we have the following relations between polynomials:

$$V_j = \sum_i X_{j,i} \mathfrak{S}_i \qquad \sum_{j,i} \gamma_{j,i} X_{j,i} + \sum_j \delta_j V_j = \sum_k \left(\sum_{j,i} \alpha_{k,j,i} X_{j,i} + \sum_j \beta_{k,j} V_j \right) \mathfrak{S}_k$$

$$= \sum_{k,j,i} \alpha_{k,j,i} X_{j,i} \mathfrak{S}_k + \sum_{k,j} \beta_{k,j} V_j \mathfrak{S}_k$$

Hence, the two polynomials are equal:

$$\sum_{j,i} \gamma_{j,i} X_{j,i} + \sum_{j,i} (\delta_j - \alpha_{i,j,i}) X_{j,i} \mathfrak{S}_i = \sum_{k \neq i, j, i} \alpha_{k,j,i} X_{j,i} \mathfrak{S}_k + \sum_{k,j} \beta_{k,j} V_j \mathfrak{S}_k$$

which leads, for all i, j, to $\gamma_{j,i} = 0$ and $\delta_j = \alpha_{i,j,i}$, and for $k \neq i$, $\alpha_{k,j,i} = 0$ and $\beta_{k,j} = 0$. Hence, $M_k \sim \sum_j \delta_j X_{j,k}$ and $\sigma \sim \sum_j \delta_j V_j$, which means that we have $(\delta_j)_j$ such that $M_k = \prod_j M_{j,k}^{\delta_j}$ and $\sigma = \prod_j \sigma_j^{\delta_j}$. $\qquad \square$

3.3 Notations and Constraints

We recall that linear combinations are seen in the exponents. Since we will mainly work on sub-vector spaces of dimension 2 (in a larger vector space), we will denote $\sigma = \mathsf{Sign}(\mathsf{sk}, (\boldsymbol{M}, \boldsymbol{M}'))$, with the verification check $\mathsf{Verif}(\mathsf{vk}, \sigma, (\boldsymbol{M}, \boldsymbol{M}')) = 1$, a signature that allows to derive a valid σ' for any linear combinations of $\boldsymbol{M}$ and $\boldsymbol{M}'$. In general, σ can be the concatenation of $\sigma_1 = \mathsf{Sign}(\mathsf{sk}, \boldsymbol{M})$ and $\sigma_2 = \mathsf{Sign}(\mathsf{sk}, \boldsymbol{M}')$, but some joint random coins may be needed, and some common elements can be merged (the tag), as it will be shown in the full instantiation.

We will also be interested in signing affine spaces: given a signature on $\boldsymbol{M}$ and $\boldsymbol{N}$, one wants to limit signatures on $\boldsymbol{M} \times \boldsymbol{N}^\alpha$ and $1 \times \boldsymbol{N}^\beta$. This is possible by expanding the messages with one more component: for $\overline{\boldsymbol{M}} = (g, \boldsymbol{M})$ and $\overline{\boldsymbol{N}} = (1, \boldsymbol{N})$, linear combinations are of the form $(g^\alpha, \boldsymbol{M}^\alpha \boldsymbol{N}^\beta)$. By imposing the first component to be g, one limits to $\alpha = 1$, and thus to $(g, \boldsymbol{M} \boldsymbol{N}^\beta) = \overline{\boldsymbol{M}} \times \overline{\boldsymbol{N}}^\beta$, while by imposing the first component to be 1, one limits to $\alpha = 0$, and thus to $(1, \boldsymbol{N}^\beta) = \overline{\boldsymbol{N}}^\beta$.

3.4 FSH Linearly-Homomorphic Signature Scheme

In [30], they proposed a *full-fledged* LH-Sign by adding a public tag during the signature. In our mix-net construction, tags will be related to the identities of the users, and so some kind of randomizability will be required for anonymity, which is not possible with their scheme. Instead, we will consider the scheme proposed in [20], which is a full-fledged LH-Sign version of our previous scheme. We can describe it as follows, using our notations:

Setup(1^κ): Given a security parameter κ, let $(\mathbb{G}_1, \mathbb{G}_2, \mathbb{G}_T, p, g, \mathfrak{g}, e)$ be an asymmetric bilinear setting, where g and $\mathfrak{g}$ are random generators of $\mathbb{G}_1$ and $\mathbb{G}_2$ respectively. The set of tags is $\mathcal{T} = \mathbb{G}_1 \times \mathbb{G}_2$. We then define param $= (\mathbb{G}_1, \mathbb{G}_2, \mathbb{G}_T, p, g, \mathfrak{g}, e; \mathcal{T})$;

Keygen(param, n): Given the public parameters param, one randomly chooses $\mathsf{sk}_i = s_i \xleftarrow{\$} \mathbb{Z}_p$, for $i = 1, \ldots, n$, which defines the signing key $\mathsf{sk} = (\mathsf{sk}_i)_i$, and the verification key $\mathsf{vk} = (\mathfrak{g}_i)_{i=0}^n$ for $\mathfrak{g}_i = \mathfrak{g}^{s_i}$ and $\mathfrak{g}_0 = \mathfrak{g}$;

NewTag(sk): It chooses a random scalar $R \xleftarrow{\$} \mathbb{Z}_p$ and sets $\tau = (\tau_1 = g^{1/R}, \tau_2 = \mathfrak{g}_0^{1/R})$ and $\tilde{\tau} = R$;

VerifTag(vk, τ): Given a verification key $\mathsf{vk} = (\mathfrak{g}_i)_{i=0}^n$ and a tag $\tau = (\tau_1, \tau_2)$, it checks whether $e(\tau_1, \mathfrak{g}_0) = e(g, \tau_2)$ holds or not;

Sign(sk, $\tilde{\tau}$, $\boldsymbol{M} = (M_i)_i$): Given a signing key $\mathsf{sk} = (s_i)_i$ and a vector-message $\boldsymbol{M} = (M_i)_i \in \mathbb{G}_1^n$, together with some secret tag $\tilde{\tau}$, one sets $\sigma = (\prod_i M_i^{s_i})^{\tilde{\tau}}$;

DerivSign(vk, τ, $(\omega_i, \boldsymbol{M}_i, \sigma_i)_{i=1}^\ell$): Given a verification key vk, a tag τ and ℓ tuples of weights $\omega_i \in \mathbb{Z}_p$ and signed messages $\boldsymbol{M}_i$ in σ_i, it outputs $\sigma = \prod \sigma_i^{\omega_i}$;

Verif(vk, τ, $\boldsymbol{M} = (M_i)_i$, σ): Given a verification key $\mathsf{vk} = (\mathfrak{g}_i)_i$, a vector-message $\boldsymbol{M} = (M_i)_i$, and a signature σ under the tag $\tau = (\tau_1, \tau_2)$, one checks if the equalities $e(\sigma, \tau_2) = \prod_{i=1}^n e(M_i, \mathfrak{g}_i)$ and $e(\tau_1, \mathfrak{g}_0) = e(g, \tau_2)$ hold or not.

When the secret keys for tags are all privately and randomly chosen, independently for each signature, unforgeability has been proven in [20], under Chosen-Message Attacks, in the generic bilinear group model. The intuition is the following: first, under the Knowledge of Exponent Assumption [16,22,26], from a new pair (τ_1, τ_2), on the input of either $(g, \mathfrak{g})$ or any other honestly generated pair $(g, \mathfrak{g}_0)$, one can extract the common exponent $1/R$ in the two components. Then, one can see σ as the signature with the secret key $(Rs_i)_i$, with the generator $\mathfrak{g}_0^{1/R}$, instead of $\mathfrak{g}_0$ in the previous construction.

However, if one knows two signatures σ and σ' on $\boldsymbol{M}$ and $\boldsymbol{M}'$ respectively, under the same tag $\tau = (\tau_1, \tau_2)$ with private key $\tilde{\tau}$, and the same key vk, then $\sigma^\alpha \sigma'^\beta$ is a valid signature of $\boldsymbol{M}^\alpha \boldsymbol{M}'^\beta$, still under the same tag τ and the same key vk: this is thus a LH-Sign, where one can control the families of messages that can be combined. In addition, one can define a tag randomizable property:

Property 11 (Tag Randomizability). Given a valid tuple $(\mathsf{vk}, \tau, \boldsymbol{M}, \sigma)$, one can derive a new valid tuple $(\mathsf{vk}, \tau', \boldsymbol{M}, \sigma')$, for a tag τ' unlinkable to τ.

Our LH-Sign has the tag randomizability property, with the algorithm RandTag defined by:

RandTag(vk, τ, $\boldsymbol{M}$, σ): Given a verification key vk, a tag $\tau = (\tau_1, \tau_2)$ and a signature σ on a vector-message $\boldsymbol{M} = (M_i)_i \in \mathbb{G}_1^n$, it chooses $\mu \in \mathbb{Z}_p^*$ and outputs $\tau' = (\tau_1^{1/\mu}, \tau_2^{1/\mu})$ and adapts $\sigma' = \sigma^\mu$.

Indeed, from a signature σ on $\boldsymbol{M}$ under the tag $\tau = (\tau_1, \tau_2)$ for the key vk, $\sigma' = \sigma^\mu$ is a new signature on $\boldsymbol{M}$ for the same key vk under the tag $\tau' = (\tau_1^{1/\mu}, \tau_2^{1/\mu})$, perfectly unlinkable to τ, as this is a new random Diffie-Hellman tuple in basis $(g, \mathfrak{g}_0)$ with $\tilde{\tau}' = \mu\tilde{\tau}$, for $\mathfrak{g}_0$ in vk.

As already explained above, we will essentially work on sub-vector spaces of dimension 2: we will thus denote $\sigma = (\sigma_1, \sigma_2) = \mathsf{Sign}(\mathsf{sk}, \tilde{\tau}, (\boldsymbol{M}, \boldsymbol{M}'))$, under the tag $\tau = (\tau_1, \tau_2)$, where $\sigma_1 = \mathsf{Sign}(\mathsf{sk}, \tilde{\tau}, \boldsymbol{M})$ and $\sigma_2 = \mathsf{Sign}(\mathsf{sk}, \tilde{\tau}, \boldsymbol{M}')$, for a common private key $R = \tilde{\tau}$ which led to $\tau = (\tau_1, \tau_2)$.

Note that in the following, the use of this LH-Sign signature scheme will swap $\mathbb{G}_1$ and $\mathbb{G}_2$, as the messages to be signed will be the verification keys of the previous OT-LH-Sign signature scheme, and thus in $\mathbb{G}_2$. Then the verification keys of this LH-Sign scheme will be in $\mathbb{G}_1$.

4   Mix-Networks

A mix-net is a network of mix-servers [14] that allows to shuffle ciphertexts so that all the input ciphertexts are in the output set, but cannot be linked together. Whereas it is easy for a server to apply a random permutation on ciphertexts and randomize them, it is not that easy to provide a proof of correctness that is publicly verifiable, and compact. In this section we present our mix-net where the proof of correctness will be implicit thanks to the properties of the (linearly-homomorphic) signatures and two proofs of Diffie-Hellman tuples.

In a first step, we provide a high-level description of our construction to give the intuitions of our new method. However, this high-level presentation suffers several issues, which are then presented in the second step, while the third step details the solutions, with the full scheme. At this point, the global proof of mixing, after several mix-servers, is linear (and verification thus has a linear cost) in the number of mix-servers. In the fourth and last step, we explain how to obtain a constant-time overhead for the proof to publish, and thus for the verification.

4.1   General Description

We first provide a high-level description of our mix-net in Fig. 1. As said above, the goal of this presentation is just for the intuition: there are still many problems, that will be highlighted and addressed in the next sections. We need two signature schemes:

- any OT-LH-Sign scheme (Setup,Keygen,Sign,DerivSign,Verif), with additional DerivSignKey, that will be used to sign ElGamal ciphertexts in $\mathbb{G}_1$: the ciphertexts C_i and the signatures σ_i belong to $\mathbb{G}_1$ and are verified with the user' verification keys $\mathsf{vk}_i = (\mathfrak{g}_k)_k$ in $\mathbb{G}_2$;
- and any LH-Sign with randomizable tag scheme (Setup*, Keygen*, NewTag*, RandTag*, VerifTag*, Sign*, DerivSign*, Verif*) that will be used to sign users' verification keys vk_i in $\mathbb{G}_2$: the signatures Σ_i also belong to $\mathbb{G}_2$ and are verified with Certification Authority's verification key $\mathsf{VK} = (g_k)_k$ in $\mathbb{G}_1$.

Each user $\mathcal{U}_i$ generates a pair $(\mathsf{sk}_i, \mathsf{vk}_i) \leftarrow \mathsf{Keygen}()$ to sign vectors in $\mathbb{G}_1$. $\mathcal{U}_i$ first encrypts his message M_i under an ElGamal encryption scheme, with encryption key EK and signs it to obtain the signed-encrypted ballot $(C_i, \sigma_{i,1})$ under vk_i. Obviously, some guarantees are needed.

In order to be sure that a ballot is legitimate, all the verification keys must be certified by the system (certification authority CA) that signs vk_i under SK, where $(\mathsf{SK}, \mathsf{VK}) \leftarrow \mathsf{Keygen}^*()$, into Σ_i. Then, anyone can verify the certified keys $(\mathsf{vk}_i, \Sigma_i)_i$ are valid under the system verification key VK. Since we want to avoid combinations between verification keys, we use $\mathsf{LH\text{-}Sign}$ with randomizable tags to sign the verification keys with a tag τ_i per user $\mathcal{U}_i$.

Because of encryption, M_i is protected, but this is not enough as it will be decrypted in the end. One also needs to guarantee unlinkability between the input and output ballots to guarantee anonymity of users. As the ballot boxes contain the ciphertexts, as well as the verification keys, the ballots must be transformed in an unlinkable way, then they can be output in a permuted way.

To have C_i' unlinkable to C_i, C_i' must be a randomization of C_i. With an ElGamal encryption, it is possible to randomize a ciphertext by multiplying by an encryption of 1. Thus, anyone can compute an encryption C_0 of 1, and as we use an $\mathsf{OT\text{-}LH\text{-}Sign}$ scheme, from a signature $\sigma_{i,0}$ of C_0 under the user's key, one can adapt $\sigma_{i,1}$ by using the message homomorphism (Property 7) with

CA = Certificate Authority, $\mathcal{U}_i$ = User$_i$, $\mathcal{S}_j$ = Mix-Server$_j$
Keys
CA's keys: $\begin{cases} (\mathsf{SK}, \mathsf{VK}) \leftarrow \mathsf{Keygen}^*() & \text{Authority } \mathsf{LH\text{-}Sign} \text{ signing key} \\ (\mathsf{EK}, \mathsf{DK}) \leftarrow \mathsf{EKeygen}() & \text{Authority homomorphic encryption key} \end{cases}$
$\mathcal{U}_i$'s keys: $\quad (\mathsf{sk}_i, \mathsf{vk}_i) \leftarrow \mathsf{Keygen}() \qquad$ User $\mathsf{OT\text{-}LH\text{-}Sign}$ signing key
CA signs vk_i: $\quad (\tilde{\tau}_i, \tau_i) \leftarrow \mathsf{NewTag}^*(\mathsf{SK}) \qquad \Sigma_i \leftarrow \mathsf{Sign}^*(\mathsf{SK}, \tilde{\tau}_i, \mathsf{vk}_i)$
Ciphertext for randomization: $C_0 \leftarrow \mathsf{Encrypt}(\mathsf{EK}, 1)$
Initial ballots (for $i = 1, \dots, n$)
$\mathcal{U}_i$ generates: $\begin{cases} C_i \leftarrow \mathsf{Encrypt}(\mathsf{EK}, M_i) & \text{User's ballot encryption} \\ \sigma_{i,0} \leftarrow \mathsf{Sign}(\mathsf{sk}_i, C_0) & \text{User's signature on randomization} \\ \sigma_{i,1} \leftarrow \mathsf{Sign}(\mathsf{sk}_i, C_i) & \text{User's ballot signature} \end{cases}$
$\mathcal{BB}\mathsf{ox}^{(0)} = (C_i, \sigma_{i,0}, \sigma_{i,1}, \mathsf{vk}_i, \Sigma_i, \tau_i)_i$
Mix (j-th mix-server, for $i = 1, \dots, n$)
From $\mathcal{BB}\mathsf{ox}^{(j-1)} = (C_i, \sigma_{i,0}, \sigma_{i,1}, \mathsf{vk}_i, \Sigma_i, \tau_i)_i$, $\mathcal{S}_j$ makes, for all i:
Randomization of the ballot:
$\quad C_i' = C_i \cdot C_0^{\gamma_{j,i}} \qquad \sigma_{i,1}^* = \mathsf{DerivSign}(\mathsf{vk}_i, \{(1, C_0, \sigma_{i,0}), (\gamma_{j,i}, C_i, \sigma_{i,1})\})$
Randomization of the keys:
$\begin{cases} \mathsf{vk}_i' = (\mathsf{vk}_i)^{\alpha_j} & \Sigma_i^* = \mathsf{DerivSign}^*(\mathsf{VK}, \tau_i, (\alpha_j, \mathsf{vk}_i, \Sigma_i)) \\ (\mathsf{VK}, \tau_i', \mathsf{vk}_i, \Sigma_i') = \mathsf{RandTag}^*(\mathsf{VK}, \tau_i, \mathsf{vk}_i, \Sigma_i^*) \end{cases}$
Adaptation of the signatures:
$\quad\quad\quad\quad \sigma_{i,0}' = \mathsf{DerivSignKey}(C_0, (\alpha_j, \mathsf{vk}_i, \sigma_{i,0}))$
$\quad\quad\quad\quad \sigma_{i,1}' = \mathsf{DerivSignKey}(C_i', (\alpha_j, \mathsf{vk}_i, \sigma_{i,1}^*))$
$\mathcal{BB}\mathsf{ox}^{(j)} = (C_{\Pi(i)}', \sigma_{\Pi(i),0}', \sigma_{\Pi(i),1}', \mathsf{vk}_{\Pi(i)}', \Sigma_{\Pi(i)}', \tau_{\Pi(i)}')_i$

Fig. 1. High-level description (insecure scheme)

DerivSign to obtain $\sigma_{i,1}^*$. In the same way, vk_i' and τ_i' must be randomizations of respectively vk_i and τ_i. If $\mathsf{vk}_i' = \mathsf{vk}_i^\alpha$, its signature must be derived from Σ_i with DerivSign* and τ_i' is obtained with the randomizable tag (Property 11) with RandTag*. Eventually, as we change the verification key, $\sigma_{i,0}'$ and $\sigma_{i,1}'$ must be adapted, which is possible thanks to the weak key homomorphism (Property 9) with DerivSignKey.

Then one generates a random permutation Π to output a new ballot-box with permuted randomized ballots $(\mathsf{vk}_{\Pi(i)}', \Sigma_{\Pi(i)}', C_{\Pi(i)}', \sigma_{\Pi(i),0}', \sigma_{\Pi(i),1}')_i$.

4.2   Difficulties

The above high-level scheme gives intuitions of our main approach. However, to get the required security, we still face a few issues that will be explained below and which motivate the full scheme described in the next section.

Expanded Vectors. From the signatures $\sigma_{i,0}$ and $\sigma_{i,1}$ with an OT-LH-Sign scheme, anyone can compute $\sigma = \mathsf{DerivSign}(\mathsf{vk}_i, \{(\alpha, C_0, \sigma_{i,0}), (\beta, C_i, \sigma_{i,1})\})$ for any α, β. As explained in Sect. 3.3, we can impose $\beta = 1$ and the right format of C_i'.

Non-Trivial Transformation. The weak key homomorphism allows to randomize vk_i into $\mathsf{vk}_i' = \mathsf{vk}_i^\alpha$ but, with our scheme, $\mathsf{Verif}(\mathsf{vk}_i^\alpha, C_i, \sigma_{i,1})$ is valid for any $\alpha \neq 0$ if and only if $\mathsf{Verif}(\mathsf{vk}_i, C_i, \sigma_{i,1})$ is valid. This provides a link between vk_i' and vk_i. To solve this issue, we introduce a randomizer vk_0, as for the ciphertext. This is a special vector also signed by CA to randomize vk_i in a non-trivial way: $\mathsf{vk}_i' = (\mathsf{vk}_i \cdot \mathsf{vk}_0^{\delta_i})^\alpha$. We will thus also have the signature $\Sigma_{i,0}$ of vk_0 and the signature $\Sigma_{i,1}$ (instead of Σ_i) of vk_i, both under the same tag τ_i to allow combinations.

Legitimate Ballots. Whereas all the ballots must be signed, nothing prevents a mix-server to delete a ballot or to add a ballot signed by a legitimate user (that owns a valid key vk_i). If one first checks that the number of ballots is kept unchanged, it is still possible that a ballot was replaced by a new legitimate ballot. Since we will consider honest and corrupted users (and so honest and corrupted ballots), four cases are possible: one replaces an honest or corrupted ballot by another honest or corrupted one. Our scheme will not provide guarantees against the replacement of a corrupted ballot by another corrupted ballot. Nonetheless, by adding a zero-knowledge proof of Diffie-Hellman tuple between the products of the verification keys before and after the mix, we can avoid all the other cases involving honest users.

Multiple Servers. After the last round, one gets a proof that the output ballot-box contains a permutation of randomized ciphertexts from the input ballot-box. However, the last mix-server could start from the initial ballot-box instead of the previous one, and then know the permutation. This would break anonymity, as soon as the last mix-server is dishonest. We will ask the mix-servers to sign their contributions to prove the multiple and independent permutations: each

CA = Certificate Authority, $\mathcal{U}_i$ = User$_i$, $\mathcal{S}_j$ = Mix-Server$_j$

MixSetup(1^κ):
Let param $= (\mathbb{G}_1, \mathbb{G}_2, \mathbb{G}_T, p, g, \mathfrak{g}, e) \leftarrow$ Setup(1^κ) and param$' = \{$param$, \mathcal{T} = \mathbb{G}_2 \times \mathbb{G}_1\}$;
Let NIZK$_{\mathsf{DH}}$-param $\leftarrow$ NIZK$_{\mathsf{DH}}$-Setup(1^κ) and Sparam $\leftarrow$ SSetup(1^κ);
Let (DK $= d$, EK $= h = g^d) \leftarrow$ EKeygen(1^κ) and $\overline{C}_0 = (1, \ell, g, h)$ for $\ell \overset{\$}{\leftarrow} \mathbb{G}_1$;
It outputs Mix-param $= ($param$'$, NIZK$_{\mathsf{DH}}$-param, Sparam, EK, ℓ).

MixKeygen(Mix-param):
CA: $\begin{cases} \mathsf{SK} = (S_1, S_2, S_3, S_4, S_5) \overset{\$}{\leftarrow} \mathbb{Z}_p^5, \mathsf{VK} = (g, g^{S_1}, g^{S_2}, g^{S_3}, g^{S_4}, g^{S_5}) \\ \text{and for each user } \mathcal{U}_i, \tilde{\tau}_i = R_i \overset{\$}{\leftarrow} \mathbb{Z}_p, \tau_i = (\tau_{i,1} = \mathfrak{g}^{1/R_i}, \tau_{i,2} = g^{1/R_i}) \end{cases}$
$\mathsf{vk}_0 = (1, 1, \mathfrak{g}_0 = \mathfrak{g}, 1, 1)$
$\mathcal{S}_j$: $\{ (\mathsf{SK}_j, \mathsf{VK}_j) \leftarrow \mathsf{SKeygen}()$
$\mathcal{U}_i$: $\begin{cases} \mathsf{sk}_i = (u_i, v_i, x_i, y_i) \overset{\$}{\leftarrow} \mathbb{Z}_p^4, \mathsf{vk}_i = (\mathfrak{g}_0 = \mathfrak{g}, \mathfrak{f}_i = \mathfrak{g}_0^{u_i}, \mathfrak{l}_i = \mathfrak{g}_0^{v_i}, \mathfrak{g}_i = \mathfrak{g}_0^{x_i}, \mathfrak{h}_i = \mathfrak{g}_0^{y_i}) \\ \Sigma_i = \left(\Sigma_{i,0} = \mathfrak{g}^{S_3 \tilde{\tau}_i}, \Sigma_{i,1} = (\mathfrak{g}_0^{S_1} \mathfrak{f}_i^{S_2} \mathfrak{l}_i^{S_3} \mathfrak{g}_i^{S_4} \mathfrak{h}_i^{S_5})^{\tilde{\tau}_i} \right) \end{cases}$

MixInit($\mathsf{sk}_i, M_i, \mathsf{vk}_i, \Sigma_i, \tau_i$):
$\mathcal{U}_i$ chooses $r_i \overset{\$}{\leftarrow} \mathbb{Z}_p$ and $\ell_i \overset{\$}{\leftarrow} \mathbb{G}_1$ and computes
$$C_i = (a_i = g^{r_i}, b_i = h^{r_i} M_i) \qquad \overline{C}_i = (g, \ell_i, a_i, b_i)$$
$$\sigma_i = (\sigma_{i,0} = \ell^{v_i} g^{x_i} h^{y_i}, \sigma_{i,1} = g^{u_i} \ell_i^{v_i} a_i^{x_i} b_i^{y_i})$$
It outputs $\mathcal{B}_i = (C_i, \ell_i, \sigma_i, \mathsf{vk}_i, \Sigma_i, \tau_i)$.
$$\mathcal{BBox}^{(0)} = (\mathcal{B}_i)_{i=1}^N$$

Mix($\mathsf{SK}_j, \mathcal{BBox}^{(j-1)}, (\mathsf{proof}^{(k)}, \mathsf{sig}^{(k)})_{k=1}^{j-1}, \Pi_j$):
From $\mathcal{BBox}^{(j-1)} = (C_i, \ell_i, \sigma_i, \mathsf{vk}_i, \Sigma_i, \tau_i)_i, (\mathsf{proof}^{(k)}, \mathsf{sig}^{(k)})_{k=1}^{j-1}$,
$\mathcal{S}_j$ chooses $\alpha \overset{\$}{\leftarrow} \mathbb{Z}_p$ and for each ballot i, $\gamma_i, \delta_i, \mu_i \overset{\$}{\leftarrow} \mathbb{Z}_p$ and computes
$$a_i' = a_i \cdot g^{\gamma_i} \quad b_i' = b_i \cdot h^{\gamma_i} \quad \ell_i' = \ell_i \cdot \ell^{\gamma_i} \quad \sigma_{i,1}' = \sigma_{i,1} \cdot \sigma_{i,0}^{\gamma_i} \cdot \ell_i'^{\delta_i} \quad \sigma_{i,0}' = \sigma_{i,0} \cdot \ell^{\delta_i}$$
$$\mathfrak{g}_0' = \mathfrak{g}_0^\alpha \quad \mathfrak{f}_i' = \mathfrak{f}_i^\alpha \quad \mathfrak{l}_i' = (\mathfrak{l}_i \cdot \mathfrak{g}_0^{\delta_i})^\alpha \quad \mathfrak{g}_i' = \mathfrak{g}_i^\alpha \quad \mathfrak{h}_i' = \mathfrak{h}_i^\alpha$$
$$\Sigma_{i,1}' = (\Sigma_{i,1} \cdot \Sigma_{i,0}^{\delta_i})^{\alpha \mu_i} \quad \Sigma_{i,0}' = \Sigma_{i,0}^{\alpha \mu_i} \quad \tau_{i,1}' = \tau_{i,1}^{1/\mu_i} \quad \tau_{i,2}' = \tau_{i,2}^{1/\mu_i}$$
$\begin{cases} \mathsf{proof}^{(j)} = \mathsf{NIZK}_{\mathsf{DH}}\text{-}\mathsf{Proof}((\mathfrak{g}_0, \mathfrak{g}_0', \prod \mathfrak{f}_i, \prod \mathfrak{f}_i') \text{ and } (g, h, \prod a_i'/\prod a_i, \prod b_i'/\prod b_i)) \\ \mathsf{sig}^{(j)} = \mathsf{SSign}(\mathsf{SK}_j, \mathsf{proof}^{(j)}) \end{cases}$
$\mathcal{S}_j$ outputs $\mathcal{BBox}^{(j)} = (C'_{\Pi_j(i)}, \ell'_{\Pi_j(i)}, \sigma'_{\Pi_j(i)}, \mathsf{vk}'_{\Pi_j(i)}, \Sigma'_{\Pi_j(i)}, \tau'_{\Pi_j(i)})_i, (\mathsf{proof}^{(k)}, \mathsf{sig}^{(k)})_{k=1}^j$

Fig. 2. Detailed shuffling of ElGamal ciphertexts

mix-server j generates the Diffie-Hellman proofs from $\mathcal{BBox}^{(j-1)}$ to $\mathcal{BBox}^{(j)}$, and signs them. We will then detail this solution in the next section, which will provide a proof linear in the number of ballots and in the number of mix-servers (because of the multiple signature). Thereafter, with specific multi-signature, one can become independent of the number of mix-servers.

4.3 Our Scheme

With all the previous remarks and explanations, we can now provide the full description of our scheme which is given in Fig. 2.

Keys. As we will sign expanded ciphertexts of dimension 4 (see below), each user needs a secret-verification key pair $(\mathsf{sk}_i, \mathsf{vk}_i) \leftarrow \mathsf{Keygen}(\mathsf{param}, 4)$ in $\mathbb{Z}_p^4 \times \mathbb{G}_2^5$. With our OT-LH-Sign, the first element of vk_i is common for all the users and initialized to $g_0 = g$. Then, one also needs a signature $\Sigma_i = (\Sigma_{i,0}, \Sigma_{i,1})$ with our LH-Sign from the certification authority of the pair (vk_0, vk_i) where $vk_0 = (1, 1, g_0, 1, 1)$ is used to make the non-trivial transformation on vk_i during the mixes. This signature is signed by the authority possessing $(SK, VK) \leftarrow$ Keygen*(param', 5) in $\mathbb{Z}_p^5 \times \mathbb{G}_1^6$ with a specific tag τ_i per user. Eventually, each mix-server has a pair of (standard) signature scheme $(SK_j, VK_j) \leftarrow$ SKeygen() just to sign with SSign its mixing contribution. The keys VK and $(VK_j)_j$, as well as $EK = h = g^d \in \mathbb{G}_1$ and the random $\ell \xleftarrow{\$} \mathbb{G}_1$, are assumed to be known to everybody.

As we are using ciphertexts with ElGamal, the ciphertext for randomization is $C_0 = (g, h)$, the trivial encryption of $1 = g^0$, with random coin equal to 1.

Initial Ballots. Each user encrypts his message M_i under EK to obtain $C_i = (a_i, b_i)$. With the remarks we already made, one needs to expand C_i into $\overline{C_i} = (g, \ell_i, a_i, b_i)$ and C_0 into $\overline{C_0} = (1, \ell, g, h)$. The addition of the first element is due to the affine space we want in the signature σ_i (see Sect. 3.3) and the second element is because we randomize the third position of vk_i with $vk_0 = (1, 1, g_0, 1, 1)$ and because the first position of vk_i is used for the verification but not to sign (the last four elements of vk_i are used to sign). Finally, $\sigma_i = (\sigma_{i,0}, \sigma_{i,1})$ is simply the OT-LH-Sign of $(\overline{C_0}, \overline{C_i})$ under the signing key sk_i.

Mix. To make a mix, the j-th mix-server computes the randomized verification keys $vk_i' = (vk_i \cdot vk_0^{\delta_i})^\alpha$, the randomized ciphertexts $\overline{C_i'} = \overline{C_i} \cdot \overline{C_0}^{\gamma_i}$ and the randomized tags $\tau_i' = \tau_i^{1/\mu_i}$, and updates the signatures σ_i' and Σ_i', thanks to the properties of the signatures. The random scalar α is common to all the ballots, but $\gamma_i, \delta_i, \mu_i$ are independent random scalars for each ballot. Then, the mix-server chooses a permutation Π and sets the j-th ballot-box $\mathcal{BBox}^{(j)}$ with all the randomized and permuted ballots $(C'_{\Pi(i)}, \ell'_{\Pi(i)}, \sigma'_{\Pi(i)}, vk'_{\Pi(i)}, \Sigma'_{\Pi(i)}, \tau'_{\Pi(i)})_i$. As already explained, the mix-server also needs to make a proof $\mathsf{proof}^{(j)}$ from $\mathcal{BBox}^{(j-1)}$ to $\mathcal{BBox}^{(j)}$, to guarantee the proper relations between the products of the verification keys and the products of the messages, and signs it in $\mathsf{sig}^{(j)}$. Finally, the output of the mix contains $\mathcal{BBox}^{(j)}$ and $(\mathsf{proof}^{(k)}, \mathsf{sig}^{(k)})_{k=1}^j$ the set of proofs and mix-server signatures of the previous mixes until the j-th mix.

Proofs. Let us denote $\mathfrak{F} = \prod \mathfrak{f}_i = \mathfrak{g}_0^{\sum u_i}$ and $\mathfrak{F}' = \prod \mathfrak{f}_i' = \mathfrak{g}_0'^{\sum u_i}$ the product of the second element of the user's verification key on all the input ballots and output ballots. If the input and output ballot-boxes contain the same ballots (with the same secret u_i), then $\mathfrak{F}' = \mathfrak{F}^\alpha$, with $\mathfrak{g}_0' = \mathfrak{g}_0^\alpha$. Hence one adds a proof of Diffie-Hellman tuple for $(\mathfrak{g}_0, \mathfrak{g}_0', \mathfrak{F}, \mathfrak{F}')$. Together with the verification that there is the same number of ballots in the input and output of the mix, we will show that the same (honest) users are represented in the two ballot-boxes. Since we cannot allow multiple ballots from the same user, we have the guarantee that the same messages from all the honest users are represented in the two ballot-boxes.

The additional proof of Diffie-Hellman tuple for $(g, h, \prod a_i' / \prod a_i, \prod b_i' / \prod b_i)$ will limit the exchange of ballots for corrupted users, as the products of the

$\mathsf{MixVerif}(\mathcal{BB}\mathsf{ox}^{(0)}, \mathcal{BB}\mathsf{ox}^{(N)}, (\mathsf{proof}^{(k)}, \mathsf{sig}^{(k)})_{k=1}^{N})$:

After N mixes, the input of the verifier is:

$$\mathcal{BB}\mathsf{ox}^{(0)} = (\overline{C}_i, \sigma_{i,1}, \mathsf{vk}_i, \Sigma_{i,1}, \tau_{i,1})_{i=1}^{n}$$

$$\mathcal{BB}\mathsf{ox}^{(N)} = (\overline{C}'_i, \sigma'_{i,1}, \mathsf{vk}'_i, \Sigma'_{i,1}, \tau'_{i,1})_{i=1}^{n'}, (\mathsf{proof}^{(k)}, \mathsf{sig}^{(k)})_{k=1}^{N}$$

It outputs 1 if: $n = n'$, the $(\mathsf{vk}_i)_i$ are all distinct

$\forall k$, $\qquad\qquad \mathsf{NIZK_{DH}\text{-}Verif}(\mathsf{proof}^{(k)}) = 1$

$\qquad\qquad \mathsf{SVerif}(\mathsf{VK}_k, \mathsf{proof}^{(k)}), \mathsf{sig}^{(k)}) = 1$

and $\forall i$, $\mathsf{Verif}(\mathsf{vk}_i, \overline{C}_i, \sigma_{i,1}) = 1 = \mathsf{Verif}^*(\mathsf{VK}, \tau_i, \mathsf{vk}_i, \Sigma_{i,1})$

$\qquad\quad \mathsf{Verif}(\mathsf{vk}'_i, \overline{C}'_i, \sigma'_{i,1}) = 1 = \mathsf{Verif}^*(\mathsf{VK}, \tau'_i, \mathsf{vk}'_i, \Sigma'_{i,1})$

Fig. 3. Detailed verification of shuffling

plaintexts must remain the same: $\prod M'_i = \prod M_i$. Since we already know these products will be the same for honest users, this products must be the same from corrupted users. This will limit the impact of the attack of Cortier-Smyth [15].

With these two Diffie-Hellman proofs, the output ballots are a permutation of the input ones. We could use any non-interactive zero-knowledge proofs of Diffie-Hellman tuples ($\mathsf{NIZK_{DH}\text{-}Setup}, \mathsf{NIZK_{DH}\text{-}Proof}, \mathsf{NIZK_{DH}\text{-}Verif}$) and any signature ($\mathsf{SSetup}, \mathsf{SSign}, \mathsf{SVerif}$) to sign the proofs but the next section will provide interesting choices, from the length point of view.

Verification. The complete verification process, after N mix-servers, is presented in Fig. 3. After all the mixes are done, it just requires the input ballot-box $\mathcal{BB}\mathsf{ox}^{(0)}$, the output ballot-box $\mathcal{BB}\mathsf{ox}^{(N)}$, and the signed proofs ($\mathsf{proof}^{(k)}, \mathsf{sig}^{(k)}$), for $k = 1, \ldots, N$ without the elements that were useful for randomization only. The verifier checks the number of input ballots is the same as the number of output ballots, the verification keys (the f_i's) in input ballots are all distinct, the signatures $\sigma_{i,1}, \sigma'_{i,1}, \Sigma_{i,1}$ and $\Sigma'_{i,1}$ are valid on individual input and output tuples (equations recalled in the full version [27]) and all the proofs $\mathsf{proof}^{(k)}$ with the signatures $\mathsf{sig}^{(k)}$ are valid with $\mathsf{NIZK_{DH}\text{-}Verif}$ and SVerif respectively. For that, we suppose that the statement is included in each zero-knowledge proof. Thus, even if the intermediate ballot-boxes are not given to the verifier, it is still possible to perform the verification.

4.4 Constant-Size Proof

From Fig. 3, one can note that our mix-net provides a quite compact proof, as it just requires $\mathcal{BB}\mathsf{ox}^{(0)}$ and $\mathcal{BB}\mathsf{ox}^{(N)}$, and the signed proofs ($\mathsf{proof}^{(k)}, \mathsf{sig}^{(k)}$), for $k = 1, \ldots, N$. The size is thus linear in n and N. This is the same for the verification complexity.

Whereas the linear complexity in n cannot be avoided, as the ballot-box must be transferred, the part linear in N could be avoided. Indeed, each proof $\mathsf{proof}^{(j)}$ ensures the relations from the $j-1$-th ballot-box to the j-th ballot-box. The global chain of proofs ensures the relations from the initial ballot-box to the last ballot-box. From the soundness point on view, a compact global proof would be enough. But for privacy, one wants to be sure that multiple mix-servers contributed, to get unlinkability as soon as one server is honest.

To avoid the dependence in N, one can use Groth-Sahai proofs [25] (see the full version [27] for details) to combine together the proofs into a unique one as already used in Chase *et al.* [13]. However, to be sure that all the mix-servers contributed: each mix-server does as above, but also receives a partial proof $\mathsf{proof}'^{(j-1)}$ from the initial ballot-box to the $j-1$-th ballot-box and, thanks to the homomorphic properties of the Groth-Sahai proof, updates it into $\mathsf{proof}'^{(j)}$, to prove the relation from the initial ballot-box and the j-th ballot-box, as shown in the full version [27] for the Diffie-Hellman proof between the products of the keys (the proof is similar for the product of the ciphertexts but with $\mathbb{G}_1$ and $\mathbb{G}_2$ swapped). At the end of the mixing steps, one has the same elements as above, plus the global proof $\mathsf{proof}'^{(N)}$. All the mix-servers can now verify the proofs and the contributions of all the servers. Only this global proof can be kept, but signed by all the servers: using the multi-signature of Boneh-Drijvers-Neven [7], that is recalled in the full version [27], the size of the signature msig keeps constant, whatever the number of mix-servers. Hence, after multiple mixing steps, the size of the mixing proof (with the input and output ballot-boxes) remains constant.

4.5   Efficiency

We consider VK and $(\mathsf{VK}_j)_j$ are long-term keys known to everybody, as well as EK and ℓ. However, for fair comparison, we do not consider vk_i as long-term keys, and consider them as part of the input of the verifier. But we insist that the f_i's in the input ballot-box must be all distinct.

Size of Verifier's Input: The verifier receives:

$$(\overline{C}_i, \sigma_{i,1}, \mathsf{vk}_i, \Sigma_{i,1}, \tau_i)_{i=1}^n \quad (\overline{C}'_i, \sigma'_{i,1}, \mathsf{vk}'_i, \Sigma'_{i,1}, \tau'_i)_{i=1}^n \quad (\mathsf{proof}'^{(N)}, \mathsf{msig}'^{(N)})$$

As the first element $\mathfrak{g}_0$ of vk_i is common to all the users (as well as $\mathfrak{g}'_0$ of vk'_i), the set of all the users' verification keys is represented by $4 \times n + 1$ elements of $\mathbb{G}_2$. Then, all input or output ballots contains $2 \times 5n$ elements from $\mathbb{G}_1$ and $2 \times (6n + 1)$ elements from $\mathbb{G}_2$.

The global proof $\mathsf{proof}'^{(N)}$ is just 4 elements of $\mathbb{G}_1$ and 4 elements of $\mathbb{G}_2$ and msig one element in $\mathbb{G}_2$. Hence, the full verifier's input contains: $10n+4$ elements of $\mathbb{G}_1$, $12n + 6$ elements of $\mathbb{G}_2$, whatever the number of mix-servers.

Verifier's Computation. Using batch verification [4,12,28], the verifier only needs to make $8n + 7$ pairing evaluations to verify together all the signatures $\sigma_{i,1}$, $\sigma'_{i,1}$, $\Sigma_{i,1}$, $\Sigma'_{i,1}$, τ_i, τ'_i, 6 pairing evaluations to verify $\mathsf{proof}'^{(N)}$ and 2 pairing evaluations to verify msig.

With some specific choices of the bases for the batch verification, as presented in the full version [27], one can improve to $8n + 14$ pairing evaluations for the global verification. This has to be compared to the $4n+1$ pairing evaluations that have anyway to be performed to verify the signatures in the initial ballot-box.

5   Security Analysis

Let us now formally prove the two security properties: the *soundness* means the output ballot-box contains a permutation of randomizations of the input ballot-box and *privacy* means one cannot link an input ciphertext to an output ciphertext, as soon as one mix-server is honest.

We stress that we are in a particular case where users have private signing keys, and ballots are signed. Unfortunately these keys allow to trace the ballots: with $\mathsf{sk}_i = (u_i, v_i, x_i, y_i)$ and $\mathfrak{g}_0'$, one can recover vk_i', which contradicts privacy for this ballot. They might also allow to exchange some ballots, which contradicts soundness for these ballots. As a consequence, we do not provide any guarantee to corrupted users, whose keys have been given to the adversary (or even possibly generated by the adversary), but we expect honest users to be protected:

- *soundness for honest users* means that all the plaintexts of the honest users in the input ballot-box are in the output ballot-box;
- *privacy for honest users* means that ballots of honest users are unlinkable from the input ballot-box to the output ballot-box.

5.1   Proof of Soundness

As just explained, we first study the soundness of our protocol, but for honest users only, in the certified key setting, where all the users must prove the knowledge of their private keys before getting their verification keys vk_i certified by the Certification Authority in Σ_i.

Definition 12 (Soundness for Honest Users). *A mix-net* M *is said* sound for honest users *in the certified key setting, if any PPT adversary* $\mathcal{A}$ *has a negligible success probability in the following security game:*

1. *The challenger generates the certification keys* $(\mathsf{SK}, \mathsf{VK})$ *and the encryption keys* $(\mathsf{DK}, \mathsf{EK})$;
2. *The adversary* $\mathcal{A}$ *then*
    - *decides on the corrupted users* $\mathcal{I}^*$ *and generates itself their keys* $(\mathsf{vk}_i)_{i \in \mathcal{I}^*}$;
    - *proves its knowledge of the secrete keys to get the certifications* Σ_i *on* vk_i, *for* $i \in \mathcal{I}^*$;
    - *decides on the set* $\mathcal{I}$ *of the (honest and corrupted) users that will generate a ballot;*
    - *generates the ballots* $(\mathcal{B}_i)_{i \in \mathcal{I}^*}$ *for the corrupted users but provides the messages* $(M_i)_{i \in \mathcal{I} \setminus \mathcal{I}^*}$ *for the honest users;*
3. *The challenger generates the keys of the honest users* $(\mathsf{sk}_i, \mathsf{vk}_i)_{i \in \mathcal{I} \setminus \mathcal{I}^*}$ *and their ballots* $(\mathcal{B}_i)_{i \in \mathcal{I} \setminus \mathcal{I}^*}$. *The initial ballot-box is thus defined by* $\mathcal{BBox} = (\mathcal{B}_i)_{i \in \mathcal{I}}$;
4. *The adversary mixes* $\mathcal{BBox}$ *in a provable way into* $(\mathcal{BBox}', \mathsf{proof})$.

The adversary wins if $\mathsf{MixVerif}(\mathcal{BBox}, \mathcal{BBox}', \mathsf{proof}) = 1$ *but* $\{\mathsf{Decrypt}^*(\mathcal{BBox})\} \neq \{\mathsf{Decrypt}^*(\mathcal{BBox}')\}$, *where* $\mathsf{Decrypt}^*$ *extracts the plaintexts (using the decryption key* DK), *but ignores ballots of non-honest users (using the private keys of honest users) and sets of plaintexts can have repetitions.*

One can note that this security game does not depend on the mixing steps, but just considers the global mixing, from the input ballot-box $\mathcal{BB}\text{ox}$ to the output ballot-box $\mathcal{BB}\text{ox}'$. The proof proof contains all the elements for proving the honest behavior. In our case, this is just the two Diffie-Hellman proofs.

Theorem 13 (Soundness for Honest Users of Our Mix-Net). *Our mix-net protocol is sound for honest users, in the certified key setting, assuming the unforgeability against Chosen-Message Attacks of the* LH-Sign *and* OT-LH-Sign *signature schemes and the* SEDL *assumption.*

Proof. For proving this theorem, we will assume the verification is successful (MixVerif($\mathcal{BB}\text{ox}$, $\mathcal{BB}\text{ox}'$, proof) = 1) and show that for all the honest ballots, in the input and output ballot-boxes, there is a permutation from the input ones to the outputs ones. And we do it in two steps: first, honest keys vk_i' in the output ballot-box are permuted randomizations of the honest keys vk_i in the input ballot-box; then we prove it for the plaintexts.

Permutation of Honest Keys. We first modify the security game by using the unforgeability against Chosen-Message Attacks of the LH-Sign signature scheme: we are given VK, and ask the Tag-oracle and the Signing-oracle to obtain Σ_i on all the verification keys vk_i and vk_0. The rest remains unchanged. Note that because of the proof of knowledge of the private keys sk_i before getting vk_i certified, one can also extract them. Actually, one just needs to extract u_i for all the corrupted users. Then one knows all the legitimate u_i's (for honest and corrupted users).

Under the unforgeability of the signature scheme (Setup*, Keygen*, NewTag*, RandTag*, VerifTag*, Sign*, DerivSign*, Verif*), for any output ballot with verification key vk_j' there exists a related legitimate verification key vk_i such that $\text{vk}_j' = \text{vk}_i^{\alpha_i} \times \text{vk}_0^{z_i}$, for some scalars z_i, and α_i.

Since in our construction $\text{vk}_i = (\mathfrak{g}_0, \mathfrak{f}_i, \mathfrak{l}_i, \mathfrak{g}_i, \mathfrak{h}_i)$ and $\text{vk}_0 = (1, 1, \mathfrak{g}_0, 1, 1)$, and $\text{vk}_j' = (\mathfrak{g}_0', \mathfrak{f}_j', \mathfrak{l}_j', \mathfrak{g}_j', \mathfrak{h}_j')$ and $\text{vk}_0' = (1, 1, \mathfrak{g}_0', 1, 1)$ with a common $\mathfrak{g}_0'$ for all the keys, α_i is a common scalar α: $\text{vk}_j' = (\text{vk}_i \times \text{vk}_0^{\delta_i})^\alpha$ and $\text{vk}_0' = \text{vk}_0^\alpha$. As a consequence, all the keys in the output ballot-box are derived in a similar way from legitimate keys (signed by the Certification Authority): $u_j' = u_i$ remains unchanged. However this does not means they were all in the input ballot-box: the adversary could insert a ballot with a legitimate verification key vk_i, which was not in the initial ballot-box.

The verification process also includes a Diffie-Hellman proof for the tuple $(\mathfrak{g}_0, \mathfrak{g}_0', \prod_i \mathfrak{f}_i, \prod_j \mathfrak{f}_j')$. This means that $\sum_i u_i$ are the same on the input ballots and the output ballots. As one additionally checks the numbers of input ballots and output ballots are the same, the adversary can just replace an input ballot by a new one: if $\mathcal{N}$ is the set of new ballots and $\mathcal{D}$ the set of deleted ballots, the sums must compensate: $\sum_{\mathcal{D}} u_i = \sum_{\mathcal{N}} u_i$.

The second game uses the SEDL assumption and the simulation-soundness of the proof of knowledge of sk_i (in the certified key setting): Let us be given a tuple $(\mathfrak{g}, \mathfrak{f} = \mathfrak{g}^u, g, f = g^u)$, as input of a SEDL challenge in $\mathbb{G}_2$ and $\mathbb{G}_1$: the simulator will guess an honest user i^* that will be deleted, and implicitly sets $u_{i^*} = u$, with $\mathfrak{f}_{i^*}$, which allows it to use $f = g^{u_{i^*}}$ in the signature of $\overline{C}_{i^*}$ on the first component g, while all the other scalars are chosen by the simulator $(v_{i^*}, x_{i^*}, y_{i^*})$, as well as all the other honest user' keys, the authority signing keys, and, for all the corrupted users, the secret element u_i can be extracted at the certification time (using the extractor from the zero-knowledge proof of knowledge) while the zero-knowledge simulator is used for i^*, thanks to the simulation-soundness.

If some honest user is deleted in the output ballot-box, with probability greater than $1/n$, this is i^*: as shown above, $\sum_{\mathcal{D}} u_i = \sum_{\mathcal{N}} u_i$, so $u_{i^*} = \sum_{\mathcal{N}} u_i - \sum_{\mathcal{D} \setminus \{i^*\}} u_i$, which breaks the symmetric external discrete logarithm assumption.

Permutation of Honest Ballots. The last game uses the unforgeability of the OT-LH-Sign signature scheme under Chosen-Message Attacks: the simulator receives one verification key vk, that will be assigned at a random honest user i^*, whereas all the other keys are honestly generated. The simulator also generates $(\mathsf{SK}, \mathsf{VK})$ and $(\mathsf{DK}, \mathsf{EK})$, as well as all signatures Σ_i and the honest ballots (with a signing query for σ_{i^*}). Then, the adversary outputs a proven mix of the ballot-box. We have just proven that there exists a bijection Π from $\mathcal{I}$ into $\mathcal{J}$ such that $\mathsf{vk}'_{\Pi(i)} = (\mathsf{vk}_i \times \mathsf{vk}_0^{\delta_i})^\alpha$ for some scalar δ_i, for all the honest users i among the input users in $\mathcal{I}$.

From the signature verification on the output tuples, $C'_{\Pi(i)}$ is signed under $\mathsf{vk}'_{\Pi(i)}$ in $\sigma'_{\Pi(i),1}$, for every i: $e(\sigma'_{\Pi(i),1}, \mathfrak{g}'_0) = e(g, \mathfrak{f}_i^\alpha) \cdot e(\ell'_{\Pi(i)}, \mathfrak{l}_i^\alpha \mathfrak{g}_0^{\alpha\delta_i}) \cdot e(a'_{\Pi(i)}, \mathfrak{g}_i^\alpha) \cdot e(b'_{\Pi(i)}, \mathfrak{h}_i^\alpha)$, and since the same α appears in $\mathfrak{g}'_0 = \mathfrak{g}_0^\alpha$, then for every i, we have

$$e(\sigma'_{\Pi(i)}, \mathfrak{g}_0) = e(g, \mathfrak{f}_i) \cdot e(\ell'_{\Pi(i)}, \mathfrak{l}_i \mathfrak{g}_0^{\delta_i}) \cdot e(a'_{\Pi(i)}, \mathfrak{g}_i) \cdot e(b'_{\Pi(i)}, \mathfrak{h}_i)$$
$$= e(g, \mathfrak{f}_i) \cdot e(\ell'_{\Pi(i)}, \mathfrak{l}_i) \cdot e(a'_{\Pi(i)}, \mathfrak{g}_i) \cdot e(b'_{\Pi(i)}, \mathfrak{h}_i) \cdot e(\ell'^{\delta_i}_{\Pi(i)}, \mathfrak{g}_0)$$

and so $\sigma'_{\Pi(i)}/\ell'^{\delta_i}_{\Pi(i)}$ is a signature of $\overline{C}'_{\Pi(i)} = (g, \ell'_{\Pi(i)}, a'_{\Pi(i)}, b'_{\Pi(i)})$ under vk_i: under the unforgeability assumption of the signature scheme, $C'_{\Pi(i^*)}$ is necessarily a linear combination of the already signed vectors under vk_{i^*}, which are C_{i^*} and C_0, with some coefficients u, v: $a'_{\Pi(i^*)} = a_{i^*}^u g^v$, $b'_{\Pi(i^*)} = b_{i^*}^u h^v$, and $g = g^u 1^v$. Hence, $u = 1$, which means that $C'_{\Pi(i^*)}$ is a randomization of C_{i^*}.

We stress that for this property to hold, each key vk_i must appear at most once in the ballots, otherwise some combinations would be possible. Hence the test that all the $\mathfrak{f}_i$'s are distinct in the input ballot-box. □

We stress that this proposition only guarantees permutation of ciphertexts for honest users. There is indeed no formal guarantee for corrupted users whose signing keys are under the control of a mix-server. The latter could indeed replace the ciphertexts of some corrupted users, by some other ciphertexts under the same identity or even under the identity of another corrupted user. One can note that replacing ciphertexts (and plaintexts) even for corrupted users is not that easy because of the additional Diffie-Hellman proof on the ciphertexts, which implies $\prod M_i = \prod M'_i$ where the first product is over all the messages M_i

in $\mathcal{BB}$ox and the second product is over all the messages M'_i in $\mathcal{BB}$ox'. However, this property is more for the privacy, as we will see below. As a consequence, our result that guarantees a permutation on the honest ballots is optimal. We cannot guarantee anything for the users that share their keys with the mix-servers.

5.2 Proof of Privacy: Unlinkability

After proving the soundness, we have to prove the anonymity (a.k.a. unlinkability), which can also be seen as zero-knowledge property. More precisely, as for the soundness, privacy will only be guaranteed for honest users.

Definition 14 (Privacy for Honest Users). *A mix-net* M *is said to provide privacy for honest users in the certified key setting, if any PPT adversary $\mathcal{A}$ has a negligible advantage in guessing b in the following security game:*

1. *The challenger generates the certification keys* (SK, VK) *and the encryption keys* (DK, EK);
2. *The adversary $\mathcal{A}$ then*
   – *decides on the corrupted users $\mathcal{I}^*$ and generates itself their keys* $(\mathsf{vk}_i)_{i\in\mathcal{I}^*}$;
   – *proves its knowledge of the secret keys to get the certifications Σ_i on vk_i, for $i \in \mathcal{I}^*$;*
   – *decides on the corrupted mix-servers $\mathcal{J}^*$ and generates itself their keys* $(\mathsf{VK}_j)_{j\in\mathcal{J}^*}$;
   – *decides on the set $\mathcal{J}$ of the (honest and corrupted) mix-servers that will make mixes;*
   – *decides on the set $\mathcal{I}$ of the (honest and corrupted) users that will generate a ballot;*
   – *generates the ballots $(\mathcal{B}_i)_{i\in\mathcal{I}^*}$ for the corrupted users but provides the messages $(M_i)_{i\in\mathcal{I}\setminus\mathcal{I}^*}$ for the honest users;*
3. *The challenger generates the keys of the honest mix-servers $(\mathsf{SK}_j, \mathsf{VK}_j)_{j\in\mathcal{J}\setminus\mathcal{J}^*}$ the keys of the honest users $(\mathsf{sk}_i, \mathsf{vk}_i)_{i\in\mathcal{I}\setminus\mathcal{I}^*}$ and their ballots $(\mathcal{B}_i)_{i\in\mathcal{I}\setminus\mathcal{I}^*}$.*

The initial ballot-box is thus defined by $\mathcal{BB}$ox $= (\mathcal{B}_i)_{i\in\mathcal{I}}$. The challenger randomly chooses a bit $b \xleftarrow{\$} \{0,1\}$ and then enters into a loop for $j \in \mathcal{J}$ with the attacker:

– *let $\mathcal{I}^*_{j-1}$ be the set of indices of the ballots of the corrupted users in the input ballot-box $\mathcal{BB}$ox$^{(j-1)}$;*
– *if $j \in \mathcal{J}^*$, $\mathcal{A}$ builds itself the new ballot-box $\mathcal{BB}$ox$^{(j)}$ with the proof $\mathsf{proof}^{(j)}$;*
– *if $j \notin \mathcal{J}^*$, $\mathcal{A}$ provides two permutations $\Pi_{j,0}$ and $\Pi_{j,1}$ of its choice, with the restriction they must be identical on $\mathcal{I}^*_{j-1}$, then the challenger runs the mixing with $\Pi_{j,b}$, and provides the output $(\mathcal{BB}$ox$^{(j)}, \mathsf{proof}^{(j)})$;*

In the end, the adversary outputs its guess b' for b. The experiment outputs 1 if $b' = b$ and 0 otherwise.

Contrarily to the soundness security game, the adversary can see the outputs of all the mixing steps to make its decision, hence the index j for the mix-servers. In addition, some can be honest, some can be corrupted. We will assume at least one is honest.

Theorem 15. *Our Mix-Net protocol provides privacy for honest users, in the certified key setting, if (at least) one mix-server is honest, under our unlinkability assumption (see Definition 4), and the* DDH *assumptions in both* $\mathbb{G}_1$ *and* $\mathbb{G}_2$.

Proof. This proof will follow a series of games $(\mathbf{G}_i)_i$, where we study the advantage Adv_i of the adversary in guessing b. We start from the real security game and conclude with a game where all the ballots are random, independently from the permutations. Hence, the advantage will be trivially 0.

Game $\mathbf{G}_0$: This is the real game, where the challenger (our simulator) generates SK and VK for the certification authority signature, and randomly chooses $d \overset{\$}{\leftarrow} \mathbb{Z}_p$ to generate the encryption public key $\mathsf{EK} = h = g^d$. One also sets $\mathsf{vk}_0 = (1, 1, \mathfrak{g}_0 = \mathfrak{g}^A, 1, 1)$ and $C_0 = \mathsf{Encrypt}_{\mathsf{EK}}(1) = (g, h)$ expanded into $\overline{C}_0 = (1, \ell, C_0)$ with the noise parameter $\ell \overset{\$}{\leftarrow} \mathbb{G}_1$. Actually, $A = 1$ in the initial step, when the user encrypts his message M_i, but since the shuffling may happens after several other shuffling iterations, we have the successive exponentiations to multiple α (in A) for vk_0. The attacker $\mathcal{A}$ chooses the set of the initial indices of the corrupted users $\mathcal{I}^*$ and the set of the initial indices of the corrupted mix-servers $\mathcal{J}^*$, provides their verification keys $((\mathsf{vk}_i)_{i \in \mathcal{I}^*}, (\mathsf{VK}_j)_{j \in \mathcal{J}^*})$ together with an extractable zero-knowledge proof of knowledge of sk_i.

From $\mathcal{I}$ and $\mathcal{J}$, one generates the signing keys for the honest mix-servers $j \in \mathcal{J} \backslash \mathcal{J}^*$, and set J to the index of the last honest mix-server. For each $i \in \mathcal{I}$, one chooses $\tau_i = R_i \overset{\$}{\leftarrow} \mathbb{Z}_p$ and sets $\tau_i = (\tau_{i,1} = \mathfrak{g}^{1/R_i}, \tau_{i,2} = g^{1/R_i})$. For each honest user $i \in \mathcal{I} \backslash \mathcal{I}^*$, one randomly chooses $u_i, v_i, x_i, y_i, r_i, \rho_i \overset{\$}{\leftarrow} \mathbb{Z}_p$ to generate $\mathsf{vk}_i = (\mathfrak{g}_0 = \mathfrak{g}, \mathfrak{f}_i = \mathfrak{g}_0^{u_i}, \mathfrak{l}_i = \mathfrak{g}_0^{v_i}, \mathfrak{g}_i = \mathfrak{g}_0^{x_i}, \mathfrak{h}_i = \mathfrak{g}_0^{y_i})$, and eventually generates all the signatures Σ_i of $(\mathsf{vk}_i, \mathsf{vk}_0)$ under SK with respect to the tag τ_i (using SK and $(\tilde{\tau}_i)_i$).

For the corrupted users, the simulator directly receives the ballots $(\mathcal{B}_i = (\overline{C}_i, \sigma_i, \mathsf{vk}_i, \Sigma_i, \tau_i))_{i \in \mathcal{I}^*}$ while for the honest users, it receives $(M_i)_{i \in \mathcal{I} \backslash \mathcal{I}^*}$ and computes $C_i = \mathsf{Encrypt}_{\mathsf{EK}}(M_i) = (a_i = g^{r_i}, b_i = h^{r_i} M_i)$, $\overline{C}_i = (g, \ell_i = \ell^{\rho_i}, C_i)$ and the signature σ_i of $(\overline{C}_i, \overline{C}_0)$ under sk_i. The input ballot-box is then $\mathcal{BBox}^{(0)} = \{(\mathcal{B}_i)_{i \in \mathcal{I}}\}$ including the ballots of the honest and corrupted users. Let $\mathcal{I}_0^* = \mathcal{I}^*$ be the set of the initial indices of the corrupted users.

The simulator randomly chooses $b \overset{\$}{\leftarrow} \{0, 1\}$ and now begins the loop of the mixes: depending if the mix-server j is corrupted or not, the simulator directly receives $(\mathcal{BBox}^{(j)}, \mathsf{proof}^{(j)})$ from the adversary or receives $(\Pi_{j,0}, \Pi_{j,1})$. In the latter case, one first checks if $\Pi_{j,0}|_{\mathcal{I}_{j-1}^*} = \Pi_{j,1}|_{\mathcal{I}_{j-1}^*}$ using the honest secret keys to determine $\mathcal{I}_{j-1}^*$. Then, the simulator randomly chooses global $\alpha \overset{\$}{\leftarrow} \mathbb{Z}_p$ and individual $\gamma_i, \delta_i, \mu_i \overset{\$}{\leftarrow} \mathbb{Z}_p$ for all the users, as an honest mix-server would do, to compute

$$\mathsf{vk}_i' = (\mathfrak{g}_0' = \mathfrak{g}_0^\alpha, \mathfrak{f}_i' = \mathfrak{f}_i^\alpha, \mathfrak{l}_i' = (\mathfrak{l}_i \cdot \mathfrak{g}_0^{\delta_i})^\alpha, \mathfrak{g}_i' = \mathfrak{g}_i^\alpha, \mathfrak{h}_i' = \mathfrak{h}_i^\alpha) = (\mathsf{vk}_i \cdot \mathsf{vk}_0^{\delta_i})^\alpha$$
$$\mathsf{vk}_0' = (1, 1, \mathfrak{g}_0', 1, 1) = \mathsf{vk}_0^\alpha$$
$$\overline{C}_i' = (g, \ell_i' = \ell_i \cdot \ell_0^{\gamma_i}, a_i' = a_i \cdot g_0^{\gamma_i}, b_i' = b_i \cdot h_0^{\gamma_i}) = \overline{C}_i \cdot \overline{C}_0^{\gamma_i}$$

$$\sigma'_i = (\sigma'_{i,0} = \sigma_{i,0} \cdot \ell_0'^{\delta_i}, \sigma'_{i,1} = \sigma_{i,1} \cdot \sigma_{i,0}^{\gamma_i} \cdot \ell_i'^{\delta_i})$$

$$\Sigma'_i = (\Sigma'_{i,0} = \Sigma_{i,0}^{\alpha\mu_i}, \Sigma'_{i,1} = (\Sigma_{i,1} \cdot \Sigma_{i,0}^{\delta_i})^{\alpha\mu_i})$$

$$\tau'_i = (\tau'_{i,1} = \tau_{i,1}^{1/\mu_i}, \tau'_{i,2} = \tau_{i,2}^{1/\mu_i})$$

and sets $\mathcal{BBox}^{(j)} = (\mathcal{B}'_{\Pi_{j,b}(i)})_i$. Eventually, the simulator computes the proof proof$^{(j)}$ for $(\mathfrak{g}_0, \mathfrak{g}'_0, \prod \mathfrak{f}_i, \prod \mathfrak{f}'_i)$ and $(g, h, \prod a'_i / \prod a_i, \prod b'_i / \prod b_i)$, and signs it using SK_j.

After the full loop on all the mix-servers, the adversary outputs its guess b': $\mathsf{Adv}_{\mathbf{G}_0} = \Pr_{\mathbf{G}_0}[b' = b]$. One important remark is that under the previous soundness result, which has exactly the same setup, the input ballot-box for the last honest mix-server necessarily contains a randomization of the initial honest ballots (the adversary against the soundness is the above adversary together with the honest simulator up to its last honest round, that does not need any secret). Only the behavior of this last honest mix-server will be modified below.

Game $\mathbf{G}_1$: We first switch the Diffie-Hellman proofs for $(\mathfrak{g}_0, \mathfrak{g}'_0, \prod \mathfrak{f}_i, \prod \mathfrak{f}'_i)$ to the zero-knowledge setting: if the input ballot-box for the last honest mix-server is not a randomization of the initial honest ballots, that can be tested using the decryption key, one has built a distinguisher between the settings of the zero-knowledge proofs. In this new setting, one can use the zero-knowledge simulator that does not use α. Under the zero-knowledge property, $\mathsf{Adv}_{\mathbf{G}_0} < \mathsf{Adv}_{\mathbf{G}_1} + \mathsf{negl}()$.

Game $\mathbf{G}_2$: We also switch the proofs for $(g, h, \prod a'_i / \prod a_i, \prod b'_i / \prod b_i)$ to the zero-knowledge setting: as above, the distance remains negligible. In this new setting, one can use the zero-knowledge simulator that does not use $\sum_i \gamma_i$. Under the zero-knowledge property, $\mathsf{Adv}_{\mathbf{G}_1} < \mathsf{Adv}_{\mathbf{G}_2} + \mathsf{negl}()$.

Game $\mathbf{G}_3$: In this game, we do not know anymore the decryption key, and use the indistinguishability of the encryption scheme (which relies on the Decisional Diffie-Hellman assumption): in an hybrid way, we replace the ciphertexts C_i of the honest users by an encryption of 1: $C_i = \mathsf{Encrypt}_{\mathsf{EK}}(1)$. Under the DDH assumption in $\mathbb{G}_1$, $\mathsf{Adv}_{\mathbf{G}_2} < \mathsf{Adv}_{\mathbf{G}_3} + \mathsf{negl}()$.

Game $\mathbf{G}_4$: This corresponds to $C_i = (a_i = g^{r_i}, b_i = h^{r_i})$. But now we can know d, but ℓ is random: under the DDH assumption, we can replace the random value $\ell_i = \ell^{\rho_i}$ by $\ell_i = \ell^{r_i}$. Ultimately, we set $\overline{C}_i = (g, \ell_i = \ell^{r_i}, a_i = g^{r_i}, b_i = h^{r_i})$ for $r_i \xleftarrow{\$} \mathbb{Z}_p$, for all the honest users, in the initial ballot-box. Under the DDH assumption in $\mathbb{G}_1$, $\mathsf{Adv}_{\mathbf{G}_3} < \mathsf{Adv}_{\mathbf{G}_4} + \mathsf{negl}()$.

Game $\mathbf{G}_5$: In this game, one can first extract the keys of the corrupted users during the certification phase. Then, all the honest mix-servers generate random signing keys sk'_i, random tags τ'_i, and random encryptions C'_i of 1, for all the honest users (the one who do not correspond to the extracted keys), and generate the signatures using the signing keys SK and sk'_i, but still behave honestly for the ballots of the corrupted users. Then, they apply the permutations $\Pi_{j,b}$ on the randomized ballots.

Lemma 16 (Random Ballots for Honest Users). *Under the Unlinkability Assumption (see Definition 4) and* DDH *assumption in* $\mathbb{G}_2$*, the view is computationally indistinguishable:* $\mathsf{Adv}_{G_4} < \mathsf{Adv}_{G_5} + \mathsf{negl}()$.

In this last game, the i-th honest user is simulated with initial and output (after each honest mix-server) ciphertexts that are random encryptions of 1, and initial and output signing keys (and thus verification keys vk_i and vk'_i) independently random. As a consequence, permutations $\Pi_{j,b}$ are applied on random ballots, which is perfectly indistinguishable from applying $\Pi_{j,1-b}$ (as we have restricted the two permutations to be identical on ballots of corrupted users): $\mathsf{Adv}_{G_5} = 0$. Which leads to $\mathsf{Adv}_0 \le \mathsf{negl}()$. $\qquad\square$

Proof of Lemma 16. In the above sequences of games, from $\mathbf{G}_0$ to $\mathbf{G}_4$, we could have checked whether the honest vk_i's in the successive ballot-boxes are permutations of randomized honest initial keys, just using the secret keys of the honest users. So, we can assume in the next hybrid games, from $\mathbf{G}_0(j)$ to $\mathbf{G}_8(j)$, for $j = N, \ldots, 1$ that the input ballots in $\mathcal{BB}ox^{(j-1)}$ contain proper permutations of randomized honest initial keys, as nothing is modified before the generation of this ballot-box. In the following series of hybrid games, for index j, the honest mix-servers up to the $j-1$-th round play as in $\mathbf{G}_4$ and from the $j+1$-th round, they play as in $\mathbf{G}_5$. Only the behavior of the j-th mix-server is modified: starting from an honest behavior. Hence, $\mathbf{G}_0(N) = \mathbf{G}_4$.

Game $\mathbf{G}_0(j)$: In this hybrid game, we assume that the initial ballot-box has been correctly generated (with $\overline{C}_i = (g, \ell_i = \ell^{r_i}, a_i = g^{r_i}, b_i = h^{r_i})$ for $r_i \xleftarrow{\$} \mathbb{Z}_p$, for all the honest users), and mixing steps up to $\mathcal{BB}ox^{(j)}$ have been honestly generated (excepted the zero-knowledge proofs that have been simulated). The next rounds are generated at random by honest mix-servers: random signing keys sk'_i and random ciphertexts $\overline{C}'_i = (g, \ell'_i = \ell^{r'_i}, a'_i = g^{r'_i}, b'_i = h^{r'_i})$, with random r'_i, and then correct signatures, using SK and sk'_i. The following sequence of games will modify the randomization of $\mathcal{BB}ox^{(j-1)}$ into $\mathcal{BB}ox^{(j)}$ if the j-th mix-server is honest.

Game $\mathbf{G}_1(j)$: We now start modifying the randomization of the ballots by the j-th mix-server, for the corrupted users. As we assumed the signatures Σ_i provided by the certification authority from a proof of knowledge of sk_i, our simulator has access to $\mathsf{sk}_i = (u_i, v_i, x_i, z_i)$ for all the corrupted users. The mixing step consists in updating the ciphertexts, the keys and the signatures, and we show how to do it without using α such that $\mathfrak{g}'_0 = \mathfrak{g}_0^{\alpha}$ but, instead, just $\mathfrak{g}'_0$, sk_i, $\overline{C}_0 = (1, \ell, g, h)$ and the individual random coins γ_i, δ_i: from $\mathcal{B}_i$ a received ballot of a corrupted user, one can compute $\mathsf{vk}'_i = (\mathfrak{g}'_0, \mathfrak{g}'_0{}^{u_i}, \mathfrak{g}'_0{}^{v_i+\delta_i}, \mathfrak{g}'_0{}^{x_i}, \mathfrak{g}'_0{}^{y_i})$ and $\overline{C}'_i = \overline{C}_i \cdot \overline{C}_0^{\gamma_i}$, and then the signatures σ'_i and Σ'_i using the signing keys, and choosing $\tilde{\tau}'_i \xleftarrow{\$} \mathbb{Z}_p$. This simulation is perfect for the corrupted users: $\mathsf{Adv}_{\mathbf{G}_1(j)} = \mathsf{Adv}_{\mathbf{G}_0(j)}$.

Game $\mathbf{G}_2(j)$: We now modify the simulation of the honest ballots. In this game, we choose random $d, e \xleftarrow{\$} \mathbb{Z}_p$ for $h = g^d$ and $\ell = g^e$. Then we have simulated $\overline{C}_i = (g, \ell_i = \ell^{r_i}, a_i = g^{r_i}, b_i = h^{r_i})$ the ciphertext in $\mathcal{BB}ox^{(0)}$ and we can set $\overline{C}'_i = (g, \ell'_i = \ell^{r'_i}, a'_i = g^{r'_i}, b'_i = h^{r'_i})$ the ciphertext in $\mathcal{BBox}^{(j)}$ for known random scalars $r_i, r'_i \xleftarrow{\$} \mathbb{Z}_p$, where r'_i is actually $r_i + \gamma_i$: γ_i is the accumulation of all the noises. All the signatures are still simulated using the signing keys (and $\tilde{\tau}'_i = R'_i \xleftarrow{\$} \mathbb{Z}_p$), with $\mathfrak{g}'_0 = \mathfrak{g}_0^\alpha$ for a random scalar α. This simulation is perfectly the same as above: $\mathsf{Adv}_{\mathbf{G}_2(j)} = \mathsf{Adv}_{\mathbf{G}_1(j)}$.

Before continuing, we study the format of the initial and randomized ballots: by denoting σ_i the initial signature in $\mathcal{BBox}^{(0)}$ and σ'_i the signature to generate in $\mathcal{BBox}^{(j)}$, we have the following relations:

$$e(\sigma_{i,0}, \mathfrak{g}_0) = e(g, \mathfrak{g}_i \mathfrak{h}_i{}^d \mathfrak{l}_i{}^e) \qquad e(\sigma_{i,1}, \mathfrak{g}_0) = e(g, \mathfrak{f}_i(\mathfrak{g}_i \mathfrak{h}_i{}^d \mathfrak{l}_i{}^e)^{r_i})$$

$$e(\sigma'_{i,0}, \mathfrak{g}'_0) = e(g, \mathfrak{g}'_i \mathfrak{h}'_i{}^d \mathfrak{l}'_i{}^e) \qquad e(\sigma'_{i,1}, \mathfrak{g}'_0) = e(g, \mathfrak{f}'_i(\mathfrak{g}'_i \mathfrak{h}'_i{}^d \mathfrak{l}'_i{}^e)^{r'_i})$$

If we formally denote $\sigma_{i,0} = g^{t_i}$ and $\sigma_{i,1} = g^{s_i}$, then we have

$$\mathfrak{g}_0{}^{t_i} = \mathfrak{g}_i \mathfrak{h}_i{}^d \mathfrak{l}_i{}^e \text{ and } \mathfrak{g}_0{}^{s_i} = \mathfrak{f}_i(\mathfrak{g}_i \mathfrak{h}_i{}^d \mathfrak{l}_i{}^e)^{r_i} = \mathfrak{f}_i \mathfrak{g}_0{}^{t_i r_i}$$

which implies $s_i = u_i + t_i r_i$. Similarly, if we formally denote $\sigma'_{i,0} = g'^{t'_i}$ and $\sigma'_{i,1} = g'^{s'_i}$, and set α as the product of all the α's and δ_i as aggregation of all the δ_i's (with α's) in the previous rounds plus this round, from

$$\mathfrak{g}_0{}^{\alpha t'_i} = \mathfrak{g}'_0{}^{t'_i} = \mathfrak{g}'_i \mathfrak{h}'_i{}^d \mathfrak{l}'_i{}^e = \mathfrak{g}_i^\alpha \mathfrak{h}_i{}^{\alpha d}(\mathfrak{l}_i \mathfrak{g}_0^{\delta_i})^{\alpha e}$$

$$\mathfrak{g}_0{}^{\alpha s'_i} = \mathfrak{g}'_0{}^{s'_i} = \mathfrak{f}'_i(\mathfrak{g}'_i \mathfrak{h}'_i{}^d \mathfrak{l}'_i{}^e)^{r'_i} = \mathfrak{f}_i^\alpha(\mathfrak{g}_i^\alpha \mathfrak{h}_i{}^{\alpha d}(\mathfrak{l}_i \mathfrak{g}_0^{\delta_i})^{\alpha e})^{r'_i}$$

we also have $\mathfrak{g}_0{}^{t'_i} = (\mathfrak{g}_i \mathfrak{h}_i{}^d \mathfrak{l}_i{}^e)\mathfrak{g}_0^{\delta_i e}$ and $\mathfrak{g}_0{}^{s'_i} = \mathfrak{f}_i(\mathfrak{g}_i \mathfrak{h}_i{}^d \mathfrak{l}_i{}^e)^{r'_i} \mathfrak{g}_0^{e \delta_i r'_i}$ which implies $s'_i = u_i + t'_i r'_i$. As consequence:

$$\sigma_{i,1} = g^{u_i} \cdot (g^{r_i})^{t_i} = g^{u_i} \cdot a_i{}^{t_i} \text{ and } \sigma'_{i,1} = g^{u_i} \cdot (g^{r'_i})^{t'_i} = g^{u_i} \cdot a'_i{}^{t'_i}$$

Game $\mathbf{G}_3(j)$: Let us randomly choose scalars $u_i, r_i, r'_i, t_i, t'_i$ and α, then, from $(g, \mathfrak{g}_0)$, we can set $\mathfrak{g}'_0 \leftarrow \mathfrak{g}_0^\alpha$, $a_i \leftarrow g^{r_i}$, $\sigma_{i,1} \leftarrow a_i{}^{t_i} g^{u_i}$, $\mathfrak{f}_i \leftarrow \mathfrak{g}_0{}^{u_i}$, as well as $a'_i \leftarrow g^{r'_i}$, $\sigma'_{i,1} \leftarrow a'_i{}^{t'_i} g^{u_i}$, $\mathfrak{f}'_i \leftarrow \mathfrak{g}'_0{}^{u_i}$.

Then, one additionally chooses $x_i, y_i \xleftarrow{\$} \mathbb{Z}_p$ and sets

$$\mathfrak{g}_i \leftarrow \mathfrak{g}_0^{x_i} \quad \mathfrak{h}_i \leftarrow \mathfrak{g}_0^{y_i} \quad \mathfrak{l}_i \leftarrow (\mathfrak{g}_0^{t_i}/(\mathfrak{g}_i \mathfrak{h}_i{}^d))^{1/e} \quad \overline{C}_i \leftarrow (g, a_i^e, a_i, a_i^d)$$

$$\mathfrak{g}'_i \leftarrow \mathfrak{g}_0'{}^{x_i} \quad \mathfrak{h}'_i \leftarrow \mathfrak{g}_0'{}^{y_i} \quad \mathfrak{l}'_i \leftarrow (\mathfrak{g}_0'{}^{t'_i}/(\mathfrak{g}'_i \mathfrak{h}'_i{}^d))^{1/e} \quad \overline{C}'_i \leftarrow (g, a_i'^e, a'_i, a_i'^d)$$

By construction: $\mathfrak{g}_0{}^{t_i} = \mathfrak{g}_i \mathfrak{h}_i{}^d \mathfrak{l}_i{}^e$, $\mathfrak{g}_0'{}^{t'_i} = \mathfrak{g}'_i \mathfrak{h}'_i{}^d \mathfrak{l}'_i{}^e$, and

$$\sigma_{i,1} = a_i{}^{t_i} g^{u_i} = g^{t_i r_i} \times g^{u_i} \qquad \sigma'_{i,1} = a_i'{}^{t'_i} g^{u_i} = g^{t'_i r'_i} \times g^{u_i}$$

With $\sigma_{i,0} \leftarrow g^{t_i}$ and $\sigma'_{i,0} \leftarrow g^{t'_i}$, σ_i and σ'_i are valid signatures of $(\overline{C}_i, \overline{C}_0)$ and $(\overline{C}'_i, \overline{C}_0)$ respectively. Then, the verification keys $\mathsf{vk}_i = (\mathfrak{g}_0, \mathfrak{f}_i, \mathfrak{l}_i, \mathfrak{g}_i, \mathfrak{h}_i)$ and $\mathsf{vk}'_i = (\mathfrak{g}'_0, \mathfrak{f}'_i, \mathfrak{l}'_i, \mathfrak{g}'_i, \mathfrak{h}'_i)$ are correctly related for the secret keys (u_i, v_i, x_i, y_i). From $\mathfrak{l}_i = (\mathfrak{g}_0^{t_i}/(\mathfrak{g}_i \mathfrak{h}_i{}^d))^{1/e} = \mathfrak{g}_0^{(t_i - x_i - dy_i)/e}$: we have $v_i = (t_i - x_i - dy_i)/e$.

From $l_i' = (\mathfrak{g}_0'^{t_i'}/(\mathfrak{g}_i'\mathfrak{h}_i'^d))^{1/e} = \mathfrak{g}_0'^{(t_i'-x_i-dy_i)/e}$: we have $v_i' = (t_i' - x_i - dy_i)/e = (t_i' - t_i)/e + v_i$, which means that $\delta_i = (t_i' - t_i)/e$.

Using the signing key SK, we can complete and sign vk_i (with random R_i) and vk_i' (with random R_i', which implicitly defines μ_i). As shown above, this perfectly simulates the view of the adversary for the honest ballots in the initial ballot-box $\mathcal{BB}\mathsf{ox}^{(0)}$, with $\mathcal{B}_i = (\overline{C}_i, \sigma_i, \mathsf{vk}_i, \Sigma_i, \tau_i)$ and a randomized version in the updated ballot-box $\mathcal{BB}\mathsf{ox}^{(j)}$, with $\mathcal{B}_i' = (\overline{C}_i', \sigma_i', \mathsf{vk}_i', \Sigma_i', \tau_i')$: $\mathsf{Adv}_{\mathbf{G}_3(j)} = \mathsf{Adv}_{\mathbf{G}_2(j)}$.

Game $\mathbf{G}_4(j)$: Let us be given $\mathsf{Cred}(u_i, g; \mathfrak{g}_0, r_i, t_i)$ and $\mathsf{Cred}(u_i, g; \mathfrak{g}_0', r_i', t_i')$, for random $u_i \xleftarrow{\$} \mathbb{Z}_p$, which provide all the required inputs from the first part of the simulation in the previous game (before choosing x_i, y_i). They all follow the distribution $\mathcal{D}_{g,\mathfrak{g}_0}(u_i, u_i)$. As we do not need to know α to randomize ballots for corrupted users, we can thus continue the simulation as above, in a perfectly indistinguishable way: $\mathsf{Adv}_{\mathbf{G}_4(j)} = \mathsf{Adv}_{\mathbf{G}_3(j)}$.

Game $\mathbf{G}_5(j)$: Let us be given two credentials of u_i and u_i', $\mathsf{Cred}(u_i, g; \mathfrak{g}_0, r_i, t_i)$ and $\mathsf{Cred}(u_i', g; \mathfrak{g}_0', r_i', t_i')$, for random $u_i, u_i' \xleftarrow{\$} \mathbb{Z}_p$. Inputs follow the distribution $\mathcal{D}_{g,\mathfrak{g}_0}(u_i, u_i')$ and we do as above. Under the Unlinkability Assumption (see Definition 4) the view is computationally indistinguishable: $\mathsf{Adv}_{\mathbf{G}_4(j)} < \mathsf{Adv}_{\mathbf{G}_5(j)} + \mathsf{negl}()$.

Game $\mathbf{G}_6(j)$: We receive a Multi Diffie-Hellman tuple $(\mathfrak{g}_0, \mathfrak{g}_i, \mathfrak{h}_i, \mathfrak{g}_0', \mathfrak{g}_i', \mathfrak{h}_i') \xleftarrow{\$} \mathcal{D}_{\mathsf{mdh}}^6(\mathfrak{g}_0)$. So we know all the scalars, except x_i, y_i and α, which are implicitly defined by the input challenge. Then, by choosing $t_i, t_i' \xleftarrow{\$} \mathbb{Z}_p$, we can define l_i, l_i' as in the previous game, and the ciphertexts and signatures are generated honestly with random scalars $r_i, r_i' \xleftarrow{\$} \mathbb{Z}_p$: $\mathsf{Adv}_{\mathbf{G}_6(j)} = \mathsf{Adv}_{\mathbf{G}_5(j)}$.

Game $\mathbf{G}_7(j)$: We now receive $(\mathfrak{g}_0, \mathfrak{g}_i, \mathfrak{h}_i, \mathfrak{g}_0', \mathfrak{g}_i', \mathfrak{h}_i') \xleftarrow{\$} \mathcal{D}_\$^6(\mathfrak{g}_0)$. We do the simulation as above. The view of the adversary is indistinguishable under the DDH assumption in $\mathbb{G}_2$: $\mathsf{Adv}_{\mathbf{G}_6(j)} < \mathsf{Adv}_{\mathbf{G}_7(j)} + \mathsf{negl}()$.

In this game, $\mathsf{vk}_i' = (\mathfrak{g}_0', \mathfrak{f}_i = \mathfrak{g}_0'^{u_i'}, l_i = \mathfrak{g}_0'^{v_i'}, \mathfrak{g}_i = \mathfrak{g}_0'^{x_i'}, \mathfrak{h}_i = \mathfrak{g}_0'^{y_i'})$, with $x_i', y_i' \xleftarrow{\$} \mathbb{Z}_p$ because of the random tuple, $v_i' = v_i + (t_i' - t_i)/e$, for random t_i' and t_i, it is thus also random, and u_i' is chosen at random.

Game $\mathbf{G}_8(j)$: We now choose at random the signing keys $\mathsf{sk}_i = (u_i, v_i, x_i, y_i)$ and $\mathsf{sk}_i' = (u_i', v_i', x_i', y_i')$ in order to sign the ciphertexts: $\mathsf{Adv}_{\mathbf{G}_8(j)} = \mathsf{Adv}_{\mathbf{G}_7(j)}$.

With this last game, one can see that $\mathbf{G}_8(1) = \mathbf{G}_5$. Furthermore, for each round $j = N, \dots, 1$, we have $\mathsf{Adv}_{\mathbf{G}_0(j)} \leq \mathsf{Adv}_{\mathbf{G}_8(j)} + \mathsf{negl}()$, while $\mathbf{G}_0(j-1) = \mathbf{G}_8(j)$: $\mathsf{Adv}_{\mathbf{G}_4} = \mathsf{Adv}_{\mathbf{G}_0}(N) \leq \mathsf{Adv}_{\mathbf{G}_8}(1) + \mathsf{negl}() = \mathsf{Adv}_{\mathbf{G}_5} + \mathsf{negl}()$. $\qquad\square$

6   Applications

We now discuss use-cases of mix-nets: electronic voting and anonymous routing. In both cases, a mix-server can, on the fly, perform individual verifications and randomization of ballots, as well as the product of the $\mathfrak{f}_i$'s and the ciphertexts adaptively until the ballots are all sent. Eventually, at the closing time for a vote or at the end of a time lapse for routing, one just has to do and sign global proof of Diffie-Hellman tuples, and then output the ballots in a permuted order.

6.1   Electronic Voting

Our mix-net fits well the case of e-voting because after the multiple mixing steps, all the mix-servers can perform a second round to sign in a compact way the constant-size proof, certifying each of their contributions. The input size as well as the computation cost of the verifier are both independent on the number of mixing steps. To our knowledge it is the first scheme with this very nice property.

About security, as explained, soundness and privacy are guaranteed for the honest users only: honest users are sure that their votes are randomized in the output ballot-box, and their input-output ballots are unlinkable. This is of course the most important requirements. However, since the u_i's are used to guarantee that no ballots are deleted or inserted, this is important those values to be unknown to the mix-server.

In the full version [27], we propose a second construction that uses Square Diffie-Hellman tuples $(\mathfrak{g}_r, \mathfrak{A}_i = \mathfrak{g}_r^{w_i}, \mathfrak{B}_i = \mathfrak{A}_i^{w_i})$ as tags to add in any one-time linearly homomorphic signature to obtain a linearly homomorphic signature with randomizable tags. Then, one can use $\prod \mathfrak{A}_j' = (\prod \mathfrak{A}_i)^\alpha$ instead of $\prod \mathfrak{f}_j'$ and $(\prod \mathfrak{f}_i)^\alpha$, in the Diffie-Hellman tuple, to guarantee the permutation of the verification keys. Only the privacy of the w_i's is required to guarantee the soundness.

The proof that $\prod M_i = \prod M_i'$ is actually never used in the previous security proofs, as it counts for privacy in e-voting only. Indeed, in our privacy security game we let the adversary choose the messages of the honest users. In a voting scheme, the adversary could not choose them and would like to learn the vote of a target voter. The first mix-server could take the vote (ciphertext) of this voter and ask several corrupted voters to duplicate this vote. The bias in the tally would reveal the vote of the target voter: the proof on the products of the plaintexts avoids this modification during the mixing. This does not exclude the attack of Cortier-Smyth [15] if the votes are publicly sent, as the corrupted voters could simply use the ciphertext for their own ballots.

6.2   Message Routing

Another important use case of mix-nets is in routing protocols where the mix-servers are proxy servers guaranteeing that no one can trace a request of a message. In this scenario, it is not possible to perform a second round on the mix-servers to obtain the multi-signature and the efficiency is thus linear in the number of mixing steps. It is still an open problem to avoid the second round while maintaining the independence in the number of mix-servers.

Acknowledgments. This work was supported in part by the European Community's Seventh Framework Programme (FP7/2007-2013 Grant Agreement no. 339563 – CryptoCloud) and the French ANR ALAMBIC Project (ANR16-CE39-0006).

References

1. Abe, M., Fuchsbauer, G., Groth, J., Haralambiev, K., Ohkubo, M.: Structure-preserving signatures and commitments to group elements. In: Rabin, T. (ed.) CRYPTO 2010. LNCS, vol. 6223, pp. 209–236. Springer, Heidelberg (2010). https://doi.org/10.1007/978-3-642-14623-7_12

2. Ahn, J.H., Boneh, D., Camenisch, J., Hohenberger, S., shelat, a., Waters, B., et al.: Computing on authenticated data. In: Cramer, R. (ed.) TCC 2012. LNCS, vol. 7194, pp. 1–20. Springer, Heidelberg (2012). https://doi.org/10.1007/978-3-642-28914-9_1

3. Bayer, S., Groth, J.: Efficient zero-knowledge argument for correctness of a shuffle. In: Pointcheval, D., Johansson, T. (eds.) EUROCRYPT 2012. LNCS, vol. 7237, pp. 263–280. Springer, Heidelberg (2012). https://doi.org/10.1007/978-3-642-29011-4_17

4. Blazy, O., Fuchsbauer, G., Izabachène, M., Jambert, A., Sibert, H., Vergnaud, D.: Batch Groth–Sahai. In: Zhou, J., Yung, M. (eds.) ACNS 2010. LNCS, vol. 6123, pp. 218–235. Springer, Heidelberg (2010). https://doi.org/10.1007/978-3-642-13708-2_14

5. Blazy, O., Fuchsbauer, G., Pointcheval, D., Vergnaud, D.: Signatures on randomizable ciphertexts. In: Catalano, D., Fazio, N., Gennaro, R., Nicolosi, A. (eds.) PKC 2011. LNCS, vol. 6571, pp. 403–422. Springer, Heidelberg (2011). https://doi.org/10.1007/978-3-642-19379-8_25

6. Boneh, D., Boyen, X., Goh, E.-J.: Hierarchical identity based encryption with constant size ciphertext. In: Cramer, R. (ed.) EUROCRYPT 2005. LNCS, vol. 3494, pp. 440–456. Springer, Heidelberg (2005). https://doi.org/10.1007/11426639_26

7. Boneh, D., Drijvers, M., Neven, G.: Compact multi-signatures for smaller blockchains. In: Peyrin, T., Galbraith, S. (eds.) ASIACRYPT 2018, Part II. LNCS, vol. 11273, pp. 435–464. Springer, Cham (2018). https://doi.org/10.1007/978-3-030-03329-3_15

8. Boneh, D., Freeman, D., Katz, J., Waters, B.: Signing a linear subspace: signature schemes for network coding. In: Jarecki, S., Tsudik, G. (eds.) PKC 2009. LNCS, vol. 5443, pp. 68–87. Springer, Heidelberg (2009). https://doi.org/10.1007/978-3-642-00468-1_5

9. Boneh, D., Freeman, D.M.: Homomorphic signatures for polynomial functions. In: Paterson, K.G. (ed.) EUROCRYPT 2011. LNCS, vol. 6632, pp. 149–168. Springer, Heidelberg (2011). https://doi.org/10.1007/978-3-642-20465-4_10

10. Boneh, D., Freeman, D.M.: Linearly homomorphic signatures over binary fields and new tools for lattice-based signatures. In: Catalano, D., Fazio, N., Gennaro, R., Nicolosi, A. (eds.) PKC 2011. LNCS, vol. 6571, pp. 1–16. Springer, Heidelberg (2011). https://doi.org/10.1007/978-3-642-19379-8_1

11. Boyen, X.: The uber-assumption family. In: Galbraith, S.D., Paterson, K.G. (eds.) Pairing 2008. LNCS, vol. 5209, pp. 39–56. Springer, Heidelberg (2008). https://doi.org/10.1007/978-3-540-85538-5_3

12. Camenisch, J., Hohenberger, S., Pedersen, M.Ø.: Batch verification of short signatures. In: Naor, M. (ed.) EUROCRYPT 2007. LNCS, vol. 4515, pp. 246–263. Springer, Heidelberg (2007). https://doi.org/10.1007/978-3-540-72540-4_14

13. Chase, M., Kohlweiss, M., Lysyanskaya, A., Meiklejohn, S.: Malleable proof systems and applications. In: Pointcheval, D., Johansson, T. (eds.) EUROCRYPT 2012. LNCS, vol. 7237, pp. 281–300. Springer, Heidelberg (2012). https://doi.org/10.1007/978-3-642-29011-4_18

14. Chaum, D.L.: Untraceable electronic mail, return addresses, and digital pseudonyms. Commun. ACM **24**(2), 84–90 (1981). https://doi.org/10.1145/358549.358563

15. Cortier, V., Smyth, B.: Attacking and fixing Helios: an analysis of ballot secrecy. J. Comput. Secur. **21**(1), 89–148 (2013). http://dl.acm.org/citation.cfm?id=2595846.2595849

16. Damgård, I.: Towards practical public key systems secure against chosen ciphertext attacks. In: Feigenbaum, J. (ed.) CRYPTO 1991. LNCS, vol. 576, pp. 445–456. Springer, Heidelberg (1992). https://doi.org/10.1007/3-540-46766-1_36

17. Fauzi, P., Lipmaa, H., Siim, J., Zając, M.: An efficient pairing-based shuffle argument. In: Takagi, T., Peyrin, T. (eds.) ASIACRYPT 2017, Part II. LNCS, vol. 10625, pp. 97–127. Springer, Cham (2017). https://doi.org/10.1007/978-3-319-70697-9_4

18. Fiat, A., Shamir, A.: How to prove yourself: practical solutions to identification and signature problems. In: Odlyzko, A.M. (ed.) CRYPTO 1986. LNCS, vol. 263, pp. 186–194. Springer, Heidelberg (1987). https://doi.org/10.1007/3-540-47721-7_12

19. Freeman, D.M.: Improved security for linearly homomorphic signatures: a generic framework. In: Fischlin, M., Buchmann, J., Manulis, M. (eds.) PKC 2012. LNCS, vol. 7293, pp. 697–714. Springer, Heidelberg (2012). https://doi.org/10.1007/978-3-642-30057-8_41

20. Fuchsbauer, G., Hanser, C., Slamanig, D.: Structure-preserving signatures on equivalence classes and constant-size anonymous credentials. J. Cryptol. **32**(2), 498–546 (2019)

21. Furukawa, J., Sako, K.: An efficient scheme for proving a shuffle. In: Kilian, J. (ed.) CRYPTO 2001. LNCS, vol. 2139, pp. 368–387. Springer, Heidelberg (2001). https://doi.org/10.1007/3-540-44647-8_22

22. Groth, J.: Short pairing-based non-interactive zero-knowledge arguments. In: Abe, M. (ed.) ASIACRYPT 2010. LNCS, vol. 6477, pp. 321–340. Springer, Heidelberg (2010). https://doi.org/10.1007/978-3-642-17373-8_19

23. Groth, J., Ishai, Y.: Sub-linear zero-knowledge argument for correctness of a shuffle. In: Smart, N. (ed.) EUROCRYPT 2008. LNCS, vol. 4965, pp. 379–396. Springer, Heidelberg (2008). https://doi.org/10.1007/978-3-540-78967-3_22

24. Groth, J., Lu, S.: A non-interactive shuffle with pairing based verifiability. In: Kurosawa, K. (ed.) ASIACRYPT 2007. LNCS, vol. 4833, pp. 51–67. Springer, Heidelberg (2007). https://doi.org/10.1007/978-3-540-76900-2_4

25. Groth, J., Sahai, A.: Efficient non-interactive proof systems for bilinear groups. In: Smart, N. (ed.) EUROCRYPT 2008. LNCS, vol. 4965, pp. 415–432. Springer, Heidelberg (2008). https://doi.org/10.1007/978-3-540-78967-3_24

26. Hada, S., Tanaka, T.: On the existence of 3-round zero-knowledge protocols. In: Krawczyk, H. (ed.) CRYPTO 1998. LNCS, vol. 1462, pp. 408–423. Springer, Heidelberg (1998). https://doi.org/10.1007/BFb0055744

27. Hébant, C., Phan, D.H., Pointcheval, D.: Linearly-homomorphic signatures and scalable mix-nets. Cryptology ePrint Archive, Report 2019/547 (2019). https://eprint.iacr.org/2019/547

28. Herold, G., Hoffmann, M., Klooß, M., Ràfols, C., Rupp, A.: New techniques for structural batch verification in bilinear groups with applications to Groth-Sahai proofs. In: Thuraisingham, B.M., Evans, D., Malkin, T., Xu, D. (eds.) ACM CCS 2017, pp. 1547–1564. ACM Press , October/November 2017

29. Johnson, R., Molnar, D., Song, D., Wagner, D.: Homomorphic signature schemes. In: Preneel, B. (ed.) CT-RSA 2002. LNCS, vol. 2271, pp. 244–262. Springer, Heidelberg (2002). https://doi.org/10.1007/3-540-45760-7_17

30. Libert, B., Peters, T., Joye, M., Yung, M.: Linearly homomorphic structure-preserving signatures and their applications. In: Canetti, R., Garay, J.A. (eds.) CRYPTO 2013, part II. LNCS, vol. 8043, pp. 289–307. Springer, Heidelberg (2013). https://doi.org/10.1007/978-3-642-40084-1_17
31. Neff, C.A.: A verifiable secret shuffle and its application to e-voting. In: Reiter, M.K., Samarati, P. (eds.) ACM CCS 2001, pp. 116–125. ACM Press, November 2001
32. Shoup, V.: Lower bounds for discrete logarithms and related problems. In: Fumy, W. (ed.) EUROCRYPT 1997. LNCS, vol. 1233, pp. 256–266. Springer, Heidelberg (1997). https://doi.org/10.1007/3-540-69053-0_18

Efficient Redactable Signature and Application to Anonymous Credentials

Olivier Sanders[(✉)]

Orange Labs, Applied Crypto Group, Cesson-Sévigné, France
olivier.sanders@orange.com

Abstract. Let us assume that Alice has received a constant-size signature on a set of messages $\{m_i\}_{i=1}^n$ from some organization. Depending on the situation, Alice might need to disclose, prove relations about or hide some of these messages. Ideally, the complexity of the corresponding protocols should not depend on the hidden messages. In particular, if Alice wants to disclose only k messages, then the authenticity of the latter should be verifiable in at most $O(k)$ operations.

Many solutions were proposed over the past decades, but they only provide a partial answer to this problem. In particular, we note that they suffer either from the need to prove knowledge of the hidden elements or from the inability to prove that the latter satisfy some relations.

In this paper, we propose a very efficient constant-size redactable signature scheme that addresses all the problems above. Signatures can indeed be redacted to remain valid only on a subset of k messages included in $\{m_i\}_{i=1}^n$. The resulting redacted signature consists of 4 elements and can be verified with essentially k exponentiations. Different shows of the same signature can moreover be made unlinkable leading to a very efficient anonymous credentials system.

1 Introduction

Digital Signature is a major cryptographic tool that is used to attest the authenticity of a digital data, ensuring that not even one bit has been modified. This rigidity is a strength in many scenarios but it also comes with its drawbacks. One of them is that verification of a standard signature requires knowledge of the full signed message.

For example, let us consider the case of a database containing n elements $\{m_i\}_{i=1}^n$ that should be certified by some authority. If the latter signs the whole set $\{m_i\}_{i=1}^n$, there is only one signature σ but checking the authenticity of even one element requires to download the full database. Obviously, this problem could be avoided by signing separately each element but this would replace one signature by potentially billions (n) of them. Between these two solutions one can find different trade-offs, such as splitting $\{m_i\}_{i=1}^n$ into different subsets that would be signed individually, but none of them is fully satisfying. Even solutions based on hash functions, such as Merkle tree, require to download at

© International Association for Cryptologic Research 2020
A. Kiayias et al. (Eds.): PKC 2020, LNCS 12111, pp. 628–656, 2020.
https://doi.org/10.1007/978-3-030-45388-6_22

least a logarithmic number of elements. Moreover, using hash functions prevents efficient proofs of knowledge, which will cause further problems.

The problem described above is not just related to efficiency. It indeed means that, to check the validity of a signature without using hash functions, one must have access to all the signed messages which is also a privacy issue. This problem is probably more obvious in a context where a user gets his attributes (e.g. his name, birthdate, address, etc) certified by some authority and then needs to prove the authenticity of only one of them. For example, to benefit from a preferential rate, he might need to prove that he is under 25 years of age. With a standard digital signature, he needs to send all his attributes, even if the latter are totally irrelevant. This means that the merchant will not only have information on his age, but he will also know his name, address and so on.

This problem is far from new in cryptography and a very classical solution for the user is to prove knowledge of the hidden attributes and that the latter are indeed certified by a credential issued by the organization. This requires a digital signature scheme with some nice features but this is not a real problem as several such schemes [4,10,21] have already been proposed. Actually, most anonymous credentials (or attribute based credentials) systems [1,9,10,21] work this way to solve our problem. Moreover, such a primitive can provide additional security guarantees, such as unlinkability of different showings, which are particularly interesting in many contexts.

Regarding privacy, this solution is thus fully satisfying. Regarding efficiency, things got worse as the unnecessary attributes must now be hidden in proofs of knowledge whose cost is at least greater than the one of sending all the attributes in clear. We believe that this problem is inherent to constructions based on digital signatures. As we explain above the latter indeed require the whole set of signed messages to be verified and do not support efficient partial verification. It seems therefore necessary to find another building block to avoid this problem.

Another strategy could be based on cryptographic accumulators, such as the ones from [2,19]. An accumulator C indeed allows to accumulate many elements $\{m_i\} \in \mathcal{I}$ while remaining of constant size. Moreover, for any accumulated message m_i, it is possible to derive a witness w_i proving that m_i has indeed been accumulated in C. If C is further signed, then one gets efficient partial verification on a message m_i: given C, the signature on C and the witness w_i, one can indeed check the authenticity of m_i without knowing any other messages. By using appropriate zero-knowledge proofs, one could even achieve some privacy properties. Actually, this is reminiscent of the approach of [15]. The authors indeed extend Nguyen's accumulator [19] to enable efficient proof that a subset $\{m_i\}_{i \in \mathcal{I}} \subset \{m_i\}_{i=1}^n$ has been accumulated. They then show how to combine their accumulator with signatures on equivalence classes to construct an anonymous credentials system with very nice features. Unfortunately, with their solution, once elements are accumulated, one only has the possibility to disclose them, not to prove that they satisfy some relations while hiding them. Concretely, in our example with user's attributes, this means that the user can now reveal his birthdate and any other necessary attribute, but not just prove (efficiently) that he is under 25.

Compared to the previous anonymous credentials cited above, [15] thus solves the efficiency issue but by removing an important feature of anonymous credentials, which implicitly harms privacy.

Finally, the problem of checking the authenticity of parts of the signed messages while hiding the other ones has already been considered by papers on redactable signature [6,18,20]. This primitive allows the user to quote parts of the message signed under σ and yet to prove that the latter is valid on the disclosed parts. Actually, this might seem exactly what we need here but, unfortunately, most redactable signatures aim at achieving some properties, such as transparency (original signatures should be indistinguishable from redacted ones), that do not seem relevant in our context and that negatively impact efficiency. Nevertheless, in [7], Camenisch *et al.* introduce a new variant of redactable signature, called *unlinkable redactable signature* (URS), that does not consider such outlying properties and that is thus perfectly tailored for applications to privacy-preserving protocols. As an example, the authors construct from an URS an anonymous credentials system with remarkable asymptotic complexity. Unfortunately, in this case, asymptotic complexity is not indicative of concrete performances. Current instantiations are indeed still very costly and can hardly compete with the most efficient solutions in practice (see Sect. 7). Moreover, their construction makes use of a vector commitment scheme that shares commonalities with the accumulator used in [15], which leads to the same issue: attributes can be either disclosed or hidden, but proving that some of them satisfy non trivial relations cannot be done efficiently. Nevertheless, to be fair, we must note that [7] provides security in the UC framework [11], which explains in part the efficiency gap with alternative solutions

1.1   Our Contribution

In this work we follow the approach based on URS from [7], but with the aim of achieving extremely efficient protocols. To this end, we construct a very flexible redactable signature scheme, that can be made unlinkable at almost no cost. We then explain how to use it to construct an anonymous credentials system with remarkable efficiency and that still supports proof of relations about attributes, contrarily to [15].

Our starting point is the Pointcheval-Sanders (PS) signature scheme [21] that generates constant size signatures on blocks of messages $(m_1, \ldots, m_n)$. As shown in [21], it comes with a series of features that are extremely useful in a privacy preserving context, such as the ability to efficiently prove knowledge of a signature or to generate a signature on a committed message. Unfortunately, when used to construct anonymous credentials systems, this scheme suffers from the problems described above, namely the fact that non disclosed messages heavily impact complexity, because their knowledge must be proven. Concretely, if one discloses k attributes (and thus hide/redact the $n - k$ other ones), one must still send $O(n - k)$ elements to the verifier (besides the k disclosed attributes) and the latter must still perform $O(n)$ operations.

The first contribution of our paper is the construction of an efficient redactable signature scheme RS from PS signatures. At first sight, this problem might seem easy to solve due to the simple algebraic structure of PS signatures. Indeed, in a bilinear group $(\mathbb{G}_1, \mathbb{G}_2, \mathbb{G}_T)$, a PS signature on $(m_1, \ldots, m_n)$, issued with secret key $(x, y_1, \ldots, y_n)$, is a pair $(\widetilde{\sigma}_1, \widetilde{\sigma}_2) \in \mathbb{G}_2$ where $\widetilde{\sigma}_1$ is random and $\widetilde{\sigma}_2 = \widetilde{\sigma}_1^{x + \sum_{i=1}^{n} y_i \cdot m_i}$. By providing $(X, Y_1, \ldots, Y_n) = (g^x, g^{y_1}, \ldots, g^{y_n})$ for some generator $g \in \mathbb{G}_1$ in the public key, one can test the validity of $(\widetilde{\sigma}_1, \widetilde{\sigma}_2)$ using the pairing e:

$$e(X \cdot \prod_{i=1}^{n} Y_i^{m_i}, \widetilde{\sigma}_1) = e(g, \widetilde{\sigma}_2)$$

When one asks to verify the authenticity of only a subset $\{m_i\}_{i \in \mathcal{I}}$ of messages, it might be tempting to only send $(\widetilde{\sigma}_1, \widetilde{\sigma}_2)$ along with an element $\sigma_1 = \prod_{i \in [1,n] \setminus \mathcal{I}} Y_i^{m_i}$ that would accumulate all the redacted elements. The previous equation would then simply become

$$e(X \cdot \sigma_1 \cdot \prod_{i \in \mathcal{I}} Y_i^{m_i}, \widetilde{\sigma}_1) = e(g, \widetilde{\sigma}_2). \tag{1}$$

Such a scheme would be extremely efficient: only a constant number of elements[1] needs to be sent to the verifier and the later only needs to perform k exponentiations in $\mathbb{G}_1$. Moreover, the structure of the resulting scheme makes combination with Schnorr's proof of knowledge [23] trivial. One can then hide and prove relations about any m_i with $i \in \mathcal{I}$.

Unfortunately, such a scheme is not secure. We provide details on the problem in Sect. 4.1 but intuitively it stems from the fact that the adversary can hide anything in σ_1, including elements of the form $Y_i^{r_i}$ with $i \in \mathcal{I}$ that it could use to cheat the verifier. A solution could then be to prove that σ_1 only aggregates the elements $Y_i^{m_i}$ with $i \in [1, n] \setminus \mathcal{I}$, by running the classical Schnorr's protocol to prove knowledge of the corresponding m_i. Unfortunately, such a solution takes us back to square one: we need to send $O(n - k)$ elements and verification requires $O(n)$ operations.

Fortunately, we can do far better by observing that we do not really care about the elements accumulated in σ_1. If the adversary manages to add some elements to σ_1 such that the verification equation above is still verified, this is not a problem as long as the added elements are not of the form $Y_i^{r_i}$ for $i \in \mathcal{I}$ and known r_i. Actually, the ability to add random elements to σ_1 should be kept since it will be the key to achieve unlinkability, as we will explain.

To retain security, we must then force the user to prove that σ_1 does not aggregate an element of the above form. Surprisingly, this can be done very efficiently by noticing that the polynomial f defined by $e(g, \widetilde{g})^{f(y_1, \ldots, y_n)} = e(\sigma_1, \prod_{i \in \mathcal{I}} \widetilde{Y}_i)$ will necessarily contain a monomial of the form y_j^2 for some $j \in \mathcal{I}$ if the user has cheated. Conversely, with a valid σ_1, f will not contain such kind

---

[1] We here follow the convention of previous works that do not include the disclosed elements $\{m_i\}$ in the complexity evaluation.

of monomials, the only degree 2 monomials being of the form $y_i \cdot y_j$ for $i \neq j$. By providing appropriate elements in the public key we can enable the user to prove that f is of the right form by simply providing an element σ_2 in $\mathbb{G}_1$ such that $e(\sigma_1, \prod_{i \in \mathcal{I}} \tilde{Y}_i) = e(\sigma_2, \tilde{g})$. That is, we get a secure redactable signature with remarkable efficiency: redacted signatures contain 4 elements and can be verified with 4 pairings and k exponentiations, whatever the values of k and n.

We believe that such a redactable signature is of independent interest. However, although it is redactable and unforgeable, it is not unlinkable and so cannot be directly used to build an anonymous credentials system. Our next contribution is then to enhance it to construct an URS in the sense of [7].

Here, the transformation is based on our previous observation. Our "proof of validity" of σ_1 does not prove that σ_1 is of the expected form $\prod_{i \in [1,n] \setminus \mathcal{I}} Y_i^{m_i}$ but simply that it does not contain illicit elements $Y_i^{r_i}$, for $i \in \mathcal{I}$. In particular, we can aggregate anything in σ_1 as long as it is not of the latter form and Eq. (1) is verified. To satisfy both conditions, we will use the fact that PS signatures can be sequentially aggregated to add to $(\tilde{\sigma}_1, \tilde{\sigma}_2)$ a signature on a random message t under a dummy public key and then modify σ_1 and σ_2 appropriately. That is, a new derived signature on $\{m_i\}_{i \in \mathcal{I}}$ is the resulting aggregate signature whose messages $\{m_i\}_{i \in [1,n] \setminus \mathcal{I}}$ and t have been redacted. As we prove in our paper, the random elements added in the process perfectly blind the original signature and thus ensure unlinkability at almost no cost: few additional exponentiations to redact the signature, but the signature size and the verification process remain unchanged.

Once we have our unlinkable redactable signature scheme, the transformation into an anonymous credentials system is rather straightforward because we inherit most of the nice features of PS signatures. We just have to adapt the protocol to get a credential on a committed value from [21] and then to add a proof of knowledge of the user's secret key during the showing process. Regarding efficiency, there is almost no change and the resulting protocol compares favourably with the state-of-the-art (see Sect. 7). In particular, in our system, the user only has to send a constant number of elements to prove possession of k attributes and the verifier only has to perform $O(k)$ operations, even if the credential was initially issued on a much larger number n of attributes. The main difference with our URS construction is the anonymity proof that is more intricate and that now makes use of the DDH assumption.

In the end, we get a remarkably versatile system which can provide both security and privacy with very good performance.

1.2   Organisation

We recall in Sect. 2 the definition of bilinear groups and two computational assumptions that we use to prove the security of our schemes. The syntax and the security model of redactable signatures (resp. anonymous credentials) are provided in Sect. 3 (resp. Sect. 6). Our redactable signature scheme is presented in Sect. 4 along with a variant achieving additional properties. The security proofs of our main construction can be found in the same section, those for the variant are provided in the full version [22] of this paper due to lack of space. Our anonymous credentials system is described, and proved secure, in Sect. 6. Finally, we compare the efficiency of our constructions with the one of the most relevant schemes from the state-of-the-art in Sect. 7.

2 Preliminaries

Bilinear Groups. Our construction requires bilinear groups whose definition is recalled below.

Definition 1. *Bilinear groups are a set of three groups $\mathbb{G}_1$, $\mathbb{G}_2$, and $\mathbb{G}_T$ of order p along with a map, called pairing, $e : \mathbb{G}_1 \times \mathbb{G}_2 \to \mathbb{G}_T$ that is*

1. *bilinear: for any $g \in \mathbb{G}_1, \widetilde{g} \in \mathbb{G}_2$, and $a, b \in \mathbb{Z}_p$, $e(g^a, \widetilde{g}^b) = e(g, \widetilde{g})^{ab}$;*
2. *non-degenerate: for any $g \in \mathbb{G}_1^*$ and $\widetilde{g} \in \mathbb{G}_2^*$, $e(g, \widetilde{g}) \neq 1_{\mathbb{G}_T}$;*
3. *efficient: for any $g \in \mathbb{G}_1$ and $\widetilde{g} \in \mathbb{G}_2$, $e(g, \widetilde{g})$ can be efficiently computed.*

In this work, we need bilinear groups of prime order with *type 3* pairings [16], meaning that no efficiently computable homomorphism is known between $\mathbb{G}_1$ and $\mathbb{G}_2$. We stress that this is not a significant restriction since this yields the most efficient parameters [12,17].

Computational Assumptions. The security analysis of our protocols will make use of the following two assumptions.

- DL assumption: Given $(g, g^a) \in \mathbb{G}^2$, the DL assumption in the group $\mathbb{G}$ states that it is hard to recover a.
- DDH assumption: Given $(g, g^a, g^b, g^c) \in \mathbb{G}^4$, the DDH assumption in the group $\mathbb{G}$ states that it is hard to decide whether $c = a \cdot b$ or c is random.

3 Redactable Signatures

A signature σ on some set of messages $\{m_i\}_{i=1}^n$ is redactable if it is possible to derive from it a signature $\sigma_{\mathcal{I}}$ on a subset of messages $\{m_i\}_{i \in \mathcal{I}}$, with $\mathcal{I} \subset [1, n]$. The point is that the verification of $\sigma_{\mathcal{I}}$ no longer requires the knowledge of the messages m_i for $i \in \overline{\mathcal{I}}$, where $\overline{\mathcal{I}} = [1, n] \setminus \mathcal{I}$. This feature is particularly useful when one only needs to check the authenticity of a subset of the messages. However, redacting messages does not necessarily mean hiding them and so it is necessary to consider additional properties when privacy is required. This leads us to the following definition of redactable signatures, adapted from [7].

3.1 Syntax

A redactable signature consists of the 4 following algorithms.

- Keygen($1^k, n$): On input a security parameter 1^k and an integer n, this algorithm returns a key pair (sk, pk) supporting signatures on sets of n messages $\{m_i\}_{i=1}^n$.
- Sign(sk, $\{m_i\}_{i=1}^n$): On input n messages $\{m_i\}_{i=1}^n$ and the signing key sk, this algorithm outputs a signature σ.
- Derive(pk, σ, $\{m_i\}_{i=1}^n, \mathcal{I}$): On input a signature σ on $\{m_i\}_{i=1}^n$, the public key pk and a subset $\mathcal{I} \subset [1, n]$, this algorithm returns a redacted (or derived) signature σ_I on the subset of messages $\{m_i\}_{i \in \mathcal{I}}$. In this paper, we will omit the subscript $\mathcal{I}$ of $\sigma_\mathcal{I}$ if this set is clear from the context.
- Verify(pk, σ, $\{m_i\}_{i \in \mathcal{I}}$): On input the public key pk, a set of messages $\{m_i\}_{i \in \mathcal{I}}$ and a signature σ (redacted or not), this algorithm outputs 1 (valid) or 0 (invalid).

Notation. In this paper, we will consider *sets* of messages $\{m_i\}_{i=1}^n$ instead of *vectors* $(m_1, \ldots, m_n)$ to highlight the benefits of redactability. Indeed, with this notation, a redacted signature σ_I can be verified only with the knowledge of the $|\mathcal{I}|$ elements in $\{m_i\}_{i \in \mathcal{I}}$. Conversely, with a vector notation, verification of σ_I would still require to send a vector of n elements $(m_1', \ldots, m_n')$, with $m_i' = \bot$ for $i \in \overline{\mathcal{I}}$.

We nevertheless stress that it is only a notation issue. In particular, even with our notation, the position of the messages (indicated by their index) remains crucial. For example, if $m_1 = m_2'$ and $m_2 = m_1'$, then we stress that a valid signature on $\{m_1, m_2\}$ is *not* valid on $\{m_1', m_2'\}$ (this would be considered as a valid forgery in our security game). More generally, we will consider in this paper that $\{m_i\}_{i \in \mathcal{I}} \subset \{m_i'\}_{i=1}^n$ when $m_i = m_i' \ \forall i \in \mathcal{I}$.

3.2 Security Model

Correctness. Correctness requires that, for honestly generated keys, honestly generated and honestly derived signatures always verify.

Unforgeability. In [7], the authors consider a very strong notion of unforgeability. Indeed, besides the natural requirements for a signature scheme, their definition considers a signature $\sigma_\mathcal{I}$ on $\{m_i\}_{i \in \mathcal{I}}$, derived from a signature σ valid on $\{m_i\}_{i=1}^n$, as a forgery if the adversary only had access to other redacted versions $\sigma_{\mathcal{J}_k}$ of σ with $\mathcal{J}_k \neq \mathcal{I}$. Concretely, this means that the adversary succeeds if it can produce a new redacted version of a signature, even if the signer has actually signed the messages $\{m_i\}_{i \in \mathcal{I}}$. In this paper, we will call this security notion "strong unforgeability" because it is reminiscent of the eponymous notion for standard digital signature schemes.

Although we will show that our unlinkable redactable signature scheme of Sect. 4.2 satisfies this strong property, we believe that it is too strong for many scenarios. For example our anonymous credentials construction only needs a weaker version, that we simply call "unforgeability", where new derivations of a signature are no longer considered as a forgery. Moreover, the strong unforgeability notion forbids some nice features, such as the ability to further redact a redacted signature. Finally, as we will show in Sect. 4.1, we can construct more efficient schemes if we only aim at achieving our unforgeability property.

We therefore think that it is relevant to consider this new notion that we define below. However, for completeness, we also recall the original one from [7].

Our security experiments in Fig. 1 make use of a counter c and three tables, Q_1, Q_2 and Q_3, along with the following oracles:

- $\mathcal{O}\mathtt{Sign}^*(\{m_i\}_{i=1}^n)$: on input a set of n messages, this oracle returns $\mathtt{Sign}(\mathsf{sk}, \{m_i\}_{i=1}^n)$, stores $Q_1[c] = (\sigma, \{m_i\}_{i=1}^n)$ and increments $c \leftarrow c + 1$.
- $\mathcal{O}\mathtt{Sign}(\{m_i\}_{i=1}^n)$: on input a set of n messages, this oracle computes $\sigma \leftarrow \mathtt{Sign}(\mathsf{sk}, \{m_i\}_{i=1}^n)$, stores $Q_1[c] = (\sigma, \{m_i\}_{i=1}^n)$ and increments $c \leftarrow c + 1$.
- $\mathcal{O}\mathtt{Derive}(k, \mathcal{I})$: on input an index k and a set $\mathcal{I}$, this algorithm returns $\perp$ if $Q_1[k] = \emptyset$ or if $\mathcal{I} \nsubseteq [1, n]$. Else, it uses σ and $\{m_i\}_{i=1}^n$ stored in $Q_1[k]$ to return $\mathtt{Derive}(\mathsf{pk}, \sigma, \{m_i\}_{i=1}^n, \mathcal{I})$. The set $\{m_i\}_{i \in \mathcal{I}}$ is then added to Q_2.
- $\mathcal{O}\mathtt{Reveal}(k)$: on input an index k, this algorithm returns $\perp$ if $Q_1[k] = \emptyset$ and $Q_1[k] = (\sigma, \{m_i\}_{i=1}^n)$ otherwise. The set $\{m_i\}_{i=1}^n$ is then added to Q_3.

We note that the only difference between $\mathcal{O}\mathtt{Sign}^*$ and $\mathcal{O}\mathtt{Sign}$ is that the former returns the signature, contrarily to the latter that does not return anything. Our unforgeability experiment only uses $\mathcal{O}\mathtt{Sign}^*$, which makes the $\mathcal{O}\mathtt{Reveal}$ and $\mathcal{O}\mathtt{Derive}$ oracles useless. For convenience, the set of messages $\{m_i\}_{i=1}^n$ stored in $Q_1[j]$ will be denoted $\{m_i^{(j)}\}_{i=1}^n$.

A redactable signature scheme is *unforgeable* if $\mathtt{Adv}^{uf}(\mathcal{A}) = |\Pr[\mathtt{Exp}_{\mathcal{A}}^{uf}(1^k, n) = 1]|$ is negligible for any polynomial time adversary $\mathcal{A}$. A redactable signature scheme is *strongly unforgeable* if $\mathtt{Adv}^{suf}(\mathcal{A}) = |\Pr[\mathtt{Exp}_{\mathcal{A}}^{suf}(1^k, n) = 1]|$ is negligible for any polynomial time adversary $\mathcal{A}$.

Unlinkability. Unlinkability states that it should be hard to link back a derived signature $\sigma_\mathcal{I}$ to its origin σ, unless the disclosed (non redacted) messages $\{m_i\}_{i \in \mathcal{I}}$ trivially allow to do so. In particular, this implies that $\sigma_\mathcal{I}$ does not leak any information on the redacted messages $\{m_i\}_{i \in \overline{\mathcal{I}}}$, even for an adversary that has generated the public key pk. This property is formally defined by the experiment $\mathtt{Exp}_{\mathcal{A}}^{unl-b}(1^k, n)$ of Fig. 1. A redactable signature scheme is unlinkable if $\mathtt{Adv}^{unl} = |\Pr[\mathtt{Exp}_{\mathcal{A}}^{unl-1}(1^k, n) = 1] - \Pr[\mathtt{Exp}_{\mathcal{A}}^{unl-0}(1^k, n) = 1]|$ is negligible for any polynomial time adversary $\mathcal{A}$.

4 Short Redactable Signatures

4.1 Our Construction

Our main building block to construct an unlinkable redactable signature or an anonymous credentials system will be the following redactable signature scheme

	Strong Unforgeability
Unforgeability	$\text{Exp}_{\mathcal{A}}^{suf}(1^k, n)$
$\text{Exp}_{\mathcal{A}}^{uf}(1^k, n)$	

Unforgeability

$\text{Exp}_{\mathcal{A}}^{uf}(1^k, n)$

1. $c \leftarrow 0; Q_1 \leftarrow \emptyset;$
2. $(\text{sk}, \text{pk}) \leftarrow \text{Keygen}(1^k, n)$
3. $(\sigma^*, \{m_i\}_{i \in \mathcal{I}}) \leftarrow \mathcal{A}^{\text{OSign}^*}(\text{pk})$
4. Return 1 if $\mathcal{I} \neq \emptyset$
   and $\text{Verify}(\text{pk}, \sigma^*, \{m_i\}_{i \in \mathcal{I}}) = 1$
   and $\forall j < c, \exists k_j \in \mathcal{I} : m_{k_j} \neq m_{k_j}^{(j)}$
5. Else, return 0

Strong Unforgeability

$\text{Exp}_{\mathcal{A}}^{suf}(1^k, n)$

1. $Q_1, Q_2, Q_3 \leftarrow \emptyset;$
2. $(\text{sk}, \text{pk}) \leftarrow \text{Keygen}(1^k, n)$
3. $(\sigma^*, \{m_i\}_{i \in \mathcal{I}}) \leftarrow \mathcal{A}^{\text{OSign}, \text{ODerive}, \text{OReveal}}(\text{pk})$
4. Return 1 if $\mathcal{I} \neq \emptyset$
   and $\text{Verify}(\text{pk}, \sigma^*, \{m_i\}_{i \in \mathcal{I}}) = 1$
   and $\{m_i\}_{i \in \mathcal{I}} \notin Q_2$
   and $\forall \{m_i'\}_{i=1}^n \in Q_3 :$
   $\quad \exists k_j \in \mathcal{I} : m_{k_j} \neq m_{k_j}'$
5. Else, return 0

Unlinkability

$\text{Exp}_{\mathcal{A}}^{unl-b}(1^k, n)$

1. $(\text{pk}, \mathcal{I}, \{m_i^{(0)}\}_{i=1}^n, \{m_i^{(1)}\}_{i=1}^n, \sigma^{(0)}, \sigma^{(1)}) \leftarrow \mathcal{A}()$
2. If $\text{Verify}(\text{pk}, \sigma^{(0)}, \{m_i^{(0)}\}_{i=1}^n) = 0$, return 0
3. If $\text{Verify}(\text{pk}, \sigma^{(1)}, \{m_i^{(1)}\}_{i=1}^n) = 0$, return 0
4. If $\exists j \in \mathcal{I} : m_j^{(0)} \neq m_j^{(1)}$, return 0
5. $\sigma_{\mathcal{I}}^{(b)} \leftarrow \text{Derive}(\text{pk}, \sigma^{(b)}, \{m_i^{(b)}\}_{i=1}^n, \mathcal{I})$
6. $b' \leftarrow \mathcal{A}(\sigma_{\mathcal{I}}^{(b)})$
7. Return b'.

Fig. 1. Security notions for redactable signatures

RS. The latter is unforgeable but it is clearly not unlinkable. We will explain in the next section how to enhance it to achieve this property. Nevertheless, we believe that this construction might be of independent interest due to its efficiency, for scenarios where privacy is not necessary.

Intuition. The signatures output by our Sign algorithm are PS signatures [21] on the messages $(m_1, ..., m_n)$. However, such signatures do not support partial verification, on a subset of $\{m_i\}_{i=1}^n$: all the signed messages must be disclosed, or one must prove knowledge of them, which in all cases imply to send at least n elements and to perform n exponentiations to verify the signature.

When considering the verification equation of PS signatures $e(X \prod_{i=1}^n Y_i^{m_i}, \tilde{\sigma}_1) = e(g, \tilde{\sigma}_2)$, it might be tempting to circumvent this problem by simply regrouping all the elements $\{Y_i^{m_i}\}_{i \in \bar{\mathcal{I}}}$ in $\sigma_1 = \prod_{i \in \bar{\mathcal{I}}} Y_i^{m_i}$. The verification equation would then become:

$$e(X \cdot \sigma_1 \prod_{i \in \mathcal{I}} Y_i^{m_i}, \tilde{\sigma}_1) = e(g, \tilde{\sigma}_2).$$

Unfortunately, the resulting scheme would clearly be insecure. Indeed, nothing prevents a dishonest user from hiding some parts of the disclosed messages in σ_1 to deceive the verifier. For example, if one receives a signature on $\{m_i\}_{i=1}^n$, one can set $\sigma_1 = Y_1^r \cdot \prod_{i=2}^n Y_i^{m_i}$ and then claims a signature on $m_1 - r$, for any $r \in \mathbb{Z}_p$. Indeed, in such a case

$$e(X \cdot \sigma_1 \cdot Y_1^{m_1-r}, \widetilde{\sigma}_1) = e(X \cdot Y_1^{m_1-r} \cdot Y_1^r \prod_{i=2}^r Y_i^{m_i}, \widetilde{\sigma}_1)$$

$$= e(g, \widetilde{\sigma}_2)$$

so the equation would be verified. The element σ_1 cannot therefore be any element of $\mathbb{G}_1$, it is necessary to prove that it only accumulates messages whose index is not in $\mathcal{I}$. The conceptually simplest solution, that is actually used in most anonymous credentials constructions, is to prove knowledge of the undisclosed messages. However, as we have explained, this leads to a cost at least linear in the size of $\overline{\mathcal{I}}$. We therefore use here a much more efficient solution, based on the following idea. If σ is a signature that has been honestly derived for $\mathcal{I}$, then the pairing $e(\sigma_1, \prod_{i \in \mathcal{I}} \widetilde{Y}_i)$ evaluates to $e(g, \widetilde{g})^{f(y_1,\dots,y_n)}$ for some polynomial f whose monomials are of the form $y_i \cdot y_j$, for $i \neq j$. Conversely, if one tries to hide some parts of the disclosed messages in σ_1, as in the attack we sketched above, then f now contains monomials of the form y_i^2, for some $i \in [1, n]$.

These two cases can easily be distinguished by adding the elements $Z_{i,j} = g^{y_i \cdot y_j}$ to the public key, for $i \neq j$. Indeed, these elements can trivially be used to reconstruct f in the former case, whereas they will not be sufficient in the latter case. Concretely, an honest user can compute $\sigma_2 \leftarrow \prod_{i \in \mathcal{I}, j \in \overline{\mathcal{I}}} Z_{i,j}^{m_j}$ and then prove that σ_1 is well formed with our second verification equation:

$$e(\sigma_1, \prod_{i \in \mathcal{I}} \widetilde{Y}_i) = e(\sigma_2, \widetilde{g})$$

Providing a similar element for an invalid σ_1 is equivalent to computing $g^{\sum_{j \in \mathcal{J}} y_j^2}$, for some $\mathcal{J} \subset [1, n]$, which is thought to be impossible in bilinear groups, given only the elements of the public key. A formal security analysis is provided in Sect. 4.3. We nevertheless recall that our redactable signature scheme RS is *not* strongly unforgeable. Such a property is achieved by our construction URS as a (positive) side effect of unlinkability.

The Scheme.

– Keygen($1^k, n$): on input a security parameter 1^k and an integer n, this algorithm generates $(g, \widetilde{g}) \xleftarrow{\$} \mathbb{G}_1^* \times \mathbb{G}_2^*$ along with $(n+1)$ random scalars $x, y_1, \dots, y_n \xleftarrow{\$} \mathbb{Z}_p$ and computes the following elements:
  - $X \leftarrow g^x$
  - $Y_i \leftarrow g^{y_i}, \forall 1 \leq i \leq n$
  - $\widetilde{Y}_i \leftarrow \widetilde{g}^{y_i}, \forall 1 \leq i \leq n$
  - $Z_{i,j} \leftarrow g^{y_i \cdot y_j}, \forall 1 \leq i \neq j \leq n$

  The secret key sk is then $(x, y_1, \dots, y_n)$ whereas the public key pk is $(X, \{(Y_i, \widetilde{Y}_i)\}_{1 \leq i \leq n}, \{Z_{i,j}\}_{1 \leq i \neq j \leq n})$.

- Sign(sk, $\{m_i\}_{i=1}^n$): To sign n messages $m_1, \ldots, m_n$, the signer selects a random element $\tilde{\sigma}_1 \xleftarrow{\$} \mathbb{G}_2$, computes $\tilde{\sigma}_2 \leftarrow \tilde{\sigma}_1^{x+\sum_{i=1}^n y_i \cdot m_i}$ and then outputs the signature $\sigma = (1_{\mathbb{G}_1}, 1_{\mathbb{G}_1}, \tilde{\sigma}_1, \tilde{\sigma}_2)$.
- Derive(pk, σ, $\{m_i\}_{i=1}^n$, $\mathcal{I}$): on input a signature $\sigma = (\sigma_1, \sigma_2, \tilde{\sigma}_1, \tilde{\sigma}_2)$ on $\{m_i\}_{i=1}^n$, the public key pk and a subset $\mathcal{I} \subset [1, n]$, this algorithm generates:
  - $\sigma_1' = \prod_{j \in \overline{\mathcal{I}}} Y_j^{m_j}$
  - $\sigma_2' = \prod_{i \in \mathcal{I}, j \in \overline{\mathcal{I}}} Z_{i,j}^{m_j} = \prod_{j \in \overline{\mathcal{I}}} (\prod_{i \in \mathcal{I}} Z_{i,j})^{m_j}$

  where $\overline{\mathcal{I}} = [1, n] \setminus \mathcal{I}$. If $\mathcal{I} = [1, n]$, then $\overline{\mathcal{I}} = \emptyset$ and $\sigma_1' = \sigma_2' = 1_{\mathbb{G}_1}$. In all cases, the signer returns the derived signature $\sigma_I = (\sigma_1', \sigma_2', \tilde{\sigma}_1, \tilde{\sigma}_2)$ on $\{m_i\}_{i \in \mathcal{I}}$.
- Verify(pk, σ, $\{m_i\}_{i \in \mathcal{I}}$): A signature $\sigma = (\sigma_1, \sigma_2, \tilde{\sigma}_1, \tilde{\sigma}_2) \in \mathbb{G}_1^2 \times (\mathbb{G}_2^*)^2$ is valid on a subset of messages $\{m_i\}_{i \in \mathcal{I}}$ if the following equalities hold, in which case the algorithm returns 1:
  1. $e(X \cdot \sigma_1 \prod_{i \in \mathcal{I}} Y_i^{m_i}, \tilde{\sigma}_1) = e(g, \tilde{\sigma}_2)$
  2. $e(\sigma_1, \prod_{i \in \mathcal{I}} \tilde{Y}_i) = e(\sigma_2, \tilde{g})$

  If (at least) one of these equations is not satisfied, then the algorithm returns 0.

Remark 2. We add $(1_{\mathbb{G}_1}, 1_{\mathbb{G}_1})$ to the signatures returned by Sign so that they have the same structure as derived signatures, produced by Derive. We note that, for such signatures, the second verification equation is trivially satisfied and does not require pairing computations: both pairings evaluate to $1_{\mathbb{G}_T}$.

We stress that any signature derived for a subset $\mathcal{I}$ can be verified without knowledge of the redacted messages (those whose indices are in $\overline{\mathcal{I}}$). Moreover, the computational cost for the verifier does not depend on the number of redacted messages, namely $|\overline{\mathcal{I}}|$.

Remark 3. One can note that $Z_{i,j} = Z_{j,i}$ for all $1 \leq i \neq j \leq n$. Therefore the public pk contains $1 + \frac{n(n+3)}{2}$ elements. Nevertheless, we note that verification does not require the knowledge of the elements $Z_{i,j}$ that are only useful to derive signatures. In practice, one could then define a verification key vk $= (X, \{(Y_i, \tilde{Y}_i)\}_{1 \leq i \leq n})$, containing only $1 + 2n$ elements, that is sufficient to verify any signature (derived or not).

4.2   Achieving Unlinkability

The redactable scheme RS described in Sect. 4.1 is unforgeable but it is not unlinkable. As in [21], we could try to rerandomize each element by raising it to some random power, but this would only work for the $(\tilde{\sigma}_1, \tilde{\sigma}_2)$ part of the signature. Rerandomizing similarly the other half of the signature seems to be much more complex and is likely to require more elements and more pairing equations to prove validity of the resulting signature.

We therefore use two tricks to achieve unlinkability. The first one is that we can add in σ_1 any element that is not of the form Y_i^r, for $i \in \mathcal{I}$ and some known scalar r. The second one is the ability of PS signatures to be sequentially aggregated. Concretely, we will aggregate a signature on a random message t under a dummy public key to the original signature and we will then include t in the set of redacted messages. Intuitively, the randomness of t will hide any information on the messages $m_i \in \overline{\mathcal{I}}$, thus ensuring unlinkability. Moreover, it remains easy to prove well-formedness of the resulting σ_1 due to the use of a dummy public key for which we know the corresponding secret key (in practice we will define the latter value as 1, but any other value would work). We thus get unlinkable signatures of the same size as previously and whose generation only requires few additional computations.

An Unlinkable Redactable Signature. The only differences between our unlinkable scheme URS and the one described in the previous section can be found in the Derive algorithm. Therefore, we here only describe this algorithm and refer to Sect. 4.1 for the description of the other algorithms that remain unchanged.

- Derive($\mathsf{pk}, \sigma, \{m_i\}_{i=1}^n, \mathcal{I}$): on input a signature $\sigma = (\widetilde{\sigma}_1, \widetilde{\sigma}_2)$ on $\{m_i\}_{i=1}^n$, the public key pk and a subset $\mathcal{I} \subset [1, n]$, this algorithm generates 2 random scalars $r, t \xleftarrow{\$} \mathbb{Z}_p$ and computes the following elements:
  - $\widetilde{\sigma}_1' \leftarrow \widetilde{\sigma}_1^r$
  - $\widetilde{\sigma}_2' \leftarrow \widetilde{\sigma}_2^r \cdot (\widetilde{\sigma}_1')^t$
  - $\sigma_1' \leftarrow g^t \prod_{j \in \overline{\mathcal{I}}} Y_j^{m_j}$
  - $\sigma_2' \leftarrow (\prod_{i \in \mathcal{I}} Y_i)^t \prod_{i \in \mathcal{I}, j \in \overline{\mathcal{I}}} Z_{i,j}^{m_j}$

  where $\overline{\mathcal{I}} = [1, n] \setminus \mathcal{I}$. If $\mathcal{I} = [1, n]$ then $\overline{\mathcal{I}} = \emptyset$ and $(\sigma_1', \sigma_2') = (g^t, \prod_{i=1}^n Y_i^t)$.

  In all cases, the signer returns the derived signature $\sigma_{\mathcal{I}} = (\sigma_1', \sigma_2', \widetilde{\sigma}_1', \widetilde{\sigma}_2')$ on $\{m_i\}_{i \in \mathcal{I}}$.

The resulting derived signature has exactly the same size and the same structure as in the previous scheme RS. In particular, it is worthy to note that the verification algorithm remains unchanged and so that an unlinkable signature is also a valid signature for RS. Alternatively, we can see the Derive algorithm of the previous section as a particular case of this one, where $r = 1$ and $t = 0$.

Regarding the computational cost, we note that generating an unlinkable signature essentially requires 5 additional exponentiations (2 in $\mathbb{G}_1$ and 3 in $\mathbb{G}_2$) compared to the scheme RS.

Correctness. Let $\sigma_{\mathcal{I}} = (\sigma_1, \sigma_2, \widetilde{\sigma}_1, \widetilde{\sigma}_2)$ be a derived signature on $\{m_i\}_{i \in \mathcal{I}}$ outputted by this new Derive algorithm. We then have:

$$e(X \cdot \sigma_1 \prod_{i \in \mathcal{I}} Y_i^{m_i}, \widetilde{\sigma}_1) = e(g^{t + x + \sum_{i=1}^n y_i \cdot m_i}, \widetilde{\sigma}_1)$$

$$= e(g, \widetilde{\sigma}_2)$$

and

$$e(\sigma_1, \prod_{i \in \mathcal{I}} \widetilde{Y}_i) = e(g^t \prod_{j \in \overline{\mathcal{I}}} Y_j^{m_j}, \prod_{i \in \mathcal{I}} \widetilde{Y}_i)$$

$$= e((\prod_{i \in \mathcal{I}} Y_i)^t (\prod_{j \in \overline{\mathcal{I}}} Y_j^{m_j})^{\sum_{i \in \mathcal{I}} y_i}, \widetilde{g})$$

$$= e((\prod_{i \in \mathcal{I}} Y_i)^t \prod_{i \in \mathcal{I}, j \in \overline{\mathcal{I}}} Z_{i,j}^{m_j}, \widetilde{g})$$

$$= e(\sigma_2, \widetilde{g})$$

which proves correctness of our scheme.

4.3   Security Analysis

The unforgeability of the scheme URS directly relies on the one of RS, proven in the generic group model. Proving strong unforgeability of URS requires to adapt the previous proof, which is done in the full version [22] of this paper. In all cases, we recall that we only consider type 3 pairings in this paper. Regarding unlinkability, we prove that the randomness added to our derived signatures perfectly hide the undisclosed messages and the original signatures. This is formally stated by the following theorem.

Theorem 4.   – RS *is an unforgeable redactable signature scheme in the generic group model.*
   – URS *is an unforgeable redactable signature scheme if* RS *is unforgeable.*
   – URS *is a strongly unforgeable redactable signature scheme in the generic group model.*
   – URS *is an unconditionally unlinkable redactable signature scheme.*

Proofs of Unforgeability. We proceed in two steps and first show the unforgeability of the scheme RS described in Sect. 4.1. We next extend this result to the unlinkable construction URS of Sect. 4.2.

Lemma 5. *In the generic group model, no adversary can break the unforgeability of the scheme* RS *with probability greater than* $3(4q_O + q_G + \frac{1+n(n+3)}{2})^2/2p$, *where* q_G *is a bound on the number of group oracle queries and* q_O *is a bound on the number of* $\mathcal{O}\mathtt{Sign}^*$ *queries.*

Proof. The adversary has access to the group elements provided in the public key $\mathsf{pk} = (X, \{(Y_i, \widetilde{Y}_i)\}_{1 \le i \le n}, \{Z_{i,j}\}_{1 \le i \ne j \le n})$ and those contained by the signatures $\sigma^{(i)}$ returned by the $\mathcal{O}\mathtt{Sign}^*$ oracle on $(m_{i,1}, \ldots, m_{i,n})$. In the following, each group element is associated with a polynomial whose formal variables are the scalars unknown to the adversary, namely $x, y_1, \ldots, y_n$ and r_i such that $\widetilde{\sigma}_{i,1} = \widetilde{g}^{r_i}$. We must first prove that the adversary is unable to symbolically produce a valid forgery $(\sigma_1, \sigma_2, \widetilde{\sigma}_1, \widetilde{\sigma}_2)$ for some subset of messages $\{m_i\}_{i \in \mathcal{I}}$.

In the generic group model, the only way for the adversary to generate new group elements is to use the group oracle queries. This means that there are known scalars $(a, b, \{c_i\}_{i=1}^n, \{d_{i,j}\}_{1 \leq i \neq j \leq n})$, $(a', b', \{c'_i\}_{i=1}^n, \{d'_{i,j}\}_{1 \leq i \neq j \leq n})$, $(\alpha, \{\beta_i\}_{i=1}^n, \{\gamma_i\}_{i=1}^{q_O}, \{\delta_i\}_{i=1}^{q_O})$ and $(\alpha', \{\beta'_i\}_{i=1}^n, \{\gamma'_i\}_{i=1}^{q_O}, \{\delta'_i\}_{i=1}^{q_O})$ such that:

$$\sigma_1 = g^a \cdot X^b \cdot \prod_{i=1}^n Y_i^{c_i} \cdot \prod_{1 \leq i \neq j \leq n} Z_{i,j}^{d_{i,j}}$$

$$\sigma_2 = g^{a'} \cdot X^{b'} \cdot \prod_{i=1}^n Y_i^{c'_i} \cdot \prod_{1 \leq i \neq j \leq n} Z_{i,j}^{d'_{i,j}}$$

$$\widetilde{\sigma}_1 = \widetilde{g}^\alpha \cdot \prod_{i=1}^n \widetilde{Y}_i^{\beta_i} \cdot \prod_{i=1}^{q_O} \widetilde{\sigma}_{i,1}^{\gamma_i} \cdot \prod_{i=1}^{q_O} \widetilde{\sigma}_{i,2}^{\delta_i}$$

$$\widetilde{\sigma}_2 = \widetilde{g}^{\alpha'} \cdot \prod_{i=1}^n \widetilde{Y}_i^{\beta'_i} \cdot \prod_{i=1}^{q_O} \widetilde{\sigma}_{i,1}^{\gamma'_i} \cdot \prod_{i=1}^{q_O} \widetilde{\sigma}_{i,2}^{\delta'_i}$$

We do not consider separately the elements $\sigma_{i,1}$ and $\sigma_{i,2}$ because they are public combinations of $\{Y_i\}_{i=1}^n$ and $\{Z_{i,j}\}_{1 \leq i \neq j \leq n}$.

Since $(\sigma_1, \sigma_2, \widetilde{\sigma}_1, \widetilde{\sigma}_2)$ is a valid signature on $\{m_i\}_{i \in \mathcal{I}}$, we know that:

1. $e(X \cdot \sigma_1 \prod_{i \in \mathcal{I}} Y_i^{m_i}, \widetilde{\sigma}_1) = e(g, \widetilde{\sigma}_2)$
2. $e(\sigma_1, \prod_{i \in \mathcal{I}} \widetilde{Y}_i) = e(\sigma_2, \widetilde{g})$

Moreover, $(\sigma_1, \sigma_2, \widetilde{\sigma}_1, \widetilde{\sigma}_2)$ is a valid forgery only if it cannot be trivially derived from the output of the $\mathcal{O}\mathtt{Sign}^*$ oracle. Concretely, this means that, for any $\ell \in [1, q_0]$, there is at least one index $k_\ell \in \mathcal{I}$ such that $m_{\ell, k_\ell} \neq m_{k_\ell}$.

Now, if we consider the second equation we get the following polynomial relation:

$$\left(a + b \cdot x + \sum_{i=1}^n c_i \cdot y_i + \sum_{1 \leq i \neq j \leq n} d_{i,j} \cdot y_i \cdot y_j\right) \sum_{i \in \mathcal{I}} y_i = a' + b' \cdot x + \sum_{i=1}^n c'_i \cdot y_i + \sum_{1 \leq i \neq j \leq n} d'_{i,j} \cdot y_i \cdot y_j$$

Since $\mathcal{I} \neq \emptyset$, for each monomial of the left member, there is at least an index $i \in [1, n]$ such that the monomial is a multiple of y_i. Therefore me must have $a' = b' = 0$. Moreover, if one of the coefficients $d_{i,j}$ were not zero, then the left member would be of degree 3 whereas the right one would be of degree 2. We can then conclude that $d_{i,j} = 0 \; \forall 1 \leq i \neq j \leq n$ and thus get:

$$\left(a + b \cdot x + \sum_{i=1}^n c_i \cdot y_i\right) \sum_{i \in \mathcal{I}} y_i = \sum_{i=1}^n c'_i \cdot y_i + \sum_{1 \leq i \neq j \leq n} d'_{i,j} \cdot y_i \cdot y_j$$

We can then note that there is no longer any term in x in the right member, which implies that $b = 0$. Moreover, there is no term in y_i^2 in the right member which means that $c_i = 0, \; \forall i \in \mathcal{I}$. We can therefore conclude that:

$$\sigma_1 = g^a \cdot \prod_{i \in \overline{\mathcal{I}}} Y_i^{c_i}$$

$$\sigma_2 = \prod_{i=1}^{n} Y_i^{c_i'} \cdot \prod_{1 \leq i \neq j \leq n} Z_{i,j}^{d_{i,j}'}$$

Now, let us consider the first equation, which gives the following polynomial relation:

$$(x + a + \sum_{i \in \overline{\mathcal{I}}} c_i \cdot y_i + \sum_{i \in \mathcal{I}} y_i \cdot m_i)(\sum_{i=1}^{q_O} \gamma_i \cdot r_i + \sum_{i=1}^{q_O} \delta_i \cdot r_i(x + \sum_{j=1}^{n} y_j \cdot m_{i,j}) +$$

$$\alpha + \sum_{i=1}^{n} \beta_i \cdot y_i) = \alpha' + \sum_{i=1}^{n} \beta_i' \cdot y_i + \sum_{i=1}^{q_O} \gamma_i' \cdot r_i + \sum_{i=1}^{q_O} \delta_i' \cdot r_i(x + \sum_{j=1}^{n} y_j \cdot m_{i,j})$$

On the left side, there is a unique monomial of the form $\delta_i \cdot r_i \cdot x^2$, $\forall i \in [1, n]$, whereas there is no term in x^2 on the right side. We can then conclude that $\delta_i = 0$, $\forall i \in [1, n]$:

$$(x + a + \sum_{i \in \overline{\mathcal{I}}} c_i \cdot y_i + \sum_{i \in \mathcal{I}} y_i \cdot m_i)(\sum_{i=1}^{q_O} \gamma_i \cdot r_i + \alpha + \sum_{i=1}^{n} \beta_i \cdot y_i)$$

$$= \alpha' + \sum_{i=1}^{n} \beta_i' \cdot y_i + \sum_{i=1}^{q_O} \gamma_i' \cdot r_i + \sum_{i=1}^{q_O} \delta_i' \cdot r_i(x + \sum_{j=1}^{n} y_j \cdot m_{i,j})$$

One can then note that, in the right member, all the monomials of degree 1 in x are also a multiple of some r_i. Therefore, we can conclude that $\alpha = 0$ and that $\beta_i = 0$, $\forall i \in [1, n]$. It then no longer remains any constant term in the left member, which implies that $\alpha' = 0$:

$$(x + a + \sum_{i \in \overline{\mathcal{I}}} c_i \cdot y_i + \sum_{i \in \mathcal{I}} y_i \cdot m_i)(\sum_{i=1}^{q_O} \gamma_i \cdot r_i)$$

$$= \sum_{i=1}^{n} \beta_i' \cdot y_i + \sum_{i=1}^{q_O} \gamma_i' \cdot r_i + \sum_{i=1}^{q_O} \delta_i' \cdot r_i(x + \sum_{j=1}^{n} y_j \cdot m_{i,j})$$

The factor $\sum_{i=1}^{q_O} \gamma_i \cdot r_i$ on the left side implies that all monomials are a multiple of some r_i. This means that $\beta_i' = 0$, $\forall i \in [1, n]$:

$$(x + a + \sum_{i \in \overline{\mathcal{I}}} c_i \cdot y_i + \sum_{i \in \mathcal{I}} y_i \cdot m_i)(\sum_{i=1}^{q_O} \gamma_i \cdot r_i) = \sum_{i=1}^{q_O} \gamma_i' \cdot r_i + \sum_{i=1}^{q_O} \delta_i' \cdot r_i(x + \sum_{j=1}^{n} y_j \cdot m_{i,j})$$

Now, if we consider this relation as an equality between polynomials in the variables r_i, we get, for each $\ell \in [1, q_O]$:

$$(x + a + \sum_{i \in \overline{\mathcal{I}}} c_i \cdot y_i + \sum_{i \in \mathcal{I}} y_i \cdot m_i)\gamma_\ell = \gamma_\ell' + \delta_\ell'(x + \sum_{j=1}^{n} y_j \cdot m_{i,j})$$

However, we know that, for any $\ell \in [1, q_0]$, there is at least one index $k_\ell \in \mathcal{I}$ such that $m_{\ell,k_\ell} \neq m_{k_\ell}$. This implies that $\delta'_\ell = \gamma_\ell = \gamma'_\ell = 0 \; \forall \ell \in [1, q_0]$, which is impossible. The adversary cannot therefore symbolically produce a valid forgery.

It remains to assess the probability of an accidental validity, when two different polynomials evaluate to the same value. All the polynomials considered in this proof are of degree at most 3. Since there are at most $(4q_O + q_G + \frac{1+n(n+3)}{2})$ polynomials, the probability of an accidental validity is bounded by $3(4q_O + q_G + \frac{1+n(n+3)}{2})^2 / 2p$ according to the Schwartz-Zippel lemma, which is negligible. $\square$

Our next lemma shows that the unforgeability of RS implies the one of our unlinkable scheme URS from Sect. 4.2.

Lemma 6. *Any adversary $\mathcal{A}$ against the unforgeability of our unlinkable scheme* URS *can be converted into an adversary against the unforgeability of* RS, *succeeding with the same probability.*

Proof. Our reduction $\mathcal{R}$ uses $\mathcal{A}$, an adversary against the unforgeability of URS, to break the unforgeability of RS. There will be then two unforgeability games. To avoid any confusion, we will refer to the unforgeability game of our basic scheme as the "RS game" and to the one of our unlinkable scheme as the "URS game".

$\mathcal{R}$ starts the RS game and then obtains a public key pk that it forwards to $\mathcal{A}$. When it receives a $\mathcal{O}$Sign* query, it simply forwards it to the corresponding oracle of the RS game and then receives a valid signature $\sigma = (\sigma_1, \sigma_2, \widetilde{\sigma}_1, \widetilde{\sigma}_2)$ for RS. It then selects two random scalars r and t and computes:

- $\sigma'_1 = \sigma_1 \cdot g^t$;
- $\sigma'_2 = \sigma_2 \cdot (\prod_{i \in \mathcal{I}} Y_i)^t$;
- $\widetilde{\sigma}'_1 = \widetilde{\sigma}_1^r$;
- $\widetilde{\sigma}'_2 = \widetilde{\sigma}_2^r \cdot (\widetilde{\sigma}'_1)^t$.

Finally, it returns $\sigma = (\sigma'_1, \sigma'_2, \widetilde{\sigma}'_1, \widetilde{\sigma}'_2)$ to the adversary $\mathcal{A}$.

The fact that $\mathcal{R}$ forwards each query to the oracles of the RS game implies that the sets of messages stored in Q_1 are exactly the same for both games. Since the oracle of the URS game is perfectly simulated, the adversary eventually outputs a forgery which is a valid derived signature σ^* for URS. Since RS and URS have the same verification algorithm, σ^* is also a valid signature for RS. Moreover, our previous remark on Q_1 means that σ^* is also a valid forgery for the RS game. $\mathcal{R}$ then never fails when $\mathcal{A}$ succeeds, which concludes the proof.

Proof of Unlinkability. We prove here that a signature $\sigma_{\mathcal{I}}$ on $\{m_i\}_{i \in \mathcal{I}}$ derived from an original signature σ on $\{m_i\}_{i=1}^n$ is distributed independently of σ and $\{m_i\}_{i \in \overline{\mathcal{I}}}$. Since the messages output by the adversary in the unlinkability game satisfy $m_i^{(0)} = m_i^{(1)}$, $\forall i \in \mathcal{I}$, this means that the advantage of the adversary can only be negligible in this game.

Concretely, let $\widetilde{\tau}$ be a random element of $\mathbb{G}_2$ and u be a random scalar. For a signature $\sigma = (\sigma_1, \sigma_2, \widetilde{\sigma}_1, \widetilde{\sigma}_2)$ on $\{m_i\}_{i=1}^n$ and any subset $\mathcal{I} \subset [1, n]$, we define $t = u - \sum_{i \in \overline{\mathcal{I}}} y_i \cdot m_i$ and $r = \frac{v}{s}$, where v and s are such that $\widetilde{\tau} = \widetilde{g}^v$ and $\widetilde{\sigma}_1 = \widetilde{g}^s$. Since u and $\widetilde{\tau}$ are random, r and t are also random and so are distributed as specified in the Derive algorithm. Running the latter algorithm on $(\sigma, \{m_i\}_{i=1}^n, \mathcal{I})$ with these values would then lead to the derived signature $\sigma_I = (\sigma_1', \sigma_2', \widetilde{\sigma}_1', \widetilde{\sigma}_2')$ with:

- $\widetilde{\sigma}_1' = \widetilde{\sigma}_1^r = \widetilde{\tau}$
- $\widetilde{\sigma}_2' = \widetilde{\sigma}_2^r \cdot (\widetilde{\sigma}_1')^t = \widetilde{\tau}^{x + \sum_{i \in \mathcal{I}} y_i \cdot m_i} \cdot \widetilde{\tau}^u$
- $\sigma_1' = g^t \prod_{j \in \overline{\mathcal{I}}} Y_j^{m_j} = g^u$
- $\sigma_2' = (\prod_{i \in \mathcal{I}} Y_i)^t \prod_{i \in \mathcal{I}, j \in \overline{\mathcal{I}}} Z_{i,j}^{m_j} = g^{u \cdot \sum_{i \in \mathcal{I}} y_i}$

Since u and $\widetilde{\tau}$ are random, the derived signature σ_I is clearly independent of the original signature and of the messages $\{m_i\}_{i \in \overline{\mathcal{I}}}$, which concludes the proof.

5   Anonymous Credentials

Anonymous credential (also called attribute-based credential) is a broad notion that usually encompasses any system that allows some organization to issue a credential on users' attributes such that (1) the users can later prove that their attributes are certified and (2) the elements revealed by the users when they *show* their credential cannot be linked to a specific issuance (unless the revealed attributes trivially allow to do so).

However, there is no unique, commonly accepted definition of anonymous credentials, but rather several variants of the same intuitive notion. For example, some definitions [5,14] assume that the credential are only shown once, whereas others support multiple (and unlinkable) showing of a credential [10,15,21]. We follow in this section the definition from [15] that consider multiple, interactive showings.

5.1   Syntax

An anonymous credentials system is defined by the following algorithms.

- OrgKeygen($1^k, n$): This algorithm takes as input a security parameter 1^k and an integer n defining a bound on the number of attributes to certify and returns the organization key pair (sk, pk).
- UserKeygen(pk): This algorithm returns a user's key pair (usk, upk) from the organization public key pk.
- (Obtain(usk, pk, $\{m_i\}_{i=1}^n$), Issue(upk, sk, $\{m_i\}_{i=1}^n$)): To obtain an anonymous credential on a set of attributes $\{m_i\}_{i=1}^n$, the user, running Obtain, interacts with the organization, running Issue. The former algorithm additionally requires the user's secret key usk and the organization public key pk whereas the latter requires upk and sk. At the end of the protocol, Obtain returns either a credential σ or $\perp$.

– $(\texttt{Show}(\mathsf{pk}, \mathsf{usk}, \{m_i\}_{i=1}^n, \mathcal{I}, \sigma), \texttt{Verify}(\mathsf{pk}, \{m_i\}_{i\in\mathcal{I}}))$: These algorithms are run by a user and a verifier, respectively, who interact during execution. $\texttt{Show}$ enables the user to prove that a subset $\{m_i\}_{i\in\mathcal{I}}$ of his attributes, with $\mathcal{I} \subset [1, n]$, has been certified. It takes as input the credential σ, the organization public key pk, the whole set of attributes $\{m_i\}_{i=1}^n$ along with the intended subset $\mathcal{I}$. The $\texttt{Verify}$ algorithm only takes as input pk and the subset $\{m_i\}_{i\in\mathcal{I}}$ and returns either 1 (accept) or 0 (reject).

5.2 Security Model

The security model considered here is the one from [15], that we slightly modify to harmonize this section with the one on redactable signature (Sect. 3).

Besides correctness, an anonymous credentials system must achieve *unforgeability* and *anonymity* that essentially mirror the unforgeability and unlinkability notions for redactable signatures. As in Sect. 3, we define these properties by the experiments described in Fig. 2 that use the following oracles along with two sets: HU, the set containing the identities of *honest* users and CU, that contains the ones of *corrupt* users. We additionally define the set Att that stores $\{i, \{m_j\}_{j=1}^n\}$ each time a credential is generated for user i on $\{m_j\}_{j=1}^n$ by the oracles $\mathcal{O}\texttt{ObtIss}$ and $\mathcal{O}\texttt{Issue}$ below. We say that $\{i, \{m_j\}_{j\in\mathcal{I}}\} \subset$ Att if $\exists \{i, \{m'_j\}_{j=1}^n\} \in$ Att with $m'_j = m_j$ for all $j \in \mathcal{I}$.

– $\mathcal{O}\texttt{HU}(i)$: on input an identity i, this oracle returns $\perp$ if $i \in$ HU $\cup$ CU. Else it generates a key pair $(\mathsf{usk}_i, \mathsf{upk}_i) \leftarrow \texttt{UserKeygen}(\mathsf{pk})$ and returns upk_i. The identity i is then added to HU.
– $\mathcal{O}\texttt{CU}(i, \mathsf{upk})$: on input an identity i and optionally a public key upk, this oracle registers a new corrupt user with public key upk if $i \notin$ HU and returns usk_i and all the associated credentials otherwise. In the latter case, i is removed from HU. In all cases, i is added to CU.
– $\mathcal{O}\texttt{ObtIss}(i, \{m_j\}_{j=1}^n)$: on input an identity $i \in$ HU and a set of attributes $\{m_j\}_{j=1}^n$, this oracle runs $(\texttt{Obtain}(\mathsf{usk}_i, \mathsf{pk}, \{m_j\}_{j=1}^n), \texttt{Issue}(\mathsf{upk}_i, \mathsf{sk}, \{m_j\}_{j=1}^n)$ and stores the resulting output. The elements $\{i, \{m_j\}_{j=1}^n\}$ are then added to Att. If $i \notin$ HU, the oracle returns $\perp$.
– $\mathcal{O}\texttt{Obtain}(i, \{m_j\}_{j=1}^n)$: on input an identity $i \in$ HU and a set of attributes $\{m_j\}_{j=1}^n$, this oracle runs $\texttt{Obtain}(\mathsf{usk}_i, \mathsf{pk}, \{m_j\}_{j=1}^n)$ and stores the resulting output. If $i \notin$ HU, the oracle returns $\perp$. This oracle is used by an adversary impersonating the organization to issue a credential to an honest user.
– $\mathcal{O}\texttt{Issue}(i, \{m_j\}_{j=1}^n)$: on input an identity $i \in$ CU and a set of attributes $\{m_j\}_{j=1}^n$, this oracle runs $\texttt{Issue}(\mathsf{upk}_i, \mathsf{sk}, \{m_j\}_{j=1}^n)$. The elements $\{i, \{m_j\}_{j=1}^n\}$ are then added to Att. If $i \notin$ CU, the oracle returns $\perp$. This oracle is used by an adversary playing a malicious user to get a certificate from an honest organization.
– $\mathcal{O}\texttt{Show}(k, \mathcal{I})$: Let $\sigma^{(k)}$ be the credential issued on $\{m_j^{(k)}\}_{j=1}^n$ for a user i_k during the k-th query to $\mathcal{O}\texttt{ObtIss}$ or $\mathcal{O}\texttt{Obtain}$. If $i_k \notin$ HU, this oracle returns $\perp$. Else, this oracle runs $\texttt{Show}(\mathsf{pk}, \mathsf{usk}_{i_k}, \{m_j^{(k)}\}_{j=1}^n, \mathcal{I}, \sigma^{(k)})$ with the adversary playing a malicious verifier.

Unforgeability
$\text{Exp}_{\mathcal{A}}^{uf}(1^k, n)$

1. $(\mathsf{sk}, \mathsf{pk}) \leftarrow \mathsf{Keygen}(1^k, n)$
2. $\{m_j\}_{j \in \mathcal{I}} \leftarrow \mathcal{A}^{\mathcal{O}\text{HU}, \mathcal{O}\text{CU}, \mathcal{O}\text{ObtIss}, \mathcal{O}\text{Issue}, \mathcal{O}\text{Show}}(\mathsf{pk})$
3. $b \leftarrow (\mathcal{A}(), \mathsf{Verify}(\mathsf{pk}, \{m_j\}_{j \in \mathcal{I}}))$
4. If $\{i, \{m_j\}_{j \in \mathcal{I}}\} \subset \mathsf{Att}$ with $i \in \mathsf{CU}$ or if $b = 0$, return 0
5. Return 1.

Anonymity
$\text{Exp}_{\mathcal{A}}^{ano-b}(1^k, n)$

1. $(\mathsf{sk}, \mathsf{pk}) \leftarrow \mathsf{Keygen}(1^k, n)$
2. $(j_0, j_1, \{m_i\}_{i \in \mathcal{I}}) \leftarrow \mathcal{A}^{\mathcal{O}\text{HU}, \mathcal{O}\text{CU}, \mathcal{O}\text{Obtain}, \mathcal{O}\text{Show}}(\mathsf{sk})$
3. If $\{j_{b'}, \{m_i\}_{i \in \mathcal{I}}\} \not\subset \mathsf{Att}$ for $b' \in \{0, 1\}$, return 0
4. $(\mathsf{Show}(\mathsf{pk}, \mathsf{usk}_{j_b}, \{m_i^{(j_b)}\}_{j=1}^n, \mathcal{I}, \sigma^{(k)}), \mathcal{A}())$
5. $b^* \leftarrow \mathcal{A}^{\mathcal{O}\text{HU}, \mathcal{O}\text{CU}, \mathcal{O}\text{Obtain}, \mathcal{O}\text{Show}}(\mathsf{sk})$
6. If $\mathcal{O}\text{CU}$ has been queried on $j_{b'}$ for $b' \in \{0, 1\}$, return 0
7. Return b^*.

Fig. 2. Security notions for anonymous credentials

Correctness. A showing of a credential σ with respect to a set $\{m_i\}_{i \in \mathcal{I}}$ always verify if σ was honestly issued on $\{m_i\}_{i=1}^n$, with $\mathcal{I} \in [1, n]$.

Unforgeability. A credential system is *unforgeable* if $\text{Adv}^{uf}(\mathcal{A}) = |\Pr[\text{Exp}_{\mathcal{A}}^{uf}(1^k, n) = 1]|$ is negligible for any polynomial time adversary $\mathcal{A}$.

Anonymity. The anonymity property is defined by the $\text{Exp}_{\mathcal{A}}^{ano-b}$ experiment in Fig. 2, for $b \in \{0, 1\}$. A credential system is *anonymous* if $\text{Adv}^{ano} = |\Pr[\text{Exp}_{\mathcal{A}}^{ano-1}(1^k, n) = 1] - \Pr[\text{Exp}_{\mathcal{A}}^{ano-0}(1^k, n) = 1]|$ is negligible for any polynomial time adversary $\mathcal{A}$.

Our definition assumes that the organization key pair $(\mathsf{sk}, \mathsf{pk})$ is honestly generated and then sent to the adversary, contrarily to [15] that lets the adversary generates its own key pair. This modification indeed allows us to reduce the size of the public key pk in our next construction. Nevertheless, we stress that the latter can satisfy the original definition from [15] if we add a non-interactive zero-knowledge proof of knowledge of sk in pk.

6   Our Anonymous Credentials System

As noticed in [7,15], an unlinkable redactable signature scheme is very similar to an anonymous credentials system [8], also called attribute-based credentials system. Indeed, it can be used to prove that some data have been certified without being traced, while hiding (redacting) all the other signed data. To achieve all the properties expected from an anonymous credentials system, it thus essentially lacks the ability to issue credentials on the user's secret key and then to present the credentials with respect to this key.

In this paper we use the definition of anonymous credentials provided in [15] and thus consider an interactive presentation protocol. However, the latter can easily be made non interactive by using the Fiat-Shamir heuristic [13] on the proof of knowledge that it contains.

6.1 Our Construction

In our system, the user's secret key usk is simply a random scalar that defines the public key upk as $\widetilde{g}^{\mathsf{usk}}$. Using the protocols described in [21], that we slightly modify, the user is able to get a redactable signature σ on usk and a set of attributes $\{m_i\}_{i=1}^n$ without revealing usk. Such a signature σ then acts as a credential for this user. To show a credential on some attributes $\{m_i\}_{i \in \mathcal{I}}$, the user essentially runs the Derive algorithm on σ and $\{\mathsf{usk}\} \cup \{m_i\}_{i \in \mathcal{I}}$ and then prove knowledge of usk.

Our construction can thus be seen as an interactive version of our URS scheme supporting proofs of knowledge of secret attributes. However, such modifications make the security proofs more intricate. In particular, anonymity no longer holds unconditionally, but under the DDH assumption in $\mathbb{G}_2$. Intuitively, this is due to the fact that usk must be kept secret but cannot either be aggregated to the set of undisclosed messages. Therefore, the distribution of derived signatures can no longer be made independent of usk and thus we cannot rely on the same arguments as those used in the security proof of Sect. 4.3.

- OrgKeygen($1^k, n$): On input a security parameter 1^k and an integer n, this algorithm generates $(n + 2)$ random scalars $x, y_0, y_1, \ldots, y_n \xleftarrow{\$} \mathbb{Z}_p$ and computes the following elements:
  - $X \leftarrow g^x$
  - $Y_i \leftarrow g^{y_i}$, $\forall 0 \le i \le n$
  - $\widetilde{Y}_i \leftarrow \widetilde{g}^{y_i}$, $\forall 0 \le i \le n$
  - $Z_{i,j} \leftarrow g^{y_i \cdot y_j}$, $\forall 0 \le i \ne j \le n$

  The secret key sk is then $(x, y_0, y_1, \ldots, y_n)$ whereas the public key pk is $(X, \{(Y_i, \widetilde{Y}_i)\}_{0 \le i \le n}, \{Z_{i,j}\}_{0 \le i \ne j \le n})$
- UserKeygen(pk): To generate a key pair (usk, upk) for a user, this algorithm selects a random usk $\xleftarrow{\$} \mathbb{Z}_p$ and computes upk $\leftarrow \widetilde{g}^{\mathsf{usk}}$.
- (Obtain(usk, pk, $\{m_i\}_{i=1}^n$), Issue(upk, sk, $\{m_i\}_{i=1}^n$)): To obtain an anonymous credential on a set of attributes $\{m_i\}_{i=1}^n$, the user first sends her public key upk along with a proof of knowledge of usk, using for example the Schnorr's protocol [23]. If the proof is correct, then the organization selects a random $r \xleftarrow{\$} \mathbb{Z}_p$ and returns $\sigma = (\widetilde{\sigma}_1, \widetilde{\sigma}_2) \leftarrow (\widetilde{g}^r, \mathsf{upk}^{r \cdot y_0} \cdot \widetilde{g}^{r(x + \sum_{i=1}^n y_i \cdot m_i)})$ to the user.
- (Show(pk, usk, $\{m_i\}_{i=1}^n, \mathcal{I}, \sigma$), Verify(pk, $\{m_i\}_{i \in \mathcal{I}}$)): For $\mathcal{I} \subset [1, n]$, we define $\mathcal{I}_0 = \{0\} \cup \mathcal{I}$. The protocol to show a credential on a subset $\{m_i\}_{i \in \mathcal{I}}$ is described in Fig. 3.

User($\mathsf{pk}, \mathsf{usk}, \{m_i\}_{i=1}^n, \mathcal{I}, \sigma$)	Verifier($\mathsf{pk}, \{m_i\}_{i\in\mathcal{I}}$)

$k, r, t \xleftarrow{\$} \mathbb{Z}_p$

$\sigma_1' \leftarrow g^t \cdot \prod_{j\in[1,n]\setminus\mathcal{I}} Y_j^{m_j}$

$\sigma_2' \leftarrow (\prod_{i\in\mathcal{I}_0} Y_i)^t \cdot \prod_{i\in\mathcal{I}_0, j\in[1,n]\setminus\mathcal{I}} Z_{i,j}^{m_j}$

$\tilde{\sigma}_1' \leftarrow \tilde{\sigma}_1^r$

$\tilde{\sigma}_2' \leftarrow \tilde{\sigma}_2^r \cdot (\tilde{\sigma}_1')^t$

$C \leftarrow e(Y_0^k, \tilde{\sigma}_1')$

$$\xrightarrow{(\sigma_1', \sigma_2', \tilde{\sigma}_1', \tilde{\sigma}_2'), C}$$

If $(\tilde{\sigma}_1', \tilde{\sigma}_2') \notin (\mathbb{G}_2^*)^2$, return 0.

Else, $c \xleftarrow{\$} \mathbb{Z}_p$

$$\xleftarrow{c}$$

$B = e(X \cdot \sigma_1' \prod_{i\in\mathcal{I}} Y_i^{m_i}, (\tilde{\sigma}_1')^{-1})$

$$\xrightarrow{s}$$

$s = k + c \cdot \mathsf{usk}$

If $e(Y_0^s, \tilde{\sigma}_1') \cdot C^{-1} = [B \cdot e(g, \tilde{\sigma}_2')]^c$

and $e(\sigma_1', \prod_{i\in\mathcal{I}_0} \tilde{Y}_i) = e(\sigma_2', \tilde{g})$

return 1

Else, return 0

Fig. 3. A protocol to show a credential σ on a subset $\{m_i\}_{i\in\mathcal{I}}$

Correctness. For a valid credential σ issued on $(m_1, \ldots, m_n)$ and usk, we have:

$$e(X \cdot Y_0^{\mathsf{usk}} \cdot \prod_{i=1}^n Y_i^{m_i}, \tilde{\sigma}_1) = e(g, \tilde{\sigma}_2)$$

which is equivalent to:

$$e(Y_0^{\mathsf{usk}}, \tilde{\sigma}_1) = e(g, \tilde{\sigma}_2) \cdot e(X \cdot \prod_{i=1}^n Y_i^{m_i}, \tilde{\sigma}_1)^{-1}$$

Therefore:

$$e(Y_0^s, \tilde{\sigma}_1') \cdot C^{-1} = e(Y_0^{\mathsf{usk}}, \tilde{\sigma}_1')^{r\cdot c}$$

$$= [e(g, \tilde{\sigma}_2) \cdot e(X \cdot \prod_{i=1}^n Y_i^{m_i}, \tilde{\sigma}_1)^{-1}]^{r\cdot c}$$

$$= [e(g, \tilde{\sigma}_2') \cdot e(g, \tilde{\sigma}_1')^{-t} \cdot e(X \cdot \prod_{i=1}^n Y_i^{m_i}, (\tilde{\sigma}_1')^{-1})]^c$$

$$= [e(g, \tilde{\sigma}_2') \cdot e(X \cdot g^t \cdot \prod_{i\in\mathcal{I}} Y_i^{m_i} \cdot \prod_{i\in[1,n]\setminus\mathcal{I}} Y_i^{m_i}, (\tilde{\sigma}_1')^{-1})]^c$$

$$= [e(g, \tilde{\sigma}_2') \cdot e(X \cdot \sigma_1' \cdot \prod_{i\in\mathcal{I}} Y_i^{m_i}, (\tilde{\sigma}_1')^{-1})]^c$$

$$= [e(g, \tilde{\sigma}_2') \cdot B]^c$$

and

$$e(\sigma_1', \prod_{i \in \mathcal{I}_0} \widetilde{Y}_i) = e(\prod_{j \in [1,n] \setminus \mathcal{I}} Y_j^{m_j}, \prod_{i \in \mathcal{I}_0} \widetilde{Y}_i) \cdot e(g^t, \prod_{i \in \mathcal{I}_0} \widetilde{Y}_i)$$

$$= e((\prod_{j \in [1,n] \setminus \mathcal{I}} Y_j^{m_j})^{\sum_{i \in \mathcal{I}_0} y_i}, \widetilde{g}) \cdot e((\prod_{i \in \mathcal{I}_0} Y_i)^t, \widetilde{g})$$

$$= e(\sigma_2', \widetilde{g})$$

which implies correctness of our protocol.

Proving Knowledge of Attributes. As we have explained, our Show protocol essentially consists in deriving a signature on usk $\cup \{m_i\}_{i \in \mathcal{I}}$ and then proving knowledge of usk. The latter proof is very easy to produce using Schnorr's protocol because usk is an exponent in the verification equation. We note that this is also true for every attribute m_i such that $i \in \mathcal{I}$. Therefore, the protocol of Fig. 3 can easily be extended to hide and prove knowledge of the attributes $\{m_j\}_{j \in \mathcal{J}}$, for any subset $\mathcal{J} \subset \mathcal{I}$.

6.2   Security Analysis

The structure of our Show protocol makes the unforgeability proof rather straightforward: if an adversary is able to prove possession of a credential on a set of attributes that it does not own, then it is able to produce a valid forgery for our URS system or to impersonate an honest user. Since our protocol requires that the users prove knowledge of their secret key, the latter case implies an attack against the discrete logarithm. Proving anonymity of our credential system is more subtle as we cannot simply rely on the unlinkability of URS.

Theorem 7. – *Our credential system is unforgeable if* URS *is unforgeable and if the* DL *assumption holds in* $\mathbb{G}_2$.
– *Our credential system is anonymous under the* DDH *assumption in* $\mathbb{G}_2$.

Proof of Unforgeability. Let $\mathcal{A}$ be an adversary against the unforgeability of our anonymous credentials system. During the game, $\mathcal{A}$ returns a set of attributes $\{m_i\}_{i \in \mathcal{I}}$ and then proves possession of a credential on this set. Obviously, the credentials issued by oracles to corrupt users cannot be valid on $\{m_i\}_{i \in \mathcal{I}}$. However, honest users could possess a credential on such attributes, which leads to consider two different cases in our proof. Let usk be the secret key whose knowledge is proved by the adversary when it shows the credential on $\{m_i\}_{i \in \mathcal{I}}$, we distinguish two types of adversary:

– Type 1: $\exists i \in$ HU such that $\text{usk}_i = \text{usk}$
– Type 2: $\forall i \in$ HU, $\text{usk}_i \neq \text{usk}$.

Lemma 8. *Any type 1 adversary $\mathcal{A}$ succeeding with probability ϵ can be converted into an adversary against the discrete logarithm assumption in $\mathbb{G}_2$ succeeding with probability $\frac{\epsilon}{q}$, where q is a bound on the number of honest users.*

Proof. Let $(\widetilde{g}, \widetilde{g}^a)$ be a DL challenge. Our reduction $\mathcal{R}$ generates the organisation key pair using $\widetilde{g}$ as the generator for $\mathbb{G}_2$ and returns pk to $\mathcal{A}$. Since we consider a type 1 adversary, we know that there is an index i such that $\mathcal{A}$ will try to impersonate the i-th honest user. Our reduction $\mathcal{R}$ then makes a guess on $i \in [1, q]$ and proceeds as follows.

- $\mathcal{O}$HU: Let j be the index query to this oracle. If $j \neq i$, then $\mathcal{R}$ proceeds as usual. Else, it returns $\mathsf{upk}_i = \widetilde{g}^a$.
- $\mathcal{O}$CU: If $\mathcal{R}$ receives a corruption query on an honest user j, it returns usk_j if $j \neq i$ and aborts otherwise.
- $\mathcal{O}$ObtIss: $\mathcal{R}$ knows the organization secret sk and so perfectly simulates the organization's side of this protocol. It can also play the role of any honest user j if $j \neq i$. Else, it simulates the proof of knowledge of usk_i.
- $\mathcal{O}$Issue: $\mathcal{R}$ knows sk and so is perfectly able to answer any query.
- $\mathcal{O}$Show: If the queried credential belongs to $j \neq i$, then $\mathcal{R}$ is able to run the Show protocol defined in Fig. 3. Else, it runs the first steps of the protocols but simulates the knowledge of usk_i.

One can note that the game is perfectly simulated if the guess on i is correct, which occurs with probability $\frac{1}{q}$. In such a case, a successful adversary $\mathcal{A}$ proves knowledge of $\mathsf{usk}_i = a$ when it shows its credential. $\mathcal{R}$ can then run the extractor of the proof of knowledge to recover a, that it returns as a valid solution to the DL problem. The probability of success of $\mathcal{R}$ is then $\frac{\epsilon}{q}$. □

Lemma 9. *Any type 2 adversary $\mathcal{A}$ can be converted into an adversary against the unforgeability of the URS scheme succeeding with the same probability.*

Proof. Our reduction $\mathcal{R}$ runs the unforgeability game of the URS scheme for the parameter $n + 1$ and so receives a public key $(X, \{(Y_i, \widetilde{Y}_i)\}_{1 \leq i \leq n+1}, \{Z_{i,j}\}_{1 \leq i \neq j \leq n+1})$. $\mathcal{R}$ changes the indices of the elements of the public key, starting from 0 instead of 1, and then returns $\mathsf{pk} = (X, \{(Y_i, \widetilde{Y}_i)\}_{0 \leq i \leq n}, \{Z_{i,j}\}_{0 \leq i \neq j \leq n})$ to $\mathcal{A}$. It can then answers oracle queries as follows.

- $\mathcal{O}$HU: $\mathcal{R}$ proceeds as usual, and stores the corresponding secret key.
- $\mathcal{O}$CU: Here again, $\mathcal{R}$ proceeds as usual.
- $\mathcal{O}$ObtIss: Let $i \in$ HU and $\{m_i\}_{i=1}^n$ be the input of this oracle. The reduction recovers the secret key usk_i that it has generated for user i and then submits $(\mathsf{usk}_i, m_1, \ldots, m_n)$ to the signing oracle $\mathcal{O}$Sign*. It then receives a URS signature $(\sigma_1, \sigma_2, \widetilde{\sigma}_1, \widetilde{\sigma}_2)$ whose first two elements are $1_{\mathbb{G}_1}$. $\mathcal{R}$ then discards σ_1 and σ_2 and stores the resulting credential $(\widetilde{\sigma}_1, \widetilde{\sigma}_2)$.
- $\mathcal{O}$Issue: Let $i \in$ CU and $\{m_i\}_{i=1}^n$ be the input of this oracle. $\mathcal{R}$ extracts usk_i from the proof of knowledge produced by $\mathcal{A}$ and then proceeds as previously to get a URS signature on $(\mathsf{usk}_i, m_1, \ldots, m_n)$. Here again, the new credential is defined as $(\widetilde{\sigma}_1, \widetilde{\sigma}_2)$.

– $\mathcal{O}$Show: Let i and $\{m_i\}_{i\in\mathcal{I}}$ be the inputs of this oracle. A show query can only be made for a credential that has been issued through the $\mathcal{O}$ObtIss oracle. Since the latter oracle uses the $\mathcal{O}$Sign* oracle of the unforgeability game of the URS scheme, there is a corresponding signature σ on $(\text{usk}_i, m_1, \ldots, m_n)$ in the table Q_1. $\mathcal{R}$ can then run the Derive algorithm on σ and $\{\text{usk}_i\}\cup\{m_i\}_{i\in\mathcal{I}}$ and gets $(\sigma'_1, \sigma'_2, \tilde{\sigma}'_1, \tilde{\sigma}'_2)$ such that:

- $\tilde{\sigma}'_2 = (\tilde{\sigma}'_1)^{t+x+y_0\cdot\text{usk}_i+\sum_{i=1}^n y_i\cdot m_i}$
- $\sigma'_1 \leftarrow g^t \cdot \prod_{j\in[1,n]\backslash\mathcal{I}} Y_j^{m_j}$
- $\sigma'_2 \leftarrow (\prod_{i\in\mathcal{I}_0} Y_i)^t \cdot \prod_{i\in\mathcal{I}_0, j\in[1,n]\backslash\mathcal{I}} Z_{i,j}^{m_j}$

The elements σ'_1, σ'_2, $\tilde{\sigma}'_1$ and $\tilde{\sigma}'_2$ are therefore distributed as in the Show protocol of Fig. 3. It then only remains to compute $C = e(Y_0^k, \tilde{\sigma}'_1)$ for some random k and to return a valid s using usk_i.

$\mathcal{R}$ can handle any oracle query and never aborts. Therefore, at the end of the game, $\mathcal{A}$ is able, with some probability ϵ, to prove possession of a credential on $\{m_i\}_{i\in\mathcal{I}}$. Our reduction extracts from the proof of knowledge contained in the Show protocol the value usk and stores the elements σ'_1, σ'_2, $\tilde{\sigma}'_1$ and $\tilde{\sigma}'_2$. The latter constitute a valid derived signature on $\{\text{usk}\}\cup\{m_i\}_{i\in\mathcal{I}}$.

Since we here consider a type 2 adversary, usk must be different from usk_i, for any honest user i. Moreover, to be considered as an attack against unforgeability, no credential owned by corrupt users can be valid on this set of messages. This means that, for any credential on $(\text{usk}_i, m'_1, \ldots, m'_n)$ with $i \in \text{CU}$, we have either $\text{usk} \neq \text{usk}_i$ or $\exists j \in \mathcal{I}$ such that $m_j \neq m'_j$. In all cases, this means that $\sigma = (\sigma'_1, \sigma'_2, \tilde{\sigma}'_1, \tilde{\sigma}'_2)$ and $\{\text{usk}\}\cup\{m_i\}_{i\in\mathcal{I}}$ is a valid forgery against our URS scheme, which concludes our proof. $\qquad\qquad\square$

Proof of Anonymity. Let $(\tilde{g}, \tilde{g}^a, \tilde{g}^b, \tilde{g}^c)$ be a DDH challenge in $\mathbb{G}_2$. We construct a reduction $\mathcal{R}$ that uses $\mathcal{A}$, an adversary succeeding against the anonymity of our credential system with advantage ϵ, to decide whether $c = a \cdot b$.

At the beginning of the game $\text{Exp}_{\mathcal{A}}^{ano-b}$, $\mathcal{R}$ generates the organization key pair (sk, pk) and forwards it to $\mathcal{A}$ that eventually returns $(j_0, j_1, \{m_i\}_{i\in\mathcal{I}})$. $\mathcal{R}$ then makes a guess on the identity of the user i_b that will possess the credential $\sigma^{(j_b)}$ targeted by $\mathcal{A}$ and answers the oracle queries as follows.

– $\mathcal{O}$HU: Let j be the identity submitted to this oracle. If $j \neq i_b$, then $\mathcal{R}$ proceeds as usual. Else, it returns $\tilde{g}^a$ as the public key upk_{i_b} of user i_b.
– $\mathcal{O}$CU: $\mathcal{R}$ proceeds as usual, unless this oracle is queried on i_b, in which case $\mathcal{R}$ aborts.
– $\mathcal{O}$Obtain: For any $j \neq i_b$, $\mathcal{R}$ knows usk_j and so is able to run the Obtain protocol as usual. If $j = i_b$, then $\mathcal{R}$ sends the public key upk_{i_b} and simulates the proof of knowledge of a.
– $\mathcal{O}$Show: Here again, $\mathcal{R}$ proceeds as usual or by simulating the proof of knowledge of the secret key if the credential belongs to i_b.

At some point in the game, the adversary outputs the identifiers j_0 and j_1 of two users, along with a set of attributes $\{m_i\}_{i\in\mathcal{I}}$. If $j_b \neq i_b$, then $\mathcal{R}$ aborts. Else, it proceeds as follows.

$\mathcal{R}$ first selects two random scalars k and α and sets $\tilde{\sigma}_1' = g^b$. It then computes:

- $\tilde{\sigma}_2' \leftarrow (\tilde{\sigma}_1')^{\alpha+x+\sum_{i\in\mathcal{I}} y_i\cdot m_i} \cdot (g^c)^{y_0}$
- $\sigma_1' = g^\alpha$
- $\sigma_2' = (\sigma_1')^{\sum_{i\in\mathcal{I}_0} y_i}$

and simulates knowledge of a.

If $c = a \cdot b$, then, by setting $t = \alpha - \sum_{i\in[1,n]\backslash\mathcal{I}} y_i \cdot m_i$, one can see that $(\sigma_1', \sigma_2', \tilde{\sigma}_1', \tilde{\sigma}_2')$ is distributed as in the protocol of Fig. 3. Else, c is random, which means that $\tilde{\sigma}_2'$ is a random element of $\mathbb{G}_2$. Since σ_1', σ_2' and $\tilde{\sigma}_1'$ are independent of a and $\{m_i\}_{i\in[1,n]\backslash\mathcal{I}}$, $\mathcal{A}$ cannot succeed in this game with non negligible advantage. Therefore any change in the behaviour of $\mathcal{A}$ can be used to solve the DDH problem in $\mathbb{G}_2$, unless $\mathcal{R}$ aborts. The advantage of $\mathcal{R}$ is then at least $\frac{\epsilon}{q}$, where q is a bound on the number of honest users.

7 Efficiency

We describe in this section the complexity of the redactable signature schemes RS and URS before comparing the one of our anonymous credentials system with the most relevant systems of the state-of-the-art.

Redactable Signatures. Table 1 provides the most important figures regarding the size and computational complexity of the schemes RS and URS. For sake of clarity, we only consider the most expensive operations, such as exponentiations and pairings, and do not take into account the other ones. As in Remark 3, we define the subset vk of the elements of the public key pk that are necessary to verify signatures. Our efficiency analysis is based on the descriptions of the schemes from Sects. 4.1 and 4.2 that aim at minimizing the complexity in $\mathbb{G}_2$, where operations are usually less efficient and elements are larger than in $\mathbb{G}_1$. Nevertheless, we note that we can safely switch $\mathbb{G}_1$ and $\mathbb{G}_2$ if needed.

Table 1. Complexity of our Redactable Signature Schemes. The costs of Derive and Verify are provided for a set $\{m_i\}_{i\in\mathcal{I}}$ of k elements. Here, r_2 denotes the generation of a random element in $\mathbb{G}_2$, e_i denotes an exponentiation in $\mathbb{G}_i$, for $i \in \{1,2\}$, and p_i denotes an equation involving i pairings.

	vk	pk	σ	Sign	Derive	Verify
RS	$(n+1)\mathbb{G}_1$ $+n\mathbb{G}_2$	$\frac{n^2+n+2}{2}\mathbb{G}_1$ $+n\mathbb{G}_2$	$2\mathbb{G}_1 + 2\mathbb{G}_2$	$1r_2 + 1e_2$	$2(n-k)e_1$	$ke_1 + 2p_2$
URS	$(n+1)\mathbb{G}_1$ $+n\mathbb{G}_2$	$\frac{n^2+n+2}{2}\mathbb{G}_1$ $+n\mathbb{G}_2$	$2\mathbb{G}_1 + 2\mathbb{G}_2$	$1r_2 + 1e_2$	$2(n-k+1)e_1$ $+3e_2$	$ke_1 + 2p_2$

Anonymous Credentials. We compare in Table 2 the efficiency of our anonymous credentials system from Sect. 6 with the one of different approaches supporting multiple unlinkable showings of credentials. Most of the references and figures are extracted from the comparison in [15]. The latter shows that the existing solutions mostly differ in the size of the public key and of the credential and in the complexity of the showing process. For sake of clarity, we therefore only consider these features in our table and, for example, do not take into account the complexity of the Issuing process. We nevertheless note that our issuing process is among the most efficient ones. Similarly, we do not indicate in our table the computational assumptions that underlie the security of the constructions and refer to [15] for this information. We indeed note that, except for [9], all of them rely on the generic group model (GGM) or on non-standard assumptions (that are themselves proven in the GGM), which seems to be the price for efficiency and functionalities.

Table 2. Comparison of different anonymous credentials systems. The pk, vk and σ colomns refer to the size of the public key, of the verification key and of the credential, respectively. |Show| indicates the number of elements exchanged by the user and the verifier when the former shows k attributes. The Show and Verify colomns indicate the computational complexity for the user and the verifier, respectively. The last colomn indicates whether the scheme only supports *selective* (s) disclosure, or if it also allows to prove *relations* (r) about the attributes.

Scheme	pk/vk	σ	|Show|	Show	Verify	Proof
[9]	$O(n)/O(n)$	$O(1)$	$O(n-k)$	$O(n-k)$	$O(n)$	r
[10]	$O(n)/O(n)$	$O(n)$	$O(n)$	$O(n)$	$O(n)$	r
[1]	$O(n)/O(n)$	$O(1)$	$O(n-k)$	$O(n-k)$	$O(n)$	r
[21]	$O(n)/O(n)$	$O(1)$	$O(n-k)$	$O(n-k)$	$O(n)$	r
[7]	$O(n)/O(n)$	$O(1)$	$O(1)$	$O(n-k)$	$O(k)$	s
[15]	$O(n)/O(n)$	$O(1)$	$O(1)$	$O(n-k)$	$O(k)$	s
Sect. 6	$O(n^2)/O(n)$	$O(1)$	$O(1)$	$O(n-k)$	$O(k)$	r

This table shows that, for a long time, a credential issued on n attributes needed $O(n)$ operations to be verified, even if the user only showed k attributes. Moreover, it was necessary to prove knowledge of the $(n-k)$ hidden attributes, which implied to send $O(n-k)$ elements during the protocol.

Our protocol circumvents this problem and proposes a constant size credential with a constant number of elements to send during Show. Moreover, a verifier who only needs to check k attributes only has to perform k operations, which seems optimal. However one can note that our scheme is not the first one to achieve such remarkable features. We therefore need to go beyond asymptotic comparison when it comes to [7] and [15].

Regarding [7], the situation is quite simple. Although it has nice asymptotic complexity, the $O(1)$ notation for |Show| hides about 100 groups elements to show a credential (see [15]). It is therefore far less practical than our scheme and the one from [15]. Nevertheless, we must mention that it is the only one to achieve strong security in the UC framework [11], which may justify the efficiency gap.

Regarding [15], we note that our public key is larger, although it can be restricted to $O(n)$ elements if we only consider elements necessary for the verification, as explained in Remark 3. Our credential only consists of 2 elements of $\mathbb{G}_2$ and so is roughly twice shorter than the one from [15] that consists of 3 elements of $\mathbb{G}_1$, 1 of $\mathbb{G}_2$ and 2 scalars.

In our case, to show a credential, a user must send 2 elements of $\mathbb{G}_1$, 2 of $\mathbb{G}_2$, 1 of $\mathbb{G}_T$ and one scalar, contrarily to 8 elements of $\mathbb{G}_1$, 1 of $\mathbb{G}_2$ and two scalars in [15]. If we use Barreto-Naehrig curves [3] to instantiate the bilinear group, we get roughly the same complexity because of the element in $\mathbb{G}_T$ in our protocol. However, we note that the latter is the commitment of a Schnorr's proof and so could be replaced by a scalar if we choose to make our protocol non-interactive using the Fiat-Shamir heuristic [13]. In such a case, our Show protocol would be twice more efficient than the one from [15].

Finally, we believe that the main difference between these two schemes can be found in the ability to prove relations about the attributes. Indeed, in our protocol, each disclosed element is involved as an exponent of some public element in the verification equation so it is easy to hide it using Schnorr's proof of knowledge [23] and then to prove that it satisfies another relation (hence the "r" in the last column). Conversely, in [15], the disclosed attributes are roots of some polynomial $f_T(a)$ that is involved in the verification equation, with a a secret parameter of their scheme. Proving knowledge of these attributes is thus much more complex than in our case, so [15] cannot be used if one needs to efficiently prove some relations about them.

8   Conclusion

In this paper, we have provided a remarkably versatile and efficient signature scheme. Given a signature σ on a set of messages $\{m_i\}_{i=1}^n$, one can indeed disclose, prove relations about or redact any subset of $\{m_i\}_{i=1}^n$. Moreover, the number $(n - k)$ of undisclosed messages does not impact communication or verification complexity, leading to very efficient partial verification of a signature when k is small.

This ability to redact or prove relations about parts of the message is particularly useful when privacy is critical and we show that our scheme can be used to construct an anonymous credentials system with the same features. The resulting protocol then combines almost all the best properties of previous solutions, with constant-size credentials and $O(k)$ verification complexity, along with the ability to prove relations about attributes.

We believe that anonymous credentials are just an example of application of our scheme and that the latter could be useful as a building block for other primitives, in particular privacy-preserving ones.

Acknowledgements. The authors are grateful for the support of the ANR through project ANR-16-CE39-0014 PERSOCLOUD and project ANR-18-CE-39-0019-02 MobiS5.

References

1. Au, M.H., Susilo, W., Mu, Y.: Constant-size dynamic k-TAA. In: De Prisco, R., Yung, M. (eds.) SCN 2006. LNCS, vol. 4116, pp. 111–125. Springer, Heidelberg (2006). https://doi.org/10.1007/11832072_8
2. Baldimtsi, F., et al.: Accumulators with applications to anonymity-preserving revocation. In: EuroS&P 2017, pp. 301–315 (2017)
3. Barreto, P.S.L.M., Naehrig, M.: Pairing-friendly elliptic curves of prime order. In: Preneel, B., Tavares, S. (eds.) SAC 2005. LNCS, vol. 3897, pp. 319–331. Springer, Heidelberg (2006). https://doi.org/10.1007/11693383_22
4. Boneh, D., Boyen, X.: Short signatures without random oracles and the SDH assumption in bilinear groups. J. Cryptol. **21**(2), 149–177 (2008)
5. Brands, S.: Rethinking Public Key Infrastructures and Digital Certificates: Building in Privacy, January 2000
6. Brzuska, C., et al.: Redactable signatures for tree-structured data: definitions and constructions. In: Zhou, J., Yung, M. (eds.) ACNS 2010. LNCS, vol. 6123, pp. 87–104. Springer, Heidelberg (2010). https://doi.org/10.1007/978-3-642-13708-2_6
7. Camenisch, J., Dubovitskaya, M., Haralambiev, K., Kohlweiss, M.: Composable and modular anonymous credentials: definitions and practical constructions. In: Iwata, T., Cheon, J.H. (eds.) ASIACRYPT 2015, Part II. LNCS, vol. 9453, pp. 262–288. Springer, Heidelberg (2015). https://doi.org/10.1007/978-3-662-48800-3_11
8. Camenisch, J., Lysyanskaya, A.: An identity escrow scheme with appointed verifiers. In: Kilian, J. (ed.) CRYPTO 2001. LNCS, vol. 2139, pp. 388–407. Springer, Heidelberg (2001). https://doi.org/10.1007/3-540-44647-8_23
9. Camenisch, J., Lysyanskaya, A.: A signature scheme with efficient protocols. In: Cimato, S., Persiano, G., Galdi, C. (eds.) SCN 2002. LNCS, vol. 2576, pp. 268–289. Springer, Heidelberg (2003). https://doi.org/10.1007/3-540-36413-7_20
10. Camenisch, J., Lysyanskaya, A.: Signature schemes and anonymous credentials from bilinear maps. In: Franklin, M. (ed.) CRYPTO 2004. LNCS, vol. 3152, pp. 56–72. Springer, Heidelberg (2004). https://doi.org/10.1007/978-3-540-28628-8_4
11. Canetti, R.: Universally composable security: a new paradigm for cryptographic protocols. In: 42nd FOCS, pp. 136–145. IEEE Computer Society Press, October 2001
12. Chatterjee, S., Menezes, A.: On cryptographic protocols employing asymmetric pairings - the role of Ψ revisited. Discrete Appl. Math. **159**(13), 1311–1322 (2011)
13. Fiat, A., Shamir, A.: How to prove yourself: practical solutions to identification and signature problems. In: Odlyzko, A.M. (ed.) CRYPTO 1986. LNCS, vol. 263, pp. 186–194. Springer, Heidelberg (1987). https://doi.org/10.1007/3-540-47721-7_12
14. Fuchsbauer, G., Hanser, C., Slamanig, D.: Practical round-optimal blind signatures in the standard model. In: Gennaro, R., Robshaw, M. (eds.) CRYPTO 2015, Part II. LNCS, vol. 9216, pp. 233–253. Springer, Heidelberg (2015). https://doi.org/10.1007/978-3-662-48000-7_12
15. Fuchsbauer, G., Hanser, C., Slamanig, D.: Structure-preserving signatures on equivalence classes and constant-size anonymous credentials. J. Cryptol. **32**(2), 498–546 (2019)

16. Galbraith, S.D., Paterson, K.G., Smart, N.P.: Pairings for cryptographers. Discrete Appl. Math. **156**(16), 3113–3121 (2008)
17. Guillevic, A.: Comparing the pairing efficiency over composite-order and prime-order elliptic curves. In: Jacobson Jr., M., Locasto, M.E., Mohassel, P., Safavi-Naini, R. (eds.) ACNS 2013. LNCS, vol. 7954, pp. 357–372. Springer, Heidelberg (2013). https://doi.org/10.1007/978-3-642-38980-1_22
18. Haber, S., et al.: Efficient signature schemes supporting redaction, pseudonymization, and data deidentification. In: Abe, M., Gligor, V. (eds.) ASIACCS 2008, pp. 353–362. ACM Press, March 2008
19. Nguyen, L.: Accumulators from bilinear pairings and applications. In: Menezes, A. (ed.) CT-RSA 2005. LNCS, vol. 3376, pp. 275–292. Springer, Heidelberg (2005). https://doi.org/10.1007/978-3-540-30574-3_19
20. Nojima, R., Tamura, J., Kadobayashi, Y., Kikuchi, H.: A storage efficient redactable signature in the standard model. In: Samarati, P., Yung, M., Martinelli, F., Ardagna, C.A. (eds.) ISC 2009. LNCS, vol. 5735, pp. 326–337. Springer, Heidelberg (2009). https://doi.org/10.1007/978-3-642-04474-8_26
21. Pointcheval, D., Sanders, O.: Short randomizable signatures. In: Sako, K. (ed.) CT-RSA 2016. LNCS, vol. 9610, pp. 111–126. Springer, Cham (2016). https://doi.org/10.1007/978-3-319-29485-8_7
22. Sanders, O.: Efficient redactable signature and application to anonymous credentials. IACR Cryptology ePrint Archive, vol. 1201 (2019)
23. Schnorr, C.P.: Efficient identification and signatures for smart cards. In: Brassard, G. (ed.) CRYPTO 1989. LNCS, vol. 435, pp. 239–252. Springer, New York (1990). https://doi.org/10.1007/0-387-34805-0_22

Author Index

Printed in the United States
by Baker & Taylor Publisher Services